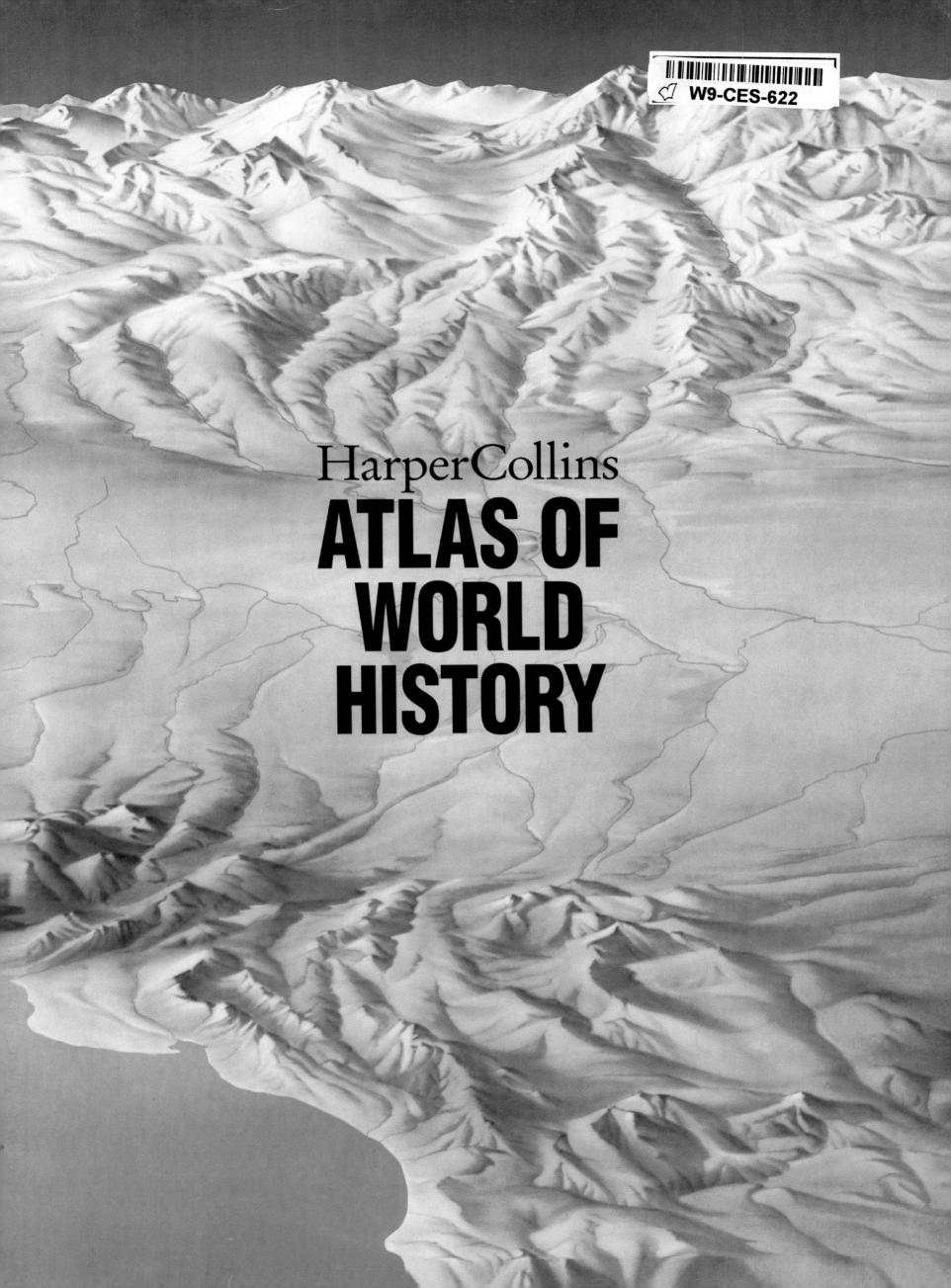

HarperCollins
ATLAS OF WORLD HISTORY

ATLAS OF

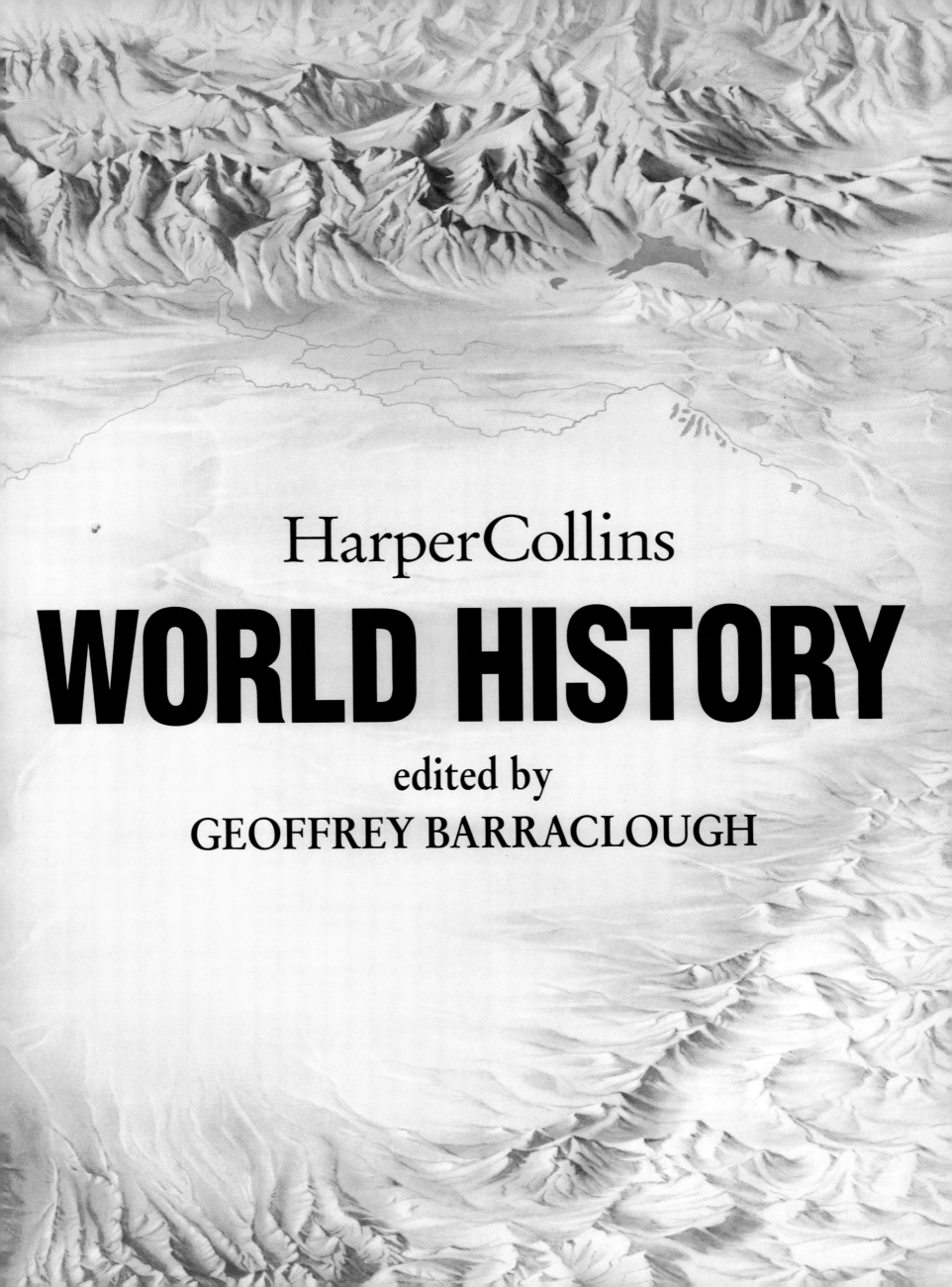

HarperCollins
WORLD HISTORY

edited by
GEOFFREY BARRACLOUGH

Published 2001 by Borders Press in association with HarperCollins.

Borders Press is a division of Borders Group, Inc. 100 Phoenix Drive, Ann Arbor. Michigan, 48108. All rights reserved.

Borders Press is a trademark of Borders Properties, Inc.

First published 1978
Reprinted with revisions 1979
Reprinted 1979, 1980, 1981, 1983
Revised edition 1984
Reprinted 1985
Reprinted with revisions 1986
Reprinted 1988
Second revised edition 1989
Copyright Times Books Ltd, London, 1978, 1979, 1980, 1981, 1983, 1984, 1985, 1986, 1988, 1989, 1998, 2001

Maps by:
Duncan Mackay, Rex Nicholls, Sue Paling, Hugh Penfold, Malcolm Swanston, Alan Wormwell of Product Support Group (Graphics) Ltd., Derby

Color separations by:
City Engraving, Hull

Editorial director: Barry Winkleman

Place names consultant: P.J.M. Geelan

Map design and layout: Peter Sullivan

Second revised edition

Artwork and typesetting by:
Swanston Graphics Limited, Derby

Color separations by:
Ensign Graphics Limited, Hull

Index set by:
Media Conversion Limited

Editorial: Elizabeth Wyse, Flair Milne, Andrew Heritage, Ailsa Hudson

Design and layout: Ivan Dodd

In addition to the contributors listed on pages 5 and 6, the publishers would also like to thank the following for their generous advice and help:

Correlli Barnett, *Fellow of Churchill College, Cambridge;* Robin Bidwell, *Secretary of the Centre for Middle East Studies, University of Cambridge;* Dr D. Brading, *Centre for Latin American Studies, University of Cambridge;* Professor Anthony Bryer, *Department of Byzantine Studies, University of Birmingham;* Professor Donald Bullough, *University of St Andrews;* Professor C.D. Cowan, *Director, School of Oriental and African Studies, University of London;* J. Morland Craig; the late Professor Michael Crowder, *University of Botswana;* Dr Elizabeth Dunstan, *International African Institute;* Professor John Erickson, *Director of Defence Studies, University of Edinburgh;* Aleksander Gieysztor; W. Grenzebach, *Brandeis University, Massachusetts;* Professor D.W. Harding, *Department of Archaeology, University of Edinburgh;* Professor David Hawkings, *School of Oriental and African Studies, University of London;* Morton Keller, *Spector Professor of History, Brandeis University, Massachusetts;* Jonathan King, *Museum of Mankind, London;* Dr Michael Leifer, *London School of Economics and Political Science;* H.A.G Lewis, *formerly of the Directorate of Military Survey;* Roy Lewis, *formerly of* The Times, *London;* George Maddocks; Professor Roland Oliver, *School of Oriental and African Studies, University of London;* Professor P.J. Parish, *Director, Institute of United States Studies, University of London;* Dr D. W. Phillipson, *Curator, Museum of Archaeology and Anthropology, University of Cambridge;* Professor M.C. Rickleffs, *Department of History, Monash University, Australia;* Dr R.L. Sims, *School of Oriental and African Studies, University of London;* Denis Mack Smith, *University of Oxford;* Professor Jan van der Houtte, *Department of History, University of Louvain, Belgium;* Roger Vielvoye, *formerly of* The Times, *London;* Dr Joachim Whaley, *University of Cambridge;* Andrew Wheatcroft; Peter Wilsher, Sunday Times, *London;* Dr L.R. Wright, *Department of Archaeology, University of Edinburgh.*

Printed and bound by Rotolito Lombarda, Italy
ISBN 0 7230 1025 0

Contributors

Editor:
Geoffrey Barraclough,
President, Historical Association, 1964-67, formerly Stevenson Research Professor of International History, University of London and Chichele Professor of Modern History, University of Oxford

Editor, Third Edition:
Norman Stone
Professor of Modern History
University of Oxford

R W Van Alstyne
Late Distinguished Professor of History
Callison College
University of the Pacific, California

Anthony Atmore
Research Fellow
School of Oriental and African Studies
University of London

John Barber
Fellow of King's College
University of Cambridge

Iris Barry
Formerly Research Student
Institute of Archaeology
University of London

Peter Bauer
Professor Emeritus
London School of Economics

Christopher Bayly
Reader in Modern Indian History
University of Cambridge

W G Beasley
Emeritus Professor of the History of the Far East
School of Oriental and African Studies University of London

Ralph Bennett
Emeritus Fellow of Magdalene College
University of Cambridge

A D H Bivar
Lecturer in Central Asian Archaeology
School of Oriental and African Studies
University of London

Hugh Borton
Formerly Professor of Japanese and Director
East Asian Institute
Columbia University, New York

A J Boyce
University Lecturer in Human Biology
University of Oxford

Warwick Bray
Reader in Latin American Archaeology
Institute of Archaeology
University of London

F R Bridge
Reader in International History
University of Leeds

Hugh Brogan
Chairman
Department of History
University of Essex

Tom Brooking
Senior Lecturer in History
University of Otago, New Zealand

Muriel E Chamberlain
Senior Lecturer in History
University College of Swansea
University of Wales

David G Chandler
Head of Department of War Studies and International Affairs
The Royal Military Academy, Sandhurst

Irene Collins
Senior Fellow in History
University of Liverpool

Jill Cook
Head of Quaternary Section
Department of Prehistoric and Romano-British Antiquities
The British Museum, London

Michael Crawford
Professor of History
University College, London

James Cronin
Associate Professor of History
University of Wisconsin

Douglas Dakin
Emeritus Professor of History
University of London

Ralph Davis
Late Professor of Economic History
University of Leicester

Frans von der Dunk
Lecturer
Department of International Law
University of Leiden

Gordon East
Emeritus Professor of Geography
University of London

I E S Edwards
Formerly Keeper of Egyptian Antiquities
The British Museum, London

R J W Evans
Lecturer in Modern History
University of Leeds

John Ferguson
Formerly President
Selly Oak Colleges
Birmingham

Stefan Fisch
Lecturer in Modern History
University of Munich

David H Fischer
Warren Professor of History
Brandeis University, Massachusetts

John R Fisher
Professor of Latin American History and Director
Institute of Latin American Studies
University of Liverpool

Michael Flinn
Late President
The Economic History Society

W J Gardner
Formerly Reader in History
University of Canterbury, New Zealand

Carol Geldart
Formerly Adviser to the House of Commons
Foreign Affairs Committee

John Gillingham
Senior Lecturer in Medieval History
London School of Economics
University of London

Martin Goodman
Solon Fellow
University of Oxford

D G E Hall
Late Emeritus Professor of South-East Asia History
University of London

Norman Hammond
Professor of Archaeology
Rutgers University, New Jersey

John D Hargreaves
Emeritus Professor of History
University of Aberdeen

G A Harrison
Professor of Biological Anthropology
University of Oxford

Ragnhild Hatton
Emeritus Professor of International History
London School of Economics
Unversity of London

M Havinden
Senior Lecturer in Social and Economic History
University of Exeter

W O Henderson
Formerly Reader in International Economic History
University of Manchester

Colin J Heywood
Lecturer in the History of the Near and Middle East
School of Oriental and African Studies
University of London

Sinclair Hood
Formerly Director
British School of Archaeology
Athens

Albert Hourani
Formerly Reader in the Modern History of the Middle East
University of Oxford

Colin Jones
Senior Lecturer in History
University of Essex

Richard H Jones
Professor of History
Reed College, Oregon

Ulrich Kemper
University of the Ruhr
Bochum, Germany

Karl Leyser
Formerly Chichele Professor of Medieval History
University of Oxford

Wolfgang Liebeschuetz
Professor of Classical and Archaeological studies
University of Nottingham

John Lynch
Emeritus Professor of Latin American History
University of London

J P Mallory
Lecturer in Archaeology
The Queen's University, Belfast

Isabel de Madriaga
Emeritus Professor of Russian Studies
University of London

James M McPherson
Professor of History
Princeton University, New Jersey

F R von der Mehden
Albert Thomas Professor of
Political Science
Rice University, Texas

A R Michell
Lecturer in Economic History
*Department of Economic and Social
History
University of Hull*

Christopher D Morris
Senior Lecturer in Archaeology
Durham University

A E Musson
Professor of Economic History
University of Manchester

F S Northedge
Professor of International Relations
*London School of Economics
University of London*

D Wayne Orchiston
Senior Lecturer in Museum Studies
*Victoria College,
Melbourne, Australia*

R J Overy
Reader in Modern History
*King's College
University of London*

Geoffrey Parker
Professor of History
University of Illinois

W H Parker
Formerly Lecturer in the
Geography of the USSR
University of Oxford

J H Parry
Late Professor of Oceanic History
Harvard University, Massachusetts

Thomas M Perry
Reader in Geography
University of Melbourne, Australia

E D Phillips
Late Professor of Greek Antiquities
Queen's University, Belfast

Sidney Pollard
Professor of Economic History
University of Bielefeld, Germany

T G E Powell
Late Professor of Prehistoric
Archaeology
University of Liverpool

John Poynter
Deputy Vice-Chancellor
University of Melbourne, Australia

Benjamin Ravid
Associate Professor of Jewish
History
Brandeis University, Massachusetts

Tapan Raychaudhuri
Reader in South Asian History
University of Oxford

B H Reid
Research Associate
*Department of War Studies
King's College
University of London*

A N Ryan
Reader in History
University of Liverpool

Gören Rystad
Professor of History
Lund University, Sweden

H W F Saggs
Professor of Semitic Languages
University College, Cardiff

S B Saul
Vice-Chancellor
University of York

Peter Sawyer
Formerly Professor of Medieval
History
University of Leeds

Chris Scarre
Faculty of Archaeology and
Anthropology
University of Cambridge

D J Schove
Late Principal
St. David's College, Kent

H M Scott
Lecturer in Modern History
*Department of Modern History
University of St Andrews, Scotland*

H H Scullard
Late Emeritus Professor of Ancient
History
*King's College
University of London*

Andrew Sharf
Professor of History
Bar Ilan University, Israel

Andrew Sherratt
Assistant Keeper of Antiquities
Ashmolean Museum, Oxford

Peter Sluglett
Lecturer in Modern Middle Eastern
History
Durham University

R B Smith
Reader in the History of South-East
Asia
*School of Oriental and African
Studies
University of London*

Frank C Spooner
Professor of Economic History
University of Durham

Jocelyn Statler
Adviser to the House of Commons
Foreign Affairs Committee

L S Stavrianos
Adjunct Professor of History
University of California, San Diego

Zara Steiner
Fellow of New Hall
University of Cambridge

W C Sturtevant
Curator of North American
Ethnology
*Smithsonian Institute,
Washington DC*

Alan Sykes
Lecturer in Modern History
University of St Andrews, Scotland

E A Thompson
Emeritus Professor of Classics
University of Nottingham

Hugh Tinker
Formerly Professor of Politics
University of Lancaster

Malcolm Todd
Professor of Archaeology
University of Exeter

R C Trebilcock
Department of History
University of Cambridge

Hugh R Trevor-Roper
Master of Peterhouse
University of Cambridge

Denis C Twitchett
Professor of East Asian Studies
Princeton University, New Jersey

Ernst Wangermann
Reader in Modern History
University of Leeds

D Cameron Watt
Stevenson Professor of
International History
*London School of Economics
University of London*

Bodo Wiethoff
Professor of Chinese History
*University of the Ruhr
Bochum, Germany*

D S M Williams
Lecturer in the History of Asiatic
Russia
*School of Slavonic and East European
Studies
University of London*

H P Willmott
Senior Lecturer in War Studies
Royal Military Academy, Sandhurst

David M Wilson
Director
The British Museum, London

George D Winius
Lecturer in the History of Spain and
Portugal
*Centre for the History of European
Expansion
University of Leiden*

Contents

Contents *CONTINUED*

SECTION 4
The world of divided regions

Contents *CONTINUED*

SECTION 6

The age of European dominance

Contents *CONTINUED*

Introduction

Significant changes have occurred during the past quarter of a century in our conception of the scope and pattern of world history. The new *Times Atlas of World History* sets out to reflect these changes and thus to present a view of world history appropriate to the age in which we live.

Most historical atlases of an earlier generation were marked by their 'Eurocentricity', that is to say by their tendency to concentrate on the history of Europe (particularly of western Europe) and to refer to other regions or countries only when and where Europe impinged upon them. In the new *Times Atlas* we have broken away from this traditional western view because we believe such an approach is misleading and untenable. Our aim has been to present a view of history which is world-wide in conception and presentation and which does justice, without prejudice or favour, to the achievements of all peoples in all ages and in all quarters of the globe.

It is, of course, true that our knowledge of the past is unequal; but while we have tried to avoid the error of allotting less space to the history of the West than its achievements demand, no people has consciously been relegated to the margin of history and none singled out for specially favoured treatment. We have laid particular emphasis upon the great world civilisations and their links and interplay; but we have not neglected the peoples outside the historic centres of civilisation – for example, the nomads of central Asia – whose impact on history was more profound than is generally appreciated.

When we say that this is an atlas of world history, we mean that it is not simply a series of national histories loosely strung together. In other words, it is concerned less with particular events in the history of particular countries than with broad movements – for example, the spread of the great world religions – spanning whole continents. There are many excellent specialised atlases of national history. It is no part of our intention to compete with them; nor would it have been possible to do so, had we wished, without dislocating the balance of the present work.

History is dynamic, not static; it is a process of change and movement in time; we have tried to avoid a series of static pictures of particular situations at particular moments in the past. In *The Times Atlas* a special effort has been made to emphasise change, expansion and contraction by the use of appropriate visual devices. In this way, we have endeavoured to convey a sense of history as a continuing process.

Any atlas seeking to present a conspectus of world history in approximately 130 plates must be selective. In singling out topics for inclusion we have adhered to the principle of selecting what was important *then* rather than what seems important *now*. Any other criterion, we believe, would put history through a distorting mirror.

If we have tried to ensure that the Atlas reflects the relative importance of different civilisations and the balance of world forces at any given moment in time, it is not merely out of piety towards the past but because we believe that, in the world as constituted today, the histories of India, China and Japan, and of other countries in Asia and Africa, are as relevant as the history of Europe. In the same way, and for the same reason, we have tried to hold a balance between eastern Europe and western Europe, and also to do justice to civilisations, such as the Ottoman Empire, which too often are treated as peripheral. It would be vain to hope that we have achieved a balance which all will find acceptable; but we believe that, granted the limits of space, this Atlas can fairly be described as comprehensive and ecumenical. Such, at least, has been our aim and endeavour.

Historical atlases have traditionally been concerned with political events and changes in political geography. Here again, the focus of interest has shifted during the past thirty or forty years. People today are more concerned with social history and with the cultural achievements of different civilisations than with political boundaries and military exploits. *The Times Atlas* pays considerable attention to such topics, and particularly to economic developments. Cultural and intellectual history does not, unfortunately, lend itself satisfactorily to cartographic documentation, and there are some subjects which ideally we should have wished to include and were forced reluctantly to omit. But we have sought in compensation to indicate the cultural connotations – and at the same time to make the presentation more vivid – by including, where space permits, visual records of the times or of historically significant tools, artefacts and other characteristic products of the peoples or civilisations with which the plates are concerned. Each plate also includes a commentary by a leading expert, providing the background to the maps and diagrams.

All atlases involve a number of specialised skills and disciplines, and none more so than an historical atlas. We have sought to make use of all available cartographic techniques, and in particular to emphasise different historical situations by employing a variety of different projections; thus the map of Islam, to take but one example, has been deliberately centred on Mecca, and the Mediterranean world has been viewed from there – as it might have been viewed by an Arab in the seventh century. In some instances we have used elaborate relief maps; in others we have deliberately simplified, sacrificing geographical detail to bring out the main historical facts. The results may not always be familiar, but we believe they may open new insights.

The original scheme for the atlas was drawn up by the present writer in 1973, and I was fortunate in being able to discuss it with L. S. Stavrianos and, before his death, with A. J. Toynbee. I am grateful to both not only for advice and criticism but also for encouragement. It is also no mere form of words to thank the contributors and other helpers (whose names are listed on pages 4, 5 and 6) for their unstinting efforts to present both familiar and unfamiliar material in an original and arresting way. Their collaboration is a guarantee of authenticity and of high scholarly standards. Finally, it is right to pay tribute to the pioneering work of our precursors, who have paved the way for us. A list of historical atlases is included in this volume. Though our purposes were often different from theirs, we have consulted them freely and they have been an indispensable source of guidance and information. Nevertheless *The Times Atlas of World History* is an entirely new venture. In particular, the plates in this volume are all original; not a few deal with topics which, to the best of our belief, have not been treated cartographically before, and all have been specially drawn to the specifications of contributors with the explicit aim of meeting the requirements and interests of present-day readers in all parts of the globe.

Geoffrey Barraclough

THE following twelve pages present a chronological synopsis of the major events in world history. The entries, necessarily abbreviated, are set out in columns under regional headings, which vary from period to period, reflecting changes in historical geography. A separate column lists important cultural events (in the broadest sense, including not only music, art and literature but also technological innovations and scientific discoveries) in all regions of the world.

Together with the Glossary and with the geographical Index (pages 297 to 360), the Chronology provides a key to the individual plates and maps, designed to help the reader to place the events there narrated in the broader context of world history. It also indicates the relative importance of different regions at different times, and the specific contributions of each to the development of civilisation and of civilised living.

The calendar of events starts with the beginnings of agriculture around the year 9000 BC. For a time-scale of prehistory readers are referred to the time chart on page 36.

A world chronology

Asia excluding the Near East

c. 6000 Rice cultivation (Thailand)

c. 3500 Earliest Chinese city at Liang-ch'eng chen (Lung-shan culture)

c. 3000 Use of bronze in Thailand

c. 2750 Growth of civilisation in the Indus valley

c. 1600 First urban civilisation in China, Shang Bronze Age culture

c. 1550 Aryans destroy Indus valley civilisation and settle in N. India

c. 1027 Shang dynasty in China overthrown by Chou; Aryans in India expand eastwards down Ganges valley

c. 800 Aryans expand southwards in India

771 Collapse of Chou feudal order in China

Europe

c. 6500 First farming in Greece and Aegean; spreads up Danube to Hungary (c. 5500), Germany and Low Countries (c. 4500) and along Mediterranean coast to France (c. 5000). Farmers cross to Britain c. 4000

3200-2000 Early Cycladic civilisation in Aegean

c. 3000 Spread of copper-working

c. 2000 Indo-European speakers (early Greeks) invade and settle Peloponnese; beginnings of 'Minoan' civilisation in Crete

c. 1600 Beginnings of Mycenaean civilisation in Greece

c. 1450 Destruction of Minoan Crete

c. 1200 Mycenaen civilisation in Greece collapses

c. 1000 Etruscans arrive in Italy

753 Traditional date for foundation of Rome

c. 750 Greek city states begin to found settlements throughout Mediterranean

c. 700 Scythians spread from central Asia to eastern Europe

c. 700-450 Hallstatt culture in central and western Europe; mixed farming, iron tools

Near East and North Africa

c. 9000-8000 Domestication of animals and crops (wheat and barley), the 'Neolithic Revolution', in the Near East; beginning of permanent settlements

8350-7350 Jericho founded: first walled town in the world (10 acres)

c. 7000 Early experiments with copper ores in Anatolia

6250-5400 Catal Hüyük (Anatolia) flourishes: largest city of its day (32 acres)

c. 5000 Colonisation of Mesopotamian alluvial plain by groups practising irrigation

c. 5000 Agricultural settlements in Egypt

c. 4000 Bronze casting begins in Near East; first use of plough

c. 3100 King Menes unites Egypt; dynastic period begins

c. 3000 Development of major cities in Sumer

c. 2685 The 'Old Kingdom' (pyramid age) of Egypt begins (to 2180 BC)

2371-2230 Sargon I of Agade founds first empire in world history

c. 2000 Hittites invade Anatolia and found empire ((1650)

c. 1800 Shamshi-Adad founds Assyrian state

c. 1750 Hammurabi founds Babylonian Empire

c. 1567 Kamose and Amosis I expel Hyksosos invaders and inaugurate Egyptian 'New Kingdom' (to 1090 BC)

c. 1200 Collapse of Hittite Empire

c. 1200 Jewish exodus from Egypt and settlement in Palestine

1166 Death of Ramesses III, last great pharaoh of Egypt

c. 1100 Spread of Phoenicians in Mediterranean region (to 700 BC)

c. 1000 King David unites Israel and Judah

c. 840 Rise of Urartu

814 Traditional date for foundation of Phoenician colony at Carthage

721-705 Assyria at height of military power

Other regions

c. 9000 Hunters spread south through Americas

c. 3000 Arable farming techniques spread to central Africa

c. 3000 First pottery in Americas (Ecuador and Colombia)

c. 2500 Desiccation of Saharan region begins

c. 2000 First metal-working in Peru

c. 2000 Settlement of Melanesia by immigrants from Indonesia begins

c. 1300 Settlers of Melanesia reach Fiji, later spreading to Western Polynesia

c. 1150 Beginning of Olmec civilisation in Mexico

c. 900 Foundation of kingdom of Kush (Nubia)

Culture and technology

c. 6000 First known pottery and woollen textiles (Çatal Hüyük)

c. 3500 Construction of Megalithic tombes and circles in Brittany, Iberian peninsula and British Isles (Stonehenge c. 2000)

c. 3500 Invention of wheel and plough (Mesopotamia) and sail (Egypt)

c. 3100 Pictographic writing invented in Sumer

c. 2590 Cheops builds great pyramid at Giza

c. 2500 Domestication of horse (central Asia)

c. 2000 Use of sail on seagoing vessels (Aegean)

c. 1500 Ideographic script in use in China; 'Linear B' script in Crete and Greece; Hittite cuneiform in Anatolia

c. 1450 Development of Brahma worship; composition of Vedas (earliest Indian literature) begins

c. 1370 Akhenaten enforces monotheistic sun worship in Egypt

c. 1200 Beginning of Jewish religion (worship of Jahweh)

c. 1100 Phoenicians develop alphabetic script (basis of all modern European scripts)

800-400 Composition of Upanishads, Sanskrit religious treatises

776 First Olympic Games held in Greece

c. 750 Amos, first great prophet in Israel

c. 750 Homer's Iliad and Hesiod's poetry first written down

Asia excluding
the Near East

c. 660 Jimmu, legendary first emperor of Japan

c. 650 Introduction of iron technology in China

c. 500 Sinhalese, an Aryan people, reach Ceylon

403-221 'Warring States' period in China

322 Chandragupta founds Mauryan Empire at Magadha, India

262 Asoka, Mauryan emperor (273-236) converted to Buddhism

221 Shih Huang-ti, of Ch'in dynasty, unites China (to 207)

202 Han dynasty reunites China; capital at Chang-an

185 Demetrius and Menander, kings of Bactria, conquer north-western India

Europe

c. 650 Rise of 'Tyrants' in Corinth and other Greek cities

510 Foundation of Roman Republic

c. 505 Cleisthenes establishes democracy in Athens

490 Battle of Marathon: Persian attack on Athens defeated

480 Battles of Salamis and Plataea (479): Persian invasion of Greece defeated

478 Foundation of Confederacy of Delos, later transformed into Athenian Empire

c. 450 La Tène culture emerges in central and western Europe

431-404 Peloponnesian War between Sparta and Athens

356 Philip II, king of Macedon

338 Battle of Chaeronea gives Macedon control of Greece

290 Rome completes conquest of central Italy

241 First Punic War (264-241) with Carthage gives Rome control of Sicily

218 Second Punic War (218-201): Hannibal of Carthage invades Italy

206 Rome gains control of Spain

168 Rome defeats and partitions Macedonia

146 Rome sacks Corinth; Greece under Roman domination

Near East
and North Africa

671 Assyrian conquest of Egypt: introduction of iron-working

612 Sack of Nineveh by Medes and Scythians; collapse of Assyrian power

586 Babylonian captivity of the Jews

c. 550 Cyrus II (the Great) of Persia defeats Medes and founds Persian Empire

521 Persia under Darius I (the Great) rules from the Nile to the Indus

c. 520 Darius I completes canal connecting Nile with Red Sea

494 Persians suppress Ionian revolt

334 Alexander the Great (of Macedon) invades Asia Minor; conquers Egypt (332), Persia (330) reaches India (329)

323 Death of Alexander: empire divided between Macedon, Egypt, Syria and Pergamum

304 Ptolemy I, Macedonian governor of Egypt, founds independent dynasty (to 30 BC)

247 Arsaces I founds kingdom of Parthia

149 Third Punic War (149-146): Rome destroys Carthage and founds province of Africa

Other regions

c. 500 Iron-making techniques spread to sub-Saharan Africa

500-AD200 Period of Nok culture in northern Nigeria

Culture
and technology

c. 650 First coins: Lydia (Asia Minor) and Greece (c. 600)

c. 650 Rise of Greek lyric poetry (Sappho born c. 612)

585 Thales of Miletus predicts an eclipse: beginnings of Greek rationalist philosophy

558 Zoroaster (Zarathustra) begins his prophetic work

550 Zoroastrianims becomes official religion of Persia

c. 540 Deutero-Isaiah, Hebrew prophet, at work during exile in Babylon

c. 530 Pythagoras, mathematician and mystic, active

528 Traditional date for death of Mahavira, founder of Jain sect

520 Death of Lao-tzu (born 605), traditional founder of Taoism

c. 500 Achaemenid Persians transmit food plants (rice, peach, apricot, etc.) to western Asia

c. 500 Caste system established in India

c. 500 First hieroglyphic writing in Mexico (Monte Albán)

486 Death of Siddhartha Gautama, founder of Buddhism

479-338 Period of Greek classical culture. Poetry: Pindar (518-438); drama: Aeschylus (525-456), Sophocles (496-406), Euripides (480-406), Aristophanes (c. 440-385); history: Herodotus (c. 486-429), Thucydides (c. 460-400); medicine: Hippocrates (c. 470-406); philosophy: Socrates (469-399), Plato (c. 427-347), Aristotle (384-322); sculpture: Phidias (c. 490-417), Praxiteles (c. 364); architecture: Parthenon (446-431)

479 Death of Confucius

350-200 Great period of Chinese thought: formation of Taoist, Legalist and Confucian schools; early scientific discoveries

312/11 Start of Seleucid era; first continuous historical dating-system

c. 290 Foundation of Alexandrian library

277 Death of Ch'ü Yüan (born 343), earliest major Chinese poet

142BC

Asia excluding the Near East

141 Wu-ti, Cinese emperor, expands Han power in eastern Asia

c. 138 Chang Chien explores central Asia

130 Yüeh-chih tribe (Tocharians) establish kingdom in Transoxania

c. 112 Opening of 'Silk Road' across Central Asia linking China to West

AD9 Wang Mang deposes Han dynasty in China

AD25 Restoration of Han dynasty; capital at Lo-yang

c.AD60 Rise of Kushan Empire

AD78-102 Kanishka, Kushan emperor, gains control of north India

AD91 Chinese defeat Hsiung-nu in Mongolia

184 'Yellow Turbans' rebellions disrupt Han China

220 End of Han dynasty: China splits into three states

245 Chinese envoys visit Funan (modern Cambodia), first major South-East Asian state

304 Hsiung-nu (Huns) invade China; China fragmented to 589

320 Chandragupta I founds Gupta Empire in northern India

c. 350 Hunnish invasions of Persia and India

Europe

133-122 Failure of reform movement in Rome, led by Tiberius and Gaius Gracchus

89 All Italy receives Roman citizenship

49 Julius Caesar conquers Gaul

47-45 Civil war in Rome; Julius Caesar becomes sole ruler (45)

31 Battle of Actium: Octavian (later Emperor Augustus) establishers domination over Rome

27 Collapse of Roman Republic and beginning of Empire

AD43 Roman invasion of Britain

AD117 Roman Empire at its greatest extent

212 Roman citizenship conferred on all free inhabitanta of Empire

238 Gothic incursions into Roman Empire begin

293 Emperor Diocletian reorganises Roman Empire

330 Capital of Roman Empire transferred to Constantinople

370 First appearance of Huns in Europe

378 Visigoths defeat and kill Roman emperor at Adrianople

406 Vandals invade and ravage Gaul and Spain (409)

410 Visigoths invade Italy, sack Rome and overrun Spain

Near East and North Africa

64 Pompey the Great conquers Syria; end of Seleucid Empire

53 Battle of Carrhae: Parthia defeats Roman invasion

30 Death of Antony and Cleopatra: Egypt becomes Roman province

AD44 Mauretania (Morocco) annexed by Rome

AD70 Romans destroy the Jewish Temple in Jerusalem

AD116 Roman Emperor Trajan completes conquest of Mesopotamia

132 Jewish rebellion against Rome leads to 'diaspora' (dispersal of Jews)

224 Foundation of Sasanian dynasty in Persia

429 Vandal kingdom in North Africa

Other regions

100 Camel introduced into Saharan Africa

c.AD50 Expansion of kingdom of Axum (Ethiopia) begins

c. 150 Berber and Mandingo tribes begin domination of the Sudan

c. 250 Kingdom of Axum (Ethiopia) gains control of Red Sea trade

c. 300 Rise of Hopewell India chiefdoms in North America and of Maya civilisation in Mesoamerica; large civilised states in Mexico (Teotihuacán, Monte Albán, El Tajín)

c. 300 Settlement of eastern Polynesia

Culture and technology

142 Completion of first stone bridge over river Tiber

79 Death of Ssu-ma Ch'ien, Chinese historian

46 Julius Caesar Reforms calendar; Julian calendar in use until AD 1582 (England 1752, Russia 1917)

31-AD14 The Augustan Age at Rome: Virgil (70-19), Horace (65-27), Ovid (43-AD17), Livy (59-AD17)

5 Building of national shrine of Ise in Japan

c. AD30 Jesus of Nazareth, founder of Christianity, crucified in Jerusalem

AD46-57 Missionary journey of St Paul

c. AD90-120 Great period of Silver Latin: Tacitus (c. 55-120), Juvenal (c. 55-c. 140), Martial (c. 38-102)

AD105 First use of paper in China

c. 125 Third Buddhist conference: widerspread acceptance of the sculptural Buddha image

150 Earliest surviving Sanskrit inscription (India)

c.150 Buddhism reaches China

c. 200 Completion of *Mishnah* (codification of Jewish Law)

c. 200 Indian epic poems: *Mahabharata*, *Ramayana* and *Bhagavad Gita*

c. 200-250 Development of Christian theology: Tertullian (c. 160-220), Clement (c. 150-c. 215), Origen (185-254)

271 Magnetic compass in use (China)

274 Unconquered Sun proclaimed god of Roman Empire

276 Crucifixion of Mani (born 215), founder of Manichaean sect

285 Confucianism introduced into Japan

c. 300 Foot-strirrup invented in Asia

313 Edict of Milan: Christianity granted toleration in Roman Empire

325 Axum destroys kingdom of Meröe (Kush)

350 Buddhist cave temples, painting, sculpture (to 800)

404 Latin version of Bible (Vulgate) completed

413 Kumaragupta; great literary era in India

426 Augustine of Hippo completes *City of God*

Asia excluding the Near East

480 Gupta Empire overthrown

589 China reunified by Sui dynasty

607 Unification of Tibet

617 China in state of anarchy

624 China united under T'ang dynasty

c. 640 Empire of Sri Harsha in northern India

645 Fujiwara's 'Taika Reform' remodels Japan on Chinese lines

658 Maximum extensions of Chinese power in central Asia; protectorates in Afghanistan, Kashmir, Sogdiana and Oxus valley

665 Tibetan expansion into Turkestan, Tsinghai

676 Korea unified under Silla

712 Arabs conquer Sind and Samarkand

745 Beginnings of Uighur Empire in Mongolia

751 Battle of Talas River: sets boundary of China and Abbasid caliphate

755 n Lu-shan's rebellion in China

794 Japanese capital moved to Kyoto from Nara

c. 802 Jayaxarman II establishes Angkorean kingdom (Cambodia)

836 Struggle for control of Indian Deccan

840 Collapse of Uighur Empire

842 Tibetan Empire disintegrates

Europe

449 Angles, Saxons and Jutes begin conquest of Britain

476 Deposition of last Roman emperor in West

486 Frankish kingdom founded by Clovis

493 Ostrogoths take power in Italy

533 Justinian restores Roman power in North Africa and Italy (552)

c. 542 Bubonic plague ravages Europe

568 Lombard conquest of north Italy

590 Gregory the Great expands papal power

610 Accession of East Roman Emperor Heraclius; beginning of Hellenisation of (East) Roman Empire, henceforward known as Byzantine Empire

680 Bulgars invade Balkans

687 Battle of Tertry: Carolingians dominate Frankish state

711 Muslim invasion of Spain

732 Battle of Poitiers halts Arab expansion in western Europe

751 Lombards overrun Ravenna, last Byzantine foothold in northern Italy

774 Charlemagne conquers northern Italy

793 Viking raids begin

800 Charlemagne crowned emperor in Rome; beginning of new Western (later Holy Roman) Empire

843 Treaty of Verdun: partition of Carolingian Empire

Near East and North Africa

531 Accession of Chosroes (died 579): Sasanian Empire at its greates extent

611 Persian armies capture Antioch and Jerusalem and overrun Asia Minor (to 626)

622 *Hegira* of Mohammed; beginning of Islamic calendar

632 Death of Mohammed: Arab expansion begins

636 Arabs overrun Syria

637 Arabs overrun Iraq

641 Arabs conquer Egypt and begin conquest of North Africa

718 Arab siege of Constantinople repulsed

750 Abbasid caliphate established

809 Death of caliph Harun al-Rashid

Other regions

c. 600 Apogee of Maya civilisation

c. 700 Rise of empire of Ghana

c. 800 First settlers reach Easter Island and New Zealand (850) from Polynesia

c. 850 Collapse of Classic Maya culture in Mesoamerica

Culture and technology

497 Franks converted to Christianity

c. 520 Rise of mathematics in India: Aryabhata and Varamihara invent decimal system

529 Rule of St Benedict regulates Western monasticism

534 Justinian promulgates Legal Code

538 S. Sophia, Constantinople, consecrated

c. 550 Buddhism introduced into Japan from Korea

563 St Columba founds monastery of Iona: beginning of Irish mission to Anglo-Saxons

607 Chinese cultural influence in Japan begins

625 Mohammed begins his prophetic mission

c. 645 Buddhism reaches Tibet (first temple 651)

c. 690 Arabic replaces Greek and Persian as language of Umayyad administration

692 Completion of Dome of Rock in Jerusalem, first great monument of Islamic architecture

c. 700 Buddhist temples built at Nara, Japan

700 Golden age of Chinese poetry: Li Po (701-62), Tu Fu (712-70); Po Chü-i (772-846)

722 St Boniface's mission to Germany

725 Bede (673-735) introduces dating by Christian era

c. 730 Printing in China

751 Paper-making spreads from China to Muslim world and Europe (1150)

760 Arabs adopt Indian numerals and develop algebra and trigonometry

782 Alcuin of York (735-804) organises education in Carolingian Empire: 'Carolingian renaissance'

788 Great mosque in Córdoba

c. 800 Temple at Borobudur (Java) constructed by Shailendra kings

853 First printed book in China

Asia excluding the Near East

907 Last T'ang emperor deposed

619 Khitan kingdom in Mongolia founded

918 State of Koryo founded in Korea

939 Vietnam independent of China

947 Khitans overrun northern China, establish Liao dynasty with capital at Peking

967 Fujiwara domination of Japan begins

979 Sung dynasty reunites China

1018 Mahmud of Ghaznisacks Kanauj and breaks power of Hindu states

1018 Rajendra Chola conquers Ceylon

1021 Cholas invade Bengal

1038 Tangut tribes form Hsi-hsia state in north-west China

1044 Establishment of first Burmese national state at Pagan

1126 Chin overrun northern China; Sung rule restricted to south

1170 Apogee of Srivijaya kingdom in Java under Shailendra dynasty

1175 Muizzuddin Muhammad of Ghazni, founds first Muslim empire in India

c. 1180 Angkor Empire (Cambodia) at greatest extent

1185 Minamoto warlords supreme in Japan

Europe

862 Novgorod founded by Rurik the Viking

871 Alfred, king of Wessex, halts Danish advance in England

882 Capital of Russia moved to Kiev

911 Vikings granted duchy of Normandy

929 Abdurraman III establishes caliphate at Córdoba

955 Otto I defeats Magyars at Lechfeld

959 Unification of England under Eadgar

960 Miesko I founds Polish state

962 Otto I of Germany crowned emperor in Roma

972 Beginning of Hungarian state under Duke Geisa

983 Great Slav rebellion against German eastward expansion

987 Accession of Capetians in France

1014 Battle of Clontarf breaks Viking domination of Ireland

1016 Cnut the Great rules England, Denmark and Norway (to 1035)

1018 Byzantines annex Bulgaria (to 1185)

1031 Collapse of caliphate of Córdoba

1054 Schism between Greek and Latin Christian churches begins

1066 Norman conquest of England

1071 Fall of Bari completes Norman conquest of Byzantine Italy

1073 Gregory VII elected Pope: beginning of conflict of Empire and papacy

1125 Renewal of German eastwards expansion

1154 Accession of Henry II: Angevin Empire in England and France

1198 Innocent III elected Pope

Near East and North Africa

936 Caliphs of Baghdad lose effective power

969 Fatimids conquer Egypt and found Cairo

1055 Seljuk Turks take Baghdad

1056 Almoravids conquer North Africa and southern Spain

1071 Battle of Manzikert: defeat of Byzantium by Seljuk Turks

1096 First Crusade: Franks invade Anatolia and Syria, and found crusader states

1135 Almohads dominant in north-western Africa and Muslim Spain

1171 Saladin defeats Fatimids and conquers Egypt

1188 Saladin destroys Frankish crusader kingdoms

Other regions

c. 990 Expansion of Inca Empire (Peru)

c. 1000 Vikings colonise Greenland and discover America (Vinland)

c. 1000 First Iron Age settlement at Zimbabwe (Rhodesia)

1076 Almoravids destroy kingdom of Ghana

c. 1000 Toltecs build their capital at Tula (Mexico)

c. 1150 Beginnings of Yoruba city states (Nigeria)

c. 1200 Rise of empire of Mali in west Africa

Culture and technology

863 Creation of Cyrillic alphabet in eastern Europe

865 Bulgars and Serbians accept Christianity

c. 890 Japanese cultural renaissance: novels, landscape painting and poetry

910 Abbey of Cluny founded

935 Text of Koran finalised

c. 1000 Great age of Chinese painting and ceramics

1020 Completion of *Tale of Genji* by Lady Murasaki

1020 Death of Firdausi, writer of Persian national epic, *The Shahnama*

1037 Death of Avicenna, Persian philosopher

c. 1045 Moveable type printing invented in China

1094 Composition of old Javanese *Ramayana* by Yogisvara

c. 1100 First universities in Europe: Salerno (medicine), Bologna (law), Paris (theology and philosophy)
c. 1100 Omar Khayyam composes *Rabaiyyat*

1111 Death of al-Ghazali, Muslim theologian

c. 1150 Hindu temple of Angkor Wat (Cambodia) built

1154 Chartres Cathedral begun; **Gothic architecture spreads throught western Europe**
c. 1160 development of European vernacular verse: Chanson de Roland (c. 1100), El Cid (c. 1150), Parzifal, Tristan (c. 1200)

1193 Zen Buddhist order founded in Japan

1198 Death of Averroës, Arab scientist and philosopher

Asia excluding the Near East	Europe	Near East and North Africa	Other regions	Culture and technology
			c. 1200 Emergence of Hausa city states (Nigeria)	
			c. 1200 Aztecs occupy valley of Mexico	
1206 Mongols under Genghis Khan begin conquest of Asia	**1204** Fourth Crusade: Franks conquer Byzantium and found Latin Empire			
1206 Sultanate of Delhi founded	**1212** Battle of Las Navas de Tolosa			
	1215 Magna Carta: King John makes concessions to English barons			**c. 1215** Islamic architecture spreads to India
c. 1220 Emergence of first Thai kingdom	**1236** Mongols invade and conquer Russia (1239)	**1228** Hafsid dynasty established at Tunis		**1226** Death of St Francis of Assisi
1234 Mongols destroy Chin Empire	**1241** Mongols invade Poland, Hungary, Bohemia			
	1242 Alexander Nevsky defeats Teutonic Order			
	1250 d. of Emperor Frederick II, collapse of Imperial power in Germany and Italy		**c. 1250** Mayapan becomes dominant Maya city of Yucatán	
1264 Kublai Khan founds Yüan dynasty in China	**1261** Greek empire restored in Constantinople	**1258** Mongols sack Baghdad; end of Abbasid caliphate		**1274** Death of St Thomas Aquinas: his *Summa Theologica* defines Christian dogma
				1275 Marco Polo (1254-1324) arrives in China
1279 Mongols conquer southern China				**1290** Spectacles invented (Italy)
	1291 Beginnings of Swiss Confederation	**1299** Ottoman Turks begin expansion in Anatolia	**c. 1300** Kanuri Empire moves capital from Kanem to Borno	
	1309 Papacy moves from Rome to Avignon		**c. 1300** Emergence of empire of Benin (Nigeria)	
	1314 Battle of Bannockburn: Scotland defeats England			
	1325 Ivan I begins recovery of Moscow		**1325 Rise of Aztecs in Mexico:** Tenochtitlán founded	**c. 1320** Cultural revival in Italy; Dante (1265-1321), Giotto (1276-1337), Petrarch (1304-71)
1333 End of Minamoto shogunate: civil war in Japan	**1337** Hundred Years War between France and England begins			**1339** Building of Kremlin (Moscow)
c. 1341 'Black Death' starts in Asia	**1348** Black Death from Asia ravages Europe			
1349 First Chinese settlement at Singapore; beginning of Chinese expansion in South-East Asia				
1350 Golden age of Majapahit Empire in Java	**1360** Peace of Brétigny ends first phase of Hundred Years War			**c. 1350** Japanese cultural revival
	1361 Ottomans capture Adrianople			
1368 Ming dynasty founded in China				
1370 Hindu state of Vijayanagar dominant in southern India	**1378** Great Schism in West (to 1417)			**1377** Death of Ibn Battuta (born 1309), Arab geographer and traveller
1380 Timur (Tamerlane) begins conquests	**1386** Union of Poland and Lithuania			**1387** Lithuania converted to Christianity
	1389 Battle of Kosovo: Ottomans gain control of Balkans			**1392** Death of Hafiz, Persian lyric poet
1392 Korea becomes independent				
1394 Thais invade Cambodia; Khmer capital moved to Phnom Penh	**1397** Union of Kalmar (Scandinavia)			
1398 Timur invades India and sacks Delhi				
c. 1400 Establishment of Malacca as a major commercial port of S.E. Asia		**1402** Battle of Ankara: Timur defeats Ottomans in Anatolia		**1400** Death of Chaucer, first great poet in English
1405 Chinese voyages in Indian Ocean	**1410** Battle of Tannenberg: Poles defeat Teutonic Knights			**1406** Death of Ibn Khalun, Muslim historian
	1415 Battle of Agincourt: Henry V of England resumes attack on France		**1415** Portuguese capture Ceuta: beginning of Portugal's African empire	
1428 Chinese expelled from Vietnam	**1428** Joan of Arc: beginning of French revival		**1430** Construction of great stone enclosure at Zimbabwe (Rhodesia)	
			1434 Portuguense explore south of Cape Bojador	**1445** Johannes Gutenberg (1397-1468) prints first book in Europe
			c. 1450 Apogee of Songhay Empire; university at Timbuktu	
	1453 England loses Continental possessions (except Calais)		**c. 1450** Monomatapa Empire founded	
	1453 Ottoman Turks capture Constantinople: end of Byzantine Empire			
1471 Vietnamese southward expansion: Champa annexed	**1475** Burghundy at height of power (Charles the Bold)		**1470** Incas conquer Chimú kingdom	
	1478 Ivan III, first Russian tsar, subdues Novgorod and throws off Mongol yoke (1480)			

Asia	Europe	Africa	New World	Culture and technology
	1492 Fall of Granada: end of Muslim rule in Spain; Jews expelled from Spain	**1492** Spaniards begin conquest of North African coast	**1492 Columbus reaches America: discovery of New World**	
	1494 Italian wars: beginning of Franco-Habsburg struggle for hegemony in Europe		**1493** First Spanish settlement in New World (Hispaniola)	
			1493 Treaty of Tordesillas divides New World between Portugal and Spain	
1498 Vasco da Gama: first European sea-voyage to India and back			**1497** Cabot reaches Newfoundland	
1500 Shah Ismail founds Safavid dynasty in Persia			**1498** Columbus discovers South America	**c. 1500 Italian Renaissance:** Leonardo da Vinci (1452-1519), Michelangelo (1475-1564), Raphael (1483-1520), Botticelli (1444-1510), Machiavelli (1469-1527), Ficino (1433-99)
		1505 Portuguese establish trading posts in east Africa		**1509** Watch invented by Peter Henle (Nuremburg)
1511 Portuguense take Malacca			**c. 1510** African slaves to America	
1516 Ottomans overrun Syria, Egypt and Arabia (1517)				
	1519 Charles V, ruler of Spain and Netherlands, elected emperor		**1519 Cortés begins conquest of Aztec Empire**	
	1521 Martin Luther outlawed: **beginning of Protestant Reformation**		**1520** Magellan crosses Pacific	
	1521 Suleiman the Magnificent, Ottoman sultan, conquers Belgrade			
1526 Battle of Panipat: **Babur conquers kingdom of Delhi and founds Mughal dynasty**	**1526** Battle of Mohács: Ottoman Turks overrun Hungary			**c. 1525** Introduction of potato from South America to Europe
	1534 Henry VIII of England breaks with Rome		**1532 Pizarro begins conquest of Inca Empire for Spain**	
	1541 John Calvin founds reformed church at Geneva			**1539** Death of Kabir Nanak, founder of Sikh religion
	1545 Council of Trent: beginning of Counter-Reformation	**1546** Destruction of Mali Empire by Songhay	**1545** Discovery of silver mines at Potosi (Peru) and Zacatecas (Mexico)	**1543** Copernicus publishes *Of the Revolution of Celestial Bodies*
1550 Mongol Altan-khan invades northern China; Japanese 'pirate' raids in China	**1556** Ivan IV of Russia conquers Volga basin			
1557 Portuguese established at Macao (China)				**1559** Tobacco first introduced into Europe
1565 Akbar extends Mughal power to Deccan	**1562** Wars of religion in France (to 1598)		**c. 1560** Portuguense begin sugar cultivation in Brazil	
	1571 Battle of Lepanto: end of Turkish sea power in central Mediterranean	**1571** Portuguese create colony in Angola	**1571** Spanish conquer Philippines	
	1572 Dutch Revolt against Spain			
1581 Yermak begins Russian conquest of Siberia		**1578** Battle of Al Kasr al Kebir: Moroccans destroy Portuguese power in north-western Africa		
1584 Phra Narai creates independent Siam	**1588** Spanish Armada defeated by English	**1591** Battle of Tondibi: Moroccans destroy Songhay kingdom		
	1598 Time of Troubles in Russia	**c. 1600** Oyo Empire at height of power		**1598** Shah Abbas I creates imperial capital at Isfahan
	1600 Foundation of English and Dutch (1602) East India Companies			**c. 1603** Beginnings of Kabuki theatre, Japan
			1607 First permanent English settlement in America (Jamestown, Virginia)	**1607** Monteverdi's *La Favola d'Orfeo* establishes opera as art form
1609 Beginning of Tokugawa shogunate in Japan	**1609** Dutch Republic becomes independent		**1608** French colonists found Quebec	**1609** Telescope invented (Holland)
				c. 1610 Scientific revolution in Europe begins: Kepler (1571-1610), Bacon (1561-1626), Galileo (1564-1642), Descartes (1596-1650)
	1618 Outbreak of Thirty Years War			**1616** Death of Shakespeare (born 1564) and Cervantes (born 1547)
1619 Foundations of Batavia (Jakarta) by Dutch: start of Dutch colonial empire in East Indies			**1620** Puritans land in New England (*Mayflower*)	**1620** First weekly newspapers in Europe (Amsterdam)
		1628 Portuguese destroy Mwenemutapa Empire	**1625** Dutch settle New Amsterdam	

Asia

1638 Russians reach Pacific

1641 Dutch capture Malacca from Portuguese

1644 Manchus found new dynasty (Ch'ing) in China

1649 Russians reach Pacific and found Okhotsk

1674 Sivaji creates Hindu Maratha kingdom

1689 Treaty of Nerchinsk between Russia and China

1690 Foundation of Calcutta by English

1697 Chinese occupy Outer Mongolia

1707 Death of Aurangzeb: decline of Mughal power in India

1736 Safavid dynasty deposed by Nadir Shah

1747 Ahmad Khan Abdali founds kingdom of Afghanistan

1751 China overruns Tibet, Dzungaria and Tarim Basin (1756-9)

1751 French gain control of Deccan and Carnatic

1755 Alaungpaya founds Rangoon and reunites Burma (to 1824)

1757 Battle of Plassey: British defeat French

1761 Capture of Pondicherry: British destroy French power in India

Europe

1630 Gustavus Adolphus of Sweden intervenes in Thirty Years War

1642 English Civil War begins

1648 Peace of Westphalia ends Thirty Years War

1649 Execution of Charles I of England; republic declared

1652 First Anglo-Dutch War: beginning of Dutch decline

1654 Ukraine passes from Polish to Russian rule

1658 Peace of Roskilde: Swedish Empire at height

1667 Beginning of French expansion under Louis XIV

1683 Turkish siege of Vienna

1688 'Glorious Revolution'; constitutional monarchy in England

1689 'Grand Alliance' against Louis XIV

1699 Treaty of Carlowitz: Habsburgs recover Hungary from Turks

1700 Great Northern War (to 1720)

1703 Foundation of St Petersburg, capital of Russian Empire (1712)

1707 Union of England and Scotland

1709 Battle of Poltava: Peter the Great of Russia defeats Swedes

1713 Treaty of Utrecht ends War of Spanish Succession

1740 War of Austrian Succession: Prussia annexes Silesia

1756 Seven Years War begins

1772 First partition of Poland (2nd and 3rd partitions 1793, 1795)

1774 Treaty of Kuchuk Kainarji: beginning of Ottoman decline

Africa

1652 Foundation of Cape Colony by Dutch

1659 French found trading station on Senegal coast

1662 Battle of Ambuila: destruction of Kongo kingdom by Portuguese

c. 1700 Rise of Asante power (Gold Coast)

c. 1730 Revival of ancient empire of Borno (central Sudan)

New World

1645 Tasman circumnavigates Australia and discovers New Zealand

1664 New Amsterdam taken by British from Dutch (later renamed New York)

1684 La Salle explores Mississippi and claims Louisiana for France

1693 Gold discovered in Brazil

1728 Bering begins Russian reconnaissance of Alaska

1760 New France conquered by British: Quebec (1759) and Montreal (1760)

1768 Cook begins exploration of Pacific

1775 American Revolution begins

Culture and technology

c. 1630 Apogee of Netherlands art: Hals (1580-1666), Rembrandt (1606-69), Vermeer (1632-75), Rubens (1577-1640)

1636 Foundation of Harvard College, first university in North America

c. 1650 Beginnings of popular literary culture in Japan (puppet theatre, kabuki, the novel)

1653 Taj Mahal, Agra, India, completed

1656 St Peter's, Rome, completed (Bernini)

c. 1660 Classical period of French culture: drama (Molière, 1622-1673), Racine, 1639-1699, Corneille, 1606-1684), painting (Poussin, 1594-1665, Claude, 1600-1682), music (Lully, 1632-1687, Couperin, 1668-1733)

1662 Royal Society founded in London and (1666) Académie Française in Paris

1687 Isaac Newton's *Principia*

1690 John Locke's *Essay concerning Human Understanding*

c. 1700 Great age of German baroque music: Buxtehude (1637-1707), Handel (1685-1759), Bach (1685-1750)

1709 Abraham Darby discovers coke-smelting technique for producing pig-iron (England)

1730 Wesley brothers create Methodism

c. 1735 Wahabite movement to purify Islam begins in Arabia

c. 1760 European enlightenment: Voltaire (1694-1778), Diderot (1713-84), Hume (1711-76)

1762 J.J. Rousseau's *Social Contract*

c. 1770 Advance of science and technology in Europe: J. Priestley (1733-1804), A. Lavoisier (1743-94), A. Volta (1745-1827). Harrison's chronometer (1762), Watt's steam engine (1769), Arkwright's water-powered spinning-frame (1769)

Asia	Europe	Africa	Americas and Australasia	Culture and technology
			1776 American Declaration of Independence	**1776** Publication of T*he Wealth of Nations* by Adam Smith (1723-90) and Common Sense by Tom Paine (1737-1809)
	1783 Russia annexes Crimea		**1783** Treaty of Paris: Britain recognises American independence	**1781** Immanuel Kant's *Critique of Pure Reason*
	1789 French Revolutions begins; abolition of feudal system and proclamation of Rights of Man		**1788** British colony of Australia founded	
	1791 Russia gains Black Sea steppes from Turks		**1789** George Washington becomes first President of United States of America	**c.1790** Great age of European orchestral music: Mozart (1756-91), Haydn (1732-1809), Beethoven (1770-1827)
	1792 French Republic proclaimed; beginning of revolutionary wars			**1792** Cartwright invents steam-powered weaving loom
	1793 Attempts to reform Ottoman Empire by Selim III			**1793** Decimal system introduced (France)
		1798 Napoleon attacks Egypt		**1793** Eli Whitney's cotton 'gin' (US)
1796 British conquer Ceylon	**1799 Napoleon** becomes First Consul and (1804) **Emperor of france**			**1796** Jenner discovers smallpox vaccine (UK)
	1805 Napoleon defeats Austria and (1806) Prussia	**1804** Fulanis conquer Hausa	**1803** Louisiana Purchase nearly doubles size of US	**1798** Malthus publishes *Essay on the Principle of Population*
	1805 Battle of Trafalgar: Britain defeats French and Spanish fleets	**1806** Cape Colony passes under British control		
	1807 Abolition of serfdom in Prussia	**1807** Slave trade abolished within British Empire	**1808 Independence movements in Spanish and Portuguese America:** 13 new states created by 1828	
	1812 Napoleon invades Russia	**1811** Mohammed Ali takes control in Egypt		**1812** Cylinder printing press invented, adopted by *The Times* (London)
	1815 Napoleon defeated at Waterloo, exiled to St Helena			
	1815 Congress of Vienna	**1818** Shaka forms Zulu kingdom in SE Africa		**1817** Foundation of Hindu college, Calcutta, first major centre of Western influence in India
1818 Britain defeats Marathas and becomes effective ruler of India			**1819** US purchases Florida from Spain	**c.1820** Romanticism in European literature and art: Byron (1788-1824), Chateaubriand (1768-1848), Heine (1797-1856), Turner (1775-1851), Delacroix (1798-1863)
1819 British found Singapore as free trade port				**1821** Electric motor and generator invented by M. Faraday (Britain)
	1821 Greek war of independence	**1822** Liberia founded as colony for freed slaves	**1823** Monroe Doctrine	**1822** First photographic image produced by J-N. Niepce (France)
1824 British begin conquest of Burma and Assam				**1825** First passenger steam railway: Stockton and Darlington (England)
1825-30 Java war: revolt of Indonesians against Dutch		**1830** French begin conquest of Algeria		**1828** Foundation of Brahmo-samaj, Hindu revivalist movement
1830 Russia begins conquest of Kazakhstan (to 1854)	**1830** Revolutionary movements in France, Germany, Poland and Italy; Belgium wins independence			**1832** Death of Goethe (born 1749)
1833 Death of Rammohan Roy (b.1772), father of modern Indian nationalism	**1833** Formation of German customs union *(Zollverein)*			**1833** First regulation of industrial working conditions (Britain)
		1835 'Great Trek' of Boer colonists from Cape, leading to foundation of Republic of Natal (1839), Orange Free State (1848) and Transvaal (1849)		**1834** First mechanical reaper patented (US)
				1836 Needfle-gun invented (Prussia), making breech-loading possible
			1840 Britain annexes New Zealand	**1837** Pitman's shorthand invented
				1838 First electric telegraph (Britain)
1842 Opium War: Britain annexes Hong Kong				**1840** First postage stamp (Britain)
1843 British conquer Sind				
1845-9 British conquest of Punjab and Kashmir	**1845** Irish famine stimulates hostility to Britain and emigration to US		**1845** Texas annexed by US	
	1846 Britain repeals Corn Laws and moves towards complete free trade		**1846** Mexican War begins: US conquers New Mexico and California (1848)	
	1848 Revolutionary movements in Europe; proclamation of Second Republic in France		**1846** Oregon treaty delimits US-Canadian boundary	**1848 Communist Manifesto** issued by Marx (1818-83) and Engels (1820-95)
1850 T'ai-p'ing rebellion in China – (to 1864), with immense loss of life			**1850** Australian colonies and (1856) New Zealand granted responsible government	**1849** Death of Chopin (b.1810); apogee of Romantic music with Berlioz (1803-69), Liszt (1811-86), Wagner (1813-83), Brahms (1833-97), Verdi (1813-1901)
1853 First railway and telegraph lines in India	**1852** Fall of French republic; Louis Napoleon (Napoleon III, 1808-73) becomes French emperor	**1853** Livingstone's explorations begin		**1851** Great Exhibition in London
1854 Perry forces Japan to open trade with US	**1854** Crimean War (to 1856)			**1853** Haussmann begins rebuilding of Paris

Asia

1857 Indian Mutiny

1858 Treaty of Tientsin: further Treaty Ports opened to foreign trade in China

1860 Treaty of Peking: China cedes Ussuri region to Russia

1863 France establishes protectorate over Cambodia, Cochin China (1865), Annam (1874), Tonkin (1885) and Laos (1893)

1868 End of Tokugawa Shogunate and Meiji Restoration in Japan

1877 Queen Victoria proclaimed Empress of India

1879 Second Afghan War gives Britain control of Afghanistan

1885 Foundation of Indian National Congress

1886 British annex Upper Burma

1887 French establish Indo-Chinese Union

1891 Construction of Trans-Siberian railway begun

1894-5 Sino-Japanese War: Japan occupies Formosa

1898 Abortive "Hundred Days" reform in China

1900 Boxer uprising in China

1904 Partition of Bengal: nationalist agitation in India

1904-5 Russo-Japanese War; Japanese success stimulates Asian nationalism

Europe

1859 Sardinian-French war against, Austria; Piedmont acquires Lombardy (1860): **unification of Italy begins**

1861 Emancipation of Russian serfs

1864 Prussia defeats Denmark: annexes Schleswig-Holstein (1866)

1864 Russia suppresses Polish revolt

1866 Prussia defeats Austria

1867 Establishment of North German confederation and of dual monarchy in Austria-Hungary

1870 Franco-Prussian war

1871 Proclamation of German Empire, beginning of Thirs French Republic: suppression of Paris commune

1875 Growth of labour/socialist parties: Germany (1875), Belgium (1885), Holland (1877), Britain (1893), Russia (1898)

1878 Treaty of Berlin: Romania, Montenegro and Serbia become independent, Bulgaria autonomous

1879 Dual alliance between Germany and Austria-Hungary

1890 Dismissal of Bismarck; Wilhelm II begins new course

1894 Franco-Russian alliance

1898 Germany embarks on naval building programme; beginning of German 'world policy'

1904 Anglo-French entente

1905 Revolution in Russia, followed by T sarist concessions

1905 Norway independent of Sweden

Africa

1860 French expansion in West Africa from Senegal

1869 Suez Canal opens

1875 Disraeli buys Suez Canal Company shares to ensure British control of sea route to India

1881 French occupy Tunisia

1882 Revolt in Egypt leading to British occupation

1884 Germany acquires SW Africa, Togoland, Cameroons

1885 King of Belgium acquires Congo

1886 Germany and Britain partition East Africa

1886 Goldl discovered in Transvaal; foundation of Johannesburg

1889 British South Africa company formed by Cecil Rhodes, begins colonisation of Rhodesia (1890)

1896 Battle of Adowa: Italians defeated by Ethiopians

1989 Fashoda crisis between Britain and France

1899 Boer War begins

1900 Copper-mining begins in Katanga

Americas and Australasia

1861 Outbreak of American Civil War

1864 War of Paraguay against Argentina, Brazil and Uruguay (to 1870

1865 End of American Civil War; slavery abolished in US

1867 Russia sells Alaska to US

1867 Dominion of Canada established

1869 Prince Rupert's Land, Manitoba (1870) and British Columbia (1871) join Canada

1876 Porfirio Diaz (1830-1915) gains control of Mexico (to 1911)

1879 War of the Pacific (Chile, Bolivia, Peru)

1885 Completion of Canadian Pacific railway

1898 Spanish-American war: US annexes Guam, Puerto Rico and Philippines

1901 Unification of Australis as Commonwealth

1903 Panama Canal Zone ceded to US

Culture and technology

1856 Bessemer process permits mass-production of steel

1859 Darwin publishes *The Origin of Species*

1859 First oil well drilled (Pennsylvania, US)

c.1860 Great age of European novel: Dickens (1812-70), Dumas (1802-70), Flaubert (1821-80), Turgenev (1818-83), Dostoyevsky (1821-81), Tolstoy (1828-1910)

1861 Pasteur evolves germ theory of disease

1861 Women first given vote (Australia)

1863 First underground railway (London)

1864 Foundation of Red Cross (Switzerland)

1867 Marx publishes *Das Kapital* (vol. 1)

1869 First trans-continental railroad completed (US)

1870 Declaration of Papal infallibility

1874 First electric tram (New York); telephone patented by Bell (US 1876) first electric streetlighting (London 1878)

1874 Emergence of Impressionist school of painting: Monet (1840-1926), Renois (1841-1919), Degas (1834-1917)

1878 First oil tanker built (Russia)

1879 F.W. Woolworth opened first '5 and 10 cent store'

1882 First hydro-electric plant (Wisconsis, US)

1884 Maxim gun perfected

c.1885 Daimler and Benz pioneer the automobile (Germany)

1888 Dunlop invents pneumatic tyre

c.1890 Beginnings of modern literature in Japan on western models

c.1890 Europe - realistic drama: Ibsen (1828-1906), Strindberg (1849-1912), Chekhov (1860-1904), Shaw (1856-1950)

1895 Röntgen discovers X-rays (Germany); Marconi invents wireless telegraphy (Italy); first public showing of motion picture (France)

1896 Herzl publishes *The Jewish State* calling for Jewish National Home

1898 Pierre and Marie Curie observe radioactivity and idolate radium (France)

1899 Howard's *Garden Cities of Tomorrow* initiates modern city plannins

1900 Planck evolves quantum theory (Germany)

1900 Freud's *Interpretation of Dreams,* beginning of psychoanalysis (Austria)

1903 First successful flight of petrol-powered aircraft (Wright Brothers, US)

1905 Einstein's theory of relativity (Germany)

Asia

1906 Revolution in Persia

1910 Japan annexes Korea

1911 Chinese Revolution: Sun Yat-sen first President of new republic

1914 German concessions in China and Colonies in Pacific taken over by Japan, Australia and New Zealand

1917 'Balfour Declaration' promises Jews a National Home in Palestine

1919 Amritsar incident; upsurge of Indian nationalism
1919 May 4th movement in China; upsurge of Chinese nationalism

1920 Mustafa Kemal (Atatürk) leads resistance to partition of Turkey; Turkish Nationalist movement
1921 Reza Khan becomes leader and takes power in Persia, becomes Shah (1925) and introduces reform
1921-2 Washington Conference attempts to regulate situation in East Asia
1922 Greek army expelled from Turkey; last Ottoman sultan deposed; republic proclaimed (1923)

1926 Chiang Kai-shek (1886-1975) begins reunification of China

1931 Japanese occupy Manchuria
1932 Kingdom of Saudi Arabia formed by Ibn Saud

1934 'Long March' of Chinese Communists begins

1936 Japan signs anti-Comintern pact with Germany
1936 Arab revolt in Palestine against Jewish immigration
1937 Beginning of full-scale war between Japan and China

1941 Japan attacks US at Pearl Harbor

1942 Japan overruns SE Asia
1942 Battle of Midway; US halts Japanese expansion

1945 US drops atom bombs on Japan, forcing surrender
1946 Civil War in China (to 1949)
1946 Beginning of Vietnamese struggle against France (to 1954)
1947 India and Pakistan independent

1948 Establishment of state of Israel; first Arab-Israeli war
1949 Communist victory in China
1949 Indonesia independent
1950 Korean War begins

Europe

1907 Anglo-Russian entente

1908 Young Turk revolution: Ottoman sultan deposed
1908 Bulgaria becomes independent; Austria annexes Bosnia and Herzegovina

1912-13 Balkan wars
1914 Outbreak of First World War

1917 Revolution in Russia: Tsar abdicates (March), Bolsheviks take over (Nov); **first socialist state established**
1918 Germany and Austria-Hungary sue for armistice: end of First World War
1918 Civil war and foreign intervention in Russia
1919 Paris treaties redraw map of Europe
1919 World-wide influenza epidemic reaches Europe

1920 League of Nations established (headquarters Geneva)

1922 Mussolini takes power in Italy
1922 Irish Free State (Eire) created
1923 French occupy Ruhr; runaway inflation in Germany
1924 Death of Lenin

1925 Locarno treaties stabilise frontiers in West
1926 General Strike in Britain
1926 Salazar takes power in Portugal
1928 First Five-Year Plan and collectivisation of agriculture in Russia

1931 Spain becomes a Republic

1933 Hitler made Chancellor in Germany; beginning of Nazi revolution

1936 German reoccupation of Rhineland
1936 Spanish Civil War begins

1938 Germany occupies Austria
1938 Munich conference: dismemberment of Czechoslovakia
1939 German-Soviet non-aggression pact; Germany invades Poland; **Britain and France declare war on Germany**
1940 Germany overruns Norway, Denmark, Belgium, Netherlands, France;
1940 Battle of Britain
1941 Germany invades Russia; declares war on US

1943 German VI army surrenders at Stalingrad; Italian capitulation
1944 Anglo-American landing in Normandy; Russians advance in E. Europe
1945 Yalta Conference, **beginning of Cold War**
1945 Defeat of Germany and suicide of Hitler

1947 Intensification of Cold War; Truman Doctrine enunciated
1947 Greek Civil War (to 1949)
1947 Marshall Plan for economic reconstruction in Europe
1948 Communist take over in Czechoslovakia and Hungary; Berlin Airlift
1949 Formation of NATO alliance

Africa

1908 Belgian state takes over Congo from King Leopold

1910 Formation of Union of South Africa

1911 Italy conquers Libya

1914 Britain proclaims protectorate over Egypt
1914-15 French and British conquer German colonies except German East Africa

1919 Nationalist revolt in Egypt

1921 Battle of Anual: Spanish army defeated by Moroccans

1926 Revolt of Abd-el Krim crushed in Morocco

1934 Italian suppression of Senussi resistance in Libya
1935 Italy invades Ethiopia

1936 Anglo-Egyptian alliance; British garrison in Suez Canal Zone

1940-1 Italian expelled from Somalia, Eritrea and Ethiopia

1941 Germans conquer Cyrenaica and advance into Egypt (1942)

1942 Battle of el-Alamein; German defeat and retreat
1942 Anglo-American landings in Morocco and Algeria

1949 Apartheid programme inaugurated in S. Africa

Americas and Australasia

1907 New Zealand acquires dominion status

1910 Mexican revolution begins

1914 Panama Canal opens

1917 US declares war on Central Powers

1918 President Wilson announces 'Fourteen Points'

1920 US refuses to ratify Paris treaties and withdraws into isolation

1921 US restricts immigration

1923 General Motors established: world's largest manufacturing company

1929 Wall Street Crash precipitates world Depression
1930 Military revolution in Brazil; Vargas becomes president
1932 Chaco War between Bolivia and Paraguay (to 1935)
1933 US President Franklin D. Roosevelt introduces New Deal

1935 Cárdenas president of Mexico: land redistribution and (1938) nationalisation of oil
1936 Pan-American congress; US proclaims good neighbour policy

1939 US proclaims neutrality in European War

1941 US begins 'lend-lease' to Britain
1941 US enters war against Germany and Japan

1944 Peron comes to power in Argentina

1945 United Nations established (headquarters New York)

1948 Organisation of American States established

1951 Australia, New Zeland and US sign Anzus Pact

Culture and technology

1907 Exhibition of Cubist paintings in Paris: Picasso (1881-1973), Braque (1882-1963)

1910 Development of abstract painting: Kandinsky (1866-1944), Mondrian (1872-1944)
1910 Development of plastics

1913 Henry Ford develops conveyor belt assembly for production of Model T automobile (Detroit, US)
1916 First birth control advice centre opened (New York)
1917 First use of massed tanks (Battle of Cambrai)

1919 Rutherford (1871-1937) slits atom (UK)
1919 Bauhaus school of design started by Gropius at Weimar (Germany)
1919 First crossing of Atlantic by air
1920 First general radio broadcasts (US and UK)
c.1920 Emergence of jazz in US: Louis Armstrong (1900-71), Duke Ellington (1899-1974), Count Basie (1904-1984)

1923 Development of tuberculosis vaccine (France)
1924 Thomas Mann (1875-1955) publishes *The Magic Mountain*
1925 Franz Kafka (1883-1924) publishes *The Trial*; Adolf Hitler publishes *Mein Kampf*
1927 Emergence of talking pictures. Rise of great film makers: D.W. Griffith (1874-1948), Chaplin (1889-1977), John Ford (1895-1973), Eisenstein (1896-1948), Clair (1898-1981), Hitchcock (1899-1980), Disney (1901-66)

1936 First regular public television transmission (UK)

1937 Jet engine first tested (UK)
1937 Invention of nylon (USA)

1939 Development of penicillin (UK)
1939 Development of DDT (Switzerland)

1942 Fermi builds first nuclear reactor (US)

1945 Atom bomb first exploded (US)

1946 First electronic computer built (US)

1947 First supersonic flight (US)

1948 Transistor invented (US)

1951 First nuclear power stations (US and UK)

Asia

1954 Geneva conference: Laos, Cambodia and Vietnam become independent states
1955 Bandung Conference
1956 Second Arab-Israeli war

1957 Civil war in Vietnam

1960 Sino-Soviet dispute begins

1961 Increasing US involvement in Vietnam

1962 Sino-Indian war

1965 Indo-Pakistan war
1965 Military take-over in Indonesia
1966 Cultural Revolution in China
1967 Third Arab-Israeli war (Six-Day War)

1971 People's Republic of China joins UN
1971 Indo-Pakistan war leads to break-away of East Pakistan (Bangladesh)
1973 US forces withdraw from South Vietnam
1973 Fourth Arab-Israeli war

1975 Civil war in Lebanon: Syria invades (1976)
1975 Communists take over Vietnam, Laos and Cambodia
1976 Death of Mao-Tse Tund; political re-orientation and modernisation under Deng Xiao-Ping
1977 President Sadat visits Jerusalem; Egypt/Israeli peace talks culminating in Camp David Peace Treaty (1978)
1977 Pakistan military coup by Zia ul-Haq
1979 Fall of Shah of Iran, establishment of Islamic Republic under Ayatollah Khomeini
1979 Afghanistan invaded by USSR
1979 Sino-Vietnamese War
1979 Vietnam invades Cambodia expelling Khmer Rouge government
1980 Military coup in Turkey, power assumed by General Evren
1980 Outbreak of Iran/Iraq War. Ceasefire 1988

1982 Israel invades Lebanon, expulsion of PLO from Beirut
1982 Israel withdraws from Sinai peninsula
1984 Indira Gandhi assassinated

1985 Israel withdraws from all of Lebanon, other than 'buffer zone' in south
1988 Palestinian uprising (intifada) against Israeli-occupied territories. PLO recognises state of Israel
1988 President Zia of Pakistan killed in air crash. Benazir Bhutto becomes President after democratic elections
1989 Withdrawal of Soviet troops from Afghanistan
1989 Death of Emperor Hiroito of Japan. Succeded by son Akihito
1989 Death of Ayatollah Khomeini
1989 Student pro-democracy demonstration crushed in Peking

1990 Iraq invades Kuwait
1991 The Gulf War: UN Coalition forces led by US attack Iraq and liberate Kuwait

Europe

1953 Death of Stalin

1955 Warsaw Pact signed
1956 Polish revolt, Gomulka in power; Hungarian revolt crushed by Russian
1957 **Treaty of Rome: Formation of European Economic Community** and (1959) of European Free Trade Association
1958 Fifth Republic in France: de Gaulle first President

1961 East Germans build Berlin Wall

1968 Liberalisation in Czechoslovakia halted by Russian invasion
1969 Outbreak of violente in N. Ireland
1970 Polish-German treaty; de facto recognition of existing frontiers

1973 Britain, Eire Denmark join EEC
1974 End of dictatorship in Portugal
1974 Turkish invasion of Cyprus
1975 Death of Franco; end of dictatorship in Spain
1975 European Security Conference, Helsinki; recognition by W. Germany of post-war states of E. Germany and Poland

1977 Democratic election held in Spain, first in 40 years

1980 Death of Marshal Tito
1980 Creation of independent Polish trade union Solidarity; martial law (1981)

1981 Mitterand elected 1st Socialist President of France since World War II
1981 Widespread demonstrations against stationing of further nuclear missiles in Europe
1981 Greece joins EEC
1981 IRA hunger strikers die in Northern Ireland
1982 Death of USSR President Brezhnev, succession of Y. Andropov

1984 Death of Andropov, succession of K. Chernenko as USSR leader (d. 1985)
1985 Gorbachov leader of USSR
1986 Spain and Portugal join EEC
1988 USSR moves towards greater freedom of information and debate (glasnost), and industrial and social re-structuring (perestroika)
1989 Democratic elections for the People's Congress held in USSR. Poland and Hungary move towards political pluralism
1989 A wave of popular protest topples Communist regimes in E. Germany, Czechoslovakia, Bulgaria and Romania (Ceausescu executed)
1989 Berlin Wall demolished
1989-90 Nationalist feelings in USSR lead to demands for secession of republics. Lithuania declares independence
1990 Communal massacres in Armenia and Azerbaijan
1990 **Unification of Germany**
1990 British prime minister Margaret Thatcher resigns

Africa

1952 Beginning of Mau Mau rebellion in Kenya
1952 Military revolt in Egypt; proclamation of republic (1953)
1954 Beginnings of nationalist revolt in Algeria

1956 Suez crisis: Anglo-French invasion of Canal Zone
1957 Beginning of **decolonisation in sub-Saharan Africa:** Gold Coast (Ghana) becomes independent

1960 'Africa's year'; many states become independent; outbreak of civil war in Belgian Congo
1961 South Africa becomes independent republic

1962 Algeria becomes independent

1965 Rhodesia declares itself independent of Britain

1967 Civil war in Nigeria (secession of Biafra) (to 1970)

1974 Emperor Haile Selasse deposed by Marxist Junta
1975 Portugal grants independence to Mozambique and Angola

1976 Morocco and Mauritania partition Spanish Sahara
1976 Establishment of Transkei, first Bantustan in S. Africa

1979 Tanzanian forces invade Uganda, and expel President Amin

1980 Black majority rule established in Zimbabwe (Rhodesia)

1981 President Sadat of Egypt assassinated

1984 Famine in the Sahel and Ethiopia; continuing war against secession
1985 Civil unrest amongst blacks and coloureds in South Africa, 'State of Emergency' declared, suspending civil rights and press freedom.
1986 President Machel of Mozambique dies in aircraft
1986 US bombs Libya in retaliation for terrorist activities

1989 UN peace-keeping forces control Namibian move to independence (independent 1990)

1990 S. African government moves towards accomodation with ANC. Mandela released
1991 S. African prime minister De Klerk announces intention to dismantle Apartheid policies

Americas and Australasia

1959 Cuban Revolution

1962 Cuba missile crisis
1963 President Kennedy assassinated
1964 US Civil Rights Bill inaugurates President Johnson's 'Great Society' programme
1966 Eruption of Black American discontent; growth of Black Power

1968 Assassination of Martin Luther King

1970 Allende elected president of Chile (killed 1973)
1971 US initiates policy of detente with China and USSR
1971 USA abandons the Gold Standard and depreciates the dollar
1973 **Major recession in US**

1974 President Nixon resigns following Watergate affair

1979 Civil War in Nicaragua, President Somoza overthrown
1979 Military junta established, continuing civil war (El Salvador)

1980 Ronald Reagan President of USA

1982 Argentina occupies South Georgia and Falkland Is.; surrenders to UK Task Force June 15th
1983 Democracy restored in Argentina
1983 Coup in Grenada; US invades

1985 Democracy restored in Brazil and Uruguay

1987 INF treaty between USSR and USA providing for elimination, over a three-year period, of all intermediate-range land-based nuclear weapons held by two nations

1989 George Bush President of USA
1989-90 US military intervention in Panama; arrest of President Noriega
1990 Democratic elections in Nicaragua end Sandinista rule

Culture and technology

1952 Contraceptive pill developed (US)

1956 Beginning of rock and roll musid (US): Elvis Presley (1935-77)
1957 First space satellite launched (USSR)

1961 First in space: Gagarin (USSR)
1961 Structure of DNA molecule (genetic code) determined (UK)
1962 Second Vatican Council reforms Catholic liturgy and dogma
1964 Publication of Thoughts of Chairman Mao

1968 World-wide student protest movement
1969 First man lands on moon: Armstrong (US)

1976 1st supersonic transatlantic passenger service begins with Concorde

1978 Election of John Paul II, first Polish pope

1980s Computer revolution: spread of computers in offices and homes in the Western world
1980s Spread of Acquired Immune Deficiency Syndrome (AIDS) throughout Africa, Europe and North
1981 First re-usable shuttle space flight (USA)

1986 Launch of world's first permanently-manned space station (USSR)
1986 Chernobyl nuclear power station in Ukraine in scene of world's worst nuclear disaster
1987 UN estimates world population at 5 billion
1988 Global recognition that the ozone layer is being depleted. Moves to ban CFCs (chlorofluoro-carbons), thought to be responsible, initiated. Global ban agreed (1990)

1989 Rushdie (British author) condemned to death for blasphemy by Khomeini
1990 Voyager space probe mission completed; last planetary encounter (Neptune)
1991 Kuwait oil fires started by Iraqi forces threaten S.W. Asian environment

The geographical background to world history

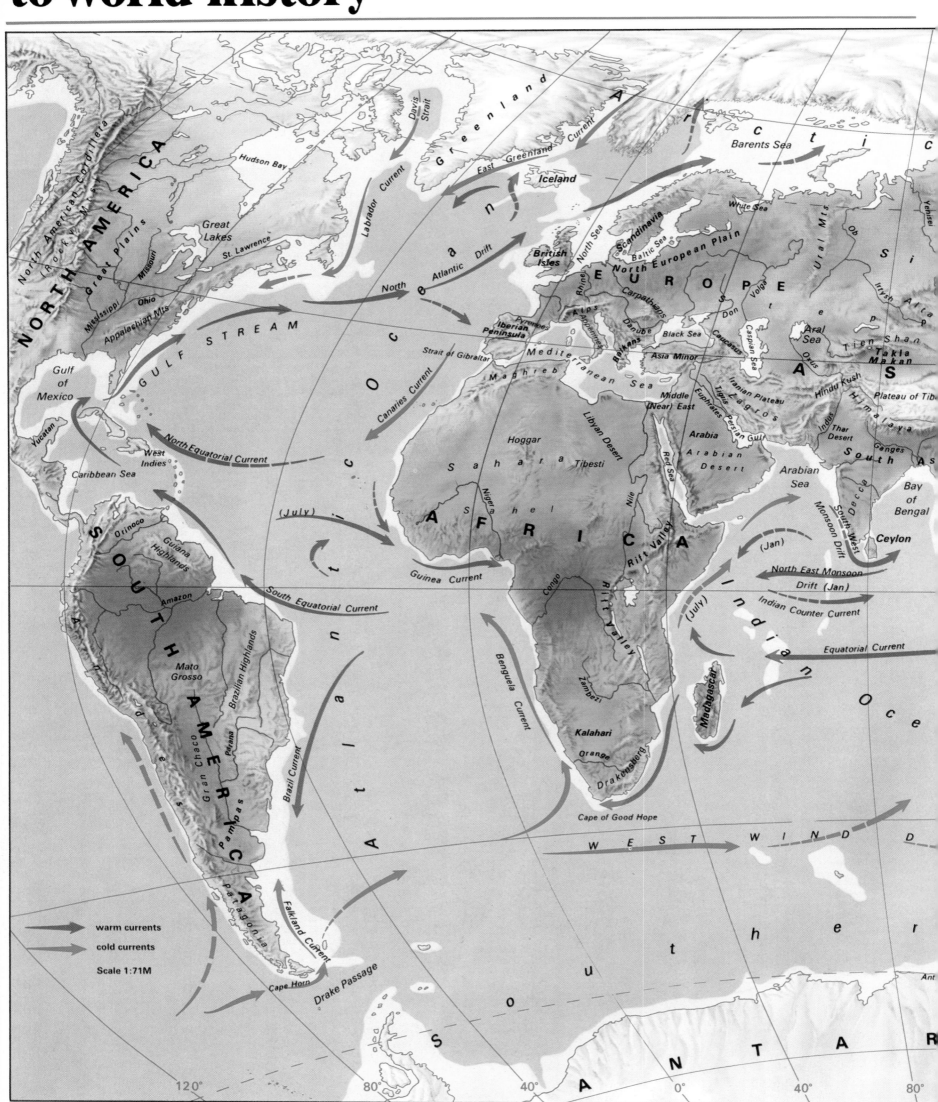

North America · (Rocky Mountains) North American Cordillera · Hudson Bay · Great Lakes · Great Plains · St. Lawrence · Missouri · Mississippi · Ohio · Appalachian Mts · Gulf of Mexico · Yucatan · West Indies · Caribbean Sea · Davis Strait · Greenland · East Greenland Current · Labrador Current · Iceland · North Atlantic Drift · British Isles · North Sea · Scandinavia · Baltic Sea · EUROPE · North European Plain · Rhine · Alps · Carpathians · Appennines · Danube · Balkans · Iberian Peninsula · Pyrenees · Strait of Gibraltar · Mediterranean Sea · Asia Minor · Black Sea · Caucasus · Caspian Sea · Don · Volga · Ural Mts · Aral Sea · Oxus · Tien Shan · Takla Makan · ASIA · Barents Sea · White Sea · Arctic Ocean · Ob · Yenisei · Irtysh · Steppe · Siberia

GULF STREAM · North Atlantic Ocean · Canaries Current · North Equatorial Current · (July) · South Equatorial Current · Guinea Current · AFRICA · Maghreb · Sahara · Hoggar · Libyan Desert · Tibesti · Niger · Sahel · Nile · Red Sea · Arabia · Arabian Desert · Iranian Plateau · Middle (Near) East · Euphrates · Tigris · Persian Gulf · Zagros · Hindu Kush · Himalaya · Plateau of Tibet · Indus · Thar Desert · Ganges · Arabian Sea · Deccan · South ASIA · Bay of Bengal · Ceylon · Monsoon Drift · South West · North East Monsoon Drift (Jan) · (Jan) · Indian Counter Current · Equatorial Current · Indian Ocean

SOUTH AMERICA · Orinoco · Guiana Highlands · Amazon · Andes · Mato Grosso · Brazilian Highlands · Gran Chaco · Parana · Pampas · Patagonia · Brazil Current · Falkland Current · Cape Horn · Drake Passage · Congo · Zambezi · Rift Valley · Benguela Current · Kalahari · Orange · Drakensberg · Cape of Good Hope · Madagascar · (July) · WEST WIND DRIFT · Southern Ocean · ANTARCTICA

warm currents
cold currents

Scale 1:71M

120° · 80° · 40° · 0° · 40° · 80°

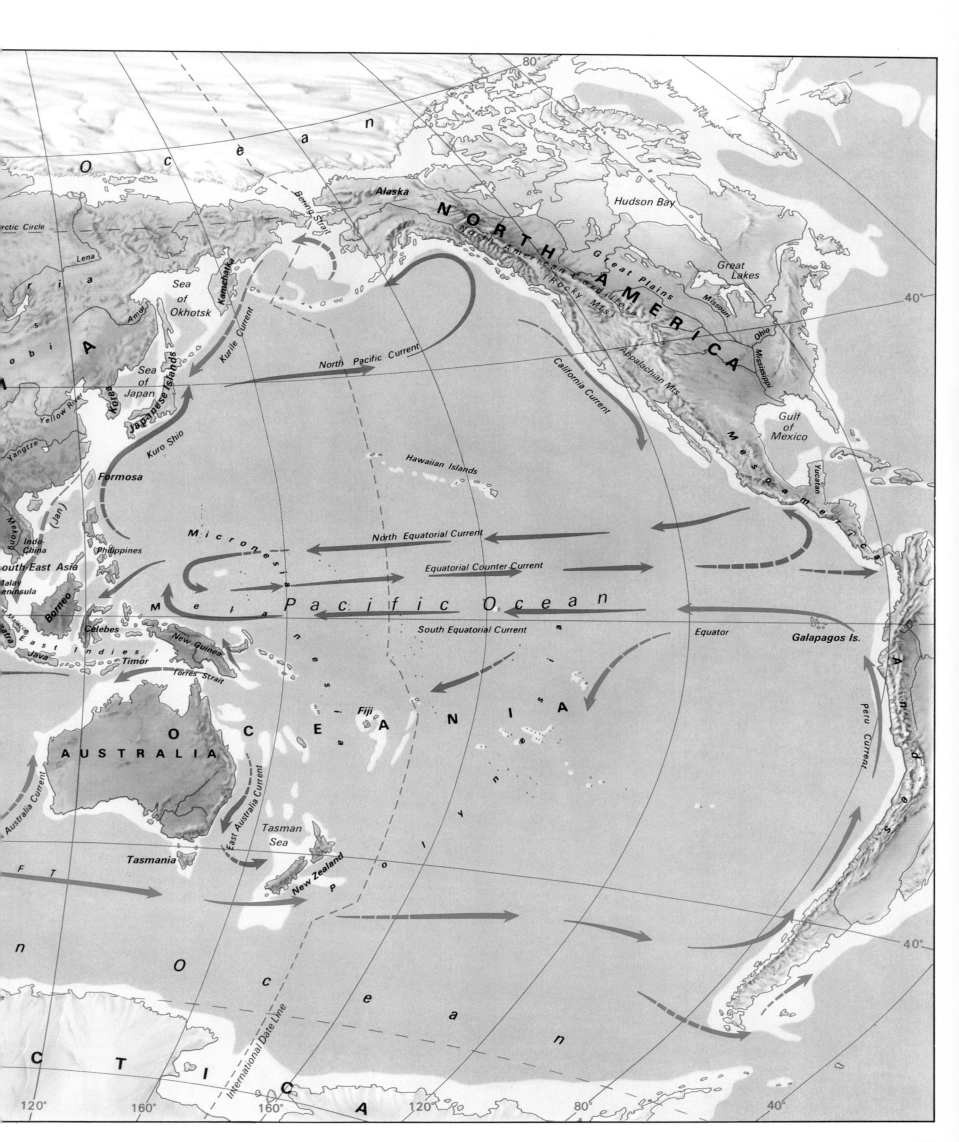

Arctic Circle

O c e a n

Lena

A

Amur

Sea
of
Okhotsk

Kamchatka

Alaska

Bering Strait

NORTH AMERICA

Hudson Bay

Great Plains

Great
Lakes

Missouri

40°

Sea
of
Japan

Korea

Yellow River

Yangtze

Japanese Islands

Kurile Current

North Pacific Current

North American Cordillera (Rocky Mts.)

California Current

Appalachian Mts

Ohio

Mississippi

Kuro Shio

Formosa

Hawaiian Islands

Gulf
of
Mexico

Yucatan

Indo-
China

(Jan)

Philippines

Micronesia

North Equatorial Current

Mesoamerica

South-East Asia

Malay
Peninsula

Borneo

Melanesia

Equatorial Counter Current

Pacific Ocean

Celebes

New Guinea

South Equatorial Current

Equator

Galapagos Is.

East Indies

Java

Timor

Torres Strait

Indonesia

Fiji

O C E A N I A

AUSTRALIA

Polynesia

Australia Current

East Australia Current

Tasman
Sea

Tasmania

New Zealand

P

Andes

Peru Current

F T

n

O

c

International Date Line

e

a

n

40°

C T I C A

120°   160°   160°   120°   80°   40°

29

RECORDED history is only the tip of an iceberg reaching back through the millennia to the first appearance on earth of the species Man. Anthropologists, prehistorians and archaeologists have extended our vista of the past by tens and hundreds of thousands of years. We cannot understand human history without taking account of their findings. The transformation of Man (or, more accurately, of certain groups of men in certain areas) from a hunter and fisher to an agriculturist, and from a migratory to a sedentary life, is the most decisive revolution in the whole of human history. The climatic and ecological changes which made it possible have left their mark on the human record down to the present day. Agriculture not merely made possible a phenomenal growth of human population, which is thought to have increased some sixteen times between 8000 and 4000 BC; it also gave rise to the familiar landscape of village communities, which was still characteristic of Europe as late as the middle of the nineteenth century and even today prevails in most parts of the world. Nowhere are the continuities of history more visible. The enduring structures of human society, which transcend and outlive political change, carry us back through the centuries to the end of the Ice Age, to the changes which began when the shrinking ice-cap left a new world for Man to tame and conquer.

1

The world

Stonehenge, Salisbury Plain, Southern England

# of early Man

Human origins

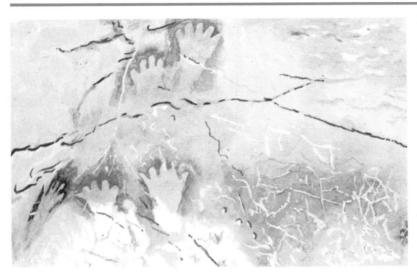

Handprints *(above)* painted by artists in the Pyrenean cave site of Gargas, France about 20,000 years ago. Paintings and engravings of animal and human subjects begin to appear in Europe, Africa, Australia and South America approximately 30,000 years ago. They reflect the activities of fully modern humans and their developing capacity for abstract thought.

2/Sites in Europe and western Asia *(below)* where fossilised human remains have been found. These sites date from c.700,000 to 14,000 years ago. The oldest (700,000–250,000 years old) are associated with the remains of an archaic form of *Homo sapiens* and the most recent (35,000–14,000 years old) with fully modern humans. Classic Neanderthals have been found at sites dating between 80,000 and 35,000 years old but some fossils with Neanderthal characteristics date back nearly 250,000 years.

WITHIN the animal kingdom, humans are most closely related to the living great apes (chimpanzees and gorillas) with whom they share the same basic anatomical structure and similar genetic make-up. These similarities were inherited from a common ancestor which, on the basis of fossil evidence and molecular research, is estimated to have lived about 10 million years ago. Stimulated perhaps by environmental change and other reasons which are still unknown, apes and humans diverged onto separate evolutionary courses between 5 and 8 million years ago. Through time, the characteristics of the common ancestor were retained or gradually changed to produce the species recognised today.

Fossilised bones and footprints show that the fundamental human adaptation of walking upright (bipedalism) on two legs had evolved in Africa by 4 million years ago. Remains were first discovered in southern Africa, mainly in the Transvaal, where they occur in the debris of former limestone caves, but the oldest known fossils which show the distinctive structure required for upright walking have been found in the Afar region of Ethiopia near Hadar. They belong to a group of early humans referred to as Australopithecines (southern apes). The Australopithecines show a combination of ape and human traits and were widespread in Africa until about 1.7 million years ago. At least four closely related species can be distinguished. It is possible that the oldest known gracile (lightly built) species *Australopithecus afarensis* may

have been ancestral to both the robust species *A. robustus* and *A. boisei* as well as the gracile form *A. africanus*. It is uncertain whether the gracile Australopithecines with their small brains, apelike faces and distinctive pelvic structure could have been ancestral to humans with their larger brains and characteristics more easily recognisable as those of our own family or genus, *Homo* (Man). It is equally feasible that Australopithecines and *Homo* represent distinct evolutionary lines stemming from a common ancestor which has not yet been recognised in the fossil record. Whichever hypothesis proves correct, the trend away from ape-like characteristics towards ever more modern attributes had certainly begun some time before 2 million years ago.

The oldest fossils attributable to the genus *Homo* have been found in East Africa in areas such as Olduvai Gorge in Tanzania and Koobi Fora in Kenya. The first fossil discovered at Olduvai was distinguished by its larger brain, rounded skull and distinctly human face. Although they vary in the extent of their similarities to Australopithecines and more modern humans, these fossils are all generally referred to a single species known as *Homo habilis*. This name means man the tool-maker. It reflects the fact that the fossils sometimes occur alongside simple, purpose-made stone tools which offer the first tangible evidence of the distinctive human ability to apply intelligence, think ahead and manipulate resources – achievements which, above all, distinguish humans from the rest of the animal Kingdom.

The trend towards more modern anatomical characteristics can be observed in African fossils dating from about 1.7 million to 200,000 years ago, which show changes in the size and shape of the skull to encase a larger, more developed brain. Indeed, the skeleton of a 12-year-old boy found at Nariokotome, Kenya, differs only slightly from that of a modern boy although it is 1.7 million years old. These fossils are currently referred to the species *Homo erectus*, a name first applied to fossils found in South-East Asia and China. This may be inappropriate as the Asian fossils from Java and sites such as Zhoukoudien in China have an unknown role in subsequent human evolution, as well as being younger and quite distinct from the African group. The latter group may be regarded as an archaic form of *Homo sapiens* (modern human) and it is from this stock that the first European populations may ultimately have stemmed.

The peopling of Europe probably began be-

tween 1 million and 700,000 years ago although the oldest sites with firm evidence of activity are about 500,000 years old. Fossilised human remains from sites such as Petralona, Mauer and Arago indicate that the people who adapted to the diverse environments of Europe were an early form of *Homo sapiens*. By about 250,000 years ago, this population was beginning to show the first signs of the characteristics which distinguish the species *Homo sapiens neanderthalensis* (Neanderthal Man). The Neanderthals were well established in Europe and western Asia between about 100,000 and 35,000 years ago. The heavily-set faces with large jaws and prominent brow ridges and the robust muscular bodies of the so-called 'classic' Neanderthals probably represent local differentiation of the early *Homo sapiens* stock and could be specialised adaptations to the cold climates of the last Ice Age.

For many years, the Neanderthals were thought to be ancestral to the first fully modern population in Europe as represented by the 30,000-year-old fossil skull from Cro-Magnon, which shows characteristics shared by all living people, such as a domed skull, flat forehead with small eyebrows, a distinct chin and rather puny skeleton. However, the discovery of much older fossils with modern characteristics, combined with the results of genetic research, suggest that modern people evolved in Africa between 100,000 and 200,000 years ago. Fossils of fully modern humans from Omo 1 in Ethiopia, Klasies River Mouth in South Africa and Qafzeh in Israel date from about 90,000 to 110,000 years ago and reflect the success and widespread dispersal of the new species. In Europe, fully modern humans seem to have replaced the Neanderthals about 35,000 years ago and it is thought that in Asia, too, older populations were replaced by modern people stemming ultimately from African stock. However, it remains to be seen whether this view will hold sway over the alternative hypothesis that *Homo sapiens sapiens* evolved separately and in parallel in both Africa and Asia.

Although a great deal remains to be discovered about their origins and dispersal, it is clear that modern humans occupied all the inhabited world by about 30,000 years ago. This included Australia which may first have been inhabited about 60,000 years ago by ancestors of the Aborigines, capable of building seacraft to cross a stretch of water at least 70 kilometres wide to reach a previously uninhabited continent. The Americas may also have been populated by waves of people periodically crossing the landbridge over the Bering Strait formed at intervals of low sea-level during the last Ice Age around 45,000, 30,000 and 20,000 years ago. Such dispersal and adaptation to new environments led to local differentiation reflected in the varying racial characteristics present within our species.

Throughout the period of human evolution from 2.5 million years to 10,000 years ago,

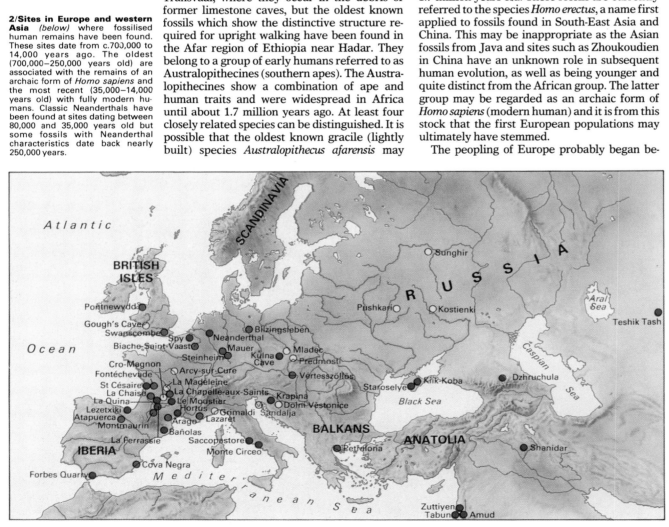

1/Traces of human origins *(right)* African, Asian and Australasian sites where important fossils of humans and ape and human ancestors have been discovered. Fossils from stratified deposits exposed by the formation of the Great East African Rift Valley which can be reliably dated, have proved particularly important in understanding human origins. The location of the remains suggests that the early humans lived away from the densely populated forests and inhabited the grasslands where a different range of resources could be exploited with less competition. A skull, discovered at Yayo in Chad, indicates that early populations also extended north of the tropics but the evidence is not forthcoming because geological conditions are less favourable for preservation or excavation.

people lived by various means of hunting and gathering but ethnicity or cultural distinctiveness is apparent in the ways in which they made different types of tools and weapons and eventually expressed themselves through the medium of art. Gradually, intelligence has made *Homo sapiens sapiens* the most successfully adapted species in the world.

The relationship between the different human species recognised from the fossil record *(right)* These relationships suggest that a trend towards modern characteristics was already apparent in African populations nearly 2 million years ago. In Asia, the ancestral relationships of *Homo erectus* and the emergence of fully modern people are less clearly understood.

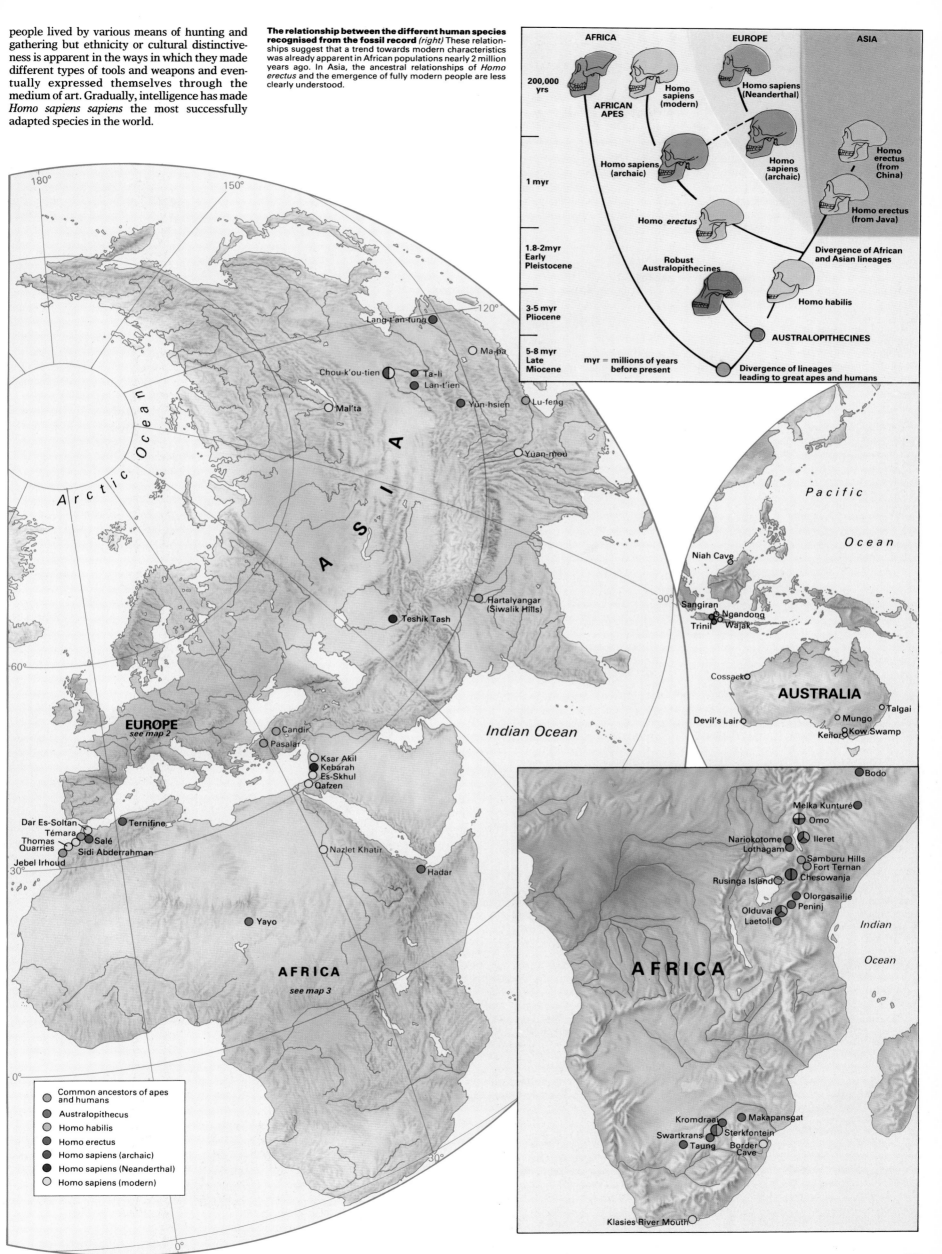

Hunters and gatherers: the economy of early Man

HUMANS capable of walking upright on two legs had evolved in Africa by 4 million years ago. The evolution of this capability involved major changes in the anatomy of the hips, legs and feet, which fundamentally remodelled the characteristics of the ape skeleton into that of the human. No such radical anatomical changes have occurred in the subsequent course of human evolution and there is no evidence to suggest that the first upright-walkers, the Australopithecines, led lives which were much different from the apes. Not having to move around on all-fours freed the hands to carry, make and use things, but this does not seem to have provided any real advantage until humans with larger, more complex, brains appeared about 2.5 million years ago. From this time forward, accumulations of stone tools and equipment made of less durable raw materials such as bone, antler, ivory, wood and leather indicate that humans were adapting successfully to widely different environments. It was as hunters and gatherers that people first colonised the earth.

Until the introduction of the first metal tools about 5000 years ago, people relied on stone artefacts for many of their daily tasks. Using stone tools, they could skin and butcher animals; dig up, cut or pulverise plant foods; cut reeds or strip bark for matting or baskets; and shape wood, bone and other raw materials into useful artefacts. It is the dependence on stone implements which has provided this earliest phase of human cultural development with the name Palaeolithic or Old Stone Age.

Millions of stone tools survived from the Old Stone Age and attest to the skills of the stoneworkers or 'knappers' who often had to work with intractable materials such as quartz, quartzite or lava cobbles. But whether they were using these materials or more suitable rocks, such as flint or obsidian which fracture with much greater regularity, the basic technique was the same. Having decided upon the size and shape of the required implement, the knapper would select a suitable nodule of stone from which to make it. (In Africa nearly 2 million years ago, raw materials were sometimes selected both from sources distant from the sites at which they were used, indicating that the capacity to think ahead and plan essential actions existed among early human groups there.) Using another stone as a hammer, the knapper would then strike off small pieces or 'flakes' from the nodule. Heavy-duty tools with strong, sharp edges could be made by removing flakes from both faces of the nodule by striking along one side, one end or all the way round the perimeter. This method was used to produce tools such as the choppers and hand-axes which formed an important component of many tool-kits in Africa and Europe until about 100,000 years ago. Light-duty tools were made from the flakes struck from the nodules which are then known as 'cores'. The sharp edges of such flakes could be used without any further modification but if stronger, purposefully-shaped and angled edges were required for specific tasks, the knapper would modify the flake by retouching it. This involved striking a series of tiny chips from the edge of the flake after it had been struck from the nodule. A great variety of tools were made in this way throughout the Stone Age and even into later prehistory and modern times.

At some sites, stone tools and the waste material from their manufacture, have remained undisturbed since they were dropped by their makers. Research on the distribution of the tools and their associations with bones, hearths or structures can give a very detailed picture of activities on a hunter-gatherer camp. Many camps were situated on open ground and some show evidence that the occupants built shelters as a home base and for protection. The oldest known shelter has been found at the 1.8 million-year-old site DK in Olduvai Gorge. It consists of a circle of stones about 4 metres across which is believed to have supported a brushwood superstructure. In addition to open sites, hunter-gatherers often took advantage of caves and rock overhangs for shelter and some of these were visisted over many millennia. Their stratified deposits provide numerous layers of information about human evolution and cultural change.

Although animal bones found with stone tools show that even the earliest tool-makers were meat-eaters, the tool-kits which survive contain no weapons, like spears or lance tips, for use in hunting and these are unknown until after about 200,000 years ago. There is a similar lack of hunting equipment in the stone assemblages predating about 35,000 years ago found in Asia and Europe and this has caused much speculation as to how early humans acquired their meat. It may be that early human groups made their weapons from organic materials which have not survived, but it seems more likely that for most of human prehistory people obtained meat by scavenging from the carcasses of animals which had died from natural causes, including those killed by other carnivores; by trapping small animals and birds; by stampeding large game into mires, over cliffs or into natural kraals and dispatching them at close range. These techniques were so successful that they persisted until between 100,000 and 35,000 years ago when the new technologies of the later Stone Age or 'Upper Palaeolithic' began to develop amongst groups of fully modern humans, *Homo sapiens sapiens*.

The stone tools of the Upper Palaeolithic were produced in a different way from those of the earlier period. Instead of using flakes, tools were made from long, narrow blades struck from nodules which had been deliberately shaped to form 'blade cores'. The artefacts produced by retouching these blades included stone tips for spears, and tools called burins used to make spear tips, spear-throwers, harpoons, fish-hooks, whistles and needles from bone, antler and ivory. These sophisticated weapons made both from stone and organic raw materials indicate that hunting had become a specialised activity, and consequently a more reliable way of acquiring a sufficient supply of meat. It also suggests that hunter-gatherer economies were becoming much more like those of recent times than their predecessors. This is confirmed by other aspects of their lifestyle which can be ascertained from the archaeological record. On the North European Plain and in the Soviet Union where caves were not available for shelter, well-organised campsites have been found to contain the foundations of substantial tents and structures made from mammoth bones. The practice of carefully burying the dead became widespread in Europe, Africa, Asia and in Australia during this period and like the art which also occurs throughout these regions, attests to an increasing capacity for abstract thought and activities beyond those essential for survival.

Between 100,000 and 10,000 years ago, fully modern humans, *Homo sapiens sapiens* colonised every continent except Antarctica. Their success was due to their capacity to adapt their hunter-gatherer lifestyle to different environments. In some areas the adaptation was so successful that the lifestyle changed little over many millennia. In Europe, where the retreat of the ice sheets of the last glaciation brought a gradual shift to warmer conditions and the frozen plains of the north were replaced by large areas of forest, there were similar shifts in the lifestyle of the hunter-gatherers. Blades were snapped and retouched to produce tiny inserts or 'microliths' which could be hafted in groups to produce tools and armatures for weapons. The use of the bow and arrow became widespread,

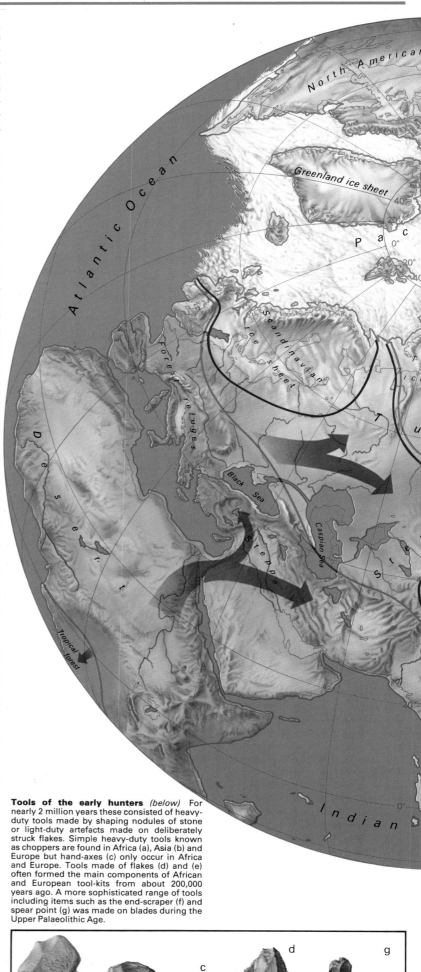

Tools of the early hunters *(below)* For nearly 2 million years these consisted of heavy-duty tools made by shaping nodules of stone or light-duty artefacts made on deliberately struck flakes. Simple heavy-duty tools known as choppers are found in Africa (a), Asia (b) and Europe but hand-axes (c) only occur in Africa and Europe. Tools made of flakes (d) and (e) often formed the main components of African and European tool-kits from about 200,000 years ago. A more sophisticated range of tools including items such as the end-scraper (f) and spear point (g) was made on blades during the Upper Palaeolithic Age.

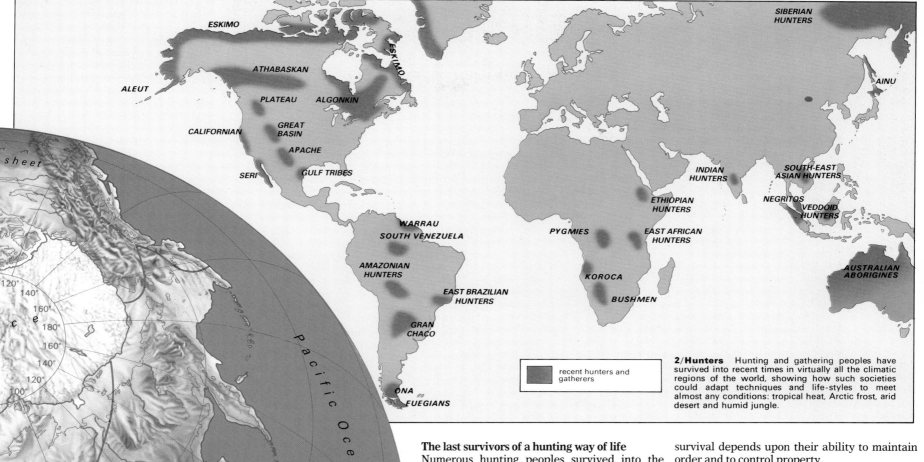

ESKIMO
ATHABASKAN
ALEUT
PLATEAU
ALGONKIN
CALIFORNIAN
GREAT
BASIN
APACHE
SERI
GULF TRIBES
ESKIMO

SIBERIAN
HUNTERS
AINU
INDIAN
HUNTERS
SOUTH-EAST
ASIAN HUNTERS
ETHIOPIAN
HUNTERS
NEGRITOS
VEDDOID
HUNTERS
PYGMIES
EAST AFRICAN
HUNTERS
KOROCA
AUSTRALIAN
ABORIGINES
BUSHMEN

WARRAU
SOUTH VENEZUELA
AMAZONIAN
HUNTERS
EAST BRAZILIAN
HUNTERS
GRAN
CHACO
ONA
FUEGIANS

recent hunters and
gatherers

2/Hunters Hunting and gathering peoples have survived into recent times in virtually all the climatic regions of the world, showing how such societies could adapt techniques and life-styles to meet almost any conditions: tropical heat, Arctic frost, arid desert and humid jungle.

120°
140°
160°
180°
160°
140°
120°
100°

sheet
ice
tundra
Coniferous
forest
Sea of
Japan
Khash
Desert
Tarim Basin
Oriental
forest
Pacific Ocean
Ocean

The last survivors of a hunting way of life

Numerous hunting peoples survived into the 19th and early 20th centuries long enough to be studied by ethnologists and anthropologists, both physical and social, but today the hunting and gathering way of life is only fully represented by the pygmies, the bushmen, the eskimos and the Australian aborigines, between them totalling only a few hundreds of thousands out of a total world population of nearly four thousand million. Nevertheless, they provide a unique and precious insight into Man's earlier way of life.

Recent studies reveal the intimacy of the relationship between hunting peoples and their natural environments; the relative simplicity of the material culture (only 94 different items exist among the Kung bushmen); the lack of accumulation of individual wealth; the mobility. The units of society, the bands or hordes, are small: groups of kinfolk and their friends who can live and work well together. Recent work contradicts the traditional view of hunting life as 'nasty, brutish and short', as a constant struggle against a harsh environment. In fact, bushmen's subsistence requirements are satisfied by only a modest effort – perhaps two or three days work a week by each adult; they do not have to struggle over food resources; their attitudes towards ownership are flexible and their living groups open. Such features set hunters and gatherers apart from more technologically developed societies whose very survival depends upon their ability to maintain order and to control property.

Evidence suggests that hunting and gathering communities often have a high percentage of old people, and that life expectancy is not necessarily short; population control is not, as is often thought, only or even mainly through high infant or child mortality, but also through long intervals between births, perhaps in part due to the long periods of breastfeeding of the infant. Indeed many hunting groups have proved highly adept at population control – not merely in the crude sense of restricting numbers, but in preserving and developing desirable social characteristics, while endeavouring to prevent (often by forced celibacy) the passing on of any personal defects that might prevent a member playing a full part in his or her small community.

Such communities frequently show great robustness and resilience in the face of normal hazards. Illness, accident, climatic change or the migration of food supplies can all be met from within the resources of the group. It is usually outside intruders, especially those introducing modern methods and economic attitudes (not to mention diseases) who shatter the delicate but essential ecological balance between the hunters and their environment. Unfortunately, given the ubiquity of contemporary technology, it seems unlikely that these life-styles will be left free to survive for more than another generation or so.

1/Hunters colonise the world *(above)* Over the last 2.5 million years, two major population dispersals have occurred. The first led to the appearance of the earliest human populations outside Africa in Europe and possibly Asia. Later, between about 200,000 and 10,000 years ago, fully modern people spread out through all the inhabitable regions of the world. Their dispersal was assisted by the expansion of ice-sheets during the last Ice Age which locked up vast quantities of water, lowering sea levels to expose land bridges and shorten sea crossings, enabling people to cross into the Americas, Japan, New Guinea and Australia. The arrows indicate the probable directions of this dispersal.

coastline at the height of the last glaciation (Ice Age), 20,000 years ago

modern coastline and rivers

Limits of human occupation in:

lower Palaeolithic (to 100,000 years ago)

middle Palaeolithic (100,000 to 40,000 years ago)

upper Palaeolithic (40,000 to 10,000 years ago)

dogs were domesticated and special equipment for fishing, including leisters, nets, harpoons, fish-hooks and basket traps came into use.

The success of the hunter-gatherers depended on intelligence and manual dexterity, as well as the ability to co-operate with, and rely upon, one another. By the time the last Ice Age came to an end around 10,000 BC modern man was one of the world's most widespread and successful species.

The art of the hunters

One of the most striking achievements of the period between 30,000 and 6000 BC was its art – cave paintings, engravings and sculptures. Animals predominate: human forms are rarely rendered with the same naturalism as the carefully observed wildlife. It seems likely that these early creative imaginings were in part a form of hunting magic, helping either to control and capture the objects of the hunt or to increase the amount of game. Perhaps they also provided a way of illustrating myths and traditions, forming a 'backdrop' for sacred and ritual purposes, or sometimes just enlivening and brightening everyday life. Whatever the impetus, it developed early in the history of *Homo sapiens sapiens* and spread almost everywhere people were able to make a living by hunting. This picture dates from c.6000 BC and shows a communal hunt for red deer. It adorns a rock-face in the Cueva de los Caballos, near Castellón in Spain. Such scenes, as opposed to representations of individual animals, are rare in the 150 or so known sites of Palaeolithic art in Europe, but are more common in the rock art of Africa.

Man and the Ice Age

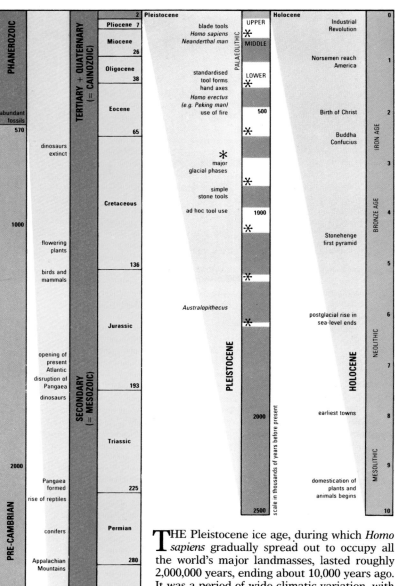

2/Geological periods and the emergence of humans
Using a complex variety of analytical techniques, it is now possible to reconstruct at least some aspects of the earth's climate as far back as the Pre-Cambrian era, more than 3000 million years ago. The chart sets out the broad patterns of change during the main geological periods down to the Cainozoic, which includes our own.

THE Pleistocene ice age, during which *Homo sapiens* gradually spread out to occupy all the world's major landmasses, lasted roughly 2,000,000 years, ending about 10,000 years ago. It was a period of wide climatic variation, with all the continents experiencing frequent alterations and extremes of heat and cold, rain and drought, far sharper than anything recorded in recent centuries. The unique human ability to adapt to such environmental change was undoubtedly a crucial factor both in the survival of the species and its greater success compared to others.

In northern latitudes throughout the Pleistocene era, the characteristics of animal and vegetable populations were determined by the advance and retreat of the glaciers. These frequently covered large parts of Europe, Asia and North America with impenetrable ice-sheets, locking up huge quantities of sea water and reducing average temperatures by 10°–12°C and ocean levels by over 450 feet – far below those of modern times. Only when they shrank back, allowing the northward spread of oak and spruce forests, and the sub-arctic vegetation on which the mammoths and reindeer browsed, was it possible for early humans to live much outside the equatorial regions; and even then it required the discovery of fire, and the ability to sew warm clothing, before they could survive a winter in the rich, but frozen, hunting grounds.

The main glacial advances have now all been accurately dated, and their associated meteorological, geographical, botanical and biological developments have been confidently established by a variety of techniques, from the study of sediments deposited in lakes and the analysis of pollen zones to the use of radiocarbon and potassium-argon decay times. But it is the probably less-known episodes of climatic variation in tropical Africa which played the first key climatic role in human history.

Early humans in Africa were living by hunting and gathering even before the Ice Age began. As the expansion and contraction of the icecaps created a succession of more favourable conditions – making the rain forests drier in the cold epochs, and bringing more rainfall to the arid savannahs as the general temperature rose again – so humans adapted their lifestyle and tool-kits and new cultures emerged: the Aterian bow-and-arrow makers in the Maghreb and the Stillbay-Magosian settlements in south and east Africa, during the wet centuries c. 20,000 years ago, and the increasingly adept craftsmen of the Sangoan, Lupemban and Tshitolian groups who inhabited the sub-Saharan forests when the rain was light enough to keep the vegetation under control.

The ability to make and use fire for protection, warmth, cooking and as a source of pleasure and social cohesion was particularly important in the process of adapting to different environments. The oldest evidence of fire in association with human activity comes from the sites of Swartkrans in South Africa and Chesowanja in Kenya which date from 2 and 1.5 million years ago respectively. There is no evidence that the occupants of these sites were able to make fire but they were able to collect it from natural sources, transport and sustain it. By the time of the first advance of the Würm glaciers in central Europe, around 75,000 years ago, the Mousterian cave-dwellers of the Dordogne, with their cooking hearths, their bone needles, and their implements for scraping and shaping furs, could already survive the bitter conditions of a northern winter; and each time the ice retreated, the peoples of Europe and Asia grew gradually more numerous and more advanced.

The water frozen into the Würm ice-sheets, and their equivalents in northern Europe and North America, the Weichsel and Wisconsin glacier-fields, reduced sea levels so far that land bridges appeared linking most major areas and many isolated islands into one single continental mainland. Helped by the three most southerly of those (see map 1) people were first able to reach Australia and Tasmania. The Bering Strait between eastern Asia and the glacier-free expanse of Alaska, which at most times has been traversable across the winter ice, now became a broad, dry land highway for the migration of peoples and animals of all kinds. The first groups to penetrate the Americas, sometime before 30,000 years ago, made little impact on their environment; and then the ice-sheets closed off the route south. An ice-free corridor opened up again about 12,000 years ago, letting the now more advanced big game hunters from Siberia through to the rich gamelands of the American plains.

Palaeolithic hunters, now making lethally

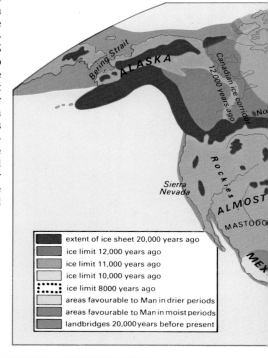

extent of ice sheet 20,000 years ago
ice limit 12,000 years ago
ice limit 11,000 years ago
ice limit 10,000 years ago
ice limit 8000 years ago
areas favourable to Man in drier periods
areas favourable to Man in moist periods
landbridges 20,000 years before present

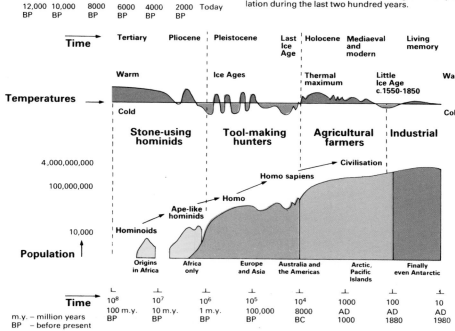

3/Climatic change and population growth The lower chart, on a logarithmic scale, plots population and climatic variation during the Pleistocene; the real-time diagram indicates the explosive growth of population during the last two hundred years.

The Berezovka Mammoth This giant animal's entire carcass was preserved in frozen Siberian mud until its discovery earlier this century. Its death probably occurred in early autumn when it slipped while feeding on a high river-bank bluff. It fell, breaking many bones, and suffocated in the ooze, probably around 40,000 years ago.

tures called casteroides, camels, ground sloths, stag-moose, two types of musk-oxen, several varieties of large, often lion-sized cats, mastodons and three mammoths, woolly, Columbian and imperial. Within a thousand years of man's large-scale arrival most of them were gone – including all the horses, which had to be reintroduced from 16th-century Europe.

No one knows to what extent the new colonists were responsible for this wholesale destruction. No evidence has appeared, though, to suggest a climatic or topographical cause and there are indications, both in cave paintings and in skeletal remains, that many of the now-extinct mammals were attacked by large groups of humans, and sometimes even stampeded in herds over high cliffs into swamps.

Whatever the explanation, there is little doubt that the greatly expanded populations of Late Palaeolithic Man, even though their hunting grounds now extended down to the far tip of South America, found their accustomed wild food-plants and wild game far sparser and more difficult to come by as the Pleistocene ice age came to its end, c. 10,000 BP.

With the vanishing of major meat sources like the mastodon, which had weighed a ton or more, and sufficed on the frozen tundra to feed a whole tribe for weeks on end, men were now driven to devise new means of subsistence. It was now, as the world slowly started to warm up again, that all over the globe small groups of people first learned to domesticate animals and plants (see page 40) and embark on the Neolithic or agricultural revolution.

accurate use of flint-tipped spears and arrows, had long since begun to accelerate the extinction of once-numerous animal species. The mastodons and mammoths started to disappear from Africa and south-east Asia at least 40,000 years ago, and the process was well advanced in Australia and northern Eurasia by 13,000 BP (meaning before the present, or more precisely before 1950). But the rolling grasslands of the American west and south-west were a different matter. Roughly 11,000 years ago they were teeming with animal life – giant bison with a six-foot horn spread, towering, beaver-like crea-

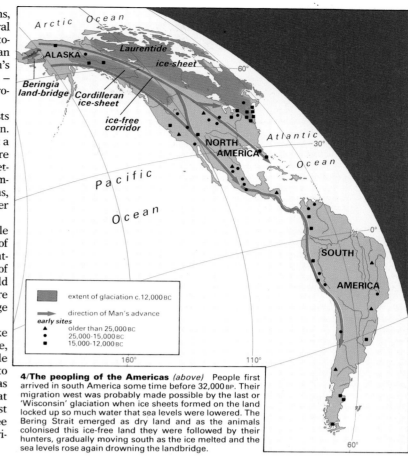

extent of glaciation c.12,000 BC

direction of Man's advance

early sites
▲ older than 25,000 BC
● 25,000-15,000 BC
■ 15,000-12,000 BC

4/The peopling of the Americas (above) People first arrived in south America some time before 32,000 BP. Their migration west was probably made possible by the last or 'Wisconsin' glaciation when ice sheets formed on the land locked up so much water that sea levels were lowered. The Bering Strait emerged as dry land and as the animals colonised this ice-free land they were followed by their hunters, gradually moving south as the ice melted and the sea levels rose again drowning the landbridge.

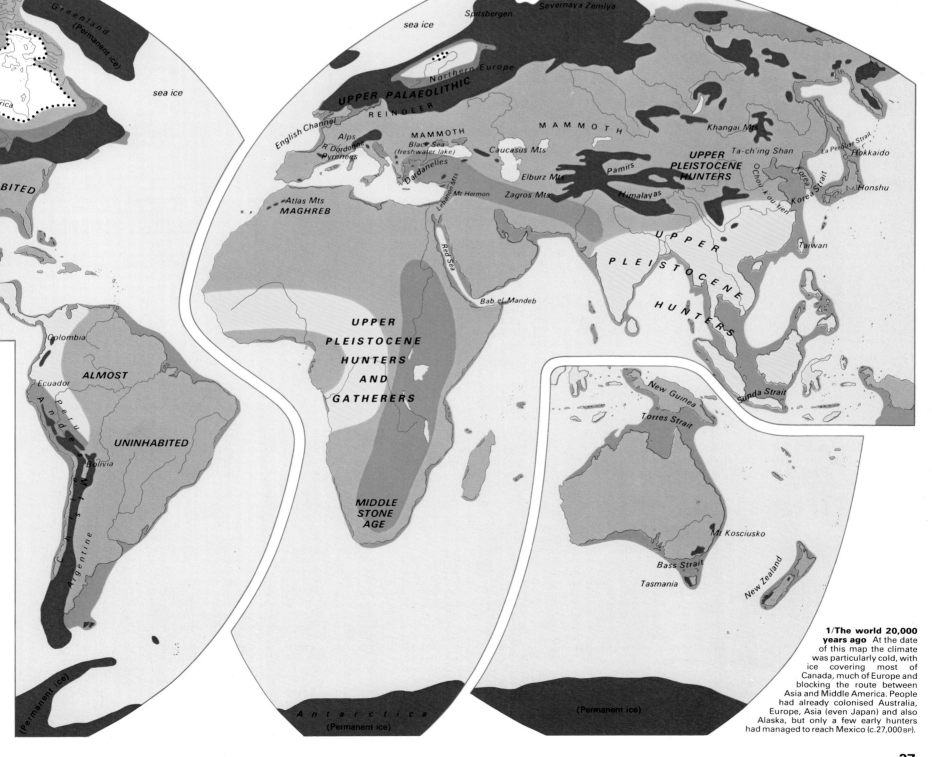

1/The world 20,000 years ago At the date of this map the climate was particularly cold, with ice covering most of Canada, much of Europe and blocking the route between Asia and Middle America. People had already colonised Australia, Europe, Asia (even Japan) and also Alaska, but only a few early hunters had managed to reach Mexico (c.27,000 BP).

From hunting to farming: the origins of agriculture

THE last ten thousand years, during which present-day climatic conditions have existed, is only the last of a dozen or so warmer phases which punctuated the Ice Age. In one respect, however, it is unique: it has seen an unprecedented explosion in the numbers of the human species, and in their impact on the world.

In 8000 BC there were still only small bands of hunters and collectors, whose scale was little different from that of their predecessors up to half a million years before. Within two thousand years, however, some substantial villages had appeared; in another two thousand years, towns and cities; two thousand years later, city-states had grown to empires; two thousand years more and the technological foundations were laid for achievements which in the next two thousand years were to include steam power, atomic energy, and man's first moon-landing.

This decisive quickening of pace in certain areas can be attributed largely to the beginnings – independently in several parts of the world, but earliest and most importantly in the Near Eastern region of the Old World – of agriculture, which is the deliberate alteration of natural systems to promote the abundance of an exploited species or set of species.

Where this involves selective breeding and genetic change, the process is called domestication; and some species are now completely dependent on man's intervention for their survival. This is especially true of the cereals, the species which more than any other has sustained the tremendous growth of population since the last glacial. The yield from cultivated cereals made possible human communities of a larger size than ever before, and thus for the first time there arose settlements which can be described as villages or even towns. Because these yields came from a limited area of land, it was possible to support a growing population by converting more and more land to crops; and the productivity of this land could be increased by intensive techniques of cultivation, such as irrigation. Because such systems demand higher levels of organisation, more complex societies were often the result. How this self-sustaining process actually started, however, is still poorly understood. Certainly, by the end of the last glaciation, man had a more complex technology and social organisation than before, and he was thus better equipped to respond to the challenge of environmental change than he had been at the beginning of previous interglacial periods. The altered distribution of rainfall and the changes in sea and lake levels after 8000 BC necessitated a greater use of the grasses which abounded in the mountain foothills; and the unconscious selection of certain forms which could be grown in lowland habitats revealed their potential as crops.

At least three major groups of cereals have independently taken part in this process, in different parts of the world becoming staple crops and causing fundamental changes in economy and society. In the Near East, and spreading out from there to Europe and India, wheat and barley formed the basis of village and city life among the most ancient civilisations. At the other end of Eurasia, in China, millet was

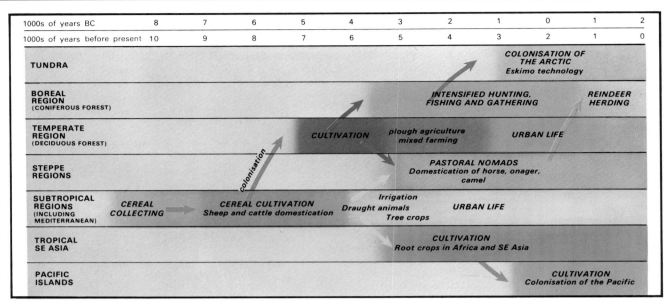

| 1000s of years BC | 8 | 7 | 6 | 5 | 4 | 3 | 2 | 1 | 0 | 1 | 2 |
| 1000s of years before present | 10 | 9 | 8 | 7 | 6 | 5 | 4 | 3 | 2 | 1 | 0 |

The cumulative consequences of the agricultural revolution *(above)* The pattern shown in map 2 developed in the ten thousand years of the post-glacial, following the initial impetus from the beginnings of cereal cultivation and the emergence of settled villages in the Near East. This diagram is based on the Old World, and shows the chain of consequences as it affected its different zones.

cultivated; and together with rice – which had been domesticated in South-East Asia – these crops supported the civilisation which has continued down to the present time. In Central America (Mesoamerica) and Peru, maize was developed from its tiny wild form to its present size, allowing the growth of the wealthy civilisations plundered centuries later by the Spanish (see page 158). Thus the initial innovation of cereal cultivation had a cumulative effect, inducing not only fundamental changes in economy and social order, but also continuing patterns of change in subsequent millennia.

In the Old World, the cultivation of plants was complemented by new forms of animal exploitation: sheep, goats, cattle and pigs came to be herded near to the permanent settlements and fields, and became domesticated through isolation from their wild populations. Later it was discovered that some of these animals could be used for wool and milk as well as meat, and also to pull ploughs and carts, so raising agricultural productivity; and that other domesticable species such as horses and asses could be used to carry loads and human riders, improving communications and the possibilities of trade. With time, also, a wider range of plants came to be used – tree-crops such as figs, dates and olives were taken into cultivation, while as agriculture spread to the tropics, techniques of vegetative propagation were applied to roots and tubers.

In the New World, where few animals were domesticated, the lack of suitable draught animals prevented the development of the plough. Nevertheless several genera of plants were domesticated, many of which were widely adopted in Europe after the discovery of the Americas, and which are of worldwide importance today – maize, squashes and several sorts of beans from Mesoamerica, and potatoes, peppers and tomatoes from the tropical region further south. The use of cotton in the New World took the place of wool in the Old World. The parallel development of domestic plants and animals in different parts of the world has provided a valuable pool of diversity, allowing modern man a wide range of choice in selecting appropriate crops and stock for particular situations.

The spread of agriculture and domestication produced important effects even outside the core areas of cereal cultivation and urbanisation. In Africa a wide range of native species of plants was domesticated in the belt on the southern margin of the Sahara, supplementing

Early milling equipment *(above)* Found wherever grain crops were cultivated, the simple saddle-quern or flat grinding stone was a basic piece of early agricultural equipment, needed to convert the hard seeds to porridge or flour. It appears in Neolithic contexts both in the Old World and in the Americas.

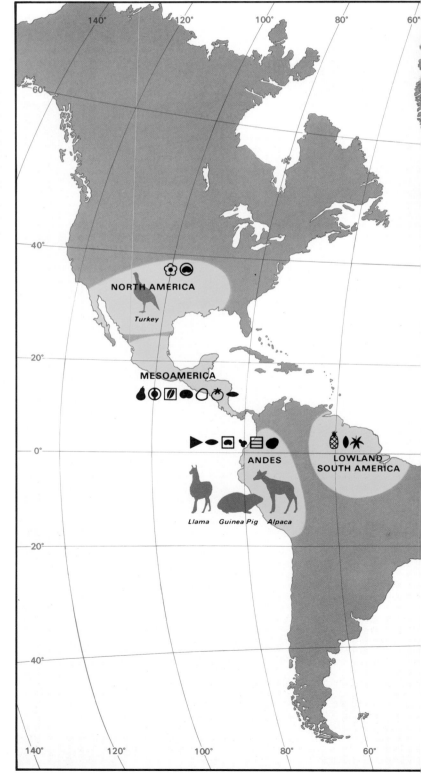

the cereals and cattle introduced up the Nile. Thereafter, expanding populations in this zone tended to move southwards, pushing the native hunting groups into more marginal territories. The native species of domesticates were further supplemented in the first millennium by the arrival of crops including the banana, which was brought by a movement of colonisation starting in coastal South-East Asia and spreading both westwards across the Indian Ocean to Madagascar and eastwards to the as yet uninhabited islands of the Pacific.

In central Eurasia, animal-keeping was more important than cultivation, especially after the domestication of the horse, and some of the techniques of milking and riding spread northwards to the Siberian tribes whose economy was still based on reindeer. In the far north, the development of more advanced technologies allowed the colonisation of the Arctic by specialised Eskimo hunters and fishers. By the time of European expansion in the 16th century AD, the world had a roughly zonal arrangement of native economies, ranging from specialised hunter-fishers in the north, through herding groups, hunting and simple agricultural groups, complex plough- or irrigation-based urban economies, and tropical cultivators, to the marginal relict hunting and gathering populations of southern South America, South Africa and Australia – the last surviving examples of the way of life (see page 34) which man had followed for thousands of years.

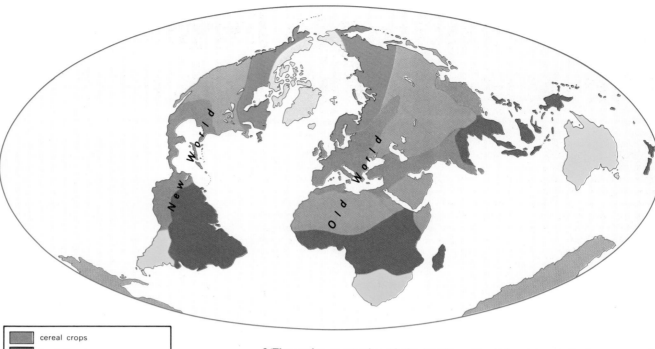

- cereal crops
- tropical root crops
- reindeer hunters and herders
- Arctic hunters
- hunters and pastoralists
- remnant hunting isolates

2/The native economies of the world *(above)* The economies of the different parts of the world, as they developed following the spread of agriculture, show a marked zonal pattern. Both at the northern and at the southern extremes, hunting economies survived — advanced Eskimo peoples in the Arctic, relict hunting groups in the often arid southern continental fringes. Cereal cultivation and root-crop cultivation are complementary to the temperate and tropical zones, with an emphasis on stock-rearing in the arid zone. A zone of reindeer-hunters completes the picture, with some herding techniques being used in the Old World where they have been learned from neighbouring pastoralists.

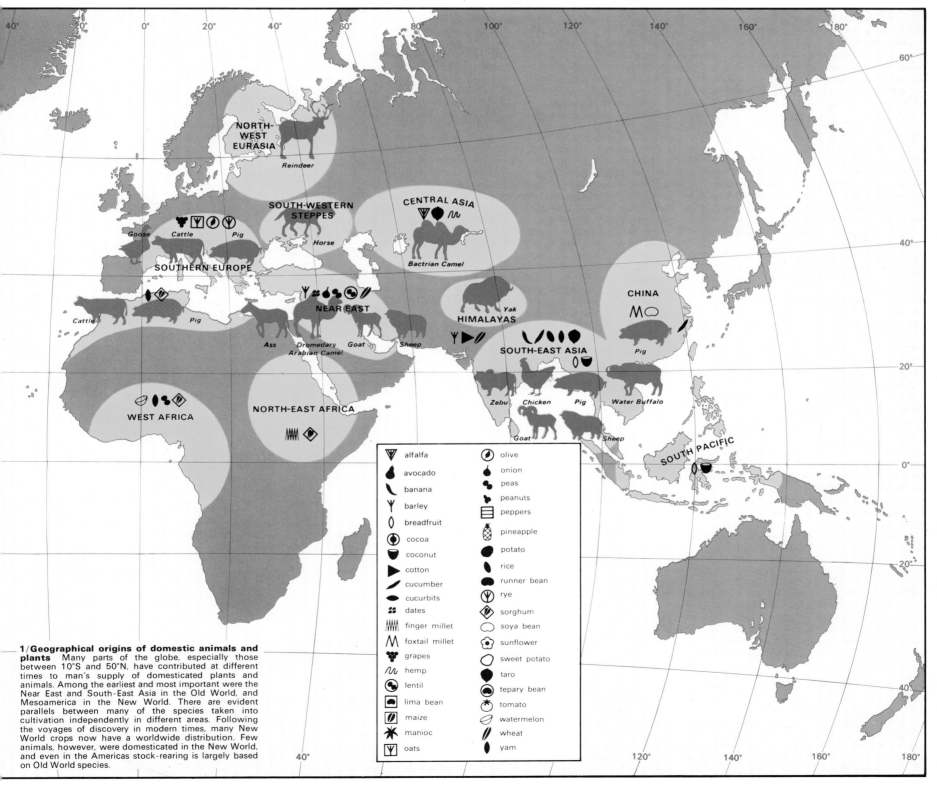

1/Geographical origins of domestic animals and plants Many parts of the globe, especially those between 10°S and 50°N, have contributed at different times to man's supply of domesticated plants and animals. Among the earliest and most important were the Near East and South-East Asia in the Old World, and Mesoamerica in the New World. There are evident parallels between many of the species taken into cultivation independently in different areas. Following the voyages of discovery in modern times, many New World crops now have a worldwide distribution. Few animals, however, were domesticated in the New World, and even in the Americas stock-rearing is largely based on Old World species.

Legend:
- alfalfa
- avocado
- banana
- barley
- breadfruit
- cocoa
- coconut
- cotton
- cucumber
- cucurbits
- dates
- finger millet
- foxtail millet
- grapes
- hemp
- lentil
- lima bean
- maize
- manioc
- oats
- olive
- onion
- peas
- peanuts
- peppers
- pineapple
- potato
- rice
- runner bean
- rye
- sorghum
- soya bean
- sunflower
- sweet potato
- taro
- tepary bean
- tomato
- watermelon
- wheat
- yam

Before the first cities: the Near East 8000 to 3000 BC

THE beginnings of cereal cultivation in the lowland areas of the Near East during the 8th and 7th millennia BC produced, for the first time, communities which were large and permanent enough to develop brick and stone architecture for both private and public buildings, and a whole range of arts and crafts which went with them. The remains of these earliest mudbrick villages – now often forming prominent mounds as a result of rebuilding over hundreds of years – are a common feature of the lowland landscape, especially where abundant springs made the area a first choice for settlement. Most Near Eastern languages have a word to describe these ancient village mounds: *tell* in Arabic, *hüyük* in Turkish, for instance.

The earliest sites were not far from the mountain ranges which had been the original home of the wild ancestors of wheat and barley, and all lay either within the critical rainfall limit of 300 mm a year, necessary for rain-fed agriculture, or in a few cases in 'oasis' situations beyond this, where floodplain cultivation was possible. Two of the most famous, because largest and most developed, of these sites are Tell es-Sultan (Jericho) in the Jordan valley and Çatal Hüyük in the central plain of Turkey.

Jericho is the older of the two, and in the 8th millennium (when Europe was still only just recovering from the last ice age) it was defended by a rock-cut ditch and stone wall with a solid circular tower. Pottery had not been invented at this stage, and the lowest levels of the town are labelled 'pre-pottery Neolithic'. Stone bowls served as containers, and stone for tools came from as far afield as Turkey. Clay ovens were used for cooking. That some public buildings existed is shown by shrines, some of which contained plaster statues, and even skulls with the faces naturalistically modelled in plaster and cowrie-shells inset for the eyes.

The site of Çatal Hüyük is even more spectacular. Covering thirty-two acres (thirteen hectares), it was not defended by walls, although the tightly-packed agglomeration of houses could only be entered through the roof. Here, too, there is evidence of long-distance trade in desirable materials: volcanic glass for tools and weapons, for instance, or light blue apatite for ornaments. The fittings of the houses indicate a comparable sophistication. Frescoes showing hunting scenes covered some of the walls, while shrines were adorned with the plastered skulls of wild oxen set into the walls.

Although these two sites were larger than most of their contemporaries, it is uncertain whether they should be described as 'towns', and although they probably were regional centres of some kind they were largely agricultural. Nor is there any continuity between these early centres of population and the temple-centred administrative and manufacturing centres of later urban civilisation, with their literate élites and monumental architecture. These developments were made possible by more intensive agricultural techniques worked out in the intervening millennia.

Çatal Hüyük came to an end around 5000 BC, some 2000 years before the earliest writing was developed. Already, sophisticated kinds of pottery were being made, and woven textiles were in use. Flax was cultivated, as well as the full range of food crops. But the area under cultivation was small – restricted by rainfall and natural groundwater. One of the most important developments of the succeeding phase was the evolution of effective techniques of irrigation, which allowed settlement to spread beyond the zone of rain-fed 'dry-farming', and make use of the great rivers which flowed through otherwise semi-desert areas.

The earliest phases of this process are evidenced in the 5th millennium by the appearance of sites on the slopes where rivers entered the plains, where simple transverse trenches could divert the wandering streams into neighbouring fields. Such small-scale water-spreading by slight ditches or breaches of stream-banks were first used only as an insurance policy in areas already rain-fed; but during the 5th and 4th millennia this innovation allowed the colonisation of areas hitherto unoccupied because they were too dry. As a result, a large number of small sites appeared which had to be supplied with essential materials obtained from distant highland areas, whose products had to be exchanged with more mobile groups of herders and pastoralists, and whose competing needs for water had to be rationalised and organised. It was religion which provided the link between these functions, and the regional religious centres grew into administrative units based on the temple. It was from such sites, like Eridu in southern Mesopotamia, that urban, literate cultures came into being in the late 4th and 3rd millennia; and the classic pattern of Near Eastern civilisation was born.

One of the technological developments of this formative period was the beginning of copper metallurgy. While this was at first of very limited practical significance, metal came to play an increasingly important role as a raw material; and the experience of copperworking led to a knowledge of the properties of other materials. Among the rocks widely traded as ornaments among the Neolithic villages of the Near East, as far back as the 8th millennium, were certain attractive green stones, found only in the highland areas. One of these was malachite – a pure, high-yielding ore of copper. The technology of these early villages also involved the controlled use of heat, either in firing pottery, or in merely baking bread in mudbrick ovens. This fertile combination of raw material and skill provided the milieu in which man's first experiments with metallurgy began. It was not until the 5th millennium, however, that effective techniques of smelting were developed, and it first became possible to cast objects like maceheads and axes. Weapons, status symbols and cult objects were the first products of this new technology; useful tools were a later application.

The output of the early copper industry was sustained by mining the rich surface ores of malachite at places like Timna, in southern Israel, where the shafts of ancient mines extend over a huge area. Production of finished objects was often under the patronage of the emerging temple centres, and the cult places were adorned by copper objects. The search for ways of moulding complex shapes led to the development of sophisticated casting processes, involving wax and clay moulds, and also led to an appreciation of the beneficial effects of certain impurities commonly found in the copper ores. Arsenical copper was the first deliberately produced alloy known to man, and produced to a consistent recipe for over a thousand years before the rarer but less dangerous metal, tin, became available through trade, and so allowed the production of bronze.

The purer copper ores such as malachite, important with simple techniques of smelting, did not last long after large-scale exploitation began. The early urban communities of the 3rd millennium had to develop ways of dealing with the more complex ores, often combined with sulphur and iron.

1/Early centres of population *(right)* The wild ancestors of the cereals – wheat and barley – on which the first agricultural revolution was based, grew in remote upland areas of the Near East. The earliest villages appeared when these crops were first cultivated in the valleys, and from 8000 BC onwards such sites appeared in the regions surrounding the natural habitats of the wild cereals. Much of the adjacent lowland area, however, was too dry for cultivation. The development of irrigation techniques allowed settlements to extend to these areas by spreading water from the rivers draining from the mountains.

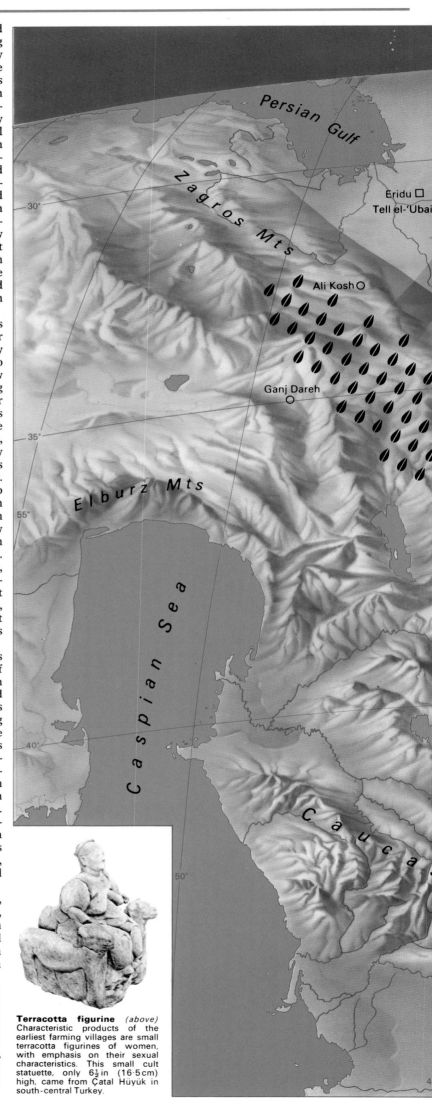

Terracotta figurine *(above)* Characteristic products of the earliest farming villages are small terracotta figurines of women, with emphasis on their sexual characteristics. This small cult statuette, only 6½ in (16·5 cm) high, came from Çatal Hüyük in south-central Turkey.

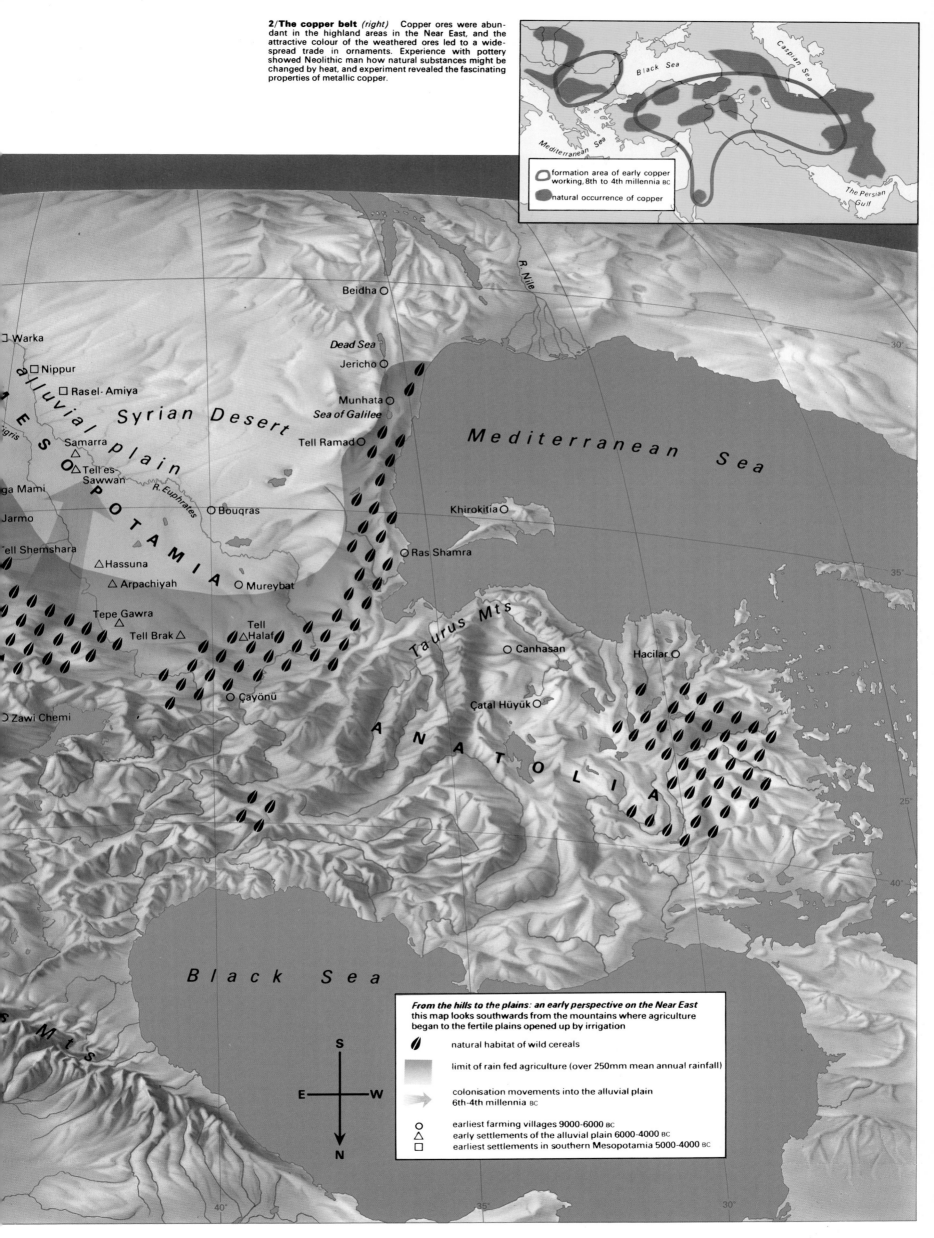

2/The copper belt *(right)* Copper ores were abundant in the highland areas in the Near East, and the attractive colour of the weathered ores led to a widespread trade in ornaments. Experience with pottery showed Neolithic man how natural substances might be changed by heat, and experiment revealed the fascinating properties of metallic copper.

formation area of early copper working, 8th to 4th millennia BC

natural occurrence of copper

Black Sea

Caspian Sea

Mediterranean Sea

The Persian Gulf

R. Nile

Beidha

Warka

Nippur

Ras el-Amiya

Dead Sea

Jericho

Munhata

Sea of Galilee

Tell Ramad

Syrian Desert

Mediterranean Sea

Samarra

Tell es-Sawwan

R. Euphrates

Bouqras

Khirokitia

Ga Mami

Jarmo

Tell Shemshara

Hassuna

Arpachiyah

Mureybat

Ras Shamra

Tepe Gawra

Tell Brak

Tell Halaf

Çayönü

Taurus Mts

Canhasan

Hacilar

Zawi Chemi

Çatal Hüyük

A N A T O L I A

M E S O P O T A M I A

Alluvial plain

Tigris

B l a c k   S e a

M t s

From the hills to the plains: an early perspective on the Near East
this map looks southwards from the mountains where agriculture began to the fertile plains opened up by irrigation

S

E — W

N

natural habitat of wild cereals

limit of rain fed agriculture (over 250mm mean annual rainfall)

colonisation movements into the alluvial plain 6th–4th millennia BC

○ earliest farming villages 9000–6000 BC

△ early settlements of the alluvial plain 6000–4000 BC

□ earliest settlements in southern Mesopotamia 5000–4000 BC

Early Europe: the colonisation of a continent 6000 to 1500 BC

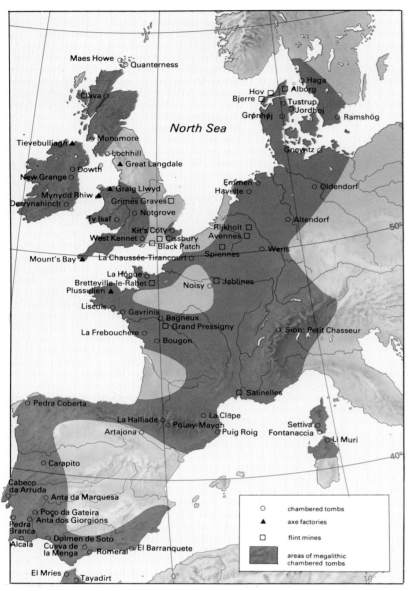

North Sea

2/Megalithic monuments
(above) The farmers of the loess-lands built their houses and cult-centres of wood. Further west, while houses continued to be mostly of wood, public monuments were constructed from large undressed boulders or slabs of stone. Such monuments, built to serve many generations, were mainly concerned with mortuary rituals and ancestor-worship. Three or four main areas began independently to build simple structures, but as the monuments grew more elaborate, ideas and techniques were exchanged. By the end of the 4th millennium BC many different kinds of monument were being built over much of western Europe, from simple cists to elaborate chambered tombs.

The cart *(above)* was introduced to Europe from the Caucasus via the steppe region in the 4th millennium BC. This small model – in fact a drinking cup – came from a cemetery at Budakalasz, near Budapest, Hungary, and dates to around 3000 BC.

THE first experiments with the cultivation of cereals and the domestication of animals began in the Near East some ten thousand years ago, and the agricultural way of life was already fully established there when farming villages appeared in adjacent parts of Europe two thousand years later. From here, farming spread rapidly across the more fertile parts of Europe at a rate of something like a mile a year, to reach the British Isles around 4000 BC.

The earliest mudbrick *tell* settlements (see page 40) in Europe, dating to about 6000 BC, are to be found on the western side of the Aegean, in the plain of Thessaly (e.g. Argissa) and on Crete (e.g. Knossos). Farming spread to these areas from Anatolia, the routes across the Aegean being already well known through the obsidian trade. The material culture of the villagers was very similar to that of their contemporaries across the Aegean: the first farmers did not use pottery, but Anatolian techniques soon spread to the new areas, and both plain and sophisticated painted pottery were in use in Greece and Bulgaria by 5500 BC, when agricultural settlement had spread up the Vardar river valley to the north Balkans and the lower Danube area. The villages consisted of clusters of square mudbrick buildings each with an identical layout of hearths, cooking and sleeping areas; though usually with one larger 'club-house' or village shrine. Their economy was based on keeping sheep and cultivating wheat and legumes. Such villages were situated in the plains, by areas of good soil with a plentiful water supply, and these sites often continued to be occupied for hundreds of years. Karanovo in Bulgaria is a good example: the mound of settlement debris is 12 metres (40 feet) high.

Villages of this kind spread inland as far as Hungary (e.g. Hódmezővásárhely), but from here northwards a new pattern developed. The square mudbrick dwellings were replaced by wooden longhouses, and the villages, like Bylany in Czechoslovakia or Köln-Lindenthal in Germany, did not build up into *tells*. Settlement spread across the whole of Europe, in a belt from north-east France to south-west Russia, on the expanses of soil produced by the weathering of loess – a highly fertile wind-blown dust laid down during the Ice Age beyond the southern margins of the glaciers. Over the whole of this area, the characteristic pottery is decorated with incised lines in spiral or meandering bands. This uniformity of culture reflects the rapid spread of settlement along the main river valleys (especially the Danube and the Rhine) which occurred around 5000 BC. In the eastern part of the area, villages continued to be grouped around a 'club-house'; but in the west, small strings of hamlets consisting of two or three longhouses were often found. Cattle seem to have been more important than sheep in the flat forested interior of Europe, but wheat continued to be the staple crop among the cereals. Where possible, settlements were placed next to small rivers or streams, and almost invariably on loess. Although small stone axes were used, the settlers did not clear wide areas of land away from the watercourses but practised an intensive horticulture in the valleys.

This pattern continued, with developments and modifications, down to 4000 BC. Meanwhile, in the Balkans, population density had increased and there had been expansion into the foothills and lower slopes of the mountains. *Tell* settlements multiplied in the plains, and these prosperous communities traded and experimented with a wide range of raw materials for tools or for decorative purposes. Pottery came to be decorated in elaborate multicoloured paints, using ochre, graphite and manganese. As in the Near East, abundant simple ores of copper in the mountains near to permanent settlements provided the opportunity of discovering the properties of metals and the techniques of simple smelting and casting. Such early developments were confined to the Balkans and the Carpathian Basin (see map 3), and their products rarely spread beyond this region. This early copper industry appears to have arisen independently from developments in Near Eastern metallurgy. Using two-piece moulds it produced small ornaments and larger forms such as axes of unalloyed copper. These were probably as much for prestige as for practical purposes. Gold was also worked at this period, and the appearance of graves especially rich in copper or gold testifies to the emergence of a stratified society.

While the process of agricultural colonisation continued, small groups of hunters, fishers and collectors continued their older way of life in areas untouched by the new economy. Hunting populations were rather sparse in the areas first selected by agriculturalists, and the rapidity with which farming spread across the loess-lands may in part reflect the lack of local competition; but where the forests were more open they were more numerous. They were especially well established in the morainic, lake-strewn landscapes created by the retreat of the ice sheets, on the Alpine foreland and on the northern edge of the North European Plain, which were rich in wild animals, fish and edible plants. The early stages of the post-glacial period – the time when the first experiments with agriculture were taking place in the Near East – had been a good time for the hunters of the European forests. As time wore on, however, life became more difficult for these hunters; the forest thickened as oak and beech moved northwards, the lakes filled in, and the coastlands were drowned by

rising sea levels. As populations grew, many of the aboriginal groups found themselves increasingly under stress, and eventually helped to swell the numbers of agriculturalists by adopting the new economy.

During the 4th and early 3rd millennia, important developments occurred which were to change the established pattern of life. New areas came into prominence; and their innovations in turn affected the older regions. The developing areas were the north European plain and the south Russian steppes and the Aegean – where fishing and maritime trade swung the emphasis from inland plains to the coasts and islands. In south-east Europe many of the *tell* settlements came to an end, and in the Carpathian Basin appeared the large grave-mounds typical of the steppe area, suggesting the arrival of nomadic elements in the population. More definite evidence of eastward links is given by metallurgy, with the appearance of Caucasian types and techniques. Wheeled vehicles are evidenced for the first time, and this may be the point at which Indo-European languages first arrived in Europe.

In large areas of western Europe farming was adopted for the first time during this period, and the clearance of fields on the rocky Atlantic shores or in the boulder-strewn moraines of northern Europe provided an opportunity for making more durable monuments as tribal mortuary shrines for the scattered hamlets of the peasants. Vast unfaced blocks were piled one upon another to create the 'megalithic' monuments which were constructed by various groups of farmers along the Baltic and Atlantic

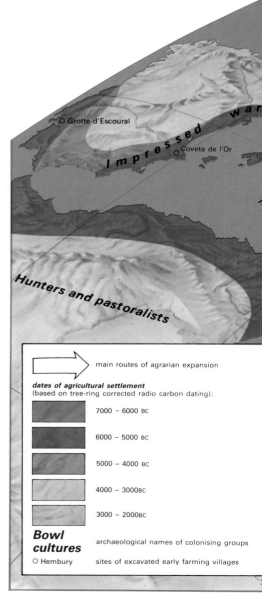

main routes of agrarian expansion

dates of agricultural settlement
(based on tree-ring corrected radio carbon dating):

	7000 – 6000 BC
	6000 – 5000 BC
	5000 – 4000 BC
	4000 – 3000 BC
	3000 – 2000 BC

Bowl cultures
archaeological names of colonising groups

○ Hembury   sites of excavated early farming villages

3/Early metallurgy (right) European copper-working began in the Balkans in the 5th millennium, producing simple objects in one-piece moulds. A similar primitive industry also began in southern Iberia in the early 3rd millennium. A little later Balkan smiths learned about alloying and two-piece moulds from the Caucasian school. The rich resources of central Europe and western Britain only came into large-scale use in the early second millennium, using local tin to make bronze.

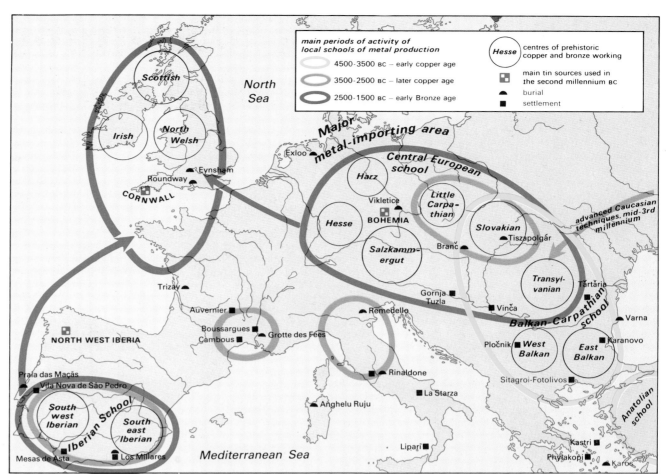

fringes of Europe (see map 2). Some of the earliest occur in Brittany in the mid-5th millennium, but particularly elaborate forms were being made in Ireland and Spain up to 2000 years later.

Such monuments were constructed with the aid of draught animals, now used both for carts and for the plough. Soils which were in general less productive than loess made the plough an essential aid in cultivating large areas of land. Widespread forest clearance became necessary, and mines for flint helped to provide the large quantities of stone needed for axes. The opening-up of northern and western Europe in this way produced a change in the cultural configuration of the continent in which the old 'Danubian' axis was less important: and with the continuing colonisation of sandy soils in northern Europe during the later 3rd and early 2nd millennia, the Balkans became something of a backwater between the rapidly-developing economy of north-central Europe and the nascent maritime civilisation of the Aegean (see page 66).

Note: All dates quoted above are based on the tree-ring correction of radiocarbon.

1/The colonisation of Europe (below) Early farmers spread from one side of Europe to the other by two main routes: the Vardar-Danube-Rhine corridor, and the Mediterranean littoral; the former was the more important. Archaeologists label the different groups involved by the characteristic kinds of pottery which each produced. For thousands of years the most 'developed' part of Europe was the south-east, which was the first to be settled.

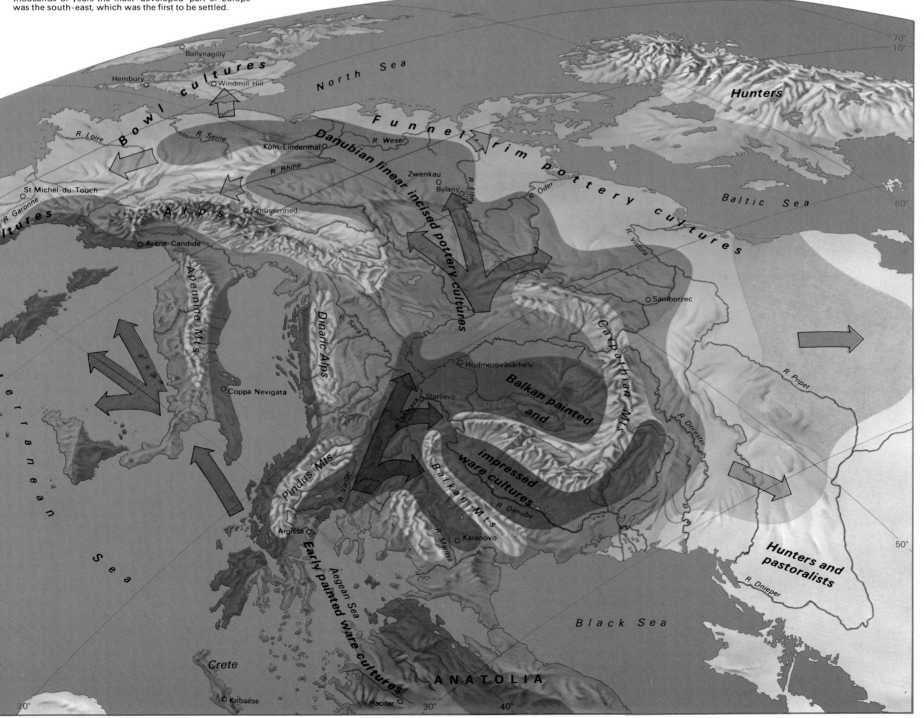

African peoples and cultures to AD 1000

THE lands of Africa south of the Equator, though possibly the original setting for the emergence of *Homo* (page 32) were for thousands of years isolated from the technological and intellectual advances that were transforming the world elsewhere. North of the Equator, the transition from hunting and gathering to food production occurred from around 8000 BC. To the south, cut off by the Sahara desert, the equatorial Nile and the almost impenetrable tropical rain forest, settled agriculture mainly developed only with the coming of iron at the beginning of the Christian era.

Domesticated cattle and cereal-growing entered the continent from western Asia. The earliest sites, dating from the 7th and 6th millennia BC, show wheat and barley being cultivated on the edges of the Nile delta, and cattle-herding near the Hoggar massif in the Sahara, which was then undergoing a pronounced wet phase in which much of the present desert was habitable parkland. The discovery of bone harpoons throughout the area indicates the temperate aspect of the climate.

Desiccation of the Sahara set in during the 3rd millennium BC, causing some pastoralists to penetrate the Nile valley and its delta, and others to move south and east. Southward expansion of cereal-growing, however, required the domestication of suitable grains, such as millet and sorghum, which could be grown in the tropics. This probably took place only during the 2nd millennium BC, although there may have been some marginal cultivation of fruits and vegetables in the forest zone before this period. The increase of Negro populations in the Sudanic belt which now took place was mainly due to the development of the tropical crops.

Small numbers of early farmers penetrated the equatorial regions of Africa, particularly in eastern Africa, where a break in the forest enabled herdsmen and perhaps cereal growers to spread down the Rift Valley from Ethiopia into central Kenya and northern Tanzania during the 1st millennium BC. Elsewhere the jungle seems to have presented a fairly effective obstacle, although probably on the eve of the Iron Age an economy based mainly on fishing, with some supporting horticulture, spread from the northern to the southern margins of the forest.

In Egypt, copper-using began in the 4th millennium BC, and in the 3rd millennium was superseded by bronze. A few copper and bronze objects have been found along the north African coast, testifying to contacts with the early metal-using societies of southern Europe. Almost everywhere else in Africa, however, iron was the first metal to be produced in any quantity. The Near East was the source of the techniques of iron smelting and working. Occasional objects of native (unsmelted) iron have come from Egyptian royal tombs of the 2nd millennium BC, but it was only in the 1st millennium that it began to be produced in north Africa from the ore, and only in the 6th century BC that it came into common use in Egypt. At about the same period, iron-using spread among the Phoenician and Carthaginian colonies of the north African coast.

Iron-using came to sub-Saharan Africa by two routes. Firstly, there was a limited spread down the Nile Valley to Meroe, which seems to have been an important centre of iron production c.500 BC. The second route took iron-working from the Carthaginian cities to Nigeria, where it is attested by 450 BC at Taruga.

The 1st millennium BC saw a decline in the fortunes of Egypt, which was conquered by a series of foreign powers. By contrast, the Kushite state of the south, with successive capitals at Napata (6th to 4th century BC) and Meroe (4th century BC to 4th century AD), experienced a period of prosperity. The cemeteries of small pyramids which mark the royal tombs of Kush illustrate the continuing importance of Egyptian influences. In the 4th century AD the kingdom of Meroe was overthrown by Axum, a trading state in northern Ethiopia. Axum derived its prosperity from the export of African ivory and maritime trade, and by the 4th century AD its fleet had become the dominant mercantile and military power in the Red Sea. The kingdom enjoyed close relations with Byzantium, and its rulers were converted to Christianity in the 4th century. In the 7th century Axum came into conflict with the rising power of Islam, and in AD 702 its fleet was destroyed by the Arabs, but the city of Axum survived until the end of the 9th century AD.

South of the Equator the earliest Iron Age sites date from around the beginning of the Christian era. This marks a revolution far more dramatic than that in the north. It not only represented an important breakthrough in itself, but in many regions was also associated with the earliest cereal agriculture, cattle-keeping and pottery. Since almost the whole of sub-Saharan Africa is now occupied by food producers, speaking closely related Bantu languages, it is probable that Bantu was disseminated by these early agriculturalists.

It appears, then, that a Negro population, related in language and physical type to the Negroes of West Africa, established itself in late Stone Age times in the Congo basin, and expanded during the early Iron Age across the rest of southern Africa. Probably the process involved both intermixture and some violence, with the better-watered and more densely settled sites of the food-producers superseding the hunters to provide linguistic and cultural foci for the region. By AD 1000 almost all of Africa was settled agricultural societies, and some quite powerful political states were emerging.

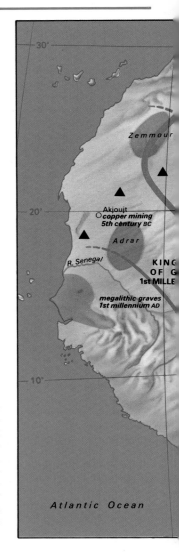

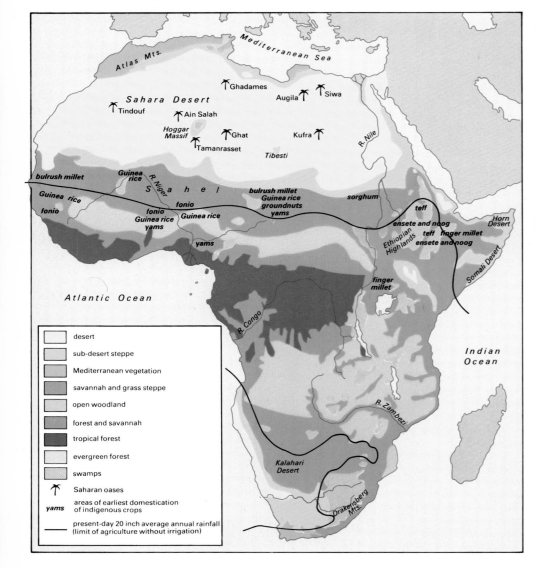

desert

sub-desert steppe

Mediterranean vegetation

savannah and grass steppe

open woodland

forest and savannah

tropical forest

evergreen forest

swamps

Saharan oases

yams areas of earliest domestication of indigenous crops

present-day 20 inch average annual rainfall (limit of agriculture without irrigation)

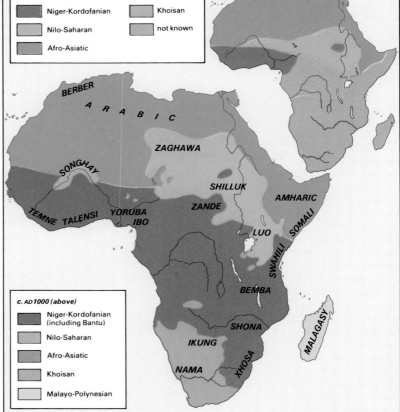

c.3000–2000 BC (right)

Niger-Kordofanian

Nilo-Saharan

Afro-Asiatic

Khoisan

not known

c. AD 1000 (above)

Niger-Kordofanian (including Bantu)

Nilo-Saharan

Afro-Asiatic

Khoisan

Malayo-Polynesian

2/Rainfall and vegetation (*left*) The peopling of Africa was crucially determined by the continent's physical constraints. Over large areas the existence of desert and equatorial jungle made agriculture and communication virtually impossible. The areas of light forest and cultivable grassland retreated in the period 2000 BC to AD 1000, forcing major changes in the established methods of food production and food distribution.

3/African languages (*above*) The analysis of languages provides a possible clue to unravelling much of ancient African history, such as the spread of population across the Sudan, the problem of linking Bantu-speakers of the south with their origins north of the Congo, and the overlaying of Bantu upon earlier Khoisan cultures. This linguistic analysis is particularly important in regions which are totally without written records.

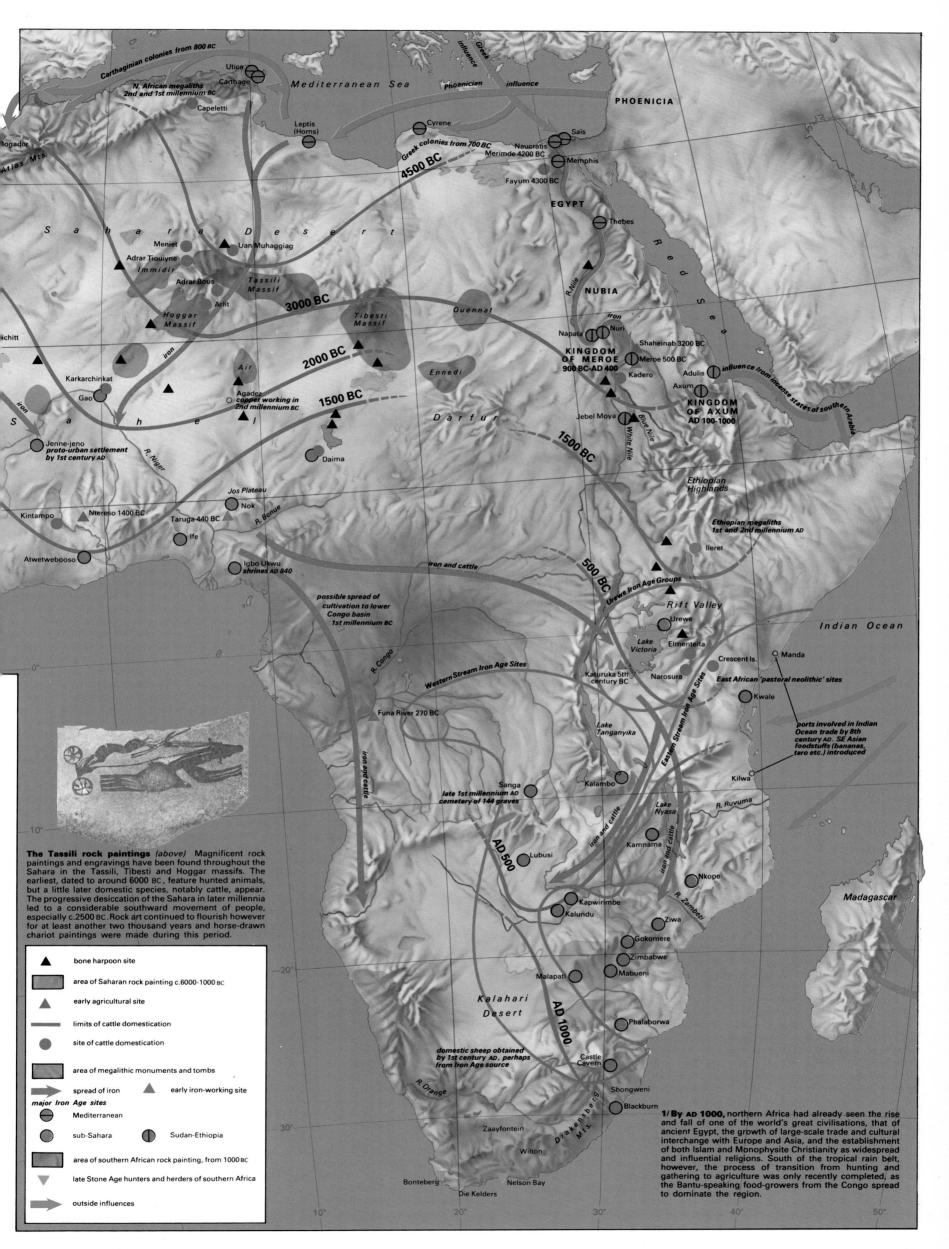

The Tassili rock paintings (above) Magnificent rock paintings and engravings have been found throughout the Sahara in the Tassili, Tibesti and Hoggar massifs. The earliest, dated to around 6000 BC, feature hunted animals, but a little later domestic species, notably cattle, appear. The progressive desiccation of the Sahara in later millennia led to a considerable southward movement of people, especially c.2500 BC. Rock art continued to flourish however for at least another two thousand years and horse-drawn chariot paintings were made during this period.

Legend

- ▲ bone harpoon site
- ▬ area of Saharan rock painting c.6000-1000 BC
- ▲ early agricultural site
- ▬ limits of cattle domestication
- ● site of cattle domestication
- ▬ area of megalithic monuments and tombs
- ➡ spread of iron   ▲ early iron-working site

major Iron Age sites
- ◐ Mediterranean
- ◐ sub-Sahara   ◑ Sudan-Ethiopia
- ▬ area of southern African rock painting, from 1000 BC
- ▽ late Stone Age hunters and herders of southern Africa
- ➡ outside influences

1/ By AD 1000, northern Africa had already seen the rise and fall of one of the world's great civilisations, that of ancient Egypt, the growth of large-scale trade and cultural interchange with Europe and Asia, and the establishment of both Islam and Monophysite Christianity as widespread and influential religions. South of the tropical rain belt, however, the process of transition from hunting and gathering to agriculture was only recently completed, as the Bantu-speaking food-growers from the Congo spread to dominate the region.

45

The peoples and cultures of the Americas to AD 900

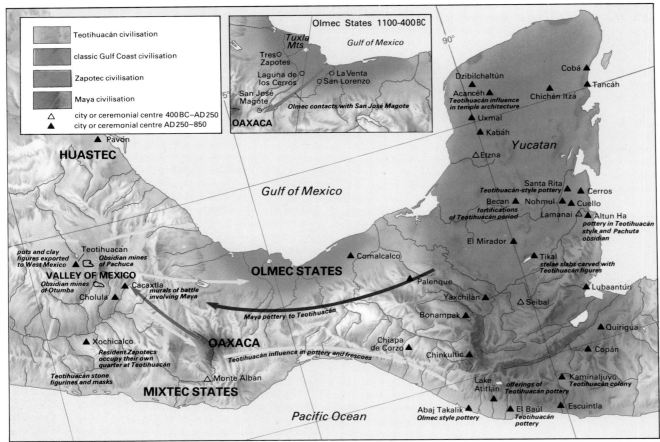

Olmec States 1100-400 BC

Legend:
- Teotihuacán civilisation
- classic Gulf Coast civilisation
- Zapotec civilisation
- Maya civilisation
- △ city or ceremonial centre 400 BC–AD 250
- ▲ city or ceremonial centre AD 250–850

2/The Classic Period in Meso-america, 400 to 900 *(above)* During this period Teotihuacán was the dominant civilisation of Mesoamerica. Although the area under its direct control may have been limited to central Mexico and parts of Guatemala, the influence of Teotihuacán was felt all over Mesoamerica. Similarly, Maya cultural influence was not limited to the Yucatán peninsula alone.

3/North America 1000 BC to AD 1000 *(below)* The Adena culture of Ohio preceded the Hopewell, when chiefs obtained ornaments and exotic raw materials from all over North America. By AD 550 Hopewell influence had waned, and c.AD 700 saw the rise of the Mississippian culture in the southwest and southeast, where temple mounds and other features derived from Mexico were built.

MAN entered the New World from Siberia some time before 20,000 BC during a period of lowered sea level, when the Bering Straits were dry land. After spending thousands of years as semi-nomadic hunters and collectors of wild plant foods, certain groups of Indians in Mesoamerica and the Andean lands began to experiment with plant cultivation until by about 1500 BC maize-farming became the basis of life. Cultivation of tropical root crops may be equally ancient, but archaeological evidence is lacking. These farmers lived in permanent villages, some of which grew into large towns during the last thousand years BC. Craftsmen worked in luxury materials imported from long distances, and there is evidence for class distinctions between rich and poor, governors and governed. Rather than bands or tribes, these communities resembled present-day chiefdoms, with control vested in a chief drawn from a single powerful lineage. Economic power derived from the chief's control over the distribution of land, foodstuffs and craft products, and his position was often reinforced by religious sanctions.

This stage of development was the takeoff point for civilisation and the growth of true states, with populations numbered in tens of thousands, with a hierarchy of social classes, an efficient civil service, professional priesthood, and specialists in all kinds of jobs from manufacturing to commerce, administration and government. Certain peoples (the Olmec of the Mexican Gulf Coast plain, the Zapotec of Monte Albán, and the inhabitants of Chavín in Peru) may have reached this stage c.1000-600 BC; by the early centuries AD most of Mesoamerica and the Central Andes was 'civilised'.

Around, and between, these nuclei of civilisation, other communities remained at the chiefdom level. Maize, beans and squashes were introduced from Mexico into north America, and the arrival of these crops initiated a period of rapid development. In Ohio and Illinois, between 300 BC and AD 550, Hopewell chiefs built elaborate burial mounds and maintained trade contacts over an area stretching from Florida to the Rockies. Most American chiefdoms were agricultural, based on plant cultivation, except along the north-west coast where unusually rich fishing grounds and an abundance of whales and seals supported large villages and a complex ceremonial life.

Towards the extremities of the hemisphere, where conditions were too harsh for farming, populations remained small and the old nomadic and tribal ways of life persisted. The conventional starting date for the Classic Period of Mesoamerican civilisation is AD 250, a time of intellectual and artistic climax. At about this date the Maya adopted hieroglyphic writing and began to erect stelae (stone slabs with carved historical or calendrical inscriptions). The Classic Maya were preoccupied with the passage of time. Their astronomers had calculated the exact length of the solar year, the lunar month and the revolution of the planet Venus, and were able to predict eclipses. These calculations demanded advanced mathematical skills, and the Mesoamericans independently invented the idea of place value and the concept of zero.

Classic Maya civilisation was not an isolated phenomenon. Important regional civilisations developed elsewhere in Mexico – along the Gulf Coast (El Tajín, etc.), in the Valley of Oaxaca (where Monte Albán became a great city), and at Teotihuacán in the Basin of Mexico. In its prime, around the year AD 600, Teotihuacán was a city of 125,000 people and covered 20 square kilometres, laid out according to a precise grid plan. The city's wealth came from agriculture, crafts and trade, in particular the export of obsidian (a natural volcanic glass used for knives and spear points) from the Otumba and Pachuca quarries. Diplomatic and commercial exchanges were kept up with the other civilisations of Mexico, and with the Maya by way of Teotihuacán colonies at Kaminaljuyú and perhaps Escuintla. All the regional civilisations of the Classic Period may be considered local variants of a pan-Mesoamerican cultural pattern. Teotihuacán was destroyed and abandoned around AD 750; Monte Albán fell into disrepair during the 10th century, and Classic Maya civilisation collapsed, for reasons still not fully understood, between AD 800 and 900.

The Central Andes were the homeland of a second group of interrelated civilisations. Although not in direct contact with Mesoamerica, the level of development was very similar, the main technological difference being that the Andean peoples had developed how to work gold, silver and copper, and were using these metals for tools as well as jewellery. This region, with its vast distances and harsh topography, was always difficult to unify under a single state, but the centuries between AD 600 and 1000 saw the rise and fall of a truly imperial power based on Huari (or Wari) in the Peruvian Andes. Many elements of Huari religion and art were first developed at Tiahuanaco in Bolivia, but were quickly adopted in Peru. From Huari, a modified version of the Tiahuanaco cult and its art style was carried by force to many parts of the coast and highlands. For a short time, Huari became the capital of a political state which embraced most of Peru, but in about AD 800 the city was overthrown and abandoned forever. The fragile artificial unity soon broke down, and local states and local art styles reasserted themselves. It was not until the Inca conquest of the 15th and 16th centuries that Peru was once more unified under the control of a single power.

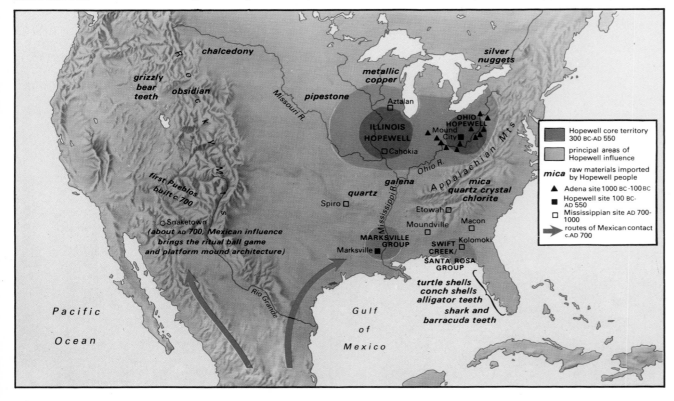

Legend:
- Hopewell core territory 300 BC-AD 550
- principal areas of Hopewell influence
- *mica* raw materials imported by Hopewell people
- ▲ Adena site 1000 BC -100 BC
- ■ Hopewell site 100 BC-AD 550
- □ Mississippian site AD 700-1000
- → routes of Mexican contact c.AD 700

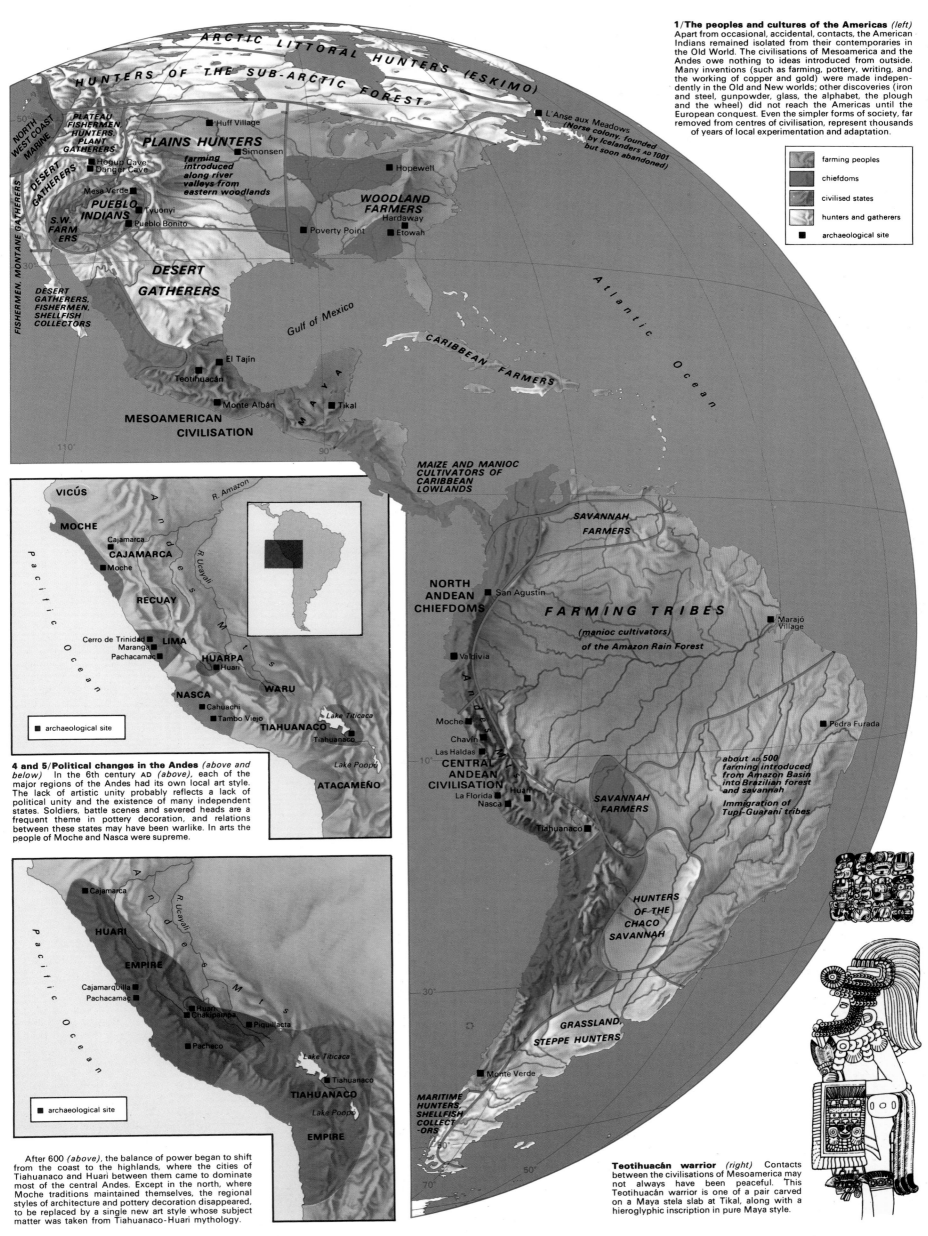

ARCTIC LITTORAL HUNTERS (ESKIMO)

HUNTERS OF THE SUB-ARCTIC FOREST

L'Anse aux Meadows
(Norse colony, founded
by Icelanders AD 1001
but soon abandoned)

NORTH WEST COAST MARINE

PLATEAU FISHERMEN, HUNTERS, PLANT GATHERERS

Huff Village

PLAINS HUNTERS

Simonsen

farming introduced along river valleys from eastern woodlands

DESERT GATHERERS

Hogup Cave
Danger Cave

Mesa Verde

Tyuonyi

PUEBLO INDIANS

Pueblo Bonito

S.W. FARMERS

Hopewell

WOODLAND FARMERS

Hardaway

Poverty Point

Etowah

DESERT GATHERERS, FISHERMEN, SHELLFISH COLLECTORS

DESERT GATHERERS

FISHERMEN, MONTANE GATHERERS

Gulf of Mexico

Atlantic Ocean

CARIBBEAN FARMERS

El Tajín

Teotihuacán

Monte Albán

Tikal

M A Y A

MESOAMERICAN CIVILISATION

MAIZE AND MANIOC CULTIVATORS OF CARIBBEAN LOWLANDS

SAVANNAH FARMERS

NORTH ANDEAN CHIEFDOMS

San Agustin

FARMING TRIBES

(manioc cultivators) of the Amazon Rain Forest

Marajó Village

Valdivia

Moche
Chavin
Las Haldas

CENTRAL ANDEAN CIVILISATION

La Florida
Nasca

Huari

Pedra Furada

Tiahuanaco

about AD 500 farming introduced from Amazon Basin into Brazilian forest and savannah

Immigration of Tupi-Guarani tribes

SAVANNAH FARMERS

HUNTERS OF THE CHACO SAVANNAH

GRASSLAND STEPPE HUNTERS

Monte Verde

MARITIME HUNTERS, SHELLFISH COLLECT-ORS

1/The peoples and cultures of the Americas *(left)*
Apart from occasional, accidental, contacts, the American Indians remained isolated from their contemporaries in the Old World. The civilisations of Mesoamerica and the Andes owe nothing to ideas introduced from outside. Many inventions (such as farming, pottery, writing, and the working of copper and gold) were made independently in the Old and New worlds; other discoveries (iron and steel, gunpowder, glass, the alphabet, the plough and the wheel) did not reach the Americas until the European conquest. Even the simpler forms of society, far removed from centres of civilisation, represent thousands of years of local experimentation and adaptation.

farming peoples
chiefdoms
civilised states
hunters and gatherers
archaeological site

4 and 5 map (above)

VICÚS
MOCHE
Cajamarca
CAJAMARCA
Moche
RECUAY
Cerro de Trinidad
Maranga
Pachacamac
LIMA
HUARPA
Huari
NASCA
WARU
Cahuachi
Tambo Viejo
TIAHUANACO
Tiahuanaco
ATACAMEÑO

R. Amazon
R. Ucayali
Andes
Pacific Ocean
Lake Titicaca
Lake Poopó

archaeological site

4 and 5/Political changes in the Andes *(above and below)* In the 6th century AD *(above)*, each of the major regions of the Andes had its own local art style. The lack of artistic unity probably reflects a lack of political unity and the existence of many independent states. Soldiers, battle scenes and severed heads are a frequent theme in pottery decoration, and relations between these states may have been warlike. In arts the people of Moche and Nasca were supreme.

5 map (below)

Cajamarca
HUARI
EMPIRE
Cajamarquilla
Pachacamac
Huari
Chakipampa
Piquillacta
Pacheco
TIAHUANACO
Tiahuanaco

R. Ucayali
Andes
Pacific Ocean
Lake Titicaca
Lake Poopó
EMPIRE

archaeological site

After 600 *(above)*, the balance of power began to shift from the coast to the highlands, where the cities of Tiahuanaco and Huari between them came to dominate most of the central Andes. Except in the north, where Moche traditions maintained themselves, the regional styles of architecture and pottery decoration disappeared, to be replaced by a single new art style whose subject matter was taken from Tiahuanaco-Huari mythology.

Teotihuacán warrior *(right)* Contacts between the civilisations of Mesoamerica may not always have been peaceful. This Teotihuacán warrior is one of a pair carved on a Maya stela slab at Tikal, along with a hieroglyphic inscription in pure Maya style.

47

Australia and Oceania before the coming of the Europeans

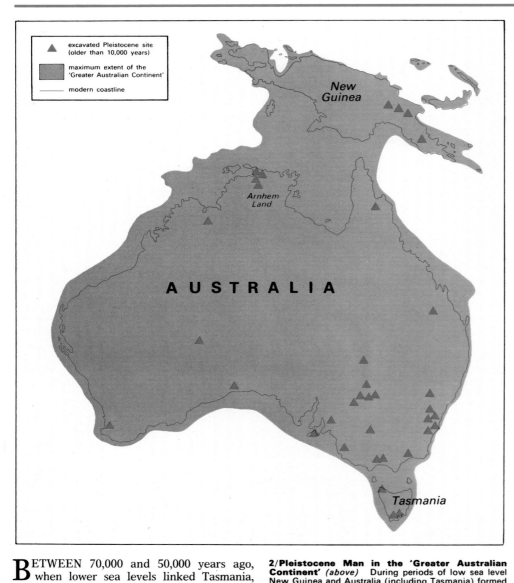

2/Pleistocene Man in the 'Greater Australian Continent' (above) During periods of low sea level New Guinea and Australia (including Tasmania) formed a single large landmass. Settlement was concentrated up the major river systems and along the coast, but Pleistocene coastal sites now lie submerged offshore. In this map, the comparative abundance of sites in south-eastern Australia is simply due to the greater attention devoted to this region by archaeologists.

B ETWEEN 70,000 and 50,000 years ago, when lower sea levels linked Tasmania, Australia and New Guinea, man first ventured onto the Greater Australian Continent. His journey, from a south-east Asian homeland, was a pioneering one, as it involved at least one major water crossing. The original Australians were therefore among the world's earliest mariners. What a strange new world greeted these newcomers: enormous beyond comprehension, and ranging from tropical north to temperate south. Admittedly, some of the edible plants found in more northerly latitudes were related to those of Asia and were therefore familiar, but this was not so of the animals. In addition to the mammals which have survived, there was a bewildering assortment of giant forms: ten-foot tall kangaroos, various enormous ox-like beasts, a large native lion, and rangy emu-like birds. Despite this terrestial abundance, it was the plentiful supply of fish and shellfish available along the coasts and in the rivers that drew most attention, and these are the areas in which Aboriginal settlements were concentrated. Regrettably, most of these sites are lost to us: between 70,000 and 5000 years ago the sea was lower than the present level and they now lie offshore, on the continental shelf. Characteristic of these Pleistocene inhabitants are bone points, and the stone core implements and crude scrapers of the Australian Core Tool Tradition. While this tradition, which underwent remarkably little change in more than 40,000 years, is pan-Australian, there are a number of regional elements that have New Guinean and Asian links. One of these is the edge-ground axe, which has been dated to 22,000 years in Arnhem Land. In Japan, similar ground stone tools have been found which are up to 30,000 years old. Ground stone tools were ultimately developed in most other parts of the world also, but only at a much later period.

Around 5000 years ago the sea rose to its present level, and while Aboriginal settlements were still concentrated along the coasts, there was rapidly increasing exploitation of inland resources. It was also at about this time that the dingo was introduced, and that a range of small, finely-finished flake implements especially developed for hafting, and known as the Australian Small Tool Tradition, appeared across the continent, superimposed on the earlier lithic forms. Political, economic and religious development continued, and by the time of settlement Europeans found that there were some 300,000 Aborigines living in around 500 tribal territories. Although their way of life was still based on hunting and gathering (the Aborigines never became agriculturalists), they had developed some very intricate relationships with their environment. In desert areas, small nomadic groups ranged over thousands of square kilometres, while in richer parts of the continent there were settled permanent villages. Fish traps were constructed, grasses and tubers replanted to assist nature, and fire was used to burn old vegetation and encourage the growth of rich new plant cover.

New Guinea was probably first occupied at the same time as Australia. A settlement on the Huon peninsula of northern New Guinea has been dated to at least 40,000 years ago, when it was covered by a deposit of volcanic ash, and New Ireland to the north is known to have been occupied by 33,000 years ago. Other sites, in the highlands of the north-west, evidence the widespread distribution of man in New Guinea by 8000 BC. Major changes took place about 6000 years ago with the introduction of domesticated Asian plants and animals and the creation of drained fields at places such as Kuk Swamp and Mugumamp Swamp. The hunting and gathering tradition of earlier times persisted into recent times, however, alongside agriculture.

Most of Island Melanesia (to the east, northeast and south-east of the New Guinea mainland) saw its first occupants during the first and second millennia BC, as maritime trading groups, bearing domesticated plants and animals, spread through the area. These Austronesian people and their distinctive pottery, belonging to the Lapita tradition, (which can be traced back to the Moluccas area of Indonesia) reached Fiji, the eastern boundary of present-day Melanesia, by 1300 BC, and soon after made their way into western Polynesia via Tonga and

Early Australian rock art (below) Rock painting was becoming more common in Australia 5000 years ago. This reconstruction shows a rock painting of Wandjina spirit beings, found in north-west Australia in 1837.

Samoa. And it was in these two island groups, but particularly in the latter, that a typically Melanesian material culture gradually evolved into a Polynesian-like one, during more than a thousand years of geographical isolation. Around 150 BC, a time when Lapita pottery was disappearing throughout Island Melanesia and western Polynesia, prehistoric Samoans ventured eastward in their canoes and settled the distant Marquesas Islands. After a brief pause, settlers spread to the Hawaiian Islands around AD 400, while at about the same time the first Polynesians reached Easter Island, there to give birth to an extraordinary and impressive culture. All the other major island groups of Polynesia, including New Zealand, were first settled, mainly from Samoa-Tonga or Society Islands-Marquesas, between 1000 and 1300, and a multitude of largely independent cultures evolved on these little 'island universes', only to be shattered by the shock of European contact during the 17th, 18th and 19th centuries.

Because of its climatic range, comparative enormity, and unfamiliar plants and animals, New Zealand presented its initial Polynesian settlers with special adaptive problems. Most of the domesticated plants and animals characteristic of the ancestral homeland were lost en route to New Zealand or else failed to withstand the more rigorous climatic conditions; the only important survivors were the dog and native rat, and the taro, yam and sweet potato, and these last three were basically restricted to coastal North Island localities. Nevertheless, the New Zealand environment offered these early set-tlers unexpected dietary compensation in the form of a whole suite of giant flightless birds, the best known of which are the moas. The original New Zealanders of the North Island and northern South Island thus became hunter-farmers, and a pattern of seasonal movement was developed to take advantage of these conditions. Settlements were predominantly coastal, and were restricted to several clearly defined regions. Meanwhile, new forms of tools were developed in response to the new environment. During the ensuing centuries the growing population expanded around the coasts of both islands, and inland resources were intensively exploited on South Island. As hunting and man-made 'fires' continued there was a gradual change in the environment, culminating in the 13th and 14th centuries with widespread deforestation, and virtual extinction of the avian megafauna.

It was probably at about this time that many of the implements derived from ancestral Polynesian types were abandoned, and that distinctly New Zealand artefacts began to emerge. So too did warfare, and with it the appearance of specially-developed fortified settlements termed *pa*. By the time of European contact, Cook and other explorers found New Zealand occupied by up to 250,000 Maoris. A hunting-farming lifestyle was still in evidence, except in the southern half of the South Island, beyond the limits of horticulture. European contact and settlement soon led to violent confrontation which resulted in the rapid breakdown of traditional Maori society and culture.

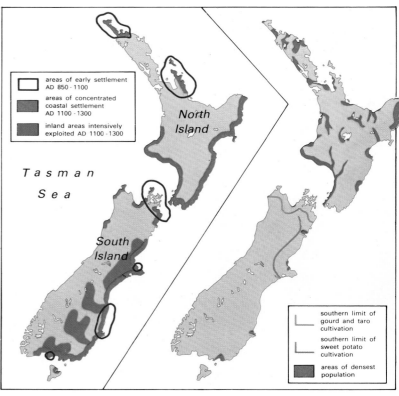

3/Early New Zealand settlement (above) New Zealand's early settlers were basically coastal hunters-gatherers, though South Island inland resources were seasonally exploited. Cultivated plants were only grown in sheltered North Island localities.

4/Maori settlement at European contact (above) By 1769 most Maoris were settled in the North Island, along the coast and rivers. Food obtained by hunting and gathering was in some areas supplemented by horticultural products.

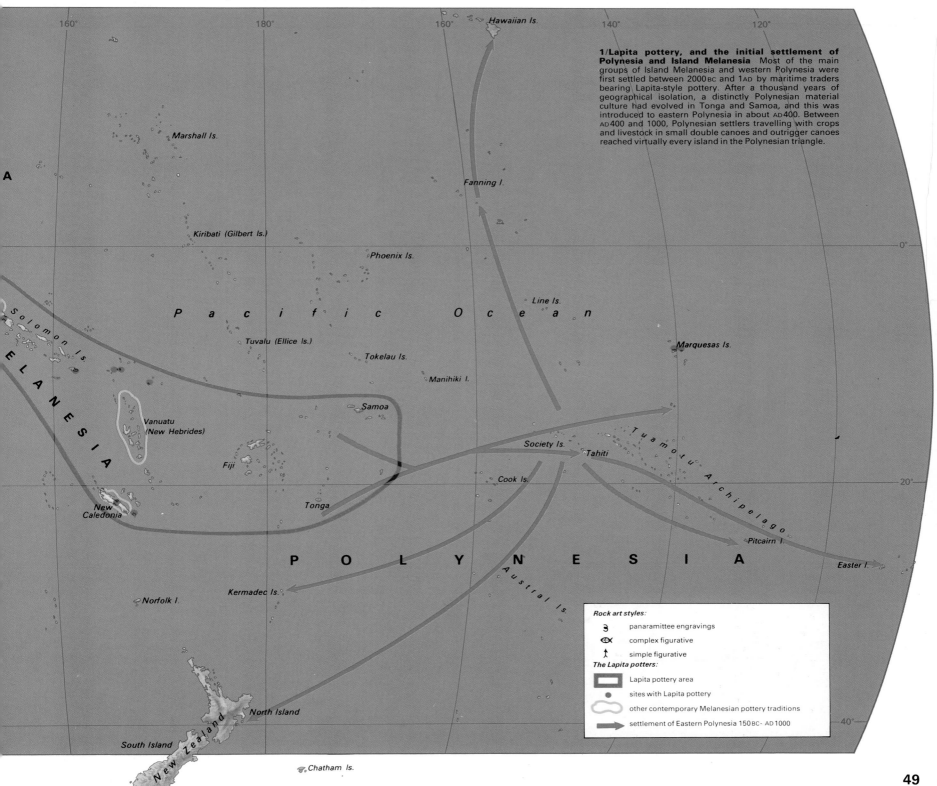

1/Lapita pottery, and the initial settlement of Polynesia and Island Melanesia Most of the main groups of Island Melanesia and western Polynesia were first settled between 2000 BC and 1 AD by maritime traders bearing Lapita-style pottery. After a thousand years of geographical isolation, a distinctly Polynesian material culture had evolved in Tonga and Samoa, and this was introduced to eastern Polynesia in about AD 400. Between AD 400 and 1000, Polynesian settlers travelling with crops and livestock in small double canoes and outrigger canoes reached virtually every island in the Polynesian triangle.

ABOUT the middle of the fourth millennium before Christ, in a few areas where agriculture was particularly intensive, the dispersed villages of Neolithic Man gave way to more complex societies. These were the first civilisations, and their emergence marks the beginning of a new phase of world history. They arose, apparently independently, in four widely dispersed areas (the early civilisations of America were considerably later in date): the lower Tigris and Euphrates valleys, the valley of the Nile, the Indus valley around Harappa and Mohenjo-Daro, and the Yellow River around An-yang. The characteristic feature of them all was the city, which now became an increasingly dominant social form, gradually eating up the surrounding countryside, until today urban civilisation has become the criterion of social progress. But the city had other important connotations as well: a complex division of labour, literacy and a literate class (usually the priesthood), monumental public buildings, political and religious hierarchies, a kingship descended from the gods, and ultimately empire, or the claim to rule over the *oikumene.* Already there was visible the dichotomy between the civilised world and the barbarian world outside. The onslaught of nomadic peoples eager to enjoy the fruits of civilisation was a recurrent theme of world history, until the introduction of firearms in the fifteenth century AD decisively tilted the balance in favour of the civilised peoples.

2

The firs

The pyramids at Giza, Egypt

civilisations

The beginnings of civilisation in the Eurasian world 3500 to 1500 BC

THE first civilisations arose in the fertile alluvial basins of the major rivers which water the otherwise arid plains of the Near East, draining from the mountain fringes where agriculture first began (see page 40). These more complex societies were the natural outcome of the increasing organisation needed to make use of these problematic, but potentially highly fertile, lowland environments.

To realise this potential, two things were necessary: a continuous flow of raw materials from neighbouring uplands to supply the stoneless, metalless and largely treeless plains, and a system of irrigation capable of spreading the copious floodwaters of the rivers over the thirsty lands nearby. As farming communities spread from the hilly flanks to the open plains and alluvial valleys, similar hierarchically organised societies sprang up – independently, but for similar reasons – in the basins of the Tigris-Euphrates, the Nile, the Yellow River and the Indus.

These societies had many features in common: the development of cities, writing, large public buildings, and the political apparatus of the state. They all stemmed from the need to organise local production and long-distance trade, and resulted from the emergence of regional centres where local produce was gathered and exchanged, trading expeditions organised, and irrigation systems planned. These functions were in the hands of either a priesthood or a secular ruler; in either case, the temple-centre with its literate élite was an important element, and large-scale public architecture a characteristic feature. Such centres supported craftsmen, and had an important role in defence. The centralised control required by these functions made necessary a specialised legal system and a standing army; they created a permanent bureaucracy, and the first division of society into classes.

The great volume of raw materials needed to supply the rapidly-expanding populations of the plains led to very extensive trading activity in the hinterlands, and to interaction with the smaller nuclei in the minor river-valleys of the intervening areas, where similar processes of urbanisation were taking place on a smaller scale. It is hard to separate cause and effect in this growing network of major and minor trading centres and city-states, which sprang up in a great arc from the eastern Mediterranean to the Indus. Only Chinese civilisation developed in relative isolation, sheltered by the Himalayas and the jungles of south-eastern Asia. Its interaction was mainly with neighbouring peasant societies, some of which already had advanced skills, for instance in bronze-working. Urban societies did not, however, appear either in the tropical zone or in temperate Europe until much later, in the Iron Age.

In northern and western Europe, copper- and bronze-working were practised on a village basis, and the population was too small and scattered to necessitate elaborate organisation. Nevertheless, there is evidence of inter-regional links, facilitated by the major river systems, and also along the coasts, suggesting the importance of boats and fishing. But the wealth of the community was not communally stored, and there is nothing to compare with the fortified centres of the Near East.

More striking changes, involving the movement of people rather than goods, were taking place in the steppe regions (see page 60), where the horse and the cart began to make possible the mobile way of life of the nomadic pastoralist.

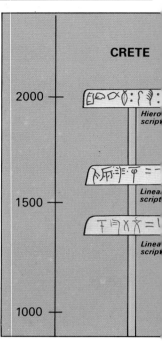

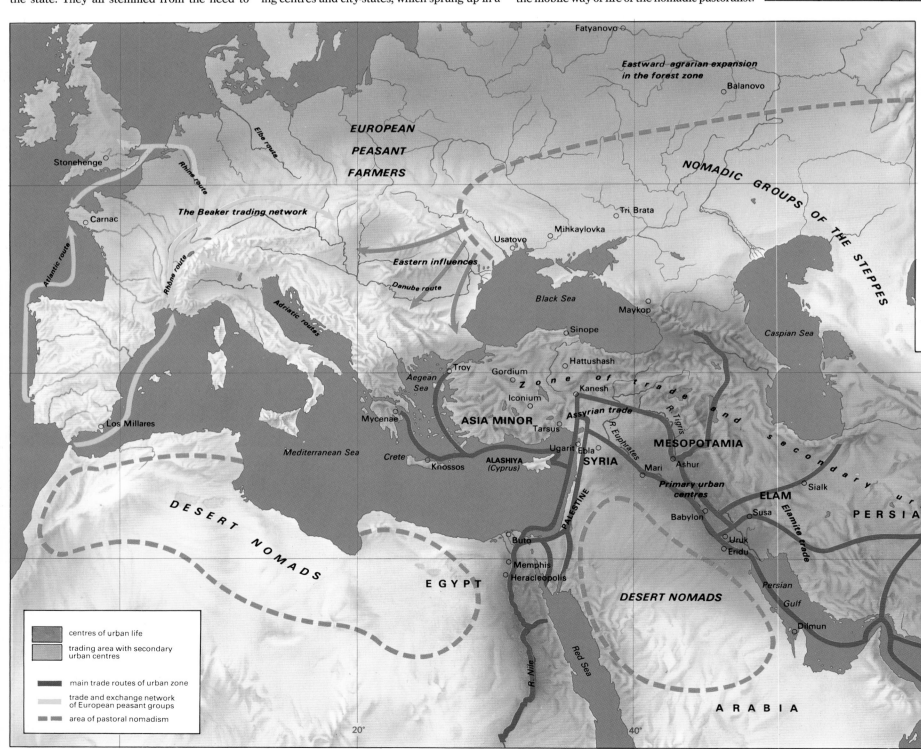

Legend:
- centres of urban life
- trading area with secondary urban centres
- main trade routes of urban zone
- trade and exchange network of European peasant groups
- area of pastoral nomadism

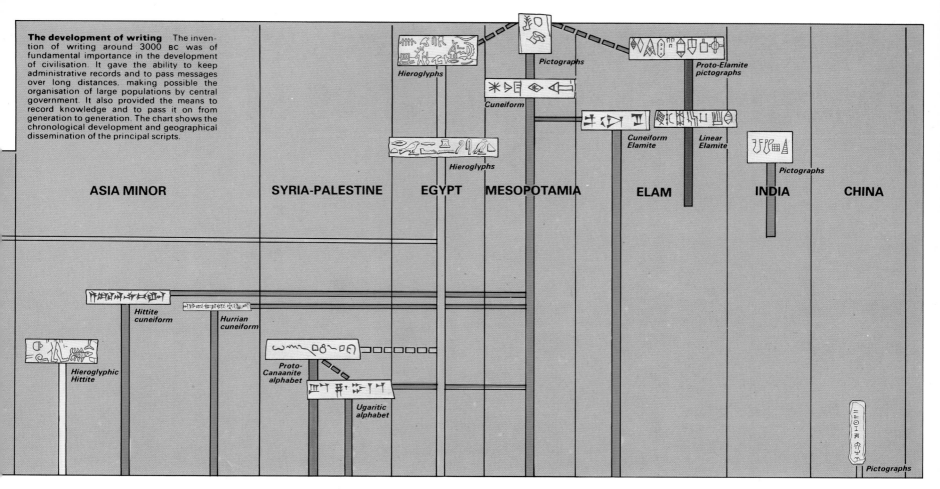

ASIA MINOR   SYRIA-PALESTINE   EGYPT   MESOPOTAMIA   ELAM   INDIA   CHINA

Pictographs

Hieroglyphs

Cuneiform

Proto-Elamite pictographs

Hieroglyphs

Cuneiform Elamite

Linear Elamite

Pictographs

Hittite cuneiform

Hurrian cuneiform

Hieroglyphic Hittite

Proto-Canaanite alphabet

Ugaritic alphabet

Pictographs

A temple of the Late Prehistoric period, c. 3000 BC (above) at Eridu, modern Abu Shahrain, in southern Mesopotamia. The main structure, built of mud brick, stood on a stone-faced platform. This architectural combination developed, in mud brick, into the ziggurat or temple tower characteristic of later Mesopotamian cities.

At the same time, groups of peasant farmers continued to push eastward along the forest belt of central Russia, using hardy types of cereals. These groups penetrated as far as the region of modern Moscow and on to the southern Urals by 2000 BC. Movements along the forest/steppe margin opened up one of the earliest contact-routes between China and north-western Eurasia by the end of the second millennium BC.

The contrast between the early civilisations and their neighbours – mobile pastoralists to the north, and peasant groups in the temperate forests of Europe or the tropical jungles of Indo-China – lay in the centralisation of their economies. In these early urban societies, goods were collected and allocated in a system of administered redistribution. To keep track of these flows of products, some kind of permanent record was needed: the development of writing systems is a characteristic feature of such societies. The earliest written records were usually no more than lists of the contents of storehouses – though once a flexible system of writing had been invented, it was used to record myths, legends and poetry, as well as for administration.

In each region, the earliest script was pictographic, i.e. symbols were used for individual words and concepts. But such a system, requiring a new sign for each new word, soon became cumbersome, and eventually symbols were used for sounds rather than ideas. The original pictures thus lost their significance as representations, and took on more arbitrary forms and meanings. One of the most successful systems was that evolved in Mesopotamia, where a stylus was used to write on clay tablets leaving wedge-shaped impressions (Latin *cuneus*=wedge: hence 'cuneiform'). This system was adopted by several groups for their own languages – initially Sumerian, then Akkadian, Babylonian and Assyrian, Eblaite (early Canaanite), Hittite and Hurrian; it thus included Semitic, non-Semitic and Indo-European languages.

It is possible that the earliest Mesopotamian pictographs spread, by way of Iran, to inspire those of the Indus – which never evolved beyond that stage. Chinese pictographs were probably an independent invention. Egyptian hieroglyphics ('priestly' pictographs) may similarly owe their initial inspiration to Mesopotamia, but developed their own strongly individual tradition. They may themselves have given the initial idea of writing to the palace-centres of Crete, which eventually developed their own 'Linear' scripts, Linear A and Linear B. Scribal inventiveness is best exemplified, however, in the creation of an alphabetic system on the basis of provincial Egyptian hieroglyphics, to write the Canaanite language. This system inspired an alphabetic cuneiform (Ugaritic) and became the ancestor of the alphabet which was taken over by the Greeks and passed on to the Romans to form the basis of the modern European script.

1/The spread of civilisation (below) As defined by urban life and writing, civilisation began in Mesopotamia and Egypt, and soon spread to Elam, the Indus Valley, and Crete and parts of Asia Minor. The spread of writing, largely from the two main stems, Mesopotamian cuneiform and Egyptian hieroglyphics (see chart above), is a good index of the spheres of influence of the two dominant centres, Mesopotamia and Egypt, and of the dissemination of civilisation from them. The beginnings of civilisation in Mesopotamia are exemplified at Warka (ancient Uruk), where several thousand pictographic clay tablets were found in levels of about 3000 BC associated with monumental architecture.

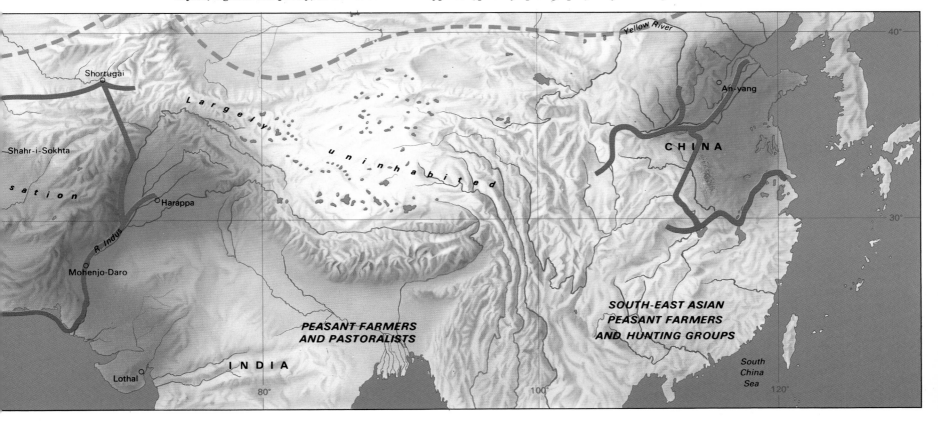

The early empires of Mesopotamia c.3500 to 1600 BC

THE fertile plains and valleys drained by the Tigris and the Euphrates offered in antiquity the richest potential farming country between the Indus and the Nile. But it was a land held always in the most delicate and fragile balance, needing constant defence both against nature and against the hungry human predators from the desert to the west and the mountains to the north and east. Unlike the regular, benevolent rise and fall of the Nile, the flow of the twin rivers, rising in the Eastern Taurus range, was irregular and unpredictable, bringing near-drought conditions in one year and violent, destructive floods the next. To establish and maintain any kind of control, dykes, canals, and organisation of the most elaborate kind were required. In meeting this challenge, many of the most significant achievements of early civilisation gradually evolved.

The pressed-mud villages dating from the first beginnings of agriculture (see page 40), whose remains have been excavated in the Zagros mountains and the northern Tigris basin, began to give way to more elaborate settlements. The potter's wheel appeared (probably invented in the region), while from about 3000 BC architecture, sculpture and metal-working reached new levels of mastery. Most far-reaching of all, writing was developed, first in the form of pictograms, later becoming cuneiform script (see page 52).

Underlying subsequent developments, during the late 4th to the mid-2nd millennium, was cultural cross-fertilisation between four major ethno-cultural groups: Sumerians, Semites, Indo-Europeans (Hittites) and Hurrians. In the Syrian area there were also significant contacts with Egypt. The underlying pattern of change involved expanding commercial contacts and the exploitation of economic resources, with initially short-lived attempts to consolidate the gains by military expansion from various centres, mainly in Mesopotamia itself.

In southern Mesopotamia it was the Sumerians, seen by some scholars as indigenous but generally taken to be immigrants via Persia from some more remote homeland (perhaps central Asia), who from 3000 BC onwards introduced writing and developed large compact social organisations which may properly be called cities. They perfected the irrigation techniques invented by their predecessors, and brought to a high standard the metal technology already developed in Anatolia and Persia.

Throughout history, Semitic-speaking peoples from the Syrian desert have filtered into Meso-

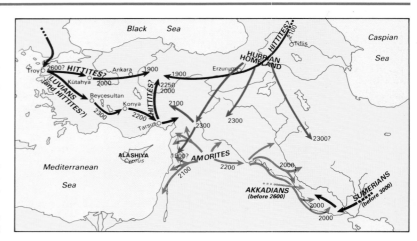

3/Ethnic movements *(above)* Long-standing controversy over the origins of, and the routes taken by, the Hittites is still unresolved: the map therefore indicates the three principal hypotheses. Very little is known for certain about the migrations of the Akkadians and Sumerians.

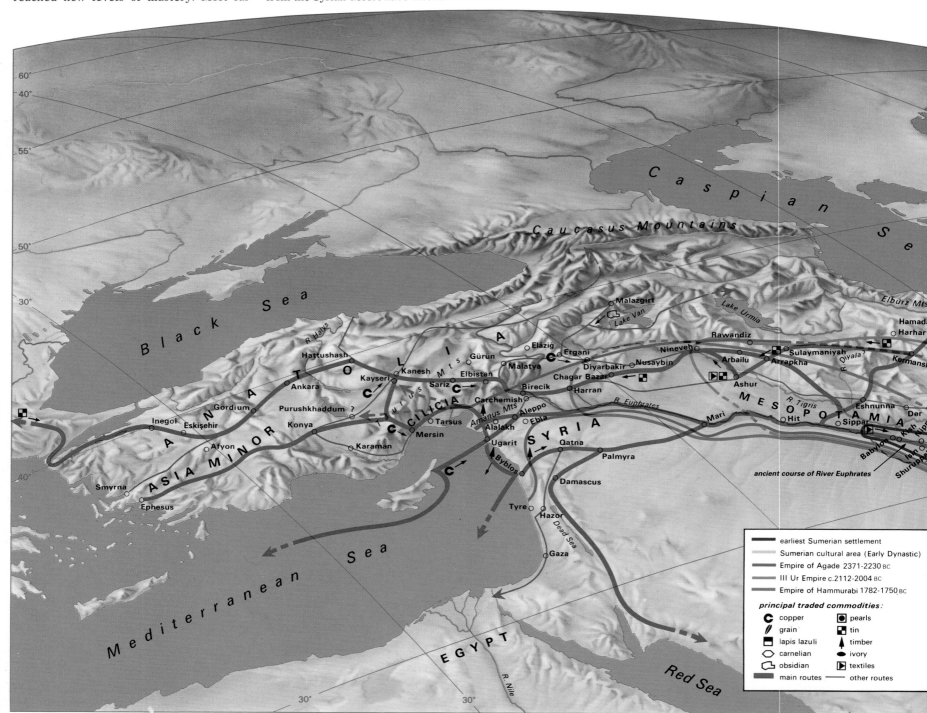

earliest Sumerian settlement
Sumerian cultural area (Early Dynastic)
Empire of Agade 2371-2230 BC
III Ur Empire c.2112-2004 BC
Empire of Hammurabi 1782-1750 BC

principal traded commodities:

C copper
/ grain
lapis lazuli
carnelian
obsidian
main routes

pearls
tin
timber
ivory
textiles
other routes

Sandstone stele of Naram-Sin *(above)* One of the greatest rulers of the third millennium Agade Dynasty, which founded the first Mesopotamian Empire. It depicts his victory over the Lullubu, a people of the Zagros. The stele, two metres high, in antiquity taken by an Elamite conqueror to Susa in south-west Persia, is now in the Louvre Museum.

potamia, but in this period there were two incursions of major significance: Akkadians in the first third of the 3rd millennium, and Amorites around the turn of the 3rd and 2nd millennia.

At least two waves of Indo-Europeans (represented later by Luvians and Hittites, the latter by far the more prominent politically) entered Asia Minor from the north before 2000 BC. The route of the Luvians in western and southern Asia Minor is generally agreed, but that of the Hittites is in dispute. The Hurrians were a people originally from the Caucasus, who began moving southwards and westwards in the 3rd millennium, becoming widespread in eastern Anatolia, Syria, and northern Mesopotamia from 1800 BC.

The political organisation of the Sumerians of the first half of the 3rd millennium (the Early Dynastic period) was based on city-states with a shifting hegemony among them. Their need of timber, metals and semi-precious stones, none of which southern Mesopotamia provides, led the Sumerians to begin exploitation of the Zagros and Amanus and to develop more distant trade routes into Persia and Asia Minor and by sea to Dilmun (Bahrain) and possibly beyond.

The first significant attempt at empire was under the dynasty of Agade, of Akkadian immigrant origin, whose rulers (most notably Sargon and his grandson Naram-Sin) reduced the importance of the old city-state system by moving towards centralised government. They undertook deliberate conquests from south-west Persia to Syria and (according to not improbable tradition) into central Asia Minor, in the interest of trade. Sea trade extended to the remote lands of Magan and Meluhha, possibly the Persian coast of the Gulf of Oman and the Indus Valley. Collapse, triggered by the invasion of hillmen (barbarous Gutians from the central Zagros) but ultimately due to internal stresses, was followed by a renaissance of the Sumerian city-state system in which Ur finally emerged as the dominant element, a highly bureaucratic empire more compact and stable than that of Agade.

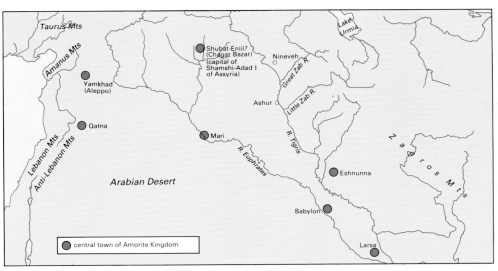

2/Principal Amorite kingdoms *(above)* Babylon's eventual supremacy under Hammurabi was not foreseen by contemporaries, one of whom wrote, 'There is no king who is unquestionably powerful by himself'. Ten or fifteen kings, he reported, followed Hammurabi, but similar numbers supported Rim-Sin of Larsa, Ibalpiel of Eshnunna and Amutpiel of Qatna, while twenty backed Yarimlim of Yamkhad (Aleppo).

This empire in turn collapsed (c. 2000 BC) under the pressure of new Semitic invaders, the Amorites, probably from eastern Syria. The Amorites gradually settled, to establish dynasties from Syria to the Diyala area and south Mesopotamia on the basis of old kingdoms and city-states. (Map 2 marks the most prominent of these.) The two of greatest eventual significance were Assyria and Babylon. Assyria, which already had trading colonies in Anatolia, passed from a native dynasty to the Amorite Shamshi-Adad I, who extended it from the Zagros mountains to the middle Euphrates to make it the most powerful state in Mesopotamia. After the death of Shamshi-Adad and towards the end of the reign of Hammurabi (1792-1750 BC), Babylon emerged pre-eminent after a period of changing coalitions among Amorite city-states, to achieve a brief empire. The enduring importance of this was the development of the ideal (not always fulfilled) of a single south Mesopotamian kingdom with Babylon as its capital.

In Asia Minor, early trading contacts, possible military expeditions by the Agade dynasty,

Assyrian merchant colonies, and indirect contacts via Syria and Cilicia, had already introduced some Mesopotamian cultural influence by the early 2nd millennium. By the 17th century BC the Hittites had crystalised into a kingdom in the Halys area, which expanded southwards from 1650 BC, eventually to control Syria north of Aleppo and west of the Euphrates. In a transitory further extension they broke past Aleppo and marched down the Euphrates to sack Babylon in 1595 BC. Further Hittite expansion towards Mesopotamia was checked by the Hurrians, by that time consolidating to the east of the Euphrates bend. After the Hittite raid, the Cassites, a people from the Zagros, seized control of Babylonia. Rapidly assimilating to its culture, it ruled for over four centuries.

1/The early empires *(below)* Throughout this period, general areas of influence and control are clear, but the exact situation of many boundaries remains uncertain, and in some cases — such as Agade's frontier south of Susa or the northern extension, of Assyria under Shamshi-Adad — completely unknown. Partly for this reason, partly because there were substantial overlaps between the empires of Shamshi-Adad and Hammurabi, the former is not shown here, though its geographical extent was at least as great.

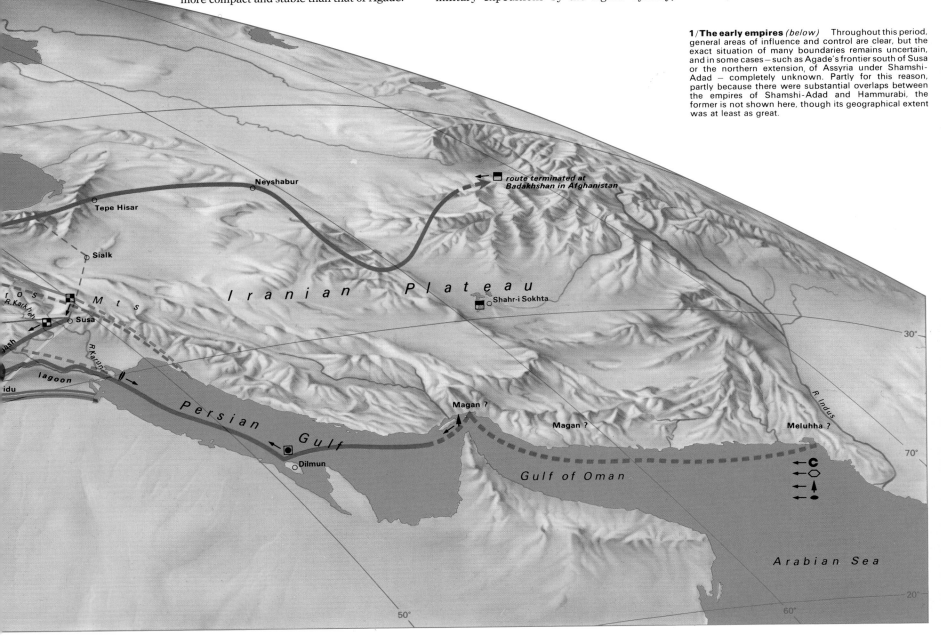

The Near East from the fall of Babylon to the fall of Assyria c.1300 to 612 BC

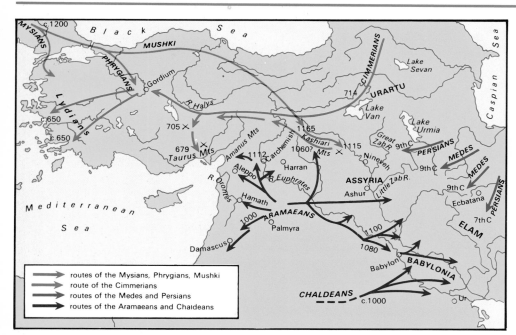

3/Catalysts of civilisation (left) The spread and unification of Near Eastern civilisation was accelerated by ethnic movements. Particularly significant were the Aramaeans. This Semitic people, the first major users of the camel, were prominent in international trade; their language and script eventually became internationally used for trade and diplomacy.

AFTER the collapse of the First Dynasty of Babylon, the centre of gravity of the Near East shifted towards Syria and north Mesopotamia, where Hittite and Hurrian zones of influence met. Syria was the junction for trade routes from the east, from Asia Minor and the Aegean, and from Egypt, and for this reason each of the major powers sought to control it.

The typical political unit in Syria at this time was the city-state. Some were fully independent, and even (as Ugarit in the 15th century and Hamath and Damascus early in the first millennium) wielded control beyond their own territory; but usually they were vassals of some great power centred outside Syria. For the first three centuries three powers come into account. Egypt, the most distant, was interested in Syria both for its mercantile importance and because control there would safeguard Egypt from a recurrence of Asiatic invasion suffered earlier in the second millennium; the port of Byblos was of particular trading importance to Egypt. The second power was the Hittites, based in central Anatolia and gradually extending control towards the Aegean. The third was Mitanni, a predominantly Hurrian state centred on the Khabur and controlling much of north Mesopotamia, including Assyria; north of it lay the associated state of Hurri. At its maximum extent during the 15th century, when the Hittites were engaged in Asia Minor, Mitanni intermittently controlled all north Syria and Cilicia (Kizzuwadna). Subsequently the Hittites resumed their drive for Syria. Internal developments had weakened Egypt's hold on south Syria, so that under Shuppiluliumash (c.1380-1346 BC), the Hittites gained control of most of Syria by a system of vassal states, cutting Mitanni off from the Mediterranean.

Assyria, centred on the Tigris from Nineveh to Ashur, was a vassal of Mitanni as long as the latter was a major power, but Hittite pressure on Mitanni allowed Assyria's re-emergence. Assyria had adopted much of the military organisation of the Hurrians, notably the use of the war-chariot, and by the second half of the 12th century intermittently controlled former Mitannian territory up to the Euphrates.

In about 1200 BC the Hittite Empire collapsed. The immediate cause was belligerent movements of migrants from the Aegean region known from Egyptian inscriptions as 'Peoples of the Sea'. A consequence of these movements was the spread of the use of iron, for the production of which the Hittite area had hitherto been the main centre. Some relics of Hittite culture survived in neo-Hittite states in north Syria, notably Carchemish and Aleppo. The later kingdom of Lydia in western Asia Minor may in-

directly represent another Hittite survival.

The vacuum left in central Anatolia by the Hittite collapse was filled not by the 'Peoples of the Sea' (although one group, the Danuna, probably settled in Cilicia) but by a new ethnic group migrating from Europe. The newcomers were the people known to the Greeks as Phrygians, with their eventual capital at Gordium. Another group, known to the Assyrians as Mushki, may (as shown here) have been a different wave of the same people, though other scholars think they came via east of the Black Sea and joined the Phrygians after an attempt to thrust southwards into Mesopotamia had been checked by Assyria in a battle in 1115 BC.

Further south another migration, in the 11th century, contributed to a significant change in the Near Eastern ethnic and political structure by the turn of the millennium. This was the migration of the Semitic Aramaeans, a people from the mountainous area east of Syria. This produced a strong Aramaean element in the Syrian states, along the Euphrates, and in north Babylonia. In south Babylonia the Chaldeans, an associated group whose earlier history is not clear, settled at this time, particularly around Ur, known henceforth as 'of the Chaldees'.

Assyria, politically the successor of Mitanni, was subject to pressures from both the northern and southern migrations. But whereas in the north Assyria deflected the Mushki, to the south and west Aramaean pressure was so persistent that although Assyria once (c.1100 BC) broke through to the Mediterranean its effective western boundary from soon after this time until the end of the 10th century was the Khabur.

In the first millennium the predominant characteristic of Assyria was its imperialism. What mainly motivated this were joint considerations of commercial interests and the quest for secure boundaries. The ultimate strength of Assyria lay in its fertile corn-plains in the rain-belt, but these had no natural defence against raids from the hillsmen to north and east. In addition, Assyria lacked metal ores and large timber. The Assyrian response to these factors was systematically to send armies through the petty states of the Zagros foothills to exact tribute in metals, timber and horses. This produced for Assyria border security, economic advantages and an efficient military organisation.

This policy, begun in the period between Mitannian decline and Aramaean pressure, was energetically resumed from the end of the 10th century. What made this possible is not wholly clear; a main factor was probably the international stability developing as many of the Aramaeans settled to form states in Syria. Ashurnasirpal II (883-859 BC) was able to force a bridge-

head through Carchemish to the Mediterranean; under his son Shalmaneser III (858-824 BC), this was extended both northwards to the Taurus (important for the trade routes to Europe and as a source of metals) and southwards to Damascus. The latter move brought Assyria directly into military conflict with the Aramaean states in Syria and their allies in Palestine, including Israel. With temporary setbacks, Assyria gradually extended control over these states, until the whole of Syria and Palestine, and for a short time in the 7th century north Egypt, were within the Assyrian Empire.

North of Assyria, the people around Lake Van, ethnically predominantly Hurrian, coalesced into a federation of states and then the kingdom of Urartu, which became notable for its metal technology and its engineering skill in irrigation works. Its developing trade, particularly in bronze objects, made it by the 8th century a serious rival of Assyria for control of northern Syria. The two states also clashed over control of the horse-rearing regions south of Lake Urmia.

Urartu was seriously weakened near the end of the 8th century by combined Assyrian pressure and invasion by Cimmerians, migrating hordes from east of the Black Sea. The Cimmerians subsequently clashed with Assyria in the Taurus, before their vanguard moved into western Anatolia, where they knocked out Phrygia in the early 7th century, and finally lost their momentum in an attack on Lydia a little later. The menace of the Cimmerians, and of the related Scythians who followed them, led to rapprochement between Assyria and Urartu.

Assyria's southern neighbour Babylonia, conquered by her in the late 13th century, was at most subsequent periods dominated politically by Assyria, even when formally independent. In turn, Assyria was strongly influenced by Babylonian culture; for example, many Assyrian royal inscriptions were written not in Assyrian but in Standard Babylonian.

To the east of Babylonia, and closely linked by economic interests, was Elam. Its political importance during this period was slight, except for a brief expansion into the Diyala area and eastern Assyria in the mid-12th century, probably seeking to gain control of the Zagros trade routes. From the late 8th century, the Chaldean tribes increasingly dominated Babylonia, requiring Assyrian military intervention there. Links of these tribesmen with Elam, and associated Elamite meddling in Babylonia, led Assyria to overrun and annex Elam in the 7th century.

Further north, east of the Zagros, Assyria had from the late 9th century been in contact with the Medes, Iranian migrants from north of the Caspian. During their two centuries as nominal vassals of Assyria, the Medes adopted features of Assyrian administrative practice and warfare which they later used against their tutors.

By the mid-7th century Assyria, attempting to control the whole Near East from Egypt to west Persia and northwards to the Taurus, was severely overstretched. Collapse began when a Chaldean, Nabopolassar, seized the kingship of Babylonia in 625, and attacked Assyria. Nabopolassar was later joined by the Medes and Scythian hordes. The Assyrian capital, Nineveh, was sacked in 612 BC, the last organised Assyrian resistance ending in 605 BC at Carchemish.

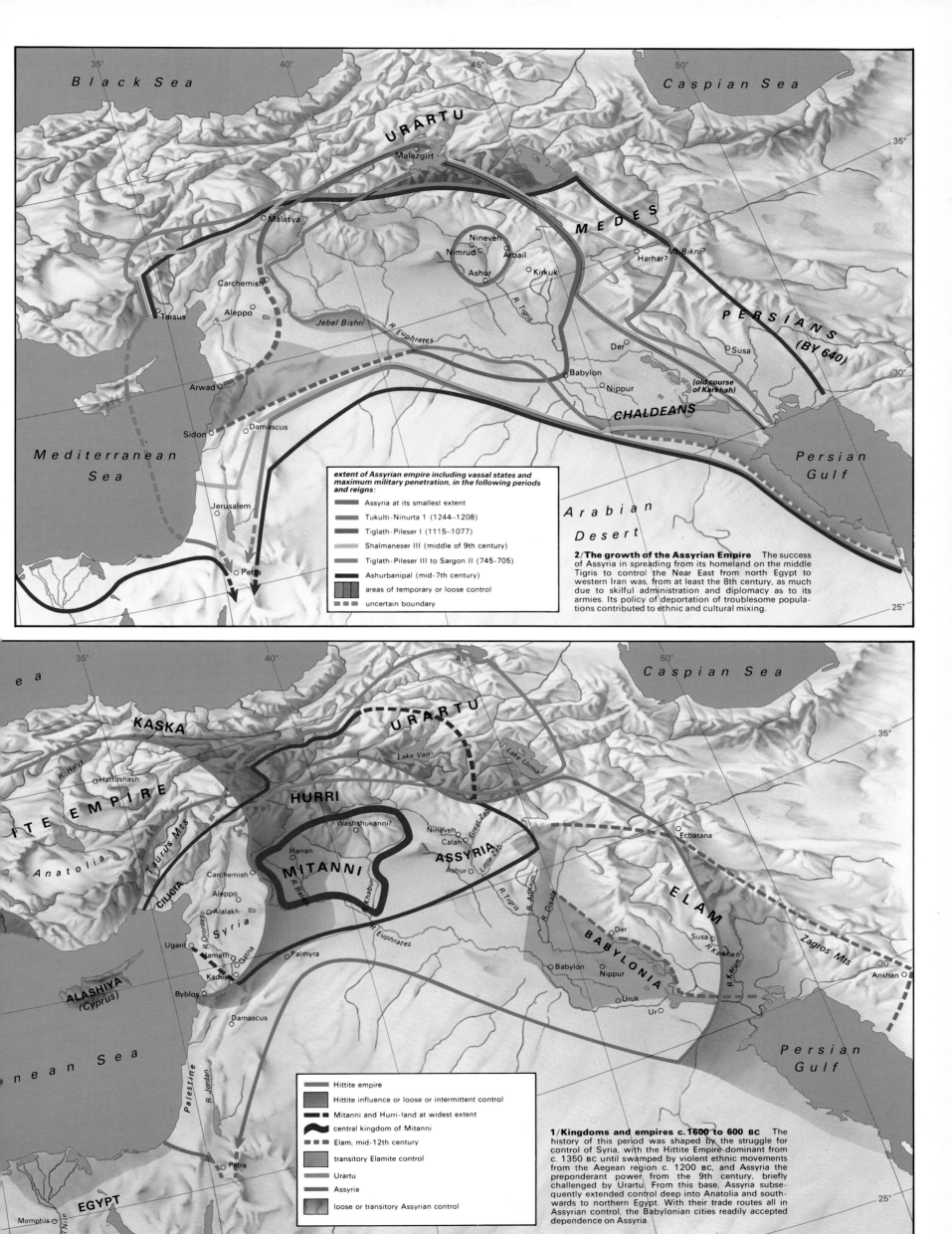

Black Sea

URARTU

Malazgirt

Caspian Sea

Malatya

MEDES

Nineveh
Nimrud   Arbail
Ashur   Kirkuk   Harhar?   Mt Bikni?

Carchemish

Aleppo
Tarsus   *Jebel Bishri*   *R. Euphrates*   PERSIANS
(BY 640)

Der   Susa

Arwad   Babylon
Nippur   *(old course of Karkhah)*

Sidon   Damascus   CHALDEANS

Mediterranean Sea   Persian Gulf

Jerusalem   *Arabian Desert*

Petra

extent of Assyrian empire including vassal states and
maximum military penetration, in the following periods
and reigns:

Assyria at its smallest extent

Tukulti-Ninurta 1 (1244–1208)

Tiglath-Pileser I (1115–1077)

Shalmaneser III (middle of 9th century)

Tiglath-Pileser III to Sargon II (745-705)

Ashurbanipal (mid-7th century)

areas of temporary or loose control

uncertain boundary

2/The growth of the Assyrian Empire   The success
of Assyria in spreading from its homeland on the middle
Tigris to control the Near East from north Egypt to
western Iran was, from at least the 8th century, as much
due to skilful administration and diplomacy as to its
armies. Its policy of deportation of troublesome populations contributed to ethnic and cultural mixing.

---

ea   Caspian Sea

KASKA   URARTU

R. Halys   Hattushash   Lake Van   Lake Urmia

HURRI

ITE EMPIRE   Washshukanni?   Ecbatana

Taurus Mts   *Anatolia*   Nineveh   ELAM
Harran   Calah
Carchemish   MITANNI   ASSYRIA
CILICIA   Aleppo   Ashur   *Little Zab*
Alalakh   *R. Balikh*   *R. Tigris*   *R. Adhaim*
Syria   *R. Khabur*   *R. Diyala*
Ugarit   *R. Orontes*   *R. Euphrates*   Der   *Zagros Mts*
Hamath   Qatna   Palmyra   BABYLONIA   Susa   *R. Karun*
ALASHIYA   Kadesh   Babylon   *R. Karkheh*
(Cyprus)   Byblos   Nippur   Anshan
Damascus   Uruk
Ur

nean Sea   Persian Gulf

Palestine   *R. Jordan*

Petra

EGYPT

Memphis   *R. Nile*

Hittite empire

Hittite influence or loose or intermittent control

Mitanni and Hurri-land at widest extent

central kingdom of Mitanni

Elam, mid-12th century

transitory Elamite control

Urartu

Assyria

loose or transitory Assyrian control

1/Kingdoms and empires c.1600 to 600 BC   The
history of this period was shaped by the struggle for
control of Syria, with the Hittite Empire dominant from
c. 1350 BC until swamped by violent ethnic movements
from the Aegean region c. 1200 BC, and Assyria the
preponderant power from the 9th century, briefly
challenged by Urartu. From this base, Assyria subsequently extended control deep into Anatolia and southwards to northern Egypt. With their trade routes all in
Assyrian control, the Babylonian cities readily accepted
dependence on Assyria.

Ancient Egypt and her empires

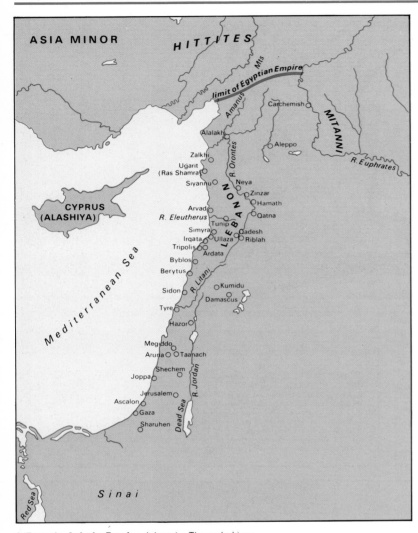

2/Egypt's Asiatic Empire *(above)* The early kings of the XVIIIth Dynasty embarked on a policy of expansion into western Asia. Having experienced the rewards of successful conquest they tried to add to what they had won. The dominion of Tuthmosis I (c. 1525-1512 BC) extended from the Euphrates to the Third Cataract in Nubia. His grandson, Tuthmosis III (c. 1504-1450 BC) fought seventeen campaigns in Palestine and Syria, taking Egypt's empire to its furthest northern limits in the region of Carchemish. After much of this empire had crumbled away in the next 130 years, the campaigns of Sethos I and Ramesses II recovered some of the lost territory, but Egyptian armies never again gained control beyond Qadesh on the Orontes.

FROM Early Palaeolithic times onwards, for very many thousands of years, the natural fauna and flora of the Lower Nile valley sustained semi-nomadic groups of hunters and food-gatherers, whose stone implements have been found in abundance in the terraces cut by the river, in the wadis adjoining the valley and on the surface of the high deserts flanking it. These primitive inhabitants were succeeded in Neolithic and pre-Dynastic times (c. 7000-3100 BC) by people who adopted a more settled mode of life, food-producers who brought arable land under cultivation and bred cattle. Their racial connections are obscure, but their artefacts are sufficiently distinctive to enable their different cultural groups to be easily distinguished and, in Upper (southern) Egypt at least, to allow their order of arrival in the Nile valley to be determined.

At first there was little intercourse between the peasant communities; each community worshipped its local deity or deities and each developed its own theological ideas. It was this insularity which was largely responsible for the multiplicity of deities and cults in historical times. When the communities were grouped into larger units (later called *nomes* by the Greeks), they retained much of their religious independence, and it was scarcely affected when, towards the end of the pre-Dynastic period, the *nomes* became two kingdoms with their respective capitals at Hieraconpolis, in Upper Egypt, and Buto. In c.3100 BC Menes, the king of Upper Egypt, subdued Lower Egypt, united the 'Two Lands' under one crown and built a new capital, later called Memphis, near the junction of the two former kingdoms. It was at about this time that writing in the hieroglyphic script was invented and also that many of the conventions employed in Egyptian art for the next three thousand years were adopted. The Early Dynastic Period (c.3100-2685 BC) was the most formative age of ancient Egypt, when proficiency advanced rapidly in stone-masonry, copper-smelting and working and technical skills of many kinds. Living conditions improved, and there can be little doubt that there was a considerable growth in the population. At the beginning of the Old Kingdom (IIIrd-VIth Dynasties, c.2685-2180 BC) Imhotep was able to assemble the necessary skill and manpower to build for

his king, Zoser, the famous Step Pyramid at Saqqara, the first monument in Egypt to be constructed entirely of hewn stone. Pyramids of step design were superseded at the beginning of the IVth Dynasty (c.2613-2494 BC) by geometrically true pyramids, the most outstanding examples of which are the Great Pyramid of Cheops and the pyramid of his son, Chephren, at Giza. Throughout the remainder of the Old Kingdom kings and high officials continued to adorn their temples and tombs with sculptures in relief and in the round which were never surpassed in strength and quality, but politically it was a period of decline which culminated, at the end of the VIth Dynasty (c.2180 BC), in the collapse of the central government. For the next 140 years (the First Intermediate Period, c.2180-2040 BC), although kings existed in name, first at Memphis and then at Heracleopolis, the real rulers were the provincial governors, the nomarchs, who recruited private armies and levied taxes for their own use in their respective *nomes*. At times famine was general and struggles for supremacy developed between the nomes.

National unity was at length restored by the nomarchs of Thebes, who first gained control of the nomes south of their own and then advanced northwards. The final victory over the Heracleopolitan king was won by Mentuhotep II, whose namesake and ancestor, Mentuhotep I, had founded the Theban dynasty four generations previously. Apart from his military achievements, which also included the expulsion of Asiatic and Libyan settlers from the eastern and the western Delta, he re-established an effective central government, at Thebes, and laid the foundations of a new age of economic and cultural progress; it marked the beginning of the Middle Kingdom (XIth and XIIth Dynasties, c.2060-1785 BC). Under the first king of the XIIth Dynasty, Ammenemes I, the capital was moved to Itj-towy, eighteen miles south of Memphis and near the entrance to the Faiyum. He and his six successors, three bearing his name and three named Sesostris, carried out important land reclamation and irrigation schemes, particularly in the Faiyum, probably in an effort to prevent a recurrence of the famines which had plagued the country since the end of the Old Kingdom. It was a time when the arts flourished, particularly sculpture and lapidary work; some

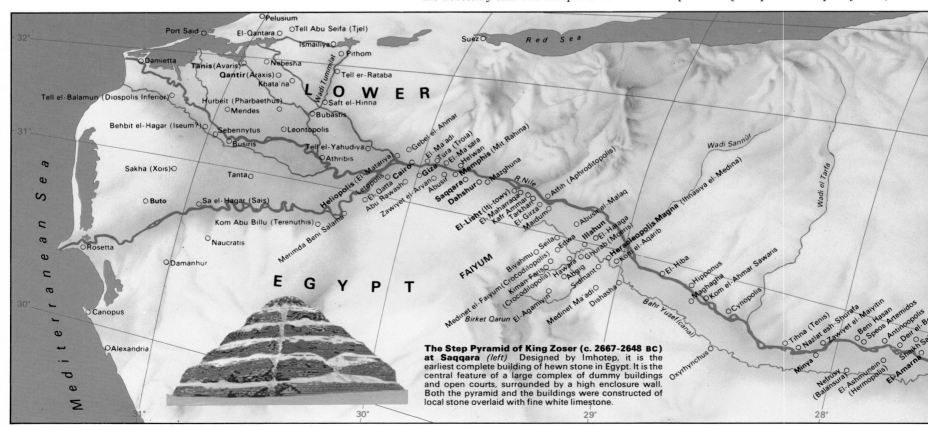

The Step Pyramid of King Zoser (c. 2667-2648 BC) at Saqqara *(left)* Designed by Imhotep, it is the earliest complete building of hewn stone in Egypt. It is the central feature of a large complex of dummy buildings and open courts, surrounded by a high enclosure wall. Both the pyramid and the buildings were constructed of local stone overlaid with fine white limestone.

of the best surviving examples are the reliefs on the peripteral chapel of Sesostris I at Karnak and the jewellery found in tombs of princesses at the pyramids of Ammenemes II at Dahshur and of Sesostris II at Illahun.

In the unsettled period which followed the XIIth Dynasty (the Second Intermediate Period, c.1785-1570 BC), a succession of, mainly ephemeral, kings failed to prevent a repetition of the infiltration of Asiatic immigrants into the northeastern Delta, this time, moreover, in large numbers. Known as the Hyksos, these intruders eventually subjected the Egyptian inhabitants of the Delta and the Nile valley as far as Cusae to their domination for more than a century. Farther south, the princes of Thebes ruled as vassals of the Hyksos kings until Kamose in c.1567 BC succeeded in recovering nearly all the occupied territory. His brother, Amosis I, completed the conquest three years later by capturing Avaris, the Hyksos capital. The traditional representation of Hyksos rule as harsh and oppressive finds little contemporary support. There can be no doubt, however, that it provided Egypt with the incentive to safeguard her territory against further foreign domination by embarking on her conquest of neighbouring lands in western Asia. In its achievement she owed much to the horse-drawn chariot and the composite bow, both of which came to her knowledge through the Hyksos.

Amosis pursued the retreating enemy through Palestine into Syria in a campaign which lasted for at least three years. Never before had Egypt exercised government over foreign territory, except in Lower Nubia, between the First and the Second Cataracts, where the kings of the XIIth Dynasty had built a series of forts. In the XVIIIth Dynasty (c.1570-1320 BC), however, the six warrior kings who followed Amosis I, each of whom was named either Amenophis or Tuthmosis, controlled an empire which ultimately stretched northwards to the Euphrates and southwards to about the Fourth Cataract. But its maintenance required frequent displays of strength and prompt action to counter threats of secession, neither of which suited the temperaments of the pleasure-loving Amenophis III or of his son, Amenophis IV, who adopted the name Akhenaten in about the fifth year of his reign. Inspired by religious fervour, Akhenaten proclaimed the god immanent in the sun's disk, Aten, to be the only god, suppressed the cults of Amun and all the other gods, confiscated their properties for the state, abandoned Thebes and built a new capital at El-Amarna. In art greater freedom was allowed in the subjects represented, and a new and distinctive style was introduced.

Akhenaten's heretical movement was already moribund when he died in c.1362 BC. Three years later the court returned to Thebes and his young successor immediately reinstated the ancient cults, signifying his own adherence to the cult of Amun by changing his name from Tutankhaten to Tutankhamun. As is evident from the Amarna letters (diplomatic correspondence, mostly written in Akkadian, between Egypt and the rulers of western Asia), much of the Asiatic empire had been lost by the time of Akhenaten's death, but Egypt still kept a foothold in Palestine; under Sethos I (c.1318-1304 BC) and Ramesses II (c.1304-1237 BC) her former possessions, as far as Qadesh on the Orontes, were regained. Some fierce but indecisive encounters with the Hittites, whose empire embraced the territory farther north, culminated in two peace treaties, the first with Sethos I and, some thirty years later, the second, a more permanent contract, with Ramesses II. Apart from being successful fighters, these two kings constructed some outstanding monuments, notably the temple of Abydus and the hypostyle hall at Karnak by Sethos I, and the rock-temples of Abu Simbel by Ramesses II.

There were still two warrior-kings to come, Merneptah (c.1236-1223 BC) and Ramesses III (c.1198-1166 BC). Their role, however, was not to expand the empire, but to defend the land of Egypt against a series of attacks, sometimes concerted, by Libyans (who had previously been defeated by Sethos I) and a mixed army of invaders from Asia Minor and the Aegean, collectively called 'peoples of the sea'. Having failed to achieve their aim by military means, the Libyans resorted to peaceful penetration, with the result that, some two centuries after the death of Ramesses III, the chief of one of their groups of settlers in the Nile Valley was able to ascend the throne as the founder of a dynasty of nine Libyan kings (the XXIInd Dynasty, c.935-730 BC).

For the next seven hundred years, until she became a province of the Roman Empire in 30 BC, Egypt was ruled in turn by Ethiopians, her former province of Nubia (the XXVth Dynasty, 751-656 BC), twice by Persians (525-404 BC and 341-333 BC) and, after the annexation by Alexander the Great in 333 BC, by Macedonians and Greeks. The two hundred years during which she was governed by native kings (the XXVIth Dynasty, c.664-525 BC and the XXVIII-XXXth Dynasties, c.404-341 BC) were periods when much attention was paid to the arts, but even under foreign rule the construction of monuments and other creative activities continued without either serious interruption or any fundamental change in character, and the same continuity can be observed in religion, government and society. No more telling tribute could have been paid to the essential worth of the Egyptian civilisation.

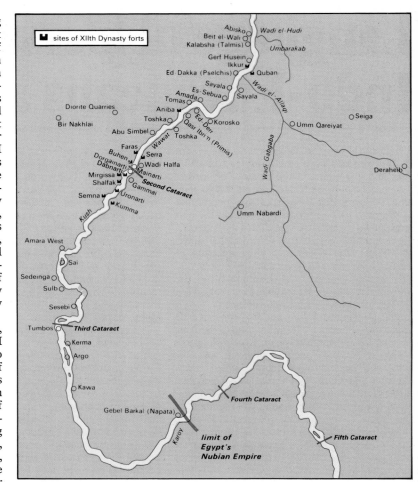

sites of XIIth Dynasty forts

3/Egypt's Nubian conquests (above) Nubia, on Egypt's southern frontier, was an important supplier, above all of gold from the region of Wadi el-Allaqi and Wadi Gabgaba, and further south between Wadi Halfa and Kerma. In the XIIth Dynasty the whole territory from the First Cataract to Semna was annexed and brick forts were built at strategic points, the most northerly being near Aswan. The XVIIIth Dynasty kings pushed the boundary further south until, under Tuthmosis III, it reached Napata, near the Fourth Cataract.

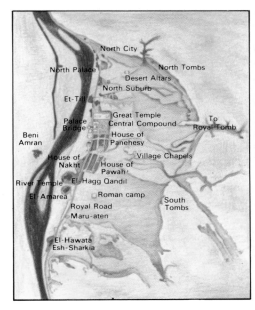

4/El-Amarna (right) Only in one instance has it been possible to reproduce the ground-plan of an ancient Egyptian city and to reconstruct the design of some of its principal buildings. This is El-Amarna, built by Akhenaten as his new capital when he abandoned Thebes. It lies on the east bank of the Nile, approximately half way between Cairo and Luxor, in a natural amphitheatre formed by the cliffs of the high desert, about eight miles long and three miles wide at the centre.

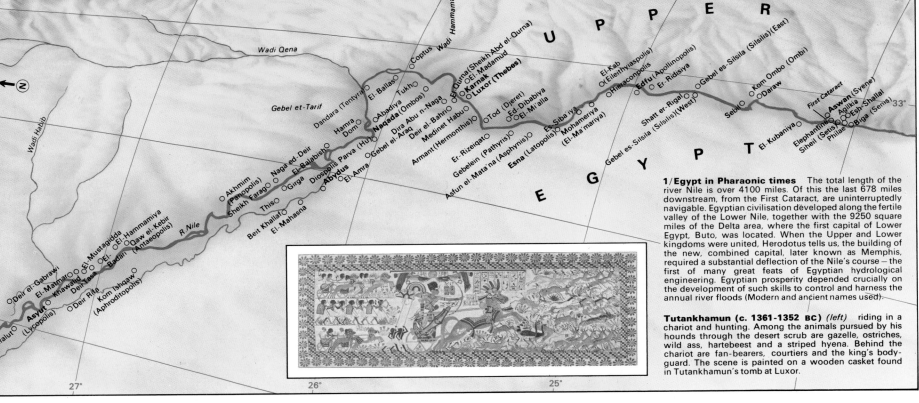

1/Egypt in Pharaonic times The total length of the river Nile is over 4100 miles. Of this the last 678 miles downstream, from the First Cataract, are uninterruptedly navigable. Egyptian civilisation developed along the fertile valley of the Lower Nile, together with the 9250 square miles of the Delta area, where the first capital of Lower Egypt, Buto, was located. When the Upper and Lower kingdoms were united, Herodotus tells us, the building of the new, combined capital, later known as Memphis, required a substantial deflection of the Nile's course — the first of many great feats of Egyptian hydrological engineering. Egyptian prosperity depended crucially on the development of such skills to control and harness the annual river floods (Modern and ancient names used).

Tutankhamun (c. 1361-1352 BC) (left) riding in a chariot and hunting. Among the animals pursued by his hounds through the desert scrub are gazelle, ostriches, wild ass, hartebeest and a striped hyena. Behind the chariot are fan-bearers, courtiers and the king's body-guard. The scene is painted on a wooden casket found in Tutankhamun's tomb at Luxor.

Language dispersals: Indo-Europeans and Semites

THE study of early languages is one of the most difficult problems faced by archaeologists and historians. In the absence of written records, the only workable approach is to combine archaeological evidence for population continuity – or conversely for invasion and migration – with the distribution of languages at the time when they are first recorded in historical records. The result is a reconstruction of language history which can usually be regarded only as tentative. Yet the development of the present day pattern of language distribution is a subject of fundamental importance.

The languages of the modern world are divided into a number of families, one of the most famous being Indo-European, which embraces both Sanskrit and Persian at one end, and such European languages as Greek, Latin, French German and English at the other. Words like *father* (Latin *pater*; Sanskrit *pitar*) for instance, show close similarities among the members of the group. The earliest-known written forms of Indo-European are the second-millennium texts from Greece, written in Mycenaean Linear B, and from Asiatic Turkey (Anatolia), written by peoples such as the Hittites and Luvians. There are also more scattered references in contemporary texts from Mesopotamia which refer to a tribe called the Mitanni, and which contain Indo-European personal names. Significantly, terms used in the training of horses turn out also to be Indo-European. Until recently, most experts agreed that these Indo-European languages had first spread to Europe from the steppes in the third millenium BC. It now seems likely, however, that the earliest farmers of Europe already spoke Indo-European languages. The spread of farming in Europe took place in two different ways. In the south-east, and in the central plains and river valleys of the Danube and Rhine, it seems that actual farming groups moved gradually across the landscape bringing the new economy and the new language with them. Thus it is possible that already by the fifth millennium BC, Indo-European was spoken throughout a broad swathe of Europe from the Balkans to the Low Countries and the Paris Basin.

In most other parts of Europe – the Baltic lands in the north, Mediterranean Europe in the south, and the Atlantic fringe (including Britain) in the west – farming seems to have been adopted without any significant movement of people. Yet by the Roman period – and perhaps long before – all these areas spoke principally Indo-European. There must therefore have been a secondary spread of Indo-European from central Europe to north, south and west. This is most likely to have occurred in the fourth and third millennia BC, when there are a number of important innovations which spread from eastern and central Europe – wheeled vehicles, the plough, copper metallurgy and the horse.

The contacts needed to ensure supplies of these and other commodities may have encouraged the adoption of Indo-European languages in western Europe. The continued survival down to relatively recent times of non-Indo-European Pictish in northern Scotland, and to the present day of non-Indo-European Basque in north-east Spain and south-west France, may represent the last vestiges of the original non-Indo-European speech of western Europe.

A basic division can be seen between the western Indo-European group, whose members had the stable agricultural life of the European farmers, and the eastern Indo-European group, whose members ranged more widely over the steppe and semi-desert areas, and whose movements may be seen in the expansion of the 'Aryan' peoples into Iran and the Indo-Aryans into northern India. Some authorities argue that the inhabitants of the Indus cities such as Mohenjo-daro and Harappa already spoke an Indo-Aryan language, though most argue that

Indo-Aryan reached India some time after the abandonment of these cities in the early second millennium BC. Eastwards, the most far-flung members of the Indo-European groups were those who reached Chinese Turkestan, where the language known as Tocharian was written down in the 8th century AD. Counter-currents also brought eastern Indo-European westwards. During the first millennium BC, groups of peoples known successively as Cimmerians, Scythians and Sarmatians pressed on the eastern frontiers of Europe, and again penetrated over the Caucasus and into north-eastern Anatolia. Many elements of Iranian art were transmitted westwards in this way, as well as superior kinds of horse-gear.

The eastern and western branches of Indo-European are today separated from one another geographically by a wedge of languages from further east, disseminated during later episodes of expansion and migration across the steppes. Down to the birth of Christ, the steppes were dominated by Indo-European tribes; but in the following millennium various tribes from the region of the Altai Mountains in Mongolia also adopted a nomadic way of life, and began to move west. The first to reach Europe were the Huns, followed by their relations the Avars: then came various Turkish tribes, led by the Khazars. The tribes which penetrated into Europe were largely driven out or assimilated by Indo-Europeans of the Slav group, but when the Seljuk Turks finally took over the remains of the Byzantine Empire, the chain of related languages from Europe to India was severed.

In the zone of urban civilisations on the southern flanks of the mountain belt and the rivers running from it, a somewhat similar interaction between settled and semi-desert areas produced another set of wide-ranging linguistic relationships, reaching down into Arabia and across into northern Africa. The distribution of the Semitic languages reflects the nomadic character of life in these areas, based at first on the ass and onager, and later on the camel. Horses, obtained from the steppe area over the mountains and used to pull light, spoke-wheeled chariots, were the equipment of richer warriors from the cities rather than the desert nomads. The earliest urban communities, those of the Sumerians (third millennium BC; see page 54) were non-Semitic, but their neighbours and second-millennium successors, the Akkadians and Assyrians, represent the north-east Semitic branch. Their north-western neighbours on the Levantine coast and adjacent areas were the urbanised Canaanites, including the Aramaeans, Phoenicians and Hebrews; while to the south-west lay the major Hamitic-speaking Egyptian civilisation, and south-east, the more nomadic Arabs – much later to carry their culture and the Islamic religion from the Atlantic to the Indian Ocean.

Even in the first millennium BC, however, Semitic languages and culture were carried well beyond the semi-arid area of the Near East by maritime expansion throughout the Mediterranean. Back in the Bronze Age, in the later second-millennium, the Levantine coast had been a noted trading area, and early in the first millennium the Phoenicians expanded their maritime trading network, setting up colonies at increasing distances from the homeland. The Greeks, recovering from the post-Mycenaean "Dark Age", soon followed suit, and great commercial and military rivalry developed. From their great Levantine ports of Tyre and Sidon, the Phoenicians sailed beyond the Greek colonial network in the Aegean and Adriatic, to found the north African cities of Carthage (814 BC) and Utica, and on to Cadiz in Spain. It was the sea-borne power of these Semitic west Mediterranean colonies that the Romans first encountered in the succession of Punic Wars.

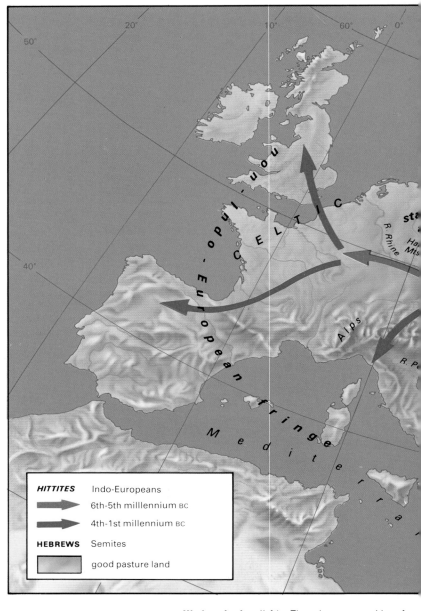

Hittite chariot *(left)* The urban communities of the Near East obtained horses from the Steppes to the north, and with their own manufacturing skills produced the spoke-wheeled chariot, as seen in this Neo-Hittite relief.

2/Trading Empires *(below)* The first millennium BC saw a great expansion of maritime activity and the foundation of overseas colonies within the Mediterranean. Bypassing the main areas of Greek influence, the Phoenicians carried Semitic languages and culture to the other end of the Mediterranean world, and even sailed beyond to explore the Atlantic coasts.

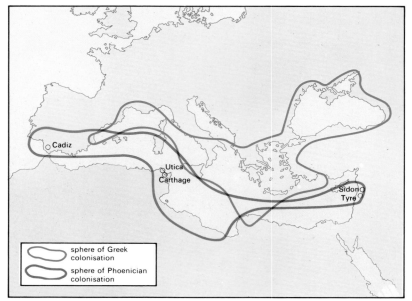

hunters of the Northern forests
(Finno-Ugrian)

BALTIC-GERMANIC

tural
Baltic Sea

ups

LAVS

LLYRIANS

THRACIANS

R. Danube

GREEKS

INDO-EUROPEAN
HOMELAND?

LUVIANS

PROTO-INDO-IRANIAN

zone of mobile pastoralists

CIMMERIANS

R. Don

Kuban Valley

R. Volga

Caucasus Mountains

Black Sea

Caspian Sea

Aral
Sea

IRANIAN COMPLEX

(ARYANS)

Amu Darya

zone of mobile pastoralists

Hindu Kush

Arctic Circle

R. Ob

R. Yenisei

L. Balkhash

Tien Shan

TOCHARIANS

Syr Darya

Pamirs

Tibetan Plateau

Himalayas

zone of mobile pastoralists

INDO-IRANIAN

R. Indus

HITTITES

Taurus Mountains

MITANNI

ASSYRIANS

ARAMAEANS

PHOENICIANS

Syrian Desert

HEBREWS

zone
of
urban
civilisations

R. Tigris

R. Euphrates

Zagros Mountains

Indus
civilisation
(Dravidian)

n

S e a

EGYPTIANS

zone
of
semi-
mobile
pastoralists

Red Sea

SOUTH SEMITES
(ARABS)

R. Nile

Arabian Sea

1/Indo-Europeans and Semites *(above)* The open
landscapes of the arid zone were the homelands of
nomadic peoples who spread their languages far and
wide. North of the Black Sea, peoples of the Indo-
European group domesticated the horse and colonised
the good grazing-grounds of the steppes. Semitic
peoples spread widely within the Near East, both as
nomads and as farmers and town-dwellers.

The beginnings of Chinese civilisation to 500 BC

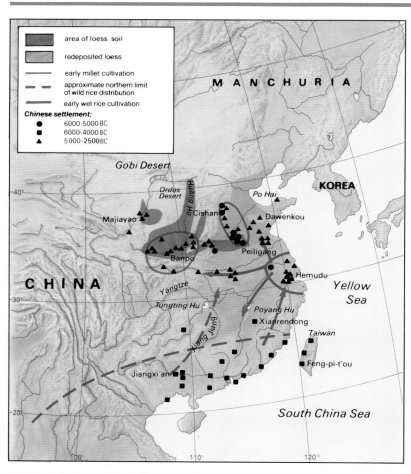

1/Early agriculture *(above)* From around 6000 BC there are numerous sites in northern China with evidence of well-established agriculture based on the cultivation of millet and on domesticated pig. Further south, rice was the principal crop. Rice grows wild in southern China, but this useful plant was soon being cultivated to the north of its natural range by the early farmers of the Yangtze Valley. In the lower Yangtze area there is already evidence of wet rice cultivation around 5000 BC.

2/Shang China *(below)* By 2500 BC there are signs of increasing social and cultural complexity among the prosperous farming communities of China. During the Lungshan period (2500-1800 BC) walled settlements and more sophisticated technology, including the potter's wheel, made their appearance. These developments were, however, only the prelude to the rise of the first Chinese civilisation, which is named after the Shang dynasty (c.1600-1028 BC). Extensive walled cities, richly furnished tombs, sophisticated craftsmanship and the earliest Chinese writing all demonstrate the wealth and originality of Shang civilisation.

CHINA has been inhabited continuously by man since very early times. Remains of early hominids, which are similar to those from Java, have been found in Kwangsi, Yunnan and Shansi. About 500,000 BC Peking Man was living around Peking, in Shansi and possibly in Hupeh and Kwangtung. *Homo sapiens* first appears in Palaeolithic cultures in the Ordos region, Hopeh, and in the south-west, about 30,000 BC. Later Mesolithic cultures flourished along the northern frontier zone, in the south and south-west, and in Taiwan.

Neolithic agricultural communities, the immediate ancestors of Chinese civilisation, arose around 7000 BC in Southern China and in the loess-covered lands of the north and north-east, where the well-drained soil of the river terraces was ideal for primitive agriculture. One of the best early sites is Banpo, where round and rectangular houses were found, as well as pottery kilns and a cemetery area. This contained only adult burials. Children were buried in pottery urns between the houses. In the valley of the Huang Ho, early Chinese agriculture depended heavily on millet, but further to the south rice-growing was important and there is evidence of rice-paddies in the Yangtze delta area as early as the 5th millennium BC. By 3000 BC, more sophisticated farming communities had developed technical skills, including the carving of jade, and settlements were larger and more permanent – small townships rather than villages – and were sometimes protected by defensive walls of rammed earth construction.

The use of bronze began around 1600 BC, and the beginning of the Bronze Age corresponded with the beginning of the first historical dynasty, the Shang. Traditionally there was a Hsia dynasty preceding Shang. This may refer to one of the later Neolithic cultures, but no site has yet been identified as from the Hsia.

The Shang (1523-1028 or 1751-1111 BC) was traditionally a powerful political regime controlling most of northern China. It was more probably a loose confederation of clan domains, many of which would have been little more than village settlements. The Shang kings moved their capital six times, and two capitals, at Cheng-chou and An-yang, have been excavated. The capital, the king's 'Great Domain', contained the court, with many royal functionaries, supported by revenues from an extensive area. The Shang had trade relations with most of northern and central China, and with the steppes to north and west. Many smaller Shang sites have been found and some are now known from

the Yangtze valley in central China. How far the Shang kings actually controlled these outer areas is uncertain.

In the 11th century BC the Shang were conquered by the Chou, a client people, possibly of different ethnic origin, living on their northwestern border. They gradually extended their sovereignty over an area much larger than the Shang, including all of Hopeh, Honan, Shansi, Shantung, much of Shensi, Hupeh and Anhwei, and parts of the middle basin of the Yangtze. At first their capital was in the vicinity of Hsi-an (Sian), with a secondary capital near Lo-yang. Their state was divided into numerous separate domains. Many of these, especially around the capitals, were possessed by the king himself as a Royal Domain. Others were granted as fiefs to members of the royal clan, to the families that had helped the Chou to power, and to the clans of important subjects and office-holders. The Shang royal family was enfiefed in eastern Honan. This system of delegated authority was something like the later European feudal system.

Until the 8th century BC the Chou kings remained powerful, and constantly extended the area under their control. About 770 BC, however, internal disorders forced them to abandon their homeland in the Wei Valley and move to their eastern capital at Lo-yang, where their power diminished and they soon became powerless figureheads. For the next two and a half centuries there was constant warfare between their former vassals. By the 5th century more than a hundred petty feudal states had been swallowed up by some twenty of the more powerful kingdoms. Real power was exercised by 'hegemon' states heading temporary alliances: from 667-632 Ch'i was predominant; after 632 Chin; during the 6th century Ch'u was the dominant power. But these alliances did not achieve political stability. Nevertheless, Chou culture and Chinese influence were consolidated and spread far beyond the political borders of early Chou times.

The Shang and early Chou periods were

3/Western Chou China: 11th to 9th centuries BC *(below)* The early Chou dominions comprised a very large number of domains. Some remained under royal control, others were granted as fiefs to supporters and servants of the Chou, in a sort of feudal tenure. Much of the area shown on the map was still occupied by peoples of different ethnic origins who were gradually assimilated and conquered by the Chou and their vassals.

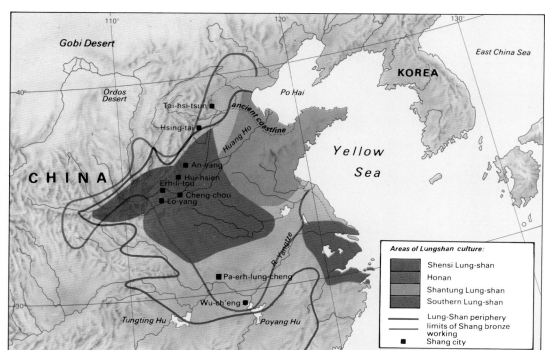

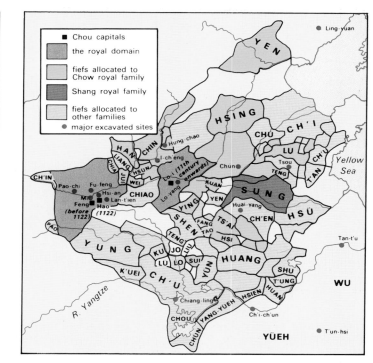

4/The Late Chou Period, c.550 BC After 770 BC the Chou lost all real power, and during the Spring and Autumn period (722-481 BC) there was constant warfare between their former vassals. At the beginning of the 8th century there were well over a hundred independent states. By the 5th century there were only about twenty. It was a period of great political instability, during which leadership was sometimes exercised by a 'hegemon king' acting as head of an alliance. The political instability, however, was the background of great advances in technology, institutions, and political ideas, and Chinese culture gradually, spread far beyond the political borders of the early Chou as can be seen from the recently excavated sites shown on the map. By the 5th century BC the Yangtze valley and the south of Manchuria were firmly integrated into the Chinese cultural sphere.

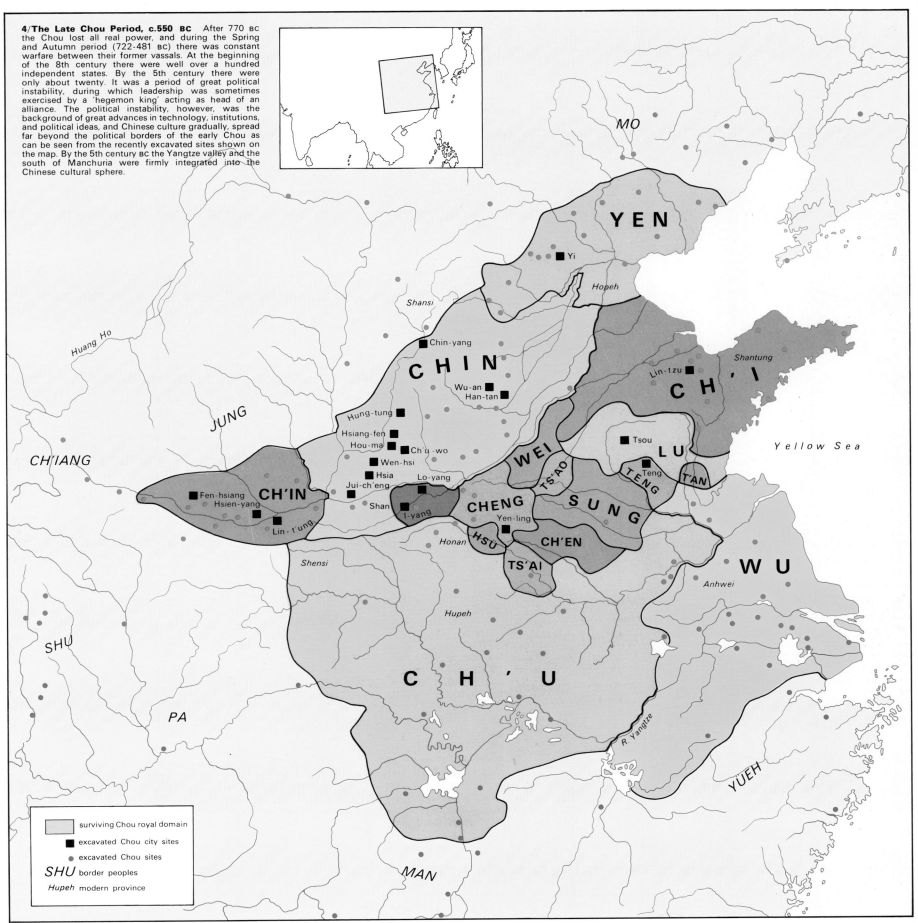

surviving Chou royal domain
■ excavated Chou city sites
• excavated Chou sites
SHU border peoples
Hupeh modern province

differentiated from their predecessors not only by their political organisation and their bronze technology, but also by the use of writing, and their culture was already recognisably 'Chinese.' Their cities maintained a hierarchy of nobles, royal officers and court servants who were all engaged in a constant round of warfare, hunting and elaborate religious ritual. They were supported by communities of craftsmen in bronze, jade, wood, stone, ceramics and textiles, many of them slaves. The peasants working the various royal domains supplied them with revenues and grain.

Although the court and the nobility enjoyed a sophisticated lifestyle, bronze remained rare and was used almost exclusively for ritual objects rather than practical tools. Farmers working in the fields continued to use stone implements and to lead much the same life as in earlier times, living in permanent settlements and cultivating lands within a fixed territory with rice, millet, barley and hemp, and raising

pigs, poultry and silkworms. There were only patches of cultivated lands, worked for a few years and then left fallow. The technology available could neither clear the dense woods on the mountains, nor drain and cultivate the heavy lands of the river valleys, so the peasants still needed the wild lands surrounding their settlements for much of their food.

Towards the end of the period the old social order began to collapse. The more powerful states employed bureaucrats rather than the hereditary nobility of older times. Religious observances decayed. A new group of state servants (*shih*) emerged, as military officers and state officials. One of their number, Confucius, formalised many of the ideas current among them, and formulated them into a new ethos, which was to have currency far into the future. He was, however, only one of many thinkers who began to ponder the philosophical and practical problems facing man in this period of insecurity and rapid change.

Shang ritual food vessel (14th-11th century BC) *(right)* The highly sophisticated bronze technology of the Shang period was devoted almost entirely to the production of ritual objects such as this. Ordinary tools continued to be made of stone rather than metal.

The beginnings of Indian civilisation

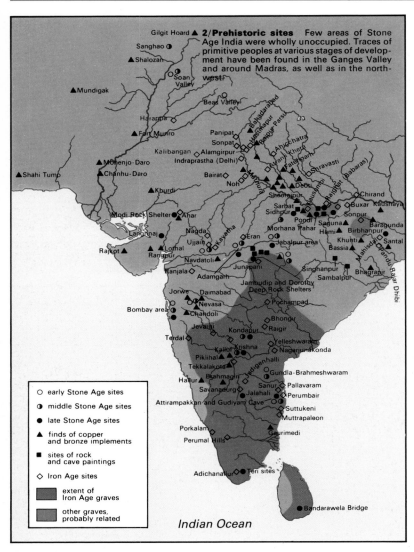

2/Prehistoric sites Few areas of Stone Age India were wholly unoccupied. Traces of primitive peoples at various stages of development have been found in the Ganges Valley and around Madras, as well as in the north-west.

○ early Stone Age sites
◑ middle Stone Age sites
● late Stone Age sites
▲ finds of copper and bronze implements
■ sites of rock and cave paintings
◇ Iron Age sites
▮ extent of Iron Age graves
▮ other graves, probably related

Indian Ocean

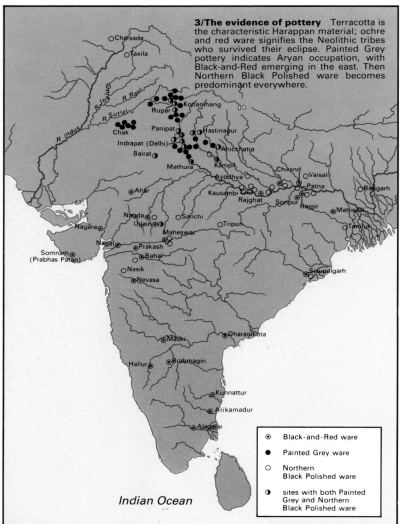

3/The evidence of pottery Terracotta is the characteristic Harappan material; ochre and red ware signifies the Neolithic tribes who survived their eclipse. Painted Grey pottery indicates Aryan occupation, with Black-and-Red emerging in the east. Then Northern Black Polished ware becomes predominant everywhere.

◉ Black-and-Red ware
● Painted Grey ware
○ Northern Black Polished ware
◑ sites with both Painted Grey and Northern Black Polished ware

Indian Ocean

MEN have lived in India since the Second Interglacial Period, from 400,000 BC to 200,000 BC. The hand-axes, chopping tools and flakes of the Early Stone Age are found in the Punjab foothills, the Soan and Beas valleys, Rajasthan, Malwa and as far south as Madras. Middle Stone Age sites, with their more delicate flake-shaped tools, occur mainly in central and peninsular India, but also in the Soan valley and at Sanghao in north-west Pakistan. There are rock paintings, depicting a vigorous hunting culture, at several places in the Narmada valley and north-east India, and the microliths and mesoliths of the Late Stone Age are distributed, apart from Pakistan, almost throughout the sub-continent.

Five of the six large ethnic groups which make up the population of India today appear to have been already well-established by the 3rd millennium BC. The earliest, probably, were the Negritos, followed by the Proto-Australoids, the Mediterranean peoples, now mainly associated with Dravidian culture, the Mongoloids, of the north-east and northern fringes, and the western Brachycephals. Their settlements, gradually evolving and growing more elaborate, were widely scattered throughout Sind, Baluchistan and Rajasthan by the end of the 4th millennium BC, and a form of urban life was already beginning to develop, with copper and bronze appearing alongside the traditional stone blades and implements. Major sites have been discovered at Mundigak in south-east Afghanistan, Kulli near the Makran coast of south Baluchistan and Amri in south Sind.

These developments came to flower in the first of the great Indian civilisations. This spread out from its leading cities, Harappa and Mohenjo-Daro in the Indus valley, to cover nearly 500,000 square miles of territory and survived for the best part of 1000 years (c. 2550 to 1550 BC). The remains of typical Harappan towns, with their high citadels, solid buildings, uniform grids of streets and elaborate drainage systems, exist as far south as Cutch and Bhagatrav, at the mouth of the Narmada river, as well as at Rupar (Punjab) and Alamgirpur (Uttar Pradesh) in the east, and Judeirjo-Daro (Sind) and the Makran coast to the south-west. The Harappan script, mainly found on seals, is so far undeciphered, but it has been deduced from the vast granaries, the large houses, the proliferation of religious figurines (many of them anticipating Hindu deities) and the absence of royal palaces that this was essentially a society of priests, merchants and peasant farmers. Many typical Harappan goods have been found in Mesopotamia, and textual references there suggest that the traders of the country known as *Meluhha* were at this time in regular commercial contact with the Middle East via the land of *Dilmun* (probably Bahrein).

The Indus civilisation vanished without trace, until digging revealed the first of its lost treasures in 1925. Its disappearance is almost certainly linked with the rise of the sixth major Indian population group, the Nordics, normally known, from their Indo-European languages, as the Aryans. Though some still argue that these were of local origin, they were most probably invaders from Bactria and northern Iran who had broken away earlier from the main nomad hordes in south Russia (see page 60). Their archaeological remains include Iranian funeral furnishings and copper hoards of a 'Caucasian' type, and their likely part in the destruction of Harappa and Mohenjo-Daro is underlined by early Vedic references to hostile, dark-skinned *dasas* (the original untouchables) living in the broken ruins (*armaka*) left behind by the great god Indra, in his role as Purandara, the breaker of cities.

The Vedas, which form the earliest Indian literature, consist largely of hymns to the Aryan gods, but together with the two enormous early Indian epic poems, the *Ramayana* and the *Mahabharata*, the *Rig-veda*, in particular, gives some notion, however selective and stylised, of life in the period from about 1500 BC to 450 BC.

At first the newcomers appear to have been hunters and herdsmen, tending cattle, which were already acquiring sacred attributes, and breeding the horses which, though unknown to the Harappan painters and sculptors, now figure frequently on the Painted Grey pottery characteristic of early Aryan settlements. Gradually they adopted the techniques of settled farming from the peoples they had conquered and particularly after the advent of iron in about 800 BC, they proceeded with extensive clearance of the forests then covering northern India. At the same time they evolved a complex and pervasive set of cultural institutions, which in many ways have shaped the sub-continent to the present day. Their language, Sanskrit, formed the basis for a literature as developed as the Greek and Latin to which it is closely related. Their metaphysical subtlety, expressed in the *Upanishads*, held the seeds of many later systems of religious thought. Their emphasis on sacrifice, and the crucial importance which they were already attaching to the notion of caste set fundamental social patterns, and at the same time created objectives of social reform, which have continued to shape life in India for almost 3000 years.

In the first phase of their expansion, down to c.1050 BC, the Rig-vedic Aryans, with their horses and light chariots extended their domain from Suvastu (the Swat valley in Pakistan) to *Sapta-Sindhava*, the land of the Seven Induses. From then on they began to move steadily eastwards towards the Ganges. Painted Grey ware has been found in quantity at the site of Hastinapur, a city largely washed away by a great Ganges flood in about 900 BC. As land clearance then spread eastwards along the valley, the river became a natural trade highway. Ships and voyages figure in the *Rig-veda*, though the Aryans probably did not venture far on the sea. Probably after 800 BC they began to penetrate increasingly further south, and though the *Ramayana*'s epic account of their conquest of Sri Lanka, generally believed to be Ceylon, has never been archaeologically substantiated, they undoubtedly moved into the Deccan, which from now on became an ever-more important route between north and south.

The physical geography of India at this time dictated a different form of development for the hilly, much-fragmented lands which make up the southern peninsula. Where the great northern plains lent themselves to large-scale agriculture and the growth of substantial kingdoms, the relatively tiny communities of the south evolved their own highly autonomous forms of religious, political and economic life. Distinctive megalithic cultures grew up around Madras, Kerala and Mysore, while the sea-faring peoples of the southern tip continued to cultivate the close maritime ties with the Middle East which had been severed, as far as northern India was concerned, with the eclipse of the Harappans.

From 600 BC to 450 BC the pattern of kingdoms and republics begins to emerge more clearly (see page 82). Archaeological evidence, largely based on pottery styles, suggests that the heartland of the Aryan peoples had by now moved east from the western Punjab to Kurukshetra and the Doab, and the texts refer to land as far eastward as Magadha. Painted Grey ware and the Black-and-Red ceramics of the eastern regions were giving way to a single Black pottery, extending throughout the Indo-Gangetic region. A culturally unified northern India was ready for her first empire, that of Chandragupta Maurya who may have met and been inspired by his contemporary, Alexander the Great.

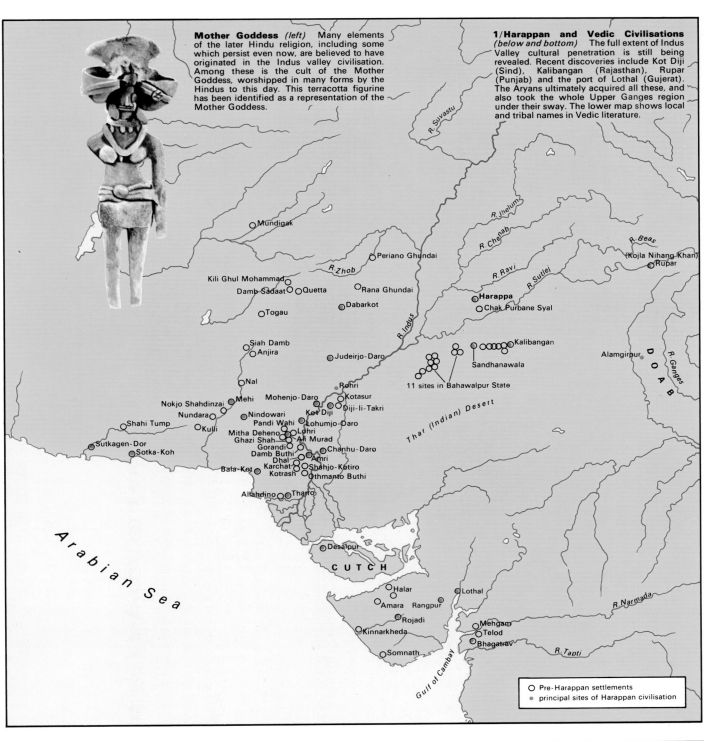

Mother Goddess (left) Many elements of the later Hindu religion, including some which persist even now, are believed to have originated in the Indus valley civilisation. Among these is the cult of the Mother Goddess, worshipped in many forms by the Hindus to this day. This terracotta figurine has been identified as a representation of the Mother Goddess.

1/Harappan and Vedic Civilisations (below and bottom) The full extent of Indus Valley cultural penetration is still being revealed. Recent discoveries include Kot Diji (Sind), Kalibangan (Rajasthan), Rupar (Punjab) and the port of Lothal (Gujerat). The Aryans ultimately acquired all these, and also took the whole Upper Ganges region under their sway. The lower map shows local and tribal names in Vedic literature.

Mundigak
Periano Ghundai
R. Zhob
Kili Ghul Mohammad
Damb Sadaat Quetta
Rana Ghundai
Togau
Dabarkot
Harappa
Chak Purbane Syal
Siah Damb
Anjira
Judeirjo-Daro
Kalibangan
Sandhanawala
Alamgirpur
11 sites in Bahawalpur State
Nal
Rohri
Kotasur
Mohenjo-Daro
Diji-li-Takri
Nokjo Shahdinzai Mehi
Kot Diji
Nindowari
Nundara
Pandi Wahi Lohumjo-Daro
Shahi Tump
Mitha Deheno Lohri
Kulli
Ghazi Shah Ali Murad
Sutkagen-Dor
Gorandi Chanhu-Daro
Sotka-Koh
Damb Buthi
Dhal Amri
Bala-Kot Karchat Shahjo-Kotiro
Kotrash Othmanto Buthi
Allahdino Tharro

Thar (Indian) Desert

R. Suvastu
R. Jhelum
R. Chenab
R. Ravi
R. Beas
(Kojla Nihang-Khan)
Rupar
R. Sutlej
D O A B
R. Ganges

Arabian Sea

Desalpur
C U T C H
Halar
Amara Rangpur
Lothal
Rojadi
R. Narmada
Kinnarkheda
Mehgam
Telod
Bhagatrav
R. Tapti
Somnath
Gulf of Cambay

○ Pre-Harappan settlements
● principal sites of Harappan civilisation

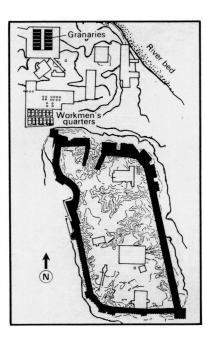

Granaries
River bed
Workmen's quarters
N

Harappa (above) and **Mohenjo-Daro** (below) are the first and most important discoveries of the Indus valley civilisation, the earliest developed urban culture on the Indian sub-continent. Excavations reveal an elaborate pattern of main roads at right-angles and houses opening onto narrow back alleys.

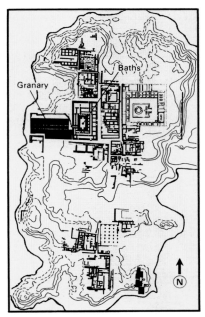

Granary
Baths
N

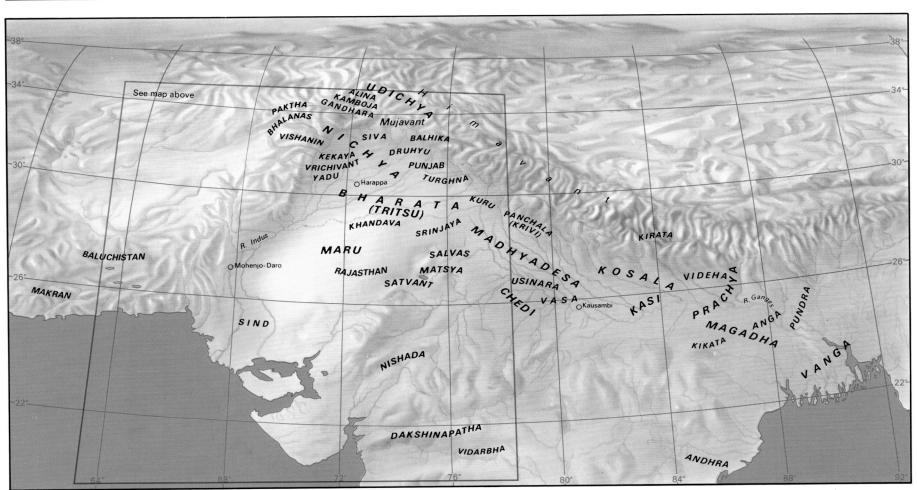

See map above

PAKTHA
BHALANAS
VISHANIN
ALINA
UDICHYA
KAMBOJA
GANDHARA
Mujavant
N I C H Y A
SIVA
BALHIKA
KEKAYA
DRUHYU
VRICHIVANT
PUNJAB
YADU
TURGHNA
Harappa
B H A R A T A
(TRITSU)
KHANDAVA
KURU PANCHALA
(KRIVI)
SRINJAYA
R. Indus
MARU
MADHYADESA
KIRATA
KOSALA
RAJASTHAN
SALVAS
MATSYA
SATVANT
USINARA
VIDEHA
KASI
CHEDI
VASA
PRACHYA
Kausambi
R. Ganges
MAGADHA
ANGA
PUNDRA
BALUCHISTAN
Mohenjo-Daro
KIKATA
VANGA
MAKRAN
SIND
NISHADA
DAKSHINAPATHA
VIDARBHA
ANDHRA

The early Mediterranean world c.3000 to 1200 BC

THE island of Crete, mountainous but fertile, saw the rise of the first high civilisation on European soil. Until less than a century ago almost nothing was known about this civilisation. It has been named Minoan, after Minos, the legendary king of Knossos, which appears to have been from the first the chief city of the island. The Cretans learned to make tools and weapons of copper, and later of bronze, and evolved a system of writing. They were ruled by kings for whom they built spacious palaces; the goddesses whom they worshipped had sanctuaries on the tops of mountains and in caves.

The peoples inhabiting the mainland of Greece and the Aegean islands in early times were probably related to the Cretans in speech and race, sharing fashions of jewellery with them and using similar tools and weapons. But the development of civilisation there was apparently delayed by invasions towards the end of the third millennium BC. The northern islands and part of the mainland were then overrun by relatively barbarous peoples from Anatolia. A century or so later, other invaders reached the Peloponnese from the north. These may have been the first Greeks; but the question of when the Greek language was introduced into Greece is much disputed, some believing that it originated in Greece itself in earlier times, others that it was brought by conquerors at the end of the Bronze Age, in about 1200 BC.

While the mainland languished after this period of invasions, the Minoan civilisation of Crete continued to develop, with exquisite pottery, superb gem-engraving and decorative wall-painting in palaces and houses.

This was evidently a period of flourishing trade. Egyptian stone vases, scarab seals and carved ivories found their way to Crete and were imitated there. Finely decorated pottery from Crete reached Egypt; some of it was recovered from the town of Kahun, built to house workmen

4/Trade connections during the Neolithic and Bronze Ages *(below)* Much of the trade in the Aegean world was probably in raw materials. This has left few traces, apart from Spondylus shell, Melian obsidian, and large copper ingots of the distinctive ox-hide shape found throughout the eastern Mediterranean.

and officials engaged in constructing a pyramid for one of the great pharaohs of the Twelfth Dynasty, Sesostris II (c.1906-1888 BC). Much of the trade in these early times was no doubt in raw materials such as copper, and the tin required to mix with it to make bronze. Crete may have imported Egyptian linen, exchanging it for timber and for woollen cloth woven with colourful designs, as depicted in representations of the dress worn by Cretan men and women. The painted decoration on the ceilings of some Egyptian tombs from the time of the Twelfth Dynasty onwards seems to reflect the influence of imported Cretan textiles. Cretan fashions spread throughout the islands and eventually penetrated the mainland. Cretans had established a settlement at Kastri on Cythera some time before 2000 BC. In the 16th century BC Cretan settlers were established on Rhodes and at Miletus, and there were evidently Cretans living in Cycladic towns like Phylakopi (Melos) and Ayia Irini (Ceos). The islands and parts of the mainland may have paid tribute to Cretan kings, as later Greek legend hints in the story of Theseus and the exploits of Minos and his sons. Mycenae became a leading centre on the mainland, and royal tombs (shaft graves) of native rulers there dating from the 16th century BC have produced treasures of gold, silver and faience, many of them made in Crete.

It is ironical that the finest products of the flourishing period of the Cretan civilisation should come from these graves of comparatively barbarous chieftains living on the fringes of the Cretan world. Among the treasures of the Mycenae shaft graves are many exquisite drinking cups of precious metal, produced in Cretan workshops or by Cretan artists living at the court of the Mycenaean rulers. The men in these graves were buried with vast quantities of swords and daggers, their hilts often adorned with gold or precious stones. The majority of these weapons were of Cretan types, and may have been imported from Crete. The most richly ornamented were the daggers, with blades inlaid with gold, silver and black niello. The more elaborate of the surviving inlays are in the form

of pictures, one showing armed men with great body shields (made of ox-hide) combating lions, which certainly lived on the Greek mainland and may have existed in Crete at the time. Another dagger is decorated with scenes of cats pursuing water fowl by silver streams stocked with fish and flanked by papyrus flowers. The ultimate source of inspiration for the scenes on this dagger was Egypt, where cats were trained, like gun dogs are now, to help in fowling in the marshes bordering the Nile. The richly mounted weapons and exquisite gold and silver vessels of the Mycenae shaft graves form a striking contrast to the barbaric splendour of most of the jewellery and of the gold masks placed over the faces of some of the dead, all clearly of local native workmanship.

About 1500 BC the flourishing settlements on the island of Thera were buried by a great eruption of the volcano there (as Pompeii was buried by Vesuvius in AD 79). Some fifty years after this, most of the important towns and cities of Crete were destroyed by fire. This havoc appears to have been the work of conquerors from the mainland, although the eruption of Thera has been falsely blamed for it. The conquerors may have been Greeks, if the system of writing afterwards found in use both in Crete and on the mainland has been correctly deciphered as Greek.

Mainland fashions in pottery, architecture and burial customs now dominate Crete. In the 14th century BC a mixed civilisation, known as Mycenaean, and related to the Minoan as was the Roman to the Greek in later times, spread throughout the Aegean. Knossos appears to have been the only centre of government in Crete after the mainland conquest of c.1450 BC, but eventually the palace there was destroyed, and the whole Aegean may have become a miniature empire ruled from Mycenae, although palaces at Tiryns, Pylos and elsewhere suggest the existence of tributary kings. The story of the siege of Troy in Homer's *Iliad* may enshrine distant memories of these times.

Shortly before 1200 BC the palaces and walled citadels on the mainland were destroyed by fire.

'Ox-hide' copper ingots *(above)* This standard shape, fashioned as a convenient way of transporting raw metal, was flat, about an inch thick, and represented a load for one man carrying it on his shoulder.

major sites
- ⊡ city with palace
- ● town or village
- ▲ sacred cave
- ▲ peak sanctuary

sites destroyed c.1450 BC
- ⊡ city with palace
- ● town or village
- ⊕ isolated home or shrine

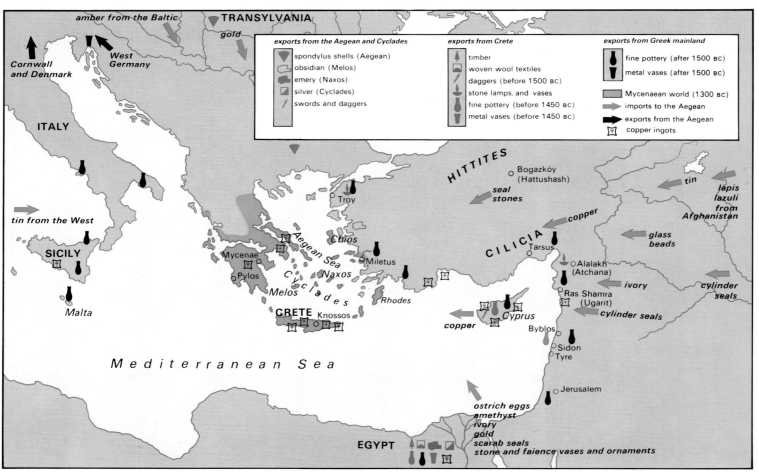

exports from the Aegean and Cyclades
- spondylus shells (Aegean)
- obsidian (Melos)
- emery (Naxos)
- silver (Cyclades)
- swords and daggers

exports from Crete
- timber
- woven wool textiles
- daggers (before 1500 BC)
- stone lamps, and vases
- fine pottery (before 1450 BC)
- metal vases (before 1450 BC)

exports from Greek mainland
- fine pottery (after 1500 BC)
- metal vases (after 1500 BC)

- Mycenaean world (1300 BC)
- → imports to the Aegean
- → exports from the Aegean
- copper ingots

The destruction seems to have been due to invaders rather than to civil war or natural causes. Refugees from the mainland settled in Aegean islands like Naxos and Crete; some travelled as far as Cyprus and Tarsus in Cilicia. The invaders may have been Greeks, or a branch of them, the Dorians, traditionally the last to enter the Peloponnese from the north, or transitory migrants like the Sea Peoples.

About this time other Indo-Europeans, Armenians and Phrygians, poured into Anatolia from the Balkans, occupying Troy and destroying the Hittite empire with its capital at Bogazköy. Peoples expelled by them moved southwards, devastating Syria and settling there. Some, from coastal regions of Anatolia – the Sea Peoples of Egyptian records – took to their ships, occupied Enkomi in Cyprus and launched a grand assault on Egypt in alliance with the Libyans on her western borders, where they were defeated by the pharaoh Merneptah in 1232 BC. Some forty years later, Ramesses III overthrew another coalition of Sea Peoples, but some of them, notably the Philistines, afterwards settled on the coast of Palestine, which still bears their name.

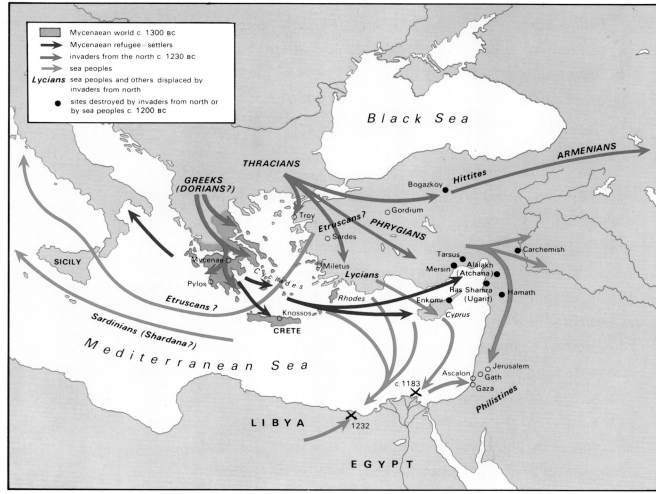

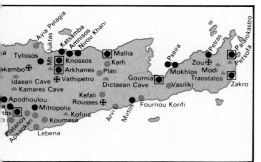

2/The island of Crete (above) Mountainous but fertile, and strategically placed in the centre of the eastern Mediterranean, Crete was the home of the first high civilisation in Europe. After a thousand or more years of undisturbed peace, it was conquered about 1450 BC by Mycenaean people from the Greek mainland, who had adopted many aspects of that civilisation.

3/Migrations in the eastern Mediterranean c. 1250 to 1150 BC (above) At the end of the Bronze Age barbarous peoples overwhelmed the Mycenaean and Hittite civilisations. Mycenaean refugees escaped overseas, while other groups, forced from homes in Anatolia and the Aegean, attacked Egypt and eventually settled in Syria, Palestine and the western Mediterranean.

1/The Aegean: main Bronze Age centres and movements of peoples c. 3000 to 1500 BC (below) Better supplied with water than today and relatively well wooded, with its genial climate and resources of olives, grapes and fish, the Aegean must always have acted like a magnet to peoples from less favoured regions. The pattern of invasions in the Bronze Age has been reproduced in historic times.

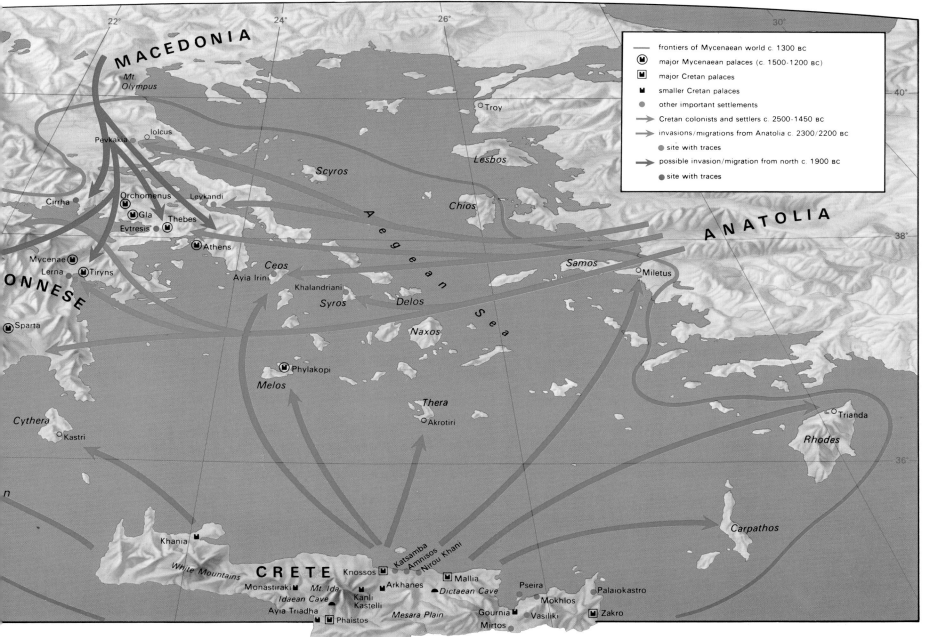

THE earliest civilisations had arisen at a few scattered points, like lighthouses in the night or oases in the vast uninhabited or sparsely inhabited Eurasian landmass. Between 1000 BC and AD 500 the pattern began to change. Although America, Australasia and Africa south of the Sahara still remained outside the mainstream of world history, and were to stay so for a further one thousand years, the civilisations of Europe and Asia now linked up in a continuous belt. By AD 100, when the classical era was at its height, a chain of empires extended from Rome, which encompassed the entire Mediterranean basin, via Parthia and the Kushan Empire to China, forming an unbroken zone of civilised life from the Atlantic to the Pacific.

This was a new and important fact in the history of the Eurasian world. The area of civilisation was still narrow and exposed to unrelenting barbarian pressures, and development in the different regions was still largely autonomous; but with the expansion of the major civilisations and the elimination of the geographical gaps between them, the way was open for inter-regional contacts and cultural exchanges which left a lasting imprint. In the west, the expansion of Hellenism created a single cultural area which extended over a period of time from the frontiers of India to Britain; in the east, the expansion of the Chinese and Indian civilisations resulted in something like a cultural symbiosis in Indo-China. These wider cultural areas provided a vehicle not only for trade but also for the transmission of ideas, technology and institutions, and above all for the diffusion of the great world religions. Beginning with Buddhism, and continuing later with Zoroastrianism, Judaism, Christianity and Islam, religion became a powerful unifying bond in the Eurasian world, with consequences that were political and cultural as well as religious.

3   The classical

The Acropolis and Parthenon, Athens

civilisations of Eurasia

The commercial and cultural bonds of Eurasia

FEW PEOPLE in the Near East, let alone in Europe, knew much about eastern Asia until the emergence of Achaemenid Persia in the 6th century BC (see page 78), and China itself remained almost unknown until shortly before the Christian era. But although there is little or no evidence of face-to-face meetings in the earlier centuries, it is clear that there were important influences and borrowings. Bronze was already giving way to iron in the west when it first appeared in China; and unparalleled technical excellence was soon achieved in the Shang and Chou kingdoms along the Huang Ho (Yellow River). Although the silk-moth was native to Assam and Bengal, it was in northern China that men first learned how to unravel a single, unbroken thread from its cocoon. Jade, the most prized material of the Chinese jewel-carvers, came from the western end of the arid and dangerous Tarim Basin. Wheat seeds originated in the west; water-buffalo and domesticated poultry in northern India; wet-rice cultivation was common throughout east and south-east Asia; cowrie shells, the first Chinese money, probably from the faraway Maldive Islands. All these, it seems, must have been introduced by nomads and itinerant merchants from beyond China's traditionally self-contained borders.

Economic and cultural contact between the extremes of the ancient world reached its height in the 2nd century AD. Although Rome and Han China never established formal diplomatic relations, each was well aware of the other's existence. Goods flowed freely, particularly from east to west, and expensive and non-bulky goods like silk and spices could be transported by caravan or ship at a cost which was only a small proportion of their market value. In return, gold and silver, mostly in coins, moved in large quantities, both by land and by sea. Between the frontiers of these great classical civilisations, the Kushan Empire and the Parthian Empire of Persia both willingly fostered this trade, maintaining and garrisoning the roads, protecting the caravans and thriving on the tolls.

To the south, in the Indian Ocean, up to 120 substantial Greek ships a year plied between the Red Sea ports and India, exploiting the monsoon, while Arab ships traded from port to port along the north-west coast of India, the Persian Gulf, the incense-bearing shore of Arabia and the spice markets of Abyssinia and Somaliland. The Roman Empire exported glass, copper, tin, lead, red coral, textiles, pottery, and above all currency. The chief imports from the east were Arabian incense, Chinese silk, and from India

Ferghana's 'Heavenly Horses' Ferghana was the homeland of the fabled 'heavenly horses' with which the Chinese were anxious to equip their cavalry as a counter to the agile ponies of the Hsiung-nu and other raiding mounted nomads north of the Great Wall. The fifth Han emperor Wu-ti sent emissaries and armies to subdue the nomad-infested areas of Sinkiang in order to control the source of these horses. China eventually received steady supplies of Ferghana stallions, and this painting from Tun-huang shows a Chinese official mounted on one of them.

precious stones, muslin and spices, especially pepper. Other spices reached the Empire from the East Indies via Madagascar and East Africa. The main land route from the East entered the Empire via Nisibis and Zeugma. Caravans moving between the Empire and the Persian Gulf ports of Charax and Apologos were owned, organised and escorted across the desert by citizens of Palmyra. Until the city was destroyed in 273 Palmyra's role as a desert entrepôt earned it the wealth to finance spectacular public buildings. Further south, Petra performed the same function for the caravans travelling to and from the Red Sea ports of Leucecome and Aelana, and the Persian Gulf port of Gerrha. The most important entrepôt of all was Alexandria, a city of about 500,000 inhabitants which received the goods of the eastern trade from the Red Sea ports of Berenice, Myos Hormus and Clysma for shipment to all parts of the Roman Empire. It also exported its own manufactures: linen, processed Arabian drugs and Indian perfumes, papyrus, glassware and – vastly the greatest shipment of all – Egyptian grain, which helped to feed the population of Rome.

In the end the horse and the Bactrian camel were the means by which the central Asian steppes were opened up as a great commercial route. During Chinese efforts to control Sinkiang, the great general Pan Ch'ao, who held the northern and western oases against all comers, defeated a massive Kushan invasion from India in AD 90, led an army across the Pamir mountains to reach the Caspian, established contact with the Parthians and was only just persuaded, in AD 97, against sending an embassy to Rome.

By that time, however, regular caravans had linked the two mighty empires for almost 200 years. Few, if any, went straight through, but there were well-established change-over points where the Greek, Arab, Roman, Iranian and Indian traders of the west exchanged goods with the nomad merchants who undertook the middle stretches of the journey, handing over in turn to the Chinese at the further frontiers.

In the 2nd century AD these trade links were cemented when the Yüeh-chih and the Tocharians combined to create the vast Kushan Empire, extending from the northern half of India to include a great part of the central Asian landmass. Even under the Achaemenids, trade, roads and safe transportation had been matters of prime concern. Darius's Royal Road ran 1677 well-garrisoned miles from Ephesus to Susa; an even longer route linked Baylon with Ecbatana, and ultimately Ortospana (Kabul). The Seleucids maintained the tradition, with a major trading network across the Persian plateau, from Seleucia through Ecbatana and Merv to Bactra. When Bactria became independent (250-139 BC) it formed the junction for a web of caravan routes joining Siberia and China with India's great trading centre of Taxila and with Persia, the Red Sea, the Persian Gulf and the Mediterranean entrepôt cities such as Antioch and Alexandria. Great trading concerns centred in Bactria kept branches and agents in China. The Parthians under Tiridates (247-212 BC) deliberately transferred their capital to Hecatompylos on the caravan road from Seleucia to Bactra. Now the Kushans, with their 'thousand cities' of central Asia, completed the chain.

The chain did not hold for long. By the opening of the 3rd century AD all parts of the 2500-mile route from Syria to the Tarim were under pressure. The Chinese were driven completely from the Tarim Basin, cutting the major routes, and both Rome and China found themselves hard pressed by the barbarians to the north (see page 94). The demand for foreign products built up during the years of peace and security did not suddenly vanish, but increasingly it had to be met by the relatively unthreatened – and for bulky cargoes very much more economical – sea

route whose traffic had grown rapidly since the Greek pilot Hippalus discovered the monsoon, probably around 100 BC. Since then ships with a carrying capacity of up to 500 tons beat with the monsoon winds across to the Indian ports, Barbaricum at the mouth of the Indus, Barygaza further south and Muziris about 200 miles north of the southern tip of India. In winter the winds reversed and the Greek ships returned laden with the products of the east. The occasional Greek merchants may have gone further east than Muziris or Ceylon, but as a rule they did not, receiving Chinese wares from Indian merchants. The Chinese Empire now reached as far south as Haiphong; it is likely that Indians and Chinese met at Oc Eo in southern Cambodia. From there the Indians shipped the goods west, portaging them across the Malay Peninsula and the southern tip of India.

The development of the sea route greatly reduced the price of silk in the Roman world and significantly increased the use of eastern spices in Roman cookery. The volume of eastern trade no doubt fluctuated according to the internal conditions of the Roman and Chinese Empires and intervening lands. From time to time war between the Roman and Persian Empires interfered with the land route, while disorders among the Arabs might impede shipping along the coast of Arabia. From the 5th century AD the progressive takeover by barbarians of the Western provinces of the Roman Empire reduced – but did not end – the demand for eastern luxuries in those areas. The oriental provinces of the Empire remained prosperous until the end of the 6th century and the age of the Arab conquests.

	trade routes from the Mediterranean used by Greeks, Phoenicians and Arabs with Roman permission
	Persian trade
	trade routes under Chinese control including nomad areas only intermittently under Chinese control
	Kushan trade
	Indian and other routes

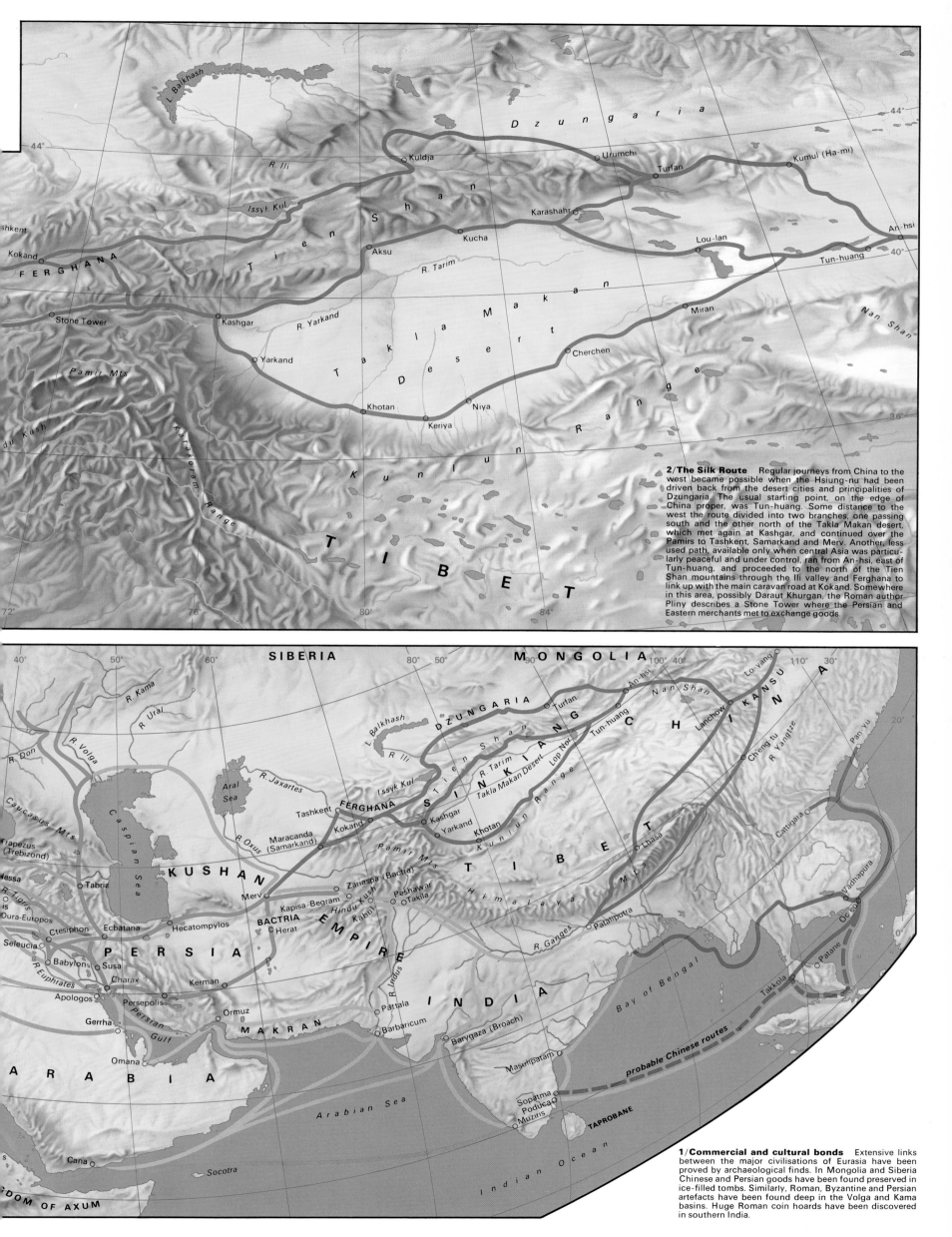

2/The Silk Route Regular journeys from China to the west became possible when the Hsiung-nu had been driven back from the desert cities and principalities of Dzungaria. The usual starting point, on the edge of China proper, was Tun-huang. Some distance to the west the route divided into two branches, one passing south and the other north of the Takla Makan desert, which met again at Kashgar, and continued over the Pamirs to Tashkent, Samarkand and Merv. Another, less used path, available only when central Asia was particularly peaceful and under control, ran from An-hsi, east of Tun-huang, and proceeded to the north of the Tien Shan mountains through the Ili valley and Ferghana to link up with the main caravan road at Kokand. Somewhere in this area, possibly Daraut Khurgan, the Roman author Pliny describes a Stone Tower where the Persian and Eastern merchants met to exchange goods.

1/Commercial and cultural bonds Extensive links between the major civilisations of Eurasia have been proved by archaeological finds. In Mongolia and Siberia Chinese and Persian goods have been found preserved in ice-filled tombs. Similarly, Roman, Byzantine and Persian artefacts have been found deep in the Volga and Kama basins. Huge Roman coin hoards have been discovered in southern India.

The religious bonds of Eurasia to AD 500

ALL the great world religions originated in Asia, and three of them – Judaism, Christianity and Islam – from a quite small area of western Asia. Equally noteworthy is the grouping of religious genius in different parts of the world in or close to the 6th century BC, an 'axial' age, as Karl Jaspers said. This was the period of Confucius and perhaps Lao-tzu in China and Zoroaster in Iran, of Gautama the Buddha in India, of the greatest of the Hebrew prophets, whom we call Deutero-Isaiah (*Isaiah* 40-59), and of Pythagoras in Greece. Possibly the emergence of civilisations which claimed to be universal called for the birth of universal religions; possibly the new religions were a response to tensions within the existing societies, and the need for a spiritual outlet and a religion which transcended a superstitious polytheism. There was a movement towards a belief in a single spiritual reality, at the same time as Greek thinkers were looking for a single principle to explain the material world. One aspect of this was the growth of monotheism.

The oldest of the world religions is Hinduism, although narrowly defined it is not a world religion at all. It is the religion of the people of India: 'Hindu' means 'belonging to the Indus'. It is comprehensive and enormously complex; it is a growth not a construction; it embraces vegetarianism and human sacrifice, asceticism and orgy, cults which express themselves in all the richness of external observance, and the devotion of internal meditation, the simplest beliefs of village folk and the abstruse ratiocinations of philosophers. Hinduism is not in any real sense a missionary religion. Buddhism, which began as a reformist movement within Hinduism, is one of the great missionary religions. Ironically, while its outreach has been so successful that it has spread over much of Asia, there are now virtually no Buddhists in India. Guatama, the Buddha (the title means 'Enlightened'), was an Indian prince who lived perhaps in the 6th and 5th centuries BC. He gave up his position in the Great Renunciation; six years later he received enlightenment under the Bo-tree. He attained Nirvana, obliteration of desire. The first great landmark in Buddhist history was the reign of the Indian emperor Asoka, 274-232 BC (see page 82).

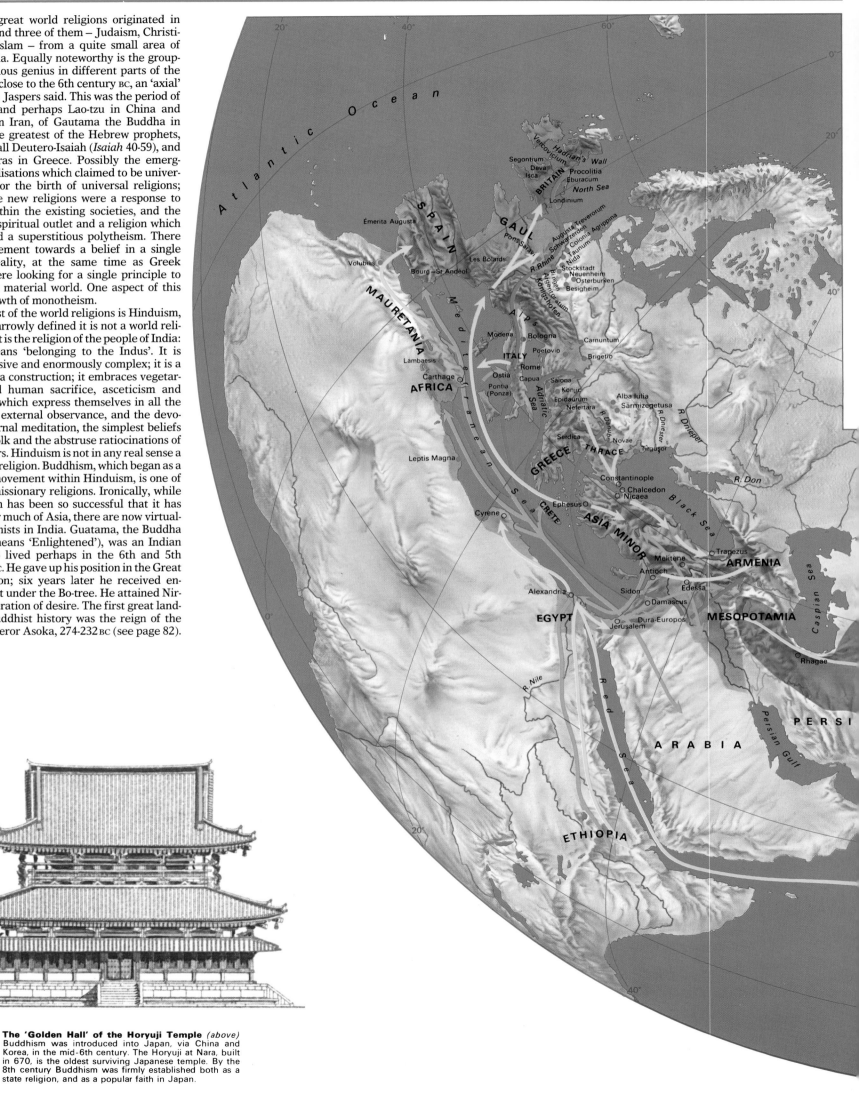

The 'Golden Hall' of the Horyuji Temple *(above)*
Buddhism was introduced into Japan, via China and Korea, in the mid-6th century. The Horyuji at Nara, built in 670, is the oldest surviving Japanese temple. By the 8th century Buddhism was firmly established both as a state religion, and as a popular faith in Japan.

He was a convert, and after his conversion became a man of peace and high principle of a kind unusual in high places; his conversion stands in marked contrast to that of the Roman emperor Constantine to Christianity. Buddhism spread early to Ceylon and Burma, and reached China by the 1st or 2nd century AD, Korea in the 4th century, and Japan in the 6th century.

Buddhism is unusual among world religions in that it does not centre upon a god. Its message is one of deliverance from suffering through the annihilation of desire. This is the Doctrine which, with the Buddha and the Community, form the focal parts of Buddhism. There has been one great schism in Buddhism, which emerged five hundred years or so after the beginning: this is between the universalist Mahayana and the more conservative Theravada. The Theravada (also called Hinayana, but the name is insulting) is strong in Ceylon, Burma and Thailand; the Mahayana tended to have more appeal further east. Buddhism spread along the coast of south-eastern Asia and also by the silk route through central Asia.

In China itself there were ancient traditions of ancestor-cult and the worship of spirits of nature. From about the 5th century BC two systems became dominant, at least among the upper classes. One was the ethical system of Kung Futzu or Confucius (551-479 BC). The other was the mystical religion of the Tao, associated with the shadowy figure of Lao-tzu. The Tao means 'the Way', the Way of the universe; man's call is to be in harmony with the Tao through the practice of quietude. These two, with Buddhism, constituted the 'three religions' of traditional China. In Japan, Buddhism challenged traditional Shinto and spirit-worship in the 6th century AD, and it was only towards the end of the Tokugawa era that Shintoism revived as the expression of Japanese national identity.

The Jews were a people, small in number, who according to tradition moved from Mesopotamia to Palestine, and whose firm history began with their escape from oppression in Egypt under a leader named Moses. They attributed their escape to a divine being named Yahweh or the Lord, with whom they made a covenant that they would be his people and he would be their god, a covenant associated with the simple but profound moral demands of the Ten Commandments, the basis of the Torah or Law. They were an exclusive people, marked off by their food-laws, circumcision, and other religious observances. The fact that Yahweh was a god who adopted them from outside had in it the seeds of universalism, and a succession of 'prophets' kept the challenge of ethical and religious righteousness before them. The Jews suffered continually from the political and military domination of others, and the consequent Dispersion carried them over much of the Mediterranean world and further east as well (see page 102). Later, as a result of Christian persecution, the Jews migrated still further.

Judaism gave birth to Christianity, which spread early over the Roman Empire and later still further afield (see pages 92 and 100). Islam too accepts the traditions of Judaism and Christianity, and sees Mohammed as standing in a line of prophets which includes Moses and Jesus. Islam was also to be a great missionary religion. In one direction it spread across North Africa, through Spain and into Europe; in another it reached India (see page 104).

One other world religion must be mentioned. This started in Persia, and is associated with the name of Zoroaster or Zarathustra, another shadowy figure. It sees life as a battleground between the forces of light and the forces of darkness, and is today represented by the comparatively small Indian sect of the Parsis. In the form of Mithraism it spread through the Roman Empire, but was ousted by the growth of Christ-ianity.

In addition, there are the tribal religions which never lasted as world religions. The Greek pantheon, adopted and adapted by the Romans, honoured a sky-god, Zeus (Jupiter), and other deities, each with a special function, who became identified with gods of conquered peoples. The Celts (whose priesthood, the Druids, was suppressed on a charge of human sacrifice), the Scandinavians (whose gods Wotan, Thor and others provided English names for the days of the week), and Germanic peoples all had their own gods, as did Syrians and Nabataeans and the peoples of Asia Minor. The Egyptian goddess Isis was worshipped far to the west. In the end all these died out, although they have sometimes influenced the religions which superseded them, and their cult-practices sometimes survive today in other religions. It was the world religions which in the end provided the bonds that linked together areas of the world previously separate.

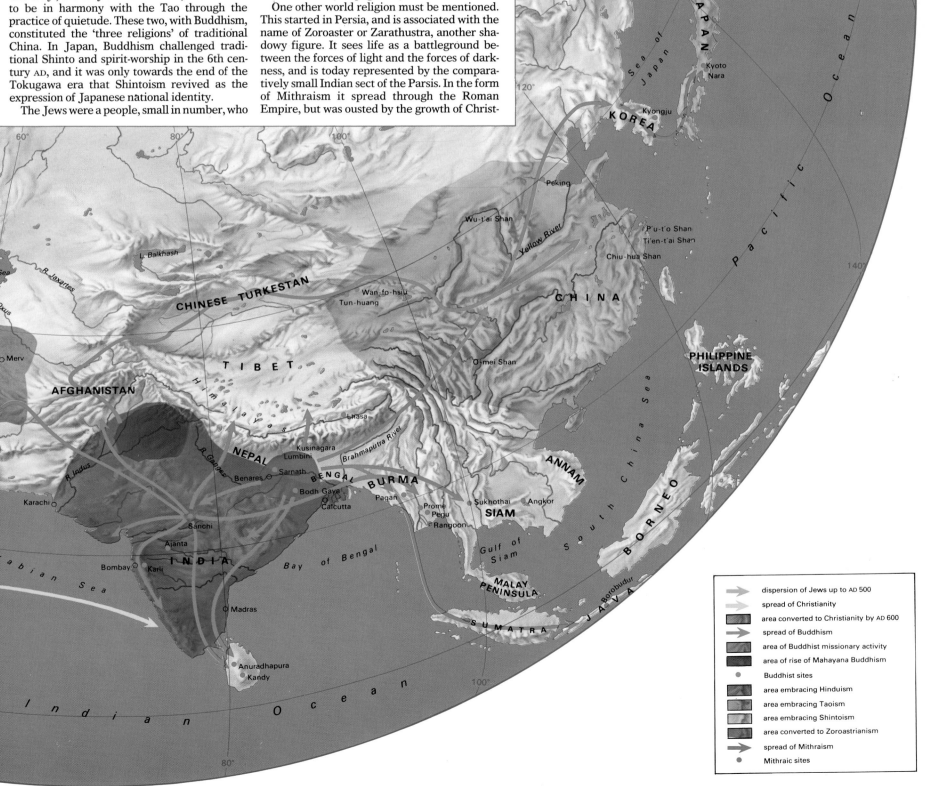

dispersion of Jews up to AD 500	
spread of Christianity	
area converted to Christianity by AD 600	
spread of Buddhism	
area of Buddhist missionary activity	
area of rise of Mahayana Buddhism	
Buddhist sites	
area embracing Hinduism	
area embracing Taoism	
area embracing Shintoism	
area converted to Zoroastrianism	
spread of Mithraism	
Mithraic sites	

The diffusion of Hellenic civilisation

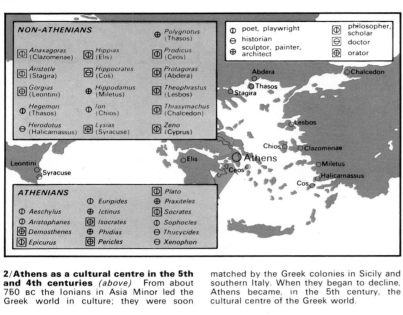

2/Athens as a cultural centre in the 5th and 4th centuries *(above)* From about 750 BC the Ionians in Asia Minor led the Greek world in culture; they were soon matched by the Greek colonies in Sicily and southern Italy. When they began to decline, Athens became, in the 5th century, the cultural centre of the Greek world.

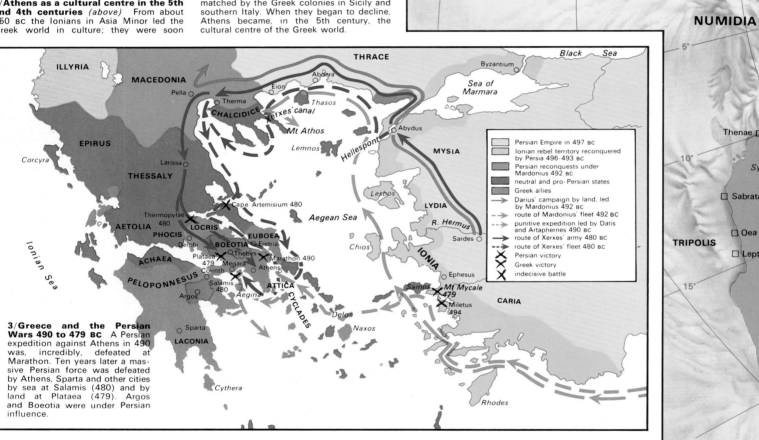

Map legend:

- Persian Empire in 497 BC
- Ionian rebel territory reconquered by Persia 496-493 BC
- Persian reconquests under Mardonius 492 BC
- neutral and pro-Persian states
- Greek allies
- → Darius' campaign by land, led by Mardonius 492 BC
- → route of Mardonius' fleet 492 BC
- → punitive expedition led by Datis and Artaphernes 490 BC
- → route of Xerxes' army 480 BC
- → route of Xerxes' fleet 480 BC
- ✕ Persian victory
- ✕ Greek victory
- ✕ indecisive battle

3/Greece and the Persian Wars 490 to 479 BC A Persian expedition against Athens in 490 was, incredibly, defeated at Marathon. Ten years later a massive Persian force was defeated by Athens, Sparta and other cities by sea at Salamis (480) and by land at Plataea (479). Argos and Boeotia were under Persian influence.

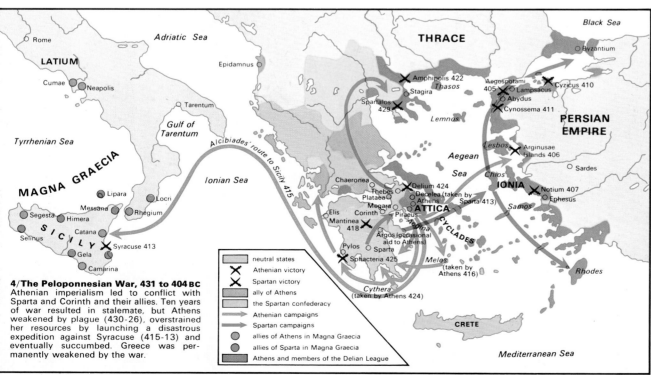

Map legend:

- neutral states
- ✕ Athenian victory
- ✕ Spartan victory
- ally of Athens
- the Spartan confederacy
- → Athenian campaigns
- → Spartan campaigns
- ● allies of Athens in Magna Graecia
- ● allies of Sparta in Magna Graecia
- Athens and members of the Delian League

4/The Peloponnesian War, 431 to 404 BC Athenian imperialism led to conflict with Sparta and Corinth and their allies. Ten years of war resulted in stalemate, but Athens weakened by plague (430-26), overstrained her resources by launching a disastrous expedition against Syracuse (415-13) and eventually succumbed. Greece was permanently weakened by the war.

THE KEY to Greek history is the *polis*, or city-state. The *polis* was a limited, independent, self-governing community which commanded the primary loyalty of its members. Its emergence was dictated by the fact of Greek geography. Greece, like Asia Minor, is a rough country, but all round the coast are comparatively small plains, separated from one another by mountain-barriers which might be impassable in winter and would be difficult to traverse at any time. These plains helped to form natural political units, often very small. Athens, for example, in her greatness with a total population of a quarter of a millon or so, was far larger than any other *polis*; many would have numbered their people in four figures rather than five, let alone six. (Aristotle said that a *polis* of 100,000 citizens – free, adult males – would cease to be a *polis*.) In the settlements of Asia Minor they protected themselves with walls; in Greece proper it sufficed for a long time to withdraw to a fortified citadel (*acro-polis*) in an emergency. Around the main centre were farms, hamlets and villages stretching as far as the mountains. The *polis* was both a political community and a religious one, as religion was, under one aspect, the life of the community.

The eighth century saw a new enlightenment. The technological development of iron-working no doubt contributed to the cultural change. Another factor was the alphabet, developed from Phoenicia. Alpha, beta, gamma are not Greek words, but come from Semitic terms for ox, house and camel. Perhaps the bardic tradition of oral poetry had its climax in the poems which go with the name of Homer, and which were preserved in writing. This was also the age of the great vases decorated with systematic geometric patterns. It was the age of a dawning consciousness that these city-states were united by a common blood, a common language, a common culture and a common religion. Throughout Greek history there is a tension between the ideal of panhellenism and the divisiveness of the *polis*. Among the forces expressing unity the Olympic Games and the Delphic Oracle, both acknowledged and respected by the whole Greek-speaking world, now appear.

The eighth century also saw the beginning of two hundred years of colonial expansion, encouraged by land-hunger, political disaffection, or the desire for adventure or profit. These were not colonies in the modern sense; they were independent of the mother city, and although there was exploitation of natives it was on a much smaller scale than the land-grabbing of the nineteenth century. The main colonising cities were few in number: Eretria and Chalcis in Euboea, Corinth and Megara on the central neck of Greece, Miletus in Asia Minor, Rhodes. They founded settlements of lasting importance: Massilia (Marseilles), Neapolis (Naples, a colony of a colony, being founded from nearby Cumae), Syracuse, Byzantium (later Constantinople, and later still Istanbul).

These centuries saw new cultural forces especially in the eastern Aegean, at the meeting-point of influences coming up the coast from Egypt and Syria, overland from Mesopotamia and even India. One finds the development of legal structures; a new individualism, especially in poetry, of which Archilochus is the revolutionary forerunner and Sappho the supreme exponent; developments in vase-painting, at first with oriental motifs in bands, and then with black figures against red clay; the beginning of stone sculpture; the emergence of coinage developed in Lydia; and right at the end of the period the first steps to a scientific philosophy.

In general there was a well-marked pattern of political development. King was challenged by baron. The barons fell out among themselves and a discontented nobleman, perhaps with the backing of the power classes, might establish himself as dictator or 'tyrant'. Good dictators were followed by bad dictators, and revolution by counter-revolution. The fifth century BC saw the Greek world oscillating between oligarchs who wished the power to be confined to a relatively few, and democrats who stood for a wider and more radical extension of power. But democracy was only extended oligarchy: women, aliens and slaves had no political rights.

By the fifth century the situation had polarised into a confrontation between Sparta and Athens. Sparta was an 'arrested civilisation'. It had retained its monarchy; power lay with a senate of two kings and twenty-eight elders, guided by five ephors or superintendents. Athens was a direct democracy, ruled by an assembly in which every citizen had the right to speak and vote, in which most of the offices were filled by lot from the whole citizen body, and in which a magistrate at the end of his year of office might find himself arraigned before a people's court.

At the beginning of the fifth century these two stood together to repel the forces of Persia. At the end they fought one another for the mastery of the Greek world in a bitter and bloody war which lasted twenty-seven years (431-404 BC); the story is told with incomparable power by the historian Thucydides. The war had arisen partly from fear and envy of Spartans and others, generated by the growth of the power of Athens, which had converted a free alliance of Greek maritime states into an Athenian empire.

Yet this century saw, especially in Athens ('the school of Greece' as her statesman Pericles called her) an unparalleled flowering of culture: the tragic drama of Aeschylus, Sophocles and Euripides; the comedy of Aristophanes; the historians Herodotus and Thucydides; the personality of Socrates; the marvellous 'red-figure' vases; the Parthenon; and the sculptures of Phidias and others. In the end it is for these achievements that Greece is of lasting importance. There is nothing else quite like it in human history – and Athens was no larger than Leicester or Miami.

The fourth century saw more jockeyings for power, with the shadow of Persia falling from the east. Plato and Aristotle produced their great metaphysical constructs, and tried to put the world back to the age of the city-state. Isocrates called vainly for the Greeks to unite. The unity which they would not find for themselves was forced upon them by the imperialistic power of Philip of Macedon. The battle of Chaeronea (338 BC) was the end of Greek liberty and the beginning, in some sense, of Greek unity.

Bronze statue of Zeus or Poseidon, more than life-size, found from a wreck off Artemisium. It is a superb example of early classical statuary (c.460 BC). It perfectly symbolises the Greek ideals of harmony, strength and moderation.

extent of Greece in 750 BC
coast under Greek influence (approximate)
coast under Phoenician influence

● Greek parent state or region
◉ Ionian colony
▲ Achaean colony
▼ Aeolian colony
● Dorian colony founded by Corinth
○ Dorian colony founded by Thera and Rhodes
⊗ Dorian colony founded by Megara or Sparta
⊙ other Greek colonies
⊞ Etruscan city
□ Punic or Phoenician city
■ Philistine city

1/Greek colonisation in the Mediterranean world, 750 to 550 BC Early Greece was not fertile enough to support a fast-growing population. The need for more land, sometimes combined with political oppression by the ruling class at home or the attractions of trade, led many Greek cities from c.750 BC onwards to send out colonists to seek new homes overseas. When established, the colonies became independent states. This epoch-making movement, which changed the whole face of the Mediterranean and spread Greek civilisation far and wide (750-600), was not paralleled again in world history until the 16th-century colonisation from Europe.

The Hellenistic world 336 to 30 BC

ALEXANDER the Great transformed the Greek world by opening up for it the resources of the Middle East. In 334 BC he crossed the Hellespont from Europe to Asia, swept through Asia Minor, past Syria to Egypt, then east and south-east down the Tigris and Euphrates, pressing on into the heartlands of Iran and then through the Caspian Gates and the Hindu Kush to the neighbourhood of Bukhara and Tashkent. Here he retraced his steps, turned south into Kashmir and east again across the Indus as far as the Beas. He hoped to reach Ocean, the great mythical river which the Greeks believed to encircle the landmass of the world, but his troops would go no further. They turned back along the Indus to its mouth, and marched, with bitter sufferings, north-westward back to Persepolis and ultimately to Susa.

Alexander died in 323 BC, just before his thirty-third birthday. His mighty empire broke up between his warring generals; among them, three major powers gradually emerged. One, with its capital at Pella, was the old kingdom of Macedon, shorn of its Asiatic conquests but still dominating northern Greece, retaining a firm foothold in Greece proper and exercising substantial authority in Greek affairs, sometimes by diplomacy and sometimes by brute force. In wealthy Egypt, whose capital was now at Alexander's new foundation of Alexandria, an able soldier-historian named Ptolemy (Soter or Saviour) established a new dynasty and extended his interests into Palestine, where he confronted the third of the great kingdoms. Seleucus had been in authority in Babylonia; from there he extended his power over Syria and established a new capital at Antioch-on-the-Orontes, whence successive sovereigns named Seleucus, Antiochus or Demetrius ruled. These Seleucid kings, like Alexander earlier, founded many Greek cities within their realm. To this triumvirate of kingdoms must be added the breakaway Pergamum, which between 264 and 133 BC maintained an independence which came to overshadow much of Asia Minor, and further east the remarkable kingdom of the Bactrian Greeks who broke away from Seleucid control.

The new developments led to a diffusion of wealth and a great expansion of trade with east Africa, Arabia, India and central Asia, while to the east there was for the first time some commerce with China. To the west Pytheas of Marseilles sailed through the Straits of Gibraltar, circumnavigating Britain, laying the foundations for the Cornish tin trade, and probably reaching Norway and the river Elbe. Within the Mediterranean, silver flowed from Spain, copper from Cyprus, iron from the Black Sea coasts, corn from Egypt, North Africa and the Crimea, olive oil from Athens, dried fruit from Palestine, dried fish from Byzantium, linen, granite and papyrus from Egypt, woollen goods from Asia Minor, timber from Macedon, Asia Minor and the Lebanon, marble from Paros and Athens. Rhodes and Delos prospered as middlemen.

Alexander had flung back the horizons. The Greeks, with their new philosophies and religions, now found themselves members not only of a local community, the *polis*, but of *cosmopolis*, the whole civilised and increasingly Hellenised world. For a century, while Stoics and Epicureans alike proclaimed the brotherhood of man, and the more radical Cynics declared themselves citizens of the universe, the great post-Alexandrian powers maintained an often uneasy, but essentially stable equilibrium. Athens, seized by the Macedonians in the course of Chremonides' War (267 to 262 BC), remained an important cultural centre, but deliberately abdicated any further large-scale political ambitions. The main growth-points were now the newer capitals: Antioch, Pergamum, to some extent Pella, and above all Alexandria. Here the Museum, like the Library of Pergamum, formed

an international centre for higher learning and the arts. Here flourished the great 3rd century poets, Apollonius of Rhodes, Callimachus and Theocritus, and far-reaching advances in medicine, astronomy, mathematics, geography and science were made. It was the age of Eratosthenes and Archimedes.

Greece itself produced a variety of political experiments: different forms of confederation, particularly in the Achaean League, and the attempts by Agis IV and Cleomenes III in Sparta to establish an early form of communism before the regime was smashed by Antigonus Doson's Macedonians at Sellasia in 222 BC. To begin with, little of this disturbed the essential underlying balance, which lasted almost throughout the 3rd century. But with Rome's second war against Macedonia (200-197 BC) increasingly significant shifts began to develop, as rulers throughout the eastern Mediterranean were forced to adjust their policies to the rising might of Rome.

Roman imperialism was henceforth to be the crucial factor in the affairs of the Hellenistic kingdoms; but under the late Republic it grew only slowly. Direct annexation, except along the barbarian frontiers, was normally regarded as a policy of last resort, acceptable only when political aims could be achieved by no other means. Not until after 150 BC was there a single Roman governor or permanent army stationed east of the Adriatic. But other forms of intervention grew progressively more forceful.

Philip V of Macedon's provocative alliance with Hannibal in 215 had led to Roman military intervention in Greece which ended in 205 with

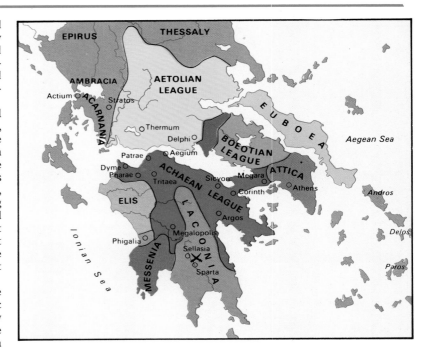

4/The Greek Leagues *(above)* Weakness in the 3rd century led to federalism. The Aetolians expanded their influence by force, while an Achaean League expanded by admitting non-Achaean members. Both Leagues were normally hostile to Macedon, but later Achaean hostility to Sparta led to reconciliation with Macedon whose king, Antigonus Doson, defeated Sparta at Sellasia (222 BC).

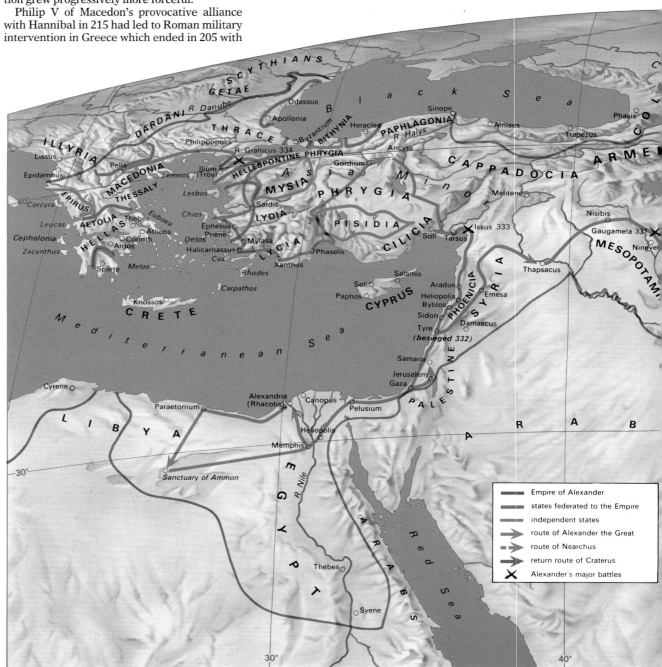

	Empire of Alexander
	states federated to the Empire
	independent states
	route of Alexander the Great
	route of Nearchus
	return route of Craterus
	Alexander's major battles

the Peace of Phoenice, a treaty of mutual coexistence. But Philip's continued expansion, both into Greece, in the Aegean and along the Adriatic, brought retaliatory action, and a heavy defeat by the army of Flamininus at the Battle of Cynoscephalae. In 190 BC, the greatest of the Seleucid monarchs, Antiochus III, after invading Greece was similarly humbled at the Battle of Magnesia, and stripped of his possessions in Asia Minor at the Peace of Apamea (188).

From then on, Rome had no serious rival in the Aegean and the Middle East. She could, and did, enhance the power of states like Pergamum and Rhodes and then, just as easily, break them. Even so, it took more than 150 years before the Hellenistic world fell fully under Roman control. Renewed Macedonian aggression, under Philip V's son Perseus, was decisively halted at Pydna (168) and the country divided into four independent territories; it only became a Roman province in 146, after further uprisings. The Seleucid Empire, weakened by internal conflicts and Parthian wars, was finally terminated by Pompey in 64 BC. Pergamum, unexpectedly bequeathed to Rome at the death of Attalus III (133), was only reluctantly accepted by the Senate; and Egypt, bestowed in an even more opulent gesture by Ptolemy Alexander I in 88 BC, was rejected outright. It was only after the defeat of Cleopatra VII, the last of the Ptolemies, at the naval battle of Actium in 31 BC, that Rome legally as well as effectively held the whole of Alexander's heritage. Long before that the framework of Greek civilisation had been broken; but its spiritual and intellectual legacy now permeated every aspect of Roman life.

1/The Empire of Alexander (below) The Macedonian conquests stretched to the limits of the known world and beyond, taking Hellenistic civilisation decisively beyond the Mediterranean and turning European minds and energies for the first time to the east; they probably also made it more vulnerable to the implacable Roman drive from the west.

2/The Hellenistic world in 240 BC (right) After two generations of war, the Ptolemies, the Seleucids and the Antigonid kings of Macedon had achieved a sustainable political and military balance. Athens had faded as a political force, but Pergamum, Rhodes, Delos, Pontus on the Black Sea were all independent rising powers, thanks not least to their commerce. Bactrian Greek rulers, breaking away from the Seleucid Empire (c. 240 BC) held Afghanistan (with parts of north-western India and Central Asia) for over a hundred years. The Parthians, whose era began in 247 BC, were beginning to build up their power, which was to stretch from the Euphrates to the Indus.

3/The Hellenistic world in 185 BC (right) With decisive victories over both the Macedonians (Cynoscephalae, 197 BC) and the Seleucids (Magnesia, 190 BC), Rome had established herself as the dominant force in the eastern Mediterranean.

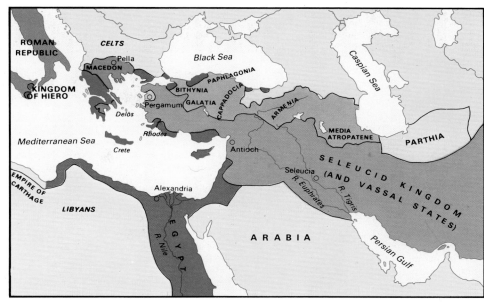

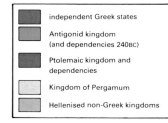

- independent Greek states
- Antigonid kingdom (and dependencies 240BC)
- Ptolemaic kingdom and dependencies
- Kingdom of Pergamum
- Hellenised non-Greek kingdoms

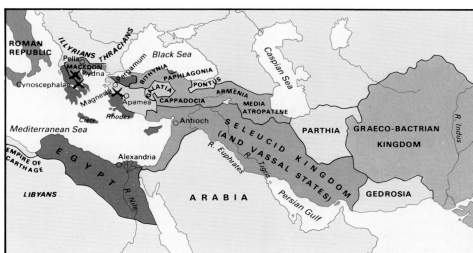

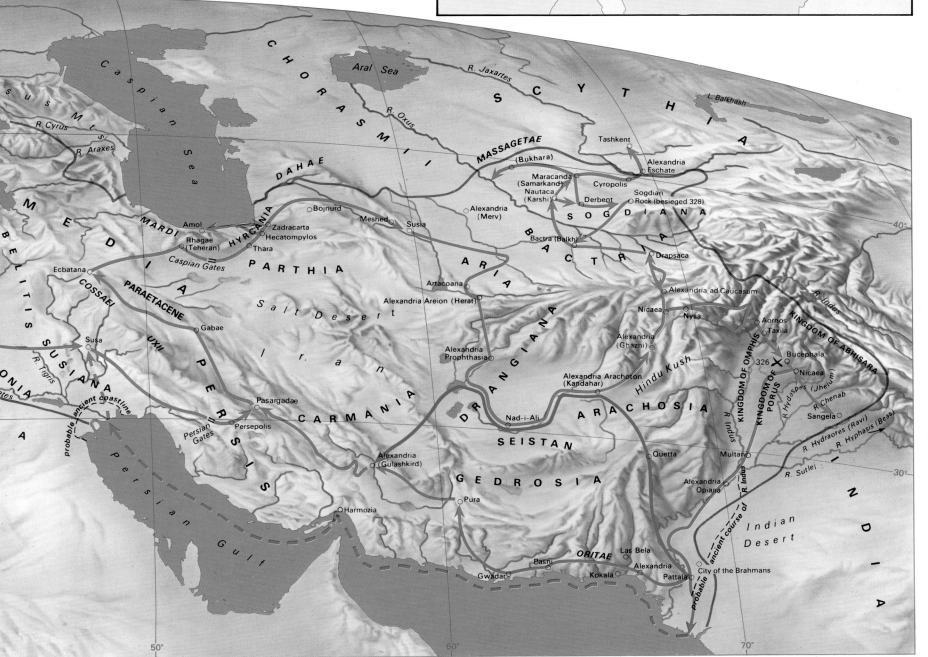

The Empires of Persia 550 BC to AD 637

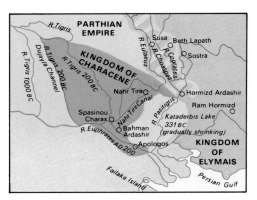

2/The Persian Gulf *(above)* With the decline of the Seleucids in the 2nd century BC, the kingdoms of Characene and Elymais arose by the Persian Gulf. Here coastlines and rivers were continually changing. Lake Kataderbis disappeared after 300 BC, and Charax near the Tigris east bank was afterwards the main port.

AFTER the destruction of Assyria and the sack of its capital, Nineveh, in 612 BC, Babylon, one of the victors, retained the Mesopotamian lowlands, while the mountain country lying westward to the river Halys (modern Kizil Irmak) was incorporated in the kingdom of its allies the Medes. In 550 BC Cyrus, then Prince of Persia, rebelled, defeated the Median king, Astyages, and welded the Medes and the Persians together to make Iran the dominant power in Asia and the Near East. Its empire, enlarged by successful military campaigns, soon incorporated Lycia, Lydia, the Ionian-Greek settlements of Asia Minor, Babylon and Afghanistan.

The Iranian peoples, newly arrived from central Asia, thus came to dominate the power centres of the Mesopotamian world. Their Iron Age technology, their ability to exploit the horse for communication and warfare, and above all their vigour and versatility, almost always gave them an edge over the forces of the more ritualised ancient civilisations. Soon after Cyrus's death, while one of his sons, Smerdis, held Iran, the other, Cambyses, defeated the last Egyptian pharaoh, Psamtik III, at Pelusium (525 BC). Later the brothers quarrelled, with fatal results, and a usurper seized the throne. But a cousin of theirs, Darius, led a group of confederates to restore the Achaemenid family line, reorganised the empire into twenty tribute-paying satrapies and established unified control, with a comprehensive code of laws, a stable currency and an efficient postal service. As organiser and financier Darius swiftly proved himself as great a genius as his uncle Cyrus had been in military affairs. His administration laid stress on regular, equitable taxes, accurate weights and measures and soundly cautious monetary policies. The Iranians' essentially ethnic religion, Zoroastrianism, sought no converts. So that tolerance, whether for Judaism or for the various Greek, Babylonian and Egyptian forms of polytheism, encouraged both communal harmony and loyalty to the king. Martial traditions, artistic sensibility and technical awareness, especially in engineering, all contributed to Iranian success, while an unshakeable national consciousness and an unusual respect for monarchic legitimacy helped the culture to survive the repeated invasions made inevitable by its position on the Asian landbridge.

This strength was soon put to the test. Darius's military enterprises were less uniformly successful than his administrative reforms. He was repulsed by the Scythians of the Ukraine in 513 BC, and his attempts to punish Athens and Eretria for their support of the rebellious Ionians led to a brusque defeat at Marathon in 490 BC. A massive invasion of Greece by his son Xerxes was similarly beaten off, both by sea at Salamis (480 BC) and by land at Plataea the following year.

Persia itself remained impregnable to the Greeks for almost another century. Its weaknesses were revealed when Cyrus the Younger, the Iranian viceroy in the west, recruited a force of Greek mercenaries, the Ten Thousand, to revolt against his brother, the Emperor Artaxerxes II, in 401 BC. The knowledge gained attacking Babylonia paved the way for the later, devastating onslaughts of Alexander of Macedon, whose defeat of the Persian army at Gaugamela (331 BC) brought the Achaemenid rule to its end.

After the break-up of Alexander's own empire (see page 76) Iran became part of the Seleucid kingdom, as it remained, apart from the appearance of the local dynasty in the region of Persis, until 247 BC. In that year Ptolemy III of Egypt invaded Syria and claimed sovereignty as far east as Bactria. The nomad Parthians on the northern borders took advantage of the resulting upheaval to tear the whole territory of Parthia and Hyrcania away from Seleucid allegiance. Further east, Diodotus, satrap of Bactria, also declared independence, and founded the Graeco-Bactrian kingdom. Valiant efforts by the restored Seleucids, notably Antiochus III the Great, in 208 BC to suppress the Parthians and Graeco-Bactrians achieved little lasting effect, and finally, in 141 BC, Mithridates I of Parthia reversed the situation and entered Seleucia.

Ten years later, however, the situation on Iran's eastern frontiers drastically changed. The Yüeh-chi nomads, or Tocharians, driven back by Huns, clashed with the Scythians, beyond the river Jaxartes. The latter then destroyed the Graeco-Bactrian kingdom on their way southward to the Punjab. The Tocharians followed more slowly, by way of northern Afghanistan, sweeping away remaining Hellenic outposts. The brief period of Indo-Parthian dominance in Taxila, the great trading city of north India, was itself ended in AD 60 with the rise of the Tocharians' mighty Kushan Empire.

In the west, the Parthian borders soon marched with Rome on the Euphrates. Invasions by the elsewhere almost invincible legions were unsuccessful, for Parthia was the only major state consistently to withstand Roman power. In 53 BC the army of Crassus was destroyed at Carrhae by the relatively modest cavalry forces of a Parthian regional commander. Mark Antony, in 36 BC, led a formidable army from Armenia to Azerbaijan (Atropatene) but quickly got into difficulties and could barely extricate the survivors of his force. Augustus, seeking better relations, effectively accepted the Euphrates boundary line, and later emperors in the main limited their intervention to dynastic intrigues. It was only in AD 114 that Trajan, exploiting a moment of Parthian weakness, formally annexed Armenia as a Roman province. He then advanced down the Euphrates and Tigris to take Seleucia and reach the Persian Gulf. In AD 165, the general Avidius Cassius again sacked Seleucia and also Ctesiphon before being forced to retreat by an attack of smallpox. This feat was repeated by Septimius Severus in AD 198, but such incursions had little lasting effect. The real threat was internal, and came to a head in about 224 when Ardashir Papakan, Prince of Persia and founder of the Sasanian dynasty, defeated his Parthian overlord, Artabanus (Ardavan) V, at Hormizdagan, north of Isfahan.

The new king replaced Parthian feudalism with a highly centralised administration and reorganised the vassal kingdoms (Characene, Elymais, etc.) as provinces, each governed by a Sasanian prince. He crushed the Kushan state to the east. His son Shapur pushed the Asiatic frontiers back as far as Tashkent and Peshawar. Immediately on his accession in 244, Shapur repelled an invasion by the Roman Gordian III near Meshik on the Euphrates, grandiloquently renaming the place Peroz Shapur. In 253 he smashed a second Roman army at Barbalissus, higher up the Euphrates, and finally, in 259,

defeated and captured the Roman emperor Valerian at Edessa. Annexing Oman on the Arabian shores of the Gulf, he firmly established Sasanian Iran as the strongest power of late antiquity, with an elaborate and efficient bureaucracy, a powerful state religion, Zoroastrianism, and a strong tradition of craftsmanship, especially in the weaving of silk, now widely imported from China.

The peak of Sasanian power and prosperity was reached under Khosrau I Anohshirvan (531-79) when he invaded Syria, captured Antioch and deported its famous metal-workers to his own lands. But his son, Khosrau II Parviz (590-628), over-reached himself. Invading the Byzantine Empire, capturing Jerusalem, overrunning Anatolia and Egypt, and camping on the Bosphorus facing Constantinople, he was forced to retreat when the Byzantine emperor Heraclius outflanked him and sacked his favourite residence at Dastagerd.

Peace came too late for the two empires, for both quickly fell victim to the newly-emergent forces of Islam (see pages 104 and 112). The Arabs scored significant victories at Dhu Qar (c.611), in the 'Battle of the Chains' and at Ullais, near the Euphrates (633), but the decisive action was at Al Qadisiya (637), when they smashed the Persians' metropolitan army and captured the capital, Ctesiphon. Yezdagird III, the last Sasanian king, fled to the Zagros, but further Arab victories at Jalula (637) and Nehavend (642) opened the road to the main Iranian plateau. Within a few years the Muslim armies reached the Oxus, and Iran became part of the Islamic world-empire.

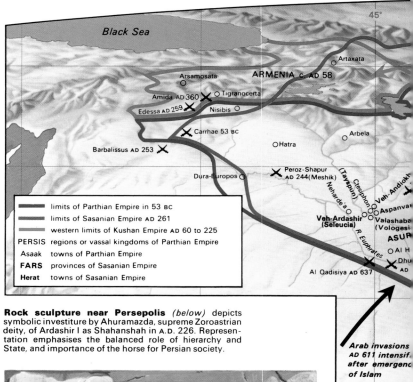

limits of Parthian Empire in 53 BC
limits of Sasanian Empire AD 261
western limits of Kushan Empire AD 60 to 225
PERSIS   regions or vassal kingdoms of Parthian Empire
Asaak   towns of Parthian Empire
FARS   provinces of Sasanian Empire
Herat   towns of Sasanian Empire

Rock sculpture near Persepolis *(below)* depicts symbolic investiture by Ahuramazda, supreme Zoroastrian deity, of Ardashir I as Shahanshah in A.D. 226. Representation emphasises the balanced role of hierarchy and State, and importance of the horse for Persian society.

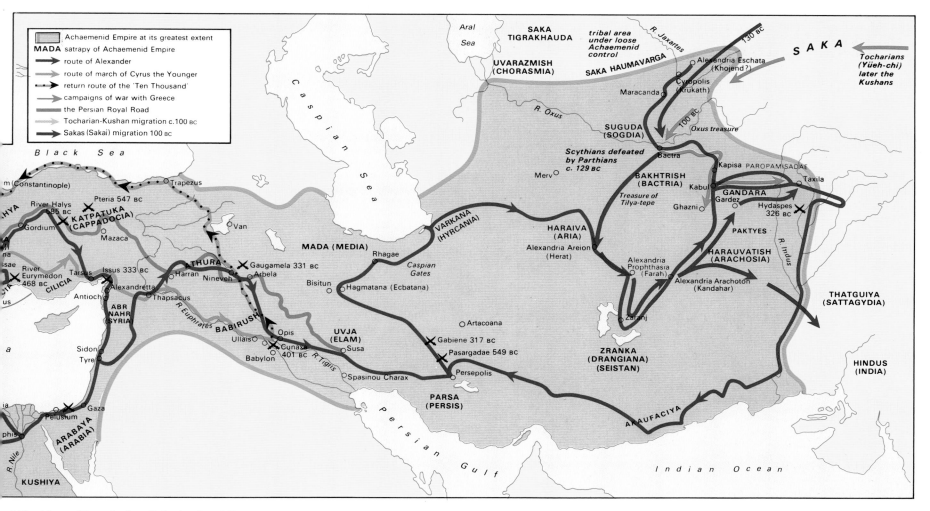

Map labels (Map 1 — The Achaemenid Empire):

Aral Sea
SAKA TIGRAKHAUDA
UVARAZMISH (CHORASMIA)
SAKA HAUMAVARGA
tribal area under loose Achaemenid control
R. Jaxartes
130 BC
SAKA
Tocharians (Yüeh-chi) later the Kushans
Alexandria Eschata (Khojend?)
Cyropolis (Krukath)
Maracanda
100 BC
SUGUDA (SOGDIA)
Oxus treasure
Bactra
Kapisa PAROPAMISADAE
Taxila
BAKHTRISH (BACTRIA)
Kabul
Caspian Sea
Scythians defeated by Parthians c. 129 BC
GANDARA
Gardez
Ghazni
Hydaspes 326 BC
Black Sea
m (Constantinople)
Trapezus
Pteria 547 BC
Treasure of Tilya-tepe
PAKTYES
Van
HARAIVA (ARIA)
Alexandria Areion (Herat)
HARAUVATISH (ARACHOSIA)
R. Indus
River Halys -85 BC
KATPATUKA (CAPPADOCIA)
Gordium
Mazaca
VARKANA (HYRCANIA)
R. Oxus
THATGUIYA (SATTAGYDIA)
na
River Eurymedon 468 BC
Tarsus
CILICIA
Issus 333 BC
THURA
Gaugamela 331 BC
Harran Nineveh
Arbela
MADA (MEDIA)
Rhagae
Caspian Gates
Alexandria Prophthasia (Farah)
Alexandria Arachoton (Kandahar)
Antioch
Alexandretta
ABR NAHR SYRIA
Thapsacus
R. Euphrates
BABIRUSH
Bisitun
Hagmatana (Ecbatana)
HINDUS (INDIA)
Sidon
Tyre
Ullais
Opis
Cunaxa 401 BC
Babylon
R. Tigris
UVJA (ELAM)
Susa
Artacoana
Gabiene 317 BC
Pasargadae 549 BC
ZRANKA (DRANGIANA) (SEISTAN)
Zaranj
ia
Pelusium
Gaza
ARABAYA (ARABIA)
R. Nile
phis
KUSHIYA
Spasinou Charax
PARSA (PERSIS)
Persepolis
Persian Gulf
ARAUFACIYA
Indian Ocean

3/Parthian and Sasanian Iran *(below)* From 247 BC when the nomad Parthians rose, under their chieftain Arsaces, and seized the Seleucid town of Nisa (Mihrdadkert), until AD 635, when the Arabs clinched their final victory. Iran, though often under attack, remained one of the richest and most powerful regions of the ancient world. The Parthians embraced the whole area from the Euphrates to northern India, but gave way, in AD 224, to the Sasanians, a Persian dynasty which only succumbed to the forces of Islam after fighting almost to the death with Byzantium.

1/The Achaemenid Empire *(above)* The Medes and Persians were Indo-European peoples from central Asia. The centre of the Medes was founded at Ecbatana, and after the sack of Nineveh in 612 they became the chief power in the East. Their cousins the Persians moved southwards to Fars province (originally Parsa), and won the leadership under Cyrus the Great (550) who extended the rule of his line from the Aegean to the Indus. Under his successors the Empire flourished mightily until 330 BC, when Alexander the Great burnt its capital, Persepolis, to the ground.

Legend (top left):
- Achaemenid Empire at its greatest extent
- MADA satrapy of Achaemenid Empire
- route of Alexander
- route of march of Cyrus the Younger
- return route of the 'Ten Thousand'
- campaigns of war with Greece
- the Persian Royal Road
- Tocharian-Kushan migration c.100 BC
- Sakas (Sakai) migration 100 BC

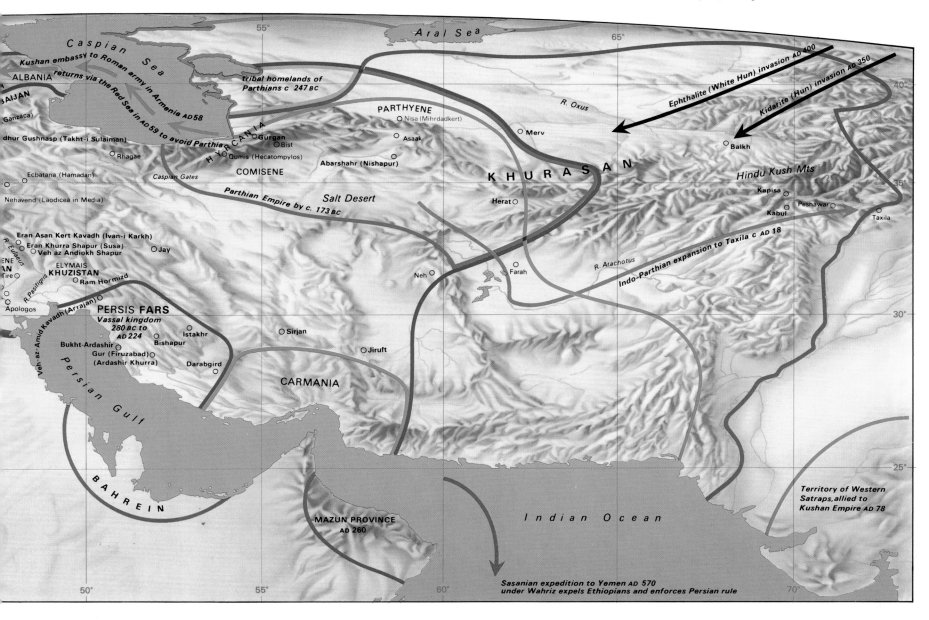

Map labels (Map 3 — Parthian and Sasanian Iran):

Caspian Sea
ALBANIA
AZERBAIJAN (BAIJAN)
Kushan embassy to Roman army in Armenia AD 58
returns via the Red Sea in AD 59 to avoid Parthia
Ganzaca)
dhur Gushnasp (Takht-i Sulaiman)
Rhagae
Ecbatana (Hamadan)
Nehavend (Laodicea in Media)
Eran Asan Kert Kavadh (Ivan-i Karkh)
Eran Khurra Shapur (Susa)
Veh az Andiokh Shapur
ELYMAIS KHUZISTAN
Ram Hormizd
Apologos
Veh-at-Amid Kavadh (Arrajan)
PERSIS FARS
Vassal kingdom 280 BC to AD 224
Bukht-Ardashir
Gur (Firuzabad)
(Ardashir Khurra)
Darabgird
Istakhr
Bishapur
Persian Gulf
BAHREIN
CARMANIA
MAZUN PROVINCE AD 260
Aral Sea
tribal homelands of Parthians c 247 BC
PARTHYENE
Nisa (Mihrdadkert)
R. Oxus
Merv
Asaak
Gurgan
Bist
Qumis (Hecatompylos)
Abarshahr (Nishapur)
HYRCANIA
COMISENE
Caspian Gates
Parthian Empire by c. 173 BC
Salt Desert
Jay
R. Euleus
R. Pasitigris
Tire
Jiruft
Sirjan
Neh
Farah
Herat
R. Arachotus
R. Arachotus
KHURASAN
Ephthalite (White Hun) invasion AD 400
Kidarite (Hun) invasion AD 350
Balkh
Hindu Kush Mts
Kapisa
Kabul
Peshawar
Taxila
Indo-Parthian expansion to Taxila c AD 18
Territory of Western Satraps, allied to Kushan Empire AD 78
Indian Ocean
Sasanian expedition to Yemen AD 570 under Wahriz expels Ethiopians and enforces Persian rule

The unification of China 350 BC to AD 220

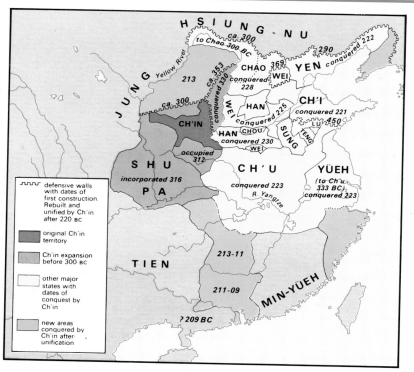

THROUGHOUT the Warring States period (403-221 BC) seven major states contended for supremacy. At first the main contenders were the old-established kingdoms of Ch'i, Ch'u, Han and Wei. Later (328-308 BC) the north-western border state of Ch'in established firm control over the north-west and west, and during the latter half of the 3rd century gradually destroyed its rivals to become master of all China in 221 BC. This was a period of constant warfare, waged on a massive scale by powerful and well-organised kingdoms which began to replace the old feudal social order with a centralised administration staffed by bureaucrats rather than hereditary nobles. They developed effective legal and fiscal systems to provide for their armies and public works.

Their emergence coincided with major economic and social changes. The introduction of iron tools from about 500 BC and the use of animal

1/The Warring States and the unification of China (left) Ch'in became a serious contender for supremacy over the other major states after her expansion and consolidation in the north-west and west from 328 to 308 BC. Later, the other states were eliminated until in 221 BC Ch'in controlled all China. Under Shih Huang-ti the Ch'in expanded its territories to the far south and north-east.

power for cultivation greatly increased agricultural productivity. The large-scale new states could undertake massive drainage and irrigation projects to bring much new land into cultivation. In these new lands a new social order arose, breaking away from the tight village community of the past. Population multiplied. Commerce and industry flourished as the states built roads and large cities emerged. It was a period of innovation in every field: in technology, science and government. There was a philosophical ferment, in which the main streams of Chinese thought, Confucianism, Taoism and Legalism, all took shape.

In the victorious state of Ch'in the old feudal aristocracy was abolished, and replaced by a rigid centralised bureaucracy. The population was organised in groups of families bearing mutual responsibility, and regimented to provide manpower for construction works and for the army. The new system was enforced through a savage penal code. When the first Ch'in emperor, Shih Huang-ti, unified China, these institutions were extended throughout the country. Although he ruthlessly eliminated all hostile factions, the burdens imposed on the people by his campaigns and vast construction works combined with surviving regional tensions to bring

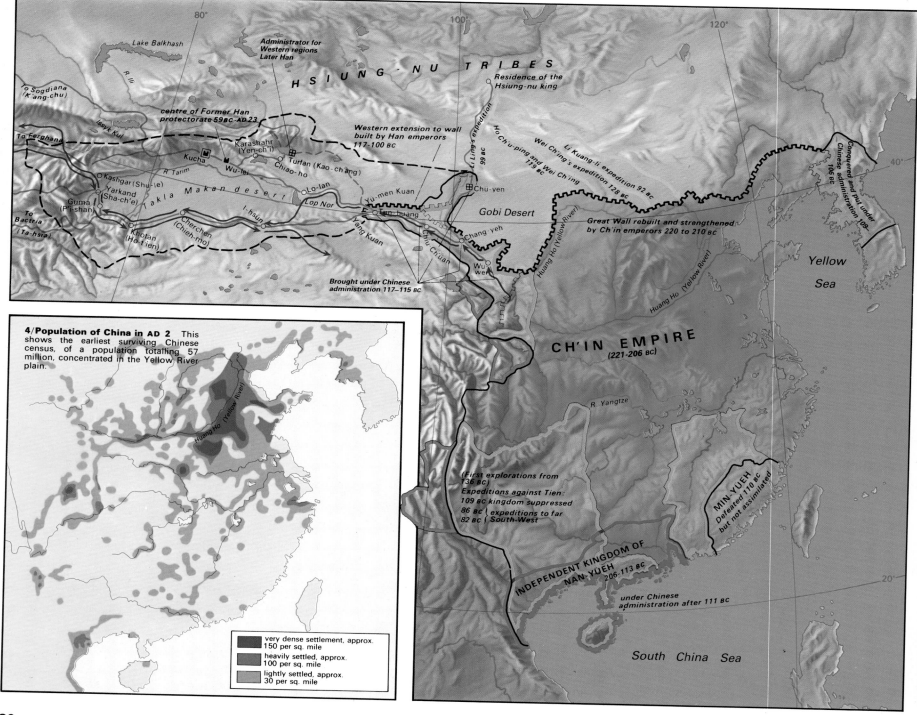

4/Population of China in AD 2 This shows the earliest surviving Chinese census, of a population totalling 57 million, concentrated in the Yellow River plain.

very dense settlement, approx. 150 per sq. mile

heavily settled, approx. 100 per sq. mile

lightly settled, approx. 30 per sq. mile

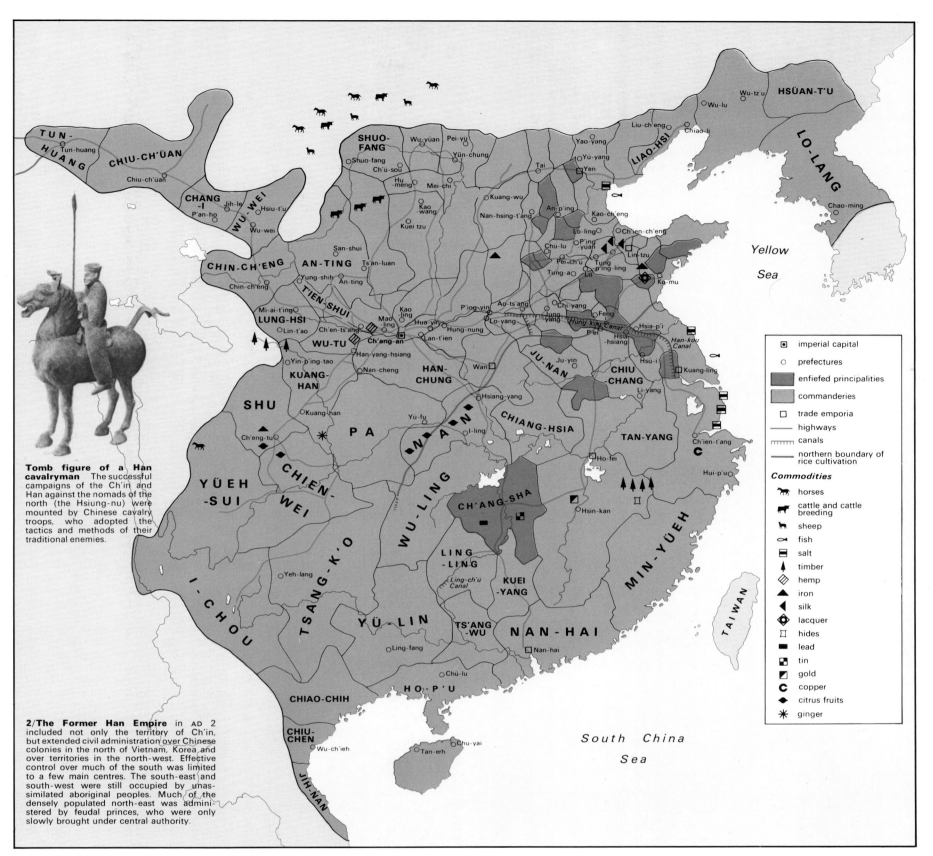

Tomb figure of a Han cavalryman (*left*) Han expansion began under Wu-ti (140-86 BC). The successful campaigns of the Ch'in and Han against the nomads of the north (the Hsiung-nu) were mounted by Chinese cavalry troops, who adopted the tactics and methods of their traditional enemies.

2/The Former Han Empire in AD 2 included not only the territory of Ch'in, but extended civil administration over Chinese colonies in the north of Vietnam, Korea and over territories in the north-west. Effective control over much of the south was limited to a few main centres. The south-east and south-west were still occupied by unassimilated aboriginal peoples. Much of the densely populated north-east was administered by feudal princes, who were only slowly brought under central authority.

Map legend:
- imperial capital
- prefectures
- enfiefed principalities
- commanderies
- trade emporia
- highways
- canals
- northern boundary of rice cultivation

Commodities
- horses
- cattle and cattle breeding
- sheep
- fish
- salt
- timber
- hemp
- iron
- silk
- lacquer
- hides
- lead
- tin
- gold
- copper
- citrus fruits
- ginger

3/The expansion of Han China (*left*) Han expansion began under Wu-ti (140-86 BC). The Chinese took the offensive against the Hsiung-nu, extended the Great Wall far to the north-west to protect the route into central Asia. For a few decades after 59 BC the Chinese controlled the Tarim basin. Missions visited Parthia and Bactria, and extensive trade with the West began. Chinese power was again briefly extended to the west after AD 94. The Han eliminated the coastal Yüeh kingdoms, occupied north Vietnam and northern Korea.

Map legend:
- China in 206 BC
- boundary of Former Han Empire
- territory added under Former Han
- boundary of Chinese protectorate of Western Regions
- journey of Chang Chien, envoy of Han Emperor 138-126 BC
- routes opened to trade by Former Han
- administrative centres under Later Han
- centre of Later Han protectorate, 73-127 AD
- territory added under Later Han
- new route opened by General Pan Ch'ao for Later Han
- expeditions against Hsiung-nu (Huns)

about the collapse of his empire in 206 BC, shortly after his death.

After a period of civil war a new dynasty, the Han, regained control of all China. Founded by a man of humble origins, the Han were forced to reintroduce a system of feudal principalities allocated to their family and supporters, and these fiefs were not brought under strong central control until about 100 BC. Copying the general outlines of Ch'in government, but softening its harshness, the Han gradually evolved a strong central government and an effective system of local administration.

The Ch'in had taken strong defensive measures against the nomad Hsiung-nu in the north, and had expanded southwards into areas occupied by non-Chinese aboriginal peoples. The Han were at first preoccupied with internal affairs. Under Wu-ti (140-87 BC) China again took the offensive against the Hsiung-nu, rebuilt the Ch'in wall and extended it far to the north-west. They opened up the route to central Asia and after 59 BC Chinese military power was briefly extended over the oasis states of the Tarim Basin. The Chinese began a large export trade, mainly in silk, to Parthia and to the Roman Empire. The Han also reaffirmed the Ch'in conquests in the Canton region, eliminated the

Yüeh kingdoms of the south-east coast at the end of the 2nd century, and occupied northern Vietnam. Chinese armies also drove deep into the south-west, establishing Han control over its native states. These southern conquests, however, led to little Chinese settlement. Away from a few main centres most of southern China remained in the hands of aboriginal peoples for centuries to come. Wu-ti's armies also occupied and placed under Chinese administration parts of southern Manchuria and northern Korea.

The Han Empire grew extremely prosperous. The rapid growth of the preceding centuries continued. During this period of stability, prosperity and growth China's population reached some 57,000,000 and many large cities grew up. The Han capital, Ch'ang-an, had a quarter of a million people, and was the centre of a brilliant culture. At the beginning of the Christian era the Han Empire rivalled that of Rome in size and in wealth.

Even the riches of the Han Empire, however, were severely taxed by Han Wu-ti's military adventures, and under a series of weak emperors during the latter half of the 1st century BC the authority of the throne was rivalled by the great court families. In AD 9 Wang Mang, an imperial relative by marriage, usurped the throne and set

up a brief dynasty (Hsin, AD 9-23) which embarked upon a drastic programme of reforms. His reign ended in widespread rebellion, and was followed by a restoration of the Han (Later Han, AD 25-220). Since Ch'ang-an had been sacked during the fighting, the capital was moved to Lo-yang and during the Later Han period the north-east of China steadily grew in importance relative to the north-west.

After some decades of consolidation, in the late 1st century the Chinese again began active hostilities against the Hsiung-nu, and in AD 94 again invaded the Tarim basin. But this revival proved short-lived. Trouble with the Chiang tribes of the north-west, the succession of several child-emperors and virulent factionalism at court had seriously weakened the Han state by about AD 160. A wave of agrarian distress culminated in the massive religious uprising of the Yellow Turbans which engulfed China from 184. Some degree of order was eventually restored by various regional warlords. Although the Han survived in name until 220, power in fact lay with these regional commanders. In 220 the last Han emperor abdicated in favour of one of them, and the empire was divided into three independent regional states. China was to remain politically fragmented until 589.

India: the first empires

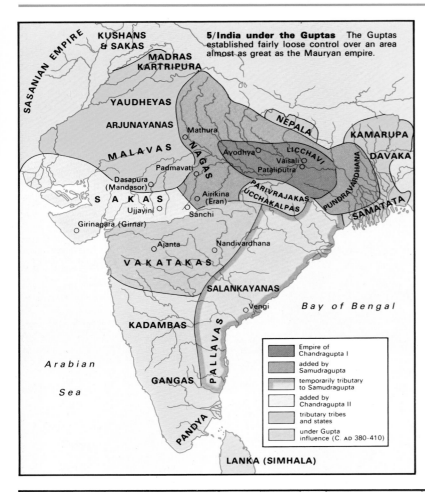

5/India under the Guptas The Guptas established fairly loose control over an area almost as great as the Mauryan empire.

Empire of Chandragupta I

added by Samudragupta

temporarily tributary to Samudragupta

added by Chandragupta II

tributary tribes and states

under Gupta influence (C. AD 380-410)

BY about 600 BC, northern India had at least sixteen well-articulated political units, some still essentially tribal republics, others already absolute monarchies, established in the rich Gangetic plain. In one of the smaller republics, Kapilavastu, Guatama Buddha, founder of Asia's most pervasive religion, was born c.566 BC, while on the Ganges itself Mahavira, his near-contemporary (born c.600 BC) was formulating the teachings of Jainism, the faith still followed by many of India's merchant community.

During the 5th century BC the number of *Mahajanapadas*, or great realms, was gradually reduced to four, and ultimately, after a century of mutual wars, these were all absorbed into the single kingdom of Magadha, with its splendid new capital of Pataliputra (Patna), strategically commanding the Ganges trade route. This was to be the nucleus of the first Indian Empire. When Alexander, having conquered Achaemenid Persia, was marching to the Indus in 327 BC, a young adventurer, Chandragupta Maurya, is said to have met him. Shortly after Alexander's invasion of India, Chandragupta seized the Magadhan throne. Then, exploiting the power vacuum left behind in the north-west after Alexander's departure, Chandragupta annexed all the land east of the Indus, swung south to occupy large parts of central India north of the Narmada river, and in 305 BC decisively defeated Alexander's successor, Seleucus Nicator, who then ceded the Greek province of Trans-Indus including a large part of Afghanistan.

The Mauryan Empire, extended by Chandragupta's son Bindusara, reached its zenith under his grandson, the Emperor Asoka, who with the conquest of Kalinga on the Bay of Bengal established his rule over the bulk of the subcontinent. Asoka's India was by this time a land of settled village agriculture, with an elaborate administrative and tax-collecting system, probably described in one of the world's earliest manuals of statecraft, the *Arthasastra*, attributed to Kautilya, Chandragupta's chief minister. Trade flourished and a special group of officials appears to have been made responsible for the building and maintenance of roads, including the Royal Highway (known to modern India as the Grand Trunk Road) from Pataliputra to the north-west. Probably neither Chandragupta nor his successors practised orthodox Hinduism, although this had now clearly established itself as the predominant religion of the Ganges plain, with the sacerdotal caste of Brahmans as the most powerful caste. After the bloody subjection of Kalinga, Asoka accepted conversion to Buddhism and abandoned the policy of conquest, *Digvijaya*, in favour of *Dhammavijaya*, the Victory of Righteousness. His ethical teachings are found inscribed on pillars and rockfaces all over India, and his emissaries visited the Hellenistic kingdoms, as well as Ceylon and the far south, to preach the new gospel of peace.

Mauryan rule, however, did not long survive Asoka's death in 232 BC. In the 2nd century BC, the north and north-west were extensively invaded, both by Greeks from Bactria and Parthia, and by new nomad groups on the move from central Asia. In particular the Kushan section of the Yüeh-chih horde (see page 78) who had settled in the Oxus valley after 165 BC, gradually extended their rule inland, reaching Benares in the 1st century AD. Large parts of Afghanistan and Khotan were included in their cosmopolitan empire, which became a melting-pot of cultures – Indian, Chinese, central Asian and Helleno-Roman. Meanwhile, various marauding families of Greek and Scythian origin established a number of kingdoms and dynasties in western and central India. Kushan emperors and Greek feudatories adopted Sanskrit names and followed Indian religions. Indian and Hellenistic influences mingled in Gandhara sculpture. Mahayana Buddhism, separating itself at this time from the fundamentalist teachings of the original Hinayana, developed a more eclectic outlook, much influenced by non-Indian faiths, with a pantheon of deities drawn from many lands. These are now the two great divisions of Buddhism, with Hinayana still dominant in Ceylon, Burma and South-East Asia, and Mahayana the leading sect in India, Tibet, China and Japan.

India's ancient trading links with the Middle East and Egypt were revitalised and greatly

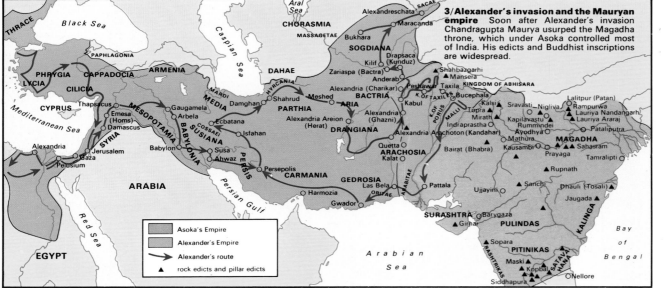

3/Alexander's invasion and the Mauryan empire Soon after Alexander's invasion Chandragupta Maurya usurped the Magadha throne, which under Asoka controlled most of India. His edicts and Buddhist inscriptions are widespread.

Asoka's Empire

Alexander's Empire

Alexander's route

rock edicts and pillar edicts

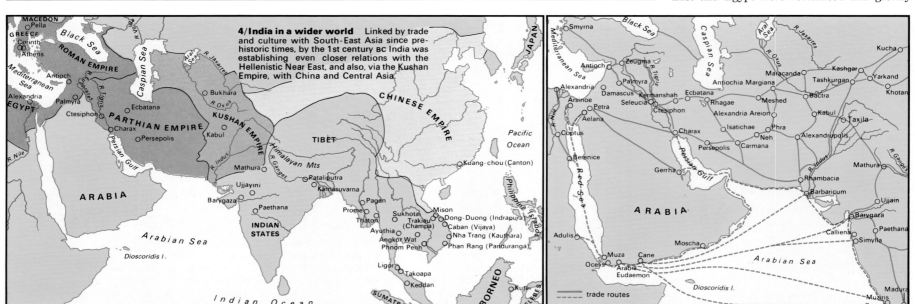

4/India in a wider world Linked by trade and culture with South-East Asia since prehistoric times, by the 1st century BC India was establishing even closer relations with the Hellenistic Near East, and also, via the Kushan Empire, with China and Central Asia.

trade routes

extended as the Hellenistic kingdoms gave way before the rising power of Rome. By the first century AD, Pliny was complaining that imports from India were costing the Romans 550 million *sesterces* a year in gold. Ports like Barbaricum, on the Indus delta, and the great entrepôt centre of Barygaza (Broach) shipped out turquoise, diamonds, spikenard, indigo, silk yarn and tortoiseshell, receiving in return an immensely varied flow of wine, pearls, copper, dates, gold and slaves, from Ethiopia, Arabia and the Mediterranean. Indian merchants, seeking spices for the Roman market, opened up agencies throughout South-East Asia, while much of the Chinese silk traffic (especially during the Roman wars with Parthia) found its way south to the trading city Taxila, in West Pakistan, before the caravans took it further west.

By the middle of the 2nd century AD the foreign kingdoms of the north were in decay, and new, indigenous groupings had begun to emerge. The Tamil-speaking peoples south of Madras had briefly occupied Ceylon and built important harbours on both sides of the southern tip, while the Satavahanas of the Deccan had become a formidable force, straddling the peninsula and driving significantly into the northern plain. Then in the 4th century, the native dynasty of the Guptas, based again on Magadha, imposed a new rule which extended, at its furthest stretch, from Sind and the Punjab to west and north Bengal. Their suzerainty was acknowledged in regions even further to the

east and the south. This was in many ways the classical age of north Indian civilisation, and it survived well beyond the political collapse of the empire, brought about by fresh invasions of Hunnish, or *huna*, nomads in the 5th century.

During this period the Puranas, recording the Hindu version of the Creation and early history of mankind, were composed in their final form, while Vedanta also began its decisive emergence as the dominant system of Hindu thought. But Buddhism, now carried far and wide by Indian merchants and travellers, proved more permanently acceptable beyond the confines of the sub-continent. In 379 it became the state religion of China, and even in South-East Asia, where Hinduism initially enjoyed much success, it persisted and flourished long after its rival's decline in the 7th and 8th centuries.

In the mid-7th century, the warrior-king Sri Harsha, ruling from Kanauj, once more established a rough feudal unity over an extensive area from Gujerat to east Bengal, but his attempts to force the Deccan were blocked by a powerful southern dynasty, the Chalukyas. For many years Hsüan Tsang, the most famous of Chinese travellers to India, lived at Sri Harsha's court, leaving a vivid account of Indian life and politics, and at his death, Chinese troops intervened to place a suitable successor on his throne. Very soon, however, India once more relapsed into a tangle of warring states.

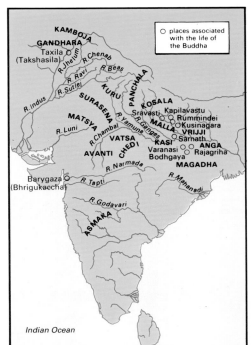

2/The Mahajanapadas (*above*) Each of the sixteen great realms of early India produced its quota of cities. Others, like Taxila and the port Barygaza were of great trading importance. By the 5th century they were reduced to four major rivals: the three kingdoms of Kasi, Kosala and Magadha, and the republic of the Vrijji, covering parts of modern Nepal and Bihar.

Lion capital (*above*) Asoka built the first of these at Sarnath where Buddha preached. The capital in its original form had a wheel of virtue atop the lions, symbolising the ascendancy of virtue over worldly pomp and power.

1/The ancient empires (*below*) The warring early kingdoms first gave way to a unified kingdom under Chandragupta Maurya, contemporary of Alexander. The domain of the Scythian Kushans stretched from Khotan to Benares, but included nothing south of the Vindhyas. The 4th century AD Guptas and the 7th century Sri Harsha established the best-known of the later northern Indian empires.

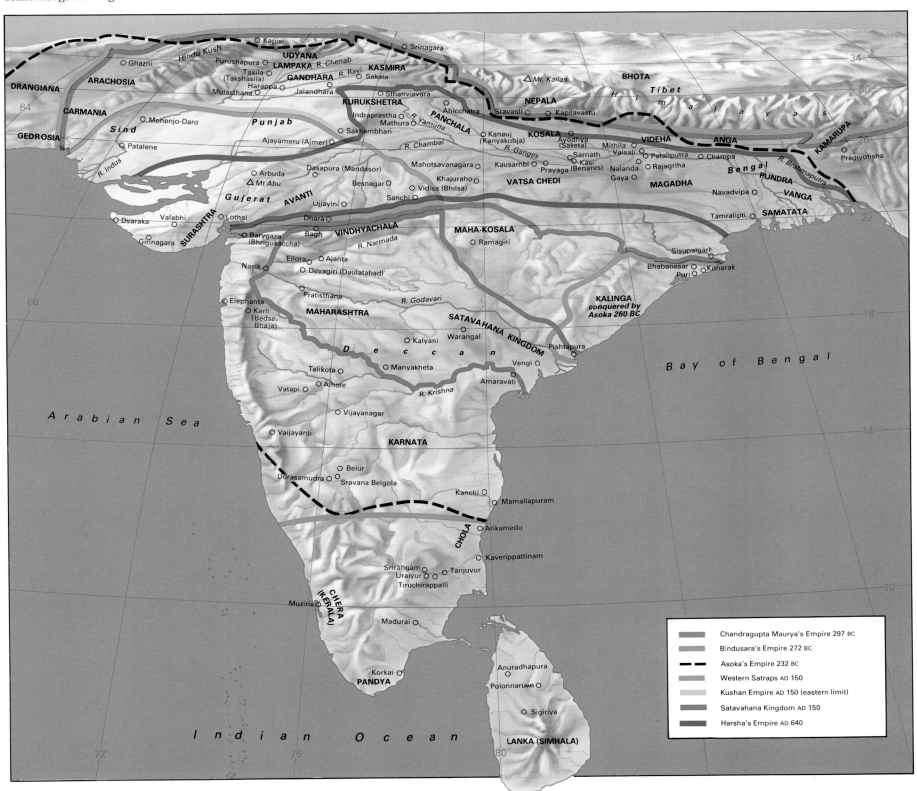

Chandragupta Maurya's Empire 297 BC
Bindusara's Empire 272 BC
Asoka's Empire 232 BC
Western Satraps AD 150
Kushan Empire AD 150 (eastern limit)
Satavahana Kingdom AD 150
Harsha's Empire AD 640

The peoples of Northern Europe

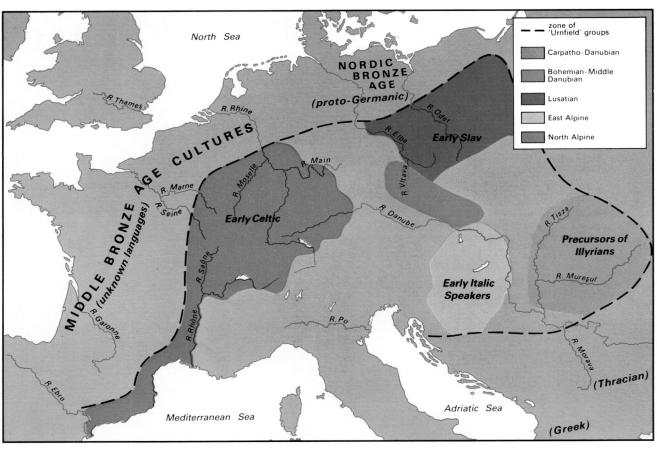

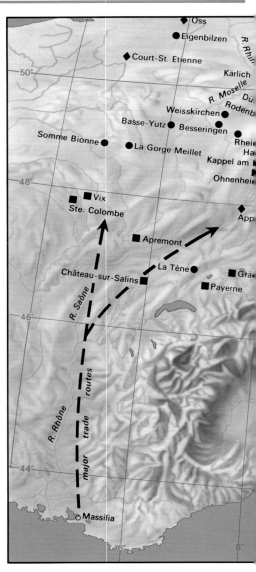

2/Middle Europe c. 800 BC *(above)* The broken line encloses the expanding groups of the Late Bronze Age 'Urnfield' complex, bordering on survivals of Middle Bronze Age cultures to the west and the proto-Germanic civilisation of the Nordic Bronze Age to the north. The North Alpine group were Celtic-speakers, and their descendants were to dominate much of Middle Europe: the Lusatian group were probably ancestors of the Slavs, and other groups of the Illyrians and Italians.

Maiden Castle *(left)* A great Celtic hill fort in Dorset, England, 400-100 BC. It was stormed by the Romans in AD 44.

3/The Expansion of the Celts *(below)* From their heartland on the Rhine and Upper Danube, Celtic groups spread to France and Czechoslovakia by the 6th century; by the 3rd century they had replaced the Scythians in the Middle Danube, and were raiding widely.

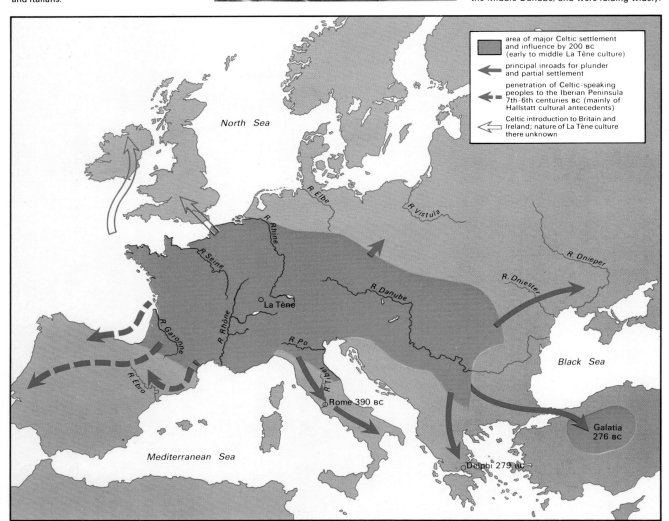

THE first millennium before Christ saw a great increase in the population of Europe north of the Alps. Many of the extensive areas of heavy land were opened up for the first time to agricultural settlement, and local expansion brought about movements of population into peripheral areas. As a result of these changes, a more centralised political system came into being, reflected in the hillforts which are found in most areas of Europe, dominating the landscape for miles around. Some of these grew to become towns and market-centres in the last two centuries before Christ. It was this growth which allowed the spread of Roman power by the conquest of one regional centre after another.

The rise in population was evident already in the Late Bronze Age, for instance in measures taken to economise in the use of bronze, even though new deep mines for copper had been opened. The adoption of ironworking when the technique became known around 800 BC was so rapid because the copper supplies no longer met the growing demand for metal. The main focus of these economic and technical developments lay in central Europe, in the territory of the various branches of the 'Urnfield' culture – a group of related tribes, with a common culture and burial practices, which dominated the Rhine/Danube axis. About 1000 BC, these tribes began to expand into adjacent areas along the main river thoroughfares. Their four main branches each gave rise to an important group of historic peoples: Celts in the west, Slavs in the north, Italic-speakers in the south, and Illyrians in the south-east. Outside this ring, to the north, lay a Nordic group of early Germans and Balts on the Baltic coast; while south-eastwards lay Dacians, Thracians and Greeks.

During the first millennium BC the Celtic

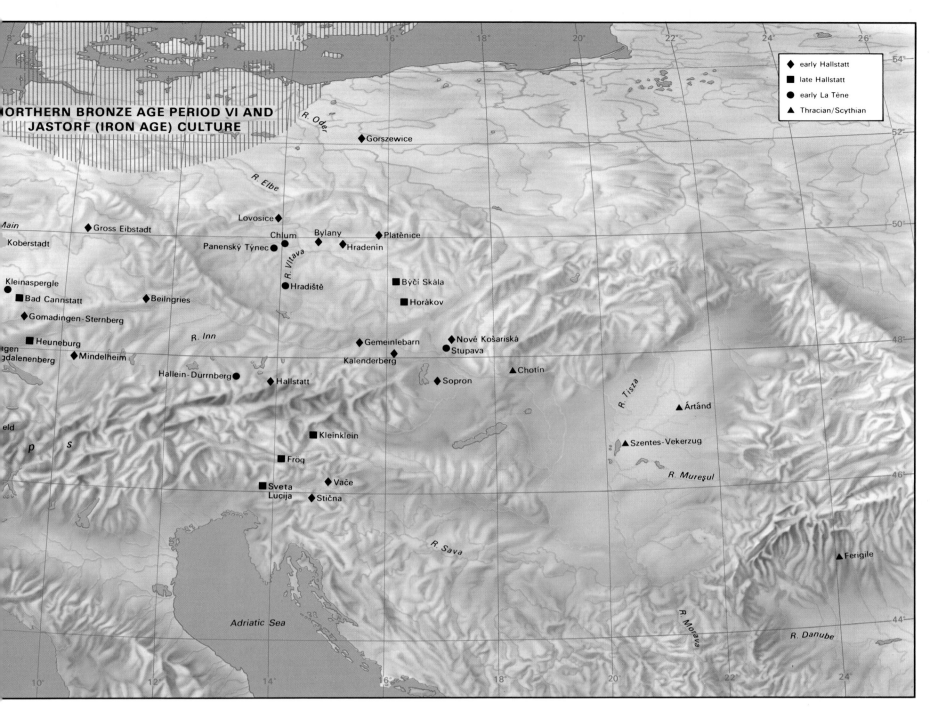

NORTHERN BRONZE AGE PERIOD VI AND
JASTORF (IRON AGE) CULTURE

Legend:
- ◆ early Hallstatt
- ■ late Hallstatt
- ● early La Tène
- ▲ Thracian/Scythian

Map labels: R. Oder, R. Elbe, Gorszewice, Main, Koberstadt, Gross Eibstadt, Lovosice, Chlum, Bylany, Platěnice, Panenský Týnec, Hradenín, R. Vltava, Kleinaspergle, Hradiště, Býčí Skála, Bad Cannstatt, Horákov, Gomadingen-Sternberg, Beilngries, Heuneburg, R. Inn, gen / agdalenenberg, Mindelheim, Gemeinlebarn, Nové Košariská, Kalenderberg, Stupava, Hallein-Dürrnberg, Hallstatt, Sopron, Chotín, Alps, Kleinklein, Árténd, Frög, R. Tisza, Szentes-Vekerzug, Vače, R. Mureşul, Sveta Lucija, Stična, Adriatic Sea, R. Sava, R. Morava, Ferigile, R. Danube

areas greatly expanded at the expense of their neighbours, just as in the first millennium AD the Germanic tribes overran large parts of western Europe (see page 98). In particular, large areas of present-day France came to be incorporated into the Celtic-speaking world. At the same time, important economic changes began to take place among the Celts as a result of growing contact with the Mediterranean world, for instance via the Greek colony of Massilia, founded in 600 BC. Some measure of the importance of commercial relations between the Greeks and their barbarian neighbours is given by the magnificent burial of a Celtic princess at Vix near Châtillon-sur-Seine, with a massive ornamented bronze punch-bowl of Italian workmanship, and other pieces of imported finery. These early Celtic aristocrats lived in hillforts such as the Heuneburg on the Upper Danube, partly designed by a Mediterranean architect, and members of their families were buried with a complete cart to carry their possessions to the grave – a burial practice followed all over the Celtic world, from Vix to Lovosice in Bohemia (see map 1).

The Celtic Iron Age is divided into two phases, named after the sites of Hallstatt in Austria and La Tène in Switzerland. The second, La Tène, phase (450 BC onwards) is characterised by an even wider extension of the area of Celtic raiding and settlement, now mainly to the east and south, though they also penetrated north as far as Britain, much of which they occupied, and by the emergence under aristocratic patronage of a characteristic decorative style known as 'Celtic Art'. This developed in the industrial and political heartland of the later Celtic world, in the Rhineland and Upper Marne. The most spectacular pieces of Celtic art are the bronze vessels and gold neck-rings with cast curvilinear

decoration, which accompany the burials of powerful chieftains in such cemeteries as Rheinheim, Basse-Yutz or Dürkheim.

The economic strength of the Celtic area was based upon growing industrialisation. Large numbers of iron ingots show the importance of the Rhineland in primary production, while the light, two-wheeled fighting chariots which were occasionally buried there with the warriors of this phase (e.g. at Somme-Bionne in France) are an indication of the skills of Celtic craftsmen. These advantages carried the Celts both eastwards, into territory which in the Hallstatt period had fallen largely under the control of the Scythians – semi-nomadic horsemen and herders whose homeland lay in the steppes of southern Russia; and at the same time southwards, to attack Rome in 390 BC and a century later to reach Delphi, and even as far as central Anatolia, where some settled, later to become the 'foolish Galatians' of St Paul's letters.

The Celts were the first of the peoples of temperate Europe to be incorporated within the Roman Empire as it spread beyond the confines of the Mediterranean. Already by the end of the second century BC, the Mediterranean part of Gaul was a Roman colony; and the intimate links northwards via the Rhône valley led Caesar into a series of campaigns which brought the western Celtic world under Roman control as far as the English Channel.

Thus the economically most advanced areas of the barbarian world were rapidly integrated within the framework of the Roman Empire. Yet beyond this frontier, and especially in Ireland, the Celtic art style survived the mass-production of the Roman world, to flower again in the early Middle Ages, in such masterpieces of manuscript illustration as *The Book of Kells* and the *Lindisfarne Gospels*.

1/Middle Europe c. 700 to 400 BC *(above)* The map shows important archaeological finds of the Iron Age Celts, and some of their Scythian neighbours to the east, including both graves with rich material, and the larger fortified centres. Note the density of finds between the Moselle and the Alps.

4/The Prelude to Germanic Expansion *(below)* Place-names between the Aller and the Somme show remnants of a language neither Celtic nor German — the last traces of a prehistoric people squeezed between expanding Celtic and Germanic groups. Even this people, however, had already adopted many features of Celtic culture.

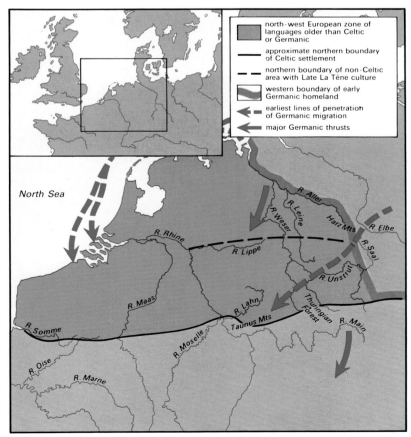

Legend:
- north-west European zone of languages older than Celtic or Germanic
- approximate northern boundary of Celtic settlement
- northern boundary of non-Celtic area with Late La Tène culture
- western boundary of early Germanic homeland
- earliest lines of penetration of Germanic migration
- major Germanic thrusts

Map labels: North Sea, R. Aller, R. Leine, R. Weser, Harz Mts, R. Elbe, R. Rhine, R. Lippe, R. Saal, R. Unstrut, R. Maas, R. Lahn, Thuringian Forest, R. Main, R. Somme, R. Moselle, Taunus Mts, R. Oise, R. Marne

The expansion of Roman power in Italy and the Mediterranean to 31 BC

ROME first grew from a cluster of villages into a city in the 6th century BC, influenced by its more civilised overlords, the Etruscans, whom in about 510 BC the Romans expelled, establishing a Republic which very slowly expanded its power. Thus while the Greeks were repelling the early 5th century Persian invasions and Athens was reaching its peak under Pericles, the Romans controlled only a small part of central Italy. But the Greeks had their own problems, and until after the days of Alexander they hardly noticed the advance of the 'barbarians' in the west. Equally the Carthaginians, with a trade monopoly and an overseas empire in the western Mediterranean, were not interested in central Italy, whose main concern was still agriculture. Rome could extend her power without much external interference. By 264 BC she led a single Italian confederacy, and little over a century later she dominated the whole Mediterranean. The contemporary Polybius felt able for the first time in Western history to write of a unified mankind.

The early Italian population was very mixed (map 2). The Bronze Age Apennine culture of the central highlands was outstripped early in the first millennium BC by an Iron Age Villanovan culture which flourished from the Po valley to Etruria and the site of Rome, and even reached Campania. In the 8th century BC a new culture emerged in Etruria, based probably on a fusion of the Villanovan population with an invading Etruscan aristocracy from Asia Minor. Other Iron Age groups included the Picentes, Veneti and Iapyges. From about 750 BC Greek settlers established colonies on the coast from Cumae southwards around the toe of Italy and Sicily.

The Etruscan empire, which at its height reached from the Po to Campania, was ultimately mastered by the Latins of central Italy. Among the Indo-European-speaking Latin towns Rome gradually gained the ascendency. Initial conflict soon developed into mutual support against the pressure of the surrounding tribes: Sabines, Aequi, Volsci and (in the 4th century BC) the Samnites. During these struggles

Rome extended both her territory (*ager Romanus*) and her alliances. By 500 BC she controlled some 350 square miles of territory; by 260 BC some 10,000 square miles. With conquest went an extension of Roman citizenship, either complete or with limited privileges. At the same time Rome built up a confederacy with special privileges for the Latins; in all, her allies controlled in 260 BC some 42,000 square miles, giving effective Roman dominance over some 52,000 square miles (map 1). By now her citizens numbered some 292,000 men, while the allies had perhaps 750,000; the total population numbered about 3 million.

With this manpower and territory Rome had become a potential world power. Her influence was strengthened by founding strategic colonies in Italy, linked by a network of roads. These colonies comprised either Roman citizens alone or Latins (originally joined by some Romans who surrendered their Roman citizenship): the former were part of the Roman state, the latter independent but privileged allies.

The emergence of this powerful confederacy was a potential challenge to Carthage, which then controlled the coast of north-west Africa, part of Spain, Sardinia and western Sicily. More by accident than design they clashed in 264 BC. In the First Punic War (264-241), Rome, still essentially agricultural, had to become a naval power; by driving the Carthaginians first from Sicily and then (238) from Corsica and Sardinia, Rome gained two overseas provinces. The Second War (218-201), when Hannibal invaded Italy, saw the Carthaginians expelled from

3/The Roman world 264 to 31 BC (below) Alexander the Great's empire split into three after his death: Macedon, Syria and Egypt. Their mutual struggles allowed Carthage to build an empire in the western Mediterranean. Rome and Carthage clashed in Sicily in 264 BC, and after three great wars Rome acquired five overseas provinces: Sicily, Corsica and Sardinia, Spain (two provinces) and Africa (roughly modern Tunisia). In the East, Rome's first annexation was Macedon (146 BC), followed by Asia (western Turkey), Cyrene, Crete, Bithynia, Pontus, Cilicia, Syria and Cyprus. But their administration overstrained the Roman constitution, which had not been designed for an overseas empire. The Republic finally collapsed in a series of civil wars, the last of which was won by Octavian (Augustus) over Antony and Cleopatra in 31 BC.

2/The peoples of Italy 500 BC (above) During the Bronze and early Iron Ages Italy contained many independent tribes. The Etruscans were the first to extend their power over a large part of the peninsula. But Etruria proper (Tuscany) was organised as independent city-states and although an Etruscan League was formed, its ties were more religious and cultural than political. It thus found concerted action difficult. Assailed by land and sea, the Etruscans were forced back into Etruria around 500 BC, and the way was left open for the more political Romans.

Lictor Fasces, thonged bundles of rods containing an axe, were carried by lictors, first before the early kings, and then in procession with the higher republican magistrates. They vividly symbolised Rome's powerful executive authority.

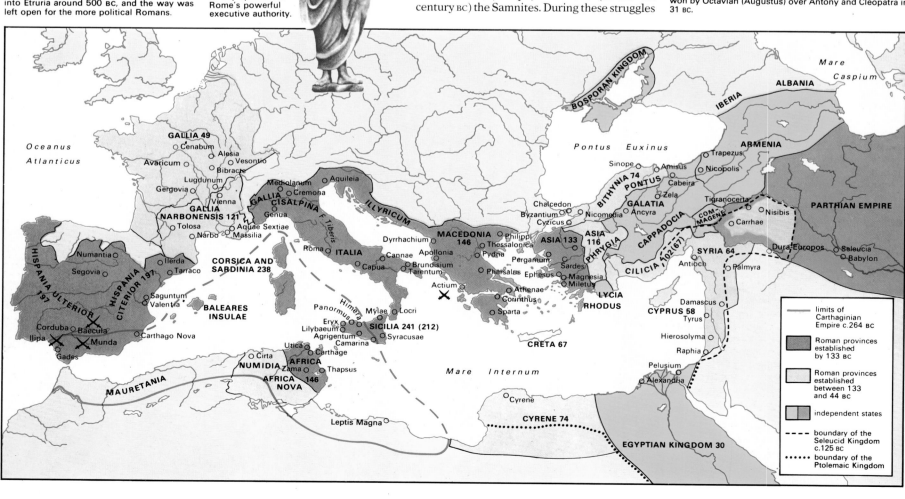

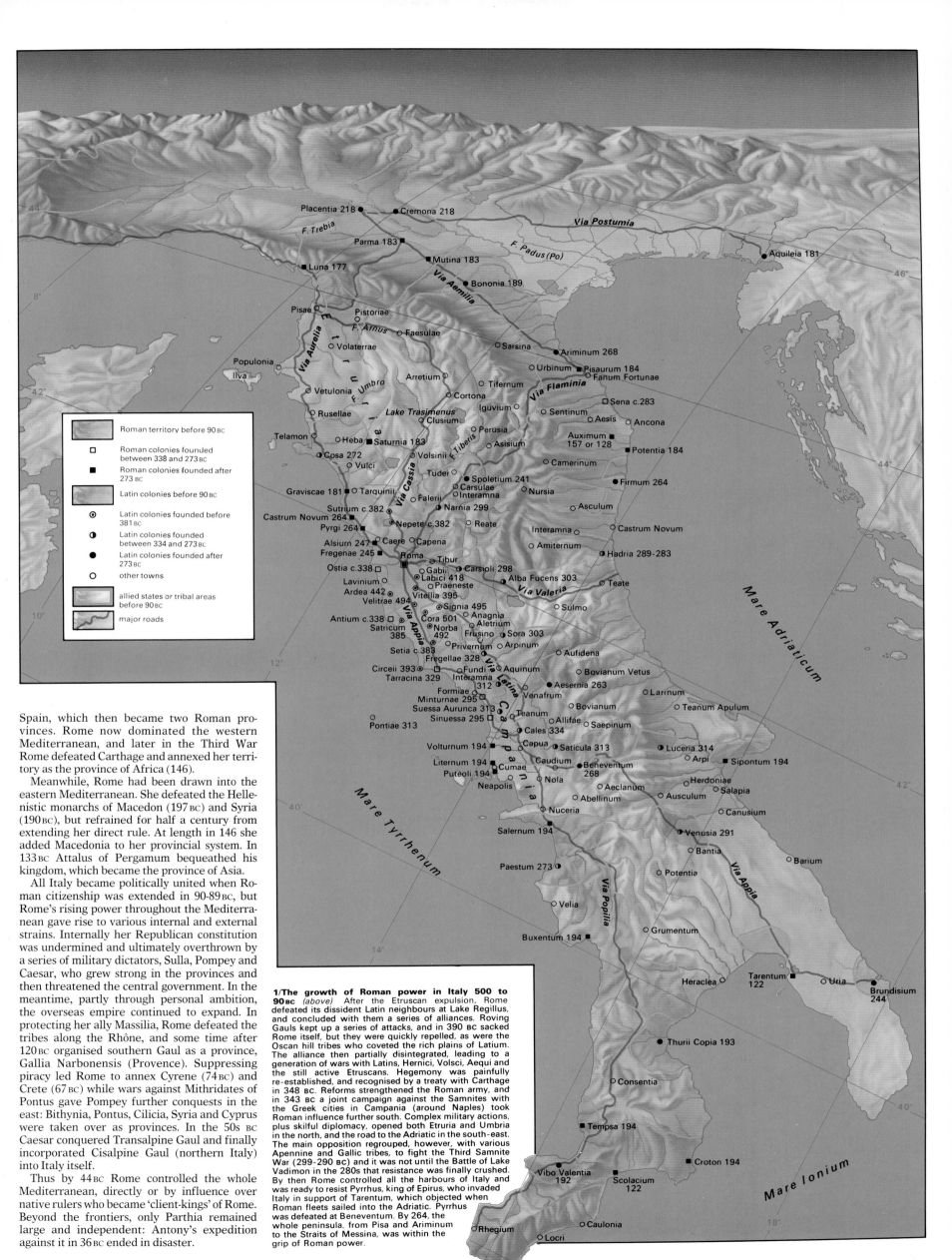

Spain, which then became two Roman provinces. Rome now dominated the western Mediterranean, and later in the Third War Rome defeated Carthage and annexed her territory as the province of Africa (146).

Meanwhile, Rome had been drawn into the eastern Mediterranean. She defeated the Hellenistic monarchs of Macedon (197 BC) and Syria (190 BC), but refrained for half a century from extending her direct rule. At length in 146 she added Macedonia to her provincial system. In 133 BC Attalus of Pergamum bequeathed his kingdom, which became the province of Asia.

All Italy became politically united when Roman citizenship was extended in 90-89 BC, but Rome's rising power throughout the Mediterranean gave rise to various internal and external strains. Internally her Republican constitution was undermined and ultimately overthrown by a series of military dictators, Sulla, Pompey and Caesar, who grew strong in the provinces and then threatened the central government. In the meantime, partly through personal ambition, the overseas empire continued to expand. In protecting her ally Massilia, Rome defeated the tribes along the Rhône, and some time after 120 BC organised southern Gaul as a province, Gallia Narbonensis (Provence). Suppressing piracy led Rome to annex Cyrene (74 BC) and Crete (67 BC) while wars against Mithridates of Pontus gave Pompey further conquests in the east: Bithynia, Pontus, Cilicia, Syria and Cyprus were taken over as provinces. In the 50s BC Caesar conquered Transalpine Gaul and finally incorporated Cisalpine Gaul (northern Italy) into Italy itself.

Thus by 44 BC Rome controlled the whole Mediterranean, directly or by influence over native rulers who became 'client-kings' of Rome. Beyond the frontiers, only Parthia remained large and independent: Antony's expedition against it in 36 BC ended in disaster.

1/The growth of Roman power in Italy 500 to 90 BC *(above)* After the Etruscan expulsion, Rome defeated its dissident Latin neighbours at Lake Regillus, and concluded with them a series of alliances. Roving Gauls kept up a series of attacks, and in 390 BC sacked Rome itself, but they were quickly repelled, as were the Oscan hill tribes who coveted the rich plains of Latium. The alliance then partially disintegrated, leading to a generation of wars with Latins, Hernici, Volsci, Aequi and the still active Etruscans. Hegemony was painfully re-established, and recognised by a treaty with Carthage in 348 BC. Reforms strengthened the Roman army, and in 343 BC a joint campaign against the Samnites with the Greek cities in Campania (around Naples) took Roman influence further south. Complex military actions, plus skilful diplomacy, opened both Etruria and Umbria in the north, and the road to the Adriatic in the south-east. The main opposition regrouped, however, with various Apennine and Gallic tribes, to fight the Third Samnite War (299-290 BC) and it was not until the Battle of Lake Vadimon in the 280s that resistance was finally crushed. By then Rome controlled all the harbours of Italy and was ready to resist Pyrrhus, king of Epirus, who invaded Italy in support of Tarentum, which objected when Roman fleets sailed into the Adriatic. Pyrrhus was defeated at Beneventum. By 264, the whole peninsula, from Pisa and Ariminum to the Straits of Messina, was within the grip of Roman power.

The Roman Empire from Augustus to Justinian 31 BC to AD 565

Trajan's column *(above)* Trajan, the first Roman emperor born outside Italy, came from Italica in Spain, near present-day Seville. His famous column, which still stands in Rome, is a unique work of art, sculptured in the form of a continuous spiral frieze, showing arms, armour, fortifications and battle scenes from the two great campaigns he fought during the Dacian Wars.

OCTAVIAN, by his defeat of Antony and Cleopatra at Actium in 31 BC, became undisputed master, not only of Egypt, which he took as his personal domain, but of the whole Roman world. In 27 BC he accepted the title of Augustus, under which, after his death, he was to become a Roman god. Without significant political rivals, and fully supported by the armies, he was able to introduce far-reaching reforms – in taxation, family and social life, the elimination of corruption at home and in provincial administration, the revival of many old Roman and Italian religious cults – which gave the now almost fully consolidated empire a new, intense surge of life. He established himself as First Citizen (*Princeps*), reshaped the internal constitution, and extended the frontiers to a point where he hoped they would remain unchanged for ever.

While keeping undivided power in his own hands, he allowed the Senate, the old republican magistrates and the business classes (the Equestrian Order) to share with him the task of administering the Empire. Thus in theory 'the Republic was restored', and the government remained civilian and not military. At the cost of some loss of personal liberties, a stable government gave to the greater part of the civilised western world some two and a half centuries of peace and prosperity, with municipalities throughout the provinces enjoying a considerable degree of local independence, and with the predominantly Latin culture of the west complementing the Hellenism of the east. This more tranquil period was threatened by two brief civil wars (in AD 69 and 193), which emphasised the increasing importance of the army and the dominance of the Princeps. As external pressures on the northern and eastern frontiers increased, the civilian gov-

The Roman Peace *(left)* This marble slab from the Altar of Peace (*Ara Pacis*) which Augustus erected in Rome, symbolises the peace and prosperity which the Roman world enjoyed for two centuries after his death. The central figure is Mother Earth *(Terra Mater)* with fruit, flowers, corn, sheep, children and a bull representing agricultural plenty.

ernment collapsed in 235, and armies in different provinces tried to set up their own commanders as emperors (the so-called Thirty Tyrants) and economic life was shattered. However, a series of strong emperors in the years 268 to 284 managed to turn back the tide of Gothic and other invaders and to restore a semblance of orderly government.

In the early days of the Augustan Empire, the long frontiers had been guarded against the less civilised peoples beyond by a permanent army of some 300,000 men, stationed in camps and mostly deployed in units along the imperial boundaries, which at first consisted mainly of natural features such as seas, rivers and mountains. This was backed by an elaborate system of military roads, while naval vessels protected Rome's widespread commercial activity. Roman citizenship gradually spread more widely, and in 212 Caracalla granted it to all free inhabitants. When expansion ceased with Trajan (d.117), permanent stone barriers were erected to protect the frontiers in northern England and Scotland, beyond the Rhine, along the Danube, in Syria and north Africa. By the mid-3rd century internal weakness threatened the whole system.

When Diocletian came to power in 284 it was obvious that one ruler could no longer hold the whole Empire together: hence his division of power between himself and a joint Augustus, with two subordinate Caesars, and his division of the empire into four prefectures and twelve dioceses. By now the principate was dead: the military had triumphed over the civilian. Further, a new basis had to be found for imperial authority: under the influence of eastern ideas the Princeps became Dominus (Lord), an absolute ruler, at the head of a vast bureaucracy. The centre of gravity was shifting eastwards: hence Constantine established a new capital and a Christian city at Byzantium, renamed Constantinople (330), while a new taxation system resulted in an economic revival. But further decline was merely postponed, not overcome. Although theoretically governed by joint rulers, the Empire gradually broke into an eastern and western half, and outlying provinces fell to barbarian invaders. Rome itself was sacked by the Visigoth Alaric (410) and the Vandal Gaeseric (455); and in 493 an Ostrogothic kingdom was established in Italy. The Western Empire had fallen to the invaders, while Justinian's attempt in the mid-sixth century to reunite the two halves led to no permanent union. Yet in the east the Byzantine Empire survived for another thousand years, until the capture of Constantinople by the Turks in 1453.

For two centuries after the breakdown of the Western Empire the Byzantine monarchy kept up Roman institutions and continued to use Latin in its courts. Although Greek then superseded Latin and the administration became less concentrated, it was the Eastern Empire that compiled the two great monuments of Roman law, the codes of Theodosius and of Justinian. Further, the east preserved and transmitted to the modern world much of the legacy of the ancient world. Even in the west many Roman traditions survived. The Latin tongue, although widely developing into the derivative 'Romance' languages, was still preserved in the Church and as the language of science; Roman law forms the basis of the law of most modern European states; the feats of Roman engineering genius are still visible in the Mediterranean world; the Roman Church lives on as a direct link with the past; and the German kings of the 'Holy Roman Empire' claimed that they were Roman rulers.

4/The Roman Empire from Diocletian to Justinian *(right)* Diocletian's major administrative reforms (see main text) put off the final splitting of the Empire which took place when Rome and the West were finally overrun by the barbarians in AD 476. The map shows the reforms (dioceses and prefectures) and the shrinkage that had occurred up to the death of Justinian. In the interim, German tribes had overrun Gaul, Spain, Britain, Italy, North Africa and Pannonia (see page 98). Justinian's partial reconquests from Vandal and Ostrogoth proved ephemeral: three years after his death the Lombards had taken Italy, Slavs soon poured into Pannonia and a century and more later the Arabs took North Africa and Spain.

1/The Roman Empire from Augustus to c.AD 280 *(below)* Augustus settled with Parthia, annexed Egypt, Galatia (25 BC) and Judaea (AD 6) and advanced over the Alps to the Danube and the Rhine, adding the provinces of Rhaetia, Noricum, Pannonia and Moesia. Settlement of colonies continued until Hadrian (d.138), after which *'colonia'* became a title for privileged *municipia*. Syria and Cappadocia were extended under the Flavians (69-96) and the German frontier advanced to the Black Forest (Agri Decumates). Trajan, whose reign marked the end of the Empire's significant territorial additions, fought wars for the annexation of Dacia (106), Armenia and Assyria (114), and Mesopotamia (115), to join Arabia Petraea, already taken in 106. His successor, Hadrian, decided to abandon these eastern acquisitions, apart from Arabia and Dacia, and to consolidate the frontiers of the Empire.

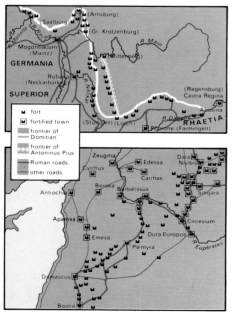

2/The frontiers in Germany *(left)* In 12 BC the Romans finally pushed across the Rhine from Gaul, to reach the Elbe in 9 BC. They failed to establish permanent occupation: in AD 9 a revolt led by Arminius (Herman) ended in the destruction of three legions in the Teutoburg Forest. In AD 74, Vespasian established Roman authority throughout the triangle known as the Agri Decumates, lying between the sources of the Rhine and the Danube and stretching to the Black Forest. Under his successor, Domitian, fortifications were erected as far as the Neckar Valley and the Taunus Mountains.

3/The Syrian 'limes' *(left)* Under Trajan and Hadrian, this once lightly-held frontier was equipped with a formidable screen of forts and military roads. It failed, however, to prevent the Sasanians sacking Antioch in AD 260, or to deter the Palmyran 'Empress' Zenobia, who won eastern Syria, Anatolia, Palestine and Egypt before her defeat by Aurelian in 272. The defences were later restored under Diocletian.

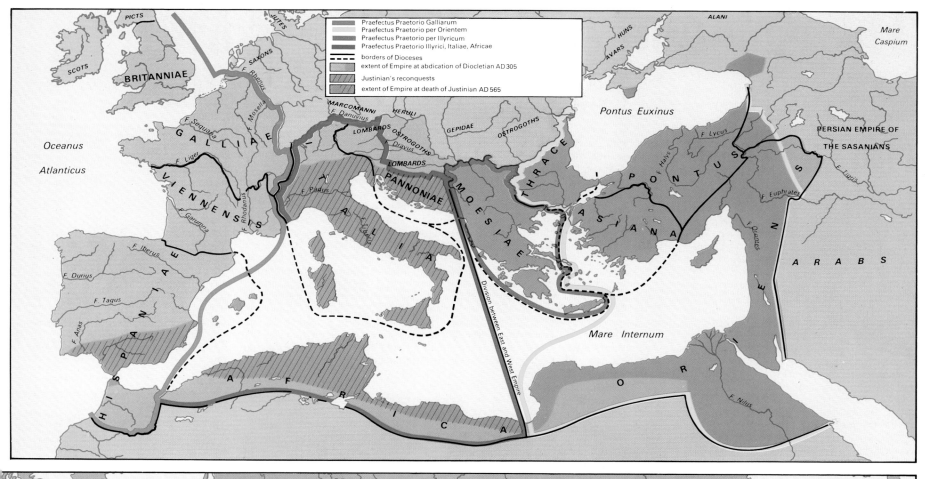

Legend (top map):
- Praefectus Praetorio Galliarum
- Praefectus Praetorio per Orientem
- Praefectus Praetorio per Illyricum
- Praefectus Praetorio Illyrici, Italiae, Africae
- borders of Dioceses
- extent of Empire at abdication of Diocletian AD 305
- Justinian's reconquests
- extent of Empire at death of Justinian AD 565

PICTS
SCOTS
BRITANNIAE
Oceanus
Atlanticus
SAXONS
UTES
MARCOMANNI
HUNS
AVARS
ALANI
Mare
Caspium
GALLIAE
F. Rhenus
F. Mosella
F. Sequana
HERULI
F. Danuvius
LOMBARDS OSTROGOTHS
GEPIDAE
OSTROGOTHS
Pontus Euxinus
PERSIAN EMPIRE OF
THE SASANIANS
VIENNENSIS
F. Ligur
F. Rhodanus
F. Garumna
LOMBARDS
PANNONIAE
THRACE
F. Lycus
PONTUS
F. Halys
HISPANIAE
F. Iberus
F. Padus
I T A L I A
ASIANA
F. Euphrates
F. Durius
F. Tagus
F. Anas
M O E S I A E
F. Tigris
ARABS
Division between East and West Empire
Mare Internum
A F R I C A
O R I E N S
F. Nilus

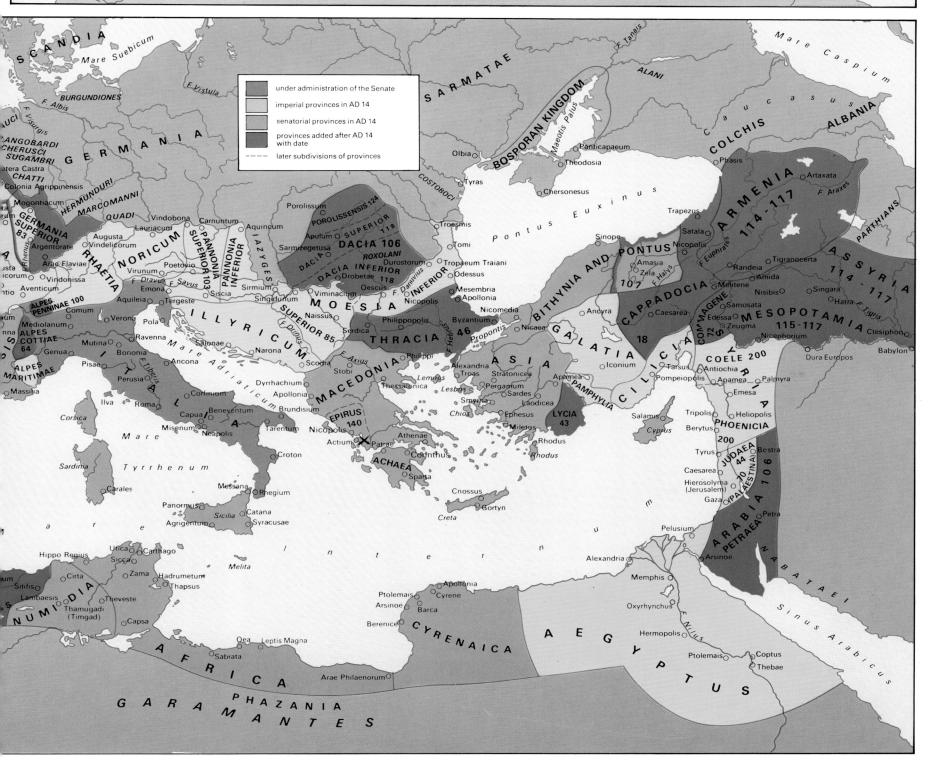

Legend (bottom map):
- under administration of the Senate
- imperial provinces in AD 14
- senatorial provinces in AD 14
- provinces added after AD 14 with date
- later subdivisions of provinces

SCANDIA
Mare Suebicum
SARMATAE
F. Tanais
Mare Caspium
BURGUNDIONES
F. Albis
F. Vistula
BOSPORAN KINGDOM
ALANI
COLCHIS
ALBANIA
ANGOBARDI
CHERUSCI
SUGAMBRI
G E R M A N I A
Batava Castra
Colonia Agrippinensis
Mogontiacum
CHATTI
HERMUNDURI
MARCOMANNI
QUADI
COSTOBOCI
Olbia
Tyras
Theodosia
Panticapaeum
Chersonesus
Caucasus
Phasis
ARMENIA
114–117
Artaxata
F. Araxes
GERMANIA
SUPERIOR 83
Argentorate
Arae Flaviae
Vindobona
Carnuntum
Aquincum
IAZYGES
Porolissum
POROLISSENSIS 124
Apulum
PONTUS
Sinope
Trapezus
Nicopolis
Satala
PARTHIANS
Tigranocerta
ASSYRIA
114–117
RHAETIA
NORICUM
Lauriacum
PANNONIA
SUPERIOR 103
DACIA 106
DACIA
ROXOLANI
Sarmizegetusa
Amasia
Zela
CAPPADOCIA
Caesarea
COMMAGENE
Melitene
Amida
Nisibis
Samosata
Singara
Hatra
ALPES
PENNINAE 100
Aventicum
Vindonissa
Augusta
Vindelicorum
Poetovio
Virunum
PANNONIA
INFERIOR
Siscia
Sirmium
DACIA INFERIOR 118
Drobetae 118
MOESIA
INFERIOR
Durostorum
Oescus
Tropaeum Traiani
Tomi
Troesmis
BITHYNIA AND PONTUS
107
Ancyra
GALATIA
18
MESOPOTAMIA
115–117
Zeugma
Nicephorium
Ctesiphon
Babylon
Dura Europos
Mediolanum
Comum
Verona
ILLYRICUM
SUPERIOR 85
F. Savus
Emona
Dravus
Viminacium
Singidunum
MOESIA
SUPERIOR 85
Naissus
Serdica
THRACIA 46
Philippopolis
Byzantium
Nicomedia
Propontis
Nicaea
ASIA
Iconium
CILICIA
Tarsus
Pompeiopolis
COELE 200
Antiochia
Apamea
Edessa
Emesa
Palmyra
ALPES
COTTIAE 64
Mutina
Aquileia
Tergeste
Salonae
Narona
ITALIA
Mare Adriaticum
Scodra
Dyrrhachium
Apollonia
MACEDONIA
Stobi
F. Axius
Philippi
Thessalonica
Propontis
Pergamum
Sardes
Laodicea
PAMPHYLIA
LYCIA 43
PHOENICIA 200
Tripolis
Heliopolis
Berytus
Tyrus
Salamis
Cyprus
ALPES
MARITIMAE
Genua
Pisae
Massilia
Ravenna
Bononia
Perusia
Roma
Capua
Beneventum
Ilva
Corsica
Sardinia
Carales
Neapolis
Misenum
Tarentum
Brundisium
EPIRUS 140
Nicopolis
Actium
ACHAEA
Patrae
Athenae
Corinthus
Sparta
Lesbos
Troas
Stratonicea
Apamea
Ephesus
Miletus
Chios
Rhodus
Rhodus
Caesarea
JUDAEA 44
SYRIA PALAESTINA 70
Hierosolyma
(Jerusalem)
Gaza
ARABIA
PETRAEA 106
Petra
NABATAEI
Sinus Arabicus
Mare Tyrrhenum
Croton
Messana
Rhegium
Panormus
Sicilia
Catana
Syracusae
Agrigentum
Melita
Cnossus
Creta
Gortyn
Mare Internum
Hippo Regius
Utica
Carthago
NUMIDIA
Sitifis
Cirta
Zama
Sicca
Thapsus
Hadrumetum
Theveste
Thamugadi
(Timgad)
Lambaesis
Capsa
AFRICA
Oea
Leptis Magna
Sabrata
PHAZANIA
Arae Philaenorum
GARAMANTES
Apollonia
Ptolemais
Arsinoe
Cyrene
Barca
Berenice
CYRENAICA
AEGYPTUS
Alexandria
Pelusium
Memphis
Hermopolis
Oxyrhynchus
F. Nilus
Arsinoe
Ptolemais
Coptus
Thebae

The economy of the Roman world c.AD 200

THE Roman Empire created a vast area, with a single currency and low customs barriers, in which commerce was hindered by neither pirates nor frontiers and was aided by an elaborate network of roads and protected harbours. While the basic needs of the great majority of the population were satisfied by local agriculture and craftsmanship, Graeco-Roman civilisation involved the long-distance movement of natural products and manufactured goods on a considerable scale. Many cities, especially those in Greece and Asia Minor, were regularly dependent on imported grain. Elsewhere, local crop failures produced a recurrent need for imports. Some parts of the Empire, notably Italy, Greece, Syria, Egypt and Africa (Tunisia) lacked local supplies of essential metals. All areas used Egyptian papyrus as a writing material. There was trade in expensive textiles from the wool and linen producing areas of the Empire. The luxuries of the eastern trade reached all provinces. Silk clothing was worn as a status symbol by the wealthiest; spices, especially pepper, seasoned the food of a wider segment of the population. The eastern trade caused a heavy drain of currency out of the Empire.

A great part of the long-distance movement of products or goods was a direct consequence of the existence of the Empire. Wealth was concentrated at Rome itself which, with a population of approximately 1,000,000, consumed most of the taxation in kind received from Sicily, Africa and Egypt as well as additional grain and a great deal of Spanish oil provided on a purely commercial basis. Stone for Roman building schemes and animals for the shows came from far afield. In addition, the armies stationed in frontier provinces created a large demand for both natural and manufactured products. As a result, these areas saw a considerable development in agriculture, mining and manufacture. Army supplies, like other goods, were if possible transported by river, notably the Rhine (Rhenus), Rhône (Rhodanus), Danube (Danuvius) and their tributaries. A number of large cities, such as Trèves (Augusta Treverorum), Lyons (Lugdunum), Aquileia and Antioch, combined the roles of a centre of administration and of distribution of supplies. In many parts of the Empire, city colonies with an attached territory were settled and farmed by the retired soldiers. Such settlements greatly contributed to the agricultural development of the Empire. Armies, colonies and the urbanisation of the wealthier of the provincials all created a new demand in the provinces of western Europe and the Balkans for commodities reflecting the Roman way of life – wine, olive oil, weapons, artistic metalware, fine pottery and glass. In the early 1st century AD Italy supplied wine, oil and metalware from Campania and pottery from Arezzo (Arretium) to Spain, Gaul, Britain and the western Balkans. Then the pottery industry moved north through

stages associated with La Graufesenque, Lezoux and the Rhineland. Glass-making grew up around Cologne (Colonia Agrippina) and metal industry in the hilly region south-west of it. Spain became a large-scale producer of wine, olive oil and other products, including a delicious fish paste (*garum*) which filled the amphorae that were shipped in very large quantities to Rome and also carried along the rivers of Gaul for destinations as far as Britain. Later, North Africa became a large-scale exporter of olive oil and fine pottery to the whole Mediterranean area. By the end of the 2nd century the export trade of Italy had dwindled and large areas of the Empire had become self-sufficient in the principal items of Roman living, but Britain and the northern Balkan provinces continued to import wine, olive oil, glassware and fine pottery from other parts of the Empire.

The distribution of cities reflects the degrees of development of different areas. Bithynia, Asia, Syria, Egypt, Africa (Tunisia), southern Spain, Greece, Italy and Provence were the most highly-developed regions. In the cities property was unequally divided, and the contributions of a small group of outstandingly wealthy men financed public building. The standing army, unoccupied in peacetime, was sometimes employed on the building of roads, bridges or fortifications. The spectacular nature of Roman remains tends to obscure the economic backwardness of the Roman Empire. It depended on a system of agriculture which required the land to lie fallow in alternate years and which could not work heavy clay soil. Development was limited by the slowness and expense of land transport, which depended on donkeys, mules and oxen rather than on horses. It was cheaper to ship grain across the Mediterranean than to cart it seventy miles.

The commerical classes were weak both in capital and in social esteem. The wealth of even the richest merchant fell below that of the local landowning notables, not to mention members of the imperial aristocracy. Much trading was carried on by humble men travelling with a small stock of goods. The shop, not the factory, was the standard unit of production; the economy was vulnerable. The political and military crisis after AD 230 permanently weakened the commercial classes in the western provinces. In order to pay its troops, the government gradually debased the silver currency. Debasement was accompanied by devaluation, which culminated in rapid inflation.

Around the year AD 300 Diocletian restored internal stability and inaugurated the Later Empire. Henceforth the government satisfied the needs of civil servants, soldiers and capital cities out of taxation in kind, the transport of which was itself a tax. A new currency based on gold was established, but rapid devaluation of the copper currency continued to the end of the 4th century. The scope of money and market economy, and thus of the private contractor and merchant, was greatly reduced. At the same time the western provinces saw a reversal of urbanisation in that both local aristocrats and craftsmen began to move into the countryside.

Throughout the imperial period slaves formed, by historical standards, a very high proportion of the population in many areas of the Empire. They provided dependent labour in domestic service, manufacture and agriculture. Positions of dependent management of, for instance, farms, workshops, ships or a bank were also normally held by slaves or freedmen. The evidence scarcely allows the establishment of quantitative trends in the employment of slaves, but it seems that a gradual decline in the social and legal status of the humbler free population worked to reduce the social and economic importance of slavery.

Seen in a global perspective, the Roman

Empire represented a single economy which was self-sufficient in all essential commodities. Its cohesion was made possible by geographical factors such as the Mediterranean Sea and the river systems flowing into it. But the development of some areas rather than others and the direction and volume of the movement of goods was largely determined by the political organisation of the area. The break-up of the Empire in the west in the 5th century AD ended the massive government-directed transfer of resources to Rome, Italy and the frontier armies. The pattern of commercial exchanges lasted longer, even though their scale declined gradually. It was only in the 7th century, with the Arab conquests in the east and the establishment of the Carolingian monarchy in France, that new patterns began to form.

A 'silver' denarius of 44 BC *(above)* The standard coin of the early Empire was progressively debased until between AD 324 and 360 it depreciated from 4350 to 4,600,000 denarii to the new gold solidus.

Amphorae *(left)* These two-handled, thin-necked pottery vessels, with pointed bases, could be either stood in a rack or stuck in the ground. They held several gallons of wine, olive oil, olives, fish sauce, salted fish, fruit, nuts, pepper, grain, flour, hair-remover or potter's clay. Their varied shapes, labels and origin-stamps give valuable information about trade.

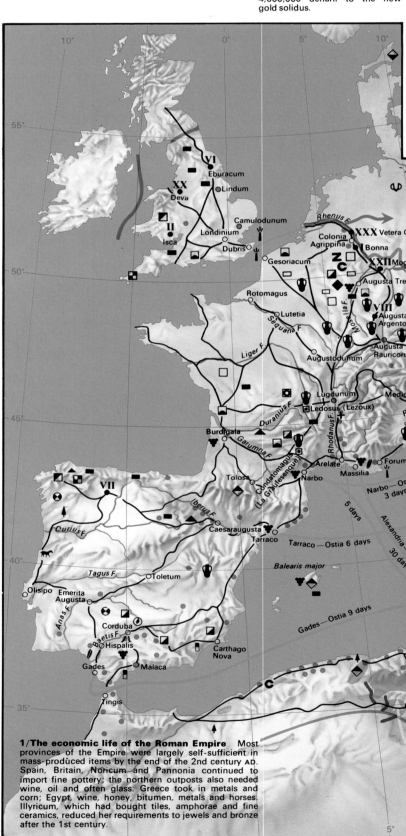

1/The economic life of the Roman Empire Most provinces of the Empire were largely self-sufficient in mass-produced items by the end of the 2nd century AD. Spain, Britain, Noricum and Pannonia continued to import fine pottery; the northern outposts also needed wine, oil and often glass. Greece took in metals and corn; Egypt, wine, honey, bitumen, metals and horses. Illyricum, which had bought tiles, amphorae and fine ceramics, reduced her requirements to jewels and bronze after the 1st century.

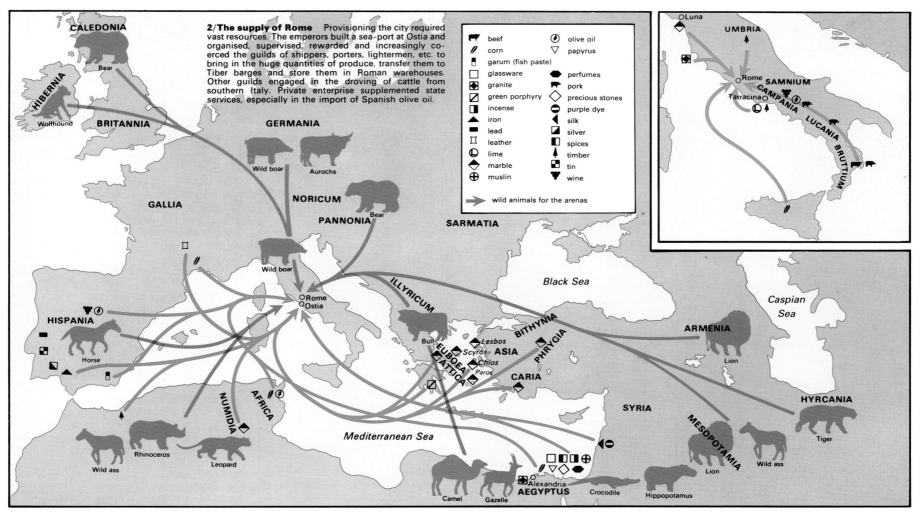

2/The supply of Rome Provisioning the city required vast resources. The emperors built a sea-port at Ostia and organised, supervised, rewarded and increasingly co-erced the guilds of shippers, porters, lightermen, etc. to bring in the huge quantities of produce, transfer them to Tiber barges and store them in Roman warehouses. Other guilds engaged in the droving of cattle from southern Italy. Private enterprise supplemented state services, especially in the import of Spanish olive oil.

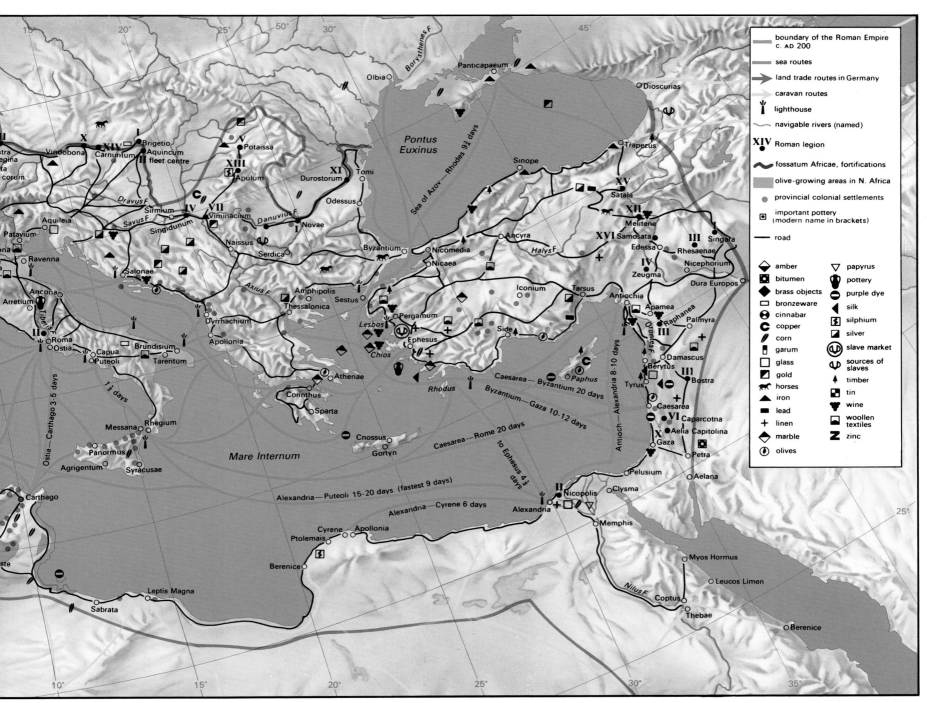

The rise of Christianity to AD 600

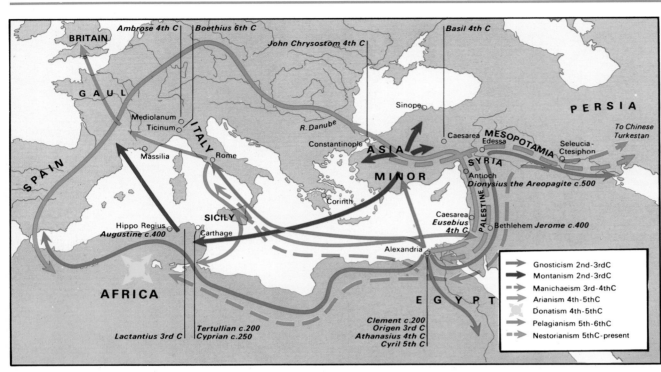

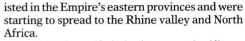

2/Writers and heresies *(above)*
As soon as Christianity became a subject of intellectual speculation in the second century AD, it was rent by doctrinal controversies, many of which represented a serious challenge to the Church's traditions and authority. The ideas of theologians like Donatus, Arius and Pelagius moved men and events almost as powerfully as the Christian revelation itself, and constantly threatened the unity of early Christendom.

The linking of pagan and Christian symbols In the pre-Constantinian inscription *(below)*, the fish, an old religious symbol used because the Greek initial letters of 'Jesus Christ God's Son Saviour' spell ΙΧΘΥΣ, fish, represents Christ; so does the anchor, a firm point in a storm. But DM is a pagan formula, and the laurel is a Roman symbol of triumph. The symbol *(above)* is from a sarcophagus of about AD 350. Here the Roman laurel wreath is combined with the *chi-rho*, the first two letters of 'Christ' in Greek, linked to a vision of Constantine and resembling the sun-wheel'.

CHRISTIANITY, the last great world religion before Islam, originated in Palestine. Little is known of its founder, Jesus of Nazareth, before he began at the age of thirty to preach that 'the kingdom of God is at hand'. It was a message for which many Jews were waiting. Their country, formally annexed by Rome in AD 6, was in turmoil; and there were many sects, some chiefly spiritual (like the Essenes), others more political (like those later called the Zealots), which hoped for the long-promised Messiah, or saviour, to liberate them. The crowds at first followed Jesus, seeing in him this Messiah; but the Jewish authorities were suspicious and his popular following soon dwindled. After three years of teaching and preaching he was seized, handed over to the Roman procurator, and crucified as a revolutionary.

The new faith proved tenacious, despite its founder's early death. His disciples, even their leader Simon Peter (the Rock), had initially abandoned Jesus, but their faith was restored by the Resurrection, when, they claimed, he appeared to them after death and charged them to proclaim the good news of God's reigning power. This revelation was at first presented in a purely Judaic context. Whether Jesus himself believed that God had sent him to convert the Gentiles remains unclear. It was left to Paul, a Jewish convert from Tarsus, to show the power and extent of Christianity's appeal as he preached in the Aegean islands, Asia Minor, Greece, Italy and perhaps as far as Spain. In all these areas there were Jewish communities (see page 102). The Christian preachers usually began with these, but the Jews in general were not won over; anti-Christian riots broke out, and the gap widened irretrievably when the Christians failed to support the Jewish uprising in AD 66.

Jesus's teaching appealed particularly – though not exclusively – to the poor and humble, who found in the kingdom of God a message of hope denied to them in the secular world. The number of converts steadily grew as economic conditions in the Empire deteriorated, though more among the urban masses than in the countryside, which largely retained its pagan beliefs. Outside the Empire, Antioch – 'the cradle of gentile Christianity' – spread its influence north and east. One disciple, Philip, is said to have converted an Ethiopian official, and there is a persistent tradition that Thomas reached India. At some point, date unknown, Edessa became a Christian stronghold. In the west, there were 1st-century churches in Puteoli, Rome, and possibly Spain; by the mid-2nd century many ex-

isted in the Empire's eastern provinces and were starting to spread to the Rhine valley and North Africa.

By this time Christianity was significant enough to attract the attention of writers like Tacitus and Pliny the Younger. The former described how Nero used the Christians to divert hostility from himself. Conversions continued, despite repeated outbreaks of repression and persecution. The Christians' refusal to worship the emperors, serve as magistrates or carry arms made them officially suspect, but their beliefs appealed strongly to the oppressed and insecure, and as traditional Roman cults withered in the stormy 3rd century they became a force to be reckoned with.

Early in the 4th century the Emperor Constantine, whose family had worshipped the Unconquered Sun, decided to accept Christianity. His reasons were partly political, but it was a momentous decision. Recognised by the Edict of Milan (313), Christianity quickly established itself as the Empire's official religion, especially in the new capital, Constantinople. There was an abortive attempt to put the clock back by the Emperor Julian (361-63), but another tough militarist, Theodosius (379-95), further strengthened the Church's power. By now Christianity had also reached the barbarians beyond the imperial frontier. Soon after 340 Ulfilas converted the Goths near the mouth of the Danube. Many of the Germanic invaders after 376 were

already Christian, though their preferred form of belief, Arianism, had been condemned as heretical at the Council of Nicaea (325).

Meanwhile, Christianity was becoming more organised. As time passed, those who had placed their faith in the second coming of Christ came to realise that this was not imminent. By the late 3rd and early 4th centuries, the sheer spread of churches demanded more complex structures to maintain discipline and safeguard doctrinal purity. The 'elders' of the early Christian communities had already been superseded by a hierarchy of bishops, and now a full-scale diocesan framework emerged.

Christianity was in any case never solely the simple faith of simple people. The great Alexandrian theologians, Pantaenus (active c.180-200), Clement (c.150-215) and Origen (c.185-254) had reconciled Christianity with Greek philosophy and made it intellectually respectable; but at the same time they opened the door to acute theological controversy. Already in the 2nd century, the mystical belief known as Gnosticism had developed at Alexandria. Other heresies and schisms which increasingly tended to split the Church were associated with Marcion (who regarded matter as evil), Novatian and Donatus (strict moralists), Arius (who subordinated the Son to the Father) and Pelagius (a moralist stressing free will). Another threat to Church unity was the withdrawal of monks and hermits by the thousand to a life of desert solitude. But Basil (c.330-79) in the east and Benedict (c.480-544) in the west curbed this trend by bringing the ascetics together in monastic communities, subject to strict ecclesiastical rules.

The Christian church modelled its structure on that of the Roman Empire. The dioceses mirrored the administrative divisions of Diocletian; bishops, based in the chief cities, met in synod in the provincial capitals, and those from the great metropolitan centres were accorded special dignity. Rome, the see of St Peter, was granted precedence in 'honour' but not in 'authority', and its bishops shared rank and power with those of Antioch and Alexandria, to which were later added Constantinople (381) and Jerusalem (451). Clear expressions of papal primacy are not found until the late 4th century.

Meanwhile important decisions, particularly the definition of doctrine, were made by the assembled clergy. In the 2nd century local synods were called in Asia Minor to deal with the Montanist heresy, and in 325 the first ecumenical council, representing the whole Church, met at Nicaea. This was followed by the councils of Constantinople (381), Ephesus (431) and Chalcedon (451). Theoretically they were the voice of the Church; but in practice Christianity as the state religion was often subjected to imperial constraint. Some emperors – notably Justinian I (527-65) – ruled the Church with a heavy hand. This was the seed of conflict between Church and State, and underlay much of the later tension between Empire and Papacy (see page 122). However, when Rome succumbed to barbarian attack, it was the Church and its bishops, with their vast estates and pervasive influence, who emerged as guardians of the classical tradition, and guided Europe, as well as Christendom, into the new age.

3/The monastic movement (above) Almost from the beginning, a significant minority of Christians adopted a life of renunciation and withdrawal. By AD 700 monasteries had become centres of piety and learning in every Christian land, as well as great landowners.

1/The Early Christian churches (below) Starting with the journeys of St Paul, Christian churches sprang up throughout the Roman world. By the time of Diocletian's persecutions (AD 304), they were thickly clustered around the Mediterranean, and scattered as far apart as Britain and the Nile.

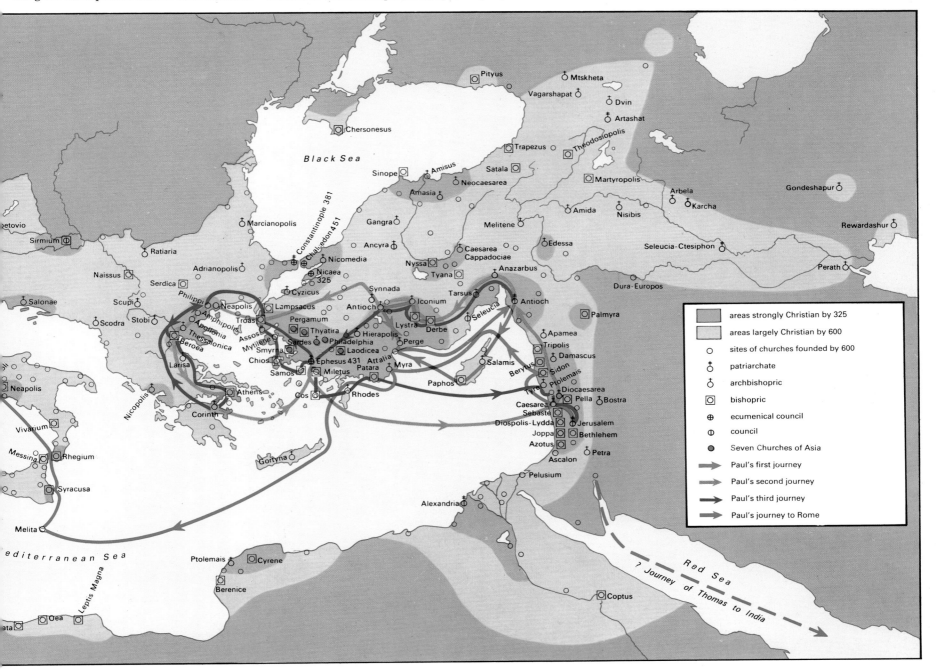

The crisis of the classical world

THE crisis of the classical world reached its height in the 5th century AD. It was prepared by earlier movements on the edge of China and affected all the great established civilisations of Eurasia, not merely the Greeks and the Romans. Its cause was the irruption of mounted nomad peoples from the north-west into the great crescent of ancient civilisations, which stretched from the Mediterranean to China. Its result was a setback to civilisation, which ushered in the so-called 'Dark Ages' not only in Europe but also in the whole of Eurasia. Only China coped successfully with the invaders; but even here their appearance saw a period of political fragmentation only ended by the Sui dynasty in AD 589.

The invading nomads whose incursions produced this crisis were no longer Indo-Europeans, though they had Indo-European peoples, mostly nomad, as subjects or allies. They were linked by common traditions and sometimes by actual kinship among their ruling groups; but they were not, unlike the Mongols seven centuries later (see page 128), under any form of central control, though their movements radiated from a common centre. Their physical type was not uniform but was often Mongoloid. Their lan-

guages were mostly of the Altaic groups of northeast Asia, now represented best by the varieties of Turkish. They all followed the pastoral mode of life with movable encampments of tents. In war they fought as mounted archers, using composite bows made of strips of bone, short, strong and convenient for riders. They also used sabres at close quarters and, when they came to possess taller horses and to use stirrups, the lance. This light and effective panoply was seldom adequately copied by civilised peoples, and accounts for the nomads' successes against them.

The centres of power among these Altaic nomads were not in arid steppe or desert, but in more favoured regions, such as the country along the Great Wall of China, and Mongolia north of the Gobi Desert. From here they struck both southward and westward. Their expansion began with the conquests of the people called Hsiung-nu in Chinese sources – a great nomad confederacy, the first to arise in eastern Asia, which grew up in continual rivalry with the Chinese empire of the Han. They were kept at bay only by a vast line of fixed fortifications. Finally the Han, using cavalry modelled on that

of the nomads, broke the power of the Hsiung-nu in the first century AD. But the Hsiung-nu did not vanish from history. Families of the ruling tribes appear to have established themselves in central Asia, where they gradually built up a new confederacy, now including Iranian nomads and some Mongoloid tribes from the Siberian forests. This revived confederacy was the origin of the Huns of later history. Mongolia, meanwhile, was ruled by other nomads, who were for the time less dangerous to the Chinese. But they finally broke into China at the beginning of the 4th century AD, after the short period of reunification under the Western Chin (265-317). Setting up an independent state in Shansi and Shensi, they took the two traditional capitals, Loyang in 311 and Ch'ang-an in 316. For the next 280 years northern China was dominated by invaders from the steppe, who established a bewildering succession of short-lived dynasties. Some of these were established by Hsiung-nu leaders, some by proto-Mongolian Hsien-pi, some by Turkic peoples, by the Avars, and by Tibetan tribes from the western borders, the Ti and Ch'iang.

These tribes had mostly had long contacts

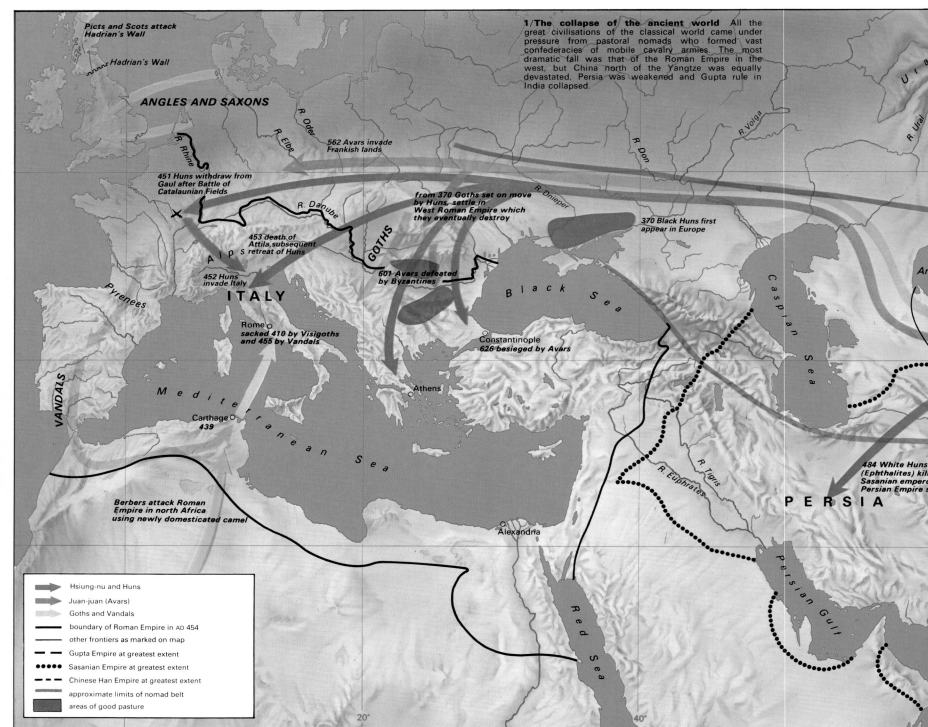

1/The collapse of the ancient world All the great civilisations of the classical world came under pressure from pastoral nomads who formed vast confederacies of mobile cavalry armies. The most dramatic fall was that of the Roman Empire in the west, but China north of the Yangtze was equally devastated, Persia was weakened and Gupta rule in India collapsed.

Picts and Scots attack Hadrian's Wall

Hadrian's Wall

ANGLES AND SAXONS

562 Avars invade Frankish lands

451 Huns withdraw from Gaul after Battle of Catalaunian Fields

from 370 Goths set in move by Huns, settle in West Roman Empire which they eventually destroy

370 Black Huns first appear in Europe

453 death of Attila, subsequent retreat of Huns

452 Huns invade Italy

601 Avars defeated by Byzantines

Black Sea

ITALY

GOTHS

Rome sacked 410 by Visigoths and 455 by Vandals

Constantinople 626 besieged by Avars

VANDALS

Mediterranean Sea

Athens

Carthage 439

Caspian Sea

484 White Huns (Ephthalites) kill Sasanian emperor Persian Empire

PERSIA

Berbers attack Roman Empire in north Africa using newly domesticated camel

Alexandria

Red Sea

Persian Gulf

Legend:
- Hsiung-nu and Huns
- Juan-juan (Avars)
- Goths and Vandals
- boundary of Roman Empire in AD 454
- other frontiers as marked on map
- Gupta Empire at greatest extent
- Sasanian Empire at greatest extent
- Chinese Han Empire at greatest extent
- approximate limits of nomad belt
- areas of good pasture

The Great Wall (below) was first built about 300 BC to prevent nomadic tribes from invading China. Under the Ch'in Emperor Shih-huang-ti the separate sections were linked up. It was further extended under the Han dynasty to protect the Kansu corridor with its highway to central Asia. By 100 BC it reached Tun-huang the beginning of the Silk Road to the west.

with the Chinese; some, like the Hsiung-nu and Ch'iang, had been allowed to settle inside the Great Wall, and had served the Chinese as mercenary troops. When they established local states of their own in Chinese territory, however, they lacked the experience needed to administer a sedentary agricultural population, and were forced to adopt Chinese methods of government and to co-operate with the local Chinese elite families. The tension between the need to adapt tribal customs to Chinese conditions, and the desire to preserve their ethnic identity proved fatal to most of these regimes.

Eventually a powerful Turkic people, the Toba (Northern) Wei 386-534, succeeded in reunifying northern China. But they did so in the end by becoming completely sinicised. In the early 6th century this led to civil conflict, and their empire was again for a time split up. During these centuries. not only did the nomadic invaders adopt Chinese customs, literary culture and political institutions, but the Chinese upper class, particularly in north-western China (Kansu, Shensi, Shansi) collaborated widely with them, and themselves intermarried with the Turks and Hsien-pi. The result was the emergence of a distinctive Sino-nomad aristocracy, many of whom spoke both Chinese and Turkish, who lived a style of life much influenced by non-Chinese customs, and among whom women played a very powerful role. It was from this aristocratic group that emerged the ruling houses of the Sui (581-617) and T'ang (618-907) dynasties, which reunified the whole of China, and extended throughout the empire the institutions and style of government which had been developed in the northern successor kingdoms to the Toba Wei. They maintained a distinctive identity as a separate aristocratic group until the late T'ang.

The political chaos of the 4th century, when northern China was fragmented into many local states, led to immense physical destruction, and widespread depopulation. Vast numbers of Chinese fled to the south, where conditions were relatively stable. The flourishing internal and external trade of Han times fell away; the use of money even disappeared, and not only was trade carried on by barter, but the states' finances were collected entirely in commodities. It was only at the end of the 5th century that the Toba carried out a redistribution of land to bring more of their territory under cultivation, and began slowly to rehabilitate the economy.

The Black Huns of Europe, as they were called, moved into south Russia in the 4th century, and advanced in the 5th century into the fertile basin of the Danube, particularly the territories later known as Hungary. There they created an east European empire which threatened both the East and the West Roman Empires until the death of its leader Attila in AD 453. Their onslaught eventually destroyed the West Roman Empire, which fell under Germanic rule, but the East Roman or Byzantine Empire survived. Meanwhile, also in the 4th, 5th and 6th centuries AD the White Huns or Ephthalites overran much of the Sasanian Empire of Iran in constant wars, and went on to set up a dynasty in northern India. Byzantine sources and Indian coins represent them as white people from central Asia, not Mongoloid, indicating that the name Hun (Khun in Iran, Huna in India) now denoted a political, rather than an ethnic, unity.

Both the Black Huns who invaded Europe, and the White Huns, have a record of devastation; the Hsiung-nu and their descendants and successors were thus the moving power in the crisis of established civilisations at the time. Not only did the effort to resist their incursions strain the resources of the states exposed to their attacks, but they also unsettled the tribes through whose territories they moved. Thus it was the Huns who set the Germanic peoples in motion (see page 98), and the withdrawal of garrisons to defend the Rhine frontier left the northern outposts in Roman Britain open to attack by the Picts. In eastern Asia, the successors of the Hsiung-nu were the Kök Türük – the Blue or Celestial Turks. They ruled during the 7th and 8th centuries over an empire which reached from Manchuria to the arid steppes west of the Syr Darya, and they appear to have driven other Turks westwards, particularly the various tribes of the Ogur, who appear in Byzantine history. They also drove out the Juan-juan of Mongolia, once their rulers. The latter passed through northern Iran to reach the Russian steppes; here they amalgamated with other nomad Turkish or Hunnish tribes and reappeared in Hungary as the Avars, who threatened Constantinople and western Europe from the 5th to the end of the 8th century, when their empire was destroyed by Charlemagne. These movements among the nomad peoples of central Asia, whose causes are obscure and can only be surmised, mark the end of one period in world history, and set the stage for another.

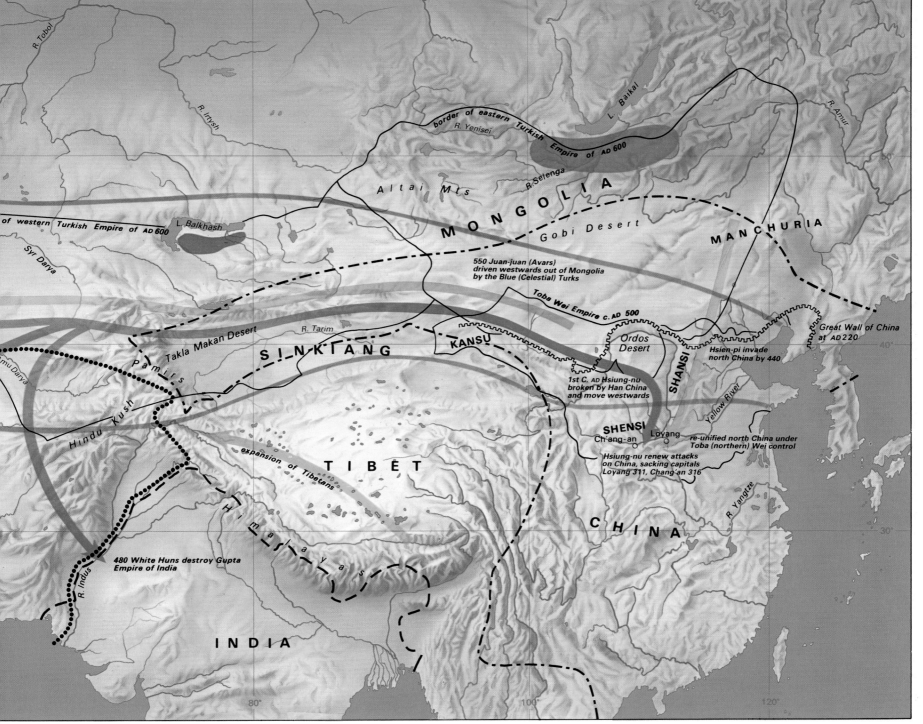

THE period around AD 500 was a time of upheaval throughout the Eurasian world, when nomads from the steppes of Asia descended upon all the existing centres of civilisation. Although the gains of the classical period were never entirely lost, there was a marked slackening of contacts between China and the West, and also between north Africa and Italy and between Byzantium and the lands of western Europe. Each region was thrown back upon its own resources to fend for itself.

In western Europe this period is traditionally known as 'the Middle Ages'. This description may be fitting in European history but makes little sense in the wider perspective of world history. Here, two outstanding events dominated the scene. The first was the rise and expansion of Islam, the second the emergence of the great Mongol Empire. After AD 632, when Mohammed died, Islam was incomparably the world's most dynamic civilisation, the true inheritor of the mantle of ancient Greece. At the same time, important developments were taking place in regions which hitherto had been isolated from the main stream. The appearance of the Maya, Aztec and Inca civilisations in America, the creation of the empires of Srivijaya and Majapahit in South-East Asia, and the rise of the empires of Ghana, Mali and Songhai in Africa, all attested to a new vitality and to the expansion of the area of civilised life.

Europe, by comparison, remained backward. Even here, however, it was a formative age, when primitive societies, such as the Anglo-Saxon heptarchy or the warbands of Frankish Gaul, were welded into feudal monarchies. But the process of consolidation was slow, interrupted by barbarian incursions and by economic setbacks. Not until the second half of the fifteenth century did Europe begin to draw level with the other world civilisations, and even then it was overshadowed by the expanding civilisation of the Ottoman Turks. If a relatively large space in this section is devoted to Europe, it is not so much because of its importance at the time, but rather because this period saw the beginnings of developments in European society which enabled it to advance to the centre of the stage in the following centuries.

4   The world o

The Dome of the Rock, Jerusalem

divided regions

Germanic and Slavonic invasions of Europe

3/The expansion of the Slavs *(above)* Following the Germanic migration westwards, the Slavs advanced into the vacated lands and also thrust south into Greece and the Balkans, accompanied by various non-Slav peoples such as Avars and Bulgars.

THE barbarian invasions of the 5th and 6th centuries and the settlement of Germanic and (later) Slav peoples on the soil of the Roman Empire are the traditional starting point of European history. Roman civilisation had been Mediterranean rather than European. With the Arab conquest of Palestine and North Africa (see page 104) and the descent of the Slavs into the Balkans, severing the links between Byzantium and the west, the Mediterranean framework of the Roman world was fractured, and the seat of power and influence shifted to the lands north of the Alps. Europe, cut off from the other civilisations of the Near East, began to go its own way under peoples who now moved from the periphery to the centre of the stage.

The Germanic peoples had moved before the Christian era, from Scandinavia to the shores of the Baltic around the mouth of the Vistula. Simultaneously the 'West Germans' were expanding into territory inhabited by the Celts east of the Rhine (see page 84). The 'East Germans' moved south c. AD 150 to the Carpathians and the lands north of the Black Sea. Pressure by both groups on the Roman frontiers began early; but it was the irruption of the Huns from Asia (see page 94) that threw the whole Germanic world into turmoil. First affected (c.370) were the Ostrogoths in the Crimea and the Ukraine. Thrown back across the Dniester, they drove the Visigoths across the Danubian frontier of the Roman Empire into lower Moesia (Bulgaria), where they received permission to settle. Their defeat of the emperor Valens at the battle of Adrianople (378) destroyed Roman powers of resistance and opened the way for other barbarians fleeing westward. The Visigoths themselves first sought to settle in Greece (369-99), then moved on to Italy, when they astonished the civilised world by sacking Rome in 410, but quickly passed over into Aquitaine (418), where they founded the kingdom of Toulouse. They were followed in 406 by Alans, Vandals and Sueves from the Theiss valley and Silesia, who broke across the frozen Rhine frontier near Mainz and ravaged Gaul for three years, until in 409 they crossed the Pyrenees and entered Spain. Behind them came the Burgundians, who founded a kingdom around the city of Worms, but were settled in Savoy in 443 after Worms had been destroyed by the Huns in 437. In Spain the Sueves founded a kingdom in Galicia, which survived from 411 to 585, when it was absorbed into the Visigothic kingdom. The Vandals and Alans crossed from Spain to Africa in 429, and in 442 the imperial government recognised their king, Gaiseric, as an independent ruler. The Vandal kingdom survived until 533, when North Africa was reconquered by Justinian's general, Belisarius. Meanwhile, the defeat of the Huns at

the climactic battle of the Catalaunian Fields near Troyes (451), the death of their leader Attila (453), and their retreat to the Russian plains, released the remaining Germanic tribes on the Danube, and the Ostrogoths moved south into Greece and subsequently into Italy, where they were in control by 493. North of the Alps, Franks and Alemans were infiltrating across the Rhine; while from about 440 Angles and Saxons were occupying the eastern and southern coastal areas of Britain, from which the Roman garrisons had withdrawn some thirty years earlier.

This great movement of peoples did not destroy the fabric of Roman civilisation. The Romans had long made a practice of settling barbarian 'confederate troops' within the empire. Salian Franks had been quartered in Belgium since c.360. The Visigoths and others only sought settlement on a larger scale. Except for the Vandals, the Germanic leaders accepted a position within the Roman heirarchy of government. Their object was not to destroy but to share in the benefits of Roman civilisation. Their greatest leaders, notably Theoderic the Ostrogoth (493-526), saw it as their task to reconcile Romans and Germans. Nevertheless, except in the Frankish kingdom (see page 106), they did not succeed. The early Germanic kingdoms were inherently unstable. There were many reasons for this, not the least being hostility between the Arian ruling class and their Catholic subjects. But the main weakness was the fact that the warbands (averaging perhaps 80,000, of whom only some 20,000 were warriors), cut off from their homeland, were too small to exercise permanent control. The exceptions were the Franks and Anglo-Saxons, both able to draw on reinforcements from Germany. Otherwise, once Justinian embarked on reconquest in 533, their instability was soon apparent, although the Ostrogoths resisted fiercely from 536 to 554.

Justinian's reconquest was the turning point. Engaged simultaneously in war with Persia, the imperial government was over-extended and unable to restore effective control. The long Gothic wars irretrievably ruined Italy. In 568, only a few years after the capitulation of the last Gothic strongholds, the defenceless country was occupied – apart from the south, which remained Byzantine – by the Lombards, another Germanic people which had moved down from the Elbe to modern Hungary. The destruction of Gothic power, removing the main obstacle to Frankish expansion, also ensured the predominance of the Frankish kingdom in the west. East of the Adriatic the Slav peoples, who had expanded from their home in the region of the Pripet marshes as the Germanic tribes moved west, crossed the Danube c.600, and descended into Greece. Just as the Germans had been propelled by the onslaught of the Huns, so it was the onslaught (beginning c.560) of another Asiatic people, the Avars, which drove the Slavs (and the Lombards) into Roman territory. Apart from Salonica, protected by its walls, Macedonia was permanently occupied by the Slavs; Salona, the Roman capital of Dalmatia, fell to them c.640. Only a few coastal cities of southern Greece and the Peloponnese remained Greek. In the eastern Balkans the Bulgars, an Asiatic people akin to the Huns, ruled over a largely Slav population and were recognised by the imperial government (681). The early history of the peoples of south-eastern Europe is obscure; but by the end of the 8th century independent Croatian, Serbian and Bulgarian kingdoms were taking shape. Meanwhile Europe had been permanently changed. The three centuries after the battle of Adrianople were a time of desperate confusion and material setbacks; but they were also a period when a new civilisation, 'Romano-Germanic' rather then Roman in character, was taking shape. Eventually it was to find its centre in the empire of Charlemagne (see page 106).

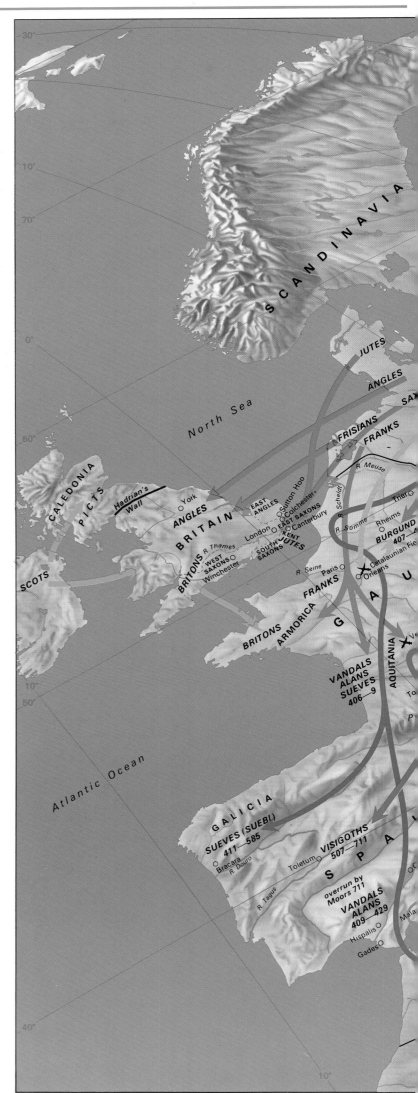

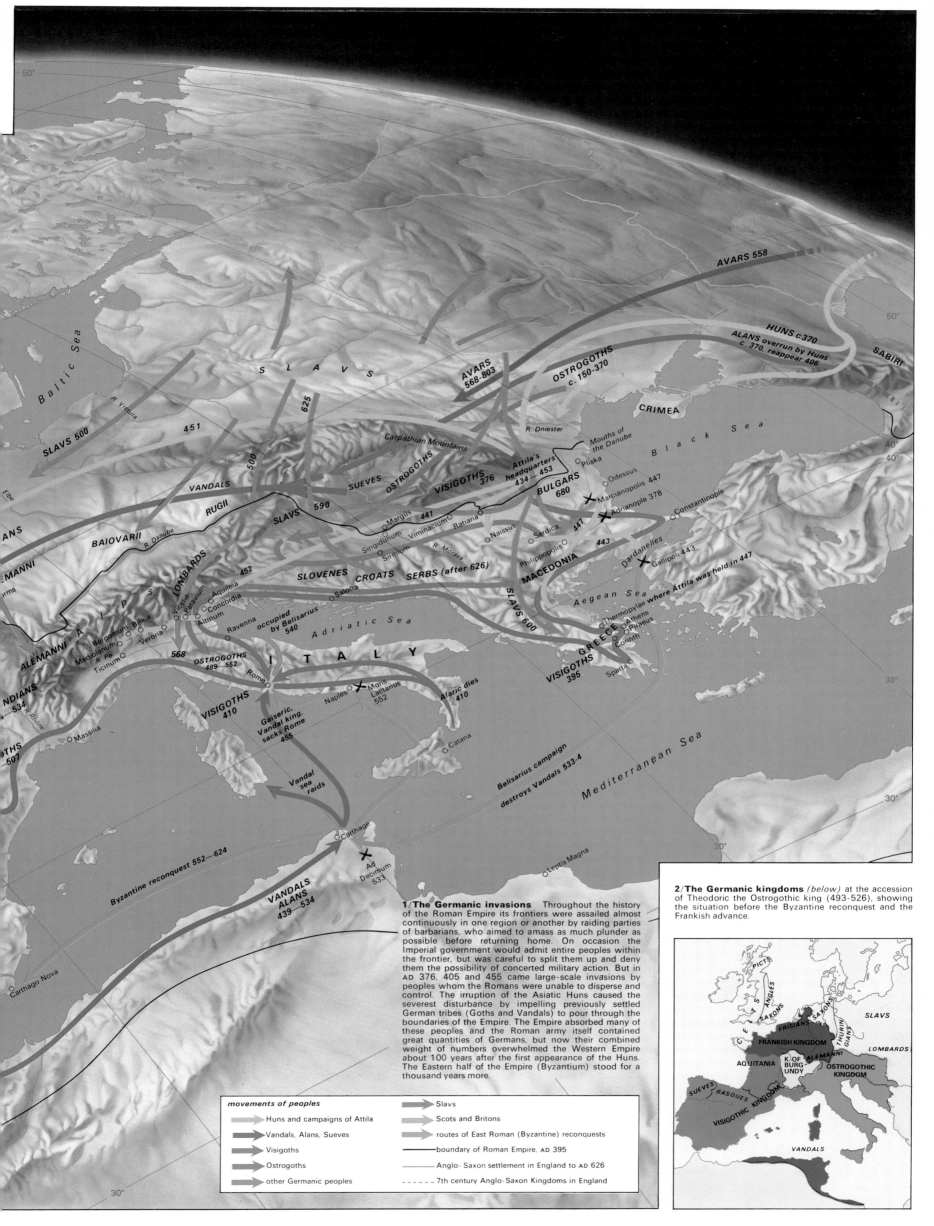

50°

Baltic Sea

S L A V S

SLAVS 500

451

SLAVS 500

VANDALS

RUGII

BAIOVARII

R. Danube

ALEMANNI

LOMBARDS

SLAVS 590

SUEVES

OSTROGOTHS

Carpathian Mountains

AVARS 568-803

625

500

AVARS 558

OSTROGOTHS c. 150-370

HUNS c 370

ALANS overrun by Huns c. 370, reappear 406

SABIRI

CRIMEA

R. Dniester

Mouths of the Danube

Black Sea

VISIGOTHS 376

Attila's headquarters 434—453

Pliska

Odessus

Marcianopolis 447

BULGARS 680

Adrianople 378

Constantinople

40°

Margus

Singidunum

Sirmium

Viminacium

Ratiaria

R. Morava

Naissus

Sardica

Philippopolis

MACEDONIA

443

Dardanelles

Gallipoli 443

SLAVS 600

SLOVENES

CROATS

SERBS (after 626)

441

452

LOMBARDS

Aquileia

Vicetia

Patavium

Concordia

Altinum

Ravenna

occupied by Belisarius 540

Adriatic Sea

Bergomum

Brixia

Mediolanum

R. Pa

Verona

Ticinum

568

OSTROGOTHS 489—552

I T A L Y

Rome

NDIANS — 534

R. Rhône

OTHS — 507

Massilia

VISIGOTHS 410

Naples

Mons Lactarius 552

Alaric dies 410

Gaiseric, Vandal king, sacks Rome 455

Catana

Aegean Sea

Thermopylae where Attila was held in 447

GREECE

Athens

Piraeus

Corinth

VISIGOTHS 395

Sparta

30°

Vandal sea raids

Belisarius campaign destroys Vandals 533-4

Mediterranean Sea

Byzantine reconquest 552—624

Carthage

Ad Decimum 533

VANDALS ALANS 439—534

Leptis Magna

20°

Carthago Nova

VANDALS ALANS 439—534

1/The Germanic invasions Throughout the history of the Roman Empire its frontiers were assailed almost continuously in one region or another by raiding parties of barbarians, who aimed to amass as much plunder as possible before returning home. On occasion the Imperial government would admit entire peoples within the frontier, but was careful to split them up and deny them the possibility of concerted military action. But in AD 376, 405 and 455 came large-scale invasions by peoples whom the Romans were unable to disperse and control. The irruption of the Asiatic Huns caused the severest disturbance by impelling previously settled German tribes (Goths and Vandals) to pour through the boundaries of the Empire. The Empire absorbed many of these peoples and the Roman army itself contained great quantities of Germans, but now their combined weight of numbers overwhelmed the Western Empire about 100 years after the first appearance of the Huns. The Eastern half of the Empire (Byzantium) stood for a thousand years more.

2/The Germanic kingdoms *(below)* at the accession of Theodoric the Ostrogothic king (493-526), showing the situation before the Byzantine reconquest and the Frankish advance.

PICTS

SCOTS

ANGLES

SAXONS

C E L T S

FRISIANS

SAXONS

THURINGIANS

SLAVS

FRANKISH KINGDOM

LOMBARDS

AQUITANIA

K. OF BURGUNDY

ALEMANNI

OSTROGOTHIC KINGDOM

SUEVES

BASQUES

VISIGOTHIC KINGDOM

VANDALS

movements of peoples

⟹ Huns and campaigns of Attila

⟹ Vandals, Alans, Sueves

⟹ Visigoths

⟹ Ostrogoths

⟹ other Germanic peoples

⟹ Slavs

⟹ Scots and Britons

⟹ routes of East Roman (Byzantine) reconquests

—— boundary of Roman Empire, AD 395

—— Anglo-Saxon settlement in England to AD 626

- - - - 7th century Anglo-Saxon Kingdoms in England

The expansion of Christianity
600 to 1500

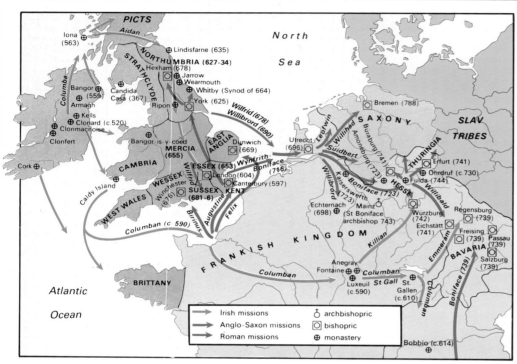

3/The Irish and the Anglo-Saxons (above) were the great missionaries of early mediaeval Europe. The impelling motive was to bring the message of the Gospel to their heathen cousins (the Saxons) on the Continent. The outstanding personality was St Boniface (c. 675-754). Though he failed to convert the Saxons, he not only restored the prestige of the Roman church but also reformed the Frankish church and transmitted to it the missionary impulse which he had inherited from his Irish forbears, St Columba and St Columban.

IN the first five centuries of its history Christianity was largely confined to the Roman Empire. Except for the missions of Ulfilas (c. 311-83) to the Goths and of St Patrick (c. 450) to Ireland, little effort was made to propagate the Gospel to the peoples outside. The decline of the Empire thus had decisive effects on the history of the Church. Already in the 5th century various attempts to shore up the tottering Empire by imposing religious orthodoxy, particularly the Council of Chalcedon (451), had alienated both the Monophysite churches of Egypt, Syria and Armenia, and the Nestorians in Upper Mesopotamia who, expelled from Edessa, took refuge in Persia. But the events which completely changed the position of the Church were the Germanic invasions of western Europe at the time of the pontificate of Pope Leo I (440-61), and the rapid advance of Islam after 635. The advance of Islam swamped three of the five patriarchates (Alexandria, Jerusalem and Antioch) and threatened a fourth (Constantinople). The western patriarchate (Rome) was similarly affected. North Africa and (later) Spain were lost; Illyria passed into the hands of heathen Slavs; while in the west most of the invaders, though Christian, were Arians and did not recognise papal authority. The Franks (though converted to Catholicism in 497) and the Anglo-Saxons were pagan.

By the time of Gregory I (590-604) Christianity was everywhere on the defensive. A century later the situation was worse. In place of a united Church in a united empire, disintegration and disruption were apparent on every side. Disputes between Rome and Constantinople over primacy compromised the Church's authority, and in the west the corrupt and secularised churches of Gaul and Spain were largely independent. Though Gregory himself sent a mission (596) to the heathen English, it accomplished little. At this crucial turning point salvation came from outside – not from the official Church, but from the Nestorians of Persia, the Copts of Egypt and the Celtic Christians of Ireland. These were the communities which initiated the expansion of Christianity at a time when, in its original Mediterranean homeland, it was under severe pressure.

In the long term the work of the Irish missionaries proved to be the most enduring, but to begin with the gains of the eastern churches were more impressive. Egypt was the home of cenobitic monasticism, and monasticism and asceticism gave the Egyptian, or Coptic, church a missionary fervour only equalled later by Celtic Christianity. Already c. 340-50 Egyptian missionaries were active in Ethiopia; a century later Coptic missions, travelling upstream along the Nile valley, converted the Nubian kingdoms between Syene (Aswan) and Khartoum. The fact that Islam was not an intolerant or persecuting religion allowed these churches to flourish. It also permitted the rapid spread of Nestorian Christianity from its centre at Ctesiphon, the Persian capital on the Tigris. The expansion of the Nestorian church between the 7th and 11th centuries placed it, in size and influence, ahead of any other Christian church of the period. By the year 1000 its adherents probably numbered millions; it had some 25 metropolitan provinces and 200-250 bishoprics, stretching from eastern Syria across central Asia into China and south into Arabia. The Christian church in India (the so-called St Thomas church) was also almost certainly an offshoot of Nestorian Christianity.

The decline of eastern Christianity began with the mass conversions to Islam in the 11th century. The Coptic church in Egypt was particularly affected. Furthermore, the appearance of crusading armies in Asia Minor after 1097 bred a new intolerance on the Muslim side. In China, Christianity never made much headway except among the tributary peoples, such as the Uighurs. In central Asia the Mongols were tolerant and the Nestorian churches flourished until the 14th century; but with the accession of Timur (1362-1405) persecution began. A few Christian communities survived in remote places, as they did in India; but by the 15th century Christianity in Asia was a dying cause. It only revived, and then not very successfully, with the arrival of Catholic and Protestant missions in modern times. The exception was Siberia, where Russian missionaries were active from the 17th century.

In the west, the impetus for revival came from the Celtic church in Ireland, another monastic missionary church which directed its attention first to its Celtic neighbours in Scotland, Wales and Brittany, then to England, and later to the heathen tribes of continental Europe. The leading figures of the first generation were Columba (d. 597) and Columban (d. 615). From Columba's

Scottish foundation at Iona, Christianity was carried south to Northumbria (634), East Anglia (653) and Mercia (655), and from 664 the English church was united under the Roman obedience. Columban went further afield, to Burgundy and to the heathen Alemanni round Lake Constance. His missionary work was continued by the leading figures of the second generation, Willibrord (658-739) and Wynfrith (or Boniface) (675-754), the former among the Frisians around Utrecht, the latter in Hesse and Thuringia. Their target was the heathen Saxons, but the conversion of Saxony only followed later (804), at the point of the sword. Henceforward the expansion of Christianity in its western form was too often linked with political expansion. Nevertheless the missionary impulse remained strong. In 826 Anskar began the mission to Scandinavia, but here again resistance was fierce and Christianity was not finally accepted before the 11th century.

The Anglo-Saxon missions inaugurated the revival of Christianity in the west. Meanwhile Rome and Constantinople, slowly drawing apart into two separate obediences, Catholic and Orthodox, were vying for the allegiance of the Slav peoples of eastern Europe. The famous mission of Cyril and Methodius in 864 misfired owing to opposition from the Frankish church, but Serbia and Bulgaria were won over to orthodoxy. Constantinople also sent missions to the northern shores of the Black Sea. By 867 there was a Christian church at Kiev, and in 988 the Russian prince Vladimir was baptised. The conversion of Russia was a capital fact, opening up to Christianity an area larger than the rest of Europe combined. After 1169, when the capital was transferred from Kiev to Vladimir, Russian missionaries, moving north and east, carried Christianity to the heathen Karelians, Lapps, Permians, Votyaks and Mari. It was a major achievement, and once again ascetic monasticism provided the impetus.

Further west, Poland (966) and Hungary (1001) opted for Catholic Christianity, but sought to escape Frankish domination by placing their churches directly under the protection of Rome. The result was to enhance the Pope's authority. From the time of Leo IX (1048-54) a reformed Papacy actively asserted leadership, and the breach between Rome and Constantinople in 1054 hardened into a permanent schism. Papal authority was enhanced as a result of the Christian counter-offensive against Islam in Spain, still more by the Pope's sponsorship of the First Crusade (1095-99). The attempt to restore Christianity in Palestine was a costly failure, but the militant crusading spirit remained alive. The propagation of Christianity was underpinned by new monastic orders, the Cluniacs (particularly in Spain) and the Cistercians (in eastern Europe), but now the monks normally followed in the wake of the conquering armies. During the 13th century the friars (Franciscans and Dominicans) undertook peaceful missions to Asia and Africa, but their results were negligible. Heathen Prussia was conquered (1231-83) by the sword. In 1387 the prince of Lithuania, the last remaining heathen state in Europe, was converted to Catholicism, but only in order to succeed to the Polish throne. This was the last success of western Christianity until the Spanish *conquistadores*, imbued with the crusading spirit, carried the Catholic faith to America and opened a new chapter.

1/Christianity in Asia (right) The expansion of Christianity, for all practical purposes the work of the Nestorian Christians of Persia, is a remarkable chapter of world history. The number of their converts cannot be accurately estimated, but they were certainly more than one million. Their missionary activity followed the trade routes of the time by land and sea. Tolerated for many centuries, they finally fell victims to the intolerance fomented by the Crusades.

2/Christianity in Europe (right) The main thrust was north and east from the line of the Rhine and Danube. In both directions the Frankish church took the lead. The 11th century saw a subsidiary thrust into Spain, and Rome and Constantinople competed for the allegiance of the Balkans. With the conversion of pagan Lithuania in 1387 the whole of Europe was at least nominally Christian; but the Russian church was still engaged in a great missionary thrust to the White Sea and the Urals.

St Andrew and St Peter (above) This portrait, from the monastery of Bawit in the Libyan desert, exemplifies the ascetic spirit of eastern Christianity and helps to explain why, for a thousand years, it was so powerful a missionary force.

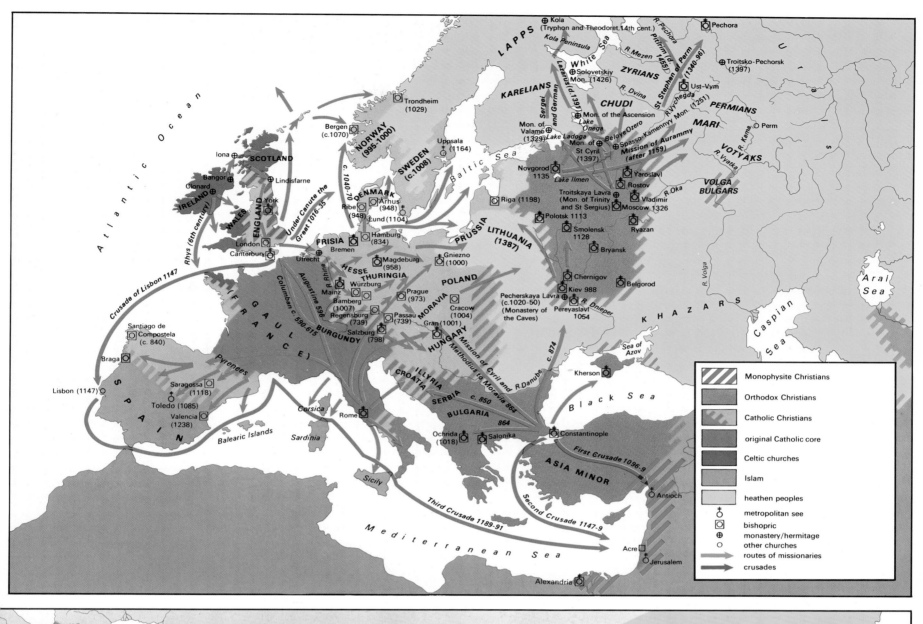

Kola
(Tryphon and Theodoret 14th cent.) ⊕

LAPPS

⊕ Pechora

White
Sea

R. Pechora

KARELIANS

R. Mezen

ZYRIANS

Troitsko-Pechorsk
(1397) ✠

NORWAY
(995-1000)

☐ Trondheim
(1029)

Bergen
(c.1070)

Iona ⊕ SCOTLAND
Bangor ✠ ⊕ Lindisfarne
Clonard
IRELAND ⊕
WALES ✠ York
ENGLAND
London ☐
Canterbury ✠

Solovetskiy
Mon. (1426)

Sergei
and German
Mon. of Valamo
(1329) Lake Ladoga

R. Dvina

Stephen of Perm (1340-96)

CHUDI

Ust-Vym
(1340-96)

R. Vychegda PERMIANS

Perm ○

R. Kama

Mon. of the Ascension

Beloye Ozero

Mission of Aurammy
(after 1159) MARI

VOTYAKS

R. Vyatka

Uppsala
(1164)

SWEDEN
(c.1008)

Baltic
Sea

Under Canute the
Great 1016-35

c. 1040-70

DENMARK

Ribe Århus
(948) (948)
Lund (1104)

Riga (1198) ☐

Hamburg
(834)

Bremen

FRISIA

Utrecht

Mon. of
St Cyril
Novgorod
1135

Troitskaya Lavra
(Mon. of Trinity
and St Sergius)

Polotsk 1113

Yaroslavl
Rostov
Vladimir
Moscow 1326

VOLGA
BULGARS

Mission of Aurammy
(1397)

R. Oka

Smolensk
1128

Ryazan

R. Volga

Aral
Sea

Santiago de
Compostela
(c. 840)

Braga

HESSE
THURINGIA
Würzburg
Bamberg
(1007) Mainz
Regensburg
(739)

Magdeburg
(958)

PRUSSIA LITHUANIA
(1387)

Gniezno
(1000)

POLAND

Bryansk

Chernigov

Belgorod

KHAZARS

Caspian
Sea

Crusade of Lisbon 1147

Columban c. 590-615

Augustine 596

R. Rhine

Prague
(973)

MORAVIA

Cracow
(1004)

Kiev 988

Pereyaslavl
1054

R. Dnieper

Lisbon (1147)

Saragossa
(1118)
Toledo (1085)

Valencia
(1238)

SPAIN

Pyrenees
(GAULE)
FRANCE

BURGUNDY

Passau
(739)

Salzburg
(798)

HUNGARY

Mission of Cyril and
Methodius to Moravia 864

Pecherskaya Lavra
(c.1020-50)
(Monastery of
the Caves)

c. 874

R. Danube

ILLYRIA
CROATIA

SERBIA c. 850

Sea of
Azov

Balearic Islands

Corsica

Sardinia

Rome ✠

BULGARIA

864

Ochrida
(1018) Salonika

Kherson

Black
Sea

Sicily

First Crusade 1096-9

Constantinople ✠

ASIA
MINOR

	Monophysite Christians
	Orthodox Christians
	Catholic Christians
	original Catholic core
	Celtic churches
	Islam
	heathen peoples
✠	metropolitan see
☐	bishopric
⊕	monastery/hermitage
○	other churches
→	routes of missionaries
⟶	crusades

Third Crusade 1189-91

Second Crusade 1147-9

Mediterranean Sea

Antioch ○

Acre ✠

Jerusalem ✠

Alexandria ☐

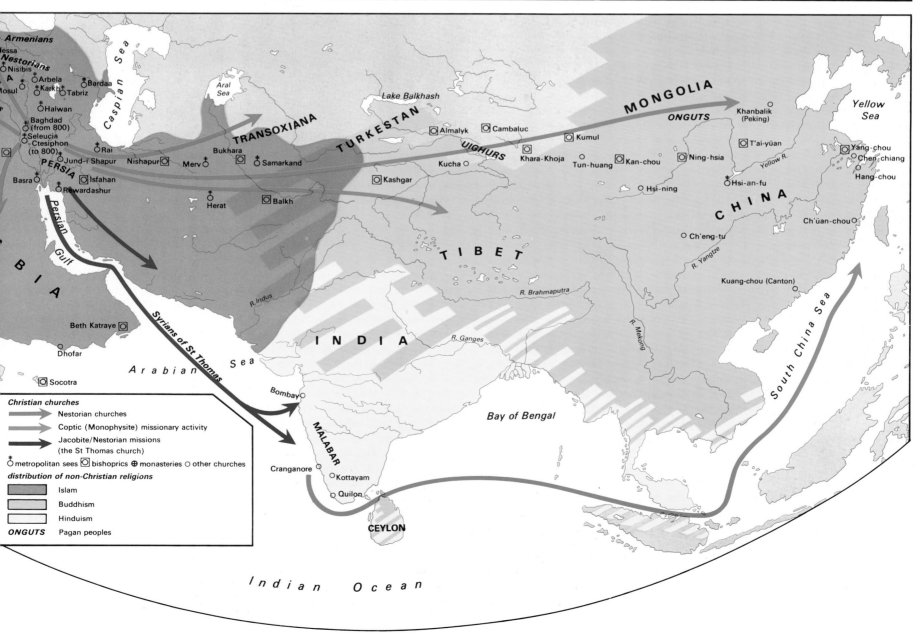

Armenians

Edessa ✠

Nestorians
○ Nisibis
Mosul ✠ Arbela
✠ Karkh Bardaa ✠
Tabriz ✠

A ✠ Halwan

Baghdad
(from 800) ✠
Seleucia-
Ctesiphon
(to 800) ✠

PERSIA

Basra ○
Rewardashur ✠

Isfahan ○
Rai ○

Jund-i Shapur ○

Persian
Gulf

Syrians of St Thomas

BIA

Beth Katraye ☐

Dhofar ○

Socotra ☐

Caspian
Sea

Aral
Sea

Lake Balkhash

TRANSOXIANA

TURKESTAN

MONGOLIA

ONGUTS

Khanbalik
(Peking)

Yellow
Sea

Nishapur ○

Merv ☐

Bukhara ☐

Samarkand ✠

UIGHURS

Almalyk ☐

Cambaluc

Kumul

T'ai-yüan

Herat ✠

Balkh ☐

Kashgar ☐

Kucha ○

Khara-Khoja ☐

Tun-huang

Kan-chou ☐

Ning-hsia ☐

Hsi-an-fu ✠

CHINA

Yang-chou ☐
Chen-chiang ○

Hang-chou

TIBET

Hsi-ning ○

Ch'eng-tu ○

Ch'uan-chou ○

R. Indus

INDIA

R. Brahmaputra

R. Ganges

R. Yangtze

R. Mekong

Kuang-chou (Canton) ○

Arabian
Sea

Bombay ○

MALABAR

Cranganore ○

Kottayam ○

Quilon ○

Bay of Bengal

South China Sea

CEYLON

Christian churches
⟶ Nestorian churches
⟶ Coptic (Monophysite) missionary activity
⟶ Jacobite/Nestorian missions
(the St Thomas church)
✠ metropolitan sees ☐ bishoprics ⊕ monasteries ○ other churches

distribution of non-Christian religions
	Islam
	Buddhism
	Hinduism
ONGUTS Pagan peoples

Indian Ocean

The Jewish diaspora AD 70 to 1497

FOR over 2000 years the history of the Jews has been a story of external dispersion and internal cohesion. From the time of the destruction of the first Temple and the Babylonian exile (586 BC), the Jewish homeland was beset by powerful, predatory empires, of which the last was Rome. Conquered by the Roman general Pompey in 63 BC, Judaea became a Roman protectorate, and in AD 6 it was placed under the direct rule of Roman procurators. The result was religious and nationalistic tension, which came to a head in AD 66 when the whole nation revolted against Rome. This uprising was crushed by Vespasian and Titus, who recaptured Jerusalem and destroyed the Temple in AD 70. Three years later the last rebel stronghold, the fortress Masada on the Dead Sea, also fell. Later, the apparent plan of the Emperor Hadrian to turn Jerusalem into a pagan city ended for over two centuries all prospects of rebuilding the Temple, and incited a second Jewish revolt in AD 132, which was finally suppressed three years later.

The political, military and religious reverses in Judaea only affected to a small extent the status of Jews in the Roman Empire, and the even larger number of Jews living in Babylonia. The movement of Jews from the main area of Jewish settlement (Palestine, Asia Minor, Babylonia, Egypt) into Europe had begun in the late Hellenistic period, and was stimulated by the incorporation of Judaea into the Roman Empire. By the middle of the first century BC, Jews already lived in the city of Rome, and later they spread out in the wake of the Roman legions. Exact figures are not known, but it has been estimated that they may have constituted as much as ten per cent of the population of the Roman Empire, playing a role in cultural and religious life, and enjoying legal privileges which facilitated their observance of Judaism.

The resilience of Judaism after the setback in AD 70 may be explained, at least in part, by the evolution of the Jewish religion following the destruction of the first Temple in 586 BC, when a system based on a Temple and sacrifices was complemented by one based on the synagogue and prayer. These new religious forms gave influence to the interpreters of biblical law. The philosophy underlying such interpretation varied. One group of interpreters, the Pharisees, became particularly influential at some time after the middle of the second century BC, and after AD 70 they evolved into Rabbis. A second important factor was the codification of Jewish law, both civil and religious, carried out in Palestine around AD 200 by Rabbi Judah the Patriarch in a work called the *Mishnah*. This code became the basis of continuous study in the academies of learning in both Palestine and Babylonia, and the discussions were preserved in the *Talmud*, still today the basis for traditional Jewish behaviour and belief.

The adoption of Christianity as the official religion of the Roman Empire in the 4th century AD brought much rhetoric by the state against Judaism and worsened the position of Jews. Restrictive legislation was enacted in the Empire and later in its successor states, particularly in Visigothic Spain, where Judaism was finally proscribed. However, the Muslim conquest of Spain in AD 711 brought a respite, which culminated in the 'golden age' of Spanish Jewry. At the same time, the break-up of the Roman Empire affected the economic activities of the Jews, which hitherto had been no different from those of other national groups. From about the 6th century this changed, and Jews became identified with international and regional trade. Internal and external factors, including the widespread dispersal of Jews both in Islamic lands and throughout Christian Europe, Jewish group solidarity, facility of linguistic communication, and a uniform system of commercial law based on the *Talmud*, accounted for this change. The trend was encouraged by the increasing exclusion of Jews from landowning, especially in northern Europe, the consolidation of the feudal system, and the constant threat of the confiscation of Jewish property and expulsion. Carolingian rulers, aware of the Jews' role in international trade, granted them special charters, assuring them of protection, commercial privileges, and the right to govern themselves according to their own law.

In the 10th and 11th centuries, Jewish settlements, apparently first consisting of merchants, were established in the Rhine valley. Later, they spread further east, and by the 13th and 14th centuries into Poland, where the Jews continued to speak their German dialect, which became known as Yiddish. But the pre-eminence of the Jews in commerce declined with the emergence of a native Christian merchant class and the exclusive policies adopted by the Christian merchant guilds. The Jews were forced more and more into the credit field (closed at least in theory to Christians by the Church's prohibition of usury), where they came to assume a dominant role, especially in northern France, England, Germany and northern Italy. As such, they were invaluable, often as a source of small-scale loans to the urban poor, and always as a source of credit and taxation to kings, princes and municipalities, who continued to grant them charters of protection, guaranteeing security of persons and property, the exercise of religious worship, and the right of communal self-government, thus making possible the development of Jewish law and institutions, the perpetuation of the religious tradition, and the evolution of intellectual and cultural life.

At the same time the Church became increasingly hostile (especially at the Third and Fourth Lateran Councils in 1179 and 1215), and as the inflammatory sermons of the wandering friars stirred the passions of the populace, the condition of the Jews deteriorated severely. They were subjected to arbitrary financial payments, severe restrictions of economic pursuits, the wearing of distinguishing badges (often yellow), confinement to special quarters known as ghettos (*ghetti*) – a term first applied to the Jewish quarter in Venice in 1516, though the institution existed earlier – and unsubstantiated charges of ritual murder, blood libel, desecration of the Host, and well poisoning (the last especially at the time of the Black Death in 1348). This combination of social, economic and religious animosity, coupled with the feeling that Jews were an alien body in a Catholic society, led to numerous expulsions. Though fairly often Jews were recalled, because their departure caused a disruption of economic life, with the emergence of alternative sources of finance and the development of the western economies they became less necessary. One by one the rulers of western Europe expelled them totally from their realms: England in 1290, France in 1394, Spain in 1492 (thereby initiating the Sephardic diaspora), Portugal in 1497 (though here large numbers, including many who had found refuge in Portugal at the time of the Spanish expulsion, were forcibly converted, though many escaped in the following decades).

Jews were also expelled from many German cities. Thus, after 1497, Jews no longer resided in western Europe or in large parts of central Europe. The centres of Jewish population and cultural life were located in northern Italy, a few cities in Germany, the Ottoman Empire, and especially in Poland and Lithuania. Not until the 17th and 18th centuries, under the impact of rationalism, mercantilism and the Enlightenment, were the Jews readmitted to England, France and the Netherlands; legal emancipation, though not always social acceptability, had to wait until the late 18th and 19th centuries.

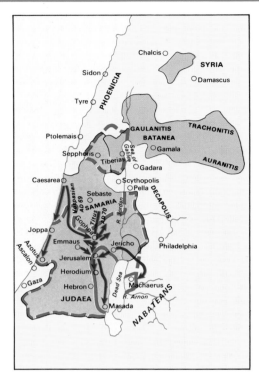

2/**Judaea in the 1st centuries BC and AD** *(left)* In 140 BC an independent Jewish state emerged under Simon the Hasmonean, a brother of Judah Maccabee. It became a Roman protectorate in 63 BC. Subsequently, the Idumaean Herod I (37-4 BC), husband of the Hasmonean princess Miriamme, divided it in his will between his three sons, Archelaus, Herod Antipas and Philip. Eventually Judaea was governed by Roman procurators from AD 6 to 66, with a brief interlude when the whole of Herod's kingdom was reunited under his grandson, Agrippa I (AD 41-44). After Agrippa's death, the rule of the procurators led to the unsuccessful revolt by Jewish nationalists of AD 66-73. Their last stand was at the fortress of Masada.

area of Roman procuratorial rule in Judaea

Agrippa II's kingdom, AD 61

area of major revolt at start of AD 66

area of revolt at end of AD 69

Roman armies

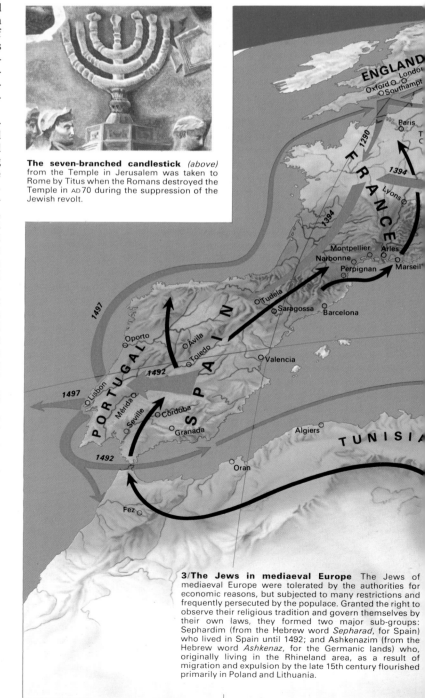

The **seven-branched candlestick** *(above)* from the Temple in Jerusalem was taken to Rome by Titus when the Romans destroyed the Temple in AD 70 during the suppression of the Jewish revolt.

3/**The Jews in mediaeval Europe** The Jews of mediaeval Europe were tolerated by the authorities for economic reasons, but subjected to many restrictions and frequently persecuted by the populace. Granted the right to observe their religious tradition and govern themselves by their own laws, they formed two major sub-groups: Sephardim (from the Hebrew word *Sepharad*, for Spain) who lived in Spain until 1492; and Ashkenazim (from the Hebrew word *Ashkenaz*, for the Germanic lands) who, originally living in the Rhineland area, as a result of migration and expulsion by the late 15th century flourished primarily in Poland and Lithuania.

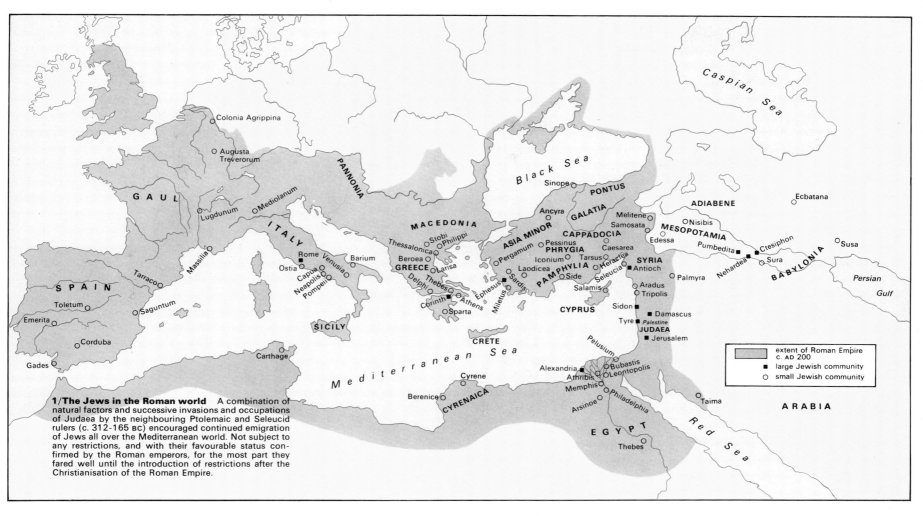

1/The Jews in the Roman world A combination of natural factors and successive invasions and occupations of Judaea by the neighbouring Ptolemaic and Seleucid rulers (c. 312-165 BC) encouraged continued emigration of Jews all over the Mediterranean world. Not subject to any restrictions, and with their favourable status confirmed by the Roman emperors, for the most part they fared well until the introduction of restrictions after the Christianisation of the Roman Empire.

extent of Roman Empire c. AD 200
■ large Jewish community
○ small Jewish community

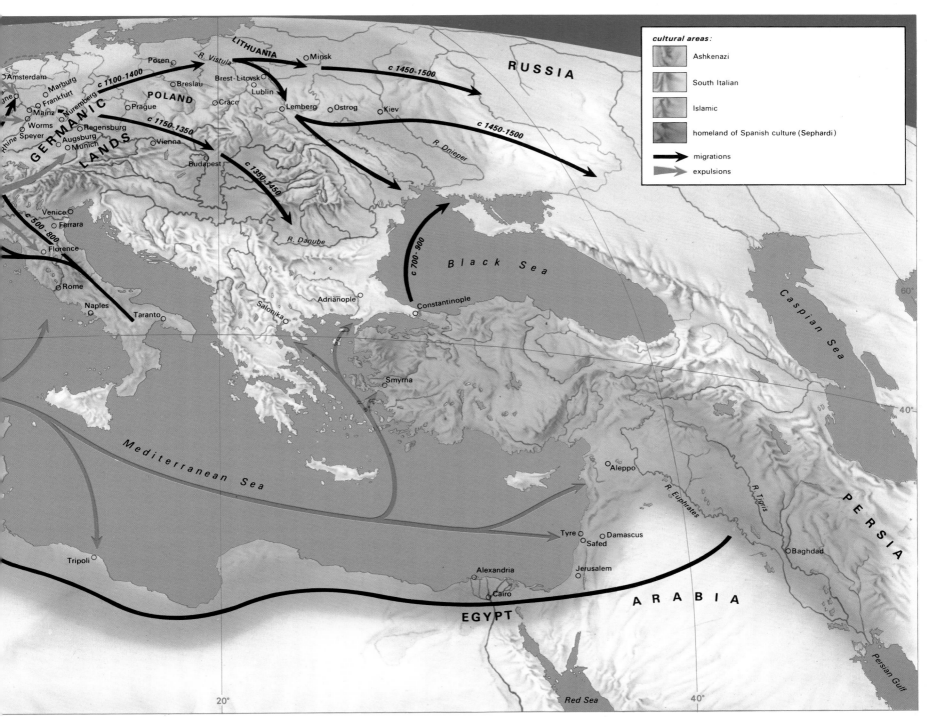

cultural areas:
Ashkenazi
South Italian
Islamic
homeland of Spanish culture (Sephardi)

→ migrations
→ expulsions

The spread of Islam from AD 632

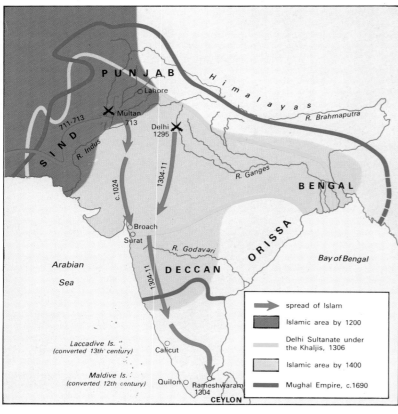

2 and 3/India and Indonesia The spread of Islam in India *(above)* was partly the result of expansion by successive waves of Muslim conquerors, partly the consequence of conversion by missionaries and traders. Indonesia and the Malay peninsula *(below)* were converted to Islam by a gradual process of proselytisation, beginning in all probability with Muslim traders from Gujerat in India, who had acquired a permanent foothold at Perlak on the northern top of Sumatra

by 1290. From there they spread to Malaya (c.1400), where the new religion quickly took hold, and also to Java and the Moluccas (c.1430-90). By the end of the 16th century most of the islands in the archipelago had accepted Islam, notably Mindanao and the Sulu archipelago in the Philippines. This process continued despite successive waves of Spanish, Portuguese and Dutch colonisation and conquest.

The minaret *(left)* from which the *muezzin* chants the call to prayer, is attached to all mosques and is a distinctive feature of Islamic religious architecture. Originally square, the minaret later assumed the slender, lofty, circular form familiar in India and Constantinople. The minaret of the famous mosque of Ahmad ibn Tulun in Cairo, built in 879 and renovated in 1267, combines both forms.

THE rise and expansion of Islam was one of the most significant and far-reaching events in modern history, and its impact continues to reverberate in our own times. Islam means 'submission to the will of God'; God's message to mankind has been expressed through a series of prophets, culminating in Mohammed, the Apostle and Prophet of God. Muslims believe that God has spoken through Mohammed, and that the Koran, which means recitation, is the Word of God. Mohammed is the Seal of the Prophets, and no others will come after him, but he is not of course divine, for divinity belongs to God alone. Mohammed's message, to his fellow citizens in the western Arabian city of Mecca, was that they should cease to worship idols, and submit instead to the will of Allah.

Mohammed was born in Mecca about AD 570, and was orphaned in early childhood. At that time Mecca was the principal commercial centre in western Arabia, and was also an important pilgrimage centre, based on the cult of the Ka'ba, the Black Stone. He received his first revelations in 610. As his followers grew in number, Mohammed aroused the hostility of the merchant aristocracy of Mecca, who feared that acceptance of his message would pose a threat to the shrine. Hostility developed into persecution, and in 622 Mohammed and his followers withdrew to Medina, some 280 miles north-east of Mecca. This 'migration', *hijra* in Arabic, on 16 July 622, marks the beginning of the Islamic era and thus of the Muslim calendar.

In Medina, Mohammed organised the Muslims into a community, and consolidated his base with the assistance of his Medinan hosts. The Meccans made every effort to dislodge him, but after a series of defeats eventually accepted his message. Mohammed returned to Mecca in triumph in 630, and cast out the idols from the Ka'ba, transforming it into the focal point of the new religion of Islam. When Mohammed died in 632, his authority extended over the Hejaz and most of central and southern Arabia.

Over the next hundred years, the Arab armies brought the religion of Islam as far west as Spain, and as far east as northern India. This expansion owed much to the enthusiasm and religious conviction of the conquerors, but it was

also facilitated by the war-weariness of the empires of Persia and Byzantium. The first of Mohammed's successors, the caliph Abu Bakr (632-34) completed the conquest of Arabia and entered southern Palestine. His successor Omar (634-44) advanced to Damascus, and victory over the Byzantines at the Yarmuk river in 636 encouraged the Muslims to advance east into Mesopotamia and north-west into Asia Minor. By 643 Persia had been overrun, and the last Persian emperor, Yazdigird, was killed in 651 after his troops had put up a final stand at Merv. The conquest of Herat and Balkh (651) and the fall of Kabul (664) opened the way to India; Sind, in north-east India, fell to the Muslims in 712.

Simultaneously, Arab forces pushed west into Egypt, occupying Alexandria in 643, and advancing across North Africa into Cyrenaica. Further progress was held up by Berber resistance, but the advance was resumed after the construction of the fortress city of Kairouan in 670. After the subjection of the Maghreb, Arab forces crossed the Straits of Gibraltar in 711 and conquered Spain. There were further advances into southern France, but the Arab armies were defeated at Poitiers in 732, and in 759 they withdrew south of the Pyrenees. In the late 7th and early 8th centuries attacks were launched against Constantinople, but the Byzantines succeeded in preventing the Arabs from capturing the city and in fact retained control of much of Asia Minor until the 11th century.

Initially, Islam did not particularly encourage, far less insist upon, conversion. The Koran enjoins Muslims to respect the 'people of the book', that is, members of the other monotheistic religions with written scriptures, and the existence of substantial Christian (and until comparative-

1/The spread of Islam outside the Arabian peninsula began almost immediately after the Prophet's death in 632. By 711, Arab armies were simultaneously attacking Sind in north-eastern India and preparing for the conquest of the Iberian peninsula. In general, the conquests in the east exceeded those in the west in size and importance. By 750, when the Abbasids ousted the Umayyad dynasty, the empire to which they succeeded was the major civilisation west of China.

ly recently, Jewish) communities throughout the Muslim world is ample evidence that this injunction was heeded. However, under the Abbasid dynasty (750-1258), large-scale conversion became common. This was partly because under the Abbasids, when the capital of the empire shifted from Syria to Mesopotamia, power passed from the conquering Arab minority to the non-Arab majority, and non-Arabs were no longer discriminated against as they had been under the Umayyads (661-750).

Although the Muslim world soon lost its original political unity – with the accession of the Abbasids and with the establishment of rival caliphates in Cairo and Córdoba in the mid-10th century it retained a considerable degree of cultural unity, largely through the Arabic language. In many ways, this unity overrode the sectarian divides which had already appeared in the first Islamic century, largely centring on the vexed question of the succession to the caliphate. With the seizure of temporal power by the Buyids in Baghdad in 936, the Abbasid caliphs were largely restricted to their religious functions. The Islamic world had split into local dynastic entities, whose acknowledgement of Abbasid suzerainty was often only nominal.

Although the Islamic empire declined as a theocratic entity, Islam itself continued to expand as a religious force (see maps 2 and 3). This expansion was partly the result of conquest, and partly – particularly in South-East Asia and West Africa – the result of missionary activity by traders and preachers. The contemporary Islamic world (map 4) covers substantial parts of Asia and Africa, and the events of the 1970s and 1980s have shown that Islam has once more emerged as a decisive factor in world politics.

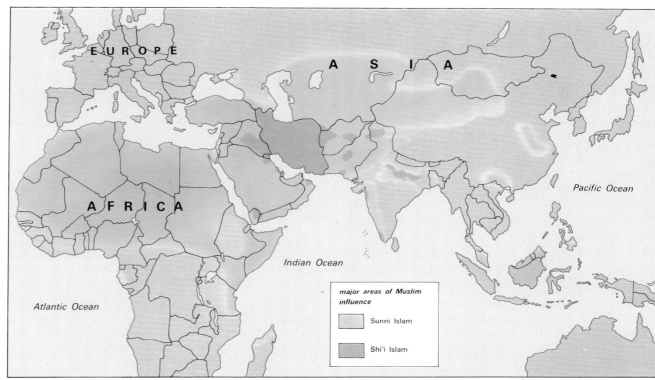

4/Islam today *(above)* Islam, the most recent of the great world religions, numbers some 400 million adherents, about one-seventh of the total population of the globe. Most Muslims are distributed in a broad band from Morocco to Indonesia, and from northern central Asia to Tanzania. The states with the largest Muslim population are Indonesia (148 million, 90% of total population), Bangladesh (88 million, 80%), Nigeria (81 million, 47%), Pakistan (80 million, 83%), India (70 million, 11%) and Egypt (41 million, 92%). The map shows the relative preponderance of Sunni (orthodox) Muslims, the Shi'i sect being largely confined to Iran, southern Iraq and Yemen.

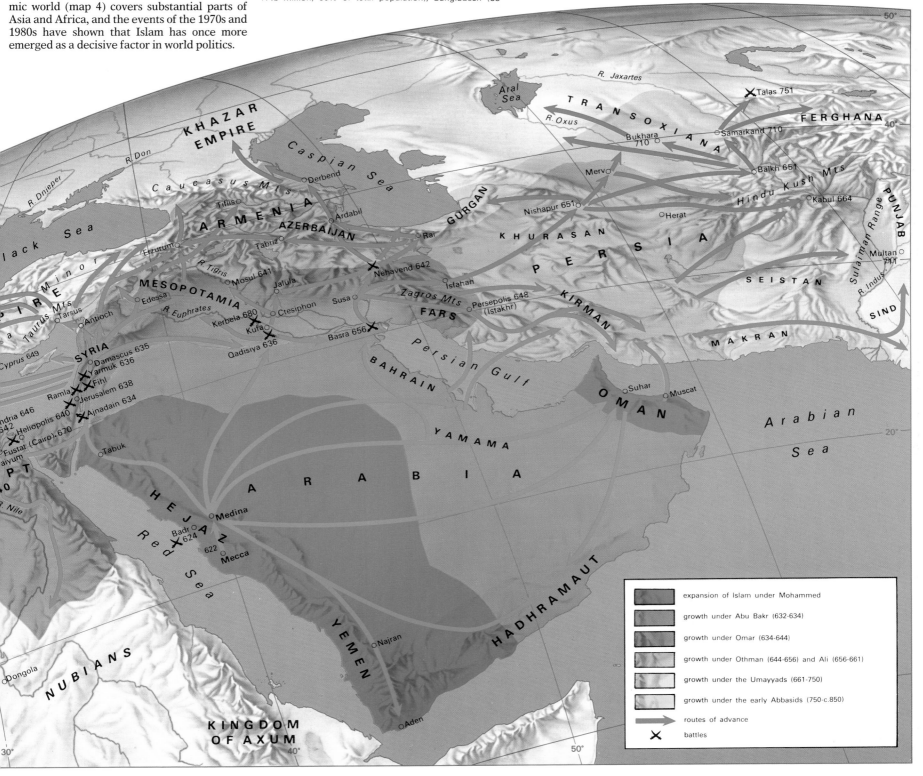

expansion of Islam under Mohammed

growth under Abu Bakr (632-634)

growth under Omar (634-644)

growth under Othman (644-656) and Ali (656-661)

growth under the Umayyads (661-750)

growth under the early Abbasids (750-c.850)

→ routes of advance

✕ battles

105

The rise of the Frankish Kingdom 482 to 814

THE conquests of Clovis, who died in 511, and his sons made the Franks the most powerful and important of all the barbarian successors of Rome, and created the basis for the Frankish hegemony that dominated western Europe for more than three centuries. The tomb of Clovis' father, Childeric, discovered in 1653, shows that he was buried with great, but not particularly barbarian, splendour in a Roman cemetery at Tournai, in the heart of the territory seized by the Franks in the 5th century. He was, however, not the only Frankish ruler, for the Franks who lived in the valleys of the Rhine, Mosel and Meuse had other chieftains or kings. Clovis not only destroyed the power of such rivals and so united the Franks under his rule, but also greatly extended his authority over neighbouring peoples to both east and west. His victories over the Thuringians and Alemans began that Frankish influence over the Germans east of the Rhine that was to be a major theme of Frankish, and of European, history; while his mastery of the greater part of Gaul was achieved by the defeat of Syagrius, 'king of the Romans', at Soissons in 486 and, some twenty years later, at Vouillé, near Poiters, of Alaric II and his

Visigoths, who were thereafter confined to Spain and the coastal district of Septimania. Clovis' kingdom was enlarged by his sons and grandsons who not only extended Frankish overlordship in the east as far as the middle Danube, but also conquered the Burgundians and drove the Ostrogoths from Provence.

This expansion was achieved more by conquest than by colonisation; some Franks did settle in northern Gaul but most of them continued to live in the north-east in those areas where Germanic languages have persisted to this day (see map 2). Clovis ruled from Paris, but in Gaul itself there was little displacement of the native population, and the French language has developed from Latin with relatively few German words (e.g. *bleu*). The government largely remained in the hands of bishops and counts drawn from the Gallo-Roman aristocracy who, as a result of Clovis' conversion to Catholic Christianity, were ready to accept Frankish rule in preference to that of Burgundians and Visigoths, who had been converted earlier to the heretical Arian form of the religion.

However valuable Clovis and his successors found such Gallo-Roman support, their power

ultimately depended on the Frankish army, and one important motive for the conquests was the need to win booty, land and revenues with which the loyalty of the warriors could be rewarded and maintained. By the middle of the 6th century the first period of expansion was over and Frankish kings had to reward followers and endow the Church by granting away their own estates and revenues. In so doing, they diminished their resources, and in time their power passed to the families that had benefited most from royal favour. There were many of these, but by the middle of the 7th century two families had emerged as particularly important and were the principal agents of the kings, holding office as mayors of the royal palace. One family came from Austrasia, the eastern, traditionally Frankish lands, while the other family was associated with Neustria, the new lands north of the Loire. The conflict between these rivals was ended at Tertry in 687 when the victor was the Austrasian, Pepin of Herstal, near Aachen. He consequently gained a dominant position in the Frankish kingdom which he retained until his death in 714, and which was quickly re-established by his son Charles Martel, 'the Ham-

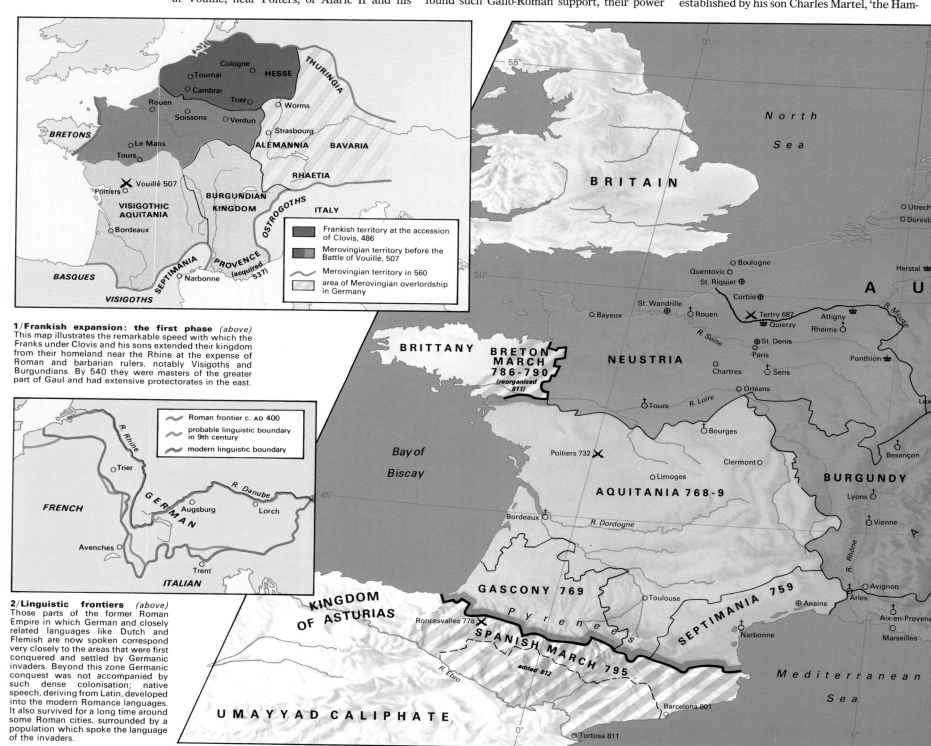

1/Frankish expansion: the first phase *(above)*
This map illustrates the remarkable speed with which the Franks under Clovis and his sons extended their kingdom from their homeland near the Rhine at the expense of Roman and barbarian rulers, notably Visigoths and Burgundians. By 540 they were masters of the greater part of Gaul and had extensive protectorates in the east.

Legend (map 1):
- Frankish territory at the accession of Clovis, 486
- Merovingian territory before the Battle of Vouillé, 507
- Merovingian territory in 560
- area of Merovingian overlordship in Germany

Legend (map 2):
- Roman frontier c. AD 400
- probable linguistic boundary in 9th century
- modern linguistic boundary

2/Linguistic frontiers *(above)*
Those parts of the former Roman Empire in which German and closely related languages like Dutch and Flemish are now spoken correspond very closely to the areas that were first conquered and settled by Germanic invaders. Beyond this zone Germanic conquest was not accompanied by such dense colonisation; native speech, deriving from Latin, developed into the modern Romance languages. It also survived for a long time around some Roman cities, surrounded by a population which spoke the language of the invaders.

mer' (d.741), who gave his name to the Carolingian family.

These men were prepared to rule while the Merovingians, so called because they traced their ancestry back to Clovis' grandfather, Meroveus, continued as kings, but in 751 the situation was transformed when, with the sanction and support of the pope, Charles Martel's son Pepin the Short (d.768) made himself king and so established the new Carolingian dynasty. The Church continued to be a pillar of the monarchy, and Alcuin of York was one of Charlemagne's main advisers. Meanwhile, the new dynasty assumed the traditional responsibilities of Frankish rulers, leading expeditions and defending their territory against such old enemies as the Frisians and the Saxons, as well as combating the new threat posed by the Muslim conquerors of Visigothic Spain. Charles Martel's most famous victory was, in fact, the battle of Poitiers in 732 against Muslim raiders, a victory that was remembered as being of the greatest moment, symbolising the role of the Franks, and of the Carolingians in particular, as defenders of Christendom. That role was first assumed by Clovis and later found its most dramatic expression on Christmas Day 800 at Rome in the imperial coronation of Pepin's son, Charlemagne (Charles the Great), who by conquering and converting the Saxons, by taking over the Lombard kingdom and so liberating the papacy from a persistent threat, and by creating a March, or buffer zone, between the Frankish lands and Muslim Spain, had created a truly imperial and Christian hegemony.

The hegemony was, however, personal. In 806

Charlemagne planned to divide his empire among three sons, a scheme that was frustrated by the death, in his lifetime, of all but one of them, thus making it possible for the survivor, Louis the Pious (814-40) to inherit the whole empire. In providing for such a division Charlemagne was following the Frankish custom of partitioning the royal demesne, a custom that had caused him to share his inheritance for three years with his brother Carloman (see map 4b). This practice can be traced back to the death of Clovis when his four sons partitioned their inheritance. The divisions, which could be very complicated, did not mean the dismemberment of the kingdom, which could still be regarded as a unit and was occasionally united, but they did create many opportunities for internal conflict which the later Merovingians appear to have preferred to external conquest.

Under the Carolingians Frankish expansion was resumed, but it was unlike that of the Merovingians for it led to the displacement of many bishops and counts of Gallo-Roman descent by Franks and Austrasia. The first generations of these Frankish agents of royal government were in general loyal to Pepin and Charlemagne, but their descendants tended to identify with the particular interests of their own localities at the expense of the kingdom, and during the 9th and 10th centuries, as they were able to free themselves from the restraints of royal authority, some established principalities over which the kings could, for a time, claim little more than a theoretical superiority. The Frankish hegemony was therefore disrupted by partition and fragmentation.

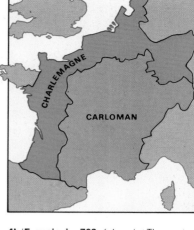

4a/Francia in 587 (above) The treaty of 587 was one of many agreements dividing the Frankish kingdom between the descendants of Clovis. Childebert's portion was in effect ruled by his mother, the Visigoth Brunhild, who dominated Frankish politics until her execution in 613.

4b/Francia in 768 (above) The custom of partitioning the kingdom was continued by the Carolingians: on the death of Pepin the Short (768) his two sons divided their inheritance. The elder, Charlemagne, held most of the key area of Austrasia until Carloman died (771), when he inherited the whole.

The Chapel at Aachen (right) Charlemagne's vast authority in western Europe was reflected by the construction of a large and complex palace in Aachen which was thought by some contemporaries to be a 'second Rome'. It included this chapel, modelled on the 6th-century church of San Vitale in Ravenna which commemorates Justinian, another great emperor who triumphed in Italy.

	Frankish realm 714
	extent of empire 814
	marches in 814 (with date of formation)
⚓	Frankish royal residences
○	archbishoprics
⊕	important monasteries

GASCONY 769 province with date of acquisition

3/The empire of Charlemagne The Frankish Empire reached its greatest extent shortly after Charlemagne's coronation in Rome when a March, or boundary province, was created beyond the Pyrenees. More important extensions of Frankish territory resulted from Charlemagne's seizure in 774 of the Lombard kingdom of Italy and his conquest and conversion of the Saxons, achieved in the face of prolonged and determined resistance.

The Eurasian world in 814

BY 814, the year of the death of the Frankish emperor, Charlemagne, Europe and Asia were recovering from the wave of barbarian invasion which, some four centuries earlier, had disrupted the civilisations of China, Rome and India and severed the trans-Eurasian ties of classical times (see page 94). It was, as events were to prove, a short-lived revival. During the century that followed all the civilisations of Eurasia suffered setbacks, some severe. But the gains at the expense of barbarism, particularly the expansion of the area of settled, civilised life, were more than temporary. By 814 a series of powerful empires stretched in unbroken sequence from the Atlantic to the Pacific, and under their shelter new states with a high level of civilisation took shape on their southern flank, among them the Srivijayan Empire of Sumatra and the Shailendra Empire of Java. In the far east the boundaries of T'ang China extended to the Tarim basin and the Pamirs. In the west the Franks had reunited the territories north of the Alps formerly a part of the Roman Empire. But the decisive factor was the astonishing expansion of Islam (see page 104) which carried the dominion of the Caliph to Bukhara and Samarkand by 710 and provided the essential link between Orient and Occident. After the Arab victory over China at the Talas river in 751 – one of the decisive battles of history – the two powers, with contiguous frontiers, dominated central Asia. Further north, at the western end of the Eurasian steppe, was the empire of the Khazars, the most civilised empire this region had seen since the collapse of Scythian power in the 3rd century BC. Converted to Judaism c.740, the Khazars ruled a vast territory extending west as far as Sambat (the future Kiev) and south to Kherson, and their capital Itil, a populous and highly civilised city, was one of the great commercial centres of the period. Only India, after the collapse of Harsha's short-lived empire (606-47), failed to reconstitute some sort of unity, and the Arabs, who had conquered Sind in 711, remained in possession.

More stable conditions were accomplished by a revival of trans-Eurasian relations. China under the T'ang dynasty was unusually open to foreign contacts, and the unification of the vast areas under Arab rule led, particularly after the succession of the Abbasids in 750, to a great expansion of trade. Diplomatic relations also became closer. The caliph, Harun al-Rashid (786-809), who probably sent embassies to Charlemagne in 797 and 801, also despatched envoys to conclude a treaty of alliance with the T'ang emperor in 798. By 758 there was a large establishment of Muslim merchants in Kanfu (Canton) and a century later we hear of Chinese in Baghdad; and in far-away England Offa of Mercia (757-96), who had fairly close diplomatic relations with Charlemagne, issued a gold coin copied from the dinar struck by the Caliph al-Mansur in 774. All this suggests active commerce from one end of the Eurasian heartland to the other. Chinese porcelain, in particular, was prized throughout the Middle East and quantities have been found in 9th-century sites as far afield as Tarsus and Cairo. The art of papermaking, learned from Chinese prisoners taken at Talas in 751, spread rapidly across the Islamic world, reaching Spain by 900; already under Harun al-Rashid the first paper mills were operating in Baghdad.

Although T'ang civilisation had passed its peak after 755, the Chinese empire was still pre-eminent in 814. Measured by almost any standard of comparison, China and Islam, even India and the countries of Indo-China, far surpassed Europe in the level of civilisation. It is characteristic that, while Chia Tan in 801 was compiling a map of China drawn to a scale of 100 *li* to an inch (2.5 cm) – a map which measured roughly 9 by 10 metres and covered an area of 16,000 by 17,600 km – geographical knowledge in the West was so embedded in myth that Jerusalem was believed to be the centre of the world, and the Nile, Euphrates and Ganges were

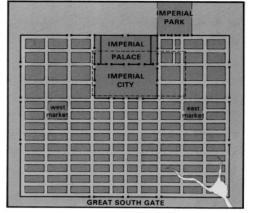

2/Ch'ang-an *(left)* Planned as a massive rectangle, 9.4 km from east to west and 8.4 km from north to south, with eleven great north-south avenues, the main avenue led from the imperial palace to the south gate. It was no less than 153 m wide, intersecting 14 east-west thoroughfares, and dividing the city into 106 separate wards. Ch'ang-an probably had a million inhabitants within the walls and another million in the suburbs outside. Already by 722 it contained 91 Buddhist and 16 Taoist places of worship, 4 Zoroastrian temples, and 2 Nestorian Christian churches.

3/Constantinople *(left)* Constantinople never grew beyond the walls of Theodosius II (c. 447) and within the walls there was much vacant space. Historians have tended to exaggerate its population, which at the beginning of the 9th century was probably less than a quarter of a million. Nevertheless it was, with the possible exception of Córdoba, the greatest city of Europe, far excelling any city in the Christian west, including Rome, which at this time was in a state of decline.

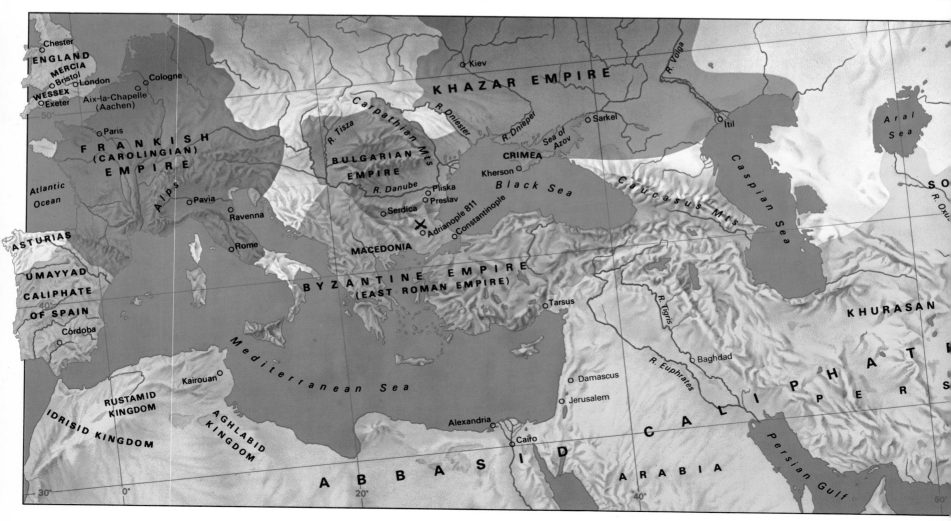

4/Baghdad *(right)* Founded in 762 by the caliph al-Mansur, who employed 100,000 men on the building. The circular city, with a diameter of 2638 metres, surrounded by a rampart with 360 towers, was almost immediately too small for the growing population. By the time of Harun al-Rashid it had expanded south to the suburb of *al-karh*, home of commerce and artisans, and east to the residential quarters near the Caliph's new palace, *Dar al-khilafa*. By 814 it was probably the world's largest city.

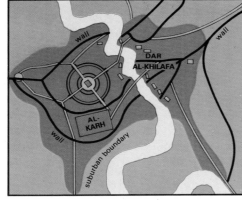

5/Córdoba *(right)* Córdoba, housing perhaps half a million Muslims, Christians and Jews, was already the leading city west of Constantinople by the end of the 8th century. Outside the original walled city, planned as a rectangle resting on the river front, with ramparts measuring about 4 km, was a series of suburbs. According to a contemporary Arab writer, Córdoba contained 471 mosques, 213,077 houses for workers and traders, 60,000 residences for officials and courtiers, and 80,455 shops. It was also the seat of a university of international repute.

6/Aix-la-Chapelle *(right)* Almost nothing is known of Charlemagne's residence before he built his palace and chapel there in the 790s. It was certainly in no sense a city, though the palace attracted a few Christian and Jewish traders, and some officials had built themselves houses by 828. The massive Romanesque church (48.6 m long and 35 m wide) is impressive, but Aix remained small, with a population probably of no more than two or three thousand, until it was destroyed by the Vikings in the second half of the 9th century. The modern city of Aachen descends from the new foundation of the 12th century.

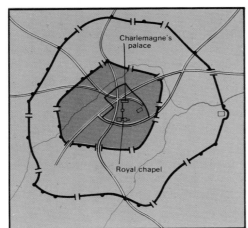

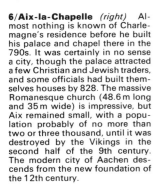

Cities in comparison *(left)* This diagram gives some idea of the comparative size of the Eurasian capitals c. 814. Clearly Charlemagne's 'royal city' does not compare with the great capitals of the Chinese and Arab empires, or even with Constantinople.

considered to have a common source in the Garden of Eden. Architecturally, also, no contemporary European building approaches in majesty the magnificent temples erected during this period at Prambanan in Java.

The Carolingian Empire, though hardly as large as the area controlled by the Khazars, was impressive in size, but, like the Bulgarian Empire flanking the Byzantine Empire in the north, it was little more than the conquest of a barbarian warband, which fell apart, only thirty years after Charlemagne's death, when its warlike energies flagged. Such empires could be dangerous militarily, as was seen in 811 when the Bulgarians under Krum (802-14) inflicted a crushing defeat on the Roman emperor Nicephorus. But, unlike China and Rome and the Caliphate, they lacked the resources and organisation – particularly the financial and bureaucratic organisation – to give them stability. The East Roman Empire, hemmed in by Arabs and Bulgars, was weak and ineffective between 780 and 820. After 751, when the Lombards conquered Ravenna and drove out the emperor's viceroy (the Exarch), its authority in Italy was only nominal, and this made it possible for Charlemagne to usurp the imperial title in 800. But the sound administration inherited from the Heraclian and Isaurian emperors enabled Byzantium not only to survive but to mount a remarkable revival under Basil I (866-86) and Leo VI (886-912). In the West, by contrast, this was the period when fuedalism, spreading from its home in northern France, became endemic. Charlemagne had attempted to hold the power of the aristocracy in check by making the counts into removable officials and sending out royal agents (*missi dominici*) to supervise their activities. But the system was too rudimentary to work; within a few years of Charlemagne's death the relationship of lord and vassal displaced that of ruler and subject as the bond of political society, and royal authority went into eclipse.

The contrast between the civilisations of Eurasia at this period is nowhere better illustrated than in their capital cities. Characteristically, the Frankish Empire, with its backward agricultural economy, had none. Rome, which Charlemagne never revisited between 800 and his death in 814, was in full decline, and there is no sign that he ever thought of reviving it. It is possible that he had a vision of creating a fixed capital at Aix-la-Chapelle, where he built himself a palace and a large and impressive chapel (see page 106) modelled upon San Vitale at Ravenna, the last capital of the Roman Empire in the west. But if so, little came of it. Carolingian writers described Aix grandiloquently as a 'royal city' (*urbs regalis*), but it is unlikely to have had more than a couple of thousand inhabitants and did not compare in any way with Constantinople, the capital of the (East) Roman Empire, or with Córdoba, the capital of Umayyad Spain, still less with Ch'ang-an, capital of T'ang China. Even after the foundation of the Abbasid capital, Baghdad, in 762 Ch'ang-an remained the outstanding city of Eurasia, so impressive that the Yamato rulers of Japan used it as a model for their capitals at Nara (710) and Kyoto (794). In the West no city equalled Córdoba, though its period of greatest renown was the 10th century (912-61). But the most astonishing phenomenon was the stupendous growth of Baghdad, which had spilled out by the death of Harun al-Rashid from the original circular city, Madinat as-Salam ('the City of Peace'), and by 814 covered an area of approximately 10 by 9km, the equivalent of modern Paris within the outer boulevards. The West had still a long way to go before it caught up.

The temple of Shiva *(above)* The great 9th-century temple of Shiva at Prambanan in Java shows both the extension of Hindu influence and the remarkable artistic and architectural achievement of Indonesian civilisation at this period. Only the great mosques of Damascus, Kairouan and Córdoba compare in scale and magnificence.

1/Eurasia in 814 The expansion of Islam and the stabilising influence it exerted in central Asia did much to restore the contacts between the eastern and western halves of the Eurasian heartland which had been disrupted by barbarian invasions in the 4th and 5th centuries. But the west was still on the periphery and its participation in the recovery was limited.

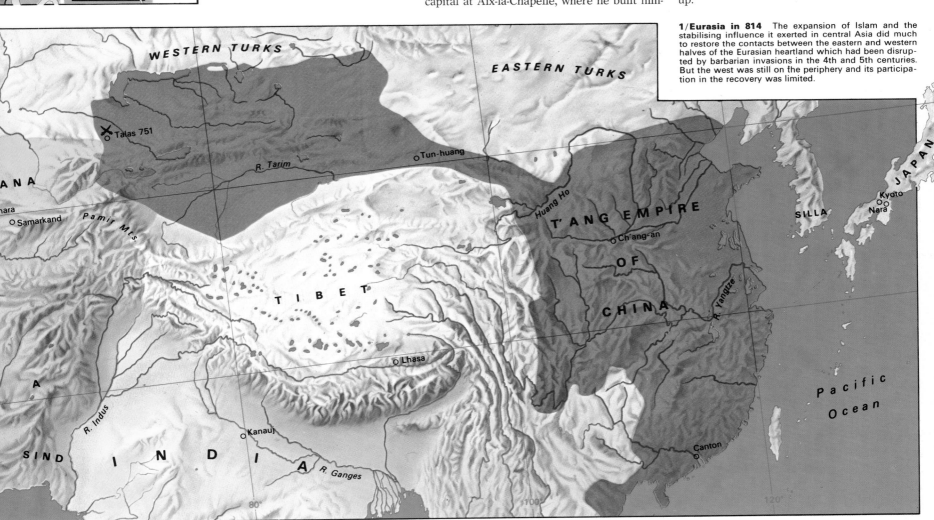

The 9th and 10th century invasions of Europe: Vikings, Magyars, Saracens

2/Scandinavian colonies in Britain and France *(above)* The first Viking colonists were Norwegians; from their new homes they raided the coasts of Western Europe. The Danes, who had tended to raid the rich lowlands of England and Francia, astonished the English in 876 by sharing out some of the conquered land and beginning to farm it, leaving a permanent linguistic mark on eastern and northern England.

T HE relatively effective rule of the Carolingians in western Europe (see page 106) and of the Mercians in England gave some assurance of security from internal attacks to both religious communities and merchants, and in the 8th century abbeys and markets were not fortified and Roman defences were not kept in repair. The accumulations of wealth in such places did, however, offer tempting bait to external raiders, men who accepted neither the religious sanctions that generally protected the holy places of the Christian west nor the authority of Christian kings, and in the 9th and 10th centuries western Europe suffered attacks from three separate groups of such strangers: Saracens, Magyars and Vikings.

The Saracen raids were an extension of Islamic conquest, and after the occupation of Sicily, completed by 827, Muslim pirates established bases on the coast of southern Italy, and later in southern Gaul, from which they were able to threaten large areas of southern Europe. Corsica and Sardinia were frequently attacked and many monasteries and towns in Italy (including Rome itself) and in Gaul were pillaged, while merchants and pilgrims were robbed or forced to pay large ransoms for their release from captivity. The main credit for driving the pirates from their Italian bases was due to the forces of the Byzantine Empire.

The Magyars posed a different kind of threat. They were horsemen who moved into the Hungarian plain in the last years of the 9th century and almost immediately began to plunder the neighbouring areas, first northern Italy, then Germany and on their longest raids deep into France. Their advantages of speed and surprise made opposition difficult, and in open country their horsemanship was markedly superior to that of their German or Italian opponents, but in mountainous country and at river crossings, especially when returning home laden with booty, they were more vulnerable and German rulers had some successes against them. The threat was finally ended by the victory of Otto I at Lechfeld near Augsburg in 955, after which the Magyar leaders were executed and the assimilation of the Magyars into western Christendom began.

The Vikings also had the advantage of surprise when they descended on the coasts and rivers of western Europe but, unlike the Magyars, they could be colonists as well as raiders. Once the Norwegians had discovered that there were islands in the North Atlantic with an environment very similar to that of their homeland, many were prepared to look for a better life overseas, particularly when Harald Fairhair tried to unify the country. The Danes also settled overseas, no doubt partly because there were better opportunities for plundering and extorting treasure in western Europe than in Scandinavia. The Norwegian and Danish leaders of expeditions appear to have been exiles who had been banished for offences, or members of unsuccessful branches of royal families who, having failed to make themselves kings, hoped to gain both wealth and reputation in the west.

The earliest Viking raids were towards the end of the eighth century – the best known though probably not the first, was on the Northumbrian monastery of Lindisfarne in 793. In the following century several Norwegian bases were established in Ireland, the most famous being Dublin, founded by 841, and from such places warrior chiefs led expeditions to plunder not only the monasteries and other centres in Ireland, but also in Britain and further afield. The Danish attacks began about a generation later than the Norwegian, with a raid on the market of Dorestad in 834, the first of a series of regular attacks on that place. By the middle of the century bands of Danes were making their way by boat and horse to attack churches and towns in many parts of Britain and the Frankish Empire. To facilitate these raids they established bases, some of which eventually became centres of permanent Scandinavian settlement, such as the Five Boroughs of the English Midlands. In such colonies the Vikings lost their advantages of mobility and surprise and were vulnerable to pressure that eventually led them to accept both the overlordship of French and English kings and conversion to Christianity.

At the same time as these western enterprises, Swedes were crossing the Baltic to visit markets, notably Bolgar on the middle Volga, in which Muslims were eager to acquire furs and slaves that the Swedes, and others, could gather in the forests of northern Russia. Swedish leaders who made themselves masters of such places as Kiev and Novgorod were soon slavicised, and maintained no more than dynastic links with Scandinavia. The rulers of Kiev came into contact with Byzantium but its influence was religious and cultural rather than economic, and the main markets for the produce of the Kiev region continued to be the Islamic east rather than the Byzantine south.

This sudden extension of Scandinavian activity overseas was in part caused by the growing demand for goods that could only be obtained from the north; walrus tusks were at that time the main source of ivory in Europe and furs from the arctic regions of Scandinavia and Russia were greatly prized. On the eve of the Viking period there was a growing commerce in coastal markets called *wics*. The greatest of these was the Wijk at Dorestad but there were many others, including Quentovic, near Boulogne, and Hamwic, later to develop into Southampton. Scandinavians were encouraged to search even further afield for fresh supplies of skins, furs and tusks and a contemporary account by a 9th-

3/Viking trade *(left)* Scandinavia and the lands east of the Baltic were important in the luxury trade of the Dark Ages as the only source of furs and ivory and a good source of slaves. In response to the demand for these goods, first in western Europe and later in the Muslim east, Scandinavians such as Ottar ventured far afield in search of new supplies.

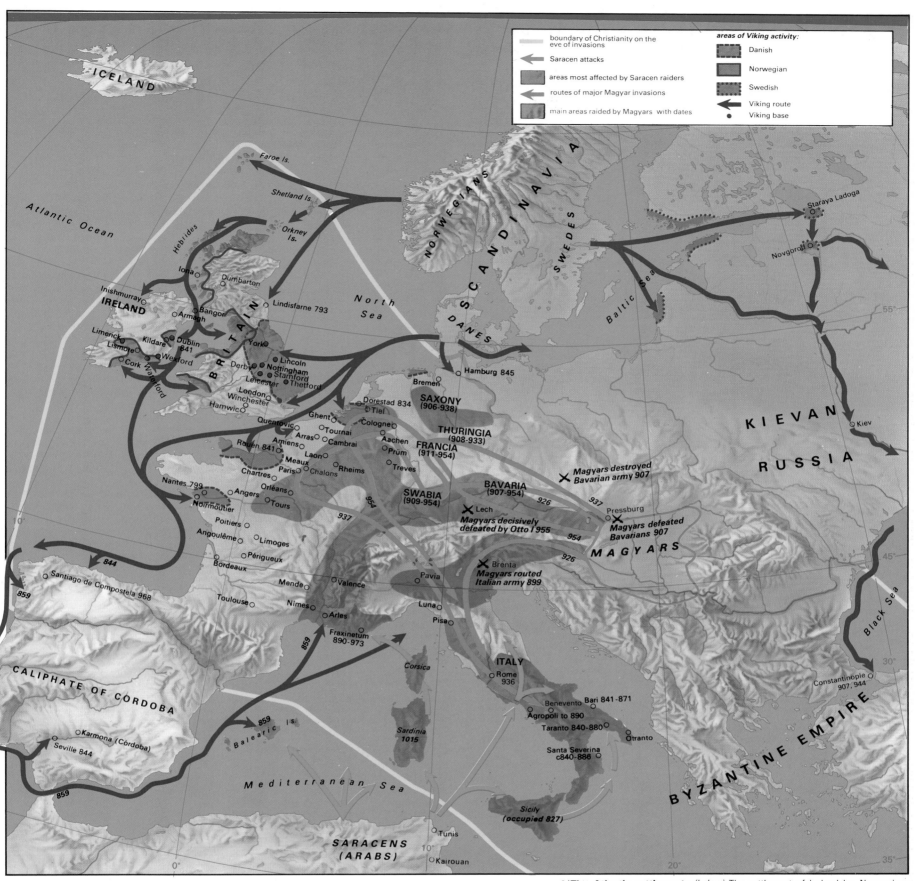

areas of Viking activity:

boundary of Christianity on the eve of invasions

Saracen attacks

areas most affected by Saracen raiders

routes of major Magyar invasions

main areas raided by Magyars with dates

Danish

Norwegian

Swedish

Viking route

Viking base

ICELAND

Atlantic Ocean

Faroe Is.

Shetland Is.

NORWEGIANS

SCANDINAVIA

SWEDES

Staraya Ladoga

Orkney Is.

Hebrides

Novgorod

Iona
Dumbarton

North Sea

DANES

Baltic Sea

Inishmurray
IRELAND
Armagh Bangor
Limerick
Lismore Kildare Dublin 841
Cork Wexford
Waterford

Lindisfarne 793

B R I T A I N

York
Lincoln
Derby Nottingham
Leicester Stamford
Thetford
London
Winchester
Hamwic

K I E V A N

R U S S I A

Kiev

Hamburg 845

Bremen

Quentovic
Dorestad 834
Tiel
Ghent Cologne
Arras Tournai Aachen
Amiens Cambrai Prüm
Rouen 841 Laon Treves
Meaux Rheims
Chartres Paris Chalons
Nantes 799 Orleans
Angers
Noirmoutier Tours
Poitiers
Angoulême Limoges
Périgueux
Bordeaux

SAXONY (906-938)

THURINGIA (908-933)

FRANCIA (911-954)

954

937

SWABIA (909-954)

BAVARIA (907-954)

Lech
Magyars decisively defeated by Otto I 955

✕ *Magyars destroyed Bavarian army 907*

926

937 Pressburg
Magyars defeated Bavarians 907

954

926

M A G Y A R S

✕ Brenta
Magyars routed Italian army 899

844

859

Santiago de Compostela 968

Mende
Toulouse Nimes Valence
Arles
Fraxinetum 890-973

859

859

Pavia
Luna
Pisa

Corsica

ITALY

Rome 936

Benevento Bari 841-871
Agropoli to 890
Taranto 840-880
Otranto
Santa Severina c840-886

Constantinople 907, 944

B Y Z A N T I N E   E M P I R E

Black Sea

CALIPHATE OF CORDOBA

Karmona (Córdoba)
Seville 844

859

Balearic Is.

Sardinia 1015

Mediterranean Sea

Sicily (occupied 827)

Tunis

Kairouan

S A R A C E N S (ARABS)

---

century Norwegian, Ottar, tells of a voyage he made from his home in northern Norway into the White Sea in search of walrus.

Although the Vikings contributed to the consolidation of early Russia (see page 114), in England the kings of Wessex, particularly Edward the Elder (899-924) and Athelstan (924-99) fought back, and in Gaul the Frankish rulers virtually capitulated, leaving defence to the local magnates. The result was the fragmentation of public authority and a great upsurge of feudalism which, though it had originated earlier in the dark days of the 7th century, had been held in check by Charlemagne. Even in England the number of free cultivators declined, as freemen commended themselves to lords for protection. In Gaul peasant freemen virtually disappeared and society was polarized between nobles and serfs. In Germany also power devolved into the hands of dukes and margraves who guarded the frontiers. From the beginning of the 10th century the map of western Europe was a feudal map, an intricate interlacing of counties, communities, principalities and lordships, and it was not until the 12th century that consolidation again got under way.

1/The invasions *(above)* No part of the Christian West was immune from external attack in the 9th and 10th centuries. From their base in the Hungarian Plain the Magyars traversed vast distances, but as they moved fast the disruption they caused was short-lived. Saracens and Vikings established bases in the West and were consequently a more persistent threat; the Saracens were eventually expelled, but the Norwegian and Danish invaders were in time assimilated, as were the Swedes, who had gone east in search of wealth among the Slavs and Finns.

4/The Atlantic settlements *(below)* The settlement of Iceland by Norwegians began in about 870 and was completed in two generations. Later emigrants travelling in ships such as that illustrated below found limited opportunities there, but after the discovery of Greenland in the last years of the 10th century some went on to create new settlements which survived for some five centuries. The Vikings reached Newfoundland, but no permanent settlements have been found either here or further south. The location of Vinland of the sagas is disputed.

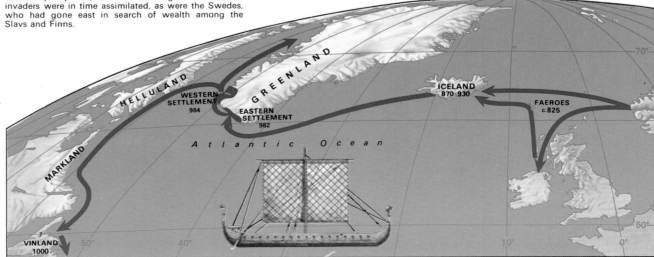

HELLULAND

GREENLAND

WESTERN SETTLEMENT 984

EASTERN SETTLEMENT 982

ICELAND 870-930

FAEROES c.825

Atlantic Ocean

MARKLAND

VINLAND 1000

The Byzantine Empire from Heraclius to the Fourth Crusade: 610 to 1204

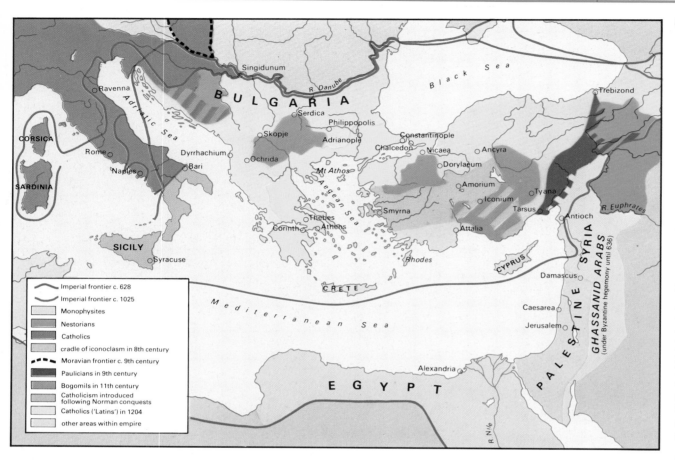

THE reign of Heraclius (610-41) marked in many ways the end of the East Roman Empire and the true beginnings of that distinctive, Greek-speaking, Christian, culturally heterogeneous form of civilisation known as Byzantine. Its first years saw the final titanic struggle with Persia, so long Rome's most formidable rival, culminating in Heraclius's crushing victory at Nineveh in 628. But before his death the Emperor saw his southern and eastern frontiers everywhere under attack, as the new forces of Islam (see page 104) burst out of Arabia, seized Palestine, Syria and the ruins of Persia, and embarked on their triumphant westward advance. For the next two centuries, increasingly isolated from the West, Byzantium was forced to mobilise its whole society for its struggle against Islam.

Constantinople withstood two long Arab sieges, from 674-8 and again 717-8. But the struggle was not only with the Arabs. About 680, the Turkic Bulgars flooded into the land now known as Bulgaria. By the 8th century they too constituted a serious threat, with armed outposts less than sixty miles from Constantinople itself. Equally seriously, the Empire was wracked with internal religious dissension. Starting with Leo III, the emperor who forced the Arabs to abandon the second siege of Constantinople, successive emperors imposed a stringent ban on Christian images. Iconoclasm produced a large crop of martyrs and exiles, and lasted, with only one break, from 726 to 843.

Soon after it was reversed, Byzantium, under a fresh and vigorous Macedonian dynasty of emperors, embarked on a new era of aggressive expansion. Its dominions, which in 610 still stretched from Gibraltar to the Euphrates, had dramatically shrunk. In the west, the only remaining toeholds were in southern Italy, Sicily and along the Dalmatian coast; Greece, though reconquest had already begun, was still largely in the hands of barbarian Slavs; in the embattled

2/The Conflict of Doctrines *(above)* Monophysite/Nestorian disputes over nature of Christ ended with Arab conquests. Paulicians and Bogomils (9th-10th centuries) preached varieties of Manicheism.

3/The 'themes' and Arab invasions *(left)* The *themes* were administrative districts and army units, peasants were granted farms in exchange for war service. They prevented Arab settlement, despite raids.

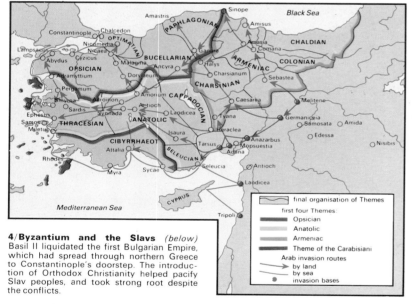

4/Byzantium and the Slavs *(below)* Basil II liquidated the first Bulgarian Empire, which had spread through northern Greece to Constantinople's doorstep. The introduction of Orthodox Christianity helped pacify Slav peoples, and took strong root despite the conflicts.

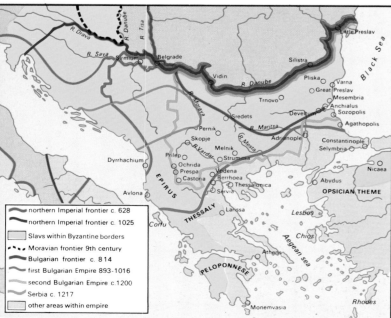

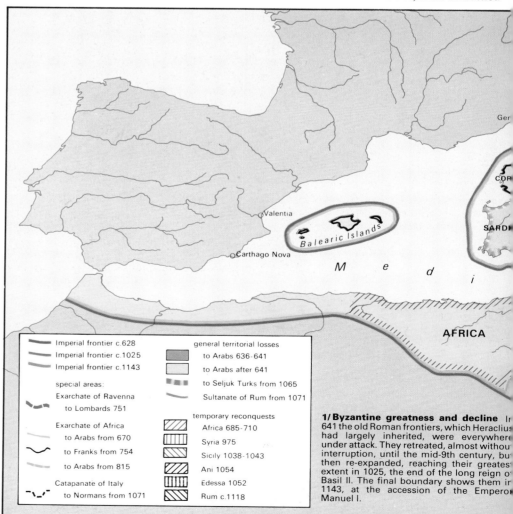

1/Byzantine greatness and decline In 641 the old Roman frontiers, which Heraclius had largely inherited, were everywhere under attack. They retreated, almost without interruption, until the mid-9th century, but then re-expanded, reaching their greatest extent in 1025, the end of the long reign of Basil II. The final boundary shows them in 1143, at the accession of the Emperor Manuel I.

and devastated wastes of Asia Minor the frontier ran roughly from Trebizond to Tarsus; and apart from Constantinople the great Roman cities of the past – Antioch, Alexandria, Beirut, Caesarea, Gaza – were all under Arab rule. But now, all this was to change.

Between 863, when a strong force of Arabs was annihilated at Poson, on the Halys river in Anatolia, and the death of the great warrior-emperor Basil II (976-1025), a series of dramatic victories pushed back the frontiers, often close to where they had been in the heyday of Rome. In the south-east the Arabs had at one stage (976) been driven back to the very gates of Jerusalem; the Russian axe-men had been held and routed at Silistra, on the Danube; Bulgaria, after long, bitter campaigning, was now reduced to a group of Byzantine provinces; and Basil, after defeating Bulgars, Armenians, Georgians, Arabs and Normans, was preparing to retake Italy, and possibly Africa beyond.

But it was not to be. Byzantium, outwardly at the height of its prosperity and power, was seriously overextended. Basil, unmarried, was succeeded by women and weaker men. The new frontiers, exhaustingly won, proved indefensible, especially as the previously invincible Byzantine military machine now found itself starved of funds by a civilian administration which feared it. Within fifty years, in 1071, a much weakened Byzantine army was smashed by a force of Seljuk Turks at the battle of Manzikert (see page 134). In the same year, the last Italian possession fell to the Normans; and the period of greatness, when Constantinople ruled the wealthiest and best-governed realm in the Christian world, was at an end.

Paradoxically, the 11th and 12th centuries were artistically and theologically among the most fertile in Byzantine history when the social and institutional links which had previously held the multilingual Empire together gradually fell into decay. Indeed, despite the disasters of 1071-81, when the Turks established permanent occupation of the Anatolian plateau and the Normans consolidated their Sicilian gains, it proved possible, under the brilliant trio of Comnenian emperors, to sustain the illusion of Byzantium's universal dominion for another hundred years. But it remained an illusion. For all their genius, Alexius I, John II and Manuel I were unable to recover much of the vast territory that had been lost; and when they had gone,

there was little spirit left to resist the final assault.

This came, not from the traditional enemy, the Muslim infidel, but from the Christian West. The real collapse, however, was from within. Byzantium's strength, apart from its religious cohesion, was two-fold – the themes with their independent freeholding peasantry, ready both to farm well and to defend its land, and an army and navy often manned by native Asian officers and troops. At least since 1000 these advantages had scarcely existed. In the 11th and 12th centuries, mercenaries (often themselves Seljuk, Muslim or Norman) formed the bulk of the armed forces, and the Empire, whose only hereditary office had been that of the Emperor himself, fell more and more into the ambitious hands of a few rich, dynastic families. These owed much of their new wealth and power to the Byzantine form of feudalism, the *pronoia* system, under which key state functions, including tax collection, were handed over to large local land-owners – originally for their lifetime, but increasingly on a hereditary basis.

It was an already seriously weakened Byzantium which saw the arrival of the First Crusade

in 1096, but hopes that Rome and Constantinople could co-exist peacefully were soon dashed. There had been tension, if not actual schism between the Roman and Orthodox churches since 1054 (see page 100). Both Seljuks and Normans resumed full-scale frontier aggression in the 1170s. By 1180 Serbia was virtually independent; Hungary absorbed Dalmatia; Bulgaria and Wallachia rose; independent feudal rulers detached whole provinces – Cyprus (1184), Philadelphia (1186), Eastern Morea (1189); and in 1204 the final blow fell when Constantinople itself was seized and ravaged by the swordsmen of the Fourth Crusade. The immediate beneficiary was the rising power of Venice, whose fleets had carried the Crusaders. But the attempt to set up a Latin Empire of Constantinople proved abortive. Now for the first time, the Greeks had become a majority within the truncated Empire, and in 1261, aided by Genoa, the rival of Venice, they drove out the westerners. But the Greek empire was only a shadow of the Byzantium of the past and, rent by civil war, was no match for the Turks when they advanced into Europe in the 14th century. It was a very different Byzantium which now entered the later Middle Ages.

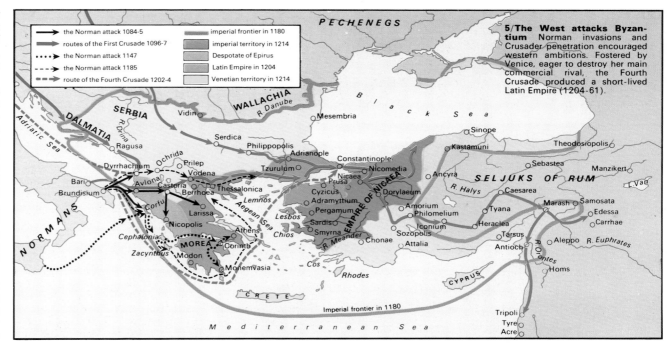

5/**The West attacks Byzantium** Norman invasions and Crusader penetration encouraged western ambitions. Fostered by Venice, eager to destroy her main commercial rival, the Fourth Crusade produced a short-lived Latin Empire (1204-61).

→ the Norman attack 1084-5	imperial frontier in 1180
→ routes of the First Crusade 1096-7	imperial territory in 1214
···▶ the Norman attack 1147	Despotate of Epirus
--▶ the Norman attack 1185	Latin Empire in 1204
--▶ route of the Fourth Crusade 1202-4	Venetian territory in 1214

The City Walls (above) Constantinople is isolated from the land by a double line, and from the sea by a single line, of turreted walls. The inner landward bastion, 30 feet high and 16 feet thick, was breached only once, in 1453.

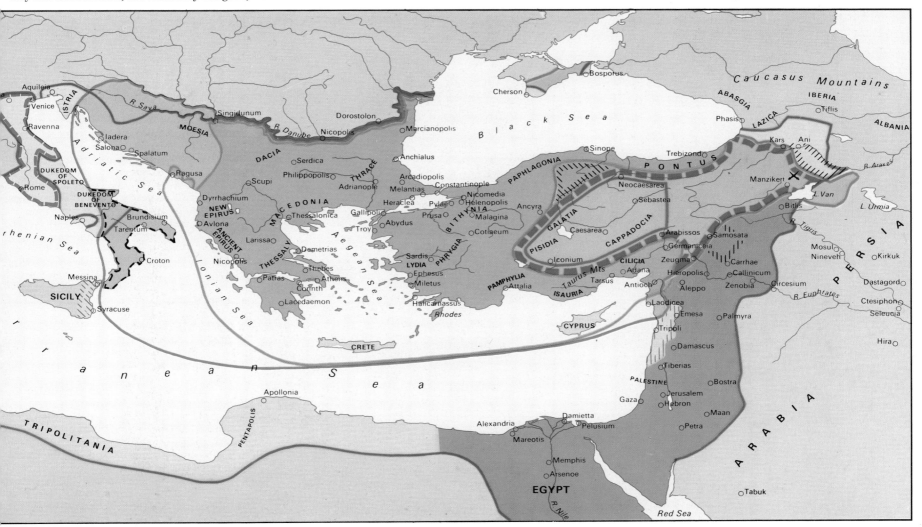

The first Russian state: Kievan Russia 882 to 1245

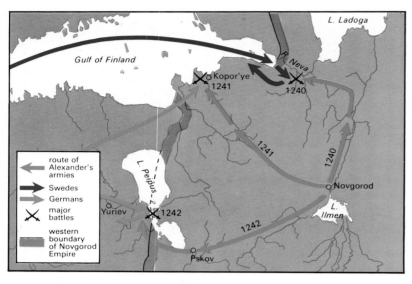

2/The campaigns of Alexander of Novgorod *(above)* An attempt by Swedes and Germans to drive Russia from the Baltic was frustrated. Alexander's decisive victory on the Neva earned him the title 'Nevsky' Two years later he defeated the Germans.

3/Vegetation belts and early migrations *(left)* The first Russian state was established by the Vikings with the Dnieper as its axis. It lay athwart the northern forest and the southern steppe. Kiev was a natural capital.

forest belt with marshes	associated waterway trade route
wooded steppe	movement of nomadic peoples
open steppe	movements of East Slavs and Russians
Viking route	

4/The Mongol onslaught on Russia *(below)* Until 1236 northern Russia was immune from the steppe nomads' raids, and its centres prospered, but in the winter of 1237-38 the Mongols struck north into the forest and subjugated its princes.

DURING the period 882 to 1242 Russia was subject to powerful external influences: as a political unit it was first hammered into shape by Vikings from the north; it then received Christianity from Byzantium in the south; and it was ultimately overthrown by the Mongol Tartars from the east.

The contrast between forest and steppe was of prime importance at this time. Before the arrival of the Vikings in the 9th century the East Slavs were pushing eastwards from Europe into the woodlands of central Russia, while hordes of nomadic horsemen moved westwards across the southern steppes from Asia. The rivers assumed significance with the coming of the Vikings, who established, dominated and exploited trade routes along the waterways; the first Russian state originated in their determination to control the lands adjoining them. Because the rivers of Russia have a general north to south and south to north direction, there was great potential for trade between northern Europe and the Baltic on the one hand, and southern Europe and the Black Sea on the other; both the main trade routes and the ensuing political unit ran north and south, across the east to west trending belts of forest and steppe which, however, proved too strong for a north-south alignment, based upon the rivers, to survive. The history of Kievan Russia, the first Russian state, is dominated by the constant struggle and ultimate failure of the Russians to hold on to their steppe territory, which became once more the undisputed realm of westward-migrating nomads. Instead, they resumed the historic eastward colonisation of the forest belt.

The principal waterway route established by the Vikings (known to the Slavs as *Varyagi* or *Varangians*) ran from the Gulf of Finland up the river Neva, through Lake Ladoga, the river Volkhov, and thence by portages to the Dnieper, and on across the Black Sea to Byzantium. This was the 'route from the Varyagi to the Greeks' referred to by the earliest writers. As the Vikings pushed their control southwards, Novgorod, Smolensk and Kiev (in 882) became in turn their headquarters. Kiev grew rapidly as the new state's flourishing capital. Its links with Byzantium, its chief trading partner, were strong, and from Byzantium it received the Christian faith during the reign of Vladimir Svyatoslavich (980-1015).

At the time of the Viking incursions the Khazars and their vassals, the Magyars, held the steppes, but by the 10th century the formerly nomadic Khazars had largely become merchants and farmers. The Russians were able to hold the lands of the lower Pruth, the Dniester and Bug, and to maintain control of the Dnieper route to the Black Sea. Grand Prince Svyatoslav (962-72) determined to strengthen and expand this Russian grip by crushing the Khazars. But by destroying the relatively peaceful Khazars, Svyatoslav opened the way to the fierce Pechenegi who henceforth dominated the south Russian steppes until displaced by the equally warlike Polovtsy. Vladimir I (980-1015) had some defensive success against the Pechenegi, but Kiev was sacked by the Polovtsy in 1093.

Weakened by its perpetual conflict with the nomads, the Kievan state broke up into a number of independent and often warring principalities after 1054. While the southern lands emptied in the face of cruel Polovtsy raids, steady colonisation of the forest increased the populations of the northern and central principalities, giving them the strength to throw off Kievan suzerainty. Novgorod, which had built up a great fur-trading empire reaching to the Urals and beyond, and Vladimir-Suzdal, which contained the fast-growing commercial centre of Moscow (first mentioned in 1147), were the foremost of these forest principalities. On the eve of the Mongol attack of 1237, Vladimir-Suzdal was about to challenge the Volga Bulgars, whose stranglehold on the middle Volga region was an obstacle to further Russian expansion eastward. Nizhni Novgorod was built as a first move in this campaign.

The Mongol invasion was perhaps the most traumatic event in Russian history. The Mongols had made an exploratory raid into the steppes in 1221, defeating a combined Russian and Polovtsy force in the Kalka river in 1223. In 1237 they returned in strength and struck first at the middle and upper Volga regions, hitherto immune from nomadic attack. In the winter of 1237-38, when the protective rivers were frozen, they overcame the Volga Bulgars and set upon Vladimir-Suzdal, destroying its prosperous towns. Only the approach of spring saved Novgorod, as the invaders dared not be caught by the thaw among its surrounding marshes. In 1239 it was the turn of south-west Russia, which suffered annihilation. Kiev itself was sacked in 1240, along with hundreds of other settlements.

Novgorod, although it escaped the Mongol fury, had to stave off incessant attacks from Swedes and Germans in the Baltic region. Prince Alexander beat the Swedes decisively on the river Neva in 1240, and the Germans on the ice of Lake Peipus in 1242; yet even he had to recognise the Mongol overlordship.

The Mongol invasion had lasting economic, social and political effects. Those peasants who survived, oppressed by the tribute the Mongols exacted, lost all hope of rising above the barest subsistence. The destruction of the leading cities, where handicrafts had flourished, reduced life to a barbarous level. The Mongols themselves soon withdrew to the steppes, and although they restricted their direct intervention to punitive expeditions when necessary, and to the appointment of local, but immensely powerful, revenue collecting agents, their influence was all-pervasive. The elimination of the urban middle classes smoothed the path of an autocracy which imitated its Mongol overlords in ruthless terror and efficient extortion.

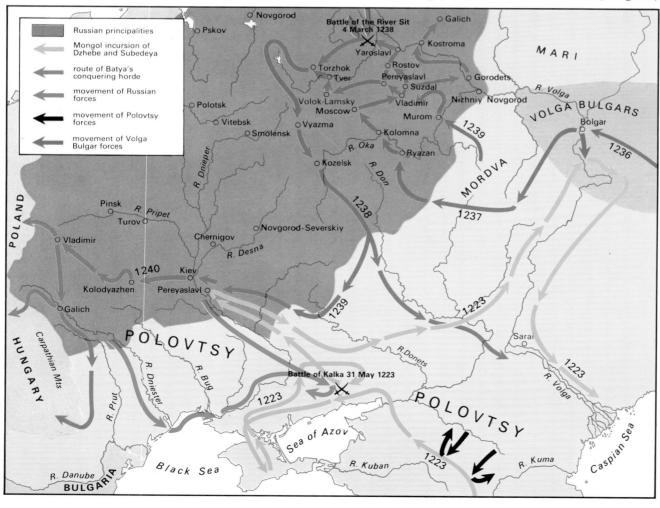

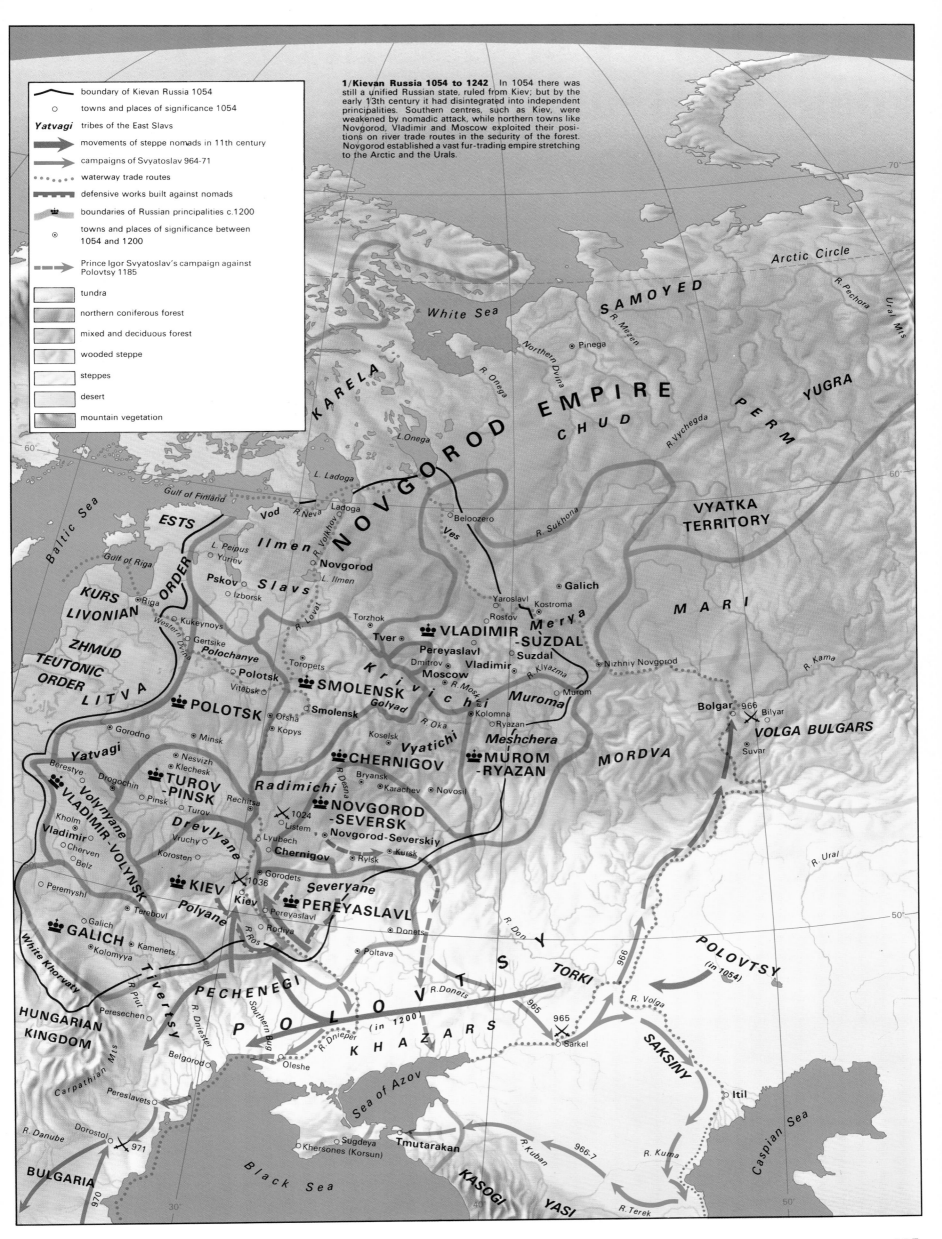

Legend

⌒⌒	boundary of Kievan Russia 1054
○	towns and places of significance 1054
Yatvagi	tribes of the East Slavs
➜	movements of steppe nomads in 11th century
→	campaigns of Svyatoslav 964-71
⋯⋯	waterway trade routes
▬▬	defensive works built against nomads
♔⌒⌒	boundaries of Russian principalities c.1200
⊙	towns and places of significance between 1054 and 1200
⇢	Prince Igor Svyatoslav's campaign against Polovtsy 1185
	tundra
	northern coniferous forest
	mixed and deciduous forest
	wooded steppe
	steppes
	desert
	mountain vegetation

1/Kievan Russia 1054 to 1242 In 1054 there was still a unified Russian state, ruled from Kiev; but by the early 13th century it had disintegrated into independent principalities. Southern centres, such as Kiev, were weakened by nomadic attack, while northern towns like Novgorod, Vladimir and Moscow exploited their positions on river trade routes in the security of the forest. Novgorod established a vast fur-trading empire stretching to the Arctic and the Urals.

Arctic Circle

R. Pechora
Ural Mts
SAMOYED
R. Mezen
White Sea
○ Pinega
KARELA
NOVGOROD EMPIRE
CHUD
PERM
YUGRA
R. Onega
Northern Dvina
R. Vychegda
L. Onega
○ Beloozero
R. Sukhona
VYATKA
TERRITORY
Gulf of Finland
Vod
R. Neva
Ladoga
Ves
○ Galich
MARI
Baltic Sea
ESTS
Ilmen
L. Volkhov
Yaroslavl
Kostroma
L. Peipus
○ Yuriev
Novgorod
Rostov ○
Merya
R. Kama
Gulf of Riga
ORDER
Pskov ○
Slavs
L. Ilmen
♔ VLADIMIR
KURS
Izborsk
Torzhok
Tver
-SUZDAL
○ Nizhniy Novgorod
LIVONIAN
○ Riga
Kukeynoys
Krivichi
Pereyaslavl
Suzdal
ZHMUD
Western Dvina
Toropets
Dmitrov
Vladimir
R. Klyazma
Bolgar ○ 966
TEUTONIC
Gertsike
Polochanye
Moscow
○ Murom
Bilyar
ORDER
Polotsk
R. Moskva
VOLGA BULGARS
LITVA
Vitebsk ○
♔ SMOLENSK
Muroma
Suvar
LITVA
Golyad
R. Oka
○ Bolgar...
♔ POLOTSK
Orsha
Smolensk
Meshchera
MORDVA
Gorodno ○
Kopys
Koselsk
Kolomna
Minsk ○
Vyatichi
Ryazan ○
Yatvagi
Nesvizh
Klechesk
○ CHERNIGOV
♔ MUROM
Berestye
Drogochin
Radimichi
R. Desna
-RYAZAN
Volynyane
Rechitsa
Bryansk ○
VLADIMIR-
Pinsk
♔ TUROV
Karachev ○ Novosil
Kholm
Turov
-PINSK
Vruchy
✕ 1024
VOLYNSK
Drevlyane
Listem
♔ NOVGOROD
Vladimir
Korosten ○
Lyubech
-SEVERSK
Cherven
Novgorod-Severskiy
Belz
✕ Kursk
Chernigov
○ Peremyshl
Gorodets
Rylsk
✕ 1036
♔ GALICH
Terebovl
♔ KIEV
Severyane
Galich ○
Kiev
Polyane
Kamenets
Pereyaslavl
♔ PEREYASLAVL
Kolomyya ○
R. Ros
Rodnya
○ Donets
White Khorvaty
Tivertsy
○ Poltava
Prut
Pereshchen
PECHENEGI
P O L O V T S Y
Peresechen
R. Dniester
(in 1200)
R. Donets
TORKI
HUNGARIAN
R. Don
R. Volga
POLOVTSY
KINGDOM
Southern Bug
R. Dnieper
965
(in 1054)
Belgorod
KHAZARS
965
✕ 965
SAKSINY
Carpathian Mts
Oleshe
Sarkel
R. Ural
Pereslavets ○
Itil
Dorostol
R. Danube
✕ 971
Sea of Azov
Caspian Sea
BULGARIA
970
Sugdeya
Tmutarakan
R. Kuban
966-7
R. Kuma
Khersones (Korsun)
Black Sea
KASOGI
R. Terek
YASI

115

The formation of states in northern and eastern Europe 900 to c.1050

THE Carolingian Empire had established some sort of political order in those parts of western Europe (except Spain) which had formerly belonged to the Roman Empire. In northern and eastern Europe it was different, and it was not until the period 900-1050 that the Scandinavian and Slav states emerged from pre-literate mists as organised, even aggressive, entities. Their emergence extended the area of civilisation, filled out the political map of Europe, and put pressure on other western European states which resulted among other things in the establishment of well-defined boundaries between kingdoms and principalities and of marches along the eastern frontiers of Germany.

As a result of the initial activity of the early Viking Age the Scandinavians were by 900 well established in the west. In England the Danelaw was only gradually reconquered and although the last Scandinavian king of York, Erik Bloodaxe, was expelled in 954, most of the incomers were apparently able to retain their land, giving permanent Scandinavian character to the customs and place-names of the region. The reconquest of the Danelaw by the kings of Wessex and an expanding economy paved the way for the unification of England and for the political and religious reforms of Eadgar (959-75). But the wealth of England soon attracted the Scandinavians again, first as organised military expeditions seeking financial rewards (the Danegeld), then as conquerors, ruling England in tandem with Norway and Denmark under a Danish king, Cnut (Canute). But Cnut's northern empire was short-lived, and with the accession of Edward the Confessor to the English throne (1042), and still more after the Norman Conquest in 1066, England turned away from its role in northern Europe and aligned itself with the culture of France and the Mediterranean. It was an historic turning-point.

With the fall of York the position of the major ports of Ireland became important to the Scandinavians. These towns had been founded by them in the 9th century, and remained economically under their control, although often politically dominated by the Irish. The Irish, like the Welsh, were a society divided by many social and political factors. Sometimes united, often in disarray, they had neither the time nor the energy to develop economically. The history of much of this period is one of continuous warfare between the various Irish dynasties. Brian Bóruma, in the few years after 1000, was the first to unite Ireland (however shakily), but his power lasted only a short time; by 1014 he was dead and his achievement in ruins. The next man to attempt to unite Ireland was Diarmat, who became King of Leinster in the 1040s. Dublin's fortunes fluctuated politically, but rarely economically. The function of Dublin, the chief of the Scandinavian towns, as a market place is emphasised by the striking of the first Irish coins there in the 990s. From the late 10th century the economic power and international connections of Dublin – the chief market of the Scandinavians in the west – grew apace. The Isle of Man, the Western Isles of Scotland and the Atlantic islands also remained under Scandinavian control throughout this period. The mainland of Scotland, apart from Galloway and the far north, was gradually taken over by the Scots in the course of the 10th and 11th centuries and, by 1050, Scottish influence also extended into the northern counties of modern England. A firm boundary was drawn only in 1237.

Although Scandinavia had been economically stable for many centuries, it consisted at the beginning of the Viking Age of many provinces speaking a more or less common tongue. Now powerful states were founded out of the disarray. Denmark under three kings (Gorm, Harald and Sven) became in the course of the

10th century a powerful kingdom and, under Cnut the Great (1014-35), the centre of a great – but impossibly large – Anglo-Scandinavian empire.

After the battle of Hafrsfjord in the 890s Norway was first reorganised as a single kingdom under Harald Finehair. After his death in the 930s, however, Norway was largely under Danish control until the death of Cnut, when a Norwegian king again succeeded. The history of Sweden is more obscure: it was gradually united, however, under the kings of Uppland towards the end of the 10th century. By 930 Iceland was an independent state (without a king) and an attempt was made to settle Greenland from about 985. Through the medium of the newly-introduced Christianity (brought to Scandinavia by a handful of English and Saxon missionaries during the 10th and 11th centuries) Scandinavia emerged from heathen obscurity into the community of European Christendom.

Meanwhile, a similar process of consolidation was taking place in eastern Europe. The first organised state in this region, Moravia, was destroyed in 906 by the Magyar invaders. A new phase of political consolidation began in the 10th century, probably in response to German pressure under Henry I and Otto I. Although the lesser Slav peoples along the Elbe successfully resisted the Germans in the great Slav revolt of 983, they remained disunited and loosely organised, and it was further east, in Poland, that a major Slav state arose. Miesko I (960-92) united the tribes of northern Poland; his son Boleslav Chrobry (992-1025) extended control of Little Poland in the south. Meanwhile, the Magyars were settling the Hungarian plain, welded into a Hungarian kingdom by Duke Geisa (972-97) and his more famous son, King Stephen (997-1038). Bohemia, caught between Germany and Poland, had also emerged as a stable political unit by the time of Boleslav I (929-67), and even though the Přemyslid dukes were vassals of the German king they exercised more or less sovereign powers internally.

The creation of Bohemia, Poland and Hungary by the Přemyslid, Piast and Árpád dynasties

2/The rise of Denmark (*above*) Denmark was the first Scandinavian kingdom to achieve full statehood in the Christian European tradition. Three kings were basically responsible: Harald Bluetooth (c.950-c.986), Sven Forkbeard (c.986-c.1014) and Cnut the Great (1014-35). Harald was instrumental in persuading the Danes to accept Christianity, while politically he countered a German threat and brought Norway under the political control of the Danish crown. Sven concentrated largely on warlike campaigns in England from which he drew large amounts of money – the Danegeld. His son, Cnut the Great, eventually came to the throne of England and ruled an empire which stretched, in theory at least, from North Cape to the Isles of Scilly. Cnut's North Sea empire collapsed at his death and Denmark was subject to the Norwegian king Magnus until 1046. Denmark then settled down within what were to become its boundaries for many centuries (including the modern Swedish provinces of Skåne, Blekinge and Halland) under Sven Estridsson. In the 10th and early 11th centuries the first towns were founded in Denmark, the first bishoprics established and a remarkable series of fortifications constructed by the central authority – including at least part of the Danevirke (the fortified southern frontier of Denmark) and the fortresses at Trelleborg, Odense, Fyrkat and Aggersborg.

The Jelling stone (*above*) is both a symbol and a fact of the unity of Denmark and its official conversion to Christianity in the 10th century. The inscription reads: 'King Harald had this monument made in memory of Gorm his father and in memory of Thyre his mother. That Harald who won for himself all Denmark and Norway, and made all the Danes Christian'. Harald died c.986.

Territories from maps 1 and 2
(right and above)

Bohemia Duchy conquered from Slavs by Otto II in 950 and made tributary to Emperor.
Brandenburg (Nordmark and Billungmark) 928 margravate under Empire; 982 reconquered by Slavs.
Brittany Independent Celtic-speaking duchy; 912-37 under Scandinavian control.
Danelaw Generic term for area of England under Scandinavian control in early 10th century.
Dublin Kingdom under Scandinavian control (although political power sometimes in Irish hands).
England Kingdom. North and east under Scandinavian control for much of first half of 9th century. Gradually united under kings of Wessex. 1016-42 under Danish rule.
Hungary Principality. After death of Kursan (904) united under one leader, Árpád. In 1001 Stephen (d.1038) became first king.
Iceland Republic.
Ireland Land of petty kings (*tuatha*). Five main kingdoms to which in this period was added a sixth, Brega. Northern dynasty of Uí Néill most important until Brian Bóruma produced semi-organised overlordship under Munster in 1002 (see also Dublin).
Man Norse kingdom; apparently independent, but in the early 10th century under Orkney control.
Moravia Empire; 906 fell to Hungarians; 1025 combined with Bohemia after a period in Polish hands.
Normandy Colonised by Scandinavian settlers; dukedom after 911.
Norway Kingdom. At first very disunited, for some time in late 10th and early 11th centuries under loose Danish control. Finally achieved independence and was united under Magnus the Good (1035).
Orkney Earldom under nominal control of Norway. For much of period also probably controlled western islands of Scotland (Sudreyjar), Shetland (Hjaltland), and also for a short period Man.
Scotland Kingdom centred in east. Edinburgh captured by Indulf (954-62), battle of Carham (1018) brought in Lothian. Strathclyde taken over after death of Owen the Bald (1015). Galloway not properly under Scottish rule; north and west controlled by Norse.
Strathclyde Kingdom incorporated in Scotland after 1015.
Sweden Political organisation obscure before c. 1000, when Olaf Skötkonung appears to have gained control.
Wales Land of petty kings (*gwiad*). Six main kingdoms struggled for power. After death of Hywel Dda (950) no consolidation until accession of Gruffydd ap Llewelyn of Gwynedd in 1039.
York Norse kingdom until 954.

3/Poland under Boleslav Chrobry *(right)* After the unification of the tribes of Great (or northern) Poland under Miesko I, his son Boleslav Chrobry ('The Brave') attempted to create a great Slav empire, including Bohemia and Moravia. Most of the gains were temporary and involved long, debilitating wars on all frontiers; but Little Poland, centring on Cracow, was permanently acquired, and it was to Cracow that Casimir I (1037-58) transferred his residence when he began the restoration of the monarchy after the setbacks under Miesko II (1025-34). Poland was already Christian and a number of bishoprics had been founded. The towns of the Baltic coast came into their own as international trading stations in this period.

respectively, was founded on agricultural development, suppression of tribal differences and of the independence of the tribal aristocracies, and on the organising and civilising influence of the Church. At this stage, despite numerous wars (particularly after 1003) there was no racial confrontation between Germans and Slavs. Miesko I worked closely with the emperor Otto III, and the Bohemian nobility gladly became vassals of Germany when threatened by the Hungarians. Moreover, all three dynasties made use of Frankish institutions (counties, castellanies) to strengthen their position. Boleslav Chrobry had ambitions of founding a great Slav state from the Baltic to the Danube, including Bohemia and Moravia and certain Russian territories in the east; but the ensuing conflicts, involving wars with Slavs and Hungarians as well as Germans, overtaxed the monarchies and enabled the nobility to reassert itself. The result in all three countries was a setback to royal authority. Nevertheless a foundation had been laid, and none of them henceforth lost its identity, though it was not until the 14th century that a new stage of advance took place.

1/The emergence of states *(below)* The 10th century was marked by the emergence of stable political organisation in northern and eastern Europe. The marauders of the previous century (the Vikings in the north, the Magyars in the east) formed settled states; in England the successors of Alfred the Great reconquered the Danelaw; in Poland the Piasts not only extended their control over Little Poland (around Cracow) but also embarked on expansion at the expense of their Slav neighbours to the south, east and west. In eastern Germany, marches were established to defend the frontiers from incursions from the east.

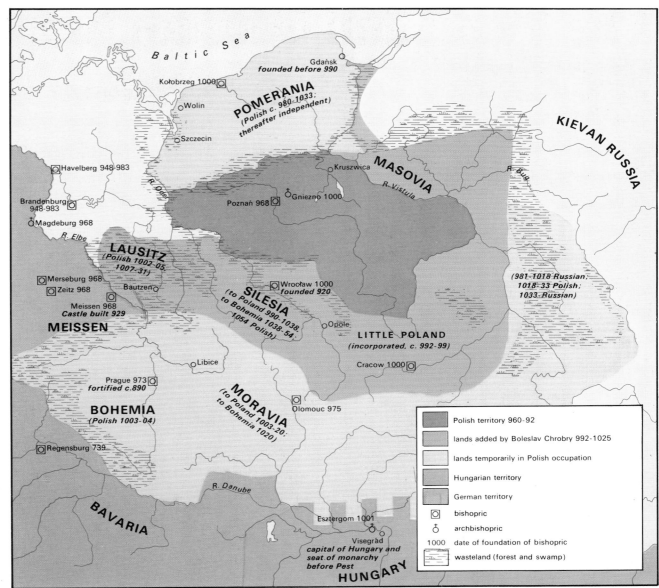

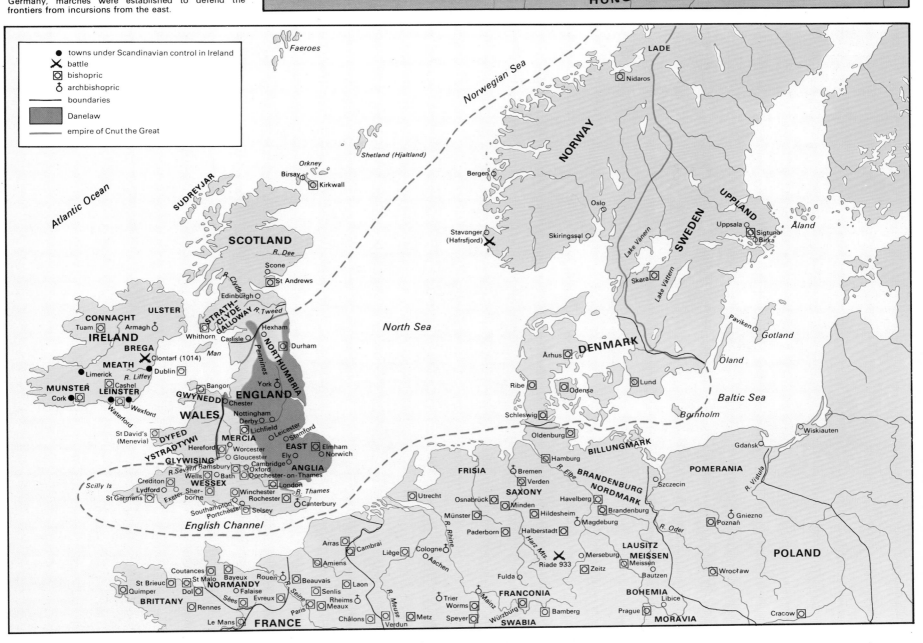

The Mediaeval German Empire 962 to 1250

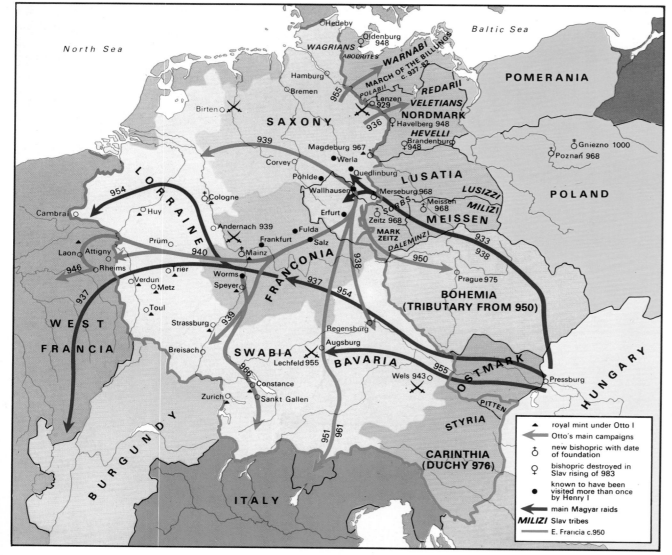

The Bamberg Rider *(above)* Bamberg Cathedral was founded in 1007. Its famous rider c. 1230 typifies the spirit of German chivalry in the drive east.

2/The Emperors' travels *(left)* Their itineraries reflect both the shifts in the focus of government and its permanent features: the central role of the Rhine valley and the fact that Burgundy, most of Bavaria, northern Saxony and the lands beyond the Elbe always lay off their beaten track.

3/The East Frankish Kingdom in the reign of Otto I *(below)* Otto I established a firm grip on the East Frankish lands. After the ducal revolts of 938-39 he was able to exercise power even in the more prosperous south and west (as shown by the distribution of royal mints). Magyar raids were halted. The drive eastward against the Slavs was normally left to the margraves, while Otto himself ranged more widely.

THE 9th century Viking, Magyar and Saracen invasions (see page 110) shook the foundations of the Carolingian Empire, already weakened by the Frankish custom of partible inheritance. After 887 the West Frankish (French) and East Frankish (German) lands went their own ways, and so did Italy. In 919 the East Frankish crown passed to Henry, Duke of the Saxons. This disputed election seemed to mark just another stage in the long-drawn out disintegration of the Carolingian world. Henry's power barely extended beyond the borders of Franconia and south-eastern Saxony. South of the Alps the imperial crown was now just a prize awarded to the most influential Italian magnate. West of the Rhine the forces of political fragmentation continued to operate for another 200 years (see page 124). But in the east the new Saxon dynasty emphatically reversed this process. By perseverance, skill and good fortune Henry I's son, Otto I, decisively extended his influence over the German duchies, defeated the Magyars at the Battle of the Lech (955), and conquered the kingdom of Italy. The imperial coronation at Rome (962) served to legitimise this vast acquisition. After the turbulence of the late 9th and early 10th centuries the Ottonian Empire emerged as the leading power west of the Adriatic, claiming equal status with Byzantium in the east.

The principle of indivisible kingship had become the rule for the Ottonian kings. They managed to pass on their Empire (extended in 1033 by the acquisition of Burgundy) to their successors in a long continuous line, helped by their control over churches and bishoprics, and by incessant itinerancy around their lands. By 1190 a partition of the Empire was unthinkable. There had been times (in 1002, 1024 and 1037) when the Italian magnates who had been emperor-makers in the early 10th century resisted the rulers thrust upon them from the north. But after 1037 they acquiesced in a custom which granted lordship over north Italy to the German king. Thus Germany, Burgundy and Italy remained together in the hands of one ruler, the emperor. Dynastic change, from Saxon to Salian (1024), and then to Hohenstaufen (1138), made little difference to the Empire's political structure. Nor, for all its high drama, did the Investiture Contest (1075-1122), when Henry IV tried to depose Pope Gregory VII, and in turn was excommunicated and forced to go in penance to Canossa, except that it cast doubt on the emperor's role as protector of the papacy.

The Empire's pre-eminence lasted until the death of Frederick II in 1250, although from the mid-12th century, with the recovery of the West Frankish territories and the rise of the Angevin Empire under Henry II of England, the balance was visibly changing. By 1200 Paris was the intellectual and artistic centre of Europe. Germany, with no capital city and no universities, lagged behind. German scholars, like Otto of Freising, studied philosophy and theology in Paris. Gothic architecture entered Germany from the West, advancing from Strassburg and Rhenish Franconia to Magdeburg and Naumburg. Although poetry, like sculpture and architecture, retained its specifically German characteristics, great poets like Wolfram of Eschenbach and Gottfried of Strassburg used French sources and subject matter.

Only gradually was the Empire's political structure undermined by the socio-economic developments of the 12th and 13th centuries: the growth of population and commerce, the clearing of waste and forest. From around 1140 internal colonisation was reinforced by the *Drang nach Osten*. But this concerned the eastern frontier princes far more than the German kings. The latter were always more interested in the West, especially the Rhineland, and in Italy. Only in these economically advanced regions were the profits of lordship sufficient to sustain an emperor and his following. Above all, there was the magnetic pull of urban wealth in Lombardy and Tuscany, the result of an unparalleled rate of economic growth. Frederick I (1152-1190) spent one-third of his reign in Italy, whereas his predecessors in the previous 150 years had averaged only one-seventh. But the growing independence of the Italian towns made it more difficult for the king to collect royal dues. The Hohenstaufen were twice involved in hostilities with Leagues of Lombard Cities (founded 1167 and 1226) and were forced to compromise. Even so, inter-communal rivalries gave the emperors many opportunities. Chroniclers' estimates of Frederick I's income from Italy make it clear that it was this source that made him the equal of the Angevins. Then Henry VI's conquest of the kingdom of Sicily (1194) made him and his son Frederick II the richest rulers in Europe.

The machinery of government remained inadequate. Only in 13th-century Sicily was there a centralised administrative system. In Germany and northern Italy the kings travelled continually, dispensing justice and supervising local government. In the 11th century they had begun to use *ministeriales* as local agents, but these men were no substitute for a salaried official class. To enforce their will, the kings had to be on the spot in person. The tremendous accession of landed wealth under Otto I had enabled the Ottonians to stay chiefly in their palaces, supplied by the produce of their estates. But the gradual alienation of royal domains forced Henry II and his successors to rely more heavily on church lands, particularly on episcopal towns and their developing markets. This meant an increasingly close relationship between king and church – and helps to explain the fierceness of the dispute over Investitures. From

1/The Mediaeval German Empire At the height of their power the emperors held sway over territories stretching from the Baltic to Sicily. Within these extended frontiers and with only a primitive apparatus of government they faced the German princes, the growing wealth and independence of the north Italian towns, and the papacy in its most creative centuries.

the second half of the 12th century, new palace building, stimulated by a surge of town growth and foundation, enabled the kings to stay more frequently in non-episcopal cities (e.g. Nuremberg, Frankfurt, Ulm, Hagenau). At the same time economic development and increasing literacy made possible a more concentrated, settled form of government. Kings were no longer driven without rest from place to place. But owing to the sheer size of the Empire this 'settling down' benefited the German territorial princes and the north Italian *signóri* rather than the monarchy. If the king profited it was as one prince among others, and by promulgating the Statute in favour of the princes (1232) Frederick II showed that he was prepared to accept a Germany of more or less autonomous principalities, though more than a century was to elapse before the Golden Bull (1356) set a seal on these developments. In Italy the Hohenstaufen conquest of Sicily had earned them the implacable hostility of the papacy. The execution of Frederick II's young grandson, Conradin, after the Battle of Tagliacozzo (1268) was the calculated triumph of papal policy and marked the extinction of the 'viper brood' of the Hohenstaufen. By this time France was encroaching on imperial territories in the west. The age of German preponderance was past.

Legend:
- eastward spread of German peasant settlement 12th century
- German settlement by 1200-1250
- city with over 10,000 inhabitants
- member of Lombard Leagues of 1167 and 1226
- member of 1167 League only
- member of 1226 League only
- German invasions 1190-94
- Henry VI's Genoese and Pisan fleet 1194
- main Hohenstaufen palaces and castles
- mountain pass ▲ monasteries

The recovery of Europe c.950 to 1150

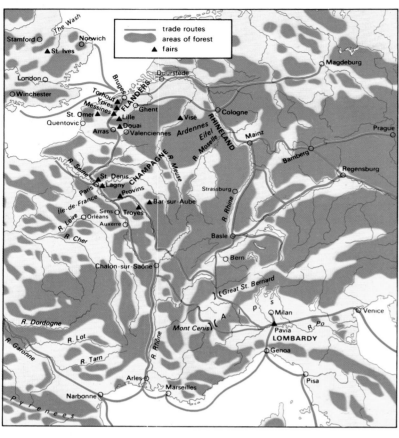

1/Western Europe, c. AD 1000 *(above)* Before AD 1000 perhaps four-fifths of Europe north of the Alps and Pyrenees was covered by dense forest. The essential work of the next two hundred years was to clear the forest and make the land available for human settlement and agriculture. Even in the Rhineland the highlands bounding the river were still largely uninhabited (see map 3). Elsewhere, forests such as the Ardennes and the Eifel constituted an almost impene-

trable barrier to communications. At this stage only the western Alpine passes were in regular use. Certain areas – Flanders, Lombardy, and the Rhine valley – were beginning by 1100 to become centres of commercial exchange. But it was only after 1150 that Italian merchants regularly attended the fairs of Champagne (Troyes, Provins, Bar-sur-Aube, Lagny), buying Flemish cloths in exchange for Oriental goods.

THE repulse of the Magyars by Otto I at the battle of Lech in 955 (see page 110) is the conventional date for the beginning of the recovery of Europe from the preceding period of devastation and economic setback. After 950 – a little earlier, perhaps, in some regions, a little later in others – the economic graph of Europe was on an upward curve until around 1300-20 (see page 142). This economic recovery, and the sharp rise in population which accompanied it, was a capital fact in European history.

The preceding period had indubitably marked a time of recession. Villages were razed to the ground and cultivated land reverted to waste. Duurstede and Quentovic, leading Carolingian ports, were destroyed, never to be rebuilt; much of Normandy was depopulated when it was handed over to the Viking chief, Rollo, in 911. In the south the cities of Marseilles, Arles, Aix, Fréjus and Genoa, the targets of Saracen raiders, were abandoned.

What is really remarkable, once the invasions were halted, is the speed with which this situation was reversed. The population of Europe in 900 was probably at its lowest level since the fall of the Roman Empire. By 1000 it may have reached a total of 30 million and 150 years later it had probably increased by 40 per cent. Most of this increase was concentrated in western Europe, in France, Germany and England. The development of eastern and northern Europe and the *repoblación* of Spain only got under way after 1150.

The basic factor in this process of recovery was the opening up of new land. In a few regions (e.g. the Po valley of northern Italy, Flanders, the country around the Wash in England) marshes were drained and land reclaimed from the sea. But there is no doubt that the bulk of new land was won by sheer hard work from the vast, impenetrable forests which still covered most of Europe in the year 1000. This is a process which

can only be followed step by step and locality by locality on large-scale maps. It took three main forms: steady encroachment by the peasants of the old villages on the woods which surrounded their fields; the migration of settlers, presumably driven by land-hunger, to the uninhabited uplands and mountains, where they carved out scattered fields and enclosures from the forest and scrub; planned development by lay lords and monasteries, wealthy promoters and speculators who founded villages and towns, at the foot of a castle or outside a monastery gate, with the aim of increasing their income. All three types of clearing are found juxtaposed in all countries, and their history is revealed by field patterns and by place-names (e.g. Newport, Neuville, Neustadt, Bourgneuf, Nieuwpoort). Occasionally the nomenclature is more fanciful. The small English market town of Baldock (Hertfordshire), founded by the Knights Templar in about 1148, was named optimistically after the great city of Baghdad.

No accurate estimate is possible of the amount of new land which was brought into cultivation in this way, but the effects of the great work of internal colonisation are indisputable. First and foremost an agricultural surplus became available for trade, and the result was to stimulate the foundation and growth of towns, markets and fairs.

Historians formerly attributed the recovery of Europe to the revival of long-distance trade at the time of the Crusades. We know today that the basis of recovery was local trade; the fairs (notably the fairs of Champagne) which became internationally renowned after 1150, still essentially served a local market in 1100. The gradual reassertion of European control over the northern shores of the Mediterranean after about 972 was a precondition for the later efflorescence of the Italian cities; but in 1000 Pisa and Genoa were only beginning to emerge from the set-

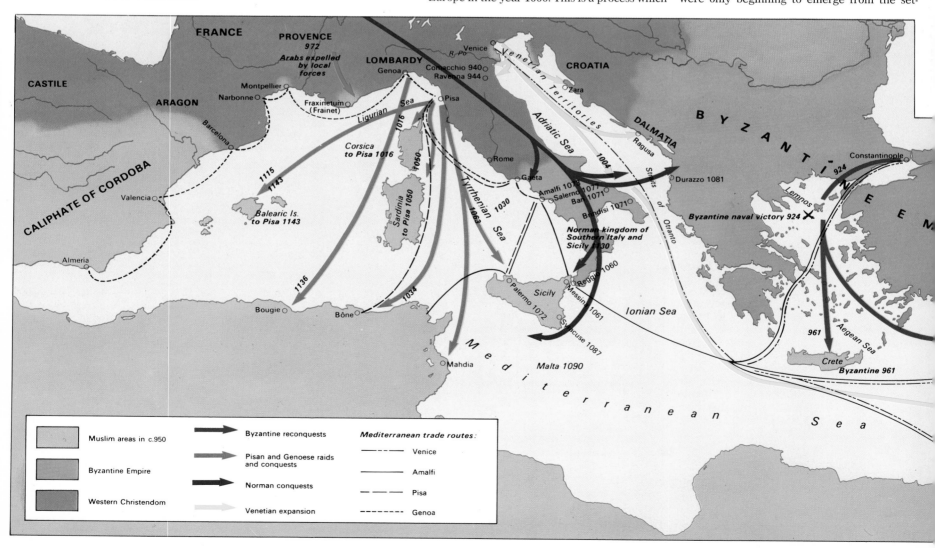

backs they had suffered at the hands of the Saracens, and Venice alone of the north Italian cities carried on a major overseas trade at the time. Significantly, the two Crusades (1096-99, 1147-49) proceeded overland to Constantinople; not until the time of the third Crusade (1189-92) did the West possess a fleet capable of transporting an army the length of the Mediterranean, from Gibraltar to Palestine.

In Europe also, though a few Roman roads remained in partial use, communications were still primitive, and rivers (Rhine, Meuse, Po, Rhône) conveyed bulk transport. Only the western Alpine passes (Mont Cenis, Great St Bernard) were in regular use; the central passes (St Gotthard, Septimer, Splügen) and the Brenner in the east were not developed before the reign of the emperor Frederick I (1155-90) or later. The Mont Cenis and Great St Bernard provided a connection with the Rhineland, and thence with the cloth-towns of Flanders, and also with the Paris region. But the Capetians were still struggling (see page 124) to assert authority in the Ile-de-France, and until this had been achieved the Rhineland remained the focus of artistic and intellectual as well as of economic life. Cologne, in particular, was at the height of its prosperity, but the cathedral-building throughout the region – e.g. at Mainz and Worms – is a testimony to the new-found wealth which 'the great age of clearing' had made available.

5, 6, 7/Urban development *(right and below)* Throughout western Europe the 12th century was a time of town-foundation. Kings, nobles and ecclesiastics all competed in setting up new towns, hoping for enhanced land values as well as profits from markets and fairs. In England and Wales *(right)* more than a hundred new towns were founded between 1066 and 1190. By no means all these ventures were a success, and many other urban centres grew from existing villages, while ancient cities such as Cologne (see map 8) got a new lease of life. The counts of Flanders were particularly active in founding new towns; so were the dukes of Zähringen (see map 3). No less than nine towns in the north-west of modern Switzerland owe their existence to their initiative *(far right)*. French kings, bishops and princes were equally enterprising. Louis VI (1108-37) and Louis VII (1137-80) planted *villeneuves* (in this case villages rather than towns) the length of the road from Paris to Orléans *(below)*, seeking in this way to consolidate their hold over the region which was the core of their domain.

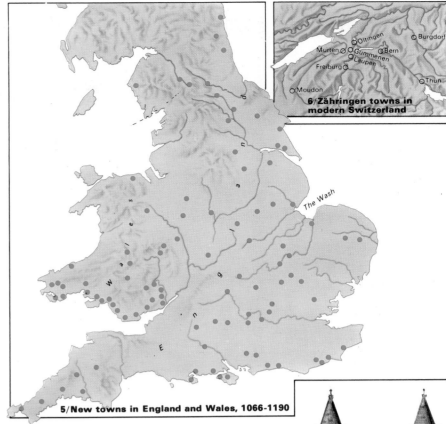

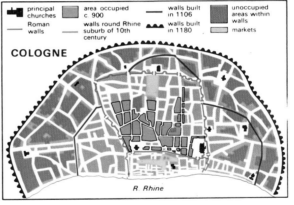

6/Zähringen towns in modern Switzerland

5/New towns in England and Wales, 1066-1190

8/Cologne *(below)*, the Roman Colonia Agrippina, was by the end of the 12th century the largest German city, commanding the trade of the river Rhine. In 900 less than half the area within the Roman walls was occupied, but a merchant quarter, with markets, was growing between the Roman city and the river. In the 10th century (presumably as protection against Viking raiders) this was enclosed by walls. In 1106 the walls were extended, but rapid growth required a new wall in 1180. This remained the city boundary until the 19th century.

principal churches	area occupied c. 900	walls built in 1106	unoccupied areas within walls
Roman walls	walls round Rhine suburb of 10th century	walls built in 1180	markets

COLOGNE

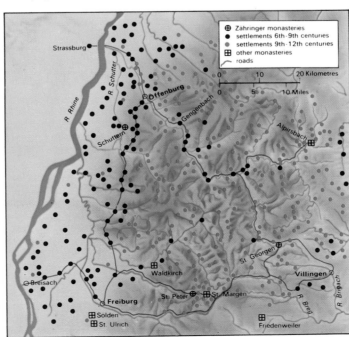

R. Rhine

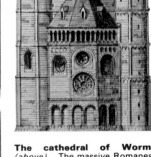

The cathedral of Worms *(above)* The massive Romanesque cathedral illustrates the new wealth generated by the economic recovery of the 11th century.

2/The reconquest of the Mediterranean *(below left)* In 950 the Mediterranean was almost entirely a Muslim lake'. Such trade as there was between western Europe and the Orient was in the hands of the cities of Byzantine Italy; Bari, Amalfi, Gaeta and Salerno. Amalfi, in particular, traded indiscriminately with Muslims (in Sicily and Egypt) and with Constantinople and Antioch. But its connections with northern Europe were at best indirect, and it was Venice, linked with the west by the Po valley, that first engaged in trade with Europe north of the Alps, once it had cleared the Adriatic of Dalmatian pirates and fought off the closure of the Straits of Otranto first by Muslims (who occupied Bari from 841 to 871) and then by Norman marauders. In the western Mediterranean trade was virtually at a standstill so long as the Saracens were in control of the Mediterranean islands and, from their base at Fraxinetum, of the Ligurian coast. Their dislodgement from Fraxinetum in 972 was therefore a capital fact. By this time Islamic unity was breaking up (see page 134), and this weakening enabled the fleets of Pisa and (later) of Genoa to wrest control of the Ligurian and Tyrrhenian seas from the Saracens. At this stage, however, these cities were freebooters and pirates rather than traders, but the loot from their raids on Saracen shipping provided capital for shipbuilding and eventually for commerce. The first Crusade (1096-99) opened up trading stations in the Levant; but it was only after the great Venetian naval victory off Ascalon in 1123 that the Italian cities came to dominate the Mediterranean from Spain to Syria.

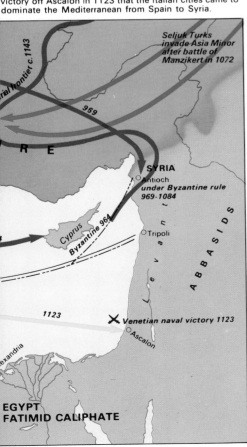

7/Villeneuves between Paris and Orléans

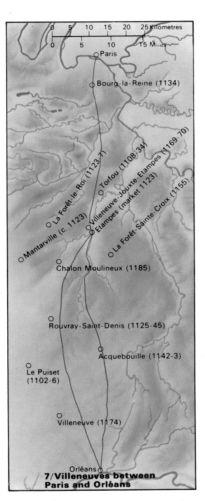

3/The colonisation of the Black Forest *(below)* The Rhineland, a main artery of communications from Roman times, was settled at an early date; but the high, heavily wooded ranges which enclosed it on both sides (Hunsrück, Taunus, Spessart, Odenwald and Black Forest) had to wait until the 11th century before clearing and colonisation took place. In the Black Forest settlement of the mountainous areas only took place after c. 1075. The agents were the dukes of Zähringen and the monasteries under their control, particularly St Peter (1093) and St Georgen (1114). The Zähringer finally asserted control over the whole region by founding (c. 1120) the towns of Freiburg, Villingen and Offenburg, which dominated the few routes traversing the forest. The advance of clearing, evidenced by the new place name, from the old-settled areas to the high woodlands is a classic example of the progress of colonisation and settlement.

4/Clearance and settlement in north-eastern France *(below)* If in some areas (e.g. the Black Forest) colonisation and the clearing of woodland and waste was planned, in others it was the result of piecemeal encroachment by individual peasants on the less fertile uplands and woods. The forest of Othe, south-east of Sens, is an example of this process. Early settlement followed in the main the river valleys and existing roads; but in the 12th century scores of new settlements opened up the intervening afforested countryside. The result was an increase in the cultivated area assessed at one-third or more for Europe north of the Alps and Pyrenees and west of the Elbe: an accretion of territory and agricultural resources which gave a major impetus to the European economy.

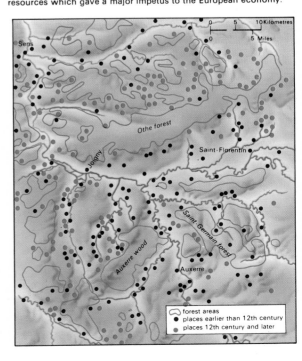

The conflict of Church and State in Europe 1056 to 1314

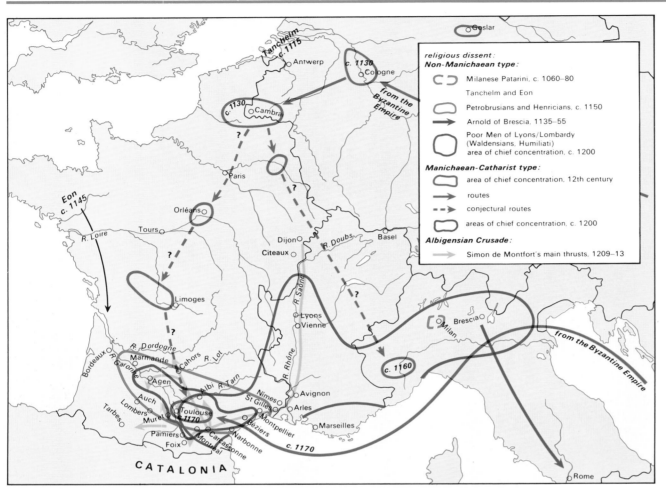

1/Movements of dissent *(above)* Almost unknown in the West since c.500, dissent spread rapidly in the late 11th century in protest against clerical worldliness; it was declared heretical in 1184. About 1130, doctrinal heresy (Manichaeism) was imported from the Middle East; it took root in southern France. Both types were repressed but not eradicated by the Albigensian Crusade (1209-13) and the Inquisition (1233).

2/Monastic reform *(below)* Reform movements began early in the 10th century, mainly in south-eastern France and Lorraine. Although Gorze influenced 10th-century Germany, monastic reform made no powerful impact east of the Rhine until after 1060.

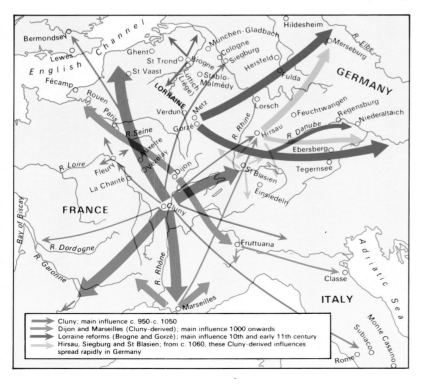

THE conflict of Church and State is a capital fact in European history. Elsewhere kings and priests tended to work in harmony, and the result was a 'monolithic' society. In Europe, particularly in western Europe, the co-existence of two powers helped to promote the emergence of 'pluralistic' societies, in which the individual had to balance the different claims made on his allegiance. Here were the distant origins of modern individualism.

From time immemorial, kings and emperors had claimed to rule by divine mandate. In imperial Rome, also, emperors assumed divine attributes and used the title 'supreme pontiff' (*pontifex maximus*); and even after the adoption of Christianity as a state religion (see page 92), old habits died hard. Constantine (324-37),

Theodosius (379-95) and Justinian (527-65) all regarded themselves as rulers of Church and State, responsible to God for the spiritual and material welfare of their subjects. So did the kings of the Germanic successor-states of western Europe. Charlemagne (page 106) saw himself as 'king and priest', and acted as the head of both aspects of a single society, in which Christianity was important not only for its religious aspirations but also as the focus of daily life.

Popes challenged this outlook from at least the 5th century, but were seldom able to do much about it. In times of stress, like those which followed the Viking and Magyar invasions (see page 110), the secular arm was uppermost. The emperor Otto I and his successors (see page 118) used bishops as instruments of government and claimed to invest them with their spiritual as well as their secular functions. Once Europe began to recover, resistance to this usurpation grew and a movement to free the Church from secular control took shape. It began in scattered monastic centres in the west, notably at Cluny, and at Brogne and Gorze in Lorraine, spread quickly, and finally reached Rome when the emperor Henry III took in hand the reform of the papacy at the Synod of Sutri in 1046.

The connection thus forged between Church reformers and the papal see inaugurated the long struggle of Empire and Papacy, which eventually destroyed the former and fatally impaired the authority of the latter. The conflict came to a head under Gregory VII (1073-85), whose combative nature and insistence on ancient but exaggerated and hitherto largely ineffective papal claims resulted in a violent explosion. Gregory deposed the emperor Henry IV in 1076 and allied with the emperor's enemies – the Normans of southern Italy, the recalcitrant German nobility, and a chain of states around the periphery which feared German power. The result was a lasting setback to German monarchy. Although Gregory failed in his immediate objects, the launching of the First Crusade (see page 100) by Urban II (1088-99) showed how rapidly papal authority was advanc-

ing. But by now both sides were exhausted, and the struggle begun in 1075 was settled in 1122 by the Concordat of Worms.

For the Church it was a pyrrhic victory. What had started as a movement to free the Church from secular control now seemed to be leading to the oppression of society by clergy and Pope. Gregory VII's legacy was a growing concern with temporal affairs, against which St Bernard warned Pope Eugenius III (1145-53). Papal centralisation caused an increasingly educated lay society to resent the clergy's privileges and stimulated popular religious movements, particularly in southern France and northern Italy, many of which ended in unorthodoxy and dissent. Nor did the Concordat of 1122 solve the question of Church and State, over which the kings of England and France as well as the German emperor frequently found themselves at loggerheads with the Pope. But now the conflict of Empire and Papacy had deteriorated from a conflict of principle to a struggle for control of Italy. The political involvement of the papacy became clear when Alexander III (1154-81) allied with the Lombard League of self-governing cities to resist Frederick I's attempts to restore German imperial authority in Italy. Once again, the issue was settled by a compromise (Peace of Constance, 1183), but the early death of Frederick's son, Henry VI (1190-97) and civil war in Germany (1197-1214) enabled Innocent III (1198-1216) to regain ascendancy for the Church.

Innocent III's pontificate marked a high point for the papacy. He established a papal state in central Italy to protect Rome; he nominated emperors; England bowed to his will, and France was his ally. He also had some success in dealing with anti-clericalism. The heretics of southern France were viciously suppressed in the Albigensian crusade (1208), but Innocent also encouraged the evangelism of the new orders of friars, the Franciscans and Domini-

3/The investiture contest *(right)* The conflict of Church and State centred round the question whether kings and emperors were entitled to invest bishops and other prelates with their offices. The question was crucial for the monarchies, because bishops and abbots were large landholders; it was crucial for the Church, because of the danger that kings would appoint bishops for temporal rather than spiritual reasons. This was the conflict that came to a head under Gregory VII and was settled by compromise in 1122. The map indicates the most consistent elements in a widely fluctuating situation: thus Lorraine changed sides several times, and England was in conflict with the Papacy after 1093. None of Gregory's allies was wholly reliable (the Normans sacked Rome in 1084, for instance) and some gave him little practical support. Countess Matilda was a prominent supporter of Pope Gregory VII.

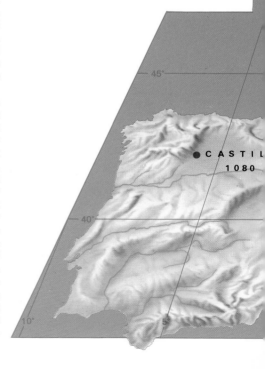

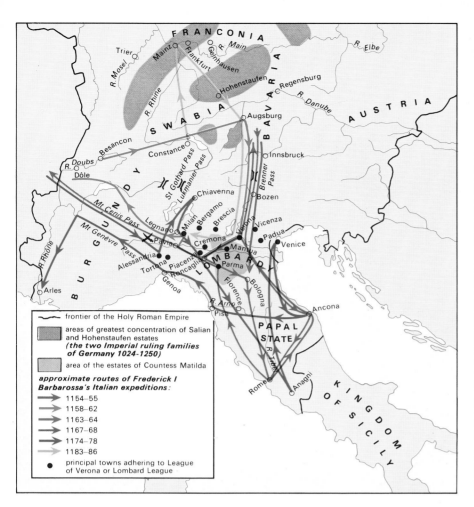

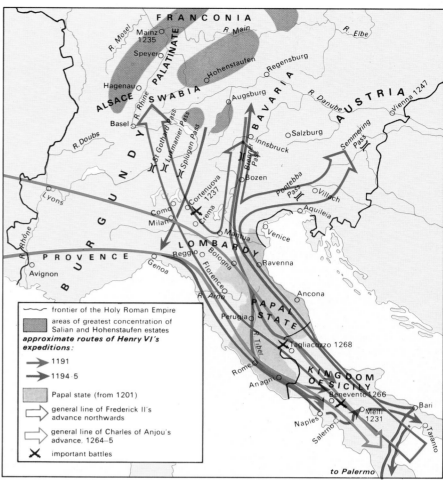

cans, who were formally approved by his successor, Honorius III (1216-27), and sought to remove the sources of discontent by reforming clerical behaviour. But his successes were greater on paper than in practice. The papal state was never effectively controlled; the reforms of the Fourth Lateran Council (1215) were ineffective; and his choice of Frederick II (1214-50) as emperor was dictated by circumstances beyond his control.

After Innocent's death decline set in. It was accelerated by renewal of the struggle with the Empire. Like Alexander III before him, Innocent IV (1243-54) allied with the Italian cities to resist Frederick II's efforts to subject the whole

of Italy to his rule (the Norman kingdom of Sicily was his by inheritance) and to unite it with Germany by controlling the lines of communication between them. The bitterness of the struggle, in which the Pope openly expressed his intention of extirpating the Hohenstaufen dynasty, produced a strong reaction, and the papacy only succeeded when Clement IV (1265-8) called in Charles of Anjou, the brother of Louis IX of France, to evict the Germans from Italy.

Charles of Anjou's victories at Benevento (1266) and Tagliacozzo (1268) brought the Empire down in ruins, but the papacy had jumped from the frying pan into the fire. After

Louis IX's death in 1270 disputes with the increasingly centralised French monarchy over taxation of the clergy and royal sovereignty led to open conflict in 1296. Boniface VIII proclaimed papal authority undiminished, but was kidnapped by his French and Italian enemies in 1303, and in 1309 his successor, Clement V (1305-14), took up residence in Avignon, directly under French supervision. Although not always a tool of France, the 'papacy of Avignon' commanded little respect, and heresy and anticlericalism were again rife. The long conflict of Church and State had still produced no final victor, for France in its turn soon collapsed in face of English invasion (see page 142).

4 and 5/Conflicts of Empire and Papacy 1152-90 *(above left)* **and 1190-1268** *(above right)* The routes of the imperial expeditions illustrate the constant pressure from Germany which led Innocent III to found the papal state. By contrast, Frederick II's bases were in Apulia and Sicily. The broad arrow suggests the stages by which he tried, after about 1230, to beat a path back northwards by controlling Italian communications, the mountain passes, and south Germany from Alsace to Austria. Charles of Anjou's invasion substituted a French for a German yoke upon Italy.

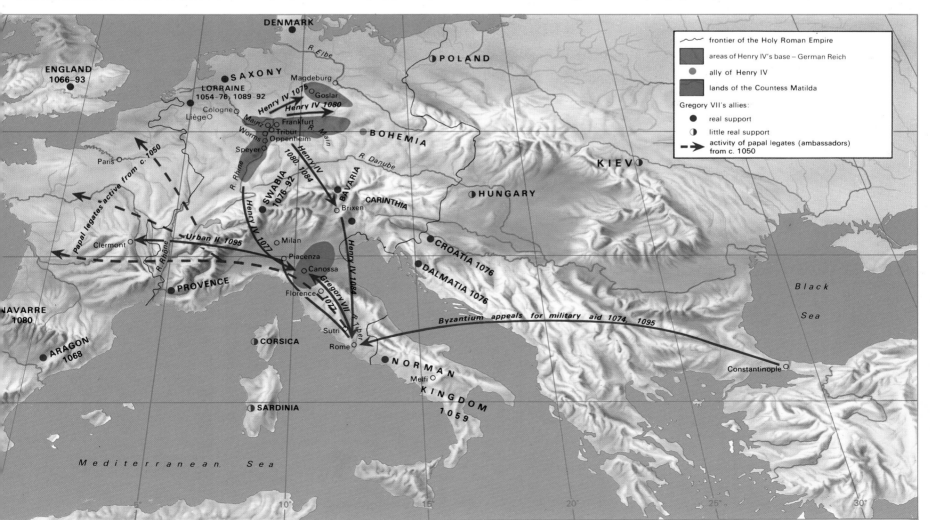

Feudal monarchy in Western Europe
1154 to 1314

2/Italy disunited *(above)* Papal-Imperial controversy and the wealth of the municipalities inhibited consolidation in Italy. After 1250, public power in independent city states was exercised by republican oligarchies or by despots who often succeeded as alternatives to the factional violence of civic politics.

3/Spain: the Reconquista *(below)* Displaced in Old Castile and León, where Christian freeholders settled, Muslims remained numerous in the Aragonese kingdoms. In Andalusia Christian military leaders, rewarded with great estates, dominated a mixed population.

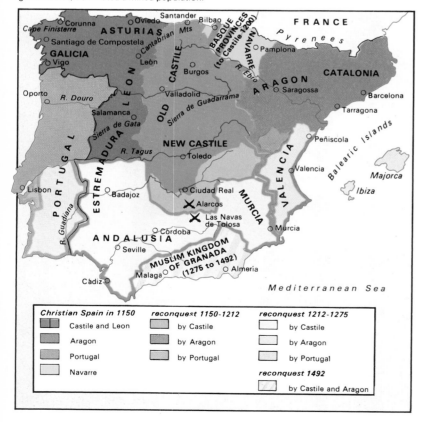

WESTERN Europe began its slow climb out of political dislocation and feudal anarchy during the 12th century. Viking and Magyar invasions (see page 110) had disrupted royal authority and strengthened the local feudatories, but kingship survived. Weak though the king might be in practice, his position was hallowed by religious sanctions, and in the 12th century kings used their position to assert their prerogatives at the head of the feudal hierarchy. They were helped by the reaction against papal attacks on the monarchy during the Investiture Contest (see page 122), when rulers turned to the arsenal of Roman law for weapons to defend their independence. In the hands of the emperor Frederick Barbarossa and later of the French Capetians, Roman law became a powerful instrument of royal authority. But the main weapons used by 12th and 13th century kings were feudal: the king's rights as 'liege lord', the duty of tenants-in-chief to render service, the theory that all land was held of the king, and all rights of justice were delegations of royal authority, and therefore reverted, or 'escheated', to the crown in case of abuse or treason. Step by step grave misdemeanours (felonies) were reserved to the king's courts as 'pleas of the crown'. By the beginning of the 13th century, at least in France and England, elective monarchy had been displaced by hereditary monarchy, and the electors, lay and ecclesiastical, shorn of their power. Much of this process was piecemeal; but by the middle of the 13th century the great lawyers (Bracton in England, Beaumanoir in France) had created a systematic structure of royal government, which kings like Edward I of England (1272-1307) and Philip IV of France (1285-1314) proceeded to exploit.

Progress was most rapid in the Norman kingdoms of England and Sicily. Since both were acquired by conquest, the aristocracy was less firmly entrenched than elsewhere and the kings' hands correspondingly free. This enabled William the Conqueror (1066-87) to retain and build up the fiscal and jurisdictional prerogatives inherited from his Anglo-Saxon predecessors in England. In Sicily also the great Norman ruler, Roger II, who united Sicily, Apulia and Calabria in 1130, retained the institutions of his Byzantine and Muslim predecessors, particularly their efficient system of taxation. By the end of the 12th century Sicily, with its control of the Mediterranean sea-routes, was the richest, most advanced and tightly organised state in Europe. In France, on the other hand, where the anarchy of the 9th and 10th centuries was greatest, progress was slower. Louis VI (1108-37) spent his reign asserting authority over the petty barons of the Ile de France, and it was scarcely before the reign of Philip Augustus (1180-1223) that expansion of the royal demesne began in earnest. The turning point was the conquest of Normandy in 1204, which effectively meant the destruction of the Angevin dominions, i.e. of the Anglo-Norman dominions across the English Channel. After 1214 English continental possessions were limited to Gascony, and a third of France was now under direct royal control. The defeat of the English also permitted the Capetians to turn elsewhere. Much of Languedoc was subdued in a campaign against the Albigensian heretics (1209-29) and royal authority now extended south of the Loire.

The other area in which monarchy made great strides was the Iberian peninsula. Here the kingdoms of Portugal (independent since 1139), Navarre, Castile and Aragon were creations of the progressive reconquest of the peninsula from the Arabs, whose decisive defeat at Las Navas de Tolosa (1212) led rapidly to the loss of Córdoba (1236), Valencia (1238), Murcia (1243), Seville (1248) and Cádiz (1262). A major role in the reconquest was taken by Castile, originally a tributary of the crown of León, with which it was

permanently united in 1230. By the middle of the 13th century Castile controlled more than half the peninsula and was gradually welded into a monarchical state by Alfonso X (1252-84). In the eastern portion of the peninsula authority was wielded by the crown of Aragon after its union with the county of Catalonia (1137) and the conquest of Valencia (1238). Hemmed in on the west by Castile, Aragon turned its expansionist energies towards the Mediterranean. The Balearics were conquered between 1229 and 1235, and Sicily wrested from Charles of Anjou, the French prince called in by the papacy, in 1282. Though the kingdom's tripartite structure left partial autonomy to the component states, the Aragonese empire was the creation of a powerful monarchy fortified by the commercial wealth of Catalonia and Valencia.

The exceptions to this process of feudal concentration were Germany and Italy. Here, despite the efforts of Frederick Barbarossa (1152-90), the monarchy never fully recovered from its setbacks during the Investiture Contest, and the long interregnum after the death of Frederick's son, Henry VI, in 1197, weakened it still further. Paradoxically, the feudal processes which strengthened monarchy in the west worked to its detriment in central Europe, where power passed to feudal princes or, in Italy, to city magistrates (*podestà*) or increasingly to tyrants (*signori*) who dominated the cities they ruled and the surrounding countryside.

In the west royal supremacy was well established before the end of the 13th century. Kings exercised powers of taxation and legislation (often in consultation with parliaments or 'estates of the realm') and controlled the administration of justice. They also used their authority to assert overlordship over neighbouring territories, where feudalism had resulted in an intricate network of overlapping rights and jurisdictions. Nowhere was the feudal map more complex than in France, where the English possessions at one time stretched from Normandy to the Mediterranean coast. The determination of the French kings to assert their overlordship over these lands and over Flanders gave rise to a series of major wars. Meanwhile the English kings were asserting similar claims in Scotland, Wales and Ireland. Henry II's attempt to conquer Ireland (1171) achieved only a precarious foothold, but Edward I subdued Wales, already harassed by marcher lords and the palatine earls of Chester, in 1284. He tried to repeat the process in Scotland in 1296 but met resistance under Wallace and Bruce, and suffered defeat at Bannockburn in 1314.

Edward I's failure in Scotland was matched by Philip IV's failure in Flanders. Defeated by the Flemings at Courtrai (1302), the French king, who had seized Gascony in 1294, was compelled to restore it to the English in 1303. War expenditure and centralisation also produced severe internal strains. In Aragon the estates forced the monarchy to grant a General Privilege in 1283. In England Edward I was compelled in 1297 to confirm and extend the charters wrested from King John in 1215. In France the States-General met for the first time in 1302. Everywhere, in short, the new monarchies had overreached themselves; the result was a powerful aristocratic reaction. When, after the middle of the 15th century, recovery began (see page 150), the foundations were no longer feudal. Sovereignty had replaced suzerainty, and a new period in the history of western monarchy had begun.

1/The growth of the French and English monarchies *(right)* Early mediaeval rulers laid claim to supreme power but they depended primarily on personal and feudal allegiances over which not infrequently they had less command than their most powerful subjects. The institutional strength of monarchy, developing in the 12th century, expanded rapidly in the 13th century. By 1300 western kings were no longer primarily feudal overlords: they had become acknowledged executors of effective public authority.

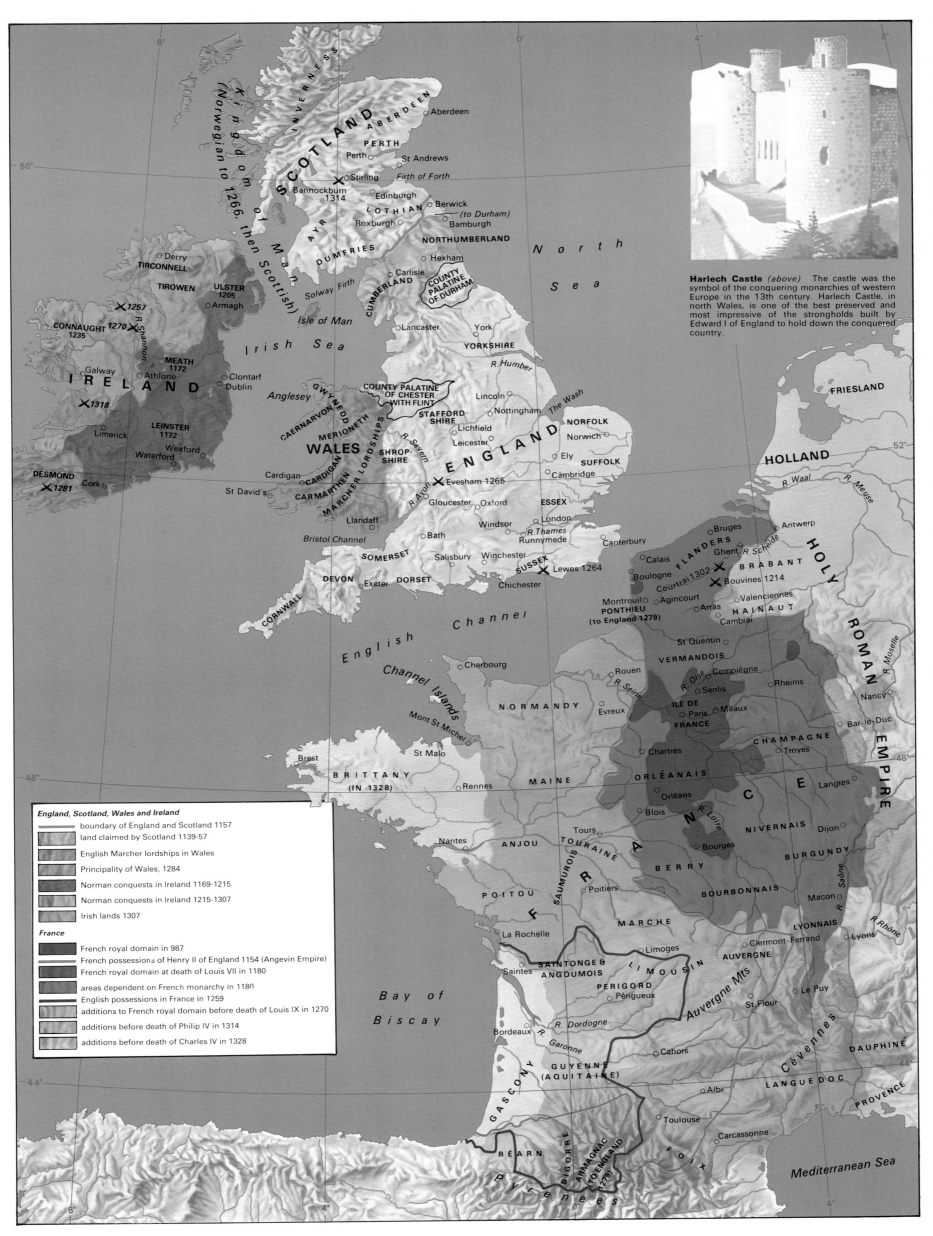

Harlech Castle *(above)* The castle was the symbol of the conquering monarchies of western Europe in the 13th century. Harlech Castle, in north Wales, is one of the best preserved and most impressive of the strongholds built by Edward I of England to hold down the conquered country.

SCOTLAND
INVERNESS
Kingdom of Man (Norwegian to 1266, then Scottish)
ABERDEEN
Aberdeen
PERTH
Perth
St Andrews
Stirling
Bannockburn 1314
Edinburgh
Firth of Forth
LOTHIAN
Berwick
(to Durham)
Roxburgh
Bamburgh
AYR
DUMFRIES
Solway Firth
NORTHUMBERLAND
Hexham
Carlisle
CUMBERLAND
COUNTY PALATINE OF DURHAM

IRELAND
Derry
TIRCONNELL
TIROWEN
ULSTER 1205
Armagh
✕1257
R. Shannon
CONNAUGHT 1235
✕1270
MEATH 1172
Galway
Athlone
Clontarf
Dublin
✕1318
LEINSTER 1172
Limerick
Wexford
Waterford
DESMOND
✕1281
Cork

Isle of Man
Irish Sea

Lancaster
York
YORKSHIRE
R. Humber
Lincoln
Nottingham
The Wash
NORFOLK
Norwich
STAFFORD-SHIRE
Lichfield
Leicester
Ely
SUFFOLK
Cambridge

WALES
GWYNEDD
Anglesey
CAERNARVON
MERIONETH
COUNTY PALATINE OF CHESTER WITH FLINT
R. Severn
SHROP-SHIRE
CARDIGAN
MARCHER LORDSHIPS
Cardigan
CARMARTHEN
St David's
✕ Evesham 1265
Gloucester
Oxford
R. Avon
ESSEX
Llandaff
Windsor
London
Bath
Runnymede
R. Thames
Canterbury
Bristol Channel
SOMERSET
Salisbury
Winchester
SUSSEX
DEVON
DORSET
✕ Lewes 1264
Exeter
Chichester
CORNWALL

ENGLAND

North Sea

FRIESLAND
HOLLAND
R. Waal
R. Meuse
Antwerp
Bruges
FLANDERS
Ghent
R. Schelde
Calais
Courtrai 1302 ✕
BRABANT
Boulogne
✕ Bouvines 1214
Montreuil
Agincourt
Valenciennes
PONTHIEU (to England 1279)
Arras
HAINAUT
Cambrai
St Quentin
VERMANDOIS
Rouen
Compiègne
Rheims
R. Oise
R. Seine
Senlis
Meaux
ÎLE DE FRANCE
Nancy
Paris
HOLY ROMAN EMPIRE
R. Moselle
Bar-le-Duc
Evreux
CHAMPAGNE
Troyes
Chartres
Langres
NORMANDY
Cherbourg
English Channel
Channel Islands
Mont St Michel
ORLÉANAIS
MAINE
Brest
Orléans
NIVERNAIS
Dijon
St Malo
Blois
BRITTANY (IN 1328)
Rennes
R. Loire
BURGUNDY
Bourges
Nantes
ANJOU
TOURAINE
BERRY
R. Saône
Macon
SAUMUROIS
BOURBONNAIS
POITOU
Tours
Poitiers
MARCHE
LYONNAIS
F R A N C E
La Rochelle
Clermont-Ferrand
Lyons
Limoges
AUVERGNE
R. Rhône
SAINTONGE & ANGOUMOIS
LIMOUSIN
Saintes
PERIGORD
Auvergne Mts
St Flour
Le Puy
Périgueux
Bay of Biscay
R. Dordogne
Bordeaux
R. Garonne
Cahors
Cévennes
DAUPHINÉ
GUYENNE (AQUITAINE)
Albi
LANGUEDOC
GASCONY
PROVENCE
Toulouse
Carcassonne
BÉARN
BIGORRE
ARMAGNAC (TO ENGLAND 1279)
FOIX
Pyrenees
Mediterranean Sea

England, Scotland, Wales and Ireland

	boundary of England and Scotland 1157
	land claimed by Scotland 1139-57
	English Marcher lordships in Wales
	Principality of Wales, 1284
	Norman conquests in Ireland 1169-1215
	Norman conquests in Ireland 1215-1307
	Irish lands 1307

France

	French royal domain in 987
	French possessions of Henry II of England 1154 (Angevin Empire)
	French royal domain at death of Louis VII in 1180
	areas dependent on French monarchy in 1180
	English possessions in France in 1259
	additions to French royal domain before death of Louis IX in 1270
	additions before death of Philip IV in 1314
	additions before death of Charles IV in 1328

Chinese civilisation from the T'ang to the Sung 618 to 1278

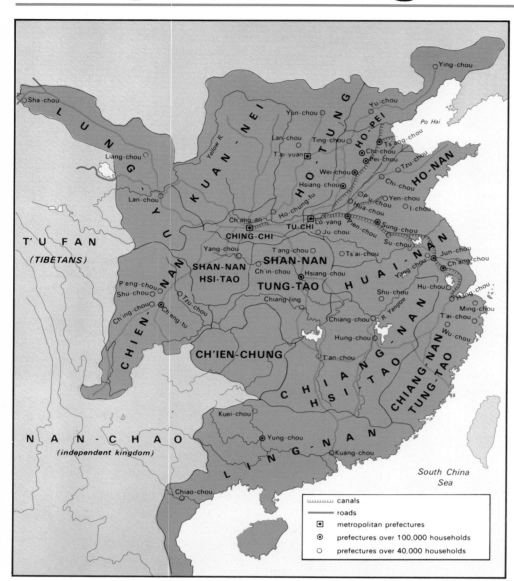

1/T'ang China *(above)* The whole of China proper, excepting the far south-west, was permanently organised under centralised administration. The empire was linked together by a network of post-roads, while transport of commodities between the rapidly developing regions of the Yangtze valley and the north was provided by an efficient system of canals and waterways. The road system centred on the capital, Ch'ang-an, which remained the political and strategic hub of the empire. However, the eastern plain and the area around the Lower Yangtze were the main economic centres.

A FTER centuries of disunion (see page 94), China was reunified in 589 by the Sui dynasty (581-617). Their empire was consolidated under the system of centrally codified institutions developed under the northern Wei and their successors, by the state patronage of a style of Buddhism acceptable in north and south alike, and by the construction of a canal system linking the Yangtze with the Yellow River (Huang Ho) and the Peking region. The Sui collapsed, partly from the burden imposed by these public works and the reconstruction of the Great Wall, partly because of repeated abortive attempts to conquer Koguryŏ (northern Korea).

After some years of widespread rebellions, the Sui were replaced by the T'ang, which was a dynasty of similar social origins and which continued most of their policies. The T'ang state was a strong centralised empire, with a simple but effective administrative system designed to be uniform. At first the system worked well, but after some years of internal consolidation the T'ang began to expand abroad, and in the 8th century the growing complexity of the state and of society, and the costs of defence, produced many changes.

By the 660s Chinese armies had intervened in India, central Asia and Afghanistan, the Chinese had occupied the Tarim Basin and Dzungaria, and briefly set up protectorates in Tukharistan, Sogdiana, Ferghana and eastern Persia. At the same period Koguryŏ was finally conquered and for a few years the T'ang occupied northern Korea. The formidable northern Turks had been defeated in 630, and in the 660s the Chinese Empire reached its greatest extent prior to the Manchu conquests of the 18th century.

While Chinese military force was establishing this vast empire, Chinese culture, its written language and political institutions, were adopted in the states which were growing up around China's eastern periphery – in Silla (Korea), in Japan, in Po-hai (Manchuria) and Nan-chao (Yunnan). Thus began the Chinese ecumene in the Far East, which persisted long after T'ang military power had decayed.

In 755 An Lu-shan, a frontier general, began a rebellion which lasted seven years and almost destroyed the T'ang. As a result the Chinese withdrew from central Asia, and the Tibetans and Uighurs occupied their former territories. Islam had meanwhile reached Ferghana and later became the dominant cultural force in Turkestan. The deep cultural links between China and central Asia were broken, and China became more inward-looking.

The rebellion also set in motion major social and economic changes. The imperial authority was much reduced, and the uniform centralised policies of the 7th century were abandoned. Power passed to the provinces, and many provincial capitals grew into large and wealthy metropolises. There was a massive movement of population to the fertile Yangtze valley, where new methods of farming produced large surpluses of grain. Trade boomed, and a network of small market towns grew up everywhere.

At the end of the 9th century massive peasant uprisings reduced central authority to a cipher, and power passed to the provincial generals, whose régimes became virtually independent. When in 907 the T'ang finally disappeared, China split into ten separate regional states, and was only reunified by the Sung in 960 to 979. In northern China there was constant warfare, and everywhere it was a period of insecurity, instability and sweeping social change, in which the diversity of China was intensified. During this period of division China lost control of the north-eastern area to the Khitan (Liao) who had overwhelmed Po-hai to set up an empire in Manchuria and Inner Mongolia. In the north-west another powerful kingdom, the Hsi-hsia, was founded by the Tanguts in Ningsia and Kansu. These areas remained completely under alien domination until 1368.

The Sung state was organised on less uniform lines than the T'ang. The emperor enjoyed greater power, and military and financial experts were given greater influence. But there was constant and bitter factional strife between those who wished to rationalise government, and the conservatives, and this weakened the Sung state, which in spite of its power and resources faced grave external threats. The Sung was a far less cosmopolitan era than the T'ang, generally on the defensive and suspicious of the outside world. In 1126-27 this attitude was hardened when the Chin, who had replaced the Liao in the north-east, overran and conquered all of northern China, with terrible devastation. From 1127 to 1279 the Sung survived in control only of central and southern China, constantly on the defensive and forced to maintain huge armies and to pay vast subsidies to their aggressive neighbours.

Nevertheless, Chinese economic growth continued under the Sung. Between 750 and 1100 the population doubled; trade reached new levels, and a great concentration of industries arose around the early Sung capital, K'ai-feng. Even after the loss of the north, Sung China was immensely prosperous. Its southern territories were far more productive than the old northern heartland of China. Population continued to in-

3/The fragmentation of China: the Five Dynasties and Ten Kingdoms 910-23 *(below)* After the widespread peasant rebellions of the 870s, culminating in the Huang Ch'ao uprising, the central power of the T'ang, already weakened since the mid-8th century, speedily collapsed, and a variety of independent local regimes developed on the basis of Late T'ang provincial regional divisions. These were finally reunified by the Sung only in 979.

2/The Chinese world, 7th-8th centuries *(right)* During the 660s and 670s Chinese military power reached a peak, and briefly extended the power of the T'ang from Sogdiana to North Korea. The Chinese remained in control of the Tarim Basin and Dzungaria until 756; the Tarim and parts of north-west China fell to the Tibetans in 763-83 after Chinese garrisons were withdrawn. Chinese institutions and literary culture extended over parts of the Far East which were never controlled by China, but became parts of the Chinese ecumene.

A foreign merchant *(above)* T'ang China was an extremely cosmopolitan society. Many of the merchants, both in large-scale international trade and in local retail trade, were central Asians, like this tomb figure of a Sogdian merchant.

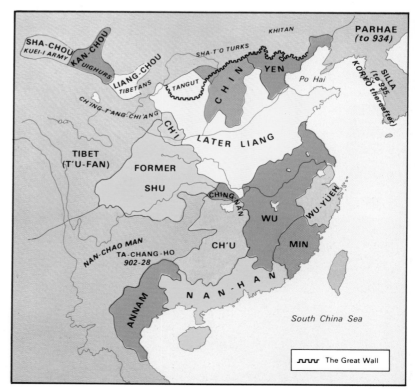

South China Sea

The Great Wall

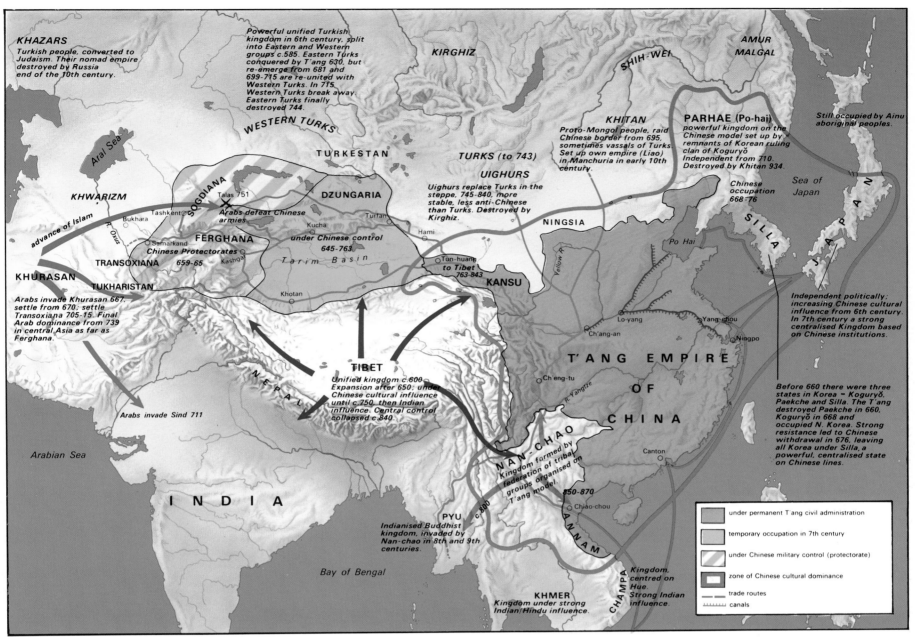

KHAZARS
Turkish people, converted to Judaism. Their nomad empire destroyed by Russia end of the 10th century.

KHWARIZM

Aral Sea

WESTERN TURKS

KIRGHIZ

SHIH-WEI

AMUR MALGAL

Powerful unified Turkish kingdom in 6th century, split into Eastern and Western groups c.585. Eastern Turks conquered by T'ang 630, but re-emerge from 681 and 699-715 are re-united with Western Turks. In 715 Western Turks break away. Eastern Turks finally destroyed 744.

TURKESTAN

TURKS (to 743)

DZUNGARIA

UIGHURS
Uighurs replace Turks in the steppe, 745-840, more stable, less anti-Chinese than Turks. Destroyed by Kirghiz.

KHITAN
Proto-Mongol people, raid Chinese border from 695, sometimes vassals of Turks. Set up own empire (Liao) in Manchuria in early 10th century.

PARHAE (Po-hai)
powerful kingdom on the Chinese model set up by remnants of Korean ruling clan of Koguryŏ. Independent from 710. Destroyed by Khitan 934.

Still occupied by Ainu aboriginal peoples.

advance of Islam

Talas 751
SOGDIANA
Arabs defeat Chinese armies

Tashkent
Bukhara
R. Oxus
Samarkand

FERGHANA
Chinese Protectorates 659-65

Kashgar
Kucha
Turfan

under Chinese control 645-763

Hami

NINGSIA

Chinese occupation 668-76

Sea of Japan

SILLA

JAPAN

TRANSOXIANA

KHURASAN

TUKHARISTAN

Arabs invade Khurasan 667, settle from 670; settle Transoxiana 705-15. Final Arab dominance from 739 in central Asia as far as Ferghana.

Khotan

Tarim Basin

Tun-huang
to Tibet 763-843

KANSU

Lo-yang
Yang-chou
Ch'ang-an
Ningpo

Yellow R.

Po Hai

Independent politically; increasing Chinese cultural influence from 6th century. In 7th century a strong centralised Kingdom based on Chinese institutions.

NEPAL

Arabs invade Sind 711

TIBET
Unified kingdom c.600. Expansion after 650; under Chinese cultural influence until c.750, then Indian influence. Central control collapsed c.840.

T'ANG EMPIRE OF CHINA

Ch'eng-tu
R. Yangtze

Before 660 there were three states in Korea — Koguryŏ, Paekche and Silla. The T'ang destroyed Paekche in 660, Koguryŏ in 668 and occupied N. Korea. Strong resistance led to Chinese withdrawal in 676, leaving all Korea under Silla, a powerful, centralised state on Chinese lines.

Arabian Sea

I N D I A

NAN-CHAO
Kingdom formed by federation of tribal groups organised on T'ang model.

Canton

c.800
850-870
Chiao-chou

ANNAM

PYU
Indianised Buddhist kingdom, invaded by Nan-chao in 8th and 9th centuries.

Bay of Bengal

CHAMPA
Kingdom centred on Hue. Strong Indian influence.

KHMER
Kingdom under strong Indian/Hindu influence.

	under permanent T'ang civil administration
	temporary occupation in 7th century
	under Chinese military control (protectorate)
	zone of Chinese cultural dominance
---	trade routes
......	canals

---

crease rapidly, trade and industry boomed, and the capital, Hang-chou, became indisputably the world's greatest city. It was also a period of great cultural achievement. In the visual arts, in literature, philosophy, science and technology, new heights were reached. Education became more widespread, aided by the dissemination of printing, which had been invented during the T'ang and was now commonplace. The prosperous cities developed an urban middle class with their own life-style and culture, who became patrons of popular drama and of storytellers.

Society was transformed. State examinations for the recruiting of officials gradually replaced the old ruling aristocratic caste with a mandarinate – a meritocracy of career bureaucrats.

Although merchants were excluded from official service, many became immensely rich and held an important place in society, forming guilds and partnerships and setting up a complex commercial organisation with banks, credit systems and paper money. In the countryside the independent peasants of T'ang times, working lands allocated by the state, were replaced by many large estates farmed by tenant farmers and labourers. A free market in land emerged.

Since the old overland routes to central Asia and the Middle East were no longer in Chinese hands, the Chinese slowly became a major sea power. Chinese shipping developed a regular trade with south-east Asia, Indonesia, India and the Persian Gulf. The southern Sung also had a powerful navy.

In the 13th century, after this period of rapid change and growth, the pace of change slowed down markedly. This was partly the result of the immense destruction and social disruption caused by the Mongol conquest (see page 128), but in part because T'ang and Sung China had evolved an abiding social stability, developing conservative and conformist intellectual and political attitudes which militated against change. But in the 13th century China remained far more populous, productive and wealthy, her society far more advanced than that of contemporary Europe. During this whole period, China was the world's greatest power, and Chinese culture the world's greatest splendour.

5/Sung China (below) The Sung suffered considerable losses of territory compared with the T'ang: Vietnam was no longer Chinese territory; in the north, the Khitan state of Liao occupied the border areas on the north-east, and the Tangut state of Hsi-hsia the north-west. The centre of the Sung state was the great commercial city of K'ai-feng, centre of the canal system and of the eastern road network, which grew into the centre of a major complex of industries. The old strategic heartland of the north-west steadily declined in importance.

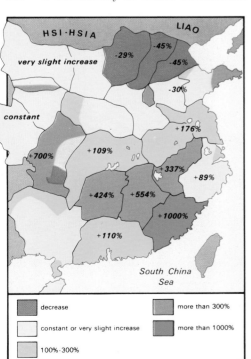

HSI-HSIA

LIAO

very slight increase -45%
-29% -45%
-30%

constant

+176%
+109%
+700% -337% +89%
+424% +554%
+1000%
+110%

South China Sea

	decrease
	constant or very slight increase
	100%-300%
	more than 300%
	more than 1000%

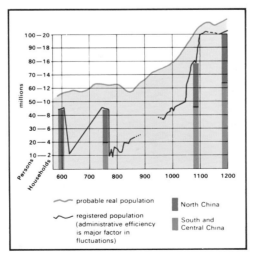

4/Population growth (above and left) The period from 750 to 1250 saw a very rapid growth of the Chinese population, which probably doubled. At the same time the distribution of the people completely changed. In the 7th century 73 per cent of the population lived in the north-east of China, and less than a quarter in south and central China. By the 13th century the situation was reversed and China's economic centre of gravity had shifted from the northern plain to the Yangtze valley.

— probable real population
— registered population (administrative efficiency is major factor in fluctuations)

North China
South and Central China

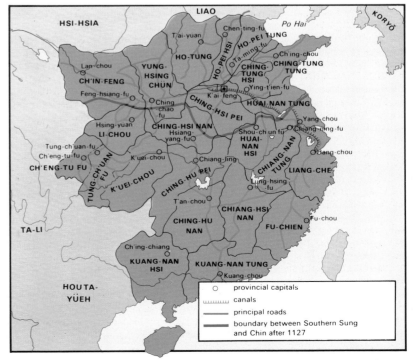

HSI-HSIA

LIAO

Po Hai

KORYŎ

T'ai-yuan
Chen-ting-fu
HO-PEI TUNG
HO-PEI HSI
Ta-ming-fu
CHING TUNG TUNG

Lan-chou
YUNG-HSING CHUN
CH'IN-FENG
Ch'ing-chou
CHING TUNG HSI
Ying-t'ien-fu

Feng-hsiang-fu
Ching-chao-fu
K'ai-feng
CHING-HSI PEI

Hsing-yüan
CHING-HSI NAN
Hsiang-yang-fu
Shou-ch'un fu
HUAI-NAN TUNG
Chiang-ning-fu
Yang-chou

LI-CHOU
Ch'eng-tu-fu
HUAI-NAN HSI
Ch'eng-tu-fu
Chiang-ling
CHIANG-NAN TUNG

CH'ENG-TU FU
TUNG-CH'UAN FU
K'UEI-CHOU
T'an-chou
CHING-HU PEI
Hang-chou
LIANG-CHE

KUANG-NAN HSI
CHING-HU NAN
Fu-chou
CHIANG-HSI NAN
FU-CHIEN

TA-LI
Ch'ing-chiang
KUANG-NAN TUNG
Kuang-chou

HOU-TA-YÜEH

○	provincial capitals
......	canals
	principal roads
	boundary between Southern Sung and Chin after 1127

127

The Mongol Empire 1206 to 1405

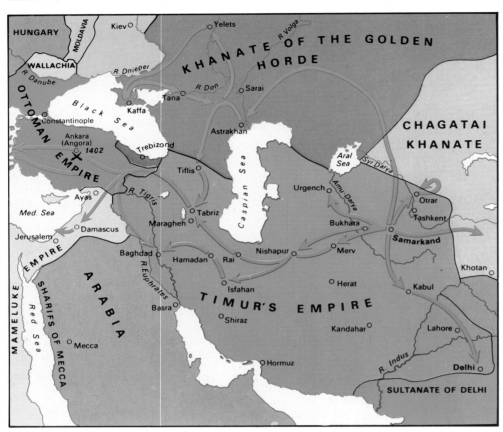

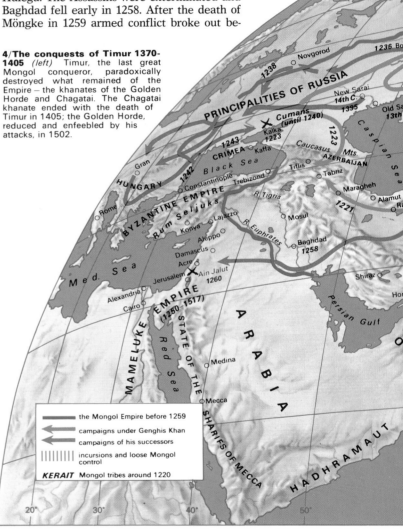

THE Mongols, a primitive nomadic people from the depths of Asia, made a tremendous impact on world history. Their conquests were of a scope and range never equalled, stretching from the eastern frontiers of Germany to Korea and from the Arctic Ocean to Turkey and the Persian Gulf. They even attempted seaborne invasions of Japan and Java. This was the last, and most violent, assault of nomadic barbarism that civilisation was called upon to endure, and its effects were considerable. The political organisation of Asia and a large part of Europe was altered; whole peoples were uprooted and dispersed, permanently changing the ethnic character of many regions; the strength and distribution of the principal religions of the world were decisively altered; European access to Asia and the Far East, interrupted for a thousand years, became possible again once the transcontinental routes were dominated by a single authority and travel made safe.

Ethnically the most striking result of the Mongol conquests was the wide dispersal of the Turkic peoples over western Asia. Since their barren land could not support a large population, the Mongols were not a numerous people, but from the outset Genghis Khan did not hesitate to augment his armies from Turkish tribes on whose fidelity he could rely, until Turks in the Mongol armies actually outnumbered the native Mongols. Thus the Turkish language advanced across Asia with the Mongol armies, the minority of Mongol speakers was absorbed by the Turkish mass and their language survived only in the original homeland. The Turks had already risen to prominence before the Mongol conquests, but the Mongols, by breaking up the old Seljuk sultanate of Rum, cleared the way for the greatest of the Turkish empires – the Ottoman.

In the course of their drive for empire the Mongols came into contact with three religions and their associated cultures – Buddhism, Islam and Christianity. Their attitude towards them was ambivalent. They professed an ancestral shamanism embodied in the *Yasa* or Law of Genghis Khan, but felt the powerful attraction of the new creeds which seemed invariably to be associated with higher cultures. Islam at first seemed unfavourably placed. Baghdad itself was captured and sacked and the caliph slain.

But the religion of the Prophet slowly established its ascendancy over the conquerors and a powerful revival began. This revival was closely bound up with the collapse of Asian Christianity, whose prospects had once looked so bright (see page 100). For a time Christianity was widely preached throughout the Asian continent, but the initial promise was never fulfilled. Buddhism, like Islam, emerged from the Mongol experience stronger than it entered it. It had little success west of the Altai mountains, but in eastern Asia the Mongol dynasty gave it a predominant place in Chinese society.

The early life of Genghis Khan is shrouded in a mist of legend. Primitive Mongol-speaking tribes had lived for centuries in the general area of present-day Mongolia, but it took an extraordinary leader to unite the Mongols and transform them into a world power. Temujin (later Genghis Khan) was born probably in 1167, the son of a tribal chief. After many years of struggle he succeeded, by 1206, in uniting all the Mongol tribes. After subduing other neighbouring tribes, in 1211 he invaded the independent Chin empire in northern China, piercing the Great Wall and opening a struggle that was to continue for twenty-three years, ending only in 1234, after Genghis' death, with the total destruction of the Chin empire. Peking fell in 1215, but Genghis was then drawn away to the west in campaigns against the Kara-Khitai and Khwarizm – the first Muslim state to experience the full fury of the Mongol onslaught. In spite of bitter resistance, the Mongols overwhelmed the Muslim states of central Asia and reached the Caucasus.

Genghis died in 1227, but his conquests were continued and extended by his successors. Before his death he made provision for the succession, dividing his empire among his four sons. Batu, a grandson of Genghis, directed the invasion of Europe. The northern Russian principalities were smashed in a lightning winter campaign in 1237-38, and the ancient city of Kiev was taken by storm and razed to the ground in 1240. The same year a two-pronged assault was

launched against Poland and Hungary. The Oder was passed at Racibórz and the Mongol army swept northwards down the river valley. Breslau was bypassed, and on 9 April 1241 a German/Polish army was annihilated at Legnica. A few days later the second Mongol army routed the Hungarians at Mohi. It is generally believed that only the death of the Great Khan Ogedei in December 1241 saved Europe. Disputes arose over the succession and Batu led the armies back to their old base on the lower Volga in the winter of 1242-43.

If Christian Europe was saved by the death of Ogedei in 1241, the death of the Great Khan Möngke in 1259 saved Muslim Asia. Möngke had resolved to extend the Mongol dominions in the east and west, against the Sung in China, and the Assassins and the Caliphate 'as far as the borders of Egypt'. Möngke himself was to take charge of the Chinese war, but the western campaign was entrusted to his younger brother, Hülegü. The Assassins were exterminated and Baghdad fell early in 1258. After the death of Möngke in 1259 armed conflict broke out be-

1/The Mongol Empire before 1259 (*below*) The greatest land empire in world history was conquered by the ruthless and brilliant cavalry armies of Genghis Khan and his successors. It stretched from Java and Korea in the east to Poland in the west, from the Arctic in the north to Turkey and Persia in the south. The armies became expert at siege warfare, learning from the Chinese, and their field intelligence and signals enabled them to mount bewildering flank attacks, encirclements and obstruction of escape routes. Byzantium and western Europe were saved by the death of Ogedei just as his advance guard reached the Adriatic, and Japan by the storms (or *kamikaze*, sacred wind) that destroyed Kublai Khan's navy.

4/The conquests of Timur 1370-1405 (*left*) Timur, the last great Mongol conqueror, paradoxically destroyed what remained of the Empire – the khanates of the Golden Horde and Chagatai. The Chagatai khanate ended with the death of Timur in 1405; the Golden Horde, reduced and enfeebled by his attacks, in 1502.

2/The Mongol invasion of Europe 1237-42 (*right*) The Mongols conquered Russia in a winter campaign – their cavalry armies moving with great speed on frozen rivers – the only successful winter invasion of Russia in history. A meticulously planned and brilliantly executed campaign against Hungary followed, penetrating from at least three different directions.

tween rival claimants, causing Hülegü to concentrate the bulk of his troops in Azerbaijan leaving only a skeleton force in Syria. This soon became known as Cairo, and the Mameluke sultan took the opportunity to march against the pagan enemies of the faith. At Ain Jalut near Nazareth on 3 September 1260 the superior Mameluke army inflicted a crushing defeat. This battle was a turning point in history. The Mongol advance in the West was never seriously renewed, and the spell of their invincibility shattered for ever.

The death of Möngke also ended the short-lived unity of the Mongol Empire. The direct authority of succeeding Great Khans was confined to the east, while the khanates of Chagatai, Persia (Il-Khan) and the Golden Horde went their several ways as independent states. In the settled kingdoms of Persia and China the Mongol dynasties came to an end in less than a century. In the khanates of the Golden Horde and Chagatai society was less urbanised and

simpler and the population partly nomadic; in consequence Mongol rule lasted longer – in Russia for more than two hundred years. Their decline can in fact be dated from the time of Timur (Tamerlane), whose rise to power marks the final end of the Mongol age of conquests.

The appearance of the Mongols on the world stage was sudden and devastating. Old kingdoms and empires went down before them in monotonous succession. Their success was probably the result of superior strategy, an excellent and highly mobile cavalry, endurance, and a disciplined and co-ordinated manner of fighting. The Mongols even had an organisation that in some ways resembled a modern general staff. On the other hand the opposing armies, especially in Europe, were usually cumbersome and uncoordinated. The invasion of Russia is a good example of Mongol methods. The strongest part of the country was conquered in a few months, and by means of a winter campaign, the Mongol cavalry moving with great speed on the frozen

rivers – the only successful winter invasion of Russia in history. The Mongols did not make any startling innovations in the ancient traditions of the steppe nomads. They used the strategy and tactics of the earlier cavalry armies of the steppe peoples, but under a military genius these were brought to the highest pitch of efficiency and produced what was certainly the most formidable instrument of war in the world at that time.

Nevertheless the social and cultural legacy of the Mongol irruption is not easy to trace. Their rule was mostly comparatively brief. In fact the Mongols never succeeded in creating a distinctive, enduring civilisation. Rather their conquests can be seen as the end of an epoch. From the dawn of civilisation, city dwellers and the cultivators of the soil had been menaced by assault from the fierce riders of the steppes. But during the life of the Mongol Empire came the invention of gunpowder and firearms; no longer would battle be decided by endurance and stamina. During the succeeding centuries Russia and China, the two nations which had suffered most from nomad aggression, steadily moved in to contain once and for all the recalcitrant herdsmen of the steppes.

The Mongol 'soldier' (above) The horsemanship of the Mongol cavalry was the most effective in military history.

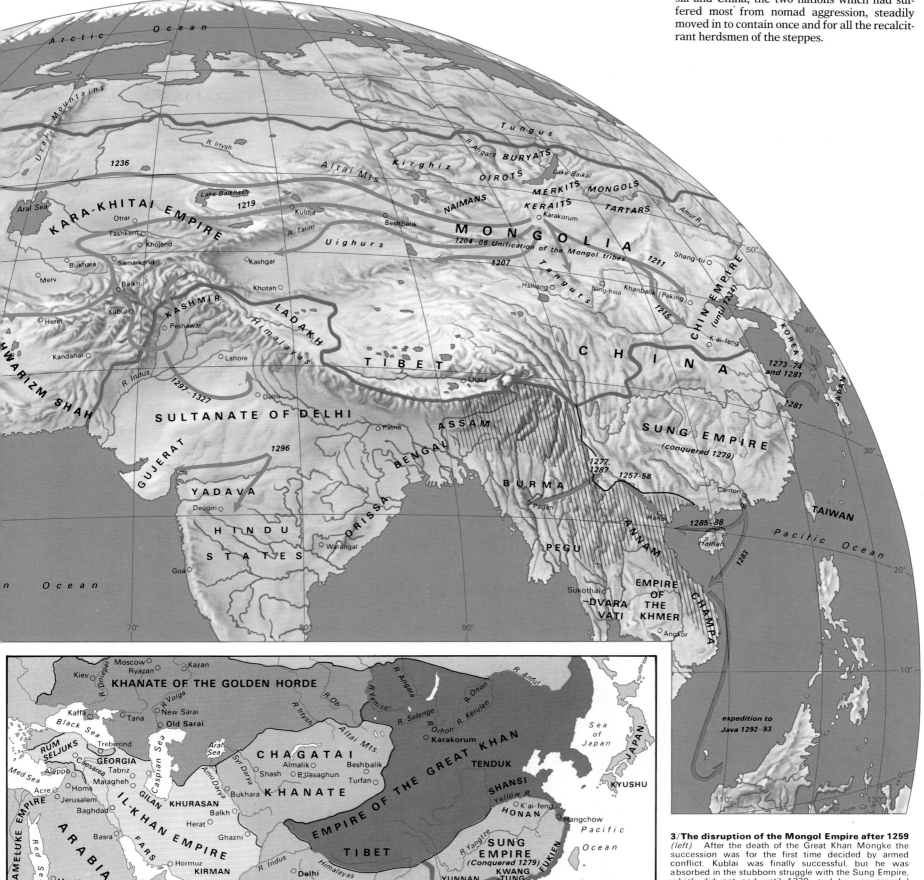

3/The disruption of the Mongol Empire after 1259 (left) After the death of the Great Khan Möngke the succession was for the first time decided by armed conflict. Kublai was finally successful, but he was absorbed in the stubborn struggle with the Sung Empire, which did not end until 1279, and by unsuccessful efforts to conquer Japan. A vast imperial realm comprising nearly all Asia and much of Europe could not be governed by one man.

India: the struggle for power and the Delhi Sultanate

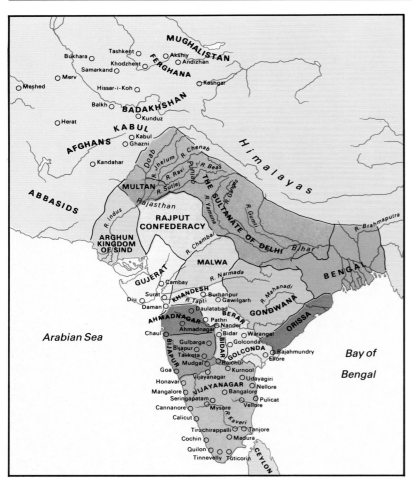

4/India on the eve of Babur's Invasion *(above)* In 1526, one of the Lodi sultans, who had assumed rule after Timur's sack of Delhi, held sway in the Punjab, and another controlled the Doab and Bihar. The Bahmani kingdom in the Deccan had broken up into five separate warring sultanates. Rajput dynasties controlled Rajasthan and also territories further to the north-west, including Delhi.

2/India in the 11th century *(below)* The conquests of Sultan Mahmud of Ghazni stretched deep into central Asia. The subcontinent is divided into two along the line of the river Narmada and the Vindhya mountains. To the south, the Chola Empire, including Ceylon, is shown at its fullest extent. But wars with the Rashtrakutas and others continually abraded the frontiers, both for the Cholas and for the Chalukyas in the west.

IN Harsha's time (see page 82) the city of Kanauj, in western Uttar Pradesh, gradually displaced the ancient dynastic capital of Pataliputra and soon came to dominate the Ganges plain. The tripartite struggle to control it (map 1) waged between the Gurjara-Pratiharas, the Palas and the Rashtrakutas, shaped north Indian history for most of the next 200 years. The Rashtrakuta kingdom, established around the year 753, constantly pressed on the lands to both north and south of its main power base in the north Deccan, and extended, at its peak, from south Gujerat, Malwa and Baghelkhand to Tanjore. The Pala Empire, maintaining strong Buddhist ties with Tibet and valuable commercial links with south-east Asia, included Bengal, Bihar, Orissa and the Andhra country. It flourished exceedingly after the election of a strong king, Gopala, ended a period of political chaos in the 8th century. The Pratiharas originated in Rajasthan and held power from 836 between the east Punjab and the north Bengal. The strengths of the three contenders proved to be almost exactly matched, and in the 10th century, after a last thrust by the Palas which reached as far as Benares, they all disintegrated into smaller warring states. The advancing Turks sacked Kanauj in 1018.

The invaders against whom the Pratiharas were guarding their territory were almost certainly the Arabs, who in the 7th century penetrated Afghanistan and Baluchistan, and in the 8th century conquered Cutch, Saurashtra and Sind. When their further progress was checked by Indian resistance, the Sind Arabs broke away from the Abbasid Empire (827) and later split up into the twin kingdoms of Multan and Mansura. These became well-known trading communities under the Delhi Sultanate, although their political significance was very small.

Events in south India, as in the past, continued to be determined largely by geography. The high, mountain-ringed plateau lands to the west of the peninsula are linked to the fertile plains south of Madras by west-to-east flowing rivers, notably the Krishna and the Godavari. During this period a succession of states and dynasties continually tried to control the waterways along their length, and out of the struggles two groups, the Tamil Cholas in the east and the Chalukyas in the west, emerged as major powers.

The Cholas were already an old people, first mentioned in the inscriptions of Asoka (page 82). Under Rajaraja (985-1014) and his son Rajendra, they now conquered most of the Tamil-nad, eastern Deccan, Ceylon and parts of the Malay Peninsula. Ceylon, involved in conflicts with assorted enemies (including the Rashtrakutas) finally expelled the Cholas in 1070, but this did not prevent the latter from successfully driving north, through Orissa and the Ganges, to take part in the dispersal of the Pala domains and threaten Bengal's independence.

The Rashtrakutas of the north were finally overthrown by the Chalukyas, who had built their kingdom on the ruins left behind by the Satavahanas (page 82) and their successors, the Vakatakas, whose fortunes had declined alongside those of their northern allies, the Guptas. In the 7th century they established control over Vengi, the land between the Krishna and the Godavari, adopted the Zoroastrians, later known as Parsees, who had been expelled by the Arabs, and spread far and wide from their homeland in north Mysore. Their power was broken, however, when the Cholas sacked their capital, Kalyani, in the early 11th century.

Civilisation flourished during this period of history despite the political disarray. Sankaracharya, a 9th-century brahmin from Kerala, set out to cleanse the ancient Vedic philosophy from its accretion of obscurities. He became a famous interpreter of Vedanta, which proclaimed that the final object of existence was the union of the individual and the Absolute Soul, and also propagated the Monist philosophy of Advaita, holding that the world is an illusion. Earlier, in the 6th and 7th centuries, the Tamil saints, known as *alvars*, preached devotion to Vishnu in exquisite poetry, while their contemporaries, the *nainars*, similarly celebrated the cult of Shiva. The Tantric form of Buddhism, with its emphasis on magic, and the substitution of female for male deities, spread its mystically erotic influence from eastern India to Nepal and Tibet. The famous temples, at Tanjore and Gangaikonda-cholapuram in the Tamil-nad, Khajuraho in central India, with its richly sexual sculptures, and the more monumental style of Bhubaneswar, in Orissa, were all built in this period. Storytellers, royal biographers, regional historians, dramatists, and the mystic erotic poets like Javadeva, with his *Gita Govinda* (Song of Krishna), preserved and developed Sanskrit literary traditions.

Early in the 11th century, new dynasties, including the Paramaras, Chandellas and Chedis from central India, and the Chalukyas from Gujerat, who now ruled in the north and northwest, came into conflict with the Yaminis of Ghazni. These former vassals of Bukhara had acquired an extensive empire in Iran and central Asia. Under their formidable leader, Mahmud of Ghazni, they repeatedly invaded as far as the Doab and the Gujerat coast, annexing parts of Baluchistan and the Punjab.

Mahmud's depredations revealed India's underlying political and military weakness. Systematic conquest by the Turkish peoples of central Asia began with the renewed annexation of the Punjab (1186) by Muizzuddin Muhammad, one of the Ghurid family who had lately overthrown their Ghaznavid suzerains. In 1191 he defeated the Rajput clans, commonly accepted descendants of earlier Hunnish invaders, and in 1206 his general, Qutbuddin Aibak, established the first Turko-Afghan dynasty in the strategically-placed city of Delhi, founded in 736. The Delhi Sultanate remained the major

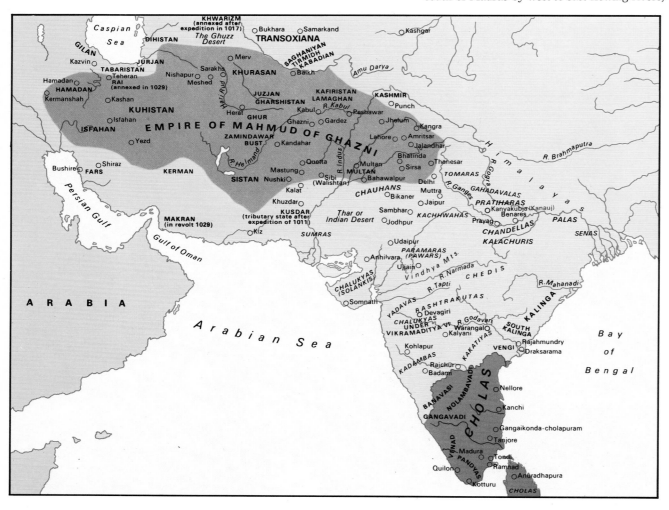

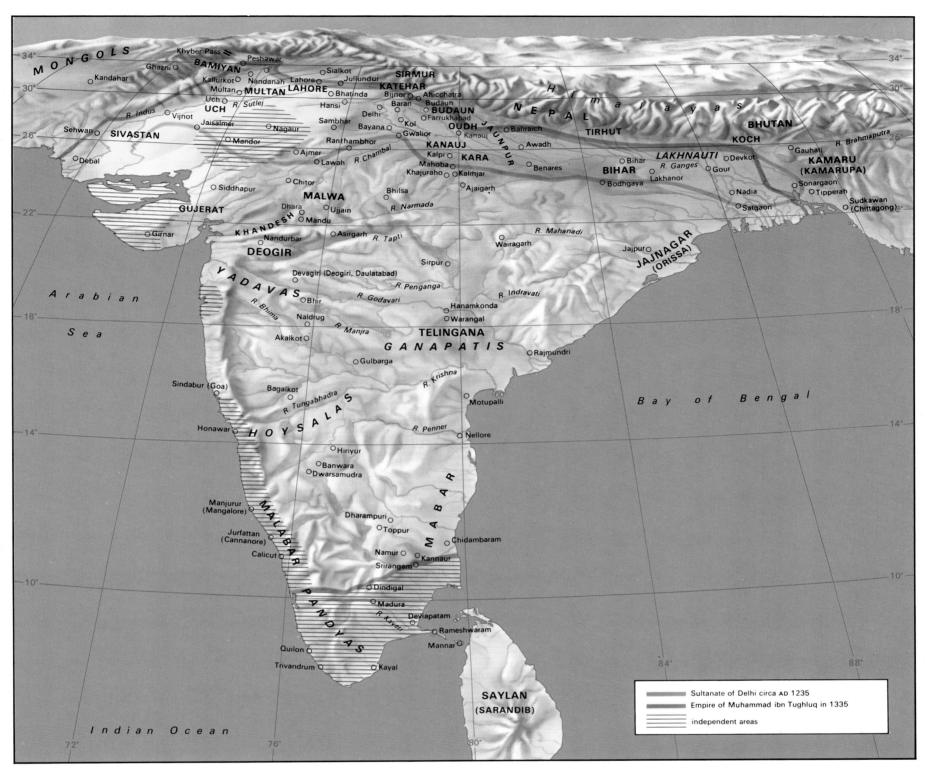

Sultanate of Delhi circa AD 1235
Empire of Muhammad ibn Tughluq in 1335
independent areas

3/The Sultanate of Delhi *(above)* Turko-Afghan rule in India started in the 12th century and reached its height with the Sultanate under Muhammad ibn Tughluq. However, by 1398 Tughluq rule barely extended beyond Delhi.

1/Regional Kingdoms and the Struggle for Empire *(right)* The fluctuating territories held by the Gurjara-Pratiharas, the Rashtrakutas, the Palas, the Cholas and the Arabs in Sind, as they struggled both on their frontiers and for control of Kanauj from c. 750 to 1018.

political factor in north India from the 13th to the 16th century, though it never controlled the whole area, and its power and territories fluctuated widely according to its current ruler's ability. By 1235, under Iltutmish, Qutbuddin's son, it stretched from Sind to Bengal (though hostilities continued in Rajputana). Iltutmish was then succeeded in turn by his daughter, Razziya (ultimately murdered) and by a former palace official, Balban. Expansion resumed when a new Turkish group, the Khaljis, succeeded. Under Alauddin Khalji they annexed Gujerat, Chitor, Ranthambhor, Ujjain, Dhar and Mandu, invaded southernmost India, and devised fiscal and administrative arrangements to support a powerful military machine. They also admitted Indian Muslims to high political office, thus easing much of the internal tension; Hindu kingdoms were reduced to vassalage.

Mongol harassment from the north started with Genghis Khan, who reached the Indus, and continued, with occasional forays to Delhi and beyond. But all were beaten back. Under Muhammad ibn Tughluq (1325-51) the Sultanate reached its maximum extent, with 23 provinces including all the southern kingdoms. But high taxes, an abortive attempt to move Delhi, with its entire population, south to a new capital at Devagiri in the Deccan (or to create a new capital, according to some authorities) and the

sheer size of the empire hastened its decline. Bengal broke away in 1341, the Deccan provinces in 1347 (to form the Bahmani kingdom), and Khandesh, Malwa, Jaunpur and Gujerat between 1382 and 1396. South of the Tungabhadra, the powerful new Vijayanagar empire was firmly established by 1374. After the invasion by Timur (Tamerlane) in 1398, Tughluq rule barely extended beyond Delhi.

During the centuries of Turko-Afghan rule, when a real *modus vivendi* between Muslim and Hindu gradually evolved, a stylistically unified architecture flourished, and a varied local literature grew up in the provincial kingdoms. Humbly-born saints, like Nanak (1469-1532) and Kabir (1440-1518), denied any contradiction between Muslim and Hindu ideas of God, and preached social egalitarianism. The cult of Bhakti, or devotion to a personal deity, revived through the efforts of preachers such as Madhva, who expounded dualism, and Chaitanya (1486-1533) led a revival of Vaishnavism in eastern and northern India. Magnificent temples were built by the Vijayanagar and Hoysala kings who now dominated the south. But much of India was fragmented into local kingdoms, Hindu and Muslim, perpetually at war with each other. When Timur's descendant, Babur, invaded from Afghanistan in 1526, only the Rajputs were organised to resist.

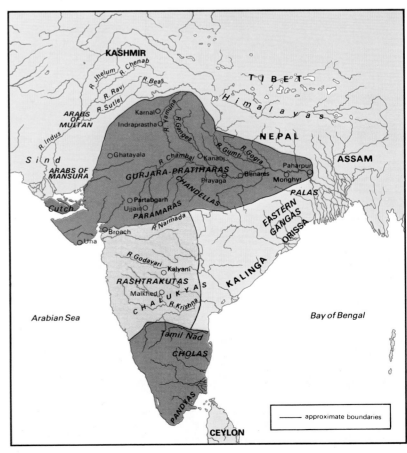

approximate boundaries

131

The early civilisations of South-East Asia to AD 1511

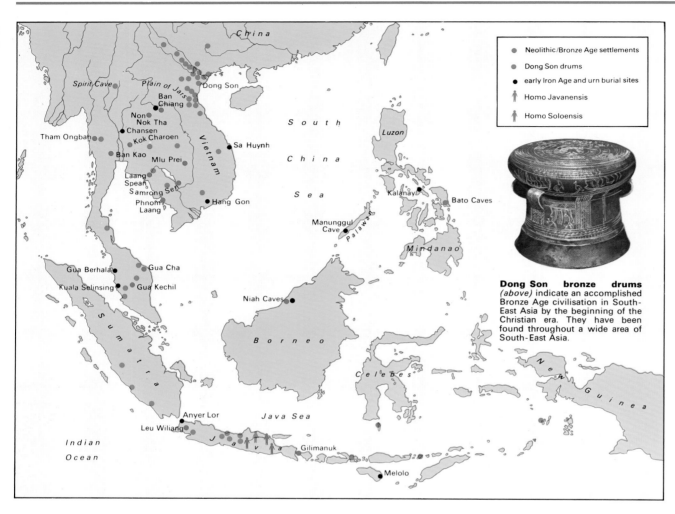

Dong Son bronze drums *(above)* indicate an accomplished Bronze Age civilisation in South-East Asia by the beginning of the Christian era. They have been found throughout a wide area of South-East Asia.

1/Prehistoric sites in South-East Asia *(above)* Neolithic and early Bronze Age sites indicate developed lowland cultures by the 2nd millennium BC. Later (late 1st millennium BC) we find more advanced cultures, characterised by 'Dong Son' bronze drums or by early Iron Age jar burials, all before the arrival of Indian and Chinese influences in the area.

Ananda Temple, Pagan Built by King Kyanzittha (1084-1112), supposedly in imitation of the great cave temple of Ananta (Orissa), of which, according to the Burmese chronicles, he learned from visiting Indian monks. The massive temple, in the shape of a perfect Greek cross, is crowned with a pinnacle rising to a height of 52 m. Inside the temple are four colossal standing Buddha images. The base and terraces are decorated with tiles depicting scenes from classic Buddhist stories.

S ITUATED at one of the world's main cross-roads, the countries of South-East Asia had their own history, with indigenous roots reaching back into early prehistory and beyond. 'Java Man', whose remains, belonging to the Middle Pleistocene, were found in the Solo Valley of central Java, may be related to the culture of 'Peking Man' in China. Java has also produced the earliest evidence of *Homo sapiens* in South-East Asia: remains of c.40,000 BC, from the Brantas Valley. A number of Palaeolithic and Mesolithic cultures have been identified in various parts of the region, notably the 'Bacsonian' and 'Hoabinhian' of Vietnam, Siam and Malaya. Early cave sites have been excavated in Sumatra, Borneo, Cambodia and Siam (Thailand), and in one (Spirit Cave, northern Siam) evidence was found suggesting rice cultivation as early as 6000 BC.

The Neolithic cultures of the region were formerly identified by axe types, including the rectangular adze which was undoubtedly of ancient origin. More recently, the excavation of burial and possibly habitation sites has provided information about specific Neolithic cultures and their highly localised pottery traditions. At sites in north-east Thailand (Ban Chiang, Non Nok Tha) there are indications of a gradual evolution towards bronze metallurgy. Attempts to date the earliest bronze, by Carbon-14 and thermo-luminescence methods, have yielded controversial results; some scholars claim a date earlier than 3000 BC, while others place it nearer to 1000 BC. A Neolithic and Early Bronze culture of around 1000 BC has also been explored in northern Vietnam. The first use of iron in the region seems to occur in central Siam, perhaps as early as 500 BC; it had spread to Borneo and Palawan by c.200 BC.

It is thus clear that South-East Asia had a number of flourishing cultures using bronze and iron before the advent of Indian and Chinese influences made itself felt in the 2nd or 3rd century AD. These influences left a permanent impact but they never obliterated the distinc-tive character of South-East Asian civilisation. Nevertheless, the next thousand years saw their assimilation to produce some distinctive South-East Asian societies.. Chinese influence was predominant in Tonking (northern Vietnam), which has its own polity down to c.110 BC, but was subsequently annexed to China and ruled as a Chinese province down to c.AD 900. The remainder of the region gradually came under Hindu-Buddhist influences from India, beginning about the 2nd or 3rd century AD. Early trade routes appear to have linked India with southern Burma, central and southern Siam, lower Cambodia and southern Vietnam, where an ancient port city (3rd-6th century) was excavated at Oc Eo. By the 5th-6th century we find Buddhist images and votive tablets, and also the earliest Sanskrit inscriptions. In addition to the above areas, early Indianisation occurred in Java and southern Sumatra. Although Indian in culture, these areas had trade and political relations with China, which welcomed tribute missions from a growing number of states whose location it is not always easy to identify.

By the 7th century, small Hindu temples were being built in lower Cambodia, notably at Angkor Borei, and also in central Java; other early temples, probably Buddhist, have been excavated in southern Burma at Peikthano and Sri Ksetra. These three areas became the principal centres of temple-building and produced a number of major temple complexes: Borobudur and Prambanan (central Java, 8th-10th centuries); Angkor (9th-13th centuries); and Pagan (11th-13th centuries). All three combined Hindu and Buddhist elements, but Buddhism was especially strong at Pagan and Hinduism at Angkor. Another series of temples belonging to the Hindu-Buddhist kingdom of Champa is found along the coast of central Vietnam. A centre of Sanskrit culture, Palembang, in south-east Sumatra, emerged in the 7th century as the probable capital of the maritime empire of Srivijaya, which for centuries controlled international trade passing through the straits of Malacca and Sunda, and across the Isthmus of Kra.

The great temple states fell into decline by the later 13th century. In Java, the area of Prambanan was superseded in importance by eastern Java, where three states developed in succession: Kediri (12th century), Singhasari (13th century) and finally Majapahit (late 13th-early 16th centuries). On the mainland, Pagan was sacked by Mongol invaders and then by Shans (late 13th century), while Angkor fell to Thai attacks from 1369 onwards and was eventually abandoned. Sukhothai, the first of the lowland Thai cities, was itself in decline by the late 14th century. In place of the old temple cities new political centres emerged: in Burma, Ava (1364) on the upper Irrawaddy, Toungoo (1347) on the Sittang, and Pegu (1369), capital of a new Mon kingdom of the south; in Siam, Ayutthaya (1350) and Chiengmai (1296); in Cambodia, Phnom Penh and other capitals along the Mekong; in Laos, Luang Prabang (1353). All were Theravada Buddhist in the Sinhalese tradition, and had stupas, not temples. Meanwhile, in Vietnam the Chinese had failed to reconquer their former province despite invasions in 1075-77 and 1285-88; a new kingdom emerged calling itself Dai Viet, and gradually absorbed the kingdom of Champa, finally annexing its capital, Vijaya, in 1471. In the meantime, Srivijaya declined and at the end of the 14th century Malacca took its place. By that time the east Javanese empire of Majapahit was declining, and the west Javanese kingdom of Pajajaran was also to go down before Muslim pressure from the northern coast ports in the early 16th century.

Political change in the 14th and 15th centuries was accompanied by significant religious developments. Thus while Theravada Buddhism

3/Cultural divisions of South-East Asia in 1500
(right) By 1500 the modern pattern of polities and cultures had begun to emerge, with the spread of Islam in the islands and Theravada Buddhism on the mainland, while Vietnam remained Confucian and Mahayana Buddhist. Malacca was the centre of a strong maritime, commercial empire which traded with the whole world, and was a main diffusion centre of Islam.

took firm root on the mainland, Islam, which had begun to influence northern Sumatra just before 1300, made its first big advances in the archipelago under the patronage of Malacca. The Malaccan empire in the peninsula and in Sumatra adopted Islam, and from it the faith was taken to the north Javanese trading ports and the Spice Islands, and also to north Borneo, and thence to Mindanao in the Philippines. Its advance in that direction was only halted by the Spanish seizure of Manila in 1571, and their introduction of Christianity. In Vietnam, this period saw the strengthening of Confucian scholarship, despite the repulse of a Chinese attempt at reconquest under the Ming. As before, Chinese cultural influence remained limited to Vietnam, but under the Ming the old system of tributary relationships was revived and strengthened, and a series of important voyages to the southern seas was made by the Muslim admiral, Cheng Ho (see page 146).

Thus by about 1500, South-East Asia had begun to take on its modern pattern of cultures and polities – on the eve of the arrival of the Europeans.

2/South-East Asia AD 500-1500 *(below)* Early Buddhist and Hindu images with isolated Sanskrit inscriptions (5th-6th centuries) were succeeded in some areas by temple complexes (8th-13th centuries) denoting major political centres, notably at Pagan and Angkor and in central Java. These were followed by Mon, Thai and Burmese kingdoms on the mainland and Malay sultanates in the maritime areas. Vietnam became Sinicised between the 1st and 9th centuries and subsequently developed as an independent kingdom absorbing the Cham kingdom to the south.

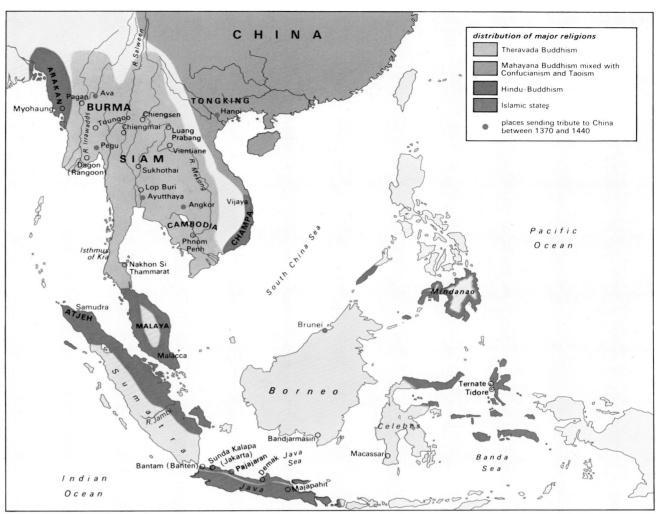

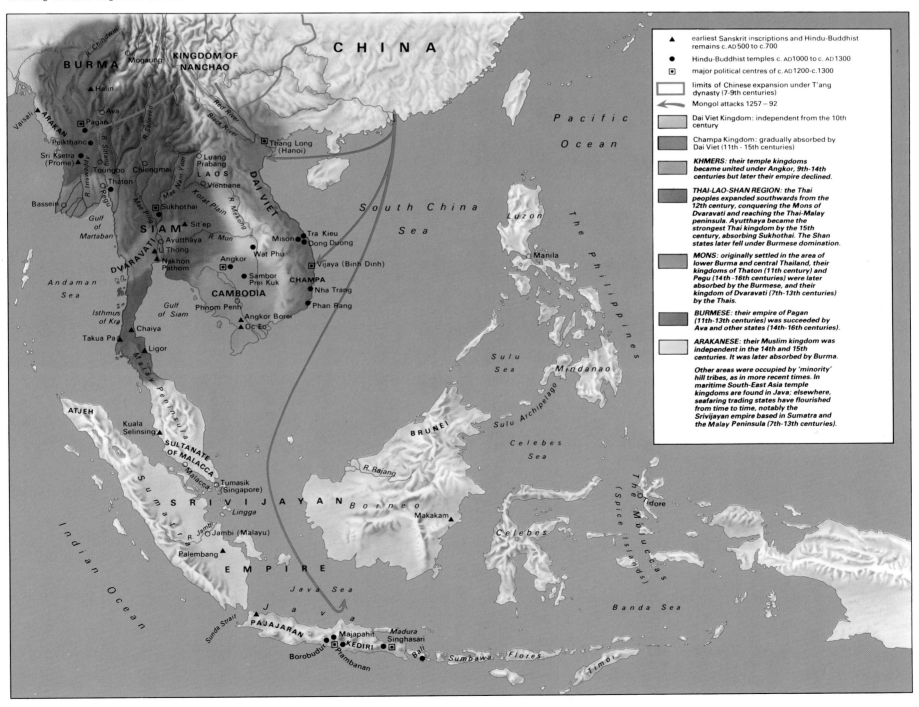

The Muslim world: the Middle East and North Africa 909 to 1517

BY the beginning of the 10th century, the efforts of the Abbasid caliphs to maintain the political unity of the Muslim world were faltering; provincial governors and army commanders were gaining local autonomy, and one military group, the Buyids, established itself in the capital, Baghdad, in 945, and ruled in the name of the Abbasids for more than a century. In some places, the bases of society were weakened; there were movements of social and political unrest, and differences concerning the succession to the caliphate and the nature of authority in Islam. These differences had emerged after Mohammed's death in 632, since the Prophet had left no guidelines for choosing his successor. The group that now forms the majority of Muslims, the Sunnis, claimed that authority passed to the caliphs, leaders whom the community designated, and who exercised supreme judicial and executive power. The Shi'is, however, believed that Mohammed's authority passed to his cousin and son-in-law Ali, and to his descendants; for the Shi'is the various imams are infallible because of their descent from Ali and from the Prophet's daughter Fatima. In political terms, the Umayyads and the Abbasids were Sunnis while many of the dynasties that challenged their authority in various parts of the Islamic world were Shi'is. In the 8th century one of these established a dynasty in Morocco, in the 9th century others created states in eastern Arabia and Yemen, and in the 10th century yet another, the Ismailis, set up a more important state, that of the Fatimids, first in Tunisia and then in Egypt and Syria. They took the title of caliph in opposition to the Abbasids; in opposition to them, so did the branch of the Umayyads who had established themselves in Spain after they had been defeated in the east by the Abbasids.

In most of the Middle East and North Africa, rainfall is scanty and irregular and vegetation sparse, and settled agriculture depends on strong government and good irrigation. In the 10th century there was some disturbance of the settled order, and a shift in the balance between sedentary cultivators and nomadic pastoralists, as Berbers expanded into Morocco, Arabs west along the North African coast, and Turks south and west from central Asia. But pastoral groups also provided the manpower and leadership which made possible a restoration of strong government. In Morocco, two successive movements of religious reform, those of the Almoravids and Almohads, gathered Berber groups around them and formed states; the former spread into Spain, the latter into Algeria and Tunisia. Another group, of Turkish origin, the Seljuks, established themselves in Baghdad. Their state was the first important example of a new type of Muslim state, based on a partnership between 'men of the sword', mainly of Turkish origin, and bureaucrats and men of the law, Persian or Arab in culture, and on an alliance with the interests of the merchant and landowning classes. In these states, officials and officers were paid by being given the right to collect and keep the tax on land in return for service; thus those who might be of alien or nomadic origin were given an interest in the prosperity of the countryside and the stability of society.

The Seljuks and their successors were called sultans, not caliphs, and ruled in the name of the Abbasid caliphs. They did not claim universal rule, but their limited kingdoms existed within a stable, international Islamic social order, which had by this time been brought into existence by gradual conversion (although Christian, Jewish and other communities still existed). This order was maintained by a common religion and law, the Arabic language and by widespread trade, the cities of Iraq, Baghdad and Basra playing an important part in this trade.

In course of time the geographical limits of this society had changed. Islam had expanded into northern India, and from the time of the Seljuks began to expand also into Anatolia. But the Normans ended Muslim rule in Sicily, and the southward expansion of the Christian states in northern Spain, checked for a time by the coming of the Almoravids and Almohads, continued after the battle of Las Navas de Tolosa (1212), until all that was left of Muslim Spain was the kingdom of Granada, and that ended in 1492. In Palestine and Syria, an attempt by Crusaders from western Europe to re-establish Christian rule led to the creation of a number of small states in the late 11th century, but a century later they were virtually destroyed by a new and strong government in Egypt and Syria, that of the Ayyubids created by Saladin.

In the 13th century the balance of Muslim society, at least in its eastern part, was again disturbed by a new conquering group, with Mongol leadership and largely Turkish manpower (see page 128); in 1258 they captured Baghdad ending the Abbasid caliphate. They were gradually converted to Islam and absorbed into Muslim society, but by this time it was in some ways a different society. The Muslim world was split into clearly defined regions. In the east, there ruled first the Ilkhanids, a branch of the conquering Mongol dynasty, and then another dynasty of similar origin, founded by Timur (Tamerlane); to the west, attempts by the Mongols to expand towards the Mediterranean were ended at the battle of Ain Jalut (1260) by a new ruling group in Egypt and Syria, the Mamelukes, an élite of soldiers from southern Russia and the Caucasus. Further to the west, North Africa fell under the control of two states: the Hafsids in Tunisia and the Marinids in Morocco.

These divisions were more than political. By now the decline of the irrigation works and a shift in trade routes had weakened the cities of Iraq; the main centres of Muslim society lay in Persia and in the Nile valley. Between these two there were deep differences of culture. The dominant Arabic culture of the west preserved its traditions of law, mysticism and literature but was no longer creative; in the east, the art of the miniature and architecture thrived, and the Persian language, revived in an Islamic form,

was the medium of great poetry. In the east, too, Turkish pastoral elements continued to play an important part in the life of society and the creation of states. In Anatolia, Turkish frontier states expanded at the expense of the Byzantines, and in one of them there emerged a new dynasty, the Ottomans.

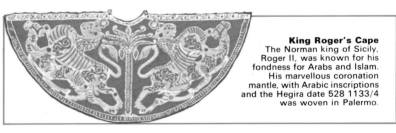

King Roger's Cape
The Norman king of Sicily, Roger II, was known for his fondness for Arabs and Islam. His marvellous coronation mantle, with Arabic inscriptions and the Hegira date 528 1133/4 was woven in Palermo.

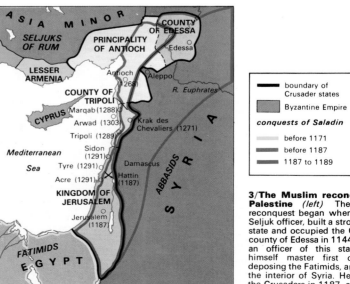

	boundary of Crusader states
▣	Byzantine Empire

conquests of Saladin

	before 1171
	before 1187
	1187 to 1189

3/The Muslim reconquest of Palestine *(left)* The Muslim reconquest began when Zengi, a Seljuk officer, built a strong Syrian state and occupied the Crusading county of Edessa in 1144. Saladin, an officer of this state, made himself master first of Egypt, deposing the Fatimids, and then of the interior of Syria. He attacked the Crusaders in 1187, and before his death in 1193 had captured Jerusalem and driven the Crusaders from all but a narrow coastal strip between Acre and Antioch.

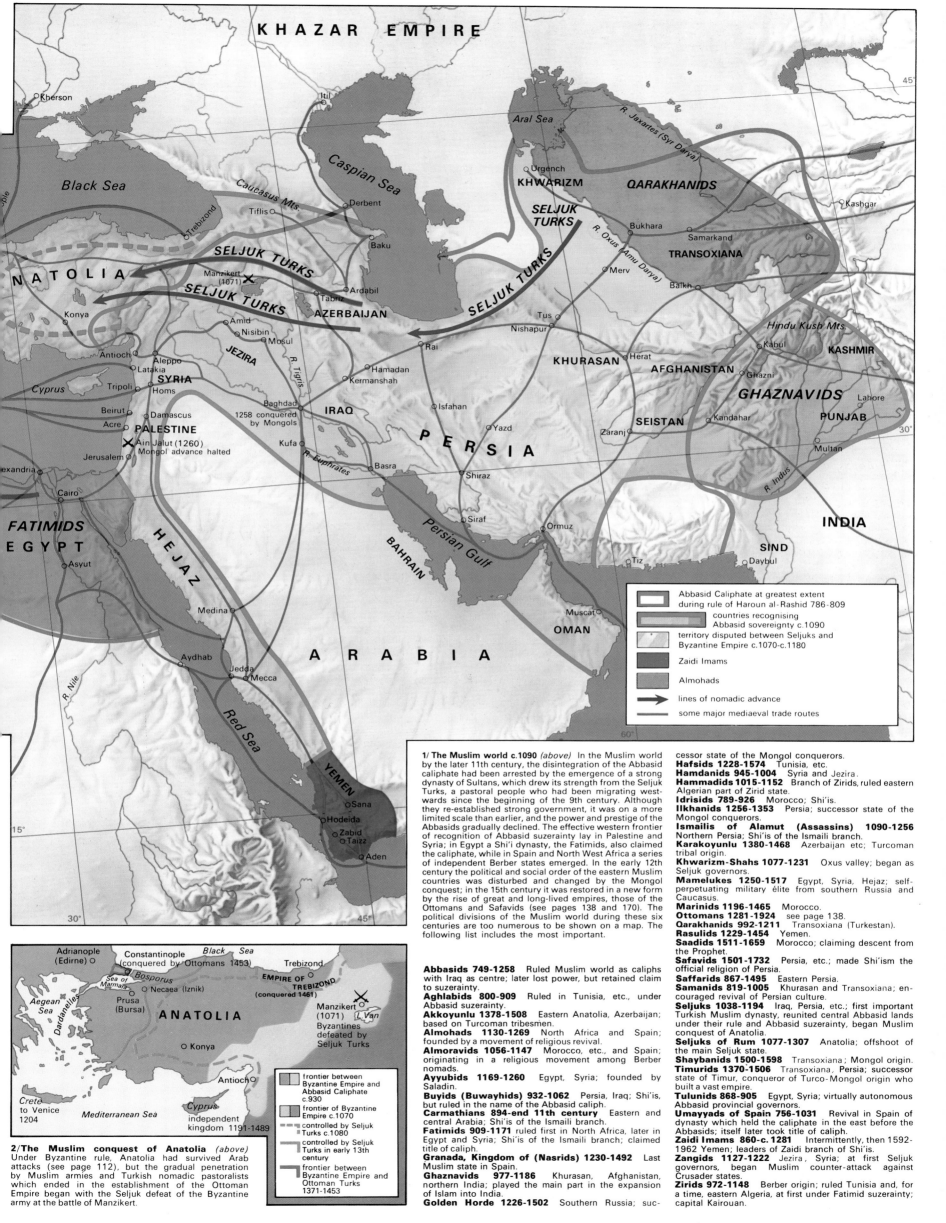

KHAZAR EMPIRE

Kherson
Itil
Black Sea
Caspian Sea
Aral Sea
R. Jaxartes (Syr Darya)
Urgench
KHWARIZM
QARAKHANIDS
Kashgar
Trebizond
Tiflis
Derbent
Bukhara
Samarkand
SELJUK TURKS
TRANSOXIANA
ANATOLIA
Manzikert (1071) X
SELJUK TURKS
SELJUK TURKS
Tabriz
Ardabil
AZERBAIJAN
Baku
R. Oxus (Amu Darya)
Merv
Balkh
Hindu Kush Mts.
Konya
SELJUK TURKS
Rai
Nishapur
Tus
KHURASAN
Herat
Kabul
KASHMIR
Amid
Nisibin
Mosul
JEZIRA
Hamadan
Kermanshah
AFGHANISTAN
Ghazni
Ghazni
Antioch
Aleppo
Latakia
SYRIA
R. Tigris
GHAZNAVIDS
Lahore
Cyprus
Tripoli
Homs
Isfahan
PUNJAB
Beirut
Damascus
Baghdad
1258 conquered by Mongols
IRAQ
PERSIA
Yazd
SEISTAN
Kandahar
Acre
PALESTINE
X Ain Jalut (1260)
Mongol advance halted
Kufa
Jerusalem
R. Euphrates
Basra
Zaranj
Multan
R. Indus
alexandria
Cairo
Shiraz
Siraf
Ormuz
SIND
Daybul
INDIA
FATIMIDS
EGYPT
HEJAZ
BAHRAIN
Persian Gulf
Tiz
OMAN
Muscat
Asyut
ARABIA
Medina
R. Nile
Aydhab
Jedda
Mecca
Red Sea
YEMEN
Sana
Hodeida
Zabid
Taizz
Aden

Legend:
- Abbasid Caliphate at greatest extent during rule of Haroun al-Rashid 786-809
- countries recognising Abbasid sovereignty c.1090
- territory disputed between Seljuks and Byzantine Empire c.1070-c.1180
- Zaidi Imams
- Almohads
- → lines of nomadic advance
- — some major mediaeval trade routes

1/ The Muslim world c.1090 (above) In the Muslim world by the later 11th century, the disintegration of the Abbasid caliphate had been arrested by the emergence of a strong dynasty of Sultans, which drew its strength from the Seljuk Turks, a pastoral people who had been migrating westwards since the beginning of the 9th century. Although they re-established strong government, it was on a more limited scale than earlier, and the power and prestige of the Abbasids gradually declined. The effective western frontier of recognition of Abbasid suzerainty lay in Palestine and Syria; in Egypt a Shi'i dynasty, the Fatimids, also claimed the caliphate, while in Spain and North West Africa a series of independent Berber states emerged. In the early 12th century the political and social order of the eastern Muslim countries was disturbed and changed by the Mongol conquest; in the 15th century it was restored in a new form by the rise of great and long-lived empires, those of the Ottomans and Safavids (see pages 138 and 170). The political divisions of the Muslim world during these six centuries are too numerous to be shown on a map. The following list includes the most important.

Abbasids 749-1258 Ruled Muslim world as caliphs with Iraq as centre; later lost power, but retained claim to suzerainty.
Aghlabids 800-909 Ruled in Tunisia, etc., under Abbasid suzerainty.
Akkoyunlu 1378-1508 Eastern Anatolia, Azerbaijan; based on Turcoman tribesmen.
Almohads 1130-1269 North Africa and Spain; founded by a movement of religious revival.
Almoravids 1056-1147 Morocco, etc., and Spain; originating in a religious movement among Berber nomads.
Ayyubids 1169-1260 Egypt, Syria; founded by Saladin.
Buyids (Buwayhids) 932-1062 Persia, Iraq; Shi'is, but ruled in the name of the Abbasid caliph.
Carmathians 894-end 11th century Eastern and central Arabia; Shi'is of the Ismaili branch.
Fatimids 909-1171 ruled first in North Africa, later in Egypt and Syria; Shi'is of the Ismaili branch; claimed title of caliph.
Granada, Kingdom of (Nasrids) 1230-1492 Last Muslim state in Spain.
Ghaznavids 977-1186 Khurasan, Afghanistan, northern India; played the main part in the expansion of Islam into India.
Golden Horde 1226-1502 Southern Russia; suc-

cessor state of the Mongol conquerors.
Hafsids 1228-1574 Tunisia, etc.
Hamdanids 945-1004 Syria and Jezira.
Hammadids 1015-1152 Branch of Zirids, ruled eastern Algerian part of Zirid state.
Idrisids 789-926 Morocco; Shi'is.
Ilkhanids 1256-1353 Persia; successor state of the Mongol conquerors.
Ismailis of Alamut (Assassins) 1090-1256 Northern Persia; Shi'is of the Ismaili branch.
Karakoyunlu 1380-1468 Azerbaijan etc; Turcoman tribal origin.
Khwarizm-Shahs 1077-1231 Oxus valley; began as Seljuk governors.
Mamelukes 1250-1517 Egypt, Syria, Hejaz; self-perpetuating military élite from southern Russia and Caucasus.
Marinids 1196-1465 Morocco.
Ottomans 1281-1924 see page 138.
Qarakhanids 992-1211 Transoxiana (Turkestan).
Rasulids 1229-1454 Yemen.
Saadids 1511-1659 Morocco; claiming descent from the Prophet.
Safavids 1501-1732 Persia, etc.; made Shi'ism the official religion of Persia.
Saffarids 867-1495 Eastern Persia.
Samanids 819-1005 Khurasan and Transoxiana; encouraged revival of Persian culture.
Seljuks 1038-1194 Iraq, Persia, etc.; first important Turkish Muslim dynasty, reunited central Abbasid lands under their rule and Abbasid suzerainty, began Muslim conquest of Anatolia.
Seljuks of Rum 1077-1307 Anatolia; offshoot of the main Seljuk state.
Shaybanids 1500-1598 Transoxiana; Mongol origin.
Timurids 1370-1506 Transoxiana, Persia; successor state of Timur, conqueror of Turco-Mongol origin who built a vast empire.
Tulunids 868-905 Egypt, Syria; virtually autonomous Abbasid provincial governors.
Umayyads of Spain 756-1031 Revival in Spain of dynasty which held the caliphate in the east before the Abbasids; itself later took title of caliph.
Zaidi Imams 860-c.1281 Intermittently, then 1592-1962 Yemen; leaders of Zaidi branch of Shi'is.
Zangids 1127-1222 Jezira, Syria; at first Seljuk governors, began Muslim counter-attack against Crusader states.
Zirids 972-1148 Berber origin; ruled Tunisia and, for a time, eastern Algeria, at first under Fatimid suzerainty; capital Kairouan.

Inset map (bottom left):
Adrianople (Edirne)
Constantinople (conquered by Ottomans 1453)
Black Sea
Trebizond
Aegean Sea
Sea of Marmara
Bosporus
EMPIRE OF TREBIZOND (conquered 1461)
Necaea (Iznik)
Prusa (Bursa)
Manzikert (1071) X
L. Van
Byzantines defeated by Seljuk Turks
ANATOLIA
Dardanelles
Konya
Crete to Venice 1204
Antioch
Mediterranean Sea
Cyprus independent kingdom 1191-1489

Legend (inset):
- frontier between Byzantine Empire and Abbasid Caliphate c.930
- frontier of Byzantine Empire c.1070
- controlled by Seljuk Turks c.1080
- controlled by Seljuk Turks in early 13th century
- frontier between Byzantine Empire and Ottoman Turks 1371-1453

2/The Muslim conquest of Anatolia (above) Under Byzantine rule, Anatolia had survived Arab attacks (see page 112), but the gradual penetration by Muslim armies and Turkish nomadic pastoralists which ended in the establishment of the Ottoman Empire began with the Seljuk defeat of the Byzantine army at the battle of Manzikert.

The emergence of states in Africa 900 to 1500

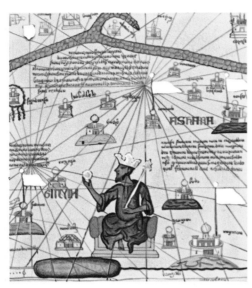

Africa's golden wealth *(above)* Western Europe abandoned the gold standard in the Dark Ages, but by the 13th century Italian city states and the Christian Spanish kingdoms were striking gold coins. Up to about 1350 at least two-thirds of the world's supply of gold came from West Africa. Mansa Musa, ruler of the great empire of Mali, epitomised the golden wealth of Africa.

THE period from the year 900 to 1500 saw the growth of states throughout much of the northern part of Africa, and coincidentally the forging of trade links. With few exceptions, we know much less about Africa south of the Equator, but even there the origins of states and of trading can be traced back to this time.

A series of foreign Muslim dynasties – the Fatimids, Ayyubids and Mamelukes – ruled Egypt, and these regimes stimulated commerce in the eastern Mediterranean, the Red Sea and the Arabian Sea. This flow of trade provided the economic basis for the revival, after the decline of Axum, of the political power of the Christian empire of Ethiopia, first under the Cushitic-speaking Zagwe dynasty in the 11th century, and then under the Amharic-speaking Solomonids in the 13th century. The Solomonids came into conflict with the Muslim coastal states of the Horn of Africa, notably Adal.

By AD 1000 the Maghreb (north-west Africa) had been Islamic land for over three centuries and was the site of the great Berber empires of the Almoravids and the Almohads (see page 134). During the period 1000 to 1500 Islam spread south: up the Nile into the Christian kingdoms of Nubia, along the northern and eastern coasts of the Horn (which faced southern Arabia), and across the Sahara into the

states in what is called the Sudanic belt (stretching from Senegal to the Nile, south of the great desert). Muslims crossed the Sahara as merchants and travellers with the caravans of camels which regularly made the hazardous journey from the trading depots on either edge of the desert, such as Sijilmassa, south of the Atlas mountains in Morocco, and Walata in Mali. This dangerous trade carried luxury goods (and in time, firearms) and salt – a vital element in the diet in tropical countries – to the black African lands south of the Sahara. In exchange, gold, leather-work and slaves went northwards. By the middle of the period, the economies of Muslim Middle East and Christian Europe depended upon African gold.

This expanding trans-Saharan trade gave an impetus to the growth of states in the Sudanic belt. Two of the greatest of these were created by Mande-speaking peoples who had spread across the western part of west Africa. Ghana, which flourished from the 8th to the 11th centuries, was established by the Soninke group of the Mande in the area north of the Senegal and Niger rivers. Its successor, Mali, founded by the Malinke Mande, was a vast empire stretching from the Atlantic right across the great bend of the Niger. In 1324 the Mali king Mansa Musa went on pilgrimage to Mecca, and took so much gold with his retinue that en route the currency of Cairo was depressed. The empire of Mali was followed by that of Songhay, which was centred on the Niger cities of Gao and Timbuktu. East of Mali were the city states of Hausaland, some of which – Zaria, Kano, Katsina – became extremely prosperous, although they never united to form a single Hausa state. Further east lay the Kanuri empire. This had been founded by desert people in Kanem, to the east of Lake Chad, but by the 14th century had shifted its political centre to Borno, west of the lake. The Kanuri kings, known as *mais*, came from one of the longest surviving dynasties in history, being finally overthrown in the 19th century.

By the late Middle Ages, therefore, when western Europe was undergoing a decline as a result of the Black Death and the ravages of the Hundred Years War, the black kingdoms of the western and central Sudan were flourishing. A numer of African kings – Mansa Musa and Sonni Ali, to name only two – were renowned throughout Islam and Christendom for their wealth, brilliance and the artistic achievements of their subjects. Their capitals were immense walled cities, to which thronged traders of many nationalities. Alongside the mosques of the Muslim townsmen grew up universities (at, for

instance, Timbuktu and Jenne) which attracted scholars and poets from far and wide. The rule of these African kings was widely acknowledged, being enforced by a mixture of military force and diplomatic alliances with local leaders. Royal judges dispensed justice, and royal bureaucracies administered taxation and controlled trade, the life-blood of these empires.

To the south of these Sudanic states, Hausa and Malinke merchants (the latter known as Dyula) traded among the peoples on the edge of the tropical forests, especially in the gold-producing regions. By 1500 the foundations had been laid of many of the famous forest states such as Oyo, Benin and the Akan kingdoms, partly as a result of contacts with the northerners. Also by 1500 these kingdoms had been visited by the first European sailors, mainly Portuguese, who had explored the way around west Africa into the Bight of Benin.

Down the east coast of Africa was a string of Muslim city states, such as Mogadishu and Kilwa Kisiwani on the mainland, and the island of Zanzibar, which were part of the Indian Ocean trading complex. Especially important to this system was the gold of the Zimbabwe region, which was shipped from the port of Sofala, south of the Zambezi. In addition to its original Indonesian colonists, Madagascar – a minor participant in the Indian Ocean trade – was being settled by mainland Africans. In 1498 Vasco da Gama sailed round Africa, and visited some of these east African ports en route for India. In a dramatic fashion, European interlopers were poaching upon a highly lucrative Indian Ocean Muslim trading preserve.

In the interior of the southern half of the continent, several African peoples were coalescing to form the nuclei of later kingdoms. These people were iron-working agriculturalists and pastoralists with material cultures known collectively as Later Iron Age; these developed into sophisticated civilisations. Many were Bantu-speakers. Centralised states, with rulers who were held to be divine, were emerging into the Kongo region south of the lower Zaire river, in Lubaland (Katanga or Shaba), Zimbabweland (Rhodesia) and the interlacustrine area between the great lakes of east Africa. By 1500 states were forming here as a result of the interaction between Bantu-speaking farmers and other Later Iron Age peoples, many of them pastoralists who had come down from the inland basin of the Nile (southern Sudan) and from the Horn of Africa, and who spoke Nilotic and other non-Bantu languages. But the great age of these Bantu African states was yet to come.

2/The trans-Saharan routes *(below)* Even with camels, which had been introduced into Africa in Roman times, the desert crossing was extremely hazardous. If the far-spread watering places dried up or if the fiercely independent desert people, the veiled Tuareg, attacked, whole caravans of hundreds of men and beasts perished; their skeletons were grisly reminders of the dangers. Yet for centuries the great trading system persisted.

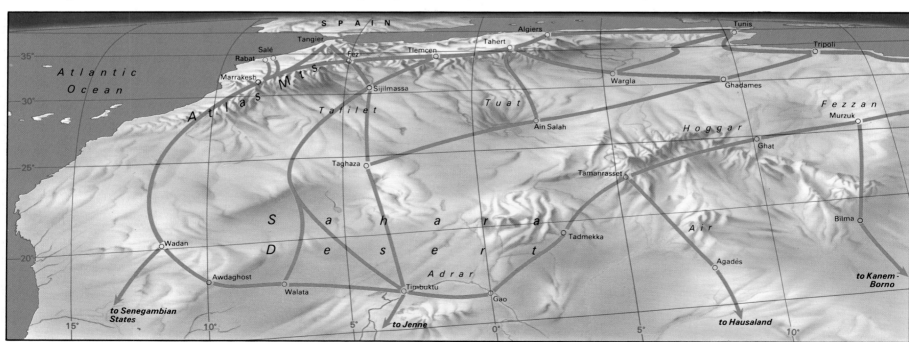

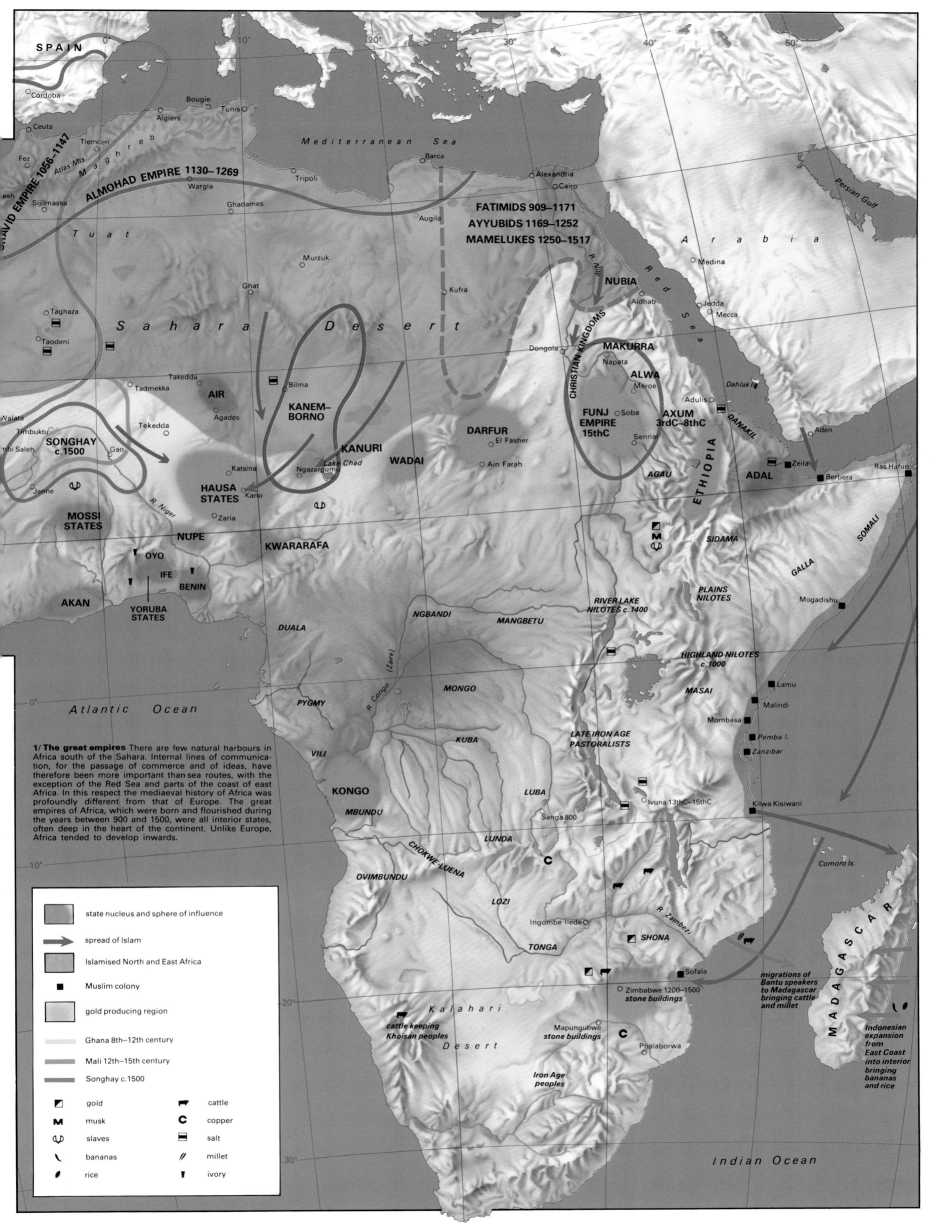

SPAIN

Córdoba
Ceuta
Fez
Tlemcen
Atlas Mts
Maghreb
ALMORAVID EMPIRE 1056–1147
ALMOHAD EMPIRE 1130–1269
Marrakesh
Sijilmassa
Tuat
Wargla
Ghadames
Algiers
Bougie
Tunis
Tripoli
Barca
Murzuk
Ghat

Mediterranean Sea

Alexandria
Cairo

FATIMIDS 909–1171
AYYUBIDS 1169–1252
MAMELUKES 1250–1517

Augila
Kufra

Sahara Desert

Taghaza
Taodeni
Walata
Timbuktu
Koumbi Saleh
SONGHAY c.1500
Gao
Jenne
MOSSI STATES
AKAN
Tadmekka
Takedda
Tekedda
R. Niger
Katsina
Zaria
Kano
HAUSA STATES
NUPE
OYO
IFE
BENIN
YORUBA STATES
KWARARAFA
AIR
Agadès
Bilma
KANEM–BORNO
Lake Chad
Ngazargumu
KANURI
WADAI
DARFUR
El Fasher
Ain Farah

Arabia
Medina
Jedda
Mecca
Red Sea
Persian Gulf

Aidhab
NUBIA
Napata
Dongola
MAKURRA
Meroe
ALWA
Soba
CHRISTIAN KINGDOMS
FUNJ EMPIRE 15thC
Sennar
AGAU
AXUM 3rdC–8thC
Adulis
Dahlak Is.
DANAKIL
Zeila
ADAL
Berbera
Ras Hafun
Aden
ETHIOPIA
SIDAMA
GALLA
SOMALI
PLAINS NILOTES
Mogadishu

Atlantic Ocean

DUALA
NGBANDI
MANGBETU
RIVER LAKE NILOTES c.1400
HIGHLAND NILOTES c.1000
MASAI
Lamu
Malindi
Mombasa
Pemba I.
Zanzibar

PYGMY
MONGO
KUBA
LATE IRON AGE PASTORALISTS
R. Congo (Zaire)
VILI
KONGO
MBUNDU
LUBA
Sanga 800
Ivuna 13thC–15thC
Kilwa Kisiwani

1/ The great empires There are few natural harbours in Africa south of the Sahara. Internal lines of communication, for the passage of commerce and of ideas, have therefore been more important than sea routes, with the exception of the Red Sea and parts of the coast of east Africa. In this respect the mediaeval history of Africa was profoundly different from that of Europe. The great empires of Africa, which were born and flourished during the years between 900 and 1500, were all interior states, often deep in the heart of the continent. Unlike Europe, Africa tended to develop inwards.

CHOKWE–LUENA
LUNDA
OVIMBUNDU
LOZI
TONGA
Ingombe Ilede
SHONA
R. Zambezi
Sofala
Zimbabwe 1200–1500 stone buildings
Comoro Is.

cattle keeping Khoisan peoples
Kalahari Desert
Mapungubwe stone buildings
Phalaborwa
Iron Age peoples

MADAGASCAR
migrations of Bantu speakers to Madagascar bringing cattle and millet

Indonesian expansion from East Coast into interior bringing bananas and rice

Indian Ocean

Legend:
- state nucleus and sphere of influence
- spread of Islam
- Islamised North and East Africa
- ■ Muslim colony
- gold producing region
- Ghana 8th–12th century
- Mali 12th–15th century
- Songhay c.1500

Symbols:
- gold
- M musk
- slaves
- bananas
- rice
- cattle
- C copper
- salt
- // millet
- ivory

137

The rise of the Ottoman Empire 1301 to 1520

ORIGINALLY a petty principality in Western Anatolia, the Ottoman state rose to become a world empire, which lasted, through many vicissitudes, from the late 13th century to 1924. Like that of the Habsburgs, its eventual rival, the Ottoman Empire was dynastic; its territories and character owed little to national or ethnic boundaries, and were determined by the military and administrative power of the dynasty at any particular time.

The rise of the Ottoman state, like the rise of Islam itself nearly seven centuries earlier, owed much to the weakness of the empires which surrounded it. The damage to the structure of the Byzantine Empire caused by the fourth crusade in 1204 facilitated the Ottomans' rapid advance into the Balkans in the course of the 14th century; the defeat of the Seljuks by the Mongols at the battle of Kösedag in 1243 gravely weakened that dynasty's power, and the gradual retreat of the Mongols from Anatolia into Iran created a vacuum in Anatolia which was filled by a number of small Turcoman states, each vying with the other for political supremacy in the area. The first recorded member of the Ottoman family, Ertoghrul, was the ruler of a small state around the town of Söğüt, then on the 'frontier' between the Seljuks and the Byzantines. In about 1281, Ertoghrul was succeeded by his son Osman, after whom the dynasty was named, and under whom the territory of the state first underwent significant expansion.

The Ottomans justified their conquests by describing themselves as *ghazis*, waging the Holy War against non-Muslims, and attempting to bring as much territory as possible into the Islamic fold, the Dar al-Islam. The non-Muslims living in these areas were then absorbed into the Empire as *dhimmis*, protected subjects. Under Osman I and his successors Orkhan (c.1324-60) and Murad (1360-89) the state gradually expanded; in 1326 Bursa was captured after a long siege, and became the Ottoman capital; the absorption of the emirate of Karasi in 1345 brought the Ottomans to the Dardanelles, and in 1354 they gained their first foothold in Europe with the capture of Gallipoli.

By 1361 Murad and his followers had taken Adrianople (Edirne), and transferred the capital there. Much of the first period of expansion in the Balkans seems to have been undertaken by quasi-independent Turkish warrior leaders rather than by forces directly controlled by the Ottomans, but with the accession of Bayezid I in 1389 and the decisive defeat of the Serbians and Bosnians at Kosovo in the same year, Ottoman supremacy was definitively established. By 1393 the kingdom of Bulgaria had become part of the empire, and by the end of the century most of the independent emirates of Anatolia had also been absorbed into the Ottoman state, which now stretched from the Danube to the Euphrates. However, Bayezid's achievement was short-lived; his army was destroyed at Ankara in 1402 by Timur (Tamerlane), the last of the Mongol invaders to reach as far west as Anatolia. There followed an eleven-year hiatus between 1402 and 1413, when the Balkan states and the Anatolian emirates took advantage of the opportunity provided by the Mongol victory to shake off Ottoman rule, although further Mongol advance ceased after Timur's death in 1405.

The reconstruction of the Ottoman state by Mehmed I (1413-21) and the revival of the conquests in the reign of his son Murad II (1421-51) again brought most of eastern and central Anatolia and the southern and eastern Balkans under direct or indirect Ottoman control. However, Ottoman rule in the Balkans was far less oppressive than the system it superseded, in which feudal dues and compulsory labour services weighed heavily upon the peasantry; in consequence, the Ottomans were often welcomed as deliverers. The rounding off of these conquests, and the emergence of the Ottoman state as a world power, was the work of Mehmed II al-Fatih, The Conqueror (1451-81), whose conquest of Constantinople in 1453 removed the last major barrier to expansion into northern Anatolia and enabled the Ottomans to dominate the Straits and the southern shore of the Black Sea. The disappearance of the Serbian kingdom, followed by the absorption of Herzegovina and much of Bosnia, left Hungary as the major European power facing the Ottomans. Mehmed's failure to take Belgrade in 1456 left the line of the middle Danube and lower Sava as the Ottoman boundary with Hungary for over sixty years. With the final re-absorption of Karaman in 1468 the last of the independent emirates disappeared, leaving the Turcoman confederation of the Akkoyunlu (White Sheep) as the Ottomans' major opponents in the area until their destruction by the Safavids of Iran in the early 16th century. Further north, Mehmed established a bridgehead in the Crimea by the capture of Caffa (Kefe) from the Genoese in 1475, thus bringing the Khanate of the Crimea, the most important of the successor states of the Golden Horde, under Ottoman control.

In Europe, the middle years of Mehmed's reign saw the ending of Byzantine and Frankish control over the Morea, and the gradual erosion of Venetian and Genoese power in the Aegean and the Black Sea. Mehmed's death in 1481 brought a temporary halt to these advances, and the struggle over the succession between Bayezid II (1481-1512) and Sultan Jem meant that the Ottomans were unable to undertake major campaigns against the west for many years. However, the securing of the land route from Constantinople to the Crimea was achieved in 1484 with the conquests of Akkerman and Kilia, and the Ottoman-Venetian war of 1499-1502 showed that the Ottomans had now become a major naval power.

The last years of Bayezid II's reign, and most of that of his successor Selim I (1512-20), were largely taken up with events in the east, in Iran, Egypt and the western fertile crescent. The rise of the Safavids in Iran had brought to power a state both militarily strong and ideologically hostile to the Ottomans as their eastern neighbour. Shi'ism, the form of Islam favoured by the Safavids, was also attractive to dissident forces and groupings within the Ottoman state, who rallied to support the new dynasty in Iran. A series of Shi'i-inspired risings among the Turcoman tribes of eastern Anatolia in the last years of Bayezid II's reign was a prelude to the war which broke out in the reigns of Selim and Shah Isma'il (1501-24), culminating in the defeat of the Safavids at the battle of Çaldiran in 1514. For a time, eastern Anatolia was secured and the threat of religious separatism removed.

Selim's annexation of the emirate of Dhu'l-Qadr in 1515 brought the Ottomans into direct contact with the Mameluke empire for the first time. Over the next two years Selim destroyed the Mamelukes politically and militarily, conquering Aleppo and Damascus in 1516, and taking Cairo in 1517. As well as bringing Syria and Egypt under Ottoman control, this campaign also added the Holy Places of Christendom and Islam to the empire, thus adding to the prestige and authority of Selim and his successors. At Selim's death in 1520 the Empire stretched from the Red Sea to the Crimea, and from Kurdistan to Bosnia, and had become a major participant and contender in the international power politics of the day. Furthermore, substantial Turkish Muslim migration to the Balkans had begun to make permanent changes in the demographic and ethnic structure of that area.

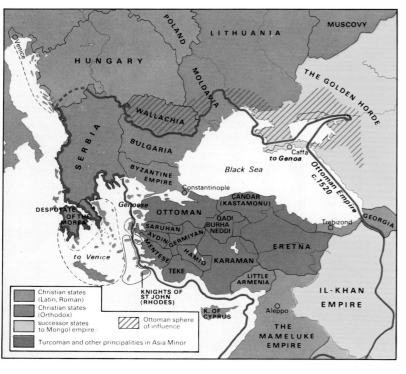

The siege of Rhodes 1522 *(right)* The élite of the Ottoman army is seen here storming the walls of the city, being defended by knights of St John. The élite was formed by the Janissaries, the famous infantry corps founded early in the Ottoman state's history, and the *sipahis*, the Muslim feudal cavalry. The Janissaries, seen here with firearms, were raised by the *Devshirme*, a compulsory levy of Christian boys begun late in the 14th century which soon became a fundamental institution of the Empire. They were regarded in Christian Europe as the most formidable component of the Ottoman army.

2/Before the Ottomans *(left)* Invasion and war between Latins, Byzantines and Muslims, and Mongols had destroyed the last shreds of the former Byzantine and Muslim empires in the Middle East. The Balkans and Anatolia, entirely fragmented by the early 14th century, were to become under the Ottomans the provinces of a single empire.

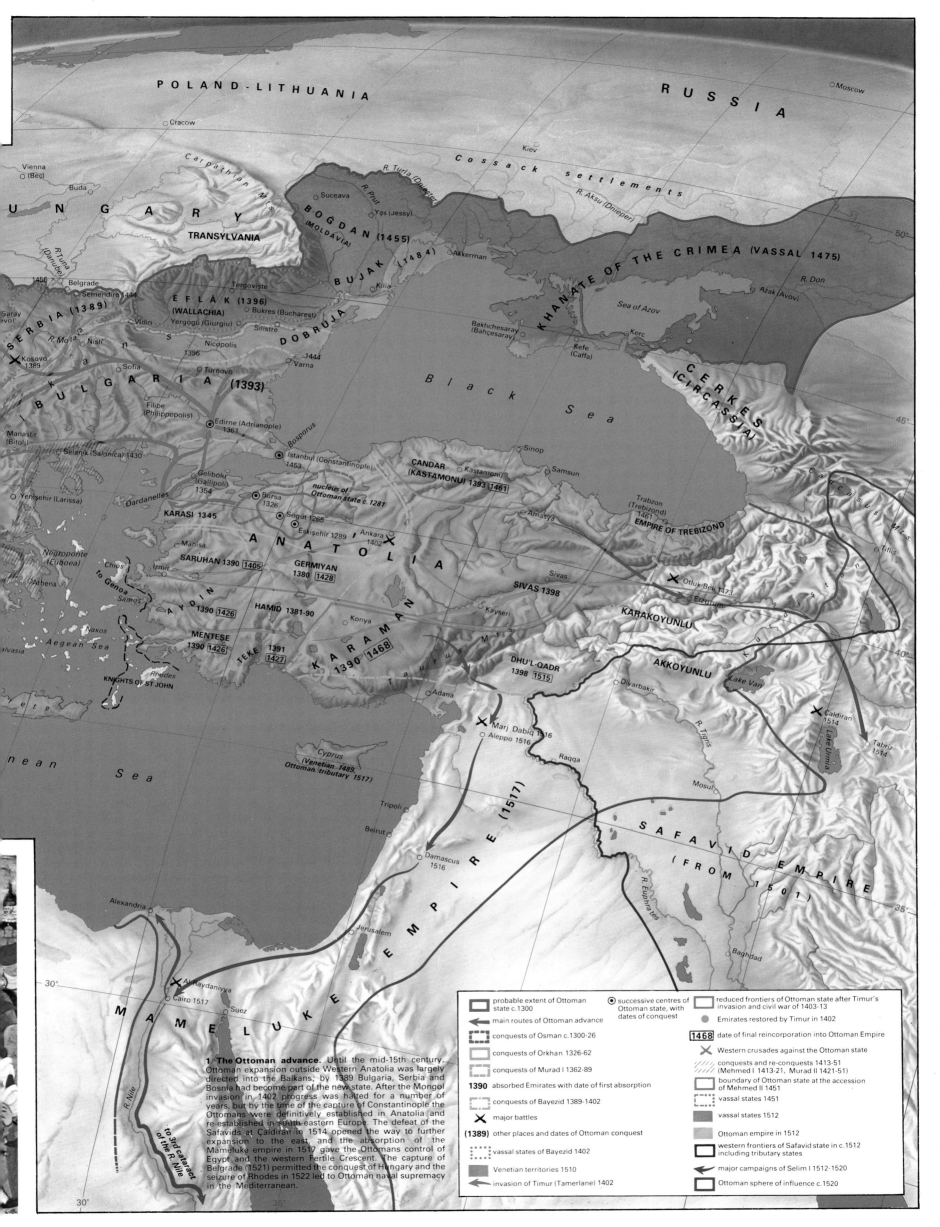

POLAND - LITHUANIA

RUSSIA

○ Cracow

○ Moscow

○ Kiev

C o s s a c k   s e t t l e m e n t s

R. Turla (Dniester)

R. Aksu (Dnieper)

Vienna
(Bec)

○ Suceava

R. Prut

Yas (Jessy)

BOGDAN
(MOLDAVIA) **(1455)**

50°

Buda

Carpathian Mts

H U N G A R Y

TRANSYLVANIA

BUJAK **(1484)**

○ Akkerman

KHANATE OF THE CRIMEA (VASSAL 1475)

R. Don

1456
Belgrade

Tergoviște

EFLÂK **(1396)**
(WALLACHIA)

Killa

Azak (Azov)

Sea of Azov

Semendire 1444

Saray
evo

SERBIA **(1389)**

R. Mo¹a

Nish

Vidin

○ Bukreş (Bucharest)

Sillistre

DOBRUJA

Bakhchesaray
(Bahçesaray)

Kerc

CERKES
(CIRCASSIA)

Kosovo
1389

B U L G A R I A

Sofia

Nicopolis
1396

1444

○ Kefe
(Caffa)

45°

Manastir
(Bitoli)

(1393)

Turnovo

Varna

B l a c k   S e a

Filibe
(Philippopolis)

Edirne (Adrianople)
1361

Bosphorus

Sinop

Trabzon
(Trebizond)
1461

C a u c a s u s   M t s

Selanik (Salonica) 1430

○ Istanbul (Constantinople)
1453

CANDAR
(KASTAMONU) **1393** 1461

Kastamoni

○ Samsun

EMPIRE OF TREBIZOND

Yenişehir (Larissa)

Gelibolu
(Gallipoli)
1354

Bursa
1326

nucleus of
Ottoman state c.1281

Amasya

Tiflis

Dardanelles

KARASI 1345

Söğüt 1265

Eskişehir 1289

Ankara
1402

A N A T O L I A

Negroponte
(Euboea)

Chios

Manisa

SARUHAN 1390 1405

GERMIYAN
1380 1428

SIVAS 1398

Sivas

Otluk-Beli 1473

Erzurum

Athens

to Genoa

Izmir

Samos

AYDIN 1390 1426

HAMID 1381-90

Kayseri

KARAKOYUNLU

Aegean Sea

Naxos

MENTEŞE
1390 1426

Konya

KARAMAN
1390 1468

AKKOYUNLU

Lake Van

Çaldıran
1514

40°

TEKE 1391
1427

DHU'L-QADR
1398 1515

Diyarbakir

Tabriz
1514

KNIGHTS OF ST JOHN

Rhodes

Adana

R. Tigris

Lake Urmia

Crete

Marj Dabiq 1516
○ Aleppo 1516

Cyprus
(Venetian 1489,
Ottoman tributary 1517)

Raqqa

Mosul

S A F A V I D

n e a n   S e a

Tripoli

Beirut

E M P I R E **(1517)**

R. Euphrates

(F R O M   1 5 0 1)

35°

Damascus
1516

Alexandria

Jerusalem

Baghdad

30°

Al-Raydaniyya

○ Cairo 1517

M A M E L U K E   E M P I R E

Suez

R. Nile

to 3rd cataract
of the R. Nile

30°

35°

1 The Ottoman advance. Until the mid-15th century, Ottoman expansion outside Western Anatolia was largely directed into the Balkans; by 1389 Bulgaria, Serbia and Bosnia had become part of the new state. After the Mongol invasion in 1402 progress was halted for a number of years, but by the time of the capture of Constantinople the Ottomans were definitively established in Anatolia and re-established in south-eastern Europe. The defeat of the Safavids at Çaldıran in 1514 opened the way to further expansion to the east, and the absorption of the Mameluke empire in 1517 gave the Ottomans control of Egypt and the western Fertile Crescent. The capture of Belgrade (1521) permitted the conquest of Hungary and the seizure of Rhodes in 1522 led to Ottoman naval supremacy in the Mediterranean.

▢	probable extent of Ottoman state c.1300
←	main routes of Ottoman advance
▢	conquests of Osman c.1300-26
▢	conquests of Orkhan 1326-62
▢	conquests of Murad I 1362-89
1390	absorbed Emirates with date of first absorption
▢	conquests of Bayezid 1389-1402
✕	major battles
(1389)	other places and dates of Ottoman conquest
▢	vassal states of Bayezid 1402
▩	Venetian territories 1510
←	invasion of Timur (Tamerlane) 1402

◉	successive centres of Ottoman state, with dates of conquest
●	Emirates restored by Timur in 1402

▢	reduced frontiers of Ottoman state after Timur's invasion and civil war of 1403-13
1468	date of final reincorporation into Ottoman Empire
✕	Western crusades against the Ottoman state
▨	conquests and re-conquests 1413-51 (Mehmed I 1413-21, Murad II 1421-51)
▢	boundary of Ottoman state at the accession of Mehmed II 1451
▢	vassal states 1451
▨	vassal states 1512
▨	Ottoman empire in 1512
▢	western frontiers of Safavid state in c.1512 including tributary states
←	major campaigns of Selim I 1512-1520
▢	Ottoman sphere of influence c.1520

Eastern Europe in the 14th century

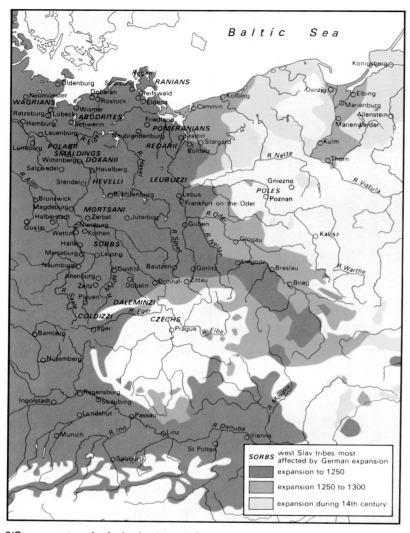

2/German eastward colonisation *(above)* For two centuries after 1125 peasants, soldiers and merchants moved in a steady German-speaking stream into the rich, welcoming land between the rivers Elbe and Oder, swamping the local Slav tribes, developing the land and opening up the Baltic to new, profitable international trade. Monasteries, particularly the Cistercians, undertook large-scale land-drainage schemes, for which they called in peasants from Flanders.

3/The conquest of Prussia by the Teutonic Knights *(below)* In 1231 Hermann Balke crossed the river Vistula with a crusading army, swiftly founding new fortified cities such as Königsberg (1255). Systematic subjection of the pagan Prussian tribes gave way, after 1309, to 100 years of prosperity. In 1202, another military order, the Brethren of the Sword, was founded in Latvia by the bishop of Riga, but in 1237 amalgamated with the Prussian Knights.

THE 14th century saw an important shift in the centre of gravity in Europe. The onset of economic depression, the prolonged and devastating wars between England and France (see page 142), and the political dislocation of Germany after the death of Frederick II in 1250 (see page 118), all resulted in a period of instability, weak government and unrest in western Europe. In eastern Europe the same period saw the rise and consolidation of powerful states with modern institutions. Under Charles the Great of Bohemia (1333-78), Casimir the Great of Poland (1339-70) and Louis the Great of Hungary (1342–82), the lands north of the Carpathians and east of the Elbe entered the mainstream of European history. Their cultural integration is symbolised by the foundation of the universities of Prague (1348), Cracow (1364), Vienna (1365) and Pécs (1367).

The early states established in eastern Europe had proved unstable. Like Kievan Russia (see page 114), they broke apart in the 12th century into warring principalities, and the Mongol invasions were a further setback, particularly in Hungary. After 1250 a new phase of concentration began. First in the field was Bohemia under Ottocar II (1253-78), who set out to build up a great territorial state including Austria and extending to the Adriatic. But Ottocar's ambitions provoked the opposition of the Bohemian nobility and of the German princes, and his defeat and death in 1278 left the way open for the Habsburgs to establish their power in Austria. Confusion and conflict in Germany, the bitter struggle between Ludwig IV of Bavaria (1314-47) and Pope John XXII (1316-34) over the imperial succession, and the extinction of the Premyslid dynasty in Bohemia (1306) and the Arpad dynasty in Hungary (1301), all helped in the process. By the time of Rudolf IV (1356-65) the Habsburgs had consolidated their position, and Austria, along with Poland, Hungary and Bohemia, was a major territorial power. At the same time, in south-east Europe Stefan Dushan (1331-55) assumed the title of 'Tsar of the Serbs and Greeks' and put together a great Serbian empire which reached from the Mediterranean coast opposite Corfu to Salonica and controlled the whole of the Bulgarian hinterland.

The half-century between 1330 and 1380 saw a remarkable upsurge of government and civilisation in east and east-central Europe. In the case of Serbia, the foundations soon proved extremely fragile. After Dushan's death the Serbian empire was torn by separatism and faction, and succumbed to the Ottoman Turks at the famous battle of Kosovo in 1389. The foundations on

which the Polish, Bohemian and Hungarian rulers built were more solid. Bohemia's financial strength and early prominence owed much to the opening of the silver mines of Kutna Hora in the 13th century, and to Prague's strategic position on the trade routes from east to west. Poland profited from the opening of the Baltic sea-route by German merchants, and became a major exporter of timber and grain. Using their new-found economic power, the rulers of the period – Charles IV, Casimir III and Louis of Hungary – set about building centralised states on the western model. Their object was to curb the nobility, encourage new classes dependent upon themselves, codify the law, and set up royal tribunals to which all classes – particularly the nobility – would be subject. *The Statutes of Casimir the Great* (1347) and the *Majestas Carolina* are a monument to their efforts; Stefan Dushan also promulgated a code of laws, the *Dušanov Zakonik*, in 1349.

The decisive factor in the transformation of eastern Europe, however, was the influx of German and Flemish settlers, who cleared forest and waste land, drained swamps, founded villages, and created vast reserves of arable land capable of sustaining a rapidly growing population. German eastern colonisation, checked by the great Slav revolt of 983 (see page 116), began again around 1125 as a result of population pressure, and quickly submerged the small west Slav peoples (Wagrians, Abodrites, Sorbs, Lusatians) inhabiting the country between the Elbe and the Oder. Military and predatory at first, it soon developed into a vast movement of peasants, often called in by Slav princes anxious to develop their territories, who granted the settlers the privilege of living under German law. A second thrust was by sea. The conquest of Wagria opened the Baltic to the Germans, and after the foundation of Lübeck (1143) a string of German cities (Wismar, Rostock, Stralsund, Greifswald, Stettin, Cammin, Kolberg) sprang up along the Baltic coast. From these emerged the later Hanseatic League, established in 1358. The immediate consequence was a series of expeditions, beginning in 1186, intended to extend German sway as far as the Gulf of Finland. But although Livonia was formally subdued (1207), there was no appreciable German colonisation except in the cities (Riga, Dorpat, Reval) where German merchants played a prominent role in the Russian trade. German enclaves remained an important element in the Baltic states, right down to the 20th century, but the bulk of the peasantry retained their national characters.

Colonisation reached its peak in the half-century after 1220. By 1300 it was slowing down, except in the territories of the Teutonic Knights, who had been called in as auxiliaries in 1226 by the Polish duke of Masovia against the heathen Prussians. That same year East Prussia was granted by the Emperor Frederick II to the Master of the Teutonic Order, who was also made an Imperial Prince. The conquest of Prussia, unlike German colonisation elsewhere beyond the Oder, was a ruthless military operation, followed by systematic settlement. Some 1400 villages and 93 towns were founded between 1280 and 1410. Under Winrich of Kniprode (1351-82), the greatest of the Grand Masters of the Order, the Teutonic Knights reached the zenith of their power. But their efforts to link up their territory in Prussia with Pomerania in the west and with Livonia in the north-east inevitably provoked hostile reactions. Poland, in particular, saw itself threatened, and further east, Lithuania, the largest territorial state of 14th-century Europe, took shape in response to German pressure. Gedymin (1316-41) and Olgierd (1345-77) were the founders of modern Lithuania, and when Poland and Lithuania were united in 1386, under Wladislaw II, the first of

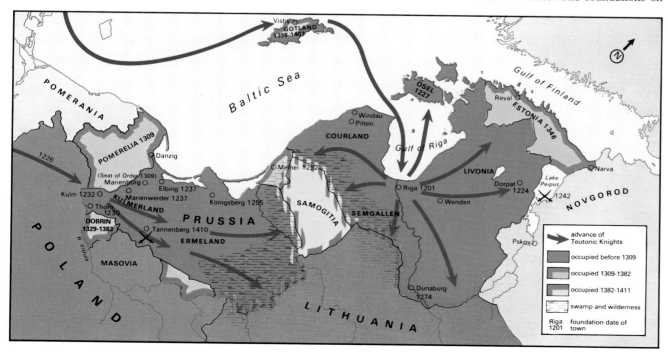

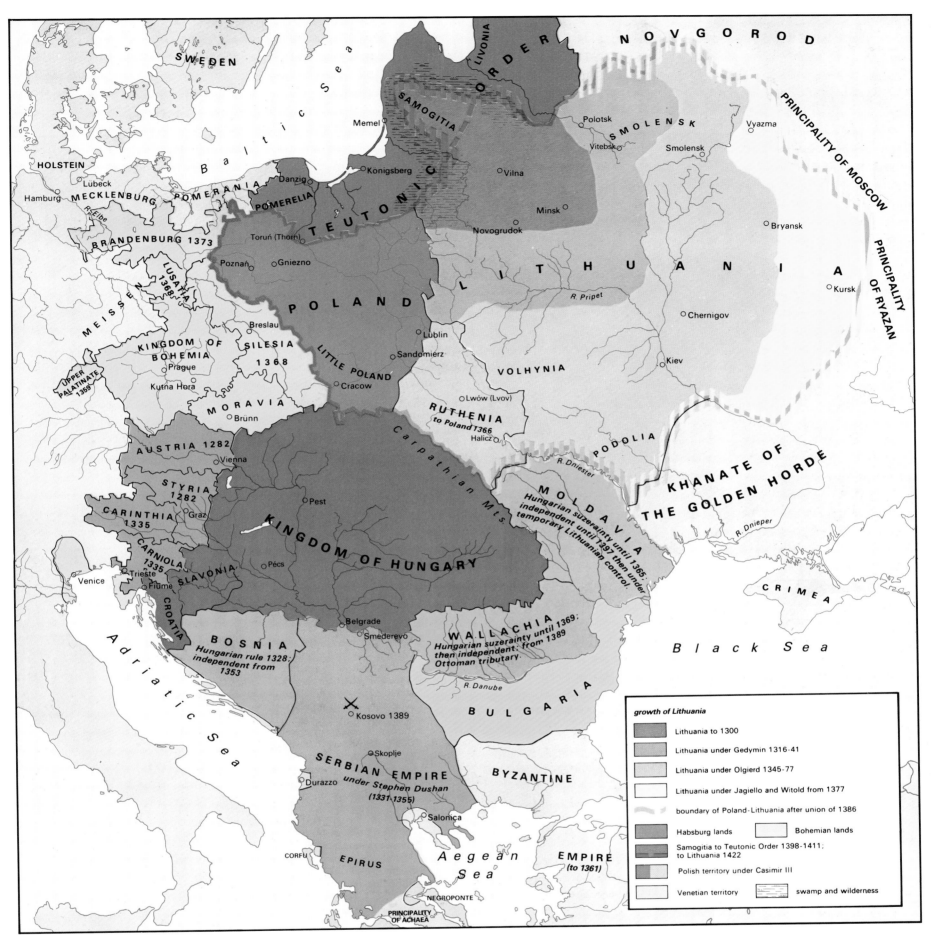

SWEDEN

HOLSTEIN
Hamburg Lübeck
MECKLENBURG POMERANIA
BRANDENBURG 1373
R.Elbe
MEISSEN
UPPER PALATINATE 1369
LUSATIA 1388
KINGDOM OF BOHEMIA
Prague
Kutná Hora
MORAVIA
Brünn
AUSTRIA 1282
Vienna
STYRIA 1282
Graz
CARINTHIA 1335
CARNIOLA 1335
Trieste
Fiume
SLAVONIA
Venice
CROATIA

Baltic Sea

POMERELIA
Danzig
Königsberg
Memel
SAMOGITIA
TEUTONIC ORDER
LIVONIA

Toruń (Thorn)
Poznań Gniezno
POLAND
Breslau
SILESIA 1368
LITTLE POLAND
Cracow
Lublin
Sandomierz

LITHUANIA

Polotsk
Vitebsk
Vilna
Minsk
Novogrudok
Smolensk
Vyazma

SMOLENSK

NOVGOROD

PRINCIPALITY OF MOSCOW

Bryansk

Kursk

Chernigov

Kiev

PRINCIPALITY OF RYAZAN

VOLHYNIA
Lwów (Lvov)
RUTHENIA to Poland 1366
Halicz
PODOLIA
R.Dniester
MOLDAVIA
Hungarian suzerainty until 1365; independent until 1387, then under temporary Lithuanian control.

KHANATE OF THE GOLDEN HORDE

R.Dnieper

CRIMEA

Carpathian Mts.

Pest

KINGDOM OF HUNGARY

Pécs
Belgrade
Smederevo

WALLACHIA
Hungarian suzerainty until 1369; then independent; from 1389 Ottoman tributary.

R.Danube

BULGARIA

Black Sea

Adriatic Sea

BOSNIA
Hungarian rule 1328; independent from 1353

× Kosovo 1389

SERBIAN EMPIRE
under Stephen Dushan (1331-1355)

Skoplje

Durazzo

Salonica

BYZANTINE EMPIRE (to 1361)

Aegean Sea

CORFU
EPIRUS

NEGROPONTE

PRINCIPALITY OF ACHAEA

growth of Lithuania

Lithuania to 1300

Lithuania under Gedymin 1316-41

Lithuania under Olgierd 1345-77

Lithuania under Jagiello and Witold from 1377

boundary of Poland-Lithuania after union of 1386

Habsburg lands   Bohemian lands

Samogitia to Teutonic Order 1398-1411; to Lithuania 1422

Polish territory under Casimir III

Venetian territory   swamp and wilderness

---

the long-lasting Jagiello dynasty, Prussia was outmatched. Defeated by the Poles at Tannenberg (1410), it entered a period of decline which culminated in the Peace of Toruń (1466) under which Pomerelia, Danzig and other parts of the former *Ordensland* passed under Polish rule.

The long conflict with Prussia also adversely affected Poland. To gain support in the wars, the Jagiellonian rulers were forced to make concessions to the gentry (*szlachta*). Furthermore, the union between Poland (which was predominantly Catholic) and Lithuania (which was predominantly Orthodox) was far from untroubled. With the rise of Muscovy under Ivan III (1462-1505) and the inception of the policy of the 'reassembly of the Russian land' (see page 162), Poland came under pressure from the east, particularly as Casimir the Great, checked by the Prussian Knights on the Baltic, had expanded in the south-east and annexed the White Russian territories of Ruthenia and Galicia (1366). Hungary,

meanwhile, was exposed to Ottoman attacks (see page 138), and in Bohemia social and religious unrest beginning under Charles IV's son, Wenceslaus (1378-1419), undermined the power of the crown. After the condemnation and burning of Jan Hus, the Bohemian reformer, at the Council of Constance (1415), the long Hussite wars (see page 142) quickly took on nationalist, anti-German overtones and divided and ruined the country, preparing the way for the eventual rise of Austria (see page 150) to the leading position in eastern Europe.

Nevertheless the changes of the 14th century were of lasting importance. Just as the centre of political power in Germany had moved east from the Rhine to the Elbe and from the Elbe to the Oder, so the rise of Poland, Lithuania, Hungary and Bohemia marked the beginning of a new phase in which Moscow, Vienna, Sweden and Turkey struggled in the 17th and 18th centuries for a new power system.

1/Eastern Europe in 1386 *(above)* The marriage of Queen Jadwiga of Poland (1382-99) to Wladislaw II of Lithuania in 1386, brought the 'personal union' of these two already powerful kingdoms, and created a formidable new political force, threatening the Teutonic Knights.

Prague *(below)* Under Charles IV (1316-78), Prague became one of the great capitals and a symbol of the new eastern Europe. The St Veit cathedral and the famous royal residence, the Hradschin, were embellished and extended, the Charles University founded (1348) and lavish efforts made to attract merchants and trade.

PRAGA

The crisis of the 14th century in Western Europe

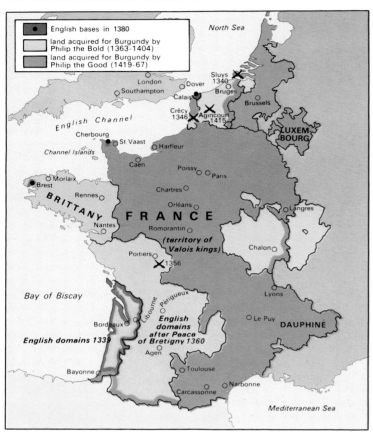

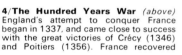

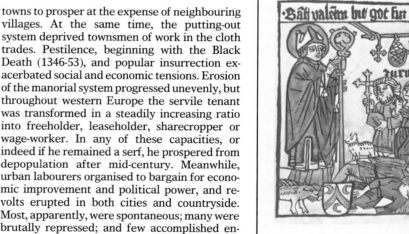

Abbreviation
SCH. SCHWYZ

3/The Swiss Confederat *(above)* Characteristic of the integration of the 14th century the success of the Swiss mount cantons in throwing off Habsb rule. The three cantons wh formed the original Confederat in 1291 were joined by five oth before the end of the 14th cent after the decisive defeat of Aus at the battle of Morgarten.

The Black Death *(below)* 1347, plague of Asiatic origin spr from the south-east across European continent, wiping perhaps a third of the we population in about two years. U the early 18th century scarcel decade went by without a recurr outbreak. Unlike famine, the pe lence affected every social rank class, and the psychological imp was profound. The disease, spr by infected fleas carried by rats, particularly virulent, and few v caught it ever recovered. German print shows the holy m of the Church praying for pla victims.

4/The Hundred Years War *(above)* England's attempt to conquer France began in 1337, and came close to success with the great victories of Crécy (1346) and Poitiers (1356). France recovered after 1360 (Peace of Bretigny), but Henry V's invasion in 1415 again gave England control of northern France (see page 150). The last English garrisons except Calais were expelled in 1453.

2/The Anglo-Scottish Wars *(above)* The effort of Edward I of England (1272-1307) to subjugate Scotland culminated in Edward II's disastrous defeat at Bannockburn in 1314. Throughout the century and beyond, the Scots, often fighting in alliance with France, were a threat to English security.

THE monarchies of western Europe were confronted in the 14th century by an aristocracy eager to reassert position and privilege though not to dismember the state. Fragmentation was, nonetheless, a threat everywhere, conspicuously so in France after 1337, where the Hundred Years War exacerbated particularist dissension. French expansion to the east (Dauphiné, 1353) was checked by a royal fief, the Duchy of Burgundy, swollen by acquisition of the imperial county of Burgundy (1363) and Flanders (1384). Military successes in France under Edward III (1327-77) and Henry V (1413-22) eased English aristocratic restlessness, but in the long run the French wars only sharpened tensions of which Edward II (1307-27) and Richard II (1377-99) were victims. In England, war with the Scots was an ever-present threat and a frequent reality. In Germany, the Golden Bull of 1356 defined the pattern for a century of political strife: a king without real power and princes incapable of preserving peace in their separate domains. The Wittelsbachs, Habsburgs and Luxembourgs, who contested for the crown, were more concerned with strengthening their own patrimonies than with stabilising German monarchy. Papal intervention contributed to monarchical weakness. A web of leagues and confederations emerged to fill the political vacuum. Of these, the Swiss Confederation (after 1291) was the most successful and enduring.

By 1400 five Italian states were predominant: Florence, Venice, the Papal States, Naples and Milan, most powerful of the *signorie* under its Visconti lords, a threat to the security of the rest. Transfer of the papacy to Avignon (1305-77) and the Great Schism (1378-1417) which followed gravely diminished papal prestige, though Avignonese popes were no mere puppets of French kings. At the same time, failure to check corruption and incompetence in the Church inspired reformers, who advanced from complaints about abuses to assaults on hierarchical authority and even on orthodox doctrine. Religious and political objectives mingled in England and Bohemia among followers of John Wyclif and John Hus.

Spain, like Italy, was a theatre of operation for bands of mercenaries employed by every side in dynasty wars. Aristocratic reaction to Castilian royal authority triumphed in the Trastamara usurpation (1369). Regionalism surfaced after the death of Martin IV of Aragon in 1410, but the settlement of 1412 acknowledged the importance of monarchy to all component sections. Iberian boundaries in fact remained essentially unchanged despite intermittent warfare including a Trastamara threat to overwhelm Portugal, decisively terminated at Aljubarrota (1385). In Denmark, Norway and Sweden the crisis for monarchy loomed not as a prospect of domination by special interests but as a threat to the existence of more than a titular kingship. By 1400 what power remained to the three crowns had fallen to one ruler, Margaret of Norway (Union of Kalmar, 1397). Yet the northern kingdoms were not united and the overriding strength of the aristocracy was undiminished.

Though growth in population and productivity was steady until after the middle of the 13th century, both began to decline prior to the Great Famine of 1315-17. Textile manufacture in Flemish and Italian cities and maritime trade fell off sharply before 1330. Banking failures, beginning with the Buonsignori of Siena (1298), culminated in the collapse of the great Florentine banking houses in the 1340s. Mineral production slumped; in many regions reclamation and colonisation virtually ceased while land went out of cultivation and timber supplies were exhausted. Resources and wealth were redistributed as established commercial and industrial centres passed their peak and new rivals prospered. English producers gained a substantial share of a diminishing cloth industry. Portuguese and Castilian shipping burgeoned in 1400. Farmland was converted to pasturage for sheep in England and Castile and for cattle in the Netherlands and northern Germany. Monopolistic restrictions designed to secure established positions in a waning market adversely affected the volume of trade and enabled some large

towns to prosper at the expense of neighbouring villages. At the same time, the putting-out system deprived townsmen of work in the cloth trades. Pestilence, beginning with the Black Death (1346-53), and popular insurrection exacerbated social and economic tensions. Erosion of the manorial system progressed unevenly, but throughout western Europe the servile tenant was transformed in a steadily increasing ratio into freeholder, leaseholder, sharecropper or wage-worker. In any of these capacities, or indeed if he remained a serf, he prospered from depopulation after mid-century. Meanwhile, urban labourers organised to bargain for economic improvement and political power, and revolts erupted in both cities and countryside. Most, apparently, were spontaneous; many were brutally repressed; and few accomplished enduring results. The Sicilian Vespers (1282), spreading from Palermo, drove the Angevins from Sicily. Hostility to the French also mingled with bitter antagonism toward burgher oligarchies and landlords in Flemish uprisings such as the Matins of Bruges (1302) and the ensuing battle of Courtrai. Non-violent takeovers of power by Jacques van Artevelde (Ghent, 1337), Cola di Rienzi (Rome, 1347), and Etienne Marcel (Paris, 1357) were bourgeois movements with popular support in which the leaders were ultimately victims of mob violence. Marcel attempted to collaborate in the best known of mediaeval peasant insurrections, the Jacquerie. Undercurrents of religious sentiment and anti-clericalism permeated much popular protest. In the Great Revolt of 1381 in England, it was radically reformist; in the popular frenzy against the Jews in Spain (1390-92), it combined outrage over social inequity with orthodox bigotry. Although these outbursts were assaults on privilege and exploitation – whether feudal and manorial vestiges, legal chicanery, clerical abuse, royal taxation or guild monopoly – demands in many instances were either visionary or unrelated to actual causes of complaint. Foreigners (French, Hansa merchants, Jews, Flemings) were often the victims.

extent of spread of the Black Death

	1346
	1347
	mid 1348
	end 1348
	mid 1349
	end 1349
	1350
	c.1351
	c.1353
	little or no plague mortality

political change

- union of Kalmar 1397
- Milanese territory under Giangaleazzo Visconti 1378-1402
- territory under Florentine control, end 14th century
- Luxemburg lands c.1400
- Wittelsbach lands
- Habsburg lands
- Swiss Confederation (inset map left)

social unrest

- areas of disturbance during Great Peasant Revolt in England, 1381
- centre of urban revolt
- rural uprisings
- ⊗ defeats in battle of lower class   ✕ battle

religious unrest

- spread of Lollardry in England to death of Richard II, 1399
- area of Hussite influence
- □ Hussite centre

the Great Schism 1378-1417 (inset map right)

- areas giving allegiance to Pope in Rome
- areas giving allegiance to Pope in Avignon
- allegiance officially to Rome but shifting local allegiances

the Great Schism 1378-1417

Avignon
Rome

1/Famine, plague and popular unrest Inadequately financed and weakened by war and internal dissension, western European monarchy underwent severe strains throughout the 14th century. Recession, compounded by famine and pestilence, led to conflicts in all countries between the autocracy and the urban oligarchies on the one hand, and the peasants and urban proletariat on the other. The Western Church was also rent with schism.

Merchants and finance in Europe c.1500

The Seal of the City of Lübeck (1258)
(left) The deputies of the Hansa towns met in Lübeck to co-ordinate policies and regulate trade. The Hanseatic ship, or cog, symbolising their activities, featured in the Lübeck seal, which once set on their decisions gave them authority throughout the Baltic.

2/Speed of communications with Venice
(above) Communities and regions were isolated by distance, poor communications, frontier and internal tolls and largely unpoliced roads. Even from Venice most journeys had to be measured in weeks. Few European cities in 1500 boasted more than 100,000 inhabitants.

Map legend:
- over 100,000 people
- between 60,000 and 100,000
- between 40,000 and 60,000
- less than 40,000

EVENTS in the closing years of the 15th century opened a new economic future for Europe. With Spain's discovery of the Americas and the Portuguese arrival in India, trade and finance, which before had rarely reached far beyond the Continent itself, rapidly extended their horizons to the far corners of the globe. The new opportunities for profit soon transformed the traditional patterns of mediaeval business into the basic structures of the modern commercial world.

In 1500, wealth and urban development was concentrated largely round the Mediterranean, and Italy in particular. Here, with the exception of Paris, were the only cities with more than 100,000 inhabitants: Naples, Venice, Milan and Constantinople. Here was held the balance, between north and south and between Europe and the East. Overland from Asia and the Levant, heavily burdened by the costs of the middlemen, the Arab caravans brought spices, silks, cotton and drugs. Across the Sahara came gold and ivory. At sea, Venice underwrote the voyages, and organised the fleets of merchant galleys which plied the Mediterranean, and even ventured beyond Gibraltar to England and Flanders.

To the north, trade and settlement were much more thinly spread. Even among the famous *Reichsstädte* of the Holy Roman Empire, only Augsburg and Cologne could muster more than 40,000 citizens. Poor roads, indifferent transport and the slow pace of news and communications accentuated regional disparities and isolated areas into a kaleidoscope of local markets. From Venice, an important centre for Europe, the

1/The Hanseatic League Venice and the Hansa provided sea-links between the Mediterranean and northern Europe. Venetian galleys brought spices, wines and fruit; Hanseatic counting houses *(kontore)* held ready stocks of metals, fish, textiles and Russian furs. Their meetings in Flanders joined two huge zones of commercial activity. The resulting trade-flows brought great profit to Italy's merchant-financiers. Genoa, like Venice, had a long history of trade in the Mediterranean and across Europe. In the early 16th century Genoese merchants were firmly established in numerous commercial centres, above all, Seville, and were ready to take a leading part in developing the machinery of growth and empire.

average journey took 9 days to Naples, 27 to London, 46 to Lisbon and 65 to Alexandria.

Despite the difficulties, however, Italian connections reached far and wide. The Medici of Florence, following the example of the Bardi and Peruzzi a century and a half earlier, controlled substantial banking agencies in the principal northern capitals. The north itself specialised in the products of sea, farm, mine and forest, many of them monopolised by the merchants of the Hanseatic League. The Hansa was an association of German cities which promoted trading monopolies and successfully sought exclusive privileges in Scandinavia, the Low Countries, Russia, Germany and England. Its activities were principally based on a network of towns in Germany and four great trading posts or *kontore*: the Tyskebrugge in Bergen (timber and fish); the Peterhof in Novgorod (furs); the Steelyard in London (wool and cloth); and the Assemblies in Bruges (cloth). Until its harbour silted up in the late 15th century, this last was the main *entrepôt* market, linking Mediterranean interests with those of the Baltic and the North Sea. Meanwhile, the substantial payment and credit requirements needed to facilitate the physical movement of goods were still mainly met by the great periodic fairs, which had emerged in the Middle Ages. After the brief prosperity of Geneva, the most famous of these in the 15th century was Lyons, strategically placed on the great trade route through the Rhône valley. There the merchants of Florence, Lucca, Genoa and Germany met, four times a year, under the freedom of the fairs from certain taxes and tolls, to settle accounts and clear bills of exchange from the principal markets of Europe.

But now the traditional mercantile structure was proving progressively less adequate. It could no longer cope fully with the opportunities presented by the Atlantic, the increasing flows of gold and silver, and the commercial exploits of the merchants of Portugal and Spain (see page 158). By the 1550s, these two great colonial powers had not only opened up the world, but also created huge demands for investment in new methods and institutions. A more advanced technology had to be developed to conquer the oceans, discover the most profitable sea routes, and train seamen to cope with winds and currents different from those of the Adriatic and Aegean seas. New market structures emerged to cater for changing needs and demands. The intermittent fairs gradually gave place to more permanent markets and bourses, open each weekday throughout the year. With the eclipse of Bruges, the merchant community moved to Antwerp, on the Scheldt, with its access to the Rhine and the cloth towns of southern Flanders, and its versatile and convenient financial facilities, now a meeting point for Europe.

With growing, changing trade came a fresh generation of rich merchants and bankers, foremost among them the Fuggers of Augsburg. Although the Hansa and Bruges had progressively declined and the Iberian powers grown in strength, Venice managed, after an initial setback, to come to terms with the Portuguese advance. But the balance of political as well as economic forces was shifting. When Charles V bribed his way to the imperial throne in 1519, not only the Holy Roman Empire but also Spain, the Low Countries, Germany, Austria and most of the New World now came under a single ruler, and it was largely the Fuggers who had furnished the money. Starting as peasant weavers and expanding into silver, copper and mercury mining, this German family grew immensely rich and powerful as moneylenders to the Court and its aristocracy. As security, they normally demanded monopoly rights over various forms of mining trade and revenue collection. They controlled the Spanish customs, and gradually extended their influence throughout the Empire and its colonies overseas. Their operations stretched from Danzig to Lisbon, from Budapest to Rome and from Moscow to Chile. In 1552 their famous loan, made to Charles V at Villach, probably saved his military campaign from disintegration.

The private financing of great states, however, was a hazardous affair. Both the Fuggers, before their descendants turned from banking to landownership, and their thrusting Genoese competitors, were badly affected when the Spanish Court repudiated its debts, which happened on five separate occasions between 1557 and 1627. After the bankruptcy of 1575, the Fuggers increasingly withdrew from such business. The merchant bankers of Genoa, who took their place, had been forced to seek new commercial channels in the 1520s when their city chose the Emperor's side in France's Italian wars and they were barred from the Lyons fairs. Charles V compensated them for a while with the fairs of Besançon, which later moved to Piacenza, but such periodic meetings, as elsewhere, could no longer cater for the growing scale and volume of business. Nevertheless, their enterprise in the corridors of Spanish power helped to pave the way to modern finance, in the Atlantic markets of Amsterdam and London.

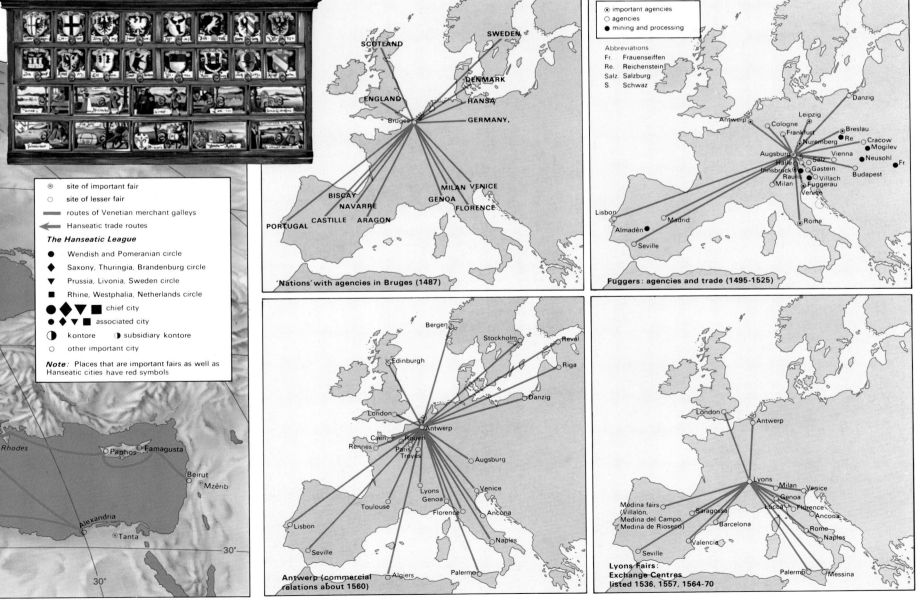

145

Eurasian trade routes from the Crusades to Bartolomeu Dias

AS LONG as the oceans of the world were thought to be unnavigable, they acted as barriers to the movement of men over the earth's surface, and the vast majority of the human race lived in ignorance of conditions in distant places. The great break through the barriers of ignorance and isolation came with the 15th-century voyages into the Atlantic and Indian Oceans, which brought European ships to the unknown shores of America, to hitherto unknown parts of Africa, and to Asia.

European interest in Asia, rekindled during the Crusades, developed considerably in the 13th century as the Mongols expanded their conquests and imposed order and relative security for travellers over an area extending from China to the Black Sea region. Suddenly Asia was open to European missionaries and merchants, the most famous traveller being the Venetian Marco Polo, whose *Description of the World* was based on a journey which lasted from 1271 to 1295 and included a period of service at the court of Kublai Khan. Colonies of Italian merchants, mostly Genoese, were established at Constantinople, Kaffa, Tana and Trebizond, the south-western termini of the 'silk roads' to Tabriz, Samarkand, and thence to China. Southwards from Tabriz ran the road to Baghdad and Ormuz.

Ormuz was one of the main entrepôts of the spice trade. Europe, like China, was dependent upon the spice-producing regions of Asia – south India, Ceylon, the Moluccas and the Malay archipelago – for cosmetic, culinary and other related products. As a result, Malacca became an international port shipping spices to China and to the Malabar cities of India, where they were purchased by Arab, Indian and Persian dealers for transit to Aden and Ormuz. From there they found their way to the Black Sea and the Mediterranean. But the roads opened by the rise of the Mongol Empire were closed by its decline in the mid-14th century. The chief victim was the traffic in Chinese silk, which wilted and dried up after the establishment of the proudly isolationist Ming dynasty in China. The steppe routes to Muscovy, Novgorod and the eastern outposts of the Hanseatic League, which dominated the Baltic trade, also fell out of use, and the spice trade was adversely affected. Plague, brigandage and hostility to Christians, as Islam spread in the disintegrating Mongol khanates, reduced to a trickle trade between Ormuz and the Black Sea. As a result, Europeans became heavily dependent upon Alexandria for spices, but the precariousness of the situation encouraged a search for alternative routes.

Dependence upon Alexandria also stimulated gold hunger in Europe, for there was little demand for European goods in the Levant and Egypt and payment for the most part had to be made in specie. The chief known source of gold was the Niger region of Africa. It was carried to the Mediterranean in trans-Saharan caravans to pay for European manufactures, particularly cloth. Some attempts were made by Italian merchants, such as the Genoese Malfante, to reach the African gold markets direct across the desert. But far more important and successful was the alliance of Italian finance and Portuguese seamanship to work down Africa's west coast in search of a reliable seaborne supply.

Many motives impelled Portugal to look beyond its own remote and impoverished shores: not only gold hunger, but shortages of grain, fish, and above all of slaves for its labour-starved sugar plantations in Madeira and elsewhere. Following the capture of Ceuta, one of the great North African gold ports, in 1415, Portuguese sea-captains pressed south, along the coast of Morocco, past the dreaded Cape Bojador (1434), finally reaching the Gold Coast where, from the 1480s, fortresses were built to protect Portugal's new-found wealth. By the end of the 15th century some 700 kilograms of gold and around 10,000 slaves were arriving in Lisbon every year from west Africa. Meanwhile exploration continued. Angola was reached and 'annexed' in 1484, and in 1487 two further important expeditions of discovery were despatched. The first, under Bartolomeu Dias, was sent to explore the coast of Africa until a southern passage to the Indies was discovered. The second, under Dom Pero de Covilhã, was sent to Ethiopia to establish contact with 'Prester John', the legendary Christian ruler, and to discover how the trade of the Indian Ocean was organised. Both ventures were successful. Dias rounded the Cape of Good Hope in 1488 and saw the coast running north-east; Covilhã reached Sofala near the mouth of the Zambezi, only 1500 miles from the Cape, and saw the coast running south-west.

The Portuguese government – confused by the claim of Christopher Columbus to have found 'the Indies' by a westerly sea-voyage –

1/Eurasian trade routes *(right)* Land trade across central Asia enjoyed a renaissance under the Mongols, but dwindled away as various 14th-century crises affected routes, customers and sources of supply. The Chinese, under Admiral Cheng Ho, took ambitiously to the open sea in the early 15th century but soon retired, leaving what international exchange there was largely in the hands of coast-hugging Indian and Arab merchants. Alexandria and Venice almost monopolised the spice flow to Europe. It should be remembered that Marco Polo and Cheng Ho travelled along already established trade routes. (For routes within Europe see page 144.)

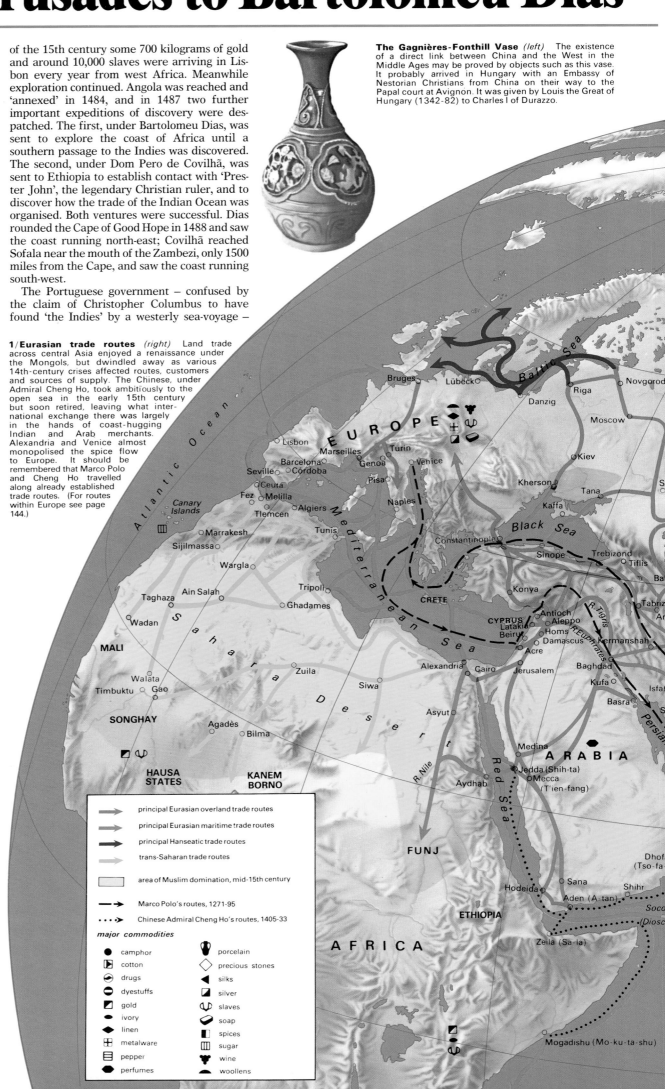

The Gagnières-Fonthill Vase *(left)* The existence of a direct link between China and the West in the Middle Ages may be proved by objects such as this vase. It probably arrived in Hungary with an Embassy of Nestorian Christians from China on their way to the Papal court at Avignon. It was given by Louis the Great of Hungary (1342-82) to Charles I of Durazzo.

principal Eurasian overland trade routes
principal Eurasian maritime trade routes
principal Hanseatic trade routes
trans-Saharan trade routes
area of Muslim domination, mid-15th century
Marco Polo's routes, 1271-95
Chinese Admiral Cheng Ho's routes, 1405-33

major commodities

● camphor		⬮ porcelain	
cotton		◇ precious stones	
drugs		silks	
dyestuffs		silver	
gold		slaves	
ivory		soap	
linen		spices	
metalware		sugar	
pepper		wine	
perfumes		woollens	

to Kilwa, Malindi, Mombasa

hesitated at first, but in December 1496 concluded that Columbus could not possibly have found India and therefore decided to send an expedition there by the newly discovered route round Africa. A fleet of four ships, armed with twenty cannon, left Lisbon under Dom Vasco da Gama in July 1497. It was fortunate to meet little resistance. Earlier in the century, between 1405 and 1433, the Chinese admiral Cheng Ho had made seven voyages of discovery into the Indian Ocean, bringing back tribute and exotic products from as far afield as Java, Ceylon and east Africa. If the Chinese had persisted, the Portuguese would have found formidable rivals, for the Chinese were better equipped and their fleet, comprising 62 ships and 28,000 men, was far larger. But their maritime enterprises ceased with Cheng Ho's death in 1434, and when the Portuguese arrived at Calicut on 17 May 1498 the sea route to India lay wide open. The 'Age of Vasco da Gama' in Asian history had begun.

2/The Portuguese in Africa *(right)* Under the patronage of Prince Henry the Navigator (1394-1460), Portuguese explorers steadily penetrated southwards in search of gold, spices and slaves. In 1488 one Portuguese expedition reached the Cape of Good Hope while another reconnoitered east Africa, preparing the way for Vasco de Gama's first direct seaborne journey to India in 1497.

Key (inset map):
— coast revealed during life of Henry the Navigator, 1418-60
— coast revealed under contract of Fernao Gomes, 1469-75
— coast revealed by Diogo Cão
— journey of Pero de Covilhã, 1487-90
— route of Bartolomeu Dias, 1487-8
— principal trans-Saharan caravan routes

147

The Americas on the eve of European conquest

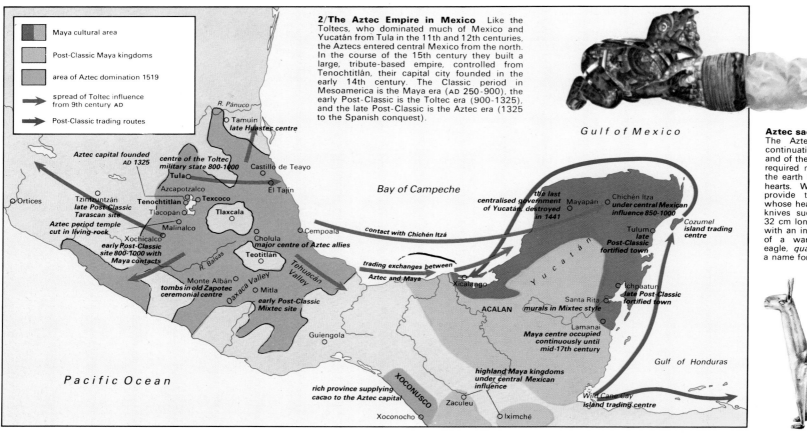

Maya cultural area

Post-Classic Maya kingdoms

area of Aztec domination 1519

spread of Toltec influence from 9th century AD

Post-Classic trading routes

2/The Aztec Empire in Mexico Like the Toltecs, who dominated much of Mexico and Yucatán from Tula in the 11th and 12th centuries, the Aztecs entered central Mexico from the north. In the course of the 15th century they built a large, tribute-based empire, controlled from Tenochtitlán, their capital city founded in the early 14th century. The Classic period in Mesoamerica is the Maya era (AD 250-900), the early Post-Classic is the Toltec era (900-1325), and the late Post-Classic is the Aztec era (1325 to the Spanish conquest).

Aztec sacrificial knife *(above)* The Aztecs believed that the continuation of human society and of the present (fifth) creation required nourishing the sun and the earth with human blood and hearts. War was necessary to provide the sacrificial victims, whose hearts were removed with knives such as this one, about 32 cm long, made of chalcedony with an inlaid handle in the form of a warrior costumed as an eagle, *quauhtli*, which was also a name for the sun.

Inca silver *(above)* This Inca-made silver llama with gold and red stone inlay, about 21 cm high, illustrates both fine Inca metallurgy and the Andean domestication of the llama and alpaca. Guinea pigs were also domesticated here. In other regions of the Americas the only domesticated animals were the dog, brought from Asia by early immigrants, and turkeys domesticated in Mesoamerica and the south-west.

THE native inhabitants of the Americas had, despite their common Asiatic origin, achieved widely varying levels of development by the second millennium AD. In the Amazonian jungles, the Chaco and the sub-Arctic most were still nomadic Stone Age hunters, but in eastern North America and much of South America farming was well established. The Apaches and the Araucanians continued a gathering existence, but agriculture was being introduced to the plains hunters of North America from the east, while groups such as the Chibcha and the Caribs had formed settled societies with some degree of political organisation. All these cultures were overshadowed, however, by the more advanced civilisations of Mesoamerica and the central Andes, where the mighty Aztec and Inca empires were at their most powerful by the late 15th century.

Like their Toltec predecessors, who controlled much of Mexico in the 11th and 12th centuries, the Aztecs came from the north, probably in the early 13th century, to a land being fought over by the semi-civilised tribes, known collectively as Chichimecs, which had destroyed the Toltec city of Tula. In this period of confused, continuous warfare they took refuge on a muddy island in Lake Texcoco, and founded there their town of Tenochtitlán as a place of safety rather than a centre of power. The surrounding swamps were drained, artificial islands were constructed to form gardens, and canals and causeways were built. By the end of the 14th century, following the transfer of religious and political authority from the tribal elders to a single ruler, Tenochtitlán had become the centre for a policy of aggression, first against overlords in Azcapotzalco, then against other neighbouring tribes. The Aztec strategy was brilliantly simple: they allied with their most powerful neighbours in the towns of Texcoco and Tlacopán against smaller groups, and then made war upon their former allies. This policy was particularly successful during the reign of Montezuma I, and by the second half of the 15th century the Aztecs, already in control of the greater part of Mexico, were beginning to enter Maya territory, where the inhabitants had reverted to a simpler way of life and the great cities of the Classic period had disappeared into the jungle.

The Aztecs allowed conquered tribes to retain their own gods and leaders, but failure to provide Tenochtitlán with an ever-growing volume of basic foods, textiles, pottery, metal goods and the other items required to support its nobles, priests and administrators (who numbered perhaps 100,000), would bring rapid retribution from the powerful imperial army. Increasingly war was waged simply to ensure an adequate supply of captives for sacrifice to the principal Aztec god, Huitzilopochtli. It is estimated that at least 10,000 victims a year, rising to 50,000 on the eve of the Spanish conquest, had their still throbbing hearts pulled from their chests by Aztec priests.

Despite its material wealth, this civilisation had neither the wheel nor a written language, but its agriculture, although primitive in equipment, was intensive and produced a wide range of crops. Surviving pictorial tribute lists show that millions of peasants – total population was probably at least twelve millions – were expected to provide a surplus of some 20,000 tons of foodstuffs alone from their communal holdings for annual delivery by the empire's complex trading network to Tenochtitlán and its satellites. Facts such as this explain why it was that subject tribes like the Totonacs and the Tlazcalans welcomed the Spanish *Conquistador*, Hernan Cortés, as a deliverer from Aztec oppression when he landed in Mexico in 1519.

The Incas were empire-builders, with an imperial ideal rather more comprehensive and coherent than that of the Aztecs. They imposed their culture, their socio-economic organisation, and, to a degree, their religion on conquered tribes as they pushed forward their frontiers from the southern Andes in the 15th century. By 1600 they had overcome the distinctive regional cultures which had emerged in Peru following the demise of the Huari empire in the 9th century, and had created an empire 200 miles wide and 2000 miles long, with a population of perhaps 10 millions. The origins of this mighty civilisation are shrouded in mystery. According to Inca legend the first emperor, Manco Capac, had been sent to Earth by his father, the sun (Inti), with instructions to found a city at the spot where a golden rod he was carrying could be pushed deep into the ground. He wandered northwards from Lake Titicaca to the Valley of Cuzco, where he found soil rich enough for this purpose. This settlement seems to have occurred in the 12th century. For the next two hundred years the Incas were simply one of several small groups, vying for supremacy with their neighbours – the Chanca, the Colla, the Lupaca and others – in the southern Andes. Their expansion out of the Cuzco region began early in the 15th century under the eighth emperor, Viracocha, and was continued by his son Pachacuti, who completed the conquest of the Titicaca basin. Pachacuti's son, Topa, led the Inca armies northwards to subdue the powerful coastal Chimú civilisation, and then following his accession as emperor in 1471, pushed forward the frontiers of his empire into Chile and northern Argentina. Huayna Capac, emperor from 1493, concentrated his efforts in the north, where he founded Quito (in modern Ecuador) as a second capital. This decision, dictated by the need to decentralise an already over-large empire, proved fatal, for after Huayna Capac's death in 1525 it provoked a bitter civil war between the northern and southern halves of the empire, led respectively by his sons Atahuallpa and Huáscar.

As new territories were incorporated into the Inca Empire, large-scale movements of population occurred, with thousands of loyal colonists moving in to replace traditional inhabitants transferred to more secure areas. An impressive network of paved highways and bridges provided the means for rapid movement of troops through the hostile terrain. In Cuzco the divine emperor lived in great splendour, ruling through four members of his family, each responsible for one quarter of the empire. These nobles in their turn delegated authority to provincial rulers, in a highly-stratified political structure which descended through a complex hierarchy to officials responsible for every ten families at village level. Here the life of the common Indian was dominated by the need to provide tribute for local and central rulers, to work on a rota basis on road and bridge maintenance, and periodically to serve in the army. In exchange he was guaranteed freedom from famine – massive, state-owned food stores insured against bad

Navajo sand painting *(above)* Maise (corn), beans and squash formed a triad of domesticated plants on which settled life depended over much of the Americas. Maise, especially, is a sacred plant, as is illustrated by this 'corn person' from a 20th-century painting.

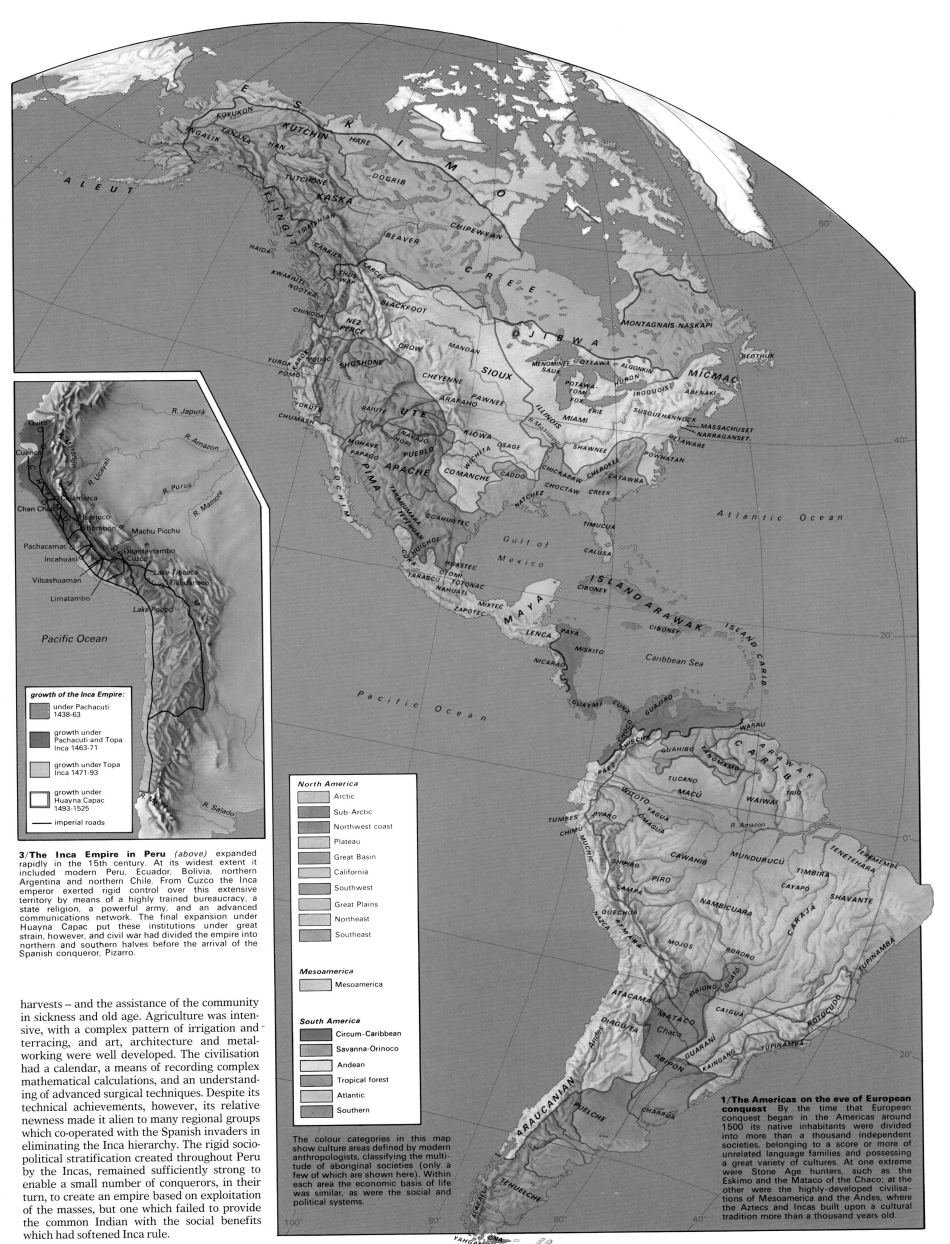

growth of the Inca Empire:

- under Pachacuti 1438-63
- growth under Pachacuti and Topa Inca 1463-71
- growth under Topa Inca 1471-93
- growth under Huayna Capac 1493-1525
- imperial roads

3/The Inca Empire in Peru (above) expanded rapidly in the 15th century. At its widest extent it included modern Peru, Ecuador, Bolivia, northern Argentina and northern Chile. From Cuzco the Inca emperor exerted rigid control over this extensive territory by means of a highly trained bureaucracy, a state religion, a powerful army, and an advanced communications network. The final expansion under Huayna Capac put these institutions under great strain, however, and civil war had divided the empire into northern and southern halves before the arrival of the Spanish conqueror, Pizarro.

harvests – and the assistance of the community in sickness and old age. Agriculture was intensive, with a complex pattern of irrigation and terracing, and art, architecture and metalworking were well developed. The civilisation had a calendar, a means of recording complex mathematical calculations, and an understanding of advanced surgical techniques. Despite its technical achievements, however, its relative newness made it alien to many regional groups which co-operated with the Spanish invaders in eliminating the Inca hierarchy. The rigid sociopolitical stratification created throughout Peru by the Incas, remained sufficiently strong to enable a small number of conquerors, in their turn, to create an empire based on exploitation of the masses, but one which failed to provide the common Indian with the social benefits which had softened Inca rule.

North America
- Arctic
- Sub-Arctic
- Northwest coast
- Plateau
- Great Basin
- California
- Southwest
- Great Plains
- Northeast
- Southeast

Mesoamerica
- Mesoamerica

South America
- Circum-Caribbean
- Savanna-Orinoco
- Andean
- Tropical forest
- Atlantic
- Southern

The colour categories in this map show culture areas defined by modern anthropologists, classifying the multitude of aboriginal societies (only a few of which are shown here). Within each area the economic basis of life was similar, as were the social and political systems.

1/The Americas on the eve of European conquest By the time that European conquest began in the Americas around 1500 its native inhabitants were divided into more than a thousand independent societies, belonging to a score or more of unrelated language families and possessing a great variety of cultures. At one extreme were Stone Age hunters, such as the Eskimo and the Mataco of the Chaco; at the other were the highly-developed civilisations of Mesoamerica and the Andes, where the Aztecs and Incas built upon a cultural tradition more than a thousand years old.

The new monarchies: Europe at the close of the 15th century

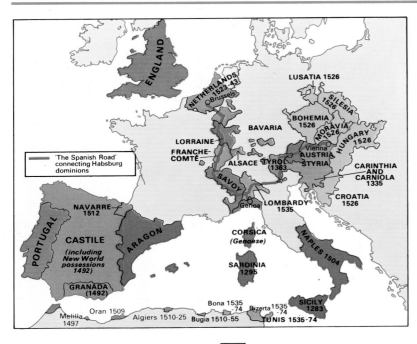

2/The Habsburg Empire in Europe (above) The emperor Charles V was heir to four separate inheritances, one from each of his grandparents. From Ferdinand of Aragon he acquired Sicily, Naples, Sardinia and Aragon, adding Milan and Tunis in 1535. The legacy of Isabella the Catholic provided Castile, Granada and the West Indies; Charles added Mexico (1519) and Peru (1533). Mary of Burgundy provided most of the Netherlands, Charles adding a number of provinces (see map 3). Maximilian of Habsburg's legacy gave him Austria, Tyrol, Carinthia, Alsace and the title of Holy Roman Emperor; he added Bohemia, Moravia, Silesia and parts of Hungary in 1526.

Key:
- Aragonese inheritance of Charles V
- acquisitions by Charles V, with date
- Castilian inheritance of Charles V
- Austrian inheritance of Charles V
- acquisitions by Charles V, with date
- Burgundian inheritance of Charles V
- acquisitions by Charles V, with date
- states favourable to Charles V

A S A RESULT of the economic and political setbacks of the 14th century (see page 142), by about 1400 there was no dominant state in Europe. Germany and Italy were already fragmented, and in neither was there any clear preponderance. In the east, the powerful states of the 14th century (see page 140) crumbled and new empires, such as those of Casimir IV of Poland (1447-92) or Matthias Corvinus of Hungary (1458-90), proved ephemeral. In the west, the Iberian peninsula was a prey to civil war, while France was torn apart by the feud between Burgundians and Armagnacs, a situation made far worse when Henry V of England (1413-22), the ally of Burgundy, invaded Normandy in 1415 and extended English control to the Loire.

This unstable balance was destroyed after 1450. The Muscovites and the Ottoman Turks rapidly subjugated large areas of the steppes and plains of eastern Europe (see map 1, and pages 138 and 162). In the west, Burgundy, the rising star of the 15th century, which seemed destined to become a major power between France and Germany, was partitioned after Charles the Bold was killed in battle in 1477 (see map 3), and the English were expelled from French soil (except from Calais) by 1453. In Spain, the warring kingdoms of Castile and Aragon were united in 1479, and in 1492 their combined forces completed the reconquest of the last Islamic strongholds in Spain. In England, failure in France and the loss of Normandy (1453) provoked civil war ('The Wars of the Roses'), but after 1485 a new dynasty, the

Tudors, succeeded in restoring order and extended royal control in the turbulent outlying regions through the Council of the North and the Council of the March of Wales. In Germany, a series of dynastic alliances united the Habsburg lands with those of Luxemburg (1437) and Burgundy (1477). All these possessions, and later those of the Spanish royal family, came to the Emperor Charles V (1519-56), making him the greatest Christian ruler since Charlemagne. He systematically expanded each of these inheritances (see maps 2 and 3) and fear of Habsburg hegemony dominated Europe for two centuries.

The states which achieved these territorial successes were very different from the 'feudal monarchies' of the 12th and 13th centuries (see page 124). New conceptions of statecraft, exemplified for later generations by Machiavelli's famous treatise, *The Prince*, were in the air, and new institutions were created to enhance the king's authority. New courts, such as the English Star Chamber, were set up to impose law and order; new taxes were introduced, such as the French *taille* (1439), and new machinery to collect them; permanent ambassadors monitored the actions of neighbouring states. There was also a marked expansion of armies and navies. In France, regular royal regiments, the beginning of the standing army, were raised after 1445, and Louis XI (1461-83) could rely, in his struggles with foreign enemies and overmighty vassals, on the best train of artillery in Europe. The armed forces of the king of Spain numbered about 30,000 in the 1470s, but 150,000

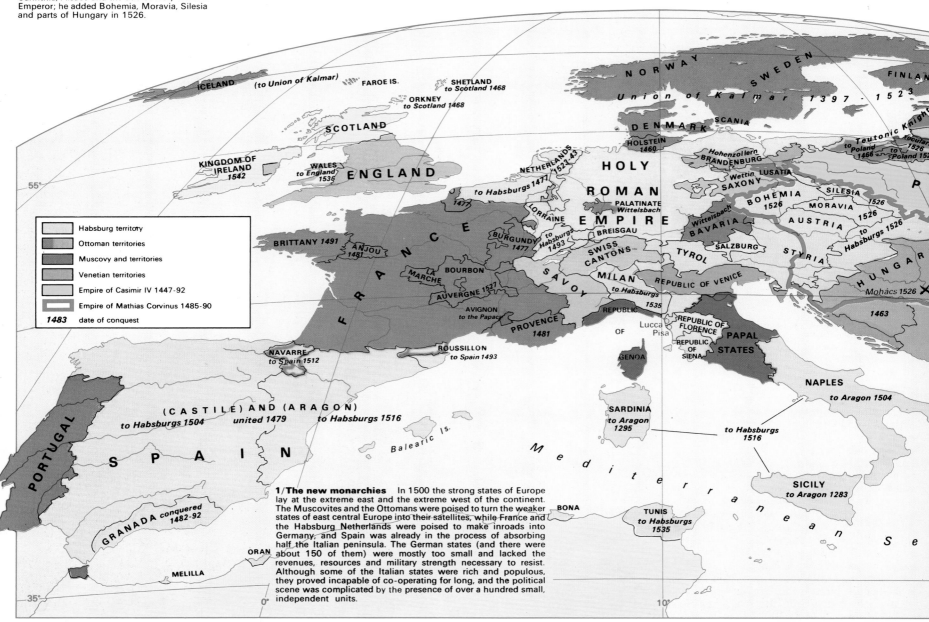

1/The new monarchies In 1500 the strong states of Europe lay at the extreme east and the extreme west of the continent. The Muscovites and the Ottomans were poised to turn the weaker states of east central Europe into their satellites, while France and the Habsburg Netherlands were poised to make inroads into Germany, and Spain was already in the process of absorbing half the Italian peninsula. The German states (and there were about 150 of them) were mostly too small and lacked the revenues, resources and military strength necessary to resist. Although some of the Italian states were rich and populous, they proved incapable of co-operating for long, and the political scene was complicated by the presence of over a hundred small, independent units.

Key:
- Habsburg territory
- Ottoman territories
- Muscovy and territories
- Venetian territories
- Empire of Casimir IV 1447-92
- Empire of Mathias Corvinus 1485-90
- *1483* date of conquest

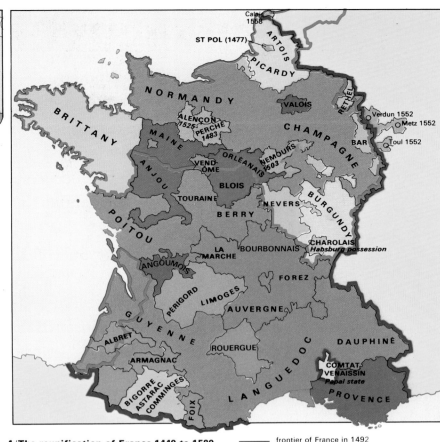

M. METZ
T. TOUL

RAVENSBERG

4 LINGEN 1543

CALAIS

LIEGE

M.
Nancy
T.
1477

Morat 1476

Grandson 1476

Charles the Bold's possessions, 1477

Burgundian possessions lost at the death of Charles the Bold, 1477

Emperor Charles V's Burgundian possessions, 1548

provincial frontiers

some sixty years later.

The attitude of the new monarchs was expressed by Matthias Corvinus when he told a Silesian assembly in 1474 that he was 'lord and king' and that 'what he with his councillors held to be best, it was for them as dutiful subjects to perform'. The inhabitants of many countries, particularly the commercial classes, were prepared to tolerate this form of royal absolutism in return for security and the suppression of civil war. The economic recovery visible from c.1450 also helped by providing more taxes. Civil war and economic setbacks had weakened the old nobility, and the church also was brought increasingly under royal control. In 'concordats' with Austria (1448), France (1516) and Spain (1526), the papacy was forced to concede far-reaching rights over the national churches, and in a number of Protestant countries the ruler openly assumed control of spiritual affairs. Henry VIII of England, for example, declared himself 'Supreme Head' of the church in England in 1534. Nevertheless the institutional armature of the 'new monarchies' was more fragile than it seemed, their apparent modernity often superficial. The new exalted sense of the prince's authority might point to the future, but rulers like Charles the Bold of Burgundy and Maximilian I of Austria, even Charles V himself (who abdicated in 1556 and spent his last years in monastic seclusion), clung to the ideals of the age of chivalry which was passing. The secular state, in which politics are divorced from religion and organised around an impersonal, centralised and unifying system of government, was still two centuries away (see page 184); the 'new monarchies' were at best its forerunner.

3/State-building in the Low Countries *(above)* In the 15th century the dukes of Burgundy succeeded in building up a compact territory at the expense of France and the Empire. Including Flanders and Brabant, it was the richest land in Europe and effectively an independent state, very active in European politics. Duke Charles the Bold (1467-77) was defeated by the Swiss at Morat and Grandson (1476) and killed at the battle of Nancy (1477). His French fiefs (Burgundy and Picardy) were confiscated by Louis XI, but the rest of the Burgundian inheritance passed to Maximilian I of Austria, husband of Charles's heiress, and thence to their son, the emperor Charles V, who added further territories in the north-east.

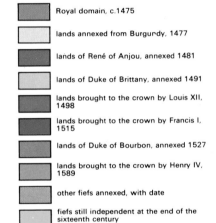

Calais 1558

ST POL (1477)

ARTOIS

PICARDY

NORMANDY

VALOIS

RETHEL

BRITTANY

MAINE
ALENÇON
PERCHE 1483
1525

CHAMPAGNE

Verdun 1552
Metz 1552

ANJOU
ORLEANAIS
NEMOURS 1503

BAR
Toul 1552

VENDÔME

BLOIS

NEVERS

BURGUNDY

TOURAINE

POITOU

BERRY

LA MARCHE
BOURBONNAIS

CHAROLAIS
Habsburg possession

ANGOUMOIS

FOREZ

PÉRIGORD

LIMOGES

AUVERGNE

GUYENNE

ALBRET

ROUERGUE

DAUPHINÉ

ARMAGNAC

LANGUEDOC

COMTAT VENAISSIN
Papal state

BIGORRE
ASTARAC
COMMINGES

FOIX

PROVENCE

4/The reunification of France 1440 to 1589 *(above)* The possessions of the French monarchy in the mid-15th century were surprisingly small. Until 1430, most of the land north of the Loire was in the hands of English and Burgundian forces, and even in the remaining area to the south the actual domain was less than half the total territory. The reconquest of Normandy, Gascony and the other areas held by the English in the 1440s doubled both the area obeying Charles VII and the royal domain. But the area under the crown's direct control was still relatively small until a series of confiscations brought in the lands of the dukes of Burgundy (1477), Anjou (1481), Brittany (1491) and Bourbon (1527). This left only a handful of semi-independent fiefs (of which many came to the crown when Henry of Navarre became King Henry IV in 1589).

frontier of France in 1492

Royal domain, c.1475

lands annexed from Burgundy, 1477

lands of René of Anjou, annexed 1481

lands of Duke of Brittany, annexed 1491

lands brought to the crown by Louis XII, 1498

lands brought to the crown by Francis I, 1515

lands of Duke of Bourbon, annexed 1527

lands brought to the crown by Henry IV, 1589

other fiefs annexed, with date

fiefs still independent at the end of the sixteenth century

lands recognising English suzerainty,1429

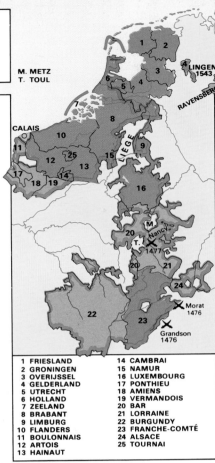

PSKOV

acquired by Ivan III 1462-1505

LITHUANIA

Moscow 1462

MUSCOVY

acquired by Vassily III 1505-33

TRANSYLVANIA 1541

MOLDAVIA 1504

1520's

1504

WALLACHIA

T A R T A R S

B l a c k S e a

1478

OTTOMAN EMPIRE
in 1451

ANATOLIA

EUBOEA 1470

Lesbos 1462

Chios (Genoese)

MOREA 1460

1453

1461

conquered 1470s

1488

1514-17

Rhodes 1522

CRETE
(Venetian)

CYPRUS
(Venetian)

20°   30°   40°

The Renaissance *(below)* The 'new monarchs' of Europe left lasting monuments to their wealth and power. Patronage on an unprecedented scale produced the rich cultural harvest known as the Renaissance. The movement began in two areas at the end of the 14th century: in the Netherlands, at the court of the Dukes of Burgundy and in the great commercial centres such as Bruges and Antwerp; and in the major city-states of Italy — Florence, Milan, Venice, Naples and Rome. From these centres new styles in art, architecture, literature and music soon spread over the whole continent, as far as Moscow. Italian architects had been employed by Ivan III since the 1470s. The purest Renaissance building in Moscow is the Cathedral of the Archangel Michael *(below)* designed by Alevisio Novi, in the Kremlin. The external decoration is distinctly Italianate, although the main structure was Russian in inspiration.

For most of the 16th century Italians continued to dominate architecture as Netherlanders dominated music, and both were prominent in art; but the Renaissance brought a flowering of vernacular literature in every country, from Spain to Sweden. Thanks to the spread of printing after 1455, the new cultural advances could be shared and improved upon by others.

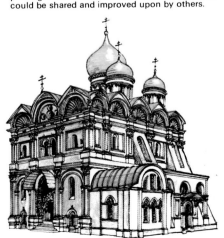

THE Indian historian Panikkar described the period from 1498 to 1947, from Vasco da Gama's discovery of the sea route to India to the declaration of Indian independence, as the European age in history. Other historians have pointed out the element of exaggeration in this definition. If the Europeans had withdrawn from their settlements on the Asian coastlands in 1750, they would have left behind 'a few relics of historical curiosity', but nothing more substantial. Nevertheless, round about 1500 the balance, which hitherto had weighed heavily on the side of Asia, began to change, and by 1750 the change was momentous.

Before 1500 civilisation had been essentially land-centred, and contacts by sea were relatively unimportant. If the year 1500 marks a new period in world history, it is because henceforward direct sea contact was established between the different continents. This resulted not only in an extension of the stage of history to regions which hitherto had gone their way in isolation, but also in a challenge to the age-old land-centred balance between the Eurasian civilisations. Only Australia and the smaller islands of the Pacific remained immune; but even they fell into European clutches before the end of the eighteenth century.

Even so, the speed of European expansion should not be exaggerated. The sixteenth century saw a remarkable resurgence of Muslim power in the Ottoman Empire, Safavid Persia and Mughal India. China and Japan closed their doors to the western barbarians. As late as the days of Voltaire, Turkey and China were the exemplars of civilised living, to which Europe could only look with envy and respect. The advent of the Industrial Revolution put Europe ahead; but the fruits of that – some of them poisonous fruits – were only garnered in the nineteenth century. The period from 1500 to 1815 was a transitional period in world history, and European society, for all its thrusting novelty, was still essentially an agricultural society of lords and peasants, closer to its agrarian past than to its industrial future.

5 The world o

The main façade of the Palace at Versailles

the emerging West

The world on the eve of European expansion c.1500

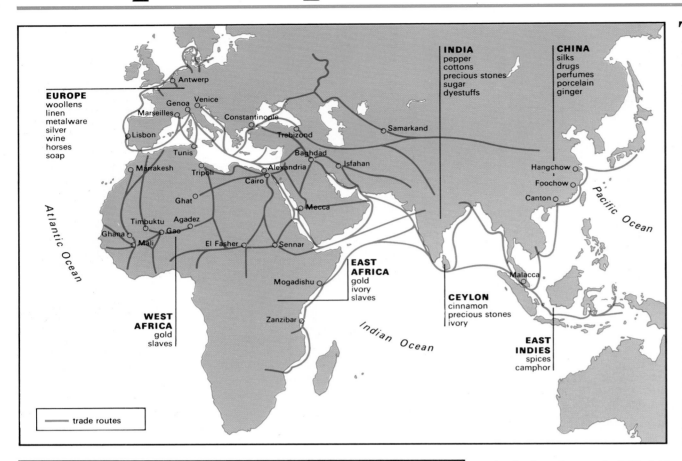

THE central feature of world history between 1500 and 1815 was the expansion of Europe and the spread of European civilisation throughout the globe. Down to 1500 the world had, on the whole, pressed in on Europe; after 1500 Europe pressed out into the world. By 1775 a new global balance was in existence.

In 1500 western Europe still stood on the periphery of the civilised world, overshadowed by the Ming Empire of China, the most powerful and advanced state of the period, and by the rising Ottoman and Safavid empires of the Middle East. Both in wealth and in population China, with over 100 million inhabitants (more than the whole of Europe), loomed far ahead, while the most expansive of the great world religions was Islam, still actively making converts in central and south-east Asia and among the peoples of sub-Saharan Africa.

The area occupied by the major civilisations, roughly equivalent to the area of plough cultivation, was nevertheless still relatively small in 1500. Over three-quarters of the world's surface was inhabited either by food gatherers and herdsmen – as in Australia and most of Siberia, north America and Africa – or by hand cultivators, especially in south-east Asia, Africa and central and south America. But the plough cultivators were far more productive, and it

2/Trade on the eve of Portuguese expansion *(left)* When Vasco da Gama set out for India, the world's richest trade routes ran from East to West. They made fortunes for the Muslim kingdoms of the Near East and for ports handling the western end.

3/Distribution of races in 1500 *(left)* **and subsequent diffusion** *(below)* Before 1500 there existed, in effect, worldwide racial segregation. The Negroids were concentrated in sub-Saharan Africa and a few Pacific islands; the Mongoloids in central Asia, Siberia, Madagascar and the Americas; the Caucasoids in Europe, north Africa, the Middle East and India; and the Australoids in Australia and India. By 1775 this pattern had fundamentally altered as the result of six principal intercontinental migrations: from Europe to north, central and south America; from Great Britain and other northern European countries to Africa (and later Australia). There was also an enforced movement of African slaves to the Americas; a steadily growing trickle from Russia across the Urals into Siberia; and a substantial flow from India to east Africa, south Africa and the Caribbean, and from China into south-east Asia. By far the greatest change occurred in the Americas, where the native population declined by 90 per cent within a century, to be replaced by white Europeans, black Africans and a mixed race of *mestizos*.

Mongoloid
Caucasoid
Australoid
Negroid

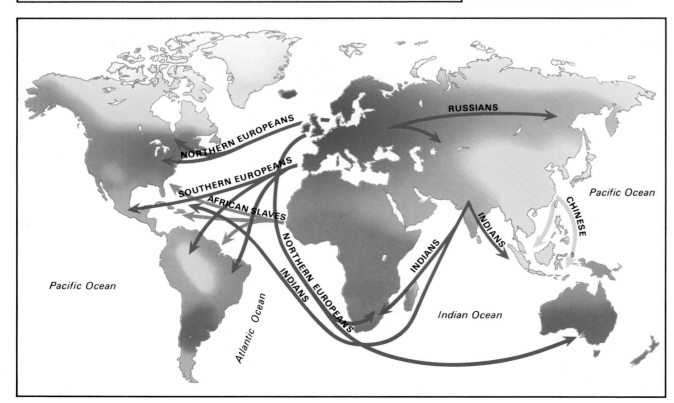

seems probable that between two-thirds and three-quarters of the total population was concentrated in the relatively small area which had been brought under the plough.

This concentration of both people and wealth closely matches the location of the major Eurasian civilisations. The comparative fragility of the Aztec and Inca civilisations in the Americas, and of the African kingdoms immediately south of the Sahara, which were outstanding in many respects, may be partly explained: first, by their geographic isolation and lack of external stimulus, which bred retardation; and second, by their dependence on hand cultivation. After 1500, when the expansion of Europe brought all continents for the first time into direct contact with each other, these non-Eurasian civilisations often found themselves unable to put up more than a feeble resistance.

It is nevertheless important not to exaggerate the tempo of change. Although in America the Aztec and Inca civilisations were destroyed by 1521 and 1535 respectively, elsewhere the political impact of Europe was extremely limited before the second half of the 18th century. China and Japan remained intact, and in India the Europeans were kept at arm's length for 250 years following the arrival of Vasco da Gama in 1498. There, as in west Africa and south-east Asia, the European presence was largely confined to trading stations along the coast. The cultural influence of Europe was even more negligible, and Christianity made little headway, except where it was imposed by the Spanish conquerors in the Philippines and Latin America, until it was backed by the resources of western technology in the 19th century.

On the other hand, the European discoveries not only opened up new global horizons but also led to a new global redistribution of races, and to a diffusion of animals and plants which was of first-rate importance. The diffusion of races involved a corresponding diffusion of religions and of animals (e.g. horses, cattle and sheep from the Old World to the New World), plants and food crops. The spread of food plants – almost all domesticated by prehistoric man in various parts of the world – had proceeded slowly until 1500, when they were transplanted to every continent. In addition, the American Indians were responsible for two major cash crops: tobacco and cotton (derived largely in its commercial form from varieties they had domesticated, though other species were known and used in the Orient before 1500). Cane sugar, introduced by Europeans into Brazil and the West Indies about 1640, also quickly became a staple of foreign trade.

This interchange of plants produced an enormous increase in food supplies, which made possible the unprecedented increase of human populations in modern times. It also initiated a corresponding increase in intercontinental trade. Before 1500, this trade was limited to Eurasia and Africa, and involved mostly luxury goods; after 1500, the combination of regional economic specialisation and improved sea transport made possible the gradual transformation of the limited mediaeval luxury trade into the modern mass trade of new bulky necessities – hence the flourishing 'triangular trade' of rum, cloth, guns and other metal products from Europe to Africa, slaves from Africa to the New World, and sugar, tobacco and bullion from the New World to Europe.

It was not until the 19th century, with the opening of the Suez and Panama canals and the construction of transcontinental railways in Canada, the United States, Siberia and Africa, that areas and lines of commerce which had previously been separate finally dissolved into a single economy on a world scale, but the first stages of global integration were completed in just over two centuries beginning in 1500.

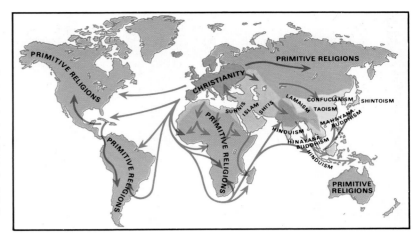

4/The diffusion of world religions *(above)* In 1500 Christianity was almost entirely a European religion, but the great Catholic powers, Spain and Portugal, imposed it, by prayer and the sword, wherever their vessels touched land, and the Anglo-Saxon Protestants soon followed suit.

5/The diffusion of plants *(below)* Wheat, originating in the Near East, had spread across Africa and Eurasia; now it spanned the globe, and was soon joined by bananas, yams, rice and the sugar cane, all from Asia, and by maize, and both sweet and ordinary potatoes, from the Americas.

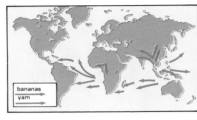

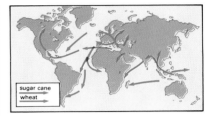

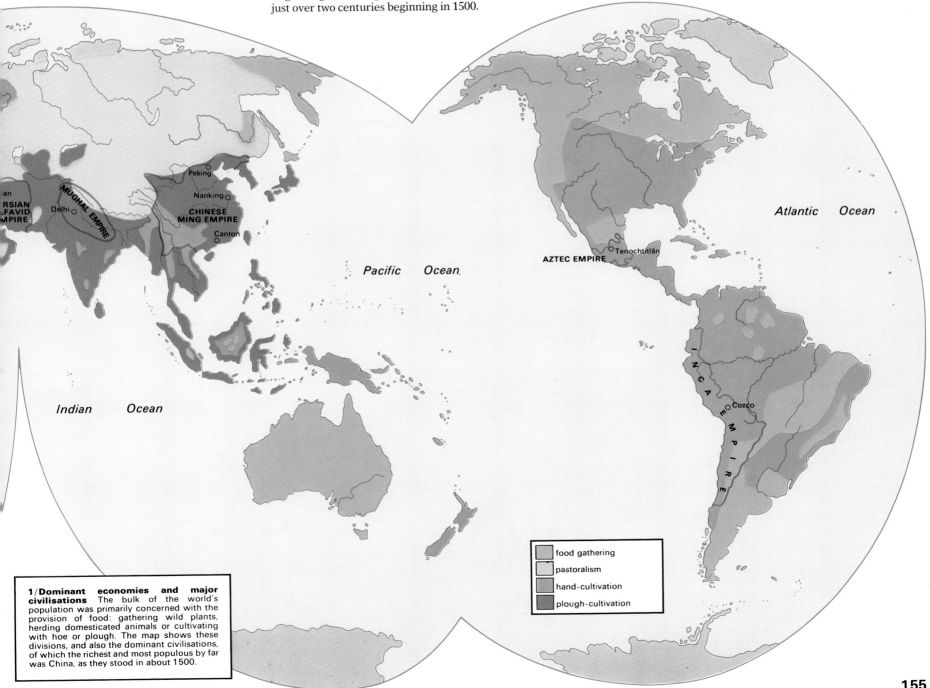

1/Dominant economies and major civilisations The bulk of the world's population was primarily concerned with the provision of food: gathering wild plants, herding domesticated animals or cultivating with hoe or plough. The map shows these divisions, and also the dominant civilisations, of which the richest and most populous by far was China, as they stood in about 1500.

food gathering
pastoralism
hand-cultivation
plough-cultivation

The European voyages of discovery 1487 to 1780

THE European voyages of discovery heralded a new era in world history. In 1480 the principal seafaring peoples of the world were separated not only by great expanses of uncharted sea but also by continental landmasses whose extent and shape were unknown. Regular European shipping was still mainly confined to the North Atlantic, the Mediterranean and the Baltic. The West African coast had been explored cursorily, and only very recently, by Europeans, but from the Gaboon to Mozambique the coast was unknown to any shipping. In the Americas, there were limited areas of raft- and canoe-borne navigation on the Pacific coasts of Ecuador and Peru and in the Caribbean, but no communication with Europe nor – so far as is known – with other parts of the Pacific. In the East several seafaring peoples overlapped. Indian, Persian and Arab shipping plied in the northern Indian Ocean. Chinese shipping – which in the past had sailed intermittently to East Africa – in 1480 usually went no farther west than Malacca, but shared the shallow seas of the Malay archipelago with local shipping, chiefly Javanese. No shipping used the southern Indian Ocean; Javanese contacts with Madagascar had long ceased. Chinese shipping, dense in the China Seas and the archipelago, went no further east than the Philippines. The great areas of the central Pacific were crossed only occasionally and perilously by Polynesian canoes. In the north Pacific, except in Japanese coastal waters, there was no shipping at all.

In the course of three centuries, approximately between 1480 and 1780, European seaborne explorers linked together the separate areas of maritime communication, and opened all seas, except in the regions of circumpolar ice, to European ships. In this long process of discovery, several distinct stages can be distinguished: initially, in the late 15th century, two series of voyages intended to find a sea passage to southern Asia, in the hope of opening direct trade for spices. One series, based on Portugal, sailing by a south-eastern route, and employing local navigators in the East, soon reached its declared destinations: the entrance to the Indian Ocean (1488), Malabar (1498), Malacca (1511), and the Moluccas (1512). The other series, based on Spain, sailing by a western or south-western route, was less successful in its immediate purpose but more fruitful in incidental discovery. The Spaniards hit upon the West Indian islands (1492) and the Spanish Main (1498). Eventually they reached south-eastern Asia (1521), but by a route too long and arduous for commercial use. In the process of search they proved the Pacific to be a great ocean and not, as some respected authorities had supposed, a mere arm of the Indian Ocean. To reach the Pacific they had to circumvent an immense landmass, which they believed initially to be a peninsula of Asia, but which by the 1520s they accepted as a New World; though its complete separation from Asia was not proved until the 18th century. They immediately began to settle their new world, and for more than a hundred years kept it effectively an Iberian preserve.

The combined effect of Spanish and Portuguese discovery was to show that all the oceans of the world, at least in the southern hemisphere, were connected. For a hundred years or so Spain and Portugal, by the use of force and threat of force, prevented other Europeans from using the connecting passages, except for occasional raids. The third great series of voyages, therefore, mostly English, French or Dutch in inception, looked for corresponding passages to Asia in the northern hemisphere, in the west, north-west or north-east. Unsuccessful in their primary purpose, they revealed another continental landmass with a continuous coast from the Caribbean to the Arctic, and opened the way for the exploration and settlement of eastern

North America by northern Europeans.

After 1632 the search for the northern passages was abandoned. By that time influential groups in England and the Netherlands had defied the Iberian monopoly and opened trade with Asia by the south-eastern route. The last three-quarters of the 17th century and the first quarter of the 18th century was a period of settlement and of commercial consolidation rather than of new discovery; the brief encouragement which the Dutch East India Company gave to Tasman was exceptional, and was openly regretted by the directors of the Company. A series of circumnavigations by buccaneers or privateers, shortly before and shortly after the turn of the century, was similarly barren of practical results.

A second, a Silver Age of discovery began in the 18th century, inspired as much by scientific curiosity as by hope of commercial advantage. The voyages were organised by governments rather than by private investors, and were made by warships commanded by naval officers, often accompanied by scientists and painters. The objects were, in general, the exploration of the Pacific; in particular the location of a great southern continent believed, on the authority of Ptolemy, Ortelius and others, to extend north of the Tropic of Capricorn in the southern Pacific; and the discovery of a strait between north-eastern Asia and north-western America leading to the Arctic Ocean and thence, possibly, round to the Atlantic – the old North-west Passage from the opposite side. The results, in part at least, were negative: there is no habitable southern continent, other than Australia; the passage to the Arctic, though it exists, is choked with ice. On the other hand, many unknown island groups were discovered; the insularity of New Zealand was established and its coasts charted; the attractive and habitable east coast of Australia was explored, and shortly afterwards settled; the general configuration of the American and Asian coasts of the North Pacific was revealed; and the old problem of keeping men alive and healthy on long ocean voyages was, in large measure, solved. After Cook's death in 1779 – as La Pérouse complained – few of the world's coastlines remained to be explored.

Voyages in the Caribbean:
30/Bastidas & La Cosa 1501-02 explored coast from Gulf of Maracaibo to Gulf of Urabá.
31/Pinzón & Solís 1508 sent from Spain to find strait to Asia, coasted E. coast of Yucatán.
32/Ponce de León 1512-13 sailed from Puerto Rico, explored coast of Florida from N. of Cape Canaveral to (possibly) Pensacola. May have sighted Yucatán on return. First explorer to note force of Gulf Stream.
33/Hernández de Córdoba 1516 sailed from Cuba, explored N. and W. coasts of Yucatán. First report of Maya cities.

34/Grijalva 1517 followed S. and W. coasts of Gulf of Mexico as far as River Pánuco.
35/Pineda 1519 explored N. and W. coasts of Gulf of Mexico from Florida to River Pánuco. Finally ended hope of strait to Pacific in that region.

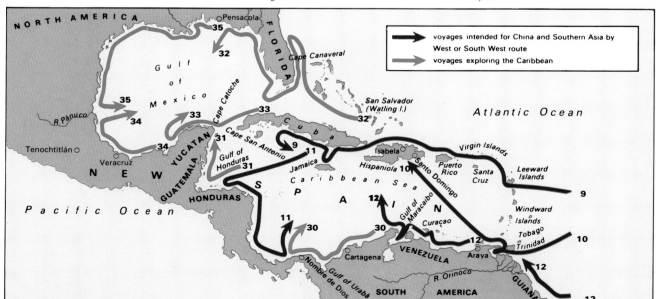

2/Voyages in the Caribbean, 1493 to 1519 (below) Spanish expeditions explored the Caribbean searching for a seaway to China, India and the Golden Chersonese. They found it landlocked on the west; took to slaving, pearling and plunder; encountered settled, city-building peoples; and founded a European empire.

1/Major European voyages of discovery from about 1480 to 1630 (below)
Explorers seeking sea routes to Asia found, in addition, a continent hitherto unknown to Europe, and an ocean of unsuspected extent. They proved that all the oceans were connected, and that the world was much bigger than accepted authorities had taught.

Voyages intended for S. Asia by S.E. Route:
1/Dias 1487-88 (outward) discovered open water S. of Cape Agulhas; entered Indian Ocean; reached Great Fish River.
2/Vasco da Gama 1497-99 (outward) discovered best use of Atlantic winds on way to Cape of Good Hope; reached India, navigated by local pilot.

3/Cabral 1500 (outward) the second Portuguese voyage to India, sighted coast of Brazil at Monte Pascoal, probably accidentally.
4/First Portuguese voyage to Malacca, 1509.
5/Abreu 1512-13 visited Moluccas.
6/First Portuguese visits to Canton River, 1514.

Voyages intended for China and S. Asia by W. or S.W. Route:
7/Da Mota, Zeimoto and Peixoto 1543 Portuguese discovery of Japan.
8/Columbus 1492-93 (outward and homeward) discovered islands in Bahama group, explored N. coasts of Cuba and Hispaniola; interpreted discoveries as part of Asia; found best return route.
9/Columbus 1493-94 (outward) explored S. coast of Cuba; reported it as peninsula of mainland China.
10/Columbus 1498 (outward) discovered Trinidad and coast of Venezuela; recognised coast as mainland, surmised it to be terrestrial paradise.
11/Columbus 1502-04 explored coast of Honduras, Nicaragua and the Isthmus. Believed Honduras to be Indo-China.
12/Ojeda & Vespucci 1499-1500 (outward) reached Guiana coast, failed to round Cap São Roque, coasted W. to Cape de la Vela. First report of Amazon.
13/Coalho & Vespucci 1501 (outward) coasted S. from Cape São Agostinho to (possibly) 35°S.
14/Solis 1515 entered River Plate estuary and investigated N. bank.
15/Magellan & Elcano 1519-22 discovered Strait of Magellan, crossed Pacific, reached Moluccas via Philippines. Revealed Pacific as separate ocean of immense size. First circumnavigation.

16/Saavedra 1527 discovered route from coast of Mexico across Pacific to Moluccas.
17/Urdaneta 1565 found feasible return route Philippines to Mexico in 42°N. using W. winds.
18/Schouten & Le Maire 1616 discovered route into Pacific via Le Maire Strait and Cape Horn.

Voyages intended for Asia by Northern Route:
19/Cabot 1497 (outward) rediscovered Newfoundland, first sighted by Norsemen in 11th century; took it for N.E. extremity of Asia.
20/Corte-Real 1500 rediscovered Greenland.
21/Verrazzano 1524 traced E. coast of N. America from (probably) 34°N. to 47°N.; revealed continental character of N. America.
22/Cartier 1534 and 1535 explored Strait of Belle Isle and St. Lawrence as far as Montreal.
23/Willoughby & Chancellor 1553 rounded North Cape and reached Archangel.
24/Frobisher 1574 reached Frobisher Bay in Baffin Island, which he took for a 'strait'; diverted from further exploration by spurious gold strike.
25/Davis 1587 explored W. coast of Greenland to the edge of the ice in 72°N.
26/Barents 1596-97 discovered Bear Island and Spitsbergen and wintered in Novaya Zemlya.
27/Hudson 1610 sailed through Hudson Strait to the S. extremity of Hudson Bay, which he and others took to be the Pacific.
28/Button 1612 explored W. coast of Hudson Bay, concluded Bay landlocked on the W.
29/Baffin & Bylot 1616 explored whole coastline of Baffin Bay and came to the conclusion that no navigable N.W. passage existed in that area.

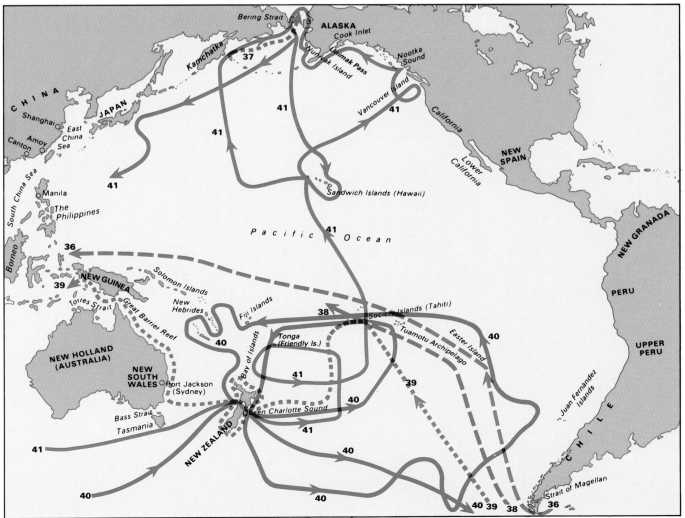

The ships of the discoverers (below) The outstanding characteristics of European ships employed in exploration were a stout pre-constructed frame to which carvel planking was fastened; and a rig combining square and lateen sails in the same vessel, giving driving power when running, adequate performance on a wind, and manoeuvrability. The engraving shows Elmina Castle, two lateen caravels, and a ship with the combined rig.

3/European exploration of the Pacific, 1720 to 1780 (right)
Most 18th-century voyages of discovery were searches for a habitable southern continent or for a usable northern strait. Both proved imaginary. The expeditions revealed instead an insular New Zealand, a habitable eastern Australia, many attractive islands and a valuable whale fishery.

Voyages in the Pacific:
36/Roggeveen 1721-22 discovered Easter Island and some of the Samoan group. Circumnavigation.
37/Bering 1728 sailed from Kamchatka, discovered strait separating N.E. Asia and N.W. America.
38/Wallis 1766-68 discovered Society Islands (Tahiti), encouraged hope of habitable southern continent. Circumnavigation.
39/Cook 1768-71 charted coasts of New Zealand, explored E. coast of Australia, confirmed existence of Torres Strait. Circumnavigation.
40/Cook 1772-75 made circuit of southern oceans in high latitude, charted New Hebrides, discovered many islands, ended hope of habitable southern continent. Circumnavigation.
41/Cook & Clerke 1776-80 discovered Sandwich Islands (Hawaii), explored N.W. coast of N. America from Vancouver Island to Unimak Pass, sailed through Bering Strait to edge of pack ice, ended hope of navigable passage through Arctic to Atlantic.

European expansion overseas: Spain and Portugal 1500 to 1600

AT the end of the 15th century Portuguese possessions outside Europe included several island groups in the Atlantic and the Gulf of Guinea, and a few trading stations on the west coast of Africa, of which the fortress-factory of Elmina was the most important. Cloth and hardware were bartered for slaves and gold dust, a dozen or so ships making the voyage between Portugal and Guinea every year.

After the discovery of the sea route to India the Portuguese, in their endeavour to become suppliers of spices to Europe, quickly acquired, by capture or lease, trading posts and fortified bases on the east coast of Africa, round the northern shores of the Indian Ocean, and in the Malay archipelago. By the middle of the 16th century they had more than fifty forts and factories, in a tenuous string from Sofala to Nagasaki. Strategically the most important bases were Mozambique, on the east coast of Africa opposite Madagascar; Goa (1510) on the west coast of India, headquarters of the Portuguese governor-general in the East; Ormuz island (1515) at the mouth of the Persian Gulf, a major port of trans-shipment in the international spice trade; and Malacca (1511), also a major spice market, on the strait connecting the Indian Ocean with the shallow seas of the archipelago. All these were outright Portuguese possessions. East of Malacca, the position of the Portuguese was precarious and their activity purely commercial. Their settlement at Macao was first occupied in 1557, through the connivance or indifference of Chinese officials. From there they traded to Nagasaki, where they were welcomed as carriers of Chinese goods, since the Chinese government forbade its own subjects to trade directly with the Japanese. At Ternate they maintained a fortified warehouse, built to collect cloves produced in the Moluccas (and at that time nowhere else) but a league of Muslim princes expelled them and restored the site to the local ruler in 1575.

All these Far Eastern trades, and the trade in the gold of the Zambezi drainage through Sofala, provided means of paying for the cargoes of pepper and other spices shipped annually from Goa to Lisbon, for distribution to western Europe. The Portuguese never achieved anything like monopoly. Large quantities of pepper, carried across the Indian Ocean in Arab, Persian and Indian ships, still reached Europe through the Red Sea, Cairo and Alexandria. Portuguese attempts to control this route, by seizing Aden as a base, were unsuccessful. Nevertheless, the Portuguese were formidable enough throughout the Indian Ocean to channel much of the trade of the area through harbours under their control, and to extort tolls or duties from the local shipping by threat of sinking or plundering those who refused to pay. If they could not fully control the trade of the Indian Ocean, they successfully preyed upon it, and for a hundred years had no European rivals.

The Spaniards, like the Portuguese, moved quickly to exploit their late 15th-century discoveries. The settlement of Hispaniola began in 1493, partly in the hope of finding gold, partly with the intention of developing a base for trade with China, supposedly nearby. The discovery of the Main coast opened alternative opportunities, for slaving and for acquiring pearls and gold trinkets by trade or plunder. Mainland settlement began in 1509-10, on both shores of the Gulf of Urabá and along the Isthmus coast.

1/Iberian trade, establishments and settlement by c.1600 *(below right)* In the East, the Portuguese 'empire' consisted of fortified bases and trading posts, few of them bigger than a single city and its immediate surrounding country, some of them mere warehouse compounds; by 1600 there were more than fifty such establishments. In the West, however, because of the considerable numbers of Spanish and Portuguese who emigrated to the Americas during the 16th century, they had by 1600 occupied all the areas of dense native population, had built impressive cities and towns, and had created an elaborate territorial administration centred in Europe.

3/The Spanish invasion of Peru 1531-33 *(above)* showing Tumbes, where Pizarro landed; Cajamarca, where Atahuallpa was seized at his first meeting with Pizarro; Jauja, the site of the first serious battle; Vilcaconga, where Soto was ambushed; and Cuzco, the Inca highland capital.

→ route of Francisco Pizarro's army to Cajamarca and Cuzco
⇢ route of Hernando Pizarro to Pachácamac and Jauja
✗ battles

Acapulco Small, unhealthy harbour town, sheltered anchorage. Terminus of annual Manila Galleon voyages.

Aden Major harbour at entrance to Red Sea; successfully resisted an attack by Portuguese fleet 1513.

Arequipa Principal Spanish city of southern Peru, founded 1540 by Pizarro.

Arica The port for Arequipa and Potosí.

Asunción Capital of province of Paraguay; the earliest surviving Spanish settlement in Plate River drainage, founded 1535.

Bahia Capital of Bahia province and of vice-royalty of Brazil; founded 1549.

Buenos Aires Founded 1580 by Juan de Garay, governor of Paraguay, to provide access to the sea.

Calicut First town in Malabar visited by Portuguese 1498.

Callao Port for Lima.

Cartagena Strongly fortified harbour and naval base. Founded 1533 by Pedro de Heredia.

Cochin Portuguese *feitoria*, occupied 1502, fortified 1503. Early allied with Portuguese against Calicut.

Colombo Portuguese *feitoria*, occupied 1517, fortified 1520. Principal centre for collection of cinnamon. 1600 Portuguese controlled most of Ceylon coast.

Cuzco Inca capital of Peru, captured and occupied by Spaniards 1533.

Diu Island. Portuguese *feitoria* and major base, heavily fortified; acquired 1535 by treaty with ruler of Gujerat.

Elmina Principal Portuguese settlement on Gulf of Guinea, founded and fortified 1481. Centre for collection and shipment of Ashanti gold. By 1600 important as slave barracoon.

Goa Administrative, commercial and spiritual headquarters in east.

Guadalajara Capital of New Galicia, Spanish foundation 1531.

Guatemala Founded 1542 by Pedro de Alvarado.

Guayaquil Harbour for Quito region; principal ship-building centre on Pacific coast.

Havana Assembly point for combined annual convoys for return to Spain. Good, almost land-locked harbour, heavily fortified.

Hooghly (Ugolim) Founded 1599 by Portuguese traders – seemingly without fort. Silk and cotton collection centre.

Lima (Ciudad de los Reyes) Capital of vice-royalty of Peru; Spanish city, founded 1535 by Francisco Pizarro.

Luanda Principal centre for export of slaves from Angola to Brazil, founded 1576.

Macao Portuguese town and *feitoria*, established c. 1557 with tacit permission of local Chinese authorities. Unfortified. Collection centre for Chinese silk.

Malacca Portuguese *feitoria*; captured and occupied 1511; fortified; principal centre of spice trade.

Malindi First Swahili town to welcome Portuguese (1498).

Manila Spanish town and fortress in Luzon, Philippines. Founded 1571; by 1600 a major commercial harbour and administrative centre. Connected by annual sailings with Acapulco, with silver westbound, silk eastbound.

Mérida Spanish capital of province of Yucatán, founded 1542 by Francisco de Montejo on site of antecedent Maya town.

Mombasa Island; Portuguese *feitoria* occupied 1505; before and after occupation a major trading centre; persistently resisted Portuguese: sacked 1505, 1529, 1587. Major fortress (Fort Jesus) constructed 1593-95.

Mozambique Major Portuguese base, occupied 1507; port of call for outbound fleets of *Carreira da India*.

Nagasaki Only Japanese port where Portuguese had permission to trade.

Nombre de Dios Shanty town on north coast of Isthmus of Panama, important as terminus of convoys from Spain and as starting point of portage to Panama.

Olinda Capital of Pernambuco province, founded c. 1535. Recife, the port for Olinda, was already in 1600 a larger town.

Ormuz Portuguese *feitoria*, and major strategic base, occupied 1515. A major market and port of trans-shipment in spice trade.

Potosi Principal silver mining centre of vice-royalty of Peru; silver discovered 1545; in 1600 probably the biggest concentration of Europeans in the Americas.

Puebla Prosperous Spanish city, founded 1532, by 1600 important for provisioning convoys returning from Vera Cruz to Seville.

Quito Indian city occupied by Benalcázar 1533; Spanish city incorporated 1534.

Saltillo Capital of province of Nuevo León; Spanish foundation 1586; cattle town.

San Agostín Small, isolated fortress on south-east coast of Florida, founded 1565 to cover passage of convoys through Straits.

San Juan del Puerto Rico Windward defence of Spanish Caribbean and of trans-Atlantic convoys. Immense fortifications were planned and started by Antoneli in 1591.

Santa Fe de Bogotá Province capital New Granada; founded 1538.

Santa Marta Prosperous port and base for hinterland expeditions. Founded 1525.

Santiago Capital of captaincy-general of Chile. Founded 1541 by Pedro de Valdivia.

Santo Domingo Founded 1496 by Bartholomew Columbus; capital of Hispaniola, administrative centre for Spanish Caribbean.

São Tomé Portuguese island plantation; important source of sugar and of provisions.

Sofala Portuguese *feitoria*, occupied 1505; port of outlet for gold of Zambezi drainage (Monomatapa) mostly shipped to Mozambique, thence to Goa.

Spice Islands (Moluccas) Portuguese *feitorias* with light fortification in Ternate (1513) Tidore (1529), Amboina and the Banda islands; collection centres for cloves, nutmeg and mace; all still occupied with local permission in 1600, except Ternate from which the Portuguese were expelled in 1575.

Tenochtitlán Capital of vice-royalty of New Spain. Large Spanish and Indian city, captured 1521.

Timor Portuguese *feitoria*, in 1600 administrative and collection centre for sandalwood destined for sale in China.

Veracruz Most important harbour on Gulf of Mexico. Terminus of annual convoys from Spain; founded by Cortés 1519.

Zacatecas Principal silver mining centre, Spanish foundation 1546.

Panama, the first Pacific settlement, was established in 1519. In the 1520s the news of Cortés' conquest of central Mexico, and descriptions of the elaborate culture and dense population he encountered there, attracted a rush of emigrants to Mexico both from Spain and from the islands. A similar rush followed the conquests of Pizarro in Inca Peru in the early 1530s, though Peru was less accessible than Mexico and could be reached only by trans-shipment and a troublesome portage across the Isthmus of Panama. Hispaniola had been the base for the settlement of central America, Cuba for that of Mexico, Panama for that of Peru; each in turn was to some extent depopulated by emigration to the new conquests. Mexico and Peru became the chief centres of Spanish population in the New World, initially because they were, before the Spaniards arrived, the chief centres of settled, organised native population; and subsequently because they were the areas where precious metals were chiefly found. None of the other major conquests – Guatemala (1523-42), New Granada (1536-39) or central Chile (1540-58) – compared with them in either respect. Their pre-eminence was recognised: a vice-regal administration was formally established in Mexico in 1535. Administrative organisation in Peru was delayed by faction among the conquerors, but there too vice-regal government was firmly established by the middle of the century.

Spanish population in the New World was largely concentrated in towns and initially wholly parasitic upon Indian society; but Spaniards soon developed characteristic economic activities, chiefly ranching and mining, employing Indian labour. Immensely productive silver mines were discovered, both in Mexico and in Peru, in the 1540s. Potosí in Upper Peru became, and for a hundred years remained, the biggest single source of silver in the world. By the 1560s silver had become the chief export to Spain, with cochineal, hides, tallow, and sugar a long way behind. These immensely valuable shipments necessitated, from 1564, a rigid system of trans-Atlantic convoys, escorted by warships, and later in the century heavy fortification of principal harbours and strategic points: Cartagena, Veracruz, Havana, San Juan del Puerto Rico. From 1564 also, Spaniards established themselves in Cebu and Luzon in the Philippines, and large quantities of silver began to be shipped annually from Mexico to Manila, chiefly to

purchase Chinese silk, of which some was used in Mexico, some re-exported to Peru, and some even, after portage across Mexico, carried to Spain.

At the end of the 16th century the whole vast, cumbersome empire was at the height of its power and prosperity. French, English and latterly Dutch raids harassed its harbours, its shipping and its colonial outposts; but none had yet succeeded in causing major damage.

The line of demarcation established by the Treaty of Tordesillas in 1494, though its precise position could not be determined, clearly excluded Spaniards from a great area in eastern South America. The Portuguese did nothing to settle Brazil until the 1530s, when they were impelled to it by fear of being forestalled by the French. Bahia was founded as an administrative capital in 1549; the first slave-worked sugar plantations and mills, on a pattern already familiar in São Tomé in the Gulf of Guinea, were established shortly afterwards. Between 1575 and 1600 coastal Brazil became the foremost sugar-producing territory in the western world, and attracted many land-hungry emigrants from Portugal and the Azores. The Brazilian demand for slave labour gave new importance to the Portuguese trading stations in West Africa, where the gold trade had dwindled as the gold became exhausted, and caused the Portuguese slavers to extend their operations from Guinea south to Angola. The Portuguese town and barracoon of Luanda was founded in 1575. Slave ships shuttled directly between Angola and Brazil, the slaves were paid for in low-grade tobacco grown in Brazil. Any surplus could easily be disposed of in Spanish America, as the Spaniards had no direct access to the source of slaves, and were able to pay in silver; and because from 1580 Spain and Portugal were united under a common crown. Thus the Iberian crown ruled not one overseas empire, but three: the silver empire of Spanish America, the spice empire of the Indian Ocean, and the sugar empire of the South Atlantic. No other European group had achieved anything permanent in the field of overseas settlement.

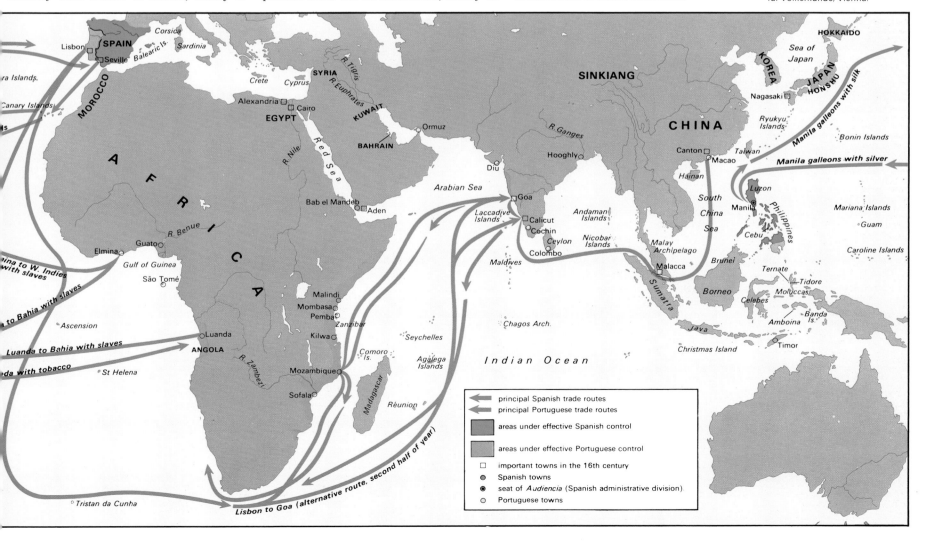

European expansion overseas: Holland, Britain and France 1600 to 1713

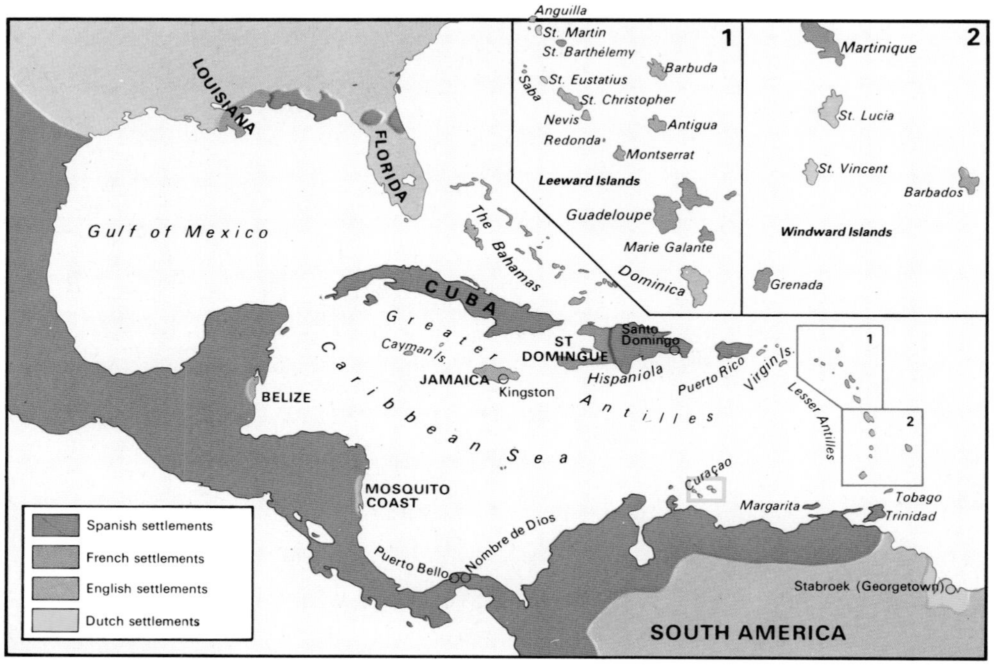

3/European settlement in the West Indies *(above)* Sugar was the most profitable of all the exotic products imported into Europe in early modern times. From the middle of the 17th century until after the end of the 18th, sugar-producing islands in the West Indies were considered by Europeans the most desirable of all overseas possessions.

Bahamas English from 1670 (Treaty of Madrid).
Belize Acknowledged as Spanish territory, but occupied c. 1660 by English logwood cutters.
Curaçao Captured from Spaniards by Dutch, 1634, formally ceded 1648 (Treaty of Münster).
Jamaica Captured from Spain by English 1655. Formally ceded 1670 (Treaty of Madrid).
Leeward Islands Anguilla (1650), Barbuda (1628), Antigua (1632) and Nevis (1628) were continuously English from first settlement. Monserrat (1632), taken by French in 1664, restored in 1668. St Christopher, shared by English and French settlers, 1625-1713, wholly English in Treaty of Utrecht. St Barthélemy, Guadeloupe and Marie Galante, French from first settlement (1648, 1635, 1648). St Eustatius (1632), Saba (1640) and St Martin (1648) confirmed to the Netherlands in 1648 (Treaty of Münster), though subsequently changed hands several times. Dominica, claimed by both England and France, inhabited only by Caribs in 1713.
Mosquito Coast English alliance with local Indians; a few English settlers; claimed by Spain.
Saint-Domingue Evacuated by Spaniards c. 1605; occupied by French buccaneers; formally ceded to France 1697 (Treaty of Ryswick).
Tobago French from 1677.
Virgin Islands Tortola English from 1666; St Thomas Danish from 1671.
Windward Islands Martinique continuously French since first settlement (1635); Grenada claimed by France 1650, in 1713 had a few French settlers; St Lucia and St Vincent, disputed between England and France, inhabited in 1713 only by Caribs.

IN THE early 17th century northern Europeans, already experienced in Caribbean smuggling, in raids on Spanish shipping and minor harbours, and in attempts, occasionally successful, on returning Portuguese Indiamen, began to establish permanent colonies of their own in the Americas and to develop eastern trades on their own account. In competing with the traditional Iberian enemy in these fields of activity, they possessed important advantages: fewer political commitments and less dispersed interests in Europe; easier access to sources of ship-building material, especially in the Baltic; thus, cheaper ships and, increasingly as the century progressed, more and better ships; a more strictly commercial attitude towards overseas endeavour; and more sophisticated devices for concentrating investment capital and spreading financial risk. The organisation which they used most commonly for distant trade or settlement, or both combined, was the chartered joint-stock company, a device earlier developed on a limited scale in northern Italy, but virtually unknown in Spain and Portugal. The companies might be empowered to trade, settle, conquer, administer and defend.

In the East, the most formidable European group throughout the 17th century was the Dutch East India Company, first formally incorporated in 1602. In 1619 this huge concern, the biggest trading corporation in Europe, established its eastern headquarters at Batavia, well to windward of Malacca and Goa, so acquiring a permanent strategic advantage. Its captains pioneered a direct route to Batavia, provisioning (after 1652) at the new Dutch settlement at the Cape, then running east before the prevailing wind in the forties of south latitude, and entering the archipelago by way of the Sunda Strait. The company never became in the 17th century – nor did its directors wish it to become – a major territorial power; but by acquiring bases in strategic locations, by bringing pressure on local rulers, and by squeezing other Europeans out, it established a monopoly of the more valuable trades of the archipelago. Elsewhere in the East it traded, as all Europeans did, in competition with other merchants, native and European, on terms laid down by Asian rulers; but throughout the 17th century it held its own against all European rivals.

The English East India Company, incorporated in 1600, was a somewhat smaller concern which was rarely able to resist Dutch pressure in the archipelago, principally engaged in trade in cotton goods and pepper from India, first at the Mughal port of Surat, subsequently at stations of its own at Madras, Bombay and Calcutta. In 1685 it began a modest trade to China, purchasing tea and porcelain at Amoy, and later at Canton, where from 1698 its factors found themselves in competition with the French *Compagnie de Chine*.

As a result of the commercial competition and naval aggression of these corporations, which continued irrespective of formal war or peace in Europe, the Portuguese *Estado da India* shrank both in territorial possession and in commercial profit; and many native trades, by sea or by land caravan, which the Portuguese had hardly touched – or had touched only to the extent of levying tolls – also began to dry up. The Red Sea and the Persian Gulf both became commercial backwaters as the companies gathered more and more of the trade between Europe and Asia into their own capacious, well-armed ships.

In America the Portuguese fared better. The Dutch West India Company – less well entrenched than its eastern counterpart, but formidable nonetheless – conquered Pernambuco in 1630 and in the next few years seized the Portuguese slaving stations in West Africa, without which the Brazilian plantations were unworkable; but in the 1640s the Portuguese, having made themselves independent of Spain, recovered the Angola barracoons, and in 1654 they drove the Dutch from Brazil. The West India Company turned to the West Indies, though many Dutch private merchants continued its trade, and much Brazilian sugar continued to flow through Amsterdam. Brazil, however, was not wholly dependent on sugar; in the 1690s a series of gold strikes in Minas Gerais made it a principal supplier of gold as well.

For Spaniards the 17th century was a period of industrial, commercial and financial debility, of faltering government and of repeated military defeat. The weight of misfortune fell much more heavily on Spain itself than upon the Spanish Indies, which remained relatively prosperous and – outside the Caribbean sea lanes – relatively peaceful. In the 1620s and 1630s a powerful offensive by the Dutch West India Company against Spanish shipping in the Caribbean interrupted the flow of silver to Spain and provided a screen for English and French settlements in unoccupied islands in the Lesser Antilles. These settlements in a few decades became prosperous sugar plantations, using Brazilian methods, employing African slave labour, and initially selling their crop to Dutch carriers. In the second half of the century, buccaneering raids, often undertaken with the connivance of French and English colonial governors, caused much damage to minor Spanish harbours, and some islands actually in Spanish possession changed hands. By the end of the century, a long string of modest but growing colonies, English, French and Dutch, stretched intermittently along the American seaboard from Barbados to Quebec. Many of them, the sugar islands especially, had themselves become objects of contention between the metropolitan governments. Every major European war was reflected by fighting in the Americas. The treaties of Münster (1648), Breda (1667),

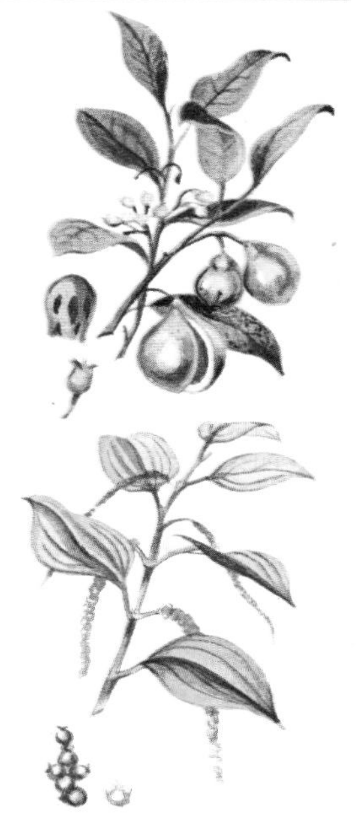

The importance of spices *(above)* In northern Europe, before the development of winter feed for cattle in the late 17th century, many beasts had to be slaughtered every autumn and the meat preserved for winter eating. Hence the eager demand for spices, both as condiments and as preservatives, and the large profits to be made by importing them to Europe. Of the most important spices, pepper *(above)* grew in many places in southern Asia; cinnamon was virtually confined to Ceylon, cloves to the Moluccas and nutmeg *(top)* to Amboina and the Banda Islands. In the 16th century, the Indian Ocean trade in these commodities had been shared between Malay, Indian, Persian, Arab and Portuguese merchants. In the course of the 17th century the Dutch East India Company, by a combination of force and diplomacy, seized control of the sources of the most valuable spices, and established a virtual monopoly of their shipment to Europe.

1/Commercial expansion to the East *(below right)* During the 17th century northern European commercial companies – Dutch, French, English and others – established trading stations throughout the East. The Portuguese lost much of their former trade and some territory; and the overland caravan trade between Europe and Asia almost disappeared.

Achin (Atjeh) Early visited by Europeans (Dutch 1577, English 1602, French 1623) but resisted European penetration. Important commercial harbour and source of gold, but decayed by 1713.
Amoy First Chinese port visited by English traders, 1685.
Bassein (Baçaim) Economic capital of Portuguese Province of the North. Still prosperous in 1713.
Bandar Abbas (Gombroon) Successor to Persian trade of Ormuz. Dutch and English East India Companies maintained factories there.
Bantam Dutch factory established 1598, English 1602; Dutch expelled English 1682, reduced sultan to vasselage 1683.
Batavia Eastern headquarters of Dutch East India Company, established 1619 on site of small town of Jakarta, acquired by conquest from Bantam.
Bombay Principal English station in western India, acquired by treaty from Portuguese 1660. Fortified.
Calcutta Principal English station in Bengal, founded 1690 on uninhabited site, after English withdrawal from Hooghly; fortified.
Canton Principal Chinese harbour in which (after 1684) Europeans were allowed to trade. All the East India Companies maintained factories there.
Cape of Good Hope Settlement begun by Dutch East India Company 1652; victualling station for its ships.
Chandernagore Principal French station in Bengal; acquired 1688; in 1713 still very small.
Chinsura Principal Dutch station in Bengal, acquired 1656 after Dutch withdrawal from Hooghly.
Cochin Principal harbour of Malabar. Taken by Dutch from Portuguese 1663.
Colombo Principal harbour of Ceylon. Taken by Dutch from Portuguese 1656.
Macao Portuguese settlement. After loss of Malacca to Dutch, Macao merchants altered business, becoming chief suppliers of silk to Manila for export in the galleons.
Macassar Taken by Dutch fleet 1669; sultan remained as Dutch vassel.
Madras Principal English station on Coromandel coast; occupied 1640 by treaty with local ruler; successor to Masulipatam (occupied 1611); fortified.
Malacca Taken from Portuguese by Dutch with Achinese help, 1641.
Manila Only significant Spanish harbour in the East, terminus of Acapulco-Manila galleons and administrative centre of Spanish Philippines.
Mocha Harbour for Beit el Fakih, marketing centre for Arabian coffee.
Mombasa Major harbour; Portuguese defeated and expelled by forces of Imam of Oman, 1698 (see page 158).
Mozambique Portuguese town and factory; repelled Dutch attempts at conquest in early 17th century.
Nagasaki Only Japanese port in which Europeans were allowed to trade; privilege restricted to Dutch East India Co. from 1639.
Negapatam Principal Dutch station on Coromandel coast, taken from Portuguese by Dutch 1659.
Ormuz Portuguese expelled by Shah Abbas with help of English fleet, 1622. In 1713 almost deserted.
Pondicherry Principal French station in India, occupied 1683 by treaty with local ruler.
Spice Islands (Moluccas, Amboina, Banda Islands) Dutch East India Co. held some islands, having expelled Portuguese early in 17th century, and monopolised spice trade in all.
Surat Major harbour of Mughal Empire. All East India Companies had factories there.
Tellicherry Principal English station on Malabar coast; small fortified factory, outside native town, built 1683, Centre for collection of pepper.
Tenasserim Disputed territory between Ayutthaya (Siam) and Pegu (Burma), with several good harbours and busy trade.
Zanzibar Portuguese island, town and factory.
Zeelandia Dutch factory in Formosa, operated from 1624 to 1662, when island occupied by Ming forces and Dutch expelled.

Nijmegen (1678), Ryswick (1697) and Utrecht (1713) all included cessions of American territory. Mainland colonies were less esteemed by governments and by orthodox economists in France and England than were the islands. Colbert was almost alone among leading statesmen in actively encouraging North American settlement, by making *seigneuries* conditional on occupation, by granting land, on the St Lawrence river and elsewhere, to demobilised soldiers, by assisting passages and providing tools, seed and stock. As a result of his efforts the population of New France, though never more than a tenth of that of the English colonies, was militarily very formidable. Nova Scotia (Acadia) in French hands was considered a serious threat to New England; it was the object of repeated attack and counter-attack, especially during King William's War and the War of the Spanish Succession; even after its annexation in 1713 the English hold on it was precarious. The chain of French trade forts on the Great Lakes and in the Ohio-Mississippi valleys, because it threatened to block westward expansion, alarmed the English colonists and their metropolitan government. The emergence of French explorers on the shore of the Gulf of Mexico in 1682 caused grave concern in Spain.

The major Spanish colonies, however, despite widespread foreign smuggling and occasional interruption of communications, were never seriously threatened. They owed their safety partly to their inaccessibility, partly to their own capacity for resistance, partly to increasing fear of French domination which towards the end of the century caused both English and Dutch to seek insurance by accommodation with Spain.

In 1700, the childless Carlos II of Spain died as the last of its Habsburgs; as feared by England, Holland and Austria, he bequeathed his crown and empire to France. Unwilling to tolerate the huge colonial empire and agglomeration of power which would have resulted from a union of the two countries and their possessions, the three countries allied to fight in a succession war which lasted for a dozen years and ended in a French promise that the new Bourbon king of Spain would never wear the crown of France. It also resulted in a number of colonial gains and commercial concessions for England.

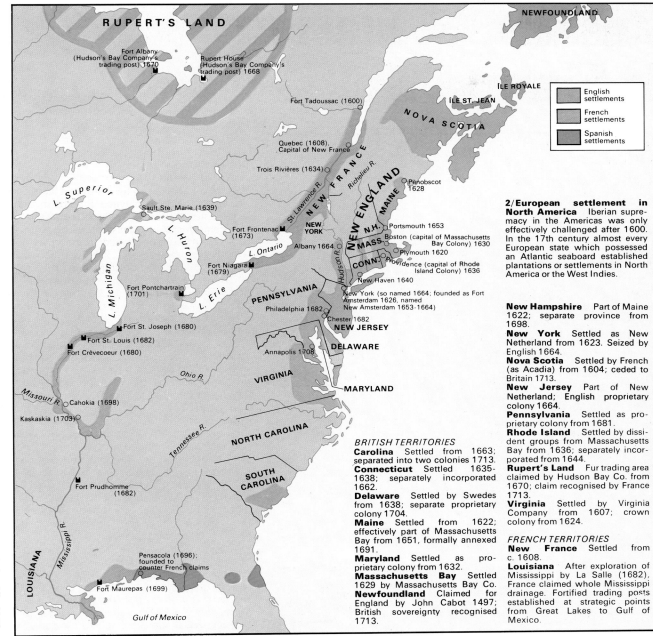

2/European settlement in North America Iberian supremacy in the Americas was only effectively challenged after 1600. In the 17th century almost every European state which possessed an Atlantic seaboard established plantations or settlements in North America or the West Indies.

New Hampshire Part of Maine 1622; separate province from 1698.
New York Settled as New Netherland from 1623. Seized by English 1664.
Nova Scotia Settled by French (as Acadia) from 1604; ceded to Britain 1713.
New Jersey Part of New Netherland; English proprietary colony 1664.
Pennsylvania Settled as proprietary colony from 1681.
Rhode Island Settled by dissident groups from Massachusetts Bay from 1636; separately incorporated from 1644.
Rupert's Land Fur trading area claimed by Hudson Bay Co. from 1670; claim recognised by France 1713.
Virginia Settled by Virginia Company from 1607; crown colony from 1624.

BRITISH TERRITORIES
Carolina Settled from 1663; separated into two colonies 1713.
Connecticut Settled 1635-1638; separately incorporated 1662.
Delaware Settled by Swedes from 1638; separate proprietary colony 1704.
Maine Settled from 1622; effectively part of Massachusetts Bay from 1651, formally annexed 1691.
Maryland Settled as proprietary colony from 1632.
Massachusetts Bay Settled 1629 by Massachusetts Bay Co.
Newfoundland Claimed for England by John Cabot 1497; British sovereignty recognised 1713.

FRENCH TERRITORIES
New France Settled from c. 1608.
Louisiana After exploration of Mississippi by La Salle (1682), France claimed whole Mississippi drainage. Fortified trading posts established at strategic points from Great Lakes to Gulf of Mexico.

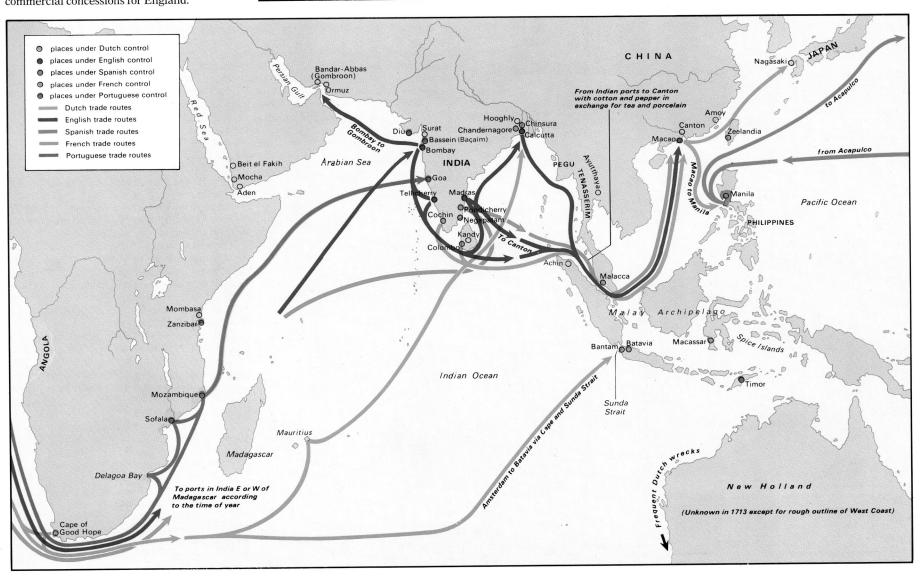

Russian expansion in Europe and Asia 1462 to 1815

2/Economic activity in 1600, 1725, 1815
(above) By 1600 industry had concentrated in and around Moscow consisting mainly of the processing of animal and vegetable products. By 1725, thanks to Peter the Great's initiative, the extensive smelting of copper and iron was established in the Urals. By 1815 a third industrial area had arisen around St Petersburg.

3/Russian expansion in Siberia *(below)*
Rivers facilitated rapid exploration, soon reinforced by strategic forts. Foundation dates show the dramatic speed of assimilation. Although most of this vast expanse was acquired from primitive peoples, the Amur was annexed from China though returned by the Treaty of Nerchinsk in 1689.

Master and serfs *(above)* From 1497 to 1861 Russian peasants were tied to the land. Initially they had two weeks of free movement each November. This was withdrawn under Godunov (1593). A 1648 decree then removed all limits to forcible reclamation of runaway serfs.

THE state created by the Grand Princes of Moscow in the north-eastern part of the Russian territory, known as Muscovy, expanded during 350 years at the expense of Sweden, Poland and Lithuania in the north and west, of the Tartars and the Ottoman Empire in the south and across the whole of northern Asia.

After the Mongol invasion of the 13th century, the Russian lands which had formed part of Kievan Russia were split. The east became subject to Mongol overlordship, under the shadow of which the principality of Moscow rose to dominate its neighbours and eventually to throw off the Tartar yoke. The west was absorbed by the neighbouring Lithuanian principality, and was eventually joined to Poland.

Muscovy in 1462 was virtually isolated: it was cut off from almost all contact with the western world by the hostility of its neighbours. It was unable to share in the scientific and cultural advance of Europe and experienced neither the Renaissance nor the Reformation, though some artistic and intellectual influences did penetrate the Church and the Court. Muscovite isolation was increased by the growth of the religious schism between the Eastern and Western Christian churches. Since 1054 the Russian Orthodox Church had viewed Roman catholicism with deep suspicion and distrust and, in 1448 it declared its independence from Constantinople, soon to fall to the Ottoman Turks, by electing its own metropolitan.

The growing power of Muscovy was manifested in the ruthless annexation of the great city republic of Novgorod by Ivan III in 1478, and this was followed by the proclamation of independence from the Tartars in 1480. In the 16th century the republic of Pskov was annexed, and Muscovy began the great advance eastwards with the conquest of the khanate of Kazan in 1552 and of the khanate of Astrakhan in 1556 which gave it control of the Volga down to the Caspian Sea. But Muscovy was still not safe from the Crimean Tartars who sacked Moscow in 1571, and failed in the attempt to extend its hold on the Baltic Sea in the long and debilitating Livonian wars conducted by Ivan the Terrible.

It was the lucrative fur trade which lured enterprising Russians deeper and deeper into Siberia until the Pacific coast was reached in 1639, and a number of forts were erected,

Tobolsk, Yeniseisk, Yakutsk, Nerchinsk, which established Russian control over northern Asia and opened the silk trade with China which also developed along the Volga with Persia.

During the late 16th and 17th centuries Russian colonization also spread southwards across the Oka River, and Ukrainians migrated eastwards from Poland into the forest-steppe zone. Here too many frontier posts were established which developed into towns, e.g. Orel (1564), Kursk (1586) and Voronezh (1586).

In 1613, after the 'time of troubles' which followed the extinction of the old Muscovite ruling house and the death of Boris Godunov, Michael, the first of the Romanov dynasty was elected tsar. During the rest of the 17th century the Muscovites turned their attention to the conquest of the lands lost earlier to Lithuania and Poland, and in spite of a number of setbacks, made substantial gains between 1640 and 1686. In 1648 the Cossacks of the Ukraine rose against Poland and transferred their allegiance to the tsar thus inaugurating a long and confused period of warfare in which Poland, Russia, Sweden and the Ottomans took part, and which ended in 1686 when the treaty of perpetual peace between Russia and Poland was signed, confirming the cession of Kiev and the lands of the middle Dnieper to Russia in 1667.

Isolation remained Russia's great problem. There was great potential foreign demand for the products of the Russian forests, but Muscovy could not benefit from this for hostile Swedes, Poles and Turks blocked sea and land communications with Europe. British merchants had opened up the White Sea route to Archangel (founded by Ivan IV in 1584), but it was navigable only in the brief summer season.

Having failed to advance to the Black Sea, Peter I concentrated in 1700 on achieving his 'window on the west', and in a long war, marked by the great victory of Poltava in 1709, he finally wrested Estonia and Livonia from Sweden at the treaty of Nystad in 1721, acquired the ancient port of Riga, and founded the new one of St Petersburg (1703). Russia's new status was proclaimed to Europe, when the title of tsar was formally changed to that of emperor in 1721.

Peter's successors reverted to his policy of expansion on the Black Sea, which was carried to a successful conclusion by Catherine II in the first (1768-74) and second (1787-92) Turkish wars of her reign. The Tartar khanate of the Crimea was annexed, and Russia now controlled the northern shore of the Black Sea from the Dniester to the Caucasus. Odessa, founded in 1794 rapidly became the principal port for Russian exports to the Mediterranean.

The period from 1772 to 1815 saw the Russian land frontier advanced 600 miles at the expense of Poland. By the partitions of 1772, 1793 and 1795 Russia obtained much of the former Polish Lithuanian Commonwealth, and after the interlude of Napoleon's Grand Duchy of Warsaw, the Congress of Vienna agreed to the Tsar becoming king of a reconstituted Polish kingdom.

Between 1772 and 1875 the Russian land frontier advanced 600 miles to the west. The 18th century wars required a large armaments industry and a correspondingly productive metallurgical base. This was established by Peter I, mainly in the Urals, which abounded in iron and copper ores and were clad in extensive forests suitable for the charcoal making. Peter I founded factories, gave investment incentives, encouraged new management, and established a form of industrial serfdom.

The population of the empire grew both by territorial acquisition and by natural increase. The total was estimated at 10 million for 1600, and 15.5 million for 1725. The census of 1811-12 gave the greatly enlarged Russian empire a population of 42.75 million.

Barents Sea

boundary of Russian territories in 1462
boundary of Lithuania in 1462
the expansion of Muscovy

Moscow territory at end of 13th century
1478 date of acquisition by Muscovy
acquisitions to 1462
acquisitions under Ivan III 1462-1505
acquisitions during 16th century (1505-86)
acquisitions during 17th century
acquisitions during 18th century
acquisitions 1801-15
territory ceded to Sweden 1617 and Poland 1618
recovered from Poland 1634
recovered from Poland 1667
area affected by Pugachev uprising 1773-74
route of Pugachev rebels
Orel 1564 date of foundation of new town

Kola Peninsula

PECHORA

Obdorsk 1595

White Sea

1478

YUGRA

Berezov 1593
1501

FINLAND

1809

1478

Archangel 1584

Kholmogory

NOVGOROD TERRITORY

Solvychegodsk

Ustyug

R. Kama

1472

Solikamsk

1743 *1721*
Vyborg

Gulf of Finland

L. Ladoga

1478

L. Onega

Kargopol

1478

Nizhniy Tagil 1724

Kronstadt 1704

Narva

St Petersburg 1703

1362-89

1393-1425

Vologda

Soligalich

Perm 1724

Yekaterinburg 1725

Baltic Sea

ESTONIA
1721

LIVONIA

Riga

1478

Pskov

Novgorod
L. Ilmen

1389-1425

1364

Galich

1489

Kungur

SIBERIA

COURLAND

1510

1364

Yaroslavl

Vyatka

MARI

UDMURTY

1772

Velikiye Luki

1503

1389-1425

R. Lovat

R. Volga

1302

Kostroma

1451

1364

Kazan

R. Belaya

Ufa 1586

BASHKIRS

Memel

LITHUANIA

Polotsk

1514-21

Vyazma

1494

Tver

Dmitrov

Vladimir

1364

Nizhniy Novgorod

KHANATE OF KAZAN

R. Niemen

Vilna

Vitebsk

Smolensk

1494

Moscow

1364

Murom

1393-1425

CHUVASHI

1552

Kovno

Grodno

Minsk

Mogilev

1634

Mozhaysk

1301

Serpukhov

1393

MESHCHERA

Arzamas

1393

Simbirsk 1648

R. Vistula

1807

1353-59

Kaluga

1425-62

Kolomna

Ryazan

MORDVA

Samara 1586

Kalish

1793

1772

Bryansk

Tula

1521

Penza 1650

R. Sura

Syzran 1683

Warsaw

POLAND

Pinsk

R. Pripet

Gomel

1503

Deana

Orel 1564

Yelets 1592

Tambov 1636

R. Khoper

Orenburg 1743

Lublin

1815

Chernigov

1634

R. Seym

Kursk 1586

1503

Voronezh 1586

R. Volga

NOGAI TARTARS

Lvov

Novograd-Volynskiy

Kiev

R. Dnieper

Belgorod 1593

R. Don

Saratov 1590

Pereyaslavl

1793

1667

Poltava

Kharkov 1654

R. Donets

Kamyshin

KHANATE OF ASTRAKHAN *1556*

KALMYKS

R. Dniester

Kamenets

BESSARABIA

ZAPOROZH'YE

Yekaterinoslav (Kodak) 1786

DON COSSACKS

R. Don

1739

Cherkassk

1589
Tsaritsyn

Guryev 1645

MOLDAVIA

Bratslav

Kishinev

1791

Sech

Nikolayev 1789

1774

Azov

Taganrog

1783

KALMYKS

Ochakov

Odessa 1794

1812

Kherson 1774

1783

KUBAN COSSACKS

R. Kuma

Caspian Sea

OTTOMAN EMPIRE

R. Danube

Akkerman

KHANATE OF CRIMEA

Sea of Azov

Yevpatoriya

Karasubazar

Kerch

Feodosiya (Kaffa)

Stavropol

Yekaterinodar 1792

Bakhchisaray

Simferopol (Ak-Mechet) 1784

Sevastopol 1783

Pyatigorsk

R. Terek

1784
Vladikavkaz

Derbent

Black Sea

1810

Sukhum-Kale

1806

DAGHESTAN

1806

Poti

1804

Kutaisi

1801

Tiflis

GEORGIA

R. Kura

Baku

Map1

Map2

Map3

1805

AZERBAIJAN

1813

ceded temporarily by Persia 1723-32

1/The evolution and expansion of Muscovy
(above) This map portrays the division of Russia after the Mongol conquest, into West Russia or Lithuania, and East Russia. It shows how East Russia, as a result of the increasing preponderance of Moscow, came to be known as Muscovy. Finally, it demonstrates the expansion of Muscovy in all directions: westwards, to absorb Lithuania and much of Poland; eastwards into Siberia; south-eastwards to the Caspian Sea; southwards to the Black Sea; and north-westwards to the Baltic Sea and into Finland.

Colonial America
1535 to 1783

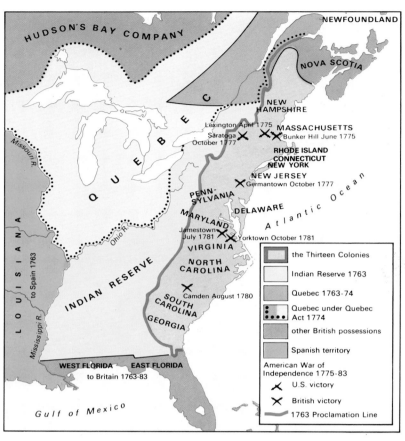

3/British North America
(above) With the Capitulations of Montreal, 1760, France abandoned her vast American territories to Britain. But the resulting Proclamation of 1763, failing either to halt encroachment on Indian land or to impose acceptable rule, helped to trigger the American Revolution. By 1783 the original Thirteen Colonies had decisively established themselves as the new United States.

A rich inhabitant *(below)* of Bahia, the capital of colonial Brazil until the mid-18th century, being carried in a litter by Negro slaves.

vigorous policy in this period. As her miners, soldiers and priests gradually moved further into the savage, semi-desert lands of the American south-west, new military governments were organised: in Texas (1718), Sinaloa (1734), New Santander (1746) and California (1767). By then Spanish authority extended as far east as the Mississippi, and northward to Monterrey and San Francisco, halting only where it came face to face with the Russians, now probing south from Alaska along the Pacific coast.

Meanwhile the French, whose first explorers, like Cartier, had already penetrated far up the St Lawrence river by 1535, were extending their North American territories in a vast sweep from the harsh northern shores of Acadia (later Nova Scotia) beyond the Great Lakes and down the eastern banks of the Mississippi to the Gulf of Mexico and the new settlement of New Orleans (founded 1718). In quest of skins and furs, New France's trappers, soldiers and Catholic missionaries thrust far into the forest wilderness, fighting and converting the Indians and starting future cities (Quebec, 1608; Ville-Marie, later Montreal, 1642; Detroit, 1701).

The French, like the Spaniards, were few and widely dispersed. The highly profitable fur trade not only discouraged formal colonisation but inevitably brought conflict: first with the Dutch and their Indian allies, the Iroquois; then, after the fall of New Amsterdam (New York) to the English in 1664, with the far more numerous Anglo-Saxon colonists of the eastern seaboard.

After a false start in the 1580s, serious development had begun here with the founding of Jamestown, Virginia (1607) and the Mayflower landing in Massachusetts Bay (1620). By the end of the 17th century the twelve so-called 'continental colonies' (Georgia was added in 1733) already possessed a prosperous agricultural, commercial and fishing economy, with the beginnings of a manufacturing industry and a population of some 250,000 souls. Fifty years later British North America, including its well over 100,000 Negro slaves, was almost one-third as populous as England itself, with Massachusetts alone having as many settlers as the whole of 'New France'.

The Anglo-French struggle for continental supremacy began very early. Quebec was first stormed by the English in 1629, and Acadia changed hands many times, even before 1700. Hostility deepened as England, starting in 1670, built up her own formidable fur-trading empire, based on the rich hunting grounds around Hudson Bay; and each major European war of the period had its parallel beyond the Atlantic. The peace of Utrecht in 1713 gave Britain Nova Scotia, Newfoundland and a clear field for the Hudson's Bay Company; but it was the French and Indian War of 1754-60, pre-dating and then forming part of the near-global Seven Years War (1756-63) between the two powers, which finally extinguished France's American ambitions. With the Treaty of Paris (1763) all Canada and the land east of the Mississippi were ceded to Britain, while Louisiana went to Spain in compensation for France's earlier transfer, to England, of the once-Spanish area of Florida.

Three new British colonies were now created; East Florida, roughly matching the present state; West Florida, stretching along the Gulf; and a much-shrunken Quebec. But the policies devised in London to administer and defend these and the vast new territories beyond were to contribute directly to the outbreak of the American Revolution in 1775.

The English colonial attitude to the Indians had always been ambivalent. Where the Spaniards willingly assimilated and intermarried – hence their extensive native and *mestizo* populations, especially in Peru and Mexico – Anglo-Americans preferred to eliminate or expel to make way for farms and plantations. Now, in

THE foundation of the city of Lima, capital of Peru, in 1535 marked the end of the first dramatic phase of colonisation in America. The task of pushing forward frontiers into unexplored territory was to continue, however, throughout the colonial period.

Until the 17th century the initiative lay primarily with the Iberian nations. Spain rapidly built up an impressive presence in America on the basis of the silver mines of Peru and New Spain, although her settlers showed less interest in territory which contained neither civilised Indians nor precious metals, a factor which allowed Portuguese adventurers to extend the frontiers of Brazil well beyond the line established at Tordesillas in 1494. Portugal, in her turn, faced threats to her authority from the French and the Dutch. Determined defensive measures ultimately succeeded, however, in pushing these intruders away from northern Brazil to the less important Guiana region. By the mid-17th century the maritime nations of northern Europe had adopted the new strategy of seizing Spanish islands in the Caribbean – thus providing themselves with bases for buccaneering and contraband trade, and eventually with the means of producing their own sugar and tobacco. This competition harmed Brazil's economy, but the damage was more than balanced by rich gold and diamond strikes in the early 18th century. Despite the stagnation of her imperial economy, Habsburg Spain succeeded in defending the territorial integrity of her major American possessions and in the 18th century a more positive strategic and commercial policy led her to create two new viceroyalties – New Granada (1739) and Rio de la Plata (1776) – and to liberalise trade.

In North America, too, Spain adopted a more

1763, the Crown established the so-called Proclamation Line, near the crest of the Allegheny mountains, and declared all land to the west to be a huge Indian reserve. But the line, lacking any geographical reality, had little effect in stemming the westward surge of the settlers and land-speculators: it merely irritated the independent-minded colonists, thus compounding their already mounting resistance to English tax demands and trade controls. By 1768 the line had been revised to open up large new areas, but

2/Population and Settlement *(below)* Three main strands have created the ethnic pattern of the Americas: the settlers, primarily west European; the negro slaves, from west and east Africa; and the indigenous Indian races, some savage, some civilised. The map shows the frontier between European settlement and Indian land. The colours on the colonies are explained in the key to map 1 *(right)*.

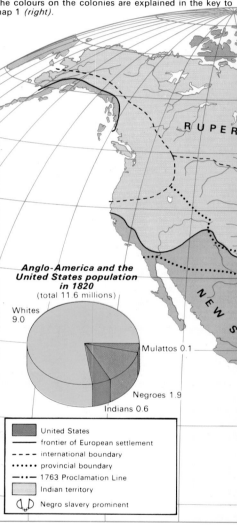

Anglo-America and the United States population in 1820
(total 11.6 millions)

Whites 9.0
Mulattos 0.1
Negroes 1.9
Indians 0.6

United States
frontier of European settlement
international boundary
provincial boundary
1763 Proclamation Line
Indian territory
Negro slavery prominent

this still did not satisfy demand; in 1774 the Quebec Act, re-expanding the boundaries of the new Canadian colony to the Mississippi and Ohio rivers, was interpreted as damaging to the interests of Virginia and Pennsylvania. Coinciding with the bitterly resented Coercive Acts, this move helped light the fuse for the American War of Independence (1775-83).

Fighting began at Lexington and Concord, Massachusetts, in April 1775. In June the colonies' Continental Congress created a Continental Army under General Washington. Despite several defeats, and the loss of New York in September 1776, Washington hung on, and at Christmas 1776, with the successful crossing of the Delaware, inaugurated a series of victories, culminating in Saratoga (1777). Final triumph was only assured, however, with the signing of a Franco-American alliance in 1778 (joined by Spain the next year). Reinforced by French troops and naval support, Washington forced the British to surrender at Yorktown on 19 October, 1781. The resulting Treaty of Versailles in 1783 recognised the Great Lakes in the north and the Mississippi in the west as the frontiers of the newly-born United States.

Legend:
- French territory
- Spanish territory
- Portuguese territory
- Dutch territory
- Russian territory
- British by 1763
- ceded by France to Britain 1763
- ceded by France to Spain 1763
- United States 1783
- --- international boundary
- ···· provincial boundary
- → *major export*

colonisation routes
- Spanish
- Portuguese
- British
- Russian
- French

Arctic Ocean

GREENLAND

U n e x p l o r e d

RUPERT'S LAND
(Hudson's Bay Company)

Hudson Bay

Disputed

by Russia
and Spain

QUEBEC

furs

NEWFOUNDLAND

ceded to Britain 1763

NOVA SCOTIA

whales, fish

St Lawrence R.
Quebec
Montreal
Boston
New York

San Francisco

LOUISIANA

Interior Provinces

Detroit
Ohio R.

UNITED
STATES
OF
AMERICA
1783

Philadelphia
Jamestown

*naval stores,
furs, fish, grain*

Los Angeles (1780)

Rio Grande

Mississippi R.

THE THIRTEEN COLONIES

*tobacco,
grain*

skins

WEST FLORIDA
New Orleans

EAST
FLORIDA (Br.1763-83)

N o r t h

N E W

Gulf of Mexico

BAHAMA
ISLANDS
(Br.1783)

A t l a n t i c

sugar, tobacco

S P A I N

silver

CUBA

WEST INDIES

O c e a n

Mexico

SANTO DOMINGO

SAINT
DOMINGUE
JAMAICA
(Br. 1655)

GUADELOUPE (Fr.)

MARTINIQUE (Fr.)

Belize (Br. 1683)

Central
America

*cochineal,
gold*

*silver,
cochineal*

C a r i b b e a n   S e a

CURAÇAO
(Dutch 1634)

*tobacco
cocoa beans, hides*

Caracas

QUEBEC

gold

Venezuela
R Orinoco

GUIANA

Paramaribo

Cayenne

U.S.

Santa Fé de Bogotá

P a c i f i c   O c e a n

NEW GRANADA
1739

*drugs,
rare plants*

Quito

Slave
trade
from
Africa

Venezuela

NEW GRANADA

*gold,
naval stores*

R. Amazon

B R A Z I L

*dyewoods,
sugar,
tobacco,
cotton*

P E R U

B R A Z I L

*silver,
drugs*

Lima

Cuzco

U P P E R

P E R U

Potosí

R São Francisco

Treaty of Tordesillas 1494

Bahia

*gold,
diamonds*

*copper,
grain*

R Paraguay
R Paraná

Rio de Janeiro

beef

C H I L E

RIO DE
LA PLATA

*hides,
silver*

C H I L E

RIO DE LA PLATA
1776

Indian frontier

Buenos Aires

**Spanish American
population in 1800**
(total 16.9 millions)

Whites 3.3

Indians 7.5

Negroes 0.8

Mestizos 5.3

FALKLAND Is.

South Atlantic Ocean

1/Colonial America *(above)* Two great
empires and three only relatively smaller ones
flourished in the western hemisphere in the
16th to 18th centuries. Richest by far were
the Spanish conquests, whose bullion directly
or indirectly (through contraband trade and
piracy) financed most European governments
of the period; but England too grew wealthy
on her American and Caribbean trade, as
Holland and France faded and Portugal
remained content with Brazil.

165

Trade and empire in Africa 1500 to 1800

THREE main processes dominate the history of Africa during the period from 1500 to 1800. One was the growth of large political units, which gathered momentum in much of black Africa. During these three centuries, independent African political and cultural achievements reached their zenith. Across the Sudanic belt of west Africa, these states were the successors of those established much earlier, such as Ghana and Mali (see page 136). In 1464 one of Africa's most renowned kings and military heroes, Sunni Ali, became ruler of the Songhay people who lived along the eastern part of the Niger bend, around the city of Gao. Sunni Ali conquered far and wide, and built up a huge Songhay Empire; but his son was deposed as ruler by an even greater leader, Askia the Great, who reigned from 1493 to 1528. This was a time of flourishing trade – especially that carried across the Sahara. The Songhay Empire incorporated a number of great commercial cities, including Timbuktu, Jenne and Gao, which became centres of learning and Muslim piety.

Trading communities from the rich Hausa city states, and others of the Manding people called Dyola, from Mali and Songhay, were instrumental in the rise of a series of states in the savannah and forest country to the south of the Niger. These were the Mossi-Dagomba states on the one hand, and the Akan-Asante states on the other. By 1500 Oyo and Benin, two of the great states of present-day Nigeria, had emerged in the woodlands to the west of the Niger delta. It was in this region that the supreme examples of the plastic arts of Africa were produced, such as the Ife and Benin terracottas and bronzes.

Elsewhere in black Africa similar processes were at work, leading to the emergence of powerful kingdoms out of societies of iron-working agriculturalists and cattle-keepers. In favourable environments, the number of people

(and their cattle) increased, their economies became more diverse, giving rise to trade in iron and copper goods and other wares, all of which provided the basis for stronger political control over a larger area. When the Portuguese arrived off the coast south of the estuary of the Congo (Zaire) river in 1484, they found the brilliant Kongo kingdom just inland. South of the Congo basin forests was a string of Bantu-speaking African states, such as the Luba and Lunda kingdoms. Likewise in the fertile lands between the lakes of east Africa – the interlacustrine region – there developed a whole series of states, the most prominent of which were Rwanda and Buganda. Another prosperous region was the plateau of present-day Rhodesia, with kingdoms based upon Zimbabwe; the Mwenemutapa empire, well known to the Portuguese and other early Europeans, was centred upon the area to the north-east of modern Salisbury. In between these great kingdoms, and over much of southern Africa lived numerous peoples slowly evolving smaller, less flamboyant states.

The first occupation of Zimbabwe can be traced back to early Iron Age farmers around the 4th century AD. It was reoccupied in the 10th century by people who traded in copper and gold. Two hundred years later stone was being used for the buildings of Zimbabwe. There was then a great fire, and the site had to be rebuilt from about the middle of the 14th century. These are the ruins which are so impressive now, and which have given their name to the African version of Rhodesia. In the valley there is a huge palace with a girdle wall more than 30 feet high, constructed of dressed stone. On the hill overlooking the palace is a massive temple or acropolis. Zimbabwe was the political and religious centre of a mighty trading state with connections as far distant as China.

The second predominating historical process was the continual expansion of Islam. Not only was northern Africa fully Islamised, but during the period 1500 to 1800 Islam consolidated its position in the Sudanic lands, and spread even further south and down the coast of east Africa. In the Horn of Africa what started as a trading rivalry between Christian Ethiopia and the

1/Developments in trade and empire (right) During the 300 years from 1500 to 1800, the course of African history developed along both well-established lines and in new ways. The interaction between Mediterranean and Sudanic Africa, which had begun in pre-Roman times, continued with Islam making deeper inroads into tropical Africa. African states and cultures, generally deep in the interior of the continent, also continued their mainly slow and steady – but sometimes most dynamic – growth. However, many parts of Africa came increasingly under the economic influence of western European states; coastal peoples were affected by this both politically and economically.

Muslim coastal states, especially Adal, became a long, bitter religious and political conflict. The sultan of Adal, Ahmad Gran, launched a fierce attack in the 1520s, and Muslim armies pushed into the heartlands of Ethiopia. The exhausted Christian empire was then invaded and settled by pagan Galla from the south and east, as indeed was Adal itself. Meanwhile in 1517 the Ottomans conquered the Mamelukes in Egypt, and subsequently Ottoman control was extended over Tripoli and Tunis; Algiers was ruled by the Corsairs, who owed allegiance to the Ottomans. Only Morocco remained independent, ruled during much of this period by factions of the Sharifian dynasty. In the 16th century much of coastal north Africa was the scene of a prolonged religious and economic conflict between the Christian powers, especially Spain and Portugal, and the Ottoman Empire and Morocco. In 1590, when at the height of its power, Morocco invaded the Songhay Empire, and set up a client state in the Sudan; this invasion disrupted the economic life of the whole region. By the beginning of the 18th century the politics and commerce of Muslim west Africa were being revived by a burst of Islamic proselytising which reached its zenith with the great Holy Wars of the 1790s.

The last great historical movement was the trade in human beings from Africa to the New World. This terrible trade was inaugurated by the Portuguese explorers of the western coast of Africa (see page 147); but the Dutch, British, French and other European nations soon joined in, setting up trading 'factories' along the coast. During the 400 years of the trade – from about 1450 to 1870 – over ten million Africans were transported to the Americas, from all over the western part of the continent as far south as Angola and, by the 19th century, from much of east Africa and Madagascar. At the same time, African slaves were carried across the Sahara and from east Africa to the Muslim world.

The effects of this vast, forced demographic change are hotly debated. Certainly a number of African states engaged in the trade gained in political importance and power – Asante, Dahomey and Benin are examples. Certainly the European slave traders and their countries made huge profits from the exploitation of human beings. Certainly what was the Americas' gain was Africa's loss. But all these gains and losses are difficult to quantify, and none of them overrides the cruelty and indignity inflicted on the slaves themselves. Later, after the abolition of the trade and the emancipation of the slaves in the 19th century, many of the ideas generated by blacks in the New World, such as the concept of Black Power, became crucial ingredients of modern African nationalism.

In spite of the shadow of the slave trade which falls over so much of the history of Africa in this period, the peoples of Africa had made tremendous political and cultural strides by 1800. Most of the continent still remained independent of external control, if not of influence. Only parts of north Africa, some scattered factories in west Africa, a few Portuguese outposts, and the Dutch East India Company settlement at the Cape (established in 1652) were occupied by foreigners. Elsewhere, particularly in the interior, political and social development followed its own established pattern.

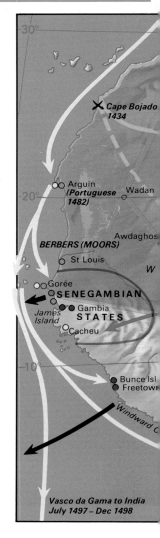

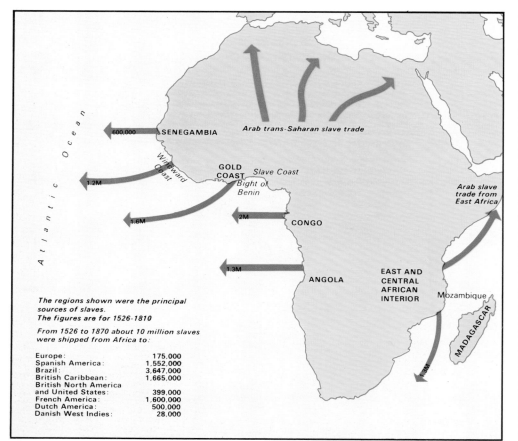

2/The growth of the slave trade (below) In the 15th century a few hundred slaves were taken from west Africa to Europe and the Atlantic islands. From the 1520s, slaves began to be transported by Europeans to the New World. The trans-Atlantic trade was at its peak during the 18th century, when between six and seven million slaves were shipped to the Americas; it came to an end in 1870.

Atlantic Ocean

600,000 SENEGAMBIA

Arab trans-Saharan slave trade

Windward Coast

1.2M

GOLD COAST Slave Coast

Bight of Benin

1.6M 2M CONGO

Arab slave trade from East Africa

1.3M ANGOLA

EAST AND CENTRAL AFRICAN INTERIOR Mozambique

MADAGASCAR

The regions shown were the principal sources of slaves. The figures are for 1526-1810

From 1526 to 1870 about 10 million slaves were shipped from Africa to:

Europe:	175,000
Spanish America:	1,552,000
Brazil:	3,647,000
British Caribbean:	1,665,000
British North America and United States:	399,000
French America:	1,600,000
Dutch America:	500,000
Danish West Indies:	28,000

Ife sculpture (above) During the golden age of African kingdoms, art forms, especially that of sculpture, flourished. Some of the most sublime African sculpture came from the forest kingdoms of Ife and Benin, in present-day Nigeria. The Ife terracotta and bronze heads began to be made in the 13th century, and the tradition continued for several hundred years. In nearby Benin, the bronze sculptures produced in the 16th and 17th centuries were more powerful and robust than the beautifully refined and naturalistic Ife figures.

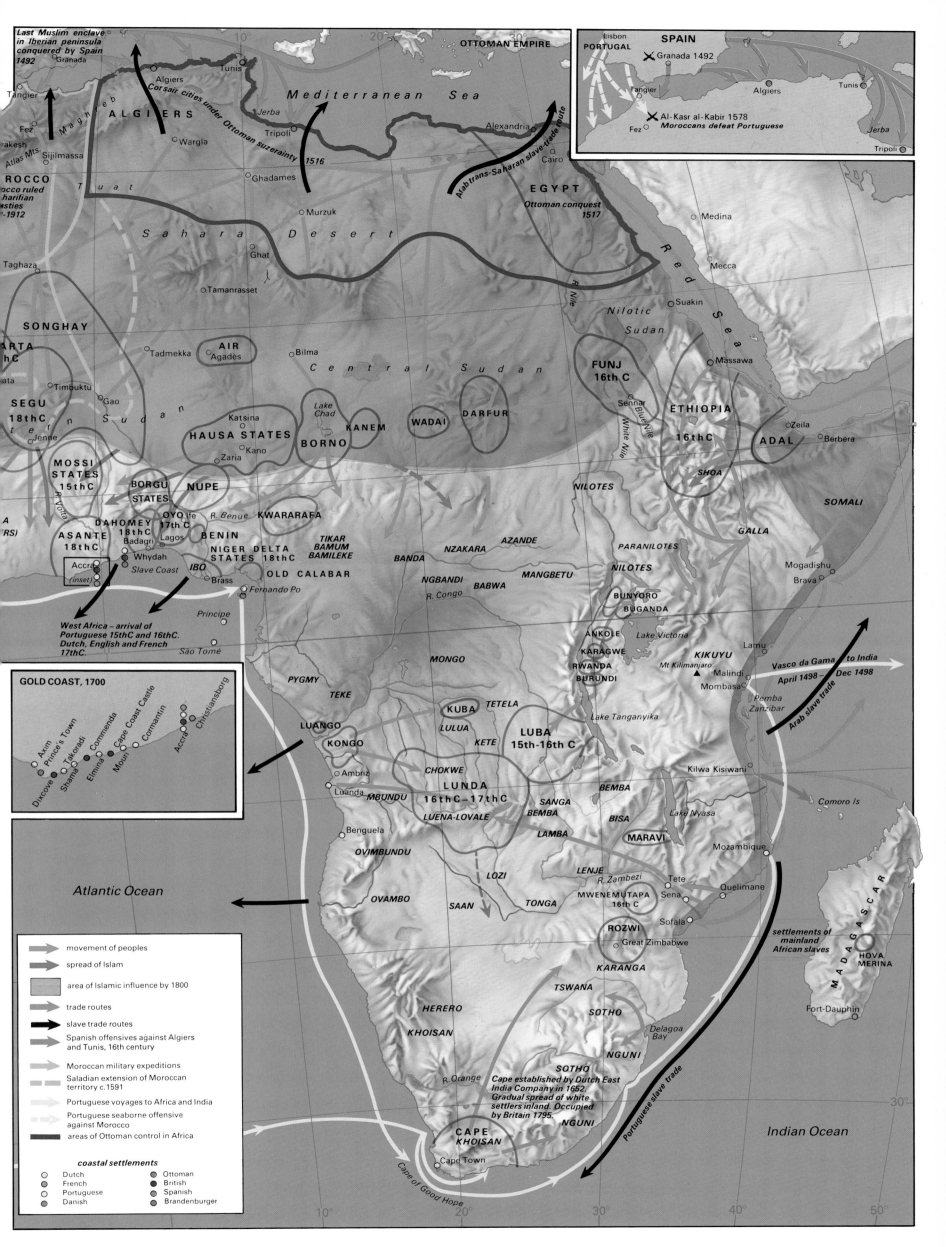

Last Muslim enclave in Iberian peninsula conquered by Spain 1492

Granada

Tangier

Fez

rakesh

Atlas Mts.

ROCCO
occo ruled
harifian
sties
-1912

Algiers
Corsair cities under Ottoman suzerainty

ALGIERS

M a g h r e b

Sijilmassa

T u a t

Tunis

Jerba

Tripoli

Wargla

Ghadames

Murzuk

1516

Ghat

Tamanrasset

S a h a r a   D e s e r t

Taghaza

Bilma

Tadmekka

AIR
Agadès

SONGHAY

ARTA
h C

ata

Timbuktu

Gao

SEGU
18thC
er

Jenne

Katsina

HAUSA STATES

Kano

Zaria

Lake
Chad

KANEM

BORNO

WADAI

C e n t r a l   S u d a n

DARFUR

MOSSI
STATES
15thC

BORGU
STATES

NUPE

OYO
17th C

DAHOMEY
18thC

ASANTE
18thC

Badagri

Lagos

BENIN

Ife

R. Benue

KWARARAFA

NIGER DELTA
STATES 18thC

Accra
(inset)

Whydah
Slave Coast

IBO

Brass

OLD CALABAR

TIKAR
BAMUM
BAMILEKE

BANDA

NZAKARA

NGBANDI

AZANDE

BABWA

MANGBETU

Fernando Po

Principe

West Africa – arrival of
Portuguese 15thC and 16thC.
Dutch, English and French
17thC.

São Tomé

R. Congo

PYGMY

MONGO

TEKE

KUBA

LULUA

TETELA

KETE

KONGO

LUANGO

Ambriz

Luanda

MBUNDU

CHOKWE

LUENA-LOVALE

LUNDA
16thC–17thC

LUBA
15th-16th C

SANGA

BEMBA

BISA

BEMBA

Lake Tanganyika

LAMBA

OVIMBUNDU

Benguela

LOZI

SAAN

LENJE

TONGA

MARAVI

Lake Nyasa

MWENEMUTAPA
16th C

R. Zambezi

Tete

Sena

Quelimane

Mozambique

Atlantic Ocean

HERERO

OVAMBO

KHOISAN

ROZWI

Great Zimbabwe

KARANGA

TSWANA

SOTHO

NGUNI

Delagoa
Bay

SOTHO

R. Orange

Cape established by Dutch East
India Company in 1652.
Gradual spread of white
settlers inland. Occupied
by Britain 1795.

NGUNI

CAPE
KHOISAN

Cape Town

Cape of Good Hope

O T T O M A N   E M P I R E

M e d i t e r r a n e a n   S e a

Alexandria

Cairo

EGYPT
Ottoman conquest
1517

Arab trans-Saharan slave-trade route

R. Nile

Medina

Mecca

Suakin

Massawa

N i l o t i c   S u d a n

Sennar

Blue Nile

White Nile

FUNJ
16th C

ETHIOPIA
16thC

Zeila

SHOA

ADAL

Berbera

NILOTES

SOMALI

GALLA

PARANILOTES

NILOTES

BUNYORO

BUGANDA

ANKOLE

KARAGWE

RWANDA

BURUNDI

Lake Victoria

KIKUYU

Mt Kilimanjaro

Malindi

Mombasa

Lamu

R e d   S e a

Vasco da Gama to India
April 1498 – Dec 1498

Arab slave trade

Pemba
Zanzibar

Kilwa Kisiwani

Comoro Is

Sofala

settlements of
mainland
African slaves

M A D A G A S C A R

HOVA
MERINA

Fort-Dauphin

Portuguese slave trade

Indian Ocean

PORTUGAL

Lisbon

SPAIN

X Granada 1492

Tangier

Fez

X Al-Kasr al-Kabir 1578
Moroccans defeat Portuguese

Algiers

Tunis

Jerba

Tripoli

GOLD COAST, 1700

Axim

Prince's Town

Dixcove

Takoradi

Shama

Commenda

Elmina

Mouri

Cape Coast Castle

Cormantin

Accra

Christiansborg

Legend

→ movement of peoples

→ spread of Islam

▢ area of Islamic influence by 1800

→ trade routes

→ slave trade routes

→ Spanish offensives against Algiers
and Tunis, 16th century

→ Moroccan military expeditions

→ Saladian extension of Moroccan
territory c.1591

→ Portuguese voyages to Africa and India

→ Portuguese seaborne offensive
against Morocco

▬ areas of Ottoman control in Africa

coastal settlements

○ Dutch   ● Ottoman
○ French   ● British
○ Portuguese   ● Spanish
○ Danish   ● Brandenburger

East Asia at the time of the Ming Dynasty 1368 to 1644

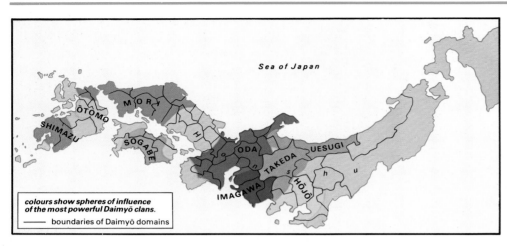

colours show spheres of influence of the most powerful Daimyō clans.
— boundaries of Daimyō domains

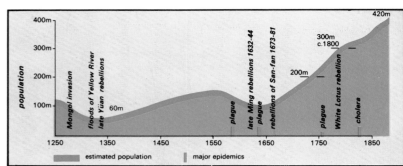

estimated population   ▌ major epidemics

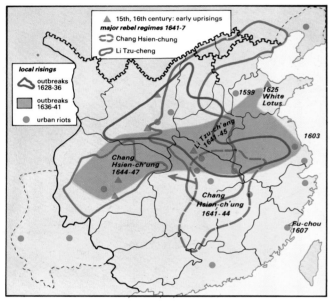

4/Japan's century of civil war. 1467 to 1590 (above) The powerful centralised regime established by the Kamakura shōguns was destroyed in the 1330s, to be replaced by the Ashikaga, a new dominant military family, until 1400, when their power declined. The Onin War (1467-77) began a century of strife between the feudal lords. The map shows the political fragmentation of the country in about 1560; Oda Nobunga and Hideyoshi Shige-kuni gradually reunified Japan by 1590, preparing the way for the powerful state of the Tokugawa, set up in 1603.

3/Rebellions under the Ming (left) Rural distress produced a number of rebellions during the 15th century, mostly in central and south-eastern China. In the early 17th century taxation and economic pressures produced urban risings in the great cities, and from the 1620s great numbers of peasant rebellions in central and northern China. In the 1640s two rebels, Li Tzu-ch'eng and Chang Hsien-chung, became contenders to found a new dynasty.

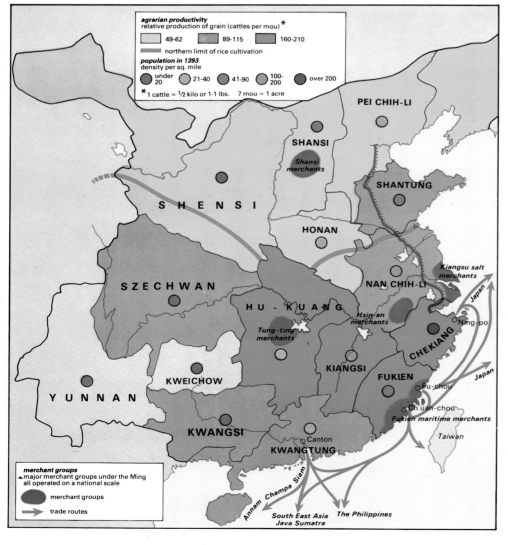

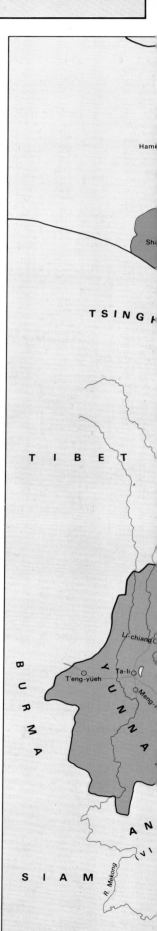

THE Mongols caused immense destruction in China, esepcially during the conquest of northern China before 1241. Much of the land went out of cultivation, its cities and industries were largely destroyed. Countless numbers died, many more were enslaved. In the south Mongol rule was less harsh after 1279, but during the Mongol (Yüan) dynasty (1280-1367) the Chinese were ruthlessly exploited, productivity fell, and commerce was badly disrupted. Popular resentment erupted in a wave of popular risings from 1335 onwards. In 1354-59 disastrous floods in the eastern plain caused further distress, and major rebellions flared up in Chekiang, the Yangtze valley, Shantung and Honan. One of the rebel leaders, Chu Yüan-chang, gradually overcame his rivals and established his new dynasty, the Ming, in Nanking in 1368. It was not until 1387 that all of China was conquered, and the Mongols were finally defeated in 1388.

Until the end of the 14th century the Ming were preoccupied with the restoration of normal life. The first priority was the revival of agriculture: irrigation and drainage works were rebuilt in great numbers, reafforestation carried out on a grand scale, and vast numbers of people moved to repopulate the devastated areas of the north. An attempt was made to break the power of the large landowners and encourage small peasants. Unlike the Sung, who had relied heavily on trade and merchants as sources of revenue, the Ming reverted to the ancient system of reliance on agriculture for revenues. They also attempted to revive the ancient concept of a self-sufficient army, and established a class of hereditary military families settled in 'military colonies' on the frontiers and in other strategic places. A new canal system was built linking Peking with the Yangtze valley, and the capital was moved to Peking in 1421.

In 1393 the Chinese population was just over 60,000,000, 40 per cent less than in the late Sung. With peace and internal stability it began again to increase, and by 1580 was probably about 130,000,000, although a drastic reduction was caused by major plagues in the late 16th century and again in the 1640s. Improved agricultural techniques enabled China to feed this growing population. New crops were introduced; cotton had become common under the Mongols and was widely grown in the Yangtze valley and the north of Chiang-su (Kiangsu). In the dry west and north-west sorghum became a common grain crop. In the 16th and 17th centuries Spanish and Portuguese traders reached the Chinese coast and introduced more new crops: sweet potato, maize, peanuts, Irish potato and tobacco, which could be grown on soils unsuited to traditional crops.

The Ming government took a negative attitude towards trade. It abandoned the use of paper money, by the misuse of which the Mongols had seriously damaged the economy. The government itself monopolised some important

2/The Ming economy (left) Chinese silk and cotton textiles and ceramics were exchanged in Manila for Spanish silver from the New World; and from the early 17th century tea was exported to Europe via Dutch traders. China imported silver, spices, sulphur, sandalwood, and copper from Japan.

Ming naval power (above) As this detail from a painting showing the defence of Korea illustrates, the Ming were a considerable naval power, capable of intervening in the affairs of distant nations.

Population fluctuations (left) At the beginning of the Ming, China still suffered from the effects of Mongol rule. Population had fallen drastically, especially in the north. With extensive reconstruction, population rose steadily, and agriculture became more productive. Outbreaks of plague in the 1580s and the 1640s, however, again reduced the population in many areas.

industries. Nevertheless industry boomed, and the great cities of the Yangtze delta, Nanking, Suchou, Wu-hsi, Sung-chiang and Hang-chou became major industrial centres, particularly for textiles. They were supplied with grain and raw cotton from the north, by the grand canal, and from Hunan and Hupeh by the Yangtze. Large movements of goods were also needed to supply Peking and the garrisons on the northern borders, for the system of self-sufficient military colonies soon decayed. To handle this huge volume of trade several powerful groups of merchants arose (see map 2). In the late 16th century commerce was stimulated by the inflow of silver from the New World, used to pay for Chinese exports of tea, silk and ceramics.

The Ming state reverted to the institutions of T'ang times, abandoning many Sung innovations. Government was simple; control over the vast population was effected largely through a new social group, the 'gentry' (shen-shih), degree-holders who had been through the examination system and shared the values of

the officials without holding office. The new system discouraged innovation and was over-centralised. The abolition of the post of chief minister made all decisions dependent upon the emperor.

At first the Ming engaged in an aggressive foreign policy. Campaigns against the Mongols in the far north, the restoration of Korea to vassal status in 1392, the occupation of Annam from 1407 to 1427 and immense seaborne expeditions (see page 146) extended Chinese power to new limits. These ventures proved costly, and after an attempted invasion of Mongolia in 1449 ended in the emperor's capture, the Ming reverted to a defensive strategy. In the 16th century they were under constant pressure from revived Mongol power under Altan Khan (1550-73) and from attacks from the sea. Japanese pirates constantly harassed the coasts, and after 1550 invaded coastal districts in force, sailed up the Yangtze, and attacked major cities. The Portuguese, by comparison a minor irritant, first appeared in 1514 and from 1557 were per-

manently established in Macao.

The threat from Japanese pirates was diminished when, in 1590, Japan was reunified after over a century of civil war and political disunion. But this Japanese revival brought new dangers. In 1592 the Japanese under Hideyoshi invaded Korea, and the Chinese had to send huge armies to aid the Koreans. Another expedition against Korea, in 1597-98, again caused terrible destruction, and required Chinese involvement.

These major threats coincided with a decline in Ming government. After 1582 the emperors refused to conduct court business or even to see their ministers. Power passed into the hands of the eunuchs who, with their own army and secret police, were able to terrorise officials and populace alike, and to extort heavy taxes. Reformist officials attempted to counter them, but this led to purges and factional discord.

The Ming had suffered rebellions before. An uprising in Fukien and Chekiang in 1448-49 had led to a million deaths. After 1627, however, a wave of rebel movements broke out, following repeated crop failures in the north-west. By 1636 much of central, northern and north-western China was in rebellion. The main contenders for power were Chang Hsien-cheng, who ravaged the eastern plain and the Yangtze valley before setting up a kingdom in Szechwan, and Li Tzu-ch'eng in Shan-hsi, Hupeh and Honan. Li took Peking in 1644, and the last Ming emperor committed suicide. But Li's ambition to found a dynasty was thwarted by the intervention of the Manchus, who in the previous quarter century had established a powerful state in Liao-tung with the aid of Chinese defectors.

1/The Ming period began with the new régime consolidating its control both in China and in the south-west, which the Mongols had incorporated into China for the first time. The first half of the 15th century was one of active expansion: great sea voyages, invasions of Mongolia and of Vietnam. Thereafter, Ming China retired to the defensive, protected by vast armies along the rebuilt Great Wall. In the 16th century the Ming were beset by attacks from the resurgent Mongols and from Japanese pirates, while the first western trading mission, led by the Portuguese Tomé Pires, appeared on the coast in 1517.

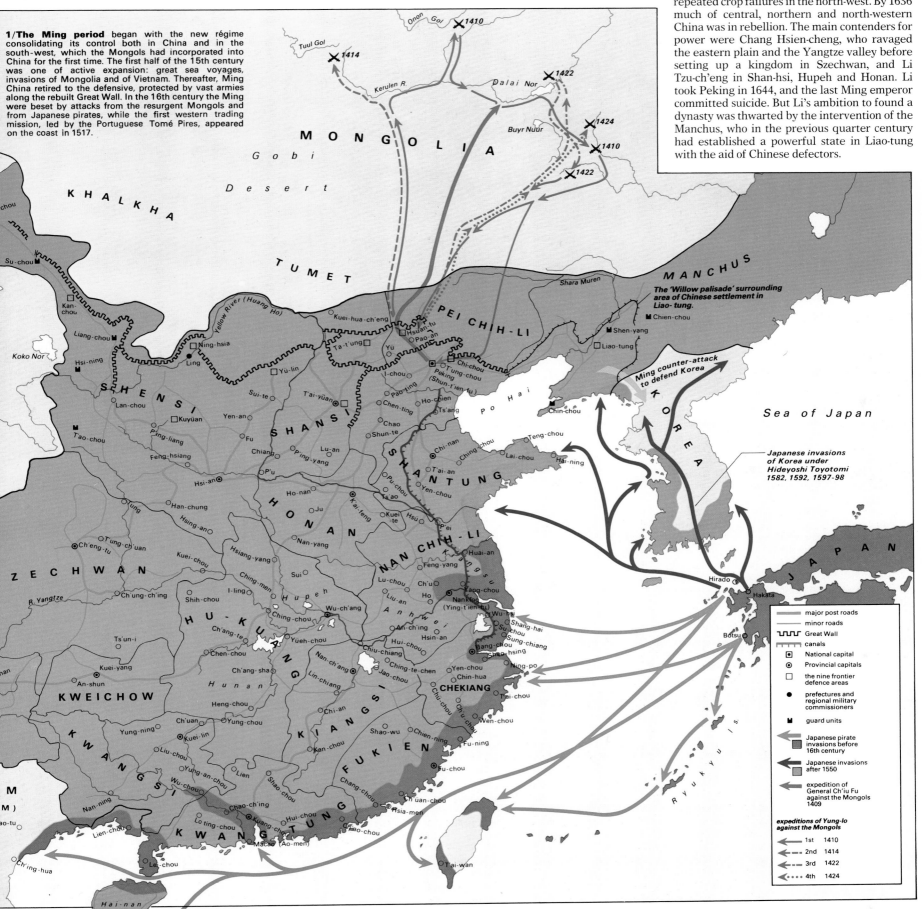

	major post roads
	minor roads
	Great Wall
	canals
■	National capital
◉	Provincial capitals
□	the nine frontier defence areas
●	prefectures and regional military commissioners
⬛	guard units
	Japanese pirate invasions before 16th century
	Japanese invasions after 1550
	expedition of General Ch'iu Fu against the Mongols 1409

expeditions of Yung-lo against the Mongols

	1st	1410
	2nd	1414
	3rd	1422
	4th	1424

Japanese invasions of Korea under Hideyoshi Toyotomi 1582, 1592, 1597-98

Ming counter-attack to defend Korea

The 'Willow palisade' surrounding area of Chinese settlement in Liao-tung.

The resurgence of Muslim power 1520 to 1639

1 / The Ottoman, Safavid and Mughal Empires *(right)* The great Muslim victories of Mohács on the Danube and Panipat in the Ganges basin took place in the same year, 1526. Subsequently, the Ottoman frontier advanced still further into Europe, and the Mughals in India extended their domains southwards until the end of the 17th century. The Ottoman triumph was less enduring; weakened by internal revolts, and challenged by the Habsburgs in Europe, Muscovy in southern Russia and the Safavids in Iran, they gradually retreated from Hungary, the Caucasus and Iraq; by the end of the 17th century many of the gains realised in the reign of Suleiman the Magnificent (1520-66) had been lost.

THE first half of the 16th century saw a great advance in the power of the three major Muslim states of the period: the Ottoman Empire, the state founded by the Safavid dynasty in Persia, and the Mughal Empire in India. In the middle of the 16th century these three polities occupied or controlled a broad belt of lands and seas, extending from the frontiers of Morocco, Austria and Ethiopia to the fringes of central Asia, the foothills of the Himalayas, and the Bay of Bengal. Much of central Asia was in the possession of another dynasty of Turkish origin, the Uzbek Shaybanids, who ruled in Bukhara. Khanates with Muslim rulers still existed in the Crimea and on the Volga at Kazan and Astrakhan, and continued to do so for many generations in the lands along the ancient Silk Road. All these states were the creation of Turkish-speaking Muslim dynasties of a strongly military character. All, with the exception of the Safavid state in Persia, affirmed their adherence to orthodox (Sunni) Islam; the Safavids, however, followed Shi'ism, a fact which encouraged bitter rivalry and intermittent warfare between them and their Ottoman and Uzbek neighbours throughout the 16th and early 17th centuries.

By the death of Mehmed II (1481) the Ottomans had conquered Constantinople and overrun the Balkans. Some time after that the sudden revival of Persia under Ismail I (1500-24) drew them back to Asia. Ismail was defeated in 1514, Syria and Egypt conquered in 1516-17. With the accession of Suleiman I (1520-66) the assault on Europe was renewed. After the battle of Mohács (1526) Hungary was overrun and Vienna besieged (1529); but Persia still remained independent. Nevertheless the Ottoman Empire, buttressed by the wealth acquired from the conquest of Egypt, was indisputably the

greatest Muslim power of the age. In the early years of Suleiman's reign the subjects of the Sultan numbered perhaps 14 million (compare this with Spain who at this time had 5 million inhabitants whilst England had 2.5 million). The population of Constantinople itself, which at the time of the Ottoman conquest had been no more than 40,000, increased tenfold, and Ottoman and European writers alike testified to the splendour of its public works, the impressiveness of the imperial mosques and the outstanding quality of administrative, charitable and educational institutions. To European observers, such as the Habsburg Emperor's ambassador Busbecq, the magnificence of the Ottoman state, and the strength and discipline of the Ottoman army, were matters for admiration – and concern.

Persia, also, under the new dynasty enjoyed a remarkable revival of art, architecture and trade, which reached its culmination in the reign of Abbas I (1587-1629), while in India Babur, an

adventurer from central Asia who had seized power in Afghanistan in 1504, swept aside the effete sultanate of Delhi and founded the Mughal Empire in 1526. Here again (see page 172) there was a great efflorescence of culture, which reached its peak during the reign of Akbar (1556-1605). But the vast extension of Muslim power and influence concealed a number of flaws. The most serious problem was the continuing clash between Sunni Turkey and Shi'i Persia – which drove a wedge into the Muslim world. Just as the Ottomans allied with

Suleiman I at Mohács *(right)* The military might, order and discipline of the Ottoman army in the first half of the 16th century are vigorously depicted in this miniature. Suleiman I is shown surrounded by his vezirs, sipahis and janissaries and the heads of the decapitated Hungarians he defeated at the Battle of Mohács in 1526.

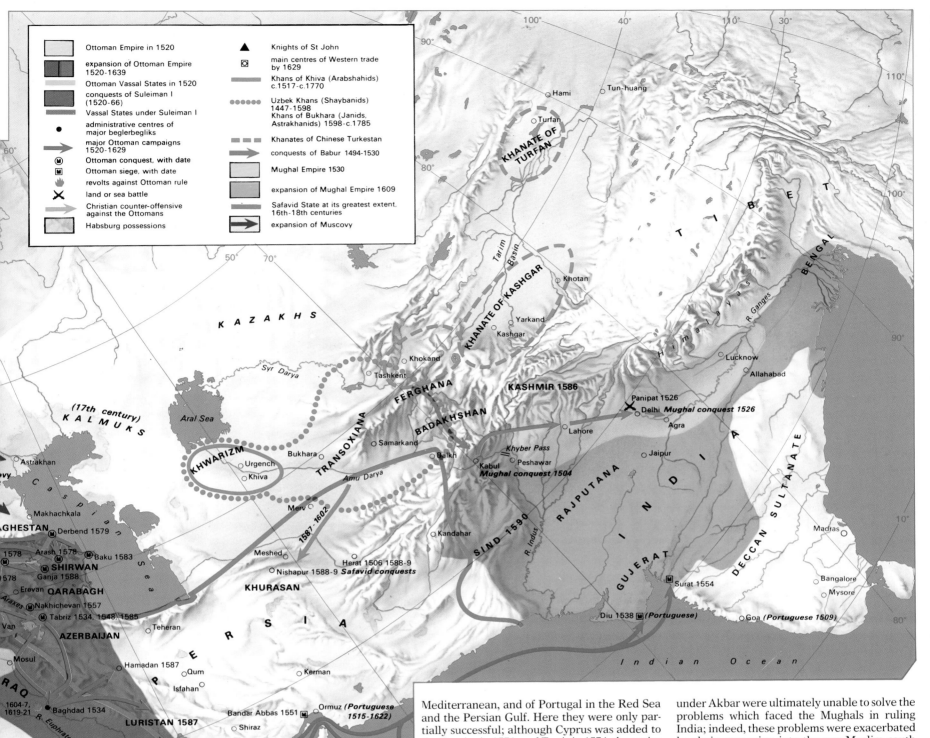

Legend:

- Ottoman Empire in 1520
- expansion of Ottoman Empire 1520-1639
- Ottoman Vassal States in 1520
- conquests of Suleiman I (1520-66)
- Vassal States under Suleiman I
- administrative centres of major beglerbegliks
- major Ottoman campaigns 1520-1629
- Ⓜ Ottoman conquest, with date
- Ⓜ Ottoman siege, with date
- ✋ revolts against Ottoman rule
- ✕ land or sea battle
- Christian counter-offensive against the Ottomans
- Habsburg possessions
- ▲ Knights of St John
- ◪ main centres of Western trade by 1629
- Khans of Khiva (Arabshahids) c.1517-c.1770
- Uzbek Khans (Shaybanids) 1447-1598
  Khans of Bukhara (Janids, Astrakhanids) 1598-c.1785
- Khanates of Chinese Turkestan
- conquests of Babur 1494-1530
- Mughal Empire 1530
- expansion of Mughal Empire 1609
- Safavid State at its greatest extent. 16th-18th centuries
- expansion of Muscovy

Mediterranean, and of Portugal in the Red Sea and the Persian Gulf. Here they were only partially successful; although Cyprus was added to the Empire in 1571, and Tunis in 1574, the major defeat at Lepanto in 1571 was a serious setback for the Ottoman navy. Further east they had been unable to prevent the capture of Socotra (1507) and Ormuz (1515) by the Portuguese, still less the establishment of a Portuguese presence in India itself.

For the Ottomans, the year 1538, when the armies and fleets of the Sultan in one season reduced Moldavia to vassal status, defeated a poorly-led Christian armada at Preveza, and appeared against the Portuguese under the walls of Diu, was certainly an *annus mirabilis*. However, the conflicts on the Hungarian and Persian frontiers both began to lose their momentum in the last two decades of Suleiman's reign. In the second half of the 16th century, the wars against the Safavids (1578-90 and 1603-19) and against the Habsburgs (1593-1606) ended in the loss of the Caucasus territories and the Habsburgs' last payment of tribute for Hungary. Furthermore, during these wars the life-blood of the Empire, its traditionally-recruited ruling class and its army, was drained away. The changing conditions of war, the effects of inflation after 1584, and the insoluble problem of a rising population, a shrinking economy, and a static frontier, had by the early decades of the 17th century produced a crisis in the Ottoman state.

In Persia the political weakness of the Safavids in the latter part of the 16th century was redressed by Abbas I, but after his death in 1629 the Safavid dynasty, too, entered a period of weakness, leading to ultimate demise. Following a similar pattern, in India the administrative reorganisation and religious experimentation under Akbar were ultimately unable to solve the problems which faced the Mughals in ruling India; indeed, these problems were exacerbated by their expansion into the non-Muslim south during the 17th century.

It was on the fringes of the Muslim world that the changes in this period were the most ominous. At sea, the Portuguese circumnavigation of Africa and their attempt to put a stranglehold on the indigenous trade of the Indian Ocean had not gone unnoticed by the Ottomans; as successors to the Mamelukes they were able at least to hold the Portuguese at bay during the 16th century. However, the arrival of the English, and later the Dutch, brought into the region powers economically stronger and politically more ruthless than the Portuguese. Their effect was increasingly felt during the remainder of the 17th century. Meanwhile, to the north, the Muslim successor states of the Mongol Empire had by the middle of the 16th century for the most part entered on the last stages of decline and decay. The khanates of Kazan and Astrakhan were annexed by Muscovy in 1552 and 1556. This brought Russian forces to the mouth of the Volga, thus driving a wedge between the Ottomans and the Uzbeks. On the other hand, the khanate of the Crimea, another successor state of the Golden Horde, continued in existence and was at times a useful military auxiliary of the Ottomans as well as a barrier closing off the Black Sea from hostile Christian states to the north. By the 1620s, however, Cossack raiders were appearing on the Black Sea and ravaging its shores. Within less than a hundred years the Islamic world had passed from the offensive to the defensive, and the great Islamic empires, which had seemed so formidable in the 16th and 17th centuries, failed to make the transition to the modern world.

France against the Habsburgs, so the Persians allied with Austria against the Turks. Secondly, the Mughal and Safavid empires were essentially based on land, and when the Portuguese appeared in the Indian Ocean, hitherto a Muslim lake, they were unable to cope. After their conquest of Egypt, the Ottomans assumed the defence of their territories against the seapower of Spain and the Italian city states in the

The Mughal Empire and the growth of British power in India

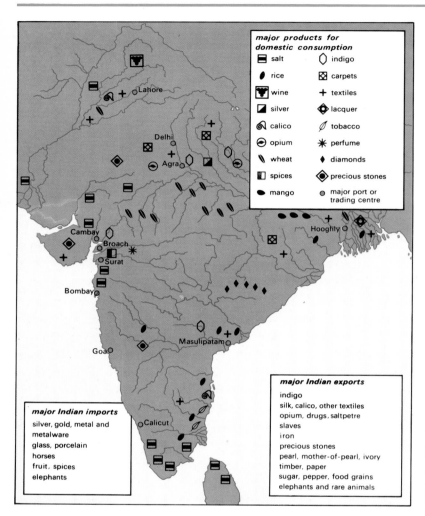

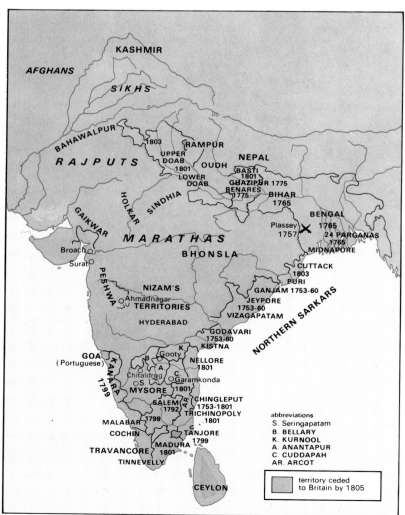

2/Mughal India: economic products and trade *(above)* Textiles from Bengal, Gujerat and Coromandel were India's main export; also sugar to Japan and Persia and pepper and saltpetre to Europe. The main imports were gold and silver.

3/The growth of British Power to 1805 *(below)* **and principal Maratha States in 1795** *(below right)* After Tipu's death at Seringapatam (1799) the Marathas represented the only major obstacle to British supremacy, largely achieved by 1805.

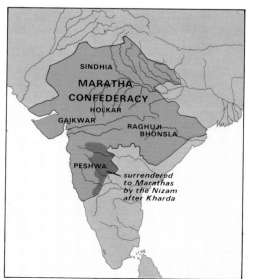

BABUR, fifth in line from Tamerlane, entered India in 1523 from Afghanistan. With his victory at Panipat in 1526 he established the Mughal Empire, but it took some time to make the foundations firm. After his death, the Mughals were expelled by the Afghans of South Bihar, under their leader Sher Shah, and it took a full-scale new invasion, brilliantly consolidated by Babur's grandson, Akbar (1556-1605), to restore their rule. This now extended to Bengal in the east and Godavari in the south, as well as Kashmir, Baluchistan, Sind and Gujerat. Most of the Rajput princes became tributary allies, and the empire, divided into *subahs* (provinces) was administered by a new class of bureaucrats, the *mansabdars*, ranked in a military hierarchy on lines first planned by Sher Shah. A standardised tax system, and tolerance towards the non-Muslim majority, helped to foster one of the great flowerings of Indian civilisation, particularly in painting and architecture. The reign of Akbar is considered one of the golden ages in India's past. Unlike his descendants, who, thanks to his policy of marriage alliances with the Rajput princely families were half Indian, Akbar was entirely a foreigner in India. Yet his sense of identification with the life and culture of the country he reconquered was total. The popular acclaim, 'Dillisvaro va jagadisvaro va' – 'the Ruler of Delhi is the same as the Lord of the Universe' – testified to the masses' enthusiastic acceptance of his benevolent autocratic rule. The artists and savants at his court recalled, in popular imagination, the glories of the mythical Vikramaditya's court with its 'nine jewels' (*navaratna*). The Mughal school of miniature painting, which combined the traditions of the Persian and Rajput schools, flourished under his patronage. His red sandstone capital at Fatehpur Sikri similarly expressed a striking synthesis of Hindu and Islamic traditions of architecture. The new style reached its climax in the days of his grandson, Shahjahan, the builder of the Taj Mahal.

Akbar's political inheritance included a ceaseless thrust towards territorial expansion, especially towards the south. New territories were added under Shahjahan (1627-56) and the Mughal domains reached their furthest extent under Aurangzeb (1656-1707), who had seized the throne after a fratricidal war. Bijapur and Golconda were annexed, Assam briefly occupied, and Chittagong wrested from Arakan. But the southern conquests led to confrontation with a new Hindu power, the Marathas, who under Sivaji (1627-80) had established an independent kingdom on the Konkan coast, with outposts in Coromandel and Mysore. The execution of Sivaji's son in 1689 failed to check the Maratha depredations, and by now religious intolerance and administrative decay were stirring up

opposition on all sides. By 1700 the Marathas were ravaging the Deccan and the eastern provinces, the former Rajput allies were at war, and near the capital Sikhs, Jats and Satnamis were all in revolt.

During the previous 150 years of Mughal peace and prosperity, foreign trade had attracted new, and now increasingly powerful European interest in India. Following Vasco da Gama's first landfall at Malabar in 1498, the spice-seeking Portuguese soon acquired territories – Goa, Daman and Diu Island – from which they tried to monopolise spice and textile sales, as well as the pilgrim voyages to Mecca. In the 17th century they were joined by less unpopular Dutch, English, French and Danish companies, all eager to set up coastal trading centres, exporting textiles, sugar, indigo and saltpetre to markets as far away as Japan and the New World.

Shortly after Aurangzeb's death, Oudh, the Deccan and the eastern provinces became effectively independent, owing only nominal allegiance to Delhi. The Peshwas, officially the chief ministers of Sivaji's house, presided over a confederacy of Maratha chiefs, the Sindhias, Gaikwars, Holkars and Bhonslas. Their territories stretched deep into north, west, central and eastern India, while in the south, Mysore, under Haidar and Tipu, had grown into a formidable power. By the late 18th century, the Mughal emperor had become a Sindhia protégé. The Marathas at this time seemed destined to succeed the Mughals. Such hopes were effectively destroyed at the Third Battle of Panipat (1761) where the Afghan Ahmad Shah Abdali decisively defeated the Peshwa's forces.

The War of the Austrian Succession (1740-48) saw the French and English trading companies in armed conflict along the Carnatic coast. With the death of the local ruler, the Nizam, this developed into open war (1744-63), ending in British victory and the eclipse of France's Indian ambitions. Robert Clive's triumph at Plassey in 1757 brought effective control of Bihar, Orissa and Bengal (where the East India Company had established its new trading centre of Calcutta in 1690). By 1768 the Northern Sarkars were secured from the Nizam. Benares and Ghazipur were wrested from Oudh in 1775. But British supremacy was only assured after a series of battles with the Marathas and Mysore, of which the outcome was frequently uncertain. However, the company's possessions were steadily expanding – particularly with the victory over Tipu in 1792 and his fall in 1799 – and by the turn of the century they formed a continuous block from Malabar to Coromandel.

In Britain, the Regulating Act of 1773 and the Younger Pitt's India Act in 1784, had placed these new Indian acquisitions firmly under English parliamentary control (and also led to the impeachment of Warren Hastings, the first Governor-General of Bengal). Now, under Richard Wellesley, brother of the Duke of Wellington, they were to be consolidated into the beginnings of an imperial realm.

Wellesley, given a virtually free hand by the Napoleonic Wars at home, swiftly defeated Tipu, the most effective of the Indian leaders, and embarked on the Second Maratha War. Both these produced large accretions of territory, alongside important but subsidiary annexations in Gooty, Garamkonda, Surat, Tanjore, the Carnatic, and large parts of Oudh and Chitaldrug. The Maratha defeats delivered the Upper Doab, Rajputana, Broach, Ahmadnagar and the south-west Deccan, while subsidiary alliances, another important policy instrument, won recognition of British suzerainty from nearly all the major Indian rulers. In 1803, the Mughal emperor himself accepted Wellesley's protection, and when he left India in 1805, the Company's supremacy was an acknowledged fact.

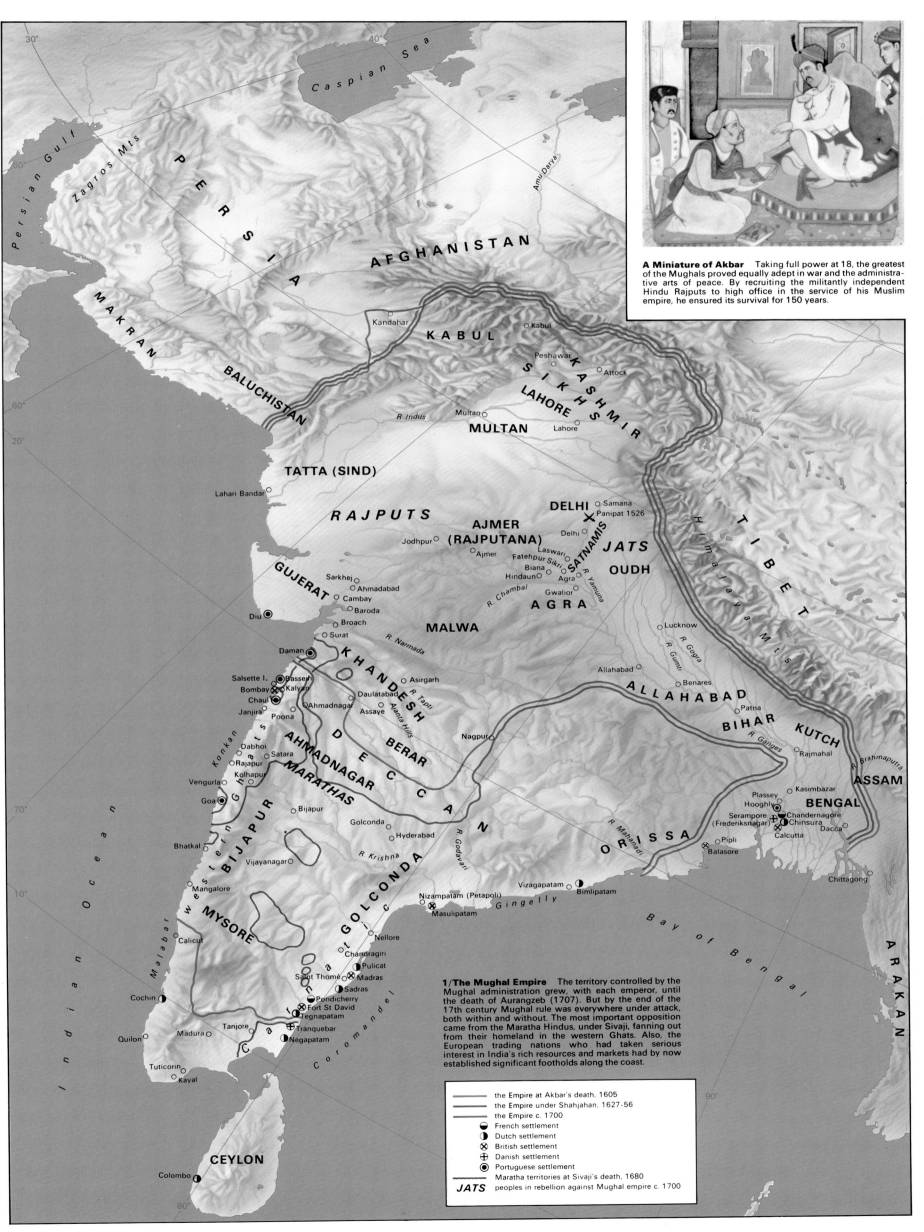

A Miniature of Akbar Taking full power at 18, the greatest of the Mughals proved equally adept in war and the administrative arts of peace. By recruiting the militantly independent Hindu Rajputs to high office in the service of his Muslim empire, he ensured its survival for 150 years.

Caspian Sea

Persian Gulf

Zagros Mts

PERSIA

AFGHANISTAN

MAKRAN

BALUCHISTAN

Kandahar

KABUL

○ Kabul

Peshawar

○ Attock

KASHMIR

SIKHS

LAHORE

R. Indus Multan ○

MULTAN

○ Lahore

Amu Darya

TIBET

TATTA (SIND)

Lahari Bandar ◉

RAJPUTS

AJMER
(RAJPUTANA)

Jodhpur ○

○ Ajmer

DELHI   ○ Samana
       Panipat 1526 ✕

○ Delhi

SATNAMIS   JATS

Laswari
Fatehpur Sikri ○

Biana
Hindaun ○ Agra

OUDH

R. Yamuna

Himalaya Mts

GUJERAT

Sarkhej ○
○ Ahmadabad

Cambay ○
○ Baroda

Diu ◉

Broach ○
○ Surat

R. Chambal

Gwalior ○

AGRA

MALWA

R. Narmada

Daman ◉

KHANDESH

Asirgarh

R. Tapti

Salsette I.
Bombay ✕ Bassein ◉
        Kalyan
Chaul ◉
Janjira ○ Ahmadnagar
        Poona

Daulatabad
Ajanta Hills
Assaye

BERAR

DECCAN

○ Lucknow

R. Gogra

R. Gumti

Allahabad ○

ALLAHABAD

○ Benares

BIHAR

KUTCH

○ Patna

R. Ganges

Rajmahal ○

Brahmaputra

ASSAM

Dabhoi
Rajapur ○ Satara
Kolhapur

AHMADNAGAR

MARATHAS

Konkan

Western Ghats

Vengurla ○
Goa ◉

Bijapur ○

BIJAPUR

Bhatkal ○

Vijayanagar ○

Mangalore ○

MYSORE

Malabar

Calicut ○

Cochin ○

Quilon ○

Madura

Tuticorin ○
Kayal ○

CEYLON

Colombo ◐

Nagpur ○

Golconda ○

Hyderabad ○

GOLCONDA

R. Krishna

R. Godavari

Nellore ○

Chandragiri ○
Pulicat ◐
Saint Thomé ✕ Madras
        Sadras
Pondicherry ◐
Fort St David ✕
Tegnapatam
Tanjore
Tranquebar ✚
Negapatam ◉

Coromandel

R. Mahanadi

ORISSA

Pipli
Balasore ✕

Plassey
Hooghly ○
Serampore ✚ Chinsura
(Frederiksnagar) ✕ Chandernagore
        Calcutta ✕ Dacca

Kasimbazar ○

BENGAL

Chittagong ○

ARAKAN

Bay of Bengal

Vizagapatam ◐
Bimlipatam ◐

Nizampatam (Petapoli) ○
Masulipatam ✕

Gingelly

Indian Ocean

1/The Mughal Empire The territory controlled by the Mughal administration grew, with each emperor, until the death of Aurangzeb (1707). But by the end of the 17th century Mughal rule was everywhere under attack, both within and without. The most important opposition came from the Maratha Hindus, under Sivaji, fanning out from their homeland in the western Ghats. Also, the European trading nations who had taken serious interest in India's rich resources and markets had by now established significant footholds along the coast.

———	the Empire at Akbar's death, 1605
———	the Empire under Shahjahan, 1627-56
———	the Empire c. 1700
◐	French settlement
◑	Dutch settlement
✕	British settlement
✚	Danish settlement
◉	Portuguese settlement
———	Maratha territories at Sivaji's death, 1680
JATS	peoples in rebellion against Mughal empire c. 1700

East Asia at the time of the Ch'ing Dynasty

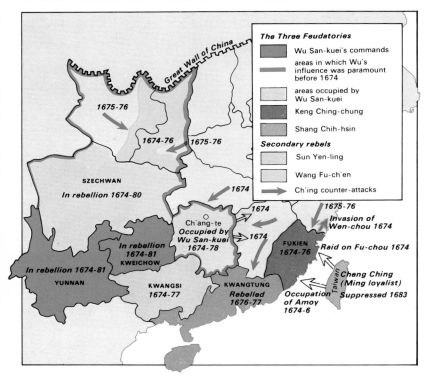

2/Rebellion of the Three Feudatories *(above)* The southern provinces, where resistance to the Ch'ing continued, were allowed to become the personal domains of various generals. Most important of these was Wu San-kuei, governor of Yunnan and Kweichow, who exercised great power over all the western provinces. In 1674 the Ch'ing government attempted to reassert control over Kwangtung. As a result the governors of all the southern and western provinces rose in a rebellion which lasted until 1681. For a time most of southern and western China was in rebel hands, but by 1677 only the south-west remained. After Wu San-kuei's death in 1678 the government slowly reduced the remaining rebels, and in 1683 occupied Taiwan, whose Ming loyalist leader Cheng Ching had supported the rebels.

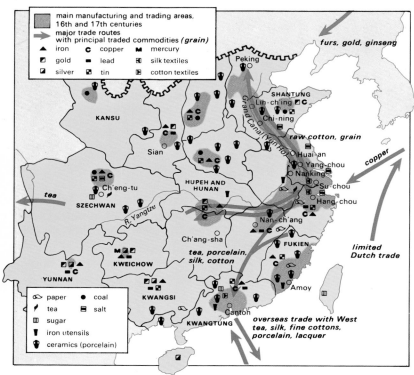

3/The Ch'ing economy *(above)* By the 17th century China had developed considerable regional specialisation and a nation-wide marketing system. Some cities in the lower Yangtze sustained large and varied handicraft industries. These industries drew their raw materials, and food for their populations, from great distances by the Yangtze and by the Grand Canal, which also supplied food and manufactured goods to the capital city, Peking.

The Chinese economy in the 19th century *(left)* Chinese exports of tea increased by over 50% in the period shown. Silk exports were increased fourfold. But ever-increasing imports of opium converted a net inflow of silver into a net outflow from the mid-1820s, with serious effects on the Chinese internal economy.

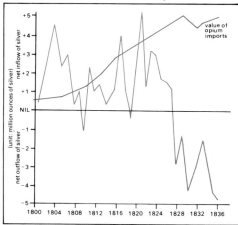

THE Ch'ing dynasty (1644-1911) was established by a non-Chinese people, the Manchus. From their homeland in the mountains of south-eastern Manchuria they gradually expanded, in the first decades of the 17th century, into the modern provinces of Liaoning and Kirin. With the aid of many Chinese, they established a stable Chinese-style state with its capital at Mukden (modern Shenyang) from 1625 to 1644; from this base they invaded Korea, reducing it to vassal status in 1637, and Inner Mongolia, which became a Manchu dependency in 1629-35. When the Ming were toppled by the rebel Li Tzu-ch'eng in 1644, the Manchus invaded China, proclaiming a new dynasty. In spite of Ming loyalist resistance in the south, most of the country was under Manchu control by 1652. Resistance continued in the south-west until 1659, and on the south-east coast Ming loyalists in 1662 occupied Taiwan (never previously under Chinese control), where they remained until 1683.

After the suppression of the rebellion of the Three Feudatories (see map 2), the Ch'ing enjoyed more than a century of internal peace and prosperity under a succession of very able rulers. The Manchus maintained their predominant place in government, and above all in the military. But they established a good working relationship with their Chinese officials, and by the end of the 18th century, deeply influenced by Chinese education and culture, had begun to lose their sharp identity. There was a number of risings of minority peoples, who were harshly exploited by Chinese and Manchus alike. There were tribal risings in Yunnan in 1726-9, among the Miao people of Kweichow in 1795-7 and again in 1829, among the Yao people of Kwangsi in 1790. The Chinese Muslim minority in Kansu rebelled in 1781-4. Most serious were the massive Chin-ch'uan tribal rebellions in western Szechwan. These first broke out in 1746-9, and after simmering for years were renewed in 1771-6, when order was finally restored after ruinously expensive military operations. A further rising occurred in the newly-occupied territory of Taiwan in 1787-8. All these risings were, however, in peripheral areas and posed no major threat to the dynasty.

At the end of the 18th century, rebellion took on a new form. By this time, although China remained immensely powerful, productive and populous, a major economic crisis loomed ahead. The area available for agriculture, which had been expanded by the introduction of new crops (maize (corn), sweet potato, groundnuts, tobacco) in the 16th and 17th centuries, was now almost totally occupied. The only vacant area suitable for Chinese-style agriculture was Manchuria, which was deliberately preserved as a Manchu homeland, and Chinese settlement in it banned. Meanwhile the population, held in check by the epidemics of the late 16th and the 17th centuries, and by the rebellions and hostilities of the late Ming and early Ch'ing, had trebled, from 100 million to 300 million, between 1650 and 1800, and continued to increase at a headlong pace. By 1850 it was 420 million. This constantly growing population had to be fed by ever more intensive cultivation of a limited area, and by the end of the 18th century population pressure was beginning to generate widespread hardship and impoverishment.

This hardship began to produce risings and rebel movements, usually inspired by secret societies, among the Chinese population. The first major outbreak was the series of risings known as the White Lotus rebellion, which erupted in the mountainous borderlands of Szechwan, Shensi and Hupeh in 1795-1804, and again on a lesser scale some years later. In Shantung a rebellion of the Eight Trigrams sect broke out in 1786-8, and in 1811 a large-scale rising of the sect of the Heavenly Principle broke out in Honan, Hopeh (Chihli) and Shantung, which was accompanied by an attempted coup in Peking before its final suppression in 1814. More risings occurred among the border peoples: the Tibetans near Koko Nor in 1807, the Yaos in Kweichow in 1833, and in Sinkiang, where the oases of Yarkand and Kashgar were in open rebellion from 1825 to 1828.

The basic economic problems of the country were made more severe by government policies of external expansion, which placed a great strain on the empire's very inefficient financial administration. Another contributory factor was foreign trade. During the 17th and 18th centuries extensive export trades, mostly in tea, silk, porcelain and handicraft goods, were built up under government licence at Canton and with the Russians at Kyakhta. Since the Chinese economy was largely self-sufficient, these exports were paid for mostly in silver, the standard medium of currency in China. Late in the 18th century the foreign powers began to import opium into China from India and the Middle East to pay for their exports. By the 1830s opium imports had outstripped the Chinese exports of tea and silk, and a drain of silver out of China began, which had increasingly serious effects upon the Chinese economy, and further impoverished the state finances.

Moreover, the quality of Ch'ing government began sharply to decline. In the late 18th century corruption became rife at every level of government from the court downwards, affecting both the civil administration and the Manchu armies, whose demoralisation, lack of supplies and equipment were shown up by the White Lotus rising. Moreover, the administration did not increase to keep pace with the vast growth of population; by the early 19th century the bureaucracy was grossly understaffed, and government came to delegate more and more power to the members of the local gentry, who acted as their unpaid agents.

By the 1820s, Manchu China was the world's largest and most populous empire, directly controlling vast territories in inner Asia, and treating as tributary states still larger areas: Korea, Indochina, Siam, Burma, Nepal. But within this huge empire, effective Ch'ing administrative and military control was gradually declining, while inexorable economic pressures built up which could be cured only by large-scale technological innovation and radical reorganisation. Neither was likely to be forthcoming, and in the meantime China faced new pressures from the expansionist Western powers.

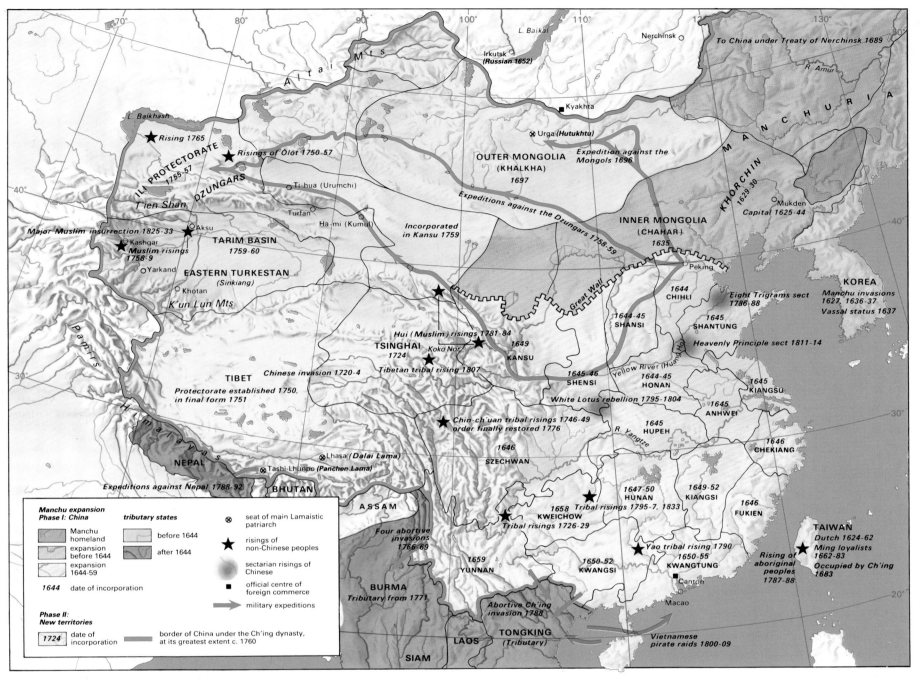

1/Chinese imperial expansion *(above)* Throughout the late 17th and the 18th centuries the Manchus pursued an expansionist policy, which left them in control of the Amur region in the north-east, Mongolia, Dzungaria, the Tarim Basin, the Ili region east of Lake Balkhash, and Tibet. Only a small part of these vast regions was incorporated under Chinese administration, and apart from military garrisons few Chinese or Manchus settled there. But these campaigns of conquest, triggered off in part by the fear of Russian expansion into Siberia and of British and French expansion into India, were immensely expensive. Chinese military expeditions went still further. Four abortive invasions of Burma were mounted in 1766-69, an expedition into Nepal in 1788-92, and a large-scale invasion of Tongking was undertaken in 1788, only to end in failure. There was a series of widespread peasant rebellions in the late 18th and early 19th centuries, usually inspired by millenarian sects. In almost every case they broke out in areas severely affected by the economic problems caused by population pressure.

4/Japan in isolation *(below)* In 1603 Tokugawa Ieyasu, who had established military dominance over the Japanese state reunified in 1590 by Hideyoshi, was made Shogun (Military Leader) by the powerless imperial court. The shogunate he founded lasted until 1868 and gave Japan a much-needed period of political stability. A complex government emerged in which the many fiefs (han) of feudal lords (daimyo) – some 250 in number – were dominated and regulated by the Shogun's government (Bakufu) in Edo. Society was organised in a hierarchy of classes, and a legal code enacted. The Christian missionaries active in the late 16th century were banned after 1612, and Christians systematically persecuted in the 1630s. Japanese were forbidden to travel abroad, and foreign contacts were limited to the Dutch, who maintained a post at Nagasaki, the Chinese and Koreans. Despite this isolation, Tokugawa Japan was extremely prosperous. Trade and cities grew rapidly. The population rose from about 20 million in 1600 to about 30 million in the 18th century. By the 19th century Japan was prosperous, well governed, had a high standard of literacy, and was far better prepared than China to meet the challenge of Western expansion.

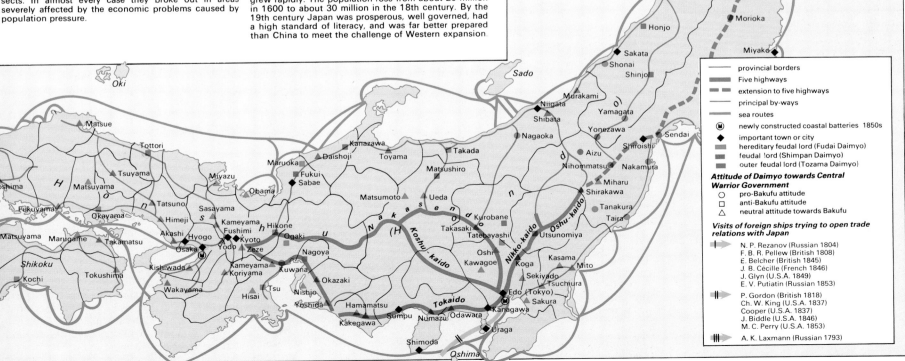

South-East Asia and the European powers 1511 to 1826

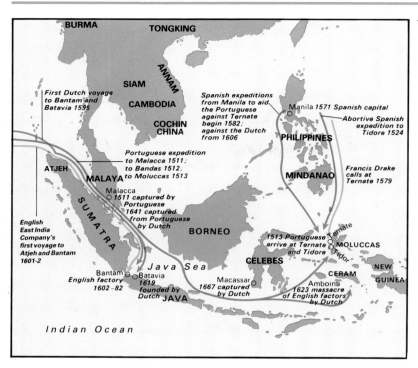

2/The spice routes (above) The Portuguese first appeared in the Moluccas and Bandas in 1512-13. Francis Drake visited Ternate in 1579. The Dutch began to trade with them in 1599; though the Anglo-Dutch treaty of 1619 provided for joint trading, the Dutch forced their partners out. The Spaniards of Manila came to the aid of the Portuguese in the Moluccas, and there was a long struggle before the Dutch gained full control.

4/The Malay states in 1826 (left) By the Treaty of London (1824) the Dutch withdrew from the Malay peninsula. The British settlements there – Penang, Singapore and Malacca – were bound by the doctrine of non-intervention laid down in Pitt's India Act. The immediate danger to the independence of the Malay states in 1826 lay in Siamese expansionism; the Burney Treaty in that year halted Siam's pressure upon them, though only after two incidents in which the Penang government safeguarded Perak's independence.

3/Dutch expansion in Java (below) Dutch territorial expansion in Java began through Sultan Agung of Mataram's attempts to capture Batavia. After his death in 1646 the Dutch East India Company, by intervening in succession disputes, gradually became the strongest political force in the island, with the ruling houses coming under its control and paying their debts by cessions of territory. The maintenance of its trade monopoly played a vital part in this expansion.

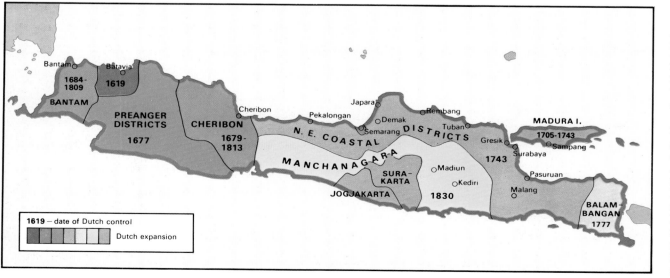

1619 – date of Dutch control

Dutch expansion

WHEN the 16th century dawned, the present Union of Burma consisted of four monarchies: Arakan (capital Myohaung), Burmese Ava, dominating the main Irrawaddy valley, Burmese Toungoo, dominating the Sittang valley, and Mon Pegu, dominating the Irrawaddy delta and Tenasserim. To the north and east of Ava a number of formidable Shan states threatened Burmese independence. Half a century later the Toungoo dynasty was to conquer both Shans and Mons. In the valley of the Chao Phraya the ruler of Ayutthaya headed a powerful Thai kingdom which controlled much of the eastern coast of the Malay peninsula. The Laos kingdom of Luang Prabang stretched along the upper and middle Mekong. The Vietnamese of Tongking and northern Annam had in 1471 annexed Cham territories down to Qui Nhon. Later they were to absorb the remaining Cham lands to the south and wrest the Mekong delta from Cambodia. Phnom Penh, not Angkor, was the capital of the much reduced Khmer kingdom. In the Malay archipelago the Javanese empire of Majapahit was little more than a memory; there were hundreds of small states with little cohesion. Islamisation was proceeding in Sumatra, Java and Borneo, chiefly from Malacca, which was the capital of an empire which included the Malay states of the peninsula and of Sumatra's east coast.

In 1511 Albuquerque conquered the great emporium of Malacca for the king of Portugal. Its ruling family escaped and established the sultanate of Johore further south, with much the same territorial sway as Malacca had exercised over the mainland Malay states and those of the Sumatran coast opposite. The Portuguese objective was to dominate the spice trade through a chain of forts linked by naval power.

Had they united, the Malay states might have driven out the invaders, but Atjeh in Sumatra strove against Johore for the leadership of the Malay world, and it was left to the Dutch East India Company, formed in 1602, to conquer the Portuguese settlements. Before then, the Spaniards had established themselves in the Philippines, making Manila, captured in 1571, their capital. From their centre at Batavia in western Java the Dutch controlled the Moluccas and Banda islands, the 'Spice Islands', making the local rulers their pensioners. They captured Malacca in 1641, but their many attempts to take Manila all failed. At the time of the Spanish occupation, the Philippines had no political organisation except for the Muslim states on Mindanao; these, in alliance with the sultans of the Sulu archipelago, maintained their independence until the 19th century.

Like the Portuguese, the Dutch empire began as one of fortified trading posts based upon sea power. But Sultan Agung of Mataram (1613-46), campaigning for supremacy over Java, failed twice to conquer Batavia, and from the 1670s his successors became dependent upon Dutch aid in their constant succession struggles, and paid for it by cessions of territory. The sultanate of Bantam, with its immensely valuable pepper trade, came under Dutch control in the same way in 1684. This involved the expulsion of the staff of the weaker rival of the Dutch, the English East India Company, from its factory there, and the transfer of its settlement to the pepper port of Benkulen on the west coast of Sumatra. After the 'Massacre of Amboina' in 1623 it had abandoned direct trade to the Spice Islands and relied upon obtaining spices indirectly through Macassar in Celebes (Sulawesi); in 1667 that source was dammed up through the Dutch conquest of the port.

The mainland monarchies of Arakan, Burma, Siam, Cambodia, Luang Prabang and Annam had little interest in European trade. They employed Portuguese adventurers as mercenaries in the 16th century, but the attempts of the latter to seize power in Lower Burma and Cambodia at the end of the century caused strong xenophobia. This increased in the next century as a result of the behaviour of the Portuguese freebooters (*feringhi*) and the attempts of the Dutch to monopolise Siam's foreign trade. To check the Dutch, King Narai (1661-88) and his Greek adviser, Constant Phaulkon, made the mistake of invoking French aid. Louis XIV's takeover bid, involving the planting of French garrisons at Bangkok and Mergui, stirred up strong popular reaction which led both to a change of dynasty at Ayutthaya and to the expulsion of the French, with heavy loss. Burma became the scene of dramatic events when the Mons rebelled in 1740 and set up a king of their own at Pegu. Their capture of the Burmese capital Ava in 1752 brought a new Burmese leader, Alaungpaya, to the fore. Josef Dupleix at Pondicherry intervened on the side of the Mons, and the English East India Company at Madras in reply seized the island of Negrais at the mouth of the Bassein river as a naval base. Alaungpaya defeated the Mons and their French allies, founding Rangoon in 1755 as the southern port of a reunited Burma. In 1759 he captured Negrais and the British left Burma.

By that time the English East India Company's expanding trade with China was causing it to look for a more southerly site for a naval station: ultimately in 1786 Penang was acquired for this purpose from the Sultan of Kedah. The conquest of Holland in 1795 by French revolutionary armies led to the British occupation of Malacca and of a number of Dutch settlements in the archipelago. In 1811 Java was conquered. After the fall of Napoleon in 1815, however, the British restored their possessions in South-East Asia to the Dutch. Trouble arose with the Dutch when Raffles acquired Singapore for the British, which was only settled by the Anglo-Dutch treaty of 1824 which drew a dividing line through the Straits of Malacca. As a result the British abandoned their west Sumatran settlements and the Dutch handed over Malacca and recognised British possession of Singapore. Borneo, omitted from the treaty, was to become the subject of further disagreement between the two parties when, in the 1840s, James Brooke became Rajah of Sarawak.

The aggressive dynasty founded by the Burmese leader Alaungpaya, after failing to make good its conquest of Siam in 1767, switched its efforts westwards to Arakan, Manipur and Assam, which it conquered and from which it threatened Bengal. Hence the first Anglo-Burmese war of 1824-26, which resulted in the annexation of Assam, Arakan and Tenasserim to British India and measures to stabilise India's north-eastern frontier. Arakan's once-famous rice industry revived through contact with India, but the great development of Burma's rice production only began after the British occupation

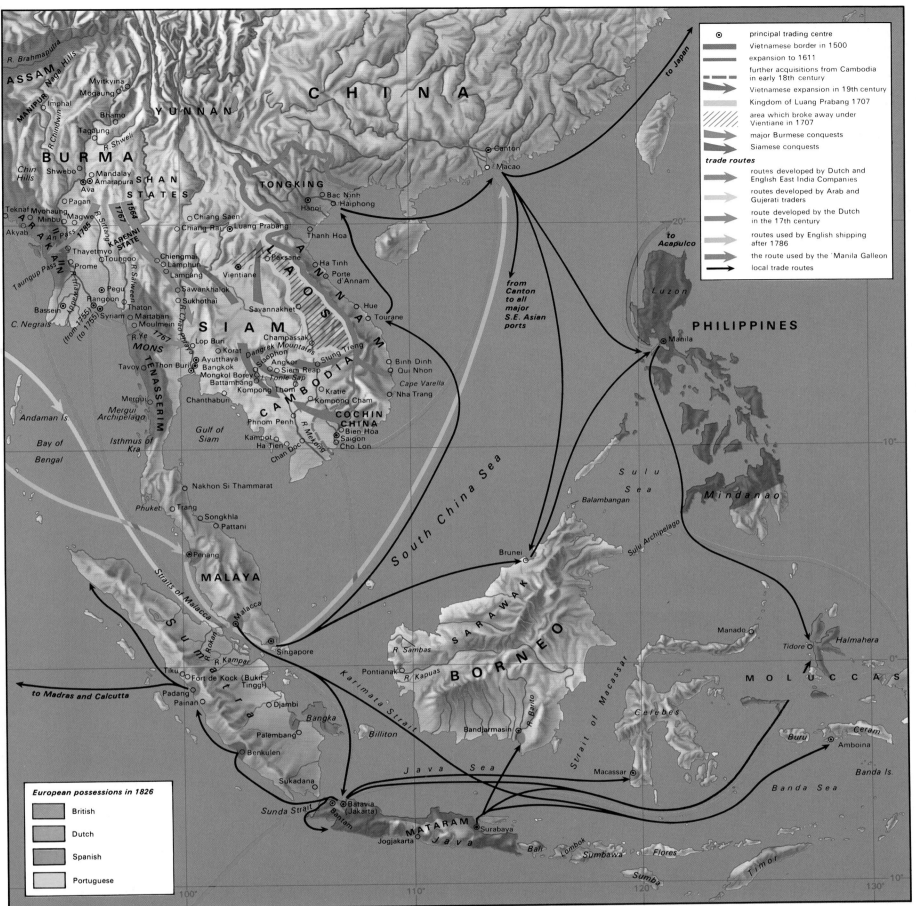

The map legend

⊙	principal trading centre
	Vietnamese border in 1500
	expansion to 1611
	further acquisitions from Cambodia in early 18th century
	Vietnamese expansion in 19th century
	Kingdom of Luang Prabang 1707
	area which broke away under Vientiane in 1707
	major Burmese conquests
	Siamese conquests

trade routes

	routes developed by Dutch and English East India Companies
	routes developed by Arab and Gujerati traders
	route developed by the Dutch in the 17th century
	routes used by English shipping after 1786
	the route used by the 'Manila Galleon
	local trade routes

European possessions in 1826

	British
	Dutch
	Spanish
	Portuguese

1/The Europeans in South-East Asia *(above)* The increasing European demand for spices and pepper led the maritime powers to seek direct trade with the islands producing them, thereby opening new fields for the missionary and the adventurer. The Dutch drove all their rivals out of the spice trade; Spain took over the Philippines. European activities made little impact upon the mainland monarchies, but in the 18th century brought coffee, China tea and chinoiserie into European social life.

of the Irrawaddy delta region after the second Anglo-Burmese war of 1852, as did the systematic exploitation of its teak forests.

European activities had comparatively little effect upon the economies of the South-East Asian states before the 19th century, when the Industrial Revolution created an increasing demand for raw materials, markets and openings for capital investment. Great Britain's impact was minimal until the foundation of Singapore in 1819 as a free trade port. Earlier, the Spaniards had sought to keep the Philippines *incommunicado*, but the Manila Galleon, trading with Acapulco (Mexico), brought the silver dollar into the international trade of the western Pacific. After the British occupation of 1762-64 had temporarily opened Manila to world commerce, the Spaniards began to foster the cultivation of tobacco, sugar, hemp and other commercial products, some of which became important in world markets, though not until 1834 was Manila officially opened to foreign traders.

At an earlier stage the Portuguese and the Dutch had forced their way into the long-established spice and pepper trades and their counterpart, the import of Indian textiles into South-East Asia. In the 18th century the Dutch introduced coffee cultivation into the parts of Java they directly controlled, but their policy of 'buy cheap, sell dear' bore heavily upon the peasantry. Nevertheless the principle of free peasant cultivation was maintained until 1830 when, with the introduction of the so-called 'Culture System', the Javanese were compelled to devote one-fifth of their land to export crops designated by the government.

Raffles *(right)* Appointed at the age of thirty as lieutenant-governor of British-occupied Java (1811-16), Raffles determined, after the restoration of the island empire of the Dutch, to seek a new focus for British power 'within its gates'. In 1819 he founded Singapore, permanently breaking the Dutch trading monopoly.

The European economy: agriculture and agricultural society 1500 to 1815

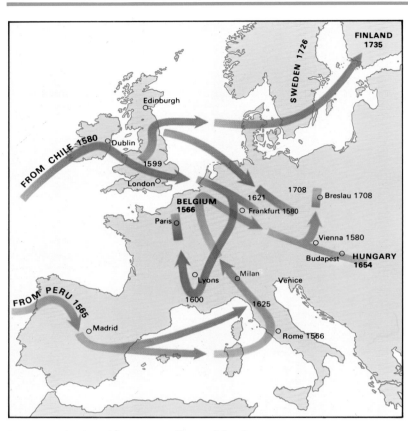

2/The introduction of the potato to Europe *(above)*
Yielding four times as much carbohydrate per acre as wheat, this South American import spread rapidly after its arrival in 1525 – first in gardens and small farms, then as a key field crop after 1700.

3/Land Reclamation in the Netherlands *(left)* Between 1540 and 1715 the people of Friesland, Zeeland and Holland wrested 364,565 acres from the sea, mainly around the river estuaries, and another 84,638 acres from around the edges of their inland lakes. Their capital-intensive methods, based on widespread use of windmills and pumps, were adapted, with great success, to draining the English Fenlands, and also more patchily in France, Italy and North Germany.

DURING this period Europe's agricultural economy as a whole improved only slowly, mainly in response to the needs of the steadily rising population. This is estimated to have grown from 69 to 188 million between 1500 and 1800, mainly in the towns and cities. But there were sharp regional contrasts. Whereas the majority of European farmers were subsistence peasants on smallholdings of from 2 to 10 hectares, the situation in north-west Europe, especially Belgium, Holland and Britain, was quite different. There an agricultural revolution, beginning in the 16th century, had produced a highly efficient, commercialised farming system by 1800. Most farms elsewhere, though, still consisted of many small parcels of ground distributed throughout the village lands. Each farm usually had a small adjacent enclosed paddock and sometimes an orchard. Techniques and levels of productivity had hardly changed since Roman times. Most peasants probably produced only about 20 per cent more each year than they needed to feed their families, their livestock and to provide for next year's seed. Consequently, in most countries about 80 per cent of the people worked on the land. But in Britain and the Low Countries, this fell rapidly in the 19th century. By 1811 the British proportion was already down to 33 per cent, releasing a huge workforce for the new mines, iron works and textile factories.

Most improvements in this period, apart from Britain and the Netherlands, came from the introduction of new, more productive crops, mainly from America. Thus the potato became a basic staple in western Europe. In Ireland it allowed so massive an increase in population (from 2.5 to 8 million) that disaster struck when the crop failed in 1846.

American maize, similarly introduced into southern Europe, gave a far higher yield per hectare than the old regional cereals – barley, millet and sorghum. Buckwheat, useful on poor soils, entered northern Europe from Russia. In the Mediterranean, sugar cane, rice and citrus fruits had arrived from Asia before 1500. Sugar production declined after 1550 in face of competition from Madeira, the Canaries and, after 1600, the West Indies and Brazil.

These slow crop changes contrasted strongly with the rapidly developing north-west. The Dutch began the process by pouring capital into reclaiming land from the sea. Naturally wishing to avoid leaving land fallow every third year (as under the old system), they discovered that fertility could be maintained by an elaborate rotation of crops, each removing different chemicals from the soils. Specially important were turnips (on which sheep could be grazed in winter, giving manure as well as mutton and wool), and peas, beans and clovers which actually restored nitrogen to the soil (though no one understood this at the time). England took these innovations much further. English farming was transformed by improved farm implements such as iron ploughs and Jethro Tull's seed drill, and such projects as extensive liming to neutralise soil acidity, irrigation and massive drainage. By 1750, 17 per cent of England's exports were foodstuffs and the old fear of famine had been banished.

Such techniques gradually spread as the growth of towns encouraged more specialisation in food production. Holland concentrated on dairy products and was exporting 90 per cent of her cheese by 1700. The Danes were sending 80,000 head of cattle a year to Germany, and the Dutch, German and Italian cloth industries were sustained by massive imports of Spanish wool. Spain, with 3 million sheep in the 16th century, gradually lost her lead to German wool and imported cotton. Trade grew between the cereals and timber of northern Europe and the fruit

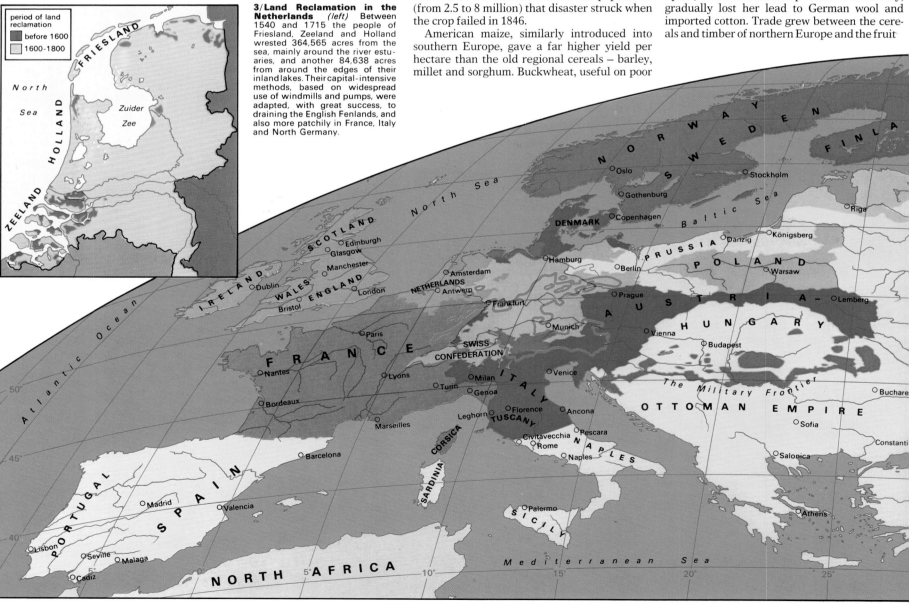

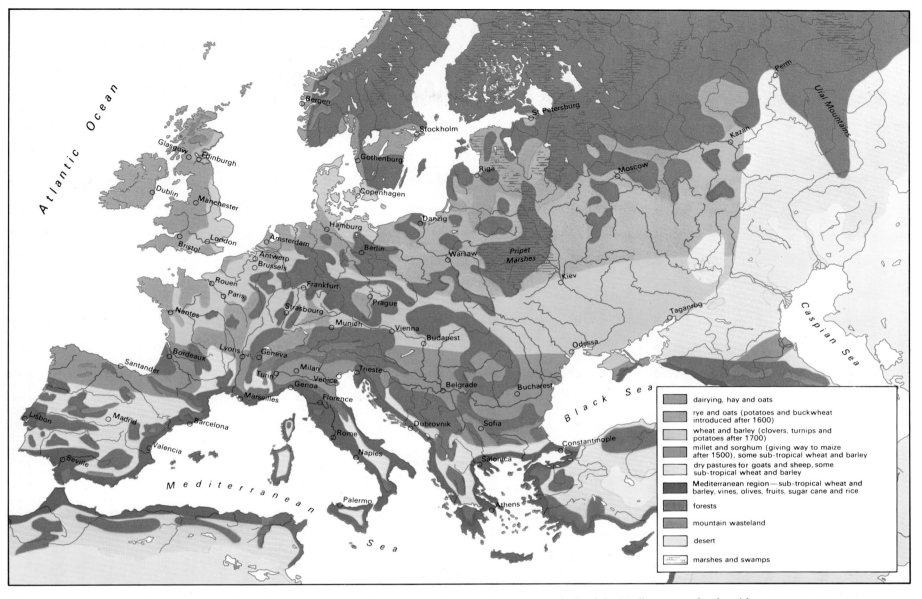

dairying, hay and oats

rye and oats (potatoes and buckwheat introduced after 1600)

wheat and barley (clovers, turnips and potatoes after 1700)

millet and sorghum (giving way to maize after 1500), some sub-tropical wheat and barley

dry pastures for goats and sheep, some sub-tropical wheat and barley

Mediterranean region—sub-tropical wheat and barley, vines, olives, fruits, sugar cane and rice

forests

mountain wasteland

desert

marshes and swamps

4/The agricultural regions of Europe *(above)* The main areas are shown as they were in 1600, distinguished by predominant activity or crops. Boundaries are only approximate. Potatoes gradually took over from cereals in many parts of northern and central Europe, while maize in the south replaced millet and sorghum.

1/The emancipation of the peasantry *(below)* By 1812, the peasants of Britain, Scandinavia and the Netherlands had long been free. Those of Denmark and the Habsburg's Austrian Empire, were encouraged in their efforts by the revolution of 1789, which unshackled the French peasantry and revivified emancipation movements in Poland and Germany, scene of the most famous peasant revolt (1525). Only Russia, Spain, Portugal and Southern Italy remained fully under the landlords' yoke.

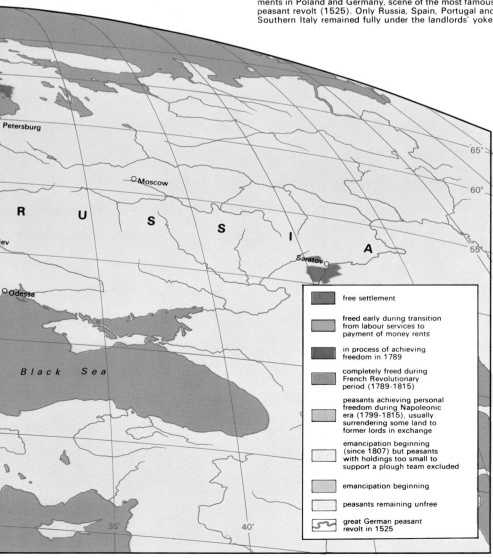

free settlement

freed early during transition from labour services to payment of money rents

in process of achieving freedom in 1789

completely freed during French Revolutionary period (1789-1815)

peasants achieving personal freedom during Napoleonic era (1799-1815), usually surrendering some land to former lords in exchange

emancipation beginning (since 1807) but peasants with holdings too small to support a plough team excluded

emancipation beginning

peasants remaining unfree

great German peasant revolt in 1525

wines and oils of the Mediterranean lands, with Danzig becoming a great export port, as did Leghorn, handling wine and fruit. Better farming not only released labour for industry but also helped to provide both capital and markets. In the 18th century, 15 per cent of British iron production was for horseshoes.

All improvements in productivity depended on breaking the old feudal relationships which oppressed the peasants. Here there was a sharp east-west cleavage. Prior to 1500 feudalism had been stronger in the older settled areas of western Europe than in the sparsely peopled lands of eastern Europe and Russia, where herdsmen still roamed. After 1500 this was completely changed. Peasants in north-west Europe exchanged the old labour services on the lords' land for a money rent (especially in England and the Netherlands) or for share-cropping tenancies *(métayage)* in France and further south. They also gradually freed themselves from burdensome personal services and dues, though this required revolutionary action, inspired by France in 1789, before it was complete.

In total contrast feudal power grew and spread in eastern Europe till it became almost slavery. Feudal lords increased their power, halting migration to empty lands further east (as in Russia) and increasing grain-export profits (as in eastern Germany and Poland-Lithuania). Free peasants only survived in newly conquered lands, when they agreed to perform military service instead of paying rent. Notable examples were the Volga Cossacks around Saratov and the settlers on the 'military frontier' in Hungary after it was freed from the Turks c. 1700-1710.

The peasants of western Germany occupied a middle position. They had tried to win complete freedom in a great revolt in 1525, partly inspired by Luther and the Swiss example. For a short time they controlled most of southern Germany before their revolt was savagely crushed. Yet the worst east European excesses were averted, and the peasants gradually moved towards greater freedom between 1600 and 1800. Their slow emancipation was, however, an important reason for the German industrial revolution coming so late.

Jethro Tull's Seed Drill *(above)* Described in Tull's *Horse Hoeing Husbandry* (1733) this machine gradually ousted the wasteful hand-scatterer.

Developments in Animal Breeding *(above)* Robert Bakewell's New Leicester long-wool sheep and greatly improved shire horses. John Ellman's short-wool breeds and the Colling brothers' short-horn cattle started a new world industry.

Crop Rotation *(above)* Fields, once left fallow one year out of two or three, now produced continuous yields.

The European economy: trade and industry 1500 to 1775

Baling press (above) from a German textile mill was used for preparing cloth for transportation. Even before 1700 expanding woollen and linen industries in Saxony and Bohemia began to encroach on the old English and Flemish markets.

3/Atlantic trade in the 18th century (left) Slaves and tropical produce from the new colonial empires made fortunes for all the main west European ports, from Cadiz to Glasgow shown here according to the size of their trade.

EUROPE'S population, expanding fast in the 16th century, was retarded by famine, plague and large-scale war in the 17th, and rapid growth was not resumed before the middle of the 18th century. The total nearly doubled overall during this period, and towns and cities grew even faster. In 1500 only four cities – Paris, Milan, Naples and Venice – had more than 100,000 inhabitants. By 1700 this number had trebled, and London, Paris and Constantinople had passed the half-million mark.

Increased complexity of government, a marked stepping-up of trade and finance, a growing taste for organised pleasure and conspicuous consumption, and a feeling that survival was better assured in the cities, all helped to hasten this trend. The resulting problems, particularly the need to guarantee large and reliable urban food supplies, also created new opportunities. Most notably, they generated a massive demand for eastern Europe's wheat and rye. In the century down to 1650, great quantities were going to western Europe, reaching even as far as Portugal, Spain and Italy. This trade fed the burgeoning economic strength of Holland, now nearly monopolising the Baltic carrying trade.

The Netherlands, whose shipbuilders, merchants and manufacturers consistently maintained a leading position in this period, formed the hinge for a gradual but decisive shift in commercial power. In 1500 industry remained largely concentrated in the narrow corridor running from Antwerp and Bruges, through Ulm and Augsburg, thence to Florence and Milan. Although English woollens, French linens and Spanish iron all possessed international reputations and markets, the main non-agricultural activity, whether it was in textiles and weapons, or in newer developments like paper, glass, printing and cloth-making, all lay along this north-south line. By 1700 this north-south axis had swung almost through ninety degrees. At one end stood England and Holland, the greatest textile producers of Europe, and also owners of the greatest merchant fleets, the most active traders, and with fast-developing manufacturers of ships and metalwares; eastward the line extended through the metal and woollen districts of the lower Rhine to the great industrial concentrations in the hills of Saxony, Bohemia and Silesia. Even huge and backward Russia was beginning to build up, for the first time since the Mongols, its own industrial base. But the great trading cities of northern Italy and the southern Netherlands, dominant two centuries earlier, were mostly stagnant after a severe decline.

The advance of technology was patchy and intermittent. The power-driven silk mills of the Po valley were the mechanical wonders of the

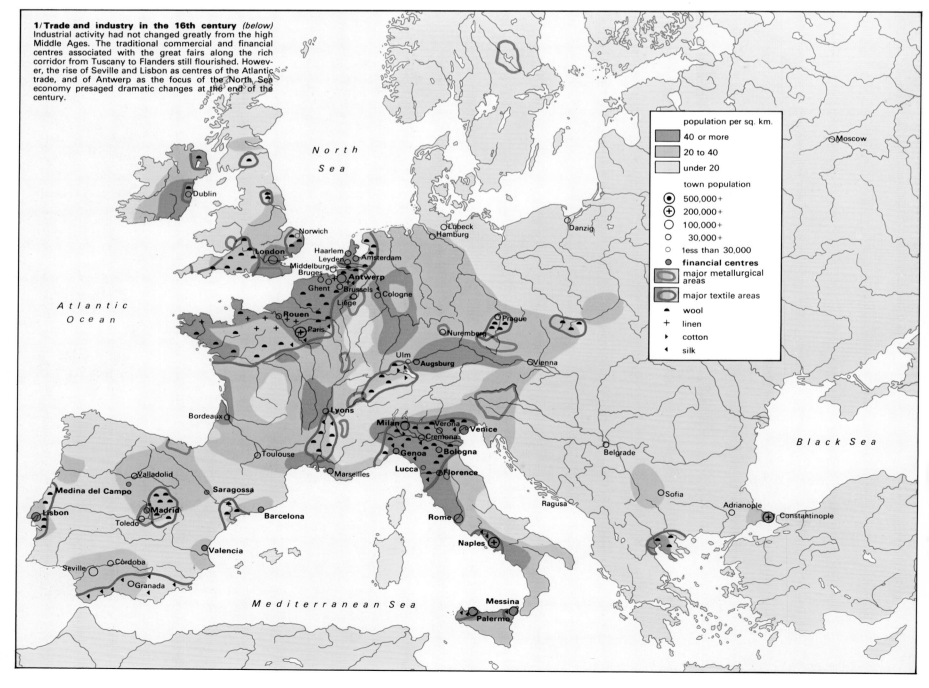

1/Trade and industry in the 16th century (below) Industrial activity had not changed greatly from the high Middle Ages. The traditional commercial and financial centres associated with the great fairs along the rich corridor from Tuscany to Flanders still flourished. However, the rise of Seville and Lisbon as centres of the Atlantic trade, and of Antwerp as the focus of the North Sea economy presaged dramatic changes at the end of the century.

population per sq. km.
- 40 or more
- 20 to 40
- under 20

town population
- 500,000+
- 200,000+
- 100,000+
- 30,000+
- less than 30,000
- financial centres
- major metallurgical areas
- major textile areas
- wool
- linen
- cotton
- silk

17th century, but produced little imitation. The spread of watch-making in the early 18th century created a repository of precision skills, and Newcomen's mine pump opened the way to the advance of the steam engine. But the crucial breakthrough to the age of steam, James Watt's separate condenser (1769), made its industrial impact only in the last years of the century. Industrial expansion was achieved by increasing the number of workers while still using the old methods. Even this, however, helped improve industrial organisation, by splitting up production processes, developing production in rural areas free of urban restriction, and drawing on the cheap part-time labour of peasant families. Wool, linen and much metal manufacture was controlled by traders who organised a scattered cottage labour force. By the 18th century this had become the typical form of all but local and luxury industry.

More impressive than the slow and erratic spread of industry was the striking increase in international trade. No longer confined to Europe, the maritime powers, with their colonies and trading ports established all over Asia and the Americas, attracted a fast-growing stream of new exotic tropical products: tea, coffee, sugar, chocolate, tobacco. They were paid for with European manufactures – the British linen and metalware industries particularly thrived on the expanding colonial markets – and with the shipping, insurance and merchanting services that built up the wealth of the western ports, all the way from Bordeaux up to London and Glasgow and even Hamburg. All these became the seats of wealthy merchant firms and great shipping interests.

Governments assisted the sectors of economic activity they favoured. Holland and England waged wars to protect and expand their shipping and trading interests, but did not consistently aid industry. The governments of France and central European states established new industries and gave protection and subsidies to old ones. Increasingly costly wars, however, had an influence even more powerful than explicit economic policies. They called for heavy taxation, with the burdens falling largely on the producing classes, and large borrowings that undermined the precarious stability of Europe's gradually evolving monetary systems. These were ruinous to Spain and damaging to France and many smaller states; only Holland and England kept their military commitments within realistic financial bounds.

Trade and war also generated an unprecedented demand for money. After being desperately short, gold and silver were amply supplied from Spanish Mexico and Peru after 1550, supported from the 1690s by Brazilian gold. This bullion was redistributed all over Europe by merchants and by Spanish government transactions, and much of it went to finance large trade deficits with the East Indies and the Levant. The money supply was supplemented by the growth of banking in western Europe. Breaking away from the older banking methods of Italy and the German towns, which were heavily engaged in government lending, Dutch and English banks served private interests with giro and foreign exchange facilities and short-term credits. For a century, almost from its opening in 1609, the Amsterdam Exchange Bank, with its links in every important commercial centre, was the undisputed focus of continental trade; England could compete with it only when, in 1694, the Bank of England provided a focus for older private banking firms. With low interest rates, free capital movement, secure international payments and an assured savings flow, the foundations of modern finance were now firmly laid in England and Holland.

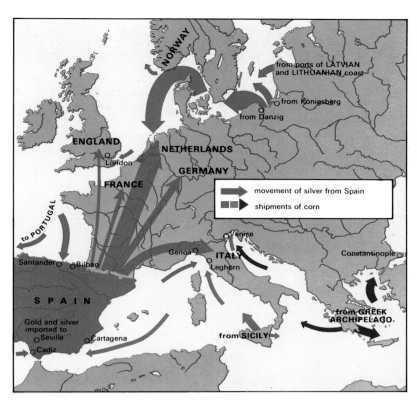

4/ Grain trade and silver flows within Europe 1550-1650 *(above)* The bullion-bearing galleons from the Indies brought a flood of liquid funds to the Spanish treasury. But it flowed out as fast as it arrived, to finance the Habsburgs and to pay for the Baltic grain now needed to victual a Mediterranean no longer able to feed itself.

2/ Trade and industry in the 18th century *(below)* Even before the Industrial Revolution, there has been a dramatic change. Italy and Spain have fallen back, while England, with major metal-working and mining interests, Holland, building ships for the whole of Europe, France behind a high protective wall, and Sweden, exploiting her mineral resources, are all developing fast.

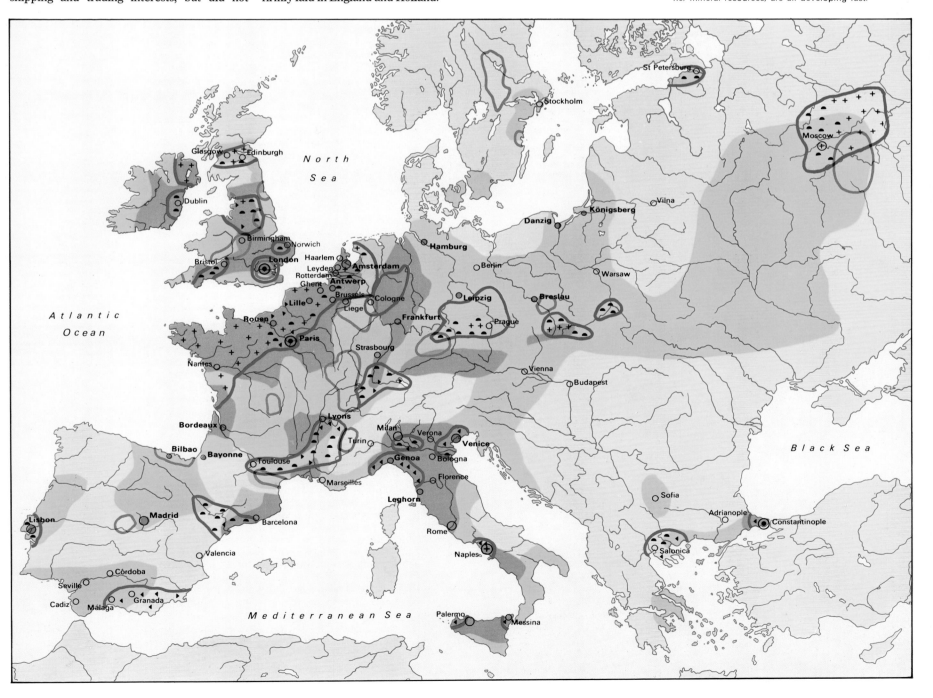

Reformation and counter- reformation: the wars of religion in Europe 1517 to 164

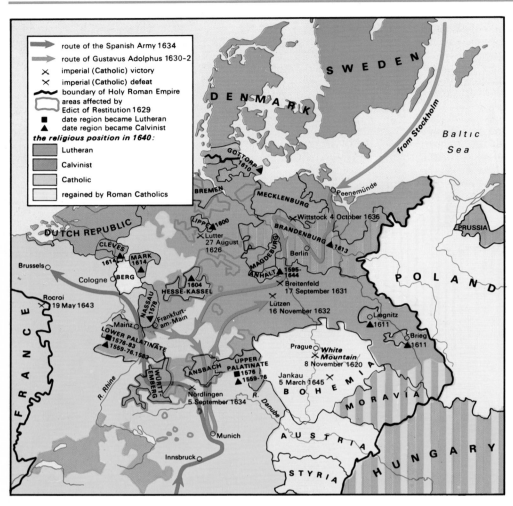

Legend:
- route of the Spanish Army 1634
- route of Gustavus Adolphus 1630-2
- × imperial (Catholic) victory
- × imperial (Catholic) defeat
- boundary of Holy Roman Empire
- areas affected by Edict of Restitution 1629
- ■ date region became Lutheran
- ▲ date region became Calvinist

the religious position in 1640:
- Lutheran
- Calvinist
- Catholic
- regained by Roman Catholics

2 and 3/Religious conflict to 1640 By 1640, the Protestant hold on Europe had weakened. Although the Mediterranean lands were still Catholic and the countries on the northern periphery were still Protestant, there were major changes in France (*below*) and the Holy Roman Empire (*above*). In the former, four decades of intermittent civil war and occasional massacres reduced the Huguenots, as French Protestants were called, to a small area around La Rochelle and a rather larger area in the south. Another period of war, from 1621-29, reduced their territories even further and in 1685 Protestantism was forbidden. The Thirty Years War (*above*) extirpated Protestantism in the Habsburgs' patrimonial lands, but not in north Germany, thanks to military intervention by Denmark (1624-29), Sweden (after 1630) and France (after 1635) on the side of the Protestants.

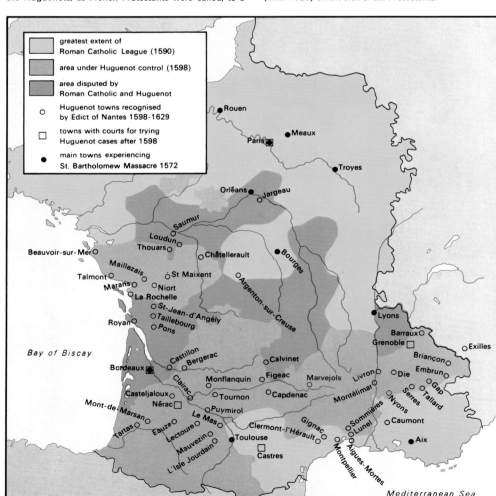

Legend:
- greatest extent of Roman Catholic League (1590)
- area under Huguenot control (1598)
- area disputed by Roman Catholic and Huguenot
- ○ Huguenot towns recognised by Edict of Nantes 1598-1629
- □ towns with courts for trying Huguenot cases after 1598
- ● main towns experiencing St. Bartholomew Massacre 1572

RELIGION held a central place in the lives of the people of early modern Europe. It elevated and dignified every major action in their lives, from birth and baptism to death and burial, and it held out the hope of salvation. The need for reassurance about the after-life appears to have been particularly acute in the years around 1500.

At first this spiritual revival was contained within the existing churches: Roman Catholic in the west and Greek Orthodox in the east, with the frontier running through Poland-Lithuania (two-fifths Orthodox) and to the south of Hungary to reach the Adriatic just south of Ragusa. The only important groups outside these two monolithic communities were the Jews, the Lollards (a small and fragmented group of English dissenters), a few Moors in southern Spain, and the Hussites (including over half the population of Bohemia and Moravia). 'Heresy' was thus virtually dead in 1500 and, faced by no substantial rivals, the Roman Catholic church became complacent and failed to deploy its wealth adequately to satisfy the 'spiritual hunger' of the early 16th century. Absenteeism, for example, was growing among the clergy and there were enough ignorant and immoral priests to discredit the Church in the eyes of many laymen. It was the conjuncture of a spiritually bankrupt yet materially acquisitive church at a time of heightened religious awareness which explains why a religious revolution occurred in the 16th century.

Within only fifty years almost 40 per cent of the inhabitants of Europe observed a 'Reformed' theology. The first reformers came from Germany and German-speaking Switzerland, led by Martin Luther (1483-1546) in Saxony and north Germany, and Huldreich Zwingli (1484-1531) in Zurich (the first state to renounce allegiance to Rome, in 1520) and the surrounding towns of south Germany. By 1570, out of every ten subjects of the Holy Roman Emperor, seven were Protestants. The Protestants already held Scandinavia, Baltic Europe, and England. There was a limited penetration of France, Spain, Italy and the Netherlands, and of the German settlements in eastern Europe.

Then came a new wave of Protestantism, the work of John Calvin (1509-64), a Frenchman, who implemented his ideas from 1541 in the city-state of Geneva. Calvinism made swift progress: in France there were over a hundred Calvinist churches by 1559 and perhaps 700 by 1562; in the Netherlands, there were perhaps 20 Calvinist churches by 1559 and over 150 by 1566; in Germany, several Lutheran states (most notably the Palatinate and Brandenburg) changed their official religion to Calvinism; and in Scotland a complete reformed polity was established by act of Parliament in 1560. Calvin's church also achieved some striking successes in eastern Europe, especially in Poland and Transylvania, two countries which also tolerated the existence of other minority groups in some numbers: Unitarians, Bohemian Brethren, Anabaptists and Jews. In Hungary and in other areas under Ottoman control, Catholic worship was prohibited and Calvinism received official protection. Calvinism also won more adherents among the Slavs, both noble and middle class, than Lutheranism.

The toleration of Protestantism was often fragile, however. In many countries, including the Holy Roman Empire, it was the product of weakness rather than strength, and it only occurred in countries where the state was not strong enough to impose the religious uniformity which in early modern times was considered essential to political survival. It was inevitable that the 'states without stakes' would perish as soon as their governments became powerful enough to enforce the chosen faith on all their subjects. What was not inevitable was that the

1/Religion in Europe in 15
The initial impact of the Reformtion was felt over almost Europe. Even Spain, Portugal Italy – which ultimately remai wholly Catholic – were affec by Protestantism. France Poland, two of the largest sta of the continent, although ev tually brought back to Rom Catholicism, seemed in 1560 to well on the way to a Protest takeover, with organised churc spread over most of the coun Only the Orthodox believers in east remained indifferent to message of Luther, Zwingli, Cal and other leading reformers.

- Roman Catholic
- Calvinist
- Lutheran
- Anglican
- Hussite
- Orthodox
- Muslim
- ■ Date of change from Cath to Lutheranism
- ▲ Date of change to Calvinis Zwinglianism
- ● Anabaptist minorities
- △ Calvinist minorities
- ▽ Lutheran minorities
- ◐ Roman Catholic minorities
- □ Muslim minorities
there were scattered Jewis communities in the Ottoman Empire, Hungary, Poland, Portugal, Bohemia and Italy

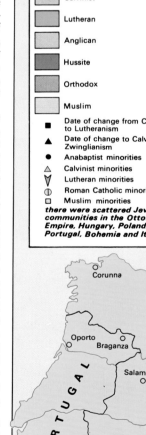

chosen faith after 1570 should so often have been Catholicism.

Not all the men who wished to reform the Church in the earlier 16th century rejected the authority of the Pope. St Ignatius Loyola (1491-1556), who founded the Jesuit order, was just one of the many who decided that the best way to achieve salvation was to remain obedient to Rome and to persuade others to do the same. From 1540 onwards, even the Papacy began to accept the need for some reforms, and a General Council of the Church was summoned to meet at Trent, on the border between Italy and Germany. There were three sessions (1545-47, 1551-52 and 1562-63) which achieved three things: the worst clerical abuses were condemned; the correct doctrine of the Church was defined (the *professio fidei tridentina*); and an efficient system of ecclesiastical supervision, to maintain clerical standards, was established. In addition, an educational offensive was mounted to promote orthodoxy among the laity.

With the aid of this revitalised organisation, the Catholic Church began to regain some of its losses. The Protestant 'share' of the European continent fell from 40 to 20 per cent between 1570 and 1650. In Poland, the largest country of eastern Europe, a succession of Catholic kings actively favoured Catholicism, and the number of Protestant churches in the country fell from around 560 in 1572 to only 240 in 1650. Much the same happened in the Habsburg lands further south: the Protestants were expelled from Austria (1597) and from Styria (1600). In France, the crown waged war for decades in order to beat off the Protestant challenge. Although there were perhaps 1¼ million Protestants in France in 1562, by 1629 there were only 1 million and by 1685, when the remainder was forced to choose between conversion to Catholicism or expulsion, there were scarcely 500,000.

The decisive phase of the struggle between Protestants and Catholics took place in the Holy Roman Empire. It began in 1618-21 when the Emperor, Ferdinand II, with the aid of troops and treasure from Spain, the German Catholics and the Papacy, defeated the Bohemian Protestants. Catholicism soon became the only permit- ted religion in Bohemia and Moravia. Encouraged by this success, the Emperor tried to reduce the power of the Protestant princes in Germany. Despite the aid sent to them by England, Denmark and the Dutch, in 1629 the Emperor's forces were victorious and an 'Edict of Restitution' was issued which reclaimed large areas of Church land held by the Protestants. The German Protestants were only saved from collapse by the arrival of substantial military aid from King Gustavus Adolphus of Sweden: the Emperor's forces were defeated at Breitenfeld (1631) and Lützen (1632). Spain soon intervened to help the Emperor; France to help his enemies. The war had become a free-for-all with fighting the political as well as the religious rivalries of over a century were settled at the great battles of Nördlingen (1634), Wittstock (1636), Rocroi (1643) and Jankau (1646), and at the peace of Münster-Westphalia which followed. The religious and political frontiers of central Europe which were then agreed lasted unchanged for a hundred years.

Spreading the word of God *(above)* Of the 250,000 or so works printed in Europe between 1447 (the date of the earliest surviving printed book) and 1600, about three-quarters were written about religion. The Reformation would have been impossible without printing-presses like this one, which graced the cover of a book printed in Paris in 1511.

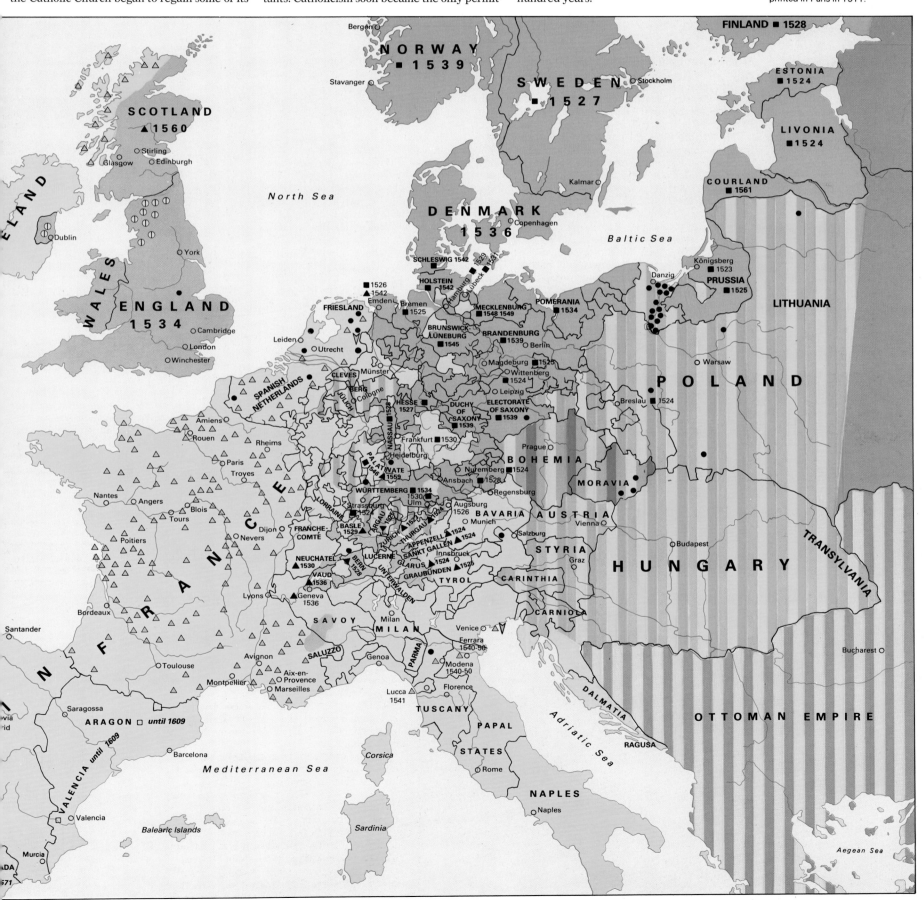

The rise of the modern state in north-west Europe 1500 to 1688

The Universal Soldier *(above)*
This cartoon, first printed in the 1640s as propaganda against the English Parliamentary army in Ireland, reflects the civilians' hatred of the ill-fed soldier who enforced government policies while taking everything he needed from the local people – down to the sausages of his shoe buckles!

DESPITE their apparent strength, until 1660 the 'new monarchies' of Europe (see page 150) never entirely escaped from the framework of government which they inherited from earlier times. Their wealth, bureaucracies, control of religion and standing armies were not sufficient to break the patterns of personal dependence which had characterised monarchy in the feudal period (see page 124). The state still relied on the goodwill of its nobles for the enforcement of its policies (in England, for example, the Tudors depended upon unpaid Justices of the Peace, always local landowners, to apply their laws), and failure to retain the support of the landed classes could provoke major revolts. The French aristocracy staged several rebellions against the crown, culminating in the Fronde (1648-53); a section of the English aristocracy rebelled against Elizabeth I in 1569-70 (the 'Northern Rising') and many English peers supported Parliament's stand against Charles I after 1640; nobles of the Netherlands opposed their 'natural prince', Philip II of Spain, in 1566 and 1576.

The Fronde, the English Civil War and the Dutch Revolt were only the most important of the rebellions which threatened the 'new monarchies' of north-western Europe: uprisings against the state were a continuing fact of life throughout the 16th and 17th centuries. Some revolts arose from attacks on the privileges of the 'estates'; others were caused by economic hardship – from taxes imposed at a time of high prices and widespread unemployment, as was the case in most French popular revolts, or from the enclosing of common land, which caused the revolts of 1549 and 1607 in England; other uprisings (the Pilgrimage of Grace in England in 1536 and the Covenanting Movement in Scotland in 1638) were triggered off by unpopular religious policies. In all cases the revolts were a response to attempts at innovation. Governments everywhere were endeavouring to create, in the words of James VI of Scotland soon after he became king of England in 1603: 'one worship to God, one kingdom entirely governed, one uniformity of laws'. The problem, however, was one of means, not ends. Neither James nor any of his fellow sovereigns had the resources to enforce such ambitious new policies. They lacked the revenues and the officials required. Even in France, which had the largest civil service in Europe, most of the 40,000 royal officials bought their offices or acquired them by hereditary succession and could pursue a course independent of the crown. They became a distinct aristocratic caste – the *noblesse de robe*.

The barriers to centralisation in early modern times were formidable. Many subjects did not speak the same language as their government (Breton and Provençal in France, Cornish and Welsh in England, Frisian in the Netherlands); there were many 'dark corners of the land' which were too inaccessible to be effectively governed; certain 'corporations', notably the Church, possessed privileges which protected them against state interference; and provinces recently annexed by the crown (see page 150) were protected by charters guaranteeing their traditional way of life. It was when the state tried to erode or remove these privileges that the most serious political upheavals occurred. The Dutch rebelled in 1566, 1572 and 1576 largely because they believed that the central government, controlled from Spain, threatened their traditional liberties; and they continued their armed opposition until in 1609 Spain in effect recognised the independence of the seven provinces still in rebellion. The Dutch Republic was born (see map 1). In England, Parliament began a civil war against Charles I in 1642 because it believed that he intended to destroy the established rights of 'free-born Englishmen'; they too maintained their armed resistance, with the help of the Scots, until the power of the king was shattered in battle, and Charles himself was tried and executed in 1649 (see map 2). The English Republic, which survived for eleven years under the Lord Protector, Oliver Cromwell, immediately set about reducing the independence of Scotland and Ireland. Although Charles' son was restored in 1660 with full powers and even a small standing army, another revolt in 1688, supported by the Dutch, drove James II into exile and ensured that the power of the crown in England would never again be absolute. Although opposition in France did not go to such lengths, the absolutist policies and fiscal exactions of Cardinal Mazarin (1602-61), chief minister of Louis XIV, so alienated the crown's officials, the nobles and the people of Paris that in 1649 they drove the king from his capital and forced him to make major concessions. Royal control was not fully restored until 1655.

In all three countries, however, the structure of the state survived. None of the rebels seriously questioned the need for strong government, only the location of that strength. 'The question was never whether we should be governed by arbitrary power, but in whose hands it should be,' wrote an English republican in 1653, and in England the 'great rebellion' gave rise to a really modern state. After 1660, even more after 1688, power was shared between Parliament, representing merchants and landowners, and the crown; but the power was absolute, even after 1707, when Scotland was incorporated to form Great Britain. In France, the failure of the Fronde cleared the way for the absolutism of Louis XIV (see page 192). In both France and England the last major effort to resist the rise of the central power and defend local autonomy had failed; there was to be no further 'great rebellion' for over a century. The Dutch Revolt, however, did protect local independence against central encroachment. Despite the preponderance of Holland within the Republic, the other six provinces retained a large measure of autonomy. But this decentralised system, reminiscent of the 15th century, seriously weakened the Dutch, particularly in commercial competition with France and Britain. The Dutch were at a permanent disadvantage in a world which permitted no profit without power and no security without war. No sooner had they broken free of Spain (the independence asserted in 1609 was formally recognised in 1648) than they were attacked on land by France (1672-78 and 1689-1713), and at sea by England (1652-3, 1665-7 and 1672-4). The strain and expense of these wars proved too much, and Dutch strength declined. The 18th century and its profits – particularly in the colonial world – would belong to the newly arisen modern states, France and Great Britain.

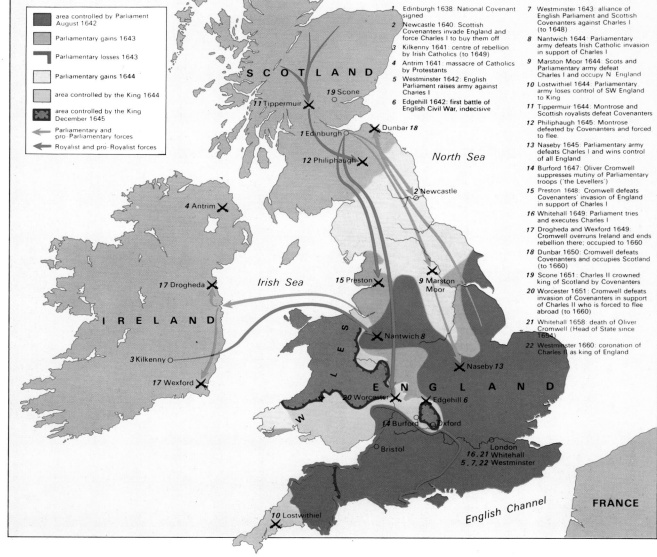

area controlled by Parliament August 1642

Parliamentary gains 1643

Parliamentary losses 1643

Parliamentary gains 1644

area controlled by the King 1644

area controlled by the King December 1645

Parliamentary and pro-Parliamentary forces

Royalist and pro-Royalist forces

1 Edinburgh 1638: National Covenant signed
2 Newcastle 1640: Scottish Covenanters invade England and force Charles I to buy them off
3 Kilkenny 1641: centre of rebellion by Irish Catholics (to 1649)
4 Antrim 1641: massacre of Catholics by Protestants
5 Westminster 1642: English Parliament raises army against Charles I
6 Edgehill 1642: first battle of English Civil War, indecisive
7 Westminster 1643: alliance of English Parliament and Scottish Covenanters against Charles I (to 1648)
8 Nantwich 1644: Parliamentary army defeats Irish Catholic invasion in support of Charles I
9 Marston Moor 1644: Scots and Parliamentary army defeat Charles I and occupy N England
10 Lostwithiel 1644: Parliamentary army loses control of SW England to King
11 Tippermuir 1644: Montrose and Scottish royalists defeat Covenanters
12 Philiphaugh 1645: Montrose defeated by Covenanters and forced to flee
13 Naseby 1645: Parliamentary army defeats Charles I and wins control of all England
14 Burford 1647: Oliver Cromwell suppresses mutiny of Parliamentary troops ('the Levellers')
15 Preston 1648: Cromwell defeats Covenanters' invasion of England in support of Charles I
16 Whitehall 1649: Parliament tries and executes Charles I
17 Drogheda and Wexford 1649: Cromwell overruns Ireland and ends rebellion there; occupied to 1660
18 Dunbar 1650: Cromwell defeats Covenanters and occupies Scotland (to 1660)
19 Scone 1651: Charles II crowned king of Scotland by Covenanters
20 Worcester 1651: Cromwell defeats invasion of Covenanters in support of Charles II who is forced to flee abroad (to 1660)
21 Whitehall 1658: death of Oliver Cromwell (Head of State since 1649)
22 Westminster 1660: coronation of Charles II as king of England

2/The English Civil War, 1642-5 *(left)*   At first, most of the north and west of England rallied to Charles I, most of the east and south supported Parliament, and Scotland stayed neutral. The campaigns of 1642 brought small Parliamentary gains in the north-west but heavy losses in the south-west, and the king seemed likely to win until in 1644 Parliament secured the support of the Scottish Covenanters (who had signed the National Covenant in 1638 to protect Scotland against the 'popish practices' imposed by Charles I). In 1645 Charles was decisively defeated at Naseby and his Scottish lieutenant, Montrose, was routed at Philiphaugh, but the king managed to ally with the Covenanters against Parliament. In 1647 the Parliamentary army was weakened by mutinies in favour of a more democratic government (the 'Leveller' movement) but the troubles were suppressed swiftly and the army moved on to defeat the Covenanters at Preston (1648), Dunbar (1650) and Worcester (1651) and to subjugate Ireland (1649). Charles I was tried and executed (1649) and the army established a Republic which controlled the entire British Isles until 1660 when monarchy was restored.

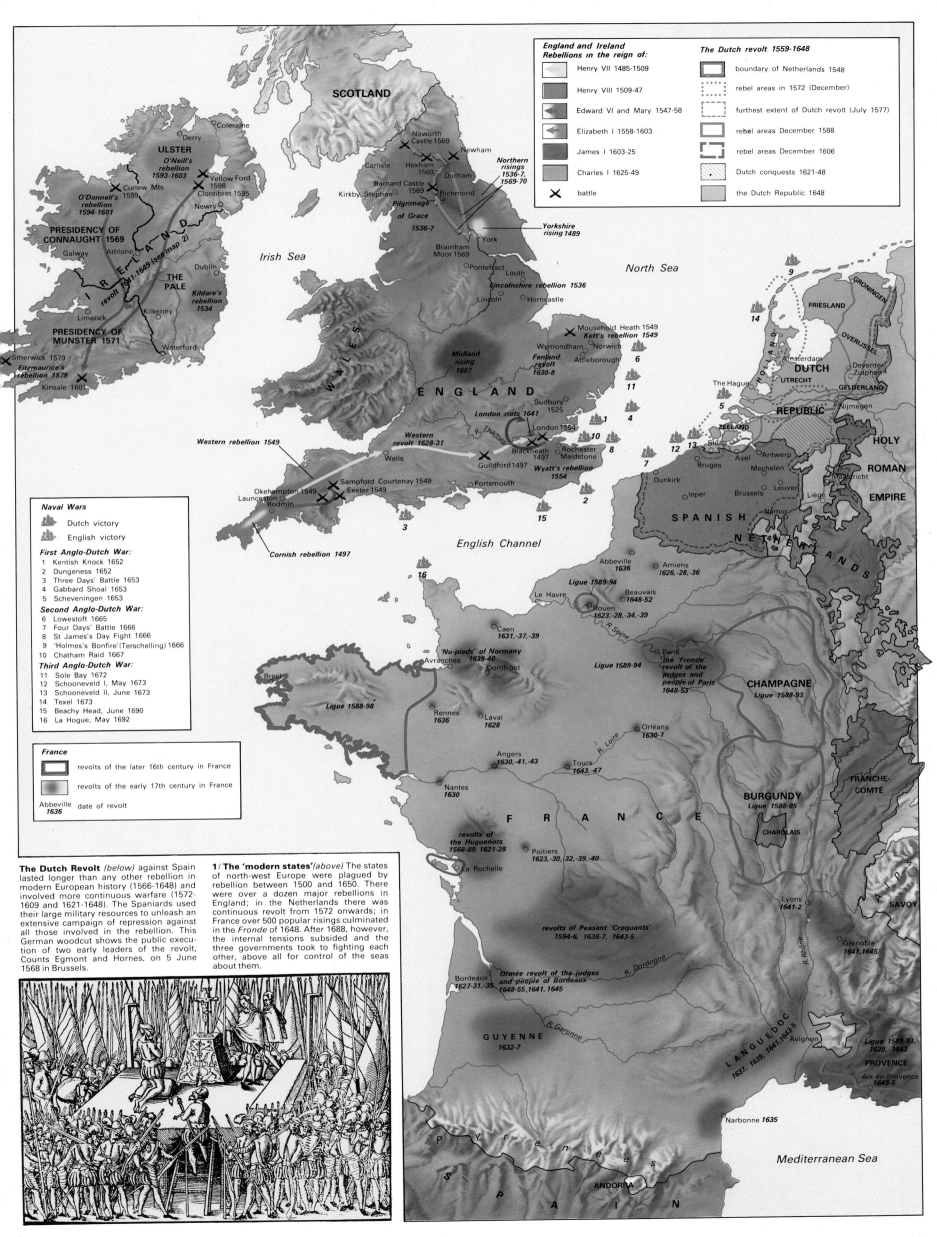

England and Ireland
Rebellions in the reign of:

Henry VII 1485-1509
Henry VIII 1509-47
Edward VI and Mary 1547-58
Elizabeth I 1558-1603
James I 1603-25
Charles I 1625-49
✕ battle

The Dutch revolt 1559-1648

boundary of Netherlands 1548
rebel areas in 1572 (December)
furthest extent of Dutch revolt (July 1577)
rebel areas December 1588
rebel areas December 1606
Dutch conquests 1621-48
the Dutch Republic 1648

Naval Wars

⚓ Dutch victory
⚓ English victory

First Anglo-Dutch War:
1 Kentish Knock 1652
2 Dungeness 1652
3 Three Days' Battle 1653
4 Gabbard Shoal 1653
5 Scheveningen 1653

Second Anglo-Dutch War:
6 Lowestoft 1665
7 Four Days' Battle 1666
8 St James's Day Fight 1666
9 'Holmes's Bonfire'(Terschelling) 1666
10 Chatham Raid 1667

Third Anglo-Dutch War:
11 Sole Bay 1672
12 Schooneveld I, May 1673
13 Schooneveld II, June 1673
14 Texel 1673
15 Beachy Head, June 1690
16 La Hogue, May 1692

France

revolts of the later 16th century in France
revolts of the early 17th century in France
Abbeville 1636 date of revolt

SCOTLAND

ULSTER
Derry
Coleraine
O'Neill's rebellion 1593-1603
Naworth Castle 1569
Newham
Curlew Mts 1599
Yellow Ford 1598
Clontibret 1595
Carlisle
Hexham 1569
Durham
O'Donnell's rebellion 1594-1601
Barnard Castle 1569
Richmond
Kirkby Stephen
PRESIDENCY OF CONNAUGHT 1569
Galway
Athlone
THE PALE
Dublin
revolt 1641-1649 (see map 2)
Kildare's rebellion 1534
Limerick
Kilkenny
PRESIDENCY OF MUNSTER 1571
Waterford
Smerwick 1579
Fitzmaurice's rebellion 1579
Kinsale 1601

IRELAND
Irish Sea
WALES
ENGLAND

Newham
Northern risings 1536-7, 1569-70
York
Yorkshire rising 1489
Pilgrimage of Grace 1536-7
Bramham Moor 1569
Pontefract
Louth
Lincolnshire rebellion 1536
Lincoln
Horncastle
Mousehold Heath 1549
Kett's rebellion 1549
Wymondham
Norwich
Attleborough
Fenland revolt 1630-8
Midland rising 1607
Sudbury 1525
London riots 1641
London 1554
Western revolt 1628-31
Blackheath 1497
Rochester
Maidstone
Wells
Guildford 1497
Wyatt's rebellion 1554
Western rebellion 1549
Sampford Courtenay 1549
Okehampton 1549
Launceston
Exeter 1549
Bodmin
Portsmouth
Cornish rebellion 1497

North Sea
FRIESLAND
GRONINGEN
OVERIJSSEL
Amsterdam
DUTCH
REPUBLIC
Deventer
Zutphen
UTRECHT
The Hague
GELDERLAND
Nijmegen
ZEELAND
Sluis
HOLY
ROMAN
EMPIRE
Antwerp
Axel
Mechelen
Maastricht
Bruges
Dunkirk
Brussels
Leuven
ieper
Liège
SPANISH
Namur
NETHERLANDS

English Channel

Abbeville 1636
Amiens 1626,-28,-36
Ligue 1589-94
Beauvais 1648-52
Le Havre
Rouen 1623,-28,-34,-39
Caen 1631,-37,-39
Paris the 'Fronde' revolt of the judges and people of Paris 1648-53
CHAMPAGNE
Ligue 1588-93
'Nu-pieds' of Normany 1639-40
Avranches
Domfront
Ligue 1589-94
Brest
Ligue 1588-98
Rennes 1636
Laval 1628
Orléans 1630-1
FRANCE
Angers 1630,-41,-43
Tours 1643,-47
Nantes 1630
BURGUNDY
Ligue 1588-95
CHAROLAIS
FRANCHE-COMTÉ
revolts of the Huguenots 1568-89, 1621-28
Poitiers 1623,-30,-32,-39,-40
La Rochelle
revolts of Peasant 'Croquants' 1594-6, 1636-7, 1643-5
Lyons 1641-2
ALPS
SAVOY
Bordeaux 1627-31,-35
Ormée revolt of the judges and people of Bordeaux 1648-55, 1641, 1645
R. Dordogne
GUYENNE 1632-7
R. Garonne
LANGUEDOC 1637, 1639, 1641/1643-5
Avignon
Grenoble 1641,1645
Ligue 1589-93, 1639, 1643
PROVENCE
Aix-en-Provence 1643-5
Narbonne 1635
PYRENEES
SPAIN
ANDORRA
Mediterranean Sea

The Dutch Revolt (below) against Spain lasted longer than any other rebellion in modern European history (1566-1648) and involved more continuous warfare (1572-1609 and 1621-1648). The Spaniards used their large military resources to unleash an extensive campaign of repression against all those involved in the rebellion. This German woodcut shows the public execution of two early leaders of the revolt, Counts Egmont and Hornes, on 5 June 1568 in Brussels.

1/ The 'modern states'(above) The states of north-west Europe were plagued by rebellion between 1500 and 1650. There were over a dozen major rebellions in England; in the Netherlands there was continuous revolt from 1572 onwards; in France over 500 popular risings culminated in the *Fronde* of 1648. After 1688, however, the internal tensions subsided and the three governments took to fighting each other, above all for control of the seas about them.

The Mediterranean world 1494 to 1797

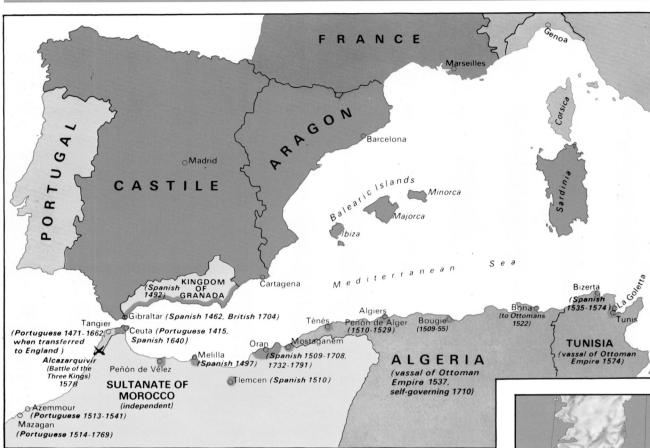

2/Spain in the Maghreb *(left)* Spanish conquests in North Africa were originally an extension of the Christian 'Reconquest'. After the capture of Granada (1492) this 'crusade' against the Moors was carried across the straits, and successive fortresses in Morocco and Algeria were taken. But after 1510 the process was halted as Spain became more deeply involved in its Aragonese inheritance in Italy. The expeditions against Tunis in 1535, after the victory in Italy, and in 1573 after Lepanto, were distinct in character: they were designed to defend the western Mediterranean against the Turks. The crusade against the Moors was now left to Portugal, which pursued it to disaster at Alcazarquivir in 1578. However, this renunciation brought its revenge: the Turks were able to extend their protection over the 'Barbary states' of Tunis and Algiers; the coastal fortresses were recovered; and the city of Algiers, under the rule of the famous corsair Barbarossa, became the capital of piracy. It was to chastise these pirates that an English fleet, under Blake, entered the Mediterranean in 1655. Blake bombarded Tunis and coerced the Bey of Algiers. This was the beginning of English naval intervention in the Mediterranean, which culminated in the capture and retention of Gibraltar (1704).

The Lion of Venice *(above)* appears on Venetian fortresses throughout the eastern Mediterranean. This flag shows the Lion standing on land as well as on water, symbolising the Republic's dominance of its hinterland as well as of the Adriatic.

IN the three centuries from 1495 to 1797 the Mediterranean world underwent two drastic changes. First, the primacy of the Italian cities was lost as the sea became the theatre of a power-struggle between two multi-national empires whose interests were only partly Mediterranean: the Spanish Habsburgs and the Ottoman Turks. Second, in the 17th century the whole area lost significance as initiative and sea-power, even in the Mediterranean, passed to the Atlantic nations.

The loss of Italian primacy was precipitated by the French invasion of Italy in 1494. In the ensuing Franco-Spanish struggle France was defeated and thereafter, by the Treaty of Cateau-Cambrésis (1559) and the French wars of religion (1562-98), effectively excluded from Italy, which was dominated by Spain. Milan was ruled by a Spanish governor; Naples, Sicily and Sardinia by Spanish viceroys. Genoa, with its colony of Corsica, was tied economically to Spain. The central Italian states, pressed between Spanish Milan and Spanish Naples, had limited freedom. There were Spanish naval bases in Tuscany, a Spanish garrison in Piacenza. Venice, which sought to preserve independence by neutrality, was nevertheless threatened by Spanish land-power in Milan and Spanish sea-power at Brindisi. As the front line of defence against the Turks, Italy was protected, and therefore dominated, by the opposite power of Spain.

While Spain pushed along the northern coast to the straits of Otranto, the Turks reached along the southern coast towards the straits of Gibraltar. At first the Spaniards made the pace here too. The Catholic kings destroyed the last Muslim kingdom in Spain, the kingdom of Granada, in 1492, and Spanish coastal garrisons were established in Morocco and Algeria. In 1535 Charles V captured Tunis and installed a puppet ruler. But Spanish resources were increasingly diverted to Italy and the north, and meanwhile Ottoman power steadily advanced. Syria and Egypt were conquered in 1517, Tripoli, Tunisia and Algeria gradually vassalised, and Spanish conquests east of Oran reversed. In 1560 Philip II's expedition against Djerba failed. In 1565 the Turks besieged Malta, to which the Knights

Hospitallers of St John had been driven back from Rhodes in 1522. However, Malta was relieved; in 1571 the great Spanish-Venetian victory of Lepanto broke Turkish sea-power in the central Mediterranean; and in 1609 the expulsion of the Moriscos (nominally converted Moors) from Spain removed a potential Turkish fifth column. By this time the Turks, engaged in Persia and on the Danube, were content to hold the eastern Mediterranean, leaving the western area as a Spanish lake. To Spain this control was now doubly necessary, for Anglo-Dutch sea-power in the Atlantic had made the traditional route from Spain to the Netherlands too dangerous. The Mediterranean route from Barcelona through Genoa to Milan was now the lifeline of the Spanish Empire in Europe: by it, troops and bullion were sent to the Spanish governors of the Netherlands and the Habsburgs of Austria.

The victims in this long struggle were the Italian mercantile republics of Genoa and Venice. Genoa lost the last of its eastern colonies, Chios and Samos, to the Turks in 1566. Venice lost its last positions in the Morea – Monemvasia and Nauplia – in 1540, Naxos in 1566, Cyprus in 1571. Genoa retained its western colony of Corsica, but only after a long revolt (1552-69), in which the insurgents received help from the Turks. Venice clung to Crete till 1669, and temporarily recovered the Morea in 1685, but was effectively reduced to an Adriatic city. Meanwhile commercial interest was bringing other powers into the Mediterranean. France had had an informal alliance with the Turks since 1525, and Marseilles grew on eastern trade; the English Levant Company established itself in Constantinople in 1581; and from 1590 Dutch fleets brought Baltic corn, Norwegian timber and colonial wares into the Mediterranean. To profit by this trade, the Grand Duke of Tuscany declared Leghorn a free port in 1593. To prey on it, international pirates invaded the sea and joined the 'Barbary corsairs' who made Algiers into a great pirate city, the Croatian Uskoks who terrorised Adriatic shipping, and the Turkish corsairs of Albania, the Morea and Anatolia. In time of war, local rulers invested in privateering and increased the need of trading nations for political stability in the sea.

	Spanish Habsburg territory
	Austrian Habsburg territory
	Spanish "client-states"
	Venetian territory
	Ottoman Empire and protectorates

In general, they achieved it. In the 17th century Spanish control was challenged in detail by France, but the effective changes were dynastic, not territorial. When a French dynasty was established in Spain (1700-14), the balance of power was preserved in the Mediterranean. The Austrian Habsburgs secured Milan. After some shuffling, a branch of the Spanish Bourbons received Naples and Sicily, and Sardinia was neutralised in the hands of Savoy. Tuscany fell, in 1737, to a branch of the Habsburgs. Lesser principalities were similarly shared out. The republics of Venice, Genoa and Lucca remained undisturbed. Venice retained its Adriatic possessions and Genoa its rule over Corsica (though challenged by another long revolt, 1755-68) till the late 18th century.

The guardian of this 18th-century stability was England. English fleets had first entered the Mediterranean in force under Cromwell, to pursue royalist vessels and to chastise the Barbary pirates. From 1662 to 1683 England held Tangier, guarding the entrance to the Mediterranean; in 1704 it took Gibraltar from Spain. Sardinia was a British base from 1708 to 1714, Minorca from 1708 to 1783. But generally the British preferred diplomacy to direct control, until Napoleon's invasion of Italy and annexation of Egypt and Malta convulsed eastern and western Mediterranean alike and brought in the British navy to dominate both.

1/The struggle for power 1495 to 1620 (below) The expanding power of Spain in the West and of the Ottoman Empire in the East frequently clashed in the Mediterranean. Spain was enriched by its new Atlantic acquisitions in the Americas, and the Ottomans by their Middle Eastern and Balkan gains. The turning point which broke the Ottoman westward advance was the Battle of Lepanto (1571), after which the central Mediterranean was left to the power of Spain.

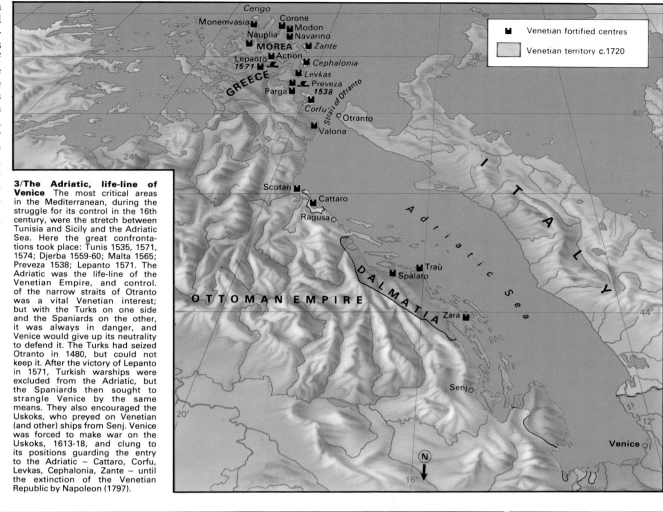

3/The Adriatic, life-line of Venice The most critical areas in the Mediterranean, during the struggle for its control in the 16th century, were the stretch between Tunisia and Sicily and the Adriatic Sea. Here the great confrontations took place: Tunis 1535, 1571, 1574; Djerba 1559-60; Malta 1565; Preveza 1538; Lepanto 1571. The Adriatic was the life-line of the Venetian Empire, and control of the narrow straits of Otranto was a vital Venetian interest; but with the Turks on one side and the Spaniards on the other, it was always in danger, and Venice would give up its neutrality to defend it. The Turks had seized Otranto in 1480, but could not keep it. After the victory of Lepanto in 1571, Turkish warships were excluded from the Adriatic, but the Spaniards then sought to strangle Venice by the same means. They also encouraged the Uskoks, who preyed on Venetian (and other) ships from Senj. Venice was forced to make war on the Uskoks, 1613-18, and clung to its positions guarding the entry to the Adriatic — Cattaro, Corfu, Levkas, Cephalonia, Zante — until the extinction of the Venetian Republic by Napoleon (1797).

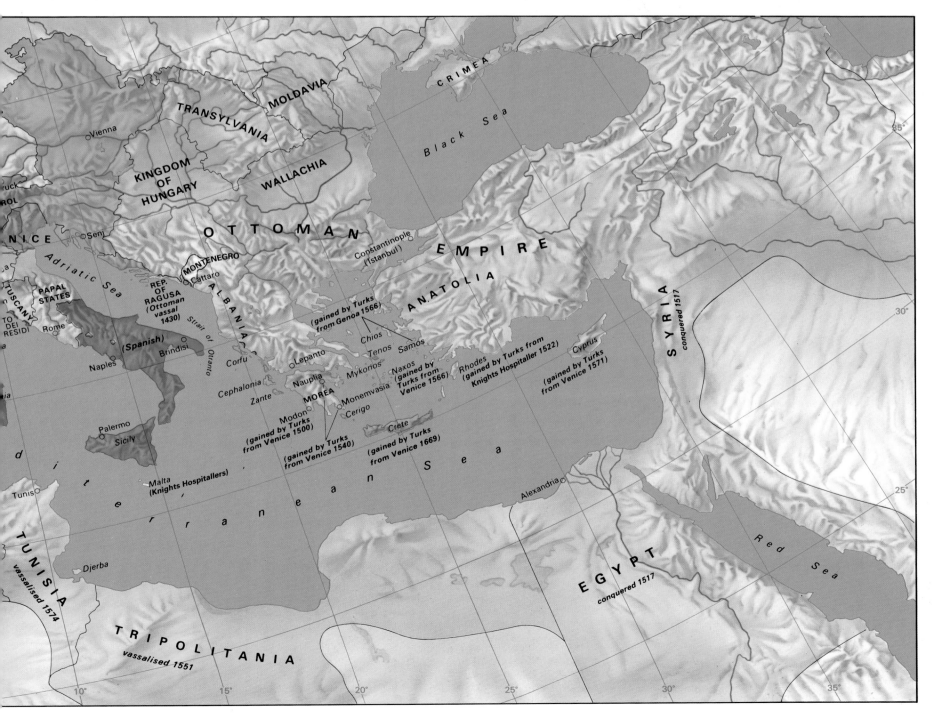

The struggle for the Baltic 1523 to 1721

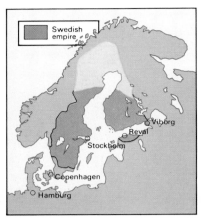

1561 Reval, an independent Hanseatic port, threatened by the commercial rivalry of Viborg and Narva and the ambitions of Poland and Denmark to control Livonia, put itself under Swedish protection.

1595 Peace of Teusina added Narva and effectively the whole of Estonia, turned the Gulf of Finland into a Swedish waterway and pushed the northern borders across the Arctic Circle.

1617 Peace of Stolbovo confirmed possession of Estonia, added Ingermanland, Karelia and the river Neva, and cut off Russia, including its great trading city of Novgorod (sacked 1616) from all access to the Baltic.

1645 All Livonia became Swedish through the Armistice of Altmark (1629); the Peace of Brömsebro transferred Ösel, Gotland, Jämtland, Härjedalen and a 30-year control over Halland from Denmark-Norway.

1648 With the Peace of Westphalia ending the Thirty Years War, Sweden gained West Pomerania, including the important port of Stettin, Wismar in Mecklenburg, and the bishoprics of Bremen and Verden.

1658 Peace of Roskilde brought Scania, Blekinge, Bohuslän, Trondheim and Bornholm; but additional Swedish demands created a Danish-Dutch alliance; renewed war, rebellion in Scania and defeat at Funen (1660).

1660 After the death of Charles X, fighting ceased. The treaty of Copenhagen returned Trondheim and the island of Bornholm to Denmark, and formally abandoned Sweden's earlier attempts to close the Baltic to foreign warships.

1721 The treaties ending the Great Northern War (1700-21) marked the effective break-up of the Swedish Empire. In the east, Karelia and the Baltic provinces were lost, and in Germany, Bremen-Verden and most of West Pomerania.

THE Baltic is a vast, almost land-locked, frequently ice-bound area of water covering over 166,000 square miles. In early modern times it provided the great bulk of the timber, tar, pitch, hemp and flax for the ships with which England, Holland, France, Spain and Portugal were building their world trading empires; also much of the grain needed to insure the rest of the continent against poor harvests, and the copper for its everyday money. The Sound Tolls, imposed on most of the commerce passing between the Baltic and the North Sea, gave Denmark (which usually controlled the narrow exit passages) a formidable source of wealth and power, but created at the same time a source of bitter rivalry with her neighbours. The resulting local struggles, with their threats to security of supply, constantly interlocked with wider European affairs – the maritime jealousies of Britain, France and the Netherlands, the dynastic confrontation of Bourbon and Habsburg, the religious conflicts between Catholic and Protestant. There was thus a much more than parochial significance in the complex Baltic power shifts of these 200 years, which saw the final decline of the Hanseatic League, Sweden's dramatic rise and eclipse, the dwindling of Denmark, the virtual elimination of Poland and the advance of Russia and Brandenburg-Prussia.

From 1397 to 1523, Denmark, Norway and Sweden were united under one crown in the Union of Kalmar. Early in the 16th century, Sweden finally broke away and re-established its independence under Gustavus Vasa (1523-60). Gustavus also promptly broke with Rome, adopted Lutheranism, and set about improving the country's economic, naval and military strength. Its position was initially extremely fragile. Its only ice-free outlet to the North Sea consisted of an eleven-mile strip of coast between the Danish province of Halland and the Norwegian province of Bohuslän, and although this was defended by the fortress of Älvsborg, it fell several times into the hands of Danish invading forces. Denmark also controlled the southern shores adjoining the Sound, and a string of strategic islands, while the Hanseatic port of Lübeck had been given, in return for its help in the wars of independence, a near-monopoly of Swedish foreign trade. This was broken, by a temporary alliance of Sweden and Denmark, as early as 1525, but the possibility of economic strangulation remained a constant threat. In the east, too, there was danger from the rising power of Muscovy, which openly coveted both Finland, under Swedish control since the 14th century, and the rapidly-disintegrating territories of the Teutonic Knights to the south of the Gulf of Finland, which represented a major trading outlet for Gustavus Vasa's new port of Helsingfors. Gradually rising tensions under Gustavus's sons, Eric XIV (1560-8) and John III (1568-92), finally erupted in the Seven Years' War of the North (1563-70). On balance Sweden held her own in this struggle, although she had to pay a crippling ransom to Denmark for the return of Älvsborg, and by 1581 she was becoming a significant force even beyond the Baltic region.

Her role was complicated by dynastic and religious considerations. John III had married a Polish (and Roman Catholic) princess, and his son ascended the Polish throne in 1587 as Sigismund III. A major constitutional crisis followed when he also became King of Sweden on his father's death in 1592. He was deposed in 1599, with his Lutheran uncle ultimately taking the crown as Charles IX; Poland and Sweden, already deeply at odds over their opposing interests in Livonia, remained open enemies for fifty years. Indeed, at the accession in 1611 of Charles's 17-year-old son, Gustavus Adolphus, Sweden was ringed by hostile states, and her constitutional and financial weaknesses, appear-

ed to make a mockery of her long-held aim to make the Baltic a Swedish lake. Amazingly, by 1660 the dream had almost become reality.

The young monarch's reign started with a serious setback. At the Peace of Knäred (1613) Sweden had to make further sacrifices to regain her fort of Älvsborg, lost to Denmark again two years before. The years from the Peace of Stolbovo to the Peace of Westphalia (1617-48) brought large new territories (see maps on left), although Gustavus was killed in 1632. Sweden was now a great international power.

Even before Westphalia, fear of Sweden's growing might had again brought war to Scandinavia. In 1643-45 Sweden fought Denmark, and in the resulting Peace of Brömsebro, Denmark lost Gotland and Ösel, together with Halland for a period of thirty years, and Norway too had to part with substantial lands. Renewed Danish attacks, while the Swedes under Charles X were

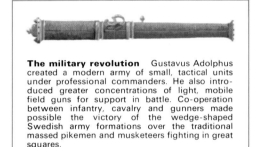

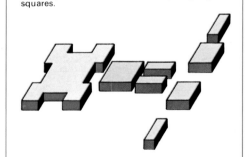

The military revolution Gustavus Adolphus created a modern army of small, tactical units under professional commanders. He also introduced greater concentrations of light, mobile field guns for support in battle. Co-operation between infantry, cavalry and gunners made possible the victory of the wedge-shaped Swedish army formations over the traditional massed pikemen and musketeers fighting in great squares.

embroiled with Russia, Brandenburg and Poland, led to further humiliation. Charles, attacking from the south, occupied Jutland, led his troops across the frozen waters of the Great Belt in the winter of 1658 and threatened Copenhagen. At the Peace of Roskilde, Sweden won Scania, Blekinge, Bornholm, Bohuslän and Halland in perpetuity.

This was the climax. From then on, Sweden's foes allied increasingly effectively against her. When Denmark invaded Scania and started the Scanian War (1676-79), Sweden was saved from territorial loss only by her French ally Louis XIV, and after a pause during the cautious reign of Charles XI (1660-97) the tide began, disastrously, to turn. The old king was succeeded by his brilliant, impetuous 15-year-old son, Charles XII, and three years later, in 1700, the Great Northern War broke out, which in twenty years was to lay the foundations for the greatness of modern Russia and to erase Sweden and Poland from the ranks of the major powers.

The war started with the deceptively crushing victory of Narva, when Charles' troops decisively defeated a Russian army five times its size. But events in Poland (see page 196) side-tracked the Swedish forces. Peter the Great recaptured Narva (1704), annihilated the Swedes at Poltava (1709), and in the final peace treaties (1719-21) gained Livonia, Estonia, all of Ingermanland, Karelia and south-eastern Finland. With minor exceptions, former Swedish areas of Germany were divided between Hanover and the newly-emergent state of Brandenburg-Prussia. Most other naval powers, for whom a prime objective had always been to prevent the Baltic becoming a 'closed sea', regarded the decay of the short-lived Swedish Empire with relief.

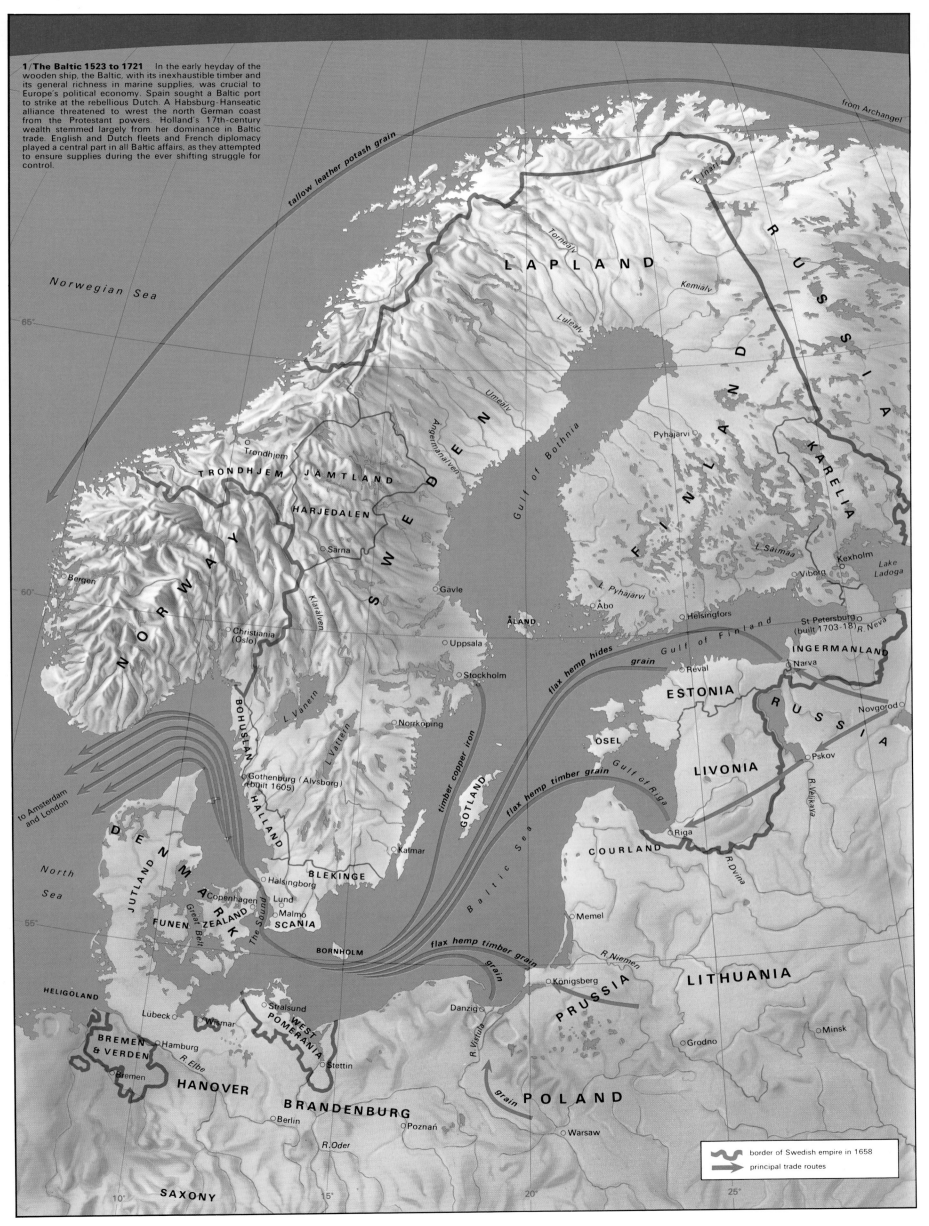

1/The Baltic 1523 to 1721 In the early heyday of the wooden ship, the Baltic, with its inexhaustible timber and its general richness in marine supplies, was crucial to Europe's political economy. Spain sought a Baltic port to strike at the rebellious Dutch. A Habsburg-Hanseatic alliance threatened to wrest the north German coast from the Protestant powers. Holland's 17th-century wealth stemmed largely from her dominance in Baltic trade. English and Dutch fleets and French diplomacy played a central part in all Baltic affairs, as they attempted to ensure supplies during the ever shifting struggle for control.

Norwegian Sea

from Archangel

tallow leather potash grain

LAPLAND

RUSSIA

65°

Torneälv

Kemiälv

Umeälv

Luleälv

KARELIA

Pyhäjärvi

FINLAND

Gulf of Bothnia

L. Saimaa

Kexholm

Lake Ladoga

L. Pyhäjärvi

Viborg

TRONDHJEM

JAMTLAND

○ Trondhjem

HARJEDALEN

○ Särna

Klarälven

SWEDEN

Angermanälven

60°

Bergen ○

○ Gävle

ÅLAND

Åbo ○

Helsingfors ○

Réval ○

St Petersburg (built 1703-18) R. Neva

Narva ○

INGERMANLAND

NORWAY

BOHUSLAN

L. Vänern

L. Vättern

○ Christiania (Oslo)

○ Uppsala

flax hemp hides

grain

Gulf of Finland

RUSSIA

Novgorod ○

ESTONIA

○ Stockholm

HALLAND

Gothenburg (Alvsborg) (built 1605)

○ Norrköping

GOTLAND

timber copper iron

OSEL

flax hemp timber grain

Gulf of Riga

LIVONIA

Pskov ○

R. Velikaya

to Amsterdam and London

flax hemp timber grain

Riga ○

Kalmar ○

COURLAND

R. Dvina

North Sea

DENMARK

○ Halsingborg

BLEKINGE

Baltic Sea

Memel ○

LITHUANIA

JUTLAND

FUNEN

Copenhagen ○

Great Belt

ZEALAND

The Sound

Lund ○

Malmö ○

SCANIA

BORNHOLM

flax hemp timber grain

R. Niemen

HELIGOLAND

grain

Königsberg ○

PRUSSIA

Minsk ○

Lübeck ○

Stralsund ○

Wismar ○

POMERANIA

WEST

Danzig ○

R. Vistula

Grodno ○

BREMEN & VERDEN

Hamburg ○

R. Elbe

Stettin ○

grain

POLAND

Bremen ○

HANOVER

BRANDENBURG

○ Berlin

○ Poznań

○ Warsaw

R. Oder

SAXONY

10°   15°   20°   25°

border of Swedish empire in 1658

principal trade routes

189

Germany disunited 1648 to 1806

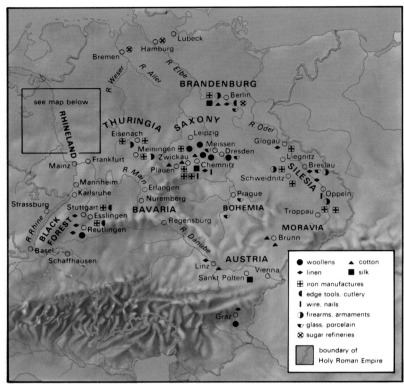

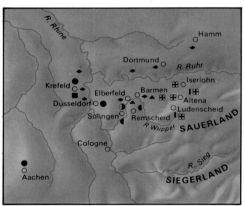

2/Industrial growth in the 18th century *(above)* Urban development centred on Vienna, Berlin, Hamburg and Bremen; textiles and iron enriched Saxony, Silesia and the lower Rhineland.

Meissen Merchant *(above)* The first Meissen factory opened near Dresden in 1710, after Böttger, an alchemist employed by the Elector of Saxony, succeeded in reproducing the translucency of Chinese porcelain with local clay. This piece, dated 1765, is now in New York's Metropolitan Museum of Art.

THE Peace of Westphalia, which in 1648 finally ended the Thirty Years War, left Germany ravaged and impoverished. The might of the Emperor was irretrievably ruined; his domains, whose political fragmentation had begun as early as the 14th century, were now split into some 300 separate principalities, bishoprics and Free Cities, with each ruler, Catholic or Protestant, lay or ecclesiastical, rich or poor, jealously defending his own sovereignty. The Empire still had common institutions, including a Diet, or *Reichstag*, which sat permanently at Regensburg (where the most important delegate was probably the French ambassador) but their effectiveness was minimal.

Among the mosaic of small, petty and 'duodecimo' states only Austria remained a major force. This was due mostly, however, to the extent of the ruling Habsburgs' possessions in Hungary, the Netherlands and Italy, rather than to those in Germany. The few other princes of any importance derived their strength – and often their titles – from outside the Empire. The Elector of Brandenburg, raised to royal dignity in 1701, took his title from Prussia (outside the imperial boundary, under Polish overlordship, from 1461 to 1657). The Elector of Hanover became King of England in 1714, and the Elector of Saxony, King of Poland (1697). Sweden ruled over Bremen and Western Pomerania, and Denmark over Holstein; while France, always alert to extending its territories at German expense, annexed Burgundy (1678), Strassburg (1681), the rest of Alsace (1697), and Bar and Lorraine (1766). Only the jealous vigilance of England, Holland, Sweden and Russia prevented her from seizing much more.

The population of Germany, between twenty and twenty-five million on the eve of the thirty-year struggle, was savagely reduced. The loss of life, variously estimated at one-third, one-half and in some regions seventy per cent, was not made good until the second half of the 18th century. War also accelerated the economic decline which had set in towards the close of the 16th century. The great south German commercial cities, Nuremberg and Augsburg (where the Fuggers had gone bankrupt in 1627) suffered, like Venice, from the rise of the Ottoman Empire and the shift in trade from the Mediter-

Austrian Habsburg
Spanish Habsburg
Wettin (Albertina)
Wettin (Ernestina)
Hohenzollern
Franconian line
Brandenburg line
Wittelsbach
Bavarian line
Palatinate line
Oldenburg lands
ecclesiastical lands
imperial cities
Holy Roman Empire 1648
Swedish from 1648

ranean to the Atlantic. The Hanseatic ports, once dominant in the Baltic and the North Sea (see page 144), failed to stem the growing power of Holland, and dissolved their League in 1669.

The rise of Prussia, begun under the Great Elector (1640-88) and continued by Frederick William I (1713-40) and his son Frederick the Great (1740-86), disguised the fragility of the Prussian state which was quickly shown by its collapse in 1806. Its real rise to great power status belongs essentially to the 19th century (see page 216). Certainly its rulers evolved a significant armoury of administrative and military institutions, as well as a highly characteristic set of social attitudes in the course of imposing order on their widely-scattered territories. However, down to 1700, Brandenburg-Prussia was outstripped by Bavaria, and until the middle of the 18th century by Saxony, in wealth and population. Though the bare framework of a kingdom existed by the end of the 17th century, it was only with the acquisition of Silesia in 1742 and the successful conclusion of the war which had been fought over it with Austria in 1763 that Prussia really began to affect the balance of power within the Empire. Not until the partitions of Poland was it possible to create a continuous Prussian territory extending from Memel to Magdeburg.

Frederick the Great's forced industrialisation programme, largely based on Silesia's iron and coal, was only a modest success. Although they were widely admired and emulated, many of his

3/The rise of Prussia The 1648 Peace, the weakening of Poland, inheritance, the Northern Wars (1655-60, 1700-21), and the War of the Austrian Succession (1740-48) enabled the Hohenzollern to extend and consolidate the territories of Brandenburg-Prussia.

Brandenburg in 1648
Prussian acquisitions 1648-1707
acquisitions 1715, 1720
acquisitions 1742, 1744, 1772

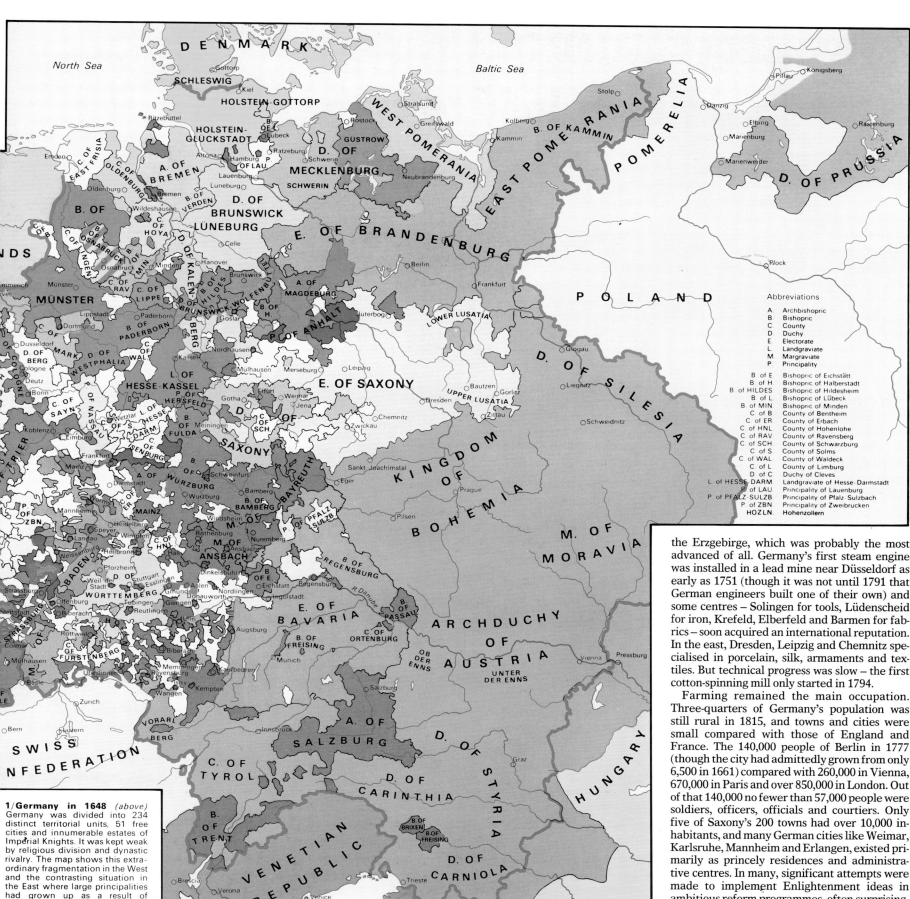

Abbreviations

A.	Archbishopric
B.	Bishopric
C.	County
D.	Duchy
E.	Electorate
L.	Landgraviate
M.	Margraviate
P.	Principality

B of E	Bishopric of Eichstätt
B of H.	Bishopric of Halberstadt
B of HILDES.	Bishopric of Hildesheim
B of L.	Bishopric of Lübeck
B of MIN.	Bishopric of Minden
C of B.	County of Bentheim
C of ER.	County of Erbach
C of HNL.	County of Hohenlohe
C of RAV.	County of Ravensberg
C of SCH.	County of Schwarzburg
C of S.	County of Solms
C of WAL.	County of Waldeck
C of L.	County of Limburg
D. of C.	Duchy of Cleves
L of HESSE DARM.	Landgraviate of Hesse-Darmstadt
P of LAU.	Principality of Lauenburg
P of PFALZ-SULZB.	Principality of Pfalz-Sulzbach
P of ZBN.	Principality of Zweibrücken
HOZLN.	Hohenzollern

1/Germany in 1648 *(above)* Germany was divided into 234 distinct territorial units, 51 free cities and innumerable estates of Imperial Knights. It was kept weak by religious division and dynastic rivalry. The map shows this extraordinary fragmentation in the West and the contrasting situation in the East where large principalities had grown up as a result of colonisation in the 13th and 14th centuries. It was the eastern provinces of Prussia and Austria that were to play the preponderant role in eventually unifying Germany.

4/Germany in 1806 *(left)* Napoleon and his armies drastically simplified the German map. Petty states were amalgamated wholesale with larger entities; new middle-sized territories emerged including Prussia, though after 1806 it had to surrender its western provinces; and France took firm control of the left bank of the Rhine.

— Confederation of the Rhine 1806
1 Wurttemberg
2 Baden
3 Wurzburg
4 Thuringian states
5 Electorate of Hesse
6 Swedish Pomerania
7 Oldenburg
8 Duchy of Hesse
9 Berg

the Erzgebirge, which was probably the most advanced of all. Germany's first steam engine was installed in a lead mine near Düsseldorf as early as 1751 (though it was not until 1791 that German engineers built one of their own) and some centres – Solingen for tools, Lüdenscheid for iron, Krefeld, Elberfeld and Barmen for fabrics – soon acquired an international reputation. In the east, Dresden, Leipzig and Chemnitz specialised in porcelain, silk, armaments and textiles. But technical progress was slow – the first cotton-spinning mill only started in 1794.

Farming remained the main occupation. Three-quarters of Germany's population was still rural in 1815, and towns and cities were small compared with those of England and France. The 140,000 people of Berlin in 1777 (though the city had admittedly grown from only 6,500 in 1661) compared with 260,000 in Vienna, 670,000 in Paris and over 850,000 in London. Out of that 140,000 no fewer than 57,000 people were soldiers, officers, officials and courtiers. Only five of Saxony's 200 towns had over 10,000 inhabitants, and many German cities like Weimar, Karlsruhe, Mannheim and Erlangen, existed primarily as princely residences and administrative centres. In many, significant attempts were made to implement Enlightenment ideas in ambitious reform programmes, often surprisingly successful precisely because the principalities were so small. Diminutive courts like Weimar were also the centres of literary revival in which Göethe and Schiller were major figures of international significance.

Attempts to simplify Germany's increasingly anachronistic pattern of tiny states were first made by the Austrian Emperor, Joseph II (1780-90). They were frustrated by Prussia, now powerful enough to block anyone else's unificatory moves but not to initiate one of her own. It was only under the impact of France's post-revolutionary wars that the redrawing of the political map seriously began. The 64 ecclesiastical principalities were secularised in 1803; 45 of the 51 Free Cities and the remaining Imperial Knights were absorbed into larger units.

These changes marked the end of the old Reich, providing a springboard for the developments of the 19th century. Their significance was formally recognised in 1806, when Francis II of Austria (1792-1806) finally abdicated his sonorous, though now almost meaningless title. He was the last Holy Roman Emperor, in a line that had lasted 850 years.

state-sponsored enterprises failed even in his own lifetime, and few survived the French occupation of 1806. Nevertheless, 18th-century Germany was not an economic backwater. Although the older cities stagnated, new industries sprang up in rural districts where they could escape the crippling guild restrictions. Apart from Silesia, where the large landowners combined with government to invest in mining, iron and textiles, the main areas were the Sauerland and Siegerland massifs in the lower Rhineland, where water power was available from the rivers Lahn, Sieg and Wupper, and Saxony, with

The ascendancy of France
1647 to 1715

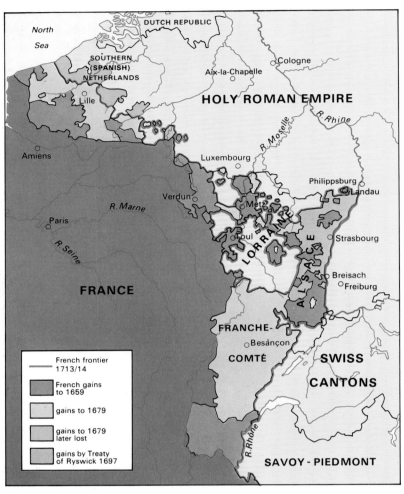

2/**The North-East Frontier** (*above*)   Louis expanded into the Spanish Netherlands. He conquered Franche-Comté, widened his hold on Alsace, and in 1681 annexed Strasbourg.

3/War of the Spanish Succession 1701/2, 1713/14 Leopold of Austria opened the struggle for the Spanish inheritance of Carlos II by invading Italy. He was encouraged by England and the Dutch Republic who also resented Louis XIV's acceptance of the will of Carlos in favour of Philip, Louis' second grandson, on condition that Spain's possessions in Europe and overseas were kept inviolate. The Holy Roman Empire, Portugal and Savoy also declared war on France. Apart from Spain, Louis' allies were the Electors of Bavaria and Cologne. Initial French successes were followed by reverses between 1704-9, but the Allies proved unable to maintain Archduke Charles, Leopold's second son, as king of Spain. A compromise peace was eventually imposed by Britain and France (Peace of Utrecht) on their respective allies. Philip retained Spain, but Spain's Netherlands and Italian territories were allocated to the Austrian Habsburgs and Savoy.

DURING the reign of Louis XIV France became so influential in Europe that other powers feared her ascendancy, regarding her – to use a contemporary expression – as an 'exorbitant' state, dangerous for the very balance of the Continent and threatening the religious as well as the political freedom of individual states and princes. Louis was suspected of plans to oust the Austrian Habsburgs from their traditional position as elected emperors of the Holy Roman Empire of the German Nation, and of spearheading a second Catholic counter-reformation. He was generally held to aim at French hegemony over Europe.

There were some solid grounds for such fears. Although war, civil and international, had for more than a century impeded progress in manufactures, in trade, overseas expansion, and in ship-building, the relatively peaceful years between 1661 and 1672 gave Louis XIV and his able ministers and administrators a chance to catch up with France's rivals in all three fields. At the same time the French army and navy were greatly expanded. The richness of French resources, including a population estimated at twenty million, played a significant part in these developments, but so did conscious effort and directives from the centre.

Louis' military objectives were, however, limited and concerned the security of France's northern and eastern frontiers. The Habsburg ring, forged by the family compacts of the Austrian and Spanish Habsburgs, was still felt to be pressing round France though the Peace of Westphalia (1648) brought sovereignty over Metz, Toul and Verdun (occupied by the French since 1552) and possession of the landgravates of Upper and Lower Alsace, and the Peace of the Pyrenees (1659) plugged the gap in the southern frontier: Spain ceded Roussillon and northern Cerdagne. Yet many *portes* (gates) remained through which France could be invaded, from the Spanish Netherlands in the north, through Lorraine and the Belfort Gap, right down to the Barcelonette valley from Italy. Spain still held Franche-Comté on the eastern border, and Louis' hold over Alsace was weakened by imperial suzerainty over its ten principal towns. The near-certainty, after 1665, that the Spanish king Carlos II would die without heirs of his own body and consequently leave his possessions to the Austrian Habsburgs raised the spectre of a resurrection of the empire of Charles V. This helps to explain the two aggressive wars of Louis' reign: the War of Devolution, fought to lay claim to part of the Spanish Netherlands in 1667-78, and the attack on the Dutch Republic in 1672. The latter, much to Louis' discomfiture, escalated into a European-wide war which was not settled till 1678-79.

Louis tried to avoid large-scale war after 1679 by resort to arbitration and multi-lateral treaties to settle European problems, but the memories of his early wars and the enormous power of France made the rest of Europe suspicious. Indeed, he preferred brief campaigns or the diplomatic isolation of those who opposed him by the use of subsidies to rulers and presents to influential ministers. His conquest of Spanish Netherlands territory (1668) and of Franche-Comté (1678) might be forgiven, but his 'reunion' policy to expand his control of German border areas was vigorously opposed; and he lost the sympathy of all Protestant powers once his anti-Huguenot measures in France began to bite. The deleterious economic effects of the exodus of over 200,000 French Huguenots in the 1670s and 1680s have been greatly exaggerated. The political consequences abroad of Louis' revocation of the Edict of Nantes (1685) were far-reaching, however, and contributed both to the Nine Years' War (1689-97) and the War of the Spanish Succession (1701-14).

The defensive element in Louis' foreign policy is still disputed among historians, but can be demonstrated in various ways: by the construction of a *barrière de fer* of Vauban fortresses around the whole of France, thickest on the ground in the north and east; by the decision, put into effect by 1696, to pull out of Italy (thus abandoning a cornerstone of the policies of Richelieu and Mazarin) to permit concentration of resources on the defensive *barrière*; by the clauses in the second partition treaty of 1700 which – while giving Spain, the Spanish Netherlands and Spain overseas to an Austrian archduke – ceded the Spanish possessions in Italy to France, but with specific provisions and plans for 'exchanges' to strengthen the eastern frontier: the duchy of Milan was to be exchanged for Lorraine, and Naples and Sicily, it was hoped, for Savoy and Piedmont.

Parallel to the preoccupation with the northern and eastern frontiers went an intense concern to catch up with the Maritime Powers (England and the Dutch Republic) in overseas settlements and commerce, and especially to have a share in the illicit trade with Spanish America. Here Louis aroused such resentment and fear that the English and the Dutch would only contemplate one of Louis' younger grandsons inheriting the Spanish throne, if they themselves were given territories and strongpoints in the West Indies, on the Spanish Main, in Spanish North Africa, on Spain's Balearic Islands and in Spain itself. The Maritime Powers were well aware that no union of the two dynasties, that of Spain and that of France, was intended; but unless they received compensation of the kind mentioned above they feared that French ascendancy in overseas trade would become a corollary of French ascendancy in Europe. They could no more free themselves from such fears than could Louis from his conviction that the Austrian Habsburgs, who between 1683 and 1699 made such vast reconquests from the Turks in Hungary, would sooner or later turn west to regain, as they loudly proclaimed, everything lost to France by their dynasty between 1552 and 1678.

French ascendancy between 1661 and 1715 was not, it should be remembered, only in the political fields which can be illustrated in an historical atlas. Indeed, in the perspective of cultural and intellectual history, Louis' work for French literature, architecture, learning, and science and the arts in general, and his pensions paid to a great number of European poets, artists and scholars, whether they studied in France or not, may seem more important than his wars. His Versailles building programme and his support for academies became models for other princes; French became the language of the educated classes all over Europe and helped to create the cosmopolitan civilisation of the late

17th and the early 18th centuries. France also made progress during his reign in the number of colleges and hospitals (a combination of what we would call hospitals, workhouses and houses of correction), in codification of laws, in administrative procedures and efficiency, and in all kinds of practical improvements from the street lighting and policing of Paris to the digging of the Languedoc canal (completed by 1684) which gave cheap and efficient communication between the Atlantic and the Mediterranean.

Taken as a whole, the reign fixed the French frontiers in Europe (though colonial cessions had to be made to Great Britain) and foreshadowed the exchange which in 1738 brought the certainty of Lorraine being incorporated with France (achieved by 1766); while, in the history of French civilisation, the reign is deservedly honoured with the title *Le Grand Siècle*.

Versailles Louis XIV's vast palace at Versailles, the centre of his government and his court, was built in 'envelope' form round three sides of his father's hunting château, preserved at the king's insistence for his private apartments. Gardens and park were enlarged and embellished. Symbolism abounded in indoor decorations and outdoor statues and sculpture. The Coysevox Vase 'War', shown here, celebrated French victories of the reign up to the Truce of Regensburg (1684).

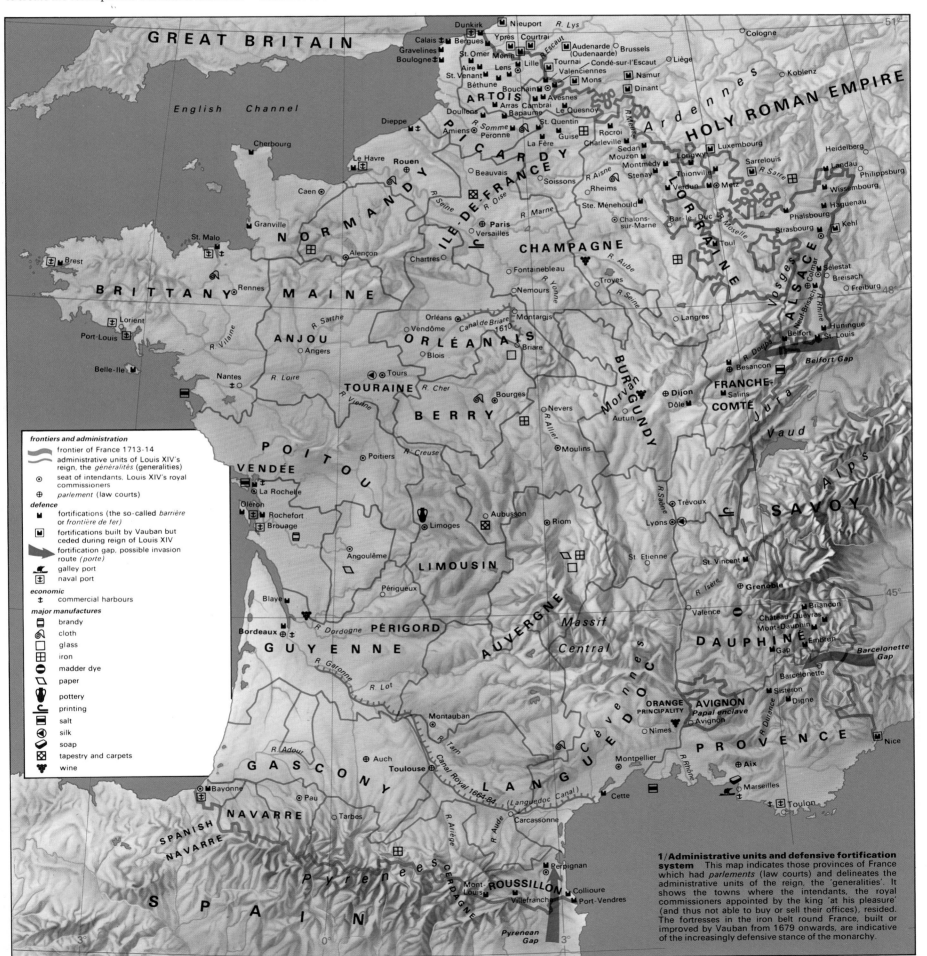

frontiers and administration

〜 frontier of France 1713-14

— administrative units of Louis XIV's reign, the *généralités* (generalities)

⊙ seat of intendants. Louis XIV's royal commissioners

⊕ *parlement* (law courts)

defence

◧ fortifications (the so-called *barrière* or *frontière de fer*)

◨ fortifications built by Vauban but ceded during reign of Louis XIV

➤ fortification gap, possible invasion route *(porte)*

⚓ galley port

⊞ naval port

economic

‡ commercial harbours

major manufactures

▯ brandy

⬠ cloth

▢ glass

⊞ iron

◖ madder dye

▱ paper

⬚ pottery

⌐ printing

▤ salt

◉ silk

◔ soap

⊠ tapestry and carpets

⟊ wine

1/Administrative units and defensive fortification system This map indicates those provinces of France which had *parlements* (law courts) and delineates the administrative units of the reign, the 'generalities'. It shows the towns where the intendants, the royal commissioners appointed by the king 'at his pleasure' (and thus not able to buy or sell their offices), resided. The fortresses in the iron belt round France, built or improved by Vauban from 1679 onwards, are indicative of the increasingly defensive stance of the monarchy.

The struggle for empire 1713 to 1815

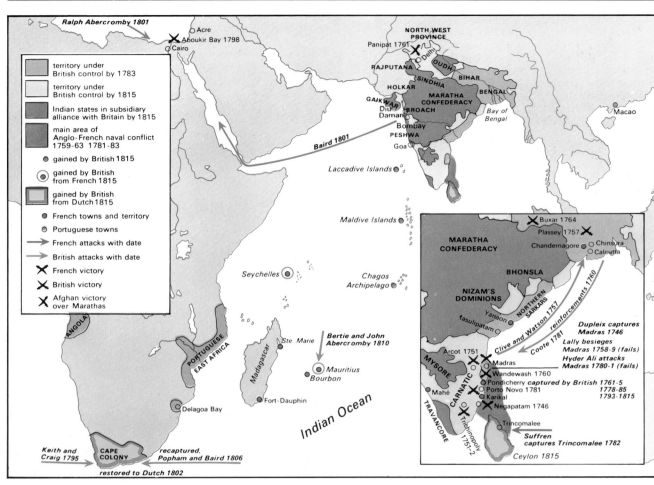

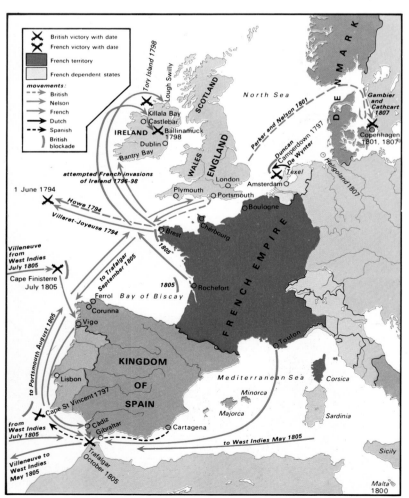

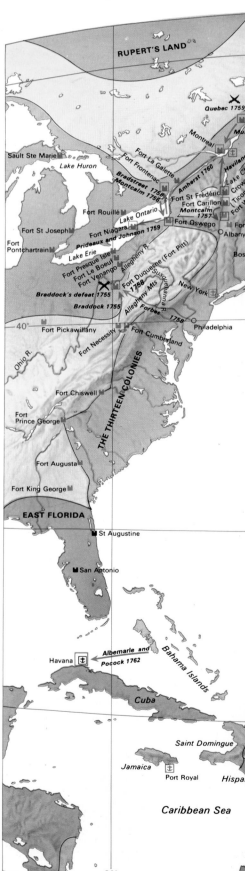

2/The Franco-British struggle for India
(above) The capture of Madras by Dupleix in 1746 began the struggle for India. As in America, British seapower proved decisive. Dupleix was checked at Trichinopoly in 1752, and after the capture of Bengal in 1757 the British could reinforce the Carnatic at will. The capture of Pondicherry in 1761 destroyed French power, and with local resources and control of the sea the British were able to hold off all subsequent challenges.

3/The British triumph in home waters, 1794-1805 *(below)* In the final confrontation between Great Britain and France the decisive battles were fought in European waters. Weakened by the French Revolution, the French fleet was no match for the British, and as successive invasion attempts foundered against British superiority at sea, Britain occupied its rival's possessions. By 1815 British possession of the key strategic colonies left it the supreme imperial power.

B Y leaving the Spanish empire and its trading monopolies substantially intact, the Treaty of Utrecht (1713) sought to establish a stable state system in Europe and overseas based upon the balance of power. Instead, it perpetuated the principal causes of colonial conflict. Territorial expansion continued throughout the 18th century, and led to serious clashes between Portugal and Spain in the Banda Oriental (Uruguay), between Spain and Great Britain in Georgia, and between Great Britain and France in North America. Trading monopolies proved an even greater source of friction. Illegal trade with the Spanish empire flourished, and Spanish attempts to suppress British and Dutch smugglers from Jamaica, St Eustatius and Curacao reduced the Caribbean to a state of undeclared war. Further north, British efforts to enforce similar restrictions upon its American colonists provoked resistance and finally open revolt.

But although dissension originated in the unsettled situation overseas, the outcome depended upon the actions of the European powers. During 1739-40 the fragile peace collapsed as Great Britain and Spain went to war in defence of their trading rights, and Frederick the Great's invasion of Silesia began the mid-century struggle for supremacy in eastern Europe (see page 196). The outbreak of war between Great Britain and France in 1744 brought the war for Caribbean trade and the war for Silesia together into a single global conflict that extended from North America to India, and from the West Indies to Russia. This struggle, which lasted intermittently until 1815, rapidly became a duel between Great Britain and France for global supremacy. European powers, American settlers, North American Indian chiefs and Indian princes all fought as subsidised and dependent allies of these two great powers. Local factors determined the nature of local struggles, but all were subordinated to the larger conflict.

The Treaty of Aix-la-Chapelle (1748) settled none of the outstanding questions, and fighting began again in North America in 1754. By 1756 France had achieved local military superiority,

its strategically sited forts preventing further British expansion. But the key to colonial victory was control of the lines of communication, and thus seapower. The outbreak of the Seven Years War in Europe transformed the local struggle; in the wider conflict of 1756-63, while France was handicapped by its continental commitments, Great Britain took control of the Atlantic and isolated the French forces in North America. Cut off from reinforcements, Louisbourg fell in 1758, Quebec in 1759. The capture of Montreal in 1760, following British naval victories at Quiberon Bay and Lagos, completed the fall of French Canada. In the West Indies, by 1763 the British were in control of Spanish Havana and all the

French islands except St Domingue. These were restored at the Treaty of Paris (1763), but Great Britain retained the North American mainland east of the Mississippi, including Florida which was ceded by Spain.

The British triumph was short-lived. Between 1763 and the American War of Independence (1776-83), France rebuilt both its navy and its alliances in pursuit of revenge. By 1781, confronted by a hostile coalition of France, Spain and the Dutch Republic, threatened by the 'armed neutrality' of the Baltic powers, and overstrained by the need to defend an empire stretching from Canada to India, Great Britain was forced to surrender control of North American waters. The French blockade of Yorktown forced Cornwallis to surrender, and although Rodney's victory off the group of islands known as The Saints in 1782 saved British possessions in the West Indies, Great Britain was obliged to recognise American independence at the Treaty of Versailles (1783). Nevertheless, the triumph of 1763 ensured that the new United States developed as an English-speaking nation. Trading contacts quickly revived, and despite occa-sional differences, the cultural link between the two countries exercised a profound influence on subsequent history.

During these same years the British found a new empire in India. The emergence of independent princes upon the ruins of the Mughal Empire forced both French and British East India Companies to intervene in local politics to protect their commerce. Here again seapower was decisive. Thus, after early French successes, Great Britain's ability to reinforce its position by sea enabled it to check Dupleix's ambitious designs for a French empire in the Carnatic. But the real foundation of the British empire in India followed Clive's victory at Plassey (1757) which, assisted by the victory of the Afghans over the Marathas at Panipat (1761), gave the British control of the rich province of Bengal (see page 172). During the Seven Years War reinforcements from Bengal enabled the British to eliminate French influence in the Carnatic. Henceforth, despite a French challenge in 1781-83, Great Britain was the predominant European power in India.

The French Revolution of 1789 shattered the French navy and, despite a partial recovery after 1794, France never regained the position as a naval power it held in 1783. This alone ruined Napoleon's plans for the invasion of Great Britain. By 1815, the French, Spanish, Dutch and Danish fleets were defeated, their colonies mostly in British hands. With the acquisition of the Cape, Ceylon and Mauritius, Great Britain secured the route to India and the East, and laid the foundations for the second British empire. It occupied a position of unrivalled power throughout large areas of the world, and its influence was to be a decisive factor in their evolution.

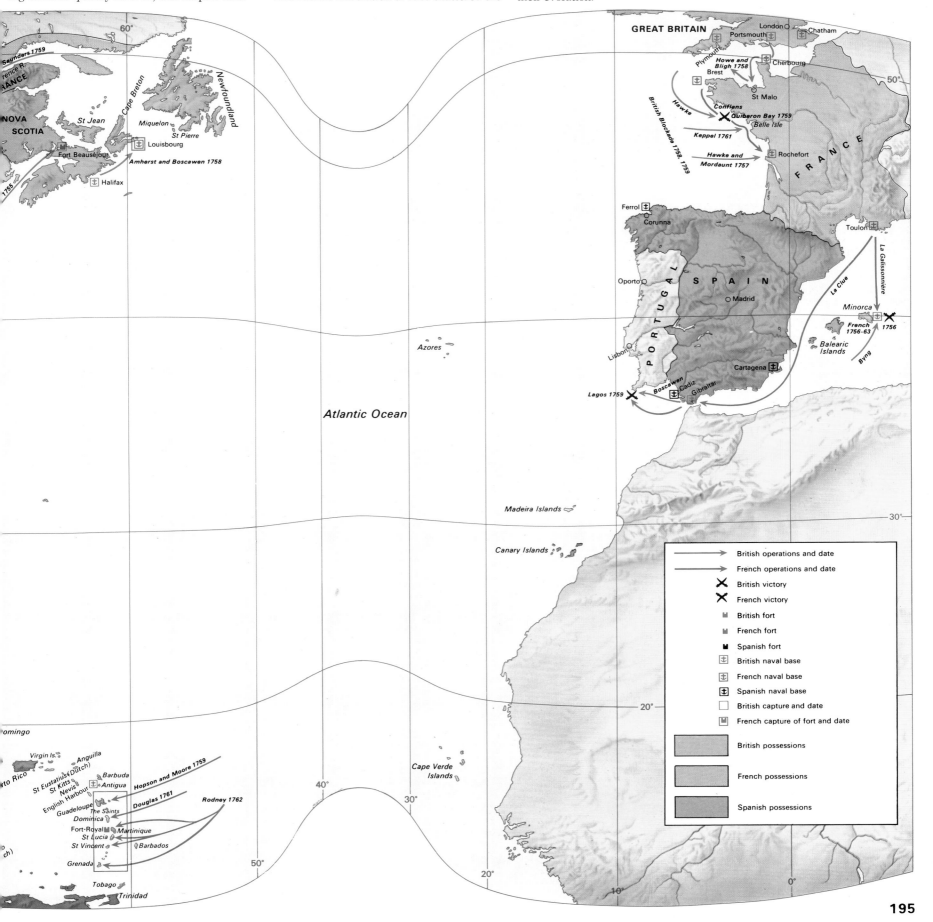

The Ottoman Empire, Austria and Russia: Eastern Europe from 1648 to 1795

1/Territorial Gains and Losses in Eastern Europe 1648-1795 *(above)* During this period the western powers began to realise that the Ottoman Empire, once the terror of Europe, was no longer an invincible force and had indeed become dangerously weak. As Austria and Russia sought advantage from the Turkish disintegration, Prussia expanded, while France and Sweden tried to maintain the traditional balance. With France increasingly paralysed, and Britain's attention concentrated beyond Europe, the eastern powers were able to contrive the Partitions of Poland (see map 5).

Legend:
- Russian conquests from Poland 1667-1795
- Russian conquests from Sweden 1700-43
- Russian conquests from Turkey 1768-92
- Prussian conquests from Austria 1740-41
- Prussian conquests from Sweden 1721
- Prussian conquests from Poland 1772-95
- Habsburg conquests from Turkey 1683-1775
- Habsburg conquests from Poland 1772-95
- Turkish conquests from Venice 1669-1718

4/The Silesian Wars *(below)* The intensive struggle began when the Prussians first won Silesia, at Mollwitz. Hohenfriedberg ended the first Austrian attempt at reconquest. In the Seven Years War, Prussians occupied Saxony and Bohemia as far as Prague (1757). Austrian victory at Kolin freed Bohemia, but recovery of Silesia was foiled at Leuthen. Though the Russians did occupy Berlin after Kunersdorf (1759) they failed to inflict a decisive defeat on Frederick II's highly mobile forces. Russian withdrawal after Peter III's accession (1762) forced Austria to renounce Silesia for good.

Legend:
- ✕ battles between Austria and Prussia
- ✕ battle between Saxony and Prussia
- ✕ battles between Russia and Prussia
- ✕ battle between Austria with Russia and Prussia

SULTAN Mehmed IV, in whose reign the Ottoman Empire launched its last major military onslaught on the west, came to the throne in 1648, just as the Treaty of Westphalia ended the Thirty Years' War. Between then and the final partition of Poland in 1795, an almost continuous series of wars, frontier changes, alliances and population movements profoundly altered the European balance of power.

Under Mehmed, and a capable dynasty of grand viziers recruited from the Köprülü family, the Turks undertook an energetic expansionist policy designed to relieve the social, religious and generally disruptive pressures that had been building up internally since the days of Suleiman the Magnificent. But Ottoman methods of warfare, triumphant in the 15th and 16th centuries, failed to take account of technical and organisational developments which had begun to transform their traditional enemies' fighting power. They achieved some naval success with the conquest of Crete at the end of a long war with Venice (1645-69), but the failure of the last vizier, Kara Mustapha, to overwhelm the defences of Vienna in 1683, started a period of spectacular decline.

The siege having been successfully raised by an anti-Ottoman coalition led by the Polish king, John III Sobieski (1674-96), the Turkish domains now came under sustained attack from all sides. The Austrian Habsburgs reconquered Hungary in 1699, and went on, in 1718, to occupy the Banat of Temesvar and part of Serbia, including Belgrade. Venice renewed her attempts to establish naval bases in the Adriatic and the Morea. Russia redoubled her efforts to break through to the Black Sea. Altogether, although there was some occasional recovery – Serbia, for example, was regained in the encounters of 1737-39 – the Turks were at war for forty-one of the 109 years between the siege of Vienna and the Treaty of Jassy (1792); most of the results were disastrous. After the peace settlements of Carlowitz (1699), the Pruth (1711), Passarowitz (1718), Belgrade (1739), Küçük Kaynarca (1774) and Jassy itself, they found themselves shorn of Hungary, the Banat, Transylvania and Bukovina. To Russia, similarly, they had lost the north coast of the Black Sea from the Dniester to the Caucasus. They had also been forced to grant her, in the Treaty of Küçük Kaynarca (1774), an ill-defined right to 'make representations' on behalf of the Russian Orthodox Christians in the Ottoman Empire, a concession which carried the seeds of future conflict, notably the Crimean War (1854-56).

The reconquest of Hungary, with the acquisitions that followed the War of the Spanish Succession, promoted the Austrian Habsburgs to the ranks of the recognised 'great powers'. But territory alone did not signify strength. Resistance by the Hungarian nobility to the extension of absolutist control hampered the full development of the country's resources. Large areas had been devastated and depopulated during the Turkish wars, and the main economic achievement of this period was the recolonisation of this land by hard-working immigrants, many from south-west Germany. Though the first settlements were successful, almost 50,000 immigrants arrived in the 1760s and 1770s, with a further 25,000 in the 1780s. Their skills and crafts made possible a more intensive and diversified agriculture.

The real weakness of the Habsburgs was revealed when the male line died out in 1740. This was the signal for Frederick II of Prussia to occupy Austria's highly-industrialised province of Silesia. He crushed the Austrian forces sent against him at Mollwitz (1741), and although after the peace of Aix-la-Chapellee, in 1748, Maria Theresa vigorously reformed her army and administration, encouraged economic development and entered into alliances with

France and Russia, the bitterly fought Seven Years' War (1756-63), failed to win her back the lost territory. Prussia had emerged as a rival, challenging the traditional pre-eminence of the Habsburg dynasty in Germany.

John Sobieski's successful participation in the alliance against the Turks had temporarily masked the growing disintegration of Poland, but in fact this process continued almost throughout the 17th and 18th centuries. The disastrous reign of John II Casimir Vasa (1648-68) saw the rebellion of the Ukrainian Cossacks, who accepted Russian suzerainty in 1654, and a Russian-Cossack invasion which detached most of eastern Poland. The Swedes, under Charles X Gustav, then occupied northern Poland and Lithuania (1655), until their brutality inspired a successful counter-attack. The Russians were also expelled (although they retained Smolensk and the eastern Ukraine). Civil War and Cossack unrest continued until 1686 when peace was signed with Russia, but even John Sobieski's successes did more to help the emergence of Austria and Russia than to strengthen his own country.

At Sobieski's death in 1696, eighteen candidates sought the votes of the nobles who had the right to elect a monarch for the Republic of Poland. The winner was Augustus the Strong of Saxony, who as Augustus II reigned until 1733. His ambition to conquer Livonia from Sweden sparked off the Great Northern War in 1700 in alliance with Peter I of Russia. The Swedes under Charles XII again devastated Poland, destroying a third of its cities, and forcing Augustus's temporary abdication. Ultimately the real victor was Peter I who restored Augustus to the throne, but seized Livonia for himself. A marsh was drained to found St Petersburg as a warm-water port, and the new city became Russia's capital in 1715.

In 1733 a French supported candidate was elected king of Poland, but Russian and Saxon troops set Augustus's son on the throne as Augustus III. Poland now ceased to count as a military power in Eastern Europe. With Frederick II's seizure of Silesia, Prussia now controlled her trade outlets to western Europe, though Poland still had direct access to the Baltic Sea through Danzig.

The decline of Poland was balanced by the rise of Russia who freely based her armies in Polish territory and made use of Polish ports in the Seven Years War. On the death of Augustus III in 1763, Catherine II of Russia procured the election of Stanislas Poniatowski as king (1764-95), but her intervention in Polish religious divisions provoked civil war in Poland and encouraged the Ottoman Porte to declare war in 1768 in order to stem the imminent Russian advance. This war was to reveal the full extent of Russia's military power. Russia's armies advanced through the Danubian principalities; her navy, making its first appearance in the Mediterranean, destroyed the Turkish fleet at Chesmé (1770) and the total collapse of the Ottoman Empire appeared a distinct possibility. From then on 'the eastern question' became a central issue in European affairs, as each great power tried to ensure that the Ottoman realms should not fall intact into one of the other's hands.

The presence of Russian forces near the mouth of the Danube in 1770 aroused the determined opposition of Austria, who tried to involve Prussia in an anti-Russian block. Frederick II, with much to lose and little to gain from a Balkan conflict, proposed the first Polish partition thus shifting the great-power conflict to an area where he had most to gain. Hence Poland paid the price for Russia's initial moderation in relation to Turkey. But further gains were in any case soon to follow. After the annexation of the Crimea in 1783, the exodus of

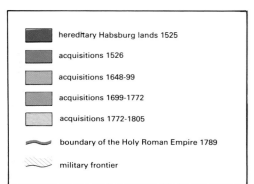

3/Growth of the Habsburg Empire (right) The Austrian branch of the Habsburg dynasty was founded by Charles V's brother Ferdinand, who took advantage of a marriage tie to have himself elected king of Bohemia and Hungary in 1526. But for nearly two centuries he and his successors had to dispute possession of Hungarian territory with the Ottomans. After the Turkish collapse following the siege of Vienna (map 2), the Habsburgs were able to expand rapidly down the Danube. Their gains were consolidated at the treaties of Carlowitz (1699) and Passarowitz (1718), though some land was lost again by the treaty of Belgrade (1739). Another consequence of the contest with the Turks was the establishment from the 16th century of a frontier area under the direct control of military authorities in Vienna, which survived until the 1870s. Austria's largest 18th-century acquisitions resulted from the First and Third Partitions of Poland (map 5), but her gains from the latter proved short-lived.

the Crimean Tartars, who preferred to live under Turkish rule, opened up all their vast, fertile, lands to Russian colonisation. Russia's next offensive against Turkey (1787-92) for the first time provoked British opposition. But at the peace of Jassy in 1792, Russia acquired the coast between the Bug and the Dniester, and control of trade in the Dniester basin.

The outbreak of the French Revolution in 1789 reduced French influence in Eastern Europe and when Poland promulgated the Constitution of 3 May 1791, she had no defence against Russia and Prussia who organised a second partition in 1793. After the Polish rising of 1794, Russia and Prussia completed the extinction of Poland in 1795 together this time with Austria.

2/Siege of Vienna (below) The Turks, advancing from the east, laid siege to the city in July 1683. The garrison and citizens held out long enough for the slow-moving German and Polish relief forces to cross the Danube and traverse the hilly country to the north and west. They finally swept down the slopes of the Wiener-wald on 12 September and destroyed the Turkish positions. The relief of Vienna marked the beginning of the Habsburg Empire's rise to great power status.

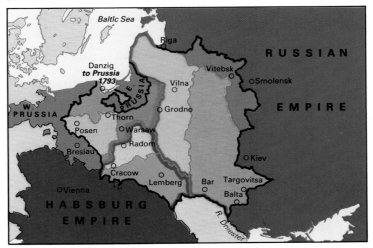

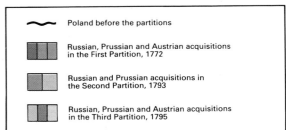

5/The Partitions of Poland (left) In the First Partition (1772), Russia made relatively modest gains, Prussia annexed the territory dividing Pomerania from East Prussia except for Danzig, Austria annexed a large area to the north of Hungary including Lemberg. In the Second Partition (1793), Russia annexed the entire eastern territory inhabited by Ukrainians and White Russians, while Prussia gained Danzig, Thorn and Posen, and pushed her frontier eastwards close to Warsaw. In the final Partition (1795) Prussia annexed Warsaw itself, Austria West Galicia, including Cracow, and Russia the remaining Polish territory, including modern Lithuania.

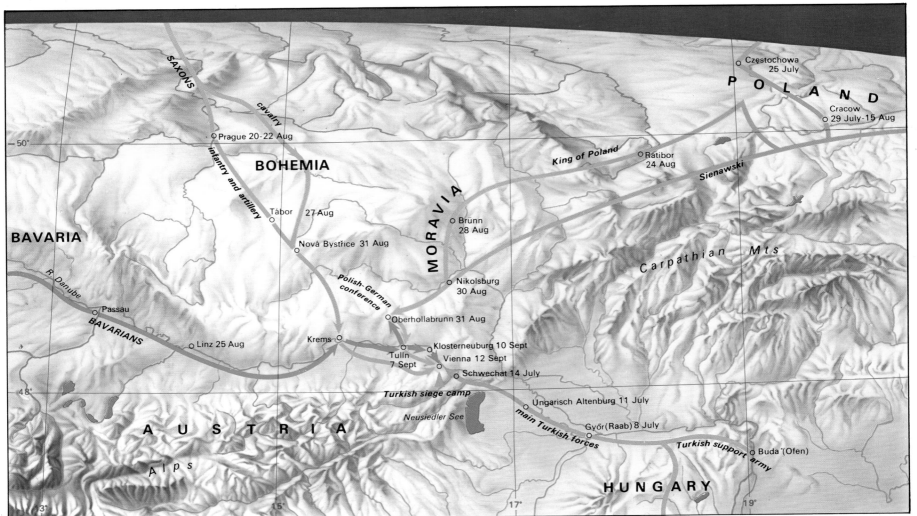

The emerging global economy 1775

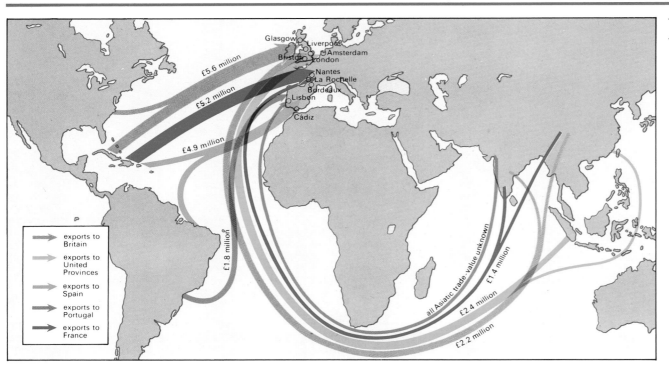

3/The main trading flows *(above)* In the 1770s Britain's total trans-Atlantic imports stood slightly ahead of France. Both now topped Spain, where over 80 per cent consisted of silver and gold. In Asia the Dutch retained their leadership, thanks mainly to the East Indies, but overall they were beginning to fall behind their larger rivals. Both Britain and France were now doing as much business with India as with China.

4/The fur trade in the North *(below)* The Russians pressed east into Siberia with even more systematic determination than the French and English into the Canadian north-west. By 1745, when there were still only isolated trading posts west of Hudson Bay, the Cossacks who had crossed the Urals 'in search of the sable' had explored the Bering Strait, established bases in the Aleutian Islands, and were beginning to penetrate Alaska.

BY the second half of the 18th century, Europe's trading connections with America and Asia were making an important contribution to its prosperity. They had begun to offer large markets for manufactures in exchange for the exotic foods and materials that Europe herself could not produce. Although the commercial links with the two distant continents were very different, the circle of trade was bound together by the transmission of South and Central American silver to Asia via western Europe.

In the Americas settlement had taken three main forms, each with its corresponding social and economic structures. In Peru (then occupying a much greater area than today) and Mexico the Spaniards had settled in small numbers as rulers over large native peasant populations; as races and skills mingled some industry grew up, and by 1700 Spanish America was essentially self-sufficient. On the outskirts of this rural economy, which engaged most of the population, were the great silver mines of northern Mexico and the Bolivian Andes, whose produce enabled the colonists to buy, at highly profitable prices, large quantities of European manufactures.

Second, there were the Caribbean and the Brazilian coastal strip, providing Europe with most of its sugar, coffee, cacao, rice, cotton and other tropical products. Here the large Indian population had almost been exterminated by conquest and disease, necessitating the massive importation of African slaves to build up the plantations. By 1775 five and a half million slaves had been brought to America; but as only a million and a half of them survived, a large replacement trade was needed to recruit scores of thousands more each year. These colonies, with their cheap tropical produce, were seen as Europe's most valuable overseas possessions.

Third, the North American mainland settlements were populated almost entirely by Europeans – English, Scots, Irish, Germans, Dutch – all breeding rapidly to a point where the original few hundred thousand immigrants had increased their numbers to over two million. Apart from the slave plantations in the southern colonies, which produced tobacco and rice, these were lands of small, independent farmers, whose grain, meat and butter duplicated those of the lands from which they had come. Unable to sell their surpluses in Europe, they found a large, rapidly-growing market in the West Indies, which now concentrated almost entirely on export crops. The bills of exchange they received in payment allowed them to buy Scots linen, Birmingham hardware and other imported manufactures. Similarly, but on a much smaller scale, Spanish farmers in the Plate river basin supplied the plantations of Brazil.

The first three-quarters of the 18th century saw enormous developments, both in the absolute size of world trade and in its geographical distribution, even before there was any real sign of the Industrial Revolution. Between 1702 and 1772, England's already healthy foreign commerce almost trebled, while that of France, starting from a much lower base, increased more than eightfold in value from 1715 to 1771 and virtually caught up. Even more significantly, Britain's trading pattern, in 1700 still largely directed towards its continental neighbours, had spread almost throughout the world by the outbreak of the American Revolution, with approximately two-thirds involving sources and destinations outside Europe.

A complex series of exchanges now tied the American colonies to Europe, to each other, and to Asia. Most of the silver brought by the Spanish bullion fleets to Cádiz, which was the monopoly port of entry until 1778, flowed out again in the ships of the Portuguese, English, Dutch and French East India Companies, or travelled overland through Turkey and Russia to China, India or the Indonesian archipelago.

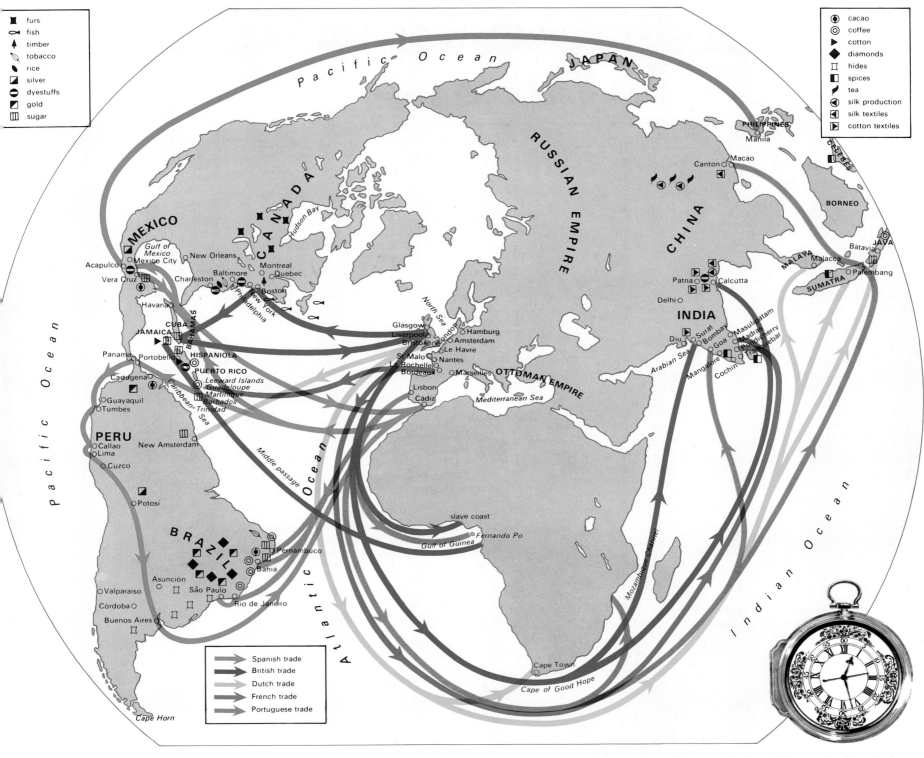

Legend (top left):
- furs
- fish
- timber
- tobacco
- rice
- silver
- dyestuffs
- gold
- sugar

Legend (top right):
- cacao
- coffee
- cotton
- diamonds
- hides
- spices
- tea
- silk production
- silk textiles
- cotton textiles

Trade route legend:
- Spanish trade
- British trade
- Dutch trade
- French trade
- Portuguese trade

1/The pattern of world trade *(above)* As the 18th century progressed, a world-wide network of trade developed. Caribbean cotton, bought with American silver, woven in France or Spain, was sold in Lima or Mexico for silver, returning to pay for more cotton.

2/The exports of the Americas *(below)* Silver, gold and foodstuffs dominated the west-to-east leg of the Atlantic trade. Only in shipbuilding did the colonies have an industry whose products were wanted in Europe.

Harrison's Chronometer *(above)* Accurate measurement of time is essential for calculation of longitude. In 1762 the Yorkshireman Harrison won the British Government's prize for his invention.

South India's spices, China's tea (in which trade was said to be more profitable than in gold) and many other commodities were increasingly in demand, as were the cotton and silk textiles that could be better and more cheaply produced in Asia than in Europe. The industries of India and China were still at least as advanced as those in the west and European manufactures made little headway; what little European export trade there was at this time was mainly involved with supplying home comforts for the small, but increasingly well-established English and Dutch trading communities. Asia wanted silver, not goods, and American silver alone made it possible to develop a large east-west trade. Even England, becoming steadily more committed to the gold standard at home (an evolution largely completed by 1774) had to spend about £30 million between 1733 and 1766 on silver bullion to cover her purchases in India and the Far East.

A handful of port cities prospered mightily on this international trade. London, the greatest, was the biggest sugar-handler and monopolised Britain's Asian commerce. Liverpool rose to dominate the slave business and much general North American commerce. Glasgow became the leading tobacco importer. In France, Bordeaux drew ahead of the other Biscay ports, though Nantes still had the largest slave trade. Amsterdam was the centre of the Dutch trade with Asia and America, and like Hamburg

combined its world-wide commerce with a large intermediary business, processing and forwarding French and English colonial produce into central Europe. Lisbon and Cádiz dominated the world trade of Portugal and Spain.

European expansion was not wholly by sea. In thinly-populated North America and northern Asia, pioneering fur traders travelled vast distances to find native trappers and the sites for future forts and trading posts. Russian expansion across Siberia, starting in the 1580s, finally established its borders in the Amur region with the first formal agreement between China and a European nation, the Treaty of Nerchinsk, in 1689, followed in 1727 with the founding of a Russian trading station in Peking.

This extra-European trade required the shipment of bulky goods over long distances, the provision of very long-term credit, the financing of large stocks and large-scale capital investment. It was responsible for making most of the great new individual fortunes of the period (apart from those of the war-financiers). This commercial revolution dominated economic thought in the hundred years prior to Adam Smith's *Wealth of Nations* in 1776.

For a century at least the merchant class was outstanding, and its importance declined only when the Industrial Revolution, with its new processes, profits, capital needs and social relationships, transformed the British economy.

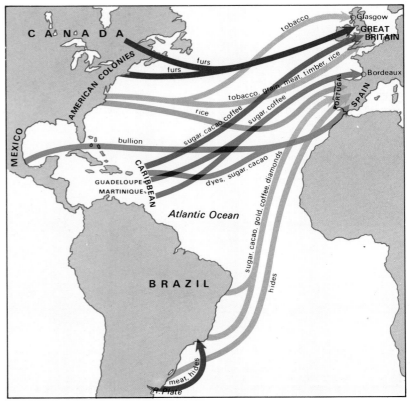

The Industrial Revolution begins: Great Britain 1760 to 1820

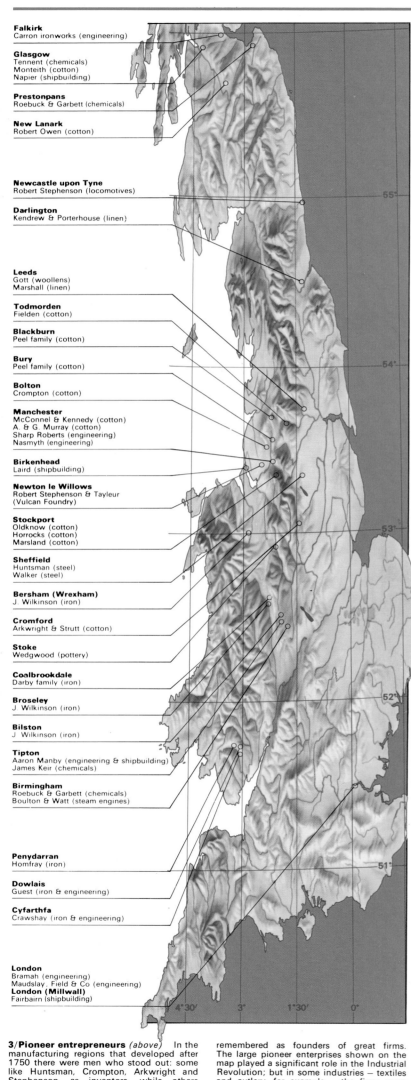

Falkirk
Carron ironworks (engineering)

Glasgow
Tennent (chemicals)
Monteith (cotton)
Napier (shipbuilding)

Prestonpans
Roebuck & Garbett (chemicals)

New Lanark
Robert Owen (cotton)

Newcastle upon Tyne
Robert Stephenson (locomotives)

Darlington
Kendrew & Porterhouse (linen)

Leeds
Gott (woollens)
Marshall (linen)

Todmorden
Fielden (cotton)

Blackburn
Peel family (cotton)

Bury
Peel family (cotton)

Bolton
Crompton (cotton)

Manchester
McConnel & Kennedy (cotton)
A. & G. Murray (cotton)
Sharp Roberts (engineering)
Nasmyth (engineering)

Birkenhead
Laird (shipbuilding)

Newton le Willows
Robert Stephenson & Tayleur
(Vulcan Foundry)

Stockport
Oldknow (cotton)
Horrocks (cotton)
Marsland (cotton)

Sheffield
Huntsman (steel)
Walker (steel)

Bersham (Wrexham)
J. Wilkinson (iron)

Cromford
Arkwright & Strutt (cotton)

Stoke
Wedgwood (pottery)

Coalbrookdale
Darby family (iron)

Broseley
J. Wilkinson (iron)

Bilston
J. Wilkinson (iron)

Tipton
Aaron Manby (engineering & shipbuilding)
James Keir (chemicals)

Birmingham
Roebuck & Garbett (chemicals)
Boulton & Watt (steam engines)

Penydarran
Homfray (iron)

Dowlais
Guest (iron & engineering)

Cyfarthfa
Crawshay (iron & engineering)

London
Bramah (engineering)
Maudslay, Field & Co (engineering)
London (Millwall)
Fairbairn (shipbuilding)

3/Pioneer entrepreneurs *(above)* In the manufacturing regions that developed after 1750 there were men who stood out: some like Huntsman, Crompton, Arkwright and Stephenson, as inventors, while others (McConnel and Kennedy, Gott, Marshall) are remembered as founders of great firms. The large pioneer enterprises shown on the map played a significant role in the Industrial Revolution; but in some industries – textiles and cutlery, for example – the firms were mostly small.

THE Industrial Revolution – the transition from a predominantly agrarian to a predominantly industrial economy – was the starting point of a new period in world history. Even in Europe, however, its impact was limited before 1820, and in many countries before the middle of the 19th century; in the wider world (see page 218) its revolutionary consequences were felt only much later. Nevertheless it is important to trace its origins in 18th century England. By 1750, Britain already had a prosperous and expanding economy. The changes to its structure which occurred during the reign of George III (1760-1820) were substantial, but they represented a continuing accumulative process of modernisation which can be traced back to the 16th century at least. Even in Britain, this process did not produce rapid growth rates in total industrial output before 1800. However, in the half-century or so before this there was striking acceleration in some sectors of manufacturing, notably cotton textiles, coal and pig iron. The first revolution of its kind in the world, it occurred in Great Britain and not on the continent of Europe for many reasons. Great Britain had valuable resources, such as coal, iron, tin, copper, stone and salt; her agriculture was highly efficient and already highly commercialised. The transport facilities – navigable rivers (Clyde, Thames, Severn, Trent, Ouse, Humber), good harbours (London, Bristol, Liverpool, Newcastle upon Tyne), and the sea – were supplemented by networks of new canals, toll roads and colliery railways. It was much cheaper to send goods, particularly bulky goods, by water than by land, and England's economic growth in the second half of the 18th century was stimulated by the heavy traffic on her inland waterways and along her coasts. A striking example was the movement of large quantities of coal from the Tyne and Wear to London. Again Lancashire had a climate which proved particularly suitable for the manufacture of cotton cloth, and this was the great growth industry in England at the time of the Industrial Revolution. The remarkable growth of London provided an expanding market for manufactured goods.

While continental Europe was plagued by one campaign after another in the 18th century, Great Britain fought her wars abroad and was free from internal strife except for two brief Jacobite revolts in 1715 and in 1745. The Wars against the French (see page 194) enabled the British to extend their empire – and to expand their overseas markets – in Canada and India. The loss of the American colonies did not, for many years, lessen the importance of the United States as a market for British manufactured goods. Again, the temporary loss of continental markets suffered during the revolutionary and Napoleonic wars was counterbalanced by the opening up of new trading opportunities across the Atlantic. The stimulus of war helped the iron, engineering, shipbuilding and textile industries which supplied the armed forces.

At a time when commerce in continental Europe was strangled by customs barriers, river tolls and local taxes, men and goods had moved freely all over Great Britain since the union of England and Scotland in 1707. The government played its part in maintaining law and order, providing a stable currency, protecting industry from foreign competition, and taking special measures to foster shipping, overseas trade and the woollen industry.

With a few important exceptions – such as mining and shipbuilding – only a modest initial capital was required to set up a new industrial enterprise. In the cotton industry, a small workshop and relatively inexpensive machines were all that the pioneer entrepreneur needed. Robert Owen had to borrow only £200 to get started. An industrialist could often expand his undertaking by ploughing back some of his

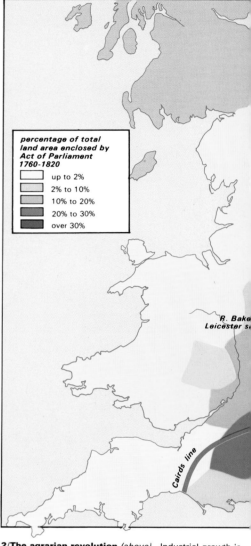

*percentage of total
land area enclosed by
Act of Parliament
1760-1820*

— up to 2%
— 2% to 10%
— 10% to 20%
— 20% to 30%
— over 30%

R. Bake
Leicester s

Cairds line

2/The agrarian revolution *(above)* Industrial growth is generally preceded by an agrarian revolution; in England after 1750 the completion of enclosure of old commons and open fields together with scientific farming increased the output of food for a growing population and of raw materials for expanding industries. Increased prosperity enabled the agricultural community to buy more manufactured goods and to invest in new industries and public works. 'Caird's Line' indicates the division between grazing and dairy lands (to the west) and the chief grain districts (to the east).

profits into the business. Although the family business or partnership which financed its own expansion was very common, enterprises were also established with capital derived from land or from commerce. Short-term loans were often available from the country (provincial) banks at low rates of interest.

A series of inventions and innovations in the second half of the 18th century greatly increased the output of consumer and capital goods. They included new spinning machines and looms, coke-smelting, puddling, and the introduction of crucible cast steel. Above all, the steam engine provided industry with a new source of power and made possible the replacement of small workshops by large factories. However this process was gradual and the factory did not become the characteristic unit of industrial organisation until after 1830.

Social conditions, too, were favourable to economic progress. The class structure in England was less rigid than in continental Europe. No social stigma prevented the landed gentry from engaging in industry or trade; no legal impediments prevented an artisan from rising in the social scale. However, the bulk of early industrialists were drawn from the wide middle ranks of British society. In spite of some sporadic violent opposition to the new order – machine-breaking and rick-burning – a labour force was set up which eventually accepted factory discipline.

Down the coalmine (left) This sketch of small boys dragging a trolley in a coalmine illustrates one aspect of the human suffering involved during the Industrial Revolution. The employment of women and children under ground was prohibited in 1842.

1/The pattern of industrial expansion (below) Rapid industrial expansion took place in regions where minerals, particularly coal and iron ore, could be exploited. Many of these natural resources were conveniently situated near ports. Thus coal from Durham and Northumberland could be shipped to London from ports on the Tyne and Wear. The manufacturing regions were linked by a network of toll roads, by navigable rivers, and by canals. The Industrial Revolution was associated with a movement of population to the coalfields, ports and new manufacturing districts.

Watt's rotative beam steam engine (above) In 1765 James Watt invented his first steam engine, which was used almost exclusively to work pumps. In 1781 he invented the rotative engine, which could turn a shaft and so drive machinery. Whilst the engines were under patent the firm of Boulton & Watt built about 200 steam pumps and over 300 rotative engines.

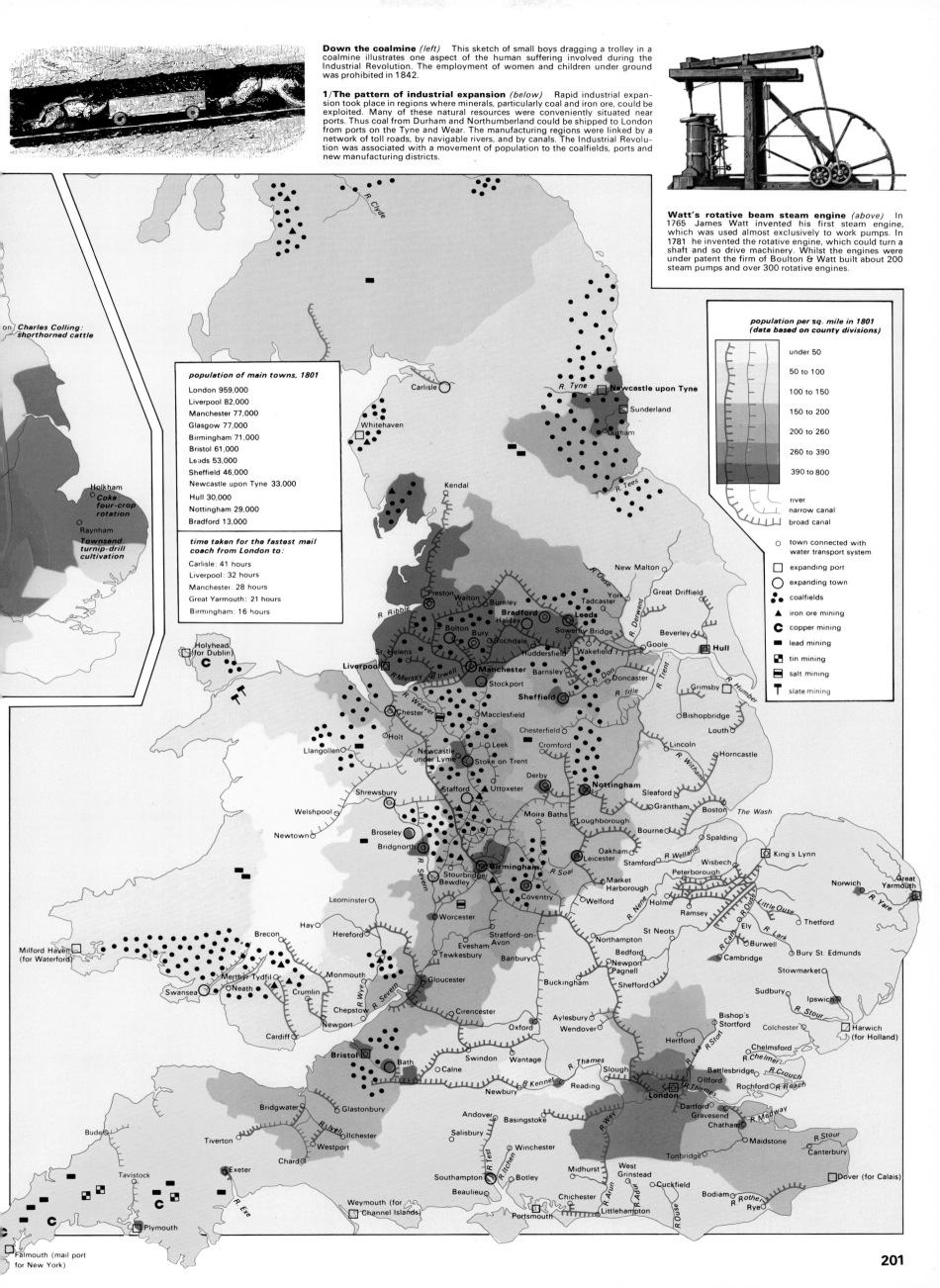

population of main towns, 1801

London 959,000
Liverpool 82,000
Manchester 77,000
Glasgow 77,000
Birmingham 71,000
Bristol 61,000
Leeds 53,000
Sheffield 46,000
Newcastle upon Tyne 33,000
Hull 30,000
Nottingham 29,000
Bradford 13,000

time taken for the fastest mail coach from London to:

Carlisle: 41 hours
Liverpool: 32 hours
Manchester: 28 hours
Great Yarmouth: 21 hours
Birmingham: 16 hours

population per sq. mile in 1801 (data based on county divisions)

under 50
50 to 100
100 to 150
150 to 200
200 to 260
260 to 390
390 to 800

river
narrow canal
broad canal
○ town connected with water transport system
□ expanding port
◯ expanding town
⦂ coalfields
▲ iron ore mining
C copper mining
▬ lead mining
tin mining
salt mining
T slate mining

Charles Colling: shorthorned cattle

Holkham
Coke: four-crop rotation
Raynham
Townsend: turnip-drill cultivation

201

The age of revolution
1773 to 1814

THE late 18th century was a time of upheaval in many parts of the western hemisphere, upheaval which can be attributed, directly or indirectly, to the ferment of ideas known as the Enlightenment. These ideas, themselves a reflection of the needs and tensions of a changing society, were based on the new scientific knowledge of the 17th century, which bred a new faith in reason and progress. On the one hand, this led to a rejection of authority and an assertion of the Rights of Man, expressed in Rousseau's famous statement that man is born free, but is everywhere in chains. On the other hand, the new ideas provided inspiration for monarchs who had already, at the close of the 17th century (see page 184), begun to draw power into their own hands and to govern through bureaucratic agents of their own choice. Centralising, enlightened rulers such as Joseph II of Austria (1780-90) or Frederick II of Prussia (1740-86) derived their ideas from rationalist philosophers such as the Encyclopaedists, for whom government was

a science leading to the efficient satisfaction of needs. But their centralising activities were opposed by all those with a vested interest in the old régime – churches, guilds and corporations, and above all the aristocracy, whose leaders drew upon the theories of Montesquieu and Burke to prove that society was an organic growth, and that its traditional groupings not only conferred inalienable rights upon their members but resulted in a balance of power which guaranteed the individual against tyranny. This, and the desire of provinces for autonomy, was the origin of unrest. But it soon became clear that the ferment could not stop here.

Open revolt was most likely to occur in areas where the aristocracy could obtain support from the peasantry; but in eastern Europe (see page 178) peasants were still serfs, and were unlikely to rebel in support of the landlords who were their immediate oppressors. However, peasants also disliked innovation and would sometimes fight fiercely to retain their traditional way of

1/The age of revolution (left and below)
1755, 1793 Corsica Local clans led by Paoli rebelled against Genoese rule and established independent democratic government. France bought island from Genoa in 1768, crushed revolt. Second attempt by Paoli to secure independence from (revolutionary) France, 1793, led to brief British occupation; rise of Bonaparte, himself a Corsican, put an end to separatist movement.
1768 Geneva Middle-class citizens of small city-state rebelled against domination by few patrician families; with French support the latter reasserted predominance 1782.
1773 South-East Russia Cossacks, peasants and Asiatic tribes rebelled in Volga and Ural region under the leadership of Pugachev, a Don Cossack. After fierce fighting, Russian army put down rebellion in autumn 1774.
1775 America Prolonged resistance by Britain's Thirteen Colonies to financial policies of mother country resulted in open warfare and Declaration of Independence, 1776 (see page 164).
1784 Dutch Netherlands Three-cornered struggle for power between Stadtholder, patrician families who controlled Estates General, and middle-class Patriot party which aimed to democratise government. In 1787 Prussian troops defeated Patriot army and restored Stadtholder with greater powers.
1787 Austrian Netherlands (Belgium) Revolt against centralising policy of Emperor Joseph II, leading to proclamation of the Republic of the United Belgian Provinces (1790). Faction fights broke out between aristocratic and middle-class rebels; Austrian Emperor reconquered area end 1790.
1789 France The States-General, summoned by Louis XVI to solve his financial difficulties, turned itself into a National Assembly, proclaimed Rights of Man, and issued constitution (1791). Risings by peasantry and Parisians overthrew feudal social and political order; Louis XVI's opposition, and attempted flight, led to abolition of monarchy (1792). King and Queen were guillotined as traitors (1793). Threat of invasion by a coalition under Austria led under the Jacobins to 'reign of terror', ended by fall and execution of Robespierre (1794). Following weak and corrupt rule of Directory (1795-99) power passed to Napoleon Bonaparte.

1789 Liège Middle-class citizens supported by workers and peasants expelled prince-bishop and abolished feudalism. Bishop restored by Austrian troops, 1790.
1790 Hungary Magyar nobles rejected edicts of Austrian emperor and demanded greater independence for Hungary within Habsburg Empire; later, frightened by peasant disturbances, accepted compromise with the monarchy.
1791 Poland King, supported by patriotic nobles, adopted constitution to modernise and strengthen government. Catherine II of Russia organised counter-revolution with support of some of greater nobles to restore old régime, invaded Poland and divided large areas with Prussia. Attempt by Kósciuszko and patriotic nobles to rise against invaders crushed, Poland was partitioned between Russia, Austria and Prussia and ceased to exist as an independent state.
1791 Haiti Slave rising in western (French) part of island (Saint Domingue) resulted in rise of Negro leader, Toussaint l'Ouverture; by 1801 had conquered rest of island from Spaniards and secured virtual independence. Island then seized by the French, rising suppressed, and independence not fully secured until 1825.
1793 Sardinia In return for expelling French revolutionary invaders, islanders demanded autonomy within combined kingdom of Piedmont-Sardinia. King re-asserted his authority when French threat subsided in 1796.
1798 Ireland Rebellion of United Irishmen seeking independence from England, put down by British army. Leading conspirator, Wolfe Tone, committed suicide.
1804 Serbia Revolt against Ottoman atrocities led to demands for autonomy within the Ottoman Empire and later for independence. Rebels under Kara George fought until the Ottoman reoccupation of Serbia in 1813.
1808 Spain After Napoleon placed his own brother, Joseph, on the throne a national rising against the French provided an opening for an expeditionary force under Wellington. Liberal constitution proclaimed by Cortes of Cadiz in 1812, but it did not survive restoration of Bourbon king in 1814.
1809 Tyrol After Austria renewed war against Napoleon, the peasants of Tyrol, whose territory had been taken from Austria by Napoleon in 1805 and given to Bavaria, rebelled against new rulers. In spite of brave stand under Andreas Hofer, an innkeeper, revolt was crushed by Bavarian and French troops.
1810 Spanish America Discontent against mother country increased after 1808, when colonists faced prospect of new imperialist policies from either Napoleon or Spanish liberals; beginning of revolutionary movement which secured independence of entire sub-continent during following two decades (see page 226).

life, as they did in Russia under Pugachev and in Hungary against Joseph II. In western Europe, a similar peasant reaction to foreign rule played a part in the Belgian revolution. But the Polish peasants had little inducement to support the gentry in the Polish revolts of 1791 and 1794, and in Ireland also middle-class nationalists who relied on peasant unrest against English landlords were disappointed and quickly succumbed to British armed force when support from France failed to arrive. On the other hand, the peasants of Serbia, who rose in 1804 in the first nationalist revolt of the Balkans, held out for three years until overwhelmed by the reorganised armies of the Sultan.

Revolution on a large scale first appeared in England's American colonies. Appealing to Locke's philosophy of natural right, the colonists refused to be taxed by a parliament in London in which they were not represented. By 1775 the dispute had led to open war (see pages 164 and 194). Moderate men, who would have retained the old structure of society, were superseded by men with more democratic aims, and the war for national independence attracted support from all classes of the population, including small farmers, town labourers, and a numerous bourgeoisie. The American example was an inspiration to rebels in the Netherlands as well as in France (whose troops had fought on the American side in the war), but in Holland and Belgium factions were too much divided between reactionary and progressive aims to succeed in face of foreign intervention.

In France, also, the revolution began as an aristocratic reaction to the centralising monarchy. But this soon proved to be merely a prelude to widespread popular revolt. This began in 1789 when the middle class took advantage of a financial crisis to establish a parliamentary type of government on a basis of wealth. This assertion of middle-class preponderance was challenged when the peasants, exploited as much by bourgeois as by aristocratic landlords, rose in a vast wave of rioting which brought about the destruction of feudal society. At the same time, the labouring population of Paris, impelled by food shortage, seized the strategic fortress of the Bastille and made it impossible for the king, Louis XVI, to recover despotic power by overawing the city. For two years the middle class retained control of the political scene and used its power to reorganise France's civil, military and religious institutions. They intended to co-operate with the king and with liberal sections of the aristocracy; but this became impossible when counter-revolutionary forces gathered strength both inside and outside the country. In 1792 the revolutionaries, confronted with the threat of armed invasion, declared war on Austria, and were soon at war with Prussia and the greater part of Europe. Early defeats produced panic measures, including the deposition and subsequent execution of the king and the slaughter of political suspects. This unification of the nation against external threat was the work of Danton, Carnot and the Girondins; but they were displaced by a more extreme set of revolutionaries, the Jacobins, who rallied support by placing government on a more democratic basis and by terrorist action against dissidents. A total call-up of the nation for war produced enthusiastic armies, superbly organised by Carnot, and the French not only expelled the foreign invaders but also attacked in their turn. Belgium and other territories were annexed to secure France's 'natural frontiers'. Army officers who owed their advancement to the revolutionary doctrine of 'careers open to talent' extended French power into Holland, Switzerland and Italy. Outstanding among them was Napoleon Bonaparte who, after a brilliant campaign in Italy, led an expedition across the Mediterranean and carried revolutionary institutions to Malta and Egypt. Only the assault on the British Isles proved unsuccessful. A raid on Wales in 1797 failed to win local support, and three expeditions to Ireland failed to meet up with local rebels.

At home, victory produced a revulsion against the Robespierrist terror, and France reverted once more to middle-class government (1794). But the corruption of the Directory and the relaxation of national effort soon led to econo-

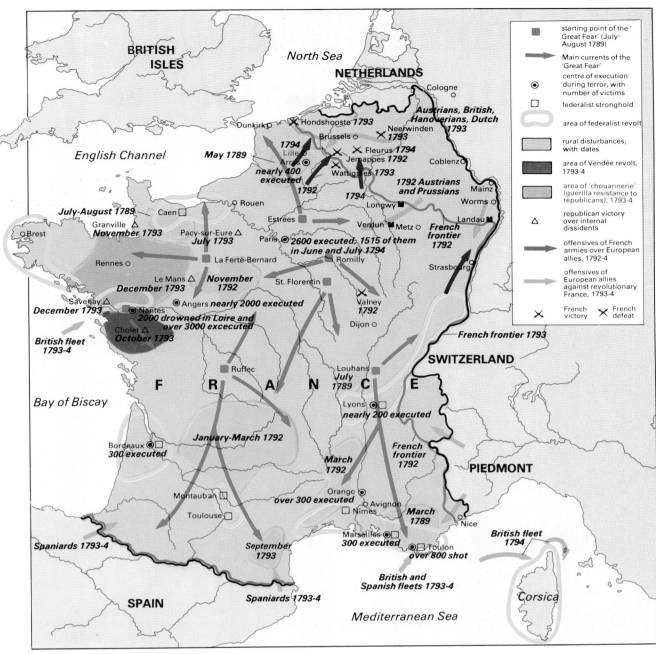

2/The revolution in France (above) The French Revolution proceeded by violence and war. In 1789 a Paris rising secured the overthrow of the government, and peasant revolt destroyed feudalism. Both were to some extent caused by food storage at a time of political excitement. In 1792-93 fear of counter-revolution led to war with the reactionary forces in Europe, led by Austria. Economic distress and military defeat encouraged royalist revolt in Vendée and federalist revolt in large terms, but the Jacobins suppressed opponents and achieved military victory.

3/The expansion of revolutionary France (right) The French Revolution produced successful armies which extended France's power and influence. Territory was annexed to secure 'natural frontiers', and beyond them 'sister republics' were established. French armies remained in occupation, but administration was in the hands of local democrats. These were too few to sustain the republics when French military power temporarily waned in 1799, but the experience of revolutionary institutions had a lasting effect.

mic crisis, political discontent and military defeat. These were the dangers from which France was rescued by Napoleon when he seized power in 1799. Napoleon not only re-established revolutionary institutions in France – even if in a modified form – but also carried them by military conquest to many other parts of Europe.

The French Revolution was a decisive turning point in European history. At the same time its vigorous assertion of personal dignity, regardless of birth or creed, was an inspiration to people as far away as Haiti, and made a lasting impact upon ideas and institutions in all quarters of the globe. Nevertheless, French attempts to impose Enlightenment by force caused resentment. Peasant resistance began in France itself at an early stage and was repeated, with nationalist implications, in the Tyrol and in Spain in Napoleonic times. Meanwhile, Spain's American colonists (see page 226) were even more determined to resist interference from a reformed mother country than from the pre-revolutionary régime, and revolutionary movements which themselves owed much to the Enlightenment eventually secured the independence of Latin America.

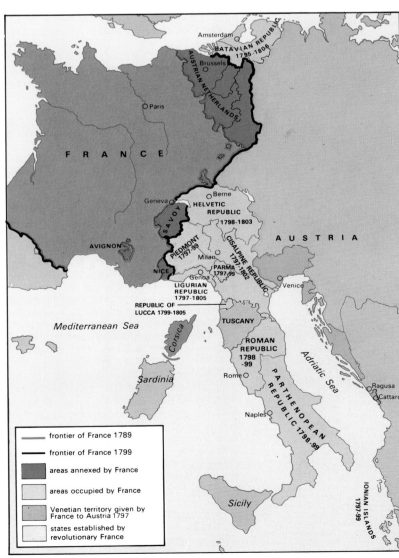

Napoleon and the reshaping of Europe

2/Napoleonic institutions *(above)*, designed to create a society based on wealth and merit rather than on prescription and privilege, were established to some degree over the whole of western Europe. Their effect varied according to the type of control Napoleon exercised (see map 1) and the length of time they operated. Spain officially received Napoleonic institutions in a modified form for about five years, but their effectiveness varied with the fortunes of war.

The Legion of Honour *(above)* was created in 1802 to reward both soldiers and civilians for outstanding service to the state. The distinction was accompanied by a pension. Critics complained that revolutionary equality had given way to elitism, but the Legion became popular throughout the French Empire. One of the recipients of the honour was Goethe.

IN 1799 the 31-year-old General Napoleon Bonaparte seized power in France. Born in Corsica, he had risen to prominence by leading French Revolutionary armies in a descent on northern Italy and an attack on Egypt. His autocratic rule as First Consul (1799-1804) and as Emperor (1804-14) was acceptable to the French people after the chaos of the last few years of the Revolution, and during his first few years of power he justified their hopes of sound government by introducing measures which were to form a lasting basis for most of France's institutions. An administrative law of 1800 reorganised the *départements* into which France had been divided by the Revolution, reducing the power of their locally elected councils and giving them prefects to carry centralised authority to every part of the country. A Concordat of 1801 brought an end to the quarrel that had broken out between revolutionary France and the Church, allowing the state to control the temporalities of the Church while the Pope confined himself to spiritual direction. An educational law of 1801 set up state grammar schools (*lycées*) for which scholarships were available and in which education was directed towards providing well-trained civil servants and army officers. More welcome still to the majority of Frenchmen was the civil code of 1804, later known as the *Code Napoléon*, which confirmed the legal equality and the property rights that had emerged from the Revolution. Members of the old nobility were allowed to share the benefits of this legislation provided they accepted the new regime. Napoleon thus consolidated the more concrete achievements of the Revolution to such an extent that they proved unshakeable even after his downfall, though in doing so he substituted efficiency for individual liberty as the goal of human endeavour. The functions of parliament were reduced to a minimum, and administrative activity took the place of politics. France became a nation of peasant farmers and landed proprietors, with a heavy top-dressing of bureaucra-

cy in which men of talent could compete for jobs and rewards.

The bureaucrats were soon joined by a military élite, for the general peace which Bonaparte secured at the outset of his career lasted only a short time, and from 1803 to 1814 war was continuous. France's armies, which had already shown their potential during the Revolution, reached the height of their achievement as a result of Napoleon's administrative genius and brilliant generalship. Abandoning the siege warfare of an earlier age, Napoleon aimed at defeating the enemy's forces in the field, after outmanoeuvring them in such a way that they were divided and thus outnumbered. Shattering defeats were inflicted on Austria at Austerlitz (1805), on Prussia at Jena (1806), and on Russia at Friedland (1807), leaving Napoleon supreme in western Europe. A lightning invasion of Spain in 1808 drove a British expeditionary force to the sea at Corunna, and renewed hostilities by Austria in 1809 produced another rapid victory for the French at Wagram. Military success was accompanied by ruthless diplomacy. Territories on the borders of France were annexed; Switzerland came under French 'protection'; the princely rulers of western Germany allied with Napoleon in return for aggrandisement of their states; Spain, north-east Italy, Naples and Westphalia became satellite kingdoms under members of the Bonaparte family; and Polish lands taken from Austria and Prussia received a Napoleonic nominee as Grand Duke. Only Austria and Prussia, greatly reduced in size, remained in precarious independence alongside the enigmatic power of Russia.

Napoleon insisted that even the remotest of his puppet rulers should establish French-style institutions if at all possible, and adopt the *Code Napoléon*. His intention was partly to carry out a social revolution in the more backward areas such as Poland, and partly to harness the resources of the whole Empire to the needs of France. The success of the new institutions in creating a society based on wealth and merit rather than on prescription and privilege was greatest in the Netherlands, the Rhinelands and north-east Italy, where feudalism had long been breaking down and where French Revolutionary armies had already laid a foundation of

1/The Empire of Napoleon *(right)* By 1812 Napoleon controlled the greater part of western Europe, exacting men and money for his armies but bringing greater opportunities for men of talent. Only Spain, supported by Britain, was in rebellion against him. In 1812, however, his invasion of Russia met with disaster. Driven back into France, he was obliged to abdicate (1814). His Empire was destroyed, but many of his ideas lived on.

French ideas, but the result was nowhere negligible. Nor was Napoleon's influence confined to the continent of Europe. His reforms, which were secular in inspiration and therefore not tied to Christianity, were adopted as a pattern by both Mohammed Ali of Egypt and the Ottoman Sultan Mahmud II later in the 19th century, and the *Code Napoléon* became a model for legal reform in South America and Japan.

Fortunately for Napoleon, national feeling at this time was almost non-existent in Germany and Italy. In spite of grievances created by France's economic exactions, many young men in annexed or allied territories appreciated the career opportunities opened up to them by Napoleonic institutions and by the fusion of petty states into larger territorial units. The only serious popular resistance to French encroachment came from Spain, where peasant guerrilla warfare encouraged a British army under Sir Arthur Wellesley (later the Duke of Wellington) to land in Portugal in 1809 and fight its way through Spain into southern France by 1813. Napoleon's chief enemies on the continent of Europe were the dynastic rulers of Austria, Prussia and Russia. All three at one time or another allied with Napoleon for the sake of expediency, but his insatiable ambition finally led him to invade Russia in 1812, and his defeat there encouraged all three monarchs to ally against him. The money for their military efforts came chiefly from Great Britain, France's most persistent enemy.

Great Britain's hostility arose from strategic and economic reasons. It had never been in her interest to allow France to dominate the whole of the Channel coast. French governments had long excluded British trade from France's territories: in an effort to bring ruin and revolution to Britain, Napoleon attempted in his Continental System to close the whole of Europe to British goods. Nelson thwarted Napoleon's invasion schemes by destroying the French and Spanish fleets at Trafalgar (1805), and British naval power in the Baltic and the Mediterranean continually undermined the Continental System, but Britain would never have been able to destroy the Napoleonic Empire without help from the eastern European powers on land. This led to the curious situation in which Britain, politically and industrially the most advanced nation in the world, allied with reactionary powers to defeat the only other modernising force in Europe.

In France, Napoleon's wars were popular for some years. Conscription could be avoided by anyone wealthy enough to buy a replacement, and for men without capital or education the army provided a welcome career in which advancement could be rapid for anyone showing courage and initiative. Only in 1814, when France was invaded by Russian, Prussian, Austrian and British armies, did the French people begin, vainly, to urge Napoleon to make peace. He was defeated and exiled to Elba. In 1815 he escaped and ruled France again for a hundred days, but he was defeated by Wellington at Waterloo and sent as a prisoner to St Helena, where he died in 1821.

3/The overseas world (right) Napoleon frequently toyed with world-wide schemes which might have threatened the British Empire had he succeeded in controlling the colonies of Spain and Holland.

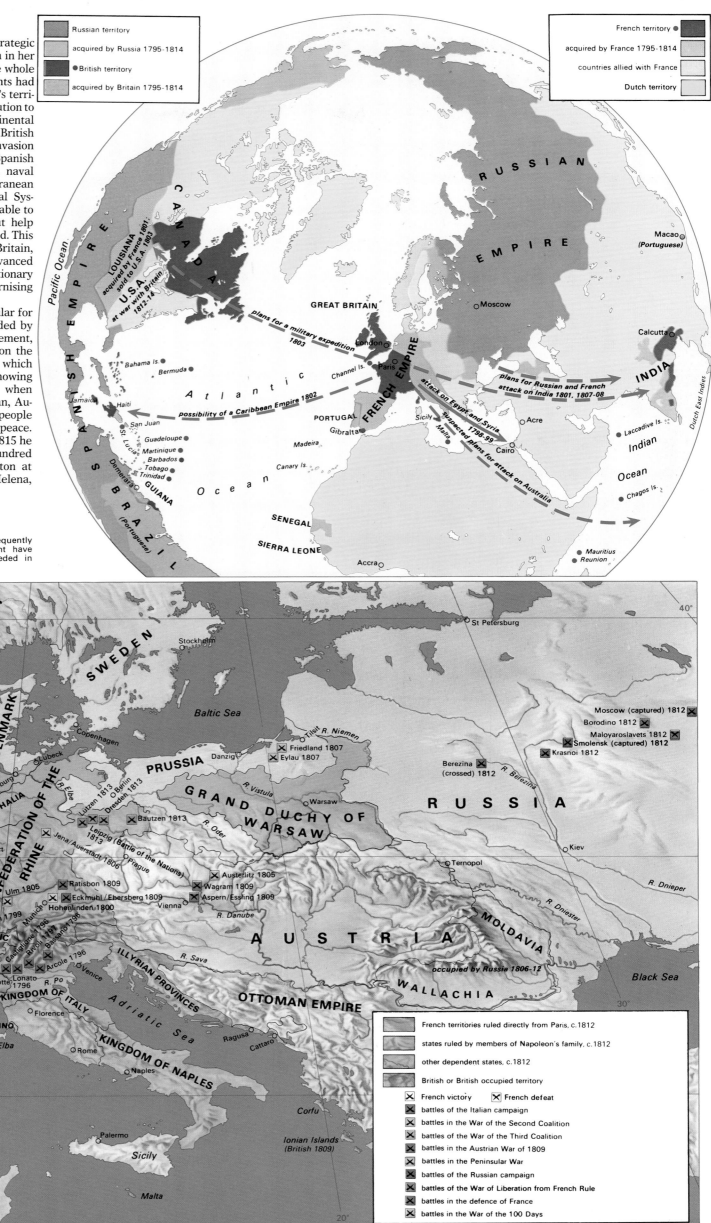

BETWEEN 1815 and 1914 Europe thrust out into the world, impelled by the force of its own industrialisation.

Millions of Europeans poured overseas and into Asiatic Russia, seeking and finding new opportunities in the wider world. Between 1880 and 1900 Africa, a continent four times the size of Europe, was parcelled out among the European powers. And when in 1898 the United States of America, following the European lead, annexed Puerto Rico, the Philippines and other islands of the Pacific, and asserted a controlling voice in Latin American affairs, it seemed as though European expansion was turning into the domination of the white race over the coloured majority. But expansion carried with it the seeds of its own destruction. Even before European rivalries plunged the continent into the war of 1914-18, the beginnings of anti-European reaction were visible in Asia and Africa, and no sooner had the United States occupied the Philippines than they were met by a nationalist uprising under the great Philippine leader, Aguinaldo.

Today, in retrospect, we can see that the age of expansive imperialism was a transient phase of history; while it lasted, it left a European imprint on the world. The world in 1914 was utterly different from the world in 1815, the tempo of change during the preceding century greater than previously during whole millennia. Though industry in 1914 was only beginning to spread beyond Europe and North America, and life in Asia and Africa was still regulated by age-old traditions, the nineteenth century inaugurated the process of transformation which dethroned agricultural society as it had existed through the ages, and replaced it with the urban, industrialised, technocratic society which is spreading – for good or for ill – like wildfire through the world today.

6

The age o

The Eiffel Tower, Paris, built in 1889 for the Centennial Exposition

European dominance

Population growth and movements 1815 to 1914

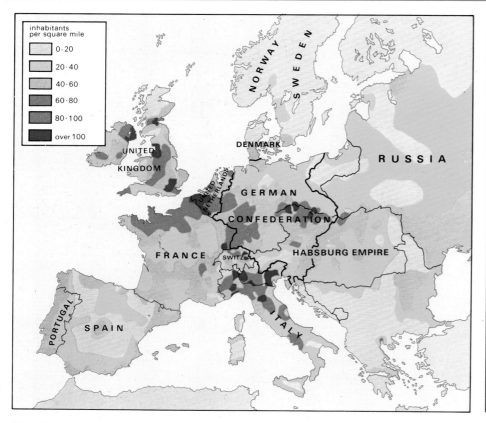

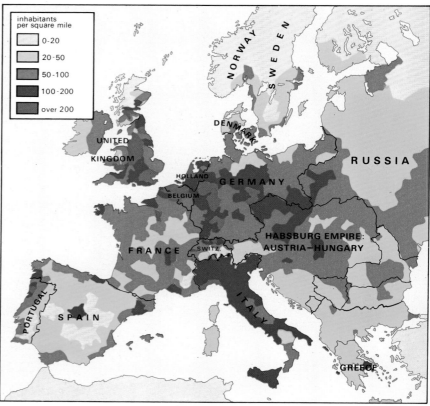

3/Europe's population in 1820 *(above)* The major centres were the industrialised regions of the United Kingdom and a few major cities and ports (London, Paris, St Petersburg, Liverpool, Bordeaux, Hamburg, Marseilles).

4/Europe's population by c. 1900 *(above)* was concentrated in the main industrial British centres: the Midlands, Yorkshire, Lancashire, south Wales, Tyneside, Clydeside; in Belgium, France and Germany (the Ruhr, Rhineland, Upper Silesia).

New York *(above)* By 1810 New York had outstripped its rivals to become the most dynamic urban centre in the New World. In 1810 the population was only 100,000, but passed 1,000,000 by 1871.

Immigration *(below)* During the 19th century more than two-thirds of the immigrants to the United States passed through the port of New York where the Statue of Liberty symbolised their hopes.

IT has been estimated that in the 19th century the population of the world expanded more rapidly than in any previous period, from about 900 million to 1600 million. (During the 20th century it was to grow four times faster.) The population of Europe increased from 190 million to 423 million; at the same time, European peoples – emigrants and their descendants – settled in North and South America, South Africa, Australia, New Zealand and Siberia, and the population of these regions grew from 5,670,000 to 200,000,000 between 1810 and 1910. In the three countries which were the leading industrial states in 1914 – the United Kingdom, Germany and the United States – the population had increased nearly five-fold in the previous hundred years. The distribution of the world's population at the beginning of the 20th century was estimated to be as follows (again in millions): Europe 423, Asia 937, Africa 120, North and South America 144, and Australia 6. There were, however, exceptions to the general growth in population. Ireland, for example, had a declining population: it fell from 8,175,000 in 1841 to 4,390,000 in 1911.

Various factors promoted the growth of the population during the 19th century. In Europe, in the United States, and in the colonies and spheres of influence of European states, the greatly improved methods of industrial and agricultural production, coupled with more efficient communications, provided work and food for expanding populations. The colonial powers established mines and plantations in their overseas territories which supplied manufacturing countries with increased quantities of raw materials and foodstuffs. Advanced industrial regions were free from the food shortages which were all too common in backward countries. There was no parallel in England, France or Germany to the famines that afflicted Ireland in 1847, India in 1866 and 1877, China in 1878 and Russia in 1891. Advances in medicine, improved sanitation and higher standards of personal hygiene resulted in a dramatic reduction in mortality from cholera, tuberculosis, smallpox,

typhus and typhoid.

Population growth was not spread evenly over urban and rural districts. The expansion of old cities and the founding of new towns were characteristic features of the industrial age. The population of some cities with a history going back to mediaeval times – London, Cologne, Lyons, Moscow and many others – increased rapidly in the 19th century. Towns which had been mere villages, or had not even existed, in the previous century sprang to life as great centres of industry, commerce or mining. Middlesbrough and Barrow in England; Gelsenkirchen, Oberhausen and Königshütte in Germany; Lodz in Poland; and a host of towns in the United States and in the English colonies were examples of this type of mushroom urban growth. In industrial countries more and more people worked and lived in towns while fewer lived in the country.

Populations not only grew more rapidly in the 19th century than ever before but also moved on a considerable scale. Millions of people moved from Europe to the United States or to British colonies in North America, South Africa, Australia and New Zealand, building up new communities of white settlers which produced foodstuffs and raw materials for the countries they had left behind. The 'Europeanisation' of vast territories overseas was a significant factor in increasing the political influence of the major European states throughout the world. Migrations within states or regions included movements of workers from one district to another, seeking employment either on the land during the harvest, or in towns, where job opportunities existed in factories and mines or in public works such as railway building. Irishmen sought work in Liverpool, Manchester and Glasgow; Poles moved to the coalmines in the Ruhr. Some migration was temporary in character. Irishmen who went to England or Scotland to dig potatoes generally returned home when the harvest was over. From Italy, there were seasonal labourers who worked in France, Germany and Switzerland – and even in the Argentine – and it has been estimated that in 1914 there were no less than three million of these migrant workers. In Russia there were peasants who secured jobs in factories in towns for the winter and then returned to work in their villages during the summer. However, emigration from one country to another – especially

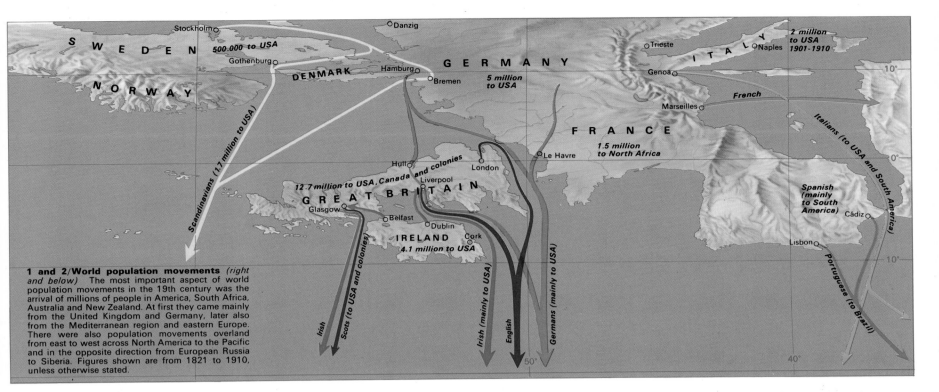

1 and 2/World population movements (right and below) The most important aspect of world population movements in the 19th century was the arrival of millions of people in America, South Africa, Australia and New Zealand. At first they came mainly from the United Kingdom and Germany, later also from the Mediterranean region and eastern Europe. There were also population movements overland from east to west across North America to the Pacific and in the opposite direction from European Russia to Siberia. Figures shown are from 1821 to 1910, unless otherwise stated.

when long distances were involved – was more usually permanent.

Some of these who left their native land had no choice in the matter. The convicts transported from England to Australia up to 1867, or from France to Devil's Island, did not go of their own accord. Nor were the Russian political prisoners who were exiled to Siberia willing migrants. Negro slaves shipped from West Africa to the Americas or from Zanzibar to Arabia were forced to leave their homes. The Atlantic slave trade, though prohibited by international agreements shortly after the Napoleonic wars, survived (though on a much reduced scale) until after the middle of the 19th century; it was not until the 1890s that the Arab slave trade on the east coast of Africa was at last stamped out.

Two factors influenced the timing of emigration and destination of the migrants. One was the fact that conditions at home were unsatisfactory, the other that the United States, Canada, Australia and New Zealand had much to offer new settlers. Some emigrated because they were persecuted on account of their religious or political beliefs. German liberals who were harassed by Metternich's police, or Russian Jews who feared for their lives, found sanctuary in the United States. But most emigrants from Europe sought a new home. And in the first half of the 19th century they braved great dangers and hardships to cross the Atlantic to North America. The Irish who emigrated at the time of the great famine of 1847, and the German peasants who gave up their smallholdings in Baden and Württemberg a year or two later because they could no longer make ends meet, had nothing to lose and everything to gain by leaving home. Whenever there was a trade slump in the industrial regions of Europe some of the unemployed emigrated. Cheap – even free – land for farmers, good prospects for employment in mines and factories and democratic institutions made the United States a promised land for those who crossed the Atlantic. The hope of making a fortune quickly brought tens of thousands of immigrants to America and Australia during the celebrated gold rushes in California (1849) and Victoria (1851).

In the first half of the 19th century the bulk of the European emigrants came from the United Kingdom (2,369,000) and Germany (1,130,000). In the second half of the century those from the United Kingdom (9.5 million) and Germany (5 million) were joined by others from Italy (5 million), the Scandinavian countries (1 million), Belgium, Spain and the Balkans. The British settled in the United States and in British colonies while the Germans went to the United States (Pennsylvania and the mid-West) and to South America (Rio Grande do Sul in Brazil). French emigrants settled in Algeria, Italians in Tunis and Argentina, and Russians in Siberia.

There were also considerable population movements in Asia and across the Indian Ocean

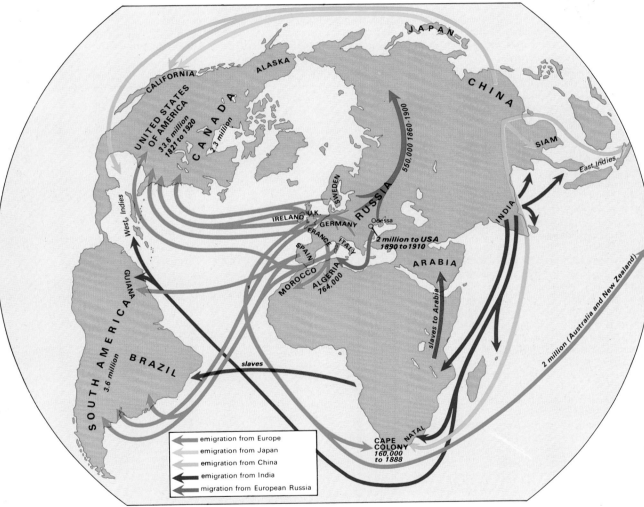

and the Pacific. From China – particularly from the southern provinces – there was a continuous flow of settlers to Siam, Java and the Malay peninsula. Chinese also emigrated to California, British Columbia and New South Wales. From India emigrants crossed the Indian Ocean to Natal and East Africa. In British East Africa they eventually surpassed the white settlers in numbers and probably in aggregate wealth. (It has been estimated that the white element in world population grew from 22 per cent in 1800 to 35 per cent in 1930.) Some of the Chinese and Indian emigrants were coolies who were engaged by contractors for a fixed term to work on plantations, in mines, and on public works. This system of indentured labour was open to grave abuses which were only gradually eradicated.

Urban growth: Berlin (right) A typical example of the expansion of a European city brought about by the construction of railways and the development of consumer industries. The court, the administration, the army and the university also contributed to population growth.

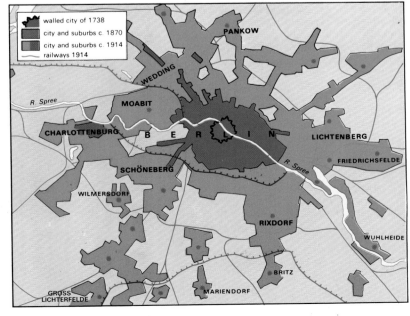

The Industrial Revolution in Europe
1815 to 1870

IN the first half of the 19th century the United Kingdom was the leading manufacturing country in the world. But modern factories, with machines driven by steam, were also to be found in some regions on the continent of Europe. As early as 1809 a visitor to the valleys of Ruhr and the Wupper described them as a 'miniature England'. On the Continent, as in Britain, the coalfields were the most important centres of industrial growth. The largest coal measures were those situated in the Nord *département* of France, the valleys of the Sambre and the Meuse in Belgium, and the valley of the Ruhr in Germany. Here modern industries developed in the first half of the 19th century. Elsewhere on the Continent progress towards industrialisation was largely confined to capital cities (Paris, Berlin), to centres of communications (Lyons, Cologne, Frankfurt am Main, Cracow, Warsaw), to major ports (Hamburg, Bremen, Rotterdam, Le Havre, Marseilles) and to particular districts such as the textile regions of Lille, Roubaix, Mulhouse, Barmen-Elberfeld (Wuppertal), Chemnitz, Lodz and Moscow, and the iron and engineering districts on the coalfields of the Loire basin, the Saar, and Upper Silesia.

Although in certain important respects the Industrial Revolution on the Continent followed a somewhat similar pattern to that in Britain, there were also significant differences. In the early 19th century the continental countries could benefit from earlier English experience. English blueprints, machinery and steam engines were installed in continental factories, and some English skilled artisans also migrated to Europe. Moreover, English entrepreneurs and financiers helped to found new industrial enterprises on the Continent. In France, Aaron Manby and Daniel Wilson founded the Charenton ironworks, Humphrey Edwards was a partner in the Chaillot engineering plant, Richard Roberts planned the layout of a cotton mill for André Koechlin at Mulhouse, while Thomas Brassey and W. and E. Mackenzie built many French railways. In time, continental countries ceased to rely upon Britain for new machines. In France, for example, several important inventions were made, such as the Jacquard loom, the Seguin multi-tubular boiler, and the Heilmann mechanical comb. And native entrepreneurs, like Alfred Krupp of Essen, showed that they had the initiative and skill to build up large enterprises without assistance from abroad. Krupp eventually became one of the largest manufacturers of armaments in Europe – a reminder that wars and preparations for war were a significant factor in the expansion of the iron and steel industries. By the 1850s and 1860s the economics of both France and the German states were capable of sustaining an autonomous industrialisation, drawing upon indigenous supplies of management, skill and capital.

While in England private investors were generally able to raise the capital to found new business undertakings and public works without government assistance, pioneer entrepreneurs on the Continent frequently had difficulty in securing the funds to build factories and to buy modern machines. Consequently the state played a more important role than it did in England in fostering industrial expansion. In Prussia, for example, the Overseas Trading Corporation (*Seehandlung*), a nationalised undertaking, was engaged in wholesale trade, operated steamships on the Brandenburg waterways, and owned or controlled textile mills, engineering plants, paper factories and chemical works. In Belgium and in some German states (Hanover, Brunswick, Baden) railways were built and operated by the state, while in France most lines were constructed jointly by the state and by private companies. However, private investment banks – institutional innovations absent in Britain – were also valuable in funding and promoting early industrialisation.

In central Europe many tariff barriers, which had long hampered economic progress, were removed between 1815 and 1870. Within the German States the customs union (*Zollverein*), established in 1834, was gradually extended so that by 1870 only Hamburg and Bremen retained their tariff independence. In the Habsburg dominions the customs frontier between Austria and Hungary was abolished in 1850. In Russia the customs frontier with Congress Poland was abolished in 1851, while Italy achieved both political and economic unity in the 1860s.

Another factor which promoted economic expansion on the Continent was the improvement in communications. Navigation on the great rivers – the Seine, Loire, Rhine, Elbe, Oder, Vistula and Danube – was improved and numerous tolls were reduced or abolished. Transport by inland waterways was of particular significance in Holland, Brandenburg, and the basin of the Seine. In France the reign of Louis Philippe (1830-48) saw the construction of several canals, while in the German states the Main-Danube and the Saar canals were important undertakings. But it

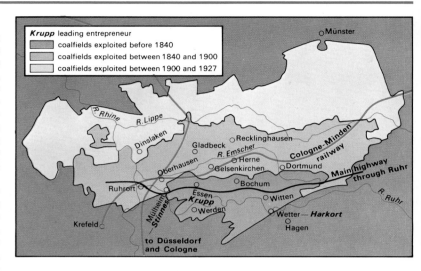

3/The expansion of the Ruhr *(above)* The exploitation of the Ruhr coalfield began in the valley of the river Ruhr. During the 19th century deeper seams to the north of the Ruhr were gradually opened up. The establishment of the Ruhrort as a coal port and the construction of the Cologne-Minden railway stimulated expansion. Mulvany established new collieries (Shamrock at Herne and Hibernia at Gelsenkirchen) while Krupp of Essen was the leading ironmaster in the district.

was the railways which really propelled the Continent into the industrial age. By 1850 the railway networks of Britain and Belgium were virtually complete, and within the German states most of the main lines had been built except for one linking Berlin and Danzig. In France, however, many main lines were still only in the planning stage, though Paris was connected by rail with Lille, Le Havre and Orléans. Substantial acceleration in French railroad construction occurred only in the 1850s and 1860s under the active encouragement of Napoleon III's authoritarian government.

On the Continent, as in Britain, a feature of the Industrial Revolution was the concentration of manufacturers in particular districts. The growth of industries in the Ruhr coalfield illustrates the expansion of such a region; but within German territory, the industrial economy was still evolving in 1870.

2/Customs unions in Europe in the 19th century *(right)* In the 18th century, trade in Europe had been hampered by tariffs. France abolished internal tariffs in 1790; German states in the early 19th century. The German customs union, founded in 1834, linked independent states and preceded political unification (1871) (see page 217).

1/Industrialisation of Europe to 1850 *(below)* The early industrial areas in Europe were mainly regions with deposits of coal or iron ore, such as Lancashire, Yorkshire, the Ruhr, and France's Nord *département*.. Relatively isolated coalfields or ironfields, such as Upper Silesia and the Donets basin, could be developed only when railways had been built. Urbanisation and industrialisation went hand in hand; except for some capital cities and ports all the large towns were in manufacturing regions.

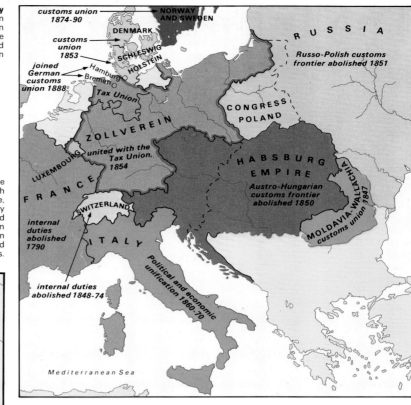

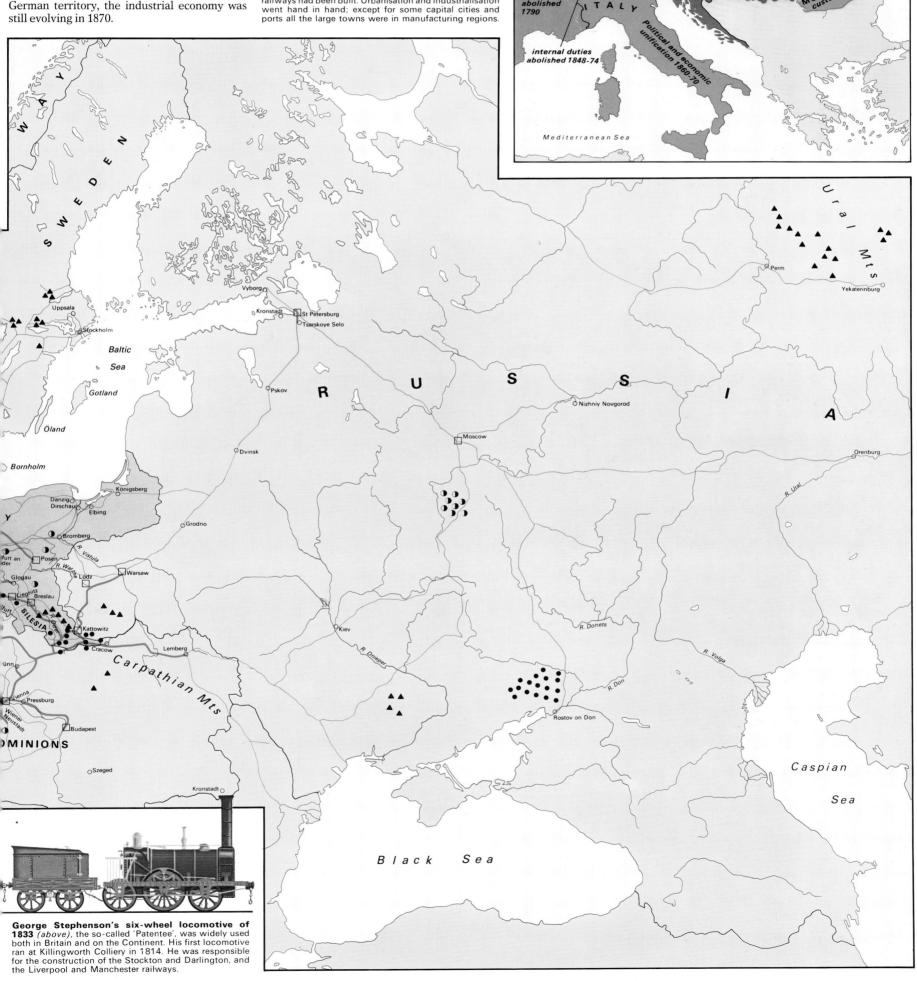

George Stephenson's six-wheel locomotive of 1833 *(above)*, the so-called 'Patentee', was widely used both in Britain and on the Continent. His first locomotive ran at Killingworth Colliery in 1814. He was responsible for the construction of the Stockton and Darlington, and the Liverpool and Manchester railways.

The Industrial Revolution in Europe 1870 to 1914

Krupp's gun at the Paris exhibition of 1867 *(above)*
In his search for new outlets for steel, Alfred Krupp of Essen had begun to experiment with armaments in the 1840s and had shown a six-pounder cannon with a cast steel barrel at the Great Exhibition in the Crystal Palace, London, in 1851. It was not until 1859 that he received an order from the Prussian military authorities for 300 steel barrels. In 1863 Krupp was awarded a large contract for steel guns from the Russian government. At the Paris Exhibition of 1867 Krupp, now established as a leading manufacturer of armaments, showed a 50-ton steel cannon; it was presented to the King of Prussia.

B ETWEEN 1870 and 1914 Europe and the United States experienced a second industrial revolution. By 1850 Great Britain had become the leading manufacturing country in the world, transformed from a predominantly agrarian into a predominantly manufacturing country. During the second industrial revolution Britain remained one of the leading manufacturing states but it was Germany, united in 1871, which now set the pace in the race for industrial supremacy. In addition to expanding its established industries – coal, iron, textiles – Germany took the lead in the development of new industries such as chemicals and electricity. At the same time there was a remarkable expansion of Germany's exports of manufactured products and of its invisible exports (banking, insurance, shipping). However, this was not a sustained expansion. The world economy experienced a 'great depression' in the 1870s and 1880s, and this affected most European economies to some extent. Germany experienced these doldrums only in the 1870s, France until 1900 and Britain perhaps until 1914. In most economies, including important new entrants such as Sweden, Italy and Russia, industrial growth was particularly pronounced in the period 1896-1914.

In the second – as in the first – industrial revolution important new machines and processes were invented in the United Kingdom. Perkin's synthetic mauve dye (the first aniline dye), the Bessemer steel converter, the Gilchrist-Thomas basic steel process, and Parsons' steam turbine were English inventions. But the invention and the development of the internal combustion engine, the diesel engine, the automobile, the electric dynamo and electric traction largely occurred in Germany, while the ring frame, the sewing machine, the typewriter, the filament lamp and the telephone were invented in the United States.

The first industrial revolution has been called a 'revolution of coal and iron', the second a 'revolution of steel and electricity'. In the first half of the 19th century steel was almost a semi-precious metal, costing between £50 and £60 a ton, compared with £3 to £4 a ton for pig iron. Initially, steel was made by the cementation process, or, alternatively, by Huntsman's crucible method. In the second half of the 19th century the new Bessemer and Siemens-Martin processes – improved by Gilchrist and Thomas – enabled the production of steel to be greatly increased. World output rose from a mere 540,000 tons in 1870 to 14,600,000 in 1895 – and there was a dramatic fall in price.

The electrical industry provided the world with a new source of energy with which to supplement steam power. When efficient dynamos were built in the 1860s electric power was used to drive machinery and trams and to light streets, factories and homes. Water power found a new use in hydro-electric power stations. Italy, in particular, with no national coal resources, turned increasingly to hydro-electric power after 1905. Another new form of energy in the second half of the 19th century was produced by the internal combustion engine, with petrol as its fuel. A new petroleum industry which exploited and refined the oil resources of the United States, Russia and the Middle East enabled stationary gas engines, motor vehicles and ships to be driven by petrol or diesel oil.

The expansion of new chemical industries was another significant aspect of the development of manufactures after 1870. For centuries chemicals had been extracted from natural substances – alkalis from vegetable ashes and dyes from madder root, indigo and so forth. Now more and more chemical substances were produced from coal by-products, nitrogen and phosphates. The soap and glass industries used soda made from ammonia (a coal by-product) while the textile industries used synthetic (aniline) dyes made from coal tar. Nitrates from natural sources and 'synthetic' nitrogen and phosphates were the raw materials for the production of explosives and fertilisers. Other branches of the chemical industries were the production of drugs, insecticides, perfumes, cosmetics, and photographic accessories. From the early 20th century, plastics, made from resins prepared from coal tar acids, were used to make a wide variety of products, while synthetic textiles, such as artificial silk, also became popular.

In the development of these new branches of industry – electricity and chemicals – Germany played a leading part. In the electrical industry two large cartels were formed, the Siemens-Schuckert group and the *Allgemeine Elektrizitäts Gesellschaft*, at the head of which were the two pioneers who dominated the industry: Werner Siemens and Emil Rathenau. The expansion of the chemical industry owed much to the invention of synthetic dyes and new drugs in the laboratories of great German firms. Two chemical cartels were formed which were merged in

1/The industrialisation of Europe 1870-1914 *(below)*
The industrial regions which had been developed in the first half of the 19th century – such as Lancashire, Yorkshire, south Wales, Clydeside, the Ruhr, the Saar, the Nord *département*, and the Sambre-Meuse region in Belgium – continued to expand after 1870; they were now joined by new industrial regions, such as the Donets basin, which were opened up when railways were developed. The construction of the Berlin-Baghdad railway as far as Ras el-'Ain, and the completion of the Trans-Siberian railway, extended Europe's economic links with the Near East and the Far East, while the opening of the Kiel Canal stimulated the trade of the Baltic region. After 1870 old-established industries (coal, iron, textiles) were joined by new branches of manufacture such as the chemical and electrical industries.

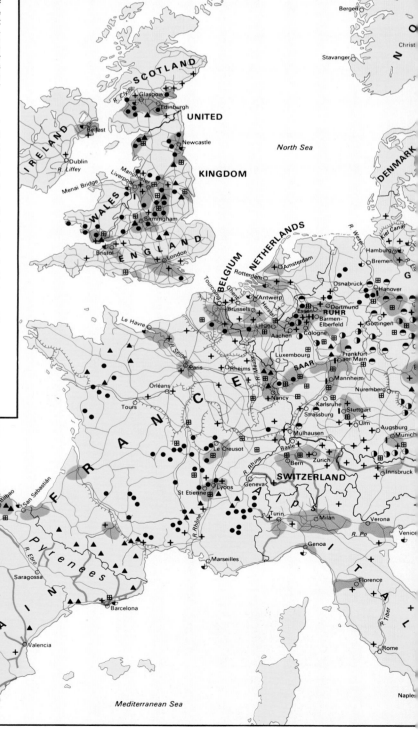

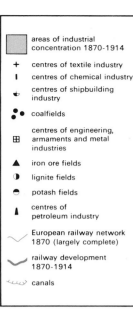

two stages in 1916 and 1925 to form the German Dye Trust (*I. G. Farben*). Germany's production of coal, iron and steel also expanded; by 1914 it produced twice as much steel and nearly as much coal as Britain. Germany's shipbuilding industry and mercantile marine both expanded in a spectacular fashion. By the outbreak of the First World War Germany's shipyards could build 400,000 tons of merchant ships a year in addition to warships and river craft, while its mercantile marine of 2,400,000 tons included some of the finest liners on the Atlantic run.

In Russia, too, striking industrial progress occurred between 1870 and 1914. At the end of this period the cotton industries had 745 mills employing 388,000 operatives and turning out products valued at 589 million roubles. The linen industry expanded rapidly in the last quarter of the 19th century with the aid of foreign capital. At the same time the woollen industry, with major centres at Moscow, Petersburg and Lodz, had 700,000 spindles, 4500 looms and 150,000 operatives. Moreover, an important

new industrial region, based on coal and iron ore resources, had developed in the basin of the Donets. Here great iron and steel works were established. The opening of the railway to Krivoy Rog in 1886 enabled high-grade iron ore to be sent from Krivoy Rog to the ironworks in the Donets basin. The exploitation of Russia's oil wells at Baku and Grozny was another factor which stimulated Russia's economic development after 1880. The Nobel brothers from Sweden were the pioneer entrepreneurs of this new industry. They built refineries at Baku and launched an oil tanker on the Caspian in 1878 to ply between Baku and Astrakhan. Again, the construction of the Trans-Siberian and Trans-Caucasian railways made it possible for Russia to tap some of the vast natural resources of its territories in Asia. The main acceleration in growth came as a result of a state-sponsored programme of industrialisation directed by the Finance Minister, Count S. I. Witte, during the 1890s. By 1914, the Russian industrial sector ranked among the four or five largest in the

world. But unlike the industrial states of western Europe, Russia also had a very large number of small domestic workshops which had survived side by side with modern plants and factories.

Nevertheless, at the end of the 19th century even in highly industrialised countries in Europe a high proportion of the population was still engaged in agriculture. In Germany, for example, the agricultural population in 1895 amounted to 18.5 million, which was just over one-third (35.5 per cent) of the total population. Most of eastern Europe (Poland, Romania, Bulgaria) and much of southern Europe (Spain, Greece, southern Italy) was still, by modern standards, under-developed. In France, industry at the end of the century was still with few exceptions small in scale; in countries such as Poland and Spain industrialisation was confined to a few small areas (Lodz; Bilbao, Barcelona) and the way of life of the bulk of the population had virtually been untouched by the great upsurge of industry elsewhere between 1870 and 1914.

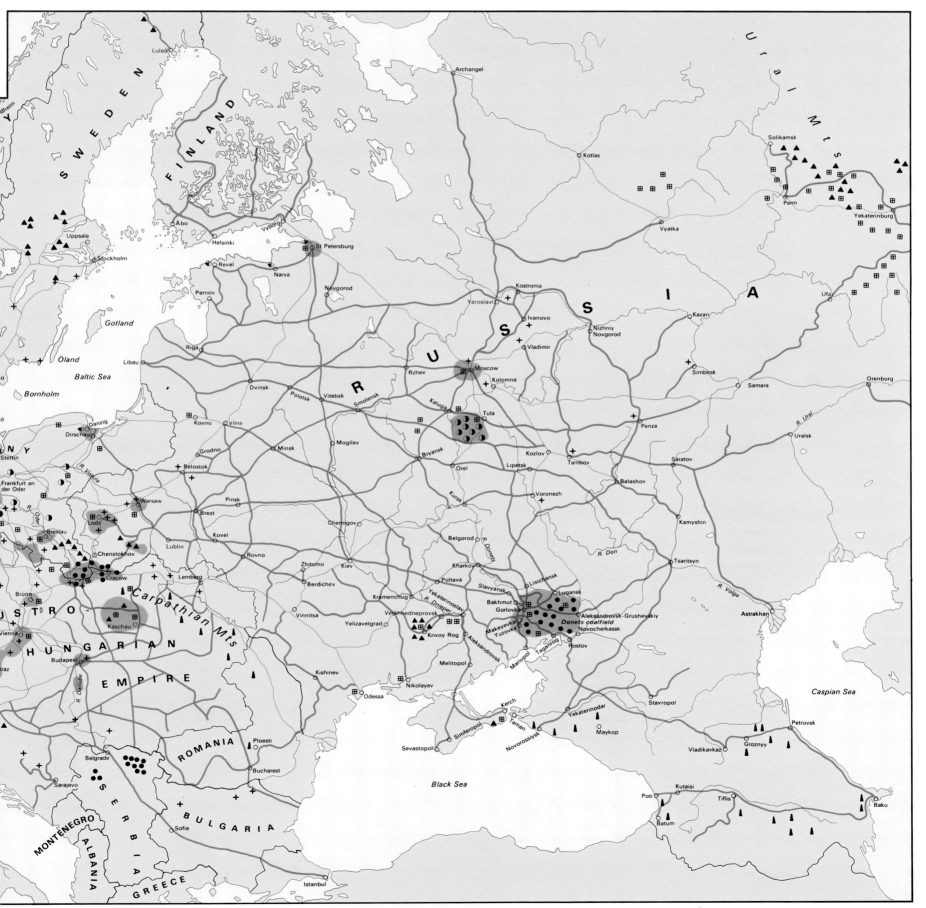

The rise of nationalism in Europe 1800 to 1914

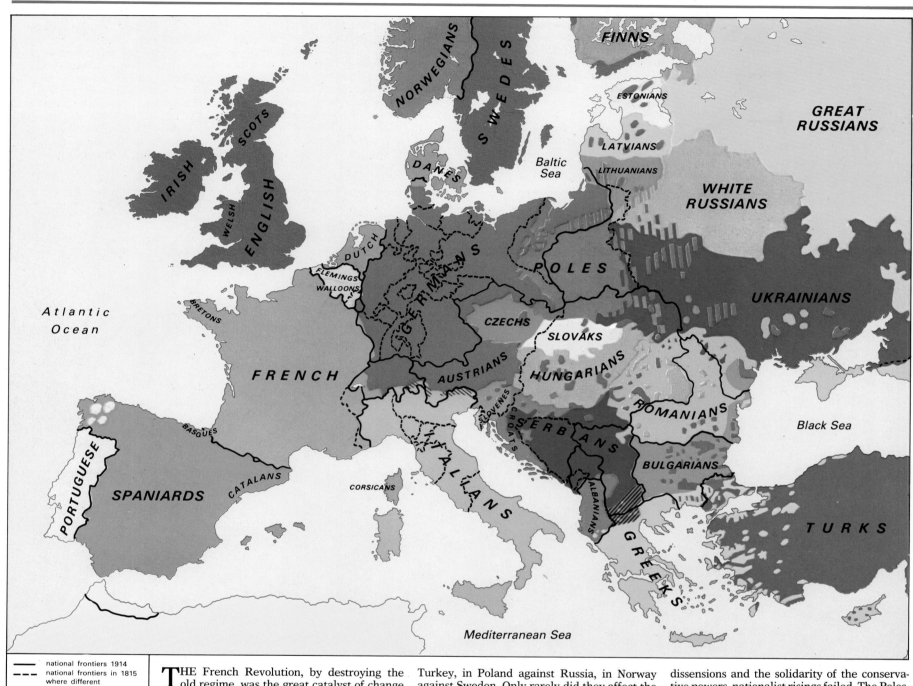

NORWEGIANS · SWEDES · FINNS · IRISH · SCOTS · ENGLISH · WELSH · ESTONIANS · LATVIANS · LITHUANIANS · GREAT RUSSIANS · Baltic Sea · DANES · WHITE RUSSIANS · DUTCH · FLEMINGS · WALLOONS · GERMANS · POLES · UKRAINIANS · BRETONS · CZECHS · SLOVAKS · Atlantic Ocean · FRENCH · AUSTRIANS · HUNGARIANS · ROMANIANS · Black Sea · SLOVENES · CROATS · SERBANS · BASQUES · PORTUGUESE · SPANIARDS · CATALANS · CORSICANS · ITALIANS · ALBANIANS · BULGARIANS · GREEKS · TURKS · Mediterranean Sea

national frontiers 1914
national frontiers in 1815 where different
Romansch
Macedonian Slavs

1/Languages, peoples and political divisions of Europe *(above)* This map of 19th century Europe shows the boundaries at the time of the Vienna Settlement of 1815 and the changes which took place between then and 1914. Linguistic boundaries were rarely precise and political frontiers often left linguistic minorities, and even majorities, under alien rule. The map shows the major languages, but some are too scattered to be included: Sorb (or Wendish, Lusatian) in Prussia and Saxony; Masurian in East Prussia; Vlach in Macedonia, Epirus and Transylvania; Gallego, a dialect of Portuguese, in Galicia, Spain; and Yiddish: there were some five million Jews, many living in the large European towns, but most in the Pale of Settlement (Lithuania, Russia, Poland, the Ukraine, Bessarabia and the Crimea).

THE French Revolution, by destroying the old regime, was the great catalyst of change in Europe. The revolutionary armies carried with them not only the slogan of 'liberty, equality and fraternity' but also the ideas of liberalism, self-government and nationalism, which were to be the central themes of 19th-century European history. Already before 1789, in reaction against the rational spirit of the Enlightenment, writers such as Herder (1744-1803) had emphasised the sense of national identity. But the state was still regarded as a dynastic patrimony, an estate to which owners of lesser estates owed allegiance and service. This conception was challenged by the French revolutionary governments, which called upon oppressed peoples to rise against their landlords and rulers. But French oppression under Napoleon produced nationalist reactions in Spain, in Russia, in the Tyrol, eventually (after 1807) in Germany. This was one source of the nationalism of the later 19th century.

Nevertheless, the strength of nationalism in the first half of the 19th century can easily be exaggerated. Down to 1866 most Germans and Italians were more attached to their provincial rulers and cultures (Bavarian, Hessian, Tuscan, Emilian) than to the ideal of national unity. Only where there was alien rule were there loud protests, chiefly from the middle classes (lawyers, teachers, businessmen), in Italy against Austria, in Ireland against England, in Belgium against Holland, in Greece against

Turkey, in Poland against Russia, in Norway against Sweden. Only rarely did they affect the peasant masses, the bulk of the European population at this time. Even in the Ottoman Empire, in spite of the corrupt, oppressive and increasingly incompetent Turkish government and the resentment of Christians against Muslim overlordship, there was little active national opposition, except in the region which during the 1820s became the core of modern Greece. In the far-flung Austrian Empire, ruling over a score of nationalities, only the Czechs and the Hungarians, both peoples with proud memories of an independent past, were restive, though they sought autonomy within the Empire, not national independence.

Furthermore, after the defeat of Napoleon in 1815, the victorious powers were hostile to nationalist aspirations, which they saw, correctly, as associated with liberalism and therefore a threat to constituted authority. At the Congress of Vienna, under the influence of Talleyrand and Metternich, the powers had adopted the principle of 'legitimacy' as a basis for redrawing the map of Europe. Metternich believed that any concessions to nationalism would be fatal to Austria, and he resisted them on all fronts down to 1848. In this period only Greece and Belgium (1830) achieved independence, and in both cases special factors – notably the rivalry of the Great Powers – were involved. Elsewhere, in Poland (1831, 1846), Germany (1848), Italy (1848) and Hungary (1849), owing to internal

dissensions and the solidarity of the conservative powers, nationalist risings failed. The Poles, dispersed within three empires, remained a subject people until 1918-19. The Hungarians, however, exploiting Austrian weakness in its war with Prussia, managed to win equal status with the German-speaking population by the *Ausgleich* (Compromise) of 1867.

In Italy and Germany provincialism and apathy were overcome by the expansionist policies of Piedmont and Prussia (see page 216). After 1854 a new generation of European statesmen no longer upheld the old order, and industrial and commercial expansion gave a new impetus to the desire for national unity. Nationality was now seen as a stabilising force; that is to say, it was thought that unified national states would have no further ambitions, and apostles of nationalism such as Mazzini (1805-72) predicted a new age when satisfied national states would co-operate peacefully in a democratic federation of peoples. After 1870 it quickly became clear that this was an illusion. Though it is true that the Czechs of Bohemia never aspired, before 1918, to more than autonomy within the Habsburg Empire, and the Slavs of Bosnia and Herzegovina were content to exchange Turkish for Austrian rule, nationalist ideas spread rapidly, particularly among the Balkan peoples. Though the standard criterion of nationality was language, linguistic groups were so mixed that a division on the basis of language was impracticable, particularly in the Balkan Peninsula.

The Balkans map showing national frontiers after the Balkan wars 1912-13

GERMAN EMPIRE

RUSSIAN EMPIRE

AUSTRO-HUNGARIAN EMPIRE

Vienna
Budapest
BESSARABIA
Jassy
MOLDAVIA semi-independent 1829

BOSNIA administered by Austria-Hungary 1878; annexed 1908
Banja Luka
R. Sava
Belgrade
Požarevac
ROMANIA
Galatz
Brăila

HERZEGOVINA
Sarajevo
SERBIA principality 1817; independent 1878
WALLACHIA semi-independent 1829
Craiova
Ploiești
Bucharest
united 1859; independent 1878; Kingdom 1881
Turtukaia
Silistria
R. Danube
DOBRUJA

Mostar
Nish
Vidin
Ruschuk
Constanza

MONTENEGRO
Kotor (Cattaro)
Podgorica
Cetinje
SANJAK OF NOVIBAZAR
Mitrovica
to Serbia 1878
Pirot
principality 1878
BULGARIA
independent 1908
Shumla
Balchik

Ipek (Peć)
to Serbia 1913
Slivnitsa
Sofia
Küstendil
Plevna
Trnovo
EASTERN RUMELIA to Bulgaria 1885
Varna

L. Scutari
Scutari
Prizren
Uskūb (Skoplje)
Kumanovo
to Bulgaria 1913
Philippopolis
R. Maritsa
Burgas

Tirana
ALBANIA principality 1913
L. Ochrida
L. Prespa
Koritsa
R. Vardar
Kočani
Strumitsa
MACEDONIA
to Bulgaria 1913
THRACE
Adrianople
Black Sea

Saseno I.
Valona
Argyrokastron
Monastir
to Greece 1913
Salonica
Kavalla
Thasos
Dede-Agach
to Bulgaria 1913
San Stefano
Constantinople
Bosporus

Cape Stylos
Corfu
EPIRUS
Yannina
R. Aliakmon
Samothrace
Imbros
Lemnos
Dardanelles

Ionian Sea
Preveza
Arta
THESSALY to Greece 1881
Larissa
Volos
Aegean Sea
Tenedos
to Greece 1913

IONIAN ISLANDS
Patras
KINGDOM OF GREECE
independent 1830
Athens
Piraeus
Lesbos
Chios
OTTOMAN EMPIRE

to Greece 1864
Tripolis
Nauplia
Samos
Nikaria

Canea
Suda Bay
CRETE independent 1898
Candia
to Greece 1913
Dodecanese (occupied by Italy 1912; ceded by Turkey 1920)
Rhodes

Legend:
- - - frontier of Ottoman empire 1800
—— proposed Bulgaria under Treaty of San Stefano 1878
━━━ national frontiers after the Balkan wars 1912-13
—— railway

Moreover, language was not always recognised by those wishing to redeem their long lost brothers, as the sole criterion of nationality. In Macedonia, Greeks, Serbians and Bulgarians made conflicting nationalistic claims and, like nationalists within the Habsburg Empire, expressed them in terms of folklore, literature, and national history as well as those of linguistic and racial theory. The result of their endeavours was that by 1913 the Turks had lost almost all their possessions in Europe. Nor was nationalist unrest confined to the Turkish and Habsburg Empires. Great Britain was faced with troubles in Ireland and Norway demanded separation from Sweden.

The activities of Serbian nationalists in Bosnia and the determination of Austria-Hungary to resist them became the immediate cause of war in 1914. This war led to the disruption of the Habsburg, German and Russian Empires and led to the formation of the states of Czechoslovakia, Poland, Yugoslavia, Hungary, Estonia, Latvia and Lithuania. Although established in recognition of the principle of 'national self-determination', two of these states, Czecho-

slovakia and Poland, contained large German minorities, the redemption of which became one of the aims of German policy.

2/The Balkans (above) From the later 18th century onwards the Russians encouraged uprisings in the Turkish Balkan provinces. The Great Powers, fearing Russian domination of the Near East and wishing to preserve the Ottoman Empire as a viable power, endeavoured to pacify the Balkans by extracting concessions to the Slavs, Greeks and Romanians. Following the Crimean War, in 1856 they imposed a settlement on Russia and Turkey and in 1878 at the Congress of Berlin they recognised the complete independence of Serbia, Montenegro and Romania, but reduced the territory which the Pan Slav Treaty of San Stefano had allocated to the new Principality of Bulgaria.

This upheaval made the Powers aware of the complexity of the rivalries between the races inhabiting the Balkan peninsula, and of the dangerous incompatibility of their own ambitions there. For the next thirty years, despite growing racial and religious strife in Macedonia and the Greco-Turkish war in 1897, the Powers clung stubbornly to the territorial *status quo*, seeking to pacify the Balkan Christians by a programme of administrative reforms under Austro-Russian supervision. But the Austro-Hungarian annexation of Bosnia (1908) revived the fires of nationalism and destroyed the unity of the Powers. In 1912 the Balkan states formed a league to expel the Turks from Macedonia; but after their victory over the old rivalries over the spoils re-emerged. The Second Balkan War left Serbia and Greece in possession of most of Macedonia and parts of Albania.

3/Scandinavia (right) The Treaty of Nystad (1721) marked the decline of Sweden as a great Northern and Baltic power.

In 1809 Sweden had ceded Finland to Russia. In 1815 her new dynasty received Norway, formerly a Danish possession, under an arrangement ensuring considerable autonomy and a separate government. During the nineteenth century, the pan-Scandinavian movement, which aimed at a close union between Denmark, Sweden and Norway, came to nothing and in 1905 Norway became completely independent with its own dynasty.

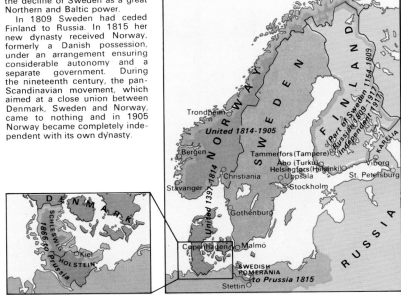

NORWAY United 1814-1905
SWEDEN
FINLAND Part of Sweden 1154-1809; Russian 1809-1917; Independent 1917
Trondheim
Bergen
Christiania
Stavanger
United 1397-1814
Tammerfors (Tampere)
Åbo (Turku)
Helsingfors (Helsinki)
Uppsala
KARELIA
Viborg
St. Petersburg
Gothenburg
Stockholm
RUSSIA

DENMARK
Schleswig Holstein 1866-70 to Prussia
Kiel
Copenhagen
Malmö
SWEDISH POMERANIA to Prussia 1815
Stettin

Germany and Italy: the struggles for unification 1815 to 1871

The Bismarck tower (above) Towering sculptures of Bismarck, the chief architect of German unity, were erected in Germany during the 1890s. Their mediaeval style recalls the period of the Teutonic Knights and the heyday of German expansion in the Middle Ages.

EVEN before the defeat of Napoleon and the Congress of Vienna (1815), demands for national unity were stirring in Germany and Italy, but they were largely confined to literary and academic circles. Only Stein in Prussia aspired to translate them into a political programme, but he was swept aside in 1808, and after 1815 Metternich, the Austrian chancellor, had no difficulty in restoring the traditional rulers. Although during the period of the 'Restoration' (1815-48) there was some unrest, fomented chiefly by ex-military personnel and officials formerly employed in the Napoleonic administration, the revolts of 1820 and 1821 (in Naples and Piedmont) and those of 1830-31 (in Parma, Modena and Romagna) had no national aims, while the liberals in Hanover, Brunswick, Hesse-Kassel and Saxony were satisfied with moderate constitutional changes. Not until 1848 did the national question, both in Germany and in Italy, come to the fore, and then only to reveal cross-purposes within nationalist ranks. In Italy, uprisings in Venice, Rome, Messina, Palermo, Reggio and Milan ended in failure, and in July 1848 Charles Albert of Piedmont was decisively beaten by the Austrians at Custoza.

1848 was a year of revolution in all major German states and in May a 'National Assembly' of deputies elected by the people from all over the Deutscher Bund (including both German and non-German parts of the Austrian Monarchy) met at Frankfurt to embark on the self-appointed task of drawing up a constitution for Germany which they hoped to unite by consent. However, they soon became divided between *Grossdeutsche* (those who wanted a federal Germany, including Austria and extending from the Baltic and the Adriatic) and *Kleindeutsche* (those who wanted a smaller Germany, excluding Austria, under Prussian leadership). The Prussian liberals denounced the provisional government of United Germany, of which the Austrian Archduke John had been proclaimed Regent, and demanded a Prussian constitution. By a small majority the Frankfurt liberals offered the German crown to the king of Prussia, which the Prussian king contemptuously turned down.

After the failure of the revolutions of 1848-49 Germany reverted to an Austro-Prussian dualistic hegemony and Italy remained divided. However, with the appointment of Cavour as prime minister of Sardinia-Piedmont (1852) and of Bismarck as chief minister in Prussia (1862), liberal nationalists in Italy and Germany showed some readiness to support the expansionist aims of Piedmont and Prussia. The policies of Napoleon III, a 'revisionist' with nationalist inclinations, gave encouragement to these aims, as did the weakening of Austria, which lost the support of Russia. After the Crimean War (1854-56), Napoleon III favoured a strong Prussia in northern Germany and a relatively powerful Sardinia-Piedmont in northern Italy within an Italian federation under the presidency of the Pope (including Tuscany, the Kingdom of Naples and the Papal States). Both powers, he hoped, would be the natural allies of France. He hoped, moreover, to create a Rhineland kingdom which would be a client state of France.

Prussia had for long been an expansionist power. Despite losses during the Napoleonic Wars, in 1815 she had been awarded a part of Saxony and territory in western Germany with the object of raising a bulwark against France and of buttressing Holland. Thereafter it was her policy to weld together her eastern and western territories. From 1828 she formed a series of customs unions (*Zollvereine*). In 1834

3/**The unification of Germany** (below) The political unification of Germany involved wars against Denmark in 1864, against Austria in 1866 and against France in 1870. Austria was excluded from the North German Confederation of 1867 which comprised the German states north of the river Main. Any influence that remained to Austria in Germany as a relic of the dualism that had obtained before 1866 was finally destroyed in 1871, when the German Southern States joined the German Empire.

	Prussia in 1815
	acquired by Prussia 1815-66
	boundary of German Confederation of 1815
	boundary of North German Confederation of 1866
	Imperial territory of Alsace-Lorraine 1871
	boundary of German Empire 1871
	Austro-Prussian forces attack Denmark 1864
	Prussian armies in the war with Austria 1866
	German armies in the Franco-Prussian war 1870-71

the German Zollverein was created, and expanded under the impact of the development of German railways and industrialisation. By the 1850s (the *Gründerjahre*) Prussia had gained an economic preponderance over Austria, but it was not until Bismarck came to power that she challenged Austria's political leadership – over the question of Schleswig and Holstein. In 1864 Austria and Prussia, acting on behalf of the German Confederation, went to war with Denmark, defeated her, and took over the administration of those two duchies (Convention of Gastein, 1865). When Austria attempted to follow a separate policy in Holstein and to deprive Prussia of her rights under the traditional dualistic arrangements, Bismarck made war on Austria, defeated her at Sadowa (1866), excluded her from Germany, and formed the North German Confederation (1867) under Prussian control. Following Prussia's defeat of France at Sedan (1870) and her annexation of Alsace and Lorraine, the German States south of the Main, through sheer economic necessity, joined the new German Reich.

In Italy, Cavour, realising that Piedmont's expansion depended on foreign support, allied with France (Plombières, 1858) against Austria, and in June 1859 the two allies won decisive victories at Magenta and Solferino. Fearing, however, the formation of a hostile European combination and the creation of a too-powerful Piedmont, Napoleon III hastily concluded preliminaries at Villafranca. At the definitive Peace of Zürich (November 1859) most of Lombardy went to Piedmont but, on being offered compensation in Nice and Savoy, Napoleon agreed to plebiscites in Tuscany, Parma and Modena, where spontaneous revolutions had broken out. These plebiscites favoured union with Pied-

mont, which was doubled in size. In June 1860 the patriot Garibaldi and his 'thousand' volunteers took Sicily and, in September, Naples. Cavour, fearing that the final stages of unification might militate against Piedmont, sent troops to the Papal States, brought Garibaldi to heel, and plebiscites were held, which resulted in the union of Sicily, Naples, Umbria, Romagna and the Marches with Piedmont-Sardinia. In 1861, an Italian parliament met in Turin and proclaimed Victor Emmanuel II king of united Italy. In April 1866 Cavour's successors made a treaty with Prussia and, following Austria's defeat at Sadowa in the Austro-Prussian war, Italy acquired Venetia from Austria. In 1870 it obtained Rome, the French having been obliged to withdraw their occupation forces as a result of defeat by Prussia.

The making of modern Italy and the creation of the German Empire, had not only changed the European balance of power but had fostered a spirit of realpolitik and militarism. Neither power was fully satisfied with its achievements. Italy had hopes of obtaining the Alto Adige, Trieste and Fiume. The new Reich, despite Bismarck's claim that Germany was a 'satiated' state, pursued expansionist policies in Posen and Elsass-Lothringen. In the period 1871-1914, however, both powers were compelled to devote attention to internal problems, to improve and expand their armed forces and to seek markets and raw materials outside Europe in competition with the other powers. While Italy remained tied to Germany and Austria by the treaty of triple alliance she was debarred from her *irredenta* and so long as Germany clung to her alliance with the Austrian-Hungarian monarchy any hopes of a Greater Germany had to be abandoned.

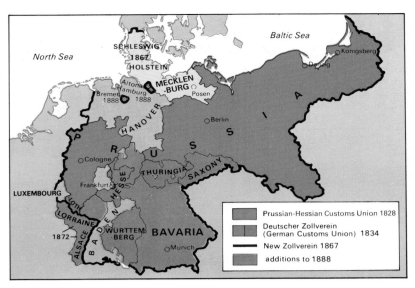

1/The economic unification of Germany (above) Well before the diplomatic skill of Bismarck and the military genius of Moltke were brought into play, the way had been prepared for the political unification of Germany by the officials responsible for the creation of the German *Zollvereine*, the developers of German roads, railways and canals, the pioneers in industry, shipping and banking.

2/The unification of Italy (below) The rapid expansion of Piedmont-Sardinia, which began with the acquisition of Lombardy in 1859, led, at the expense of the loss of Nice and Savoy, to the creation of the United Italy of 1861. The new kingdom acquired Venetia in 1866 and in 1870 Rome, which was made the capital.

The Industrial Revolution in the wider world 1850 to 1929

AFTER the middle of the 19th century the Industrial Revolution, which had radiated out from Great Britain to north-western Europe and the eastern seaboard of the United States, was spreading further afield in ever-widening circles. It did so at very different rates, depending largely on the economic, social and cultural preparation of the receiving territories.

Societies modelled on the West and formed or dominated by European settlers adopted industrialisation with no greater difficulty than the home country; the Anglo-Saxon areas of settlement being, as in Europe, well ahead of those of the Spanish and Portuguese. In most other, non-settler societies, industrialisation was a foreign transplant rather than an indigenous growth. Economic as well as political control tended to pass to Europeans, and this limited industrialisation to certain enclaves, hardly touching the lives of the majority of inhabitants.

India and China exhibited as late as 1930 all the features of such enclave industrialism. In India, 69 per cent of all cotton workers in 1919 were in Bombay Province, two-thirds of them in Bombay City. Much of the sub-continent's steel capacity was concentrated in a single firm, the Tata Iron and Steel Co. at Tatanagar in Bihar, which produced in 1926-27 650,000 tons of pig iron and 600,000 tons of steel. China was opened up in the late 19th century mainly along the lines of the railway concessions granted to foreign groups, capitalists who had no interest in the development of the country. Of the foreign-owned firms in China between 1895 and 1917, 60

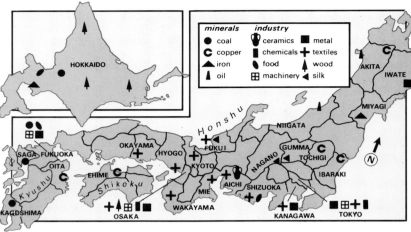

2/Japan's industrialisation *(above)* began after the Meiji restoration (1868). In spite of its poor natural endowment in such key resources as coal, iron ore and oil, it was the only non-Western society to have built a broad and varied industrial base by 1929.

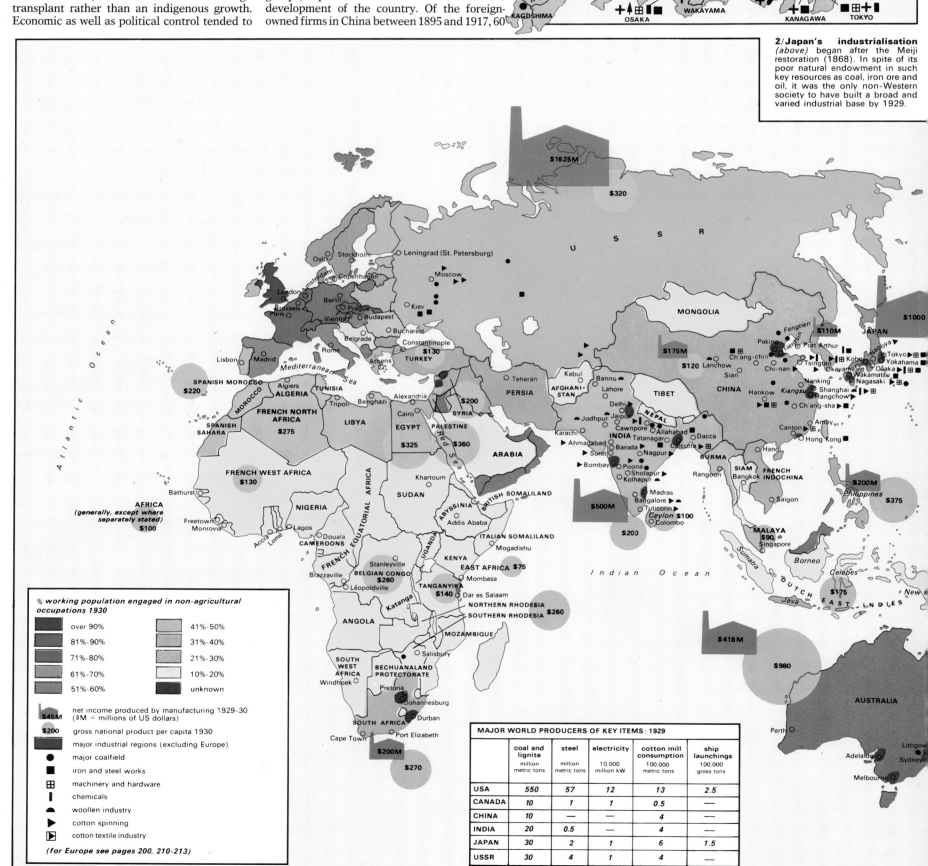

MAJOR WORLD PRODUCERS OF KEY ITEMS: 1929					
	coal and lignite *million metric tons*	steel *million metric tons*	electricity *10,000 million kW*	cotton mill consumption *100,000 metric tons*	ship launchings *100,000 gross tons*
USA	550	57	12	13	2.5
CANADA	10	1	1	0.5	—
CHINA	10	—	—	4	—
INDIA	20	0.5	—	4	—
JAPAN	30	2	1	6	1.5
USSR	30	4	1	4	

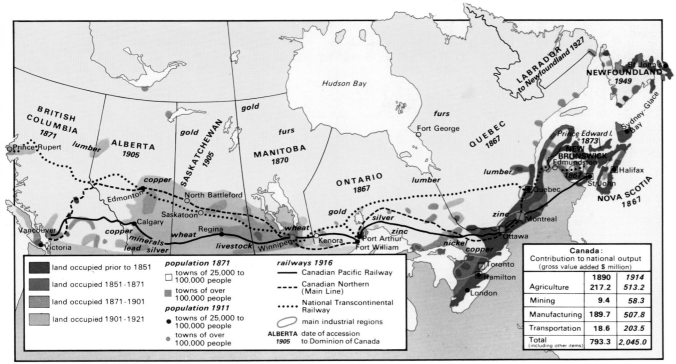

3/Canada in 1915 (*above*) after a quarter of a century of rapid economic development. Hard on the heels of expanding exports of wheat and timber, after 1890 there followed an influx of people and capital. Mining was well under way by 1914; manufacturing grew mainly after that date.

Map legend:

population 1871
- land occupied prior to 1851
- land occupied 1851-1871
- land occupied 1871-1901
- land occupied 1901-1921

population 1871
- □ towns of 25,000 to 100,000 people
- towns of over 100,000 people

population 1911
- ● towns of 25,000 to 100,000 people
- • towns of over 100,000 people

railways 1916
- —— Canadian Pacific Railway
- – – – Canadian Northern (Main Line)
- ······ National Transcontinental Railway
- ◯ main industrial regions

ALBERTA 1905 date of accession to Dominion of Canada

Canada: Contribution to national output (gross value added $ million)	1890	1914
Agriculture	217.2	513.2
Mining	9.4	58.3
Manufacturing	189.7	507.8
Transportation	18.6	203.5
Total (including other items)	793.3	2,045.0

per cent, owning 40 per cent of the capital, were in only two provinces, Kiangsu and Fengtien.

Industrial development overseas occurred generally in three overlapping stages. In the first, it was directed by westerners, usually to exploit some valuable product such as metallic ores, agricultural produce or oil. Virtually the whole world had reached that stage by 1930.

The second stage developed out of the need for servicing and repairing the major plants focussed on export production. In addition there was a growth of businesses supplying the needs of a more demanding population, but since these firms frequently merely replaced and destroyed existing traditional native handicraft industries, the proportion of the population engaged in manufacture did not necessarily grow, and may even have declined. For this reason, rather than registering the proportion engaged in manufactures, the main map shows the comparative non-agricultural population as a more sensitive indicator of the stage of development. Latin America, North Africa and many parts of Asia had reached this stage by 1930.

Such growth could sometimes be extremely fast. In Canada, which became the classic 'wheat economy' after all the land in the United States had been occupied in the early years of the 20th century, 73 million acres of land were occupied in 1900-16, and $400 million of foreign investment a year were attracted, together with streams of immigrants. The mining of coal, gold, lead, zinc, nickel and copper followed, and the country was well on the road to industrialisation.

In South Africa, gold was discovered in 1886; by 1900, the gold fields employed 100,000 workers, and Johannesburg, a place of under 100 inhabitants in 1885, had 237,000 in 1911. Katanga, where copper deposits were first recognised in 1900, produced by 1914 10,722 metric tons of copper, and by 1930 its output, together with that of Northern Rhodesia, had risen to 305,000 tons, employing 30,000 African miners.

In Malaya, tin production was first encouraged on a large scale by the abolition of the British import duties on tin in 1853. By 1900, Malaya furnished nearly half the world's tin exports. Rubber was first grown in 1894; 50,000 acres were under rubber trees in 1905, and 300,000 acres in 1910. Most tin, however, was produced neither by European nor by native enterprise but by the Chinese, and apart from the port of Singapore, the effects of the large new industries were limited and localised. In China itself, where pig iron production rose from a derisory 477,000 tons in 1928 to 5.9 million tons in 1937, steel from 30,000 tons to 5.3 million tons and coal from 25 million tons to 124 million tons in the same period, the effects on the economy were even more circumscribed.

The third stage was the development of industries which competed with manufactured goods entering world markets. Iron and steel, textiles and machinery are always the most important of such commodities, and have therefore been emphasised in the map. As the map shows, Australia and New Zealand, Japan and some very limited areas in China and Manchuria, India, the Mediterranean coastline and Latin America had reached this stage. Among them, Japan stands out as the only wholly independent non-European society which had successfully embraced the western type of industrialism before the Depression of 1929. Indeed she had been growing strongly as an industrial economy since 1885 and had established many large-scale modern industries such as ship-building, machine-building and steel-making, even before 1914. Nevertheless, the changes since 1850 in many, if scattered, parts of the globe had been scarcely less remarkable than those in Europe and the United States a hundred years earlier.

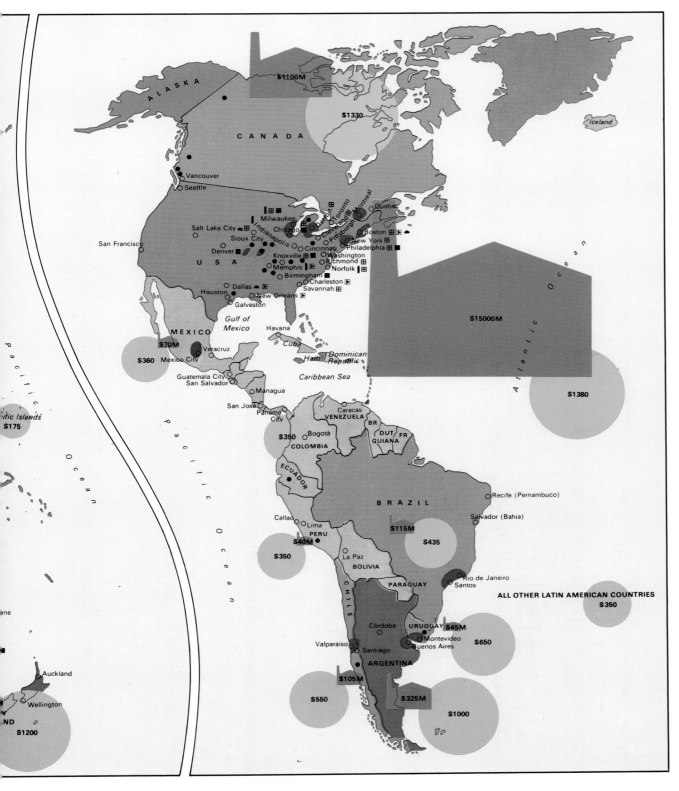

1/Industrialisation outside Europe and North America (*left*) was still the exception rather than the rule in 1929. Even after the opening of Africa in the 1880s and 1890s, the amount of European capital which flowed into the colonial world was small, and colonial governments were disinclined to invest in the infrastructure of ports, roads and railways, except in India. Even by the end of the period such transport and industry as did exist were either focussed on the ports trading with Europe or worked by European settler communities.

The making of the United States: westward expansion 1783 to 1890

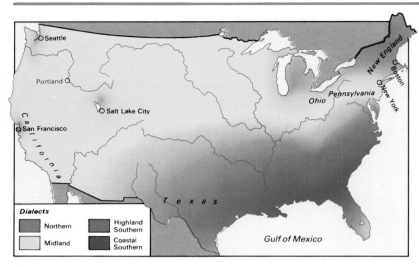

2/Migration and settlement *(above)* The American population flowed west in several distinct migration streams. The best guide to their location is the study of linguistic geography, which still preserves the history of the westward movement in the different spatial patterns of American speech. One migration stream led westward from New England to New York, Ohio and the northern plains. Another went by sea from Boston and New York to San Francisco and Seattle. Still a third went overland from Vermont and western New York to Salt Lake City. The largest migration stream rose in Pennsylvania and spread westward through the middle of the continent to California. Two southern streams flowed side by side, one south-west through the mountains, the other along the coast. They met and merged in Texas.

1/Westward expansion *(below)* There were several separate frontiers in American history – the frontier of the explorer, the fur trader, the miner, the cattleman and sheepherder, and finally the domestic frontier with which the Wild West ended. Each of those westward movements had its own special rhythm, its own settlements and routes.

IN 1783, the American republic was small and weak. Its population was a little more than three million people. Half its territory was held by hostile neighbours. Its colonial economy was still tributary to the mother country, and its polity was dangerously disordered. In less than a hundred years, the new nation had become a giant. By 1890 its population had grown larger than that of any European nation except Russia. Its economy was the most productive in the world. Its territory had grown to continental proportions. And its republican government had become strong, centralised, and highly stable.

The expansion of the American republic was sustained by its vast abundance of physical resources. As the great powers of Europe pursued their imperial dreams in Africa and Asia, the United States enjoyed the luxury of a built-in empire. The westward movement may be understood as a type of domestic imperialism, with many of the same motives as the imperialist movement in Europe but with profoundly different results. The native culture of North America was not merely conquered but destroyed; an integrated capitalist democracy developed in its place.

In 1783 the United States had an area of approximately 800,000 square miles, much of it rich arable land. That immense territory was soon enlarged by other tracts, even larger and more fertile. The Louisiana Purchase (827,000 square miles) was a mighty windfall which dropped into the hands of an astonished President Thomas Jefferson in 1803. West Florida was taken by force during James Madison's administration and East Florida (60,000 square miles) by purchase, with the threat of force, during the presidency of James Monroe.

A second set of acquisitions in the period 1845-53 completed the contiguous area of the continental United States. Protracted negotiations for the territory of Oregon (285,000 square miles) finally ended with a compromise in 1846. The Texas republic (390,000 square miles) was annexed in 1845, and the vast Mexican cession (529,000 square miles) was a spoil of war in 1848. Finally, there was the Gadsden Purchase in 1853, bought from Mexico to control a promising railroad route. Compared with other acquisitions, it was trivial in size – a mere 30,000 square miles, approximately the area of Scotland.

This enormous landmass was occupied almost

3/Land cessions and density of settlement *(below)* In 1783, the new nation occupied a space between the Atlantic coast and the Mississippi river. Its territory was enlarged in only two great expansionist movements. During the first (1803-19), three Jeffersonian presidents acquired Louisiana and the Floridas. The second (1845-53) added Texas, Oregon and California.

expansion of settled area by
1750   1790   1850   1890   largely unsettled by 1890

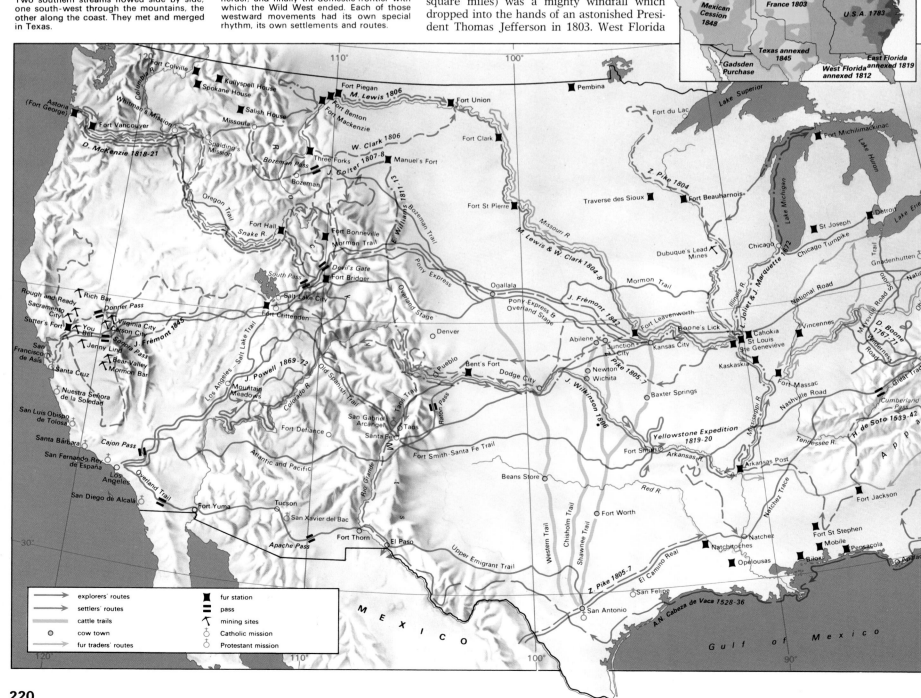

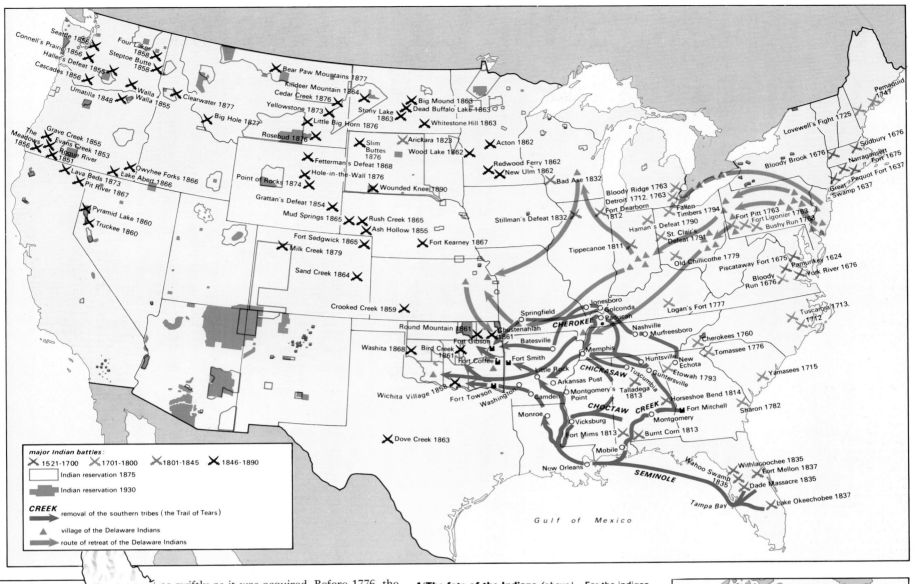

major Indian battles:
- ✗ 1521–1700 ✗ 1701–1800 ✗ 1801–1845 ✗ 1846–1890
- ☐ Indian reservation 1875
- ▨ Indian reservation 1930
- **CREEK** removal of the southern tribes (the Trail of Tears)
- ▲ village of the Delaware Indians
- ➙ route of retreat of the Delaware Indians

as swiftly as it was acquired. Before 1776, the Americans had been slow to settle the interior, which they called the 'back-country'. After 1800, the 'back-country' became 'frontier' in American speech, and the line of settlement advanced westward with astonishing speed. By its conventional definition, the 'frontier' is commonly understood to be the outer edge of the area with a population density of at least two persons per square mile. Before 1783 that line was still largely east of the Appalachian mountains except for a small settlement on the dark and bloody ground of Kentucky. Thirty years later, the great centre of the continent was occupied. By 1820 the frontier had crossed the Mississippi. And by 1840, it had reached the 100th meridian. The plains beyond were subdued after 1865 with the aid of a new technology – the steel plough, the six-shooter, and the barbed wire fence. After the census of 1890, the superintendent of the census observed that for the first time in American history, a single frontier-line was no longer visible on his map. The frontier, in that sense, had come to an end.

But as an experience, myth and symbol, the frontier continues to dominate American thought even today. The movement, progress, energy, expectation, confidence, prosperity and hope which it engendered still remain central to American culture. The unique experience of a built-in empire made it especially difficult for Americans to understand the conditions of other less fortunate people, and for others to understand America as well.

4/The fate of the Indians (above) For the indigenous Indians, every American cliché ran in reverse: expansion became contraction, democracy became tyranny, prosperity became poverty, and liberty became confinement. Before 1600, a million Indians lived north of the Rio Grande, speaking 2000 languages and subsisting in small villages on maize, game and fish. The coming of the Europeans caused a flowering of Indian culture. From whites, the Sioux obtained their horses; the Navajo, their sheep; the Iroquois, their weapons. But destruction quickly followed. The New England tribes, hard hit by disease, were broken in the Pequot War (1636) and King Philip's War (1675-6). In the middle colonies, the great Delaware nation was defeated by the Dutch in the Esopus Wars (1660), disgraced by the Iroquois (who made all the Delaware into 'honorary women'), and cheated by Quakers. The Delaware began a great diaspora; today they are scattered from Canada to Texas. For the southern tribes another fate was in store. Planters, led by Andrew Jackson obtained a law for their 'removal'. Despite the opposition of the Supreme Court, some 50,000 Cherokee were collected in concentration camps, and sent on a winter march to Oklahoma in 1838. Many died. The Choctaw, Creek and Chickasaw suffered equally. Only the Seminole resisted for long in the Florida swamps.

5/The buffalo (right) On the plains, the economic base of Indian culture was broken when the buffalo herd was cut in two by the railroad (1869). Twenty years later the buffalo, like the Indians, survived only in protected reservations.

6/Indian culture after the conquest (below right) As the material base of Indian culture crumbled, its spiritual structure was also destroyed. Many Indians created new systems of belief. The Ghost Dance was a religion of resistance, first developed in non-violent form c. 1870 by the Paiute prophet Woroke. The Sioux made it a warrior's faith; the inevitable result was the battle of Wounded Knee (1890). The Peyote drug cult, on the other hand, was a religion of accommodation, a syncretist faith which drew its doctrines from Indian and European sources, and which served as a spiritual bridge from one culture to another.

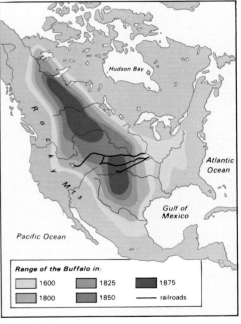

Range of the Buffalo in:
- ☐ 1600 ☐ 1825 ■ 1875
- ☐ 1800 ☐ 1850 — railroads

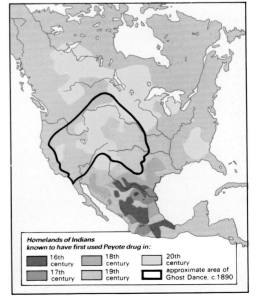

Homelands of Indians known to have first used Peyote drug in:
- ■ 16th century ☐ 18th century ☐ 20th century
- ☐ 17th century ☐ 19th century — approximate area of Ghost Dance. c.1890

Westward migration (right) by covered wagon started at the end of the 18th century and gathered pace after the breaching of the Allegheny mountains and the entry of immigrants to the mid-west by way of the great lakes and the Mississippi. The immigrants were opposed by Indian tribes driven westward by the ever increasing pressure.

The making of the United States: civil war and economic growth

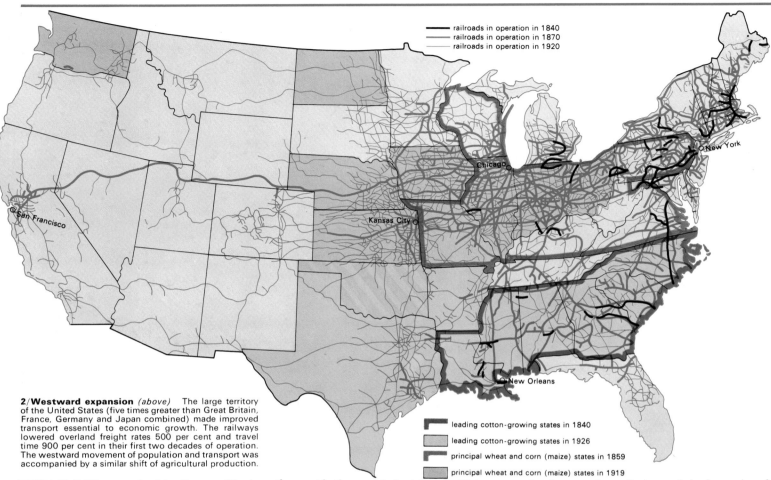

railroads in operation in 1840
railroads in operation in 1870
railroads in operation in 1920

2/Westward expansion *(above)* The large territory of the United States (five times greater than Great Britain, France, Germany and Japan combined) made improved transport essential to economic growth. The railways lowered overland freight rates 500 per cent and travel time 900 per cent in their first two decades of operation. The westward movement of population and transport was accompanied by a similar shift of agricultural production.

leading cotton-growing states in 1840
leading cotton-growing states in 1926
principal wheat and corn (maize) states in 1859
principal wheat and corn (maize) states in 1919

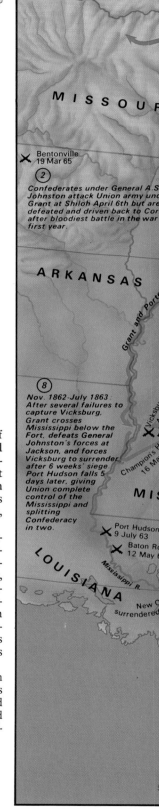

THE Civil War was the bloodiest conflict in American history. More Americans died than in all the nation's other wars combined. And the consequences equalled the cost – four million slaves emancipated, central government strengthened, and northern hegemony established.

Soon after the election of Lincoln, South Carolina left the Union. She was followed by the other six states of the lower South, which combined to form the Confederate States of America on 8 February 1861. After fighting began at Fort Sumter on 12 April, the states of Virginia, North Carolina, Tennessee and Arkansas joined their departing sisters. Although the South seceded to forestall a felt threat to slavery, the North fought at first only for the Union and not for the freedom of slaves. But by 1863 the revolutionary social and military momentum of the war, coupled with the growing power of radical Republicans in Congress, made emancipation a second Union war aim.

The massive volunteer armies mobilised by both sides were little more than armed mobs in 1861. The only major battle of the war's first year was fought at Bull Run on 21 July 1861, when the southern mob turned back a northern invasion of Virginia. Serious military operations began in the spring of 1862. Northern strategy was to deny the South vital resources by a naval blockade, to gain control of key river routes and forts in the west, and to capture the Confederate capital of Richmond. In view of the North's overwhelming superiority in manpower and resources, it may seem surprising that Union victory took four years. There were two main reasons for this: first, the South enjoyed superior generalship during the first two years of war; second, the North's war aims required occupation of the South and destruction of its armies, whereas the southern goal of independence required a primarily defensive strategy. In the east, General Robert E. Lee turned back two invasions of Virginia in 1862 and carried the war into the North. But he was stopped at Antietam, Maryland in September 1862 and decisively defeated at Gettysburg, Pennsylvania in July 1863. By the latter date the Northern strategy in

the west had succeeded, giving the Union control of the Mississippi and Tennessee rivers and opening the way for invasion of the lower South. By 1864 the Union blockade was effective, and General Grant began his invasion of Virginia which, combined with General Sherman's march through Georgia and South Carolina, destroyed the South's armies by the spring of 1865.

Northern victory was a triumph not only for the political and social goals of union and emancipation, but for economic modernisation as well. Before the war the contrasting economic systems of plantation slavery and free-labour capitalism had generated bitter ideological conflict between pro-slavery and anti-slavery partisans that was finally resolved on the battlefield. The North won the war mainly because its modernising economy could better mobilise the resources for war than could the agricultural South. Although many of the criteria for modernisation – per capita increase of agricultural and industrial output, technological innovation, urbanisation, expansion of education – were present before the war, these developments were confined mainly to the North. The war crippled the Southern ruling class and liberated its labour force, thereby removing the chief obstacle to the triumph of competitive free-labour capitalism.

From 1825 to 1910 the output of the American economy grew at an average annual rate of 1.6 per cent per capita. At the same time the population, through natural increase and immigration, doubled every twenty-seven years, giving the United States the fastest economic growth rate in the world.

Most important to this result was the growth of agricultural output. A population moving westward onto virgin lands, increased mechanisation and use of fertilisers, new strains of cotton, maize and wheat, and more efficient farm management made the United States the leading agricultural producer in the world.

Dramatic improvements in transport from 1790 to 1840 – turnpikes, bridges, canals, high-pressure steamboats and railways – lowered costs, raised volume, and created new markets

for farm products. Because of the large size of the country and because America's industrial revolution coincided with the great age of railway building, railways played a more important part in American economic development than in any other country. By 1890 the rail network was larger in the United States than in all Europe, including the British Isles and Russia.

These developments in agriculture and transport, combined with abundant resources, a literate population, technological innovation, managerial expertise, large-scale capital investment, political stability and a widely-shared entrepreneurial ethic, promoted the rapid industrialisation of the United States in the 19th century. The greatest industrial growth occurred from 1877 to 1892, when American factories tripled their output. By 1890 the United States was the world's leading industrial power.

In the 19th century the United States was an importer of capital, and much of the country's economic growth was fuelled by British and European investment. During the First World War that balance changed. After 1918 the United States became an exporter of capital.

3/Union states and Confederate states *(below)* This was a sectional Civil War, with geography determining the separation between the slave plantation and free labour economies. The five most northerly slave states remained in the Union, though part of their population supported the Confederacy.

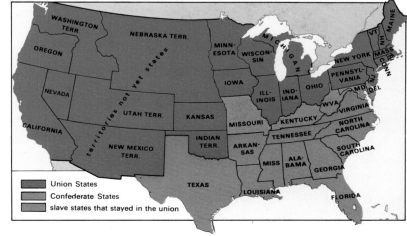

Union States
Confederate States
slave states that stayed in the union

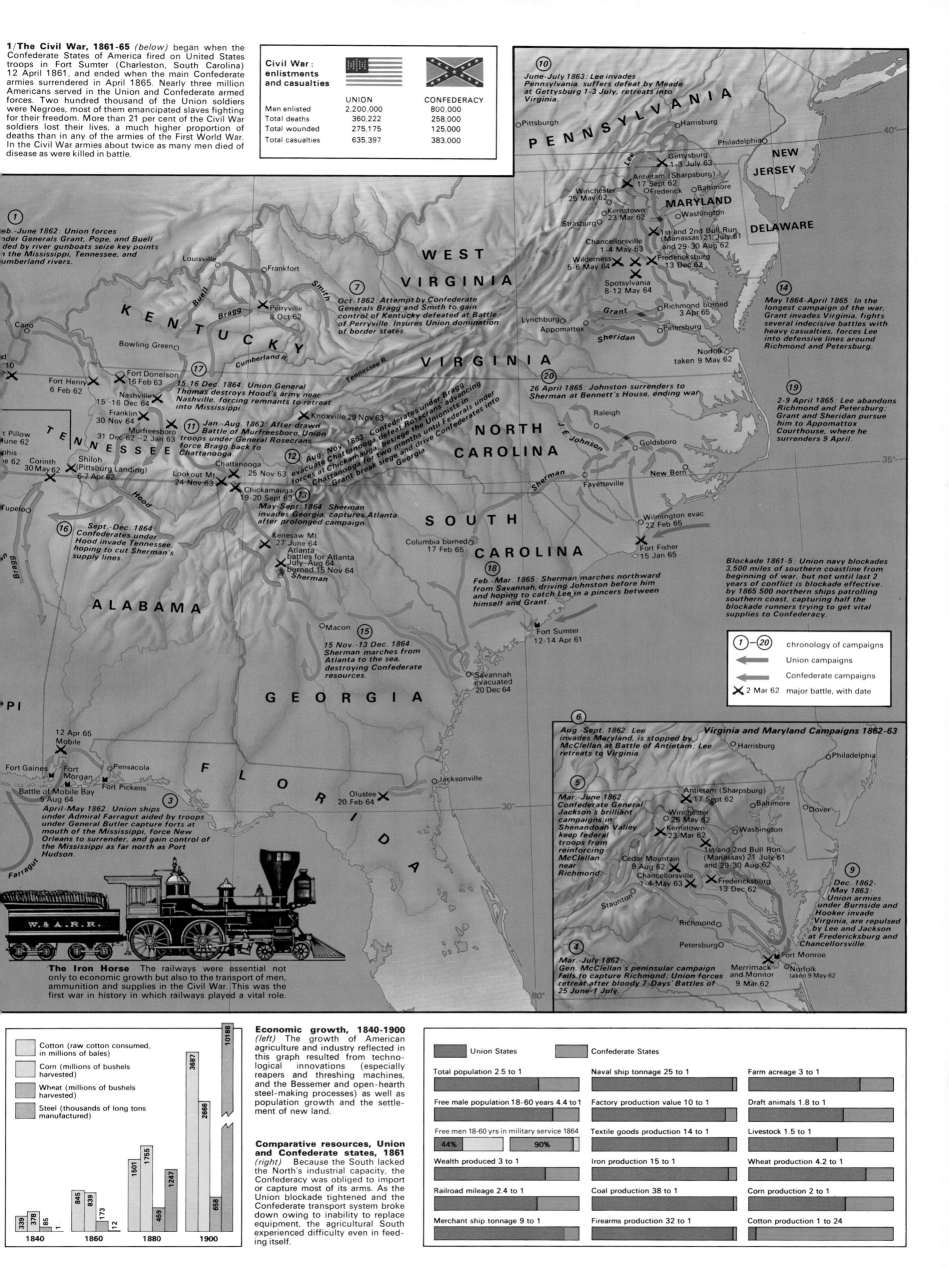

1/The Civil War, 1861-65 (below) began when the Confederate States of America fired on United States troops in Fort Sumter (Charleston, South Carolina) 12 April 1861, and ended when the main Confederate armies surrendered in April 1865. Nearly three million Americans served in the Union and Confederate armed forces. Two hundred thousand of the Union soldiers were Negroes, most of them emancipated slaves fighting for their freedom. More than 21 per cent of the Civil War soldiers lost their lives, a much higher proportion of deaths than in any of the armies of the First World War. In the Civil War armies about twice as many men died of disease as were killed in battle.

Civil War: enlistments and casualties

	UNION	CONFEDERACY
Men enlisted	2,200,000	800,000
Total deaths	360,222	258,000
Total wounded	275,175	125,000
Total casualties	635,397	383,000

The Iron Horse The railways were essential not only to economic growth but also to the transport of men, ammunition and supplies in the Civil War. This was the first war in history in which railways played a vital role.

① Feb.-June 1862: Union forces under Generals Grant, Pope, and Buell aided by river gunboats seize key points on the Mississippi, Tennessee, and Cumberland rivers.

⑦ Oct. 1862: Attempt by Confederate Generals Bragg and Smith to gain control of Kentucky defeated at Battle of Perryville. Insures Union domination of border states.

⑰ 15-16 Dec. 1864: Union General Thomas destroys Hood's army near Nashville, forcing remnants to retreat into Mississippi.

⑪ Jan.-Aug. 1863: After drawn Battle of Murfreesboro, Union troops under General Rosecrans force Bragg back to Chattanooga.

⑫ Aug.-Nov. 1863: Confederates under Bragg advancing on Chattanooga, defeat Rosecrans at Chickamauga, besiege the Unionists in Chattanooga for two months until Federals under Grant break siege and drive Confederates into Georgia.

⑬ May-Sept. 1864: Sherman invades Georgia, captures Atlanta after prolonged campaign.

⑯ Sept.-Dec. 1864: Confederates under Hood invade Tennessee, hoping to cut Sherman's supply lines.

⑮ 15 Nov.-13 Dec. 1864: Sherman marches from Atlanta to the sea, destroying Confederate resources.

③ April-May 1862: Union ships under Admiral Farragut aided by troops under General Butler capture forts at mouth of the Mississippi, force New Orleans to surrender, and gain control of the Mississippi as far north as Port Hudson.

⑱ Feb.-Mar. 1865: Sherman marches northward from Savannah, driving Johnston before him and hoping to catch Lee in a pincers between himself and Grant.

⑩ June-July 1863: Lee invades Pennsylvania, suffers defeat by Meade at Gettysburg 1-3 July, retreats into Virginia.

⑭ May 1864-April 1865: In the longest campaign of the war, Grant invades Virginia, fights several indecisive battles with heavy casualties, forces Lee into defensive lines around Richmond and Petersburg.

⑳ 26 April 1865: Johnston surrenders to Sherman at Bennett's House, ending war

⑲ 2-9 April 1865: Lee abandons Richmond and Petersburg; Grant and Sheridan pursue him to Appomattox Courthouse, where he surrenders 9 April.

Blockade 1861-5: Union navy blockades 3,500 miles of southern coastline from beginning of war, but not until last 2 years of conflict is blockade effective. by 1865 500 northern ships patrolling southern coast, capturing half the blockade runners trying to get vital supplies to Confederacy.

① — ⑳ chronology of campaigns
⟵ Union campaigns
⟵ Confederate campaigns
✗ 2 Mar 62 major battle, with date

Virginia and Maryland Campaigns 1862-63

⑥ Aug.-Sept. 1862: Lee invades Maryland, is stopped by McClellan at Battle of Antietam; Lee retreats to Virginia.

⑤ Mar.-June 1862: Confederate General Jackson's brilliant campaigns in Shenandoah Valley keep federal troops from reinforcing McClellan near Richmond.

⑨ Dec. 1862-May 1863: Union armies under Burnside and Hooker invade Virginia, are repulsed by Lee and Jackson at Fredericksburg and Chancellorsville.

④ Mar.-July 1862: Gen. McClellan's peninsular campaign fails to capture Richmond; Union forces retreat after bloody 7-Days' Battles of 25 June-1 July.

Economic growth, 1840-1900 (left) The growth of American agriculture and industry reflected in this graph resulted from technological innovations (especially reapers and threshing machines, and the Bessemer and open-hearth steel-making processes) as well as population growth and the settlement of new land.

Cotton (raw cotton consumed, in millions of bales)
Corn (millions of bushels harvested)
Wheat (millions of bushels harvested)
Steel (thousands of long tons manufactured)

Comparative resources, Union and Confederate states, 1861 (right) Because the South lacked the North's industrial capacity, the Confederacy was obliged to import or capture most of its arms. As the Union blockade tightened and the Confederate transport system broke down owing to inability to replace equipment, the agricultural South experienced difficulty even in feeding itself.

Union States   Confederate States

Total population 2.5 to 1	Naval ship tonnage 25 to 1	Farm acreage 3 to 1
Free male population 18-60 years 4.4 to 1	Factory production value 10 to 1	Draft animals 1.8 to 1
Free men 18-60 yrs in military service 1864 44% 90%	Textile goods production 14 to 1	Livestock 1.5 to 1
Wealth produced 3 to 1	Iron production 15 to 1	Wheat production 4.2 to 1
Railroad mileage 2.4 to 1	Coal production 38 to 1	Corn production 2 to 1
Merchant ship tonnage 9 to 1	Firearms production 32 to 1	Cotton production 1 to 24

The making of the United States: politics and society 1776 to 1930

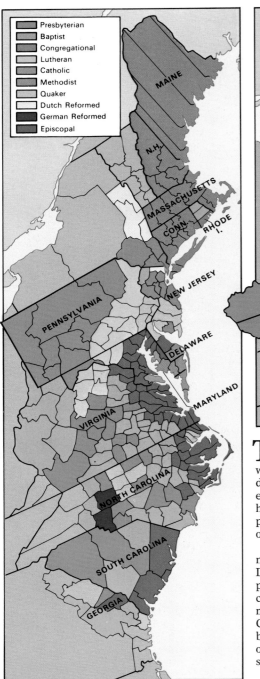

Presbyterian
Baptist
Congregational
Lutheran
Catholic
Methodist
Quaker
Dutch Reformed
German Reformed
Episcopal

1/The election of 1800 (above and above right) In the election of 1800, power passed from the ruling Federalist party to its Jeffersonian challengers. That peaceable revolution provided a foundation for stable republicanism in North America. Voting patterns reflected the distribution of ethnic and religious groups.

Adams and other Federalist candidates

Jefferson and other Democratic-Republican candidates

no returns, unsettled

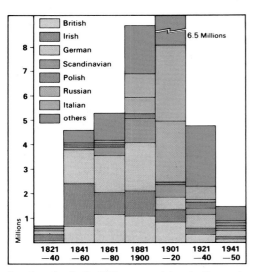

British
Irish
German
Scandinavian
Polish
Russian
Italian
others

6.5 Millions

1821 –40 | 1841 –60 | 1861 –80 | 1881 1900 | 1901 –20 | 1921 –40 | 1941 –50

Immigration in the 19th century (above) Economic change, population surplus, and famine sent millions of Europeans to North America, where scarcity of labour and virgin agricultural land provided economic opportunity. In the 1890s there was a fundamental shift in the sources of immigrants from north-western to southern and eastern Europe. Russian Jews and subject nationalities of the Austro-Hungarian Empire as well as Poles and Italians now constituted the majority of immigrants.

THE United States was a paradox in political history: a republic of imperial dimensions, which drew its unity from its multitude of differences. Any one of those differences – ethnic, regional, economic or religious – might have destroyed the nation. Instead, the multiplicity of conflicts in America prevented any one of them from polarising the nation.

In 1776, most Americans were British in national origin and Calvinist in their religion. During the next 150 years, nearly 40 million people migrated to the United States. As a consequence, the map of the nation became a mosaic of many different religions. Roman Catholics, Methodists, Baptists and Lutherans became the largest denominations, with scores of smaller rivals. The ethnic map of American society thus became more complex too.

As the country expanded, its regions also became more diverse. The difference between North and South – between a system of wage labour and bond labour – became the most dangerous difference, as it was at once economic, political and racial. Before 1860 more than 90 per cent of the black population lived below the Mason-Dixon line. Race was a regional problem. Not until the First World War did significant numbers of blacks move north. And as the economy developed the distribution of wealth became increasingly unequal between both individuals and regions. Rich and poor concentrated in urban areas, while the middling classes remained predominantly rural. With the growth of economic inequality came a corresponding growth of class consciousness.

American presidential elections reflected the interplay of these patterns of ethnicity, religion, region and class. The 1800 campaign, in which the Republican candidate Thomas Jefferson beat the Federalists' John Adams, saw a coalition of New England Congregational elites, Dutch burghers in New York, Free Blacks in the middle states lining up against the northern Baptist yeomen, Virginia Episcopalian planters, Irish immigrants in the cities and German farmers in Pennsylvania. The peaceful transfer of power was made possible by the complexity of those electoral patterns.

By 1828 the Federalist party had disappeared and the Jeffersonians had divided into the National-Republicans, headed by John Quincy Adams, and the Democratic-Republicans led by Andrew Jackson. This election prefigured the evolution of the Whig and Democratic parties. Jackson ran strongly among the common people of northern cities and the southern countryside; his opponents in 1828 and later were strongest in rural New England and the Old North-West, and among the commercial and planter elites of both North and South. National Republicans/Whigs found their greatest support among Unitarians, Congregationalists, Presbyterians and Episcopalians; Jacksonians were strongest among Baptists and Catholics; Methodists and Lutherans were divided.

Although many of these patterns persisted in 1860, the sectional conflict over slavery overshadowed them. The Democratic party, which had traditionally united different ethnic and economic groups across sectional lines, broke into two parties, one southern, one northern, with John C. Breckinridge and Stephen A. Douglas respectively for the presidency. Battered remnants of the Whigs formed the Constitutional Union party, with John Bell as its candidate, to try to unite conservatives in both sections, but Bell ran well only in the border states. The anti-slavery Republicans, entirely a northern party, nominated Abraham Lincoln on a platform of slavery containment. Carrying every county in New England and most of the counties in the other free states (but only two counties in all the south), Lincoln won the presidency with only 39 per cent of the popular vote. His election precipitated the secession of eleven slave states, and brought on the Civil War.

For a generation after the war, ethnic, religious and sectional patterns dominated American elections. As the party of Union, emancipation, and reform, the Republicans won the votes of most evangelical Protestants in the North and Negroes in the South. The Democrats were supported by most whites in the South, and many non-evangelical Protestants in the North. Class was only a minor factor in determining party allegiance, but since an increasing percentage of unskilled working men in the North were immigrants and Catholics, there appeared to be a relation between class and party in some northern states.

In the election of 1896, economic issues jolted old ethnic and religious patterns. William Jennings Bryan and the Democrats, campaigning for an inflationary policy of expanded silver coinage, carried all but three counties in the silver states of the West, as well as the farm states of Kansas, Nebraska and the South. Fearing the impact of inflation on real wages, and attracted by McKinley's repudiation of traditional Republican anti-Catholicism, northern working men of Catholic as well as Protestant faiths joined native-born middle-class Protestants in voting Republican. The Democratic party, in power when the Panic of 1893 began, became stigmatised as the party of depression. The sectional and rural/urban divisions in this election were striking: McKinley carried every county in New England (despite the region's large Catholic population), all but one county in New York, and all but two in New Jersey. He was the only Republican candidate in the 19th century to carry New York City. For twenty years before 1896 the two major parties had been evenly balanced in national elections; McKinley's success in winning many immigrant and urban votes while losing only the farmers and miners of thinly-populated Western states moved the Republican party in a more urban, cosmopolitan and progressive direction and ensured its domination until the 1930s.

2/The election of 1860 (right) In 1860 the American Union was split by the issue of slavery. The Republican candidate, Abraham Lincoln, promised to contain the westward expansion of slavery. He carried every county in New England, most of New York, and much of the north-west. John C. Breckinridge ran strongly throughout the south, but ironically the counties where slavery was strongest voted heavily for a compromise candidate, John Bell. The nominee of the northern Democrats, Stephen A. Douglas, did well in the popular vote, but carried few counties.

3/The election of 1896 (below) The main issue of this election was the monetary system. The Republican candidate, William McKinley, stood for preservation of the gold standard, while the Democrat William Jennings Bryan crusaded for a bimetallic silver and gold standard, whose expected inflationary impact would benefit farmers of the south and west. This issue, plus Bryan's fundamentalist Protestantism and McKinley's religious pluralism, help to explain the sectional pattern of the voting, with the urbanised north-east and north central states solidly Republican and the south and west solidly Democratic.

1896 Electoral results

McKinley, Republican

Bryan, Democrat, Populist and National Silver

no returns, unsettled etc.

Wealth per capita
below $500 income, rest of U.S.A. over $500

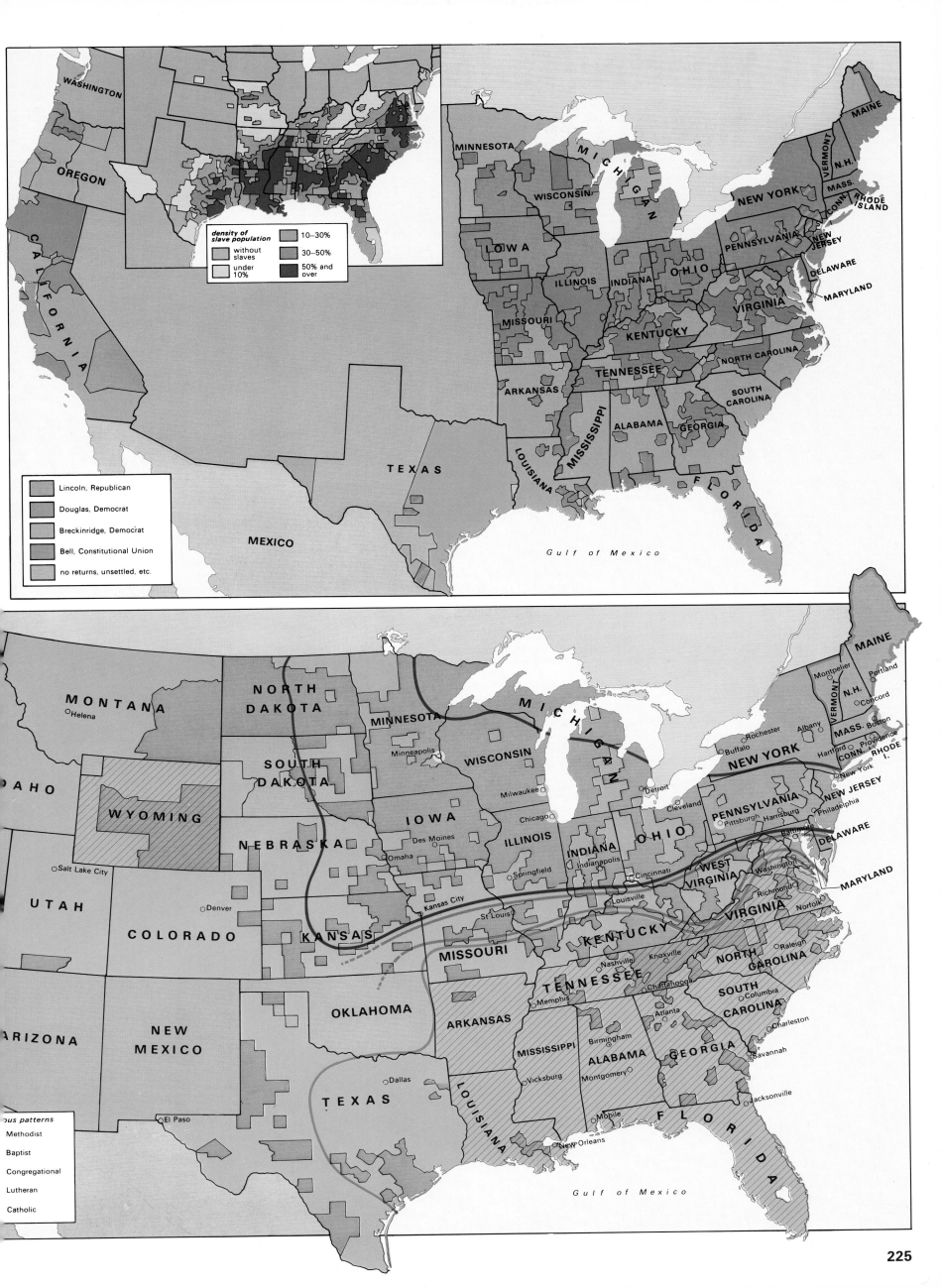

density of slave population

- without slaves
- under 10%
- 10–30%
- 30–50%
- 50% and over

- Lincoln, Republican
- Douglas, Democrat
- Breckinridge, Democrat
- Bell, Constitutional Union
- no returns, unsettled, etc.

religious patterns

- Methodist
- Baptist
- Congregational
- Lutheran
- Catholic

225

Latin America: independence and national growth 1810 to 1910

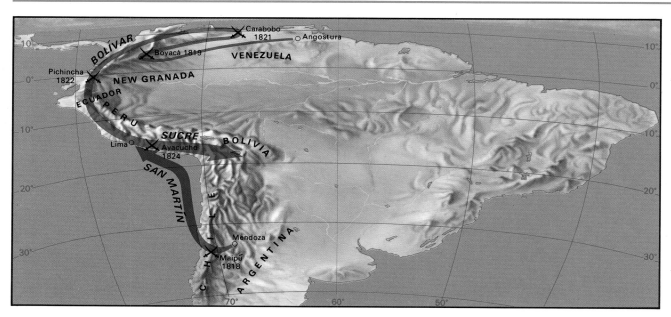

2 / Independence campaigns 1810 to 1826 (above) Latin America's main wars of liberation, against Spain, lasted until 1826. They involved two major forces: one, led by the Venezuelans, Bolívar and Sucre, converging on Peru, the central Spanish bastion; the other, the Army of the Andes, with San Martín's Argentines and Bernardo O'Higgins' Chileans, attacking the Peruvian capital, Lima.

3/Export economies and foreign investment (below) The new nations of Latin America were classic export economies, exploiting cheap land and labour to produce raw materials for a world market. Foreign competition and small, subsistence-level domestic markets held back development of national industries; characteristic economic institutions were the plantation, the ranch and the mine. From the 1880s, a massive immigration of foreign manpower and capital, reinforced by railways and improved ocean transport, accelerated economic growth.

THE emancipation of Latin America between 1808 and 1826 was precipitated by the Napoleonic subjection of Spain and Portugal, which effectively cut off the colonies from their motherlands. This merely released a long dormant nationalism, now able to express itself in demands for political freedom, administrative autonomy and economic self-determination. The Portuguese royal family met these demands by adopting them and leading Brazil peacefully into nationhood as an independent empire, with its own crown and a minimum of social change. Spain, on the other hand, sought to crush its colonies' pretensions at their source. Spanish American independence then swept across the sub-continent in two violent movements: the southern revolution advanced across the pampas from Buenos Aires and was carried by San Martín's Army of the Andes to Chile and beyond; the northern revolution, more vigorously harassed by Spanish troops, was led by Bolívar from Venezuela to the mountainous battlefield of Boyacá in Colombia (then called New Grana-

da) and back to its birthplace. Both converged on Peru, the fortress of Spain in America. In the north, Mexican insurgency followed a course of its own – first frustrated social revolution, then prolonged counter-revolution and finally a successful power-seizure by the conservative commander Iturbide, enthroned as Emperor Agustín I. Independence everywhere was essentially a political movement, involving a transfer of authority but only marginal social and economic change.

The wars caused great loss of life and property; terror and insecurity provoked a flight of capital and labour, making it difficult to organise recovery. The first decades of freedom were occupied with violent political debate – between centre and regions, between free trade and protection, between agriculturists, mine-owners and industrialists, and between supporters of cheap imports and defenders of national production. In Colombia the civil war between 'liberals' and 'conservatives' lasted well over a hundred years. On the whole, policies of primary export

and cheap imports won the day, and British (and later French and North American) merchants, bankers and shippers were ready and eager to fill the entrepreneurial vacuum left by Spain.

Prospects of national economic development were really defeated by the social structure of the new states, where impoverished rural populations offered little support for local industry. The old colonial division between a privileged minority, monopolising land and office, and a barely subsisting mass of peasants and workers, survived independence and grew even sharper. The new power base was the *hacienda*, the great landed estate; this was a social rather than an economic investment, utilising too much land and too little capital, and was ultimately carried on the back of cheap labour, seasonal or servile. The slave trade did not long survive independence, and slavery itself was abolished in all Spanish-speaking republics by the 1850s – though not in Brazil, where it lasted until 1888. But the Negro, like the majority of *mulattos* and *mestizos*, remained at the foot of the economic ladder. Such groups often became tied *peons*, allowed a strip of land on the *hacienda* in return for arduous labour service. After the wars, the new rulers sought to reduce tension by abolishing socio-racial discrimination – at least in law. They also sought to integrate the Indians into the nation by forcing them to participate in the economy; this involved dividing their communal lands among individual owners, theoretically benefiting the Indians themselves, but in practice only strengthening their powerful white neighbours.

The independence movement was a war, and inevitably nurtured warriors, giving a prepon-

4/Population and immigration (below) Latin America inherited a complex racial structure. Spanish American societies were composed in varying proportions of a great mass of Indians, a lesser number of mestizos, and a minority of whites. The Indian base of this pyramid was extensive in Peru, Mexico and Guatemala, less so in the Río de la Plata and Chile. The slave trade from Africa had also added the Negro, from whom were descended Mulattos and other mixed groups. Brazil was a slave society until 1888, blacks and mixed bloods occupied the lower part of the social scale. Both Argentina and Brazil received massive immigration from Europe in the late 19th century.

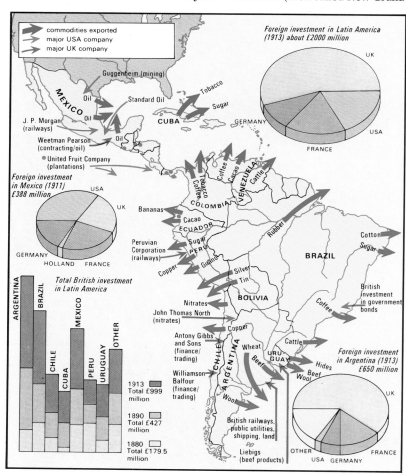

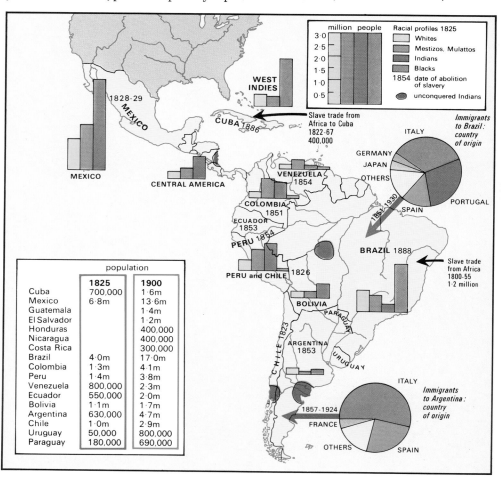

population		
	1825	**1900**
Cuba	700,000	1·6m
Mexico	6·8m	13·6m
Guatemala		1·4m
El Salvador		1·2m
Honduras		400,000
Nicaragua		400,000
Costa Rica		300,000
Brazil	4·0m	17·0m
Colombia	1·3m	4·1m
Peru	1·4m	3·8m
Venezuela	800,000	2·3m
Ecuador	550,000	2·0m
Bolivia	1·1m	1·7m
Argentina	630,000	4·7m
Chile	1·0m	2·9m
Uruguay	50,000	800,000
Paraguay	180,000	690,000

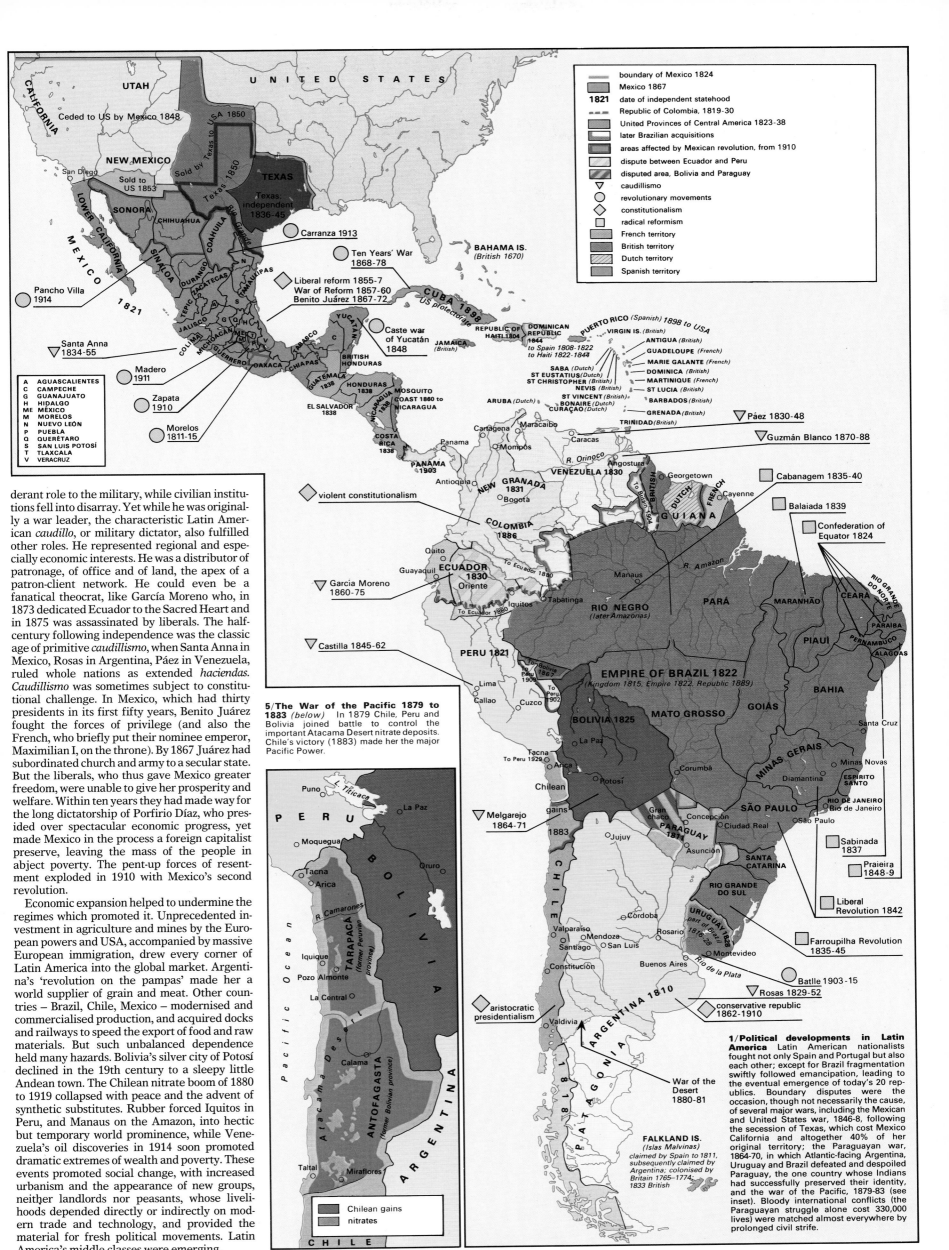

derant role to the military, while civilian institutions fell into disarray. Yet while he was originally a war leader, the characteristic Latin American *caudillo*, or military dictator, also fulfilled other roles. He represented regional and especially economic interests. He was a distributor of patronage, of office and of land, the apex of a patron-client network. He could even be a fanatical theocrat, like García Moreno who, in 1873 dedicated Ecuador to the Sacred Heart and in 1875 was assassinated by liberals. The half-century following independence was the classic age of primitive *caudillismo*, when Santa Anna in Mexico, Rosas in Argentina, Páez in Venezuela, ruled whole nations as extended *haciendas*. *Caudillismo* was sometimes subject to constitutional challenge. In Mexico, which had thirty presidents in its first fifty years, Benito Juárez fought the forces of privilege (and also the French, who briefly put their nominee emperor, Maximilian I, on the throne). By 1867 Juárez had subordinated church and army to a secular state. But the liberals, who thus gave Mexico greater freedom, were unable to give her prosperity and welfare. Within ten years they had made way for the long dictatorship of Porfirio Díaz, who presided over spectacular economic progress, yet made Mexico in the process a foreign capitalist preserve, leaving the mass of the people in abject poverty. The pent-up forces of resentment exploded in 1910 with Mexico's second revolution.

Economic expansion helped to undermine the regimes which promoted it. Unprecedented investment in agriculture and mines by the European powers and USA, accompanied by massive European immigration, drew every corner of Latin America into the global market. Argentina's 'revolution on the pampas' made her a world supplier of grain and meat. Other countries – Brazil, Chile, Mexico – modernised and commercialised production, and acquired docks and railways to speed the export of food and raw materials. But such unbalanced dependence held many hazards. Bolivia's silver city of Potosí declined in the 19th century to a sleepy little Andean town. The Chilean nitrate boom of 1880 to 1919 collapsed with peace and the advent of synthetic substitutes. Rubber forced Iquitos in Peru, and Manaus on the Amazon, into hectic but temporary world prominence, while Venezuela's oil discoveries in 1914 soon promoted dramatic extremes of wealth and poverty. These events promoted social change, with increased urbanism and the appearance of new groups, neither landlords nor peasants, whose livelihoods depended directly or indirectly on modern trade and technology, and provided the material for fresh political movements. Latin America's middle classes were emerging.

5/The War of the Pacific 1879 to 1883 (below) In 1879 Chile, Peru and Bolivia joined battle to control the important Atacama Desert nitrate deposits. Chile's victory (1883) made her the major Pacific Power.

1/Political developments in Latin America Latin American nationalists fought not only Spain and Portugal but also each other; except for Brazil fragmentation swiftly followed emancipation, leading to the eventual emergence of today's 20 republics. Boundary disputes were the occasion, though not necessarily the cause, of several major wars, including the Mexican and United States war, 1846-8, following the secession of Texas, which cost Mexico California and altogether 40% of her original territory; the Paraguayan war, 1864-70, in which Atlantic-facing Argentina, Uruguay and Brazil defeated and despoiled Paraguay, the one country whose Indians had successfully preserved their identity, and the war of the Pacific, 1879-83 (see inset). Bloody international conflicts (the Paraguayan struggle alone cost 330,000 lives) were matched almost everywhere by prolonged civil strife.

The disintegration of the Ottoman Empire 1800 to 1923

3/The Greco-Turkish War, 1920-1922 *(above)* After the First World War, the Allies proposed to dismember Turkey under the Treaty of Sèvres (1920). Nationalist opposition crystallised around the country's only unbeaten general, Mustapha Kemal, and erupted after the Greek occupation of Smyrna (1920). Turkish resistance, centred on Ankara, was at first unable to counter the Greek advance towards central Anatolia. However, the Turks rallied and drove the Greeks back after two important battles at Inönü (1921). The tide gradually began to turn in the Nationalists' favour; they concluded a border agreement with the Soviet Union (1921), and made separate pacts with France and Italy, who withdrew from the Turkish mainland. In 1922, Turkish forces reoccupied Smyrna, massacring many of the Greek population. Advancing towards the Dardanelles, they met a British detachment at Çanakkale, and confrontation appeared inevitable. Eventually, Turkish demands were met, and the Treaty of Lausanne (1923), recognised Turkish sovereignty.

Turkey's national flag provides a link with both the Ottoman and Byzantine Empires. Legend tells that the Greek city of Byzantium was saved from Philip of Macedon by the brightness of the crescent moon, which was adopted as the symbol of the later Christian Byzantine Empire and by its Muslim Ottoman conquerors.

B ETWEEN the beginning of the 19th century and the end of the First World War, the Ottoman Empire disintegrated, despite extensive efforts to reform and modernise its structure. Steady European commercial and colonial penetration into the Near East and North Africa undermined its fragile economy, and growing demands for national independence among the subject peoples caused large areas either to break away or to fall effectively under foreign control.

The Napoleonic expedition to Egypt in 1798 was the first indication of the Great Powers' new concern with the area. In spite of his defeat by Britain, Napoleon's invasion marked the beginning of an extensive period of acculturation between East and West, which brought European technical, political and philosophical ideas to an area which had known neither the Renaissance nor the Enlightenment. In Egypt itself, 1798 marked the end of effective control from Constantinople; the Ottoman commander in Egypt, Mohammed Ali, sent in 1802 to restore order, founded a dynasty in 1805 which lasted until the revolution of 1952. Mohammed Ali's son, Ibrahim Pasha, led expeditions to Nejd, to subdue the Wahabis, adherents of a puritanical form of Islam, who had challenged Ottoman authority in the Hejaz and in Iraq. Ibrahim Pasha also conquered the whole area between Egypt and what is now Turkey between 1831 and 1839, and was only dissuaded from attempting to overthrow the central authority of the Empire itself under pressure from Britain and France. Egyptian pretensions were subsequently confined to Egypt itself and Sudan, which had been ruled from Cairo since 1821.

Faced with this and other challenges to its authority, the Empire began a series of major reforms, in the armed forces, and in the fields of law, education, religion and administration. Previous efforts at reform had generally foundered on the intransigence of the traditional military forces, the janissaries, in the face of what they correctly perceived as a threat to their own position; Mahmud II (1808-1839) had dissolved the janissaries in a bloody battle in 1826, which meant that this obstacle no longer existed. Two edicts, in 1839 and 1856, stressed the subjects' rights to security of life and property, equitable taxation, and limited military service, and emphasised complete equality between Muslim and Christian subjects in the Empire. Here, as in other spheres, the gap between the ideal and the reality was apparent, and opposition to the reforms soon developed. In addition, the stress on Muslim/Christian equality provided a ready excuse for the intervention of the European powers on behalf of their Christian and other protégés: the Orthodox, supported by Russia; the Maronites and other Catholics, protected by France; and the Druzes and Jews, under British

1/The Middle East and North Africa 1798-1923 *(right)* The Ottoman Empire and the regions adjoining it broke up into a large number of political units in the course of the 19th and early 20th centuries:

Afghanistan Independent state under Durrani dynasty 1747-1842, power gradually assumed by Barakzais (c.1819-1973); remained independent in spite of Russian invasions and wars with Britain 1839-42, 1878-90, 1919.

Albania Ottoman province until independence secured late 1912 after fierce fighting; pro-Italian regime of King Zog 1928-39, followed by Italian occupation.

Armenia Western part in Ottoman Empire, eastern in Persia; east part occupied by Russia 1804; briefly a united independent republic 1918-20; autonomy promised but not given due to non-ratification of Treaty of Sèvres (1920); subsequently absorbed by Turkey and USSR.

Azerbaijan Persian until early 19th century; partly occupied by Russia 1803-1828; briefly independent 1918-20, thereafter incorporated into USSR; Azeri speakers roughly equally divided between USSR and Iran.

Bahrain Independent sheikhdom under al-Khalifa family since 1783; British protection from 1820, formalised in agreements in 1880 and 1892.

Bessarabia Ceded to Russia by Ottomans under Treaty of Bucharest (1812); southern part returned to (Ottoman) Moldavia under terms of settlement after Crimean War (1856); recovered by Russia 1878. Incorporated into Romania 1918.

Bosnia-Herzegovina Ottoman; Austrian administration from 1878; incorporated into Austro-Hungarian Empire, 1908; part of Yugoslavia after 1918.

Bukhara Independent khanate; Russian protectorate 1868; incorporated into USSR 1924.

Bulgaria Ottoman province since late 14th century; unsuccessful national rising 1875-76; given autonomy but partitioned 1878; united with Eastern Rumelia 1885; independent kingdom 1908; gained Macedonia and Western Thrace 1913; present (1989) boundaries from 1919.

Crete Ottoman province since 1669; autonomous 1898; incorporated into Greece 1913.

Daghestan Persian; Russian occupation complete by 1859; formally incorporated into USSR 1921.

Eastern Rumelia Ottoman province since 14th century; privileged province 1878; incorporated into Bulgaria 1885.

Georgia Independent kingdom under intermittent Persian control; incorporated into Russia 1801; briefly independent 1918-20; thereafter incorporated into USSR.

Greece Ottoman rule since 14th century; independent state after revolts of 1821, 1833; enlarged by additions of Crete (1913), Macedonia (1913) and Dodecanese (1947).

Iraq Formed out of three former Ottoman provinces of Basra, Baghdad and Mosul, 1920; unified as kingdom under Hashemite monarchy, 1921-58; under British mandate, 1920-32.

Kars and Ardahan Fortress of Kars occupied by Russia, 1828; returned to Ottomans after Crimea, 1856; to Russia after San Stefano,

1878; incorporated in Armenian Republic, 1918-20; re-occupied by Turkey after 1920.

Khiva Independent khanate; Russian occupation after 1873.

Kokand Independent khanate; Russian occupation after 1876.

Kuwait Autonomous sheikhdom under al-Sabah family since c.1756; treaty of protection with Britain, 1899-1961.

Lebanon Ottoman conquest, 1516-17; Mount Lebanon ruled by Ma'n princes (12th century-1697), then Shihab princes (1697-1840), both generally independent of Istanbul; 'double qaimaqamate' established after re-assertion of Ottoman control, 1840-1861; given privileged status after civil war of 1860-61 under Christian governors, 1861-1914; French occupation 1918-20; enlarged and given republican status under French mandate, 1920-46.

Macedonia Ottoman province; divided between Greece, Serbia and Bulgaria 1913.

Montenegro Autonomous region within Ottoman Empire (prince-bishops until 1851, then princes); independent 1878; kingdom 1910; incorporated into Yugoslavia after 1918.

Palestine Ottoman conquest, 1516-17; ruled by provincial governors and/or local dynasts until 1917; British conquest 1917-18, assigned to Britain as mandate (1920-47) with British obligation to facilitate creation of Jewish national home.

Persia Independent kingdom under Qajar Shahs 1779-1924; Constitutional Revolution, 1905-11; British and Russian agreement on partition into spheres of influence, 1907; under Pehlevi dynasty, 1924-79.

Qatar Autonomous sheikhdom under al-Thani family since late 18th century; treaty of friendship and protection with Britain, 1916-71.

Romania Formerly Ottoman provinces of Moldavia and Wallachia under local rulers; autonomous, united 1861; independent kingdom, 1878, enlarged by the addition of Bessarabia, 1918.

Serbia Ottoman province; autonomous from c.1817; independent kingdom, 1878; incorporated after 1918 into what later became Yugoslavia.

Syria [Name formerly applied to whole area of modern Syria, Israel-Palestine, Lebanon, Jordan] Ottoman conquest 1516-17; British conquest/occupation 1918; independent Arab state 1918-20; French occupation 1920, French mandate within present geographical boundaries (Sanjak of Alexandretta ceded to Turkey, 1939) 1920-46.

Transjordan Formerly part of Ottoman province of Damascus; princedom (Hashemite family) under British mandate for Palestine 1921-23; separate administration created 1923.

Trucial Oman Small sheikhdoms under British protection, 1820s-1971.

Tunisia Ottoman conquest, 1574; virtually independent under Husainid dynasty, 1705 to French occupation in 1881; French protectorate, 1881-1956.

Yemen Local rulers belonging to Za'idi (Shi'i) sect; nominally incorporated into Ottoman Empire, 1517, Aden occupied by Britain 1839; declaration of independence, 1918; loss of part of Asir, Najran and Tihama to Saudi Arabia, 1934.

protection. Foreign intervention contributed in particular to the Crimean War (1853-56) and the Lebanese crisis of 1860-61, while Russian and Austrian pressures were vitally important in securing the independence of Bulgaria, Montenegro, Serbia and Romania by 1878.

Thus by the outbreak of the First World War, the Ottoman Empire had been reduced to what is now Turkey, a small corner of south-eastern Europe, and the Arab provinces in Asia. Further west, North Africa was completely dominated by the Powers; the French invaded Algeria in 1830, and by 1900 there were some 200,000 French settlers installed there. Similar developments took place on a smaller scale in Tunisia after the French invasion in 1881, in Morocco – itself never a part of the Ottoman Empire – after 1912, and in Libya, invaded and colonised by Italy after 1911. In Egypt, the rise of nationalism and the dangers which this posed to some £100 million of foreign investment served as the excuse for the British occupation in 1882.

In the other Arab provinces, there were stirrings of discontent, particularly during the long and oppressive reign of Abdul-Hamid II (1876-1909). Ideas of autonomy, encouraged by the revival of Arabic literature and campaigns to reform the Arabic language, gradually gained wider currency. Abdul-Hamid had prorogued the Ottoman parliament, itself one of the major achievements of the second wave of Ottoman reformers, in 1878, and opposition to his rule culminated in the Young Turk revolution of 1908-09, which was supported by members of most of the ethnic groups in what was left of the Empire. After the revolution, however, the Turkish element in the government proceeded to 'Turkify' all administrative, legal and educational institutions, a step which succeeded in alienating many Arabs and contributed in considerable measure to their willingness to seek an accommodation with Britain in the course of the war. In this they were to be disappointed, since the effect of the peace settlement was to put most of the Middle East firmly under British and French colonial control. After Turkey's defeat, her new leader, Mustapha Kemal (Atatürk), abolished the caliphate and attempted to construct a purely secular state.

As the process of disintegration continued, new forms of trade and communications, largely funded by foreign capital had begun to transform the empire. By 1914, Turkey and Egypt had substantial rail networks, with banks and mines and public utilities such as ports, tramways, water and electricity companies. North Africa and the Middle East became important markets for European goods, and Algeria began to export wine, Lebanon to produce silk, and perhaps most spectacularly, Egypt to export cotton. Starting in 1822, demand for Egyptian cotton soared tenfold during the American civil war and almost trebled again, to £27 million, before 1914.

Parallel developments were taking place in Iran. The Qajars (1779-1924) had suffered constant British and Russian interference in their internal affairs, which culminated in the partition of the country into the spheres of influence of the two powers in 1907. However, the Tobacco Rebellion of 1896-98 and the Constitutional Revolution of 1905-11 served to arouse national consciousness and political awareness, although the Qajars were eventually to be overthrown by a military coup led by Reza Khan Pehlevi in 1924. In the interwar period it was to be oil, discovered in the Arabian peninsula, Iran and Iraq, which was to become the region's most precious and most sought after natural asset.

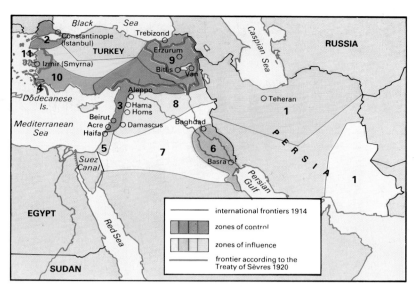

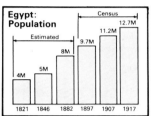

Egypt: Population

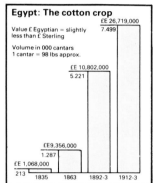

Census

Estimated

| 4M | 5M | 8M | 9.7M | 11.2M | 12.7M |
| 1821 | 1846 | 1882 | 1897 | 1907 | 1917 |

Egypt: The cotton crop

Value £ Egyptian = slightly less than £ Sterling

Volume in 000 cantars
1 cantar = 98 lbs approx.

£E 26,719,000
7.499

£E 10,802,000
5.221

£E9,356,000
1.287

£E 1,068,000
213

| 1835 | 1863 | 1892-3 | 1912-3 |

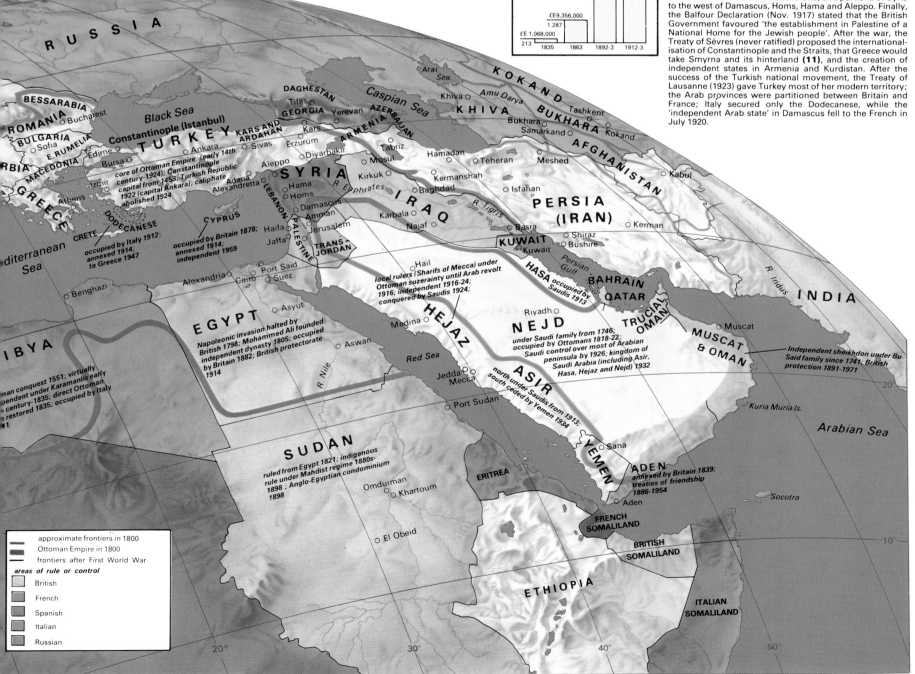

The Russian Empire: expansion and modernisation 1815 to 1917

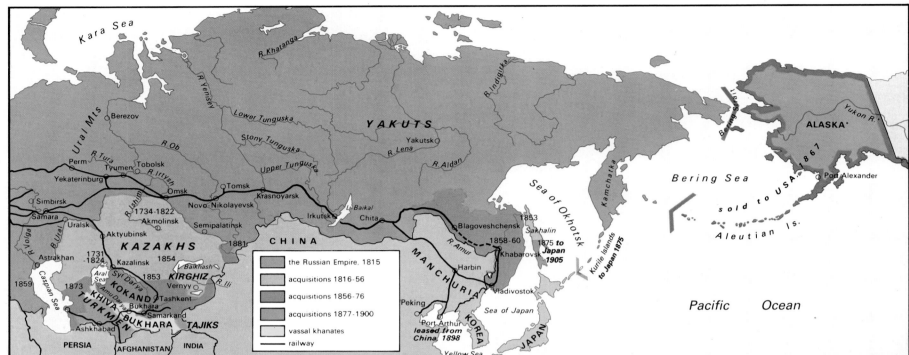

the Russian Empire, 1815
acquisitions 1816-56
acquisitions 1856-76
acquisitions 1877-1900
vassal khanates
railway

2/Russia in Asia (above) During the 19th century, Russian authority was extended southwards across the deserts of central Asia inhabited by nomadic Kazakhs, Turkmen and others, to embrace the irrigated areas at the foot of the central Asian mountains and along the Amur river. In the Far East, acquisition of the Amur territory and Sakhalin was followed by penetration of Manchuria and Korea, but the war with Japan (1904-5) expelled Russian influence from these provinces, and southern Sakhalin was abandoned.

3/Rural Population (right) Despite emigration to the steppes of the southern Ukraine, to southeastern Russia, the Volga lands and beyond into Siberia, the rich black-earth lands of the southcentral provinces became increasingly overcrowded, resulting in the subdivision of holdings and severe soil exhaustion.

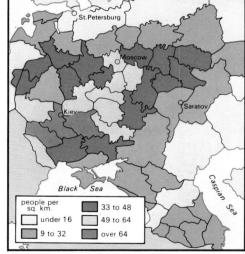

people per sq. km.
under 16   33 to 48
9 to 32   49 to 64
     over 64

4/The Crimean War (below) resulted from the determination of Britain and France, abetted by Austria, to prevent Russia benefiting from the impending dissolution of the Ottoman Empire. The war centred on the allied attempt to take the naval base of Sevastopol, which fell in September 1855 after a year-long siege.

Anglo-French forces
raids on Russian coast
Turkish forces
Russian forces
(ceded by Russia to Turkey)

FOR forty years after the Congress of Vienna, Russia remained the strongest military power in Europe, and she used her strength to maintain the order established in 1815. In this she was associated with Austria and Prussia, but Britain and France drifted away from the principles which had inspired the Congress. British public opinion became increasingly antagonistic towards the absolutism and repression which characterised the Russian system, while from France emanated the revolutionary impulses that threatened established monarchies everywhere.

Russian interests after 1815 focussed on the Balkans and on the straits leading from the Black Sea to the Mediterranean. The Turkish subjects of the Balkan countries were mostly Slavs and Orthodox, and the Russians therefore saw themselves as their natural protectors; because Turkey lay athwart Russia's link with the Mediterranean it seemed essential that Constantinople should be amenable only to Russian influence. But France, Austria and Prussia also had imperial ambitions in the Balkans or in the eastern Mediterranean, while Great Britain was opposed to any further Russian aggrandisement anywhere and regarded the maintenance of a Turkey independent of Russia as equally essential. In 1841 an international Straits Convention closed the Bosporus to Russian warships. In 1853 the Russians invaded Turkey's Danubian provinces and also gained control of the Black Sea by sinking the Turkish fleet. In 1854 Britain and France declared war, while Austria insisted on the withdrawal of Russian troops replacing them with her own. Britain and France then invaded the Crimea, and the Russians, unable to dislodge them, accepted the humiliating terms of the Peace of Paris in 1856, undertaking to keep no navy on the Black Sea and to maintain no bases on its shores.

In the 1870s spontaneous revolts of the Balkan Slavs and their ferocious repression by the Turks provoked another Russian invasion of the Balkans (1877) but, faced with the united opposition of the great powers, Russia again had to give way at the Congress of Berlin (1878). Russia, having at great cost fought what seemed to her people a thoroughly justifiable war, and having liberated fellow Slavs and co-religionaries from intolerable oppression, had to stand by while the fruits of victory were either transferred to Austria or handed back to Turkey.

Russia had meanwhile completed the acquisition of the whole of northern Asia as far as – and sometimes into – the great mountain chains which separate it from Persia, Afghanistan, India and China. Military domination over the Kazakh nomads to the east of the Caspian was secured by the building of forts, beginning with that of Akmolinsk in the north in 1830 and ending with the foundation of Vernyy (now Alma-Ata) in 1854. Mountain campaigns between 1857 and 1864 completed Russian control of the Caucasus, and the armies thus set free were used to reduce central Asia. Here the Uzbek khanates of Kokand, Bukhara and Khiva, the Turkmen nomads and the Tajik and Kirghiz mountaineers were all in turn subdued.

In the late 18th century Russian colonisation spilled over into Alaska and early in the 19th century forts were built as far south as Fort Ross in California (1812). This penetration was short-lived, but Alaska was held until 1867, when it was sold to the United States.

In the Far East the treaties of Aigun (1858) and Peking (1860) brought the Russian frontier south to the Amur river and, in the coastal region, to south of Vladivostok (founded in 1860); the southern part of Sakhalin was acquired from Japan in exchange for the Kurile Islands. In 1891 the Trans-Siberian railway was begun; but northern Manchuria stood in the way of a direct route to Vladivostok. In 1896 the Chinese conceded a strip of land for the building of the railway across Manchuria, and two years later leased Port Arthur in the Yellow Sea, giving Russia a warm-water port unimpeded by winter ice. This was also connected by railway to the main trans-Siberian line.

These advances conflicted with Japanese designs. Encouraged by the Anglo-Japanese alliance, Japan began hostilities in 1904. Russia, handicapped by fighting at such a distance from her main centres of industry and population, was compelled in the Treaty of Portsmouth (1905) to give up the concessions she had won, to leave Manchuria, and to return southern Sakhalin to Japan.

At home, serfdom was abolished in 1861 by Alexander II (1855-1881), the 'Tsar Liberator', one of a series of measures to remedy the backwardness exposed by the Crimean War. Yet the peasants were in some ways worse off, having to buy by instalments the land they had always worked, a tax they could ill afford to pay. They became increasingly impoverished and, bound still to remain in their village communes, more and more overcrowded. Unrest became widespread, culminating in violent uprisings during the revolution of 1905, which forced Tsar Nicholas II (1894-1917) to grant a parliament or *duma*. Prime Minister Stolypin's agricultural reforms (1906-11) came too late. Gradually, however, the commune lost its grip on the peasant population and during the last two decades of the 19th century and up to the Revolution, there was a mass exodus from the Russian countryside into Siberia and to the towns. With labour cheap and abundant, the Russian industrial revolution could at last begin. Railways were built and factories arose in the towns: Petersburg and Moscow became textile and metal-working centres while the metallurgical industry developed in the Ukraine. Towns grew rapidly, the urban population more than trebling – rising from 6 million to 18.6 million – between 1863 and 1914. Thus the urban proletariat, whose hardships and grievances the revolutionaries were quick to exploit, was formed (see page 258).

Legend

- ● urban population increase, 1861-1914 the circle is proportionate to the size of growth
- ■ economic activity to 1861
- ■ economic activity 1861-1914
- ⊞ metallurgical and metalworking industry
- ◆ coal mining
- ▲ iron ore mining
- ⊕ textile industry
- | sugar refining
- ▲ oil industry
- railway

Barents Sea

White Sea

FINLAND

Baltic Sea

Gulf of Finland

GERMANY

POLAND

ROMANIA

BULGARIA

TURKEY

Black Sea

Sea of Azov

Caspian Sea

PERSIA

Uleåborg
Kem
Archangel
Petrozavodsk
L. Onega
Kotlas
Solikamsk
Åbo Helsingfors
Vyborg
L. Ladoga
Kronstadt
Revel
St.Petersburg
Vyatka
Perm
Yekaterinburg
Narva
Pernov
Novgorod
Chelyabinsk
Libau
Riga
Yaroslavl
Ivanovo
Nizhniy Novgorod
Kazan
Ufa
Dvinsk
Rzhev
Vladimir
Polotsk
Moscow
Kovno
Vilna
Vitebsk
Kolomna
Simbirsk
Smolensk
Kaluga
Samara
Grodno
Minsk
Tula
Belostok
Mogilev
Lodz
Warsaw Brest
Pinsk
Bryansk
Penza
Orenburg
Chenstokhov
Lyublin
Kovel
Orel
Kozlov
Lipetsk
Tambov
Uralsk
Rovno
Kursk
Balashov
Saratov
Chernigov
Belgorod
Voronezh
Kamyshin
Zhitomir
Kiev
Berdichev
Kharkov
Vinnitsa
Poltava
Lugansk
Tsaritsyn
Kremenchug
Slavyansk
Yelizavetgrad
Bakhmut
Guryev
Yekaterinoslav
Makeyevka Gorlovka
Zaporozhye
Yuzovka
Novocherkassk
Kishinev
Nikolayev
Melitopol
Mariupol Taganrog
Rostov
Astrakhan
Odessa
Kherson
Kerch
Simferopol
Yekaterinodar
Stavropol
Sevastopol
Novorossiysk
Maykop
Vladikavkaz
Poti Kutaisi
Tiflis
Krasnovodsk
Baku

R. Pechota
R. Mezen
R. Ob
Northern Dvina
R. Sukhona
R. Kama
R. Vyatka
R. Belaya
R. Neman
R. Dnieper
R. Pripet
Southern Bug
R. Dniester
R. Don
R. Volga
R. Ural
R. Danube
Carpathian Mts.
Caucasus Mts.
R. Kura
Bosporus
Ural Mts.

1/European Russia 1815-1917 There was little economic growth in 19th-century Russia before the liberation of the serfs in 1861, although railway building had begun. From the 1860s onwards industrialisation gathered momentum, becoming a veritable industrial revolution in the 1880s and after. Concentrations of poverty-stricken workers in the towns formed the proletariat among whom revolutionary ideas flourished. There was extensive railway building, though much of this was strategic and intended to facilitate the movement of troops to frontier areas.

The collapse of the Chinese Empire 1842 to 1911

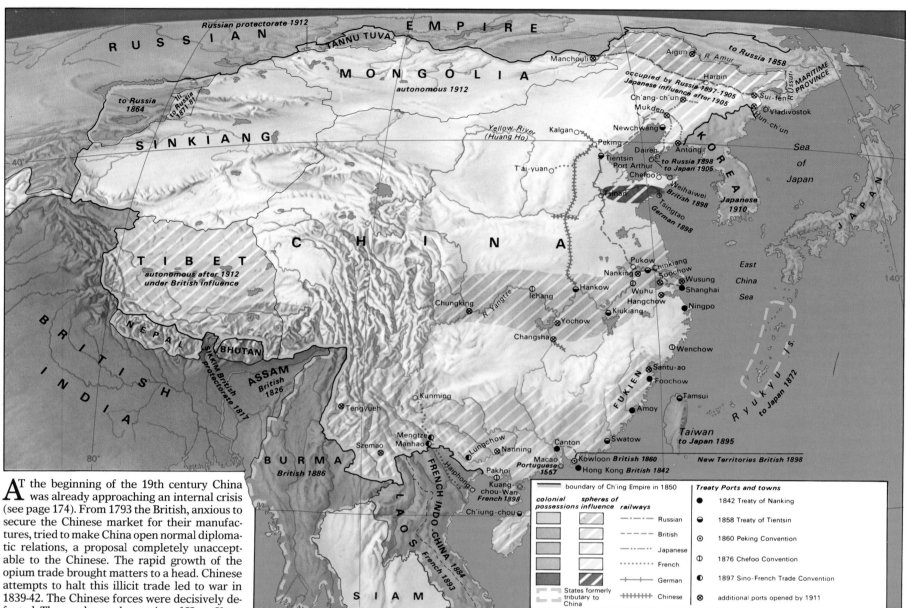

A T the beginning of the 19th century China was already approaching an internal crisis (see page 174). From 1793 the British, anxious to secure the Chinese market for their manufactures, tried to make China open normal diplomatic relations, a proposal completely unacceptable to the Chinese. The rapid growth of the opium trade brought matters to a head. Chinese attempts to halt this illicit trade led to war in 1839-42. The Chinese forces were decisively defeated. The result was the cession of Hong Kong and the opening of five Treaty Ports in which foreign residents were permitted to trade and were freed of Chinese jurisdiction. French and American treaties followed. Shanghai soon replaced Canton as the centre of foreign trade and influence. Exports of tea and silk flourished, and the opium trade continued to expand.

The Chinese failed to understand the new challenge the western powers presented. Until the 17th century China had remained superior to the West in many ways. During the 18th century the Manchu empire achieved a peak of prosperity and stability, while its armies conquered a vast new empire in inner Asia. But during this period of great success, China had been overtaken by the rapid growth of Europe. Although the empire remained self-sufficient, it was now forced to deal with expansionist Western powers enjoying technological superiority and the wealth and capacity for organisation resulting from the Industrial Revolution. As the 19th century progressed, China's ruling class, nurtured in a tradition of unquestioned Chinese cultural supremacy, proved unable to understand this new challenge, or to modernise the country. Consequently, China fell further and further behind.

Even had the Manchu government responded to this new situation and been willing to modernise the empire it could have done little, for internal developments now involved it in a desperate struggle for survival. The Chinese defeat in the Opium War weakened imperial authority, and switching the export trade from Canton to Shanghai exacerbated the economic problems of the south. In 1850 a rebellion broke out in

Kwangsi, which rapidly grew into a full-scale dynastic revolt, the T'ai-p'ing T'ien-kuo (Heavenly Kingdom of Great Peace). Moving north to the Yangtze valley the rebels took Nanking in 1853 and established control over much of central China. The rebellion was not suppressed until 1864.

The T'ai-p'ing rebellion was only the most serious of the major rebellions which erupted in the 1850s and 1860s, affecting a large part of the empire. The last of them was not finally suppressed until 1878. The Manchu armies and government again proved inadequate to deal with these internal threats. The suppression of the rebellion was largely the work of a few farsighted provincial governors who built up modern armies, founded modern arsenals and trained experts in Western technology. They were a minority, however. Most of the court and the bureaucracy remained intent on the restoration of traditional institutions rather than on change.

The rebellions caused terrible suffering. The T'ai-p'ing and Nien rebellions alone left 25 million dead, while the Muslim risings depopulated vast tracts of Yunnan and the north-west. The wealthy region around Nanking did not recover for decades. In 1877-79 there followed a terrible famine in the north during which at least ten millions starved to death.

These grave disorders favoured the foreign powers, which had still failed to open normal relations with China. When their attempts to negotiate were refused, the British and French began another war in 1856, which ended with

the occupation of Peking. The ensuing peace settlement finally secured diplomatic representation in Peking, opened more treaty ports and allowed foreign missionaries freedom of movement throughout China. Meanwhile, the Russians took advantage of the situation to occupy the Amur River region in 1858 and the Maritime Province in 1860. In 1871 they occupied the Ili valley in Turkestan, only withdrawing in 1881 when the Chinese paid an indemnity. A further defeat came in a war with France over Indo-China in 1884-85. The final humiliation came from Japan which, faced with the same challenge, had begun to transform itself into a modern industrialised power. Japan had already intervened in Taiwan, in the Ryukyu Islands and in Korea. Finally, in 1894-95 Japan overwhelmed the modernised Chinese forces in a full-scale war and Taiwan was annexed.

This defeat finally convinced many Chinese that radical changes were inevitable. In 1898 the young Emperor and a group of reformers attempted a sweeping reform programme, but the conservative Manchus, led by the Empress Dowager, carried out a coup to prevent its implementation. Meanwhile, the foreign powers, believing China on the point of collapse, joined in a scramble for further rights and concessions, carving out spheres of influence and leasing territories as bases. This produced a wave of xenophobia which inspired the Boxer Rising in north-east China. The rebels attacked first missionaries, and then the foreign legations in Tientsin and Peking. The western powers sent troops into north China, while Russia occupied

2/The dismemberment of the Ch'ing Empire (above) During the 19th century China was forced to cede Hong Kong to Great Britain, and to open ever more ports to foreign trade, in which foreigners enjoyed extra-territorial rights. At the same time she lost extensive territories in the north and north-east to the expansionist Russian empire, and was challenged in the peripheral states like Nepal, Burma, Laos, Tongking, the Ryukyus and Korea, which had been her tributary states. With the collapse of the Ch'ing Empire in 1912 China lost control of Tibet and Mongolia.

Japan defeats China (above) In the Sino-Japanese war of 1894-5 the carefully modernised western-style Japanese army disastrously routed the ill-led Chinese forces.

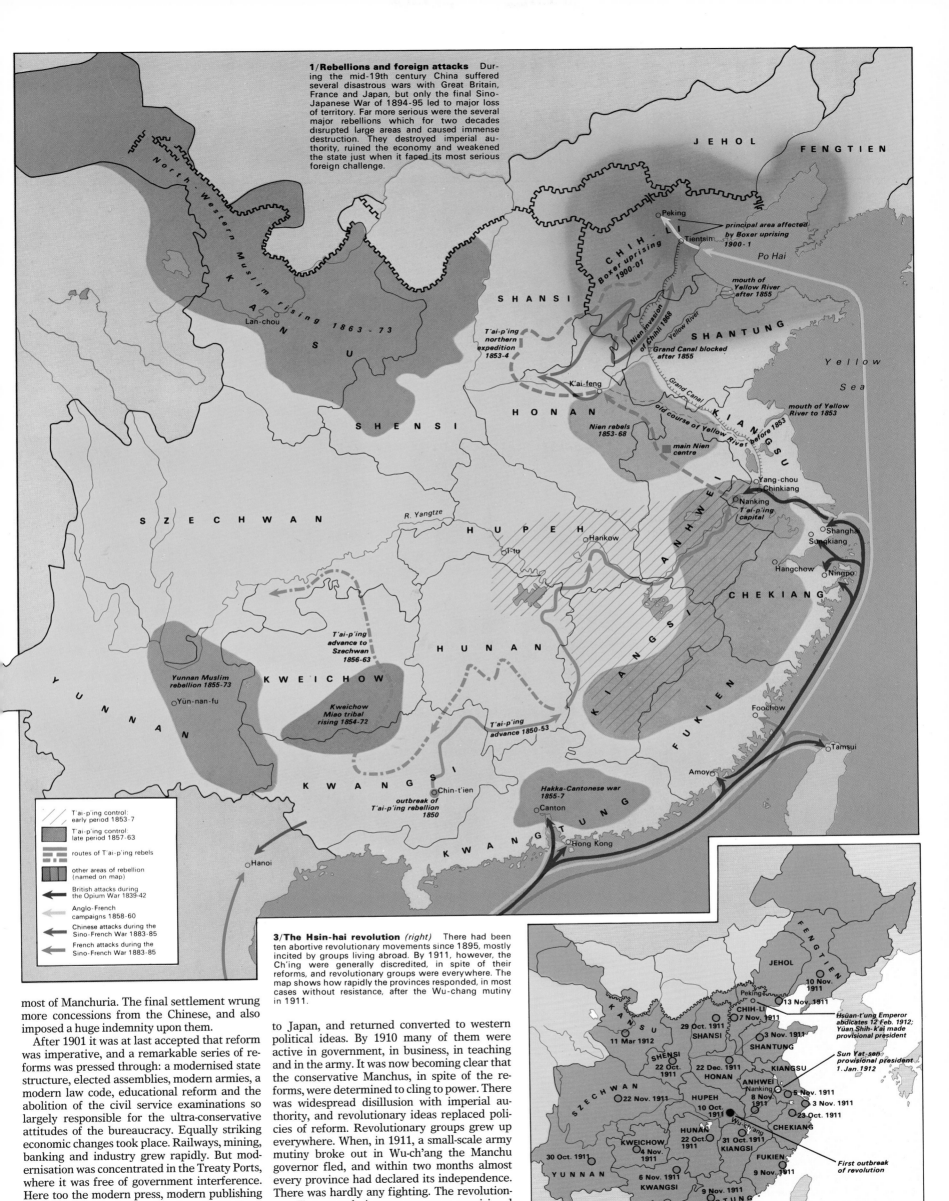

1/Rebellions and foreign attacks During the mid-19th century China suffered several disastrous wars with Great Britain, France and Japan, but only the final Sino-Japanese War of 1894-95 led to major loss of territory. Far more serious were the several major rebellions which for two decades disrupted large areas and caused immense destruction. They destroyed imperial authority, ruined the economy and weakened the state just when it faced its most serious foreign challenge.

3/The Hsin-hai revolution (right) There had been ten abortive revolutionary movements since 1895, mostly incited by groups living abroad. By 1911, however, the Ch'ing were generally discredited, in spite of their reforms, and revolutionary groups were everywhere. The map shows how rapidly the provinces responded, in most cases without resistance, after the Wu-chang mutiny in 1911.

most of Manchuria. The final settlement wrung more concessions from the Chinese, and also imposed a huge indemnity upon them.

After 1901 it was at last accepted that reform was imperative, and a remarkable series of reforms was pressed through: a modernised state structure, elected assemblies, modern armies, a modern law code, educational reform and the abolition of the civil service examinations so largely responsible for the ultra-conservative attitudes of the bureaucracy. Equally striking economic changes took place. Railways, mining, banking and industry grew rapidly. But modernisation was concentrated in the Treaty Ports, where it was free of government interference. Here too the modern press, modern publishing and modern schools flourished, and with them the revolutionary and reformist parties.

From the 1890s ever-increasing numbers of young men were sent to study abroad, especially

to Japan, and returned converted to western political ideas. By 1910 many of them were active in government, in business, in teaching and in the army. It was now becoming clear that the conservative Manchus, in spite of the reforms, were determined to cling to power. There was widespread disillusion with imperial authority, and revolutionary ideas replaced policies of reform. Revolutionary groups grew up everywhere. When, in 1911, a small-scale army mutiny broke out in Wu-ch'ang the Manchu governor fled, and within two months almost every province had declared its independence. There was hardly any fighting. The revolutionary T'ung-men-hui party set up a provisional government at Nanking, where its leader Sun Yat-sen was proclaimed president on 1 January 1912.

233

India under British rule 1805 to 1931

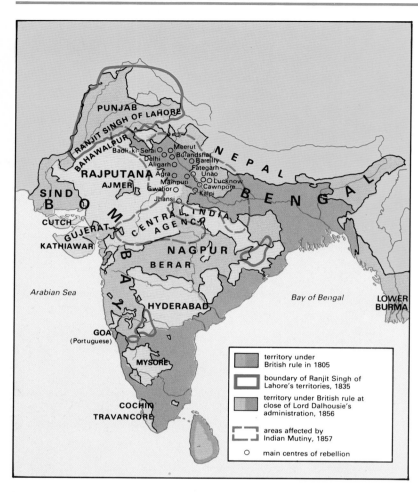

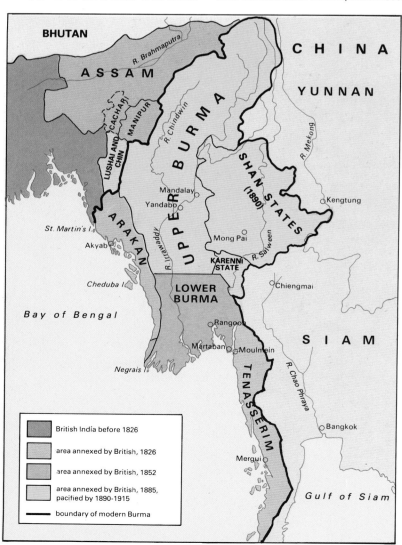

1/India in 1857 *(above)* The Mutiny began at Meerut on 10 May, spread swiftly to other parts of northern India, involving Hindus and Muslims. Sikh loyalty in the Punjab, and passivity in the Deccan and south, turned the tide in favour of the British.

2/The acquisition of Burma *(below)* Part of Britain's Indian dominion until 1935, Burma was annexed, along with her dependencies of Arakan, Manipur and Assam, as a result of three wars fought in 1826, 1852 and 1885. The Shan States were acquired in 1890.

By 1805 the English East India Company's hegemony was an established fact in the Indian sub-continent. In another fifty years the Company emerged as the paramount power. The Third Anglo-Maratha War (1813-23) marked the end of the most serious threat to the Company's supremacy. With the conquest of Sind (1843) and the Sikh kingdom of the Punjab (1849), the empire became coterminous with the country's natural frontiers in the north-west, while in the north the wars with Nepal (1814-16) had extended it into the Himalayas. To the east, the British clashed with the Burmese empire and, by 1885, annexed all its territories. Within the empire, Dalhousie's Doctrine of Lapse (1848-56) led to the absorption of autonomous but dependent states like Oudh and several Maratha kingdoms into the directly administered territories.

The hostility of dispossessed rulers and agrarian classes, as well as suspicions of intended assaults on India's traditional faiths – aroused by innovations including the prohibition of *suttee* and the introduction of cartridges greased with the fat of tabooed animals for the use of the Indian sepoys – erupted in the rebellion of 1857-59. Beginning as a mutiny of the Company's sepoys, it soon involved princes, landlords and peasants in northern and central India and was only crushed after fourteen months of bitter fighting. The direct administration of India was now taken over by the British Crown.

India soon acquired a pivotal position in the British imperial system and became involved in European rivalries, particularly after the Russian advance in central Asia (see page 230). The attempt to stabilise Afghanistan as a buffer state under friendly Amirs generated a series of wars fought with Indian armies and increasing India's debts. The third Anglo-Burmese War (1885) had as its background the growing rivalry with France in South-East Asia. Security of the Indian empire was also a major concern in Great Britain's involvement in the partition of Africa (see page 240). From Abyssinia to Hong Kong, the Indian army was freely deployed to protect British interests.

India was absorbed into the world economy as a dependency of Great Britain. The Company's monopoly over the Indian market was abolished in 1833 through persistent pressure from British commercial and business interests, which also pressed for the development of modern transport in India to facilitate the import of British manufactures and export of raw materials. By 1853, India had lost its world-wide market for textiles and was importing the products of Lancashire. The Lancashire cotton famine, generated by the American Civil War, led to a cotton boom in the Deccan and thus to regional specialisation in cropping patterns in India.

Railway development, financed by British capital, and the opening of the Suez canal in 1869, contributed to a sevenfold increase in India's foreign trade between 1869 and 1929. Despite severe British competition, a range of modern industries developed under Indian entrepreneurs; but in most areas neither the character of the economy nor traditional agriculture experienced any basic change. The gross national product increased very slowly, but with sustained population growth from 1921 onwards, per capita income declined. In short, India developed the typical characteristics of an under-developed economy while contributing substantially to the British balance of payments.

Administrative developments also contributed to India's absorption into a world order dominated by Europe. English civil servants inspired by Benthamite ideas abandoned earlier hesitations regarding interference with the indigenous social order. Tenurial systems guaranteeing property rights in land, a network of modern irrigation in parts of the country, prohibition of social customs abhorrent to humanistic ideas, and the development of a modern judiciary and civil service, were among the chief expressions of the new spirit. The net results of such policies are still a matter of debate. Probably the rural propertied classes benefited but often at the cost of the mass of producers. Periodic famines continued to take heavy tolls of life, while commercial agriculture flourished.

Professional groups, employees of the colonial administration, and landed proprietors created by the new tenurial systems constituted the new élite of colonial India. Western-style education – officially supported only from 1835 – is traceable to the material and cultural urges of these new social groups. Knowledge of the West generated social and literary movements influenced by western models but looking back, selectively, to India's past traditions. The Brahmo Samaj founded by Rammohan Roy (1819), aiming at restoring Hindu monotheism, and the frankly revivalist Arya Samaj, represent the two most important examples of this new consciousness.

The new awareness of an Indian identity, reinforced by overt British racism, soon acquired a political dimension first expressed through local political associations and public agitation over specific issues. The Indian National Congress, the first all-Indian political organisation, was founded in 1885 with official blessing as a safety valve for the growing disaffection. Beginning as a tame annual gathering of affluent public men, it soon developed an extremist wing which questioned the alien's right to rule India. In 1905, the first mass agitation – anticipating Gandhi's non-violent non-cooperation and propagating *swaraj* (self-rule) –

4 and 5/Population: social and economic change *(below)* Between 1881 and 1931 population rose from 253.9 million to 352.8 million, with a slight acceleration following the First World War. Over the same period the proportion of literates grew only from 35 to 80 per thousand; 101 people in every 10,000 were able to read and write in English. Nevertheless, the beginnings of a modern economy were emerging.

inhabitants per sq. km.

over 250	50 to 100
150 to 250	25 to 50
100 to 150	under 25

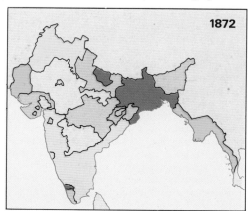

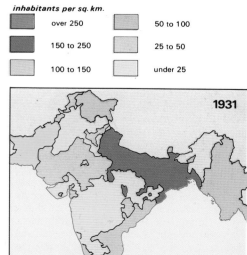

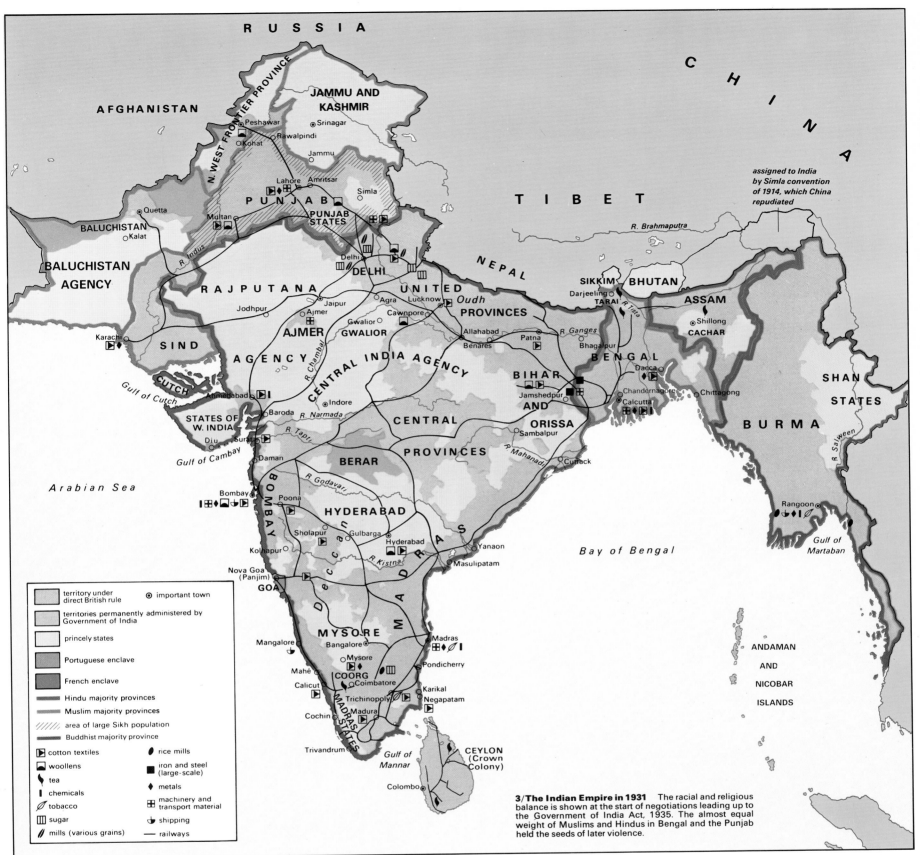

assigned to India
by Simla convention
of 1914, which China
repudiated

Legend

territory under direct British rule	⊙ important town
territories permanently administered by Government of India	
princely states	
Portuguese enclave	
French enclave	
Hindu majority provinces	
Muslim majority provinces	
area of large Sikh population	
Buddhist majority province	

▶ cotton textiles	◆ rice mills		
▬ woollens	■ iron and steel (large-scale)		
♪ tea	◆ metals		
I chemicals	⊞ machinery and transport material		
⊘ tobacco	⇙ shipping		
⫙ sugar	— railways		
⫽ mills (various grains)			

3/The Indian Empire in 1931 The racial and religious balance is shown at the start of negotiations leading up to the Government of India Act, 1935. The almost equal weight of Muslims and Hindus in Bengal and the Punjab held the seeds of later violence.

was launched to resist the decision to partition the province of Bengal, while revolutionary groups adopted terror to attain the same goal (see page 248). Political awareness and expectations were quickened by the First World War and a Ministerial Proclamation (1917) which declared the realisation of responsible government to be the goal of British rule in India. The Indian Counsels Act of 1909 had already established a provincial legislature, and the Montagu-Chelmsford reforms (1919) extended the provincial councils. But repressive legislation enacted in 1919 authorising detention without trial seemed to conflict with this goal. Against it, Gandhi deployed his weapon of *satyagraha* or non-violent mass action, first developed in his fight against racist laws in South Africa. The response included the Amritsar massacre, provoking intense racial bitterness. Indian Muslims were further incensed by the Allies' treatment of the Turkish sultan, their khalifa or spiritual head. The Non-Cooperation Movement (1920-22), aimed at redressing the 'Khalifat wrong' and winning *swaraj*, was the first all-Indian mass movement, involving sections of the peasantry as well. But the Hindu-Muslim unity achieved during the movement did not long survive its suspension. Elections to the expanded provincial councils with their communal electorates further embittered relations.

While communal riots undermined national unity in the mid-twenties, a radical wing within Congress under the leadership of the young Jawaharlal Nehru and Subhas Chandra Bose pressed for renewed militant action against the Raj, and induced Congress to adopt complete independence as its goal (1929). When in 1930 Gandhi launched the Civil Disobedience Movement (1930-39) for the attainment of *Purna Swaraj* (complete independence), he himself and some 60,000 of his followers were arrested. Nevertheless the movement was a watershed. Suspended in 1931 as a result of an agreement with Viceroy Irwin, it was resumed when Gandhi returned from the abortive constitutional discussions at the Round Table Conference in London. Negotiation had failed, and the policy of confrontation espoused by the younger leaders was reinforced.

The 1911 Durbar *(right)* King George V had his coronation as King Emperor of India at a Durbar, or assembly of notables, held in Delhi in 1911. A decision to annul the unpopular partition of Bengal was announced at this Durbar.

The development of Australia and New Zealand

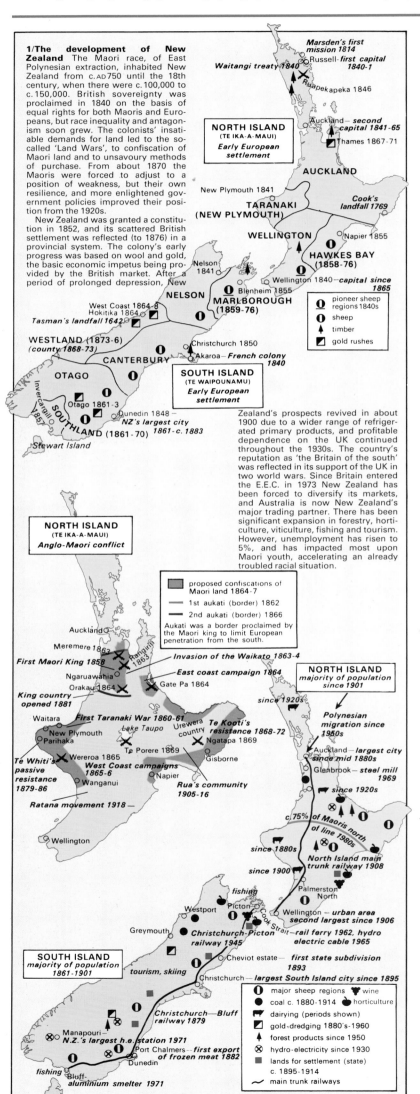

1/The development of New Zealand The Maori race, of East Polynesian extraction, inhabited New Zealand from c. AD 750 until the 18th century, when there were c. 100,000 to c. 150,000. British sovereignty was proclaimed in 1840 on the basis of equal rights for both Maoris and Europeans, but race inequality and antagonism soon grew. The colonists' insatiable demands for land led to the so-called 'Land Wars', to confiscation of Maori land and to unsavoury methods of purchase. From about 1870 the Maoris were forced to adjust to a position of weakness, but their own resilience, and more enlightened government policies improved their position from the 1920s.

New Zealand was granted a constitution in 1852, and its scattered British settlement was reflected (to 1876) in a provincial system. The colony's early progress was based on wool and gold, the basic economic impetus being provided by the British market. After a period of prolonged depression, New

Zealand's prospects revived in about 1900 due to a wider range of refrigerated primary products, and profitable dependence on the UK continued throughout the 1930s. The country's reputation as 'the Britain of the south' was reflected in its support of the UK in two world wars. Since Britain entered the E.E.C. in 1973 New Zealand has been forced to diversify its markets, and Australia is now New Zealand's major trading partner. There has been significant expansion in forestry, horticulture, viticulture, fishing and tourism. However, unemployment has risen to 5%, and has impacted most upon Maori youth, accelerating an already troubled racial situation.

B EFORE European discovery in the seventeenth century there was neither contact nor similarity between Australia and New Zealand, and their development since white settlement has been distinct, if parallel. The Maoris of New Zealand shared the civilisation of their island neighbours (see map 1). The Aboriginal inhabitants of Australia retained only tenuous contact with Asia (from which they had originally migrated) after the rising of the seas made their continent an island. Dispersed in a hot, dry habitat, they hunted and gathered plants but did not herd, cultivate or build settlements, and identified their destinies with the natural features of the land they wandered. They remained free from European interference until late in the period of European expansion.

Winds and currents guarded their isolation. Spaniards rounding the Horn sailed north-west into the Pacific avoiding the prevailing westerlies, while the Portuguese turned towards India from the Cape of Good Hope. The Portuguese may have discovered Australia before 1542, as the Dutch did after 1600 when they exploited the westerlies for a fast route to the East Indies. In 1642-43 Tasman discovered Van Diemen's Land (later Tasmania) and New Zealand, but otherwise the Dutch encountered only the inhospitable north and west coasts.

Scientific curiosity was a motive in Cook's Pacific exploration, and his discovery in 1770 of Australia's more fertile eastern coast, with its extraordinary animals and plants, excited European scientists and artists more than traders or colonists. He claimed the coast for Britain, and strategy and trade were subordinate motives when George II's government decided in 1786 to found a penal colony in New South Wales. Sydney Cove was settled in 1788, and the need for subsidiary jails, and outposts against the French – also active in exploration – led to further settlements at Norfolk Island (1788), Newcastle (1801), Hobart (1804) and Brisbane (1824). The naval officers who charted the southern coasts were followed by a marauding tribe of whalers and sealers. In 1829 Britain annexed the whole continent.

The small settlement at Sydney Cove was hemmed by mountains, and free settlers were attracted only when access to the inland plains was won after 1813. Squatters followed the explorers, settling large areas of south-eastern Australia, while private ventures at Perth (1829), Melbourne (1835) and Adelaide (1836) established bridgeheads for settlement which became the capitals of the separate colonies of Western Australia, Victoria and South Australia which, with Tasmania, Queensland and the remnant of New South Wales gained responsible government between 1855 and 1890. Despite inter-colonial rivalry, regional differences were never great enough to destroy a sense of common destiny, and the federation of the colonies into the Commonwealth of Australia in 1901 had a logic which only the far west continued intermittently to deny.

Unlike New Zealand, where the wars between European and Maori led to co-existence, if not equality, of old inhabitant and new, European settlement in Australia destroyed Aboriginal civilisation. The tribes fell before European diseases and weapons and their lands were expropriated by European law. Aboriginal institutions survived only in the centre and north, damaged even there. The settler society which seized and transformed the land was predominantly British in origin, though spiced with a different mixture of Irish and Scots, and a higher proportion of dissidents and outlaws, than at home. These factors made for social homogeneity, and for politics which have been rancorous in tone but democratic in process.

The Australian colonies, like New Zealand had to seek self-sufficiency through trade. Farm-

ing was commercial, with little subsistence agriculture. The growing world market for wool caused the inland grasslands to be settled before the richer forested eastern coastlands, which awaited the development of dairying and of sugar cultivation in Queensland. Wheat cultivation expanded after the 1860s and the development of the frozen meat trade after 1880 gave impetus to meat production. But settlement in dry areas proved hazardous and intermittent, and although most of Australia was explored and much nominally settled by 1890, effective exploitation was restricted to areas of adequate rainfall. Even irrigation rarely succeeded outside the river systems of the south-east

The commercial nature of Australia's primary industry strengthened the dominance of the major ports over the inland towns, and the transport systems consolidated their power after the railway supplanted the bullock dray and the river boat. Spectacular mineral discoveries, especially of gold in the 1850s and 1880s, brought new wealth and a more polyglot immigration, but although the gold rushes at first took population inland, the eventual beneficiaries in wealth and people were the cities, especially Melbourne and Sydney. By 1890 some two-thirds of Australians lived in urban areas. But isolation persisted; Melbourne, when Australia's largest city, faced neither Asia nor the Pacific as its true neighbours, but London and Liverpool. Isolation bred concern about national identity and exaggerated fears of foreign threats. Free (until 1942) from war at home, Australians met its realities only when they crossed the world to fight in other people's battles.

This predominantly British society persisted until the mid twentieth century, dependent on primary exports despite the growth of secondary industry behind high tariff barriers. The Second World War, and Australia's appeal to the United States rather than Britain for protection against the Japanese, signalled major changes in her policies. Post-war governments fostered non-British immigration from Europe, and gradually abandoned the White Australia Policy to admit an increasing number of Asians. Australia shared the economic growth of the West, helped by the development of a large new export trade in iron ore and coal to Japan, and local discoveries of oil and gas. Her new dependence on Pacific trading partners was confirmed after Britain joined the European Economic Community in 1973, and the British relationship rapidly receded in importance. In the 1970s inflation and recession uncovered the structural weaknesses of an economy too dependent on commodity exports and high-cost protected industries, and uncontrolled inflation helped unseat a reformist Labor government in 1975, in what was, by Australian standards, a constitutional crisis. After 1983 another Labor government moved to dismantle the regulatory mechanisms which had for decades distorted market realities. By coincidence, a Labour government in New Zealand pursued a parallel course.

Despite economic difficulties, the Bicentennial of European Settlement in 1988 was approached by a culturally richer and more varied society. Nevertheless, Australia still remains uncertain how to balance its British heritage, its recent cosmopolitan immigration, and the claims of its disinherited aboriginal remnant.

5/Settlement and Development *(right)* After 1820 settlement spread inland from scattered coastal towns, but vast arid areas of the continent remained sparsely populated, and the total population did not reach 5 million until 1918. Exports of wool, wheat and minerals enabled Australians to enjoy the highest per capita income in the world by 1900, a position not maintained despite recent extensive mineral discoveries. Most Australians depend on urban employment; in 1980, 70 per cent of the population of 14.7 million lived in 12 cities, including 3.2 million in Sydney and 2.8 million in Melbourne. Canberra, federal capital since 1927 and largest inland city, had a population of 245,500 in 1980.

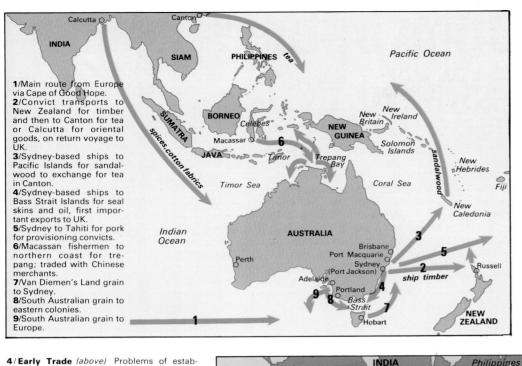

1/Main route from Europe via Cape of Good Hope.
2/Convict transports to New Zealand for timber and then to Canton for tea or Calcutta for oriental goods, on return voyage to UK.
3/Sydney-based ships to Pacific Islands for sandalwood to exchange for tea in Canton.
4/Sydney-based ships to Bass Strait Islands for seal skins and oil, first important exports to UK.
5/Sydney to Tahiti for pork for provisioning convicts.
6/Macassan fishermen to northern coast for trepang; traded with Chinese merchants.
7/Van Diemen's Land grain to Sydney.
8/South Australian grain to eastern colonies.
9/South Australian grain to Europe.

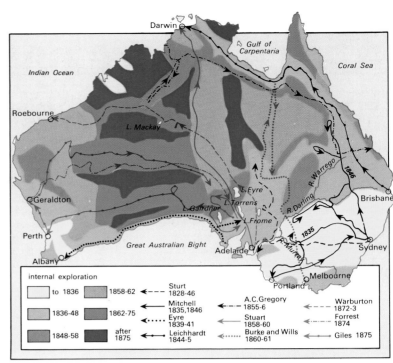

internal exploration			
to 1836	1858-62	Sturt 1828-46	A.C.Gregory 1855-6	Warburton 1872-3
1836-48	1862-75	Mitchell 1835,1846	Stuart 1858-60	Forrest 1874
1848-58	after 1875	Eyre 1839-41	Burke and Wills 1860-61	Giles 1875
		Leichhardt 1844-5		

4/Early Trade (above) Problems of establishing agriculture in an alien environment hampered the development of the first settlement, which had to rely on imported food supplies. The settlers traded sealskins, seal oil and sandalwood to pay for imports, but it was only when wool exports developed in the 1820s that the Australian colonies ceased to drain the British treasury.

2/The Discovery of Australia (right) Although the north-west and south coasts were discovered in the 17th century and the east coast in the 18th, detailed charting by Matthew Flinders and Philip Parker King came in the early 19th century.

3/Exploration (above) Because the navigators failed to discover river mouths, inland explorers searched first for an inland sea, then made attempts to reach the centre of the continent and to cross it from south to north, and finally traversed the western part between the coast and the Overland Telegraph Line (built 1870-72, see map 5).

Westward navigation by sail impeded by winds and current

Dutch discoveries to 1644	
coasts charted by 1802	

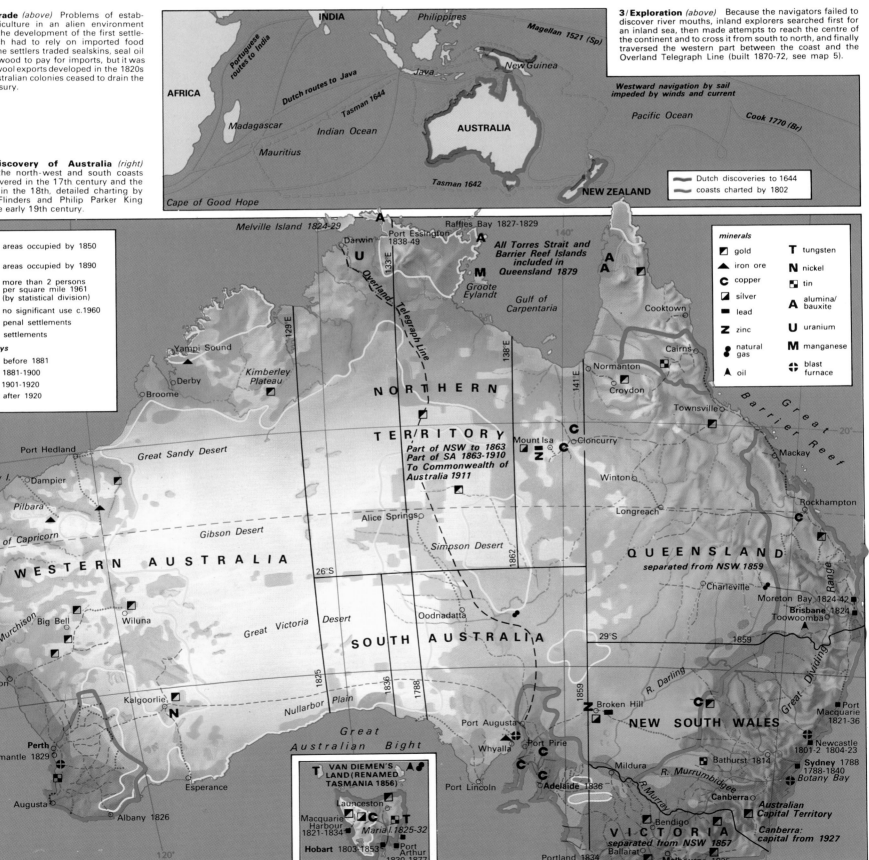

areas occupied by 1850	
areas occupied by 1890	
more than 2 persons per square mile 1961 (by statistical division)	
no significant use c.1960	
■ penal settlements	
○ settlements	

railways
— before 1881
—·— 1881-1900
--- 1901-1920
···· after 1920

minerals			
gold		T	tungsten
iron ore		N	nickel
copper			tin
silver		A	alumina/bauxite
lead		U	uranium
Z zinc		M	manganese
natural gas			blast furnace
A oil			

All Torres Strait and Barrier Reef Islands included in Queensland 1879

NORTHERN TERRITORY
Part of NSW to 1863
Part of SA 1863-1910
To Commonwealth of Australia 1911

WESTERN AUSTRALIA

SOUTH AUSTRALIA

QUEENSLAND separated from NSW 1859

NEW SOUTH WALES

VICTORIA separated from NSW 1857

VAN DIEMEN'S LAND (RENAMED TASMANIA 1856)

Canberra: capital from 1927

Australian Capital Territory

Africa before partition by the European powers 1800 to 1880

DURING the eighty years prior to the European partition of the continent, much of west Africa was dominated by a Muslim religious revival, which took the form of holy wars (*jihads*) waged mainly against backsliding Muslim (or partly Muslimised) communities. The great warriors of the *jihad* were the Fulani cattle-keepers, widely scattered among the agricultural communities of the Sudanic region. Though the Fulani were largely pagan, a section of them became Muslims, fervent in the faith of the newly converted. In the 18th century they set up theocracies in the far west – Futa Toro and Futa Jallon – and at Masina, in the former Mali and Songhay empires on the upper Niger. It was the Muslim Fulani in Hausaland, however, who set up the largest Muslim state of the 19th century. In 1804 a Fulani religious leader, Uthman dan Fodio, was proclaimed Commander of the Faithful (*Amir al-Mu'minin*), and declared a *jihad* against the infidel. Within a few years his formidable army of horsemen (many of them drawn from the pagan Fulani) conquered all the Hausa city states, and struck east into Adamawa and south-west into Nupe and Yorubaland. Uthman dan Fodio's son became the Sultan of Sokoto, an empire still in existence when the British invaded Nigeria in the 1890s.

An even fiercer *jihad* was conducted by another holy man, al-Hajj Umar from Futa Jallon, whence he conquered the Bambara kingdoms and Masina, and was only prevented from reaching the Atlantic by the French on the Senegal river. In the 1870s and 1880s a Mandingo Muslim leader, Samori, carved out another empire south of the Niger valley; he was finally defeated by the French only in 1898.

South of the area of the *jihads*, African states, among which Ashanti and Dahomey were outstanding, responded to the change in the trading requirements of the Europeans on the coast, from slaves to products such as palm oil and groundnuts, and became more wealthy and powerful. Other states, in modern southern Nigeria, such as Oyo and Benin, tended to disintegrate – partly because this was a region where the economic changeover was uneven, illegal slaving continuing there until the 1870s. By and large, much of west Africa experienced increasing instability and violence during the first three-quarters of the century.

Another huge area where new patterns of trading and political developments were disruptive and violent was central and East Africa. The western world evinced an almost insatiable appetite for ivory in the 19th century (middle class males playing billiards and females playing the piano), and the hunting of elephants and trading of their tusks became a major economic activity in much of this part of the continent. Many states and peoples grew rich on the proceeds of this activity – the Chokwe and King Msiri in central Africa, for instance, and Buganda and the Nyamwezi in East Africa. In central Africa the foreign traders were often Portuguese, from their settlements in Angola and Mozambique; in East Africa, Swahili-Arabs from Zanzibar, the island state of the Omani Sultan, made contact with the states in the interior, in many instances bringing their Muslim religion with them. Some peoples – particularly around Lakes Nyasa and Tanganyika – suffered severely from the Arab slave trade, which often went hand in hand with that in ivory.

In north-east Africa the territorial expansion of Egypt, ruled after Napoleon's invasion at the beginning of the century by Mohammed Ali, nominally viceroy of the Ottoman Sultan, brought a foretaste of the later European partition. Mohammed Ali's armies conquered the northern Nilotic Sudan, founding Khartoum as the capital of the province in 1830. Mohammed Ali had refused to sanction the Suez Canal, but after his death in 1849 construction went ahead. His grandson, the Khedive Ismail, consolidated the Egyptian hold over much of the littoral of the Red Sea and Horn of Africa. He also pushed south up the Nile towards the Great Lakes in an attempt to create a great African empire. Partly in response to this Egyptian activity, there was a revival of Ethiopian politican power under the emperors Theodorus and Johannes.

Two areas of Africa were being colonised by European powers before the partition. In 1830 the French invaded Algeria (nominally part of the Ottoman Empire), and in the course of a long and bitter struggle, conquered and settled the territory. At the other end of the continent, the British had taken over the Cape from the Dutch during the Napoleonic Wars. Coincidentally in time, but unrelated in cause, there was a major political and demographic revolution among the peoples of the interior of southern Africa, initiated by the formation of the Zulu kingdom by Shaka in 1818. Large numbers of Nguni and Sotho-speaking peoples moved away from the troubled area (the period is known as the *Mfecane*, or the Time of Troubles), the Ndebele (Matabele) into present-day Zimbabwe, the Nguni as far north as Zambia, Malawi and Tanzania, where their presence created even more disruption, and the Sotho (Kololo) into Barotseland (Zambia). No sooner had southern Africa begun to settle down after the *Mfecane* than another event disrupted the region. This was the Great Trek of Dutch or Afrikaner colonists, known as Boers (farmers) who, dissatisfied with British rule, left the Cape colony after 1836 and marched north to found settlements which became the republics of the Orange Free State and Transvaal. By 1880 whites had appropriated the greater part of the habitable land of South Africa.

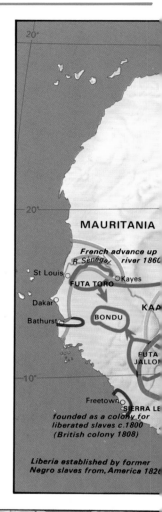

MAURITANIA

French advance up
R. Senegal river 1860

St Louis
Kayes
FUTA TORO
Dakar
KAA
Bathurst
BONDU
FUTA JALLON

Freetown
SIERRA LE
founded as a colony for
liberated slaves c.1800
(British colony 1808)

Liberia established by former
Negro slaves from America 182

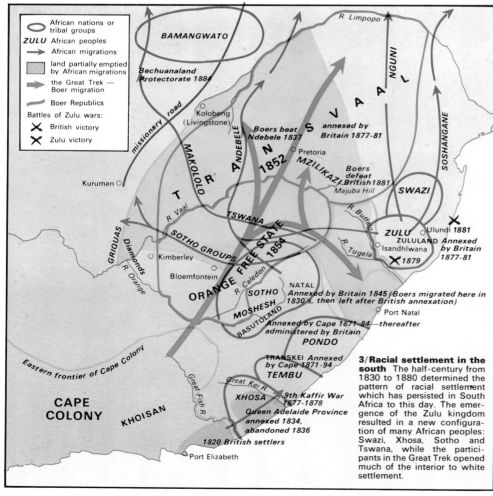

African nations or tribal groups
ZULU African peoples
→ African migrations
land partially emptied by African migrations
the Great Trek — Boer migration
Boer Republics
Battles of Zulu wars:
✕ British victory
✕ Zulu victory

R. Limpopo
BAMANGWATO
missionary road
Bechuanaland Protectorate 1884
Kolobeng (Livingstone)
MAKOLOLO
NDEBELE
N VAAL 1852 MZILIKAZI
Pretoria
Boers beat Ndebele 1837
annexed by Britain 1877-81
Boers defeat British 1881
Majuba Hill
NGUNI
SOSHANGANE
SWAZI
Kuruman
TSWANA
R. Vaal
R. Buffalo
ZULU Ulundi 1881
ZULULAND *Annexed by Britain 1877-81*
Isandhlwana
✕ 1879
GRIQUAS
Diamonds
R. Orange
SOTHO GROUPS
ORANGE FREE STATE 1854
Kimberley
Bloemfontein
R. Caledon
R. Tugela
NATAL *Annexed by Britain 1845 (Boers migrated here in 1830's, then left after British annexation)*
SOTHO MOSHESH
BASUTOLAND *Annexed by Cape 1871-84 thereafter administered by Britain*
Port Natal
PONDO
Eastern frontier of Cape Colony
TRANSKEI *Annexed by Cape 1871-94*
TEMBU
Great Kei R.
Great Fish R.
XHOSA
9th Kaffir War 1877-1878
Queen Adelaide Province annexed 1834, abandoned 1836
CAPE COLONY
KHOISAN
1820 British settlers
Port Elizabeth

3/Racial settlement in the south The half-century from 1830 to 1880 determined the pattern of racial settlement which has persisted in South Africa to this day. The emergence of the Zulu kingdom resulted in a new configuration of many African peoples: Swazi, Xhosa, Sotho and Tswana, while the participants in the Great Trek opened much of the interior to white settlement.

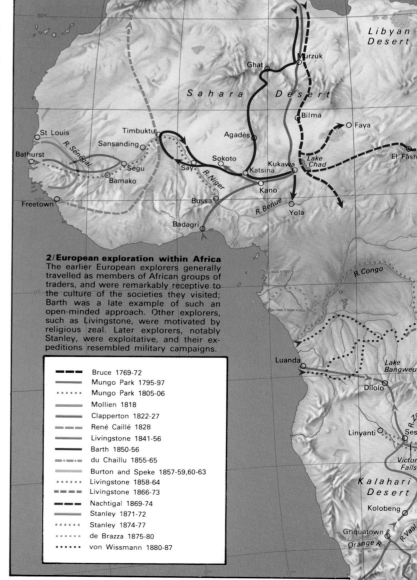

Libyan Desert
Sahara Desert
Ghat
Murzuk
Bilma
St Louis
Timbuktu
Agadès
Faya
Bathurst
R. Senegal
Sansanding
Sokoto
Kukawa
Lake Chad
El Fash
Freetown
Segu
Say
R. Niger
Katsina
Kano
Bamako
Bussa
R. Benue
Yola
Badagri

2/European exploration within Africa The earlier European explorers generally travelled as members of African groups of traders, and were remarkably receptive to the culture of the societies they visited; Barth was a late example of such an open-minded approach. Other explorers, such as Livingstone, were motivated by religious zeal. Later explorers, notably Stanley, were exploitative, and their expeditions resembled military campaigns.

R. Congo
Luanda
Lake Bangweu
Dilolo
Linyanti
Victoria Falls
Kalahari Desert
Kolobeng
Griquatown
Orange R.

– – –	Bruce 1769-72
———	Mungo Park 1795-97
·········	Mungo Park 1805-06
———	Mollien 1818
———	Clapperton 1822-27
———	René Caillé 1828
———	Livingstone 1841-56
———	Barth 1850-56
———	du Chaillu 1855-65
– – –	Burton and Speke 1857-59,60-63
·········	Livingstone 1858-64
———	Livingstone 1866-73
– – –	Nachtigal 1869-74
———	Stanley 1871-72
·········	Stanley 1874-77
———	de Brazza 1875-80
·········	von Wissmann 1880-87

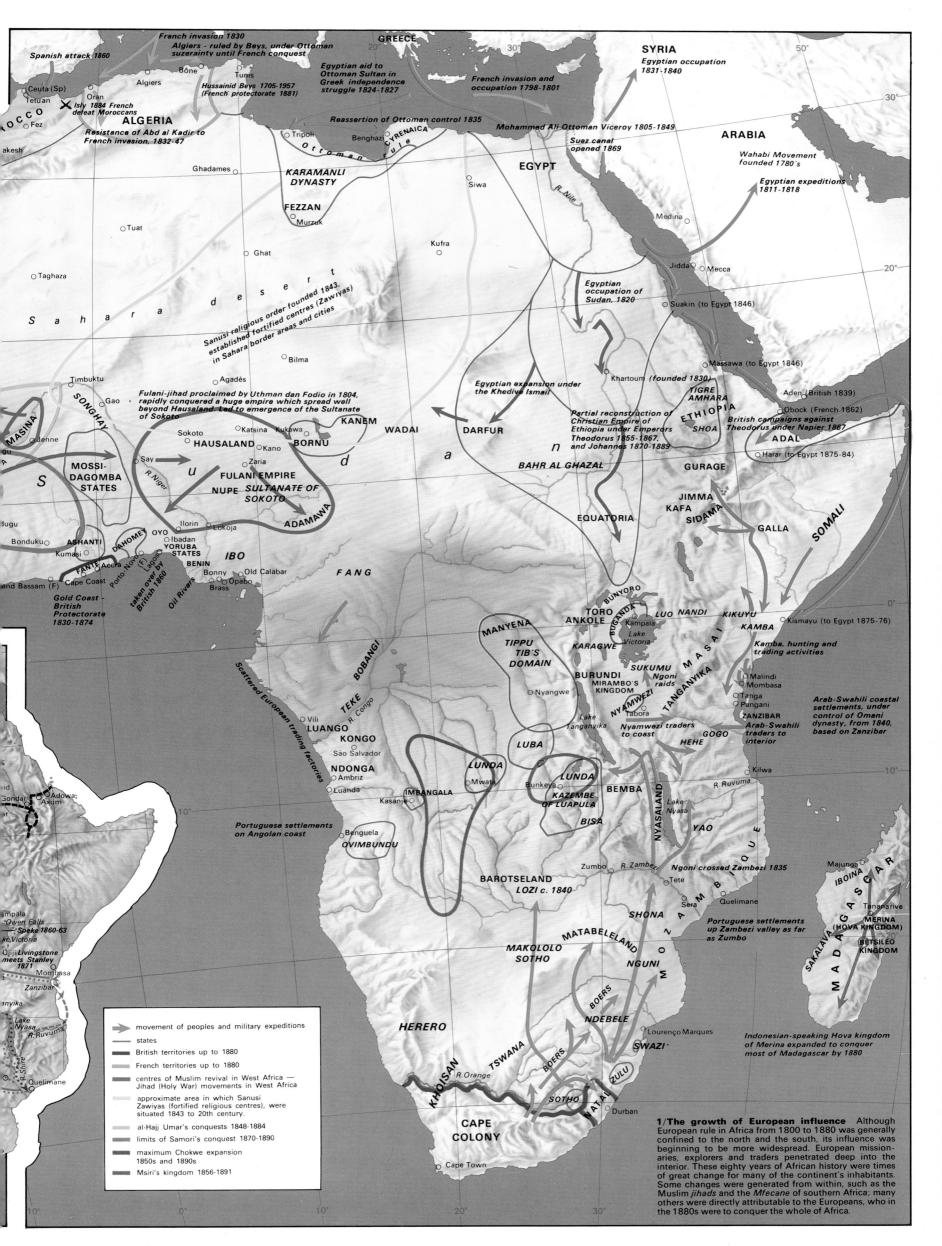

movement of peoples and military expeditions
states
British territories up to 1880
French territories up to 1880
centres of Muslim revival in West Africa — Jihad (Holy War) movements in West Africa
approximate area in which Sanusi Zawiyas (fortified religious centres), were situated 1843 to 20th century.
al-Hajj Umar's conquests 1848-1884
limits of Samori's conquest 1870-1890
maximum Chokwe expansion 1850s and 1890s
Msiri's kingdom 1856-1891

1/The growth of European influence Although European rule in Africa from 1800 to 1880 was generally confined to the north and the south, its influence was beginning to be more widespread. European missionaries, explorers and traders penetrated deep into the interior. These eighty years of African history were times of great change for many of the continent's inhabitants. Some changes were generated from within, such as the Muslim *jihads* and the *Mfecane* of southern Africa; many others were directly attributable to the Europeans, who in the 1880s were to conquer the whole of Africa.

The partition of Africa 1880 to 1913

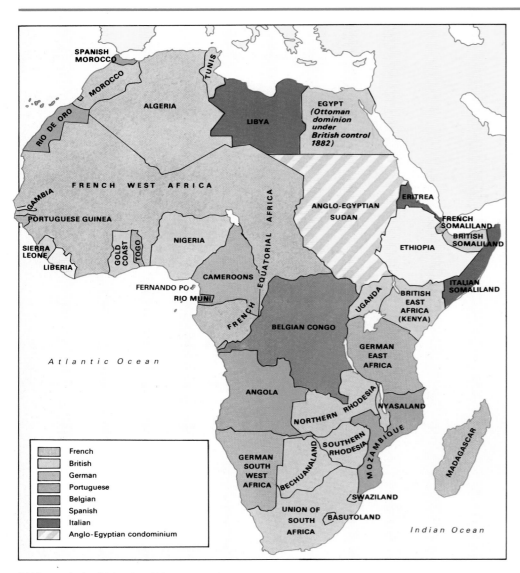

2/Alien rule in Africa in 1913 *(above)* Once the partition of Africa among the European powers got under way, the whole continent was carved up in a remarkably short period: in thirty years the scramble was complete.

AFRICA, as late as 1879, remained almost unknown territory to the European powers; an intricate kaleidoscope of tribal kingdoms and traditional hunting grounds. Before 1880 the areas of Africa under direct European control were few. In the north, the French had been engaged in conquering Algeria since the 1830s. There were small French and British colonies in West Africa – Senegal, Sierra Leone, the Gold Coast, Lagos and Gabon – and old-established but moribund Portuguese settlements in Angola and up the Zambezi valley in Mozambique; but only in the south, where the British colonists of the Cape were already locked in rivalry with the Afrikaners of the Transvaal and the Orange Free State, was penetration at all deep. Elsewhere, apart from French Algeria and the debt-ridden regimes of Egypt and Tunis, occupation and even influence were restricted to a handful of trading posts, military stations and the offshore islands of Madagascar and Zanzibar. Yet within two decades the entire continent had been seized, annexed, fought over and partitioned. Of the forty political units into which it had been divided – often with little more than a ruler and pencil, wielded in London, Paris or Berlin – direct European control extended to thirty-six. Only Ethiopia, which had fought off the Italians, and Liberia, with its financial links to the United States, claimed real independence. France, the largest beneficiary, controlled nearly 4 million out of Africa's 11.7 million square miles.

Many ingredients contributed to this imperialistic explosion. The progress of industrialisation in Europe created a demand for new markets and also set up new social tensions, for which some politicians at least (e.g. Joseph Chamberlain) saw colonisation as an outlet. The rivalries between the European states were transferred to the extra-European world, and to Africa in particular. This meant that often trivial incidents between competing European traders in Africa achieved the status of major international crises, and that initiatives undertaken locally by European agents, occurring in rapid succession, set in motion the undignified scramble for possession of the continent. To a large extent the partition of Africa resulted from the backing given by the metropolitan countries to the uncoordinated activities of their men on the spot, who decided that the best way out of minor confrontations, either with African states or with other Europeans, was to take a little more African territory under their control.

In West Africa, it was mainly the French who took these local initiatives. The most important were the exploits of the French army attempting to advance up the Senegal river towards the upper Niger. French officers, denied the chance of avenging the defeat of 1870, sought glory in the dusty savannahs south of the Sahara (the Sudan region). This brought them into conflict with the British in Gambia and Sierra Leone, and with African states such as the empires of Samory and al-Hajj Umar (see page 238). Along the West African coast there was intense Anglo-French rivalry in the regions of the Gold Coast, Togo, Dahomey and Yorubaland. French attitudes towards Great Britain hardened after the unilateral British invasion and occupation of Egypt in 1882, but it was the intervention of other European powers that exploded these squabbles all over the continent.

After the explorer Stanley's epic journey down the Congo river in 1877, the ambitious King Leopold of the Belgians took him into his personal service. In 1879 Stanley returned to the lower Congo and laid the foundations of the huge private domain the king carved out for himself in the Congo basin. Stanley's activities stimulated others in the same area. The Italian de Brazza concluded some vital treaties with African chiefs, and on his return to Europe, France readily took up his claims. The action of France brought an immediate British and Portuguese response, though this came to nothing because of pressure exercised by Bismarck. Bismarck bought off French thoughts of revenge over the loss of Alsace by allowing France a free hand in Africa: this he was able to do by black-mailing Great Britain over Egypt. Then Germany itself, under Bismarck, entered the race by grabbing territory in four widely separated regions; in Togoland, the Cameroons, South-West Africa and East Africa. French and German initiatives in West Africa led Great Britain to intervene actively, especially in securing the lands which became Nigeria. The far interior was left to the French, who by 1900 had swept right across the western Sudan region.

The German presence in southern Africa revived Portuguese ambitions, and the threat of Afrikaner expansion led to British thrusts into the interior of central Africa, into what later became Rhodesia, Zambia and Malawi. The initiative for these drives came largely from the Cape industrialist and politician Cecil Rhodes. Likewise, German colonisation in East Africa (Tanganyika) produced its British counterpart when the Prime Minister, Lord Salisbury, laid claim to the region of the Great Lakes (Uganda) and the intervening territory down to the coast, which later became Kenya. The British were also drawn from their position in Egypt to intervene in the affairs of the Sudan, which had rebelled against Egypt in 1881 under the Islamic religious leader, the Mahdi. At the same time, French successes in the west – the occupation of Gabon in the western Congo, the conquest of the ancient kingdom of Dahomey (1893) and a three-pronged drive towards Lake Chad – caused Great Britain to mobilise the resources of the Royal Niger Company, to seize the emirates of Nupe and Ilorin, and to embark on a series of armed clashes not only with the French but also, for the first time, with the African states within its trading sphere. The tension reached its height in 1898, when France's Commandant Marchand, after a two-year march from Gabon, faced the British troops at Fashoda on the White Nile, and the two countries only just averted open war.

Partition, which had begun as a fairly peaceful process, was now causing more and more bloodshed. Ethiopia inflicted a heavy defeat on the Italians at Adowa in 1896. Some 20,000 Sudanese died during the British suppression of the Mahdist state. Rhodes' settler forces engaged in bitter battles with the Matabele and Mashona as they moved north, and the white colonists everywhere came to rely increasingly on the repeating rifle and the Maxim gun.

Conflict reached its climax with the Boer War (1899-1902) in which the British, with great difficulty, won control of the Transvaal gold mines (discovered on the Witwatersrand in 1886) and absorbed the Afrikaner republics. Hostilities opened with the abortive Jameson Raid in 1896, which destroyed Rhodes' political reputation, but Chamberlain, the British Colonial Secretary, and Milner, the High Commissioner in Cape Town, continued to push Rhodes' policies to the point of war. The Africans, on the other hand, though they bitterly opposed the 'forward moves' of the European powers (see page 248), never offered concerted resistance, and were fairly easily dealt with piecemeal. Of the handful of African states still precariously independent in 1902, Libya was invaded by Italy in 1911, and Morocco survived until 1912 before being divided between France and Spain.

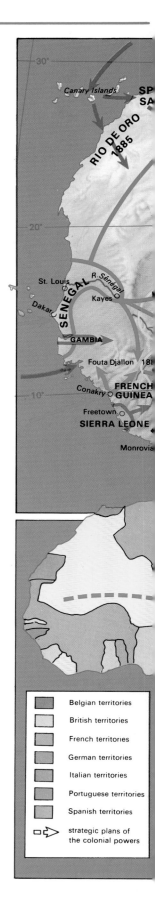

3/Colonial strategy in Africa *(above)* All the major powers involved in the scramble for Africa had wide-reaching ambitions. The Germans hoped to absorb the Portuguese colonies and at least part of the Congo, and in this way to form a solid empire extending across the centre of the continent. France had similar ambitions in the north. To counter them, the British pushed north through Bechuanaland and south from the Sudan, hoping to form a continuous belt of British territory from the Cape to Cairo. These conflicting aims brought the British and French face to face at Fashoda in 1898 and nearly led to a major war.

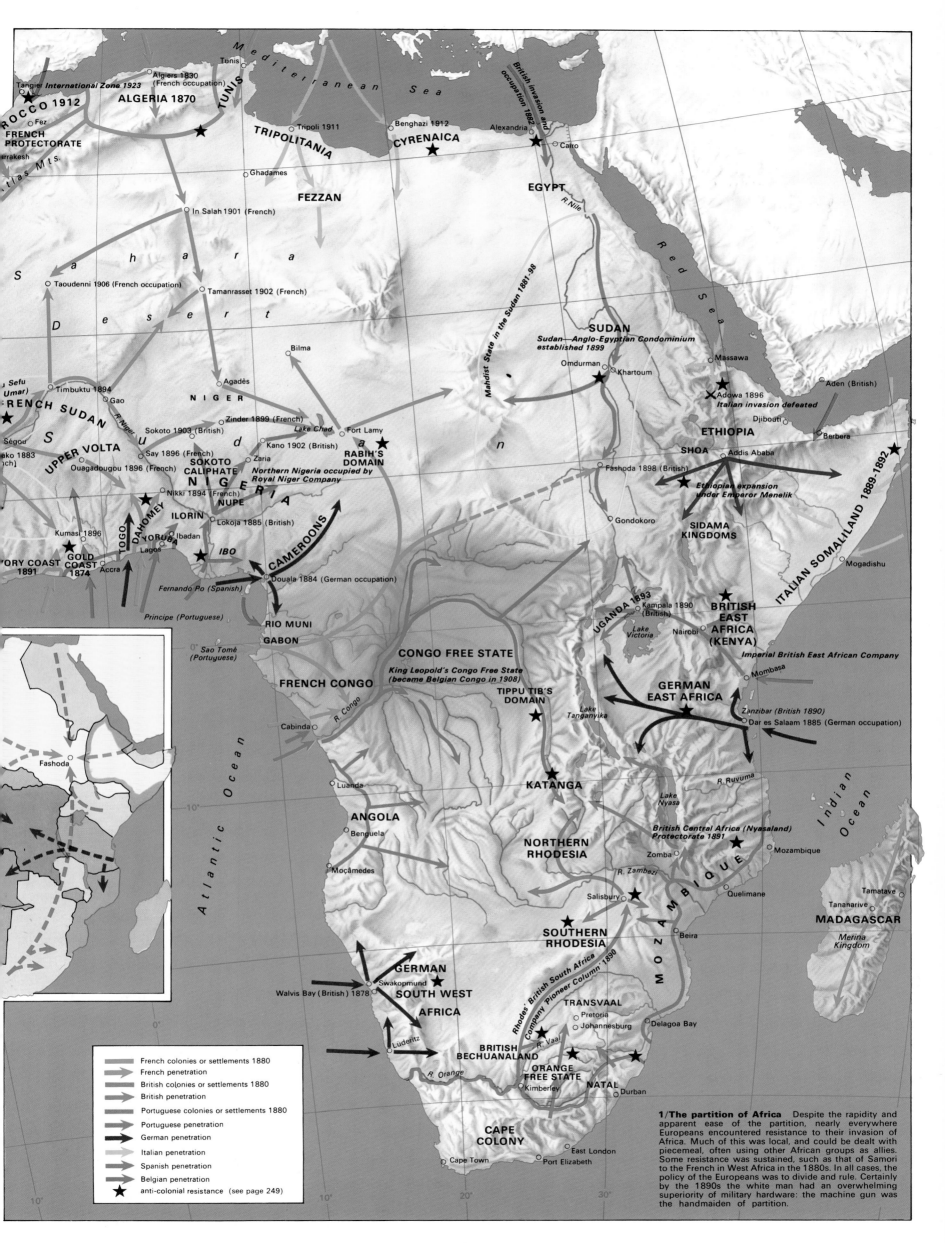

MOROCCO 1912
FRENCH
PROTECTORATE

Tangier *International Zone 1923*
Fez
Marrakesh
Atlas Mts.

Algiers 1830
(French occupation)
ALGERIA 1870
Tunis
TUNIS

Mediterranean Sea

Tripoli 1911
TRIPOLITANIA
Ghadames

Benghazi 1912
CYRENAICA

Alexandria
Cairo
British invasion and occupation 1882
EGYPT
R. Nile

Red Sea

In Salah 1901 (French)
FEZZAN

S a h a r a
D e s e r t

Taoudenni 1906 (French occupation)
Tamanrasset 1902 (French)

Bilma
Agadès

Mahdist State in the Sudan 1881-98

SUDAN
Sudan—Anglo-Egyptian Condominium established 1899

Omdurman
Khartoum
Massawa
Aden (British)

Adowa 1896
Italian invasion defeated

u Sefu Umar
Timbuktu 1894
Gao
NIGER

FRENCH SUDAN
Ségou
ako 1883 ench

Zinder 1899 (French)
Sokoto 1903 (British)
Lake Chad
Fort Lamy
Kano 1902 (British)
Zaria
RABIH'S DOMAIN

S u d a n

ETHIOPIA
SHOA
Addis Ababa
Fashoda 1898 (British)
Ethiopian expansion under Emperor Menelik

Djibouti
Berbera

UPPER VOLTA
Say 1896 (French)
Ouagadougou 1896 (French)
SOKOTO CALIPHATE
Nikki 1894 (French)
NIGERIA
Northern Nigeria occupied by Royal Niger Company

NUPE
Lokoja 1885 (British)

Gondokoro

SIDAMA KINGDOMS

Kumasi 1896
TOGO
DAHOMEY
ILORIN
YORUBA Ibadan
Lagos
IBO
CAMEROONS

ITALIAN SOMALILAND 1889-1892

Mogadishu

IVORY COAST 1891
GOLD COAST 1874
Accra
Fernando Po (Spanish)
Douala 1884 (German occupation)

Principe (Portuguese)
RIO MUNI
GABON

São Tomé (Portuguese)

CONGO FREE STATE
King Leopold's Congo Free State (became Belgian Congo in 1908)

TIPPU TIB'S DOMAIN

Kampala 1890
(British)
UGANDA 1893
Lake Victoria
Nairobi
BRITISH EAST AFRICA (KENYA)
Imperial British East African Company

FRENCH CONGO

Cabinda
R. Congo

GERMAN EAST AFRICA
Zanzibar (British 1890)
Dar es Salaam 1885 (German occupation)
Mombasa
Lake Tanganyika

Luanda
KATANGA
R. Ruvuma

ANGOLA
Benguela
Lake Nyasa
Indian Ocean

Moçâmedes
NORTHERN RHODESIA
British Central Africa (Nyasaland) Protectorate 1891
Zomba
Mozambique

Atlantic Ocean

R. Zambezi
Quelimane
Tamatave
MADAGASCAR

Salisbury
M O Z A M B I Q U E
Beira
Merina Kingdom

SOUTHERN RHODESIA

Walvis Bay (British) 1878
Swakopmund
GERMAN SOUTH WEST AFRICA

Rhodes' British South Africa Company Pioneer Column 1890
TRANSVAAL
Pretoria
Johannesburg
Delagoa Bay

Lüderitz
R. Vaal

BRITISH BECHUANALAND
ORANGE FREE STATE
R. Orange
Kimberley
NATAL
Durban

CAPE COLONY
Cape Town
East London
Port Elizabeth

Fashoda

Legend:
— French colonies or settlements 1880
→ French penetration
→ British colonies or settlements 1880
→ British penetration
→ Portuguese colonies or settlements 1880
→ Portuguese penetration
→ German penetration
→ Italian penetration
→ Spanish penetration
→ Belgian penetration
★ anti-colonial resistance (see page 249)

1/The partition of Africa Despite the rapidity and apparent ease of the partition, nearly everywhere Europeans encountered resistance to their invasion of Africa. Much of this was local, and could be dealt with piecemeal, often using other African groups as allies. Some resistance was sustained, such as that of Samori to the French in West Africa in the 1880s. In all cases, the policy of the Europeans was to divide and rule. Certainly by the 1890s the white man had an overwhelming superiority of military hardware: the machine gun was the handmaiden of partition.

The expansion and modernisation of Japan 1868 to 1918

3/The Russo-Japanese War *(above)* After surprising Tsarist ships at Port Arthur (8 February 1904), Japan's forces achieved a series of victories, culminating in the fall of Port Arthur (January 1905), the Battle of Mukden (February-March), and the destruction of Russia's Baltic Fleet in the Tsushima Straits (May). Adults and children *(left)* study together in a typical Meiji period classroom scene.

1/Industrial Japan *(below)* By 1918 the country's first major phase of modern economic growth was completed. Urban population had substantially increased. Port cities and installations had expanded to meet changes in the scale and structure of foreign trade. The main railway network, nationalised in 1906, connected all major centres. World War I, diverting the energies of all significant competitors, opened large new markets for manufactured exports. Japanese shipping was now operating worldwide.

JAPAN is of major importance in considering the expansion of Western power and civilisation to the rest of the world in the 19th and 20th centuries. First, it is the outstanding example of Western-induced political and economic modernisation in the non-Western world; second, its response was not only to modernise, but also to create an imperialism of its own, making Japan as much an influence on its neighbours as the West was on Japan.

The process began in the 1850s. Two centuries of self-imposed isolation, during which feudalism had been gradually undermined by the growth of a money economy, ended when the powers, led by the United States, demanded access to Japanese ports for trade. The 'unequal treaties' concluded under threat in 1858 aroused hostile reactions, which contributed to the overthrow of the ruling Tokugawa house in January 1868. Direct imperial rule was then restored in the name of the Meiji emperor (1867-1912).

These events brought to power new leaders, men who saw their main task as the pursuit of national wealth and strength in order to assert Japan's international independence and equality. They abolished the feudal domains (1871), creating a system of prefectures and a centralised bureaucracy. By the 1880s the pattern of official recruitment and promotion, previously based on traditional Chinese models introduced in the 7th century, had become much more comparable with those in continental Europe, especially in France and Germany, and from about 1900 staffing was increasingly from graduates of Japan's new universities. A Western-style peerage (1884), cabinet government (1885) and a bicameral legislature (1889), laid a foundation of political unity and stability on which was soon erected a modern social, economic and military structure. Samurai privilege was abolished and a conscript army created (1873). A navy was founded, equipped with modern ships. A national education system was instituted (1872), providing teaching for 90 per cent of school-age children by 1900. Legal codes, largely based on French and German models (except in traditional areas like the family system) were introduced, beginning in 1882. Land tax was reformed (1873), furnishing a regular cash revenue to replace feudal dues. Official encouragement was given to commerce and industry by a wide variety of measures: quality control of export goods such as silk; subsidies or direct government investment for strategic and import-saving industries; technical training schemes; tax advantages; the development of transport and communications.

Economic modernisation was not easy, even though Japan started with greater advantages than most Asian countries. In 1868 she already had an extensive domestic commerce. Moreover, despite a shortage of arable land, there was a highly developed intensive agriculture, capable of supporting a population of 30 million. Japan, for several centuries a major copper producer, also had adequate coal deposits, some already in use, and enough accessible ore to supply an iron industry in its initial stages (though not beyond). Japanese scholars had begun to study and experiment with Western science and technology, learning at first from books imported through the Dutch, then after 1858 directly from foreigners or in foreign countries. By 1860 they had built a Western-style ship, which crossed the Pacific with a Japanese crew. From then on, many students were sent abroad, sometimes for short training visits to Europe and America, sometimes for longer periods at Western universities. This provided knowledge not only of technical skills, but also of political and economic affairs. Later development depended heavily on Japan adopting institutions such as the joint stock company and banks, as well as the government's success in providing a stable social and financial environment.

Within this framework capitalism made rapid headway, quickly making Japan the outstanding example of large-scale industrialisation in the non-Western world. By the late 1880s there were beginnings in textiles, and after 1895 heavy industry also began to develop on a considerable scale. Further impetus came from Japan's increased penetration of foreign markets during the First World War. Foreign trade rose sharply from the 1890s, as Japan exploited major outlets in China (cotton textiles) and the United States (silk). The trade structure changed strikingly as she became a large-scale importer of raw materials and exporter of finished goods.

Predictably, these developments were reflected in considerable changes in the country's way of life. Population rose from 35 million in 1873 to 55 million in 1918. By then, although half the population was still engaged in agriculture, nearly a third lived in towns of 10,000 persons or more, especially in the major industrial areas of Honshu and northern Kyushu, and along the coastal belt that joined them. Moreover, these areas were linked to most parts of the country, even remote ones, by a railway system totalling 10,000 kilometres of government trunk routes (nationalised in 1906) connecting a network of privately-owned local lines.

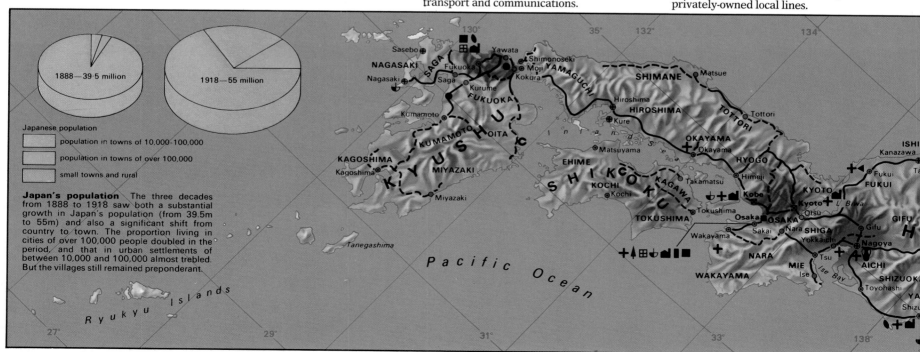

Japanese population

- population in towns of 10,000-100,000
- population in towns of over 100,000
- small towns and rural

Japan's population The three decades from 1888 to 1918 saw both a substantial growth in Japan's population (from 39.5m to 55m) and also a significant shift from country to town. The proportion living in cities of over 100,000 people doubled in the period, and that in urban settlements of between 10,000 and 100,000 almost trebled. But the villages still remained preponderant.

National strength, military and industrial, brought expansion overseas. Initially, foreign policy was preoccupied with problems of defence. The nearby islands of the Ryukyu archipelago were claimed in 1872 and were made a Japanese prefecture in 1879 despite Chinese protests. The Bonin (Ogasawara) islands were taken over by agreement with Britain and the United States in 1873. The Kuriles had been partitioned between Japan and Russia by a treaty of 1855, but in 1875 Japan relinquished a claim to part of Sakhalin in return for all the Kurile chain.

As Japan's strength and confidence grew, so did nationalist and imperialist ambitions. The 'unequal treaties' were revised in 1894, though the revisions were not fully implemented until 1911. In 1894-95 a victorious war against China, arising from disputes in Korea, led to the treaty of Shimonoseki in 1895, granting Formosa (Taiwan) to Japan. A claim to the Liaotung Peninsula was made in the treaty, but had to be withdrawn under pressure from Russia, France and Germany. From then on, Japan and Russia were in rivalry over their respective interests in Korea and South Manchuria, a rivalry culminating in war in 1904-5. Again Japan was successful. She gained land victories in Manchuria, notably at Port Arthur and Mukden, and defeated the Russian fleet in the Tsushima Straits in May 1905. The Treaty of Portsmouth (1905) gave her a lease of Liaotung (Kwantung Leased Territory), plus extensive rights in South Manchuria and a colony in southern Sakhalin (Karafuto). Korea was made a protectorate and later annexed (1910). Finally, the outbreak of war in Europe in 1914 allowed Japan to extend her rights on the Chinese mainland, this time in the former German sphere in Shantung, as well as in Manchuria and Fukien. In the Twenty-one Demands she made sweeping claims in these areas, most of which were incorporated in treaties with China in 1915. Bitterly resented by many Chinese, they were nevertheless acquiesced in by Japan's allies in a series of separate agreements which also recognised her claims to captured German islands in the northern Pacific. Most of these gains were confirmed at the Versailles Conference in 1919, when Japan emerged as a major power, with a permanent seat on the Council of the League of Nations.

There was another side to the story. The era of reform on which international success was founded had also helped to destroy the basis of stability at home. The deaths and retirement of the Meiji generation of leaders opened the way for a power struggle between fresh contenders. By 1918 the army was already showing a willingness to act independently of civil control in operations against Soviet Russia in Siberia. Party politicians, appealing to Western parliamentary ideas, sought power through the support of businessmen. Finally, cutting across previous patterns of political development, were those who rejected the whole trend of Japan's modern history: traditionalists, offended by the sacrifice of Japanese to Western-style habits and institutions; and representatives of the tenant farmer and the factory labourer, who resented the capitalist structure. Following the end of the war in 1918, Japan suffered a wave of strikes in major industrial centres, followed by widespread rural unrest. In 1921 Hara Kei, prime minister and party leader, was assassinated by a young right-wing fanatic. In these events were the seeds of future disruption, presaging a new phase of international conflict.

Nevertheless, with the rise of Japan, Asia had returned to the forefront of world history; although Japan itself continued to be divided between its Asian past and its future as one of the world's leading industrial powers.

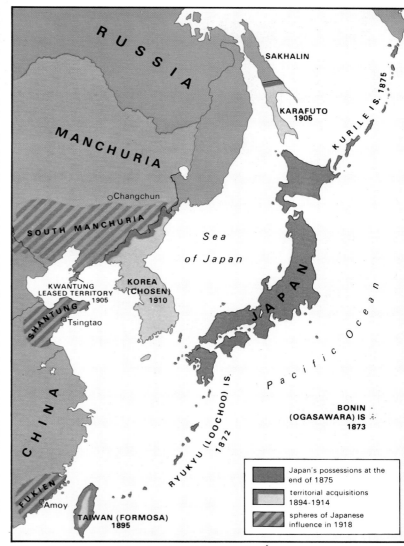

2/Growth Overseas (above) After 200 years of isolation, 1868 brought an explosion of Japanese interest both in the West and in her neighbours. By the end of 1875 Japan had successfully asserted rights in several nearby islands. Thereafter three wars (1894-95, 1904-5 and 1914-18) extended her holdings north and south and established an empire on the mainland.

Legend:
- Japan's possessions at the end of 1875
- territorial acquisitions 1894-1914
- spheres of Japanese influence in 1918

Japan's trading partners (right) The United States had already become Japan's major trading partner 1918-22, with imports and exports roughly in balance. China was more important as a customer than as a supplier, and India the reverse. Britain's dominance of China was not duplicated in Japan.

Japan's trading partners 1918-1922
- exports
- imports

The dramatic growth of Japanese trade (below right) The growth of imports and exports is shown in yen. The yen was first issued in 1871 at parity with the dollar, but it declined steadily until 1894, when the exchange rate stabilised at 2 yen to the dollar, where it remained, with small variations, until 1931.

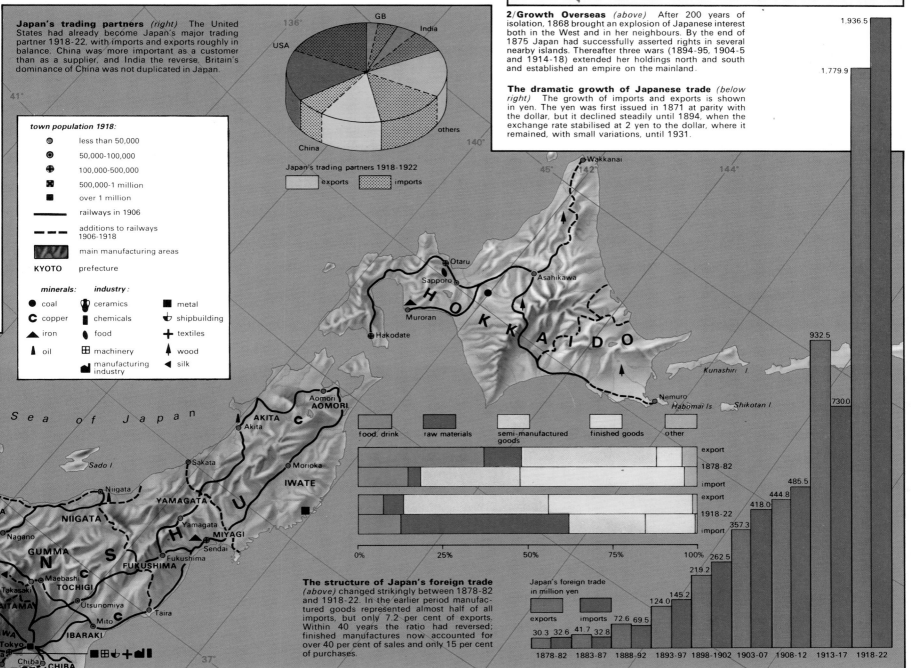

town population 1918:
- ⊙ less than 50,000
- ◉ 50,000-100,000
- ⊕ 100,000-500,000
- ⊠ 500,000-1 million
- ■ over 1 million

— railways in 1906
--- additions to railways 1906-1918
▨ main manufacturing areas
KYOTO prefecture

minerals:
- ● coal
- C copper
- ▲ iron
- ○ oil

industry:
- ♟ ceramics
- ▮ chemicals
- ▮ food
- ⊞ machinery
- ▰ manufacturing industry
- ■ metal
- ⚒ shipbuilding
- ✛ textiles
- ▲ wood
- ◀ silk

The structure of Japan's foreign trade (above) changed strikingly between 1878-82 and 1918-22. In the earlier period manufactured goods represented almost half of all imports, but only 7.2 per cent of exports. Within 40 years the ratio had reversed; finished manufactures now accounted for over 40 per cent of sales and only 15 per cent of purchases.

food, drink | raw materials | semi-manufactured goods | finished goods | other

1878-82 export / import
1918-22 export / import

0% 25% 50% 75% 100%

Japan's foreign trade in million yen

exports / imports

	exports	imports
1878-82	30.3	32.6
1883-87	41.7	32.8
1888-92	72.6	69.5
1893-97	124.0	145.2
1898-1902	219.2	262.5
1903-07	357.3	418.0
1908-12	444.8	485.5
1913-17	932.5	730.0
1918-22	1,936.5	1,779.9

243

European colonial empires 1815 to 1914

THE 19th century is often seen as the great age of European expansion or 'imperialism', and one of the main themes of 20th century history has been the anti-colonialist reaction it has provoked among the peoples of Asia and Africa. In fact the creation of large new empires occupied only the last half of the century. As late as 1871, apart from the possessions of Great Britain in India and South Africa, of Russia in Siberia and central Asia, and of France in Algeria and Indo-China, the European stake in Asia and Africa was confined to trading stations and strategic posts. Colonial struggles had played an important part in European politics in the 18th century (see page 194), but by the mid-19th century empire-building seemed to have lost its attractions. On a theoretical level, its mercantilist justification had been demolished by Adam Smith and the 'Manchester School' of economists. More practically, Great Britain's flourishing trade with both the United States and South America appeared to show that political control was not necessary for commercial success. The

future British prime minister, Benjamin Disraeli, expressed the prevailing orthodoxy when he said, in 1852, 'the colonies are millstones round our neck'.

Nevertheless, the European powers were in no hurry to abandon their existing possessions overseas. Spain and Portugal lost their empires in the western hemisphere as they became weaker at home. By 1830 their former colonies in South and Central America were virtually all independent (see page 226). Russia too surrendered her North American territories, selling Alaska to the United States in 1867. But France, who had lost most of her first empire by 1815, gradually built a new one, conquering Algeria in the 1830s and 1840s, expanding her colony of Senegal in the 1850s, taking various Pacific islands (Tahiti, the Marquesas) in the 1840s, and annexing Saigon in 1859. Great Britain was also steadily acquiring new territories. By the peace settlements of 1815 she retained the Cape of Good Hope and the maritime provinces of Ceylon from the Dutch, Malta from the Knights

of St. John, Mauritius and the Seychelles from France and some West Indian islands from France and Spain. Fearing a French challenge, she extended her claim to sovereignty over the whole of Australia in the 1830s and over New Zealand in 1840. Her power continued to expand in India (see page 234), and by 1858 the boundaries of British India and of the Princely States under British tutelage had assumed roughly the positions they were to retain until independence in 1947. Elsewhere she acquired Singapore in 1819, Malacca in 1824, Hong Kong in 1842, Natal in 1843, Labuan in 1846, Lower Burma in 1852, Lagos in 1861 and Sarawak in 1888. Many of these acquisitions were strategic points, commanding sea routes. Great Britain was particularly sensitive about the route to India as India was her most valuable overseas possession. This apparent paradox between theory and practice is explained by the fact that the British felt that their prosperity and survival depended on trade and, although they preferred to safeguard this by 'influence', they never ruled out direct poli-

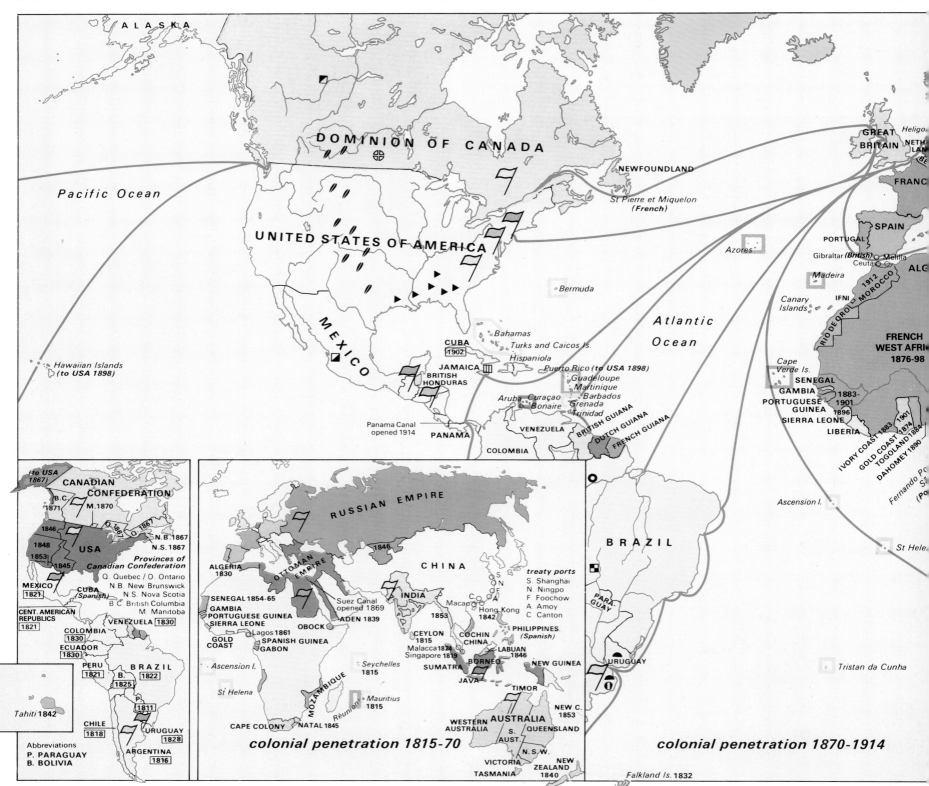

colonial penetration 1815-70

colonial penetration 1870-1914

tical or military intervention.

The late 19th century saw a new imperial outburst of an intensely competitive kind. In the scramble for territory, resources, markets and outlets for capital investment, an immense part of the world's total land area passed under European control. But many desirable areas were already pre-empted: the Monroe Doctrine discouraged further European involvement in the western hemisphere; latecomers such as Germany and Italy had to look to Africa, the Pacific or China. Great Britain, France and even Portugal re-entered the lists. The United States seized former Spanish territory in the war of 1898. Japan, emerging as a great Pacific power, began to covet Korea, Formosa and even mainland China. Of the great trading nations, the Netherlands almost alone remained content with their existing (and prosperous) possessions in the East Indies. Between 1871 and 1914 the French empire grew by nearly 4 million square miles and nearly 47 million people. Her new empire was mainly in north and west Africa and Indo-China, where Laos and Tongking were added to Cambodia and Cochin China, but she also secured Madagascar and some Pacific territories. Germany acquired an empire of 1 million square miles of territory and 14 million colonial subjects in South-West Africa, Togoland, the Cameroons, Tanganyika and the Pacific islands. Italy obtained Libya, Eritrea and Italian Somaliland but failed to secure Abyssinia. Leopold II of the Belgians got international recognition for his

Congo State (later the Belgium Congo). Portugal extended her territory in Angola and Mozambique. Great Britain made the greatest gains of all in Africa, controlling *inter alia* Nigeria, Kenya, Uganda, Northern and Southern Rhodesia, Egypt and the Sudan, and in the Pacific, where she took Fiji, parts of Borneo and New Guinea, and other islands. She added 88 million subjects to her empire and, by 1914, exercised authority over a fifth of the world's land surface and a quarter of its peoples.

Africa was completely partitioned (see page 240), China seemed likely to share the same fate. Russia joined the other European powers in competing for influence here. Her land empire in central Asia and Siberia had grown enormously since the 1860s and over 7 million Russians had emigrated from European to Asiatic Russia between 1801 and 1914. In China, the late 19th century was the time of the 'battle of the concessions', when the leading contenders manoeuvred for commercial advantage and financial and railway concessions. But the Chinese state, although debilitated, was stronger and more centralised than the divided polities of Africa. The Chinese held the West at bay until the First World War which was a watershed. Although the British empire actually grew in size after the war, with the addition of the former German colonies, indiscriminate land-grabbing was no longer considered acceptable conduct in a world supposedly ruled by the League of Nations.

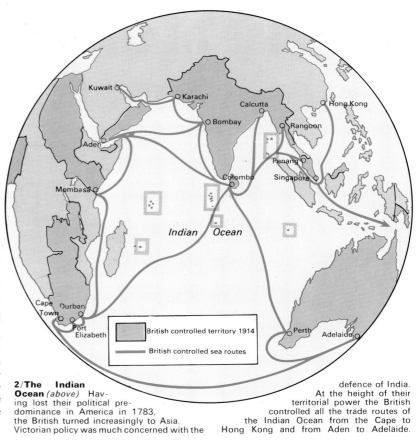

2/The Indian Ocean *(above)* Having lost their political predominance in America in 1783, the British turned increasingly to Asia. Victorian policy was much concerned with the defence of India. At the height of their territorial power the British controlled all the trade routes of the Indian Ocean from the Cape to Hong Kong and from Aden to Adelaide.

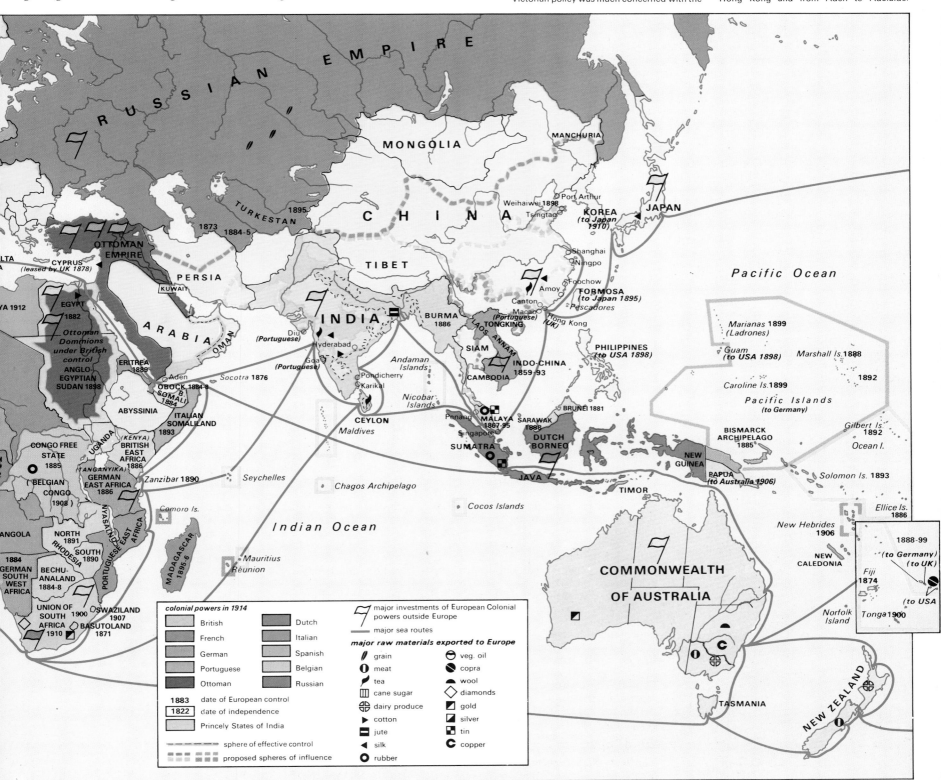

The rise of the United States to world power 1867 to 1917

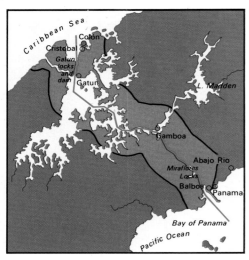

2/The Panama Canal zone *(above)* Under a treaty with Panama (1903) the US leased the zone in perpetuity, but also took possession of it as 'if it were sovereign'. However, under two treaties ratified in 1978, the Canal zone was handed over to Panama and the canal itself is to be relinquished by the US by the end of 1999.

THE United States emerged onto the world stage in 1867, followed by Germany in 1870. Between them these two imperial powers exerted a decisive influence in transforming the modern world. In 1917, by entering the war on the side of Great Britain and France, the US brought about a decisive German defeat and thereby made itself the world's greatest power.

The preceding half-century, from 1867 to 1917, was a period of intense international rivalries, of which the United States took full advantage. American ambitions had manifested themselves since the 18th century, but dissension between the northern and southern states, culminating in the Civil War of 1861 to 1865, slowed expansion to a halt. When the forward movement was resumed, industrialism and later finance capitalism appeared as potent forces superimposed upon the earliest type of empire-building which had stressed commerce and territory. This new imperialism vented itself in war against Spain in 1898, a watershed year when the US plunged into world politics; meanwhile, it had been strengthening its navy and occupying strategic outposts before claiming supremacy in the Caribbean and the Pacific.

The first step in the resumption of this new forward movement was the acquisition of Alaska in 1867 as the result of a deal with Russia. To Americans Alaska was both the back door to Canada and a 'finger pointed at Asia'. Many

3/The Alaska border dispute *(below)* The rush to the Klondike gold fields in 1897 brought this dispute near the boiling stage. Canada feared the loss of the north-west, but a politically-oriented tribunal, a British judge holding the casting vote, favoured the boundary demanded by the US (1903).

land claimed by US
land claimed by Canada
boundary agreed 1903

Americans believed that British North America, encircled in this way, would be forced into the Union, thus fulfilling the dream of a continent-wide empire. But the Canadians frustrated these hopes, first by federation (1867), then by the purchase of Rupert's Land from the Hudson's Bay Company (1869). Finally, they attracted Manitoba (1870) and British Columbia (1871) into the new Dominion, thus blunting the northward thrusts of the United States. Tensions with Britain stemming from the American Civil War were eased by the Treaty of Washington (1871).

With the Aleutian island chain stretching out toward Japan, Alaska was the natural bridge to north-east Asia. Since the mid-19th century, however, Hawaii had been the main entrepôt to the Orient. A three-power rivalry involving Britain and France had kept American relations with this native kingdom in an unsettled state, but by annexing Midway Island (1867) the United States moved ahead of the other two powers. A commercial treaty in 1875 made Hawaii a virtual American protectorate, and in 1887 the United States obtained Pearl Harbor as a coaling station and future naval base. Annexation entered its final stage in 1893, when a group of sugar planters and Honolulu businessmen, aided by American officials, overthrew the native monarchy and established a republic. The outbreak of war with Spain in 1898 furnished the impetus for formal annexation. Wake Island followed in 1899. Earlier, in 1878, a foothold had been established at Pago Pago in the Samoan group, where the British and Germans were also involved. Friction resulted in a treaty (1899) partitioning the group, but the Germans lost their share to New Zealand in 1914.

The chief fruits of the Spanish-American war in the Pacific were the Philippines and the island of Guam, formally ceded by Spain in the peace treaty of 1898. The United States now had its 'stepping stones' to China, already the focus of international rivalry as a field for capital investment (see page 232). Backed by the government, American bankers and entrepreneurs expected to get their full share. They would secure the 'Open Door', a phrase already in current use to describe the unlimited opportunities China was supposed to offer. A secret move in 1900 to obtain a lease over Samsah Bay in Fukien province, opposite Formosa, proved unsuccessful. Nevertheless, the United States was determined to outpace the European powers in the scramble. Its attention was concentrated particularly on Manchuria. Promoters like Willard Straight, who was consul-general in Mukden, conceived of Manchuria as America's 'new West', to be gridironed by railways owned and managed from the United States. These designs were thwarted by Russia and Japan, who effectively divided Manchuria between themselves by treaty in 1907 and 1910 respectively.

The other principal area of American expansion took in Mexico and the Caribbean. From Mexico the United States had wrested the provinces of Texas, New Mexico and California between 1846 and 1848. Land, mining and oil companies, competing with European interests, penetrated the country after 1880 but were checked by the revolution of 1911, which adumbrated a far-reaching programme of nationalisation. President Wilson reacted with two armed interventions: an occupation force to Veracruz in 1914, and a punitive expedition across the Rio Grande in 1916. But these actions stimulated the Mexicans to resist, and helped the initiation of a German intrigue which came to a head in 1917. Meanwhile, the war on Spain in 1898 had led to the conquest of Puerto Rico and the conversion of Cuba into a protectorate (1903). Britain, the other power chiefly interested in the Caribbean, recognised the changed situation and, in the Hay-Pauncefote treaty of 1901, gave the United States a free hand. From this agreement fol-

lowed the building of the Panama Canal (opened in 1914) under the sole ownership and control of the United States.

The ideological basis for this hegemony was the Monroe Doctrine which, even when first set forth in 1823, implied an intention to treat Latin America as a United States sphere of influence. However, with the outbreak of the Civil War (1861), expansionist ambitions were temporarily dropped, although the Monroe Doctrine was by no means forgotten. The French attempt to erect a puppet empire in Mexico (1862-67) offered it a fresh challenge, and in actually beginning work on a canal across Panama the French engineer, Ferdinand de Lesseps, builder of the Suez Canal, caused further objections. As President Hayes put it, any such canal must be regarded as 'virtually a part of the coastline of the United States' (1879).

Interfering in a British dispute with Venezuela over a boundary question, the United States, through Secretary of State Olney, in 1895 declared itself 'practically sovereign on this continent', and the British dropped the argument. Obstinacy on the part of Colombia in failing to bow to American demands for canal rights across Panama led to an insurrection accompanied by the forcible detachment of that country from Colombia. The United States then guaranteed the 'independence' of Panama but under terms that made it a protectorate. This period of dominance in the Caribbean survived under difficulties until about 1945. Mexican resistance stiffened into open defiance (1934-38), tactics had to be altered to appease the larger South American countries, intense diplomacy was undertaken to offset the activities of Nazi Germany. Interventions that occurred from time to time in the affairs of the Caribbean republics were covert or indirect, on the surface the Monroe Doctrine was transformed into the 'Good Neighbour' policy, and a battle of wits ensued to convince Latin America of US good intentions. But obviously new forces were at work, and the Monroe Doctrine continued to recede farther into the background.

An American view *(above)* of the relative importance of Uncle Sam and John Bull, from *The New York Journal* in 1898. *The Times* of London predicted, after America's crushing victory over Spain, that she would henceforth play a prominent role in world affairs.

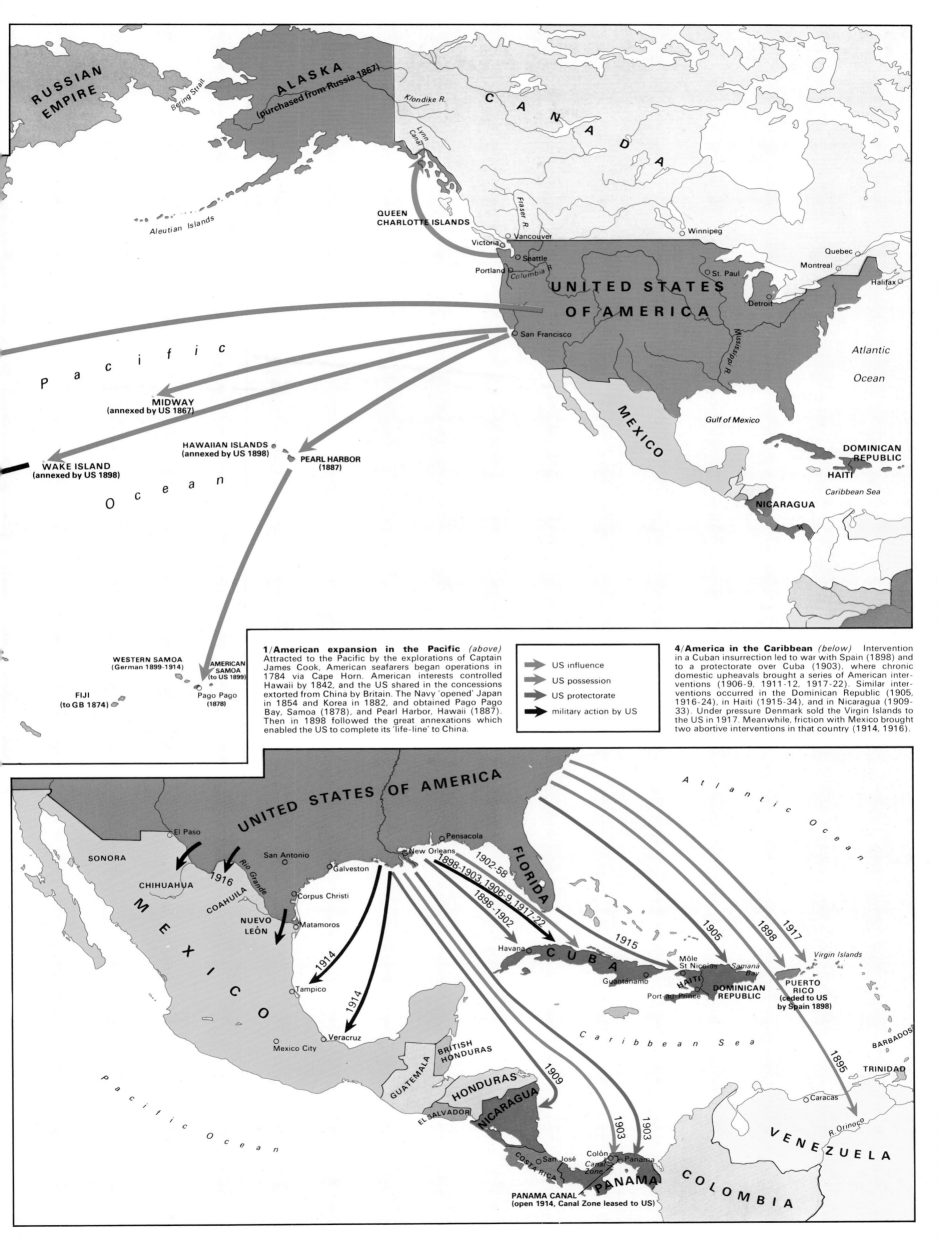

RUSSIAN EMPIRE

ALASKA (purchased from Russia 1867)

Bering Strait

Klondike R.

CANADA

Aleutian Islands

Fraser R.

Lynn Canal

QUEEN CHARLOTTE ISLANDS

Victoria

Vancouver

Winnipeg

Seattle

Portland

Columbia R.

St. Paul

Quebec

Montreal

Halifax

UNITED STATES OF AMERICA

Detroit

San Francisco

P a c i f i c

Atlantic Ocean

MIDWAY (annexed by US 1867)

MEXICO

Mississippi R.

WAKE ISLAND (annexed by US 1898)

HAWAIIAN ISLANDS (annexed by US 1898)

PEARL HARBOR (1887)

O c e a n

Gulf of Mexico

DOMINICAN REPUBLIC

HAITI

Caribbean Sea

NICARAGUA

WESTERN SAMOA (German 1899–1914)

AMERICAN SAMOA (to US 1899)

FIJI (to GB 1874)

Pago Pago (1878)

1/American expansion in the Pacific *(above)* Attracted to the Pacific by the explorations of Captain James Cook, American seafarers began operations in 1784 via Cape Horn. American interests controlled Hawaii by 1842, and the US shared in the concessions extorted from China by Britain. The Navy 'opened' Japan in 1854 and Korea in 1882, and obtained Pago Pago Bay, Samoa (1878), and Pearl Harbor, Hawaii (1887). Then in 1898 followed the great annexations which enabled the US to complete its 'life-line' to China.

→	US influence
→	US possession
→	US protectorate
→	military action by US

4/America in the Caribbean *(below)* Intervention in a Cuban insurrection led to war with Spain (1898) and to a protectorate over Cuba (1903), where chronic domestic upheavals brought a series of American interventions (1906-9, 1911-12, 1917-22). Similar interventions occurred in the Dominican Republic (1905, 1916-24), in Haiti (1915-34), and in Nicaragua (1909-33). Under pressure Denmark sold the Virgin Islands to the US in 1917. Meanwhile, friction with Mexico brought two abortive interventions in that country (1914, 1916).

UNITED STATES OF AMERICA

A t l a n t i c   O c e a n

El Paso

SONORA

San Antonio

Pensacola

New Orleans

FLORIDA

CHIHUAHUA

1916

Rio Grande

COAHUILA

Galveston

1902-58

1898-1903, 1906-9, 1917-22

1898-1902

NUEVO LEÓN

Corpus Christi

Matamoros

M E X I C O

1914

1914

Tampico

1915

Havana

CUBA

1905

1898

1917

Virgin Islands

Môle St Nicolas

Samaná Bay

PUERTO RICO (ceded to US by Spain 1898)

Guantanamo

HAITI

DOMINICAN REPUBLIC

Port-au-Prince

Mexico City

Veracruz

GUATEMALA

BRITISH HONDURAS

C a r i b b e a n   S e a

BARBADOS

P a c i f i c   O c e a n

EL SALVADOR

HONDURAS

1909

NICARAGUA

TRINIDAD

Caracas

San José

COSTA RICA

1903

1903

Colón

Panama

Canal Zone

PANAMA

COLOMBIA

R. Orinoco

V E N E Z U E L A

PANAMA CANAL (open 1914, Canal Zone leased to US)

1895

The anti-colonial reaction 1881 to 1917

Shooting the Pig and Decapitating the Sheep *(above)* This detail from a popular Chinese woodcut of the 1890s illustrates graphically the intensity of anti-western feeling in the colonial and semi-colonial world. The pig is Christ, the sheep are the Christians. This was the sentiment behind the Boxer rising of 1900, but it was duplicated in many other parts of the world.

THE 'new imperialism', beginning with the French occupation of Tunis in 1881 and the British occupation of Egypt in 1882, unleashed an anti-colonial reaction throughout Asia and Africa, the extent, intensity and significance of which have rarely been fully appreciated. In Tunisia French intervention provoked a large-scale Islamic rising, followed by spasmodic warfare in the south; in Egypt the British faced a national revolt under Arabi Pasha. Independence was not passively surrendered either in Africa or in Asia. The Italians were decisively defeated by the Abyssinians at Adowa in 1896. In Annam the emperor, Ham Nghi, took to the mountains in 1883 and resisted French occupation until 1888. The British suffered repeated setbacks in the Sudan at the hands of the Mahdi and his successor, the Khalifa, including the annihilation of the garrison of Khartoum under General Gordon in 1885. Russia, fanatically opposed in the Caucasus from 1834 to 1859 by Shamil, 'ruler of the righteous and destroyer of the unbeliever', encountered further Muslim resistance when it invaded central Asia; and when the United States occupied the Philippines in 1898, the Americans also found themselves involved in a costly war with nationalist forces under Emilio Aguinaldo, which cost them some 7000 casualties and dragged on until 1902.

Even after occupation, the European powers had to face almost continuous unrest. After the capture of Aguinaldo, the Moros of Mindanao carried on resistance in the Philippines. In Indo-China the 'Black Flags' took up the struggle after the capture of Emperor Ham Nghi in 1888, and after 1895 a new leader appeared in the person of De Tham, who resisted the French until 1913. In Africa the British met equally determined resistance from the Ashanti, Matabele, Zulu and other African tribes, and oppressive German rule provoked the great Herero and Maji-Maji revolts in South-West Africa and Tanganyika in 1904 and 1905.

Much of this resistance was a negative explosion of resentment, xenophobia and despair; it was also conservative and backward-looking, with a strong traditionalist and religious bias. In Egypt and North Africa nationalists such as Afghani and Mohammed Abduh called for an Islamic revival to expel the infidel, and the Mahdiyya, which effectively controlled the Sudan from 1881 to 1898, was a Muslim revivalist movement, directed at once against Egyptians and Europeans. A similar role in fomenting resistance was played by Hinduism in India and by Confucianism in China. But this conservative, traditionalist reaction to European imperialism, which had little prospect of success in view of the immense military preponderance of the colonial powers, was accompanied elsewhere by a more positive response, particularly in countries such as Turkey, Egypt, China and India

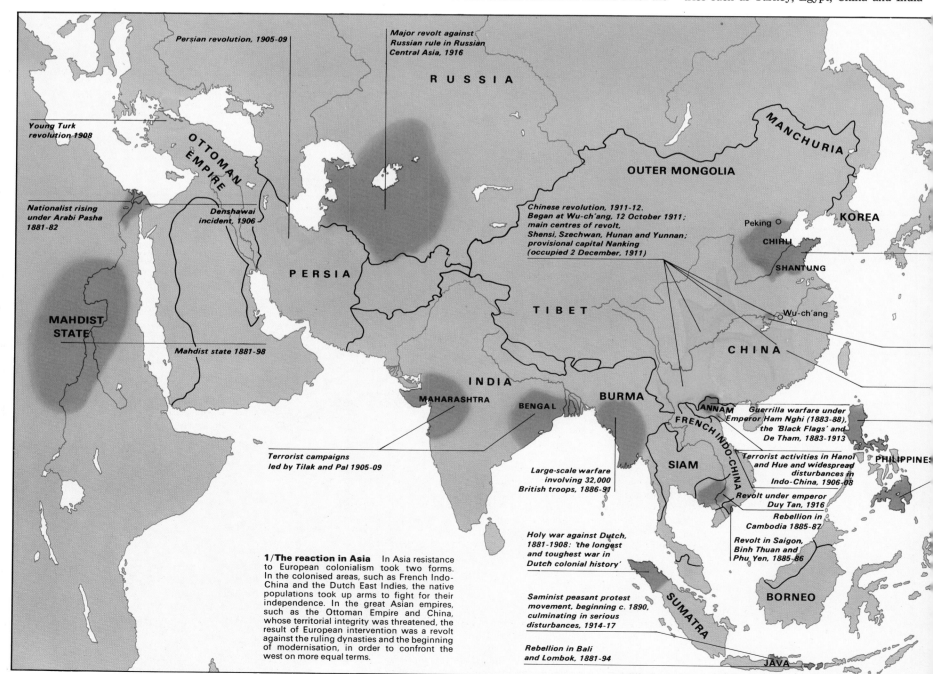

Persian revolution, 1905-09

Major revolt against Russian rule in Russian Central Asia, 1916

RUSSIA

Young Turk revolution 1908

OTTOMAN EMPIRE

MANCHURIA

OUTER MONGOLIA

Nationalist rising under Arabi Pasha 1881-82

Denshawai incident, 1906

Chinese revolution, 1911-12. Began at Wu-ch'ang, 12 October 1911; main centres of revolt, Shensi, Szechwan, Hunan and Yunnan; provisional capital Nanking (occupied 2 December, 1911)

Peking O

KOREA

CHIHLI

PERSIA

SHANTUNG

Wu-ch'ang

MAHDIST STATE

TIBET

CHINA

Mahdist state 1881-98

INDIA

BURMA

ANNAM

Guerrilla warfare under Emperor Ham Nghi (1883-88), the 'Black Flags' and De Tham, 1883-1913

MAHARASHTRA

BENGAL

FRENCH INDO-CHINA

PHILIPPINES

Terrorist campaigns led by Tilak and Pal 1905-09

Terrorist activities in Hanoi and Hue and widespread disturbances in Indo-China, 1906-08

SIAM

Large-scale warfare involving 32,000 British troops, 1886-91

Revolt under emperor Duy Tan, 1916

Rebellion in Cambodia 1885-87

Revolt in Saigon, Binh Thuan and Phu Yen, 1885-86

1/The reaction in Asia In Asia resistance to European colonialism took two forms. In the colonised areas, such as French Indo-China and the Dutch East Indies, the native populations took up arms to fight for their independence. In the great Asian empires, such as the Ottoman Empire and China, whose territorial integrity was threatened, the result of European intervention was a revolt against the ruling dynasties and the beginning of modernisation, in order to confront the west on more equal terms.

Holy war against Dutch, 1881-1908: 'the longest and toughest war in Dutch colonial history'

Saminist peasant protest movement, beginning c. 1890, culminating in serious disturbances, 1914-17

BORNEO

SUMATRA

Rebellion in Bali and Lombok, 1881-94

JAVA

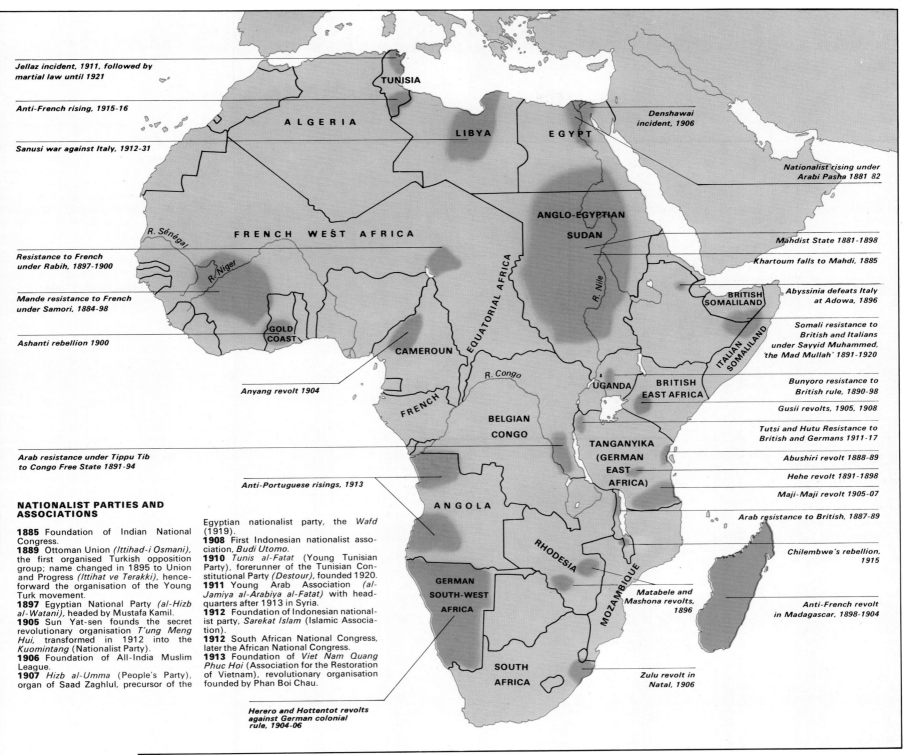

Jellaz incident, 1911, followed by martial law until 1921

Anti-French rising, 1915-16

Sanusi war against Italy, 1912-31

Resistance to French under Rabih, 1897-1900

Mande resistance to French under Samori, 1884-98

Ashanti rebellion 1900

Anyang revolt 1904

Arab resistance under Tippu Tib to Congo Free State 1891-94

Anti-Portuguese risings, 1913

Herero and Hottentot revolts against German colonial rule, 1904-06

Denshawai incident, 1906

Nationalist rising under Arabi Pasha 1881-82

Mahdist State 1881-1898

Khartoum falls to Mahdi, 1885

Abyssinia defeats Italy at Adowa, 1896

Somali resistance to British and Italians under Sayyid Muhammed, 'the Mad Mullah' 1891-1920

Bunyoro resistance to British rule, 1890-98

Gusii revolts, 1905, 1908

Tutsi and Hutu Resistance to British and Germans 1911-17

Abushiri revolt 1888-89

Hehe revolt 1891-1898

Maji-Maji revolt 1905-07

Arab resistance to British, 1887-89

Chilembwe's rebellion, 1915

Anti-French revolt in Madagascar, 1898-1904

Matabele and Mashona revolts, 1896

Zulu revolt in Natal, 1906

TUNISIA · ALGERIA · LIBYA · EGYPT · FRENCH WEST AFRICA · ANGLO-EGYPTIAN SUDAN · BRITISH SOMALILAND · ITALIAN SOMALILAND · EQUATORIAL AFRICA · CAMEROUN · FRENCH · UGANDA · BRITISH EAST AFRICA · BELGIAN CONGO · TANGANYIKA (GERMAN EAST AFRICA) · ANGOLA · RHODESIA · MOZAMBIQUE · GERMAN SOUTH-WEST AFRICA · SOUTH AFRICA · GOLD COAST · R. Sénégal · R. Niger · R. Nile · R. Congo

NATIONALIST PARTIES AND ASSOCIATIONS

1885 Foundation of Indian National Congress.
1889 Ottoman Union (Ittihad-i Osmani), the first organised Turkish opposition group; name changed in 1895 to Union and Progress (Ittihat ve Terakki), henceforward the organisation of the Young Turk movement.
1897 Egyptian National Party (al-Hizb al-Watani), headed by Mustafa Kamil.
1905 Sun Yat-sen founds the secret revolutionary organisation T'ung Meng Hui, transformed in 1912 into the Kuomintang (Nationalist Party).
1906 Foundation of All-India Muslim League.
1907 Hizb al-Umma (People's Party), organ of Saad Zaghlul, precursor of the

Egyptian nationalist party, the Wafd (1919).
1908 First Indonesian nationalist association, Budi Utomo.
1910 Tunis al-Fatat (Young Tunisian Party), forerunner of the Tunisian Constitutional Party (Destour), founded 1920.
1911 Young Arab Association (al-Jamiya al-Arabiya al-Fatat) with headquarters after 1913 in Syria.
1912 Foundation of Indonesian nationalist party, Sarekat Islam (Islamic Association).
1912 South African National Congress, later the African National Congress.
1913 Foundation of Viet Nam Quang Phuc Hoi (Association for the Restoration of Vietnam), revolutionary organisation founded by Phan Boi Chau.

Boxer uprising 1899-1900 - Shantung and Chihli

Anti-western riots, 1891

...scale republican rising, 1906-07 - Hunan, Kiangsi, Kwangtung

Nationalist revolt under Aguinaldo 1898-1902

Continuing resistance of Moros, 1898-1913

where western interference had already undermined the old order. The bankruptcy of Turkey in 1875 and of Egypt in 1879 drove home the lesson that the only hope of halting western encroachment was to get rid of archaic institutions and decadent, semi-feudal dynasties and carry through a programme of modernisation and reform. In Turkey the Russian assault in 1877 and the dismemberment of the Ottoman Empire by the European powers at the Congress of Berlin in 1878 fanned the patriotism of the Young Turks, who were to rise in revolution in 1908. In China the disastrous war with Japan in 1894-95, and the threat of partition which was its immediate consequence, led to the abortive Hundred Days' Reform of 1898 and, after its failure, to the bitterly anti-foreign Boxer rising. In Egypt the revolt of Arabi Pasha, directed first against the khedive Tewfik, a pliant tool of European interests, turned against the foreigner after the British occupation in 1882. In India the National Congress, founded in 1885, which pursued a moderate policy of constitutional reform, was overtaken after 1905 by a militant, Hindu-inspired, terrorist movement led by the Maharashtrian Brahmin, Bal Gangadhar Tilak.

All these movements were 'proto-nationalist' rather than nationalist in character; the disparate elements they brought together lacked unity and clearly defined objectives, and none achieved lasting results. In the Ottoman Empire the Young Turks deposed Sultan Abdul Hamid in 1908, but their attempts at reform floundered. In China the republic proclaimed in 1912 gave way a year later to the dictatorship of Yüan Shih-k'ai. In Persia strikes and riots in 1906 forced the Shah to convoke a national assembly, the majlis, which drew up a liberal constitution, and when his successor attempted to revoke it, he was deposed in 1909; but only two years later Mohammed Ali was restored and the majlis was suppressed. In spite of these and other setbacks the movement of protest and resistance should not be written off as a failure. Though xenophobic and anti-foreign in origin, already before 1914 it was being transformed into a modern nationalist movement. The clearest evidence of this change is the appearance of nationalist associations and political parties. Many of these were small groups of the disaffected intelligentsia; but a few already had a mass following. The membership of Sarekat Islam, the first politically-based Indonesian nationalist organisation, founded in 1912, was 360,000 in 1916 and had risen to over two million by the end of the First World War.

The First World War gave new impetus to the incipient nationalist stirring in Asia and Africa before 1914. Even earlier the flame of resistance had been fanned by the Japanese victory in the Russo-Japanese war of 1904-5, which showed that the European powers were not invincible. Chinese nationalists, Sun Yat-sen later recalled, 'regarded the Russian defeat by Japan as the defeat of the West by the East', and the repercussions were felt throughout Asia from Persia to Indo-Chieu, where it sparked off the Chieu conspiracy against France in 1906. By diverting the imperialist powers' attention from their colonies, the outbreak of war in Europe in 1914

2/The reaction in Africa (above) The partition of Africa among the European powers, inaugurated at the Berlin Conference of 1884, provoked a movement of resistance among the African peoples, which was never quelled, in spite of harsh repression. The map shows how widespread and continuous rebellion was during the whole period from 1887 to 1917.

created new opportunities. When in 1914 the British proclaimed a protectorate over Egypt, they united Egyptian opposition and gave the final impetus to anti-British sentiment, already inflamed by the notorious Denshawai incident of 1906. In Russia a major revolt broke out among the Muslim peoples of central Asia in 1916. In North Africa there were risings against the French in Tunisia in 1915-16, supported by the Sanusi tribesmen of the Sahara who had been waging war against the Italians ever since the Italian occupation of Tripolitania and Cyrenaica in 1911 and 1912. France also had to face disaffection in Annam in 1916, and in Nyasaland the withdrawal of regular troops to fight the Germans on the northern frontier made it possible for Chilembwe to stage a revolt against the British settlers in 1915. The remarkable fact is the persistence of opposition in spite of disheartening setbacks and harsh repression. None of the powers which had launched the scramble for colonies in 1884 was secure in its possessions; nowhere was the finality of European rule accepted. The tangible achievements of nationalists in this period were negligible; but by keeping the flame of resistance alive, they inaugurated the process which led, a generation later, to the collapse of the European empires and the emancipation of the colonial peoples.

European rivalries and alliances 1878 to 1914

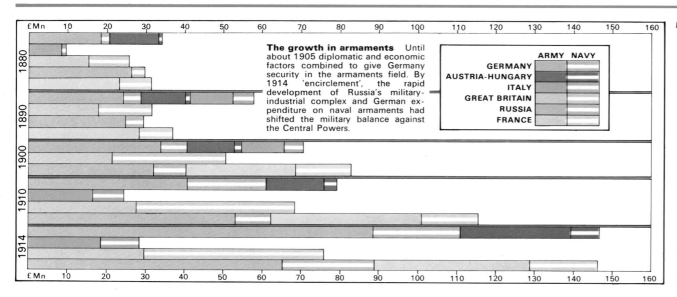

The growth in armaments Until about 1905 diplomatic and economic factors combined to give Germany security in the armaments field. By 1914 'encirclement', the rapid development of Russia's military-industrial complex and German expenditure on naval armaments had shifted the military balance against the Central Powers.

	ARMY	NAVY
GERMANY		
AUSTRIA-HUNGARY		
ITALY		
GREAT BRITAIN		
RUSSIA		
FRANCE		

1a/The Dual Alliance: October 1879 *(below)* recognised the fact that Germany could never afford to let Austria-Hungary succumb to a Russian attack, but Germany, as a conservative Empire with an interest in keeping Poland down still had much in common with Russia. Bismarck sympathised with Russia's efforts to consolidate its position in Bulgaria, and even exploited Germany's new role as an ally to force Austria-Hungary into line, pouring scorn on its attempts to enlist the support of Britain, Italy and Germany against Russia.

1b/Bismarck's system at its zenith: 1883 *(below)* Austria-Hungary, rebuffed by Gladstone, fell back on co-operation with Germany and Russia in the Three Emperors' Alliance (1881). But the Dual Monarchy still reinsured itself with the Triple Alliance (1882), which assured it of Italy's neutrality in a war with Russia; while its alliances with Serbia and Romania lessened the risk of Russia exploiting Serbian and Romanian irredentism against it. The Triple Alliance was worth more to Germany, providing for Italy's assistance in the event of a French attack.

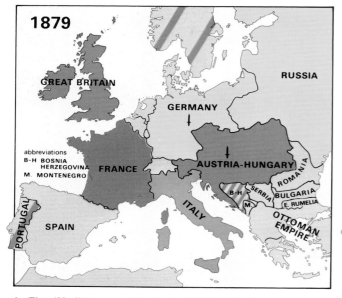

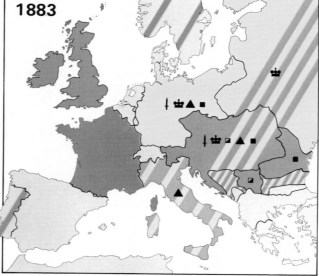

1c/The 'Mediterranean' Entente: 1887 *(below)* The Three Emperors' Alliance survived the crisis over the union of Bulgaria and E. Rumelia in 1885, but the Austro-Russian contest for control of Bulgaria (1886-87) destroyed it. Bismarck had promised the Russians his continued support in the Reinsurance Treaty, but the 'Mediterranean' agreements of Feb.-Mar. and Dec. 1887 between Britain, Italy and Austria-Hungary (Spain acceding in May), to resist supposed French and Russian designs in the Mediterranean and at the Straits, annihilated Russian influence in Bulgaria.

1d/The 'New Course' in Germany: 1891 *(below)* Italy acceded to the Austro-German-Romanian alliance in 1888, and between 1889 and 1894 Germany, with a new emperor and chancellor, swung into line behind the Mediterranean Entente. Already, before the Reinsurance Treaty was dropped after Bismarck's fall in 1890, Russo-German relations had deteriorated sharply as a result of disputes over tariffs and loans after 1887. France drew steadily closer to Russia; the first of a series of loans was concluded in 1888 and a military convention was signed in 1892.

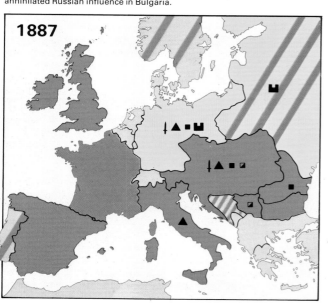

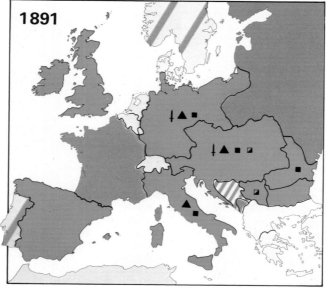

THE years 1871 to 1914 saw the apogee of the European state system. The Great Powers established their control of the non-European world to an extent never witnessed before or since; within Europe they sought security in a multi-faceted system of diplomatic alignments and alliances. Although always implying threats of war, as long as it remained flexible the system made for the peaceful adjustment of rivalries.

Four wars in a dozen years had solved the Italian and German questions and revised the map of Europe from Denmark to Sicily; for four decades after 1871 there were no more wars between the Great Powers, and although irredentist and nationalist grievances continued to fester, territorial questions had ceased to be an issue for most governments.

Of the Great Powers, only France was unable to reconcile itself to the rise of the new German Empire, which had robbed it of the primacy of Europe; this, rather than the cession of Alsace-Lorraine in 1871, was the basic cause of Franco-German estrangement. This was the one fixed point in the shifting alignments of the Great Powers during the armed peace of 1871 to 1914, but in itself it was not a threat to peace. France was in no position to challenge a Germany which had developed by the end of the century into the strongest military-industrial power in the world; nor for the first half of the period could it find an ally to provide even a diplomatic counterweight to German power.

The other five powers of Europe all accepted the changed balance of power set up in 1871. Neither Austria-Hungary nor Russia was inclined to support France because all the three eastern empires were united by a common conservative ideology of co-operation against the threat of proletarian revolution which they discerned in the Paris commune of 1871, the activities of the Second International after 1889, and the progress of social democracy consequent upon the progress of industrialisation. In 1882 even the Italian government joined the conservative camp, and clamped down firmly on irredentist propaganda about Italians still languishing under Habsburg rule. Nor could France find support elsewhere. By the 1880s a variety of economic, social, political and strategic factors was driving the European powers (except Austria) to intensify their 'imperialist' activities outside Europe; and disputes over Tunis (1881) and Egypt (1882) ensured that France's relations not only with Italy but also with Britain became as cool as her relations with Germany. Finally, dynastic links between the Hohenzollerns and the Romanovs and a community of interest in suppressing Polish nationalism, still counted for much in Russo-German relations. Altogether, Germany succeeded for twenty years after 1871 in convincing most of Europe of her conservative and pacific intentions, and France remained safely isolated.

Less intractable than the Franco-German estrangement, but equally permanent and sometimes threatening to combine with it, was the potential clash of Austro-Hungarian and Russian interests in south-east Europe, where a combination of misgovernment and insurgent nationalism threatened to destroy the Ottoman Empire (see page 214). For Russia, it was essential to ensure that no other power achieved a position from which it could control the Straits

✝	Austro-German alliance 1879-1918
♛	three Emperors' alliance 1881-7
⬙	Austro-Serbian alliance 1881-95
▲	triple alliance 1882-1915
■	Austro-German-Romanian alliance 1883-1916
⬓	reinsurance treaty 1887-90
○	Franco-Russian alliance 1894-1917
⬋	Russo-Bulgarian military convention 1902-13

Stripes, similar and identical colours indicate an entente or community of interests.

at Constantinople – through which passed much of that grain export trade on which Russia's economy and Great Power status depended. Russia's fundamental aim was therefore defensive; but its tactics varied from trying to bolster up and influence the Ottoman government, to assisting its Christian subjects against it in the hope of replacing the empire by a string of docile satellites.

To Austria-Hungary, Russia's efforts to achieve security by extending its influence in the Ottoman Empire seemed dangerous and offensive, either as threatening Austria-Hungary's 'colonial' markets in the Balkans, or as portending the encirclement of the Habsburg monarchy by a crowd of irredentist states under Russian protection. Nevertheless, for most of the period the Austrians were able to achieve a conservative understanding with the Tsarist government against revolutionary nationalism in both Russia and the Ottoman Empire. But when these agreements broke down (1878, 1886, 1908) Austria-Hungary sought salvation in trying to establish its own economic and diplomatic control of the Balkan states; and in building up blocs to oppose Russia.

In this policy Austria-Hungary could usually count on support from the United Kingdom, where many people regarded Russia's interest in the Ottoman Empire as a threat to the overland and Suez routes to India, already threatened (as they thought) by Russian expansion towards Persia and Afghanistan. Until the Anglo-Russian agreement of 1907 removed these fears, Anglo-Russian rivalry in the Near East, in central Asia and, in the 1890s, in China, was perhaps the chief determinant of diplomatic relations between the island empire and the continental Powers. The Anglo-Italo-Austrian entente of 1887-97 against Russia (and France) was, Salisbury told Queen Victoria, 'as close an alliance as the Parliamentary character of our institutions will permit'.

In the early 1890s even Germany lent her support to this combination. Already in 1887 Bismarck had increased the tariffs against Russian grain exports in order to protect the economic interests of Prussian landowners, and it was he who put a stop to Russia's borrowing on the Berlin stock exchange the money to finance potentially threatening armaments and strategic railways. When France made the Paris *bourse* available the foundations were laid for the Franco-Russian alliance of 1894. Germany's attempts to parry this by co-operating with Russia in the Far East after 1895 were only partially successful; but Russia's concentration at this period on its Far Eastern interests at least allowed the Austrians to re-establish the conservative entente in 1897. By the end of the 1890s, therefore, there were three groups of Powers in Europe: the British Empire; its chief opponent, the Franco-Russian alliance; and the Triple Alliance (Germany, Austria-Hungary, Italy) – an unstable equilibrium which allowed for endless diplomatic manoeuvring and was therefore probably conducive to peace.

The dangerous simplification of alignments into a bi-polar system started with the development of German *Weltpolitik*, a challenge to all three established imperial Powers, and one which convinced Great Britain in particular that Germany was out to dominate the European continent. By 1907 Great Britain had made up its differences with France and Russia, and joined with them in a Triple Entente to contain – or in Berlin's view to 'encircle' – Germany. By 1914 the Germans and their Austrian allies were deeply concerned about this 'encirclement', particularly in the Balkans, the most unstable area of Europe. The breakdown of the Austro-Russian entente when Austria-Hungary annexed Bosnia and the Herzegovina in 1908, and the Balkan wars of 1912 and 1913 which replaced Turkey-in-Europe by a complex of dissatisfied and mutually antagonistic Balkan states, created a highly volatile situation, and when, in 1914, it looked as though Serbian ambitions were reopening the issue, Vienna decided that it was now or never. When Berlin, impelled by the fear of 'encirclement', decided to support Vienna far beyond the terms of the defensive alliance of 1879, the fuse was lit which exploded in the First World War.

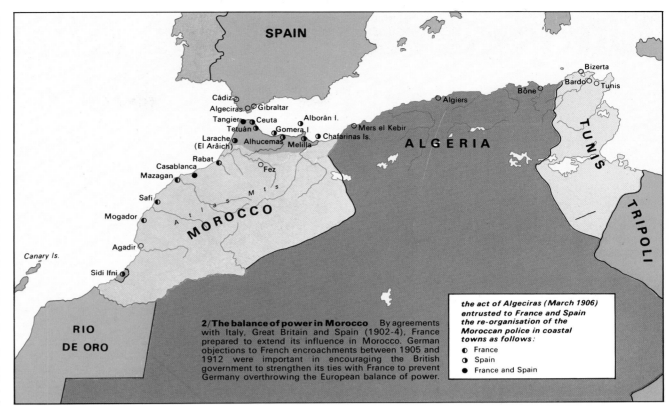

2/The balance of power in Morocco By agreements with Italy, Great Britain and Spain (1902-4), France prepared to extend its influence in Morocco. German objections to French encroachments between 1905 and 1912 were important in encouraging the British government to strengthen its ties with France to prevent Germany overthrowing the European balance of power.

the act of Algeciras (March 1906) entrusted to France and Spain the re-organisation of the Moroccan police in coastal towns as follows:
○ France
◑ Spain
● France and Spain

1e/The Austro-Russian Entente: 1897 *(below)* The Germans now abandoned the 'New Course', ceasing to underwrite Austria-Hungary in the Balkans and co-operating in the Far East with Russia and France. Britain, after the Armenian massacres, refused to promise to fight for the Sultan. Austria-Hungary, torn by domestic strife, and with its Balkan alliances in decay, settled for an entente with Russia to put Balkan problems 'on ice' (1897). Russia still improved its position in Bulgaria, signing a military convention (1902); and in Serbia, after a coup by nationalist army officers in 1903.

1f/The Anglo-French Entente: 1904 *(below)* By 1902 France – partly to weaken the Triple Alliance – had settled the 20-year dispute with Italy; in 1904 it reached agreements about Egypt and Morocco with Britain. Meanwhile, Russia and Austria-Hungary extended their entente. Germany's clumsy efforts to exploit Russia's embarrassments over Japan in order to renew formal ties with St Petersburg and to browbeat France out of recent agreements with Britain failed; the Anglo-French link was even strengthened when Russia settled its own extra-European disputes with Britain in 1907.

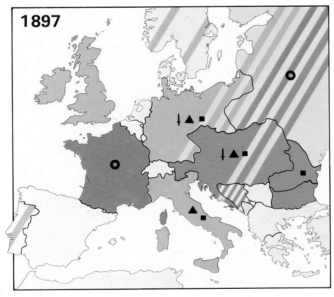

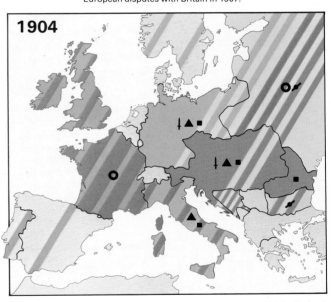

1g/Europe after the Bosnian crisis: 1909 *(below)* Between the Moroccan crises of 1905-6 and 1911, Anglo-German relations, complicated by the naval issue, reached their nadir. Friction between Russia and Austria-Hungary over the Austro-Serbian 'Pig War' (1906-11), the Sanjak railway project and the annexation of Bosnia and the Herzegovina put an end to the entente of 1897 and severely strained Russo-German relations (although the Potsdam agreement over Persia and the Baghdad railway in Nov. 1910 showed that the German 'wire to St Petersburg' had not been broken).

1h/Europe on the eve of war: 1914 *(below)* Between 1911 and 1914 the fronts between Triple Alliance and Triple Entente hardened, the grudging attitude of the latter towards Italy's ambitions in Tripoli and Albania helping restore links between Italy and her allies. In 1912-13 Austria-Hungary watched in alarm while a Russian-sponsored Balkan League expelled the Turks from Europe. The Austro-Romanian alliance was a dead letter. Although there were signs of Anglo-German co-operation on Balkan and colonial issues, Russo-German relations deteriorated sharply.

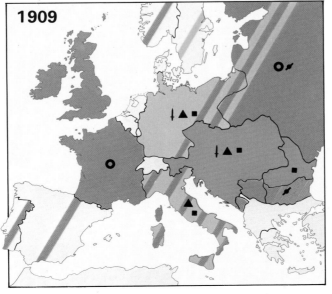

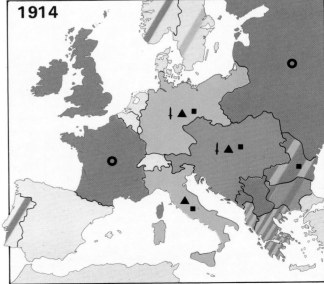

The First World War 1914 to 1918

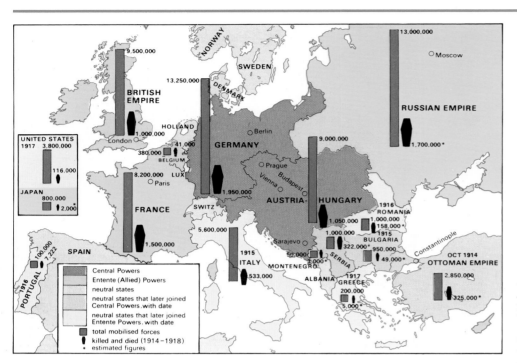

UNITED STATES
1917 3,800,000
116,000

JAPAN
800,000
2,000

Central Powers
Entente (Allied) Powers
neutral states
neutral states that later joined Central Powers, with date
neutral states that later joined Entente Powers, with date
total mobilised forces
killed and died (1914–1918)
estimated figures

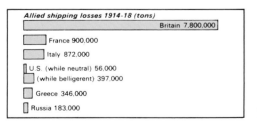

Allied shipping losses 1914-18 (tons)

Britain	7,800,000
France	900,000
Italy	872,000
U.S. (while neutral)	56,000
(while belligerent)	397,000
Greece	346,000
Russia	183,000

The naval war *(above)* After the battle of Jutland (1916) in which the Germans inflicted heavier losses but the British retained command of the North Sea, both sides used naval means to cut the other's supply lines in a war of attrition. The British instituted an open blockade of the Central Powers which became effective by the end of 1916. In that year, there were fifty-six food riots in German cities. In reply, the Germans resorted to unrestricted submarine warfare in February 1917 and one out of every four ships leaving British ports was sunk *(above)*. This assault was only checked by the convoy system, first used in May 1917.

T HE war which began in August 1914 – to contemporaries the 'Great War', to posterity the 'First World War' – marked the end of one period of history and the beginning of another. Starting as a European war, it turned in 1917 into a world war, and thus can be seen as a bridge between the age of European predominance and the age of global politics. The spark that triggered it off was the assassination of the Austrian heir-presumptive, Archduke Franz Ferdinand, by Bosnian terrorists at Sarajevo on 28 June 1914. In the ensuing crisis, none of the powers was prepared to accept diplomatic defeat; war replaced diplomatic manoeuvre.

Everyone expected a short war, over by Christmas 1914. The Germans knew that their chances in a long war on two fronts were slender. Their war plan, drawn up by Schlieffen in 1897, was to trap and annihilate the French army by a great encircling movement through Belgium, before the Russians had time to mobilise. But the Russians mobilised unexpectedly quickly, invaded East Prussia, defeated the German 8th Army at Gumbinnen (20 August), and drew off German reserves from the west. However, the Germans defeated the Russian invasion at Tannenberg (26-29 August), but were not strong enough to exploit their victory. In the west the Allies outmanoeuvred the Germans in the Battle of the Marne (see map 2), 5-8 September. The Schlieffen Plan was always a gamble; when it failed the Germans had no alternative strategy. On 8-12 September the Russians won a crushing victory over Austria at Lemberg. A last, mutual, attempt by the German and Allied armies to outflank each other in Flanders failed in November, and both sides dug in on a line 400 miles

1/The line-up of the Powers *(above)* By 1914 the European powers were already divided into two rival camps (see page 251). After the outbreak of war both groups sought allies. Germany and Austria-Hungary were joined by Turkey and Bulgaria. Russia, France and Great Britain sought and gained the support of Japan, Italy, Romania and, after a long struggle, Greece. By far the most important adherent to the Allied cause was the United States, which declared war on Germany on 6 April 1917. In Europe, the price in terms of human life and material destruction changed men's conception of war; it is estimated that over eight million combatants were killed.

long from the Channel to the Swiss frontier. In the east, mobile warfare was still possible because of the far lower density of men and guns – a possibility brilliantly exploited by the Germans at Gorlice-Tarnow in 1915, and by the Russian general Brusilov in 1916.

In the west, from the beginning of 1915 the dominant factors were trenches, barbed wire, artillery, machine-guns and mud. The war of mobility gave way to a war of attrition. One entrenched man with a machine-gun was more than a match for a hundred advancing across open country. Railways could bring up defenders faster than slowly-moving troops could advance into the front-line gaps which they had created at such high human cost.

Yet the German occupation of Belgium and northern France made it inevitable that the Allies should seek to expel them. This meant repeated French offensives in Artois and Champagne in 1915, assisted by small British offensives at Neuve Chapelle and Loos. For 1916 the Allies planned a joint offensive on the Somme, but the Germans struck first, at Verdun, with the intention of bleeding the French army to death. Casualties ran to over 700,000. On 1 July 1916, the British launched their first mass offensive of the war, on the Somme. The fighting lasted until November and the casualties totalled at least 1,000,000. It failed to break the stalemate.

By now the conflict was becoming a total war demanding mobilisation of industry, carried out in Germany by Rathenau and in Britain by Lloyd George. Answers to the trench stalemate were sought in technology; poison gas was first used by the Germans at Bolinów in January 1915; the British invented the tank and fielded 32 of them in the closing stages of the Somme battle, but due to manufacturing difficulties it was only in November 1917, at Cambrai, that the first mass tank attack took place – also proving indecisive.

The struggle spread to the skies, where the handful of reconnaissance aircraft of 1914 gave place to fighters, bombers and artillery-spotters. With the Zeppelin airship and the Gotha long-range bomber the Germans introduced strategic bombing of enemy towns. Using naval blockades

the Allies sought to starve the industries and peoples of the Central powers; Germany riposted by U-boat attacks on British shipping.

Confronted by failure in the west, the Allies sought successes on other fronts: the Dardanelles (April 1915 - January 1916); an offensive in Mesopotamia against the Turks; a landing at Salonika to help the Serbs. All ended in failure. Italy, which entered the war on the Allied side on 23 May 1915, likewise failed to break the Austrian front on the Isonzo.

On the Eastern Front, too, there was no decision, despite the German-Austrian offensive at Gorlice-Tarnow in 1915 and a far-reaching Russian advance under General Brusilov in 1916. Serbian resistance was crushed, but the Germans were now embedded in the prolonged two-front war they had dreaded. By the end of 1916 all the combatants recognised that victory was far off. There were peace feelers, but annexationist demands ruled out a compromise peace. The war went on – under new and ruthless leaders: the soldiers Hindenburg and Ludendorff in Germany, the civilians Lloyd George in Britain and later Clemenceau in France. On 1 February 1917 Germany declared unrestricted U-boat warfare, in the hope of bringing Britain to her knees. This was narrowly averted by the introduction of the convoy system in May 1917. But the U-boat offensive brought the United States into the war on 6 April 1917 – a potentially decisive help to the Allies.

In March, revolution broke out in Russia, sparked by heavy losses, war-weariness and economic dislocation. On 15 March 1917 the Tsar abdicated. The future of Russia as an ally lay in doubt. By May France was in deep trouble too. An offensive by the new Commander-in-Chief, Nivelle, failed to achieve his promised object of a breakthrough leading to peace. Widespread

2/The German attack in the west and the battle of the Marne *(left)* 1 Germans invaded Belgium, successfully taking Liège on 16 August; the French offensive in Alsace was defeated with heavy loss. 2 A further French offensive towards the Ardennes was defeated, and the British and one French army were forced to retreat from the Mons area to avoid encirclement. 3 The Germans were too weak to go west of Paris as they planned, and passed north-east of Paris to cross the Marne. 4 The exposed German army north of Paris was attacked by the French army on 5 September, and in manoeuvring to oppose the French attack left a gap on its own eastern flank. 5 British and French advanced into the gap. 6 The German army retired to the Aisne to regroup.

German "Schlieffen Plan" to encircle Paris
actual route of German armies

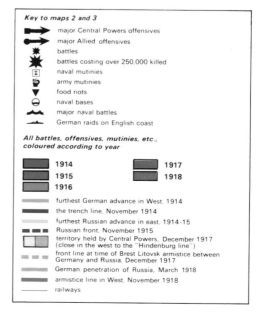

Munitions factory in England *(above)* As a result of the labour shortage, the British used women to do men's work in offices, factories and behind the front lines in France. Political emancipation came immediately after the war.

Key to maps 2 and 3

major Central Powers offensives
major Allied offensives
battles
battles costing over 250,000 killed
naval mutinies
army mutinies
food riots
naval bases
major naval battles
German raids on English coast

All battles, offensives, mutinies, etc., coloured according to year

	1914		1917
	1915		1918
	1916		

furthest German advance in West, 1914
the trench line, November 1914
furthest Russian advance in east, 1914-15
Russian front, November 1915
territory held by Central Powers, December 1917 (close in the west to the "Hindenburg line")
front line at time of Brest Litovsk armistice between Germany and Russia, December 1917
German penetration of Russia, March 1918
armistice line in West, November 1918
railways

mutinies erupted in the French army with parallel civilian unrest on the home front. The British planned an offensive at Ypres as the best means of keeping German pressure off the French and encouraging Russia. The 'Passchendaele' offensive, dogged by bad weather, failed to break the German front; each side suffered some 250,000 casualties.

In November 1917 the Bolsheviks seized power in Russia (see page 258) and in December sued for peace at Brest-Litovsk. At last the Germans could concentrate the bulk of their strength on the Western Front. On 21 March 1918 Hindenburg and Ludendorff launched a series of offensives aimed at victory in the West before the Americans could arrive in strength. They failed, despite impressive initial success. On 18 July the new Allied generalissimo, Foch, launched a French counterstroke. On 8 August Haig followed with a brilliant success on the Somme. From then on the Allies hammered the enemy without respite, breaking the Hindenburg Line on 27-30 September. Meanwhile Germany's allies, Austria, Turkey and Bulgaria were beginning to collapse under Allied offensives. On 29 September Ludendorff acknowledged defeat and urged his government to ask for an immediate armistice. In October the German fleet mutinied; revolution and the abdication of the Kaiser followed, and the new German gov-

ernment accepted the Allies' armistice terms. Fighting stopped on 11 November 1918.

The material and human cost of the war had been immense; the political and social consequences were incalculable. The Europe of 1914 had vanished.

4/The war in the Middle East *(right)* The war was not confined to Europe. In order to protect the Persian oil wells an Anglo-Indian force occupied Basra (22 Nov. 1914), and marched on Baghdad (Oct. 1915); they were forced to retreat and surrendered to the Turks at Kut (April 1916). Meanwhile, the British had repelled a Turkish attempt to cross the Suez Canal (1915), and a counter-offensive force entered Palestine in 1916. Here they were assisted by the British-sponsored Arab revolt against Ottoman rule, which broke out in June 1916 under Sherif Hussein of Mecca, but they were checked by the Turks at Gaza in 1917. To the north, the Russians occupied Turkish Armenia (July 1916), and held it until the Russian revolution restored initiative to the Ottomans. In Autumn 1917, British forces under General Allenby rallied, and pushed through Gaza to Jerusalem (11 Dec.). In Mesopotamia Kut was retaken, and Baghdad was finally captured (10 March 1917); Mosul was occupied shortly after the Anglo-Turkish Armistice (29 Oct. 1918), while Damascus had fallen to British and Arab troops at the beginning of the same month.

The war spilled over into Africa and the Far East where Germany quickly lost its colonial possessions (see page 244). The South Africans conquered German South-West Africa in July 1915; the British and French took the Cameroons and Togoland. In German East Africa the British had a far more difficult task because of the determined German defence under General von Lettow-Vorbeck. In the Pacific, Australian, New Zealand and Japanese troops captured the German colonies within four months of the outbreak of war, and the concessions in China also fell to Japanese and British forces.

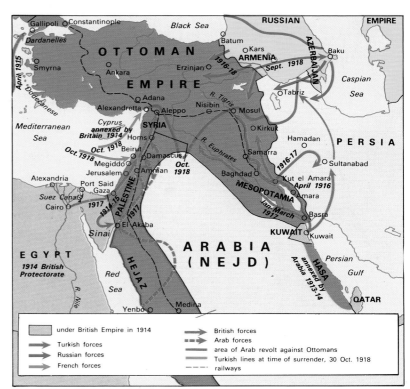

under British Empire in 1914	British forces
Turkish forces	Arab forces
Russian forces	area of Arab revolt against Ottomans
French forces	Turkish lines at time of surrender, 30 Oct. 1918
	railways

3/The Great War in Europe *(below)* On the Western Front only the opening and closing stages (see map 2) saw a war of movement. From late 1914 to Spring 1918, the superiority of defence based on trench-systems and machine-guns over slow-moving offensives by infantry, preceded by the fire of immense concentrations of artillery, imposed a stalemate. Only when armies had been weakened by years of attrition did sweeping advances again become possible. In Eastern Europe and the Balkans, with a lower density of manpower and weaker defences, the war was more mobile. The Italian front along the River Isonzo saw another stalemate despite eleven Italian offensives against the Austrians; a stalemate broken in October 1917 by the German-Austrian victory at Caporetto, and the Italian victory at Vittorio Veneto a year later.

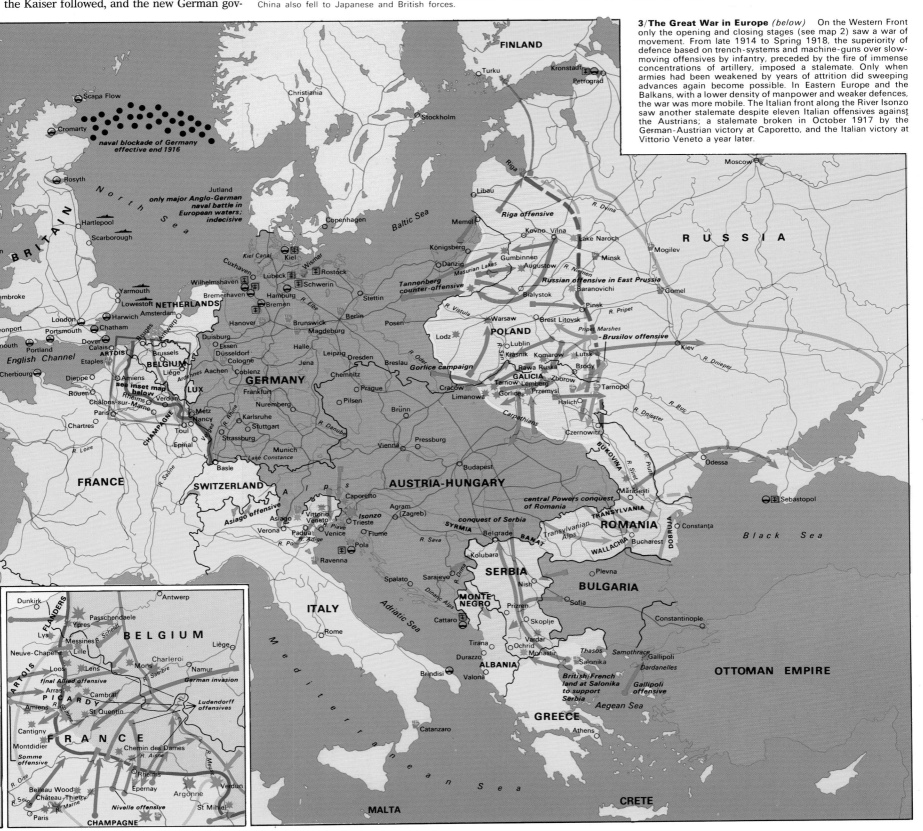

THE date at which the European age was succeeded by the age of global civilisation is a matter of debate. Some historians have picked out 1917 as a year of destiny. Others have seen 1947, the year of Indian independence, and 1949, the year of the Chinese revolution, as decisive turning points. The United States' declaration of war in 1917 turned a European conflict into a world war; the Bolshevik revolution in Russia, challenging the existing social and political order, split the world into two conflicting ideological camps; the independence of India and the revolution in China symbolised the resurgence of Asia and the gathering revolt against the west. All were important events in world history; but even earlier a single world economy was in existence, and the rise of the United States to world power between 1867 and 1917 was an omen of things to come.

Today it is obvious that we are in a post-European age. By making the whole world one, the European powers stirred up forces which spelled their own eclipse. The European civil war – or what has been called the second Thirty Years War, from 1914 to 1945 – whittled away the resources of the European powers, and only the healing of the wounds, symbolised by the formation of the European Economic Community in 1957, restored their fortunes. The residuary legatees, when the Second World War ended in 1945, were the Soviet Union and the United States, the two superpowers on the eastern and western flanks, whose rivalry seemed for twenty years to herald an age of bipolarity. But bipolarity may prove to be a temporary phenomenon. The recovery of Europe, the emancipation of Asia and Africa, and the rise of Japan to the first rank among the industrial powers, brought a new constellation into being, and with it the threat of a confrontation between rich nations and poor nations, and between the white and coloured peoples. Whether this is the shape of things to come, no one can foretell. All this section can do is to show, in historical perspective, how the world balance changed during the past fifty or sixty years, and the new factors in the situation.

7

The age o

The Statue of Liberty and World Trade Center, New York

global civilisation

The formation of a world economy 1870 to 1914

ONE of the main features of the period between 1870 and 1914 was the way in which the world's economy became knitted together into a single interdependent whole, to an extent inconceivable in earlier ages. The focus of this process was Europe, with the United States as a subsidiary centre, and it was from there that the impulses went out which opened up the last unknown landmasses of the globe to European exploration and penetration, as well as linking the continents, settled and unsettled, colonial and independent, with the industrial and commercial capitalism which had conquered most of Europe and North America in the preceding age.

Three closely interrelated aspects of this process are illustrated here. One was the development of means of communication, with railways and shipping taking a main share, but canals and river navigation as well as roads also playing a significant part in some areas of the globe. The basic technical problems of railways had been solved well before 1870, though improvements in speed, capacity, safety, reliability and comfort were continuously being made afterwards. Yet at that date they were limited almost wholly to Europe and the United States, and even there complete networks could be said to have existed only in north-western Europe and in the eastern states of the USA: indeed, the first United States 'transcontinental' link between the Pacific and Atlantic Oceans had been forged only in 1869, though others were to follow in 1881, 1883 and 1893. In 1870, Europe had 60,400 miles of track open, the United States and Canada 56,300 miles, and the rest of the world 9,100 miles – most of which had been built by European or North American engineers. By 1911 the world's network of tracks had increased to 657,000 miles, the areas outside Europe, the United States and Canada now accounting for 175,000 miles. Among the most striking achievements were the completion of transcontinental lines in Canada (1886), in Russia to the Pacific coast at Vladivostok (1904) and in South America, to cross the Andes, in 1910. Railways also breached many other mountain barriers which had hitherto inhibited traffic flows between adjacent countries: the main lines and tunnels across the Alps are illustrated here in map 2. Yet it will be noticed that despite its relatively rapid growth, the rest of the world's mileage still largely consisted of single trunk lines instead of the dense network of the industrial countries. This reflected the differing role of the railways in regions outside Europe and North America, where they were often built primarily as strategic lines, or as a means of tapping certain exportable primary products, rather than as an integral part of an industrialised community.

The expansion of world shipping was equally striking. It was in fact greater than the statistics indicate, as in 1870 most of the world's tonnage, apart from the British, still consisted of sailing vessels, whereas by 1913 it was composed mostly of steamers. Because of the higher speed and greater regularity obtainable in powered ships, one steam ton was generally reckoned to be the equivalent of four sailing tons, while steamers themselves greatly increased in speed and efficiency. For passengers, comfort and safety also improved. The diagram (far right) contrasts the conditions and amenities available in one of the earlier passenger liners with one of the finest vessels of the immediate pre-war years. By such developments the hardships of the crossing, which once held back emigration except among the poor and desperate, were largely removed for the millions who now flocked to North and South America, while for first-class passengers crossings on regular liners became indulgences of luxury. Again, it will be observed, the main shipping traffic was to be found among the advanced countries and the white dominions, or

between them and their producers of raw materials. The traffic among the latter had grown but little.

Canals were also built in this period, particularly in Europe. Those of the greatest significance for world trade were the ship canals that broke through important land barriers. The Suez Canal, completed in 1869, carried 437,000 net register tons in 1870 and 20,034,000 net tons in 1913; the Panama Canal, opened in August 1914, carried 4,900,000 tons of cargo in its first year. The savings in miles achieved by these two canals were particularly significant for the journeys from Europe to India, and for the routes from the east coast to the west coast of the United States.

These developments in transport reflected the concurrent developments in trade. Foreign trade, as a proportion of world output, increased from 3 per cent to 33 per cent between 1800 and 1913. It grew some threefold in volume between 1870 and 1914, and again we observe its concentration on the links among the industrialised countries, or between them and their suppliers of primary materials, and the varied markets now opening up for their manufactures: only 11 per cent of the world's trade was carried on among the primary producers themselves in 1913. Among industrial nations, trade permitted specialisation, with some advantages to consumers' choice and a very considerable contribution to furthering large-scale production. But trade between them and the primary producers was of a different nature. While in a sense it 'opened up' the latter to receive western influences of all kinds, it was not in any way directed by them, nor did it reflect their needs, except accidentally. The initiative came from entrepreneurs in the West, looking for markets, food and raw materials.

The operation of a single multi-national system of world trade, pivoting on London, was made possible by the adoption of a gold stan-

Suez and Panama *(above)* Not until the advent of the commercial aeroplane was the world again so significantly shrunk as by the opening of these two great canals.

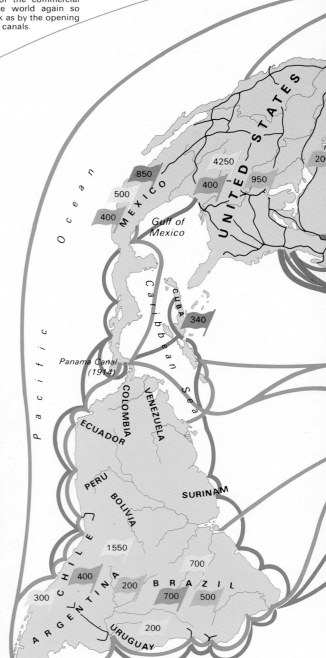

		Europe	N. America	S. America	Asia	Africa
UNITED KINGDOM	imports 1860	419	252	96	143	80
	exports 1860	358	132	74	139	36
	imports 1913	1,548	848	393	458	220
	exports 1913	917	265	272	620	248
USA	imports 1860	217	—	80	29	—
	exports 1860	249	—	46	11	—
	imports 1913	893	199	381	298	26
	exports 1913	1,479	469	294	140	29
FRANCE	imports 1860	234	47	41	16	34
	exports 1860	293	49	53	3	45
	imports 1913	880	187	183	192	148
	exports 1913	937	89	94	36	181
HOLLAND	imports 1860	92	5	3	32	—
	exports 1860	87	2	1	14	—
	imports 1913	624	190	87	274	14
	exports 1913	1,131	57	9	73	14
GERMANY	imports 1913	1,402	423	290	250	118
	exports 1913	1,828	184	183	130	50
RUSSIA	imports 1913	556	—	—	—	—
	exports 1913	719	—	—	—	—

figures in million dollars US

Balance of world trade *(diagram left)* and **share of world trade 1860 and 1913** *(diagram right)* Great Britain was the world's biggest trading nation in 1860 but by 1913 Germany had twice the exports to Europe and America was catching up just as fast. British, Dutch and French networks in the wider world were still predominant.

1860
share of world
total $8 billion

dard for the currencies of the chief European nations between 1863 and 1874. It was also intimately connected with the third type of international linkage shown here: foreign investment. Normally flowing from the more advanced to the poorer regions, the transfer of capital had earlier in the 19th century been largely a phenomenon occurring within Europe and North America, and indeed much of it was still of this kind in 1914. In this setting, the process undoubtedly assisted and speeded economic advancement, especially when devoted to building up the costly infrastructure, such as railways and other public works, for developing nations which could then ultimately repay their international debts. But increasingly, as these investments flowed into the non-industrial regions of Europe such as Russia, the Balkan countries and the Ottoman Empire, and then to overseas territories which were without either the knowledge or the power to direct the capital flow, it did not help to develop them, but rather

to colonise them, often destroying what native industry there was. Where the loans were made to governments, or to enterprises guaranteed by government, as many inevitably were, they raised serious quesions of political control, and as rival European powers fought for concessions and controls in overseas areas, the rivalries and conflicts engendered thereby became part of the drive to 'imperialism' and to war.

Britain was the largest source of foreign investment, and London a highly important centre of banking. British overseas assets in 1914 totalled nearly £4000 million. France and Germany were the other chief lenders, but the total foreign investments of France, Germany, Belgium, Holland and the United States put together amounted to less than £5500 million. The United States and Russia were still, in fact, net borrowers of foreign capital.

Closely associated with the movement of capital was the large-scale migration of labour illustrated on page 208.

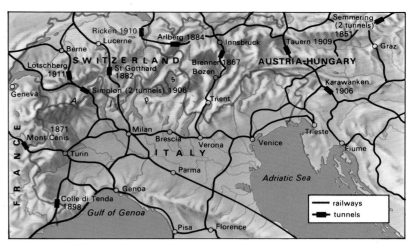

2/Alpine tunnels and railways *(above)* Only two rail routes pierced the Alps in 1870, but in the next forty-one years they were joined by another ten, many of them involving feats of tunnel-building and civil engineering on a previously unparalleled scale.

1/The development of the world economy *(below)* Between 1870 and 1914 the whole world became closely connected by an intricate web of transport routes, communication channels, trading relationships and financial flows. The major benefits, however, remained concentrated where the network was at its most dense — among the industrial nations of Europe and North America.

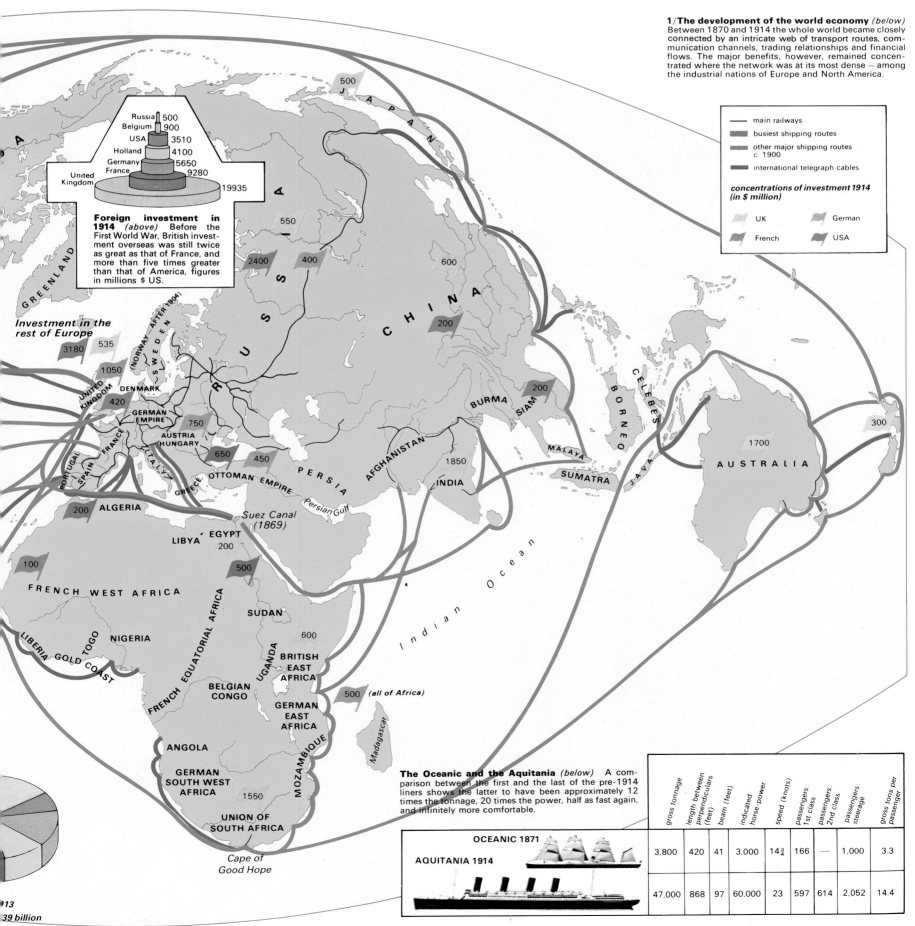

Foreign investment in 1914 *(above)* Before the First World War, British investment overseas was still twice as great as that of France, and more than five times greater than that of America, figures in millions $ US.

| main railways |
| busiest shipping routes |
| other major shipping routes c. 1900 |
| international telegraph cables |

concentrations of investment 1914 (in $ million)
| UK | German |
| French | USA |

The Oceanic and the Aquitania *(below)* A comparison between the first and the last of the pre-1914 liners shows the latter to have been approximately 12 times the tonnage, 20 times the power, half as fast again, and infinitely more comfortable.

	gross tonnage	length between perpendiculars (feet)	beam (feet)	indicated horse-power	Speed (knots)	Passengers 1st class	Passengers 2nd class	Passengers steerage	gross tons per passenger
OCEANIC 1871	3,800	420	41	3,000	14¾	166	—	1,000	3.3
AQUITANIA 1914	47,000	868	97	60,000	23	597	614	2,052	14.4

The Russian Revolution
1917 to 1925

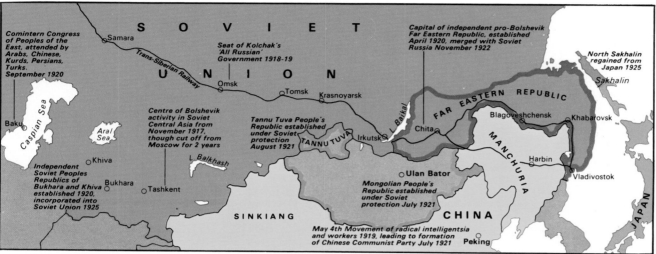

Comintern Congress of Peoples of the East, attended by Arabs, Chinese, Kurds, Persians, Turks. September 1920

Seat of Kolchak's 'All Russian' Government 1918-19

Capital of independent pro-Bolshevik Far Eastern Republic, established April 1920, merged with Soviet Russia November 1922

North Sakhalin regained from Japan 1925

Centre of Bolshevik activity in Soviet Central Asia from November 1917, though cut off from Moscow for 2 years

Tannu Tuva People's Republic established under Soviet protection August 1921

Independent Soviet Peoples Republics of Bukhara and Khiva established 1920, incorporated into Soviet Union 1925

Mongolian People's Republic established under Soviet protection July 1921

May 4th Movement of radical intelligentsia and workers 1919, leading to formation of Chinese Communist Party July 1921

3/Red Star over Asia *(left)* ' ...the east has been definitely drawn into the revolutionary movement... In the last analysis, the outcome of the struggle will be determined by the fact that Russia, India, China, etc. account for the overwhelming majority of the population of the globe.' (From Lenin's last article, March 1923). As the prospects of revolution dimmed in the west, Lenin looked eastwards to the backward countries colonised by the great powers. Here the struggle for national independence might be combined with the fight for socialism. Victory, though perhaps far off, would fatally weaken the capitalist world.

Architect of revolution *(left)* From its foundation in 1903, Lenin dominated the Bolshevik party. His combination of theoretical originality, political decisiveness and passionate dedication to the socialist cause made him the greatest revolutionary leader of modern times. Trotsky *(bottom right of picture),* the only other Bolshevik whose stature approached Lenin's during the revolution and civil war, himself acknowledged that without Lenin the Bolshevik revolution would have been impossible.

2/Red Star over Europe *(below)* 'If we come out now, we shall have all proletarian Europe on our side.' (Lenin, October 1917). The Bolsheviks seized power firmly convinced that socialist revolution was imminent in advanced western countries. These, they believed, would come to the aid of backward Russia. At first events in central and eastern Europe seemed to justify their optimism. By 1921, however, revolution was on the retreat, and Soviet Russia isolated.

NO other single event has had such decisive impact upon the modern world as the Russian Revolution of 1917. It opened a new epoch in Russia's history, transforming an under-developed country into an industrial and military superpower, fundamentally altering the pattern of international relations. Above all, it inaugurated the age of modern revolutions. By showing that Marxists could gain power and begin the construction of a socialist society, the Bolsheviks inspired revolutionaries everywhere to emulate their victory. After 1917 the world could never be the same again.

By March 1917 the strain of war had fatally weakened the Tsarist government. Liberals, socialists, businessmen, generals, nobles – all were plotting its overthrow. Yet the disturbances in Petrograd which in four days destroyed the regime owed little to organised opposition. Sheer hunger turned wage demands into a general strike and bread queues into anti-government demonstrations. Ordered to disperse the crowds, the garrison mutinied. Nicholas II set out for the capital from his headquarters at Mogilev, but was prevented from arriving by railway workers. On 15 March at Pskov he abdicated. Authority now passed to a Provisional Government established by prominent Duma politicians. But its power was limited by the existence of the Petrograd Soviet (or Council) of Workers' and Soldiers' Deputies. The latter, looked to for leadership by Soviets throughout Russia, effectively constituted an alternative government. At first, however, the instability of 'dual power' was not apparent. The Soviet's moderate, Menshevik and Socialist-Revolutionary leaders supported the Government, and in May entered it. Even the Bolsheviks initially gave their qualified support.

Their policy was dramatically reversed in April when Lenin returned to Petrograd. All Europe, he declared, was on the brink of socialist revolution. Marxists should therefore destroy the Provisional Government and transfer all power to the Soviets. This was a crucial turning-point. The Government, struggling to maintain order amid mounting chaos, was now faced with outright opposition. As the war dragged on, the desire for peace spread, and desertions from the army escalated. Impatient with official procrastination over agrarian reform, the peasants began to seize the land, Urban workers, discontented about failures to improve their conditions, became increasingly militant. Support grew for the Bolsheviks, with their promise of peace, land and bread. In September they won control of the Petrograd and Moscow Soviets, and in October gained a majority at the Second All-Russian Congress of Soviets. The outcome was inevitable – a coup by Left or Right. In September the Commander-in-Chief, General Kornilov, marched on the capital, only to be abandoned by his troops. Two months later, on 7 November (25 October according to the old calendar), the Bolsheviks struck. Organised by Trotsky, they seized strategic points in Petrograd, arrested the Provisional Government and in the name of the Soviets, assumed power.

But could they retain it? Few people thought so. Even the Bolsheviks believed only revolution in western Europe could guarantee survival. When Germany demanded humiliating territorial concessions in return for peace, a majority wanted to fight on, however hopelessly, rather than capitulate. Nevertheless, Lenin's determination to gain time prevailed, and the Treaty of Brest-Litovsk was signed. Almost immediately, White Russian armies, assisted by foreign powers, attacked the young Soviet republic. After three years of brutal civil war, the Bolsheviks emerged victorious – but at enormous cost. Thirteen million people perished in the war and subsequent famine. The economy was shattered, with industrial production in 1920 at only a seventh of its 1913 level. Money lost significance and was replaced by a barter system which, combined with an attempt at state direction of the economy, was dignified by the title 'War Communism'. In the battle with counter-revolution democracy vanished, dictatorial power exercised by the Communist Party replacing rule by Soviets in all but name. As the war ended, a wave of strikes and riots broke out, culminating in mutiny at the Kronstadt naval base in February 1921. The regime was in no mood for political concessions and ruthlessly suppressed rebellion. Economic concessions, however, were granted. In March 1921, Lenin announced the New Economic Policy (NEP). Food requisitioning was replaced by a 'tax in kind', with peasants allowed to sell surplus produce on the free market. Private firms were freed from government control; the retail trade largely returned to private hands. In effect, a market economy was restored.

Again the Bolsheviks won a breathing-space. By late 1925, industrial production had virtually regained its pre-war level. Relative prosperity created a more relaxed atmosphere, reflected especially in cultural life. Despite the failure of revolutionary movements elsewhere, greater security resulted from resumption of relations with the outside world. A trade agreement with Britain in 1921 was followed by the Rapallo Treaty of 1922 with Germany, and by diplomatic recognition in 1924 from Britain, France and other European countries.

This new-found stability could not last. Soviet Russia was isolated and surrounded by hostile capitalist powers. The majority of the population were still peasants wedded to their land, sharing few of their rulers' socialist aims. How could Russia advance? Was NEP a pause before renewal of the socialist offensive, or a long-term programme for acquiring the economic preconditions for socialism? Lenin provided no answer before his death in January 1924. During the struggle for the succession, two distinct lines emerged: Trotsky's policy of encouraging revolution abroad and industrialising rapidly at home, and Stalin's strategy of gradual economic growth plus recognition of capitalism's temporary stabilisation – 'permanent revolution' versus 'socialism in one country'. Labelled an extremist, by 1925 Trotsky had been manoeuvred out of high government office. Stalin and Bukharin now dominated Soviet politics. Moderation, it seemed, had triumphed.

Civil war Jan.-May 1918 Marxists defeated

Communists control Riga Jan.-May 1918

Unsuccessful Communist uprising October 1923

A Soviet Republic proclaimed January 1919. Lasts 4 weeks

German revolution overthrows Kaiser, brings socialists to power November 1918. Communist (Spartakist) uprising crushed January 1919

Unsuccessful Communist insurrection March 1921

Red Army, attacking Poland after Polish invasion of the Ukraine, defeated outside Warsaw August 1920

Bavarian Soviet Republic proclaimed April 1919. Lasts 4 weeks

Slovakian Soviet Republic proclaimed July 1919. Lasts 3 weeks

Hungarian Soviet Republic headed by Bela Kun March-August 1919

Communist uprising crushed September 1923

Legend:
- boundary of the Russian Empire, 1914
- front between Russia and Central Powers, March 1917
- principal towns where Bolsheviks took power, Nov. 1917 – Feb. 1918 (dates in new calendar)
- boundary of Russian territory occupied by Central Powers following the Treaty of Brest-Litovsk, March 1918
- boundary of area controlled by the Bolsheviks, August 1918
- eastern boundary of area controlled by the Bolsheviks, April 1919
- area controlled by the Bolsheviks, October 1919
- boundary of Soviet Territory, March 1921
- boundary of areas controlled by anti-Bolshevik forces, May 1920
- White Russian armies
- non-Russian anti-Bolshevik forces

NORWAY

SWEDEN

Entente fleet

Barents Sea

Murmansk

BRITISH FRENCH CANADIANS ITALIANS SERBS

White Sea

CANADIANS AMERICANS

BRITISH FRENCH

Archangel
17 Feb 1918

FINLAND

FINNS

Independence of Finland recognised December 1917

Petrozavodsk
17 Jan 1918

L. Ladoga

L. Onega

Helsinki

Kronstadt

British fleet

Revel (Tallinn)
8 Nov 1917

ESTONIA

Yudenich

Petrograd (Leningrad)
7 Nov 1917

Kornelov's attack on Petrograd September 1917

Novgorod
27 Nov 1917

Vologda
8 Feb 1918

BOLSHEVIK   RUSSIA

Vyatka
8 Dec 1917

Perm
14 Nov 1917

Nicholas II and family shot by Bolsheviks July 1918

Yekaterinburg (Sverdlovsk)
8 Nov 1917

LETTS

Riga

LATVIA

BALTIC GERMANS

Pskov
15 Nov 1917

Kostroma
15 Dec 1917

Yaroslavl **9 Nov 1917**

Izhevsk
9 Nov 1917

Kolchak 1918-19

LITHUANIA

GERMANY (E PRUSSIA)

Vitebsk
9 Nov 1917

Tver (Kalinin)
10 Nov 1917

Ivanovo
7 Nov 1917

Nizhny Novgorod (Gorkiy)
10 Nov 1917

Kazan
8 Nov 1917

Ufa
8 Nov 1917

CZECHS

Warsaw

Minsk
7 Nov 1917

Smolensk
12 Nov 1917

Moscow
15 Nov 1917

Government moved from Petrograd March 1918

Kaluga
11 Dec 1917

POLAND

Brest-Litovsk

Mogilev
1 Dec 1917

Tula
20 Dec 1917

Trans-Siberian Railway

Samara
9 Nov 1917

POLES

Gomel
12 Nov 1917

Orel
14 Nov 1917

Tambov
13 Feb 1918

Penza
4 Jan 1918

Orenburg
31 Jan 1918

CZECHOSLOVAKIA

Zhitomir
22 Jan 1918

Kiev
8 Feb 1918

Denikin 1919

Voronezh
12 Nov 1917

Saratov
9 Nov 1917

HUNGARY

ROMANIANS

Poltava
19 Jan 1918

Kharkov
24 Dec 1917

Don Cossacks
1917-19

Ural Cossack Army 1918-20

BESSARABIA

Yekaterinoslav (Dnepropetrovsk)
11 Jan 1918

R. Don

Tsaritsyn (Stalingrad, Volgograd)
27 Nov 1917

ROMANIA

Kishinev
10 Dec 1917

FRENCH

Nikolayev
27 Jan 1918

Novocherkassk
25 Feb 1918

Rostov-on-Don
10 Nov 1917

Odessa
31 Jan 1918

Wrangel 1920

Cossacks

R. Volga

Astrakhan
7 Feb 1918

BULGARIA

Sevastopol
29 Dec 1917

Simferopol
26 Jan 1918

FRENCH

Novorossiysk
14 Dec 1917

BRITISH

Black   Sea

Entente fleet

BRITISH

Batum

Georgians

1919-20

Mensheviks

Caspian Sea

Baku
15 Nov 1917

Krasnovodsk

Kars

Tiflis (Tbilisi)

BRITISH

BRITISH

TURKEY

Tabriz

1918-19

PERSIA

1/Russia in War and Revolution Under the intolerable pressure of war, first the Tsarist regime and then the Provisional Government collapsed. Their Bolshevik successors brought only temporary peace. From the summer of 1918, White armies moved towards the heart of Russia, and within a year Soviet Russia was in extreme peril. Eventually, Bolshevik control of interior lines of communication, the Whites' disunity and the half-heartedness of the Allied intervention told. In 1921, after seven years of war, peace finally came to Russia.

Imperialism and nationalism 1919 to 1941

B Y the 1920s the European empires in Asia and North Africa had reached their greatest extent. At the end of the First World War, France gained control of Syria and Lebanon. Iraq, Palestine and Transjordan were drawn into the area of British control which already included Egypt, the Sudan, the southern and eastern fringes of Arabia, India, Burma, Ceylon and the Malay states. The Dutch remained in the East Indies, the Spaniards consolidated their control over the northern zone of Morocco, and the Italians theirs over Libya. After this, the only important addition was Ethiopia, conquered by Italy in 1936. Turkey, Persia, Saudi Arabia, Yemen, Afghanistan and Siam were independent, but only within limits: the military power of Europe and the domination of world markets by the industrial states of the West were facts which even independent countries had to take into account. Moreover, this situation began to assume a new dimension with the increasing demand for oil for armies and industry, and the discovery and exploitation of large oil resources in the Middle East, especially in Persia and Iraq. The position of the imperial powers was weaker than it seemed, however. The exhaustion of the victors in the First World War; the growth of a new conception of imperial rule as something temporary and limited, expressed both in the British idea of progress towards 'dominion status' and in the mandate system of the League of Nations; criticism and challenges coming from the United States, the USSR and later from Nazi Germany: all these limited the freedom of action of Great Britain and France. The countries of Asia and North Africa were for the most part also countries of ancient literate civilisation,

with a tradition of independence or participation in their own government; in some of them, several generations of modern education had produced an élite which was playing some part in colonial administration and wished to obtain greater autonomy as a step towards independence.

Thus the colonial powers were faced with increasing opposition in Asia and North Africa, though not yet in sub-Saharan Africa. Reaction to it was a mixture of repression and concession. Opposition was of two kinds either led by traditional rulers or élites making use of indigenous social forces. Thus in Morocco first Spanish and then French rule was threatened by a revolt in the Rif Mountains, led by Abd el-Krim and only suppressed with difficulty (1921-26); and in Cyrenaica, the Italian conquest met with prolonged resistance from the Sanusi tribesmen. The ruler of Afghanistan, long dependent on British India in foreign affairs, threatened the British position on the troubled North-West Frontier in 1919, and secured his independence by the treaty of 1921.

In other places, the new educated élite espoused the idea that each nation (whether defined in territorial or in ethnic terms) should have its own independent state. But in this period nationalist movements could only pre-

sent a serious challenge in countries where they were able to mobilise wider support. This occurred first in Turkey, where the nationalists, led by Mustafa Kemäl (Atatürk), were able to defeat Anglo-French plans for the partition of the Ottoman Empire, to abolish their own traditional system of government, and to create an independent Turkish republic in 1923.

In the former Arab regions of the Ottoman Empire similar attempts to secure independence had less success. In Syria, a nation-wide revolt beginning in the Jebel Druze was eventually suppressed (1925-27), and the French made only minor concessions before the end of the Second World War. In Iraq, a revolt in 1920 helped to persuade the British to create an autonomous government under an Arab king, Faisal, of the Hashemite dynasty of the Hejaz, which some nationalists were willing to accept as a first step; by 1932, Iraq had secured formal independence and membership of the League of Nations, but the British military presence continued under the new treaty. In Palestine, the conflict resulting from Britain's support for the creation of a Jewish national home led to dis-

The Indian national flag *(above),* adopted by the Congress Party in 1930, showed a spinning wheel, the symbol of Gandhi's appeal to Indians to revive their traditional way of life and win economic independence. It was first hoisted by Nehru as President of Congress on 1 January 1930 to launch the civil disobedience campaign.

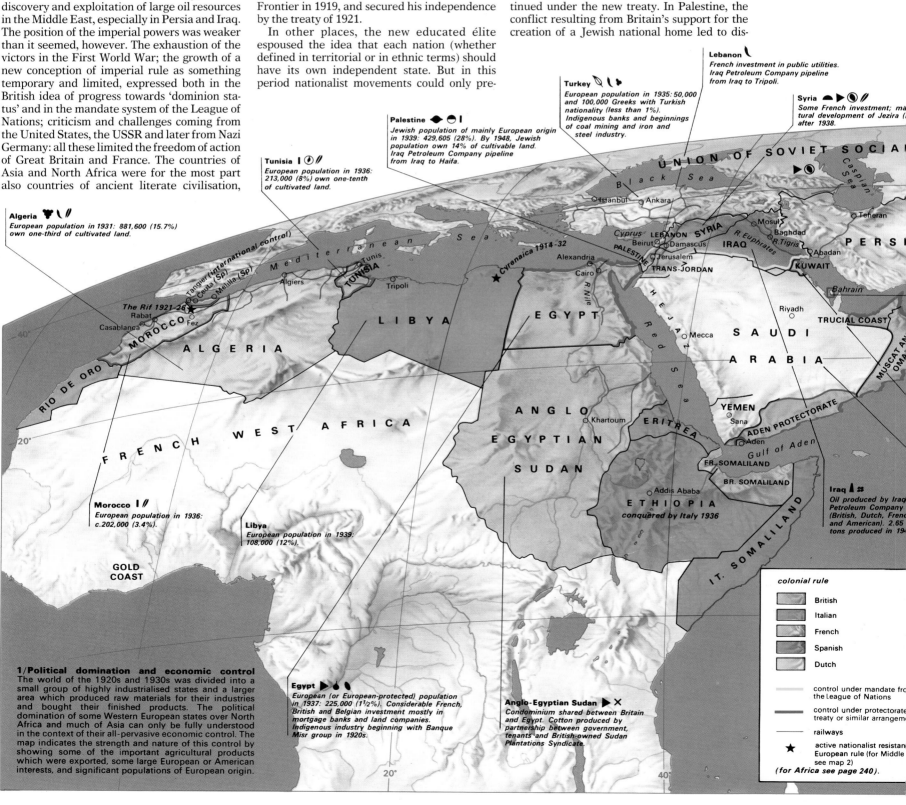

Lebanon
French investment in public utilities. Iraq Petroleum Company pipeline from Iraq to Tripoli.

Turkey
European population in 1935: 50,000 and 100,000 Greeks with Turkish nationality (less than 1%). Indigenous banks and beginnings of coal mining and iron and steel industry.

Syria
Some French investment; natural development of Jezira (after 1938.

Palestine
Jewish population of mainly European origin in 1939: 429,605 (28%). By 1948, Jewish population own 14% of cultivable land. Iraq Petroleum Company pipeline from Iraq to Haifa.

Tunisia
European population in 1936: 213,000 (8%) own one-tenth of cultivated land.

Algeria
European population in 1931: 881,600 (15.7%) own one-third of cultivated land.

Morocco
European population in 1936: c.202,000 (3.4%).

Libya
European population in 1939: 108,000 (12%).

Iraq
Oil produced by Iraq Petroleum Company (British, Dutch, French and American). 2.65 tons produced in 19...

Egypt
European (or European-protected) population in 1937: 225,000 (1½%). Considerable French, British and Belgian investment mostly in mortgage banks and land companies. Indigenous industry beginning with Banque Misr group in 1920s.

Anglo-Egyptian Sudan
Condominium shared between Britain and Egypt. Cotton produced by partnership between government, tenants and British-owned Sudan Plantations Syndicate.

1/Political domination and economic control
The world of the 1920s and 1930s was divided into a small group of highly industrialised states and a larger area which produced raw materials for their industries and bought their finished products. The political domination of some Western European states over North Africa and much of Asia can only be fully understood in the context of their all-pervasive economic control. The map indicates the strength and nature of this control by showing some of the important agricultural products which were exported, some large European or American interests, and significant populations of European origin.

colonial rule
British
Italian
French
Spanish
Dutch

control under mandate from the League of Nations
control under protectorate treaty or similar arrangeme...
railways
★ active nationalist resistance European rule (for Middle see map 2)
(for Africa see page 240.)

turbances in the 1920s, and opposition to the rise in Jewish immigration after Hitler's seizure of power in Germany in 1933 led to a widespread Arab revolt between 1935 and 1939. In Egypt, the main nationalist party, the Wafd under Saad Zaghlul, succeeded in mobilising considerable popular support. A national revolt in 1919 ultimately led to Britain conceding independence in 1922, although a number of important matters were 'absolutely reserved to the discretion of His Majesty's Government'. In 1936 an Anglo-Egyptian treaty gave Egyptians wider control over their affairs, but military control and the management of the Suez Canal remained outside Egyptian hands. Further west, in the European colonies of North Africa, nationalist feeling was less developed; the Moroccan and Algerian movements were only beginning in the 1930s, and the pressures exerted on the French by the Néo-Destour in Tunisia were insufficient to change basic policies.

In India, too, the main nationalist party, the Indian National Congress, was by now gathering wide popular support, thanks largely to the leadership of Mahatma Gandhi. By linking the idea of nationalism with traditional Hindu thought and action, Gandhi propelled India into the age of mass politics. His first civil disobedience campaign in 1920 misfired, and was followed by a period of repression. But in 1930, profiting from the unrest caused by unemployment and the world economic depression, he launched a second campaign which went on for some years and played a part in inducing the British to introduce the Government of India Act in 1935. This provided a framework of participation, in central and still more in provincial governments, which the more conservative elements in Congress were able to accept, but was less to the liking of more radical nationalists such as Jawaharlal Nehru; in 1937 Congress controlled the

majority of the fourteen provincial governments. This phase, however, came to an end with the Second World War; Congress decided not to participate in the war effort, and its ministers resigned. By this time, moreover, leaders of the Muslim population were developing their own movements; in 1940 their most powerful group, the Muslim League, which aimed at a special status for the Muslim parts of India, passed a resolution calling for an autonomous Pakistan.

In other areas of the colonial world the distress of the 1930s was a catalyst, providing nationalist leaders with the popular support hitherto for the most part lacking. This was the case in the Gold Coast, where the cocoa farmers, hit by falling world prices were stirred into action; and throughout the West Indies, beginning in St Kitts in 1935, there were riots and strikes. In some cases, the result was concessions which created a temporary balance of forces, as in Ceylon, where a new constitution was in force from 1931, and in Burma, which was separated from India and given a limited kind of responsible government in 1935. In the Dutch East Indies a phase of revolutionary movements, beginning with the Communist revolt of 1926 was suppressed with only limited changes in provincial government, and the Dutch were able to ride out the storm until the arrival of the Japanese in 1941. In French Indo-China no concessions were made, and the policy of retaining firm French control led to outbreaks in the 1930s, and the creation of the Viet Minh by Ho Chi Minh in 1941. But the period as a whole saw the rise of new, more radical nationalist leaders – Azikiwe in West Africa, Ho Chi Minh in Vietnam, Nehru in India, Sukarno in Indonesia, Bourguiba in Tunisia – who understood better than their predecessors how to manipulate popular forces and who were destined to make their mark after the end of the Second World War.

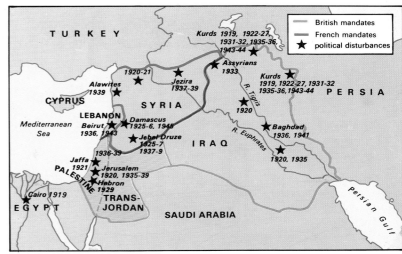

2/Disturbances in Egypt and the mandated territories of the Middle East, 1919 to 1945 (above) These included instances of opposition to British and French imperialism and also attempts by rural or minority populations to resist the newly-created central governments.

Egypt 1919 Nation-wide revolt, organised by the Wafd Party, against British refusal to consider an Egyptian request for independence and the end of the British protectorate.

Palestine 1920, 1921, 1929, 1935-39 Riots and disturbances and Arab Revolt (1935-39): expressions of opposition by indigenous Arab population to Jewish immigration, land purchase and exclusivist labour policy. Nation-wide strikes and rural rising 1936-39. Jewish agitation for increased immigration.

Syria/Lebanon 1920-21, 1925-27, 1936-39, 1943-45 Local rebellions (Aleppo 1920-21, Jebel Druze 1925-27) against French administ-

ration; national risings against the mandate (1925-27); further revolt against French failure to grant independence (1943-45). Local revolts against centralised government in Jebel Druze (1937-39), Jezira (1937-39) and Alawite area (1939). Local disturbance in Beirut in 1936 between anti-French Muslims and pro- French Armenian Christians.

Iraq 1920, 1933, 1935, 1936, 1941 Revolt of rural tribes against British military rule (1920); massacre of Assyrian Christians (community closely associated with British rule) (1933); major tribal rising in the Euphrates basin against centralised government (1935); military coup (1936); attempted seizure of power by pro-Axis politico-military group (Baghdad 1941).

Iraqi Kurdistan 1919, 1922-27, 1931-32, 1935-36, 1943-44 Kurds promised (and subsequently denied) autonomy under unratified Treaty of Sèvres (1920); revolts in northern Iraq led by Sheikh Mahmud Barzinji, later by Mulla Mustafa Barzani.

Anti-colonial uprisings (below)
Afghanistan 1919 Anglo-Afghan war May-June 1919 precipitated by King Amanullah's declaration of Afghan independence, following recognition by Soviet Russia; British acquiescence, August 1919.

The Rif 1921-26 Attempt by Berber tribesmen under Abd el-Krim to establish state independent of Spanish, and later French, rule.

Cyrenaica 1914-32 Long, drawn-out attempt by Arabs of Cyrenaica, within the framework of the Sanusi religious brotherhood, to resist Italian occupation.

India 1919-41 Most populous and complex society to be wholly colonised, its nationalist movement was the most articulate and highly

organised. General disturbances, characterised by Gandhi's civil disobedience campaigns: first in 1920, called off in 1922 after violence and bloodshed; second in 1930, inaugurated by famous 'march to the sea', called off in 1934. Important disturbances took place in Amritsar (1919) when British troops dispersed urban demonstration with considerable loss of life, and in Bengal (1923-32) which had a long period of intermittent terrorist activity.

Dutch East Indies 1926 Attempted rebellion by the Communist party in support of nationalist demand for self-rule.

Indo-China 1930 Urban strikes and rural rebellion, aiming at national independence and mainly organised by the Communist party led by Ho Chi Minh.

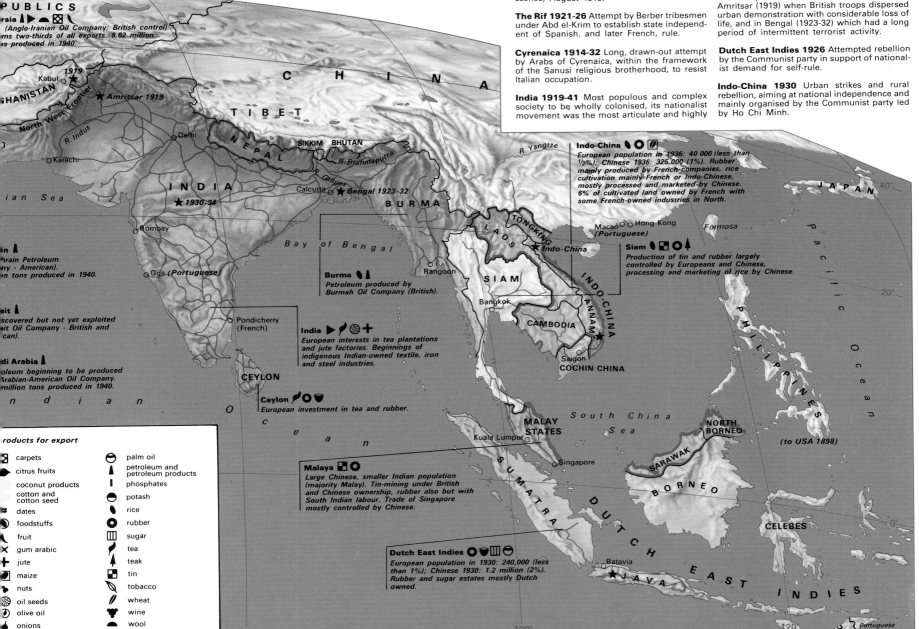

...PUBLICS
...rsia ▲ ▶ · ▨ ▮
(Anglo-Iranian Oil Company; British control)
...ms two-thirds of all exports. 8.62 million
...s produced in 1940.

...HANISTAN ▲

...in ▲
...hrain Petroleum
...ny - American).
...n tons produced in 1940.

...it ▲
...covered but not yet exploited
...it Oil Company - British and
...can).

...di Arabia ▲
...oleum beginning to be produced
...rabian-American Oil Company.
...million tons produced in 1940.

Indo-China ◖ ● ◪
European population in 1936: 40 000 (less than ½%); Chinese 1936: 325,000 (1%). Rubber mainly produced by French companies, rice cultivation mainly French or Indo-Chinese, mostly processed and marketed by Chinese. 5% of cultivated land owned by French with some French-owned industries in North.

Siam ▮ ◪ ● ▲
Production of tin and rubber largely controlled by Europeans and Chinese, processing and marketing of rice by Chinese.

Burma ◖ ◖
Petroleum produced by Burmah Oil Company (British).

India ▶ ✦ ◉ ✚
European interests in tea plantations and jute factories. Beginnings of indigenous Indian-owned textile, iron and steel industries.

Ceylon ✦ ● ▼
European investment in tea and rubber.

Malaya ▮ ◪ ●
Large Chinese, smaller Indian population (majority Malay). Tin-mining under British and Chinese ownership, rubber also but with South Indian labour. Trade of Singapore mostly controlled by Chinese.

Dutch East Indies ● ▼ ▥ ◭
European population in 1930: 240,000 (less than 1%); Chinese 1930: 1.2 million (2%). Rubber and sugar estates mostly Dutch owned.

...roducts for export

▨ carpets	◖ palm oil
◗ citrus fruits	◭ petroleum and petroleum products
coconut products	◓ phosphates
cotton and cotton seed	◣ potash
◗ dates	● rice
foodstuffs	● rubber
◖ fruit	▥ sugar
✦ gum arabic	✿ tea
✚ jute	◈ teak
◪ maize	◩ tin
◗ nuts	◭ tobacco
◉ oil seeds	▼ wheat
◭ olive oil	▼ wine
onions	▼ wool

The Chinese Revolution 1912 to 1949

1/The Northern Expedition 1926-27 In 1926 the Kuomintang and their Communist allies launched a major expedition to unify the country. Their government was moved to Wuhan, which became the centre of the Left. In April 1927 Chiang Kai-shek carried out a purge of the Communists, and transferred the capital to Nanking. Subsequent operations against the Feng-tien faction in the north were joined by Yen Hsi-shan, warlord of Shansi, and Feng Yu-hsiang leader of the Kuo-min-chün faction. Although the Kuomintang now claimed to control China, many areas remained outside their effective control.

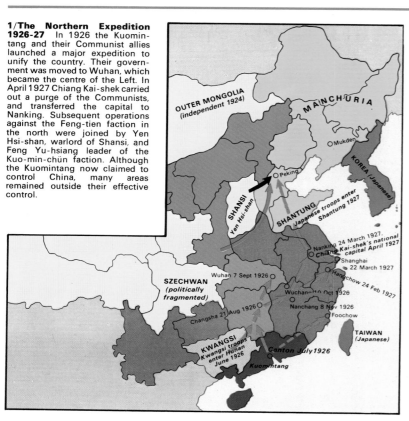

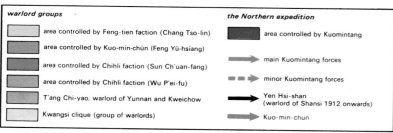

warlord groups	the Northern expedition
area controlled by Feng-tien faction (Chang Tso-lin)	area controlled by Kuomintang
area controlled by Kuo-min-chün (Feng Yü-hsiang)	main Kuomintang forces
area controlled by Chihli faction (Sun Ch'uan-fang)	minor Kuomintang forces
area controlled by Chihli faction (Wu P'ei-fu)	Yen Hsi-shan (warlord of Shansi 1912 onwards)
T'ang Chi-yao, warlord of Yunnan and Kweichow	Kuo-min-chün
Kwangsi clique (group of warlords)	

2/The Nationalist (Kuomintang) regime (1928-37) only controlled part of China. The north-east was occupied by Japan from 1931 and the Japanese constantly attempted to gain complete control of northern China. Warlords remained in control of many provinces; other areas were in a state of anarchy. Large areas of Kiangsi were under a Communist regime from 1931 to 1934, and by 1936 the Communists had a new base in the north-west at Yenan.

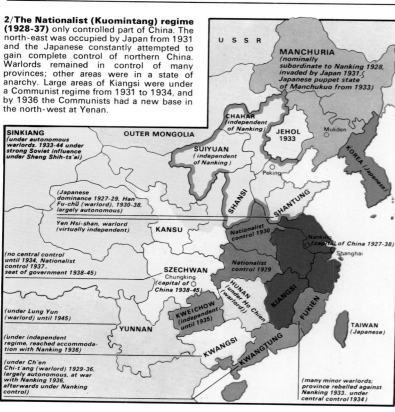

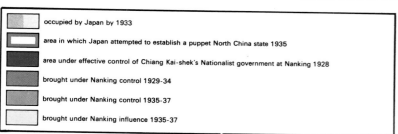

occupied by Japan by 1933	
area in which Japan attempted to establish a puppet North China state 1935	
area under effective control of Chiang Kai-shek's Nationalist government at Nanking 1928	
brought under Nanking control 1929-34	
brought under Nanking control 1935-37	
brought under Nanking influence 1935-37	

THE foundation of the Republic in 1912 failed to produce a lasting political solution for China's problems. Within weeks Sun Yat-sen, the revolutionary who had been elected China's first president, was replaced by Yuan Shih-k'ai, China's most powerful military figure under the old order. Yuan and the revolutionary leaders were soon involved in bitter political struggles; Yuan suppressed a 'Second Revolution' that broke out in the provinces in 1913, and by 1914 was a virtual dictator.

China's position was seriously weakened. The government was forced to borrow huge sums abroad to offset the lack of a modern revenue system, and the whole customs revenue passed into foreign hands. Tibet and Mongolia broke away, becoming autonomous, under British and Russian dominance respectively, and in 1924 Mongolia finally became independent. More serious were the expansionist plans of Japan. When the outbreak of the First World War diverted the attention of the Western powers from Asia, Japan seized the German leased territory and sphere of influence in Shantung, and then presented China with a set of demands which would have reduced her to a Japanese dependency. Yuan resisted the more extreme demands, but in 1915 a treaty was signed establishing Japanese dominance in Shantung, Manchuria and Inner Mongolia. This provoked a massive upsurge of nationalist feeling.

Yuan died in 1916, after attemping unsuccessfully to have himself made emperor. His regime left China with a weak and unstable central government, and real authority in the provinces passed increasingly into the hands of the generals. For the next decade, although the government in Peking claimed to govern China, it was the puppet of one group of generals or another, and the country was divided between rival warlords. Some of these, as in Shansi, Kwangsi and Manchuria, established relatively stable regimes, sometimes instituting reformist programmes. In other areas, such as Szechwan, anarchy prevailed, with a host of petty generals living off the countryside. Even some of the most powerful warlord leaders, such as Feng Yü-hsiang, never found a permanent territorial base. In the 1920s there was a series of devastating wars between the major warlord coalitions, which not only destroyed orderly civil government but also caused millions of casualties and untold physical damage and disruption. Only the Treaty Ports were secure under foreign protection.

The early 1920s saw an upsurge of revolutionary activity. Both the revolutionaries and the nascent Communist party benefited from widespread popular reaction against foreign interference, the grossly unfair terms of the Paris Peace Conference, which reinforced Japan's position in Shantung, and economic exploitation. In 1919 this upsurge of nationalism erupted in the 4 May Movement, in which a new generation of Western-orientated students and intellectuals, together with urban workers, first made themselves a force in politics, forcing the government to refuse to sign the Treaty of Versailles.

Sun Yat-sen's revolutionary party had established a regional regime in Canton. From 1923 Sun reorganised the Nationalist (Kuomintang) Party and its army, with aid and advice from the Comintern, and entered into an alliance with the still minuscule Communist Party. Sun died suddenly in 1925, and in that year anti-foreign feeling reached a new peak with widespread strikes and boycotts in which both organised labour and the merchant class joined. Communist influence rapidly gained ground in the industrial cities. In 1926 Chiang Kai-shek, the principal general of the Kuomintang army, led a 'Northern Expedition' aimed at the elimination of the warlords and the unification of the nation. At the end of 1926 the nationalist government

moved to Wuhan, while its armies moved into the lower Yangtze, taking Nanking and Shanghai in April 1927. Chiang Kai-shek now instigated a purge of his Communist allies, and set up a regime of his own in Nanking. Communist troops rose against Chiang in Nanchang in August 1927, but were easily put down, as was a peasant rising in Hunan. In 1928 Chiang's armies again turned north and took Peking.

Although the Nationalists now dominated China, and were recognised as the national government, the warlords were not eliminated. Even after the most powerful warlords, Yen Hsi-shan and Feng Yü-hsiang, were defeated in a major war in 1929-30, many provinces retained a great degree of autonomy, and warfare with provincial armies repeatedly broke out. Chiang's government held firm centralised control only over the rich provinces of lower Yangtze, where they modernised the administration and the army, built a road system and railways, and established new industry in spite of world depression and constant Japanese pressure. But much of this development was concentrated in the cities, particularly in Shanghai and Nanking.

In addition to continued warlord power, Chiang had to face the far more serious threat of Japanese expansion. The Japanese had constantly intervened in warlord politics, especially in the north-east. In 1931 they occupied Manchuria, in 1933 establishing there a puppet state of Manchukuo under the last Manchu emperor. They then occupied the neighbouring province of Jehol, and in 1935 unsuccessfully attempted to establish a puppet regime controlling all northern China. In Manchuria they rapidly built up the basis of a modern economy, with a dense railway network and various heavy and light industries, on a scale unmatched elsewhere in China. This economic growth was intensified after the outbreak of war in 1937.

The second threat to Chiang's position was the Communists. After the purges of 1927 and a series of abortive insurrections, the power of the Communist Party in the cities was systematically broken, and the Communist leaders retreated to remote mountain areas where they established local regimes. Most important of these was the Kiangsi soviet, based at Jui-chin, where from 1929-34 the Communist Party controlled an area with several million people and developed reform programmes as a peasant-based party rather than a party based on an urban proletariat on the Russian model. Chiang's armies repeatedly attacked Kiangsi, and in 1934 the Communist leaders decided to abandon the area. The ensuing Long March led them to the north-west, where another minor Communist base had been established since 1930 in Pao-an. At the Tsunyi conference during the Long March, the party's peasant-based wing, led by Mao Tse-tung, finally established its leadership. His policies were put into practice in the new Communist base area centred on Yenan.

Even now, Chiang's first priority was to crush the Communists and his provincial rivals, rather than resist the Japanese, but in 1936 he was forced, under threat of deposition if not of assassination, to form a united front against the common enemy. The Japanese responded by invading China in force, and by the end of 1938 they occupied most of north and central China, together with the main coastal ports and all the centres of modern industry. The Nationalists retreated into the impregnable mountains of Szechwan and the south-west, and the fighting subsided until the Japanese offensives of 1944, which led to further areas falling into their hands.

Although they occupied a large part of China, the Japanese controlled only the major cities and lines of communication. In the occupied zones there were many centres of Chinese resistance, often dominated by Communists

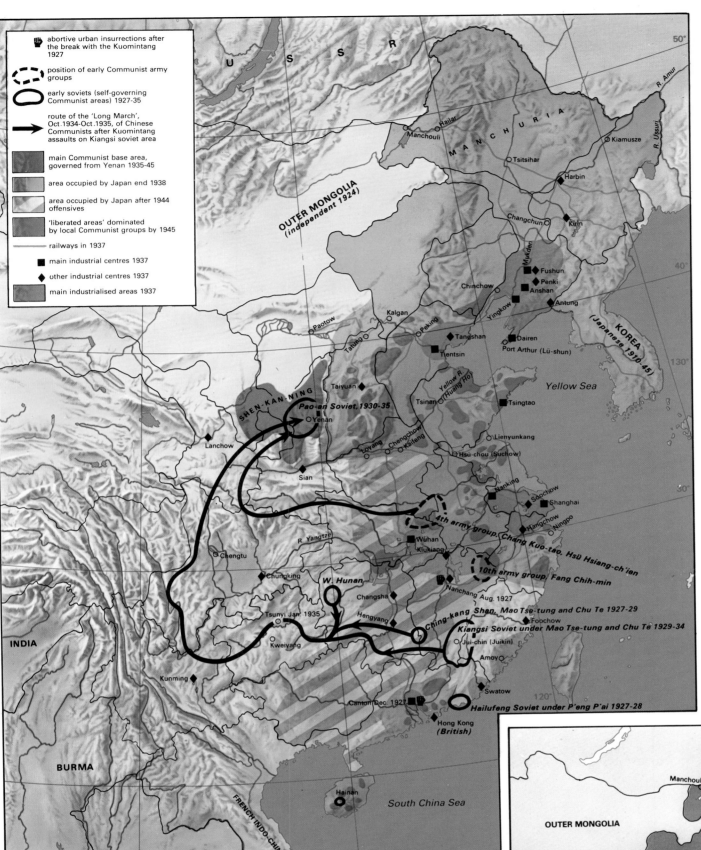

3/The Chinese Communist movement to 1945 *(left)* After the break with the Kuomintang (KMT) in 1927 there were abortive risings in Nanchang and Canton. The first Communist regime was that at Hailufeng, 1927-28. Various small bases emerged in remote mountain areas in central China in 1927-1930. Most important was Mao Tse-tung's base at Ching-kang shan. In 1929 he moved to southern Kiangsi where a stable soviet government survived repeated KMT campaigns until 1934 when the Communist forces withdrew from their southern bases and travelled to the north-west on the famous Long March. From 1937, during the Japanese war the Chinese Communist regime in Yenan and the Nationalist government in Chungking were at least nominally united in resistance to the Japanese. By the end of 1938 Japan had occupied a very large part of north and central China, including all the major industrial centres and ports. However, Japanese control was only fully effective in the cities and along the main rail lines. In rural areas many centres of resistance grew up, many of them Communist-organised. Only a few of the centres had any real territorial control, but all were centres of Communist political influence among the rural population. In 1937 China's industries, poor and largely foreign-owned, were concentrated in the Treaty Ports: Shanghai alone had about 60 per cent of all industrial plant. Much of the rail network and well-planned industry was built up in Japanese-controlled Manchuria. By 1945, in spite of some wartime development in the west (Chungking, Kunming), the industrial situation had changed little.

4/Communist victory in the Civil War 1945-49 *(below)* After the defeat of Japan, Manchuria was occupied by Russian armies; in the rest of China, Communist and Nationalist forces competed in guerrilla operations for control of former Japanese territory. By 1947 the Communists controlled most of the north apart from the Peking-Tientsin area, some major cities and rail-lines. After 1948 the Communists were strong enough to engage the Nationalists in major battles: the main Nationalist armies were destroyed in Manchuria in 1948 and at Hsü-chou in 1948-9, and after the rapid fall of northern China no serious attempt was made to hold China south of the Yangtze.

who gained widespread credibility as the party actively pursuing guerrilla warfare, and won the sympathy of the peasant farmers by the reform programmes practised in their base area around Yenan. By 1945 the Communists claimed to control numerous 'liberated areas', but only in a few of these did they have real administrative power.

When the Second World War ended in 1945 the Nationalist government returned to Nanking. During the war years it had become increasingly dependent upon American aid and finance, more and more reactionary and corrupt. by 1945 it was widely discredited; inflation was rampant, its armies were demoralised. After the Japanese surrender the Nationalist and Communist forces raced to take possession of former Japanese-held territory; the Communists gained control of much of the north and most of Manchuria, which had been occupied by the Russians in 1945. For some time negotiations went on in an attempt to reach a political settlement and to create a national government, but hostilities continued between Nationalist and Communist forces, and in 1947 this broke into open civil war. By 1948 the initiative had passed to the Communists, who defeatd the crack Nationalist armies in Manchuria and entered Tientsin and Peking in January 1949. Further south a major battle around Hsü-chou raged from November 1948 to January 1949 with half a million troops engaged on each side. The Nationalists were defeated; Nanking fell in April, Shanghai in May, Canton in October 1949. On 1 October 1949 the People's Republic of China was founded. By May 1950 the Nationalist government had fled to Taiwan.

The civil war completed the destruction that had taken place during the warlord period and the Japanese war. In 1949 most of the Chinese industrial plant was in ruins; the Japanese industrial base in Manchuria had been looted by the Russians; much of the rail system was inoperative. Years of hyper-inflation had destroyed the currency, the banking system and urban business. But for the first time since 1911 a strong regime controlled all Chinese territory, and moreover had plans, already tested in limited areas, for the regeneration of the economy and the transformation of the country.

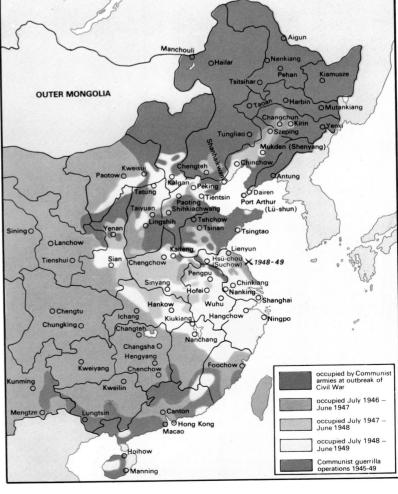

	occupied by Communist armies at outbreak of Civil War
	occupied July 1946 – June 1947
	occupied July 1947 – June 1948
	occupied July 1948 – June 1949
	Communist guerrilla operations 1945-49

European political problems 1919 to 1934

THE collapse of the Central Powers in the autumn of 1918 and the subsequent peace treaties of Versailles (28 June 1919) between the Allies and Germany, of St Germain (10 September 1919) with Austria, of Neuilly (27 November 1919) with Bulgaria, and of Trianon (4 June 1920) with Hungary, brought about major frontier changes, the emergence of a number of new states and the enlargement of others fortunate enough to be on the victorious side. New states included Finland, Estonia, Latvia and Lithuania (all now independent of their former Russian overlords); Poland (reconstituted from the three empires which had shared in its partition at the end of the 18th century); Czechoslovakia, comprising the old Habsburg 'crown lands' of Bohemia, Moravia and Silesia, together with Slovakia and Carpathian Ruthenia from former Hungarian territory; and Yugoslavia, comprising the territories of the former independent kingdoms of Serbia and Montenegro, the former crown land of Croatia, the former Turkish provinces of Bosnia and the Herzegovina, and the Habsburg provinces in Slovenia and Dalmatia. Romania enlarged itself greatly, taking Transylvania from Hungary, Bukovina from Austria and Bessarabia from Russia and southern Dobruja from Bulgaria. Italy took the South Tyrol (Alto Adige) and the Triestino, the former Habsburg province of Istria. France recovered Alsace-Lorraine, and Belgium took the small frontier areas of Eupen and Malmédy. Plebiscites held in the disputed areas of Upper Silesia, Marienwerder, Allenstein and Schleswig resulted in more or less satisfactory solutions on ethnic lines, although the Poles did their best to annex Upper Silesia by force of arms.

The ethnic elements in the other settlements were far from satisfactory, *irredenta* being scattered wholesale across the map of eastern Europe, save only on the boundary between Greece and Turkey, where at the end of the Greco-Turkish war of 1920-22 (see page 228) a wholesale exchange of populations was negotiated. Danzig and the Saarland were set up under League of Nations High Commissioners, the Saarland reverting to Germany by plebiscite in January 1935. Peace with Turkey was delayed until the Treaty of Lausanne (24 July 1923), owing to the inability of the Allies to impose their terms on a renascent Turkish national movement despite their enlisting the help of the Greeks. On Europe's eastern frontiers settlement had to await the victory of the Bolsheviks in the Russian civil war, and the repulse first of the Polish invasion of Russia and then of the Soviet invasion of Poland. The Western Powers proposed a mediated frontier along the Curzon Line (Spa Conference, July 1920). The frontier finally settled at the Treaty of Riga (October 1920) gave Poland a large minority of White Russians and Ukrainians.

The destruction of the Habsburg Empire, the disarmament of Germany and the effects of the Russian Revolution and the civil war completely altered the balance of power in Europe. Potentially Germany, in terms of population and industrial strength, was now without any counterbalance in central Europe. The only hope of those powers who stood to lose by a revision of the peace treaties was the maintenance of overwhelming military strength in alliance against any revival of German power. France tried to restrain Germany by signing alliances with the new states of Poland and Czechoslovakia, and by using the issue of reparations to hold Germany down. But France's efforts to promote a separatist movement in the Rhineland, and its occupation of the Ruhr to enforce reparations deliveries in 1923, proved disastrous. Thereafter Germany and France came much closer together, and the Treaty of Locarno (1925) established a system of guarantees along the Franco-German and Belgian-German frontiers. Germany joined the League of Nations (1926), but at the same time signed a pact of friendship and non-aggression with the USSR; French and British forces occupying the Rhineland were steadily withdrawn, and the European powers began discussions intended to lead to a world disarmament agreement.

Superficially, Europe in 1929 presented the appearance of a stable system secured against war by the sanctions clauses of the Covenant of the League of Nations. But the illusory nature of that security had been shown when Italy's naval action against the Greek island of Corfu in 1923, and Poland's seizure of Vilna from Lithuania in 1920, went unpunished. Another weakness was the lack of stability in the domestic politics of many European powers, particularly in Eastern Europe, and the weakness of the economic underpinning of the international system. The strains of the war of 1914-18 and the defects of the peace settlements, coupled with the major and occasionally disastrously inflationary strains of economic adjustment, combined to strengthen anti-parliamentary (see page 258) and revolutionary groups, parties and movements of both left and right throughout Europe. The Russian Revolution led to the setting up of a new Third Socialist International (the Comintern). Russian insistence that all parties and movements affiliating themselves to it should follow its leadership and organisational model split the socialist parties of Europe into rival parliamentary socialist and revolutionary Communist sections, and made their defeat by the right inevitable. Some of the new regimes and movements were organised on nationalist totalitarian lines on the model of Italian Fascism, which achieved power in 1922. Others (Poland, Yugoslavia, Greece) were simply military-bureaucratic tyrannies. In Germany armed risings and major breakdowns of public order created an atmosphere of incipient civil war until the economic recovery of 1924. Great Britain experienced a series of strikes, culminating in the General Strike of 1926; and in Ireland from 1919 to 1922 violent guerrilla-style warfare raged between the forces of the Irish nationalists, who set up their own underground government in 1919, and the British forces. The settlement of 1921 preserved the Loyalist (and Protestant) stronghold of Ulster under British rule, made Ireland a Dominion of the Empire, but led to a bitter conflict within the new Irish Free State between radicals and moderates, settled in 1923.

The stabilisation of 1925-29 was more apparent than real, and with the onset of the Depression (see page 266), financial and economic chaos returned to Europe. Unemployment mounted drastically in Germany and Great Britain. In Germany after 1930 the anti-parliamentary movements of right and left, Nazis and Communists, increased their strength enormously. In Great Britain a 'national' government, with a huge majority in the 1931 general election, maintained parliamentary control. In

2/The European Security System, 1921-34 (*left*) The peace settlements of 1919 were supported by a series of pacts and alliances with three main purposes: to prevent Germany from seeking to reverse the verdict of the First World War; to build up a *cordon sanitaire* against Bolshevik Russia; to maintain the territorial settlement in Eastern Europe and forestall treaty revision, particularly on the part of Hungary. The map shows clearly the key position of France, in alliance with Poland, as the main support of the Little Entente, and the comparative isolation of the two 'outsiders', Germany (which only recovered freedom of manoeuvre after 1934) and the Soviet Union. It also shows the ambition of Italy under Mussolini to play a major role in the Mediterranean and in the Danubian basin. Nevertheless, the French security system operated effectively until the onset of Depression (see page 266), which weakened France and after 1936, if not before, undercut its alliances in Eastern Europe. The decisive change came with the German-Polish Neutrality Pact (1934), which knocked the lynch-pin out of France's defensive system. After 1936, when Germany repudiated the Locarno treaties of 1925, a new period began, leading to the outbreak of war in 1939 (see page 268).

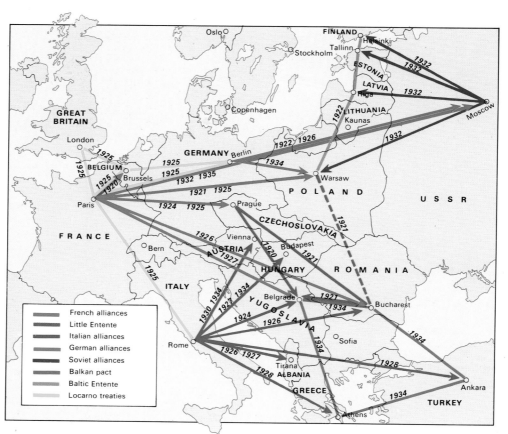

French alliances
Little Entente
Italian alliances
German alliances
Soviet alliances
Balkan pact
Baltic Entente
Locarno treaties

1920 Franco-Belgian military convention.
1920 Czechoslovak-Yugoslav defensive alliance (against Hungarian revisionism), converted **1921** into 'Little Entente' by alliances between Czechoslovakia and Romania and between Romania and Yugoslavia. The system further cemented by Franco-Polish alliance (19 February 1921) and alliance between Poland and Romania (against U.S.S.R.), later by treaties between France and Czechoslovakia (1924), France and Romania (1926), and France and Yugoslavia (1927).
1922 Baltic Entente between Poland, Estonia, Latvia and Finland (defensive alignment against U.S.S.R.).
1922 Rapallo Treaty between Germany and Soviet Union, consolidated by Treaty of Berlin, **1926**.
1924 Adriatic Treaty (Italy and Yugoslavia) confirming *status quo* in Adriatic.
1925 Locarno treaties: Germany, France, Belgium, Great Britain, Italy guarantee frontiers in West. Treaties of mutual assistance in event of German aggression between France and Poland and France and Czechoslovakia.
1926 Pact between Italy and Albania, converted into alliance (1927).
1926 Treaty of Friendship between Italy and Romania.
1927 Italian-Hungarian treaty (putting Italy on side of revisionist powers).
1928 Treaties between Italy and Turkey and Italy and Greece.
1930 Treaty of Friendship between Italy and Austria.
1932 Non-aggression Pact between France and U.S.S.R., leading to Franco-Russian Mutual Assistance Treaty, **1935**. Further non-aggression treaties concluded between U.S.S.R. and Finland, Estonia, Latvia and Poland (to protect Russia's western frontier).
1934 Balkan Pact (Yugoslavia, Romania, Turkey, Greece) to forestall German and Russian revisionist pressures.
1934 Rome Protocols (Italy, Austria, Hungary) to strengthen Italy's position in Danubian region in face of National Socialist Germany.
1934 German-Polish Non-Aggression Treaty (beginning of collapse of French security system in Eastern Europe).
1936 Germany denounces Locarno treaties.

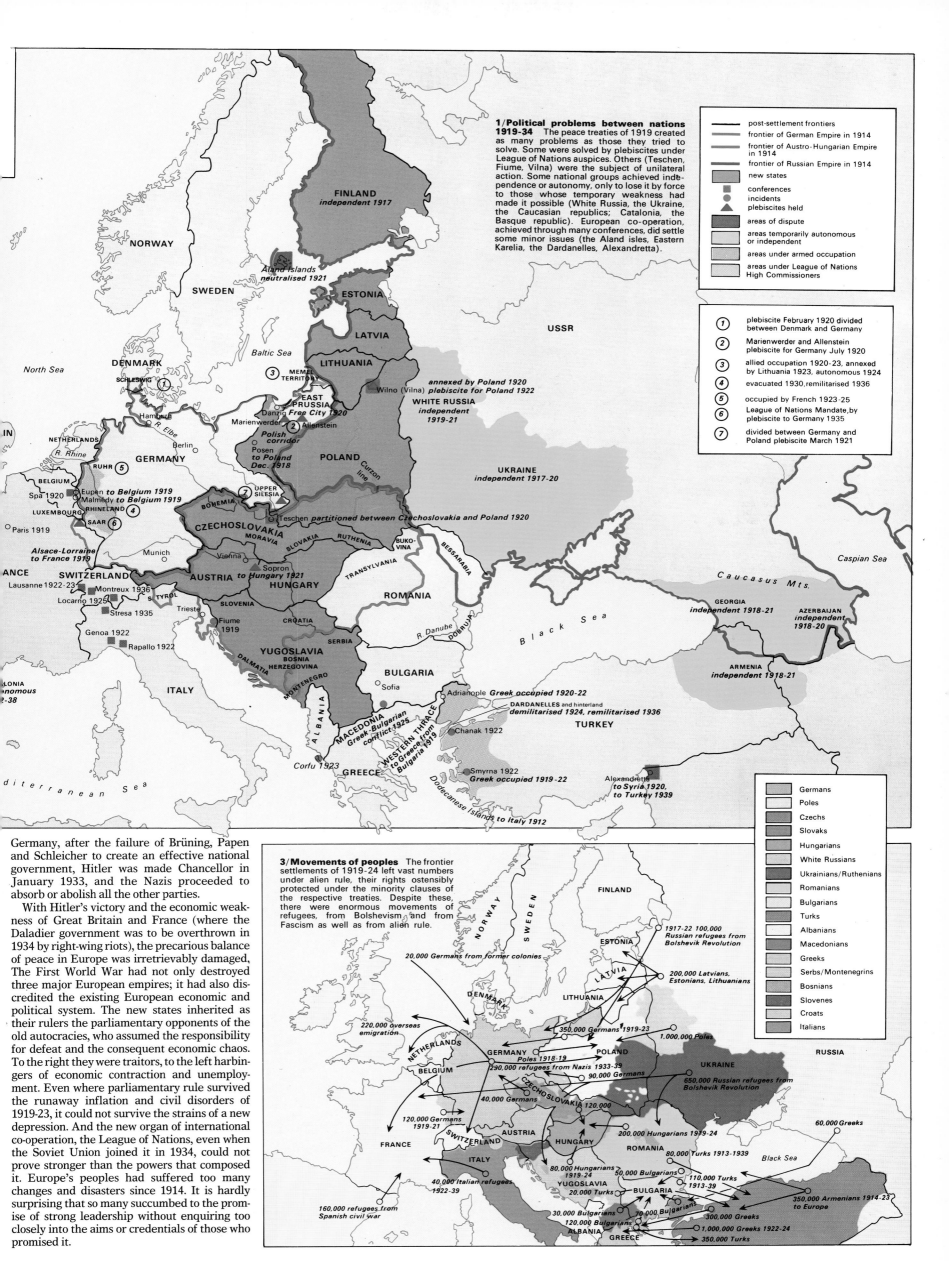

1/Political problems between nations 1919-34 The peace treaties of 1919 created as many problems as those they tried to solve. Some were solved by plebiscites under League of Nations auspices. Others (Teschen, Fiume, Vilna) were the subject of unilateral action. Some national groups achieved independence or autonomy, only to lose it by force to those whose temporary weakness had made it possible (White Russia, the Ukraine, the Caucasian republics; Catalonia, the Basque republic). European co-operation, achieved through many conferences, did settle some minor issues (the Aland isles, Eastern Karelia, the Dardanelles, Alexandretta).

post-settlement frontiers
frontier of German Empire in 1914
frontier of Austro-Hungarian Empire in 1914
frontier of Russian Empire in 1914
new states
conferences
incidents
plebiscites held
areas of dispute
areas temporarily autonomous or independent
areas under armed occupation
areas under League of Nations High Commissioners

1 plebiscite February 1920 divided between Denmark and Germany
2 Marienwerder and Allenstein plebiscite for Germany July 1920
3 allied occupation 1920-23, annexed by Lithuania 1923, autonomous 1924
4 evacuated 1930, remilitarised 1936
5 occupied by French 1923-25
6 League of Nations Mandate, by plebiscite to Germany 1935
7 divided between Germany and Poland plebiscite March 1921

3/Movements of peoples The frontier settlements of 1919-24 left vast numbers under alien rule, their rights ostensibly protected under the minority clauses of the respective treaties. Despite these, there were enormous movements of refugees, from Bolshevism and from Fascism as well as from alien rule.

Germans
Poles
Czechs
Slovaks
Hungarians
White Russians
Ukrainians/Ruthenians
Romanians
Bulgarians
Turks
Albanians
Macedonians
Greeks
Serbs/Montenegrins
Bosnians
Slovenes
Croats
Italians

Germany, after the failure of Brüning, Papen and Schleicher to create an effective national government, Hitler was made Chancellor in January 1933, and the Nazis proceeded to absorb or abolish all the other parties.

With Hitler's victory and the economic weakness of Great Britain and France (where the Daladier government was to be overthrown in 1934 by right-wing riots), the precarious balance of peace in Europe was irretrievably damaged. The First World War had not only destroyed three major European empires; it had also discredited the existing European economic and political system. The new states inherited as their rulers the parliamentary opponents of the old autocracies, who assumed the responsibility for defeat and the consequent economic chaos. To the right they were traitors, to the left harbingers of economic contraction and unemployment. Even where parliamentary rule survived the runaway inflation and civil disorders of 1919-23, it could not survive the strains of a new depression. And the new organ of international co-operation, the League of Nations, even when the Soviet Union joined it in 1934, could not prove stronger than the powers that composed it. Europe's peoples had suffered too many changes and disasters since 1914. It is hardly surprising that so many succumbed to the promise of strong leadership without enquiring too closely into the aims or credentials of those who promised it.

The Great Depression 1929 to 1939

THE chronology of the 'Slump' is by now well known, but its causes are still debated. What is certain is that the stock market crash of 1929, and the ensuing world-wide financial collapse, were only the manifestation of deeper weaknesses in the world economy. The sources of instability were several: the First World War caused a dramatic increase in productive capacity, especially outside Europe, but there was no corresponding increase in demand. Above all, there was a world-wide imbalance between agriculture and industry. The rewards of growth accrued disproportionately to the industrialised countries and, within these countries, to their industrial and financial sectors. Increased production allowed food and raw material prices to decline throughout the 1920s, worsening the terms of trade for countries dependent on the export of such commodities, and decreasing their ability to buy the industrial products of Europe and the United States. Within the latter, wages lagged behind profits, impairing the development of domestic markets, and limiting the potential of new industries, such as automobiles, to replace declining ones, like textiles. International finance never fully recovered from the dislocations of the First World War. The pre-war system of fixed exchange rates and free convertibility (see page 256) was replaced by a compromise – the Gold Exchange Standard – which never achieved the stability necessary to rebuild world trade.

The slump was touched off by financial crisis. The great Bull Market of 1928 – itself a sign of weakness, of shrinking opportunities for investment – gave way to a precipitous fall in stock prices in October 1929. In the ensuing scramble for liquidity, funds flowed back from Europe to America, and the shaky European prosperity collapsed. In May 1931, the Austrian Credit-Anstalt defaulted. When England left the Gold Standard, allowing sterling to depreciate in September 1931, virtually the entire world was affected.

In many industrial countries, over a quarter of the labour force was thrown out of work. Industrial production fell to 53 per cent of its 1929 level in Germany and the United States, and world trade sank to 35 per cent of its 1929 value. For many the Depression seemed endless: as late as 1939, the world average of unemployment was over 11 per cent. But the impact of the slump was uneven. Some economies rebounded relatively quickly; others languished throughout the decade. In retrospect, it is evident that considerable structural changes took place in the 1930s. New industries continued to progress, consumption patterns shifted, peripheral areas increased their output of industrial goods, and real wages rose. A new economic world order, anchored on Wall Street and Detroit, was struggling to be born. But even by 1939 the lynchpin of this new system had not yet regained the level of industrial output of 1929, and it ultimately required a Second World War to pull the United States out of depression.

Government reactions to the Depression were unenlightened. The first response was to deflate and to try to preserve the value of the currency. Soon, however, the dire consequences led one government after another to attempt to stimulate the domestic economy by reflation (e.g. public works), devaluation (in the hope of increasing exports), protective and preferential tariff arrangements (e.g. the Ottawa Agreements, 1932), or by some combination of these policies. Even the most economically conservative regimes were forced to abandon *laissez faire* in favour of some degree of state intervention.

These measures achieved mixed results. Success hinged on applying consistent and firm stimulants and, more importantly, on how soon and how thoroughly rearmament was undertaken. Germany and the United Kingdom rearmed early, stimulating their own economies and those of the Commonwealth, Scandinavia and eastern Europe. France and the United States rearmed late, and suffered much more severely in the recession of 1937-38. Internationally, government policies led to a decrease and redirection of trade. By 1935, much of the world had divided into five currency blocs: the sterling and dollar areas, the gold and yen blocs, and the German-dominated exchange control area. Though plagued by instability, these groupings corresponded roughly to the new patterns of trade and influence.

The revival of economic nationalism was paralleled by a new intensity in international politics. The Japanese export offensive had its political reflex in military aggression against China. Hitler, Mussolini and the Japanese exploited the disarray which the economic collapse had brought about, and gradually the world polarised into two armed camps, the Axis (Germany, Italy and Japan) and the 'democracies' (led by the United Kingdom, France and the United States). In between stood the Soviet Union, the one country which, isolated from the world market, had managed to sustain economic growth throughout the 1930s, and which both sides tried, alternately, to ally with or to isolate.

Few countries emerged from the Depression without undergoing some dramatic domestic transformation. In Africa, Asia and Latin America, nationalist and revolutionary movements gained new bases of support, as the crisis radicalised urban workers, poor peasants and agricultural labourers. The developed world followed one of two patterns. The first was liberal and democratic, typified by Roosevelt's New Deal in the United States, and by the Popular Front government in France. In both countries, the election of the left- or liberal-minded administrations unleashed enormous waves of strikes and trade union organisation, and stimulated numerous efforts at reform. Much more common was the path to the right. The resignation of the Hamaguchi Cabinet in 1931 marked the effective end of Japan's weak experiment in constitutional democracy. With the coming of the Depression, fascist movements spread throughout Europe, carrying Hitler to power in Germany in January 1933, followed two months later by Dollfuss in Austria. Most of eastern Europe quickly followed suit. Even in France, the United Kingdom and the USA, fascist movements arose, pressurising governments from the right and harassing reform movements.

In summary, the Great Depression brought the collapse not only of economic liberalism, but also of liberal political institutions. Yet the triumph of the authoritarian regimes proved short-lived. They were incapable of restoring the old order, or of establishing a stable new one, and ultimately perished in the Second World War.

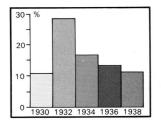

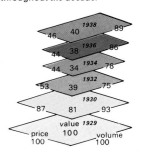

World unemployment *(above)*
In the early 1930s unemployment reached record levels in just about every industrialised country, and many workers remained jobless throughout the decade.

Indices of world trade *(above)*
A drastic drop in the level of prices, coupled with a moderate decrease in volume, produced a sharp decline in the value of world trade.

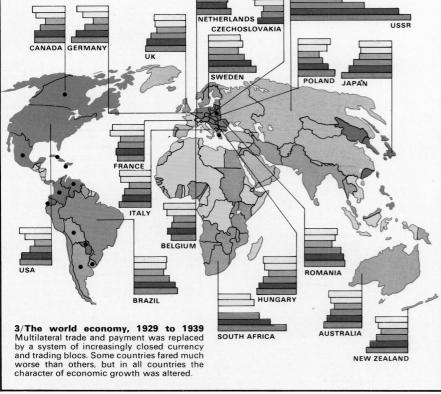

3/The world economy, 1929 to 1939
Multilateral trade and payment was replaced by a system of increasingly closed currency and trading blocs. Some countries fared much worse than others, but in all countries the character of economic growth was altered.

major currency blocs
- gold bloc
- yen bloc
- German-dominated exchange control area
- dollar area
- sterling area
- areas of shifting or dubious allegiance due to German–American rivalry
- • areas of loose currency bloc allegiance

production indices
- 1929 = 100
- 1930
- 1932
- 1934
- 1936
- 1938

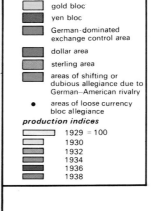

Commodity production 1926 to 1938 *(above)* The movement of commodity prices, stocks and production, especially in the drastic price decline, caused severe hardship and dislocation in many countries, particularly those dependent upon agricultural and raw materials exports.

US statistics *(below)*
These statistics, especially for the years 1937-38, show both the extreme depth of the Depression in the United States and the country's weak, slow and halting recovery.

	unemployment (no. in 000's)	Federal budget surplus + or deficit − (millions of $)	days lost through strikes (000's)	no. of union members (000's)
1930	4340	+737	3320	3632
1932	12060	−2,735	10500	3226
1934	11340	−3,689	19600	3249
1936	9030	−4,424	13900	4164
1938	10390	−1,176	9150	8265

1/The depression in the
1929 Oct. Wall Street Crash.
1930 Hawley-Smoot Tariff pass
1931 Hoover declares moratori on war debts.
1932 Jan. Reconstruct Finance Corporation establish with power to use $2 billion underwrite banks and business **July** Federal Home Loan Ba Act provided $125 million prevent foreclosures. **N** Roosevelt elected presid promising 'New Deal'.
1933 4 Mar. Roosevelt inau rated. **9 Mar.** to **16 June** 'H dred Days' of reform:
Bank Holiday. Glass-Steagall (reform of banking). Fede Securities Act. US goes off g

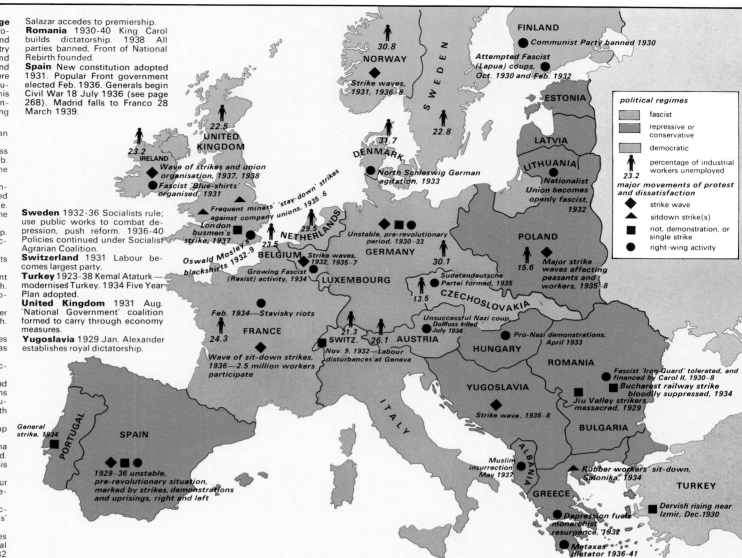

2/Social and political change in Europe, 1929 to 1939 Protest movements of the left and right arose in almost every country in response to the slump, and severely tested the social and political fabric. In countries where democratic traditions and institutions were weak — and this included most European countries — some form of right-wing dictatorship resulted.

Albania 1927 Nov. Virtual Italian protectorate established.
Austria 1933 March. Dollfuss dictatorship established. 1934 Feb. Parties banned, destruction of the Austrian Socialists.
Belgium 1935 March. 'Government of National Union' formed under van Zeeland. 1936 June. Social Improvement Programme stimulates reform.
Bulgaria 1935 May. Army coup. 1936 Boris establishes royal dictatorship.
Estonia 1934 March. Päts dictatorship established.
France 1936 June. Popular Front government installed. 1937 March. 'Breathing Spell' from reform proclaimed.
Germany 1933 Jan. Hitler appointed chancellor. 23 March. Enabling Act passed.
Greece 1935 George II restores monarchy. 1936 Aug. Metaxas establishes dictatorship.
Hungary 1931-35 Gömbös Dictatorship.
Ireland 1932 De Valera, at head of republican Fianna Fail, wins election. Oath of allegiance repudiated. 1932-33 Tariff war with United Kingdom.
Latvia 1934 May. Ulmanis coup established dictatorship.
Lithuania 1926 Dec. Smetona coup. 1936 Feb. All parties banned.
Netherlands 1933-39 'Crisis Cabinet' formed under H. Colijn.
Norway 1935 Second Labour government institutes major reforms.
Poland 1926-35 Pilsudski dictatorship. 1935-39 Colonels' Regime.
Portugal 1928 Salazar becomes Finance Minister. 1930 'National Union' becomes only party. 1932 Salazar accedes to premiership.
Romania 1930-40 King Carol builds dictatorship. 1938 All parties banned, Front of National Rebirth founded.
Spain New constitution adopted 1931. Popular Front government elected Feb. 1936. Generals begin Civil War 18 July 1936 (see page 268). Madrid falls to Franco 28 March 1939.
Sweden 1932-36 Socialists rule; use public works to combat depression, push reform. 1936-40 Policies continued under Socialist Agrarian Coalition.
Switzerland 1931 Labour becomes largest party.
Turkey 1923-38 Kemal Ataturk—modernises Turkey. 1934 Five Year Plan adopted.
United Kingdom 1931 Aug. 'National Government' coalition formed to carry through economy measures.
Yugoslavia 1929 Jan. Alexander establishes royal dictatorship.

political regimes
- fascist
- repressive or conservative
- democratic
- percentage of industrial workers unemployed 23.2

major movements of protest and dissatisfaction
- ◆ strike wave
- ▲ sitdown strike(s)
- ■ riot, demonstration, or single strike
- ● right-wing activity

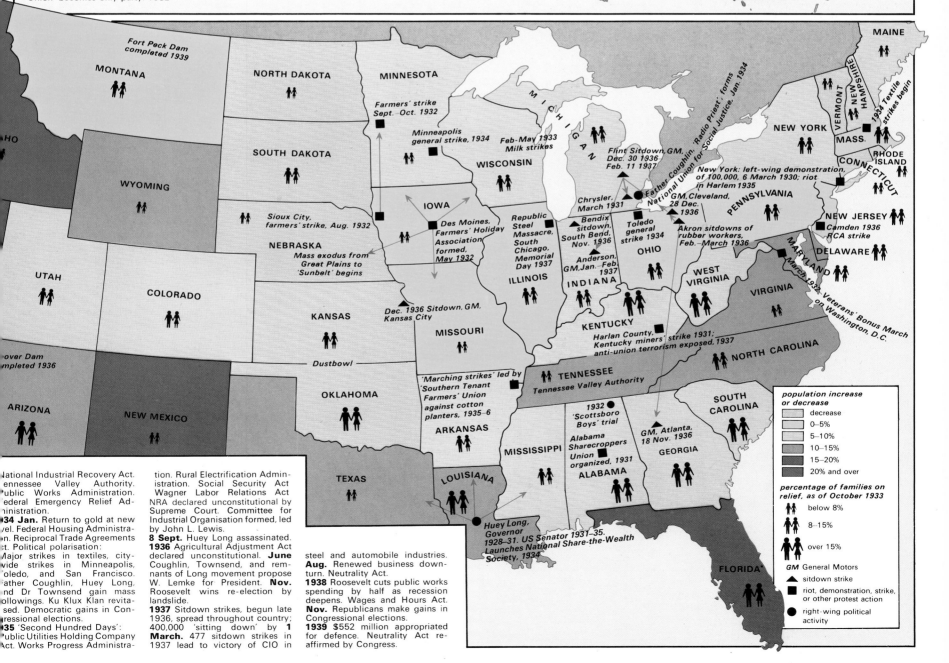

National Industrial Recovery Act. Tennessee Valley Authority. Public Works Administration. Federal Emergency Relief Administration.
1934 Jan. Return to gold at new level. Federal Housing Administration. Reciprocal Trade Agreements Act. Political polarisation: Major strikes in textiles, citywide strikes in Minneapolis, Toledo, and San Francisco. Father Coughlin, Huey Long, and Dr Townsend gain mass followings. Ku Klux Klan revitalised. Democratic gains in Congressional elections.
1935 'Second Hundred Days': Public Utilities Holding Company Act. Works Progress Administra-tion. Rural Electrification Administration. Social Security Act Wagner Labor Relations Act. NRA declared unconstitutional by Supreme Court. Committee for Industrial Organisation formed, led by John L. Lewis.
8 Sept. Huey Long assassinated.
1936 Agricultural Adjustment Act declared unconstitutional. **June** Coughlin, Townsend, and remnants of Long movement propose W. Lemke for President. **Nov.** Roosevelt wins re-election by landslide.
1937 Sitdown strikes, begun in 1936, spread throughout country; 400,000 'sitting down' by **1 March.** 477 sitdown strikes in 1937 lead to victory of CIO in steel and automobile industries. **Aug.** Renewed business downturn. Neutrality Act.
1938 Roosevelt cuts public works spending by half as recession deepens. Wages and Hours Act. **Nov.** Republicans make gains in Congressional elections.
1939 $552 million appropriated for defence. Neutrality Act reaffirmed by Congress.

population increase or decrease
- decrease
- 0–5%
- 5–10%
- 10–15%
- 15–20%
- 20% and over

percentage of families on relief, as of October 1933
- below 8%
- 8–15%
- over 15%

GM General Motors
- ▲ sitdown strike
- ■ riot, demonstration, strike, or other protest action
- ● right-wing political activity

The approach of the Second World War 1931 to 1941

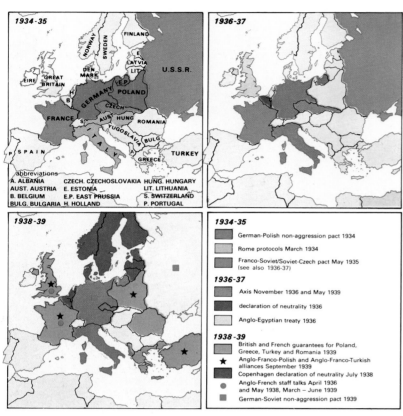

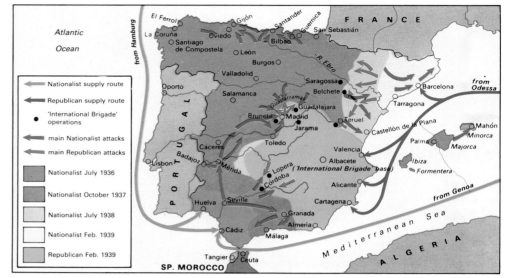

1/European alliances and alignments *(above)* France and Great Britain sought associates to deter German or Italian aggression. Hitler tried either to isolate or, as with the Axis and the Anti-Comintern Pact, to distract potential opponents. Mussolini hoped to control Hitler's rate of expansion to match Italy's capabilities. Other countries concluded non-aggression pacts with Hitler or joined in the 'neutralist' Declaration of Copenhagen, hoping to contract out of war.

2/The expansion of Japan, 1931-41 *(below)* Japanese expansion in Manchuria and northern China before 1936 was designed to control China's potentialities and eliminate British, American and Soviet influence. From 1937 to 1940 Japan sought victory in China through isolating China from external aid. American economic counter-pressure led in 1941 to the decision to conquer and hold 'Greater East Asia', seen as a self-sufficient, defensible empire.

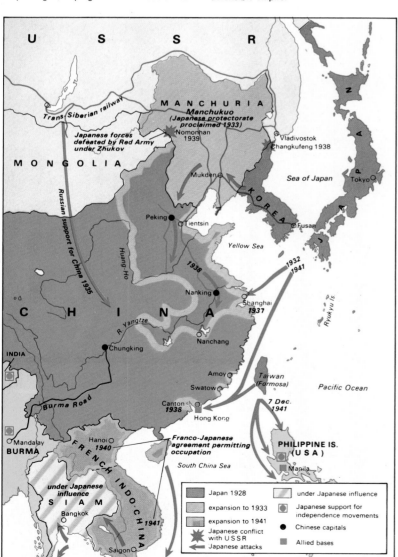

3/The Spanish Civil War, 1936-39 *(above)* The Civil War grouped the military, the political right and the Roman Catholic Church (with German and Italian 'volunteers' and military aid) against the 'Popular Front' government, republicans, anti-clericals, anarchists, socialists and Communists, Basque and Catalan autonomists (with Soviet military aid). Against widespread criticism, Great Britain and France initiated an international Non-Intervention Agreement to prevent escalation into a Mediterranean conflict with Italy.

THE events of the years 1931 to 1941 marked the breakdown of the international security system set up in 1919. This system, centred round the League of Nations, was designed to prevent a dispute between two states escalating, as in 1914, into a general war. It could not rely on American support, and the Soviet Union, though a member of the League from 1934 to 1939, never played a major role. Leadership therefore fell to Great Britain and France. Italy alone, and possibly Japan, might have been deterred or dissuaded from expansion, but Germany under Hitler was, in the last resort, irrationally set on world power or defeat. When all three joined together in the Anti-Comintern Pact and then in the Tripartite Pact, the democratic powers were thrown on to the defensive.

Japanese expansionism was fuelled by exclusion from vital markets and by a sense of racial discrimination on the part of the 'whites'. The ruling groups were also driven by fear of conspiracies among nationalist extremists, especially in the officer corps, such as those who provoked the expulsion of Chinese authority from Manchuria in 1931 and mutinied in 1936. Japanese expansion began with pressure on northern China, continued with open conquest of central China and the Chinese coastline in 1937-39, spread into northern Indo-China and finally, under the pressure of the American economic embargo imposed in July 1941, culminated in the attack on Pearl Harbor and the seizure of the central Pacific and South-East Asia.

Japanese expansion was opposed by the Soviet Union, Great Britain and the United States, at first in the form of aid to China; after 1939 the United States steadily escalated economic pressure on Japan and refused to discuss anything but total Japanese withdrawal. Japan sought German assistance, in the Anti-Comintern Pact of 1936, against the Soviet Union. After the Nazi-Soviet Pact (1939), and the Soviet defeat of Japan at Nomonhan in Mongolia, in 1941 Japan signed a non-aggression pact with the Soviets. German aid was now sought, in the Tripartite Pact of 1940, against the United Kingdom and the United States.

Italian expansionism was inspired by Mussolini's need to fulfil the nationalist ambitions his democratic predecessors had failed to meet and to maintain his prestige as a world leader. This led him to build up Italy's position in central Europe and seek a colonial empire in Ethiopia in 1935. British and French resistance, and the anti-Fascist Popular Front victory in France, induced him to intervene in Spain, and to turn to Hitler in the Rome-Berlin Axis of 1936. Thereafter imitation of Hitler inspired him to claim French territory in 1938, annex Albania in April 1939 and, after the defeat of France, attack Greece in 1940. But military and economic

weakness stultified his efforts to match Hitler's achievements, and tied him to Hitler in the Pact of Steel of 1939.

Hitler's expansionism embraced German nationalist desires to recover the losses of 1919, and looked to dominion over Europe, including European Russia, with a colonial empire in Africa and elsewhere to follow. He took advantage of Anglo-French disagreement and the Ethiopian crisis to ensure recovery by plebiscite of the Saarland and remilitarise the Rhineland. Thereafter, in the annexation of Austria, the Czech crisis and the occupation of Bohemia and Moravia in 1939, he relied on British and French unreadiness for and fear of war. Against Poland his miscalculation involved him in war, not only with Poland but also, despite his conclusion of the Nazi-Soviet Pact, with Great Britain and France. Conquest of Denmark and Norway and the defeat of France in 1940 failed to bring him the compromise peace with Great Britain he desired. He ordered preparations for the invasion of England, but the defeat of the preliminary air offensive in the Battle of Britain led him to postpone the invasion – as it happened, for good. Instead he decided to attack Soviet Russia. The directive for 'Operation Barbarossa' was issued in December 1940. The invasion of Russia was launched on 22 June 1941, after a delay caused by the need to conquer Yugoslavia and Greece. 'Barbarossa' precluded a major German effort in the Mediterranean and Middle East.

Before 1939 British and French opinion on Hitler was far from united. Their governments were inhibited by the need to repair the military, economic and financial weaknesses caused by the Depression (see page 266). Furthermore, Hitler's authoritarianism, anti-Bolshevism and anti-Semitism were widely admired, and the propertied classes in France and other European countries were not averse to co-operation with Nazi Germany. After the League's failure over Ethiopia, Belgium and other smaller European states tried to preserve their neutrality, uniting in 1938 in the Declaration of Copenhagen. It was a vain attempt, and by 1941 only Spain, Portugal, Turkey, Switzerland and Sweden remained inviolate. Meanwhile, Britain and France sought to avoid conflict by appeasing Hitler; but after the sacrifice of Czechoslovakia at Munich in 1938, this no longer seemed possible. Deterrence by a system of guarantees failed too, bringing war over Poland. The Soviets preferred to make a deal with Hitler (August

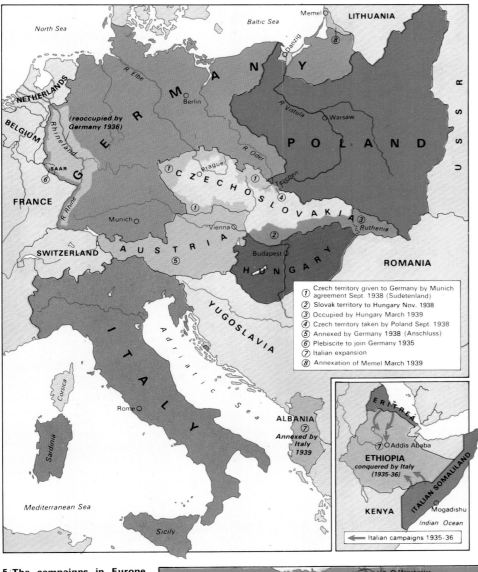

4/German and Italian expansion 1934-39 (left)

Hitler first eliminated the restrictions of Versailles (the recovery of the Saarland by plebiscite, re-militarisation of the Rhineland, annexation of Austria). Then, pretending to advocate self-determination for German minorities, he turned on France's allies, Czechoslovakia and Poland. Czechoslovakia's multi-racial composition facilitated, with British and French acquiescence at Munich, its progressive partition. Polish resistance to German claims (Danzig, the 'Corridor') led to war with Great Britain and France earlier than planned despite Hitler's agreement with the USSR to divide Poland and the Baltic States.
Mussolini's colonial ambitions (Ethiopia) changed into emulation of Hitler (Albania, Greece).

1939), by dividing Poland with him rather than defending it in alliance with a Great Britain and France they distrusted. Their reward was eastern Poland, the Baltic states and Bessarabia. Finland resisted; after victory, Stalin contented himself with limited gains.

President Roosevelt only began to take Hitler seriously after Munich. Until 1941 he thought economic pressure alone could restrain Japan. French defeat and British financial exhaustion brought him to advance his naval power into mid-Atlantic and give lend-lease aid for Great Britain. American opinion was at first both isolationist and anti-Hitler; Pearl Harbor united America in war.

The European collapse, placing the French, Dutch and British colonies in south-east Asia at Japan's mercy, turned a war which had begun in eastern Europe into a world war.

① Czech territory given to Germany by Munich agreement Sept. 1938 (Sudetenland)
② Slovak territory to Hungary Nov. 1938
③ Occupied by Hungary March 1939
④ Czech territory taken by Poland Sept. 1938
⑤ Annexed by Germany 1938 (Anschluss)
⑥ Plebiscite to join Germany 1935
⑦ Italian expansion
⑧ Annexation of Memel March 1939

5/The campaigns in Europe 1939-41 (right)

In September 1939 Hitler overran Poland; in 1940 Denmark, Norway, the Low Countries and the defeat of France followed. Great Britain, its army in France evacuated from Dunkirk, rejected Hitler's peace offers and defeated his *Luftwaffe*. Mussolini's abortive attack on Greece, British intervention and an anti-Axis coup in Yugoslavia led to German occupation of Yugoslavia, Greece and Crete (May 1941). In June 1941 Hitler attacked the Soviet Union.

Propaganda Following the rise of National Socialism, propaganda took on a new dimension. *Above:* protest against bombing of Madrid, 1937, during Spanish Civil War; *below:* exhortation to vote for Hitler in 1938 plebiscite.

Axis territory 1 September 1939
Axis satellites
Axis occupied
German advances
Italian advances
Soviet forces
Allied forces
retreat and withdrawal
airborne landings
cities severely damaged by bombing
Soviet occupied territory 1939-40
British Empire
neutral powers

The war in Asia and the Pacific 1941 to 1945

THE Great Depression (see page 266) fell heavily upon Japan. Most Japanese people became deeply disillusioned with party government. They believed that their army's conquest of Manchuria and advances in inner Mongolia and northern China indicated their nation's predestined role to become the new leader of east Asia. They were convinced that the exploitation of those regions would ease the economic stresses resulting both from a rapidly growing population and from massive military expenditure.

Chiang Kai-shek, supported by the United States and other powers with special interests in China, refused to acquiesce in Japan's advances. In July 1937, skirmishes began near Peking and quickly erupted into a full-scale war. Chiang's troops were no match for the Japanese. In December China's capital, Nanking, was ravaged by the Japanese army and Chiang's government fled into the interior. Within the next year, Japan completed its conquest of eastern and central China, and proclaimed a New Order in which the western powers would be driven from eastern Asia.

The USA and the UK replied by sending aid to Chiang over the Burma Road, strengthening his will not to capitulate. In February 1939 Japan occupied Hainan Island, and in July blockaded British and French concessions in Tientsin, prompting the United States to denounce its treaty of commerce with Japan. The rulers of Japan were convinced that its destiny depended on the acquisition of petroleum, bauxite and rubber in the Philippines, Burma, Malaya and the Indies. By joining the Tripartite Alliance, Japan secured the approval of the Axis for its New Order in east Asia. Unable to obtain its objectives through diplomacy, Japan used the opportunity provided by the German attack on Russia in June 1941 to occupy Indo-China. In October, an expansionist, General Hideki Tojo, became Prime Minister and supported plans for simultaneous surprise attacks on the Americans at Pearl Harbor and on the British in Malaya. The aim was to force the capitulation of South-East Asia within four months, and to create an impregnable Greater East Asia Co-Prosperity Sphere within two years.

The die was cast on 7 December 1941. Pearl Harbor was attacked and the American Pacific Fleet was temporarily crippled. On the same day, Japan attacked the Philippines. By the end of March, all Malaya was conquered, the Netherlands East Indies had surrendered and Burma was overrun. In May 1942 the American fortress at Corregidor fell and Allied resistance ended in the western Pacific. Japan had completed the first stage of its conquest with a minimum of loss. Churchill and Roosevelt, with a war on two fronts, gave first priority to the defeat of Germany. But they also took steps to prevent the extension of the Japanese perimeter by sending American forces to occupy the Fiji Islands and New Caledonia. In May 1942 a Japanese fleet heading for Port Moresby was intercepted by an American task force in the Coral Sea. Neither side won a decisive victory.

Then the tide turned. A great Japanese fleet was sent against the Americans at Midway Island in June 1942. In one afternoon four Japanese aircraft carriers were sunk and the momentum of war reversed. Before the Battle of Midway, Japan never lost a major battle in the Pacific; afterwards, it never won another.

In late 1942 the Allies advanced against the Japanese in four separate lines. The South-West Pacific Forces under General MacArthur began their amphibious drive against the Japanese perimeter. At Guadalcanal the Americans successfully challenged Japanese landings and reinforcements while the Australians halted an overland threat to Port Moresby. Henceforth, these South-West Pacific Forces moved north

from the Bismarck Archipelago and New Guinea to the Philippines and eventually to Okinawa.

In November 1943 the Pacific Ocean Area Forces under Admiral Nimitz began successful amphibious assaults on the Gilbert Islands, the first of a series of co-ordinated advances across the central Pacific to cut Japan's supply lines, and to provide forward American bases for the next selected target as well as airfields for bombing Japan's home islands. The fanatical stands of the Japanese defenders on their island strongholds were ineffective against the prodigious Allied sea, air and land attacks. After the great battle of Leyte Gulf, the Japanese navy no longer posed a threat to Allied advances. Their air force became so diminished that after March 1945 it was powerless against the devastating air raids on principal metropolitan areas.

At the same time, British and Indian troops stopped the Japanese advance through Burma at Imphal and began the liberation of South-East Asia. American assistance was despatched to the Chinese nationalists, and the American air force began bombing the Japanese homeland from China. The American submarines, guided to their targets by American crypto-analysts, inflicted severe damage on Japan's merchant marine and slowly strangled its island economy.

At Cairo in 1943, the Allies had announced that they would fight until Japan's unconditional surrender, stripping it of all territories acquired after 1895. Even though Japan showed no signs of giving up, post-war policy planners in the US Department of State believed that Japan might stop its fanatical resistance if it knew what the Allies really meant by 'unconditional surrender', and prepared a policy statement defining unconditional surrender in specific terms. Simultaneously, the secret work on a nuclear weapon, which Churchill and Roosevelt had sanctioned in 1942, was nearing completion. In July 1945 a special commission recommended to President Truman that the bomb be used against Japan. The American Secretary of War, Henry Stimson, argued instead that Japan should be given a chance to surrender before the bomb was used. But at Potsdam that month, the Allied leaders approved the Potsdam Declaration appealing to Japan to surrender or face destruction, confirmed the territorial limits set at Cairo, called for an Allied occupation of Japan, the elimination of its armed forces and the establishment of a peacefully inclined and responsible government. When Japan failed to reply positively to this offer, President Truman ordered the first atomic bomb to be dropped on

1/The Japanese advance 1941-1942, (below) In the first six months of the war in Asia and the Pacific, Japan, by virtue of holding the initiative, careful preparation and local air and naval superiority, inflicted a series of humiliating defeats upon the western powers. The Philippines, the Indies, Burma, Hong Kong, Malaya and Singapore were overrun by Japanese forces at minimal cost and often with contemptuous ease but in the great expanse of the Pacific, the victory that Japan needed to neutralise American power eluded her. Japan sought not to conquer the United States but to destroy both the American capacity to dispute her gains in South-East Asia and American morale. However, the preemptive attack on Pearl Harbor only temporarily crippled the US Pacific fleet, and the immunity of American industry to disruption ensured that the Americans were able to recover their strength and to fight in the Pacific the war of attrition they were certain to win.

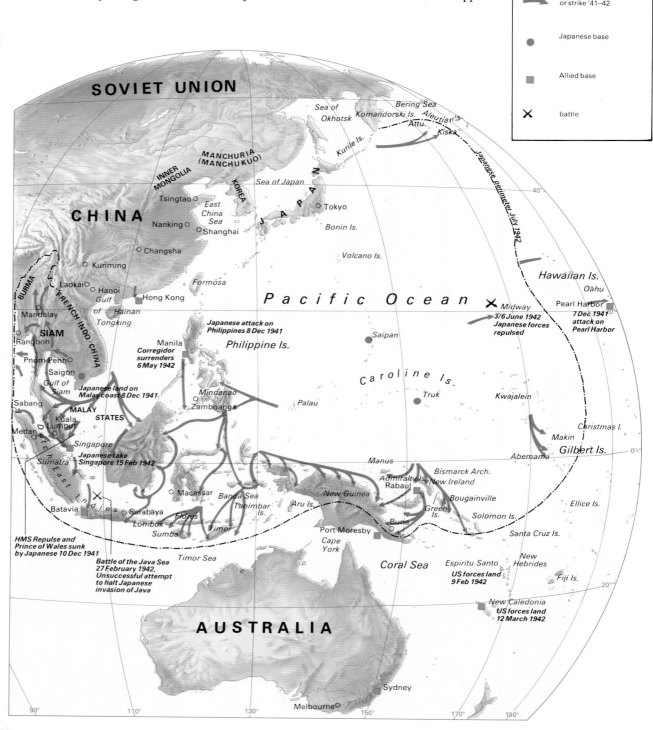

Japanese advance
or strike '41–42

Japanese base

Allied base

battle

SOVIET UNION

MANCHURIA (MANCHUKUO)

INNER MONGOLIA

KOREA

CHINA

Tsingtao

Nanking

Shanghai

Changsha

Kunming

Laokai

Hanoi

Hong Kong

Mandalay

BURMA

FRENCH INDO-CHINA

SIAM

Rangoon

Pnom Penh

Saigon

Sabang

MALAY STATES

Medan

Kuala Lumpur

Singapore

Sumatra

Batavia

Surabaya

Lombok

Sumba

Flores

Timor

Macassar

Banda Sea

Tanimbar Is.

Aru Is.

New Guinea

Rabaul

Bougainville

Solomon Is.

Port Moresby

Cape York

Timor Sea

Coral Sea

AUSTRALIA

Sea of Okhotsk

Komandorski Is.

Bering Sea

Aleutian Is.

Attu

Kiska

Kurile Is.

Sea of Japan

JAPAN

Tokyo

Bonin Is.

Volcano Is.

Formosa

Pacific Ocean

Midway
3/6 June 1942
Japanese forces repulsed

Hawaiian Is.

Oahu

Pearl Harbor
7 Dec 1941
attack on
Pearl Harbor

Saipan

Philippine Is.

Caroline Is.

Palau

Truk

Kwajalein

Christmas I.

Makin

Abemama

Gilbert Is.

Manus

Admiralty Is.

Bismarck Arch.

New Ireland

Green Is.

Ellice Is.

Buna

Santa Cruz Is.

Espiritu Santo
US forces land
9 Feb 1942

New Hebrides

Fiji Is.

New Caledonia
US forces land
12 March 1942

Japanese attack on Philippines 8 Dec 1941

Manila
Corregidor surrenders
6 May 1942

Japanese land on Malay coast 8 Dec 1941

Mindanao
Zamboanga

Japanese take Singapore 15 Feb 1942

HMS Repulse and Prince of Wales sunk by Japanese 10 Dec 1941

Battle of the Java Sea 27 February 1942, Unsuccessful attempt to halt Japanese invasion of Java

Gulf of Tongking

Hainan

Gulf of Siam

Dutch East Indies

Japanese perimeter, July 1942

Sydney

Melbourne

Hiroshima on 6 August 1945. Three days later a second bomb was dropped, on Nagasaki, and Russia entered the war against Japan. On 2 September 1945, on board *USS Missouri* in Tokyo Bay, General MacArthur, the Allied Supreme Commander, accepted Japan's surrender.

However, the end of hostilities brought neither peace nor stability to the Far East. The European defeat in 1941 and subsequent Japanese occupation had combined to fan nationalist and Communist sentiments that were to change the map of East and South-East Asia over the next three decades as the attempted restoration, after Japan's defeat, of the colonial empires gave rise to a generation of conflicts throughout the area.

The atomic bomb *(right)* The picture shows the devastation inflicted by the first atomic bomb, dropped on Hiroshima on 6 August 1945. Nagasaki suffered the same fate three days later and the combined death toll was over 150,000. The world had entered the nuclear age.

2/The Allied counter-offensive *(below)* The stages of Japanese defeat divided into two phases, the first a difficult and protracted struggle in the south-west Pacific, and then the sudden and dramatic collapse of Japanese air and naval power throughout the western Pacific. Allied gains in the south-west Pacific between July 1942 and November 1943, after the Japanese defeat off Midway in June 1942, decisively weakened Japan as she faced Allied offensives across the central as well as the south-west Pacific. In addition, the Allies successfully mounted an unrestricted submarine campaign against Japanese shipping. By November 1944 when American bombers, operating from the Marianas, first raided the Japanese home islands, the merchant fleet was all but destroyed. Allied occupation of the Philippines (late 1944) and Okinawa (April 1945) effectively severed Japan's lines of communication with South-East Asia. By mid-August, following two atomic bombings, Japan capitulated.

The war in the West 1941 to 1945

THE German attack on the Soviet Union in June 1941 was to be followed by fourteen months of German victory, interrupted by the Soviet winter offensive of December 1941 which drove the invaders, frozen and unprepared for the Russian winter, back from Moscow, and by a British offensive in November 1941 in Cyrenaica. The tide of victory turned against Germany in November 1942 with the British victory at El Alamein, the Anglo-American landings in French North Africa and the Soviet break through the German front at Stalingrad. After massive withdrawals, heroic German efforts temporarily stabilised the various fronts. Vichy France was occupied. But by February 1943 the Germans had lost their Sixth Army, surrounded near Stalingrad, and all North Africa with a quarter of a million men. In July 1943 the Allies invaded Sicily and the Russians defeated the last major German offensive at Kursk. In Italy the Fascist Grand Council deposed Mussolini (25 July) who was arrested. The new Premier sued in secret for an armistice, which was announced on 8 September. In swift reaction, Germany seized northern and central Italy, rescued Mussolini to head a puppet Fascist Republic and disarmed Italian occupation forces in Greece and Yugoslavia. Allied landings in southern Italy met bitter resistance, and they took eleven months to reach Rome. Soviet forces met equally bitter resistance, reaching the Vistula only in August 1944.

In June 1944, Anglo-American forces landed in northern France, creating the Second Front so often promised to Stalin over the two previous years. The differing political aims of the Big Three – the United States, Great Britain and the Soviet Union – were already apparent, despite the conference of the Allied leaders at Teheran (November 1943). Soviet offensives led to the conquering of all south-eastern Europe. Romania surrendered in August 1944, Bulgaria in September. A German coup prevented Hungary from doing likewise. Churchill, failing to secure a Western invasion of south-east Europe, agreed at Moscow in October to divide the area with the Soviet Union on a percentage basis. In Poland the Russians made little effort to intervene when the Germans suppressed a rising in Warsaw by the non-Communist Polish underground army. In April 1943 to 1944 they had broken relations with the Polish government in exile, recognising instead their own creation, the Lublin Committee. They also prepared a Free German movement, to work for Soviet victory in post-war Germany.

The Allied forces in northern France aimed for victory in 1944, but they failed. France and Belgium were liberated, the German border reached; but the drive for northern Germany ended with the failure to capture the Rhine bridges by airborne assault at Arnhem. Hitler chose the west for his final offensive in the Ardennes in December 1944. The major Soviet offensive against East Prussia opened in January. In February, Roosevelt, Churchill and Stalin met at Yalta. Both Roosevelt and Churchill, particularly the former, put the need to secure Russian membership of the new United Nations before everything else, accepting Soviet primacy in Poland and major changes in Poland's frontiers. By April Berlin was under assault and Hitler committed suicide on the 30th. On 7 May, Admiral Doenitz, his successor, surrendered unconditionally.

Until June 1944, the main Anglo-American attack on Germany had been by air against the cities. German air defences had gained the upper hand by late 1943, but were unable to withstand its resumption in late 1944 despite Germany's lead in developing jet engines. German guided and ballistic missiles, used from June 1944 against south-east England, came too late to be effective. At sea, the German submarine blockade, operating in mid-Atlantic beyond the range of Allied land-based aircraft, brought the Allies close to disaster, until the advent of long range aircraft and escort carriers from May 1943 onwards closed the unpatrolled 'gap'.

In German-occupied Europe, resistance forces fought against German occupation and, where they were ideologically divided, against each other. In Yugoslavia, Tito's Communist partisans won British backing. In Greece the Communist EAM rose against the British when the latter decided to restore the monarchy. In Slovakia a Communist rising was defeated by the Germans. In Italy, partisans caught and killed Mussolini in April 1945.

The conduct of war was 'total', embracing and mobilising everyone. Great Britain and the Soviet Union achieved total mobilisation, including severe food rationing from 1940 onwards. Germany only adopted full mobilisation in 1944, led by Josef Goebbels and Albert Speer. United States' unused productive capacity was so great that the American economy enjoyed boom conditions where Europe and the western USSR saw major destruction and massive movements of population. Several millions of slave and contract labourers were drawn into Germany; German settlers were sent into the Baltic states and then withdrawn. Over ten million

The Russian flag hoisted on the ruins of the Reichstag *(above)* Russian forces under Koniev and Zhukov took Berlin in May 1945. The Soviet Union bore the lion's share of all land fighting from 1941 to 1944, suffering seven and a half million military deaths alone and untold devastation throughout European Russia.

1/Hitler's 'New Order' in Europe *(below)* Hitler divided Europe into four: pure Aryan areas annexed to or occupied by Germany and integrated into the German economy; occupied 'non-incorporated' areas; puppet and satellite states; the occupied and despoiled Slavic east, earmarked for German colonisation, whose native population would become illiterate helots.

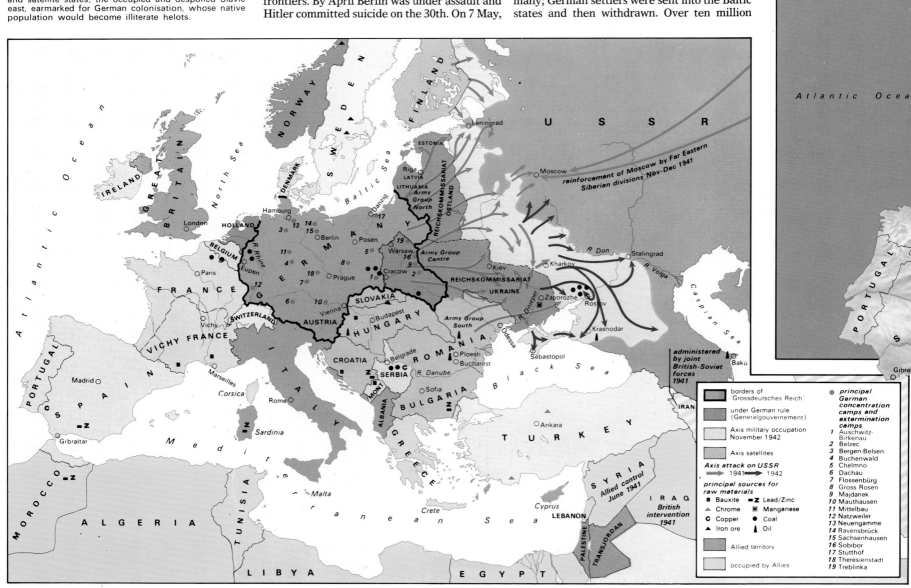

	borders of 'Grossdeutsches Reich'
	under German rule (Generalgouvernement)
	Axis military occupation November 1942
	Axis satellites

Axis attack on USSR
1941 ➡ 1942

principal sources for raw materials
- ■ Bauxite
- ▲ Chrome
- C Copper
- ▲ Iron ore
- ⚊Z Lead/Zinc
- Ⓜ Manganese
- ● Coal
- ▮ Oil

| | Allied territory |
| | occupied by Allies |

● **principal German concentration camps and extermination camps**
1 Auschwitz-Birkenau
2 Belzec
3 Bergen-Belsen
4 Buchenwald
5 Chelmno
6 Dachau
7 Flossenbürg
8 Gross Rosen
9 Majdanek
10 Mauthausen
11 Mittelbau
12 Natzweiler
13 Neuengamme
14 Ravensbrück
15 Sachsenhausen
16 Sobibor
17 Stutthof
18 Theresienstadt
19 Treblinka

Germans were expelled from Eastern Europe or fled the Russian advance. Germany rounded up Europe's Jewish and Gipsy minorities for slaughter in the death-camps. Stalin deported sixteen minority peoples from the Crimea and Caucasus for alleged collaboration with the Germans. One hundred million men and women were mobilised to fight. The dead have been estimated at fifteen million military and thirty-five million civilians (twenty million of these being Soviet citizens, six million Jews, four and a half million Poles). There are no reliable estimates of the wounded. When the war ended, the leaders of the so-called Big Three countries led the United Nations. But Great Britain and

Europe were bankrupt, and European Russia was in ruins. Only the United States, whose money and industries had through 'lend-lease' sustained and augmented the war economies of her allies, seemed the immediate and real victor.

2/The Battle of the Atlantic (right) The German campaign against British shipping began in the western approaches to Britain, moving in April 1941 to the mid-Atlantic 'gap', then beyond the range of British air-cover. The entry of the United States into the war opened further killing-grounds in US waters and the Caribbean to the new German long-range U-boats. After May 1943, patrolling of the 'gap' by very long range aircraft, with airborne radar acting on deciphered U-boat radio traffic, destroyed the existing U-boats' effectiveness.

3/The defeat of Germany (below) Hitler's failure to defeat Great Britain in the Blitz and the Atlantic and to overthrow Stalin's regime in the Soviet Union made his own defeat inevitable, as irreconcilable ideologies ruled out a compromise peace. The German armies were defeated in detail on the eastern front, the British and Americans knocked out Italy and invaded France, making German collapse under attack from east, west and south only a question of time.

6/The Normandy landings (inset below) On 6 June, 1944 American, British and Canadian armies landed in Normandy, breaching the German fortifications ('Atlantic Wall'). Allied air attack on German communications prevented German counter-attack. Artificial 'Mulberry' harbours turned the beaches into ports adequate for all necessary supplies.

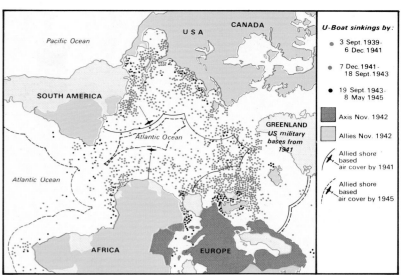

U-Boat sinkings by:
- 3 Sept. 1939 - 6 Dec. 1941
- 7 Dec. 1941 - 18 Sept. 1943
- 19 Sept. 1943 - 8 May 1945

Axis Nov. 1942
Allies Nov. 1942
Allied shore based air cover by 1941
Allied shore based air cover by 1945

4/The Battle of Stalingrad (inset below) In November 1942 the Russians encircled the German Sixth Army near Stalingrad, broke a rescue attempt and rolled the German front back to the Kharkov-Taganrog line.

5/The Battle of Kursk (inset bottom) in July 1943 was Hitler's last major offensive on the eastern front. It failed because of his own hesitation, superior Russian firepower and fears of an Italian collapse following the Allied invasion of Sicily.

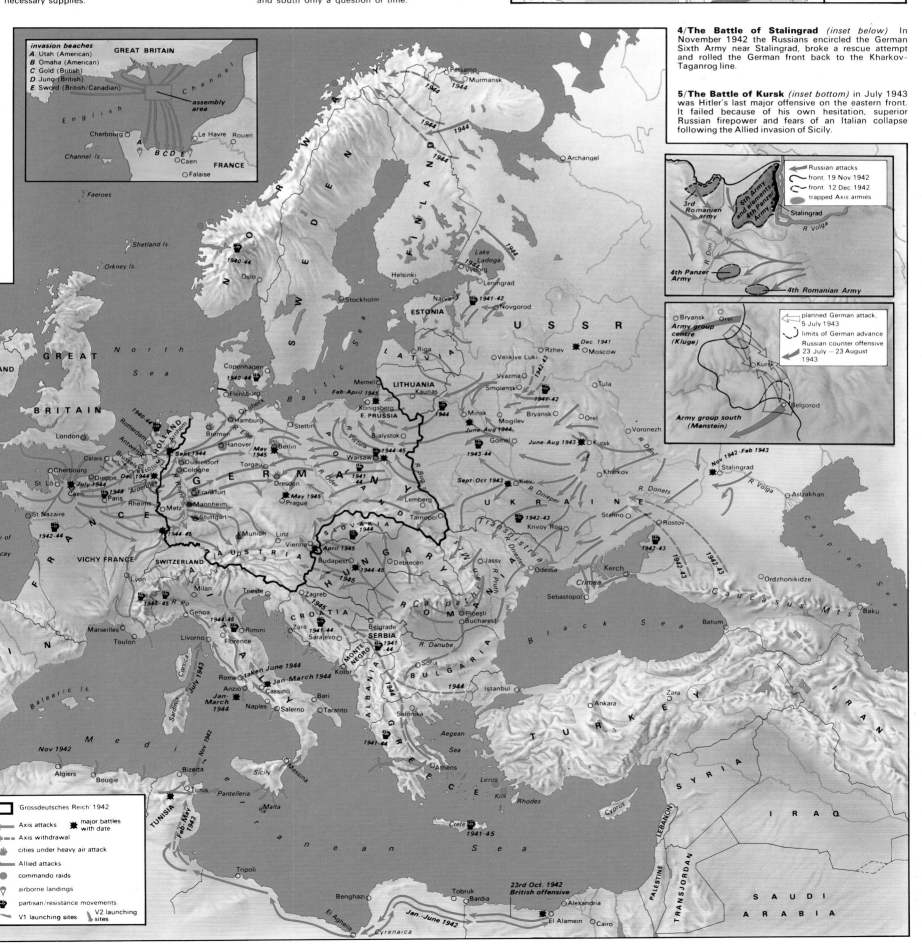

invasion beaches
A. Utah (American)
B. Omaha (American)
C. Gold (British)
D. Juno (British)
E. Sword (British/Canadian)

assembly area

Russian attacks
front. 19 Nov 1942
front. 12 Dec 1942
trapped Axis armies

planned German attack. 5 July 1943
limits of German advance
Russian counter offensive 23 July – 23 August 1943

'Grossdeutsches Reich' 1942
Axis attacks
Axis withdrawal
cities under heavy air attack
Allied attacks
commando raids
airborne landings
partisan/resistance movements
V1 launching sites
V2 launching sites
major battles with date

273

Europe since 1945

THE war left Europe in 1945 politically disorganised and economically prostrate, a situation which was greatly exacerbated by large-scale population movements. Until 1949 the outlook was bleak, and political uncertainty, fostered by the antagonism between the USA and the USSR, hampered recovery.

Meanwhile, the dismantling of the German New Order and the political reconstruction of Europe were taking place under the shadow of Russian-American conflict. The political frontiers of Europe were established at the Yalta and Potsdam conferences of the Soviet Union, the United Kingdom and the United States in February and July-August 1945 respectively. Germany and Austria (the *Anschluss* of 1938 nullified) were divided into occupation zones and placed under four-power control. It was not until 1955 that Austria re-emerged as an independent, though permanently neutralised, state or that sovereignty was fully restored to Western Germany. There was also an inter-Allied Control Council in Berlin, which, though within the Soviet zone, was itself divided into zones. This created problems for the Western powers during the 'airlift' crisis of 1948-49 and again in 1958-61, when the Soviet government sought to have the Western sectors of Berlin incorporated in a demilitarised Free City. The latter crisis ended with the building of the Berlin Wall by the East Germans in August 1961.

Of the two new German states, formed in 1949 (see map 2), the Federal Republic joined the European Coal and Steel Community (ECSC) in 1952 and the North Atlantic Treaty Organisation (NATO) in 1955, and the German Democratic Republic joined the newly-founded Warsaw Treaty Organisation. The Western Powers refused for many years to recognise the DDR, but in 1972 the West German government reversed its policy and accorded recognition, and at the Helsinki Conference on Security and Co-operation in Europe in 1975 the other Western Powers followed suit.

The two halves of Europe became strikingly different: on the one side, democracy and unparalleled consumer-prosperity with its attendant problems, on the other side regimentation, privation and shabbiness. After 1949, western Europe experienced economic miracles, with Federal Germany leading the way. Increased integration of markets, mobility of labour, flexible responses to technology and mass-education made the countries of the EEC equal and then superior in economic weight to the United States.

As a result of the 'cold war' (see page 292) Europe was divided into three blocs: Western, Communist and neutral. The six countries forming the European Coal and Steel Community in 1952 – the Benelux group (Belgium, Luxembourg and the Netherlands), West Germany,

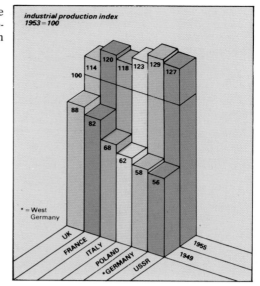

Industrial production *(left)* For Western Europe, the bleak outlook for economic recovery was ended by the injection of massive American aid (the Marshall Plan) between 1948 and 1952. A parallel recovery occurred more slowly in Eastern Europe.

1/Post-war population movements *(below)* The collapse of Hitler's Third Reich in 1945 released millions of prisoners of war and slave-workers incarcerated in Germany during the war. Furthermore, some 5 million Russian prisoners, refugees and servicemen were forcibly repatriated. A more lasting shift of population was the expulsion of Germans from some of their pre-war territories, especially in eastern Europe, and from the lands they had annexed in the late 1930s. A further movement at the end of the war was the result of the westward expansion of the Soviet Union, especially the annexation of the Baltic states, Estonia, Latvia and Lithuania.

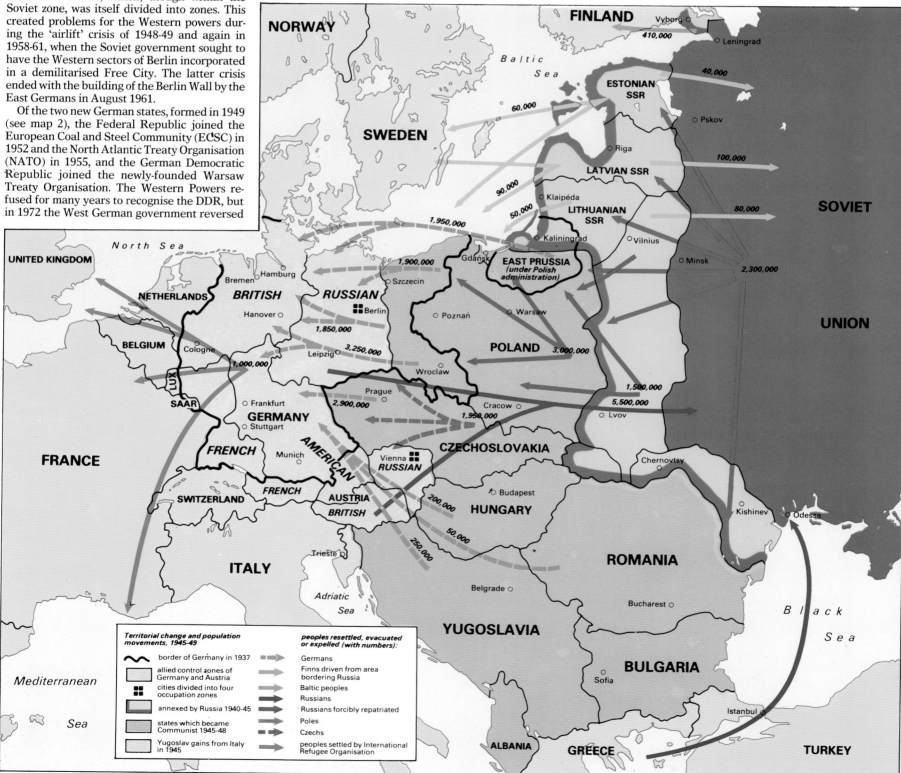

France and Italy – joined together to form the European Economic Community (EEC) and Euratom in 1957. These three Communities became the European Community and were joined by Denmark, Ireland and the United Kingdom in January 1973. It was envisaged that eventually this economic grouping would form a political unit, but problems arising over the common agricultural policy and exchange rate fluctuations made this objective optimistic.

Politically, by 1970 Europe had settled on its new course. The European Security Conference at Helsinki removed old tensions and inaugurated a period of détente and peaceful co-existence. Trade between eastern and western Europe increased rapidly. A further factor behind stabilisation was the upsurge of prosperity following the formation of the EEC. Between 1958 and 1962 trade between member states increased by 130 per cent, and in seven years Italian industrial production rose by 107 per cent. But the benefits were uneven and accrued mainly to the core countries. Southern Italy, like Spain and Portugal, and other countries on the periphery remain backward, and elsewhere there were regional pockets of persistent depression. Northern Ireland, prosperous in the immediate post-war years, suffered a sharp setback after 1970, and here economic distress coupled with long-standing religious and racial grievances, fanned by a series of bloody incidents in 1972, gave rise to a situation bordering on civil war. In France there was unrest in Brittany, where average income was only 60 per cent of that in Paris, as well as in Corsica: in Spain Basques and Catalans demanded autonomy; Belgium was beset by the conflict between Flemings and Walloons.

Although Communist Europe became heavily industrialised on Soviet lines, there was little comparison with the consumer prosperity of western Europe. Housing, wage-rates, communications, health-care remained backward, and pollution became a serious problem in most parts. Widespread discontent with this, and with the Soviet military presence, led to revolts: Hungary and Poland in 1956, Czechoslovakia in 1968, Poland in 1970 and again in 1980-81, when an underground, Catholic-inspired trade union movement, *Solidarity*, became a focus for widespread nationalist discontent. These revolts were crushed – in 1956 and 1968 by Soviet force, in 1970 and in the early 1980s by local forces. They did, however, lead to efforts towards 'reformed Communism', including experiments with market-socialism for which Hungary became a show-case. In the late 1980s popular protests led to the collapse of Communist power in Eastern Europe and free elections brought non-Communist parties into government in Poland, Czechoslovakia and Hungary. Germany was re-united on 3 October 1990, and Soviet domination came to an abrupt halt.

The decline of Communism in Eastern Europe 1980-1990

East Germany 1989 (Aug.-Sept.) Mass refugee escape to West Germany via Hungary and Czechoslovakia; (Oct.-Nov.) Mass demonstrations throughout country; (9 Nov.) Berlin Wall breached, formally opened Dec.-Jan. 1990 leading to reunification.

Poland 1980 formation of independent trade union, *Solidarity*; 1981-89 martial law imposed; 1989 (Sept.) *Solidarity* led government takes office; 1990 (Jan.) Polish Communist Party dissolves itself

Czechoslovakia 1989 (Nov.) Mass demonstrations spread from Prague leading to collapse of Communist rule

Hungary 1989 (Oct.) End of Communist rule. Hungarian Communist Party becomes a 'Socialist Party'

Yugoslavia 1988 Mass demonstrations against falling living standards and corruption; 1989 Slovenia and Croatia legalise opposition parties; 1990 (April) Non-Communists elected in Slovenia and Croatia

Romania 1989 (Dec.) Mass demonstrations lead to armed uprisings in Bucharest and Timisoara; dictatorship overthrown, President Nicolae Ceausescu executed

Bulgaria 1989 (Nov.) Dictator Todor Zhivkov removed from office by Party opponents

Ukraine 1989 (July) Ukrainian coal-miners join all-Union strike calling for improved conditions and end to Party monopoly; (Sept.) First National Congress of *Rukh* (Ukrainian Nationalist Party)

Byelorussia 1989 (June) Popular Front founded

Moldavia 1989 (May) Popular Front founded; (Sept.) Moldavian Supreme Soviet reintroduces Moldavian State language and Latin alphabet; 1990 (Feb.) Popular Front wins 75% of votes in election

Lithuania 1988 *Sajudis* (independent movement) formed; 1989 (May) Lithuanian Supreme Soviet declares sovereignty 1990 (Feb.) *Sajudis* wins 63% of seats; (Mar.) Lithuania declares independence

Latvia 1988 National Independence Movement formed; 1989 mass anti-Communist demonstrations

Estonia 1988 National Independence Party formed; (Nov.) Estonian Supreme Soviet adopts right to veto all-Union laws; 1990 (Mar.) Congress of Estonia formed

2/Post-war Germany 1945-1990 *(right)* Immediately after the war, Germany lost territory to the USSR and Poland and was split into British, American, Soviet and later, French zones. Berlin, although in the Russian sector, was further subdivided. In 1949 the Soviet zone of occupation was converted into a separate state, the German Democratic Republic (DDR) and the three Western zones of Germany formed the Federal Republic of Germany (BRD). It took until 1970 for the West Germans to recognise the post-war Polish western frontier and until 1972 before they recognised the separate existence of two German states. 1989 saw a wave of protest against the Communist Government in the DDR and the Berlin Wall began to be dismantled. The overthrow of the Communist regime of Erich Honecker brought the re-establishment of democracy in East Germany, and in October 1990 the re-unification of East and West.

3/Military and economic blocs *(right)* The Western defence group NATO (1949) is shown confronting the Warsaw Treaty Organisation (1955). Their economic counterparts are the EEC, formed in 1957, and Comecon, formed in 1949.

4/Communism in Eastern Europe 1947-1990 *(below)* The peoples of east-central Europe never accepted Communist rule, but initially were powerless to resist the police state. In the 1980s confidence grew that the time had come to oppose the ruling cliques. This new mood owed much to new Soviet leader Gorbachov's policy of *glasnost*, but was also due to the failure of Communist leaders to halt falling living standards and avert impending ecological disasters. Poland and Hungary led the way in moving towards political pluralism, and in the latter half of 1989 Communist regimes in East Germany, Czechoslovakia, Bulgaria and Romania collapsed like dominoes. Pressure towards ending the Communist party's monopoly of power was also growing within the Soviet Union, and the Baltic States were first in moves to declare their independence. The collapse of Soviet influence in Eastern Europe also brought the end of the Warsaw Pact and of Comecon.

Retreat from empire after 1939

IN 1939 the European powers with colonial possessions were Great Britain, France, the Netherlands, Italy, Belgium, Spain and Portugal. The first three powers were, to varying degrees, committed to the evolution of their colonial territories towards self-government, and this commitment was reinforced, in the case of Great Britain and France, by the terms under which they had been granted mandates by the League of Nations over territories formerly part of the German and Ottoman empires. Great Britain alone conceived the ultimate goal as going beyond self-government to independence, within a loose framework of attachment to the Commonwealth (established by the Statute of Westminster, 1931), a goal already reached in 1939 by Canada, South Africa, Australia and New Zealand, and towards which India was considered to be moving. The continental powers thought more in terms of evolution towards a common citizenship, and saw their colonies largely as overseas parts of the metropolitan territory. These commitments were, however, complicated both by the resistance of sizeable minorities of European settlers, with consequent interracial tensions, and by clashes between the European ideal of evolution along western lines (e.g. in education and in economic development) and the powerful Islamic, Hindu, Buddhist and Confucian cultures of their colonial subjects.

The need to raise western-educated élites from the colonial peoples to man at least the lower ranks of colonial administrations had already resulted in the growth of important local nationalist movements, some of which also were inspired by Soviet, Chinese or Japanese models. The unwillingness of metropolitan legislatures or electorates to finance full-scale European-manned administrations also encouraged the colonial powers to rely on indigenous local authorities wherever these were powerful enough to be used by the European governments.

The events of the Second World War had revolutionary effects on the slow processes of development within the main colonial empires. In Europe, Belgium, France and the Netherlands were overrun by Germany. The governments of Belgium and the Netherlands took refuge in England; that of France accepted defeat and compromise with Germany and Italy so completely that in part of the overseas territories an anti-capitulation movement, the Free French, sprang up, while the British and Americans felt obliged to take over Vichy-held territories in the Middle East and North Africa. Italy's African colonies passed under British occupation. In South-East Asia, Germany's Japanese ally expelled the colonial powers from Malaya, the East Indies and Burma, and established governments based on local nationalist movements in Burma in 1942 and the East Indies and Indo-China in 1945. After the surrender of Japan these governments won much popular backing and were strong enough to force the colonial power – in the case of Burma with only minimal violence, in the East Indies and Indo-China after prolonged conflict – to recognise their independence.

The war years were marked by a political impasse in India. The ill-timed Cripps' Mission, sent by a reluctant Churchill under American pressure, failed to resolve it. In 1942, Gandhi and his associates were imprisoned and the subsequent mass uprising was suppressed with great firmness. The radical leader, Subhas Bose, escaped and organised an Indian National Army under Japanese auspices. When, after the war, the unrest spread to the main army, the newly-elected Labour government in England decided to break with the tradition of holding on to the essence of power. Meanwhile the Indian Muslim demand for an autonomous region had grown strong and in 1947 power was transferred to the two states of India and Pakistan (see page 280).

In France, the Fourth Republic replaced the old Empire by a new *Union française* consisting of metropolitan France with its overseas *départements* and territories, and a group of associated states, including Laos, Cambodia and a French-inspired Republic of Vietnam. But in Vietnam the French 'satellite' administration was opposed by the forces of the Democratic Republic of Vietnam which were committed to independence, and after the defeat of Dien Bien Phu the French were forced, in 1954, to withdraw. In 1957 Great Britain took the first major step towards conferring independence in Africa, with the grant of independence to Ghana.

Attempts to solve the problem posed by white settler minorities in central Africa by the creation of a Central African Federation broke down in 1963, and Rhodesia, which had enjoyed white settler self-government since 1923, declared its independence, without British agreement, in 1965. France, after the collapse of the Fourth Republic in 1958, replaced the *Union française* with the *Communauté française*, but this was unacceptable to Guinea, which opted for complete independence; thirteen others followed its example in 1960, leaving Algeria the only French possession in Africa.

In the French territories of the Middle East and North Africa, the effects of British or American occupation and protection had helped to revitalise the independence movements. Italy's two main colonial possessions, Libya and Somalia, placed under UN mandate in 1945, became independent in 1951 and 1960; Eritrea, was absorbed uneasily into Ethiopia.

At the same time, Britain hoped to maintain her links with the Arab world after the ending of the mandates system by encouraging the formation of the Arab League, and later by the Baghdad Pact, a military alliance intended to incorporate the US, Britain, Pakistan and various pro-Western Middle Eastern states. However, Zionist victories in Palestine leading to the creation of Israel in 1948, Nasser's seizure of power in 1952, and the Anglo-French-Israeli invasion of Egypt in 1956 combined to diminish British and French influence and credibility in the region. Bitter conflicts in Cyprus and Aden led Britain to withdraw in 1960 and 1967, and the British presence east of Suez was gradually abandoned; many of the smaller Gulf sheikhdoms combined to form the United Arab Emirates in 1971. France realised its inability to sustain prolonged conflict in more than one of its North African territories; Morocco and Tunisia became independent in 1956, while Algeria suffered 8 years of war until the French capitulated in 1962.

Since the powers had tended to endow their colonial territories with political institutions with little or no indigenous roots, it is not surprising that colonial withdrawal was frequently accompanied – or soon followed – by acts of revolutionary violence, and the setting up of repressive regimes. In other cases, ethnic or tribal units extended across frontiers: Indonesian claims over all Malay-speaking areas in the 1950s and 1960s led to conflict with Malaysia, and Somalia laid claim to areas of Kenya and Ethiopia. After Belgium abandoned the Congo in 1960, most of the new African states were united against the remaining Portuguese colonial territories and supported guerrilla liberation movements which brought independence to Angola and Mozambique a year after the collapse of the dictatorship in Portugal in 1974. Spain continues to occupy a few tiny enclaves in Morocco, but abandoned the Sahara to Morocco and Mauritania in 1976, since when Mauritania has also opted out of any territorial claim. After 13 years of guerrilla warfare, white minority rule ended in Rhodesia, which became Zimbabwe in 1980, leaving South Africa as the last remaining 'colonial' state in the African continent in the late 1980s.

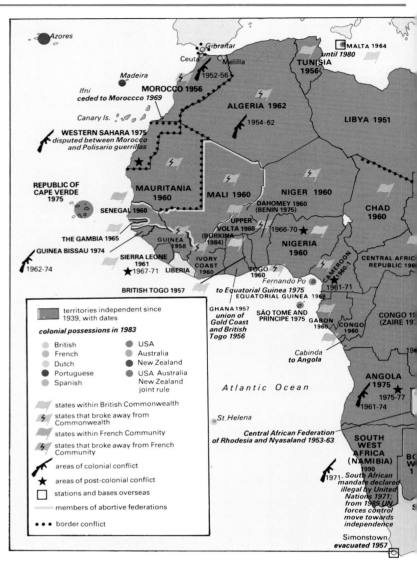

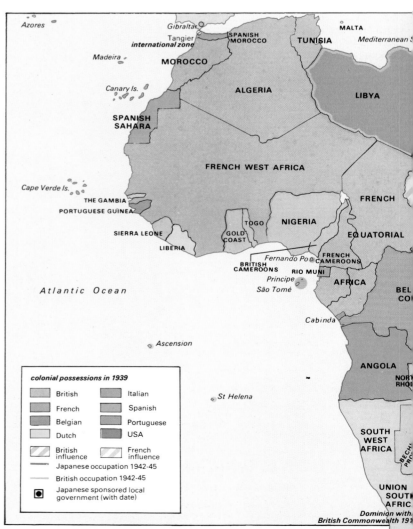

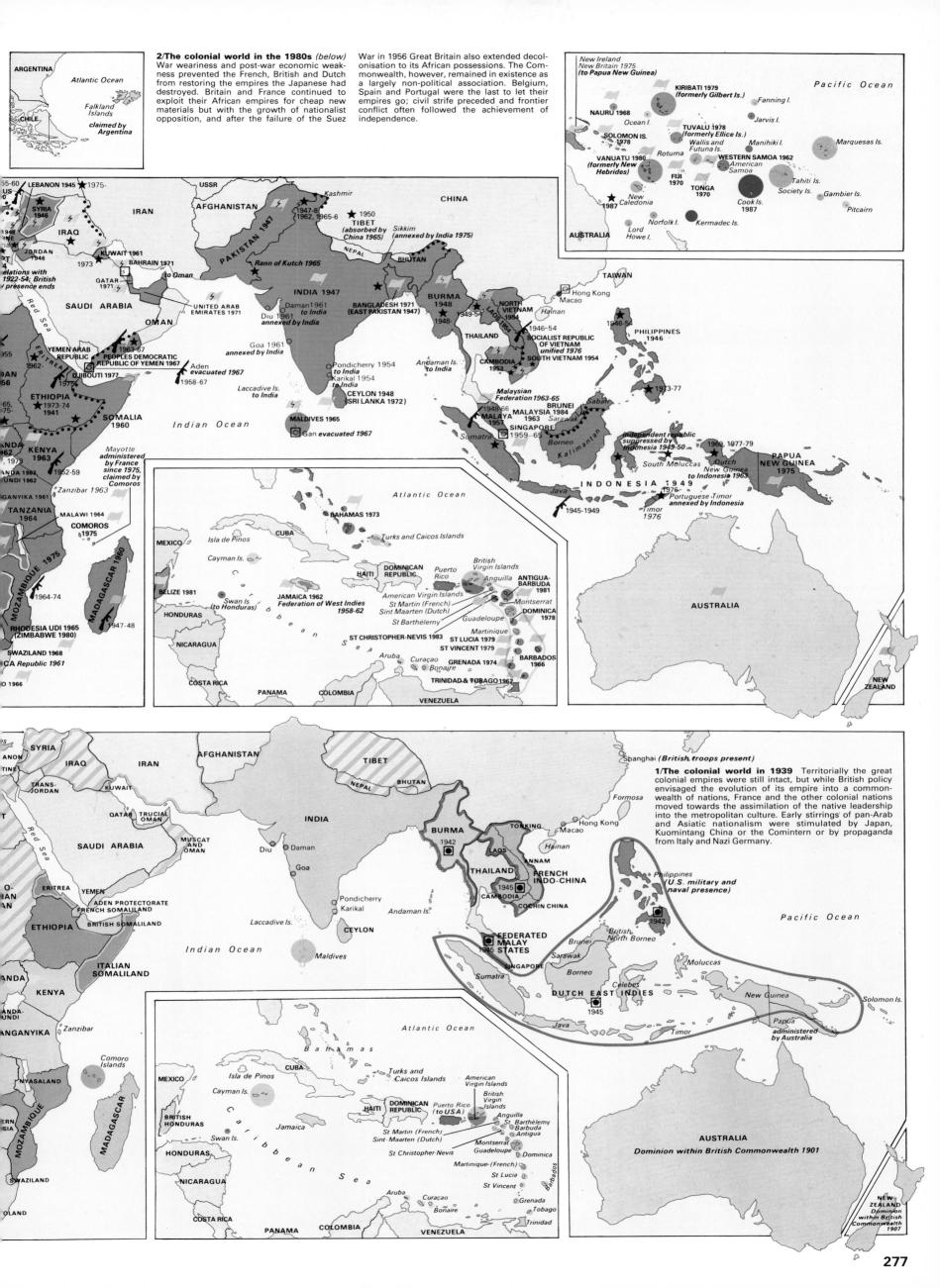

2/The colonial world in the 1980s *(below)* War weariness and post-war economic weakness prevented the French, British and Dutch from restoring the empires the Japanese had destroyed. Britain and France continued to exploit their African empires for cheap new materials but with the growth of nationalist opposition, and after the failure of the Suez War in 1956 Great Britain also extended decolonisation to its African possessions. The Commonwealth, however, remained in existence as a largely non-political association. Belgium, Spain and Portugal were the last to let their empires go; civil strife preceded and frontier conflict often followed the achievement of independence.

1/The colonial world in 1939 Territorially the great colonial empires were still intact, but while British policy envisaged the evolution of its empire into a commonwealth of nations, France and the other colonial nations moved towards the assimilation of the native leadership into the metropolitan culture. Early stirrings of pan-Arab and Asiatic nationalism were stimulated by Japan, Kuomintang China or the Comintern or by propaganda from Italy and Nazi Germany.

277

The new states of East and South-East Asia from 1945

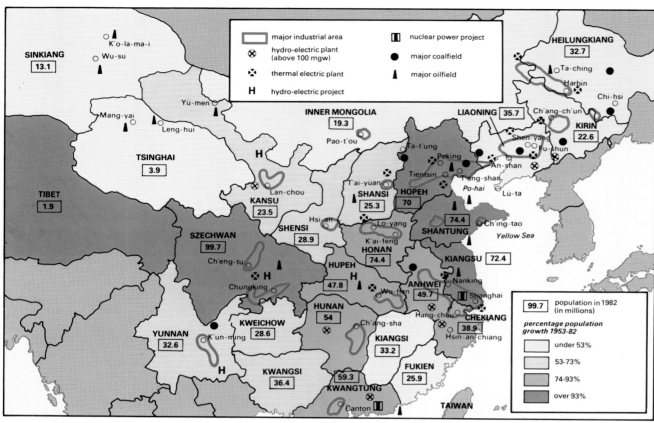

	population in 1982 (in millions)
99.7	

percentage population growth 1953-82

- under 53%
- 53-73%
- 74-93%
- over 93%

Legend: major industrial area; hydro-electric plant (above 100 mgw); thermal electric plant; H hydro-electric project; nuclear power project; major coalfield; major oilfield

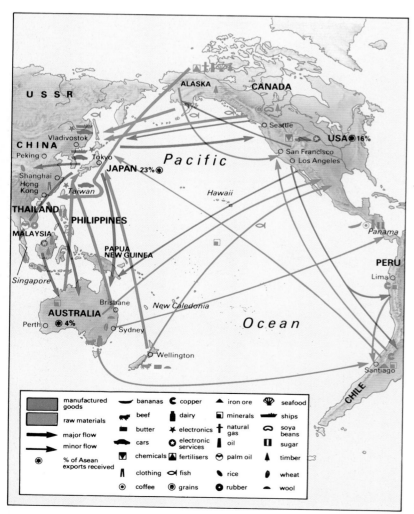

2/Trade flows around the Pacific rim (below) The post-war years saw high economic growth rates in some parts of east and south-east Asia such as Japan, S. Korea, Taiwan and Singapore. This was encouraged by American trade and political influence in the area, particularly in Japan where the Americans supported conservative governments who encouraged investment in industry, and set Japan on the road to becoming one of the largest industrial powers in the world. As many of the Asian countries developed their markets in manufactured goods they became increasingly dependent on imported raw materials. The US–Japanese trade flow, for example, is primarily one of agricultural exports to Japan and electronics and automobile imports to the States. This pattern is matched, but intensified, by the countries of South America and south-east Asia which are major exporters of agricultural or raw materials and large importers of manufactured goods, thus reflecting their relative economic status. The level of American and Japanese investment in Asia shows the importance of the Pacific rim as an economic sphere of interest and indicates an emerging informal empire of trade and investment centred on the principal trade flows – those between Japan, Taiwan, Singapore and the west coast of America.

Legend: manufactured goods; raw materials; major flow; minor flow; % of Asean exports received; bananas; beef; butter; cars; chemicals; clothing; coffee; copper; dairy; electronics; electronic services; fertilisers; fish; grains; iron ore; minerals; natural gas; oil; palm oil; rice; rubber; seafood; ships; soya beans; sugar; timber; wheat; wool

ASIA was a centre of unrest and turmoil in the generation since the Second World War, with violence and instability at many levels. Civil war developed in China, Burma, Indo-China and Korea. The Communist-Nationalist conflict in China had begun in the 1920s, coming to a head after 1945 when the Communists began the drive that brought them control of China (apart from Taiwan and Tibet) by the end of 1949. In 1950 war between North and South Korea, brought China into the battle against South Korea and the UN forces. Negotiations brought peace in 1953. Burma still suffers civil strife, on both communal and ideological issues. In 1987 this series of conflicts was in its fortieth year and showed no sign of ending. The most intense war began in Vietnam in 1948-49. It was a war which combined conflict between internal groups with anti-colonial resistance to France, and after the defeat of France in 1954 turned into a struggle between the US-sponsored Ngo Dinh Diem in Saigon and the National Liberation Front. Ultimately, the civil war brought in North Vietnamese and US armed forces and spread to other areas of Indo-China. Although a formal ceasefire was established in 1973 and US forces withdrew, in 1975 Cambodia fell to the Khmer Rouge and South Vietnam to the Viet Minh.

Clashes between Communist-led insurgents and government forces were widespread, beginning in 1947-48 with rebellions in Malaya, Burma, Indonesia and the Philippines. By 1987 there was still small-scale insurgency in Malaysia, Thailand, Burma, the Philippines and Indo-China. Communal violence based on religious, racial, regional and linguistic issues was endemic, with incidents including clashes between Christians and Muslims in the southern Philippines; Thai Buddhist government forces and Muslim Malays in southern Thailand; Burmese and Kachins, Mons, Shans, Karens and Arakanese in Burma; Vietnamese and Montagnards in southern Vietnam; Vietnamese and Cambodians; the Java-based government and dissidents in the outer islands of Indonesia; Malays and Chinese in Malaysia and Singapore; and Chinese and Tibetans in Tibet.

The post-war era saw the successful revolution in an independent China, and later victories of communist forces in Indo-China. Elsewhere, re-volts and coups were increasingly frequent. Coups have been primarily led by the military, with new states often maintaining large standing armies. In part they derived from the low levels of economic growth in a region in which – in spite of high growth rates in Japan, Singapore, Malaysia and South Korea – most countries remained extremely poor.

While outside forces were involved in domestic disputes and insurgency activities in South-East Asia, territorial disputes frequently occurred between Asian states themselves. Most of these took a legal rather than a violent form. Fighting did occur in the dispute between China and South Vietnam over the Spratly and Paracel Islands, during Indonesia's successful effort to incorporate West Irian (formerly Dutch New Guinea) and Portuguese Timor and during the 'confrontation' between Indonesia and Malaysia over the Borneo territories. The conflict over Taiwan is a carry over from the Chinese civil war. Other areas that have been in dispute are Cochin China, and surrounding waters claimed by Cambodia; the temple of Preah Vilhear acquired by Cambodia after a legal dispute with Thailand; Sabah, incorporated into Malaysia but claimed by the Philippines; the southern Kurile Islands and southern Sakhalin, taken by the Soviet Union after the Second World War and the object of Japanese irredentism; Okinawa, held by the United States after the war and finally brought under full Japanese control in 1972; Takeshima Island (Tok-do) claimed by Japan and South Korea, and three small areas on the Sino-Burmese border ceded by China to Burma in 1960. China's borders with her neighbours have been areas of contention with both Communist and Nationalist regimes producing maps claiming large areas, allegedly lost to imperialist countries.

The most serious tensions in the region followed the establishment of the new governments in Indo-China in 1975. Internally, this led to the flight of over one million refugees from Cambodia, Laos and Vietnam. More serious were the deaths of over one million Cambodians during the rule of the Communist Pol Pot from 1975 to early 1979. Internationally, tensions and border clashes led to the invasion of Cambodia by Vietnamese forces in 1978 and a new Cambodian leadership friendly to Hanoi. Since then, there have been continuous clashes between Vietnamese troops in Cambodia and opposition Communist and non-Communist insurgents. Hanoi's increased power, alleged ill-treatment of its Chinese citizens and the emerging alliance between Vietnam and the Soviet Union brought tensions between Vietnam and China to a head in 1979.

The post-war years did not only bring turmoil. Asia in 1987 had a higher standard of living than in 1947, Japan had become the third largest industrial power in the world, China had revived from decades of war, and countries such as Malaysia, Taiwan, Singapore and the Koreas had developed strong economies. On the international scene, old enemies had begun efforts to form regional organisations, the most successful being the Association of South-East Asian Nations, ASEAN. In China the government turned to a more moderate course following the turmoil of the Cultural Revolution, while most of South-East Asia displayed strong continuities in leadership. However, after decades of colonial rule and civil and international strife, in 1987 competitive democracy only flourished in three of the region's sixteen states.

The economic recovery of Japan *(right)* Japan's progress, after independence in 1951, was phenomenal. By maintaining close relations with the United States and concentrating on industrial development and new technology, in the 1970s Japan emerged as the world's third industrial nation.

1/East Asia after independence *(below right)* Post-independence East Asia experienced strife, coups and unconstitutional changes in government, while lengthy civil wars with heavy casualties took place in China, Burma, Indo-China and Korea. Major territorial disputes involved almost every state in the region.

Independent countries and colonies 1987

Brunei Oil-rich Islamic state. Internally self-governing 1959; independent 1984.

Burma Independent from Britain in 1948. Military coups 1958-62; military government since then. Insurgencies among ethnic minorities and Communists continue.

Cambodia (Kampuchea; Khmer Republic) French protectorate 1862-1953. Prince Sihanouk ousted by Lon Nol, 1970; gave way to Khmer Rouge regime of Pol Pot in 1975; invaded by Vietnam in 1978; ruled by "puppet" regime of Heng Samrin. Active Khmer-Rouge-Sihanouk insurgency on Thai border. Degree of economic recovery.

China Communist regime under Mao Tse-tung from 1949. Death of Mao in 1976 led to modernisation and a revival of a degree of private sector trade and production.

Hong Kong Vigorous private sector produced flourishing trade, light industry and a busy financial centre. Sept. 1982 Anglo-Chinese negotiations opened for reunification of Hong Kong with the mainland, which led to dislocation of the economy. Agreement reached 1986 for reunification 1997, with Hong Kong able to retain its institutions for 50 years.

Indonesia Independent 1945; Dutch control ended 1949; rebellions in 1950s. Military dominant after abortive Communist coup of 1965. "New order" of President Suharto suppressed political opponents, but social policies have ameliorated authoritarian excesses.

Japan Following end of US military rule in 1952, conservative, pro-business government policies led to spectacular economic growth. Low profile international politics.

Korea Japanese empire, 1905-45; North Korea became a "Peoples Democracy" (Communist) 1948. South Korea established constitutional government 1948. War between north and south, 1950-53, involving UN and Chinese forces ended in stalemate. Economic growth in South Korea under strong rule with military backing. Military rule relaxed after student riots 1987.

Laos French protectorate 1893-1953; coups and civil wars between Communist and non-Communist forces, with outside military involvement, until 1975 when Pathet Lao abolished monarchy. Measure of economic recovery since 1979.

Macao Former Portuguese colony now "Chinese territory presently administered by Portugal". 1987 Sino-Portuguese agreement for reunification with mainland.

Malaysia Under British protection 1874-1958; joined with Sabah and Sarawak to form Malaysia Federation 1963. Multi-racial; political stability and economic growth.

Mongolia "People's Republic" under Soviet influence from 1921; gradually modernising.

Philippines Independent 1946. Continuing Communist and Muslim insurgencies. Strong-man rule under President Marcos from 1965; martial law 1972-81. 1986 overthrow of Marcos by Mrs Aquino and popular government.

Singapore Part of Malaysia 1963; independent 1965. Economic planning brought prosperity.

Taiwan Japanese colony 1895-1945; the KMT forces retreated to Taiwan in 1949 and maintain their regime as the Republic of China. Economically prosperous.

Thailand Absolute monarchy succeeded by constitutional monarchy in 1932. Military government. Several coups 1932-76. Continuing Communist insurgency crushed by 1980. Slow economic growth.

Timor Portuguese colony 1586-1976 when it was annexed to Indonesia; smouldering insurgency.

Vietnam Under French colonial administration 1862-1954 when North Vietnam became Communist state. South Vietnam became a republic in 1955 when monarchy ended. North-South war from late 1950s with outside military involvement. North invaded south 1975: Unified Vietnam has extended power over Indo-China.

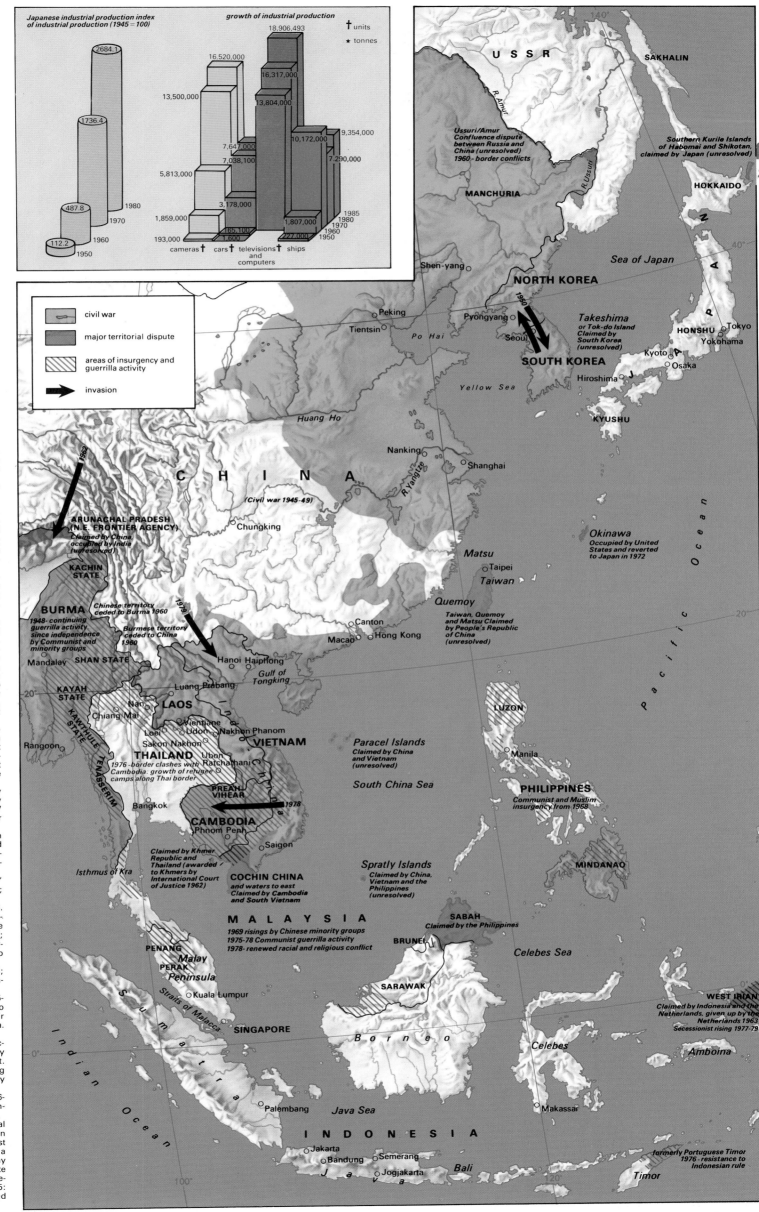

Japanese industrial production index of industrial production (1945 = 100)

growth of industrial production

† units
★ tonnes

2684.1
1736.4
487.8
112.2

1980
1970
1960
1950

18,906,493
16,520,000
16,317,000
13,500,000
13,804,000
7,647,000
7,038,100
5,813,000
10,172,000
9,354,000
7,290,000
1,859,000
3,178,000
1,807,000
193,000 165,100 227,000
1,600

1985
1980
1970
1960
1950

cameras † cars † televisions and computers † ships †

civil war

major territorial dispute

areas of insurgency and guerrilla activity

invasion

USSR

SAKHALIN

Ussuri/Amur Confluence dispute between Russia and China (unresolved) 1960- border conflicts

MANCHURIA

R. Amur

R. Ussuri

HOKKAIDO

Southern Kurile Islands of Habomai and Shikotan, claimed by Japan (unresolved)

Shen-yang

NORTH KOREA

Peking

Pyongyang

Seoul

SOUTH KOREA

Tientsin

Po Hai

Sea of Japan

Takeshima or Tok-do Island Claimed by South Korea (unresolved)

HONSHU

Tokyo

Yokohama

Kyoto

Osaka

KYUSHU

Hiroshima

Yellow Sea

Huang Ho

Nanking

Shanghai

R. Yangtze

C H I N A

(Civil war 1945-49)

Chungking

Okinawa Occupied by United States and reverted to Japan in 1972

Matsu

Taipei

Taiwan

Quemoy

Canton

Macao

Hong Kong

Taiwan, Quemoy and Matsu Claimed by People's Republic of China (unresolved)

ARUNACHAL PRADESH (N.E. FRONTIER AGENCY) *Claimed by China, occupied by India (unresolved)*

KACHIN STATE

BURMA *1948- continuing guerrilla activity since independence by Communist and minority groups*

Chinese territory ceded to Burma 1960

Burmese territory ceded to China 1960

Hanoi Haiphong

Gulf of Tongking

Mandalay   SHAN STATE

KAYAH STATE

Luang Prabang

LAOS

Nan

Chiang Mai

Loei

Udon

Nakhon Phanom

Sakon Nakhon

VIETNAM

Rangoon

KAWTHULE STATE

TENASSERIM

Vientiane

THAILAND *1976- border clashes with Cambodia; growth of refugee camps along Thai border*

Ubon

Ratchathani

Paracel Islands Claimed by China and Vietnam (unresolved)

LUZON

Manila

PREAH VIHEAR

South China Sea

PHILIPPINES *Communist and Muslim insurgency from 1968*

Bangkok

1978

CAMBODIA Phnom Penh

Saigon

Isthmus of Kra

Claimed by Khmer Republic and Thailand (awarded to Khmers by International Court of Justice 1962)

COCHIN CHINA *and waters to east Claimed by Cambodia and South Vietnam*

Spratly Islands Claimed by China, Vietnam and the Philippines (unresolved)

MINDANAO

M A L A Y S I A *1969 risings by Chinese minority groups 1975-78 Communist guerrilla activity 1978- renewed racial and religious conflict*

SABAH Claimed by the Philippines

BRUNEI

Celebes Sea

PENANG

Malay PERAK *Peninsula*

SARAWAK

WEST IRIAN Claimed by Indonesia and the Netherlands, given up by the Netherlands 1963 Secessionist rising 1977-79

Kuala Lumpur

Straits of Malacca

SINGAPORE

B o r n e o

Celebes

Amboina

Sumatra

Java Sea

Palembang

Makassar

Indian Ocean

I N D O N E S I A

formerly Portuguese Timor 1976- resistance to Indonesian rule

Jakarta

Bandung

Semerang

Bali

Timor

Jogjakarta

Southern Asia since independence

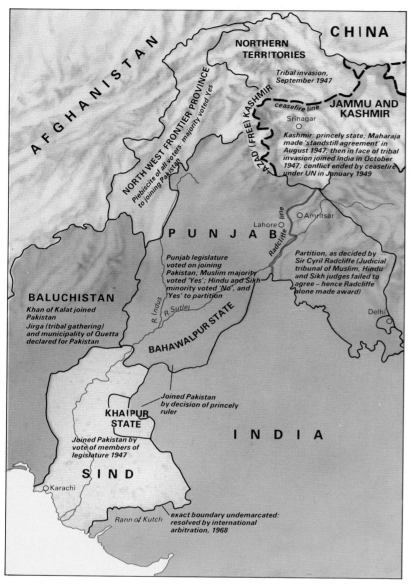

1 and 2/ The partition of Punjab *(above)* **and Bengal** *(below)* The division of the Indian sub-continent in 1947 particularly affected Punjab and Bengal. The result of partition was a great exodus. Some 6 million Muslims migrated from Punjab to the new Pakistan and about 4.5 million Sikhs and Hindus to the areas between Amritsar and Delhi. In Bengal about 1.6 million Hindus left the eastern sector (now Bangladesh); thousands of Muslims from Bihar, Calcutta and elsewhere sought shelter in east Bengal.

INDEPENDENCE came to India and Pakistan in August 1947, to Burma in January 1948, and to Ceylon in February 1948. In India it was fraught with problems from the beginning. The major part of the Indian sub-continent wished for a strong central government to implement economic development and national integration. Jinnah and the Muslim League would not accept this. But Congress's price for allowing the creation of a separate Muslim state of Pakistan was partition of the provinces of Punjab and Bengal. Hindu-Muslim rioting and the British desire to be quickly rid of the problem forced the hand of the Viceroy, Lord Mountbatten, and on 14 August 1947, the sub-continent was partitioned and the new state of Pakistan came into existence. The Princely states, over 600 in number, were left to the individual decisions of their rulers, who could in effect join either India or Pakistan, or even opt for independency.

A key question was the delimitation of frontiers between the new states. This particularly affected the provinces of Punjab and Bengal, whose very mixed population made partition seem the only feasible solution. But the boundary award cut through areas which in Punjab were occupied by rich farmlands populated by Sikhs, Muslims and Hindus as neighbours. Communal riots raged, and a two-way exodus began, with Muslims moving west and Sikhs and Hindus moving east. The partition of Bengal produced similar results. Overall as many as 500,000 people may have lost their lives. As well as the resettlement of the refugees, the governments had to integrate the 600 princely states. Most princes were persuaded to accede, promptly, to either India or Pakistan. Hyderabad resisted and was absorbed only after a 'police action'; Kashmir's ruler also hesitated, and an invasion of tribesmen from Pakistan's N.W.F. Province followed. The Maharaja then acceded to India, subject to a plebiscite of the Kashmir people, but Pakistan supported the tribal invaders and the situation was only stabilised by United Nations mediation in 1948.

Burma's start in independence was comparably troubled. Revolts by different communist groups and by minorities demanding separation almost led to the overthrow of the government in the first two years, 1948-49. Subsequently the country settled into some kind of stability under prime minister U Nu, but the army commander, General Ne Win, intervened in 1958 and the army again took over in 1962. Ne Win declared that the country must establish 'The Burmese Way to Socialism' on Marxist lines, and in January 1974, following a referendum, the Socialist People's Republic of Burma was inaugurated. (It survived until 1988 when it was shaken by mass popular protest).

Between 1956 and the present Ceylon, which became Sri Lanka in 1972, swung between conservative and populist administrations. But the main consequence was to consolidate the power of the Sinhalese majority.

All the countries of South Asia have been troubled by the special position of minorities and of regional groups, to say nothing of the persistent social problems arising from untouchability which remain an important issue in Indian society, in spite of legislation to the contrary. The Indian government's attempt to foster Hindi was soon faced by demands for a new structure of states on linguistic lines, and from 1953 onwards state boundaries were realigned. But linguistic feeling remained strong, especially in south India in Madras State, which was renamed Tamil Nadu. In Assam, various tribal groups, particularly the Nagas, sought either independence or statehood. In Pakistan linguistic and regional demands were initially resisted, and the separate provinces of West Pakistan were amalgamated as One Unit. But regional loyalties forced a return to the old provinces, representing linguistic regions, in 1970. In East Pakistan, the strength of Bengal culture and grievances against the dominant West Pakistan elite fostered a demand for autonomy. In Burma, the frontier peoples resisted the central government, and among the Karens, Shans and Kachins the separatist movements were able to take control of large areas. Ceylon also witnessed the emergence of strong separatist movements among the Tamil, Hindu population. The workers on the tea estates, whose fathers and grandfathers had arrived from India, were mostly disenfranchised and rendered stateless; those recognised as Ceylon Tamils campaigned for autonomy within a loose federal state leading to attacks by the Sinhalese in 1983. The rebels created a virtually independent Tamil state in the Jaffna Peninsula which was attacked by the Sri Lankan and Indian armies in 1987.

Conflicts in South Asia have periodically led to hostilities. The growing deterioration on the frontiers between India and China led to the outbreak of war in 1962 and defeat for India. As Sino-Indian relations deteriorated, so Sino-Pakistan relations became closer. In 1965 Pakistan attempted to infiltrate troops into the Indian-held portion of Kashmir. In the fighting which ensued India made some gains, but in the agreement afterwards reached at Tashkent under Soviet auspices both countries agreed to return to the status quo. Relations continued to be tense, however, and rapidly worsened in 1971 when Pakistan's military president, Yahya Khan, cruelly repressed the demands for autonomy in the East, which led to 10 million refugees crossing over into India. Finally, in December 1971 India supported the Bangladesh guerrillas with powerful military forces which defeated the Pakistan army within two weeks. The new state of Bangladesh then emerged under the leadership of Sheikh Majib-ur Rahman.

All the states in South Asia have attempted to function under democratic, parliamentary forms of government but gradually parliamentary institutions have been eroded. Pakistan and Burma both came under military rule in 1958. Bangladesh soon discarded parliamentary democracy after the murder of Sheikh Majib-ur in 1975. Pakistan, after a brief period of civilian government under Bhutto's leadership remained under military rule. In India, prime minister Indira Gandhi ruled by emergency decree from 1975 to 1977, but allowed elections to take place leading to her defeat. Her party was reelected in the next election. Conflicts between the central government and provincial administrations, however, allowed the emergence of guerrilla activity by extreme Sikh separatists. In 1984 the Indian Army seized the Golden Temple of Amritsar, a Sikh holy place, made into the extremist headquarters. Mrs Gandhi was assassinated in revenge and her son Rajiv became prime minister. Punjab remained disturbed and Rajiv Gandhi's difficulties with minorities and entrenched economic interests persisted, despite initial optimism. Nevertheless, India has achieved a considerable rate of industrial growth and has for some years been self-sufficient in food grains. Despite low per capita income, a large and well-educated middle class has helped to restrain centrifugal forces. Despite occasional outbreaks of intercommunal violence and Sikh demands for autonomy in the Punjab, India remains the world's largest functioning democracy. In Ceylon, as in India, the parliamentary form of government has survived though in both countries the power exercised by a single political party inhibits democratic processes. In India and Pakistan, industrial development has been substantial. India is one of the major industrial powers today, but income per head remains low and maldistribution keeps vast numbers in abject poverty.

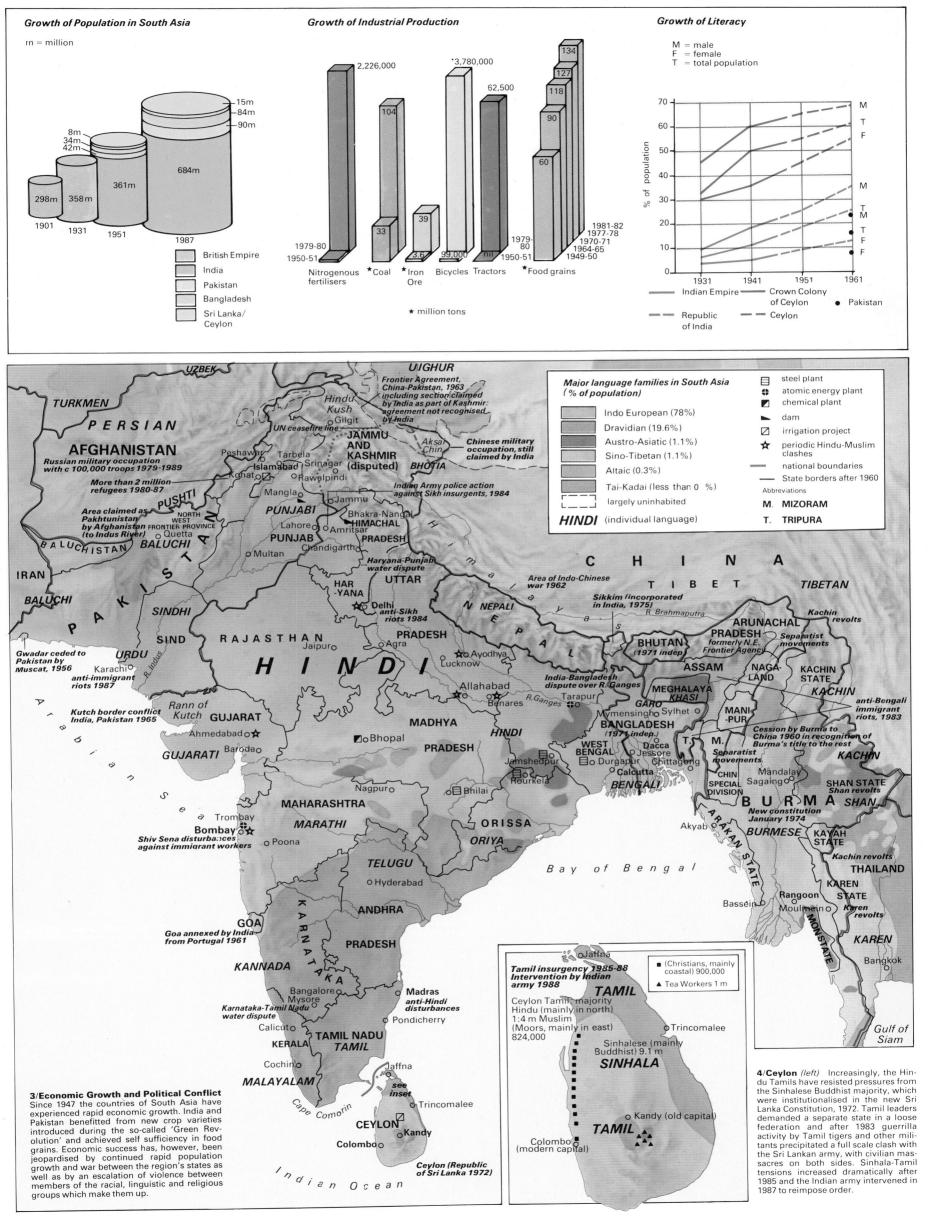

Growth of Population in South Asia

m = million

298m 1901
358m 1931
361m 1951
684m 1987

8m
34m
42m
15m
84m
90m

British Empire
India
Pakistan
Bangladesh
Sri Lanka/Ceylon

Growth of Industrial Production

	1950-51	1979-80
Nitrogenous fertilisers		2,226,000
★Coal	33	104
★Iron Ore	3.6	39
Bicycles	99,000	*3,780,000
Tractors	nil	62,500
★Food grains	60	134

1949-50 60
1964-65 90
1970-71 118
1977-78 127
1981-82 134

★ million tons

Growth of Literacy

M = male
F = female
T = total population

% of population
70 60 50 40 30 20 10

1931 1941 1951 1961

M T F   M   T M   T F   F

Indian Empire — Crown Colony of Ceylon — Pakistan ●
Republic of India — Ceylon

Major language families in South Asia (% of population)

Indo European (78%)
Dravidian (19.6%)
Austro-Asiatic (1.1%)
Sino-Tibetan (1.1%)
Altaic (0.3%)
Tai-Kadai (less than 0 %)
largely uninhabited

HINDI (individual language)

steel plant
atomic energy plant
chemical plant
dam
irrigation project
periodic Hindu-Muslim clashes
national boundaries
State borders after 1960

Abbreviations
M. MIZORAM
T. TRIPURA

Map labels:

UZBEK, TURKMEN, UIGHUR, Frontier Agreement, China-Pakistan, 1963 including section claimed by India as part of Kashmir: agreement not recognised by India

PERSIAN, AFGHANISTAN
Russian military occupation with c 100,000 troops 1979-1989
More than 2 million refugees 1980-87
Area claimed as Pakhtunistan by Afghanistan (to Indus River)

Hindu Kush, Gilgit, UN ceasefire line
JAMMU AND KASHMIR (disputed), Aksai Chin
Chinese military occupation, still claimed by India

PUSHTI, NORTH WEST FRONTIER PROVINCE
Peshawar, Kohat, Tarbela, Islamabad, Srinagar, Rawalpindi, Mangla, Jammu
Indian Army police action against Sikh insurgents, 1984

IRAN, BALUCHISTAN, BALUCHI, PAKISTAN, SINDHI
Gwadar ceded to Pakistan by Muscat, 1956
Karachi anti-immigrant riots 1987

SIND, URDU
Lahore, Multan, Amritsar, Chandigarth
PUNJABI, PUNJAB, HIMACHAL PRADESH
Bhakra-Nangal
Haryana-Punjab water dispute

HAR-YANA, Delhi anti-Sikh riots 1984
UTTAR PRADESH
Area of Indo-Chinese war 1962
NEPAL, NEPALI
Sikkim (incorporated in India, 1975)
R. Brahmaputra

CHINA, TIBET, TIBETAN
BHUTAN (1971 indep.)
ARUNACHAL PRADESH formerly N.E. Frontier Agency
Kachin revolts, Separatist movements

RAJASTHAN, Jaipur, Agra, Lucknow, Ayodhya, Allahabad
HINDI
India-Bangladesh dispute over R. Ganges, Tarapur
ASSAM, MEGHALAYA, GARO, KHASI, NAGA-LAND, KACHIN STATE

Kutch border conflict India, Pakistan 1965
Rann of Kutch, GUJARAT, Ahmedabad, Baroda
GUJARATI, Bhopal, MADHYA PRADESH, HINDI
Benares, R. Ganges
MANI-PUR, anti-Bengali immigrant riots 1983
Cession by Burma to China 1960 in recognition of Burma's title to the rest

BANGLADESH (1971 indep.), Mymensingh, Sylhet, Dacca, Jessore
WEST BENGAL, Durgapur, Jamshedpur, Rourkela, Bhilai, Nagpur
BENGALI, Calcutta, Chittagong
CHIN SPECIAL DIVISION, Mandalay, Sagaing, SHAN STATE, Shan revolts

MAHARASHTRA, MARATHI, Trombay
Bombay, Shiv Sena disturbances against immigrant workers
Poona, ORISSA, ORIYA
TELUGU, Hyderabad, ANDHRA PRADESH
Bay of Bengal
BURMA, BURMESE, ARAKAN STATE, Akyab, New constitution January 1974
KAYAH STATE, Kachin revolts, THAILAND, KAREN STATE, Karen revolts, MON STATE, KAREN

GOA, Goa annexed by India from Portugal 1961
KARNATAKA, KANNADA, Bangalore, Mysore
Karnataka-Tamil Nadu water dispute
Calicut, Madras, anti-Hindi disturbances, Pondicherry
Bassein, Rangoon, Moulmein, Bangkok, Gulf of Siam

TAMIL NADU, TAMIL, KERALA, Cochin, Calicut
MALAYALAM, Cape Comorin, Jaffna (see inset)
CEYLON, Kandy, Colombo, Trincomalee
Ceylon (Republic of Sri Lanka 1972)
Indian Ocean

Tamil insurgency 1985-88 Intervention by Indian army 1988

■ (Christians, mainly coastal) 900,000
▲ Tea Workers 1 m

Ceylon Tamil majority Hindu (mainly in north) 1:4 m Muslim (Moors, mainly in east) 824,000
Sinhalese (mainly Buddhist) 9.1 m
TAMIL, SINHALA, Jaffna, Trincomalee, Kandy (old capital), Colombo (modern capital), TAMIL

3/Economic Growth and Political Conflict

Since 1947 the countries of South Asia have experienced rapid economic growth. India and Pakistan benefitted from new crop varieties introduced during the so-called 'Green Revolution' and achieved self sufficiency in food grains. Economic success has, however, been jeopardised by continued rapid population growth and war between the region's states as well as by an escalation of violence between members of the racial, linguistic and religious groups which make them up.

4/Ceylon (left)

Increasingly, the Hindu Tamils have resisted pressures from the Sinhalese Buddhist majority, which were institutionalised in the new Sri Lanka Constitution, 1972. Tamil leaders demanded a separate state in a loose federation and after 1983 guerrilla activity by Tamil tigers and other militants precipitated a full scale clash with the Sri Lankan army, with civilian massacres on both sides. Sinhala-Tamil tensions increased dramatically after 1985 and the Indian army intervened in 1987 to reimpose order.

The emancipation of Africa from 1946

IN 1939 control over most of the African continent appeared secure but within 40 years white control was confined to a South African *laager*. The necessary impetus for change was provided by the Second World War and the consequent social changes which were often accompanied by heightened political consciousness, thus strengthening the hands of African leaders committed to the social and political advancement of their nations.

Equally important were changes taking place outside Africa. Allied victory greatly increased the prestige of the USSR, while the USA emerged determined to prevent the colonial powers from impeding the extension of American influence. In France and Britain, liberals and socialists sympathetic to African claims initiated programmes of social improvement and political reform (though these ran into difficulties in territories where they threatened the interests of white settler populations). But even reformers appreciated that colonial empire might assist Britain and France to recover some of their economic strength and political influence. From about 1947 the onset of the Cold War, and the continuing dollar famine, pointed towards a certain reassertion of colonial control; France's fierce repression of rebellion in Madagascar was only the most striking demonstration of this.

Some nationalist movements nevertheless effectively challenged these policies. In 1948 riots in Accra and other Gold Coast towns constrained the British government to initiate constitutional reforms which three years later enabled the Covention Peoples' Party of Kwame Nkrumah to achieve a striking electoral success. Meanwhile disturbances in the Ivory Coast led the French government to seek reconciliation with the *Rassemblement Democratique Africain*, which had been hitherto distrusted because of Communist influence. By 1960 both British and French governments had concluded that in their West African colonies wise policy required them to transfer responsibility to elected governments.

In Muslim North Africa longer-established nationalist movements received great stimulus from the overthrow of the Egyptian monarchy in 1952, and the subsequent rise of Gamal Abdel Nasser. In 1953-54 Britain agreed to withdraw her troops from the Suez Canal zone and to accelerate the independence of Sudan; in 1956 France accepted the independence of the protectorates of Tunisia and Morocco. But in Alger-

ia, which was considered part of Metropolitan France, French determination to maintain control had been clear since their repression of a popular rising in 1945; in November 1954 the Front de Libération Nationale began a war which continued with increasing ferocity until 1962 (see map 3) when independence was granted. In 1956 Britain and France attempted to protect their interests in the Suez Canal and reassert their power in the region by invading the Suez Canal zone; but strong opposition from the United States of America, the Soviet Union and the United Nations showed that such methods were no longer practicable.

In the south and east, the crucial event of the post-war years was the election of a Nationalist government in South Africa under D. F. Malan. This was dedicated to the establishment of an Afrikaner Republic and policies of racial *apartheid*, even though British post-war policies in east and central Africa had been directed along a different route, towards the encouragement of multi-racial 'partnership' in government. Settlers in Kenya, though numbering only about 40,000, at one time hoped for ascendency in an East African dominion; but these hopes perished after 1952, when the British government assumed responsibility for combatting the Mau Mau insurrection, which was directed against them. In Central Africa the British in 1953 enacted the federation of Nyasaland and Northern and Southern Rhodesia, with Rhodesian whites in a dominant position; but after 1960 this too collapsed under the force of what the British Prime Minister Harold Macmillan called the 'wind of change'. Ghanaian independence provided a great stimulus to African nationalists; from a pan-African conference in Accra in 1958 Dr Hastings Banda returned to lead the anti-Federation movement in Nyasaland (Malawi), while Patrice Lumumba's enthusiasm accelerated the drive to independence in the Congo (see map 2). With the achievement of independence in Nigeria and most of the former French colonies, 1960 appeared to be Africa's year.

During the 1960s this state of euphoria largely evaporated. The African economy proved fragile, and the ethnic rivalries and political disorders of Zaire were reproduced in other states; military coups and takeovers became more common, and in Nigeria led in 1967 to a destructive civil war. While the Algerian revolutionaries achieved independence in 1962 after a bitter eight-years war, the Portuguese government failed to learn its lesson; nationalists were

driven into revolutionary warfare in Angola, Mozambique and Guinea-Bissau. In 1965 Ian Smith illegally declared the independence of white-dominated Rhodesia; the British government failed to repress this rebellion, and during the 1970s African nationalists resorted to armed rebellion here also. Behind these surviving colonial regimes stood the growing economic and military power of South Africa, since 1961 a Republic outside the Commonwealth and committed to repressive measures against militant African nationalists.

In 1974 the overthrow of the Portuguese dictatorship opened the way to independence for her African colonies. By 1980 the armed struggle of nationalist guerrillas, the support of the Organisation of African Unity (united on this as on nothing else), and international pressures through the British government, interacted to replace the rebel regime in Rhodesia by the Republic of Zimbabwe. South Africa, becoming increasingly isolated, sought to protect itself by tightening its illegal control of Namibia, by military incursions into neighbouring states, and by conceding to the impoverished labour reserves known as 'Bantustans' a spurious independence which was not recognised internationally.

For the new states, whether capitalist or socialist in orientation, immediate economic prospects remained poor. For some, the exploitation of petroleum and other minerals offered short-term relief, though often at the cost of diverting resources from producing food for rapidly growing populations. Increasingly, elected governments proved unable to control problems of poverty, corruption and ethnic rivalry and were replaced by military dictatorships or single-party regimes, often with populist leanings. Almost everywhere, the fruits of political emancipation proved less sweet than had been expected.

Polisario government recognised by a majority of OAU, but occupied by Morocco since Spanish withdrawal, 1976

Dakhla (Villa Cisneros)

MAURI

War with Polisario Military rule 1978 Slavery officially abolished 1980

Senegambian Confederation formed following Gambian rising 1981

Nouakchott

Cape Verde Islands

Dakar

SENEGAL

REPUBLIC OF CAPE VERDE

Banjul (Bathurst)

Bissau

GUINE

1953-1984 Sék Touré Preside

Conakry

Freetown

SIERRA LEONE

1963-74 PAIGC war against Portuguese

Monrovia

President Tolbert overthrown b Master Sergeant Doe 1980

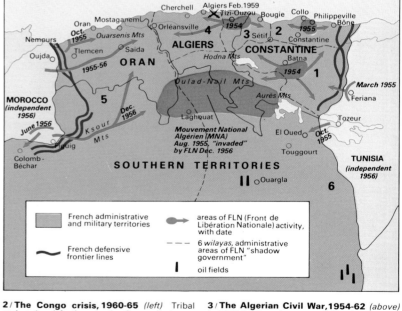

2 / The Congo crisis, 1960-65 *(left)* Tribal and regional factions in the Congo (independent 30 June 1960) led to demands for a federal constitution. However, the federalist leader, Kasavubu, of the Bakongo tribal party (ABAKO) was opposed by Lumumba's centralist Mouvement National Congolais (MNC). After a compromise central government was formed, but the army, left under Belgian officers, mutinied on 4 July. Belgium flew in troops to protect her civilians and interests. On 11 July the mineral-rich province of Katanga seceded under Moise Tshombe. Lumumba and Kasavubu, convinced that Belgium wished to regain control, called in the UN. Following the dismissal of Lumumba, and his murder in Katanga, the UN intervened with US support, but attempts to reach a compromise with Katanga were abandoned. By 1963 Katanga was overrun by the UN. Tshombe, who had withdrawn to Angola, was recalled as President in 1964 and, with Belgian and US aid, suppressed a new revolt backed by the OAU. But both he and Kasavubu were overthrown by the army under Mobutu in November 1965.

3 / The Algerian Civil War, 1954-62 *(above)* In 1945 the French assumed Algeria would be re-incorporated into the Fourth Republic. However, this assumption was challenged by nationalist demonstrations which were followed by violent repression. Subsequent reforms did not satisfy the more nationalist Algerians; in 1954 they formed the Front de Libération Nationale (FLN) and launched attacks on 1 November on French positions throughout Algeria. The French were committed to protecting oil and gas resources, but faced a formidable underground army – a revolutionary movement of socialist inspiration, capable of eliminating its rival the Mouvement Nationaliste Algérien (MNA). In 1958 the threat of a military coup by the frustrated French army brought de Gaulle to power. Holding Algeria was only possible at an unacceptable price and the FLN could not be broken, refusing offers to negotiate peace without independence. In the Evian agreements of March 1962 de Gaulle finally recognised their sovereignty, though with provision to safeguard continuing French interests.

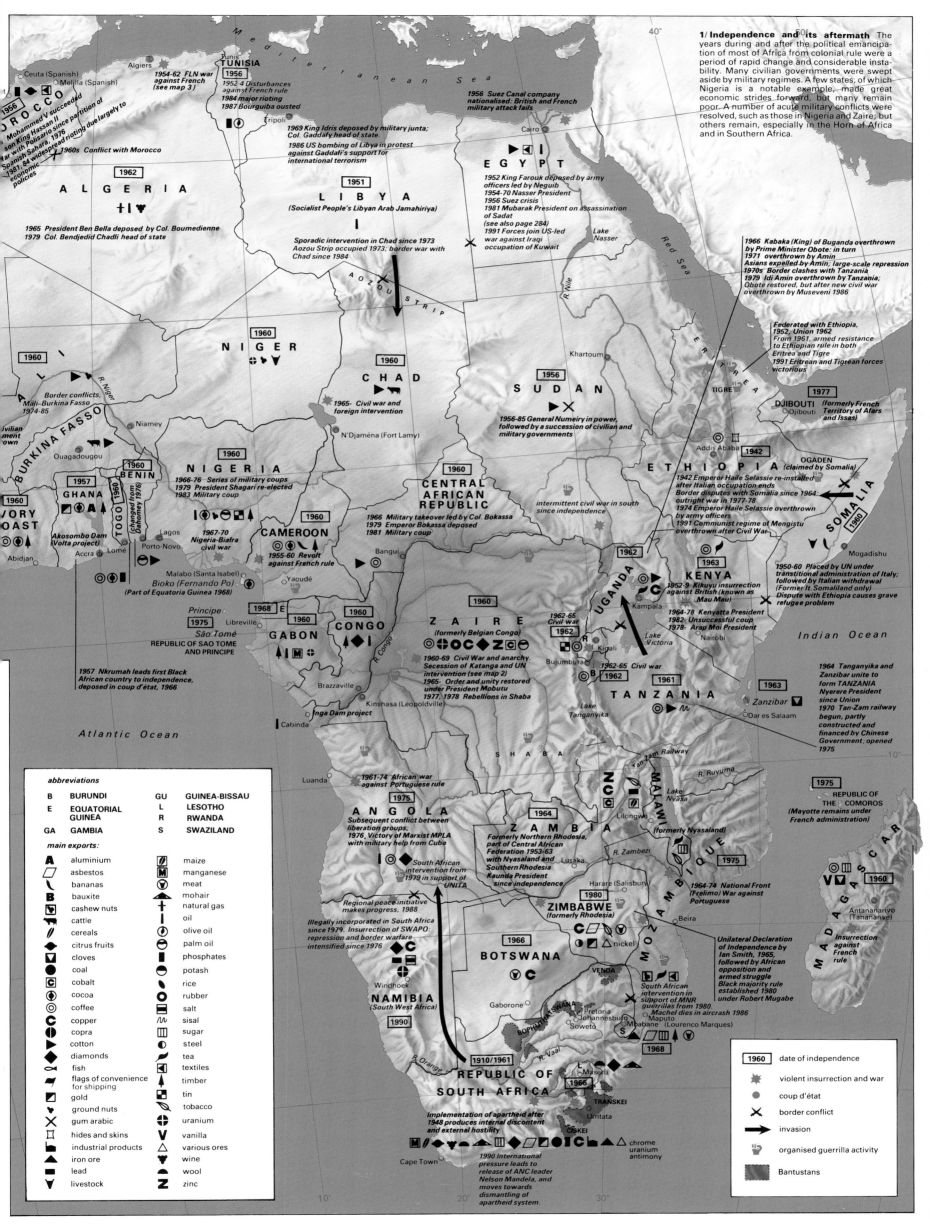

The Middle East from 1945

IN THE years since 1945, the Middle East has been in a state of almost continuous upheaval, and the last decade in particular has seen an enormous increase in the level of violence and human suffering. Most of the regimes in the area are either highly autocratic, or little more than military dictatorships; almost all are brutally repressive of minority communities, political dissidents, even of political organisations.

In the immediate post-war period, a combination of war weariness, financial pressure and local opposition gradually led to Britain and France abandoning formal control over the area. These changes were accompanied by the growing nationalist ferment of the time, which continued into the 1950s, and the ending of Soviet isolation, all factors which encouraged the US to take a more active interest in the region's affairs. Thus the Eisenhower doctrine (1957) promised US assistance to regimes apparently threatened by Soviet aggression. Covert and overt threats by the US, notably in Jordan in 1957 and Lebanon in 1958, had the effect of encouraging other states in the region to seek closer political and military ties with the USSR and with each other.

In the 1950s and 1960s, the US became the most powerful external influence in the Middle East, using the fear of Soviet expansion to increase its support to Israel, which, with Saudi Arabia, and Iran until 1979, functioned as the principal surrogates of American interests in the area. The inherent instability of the 'revolutionary states' (Egypt, Iraq, Syria) made them unreliable partners for the Soviet Union. The Arab countries were unable to combine effectively against Israel, partly because their crack troops had to be kept in the capitals in times of crisis to maintain what were often highly unpopular regimes in power. Israel thrived on inter-Arab differences, especially as it became clear in the 1970s that the Soviet Union was not prepared to risk a major confrontation with Israel. The Soviet Union's major military undertaking in the area, the invasion of Afghanistan in 1979, was more a costly aberration than symptomatic of a more general policy.

The Arab-Israeli conflict has dominated Middle Eastern politics since 1948. As well as the four main wars between the various Arab states and Israel, the conflict has also spilled into Lebanon, because of the large numbers of Palestinians living there, and because it has been used as a base for guerrilla operations against Israel by the Palestine Liberation Organisation since 1968. Since its inception, Israel has expanded beyond its 1948 boundaries into the West Bank and Gaza (1967), Sinai (1956, 1967-1982), the Golan Heights (1967: incorporated officially into Israel in 1981), and has been firmly in control of large parts of south Lebanon since 1978. President Sadat's visit to Israel in 1977, and the bilateral treaty between Egypt and Israel which followed, resulted in the return of the Sinai peninsula to Egypt in 1982. Israel has justified this expansion, and the creation of large numbers of settlements on the occupied West Bank, on the grounds that it needs to secure its borders and to protect its citizens from guerrilla attacks. Some 300 Israeli civilians were killed in such attacks between 1967 and 1982, some in particularly horrifying incidents such as the Maalot massacre in March 1978, in which the majority of the 34 killed and 78 wounded were children. However, in the invasion of south Lebanon which this attack prompted, 2000 Lebanese and Palestinian civilians were killed, and the operations surrounding the attack on Beirut in June-August 1982 resulted in the deaths of between 15,000 and 20,000 Lebanese and Palestinians.

Over the past decades attempts have been made to overcome the problems of poverty and underdevelopment in the region. Although great strides have been made in the provision of health, education and welfare services in a number of states, the combination of government policies and rising inflation has tended to increase the gap between rich and poor. The rapidity of change, the belief that the West and 'modernisation' bear a heavy responsibility for many contemporary ills, and the moral and ideological bankruptcy of most of the regimes have combined to produce a sense of bewilderment and despair. It is thus not surprising that many of the young, and the recent migrants to the cities, should find new fulfilment in a commitment to a form of 'political Islam'.

One of the most visible signs of this 'Islamic renewal' was the revolution in Iran in 1978-79, which overthrew a regime with particularly close ties to the West. The ruler of the new Islamic Republic of Iran, Ayatollah Khomeini, proclaimed a form of Islamic government in which the Shi'i authorities exercised special theocratic functions. Although it succeeded in asserting Iran's political independence, the Islamic Republic was extremely repressive, imprisoning and executing many thousands of political detainees, and in addition the wider implications of its religious militancy were feared both within and beyond the Middle East. In September 1980 Iraq invaded Iran, initiating a conflict which was to last for almost eight years, in which Iraq regularly deployed chemical weapons against Iranian forces and continued the reign of terror against its own population which it had been conducting since the mid-1970s. After the cease-fire the Iraqi government attacked the rebellious Kurdish population in the mountainous north-east of the country with bombs and chemical weapons, causing enormous casualties and forcing mass migration across the

1/The Middle East since independence (below) With the exception of the smaller states of the Arabian peninsula (which had all become independent by 1971) most of the nations of the Middle East had obtained formal independence from Britain or France by 1950, although both sought to maintain their influence through military and other alliances. During the 1950s many of the constitutional monarchies and republics established by Britain and France in the 1920s and 1930s were overthrown by nationalist-inspired military coups, ushering in regimes of varying degrees of permanence and stability. For many in the Arab world, the success of Nasser in Egypt provided a model for their aspirations for true independence, especially after his successful nationalisation of the Suez Canal in 1956. However, pan-Arab nationalism and calls for Arab unity have proved largely powerless to resolve any settlement of the outstanding problems in the area: the glaring contrasts between rich and poor, the virtual absence of democracy, and economic dependence on the outside world. Almost all the poorer states (particularly Jordan, Syria, Egypt and Turkey) suffer from chronic inflation and massive migration from rural areas to cities, and most, even the most fertile, are net importers of food.

In addition to the apparently endemic decline in living standards over the past decade, populist military dictatorship based on repression and the cult of personality has become the most characteristic form of government in the contemporary Middle East. The deep frustrations already mentioned, combined with the continuing failure to solve the Arab-Israeli conflict despite the intifada and the PLO's recognition of Israel, go some way to explain popular support for Saddam Hussein's invasion of Kuwait in August 1990, however misconceived, in terms of a display of 'Arab' defiance against the oil-rich oligarchs of the Arabian peninsula and their American backers.

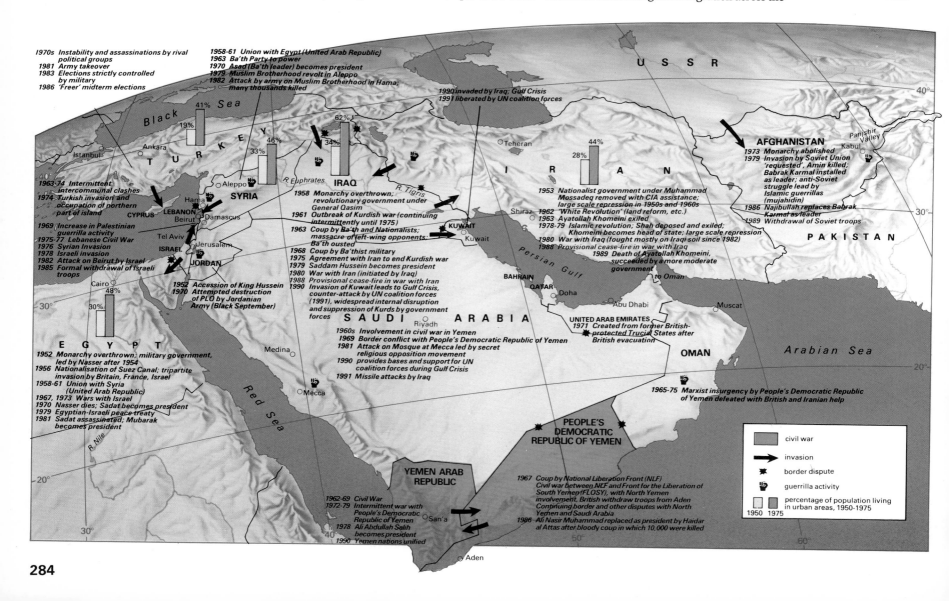

1/The Middle East since independence

2/Israel and Palestine *(right)* For many centuries Palestine had an Arabic-speaking Muslim majority and Christian and Jewish minorities, but in the late 19th century the proportions began to change as Jews from Eastern Europe began to emigrate, under the pressure of Russian persecution and of the new Zionist ideal of the recreation of a Jewish national state. In 1917, during the First World War, the British government stated that it looked with favour on the establishment of a Jewish National Home in Palestine, provided that the position of the non-Jewish population was not harmed. These two obligations were embodied in the mandate under which Great Britain administered the country, subject to supervision by the League of Nations, but they proved difficult to reconcile, particularly after the rise of Hitler, when Jewish emigration from Europe increased sharply (in 1922, Jews formed 11 per cent of the population; in 1936, 29 per cent; in 1946, 32 per cent). Arab fears led to a serious revolt before the Second World War; after the war and the holocaust of European Jewry, the Jewish demand that the survivors be allowed to immigrate, American pressure in support of it, and Arab fear that such immigration would lead to their subjection or dispossession, caused the British government to declare its intention of withdrawing. A plan to partition Palestine into a Jewish and an Arab state, while Jerusalem would be under international control, was adopted by the United Nations General Assembly on 29 Nov. 1947, but was rejected by the Arabs. On the day of British withdrawal, 14 May 1948, David Ben Gurion proclaimed the state of Israel and a war ensued between the Jews and the Palestinian Arabs, supported by the neighbouring Arab states, whose Arab armies were defeated. The greater part of Palestine became the Jewish state of Israel, most of the rest was amalgamated with Transjordan to become Jordan, and the Gaza Strip was occupied by Egypt.

During and after the fighting, two-thirds of the Palestinian Arabs became refugees in Jordan, Gaza, Syria and Lebanon to be largely replaced by Jewish immigrants from North Africa and the Middle East. After 1948, however, the Palestinian refugees' desire to return and to have their own state, the refusal of Israel to accept Palestinian claims and of the Arab states to recognise Israel, and intervention by external forces, led to three further wars: in 1956 the Israelis, following increasing guerrilla raids, attacked Egypt in secret agreement with Great Britain and France, but were compelled to withdraw under pressure from the US and the USSR; in June 1967 the Israelis moved to prevent a threat to their existence when the Straits of Tiran were closed to Israeli shipping by Nasser, and occupied the west bank of the Jordan (after Jordan allied itself with Egypt), Sinai and the Golan Heights in Syria; in 1973 an Egyptian and Syrian attack on Israel had a limited military success, and opened a new phase of negotiations. President Sadat of Egypt had little desire to continue the struggle and his visit to Jerusalem (Nov. 1977), followed by the Egyptian-Israeli Camp David accords (1978), confirmed this. However, Begin's Likud government now began to take a harder line on the West Bank (which it claimed as an integral part of biblical Israel) by greatly increasing the settlements. The focus of conflict shifted when, in 1978, Israel invaded southern Lebanon to counter Palestinian guerrilla (PLO) activity and advanced as far as Beirut in the summer of 1982 (see map 4). Later in 1982 Israel withdrew from Sinai. In 1987, the *intifada*, a movement of protest against Israeli rule in the West Bank and Gaza, began to gather momentum and in December 1988 the PLO formally recognised Israel within its 1948 boundaries. The *intifada* continued; by April 1991 Israeli military action had caused the death of some 950 Palestinians.

border to Turkey. In August 1990, Iraq invaded, and later attempted to annex Kuwait; the United States responded by posting some 500,000 troops to Saudi Arabia and forming an alliance with a number of European and Arab countries, threatening Iraq with attack if it did not withdraw. Coalition forces began bombing Baghdad on 17 January 1991 and by the end of February, after immense human and material destruction, obliged Iraq to leave Kuwait.

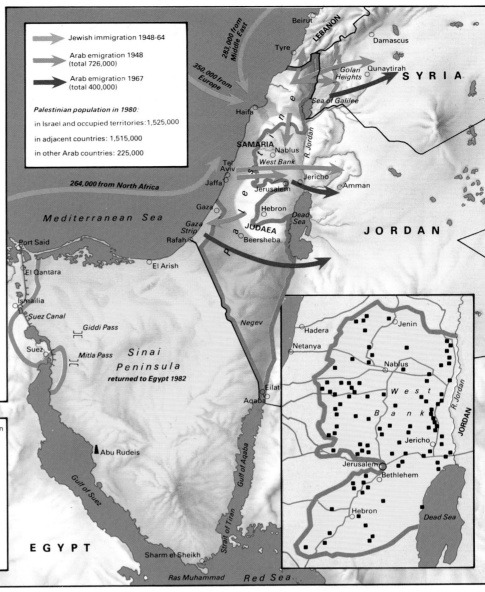

Jewish immigration 1948-64
Arab emigration 1948 (total 726,000)
Arab emigration 1967 (total 400,000)

Palestinian population in 1980:
in Israel and occupied territories: 1,525,000
in adjacent countries: 1,515,000
in other Arab countries: 225,000

283,000 from Middle East
350,000 from Europe
264,000 from North Africa

Jewish state under UN partition plan for Palestine 1947
Israel after Arab invasion and War of Independence 1948
Israel conquests 1967
Egyptian re-conquests and Israeli conquests 1973
Israeli settlements on the West Bank (see inset right)
main roads
■ Israeli settlements in 1983

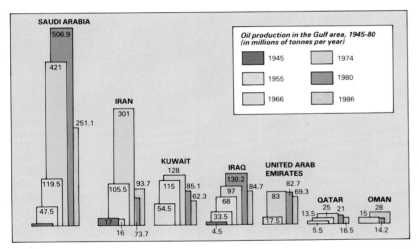

	1945	1955	1966	1974	1980	1986

Oil production in the Gulf area, 1945-80 (in millions of tonnes per year)

SAUDI ARABIA: 47.5, 119.5, 251.1, 421, 506.9
IRAN: 16, 17, 105.5, 301, 93.7, 73.7
KUWAIT: 54.5, 115, 128, 85.1, 62.3
IRAQ: 4.5, 33.5, 68, 97, 130.2, 84.7
UNITED ARAB EMIRATES: 17.5, 83, 82.7, 69.3
QATAR: 5.5, 13.5, 25, 21, 16.5
OMAN: 14.2, 15, 28

Oil production *(above)* Oil is the region's most valuable natural asset, and production and revenues have increased dramatically in recent years, most notably since the OPEC price rise in 1973. However, later figures show the impact of the war between Iran and Iraq.

Ironically, the wealth which oil has created has contributed to serious inflation in the poorer states; also, the lack of indigenous skilled labour has made large-scale labour immigration and the presence of a high proportion of foreign workers permanent features of the area.

4/The Lebanese crisis *(right)* The Lebanese political system is based on the distribution of offices between the various communities (Maronite, Orthodox, Catholic and Armenian Christians, Sunni and Shi'i Muslims and Druzes) in a way which ensured the pre-eminence of the Maronites, although by the 1970s they were no longer the largest single community. Opposition forces joined with the Palestinian (PLO) guerrillas in the mid-1970s in an attempt to force the Maronites to agree to a secular democratic Lebanon, but were both checked by Syrian intervention in 1976. Lebanon subsequently became the principal arena of the Arab/Israeli conflict. Syrian troops remained in permanent occupation, and Israeli forces have invaded twice, in 1978 and then on a more massive scale in 1982, when they expelled the PLO from Beirut. Israel's withdrawal in 1985 did little to check the de facto cantonisation of the country, and inter-factional fighting, in which the Shi'i Amal and Hezbollah forces played a prominent role, continued into the late 1980s.

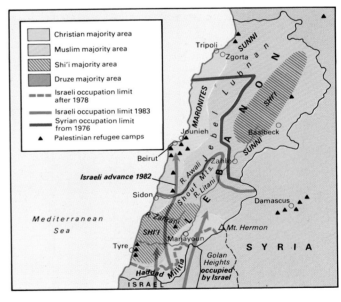

Christian majority area
Muslim majority area
Shi'i majority area
Druze majority area
- - - Israeli occupation limit after 1978
Israeli occupation limit 1983
Syrian occupation limit from 1976
▲ Palestinian refugee camps

3/The Persian Gulf remains the most valuable and most heavily exploited region of oil and natural gas resources in the world, producing 41% of the world's oil requirements in 1979. In the 1980s the strategic importance of the area became sharply defined when the war between Iran and Iraq interrupted the export of oil from the Gulf.

The invasion of Kuwait by Iraq in 1990 produced a UN embargo on oil exports from both countries. In addition, Iraqi sabotage of the Kuwait oilfields brought about a long interruption in Kuwait's oil-exporting capacity as well as inflicting serious ecological damage.

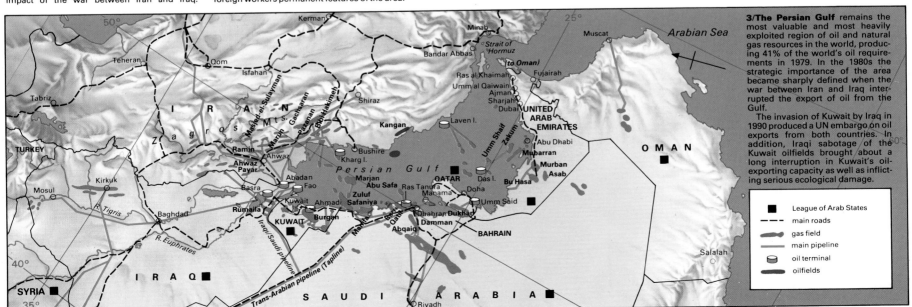

■ League of Arab States
- - - main roads
gas field
main pipeline
oil terminal
oilfields

Latin America: revolution and reaction from 1930

THE Great Depression of 1929 struck Latin America a shattering blow, cutting off supplies of foreign capital and lowering the price of its primary products in the world markets. In the long run this forced the area to look to its own resources and to undertake a programme of industrialisation. But it caused great immediate distress, especially among those who lacked the political power to protect themselves. Urban workers lost faith in the middle-class liberal or radical parties which had hitherto wooed them, and began to look to the strong man who offered immediate relief. Governments emerged appealing directly to the masses, basing themselves on the support of organised labour, and offering accelerated industrialisation. Such was the regime of Vargas in Brazil (and later that of Perón in Argentina). Instead of the vote he offered security, improved working conditions, stronger – though state-controlled – trade unions. However, populist dictators could not escape their military origins or desert the interests of the armed forces and their civilian allies. Perón, as well as Vargas, was made to realise this. Peronism rested not only on the support of urban workers, to whom it offered higher wages, a new unionism and more jobs, but also on the acquiescence of a nationalist and development-minded military. And when, in 1955, the military decided that the rival power base had become a threat to their own interests they overthrew Perón.

The prospects of further reform began to grow dim, even in Mexico, the homeland of revolution. In the 1930s, it is true, there was a radical shift to the left under Cárdenas, who expanded the distribution of land to the peasants, increased the power of organised labour and nationalised the foreign oil companies. But from 1940 land distribution and social reform declined; there was a new emphasis on industrialisation, foreign investment was encouraged and closer economic relations with the US were developed.

In the rest of Latin America, too, the first wave of change had spent itself. In some countries – Uruguay, Mexico, Brazil and Argentina – it had produced noticeable results. In most it had hardly been felt. The result was frustration, and it was stimulated by two things. Population growth, especially from the 1950s, outstripped economic development and further worsened the prospects of the under-privileged. Meanwhile, during the Second World War, Latin America was cut off from foreign sources of consumer goods and forced to industrialise still further; this brought great profit, but little went to the working-class sector, widening the gulf between the wealthy and the poor.

By this time, people were looking for new answers to economic and social problems; some found inspiration in Marxism and the example of the Soviet Union. Communist parties had existed in Latin America since the 1920s. They had few convinced adherents. The Guatemalan revolution of 1944 inaugurated basic social change. When, from 1951, President Arbenz undertook a programme of agrarian reform, only the Communists could give him the ideas and the political machine he needed. In the event his Communist allies overreached themselves, for they gained political influence without acquiring any military power, and they were unable to defend the revolution against the conservative rebellion organised, with US connivance, from Honduras in 1954. The Guatemalan revolution also underlined a common problem – at what point does investment in social welfare hinder rather than promote economic growth? The dilemma of creating a welfare state without having the economic resources to sustain it was seen above all in Bolivia, one of the worst examples of under-development in the region. In 1952 left-wing forces led a violent revolution of civilians over the military junta. The new regime nationalised the tin mines, enfranchised the Indians and imposed agrarian reform. But wage increases, productivity decline, and enormous inflation eroded many of the social accomplishments of the revolution and brought it to a halt in the 1960s.

From 1959, however, another revolution, that in Cuba, sought to bring about social change and economic growth simultaneously. This involved a decision to adopt Communism, a decision which was reinforced by the hostility of the US as well as by the need for an ideology and a political machine. Land was collectivised, businesses were nationalised and education was given a Marxist orientation. While this did bring greater social equality and some improvement in the prospects of the rural workers, it was procured at the cost of political freedom and did not resolve the problem of how to impose social change at an early stage of economic development; the Cuban economy remained rooted in sugar and dependent on an outside metropolis.

Nevertheless, Castro and his followers were convinced that it was their mission to extend the revolution throughout Latin America. There was some response; rural guerrilla movements in a number of countries posed a serious threat to security forces, culminating in the expedition of Guevara to Bolivia and his death there in 1967. An alternative revolutionary focus was then provided by urban guerrillas, but these had too narrow a political base to succeed. Meanwhile, left of centre democratic parties, including Christian Democracy, sought to prove that change could be accomplished in liberty. Their record in Venezuela and Chile was criticised for producing too little and proceeding too slowly. The election of Allende in Chile in 1970 at the head of Popular Unity brought Marxism to power and the chance to prove that structural change could be made by constitutional means. In 1973 military intervention terminated the experiment.

Meanwhile, the Latin American economies had been undergoing major structural change. Investments in mining and agriculture (though not in oil) had lost their traditional dynamism, while investments in manufacturing and commerce were expanding dramatically. This shift from the primary-export model to industrialisation by import substitution represented a new stage of modernisation and brought in its wake important social and economic changes. New social and political groups replaced or challenged the traditional landed oligarchy, explosive urbanisation took place, further concentration of income was encouraged, and acute social tensions appeared. At the same time industrialisation made Latin America dependent upon imported capital goods, raw materials, technology and finance, creating enormous foreign debts, which neither the traditional exports nor the new manufactured exports could meet.

As the 1970s advanced the military governments of the south combined political conservatism with economic liberalism, and enjoyed some support from the upper and middle sectors. The alternative model was that of democracy and regional integration, exemplified in the Andean Pact, some of whose member countries could claim economic and social gains, especially with the dramatic rise of oil revenues from 1973. In the late 1970s democracies such as Mexico and Venezuela appeared to be stable and prosperous, but the impermanence of the oil boom and excessive state expenditure cast a shadow over their future development and by 1982 Mexico was in deep trouble. The authoritarian regimes, meanwhile, saw their free market economies challenged by world recession and, in the case of Argentina, by growing political opposition. When, in 1976, the Argentine military ended the second Peronist regime they replaced populism by dictatorship, economic protection by market forces, and non-alignment by a commitment to the West. The policy failed and society was further polarised. The invasion of the Falklands, however, was intended to rally the country behind a national cause, but it worsened the economy without improving political prospects. The experience left a deep impression and called into question both the role of the military in politics and the relation of Latin America to the rest of the world.

From 1985 to 1988 three problems dominated Latin American affairs: the debt crisis continued to elude all solutions; the return to democracy in the southern cone was watched with some suspicion by the outgoing military; and in Central America it remained to be seen whether regional initiatives could succeed in ending civil conflicts where international action had failed.

2/Economic development (*below*) Latin America's traditional primary-export economy was modified, though not transformed, by the great depression and the Second World War. The search for economic development and independence met with some success in some countries and impetus was given to import substitution. But the area continued to depend upon the developed world for markets for its raw material exports, for imports of industrial capital goods, for technology, and for finance.

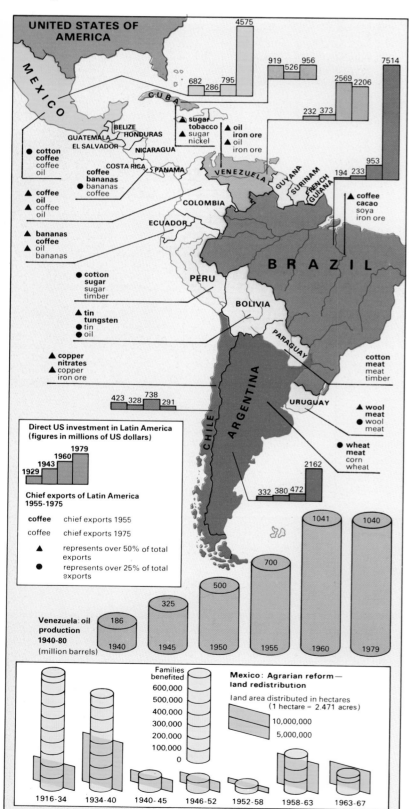

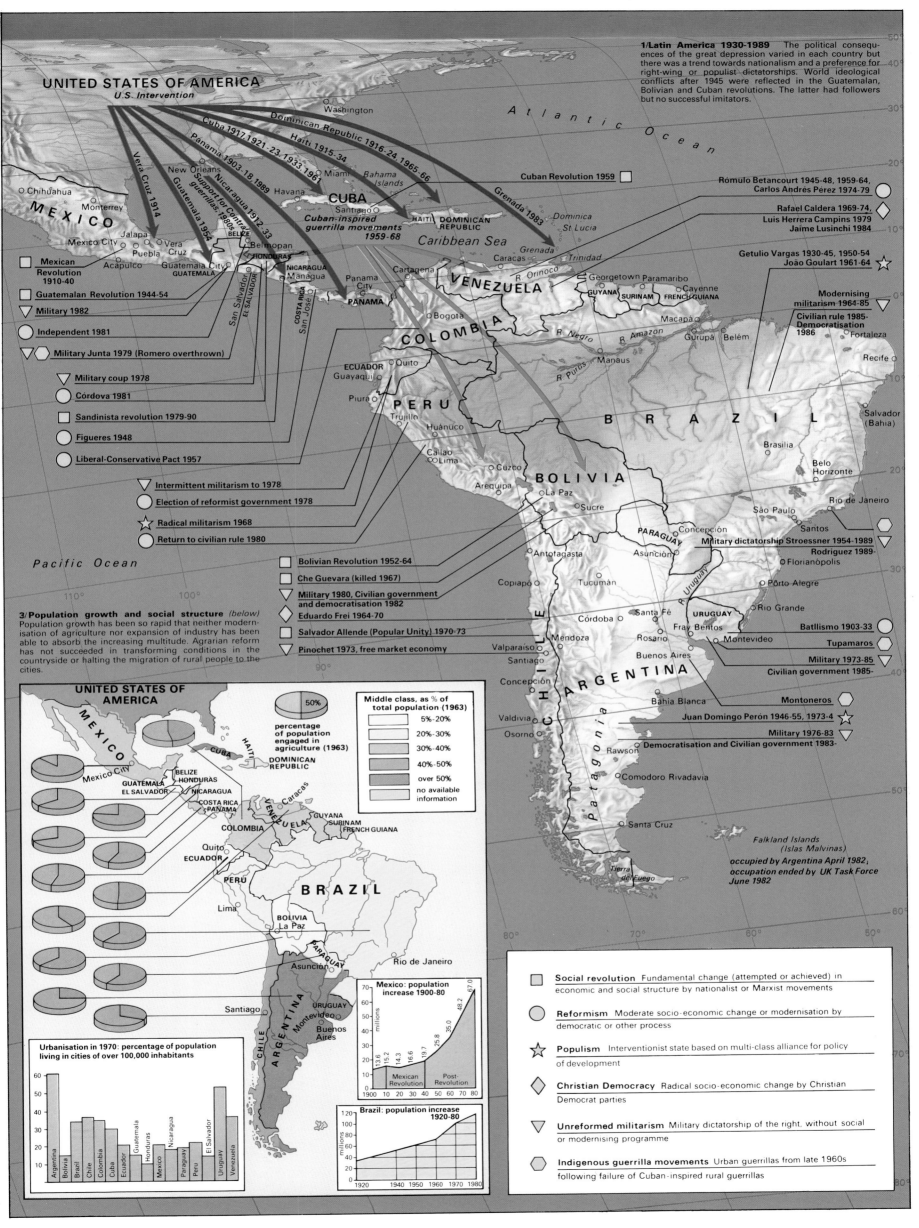

1/Latin America 1930-1989 The political consequences of the great depression varied in each country but there was a trend towards nationalism and a preference for right-wing or populist dictatorships. World ideological conflicts after 1945 were reflected in the Guatemalan, Bolivian and Cuban revolutions. The latter had followers but no successful imitators.

UNITED STATES OF AMERICA
U.S. Intervention

Dominican Republic 1916-24, 1965-66
Haiti 1915-34
Cuba 1917, 1921-23, 1933, 1961
Panama 1903-18, 1989
Support for Contra guerrillas, 1980s
Nicaragua 1912-33
Guatemala 1954
Vera Cruz 1914

Cuban Revolution 1959 □

Cuban-inspired guerrilla movements 1959-68

Rómulo Betancourt 1945-48, 1959-64, Carlos Andrés Pérez 1974-79 ◯
Rafael Caldera 1969-74, Luis Herrera Campins 1979, Jaime Lusinchi 1984 ◇
Getulio Vargas 1930-45, 1950-54, João Goulart 1961-64 ☆
Modernising militarism 1964-85 ▽
Civilian rule 1985-Democratisation 1986 ▽

□ Mexican Revolution 1910-40
□ Guatemalan Revolution 1944-54
▽ Military 1982
◯ Independent 1981
▽⬡ Military Junta 1979 (Romero overthrown)

▽ Military coup 1978
◯ Córdova 1981
□ Sandinista revolution 1979-90
◯ Figueres 1948
◯ Liberal-Conservative Pact 1957

▽ Intermittent militarism to 1978
◯ Election of reformist government 1978
☆ Radical militarism 1968
◯ Return to civilian rule 1980

Pacific Ocean

□ Bolivian Revolution 1952-64
□ Che Guevara (killed 1967)
▽ Military 1980, Civilian government and democratisation 1982
◇ Eduardo Frei 1964-70
□ Salvador Allende (Popular Unity) 1970-73
▽ Pinochet 1973, free market economy

Military dictatorship Stroessner 1954-1989 ▽
Rodriguez 1989- ▽

Batllismo 1903-33 ◯
Tupamaros ⬡
Military 1973-85 ▽
Civilian government 1985-

Montoneros ⬡
Juan Domingo Perón 1946-55, 1973-4 ☆
Military 1976-83 ▽
Democratisation and Civilian government 1983-

Falkland Islands (Islas Malvinas)
occupied by Argentina April 1982; occupation ended by UK Task Force June 1982

3/Population growth and social structure *(below)*
Population growth has been so rapid that neither modernisation of agriculture nor expansion of industry has been able to absorb the increasing multitude. Agrarian reform has not succeeded in transforming conditions in the countryside or halting the migration of rural people to the cities.

UNITED STATES OF AMERICA

50% percentage of population engaged in agriculture (1963)

Middle class, as % of total population (1963)
- 5%-20%
- 20%-30%
- 30%-40%
- 40%-50%
- over 50%
- no available information

Mexico: population increase 1900-80
13.6 15.2 14.3 16.6 19.7 25.8 35.0 48.2 67.0
| Mexican Revolution | Post-Revolution |
1900 10 20 30 40 50 60 70 80

Urbanisation in 1970: percentage of population living in cities of over 100,000 inhabitants
Argentina, Bolivia, Brazil, Chile, Colombia, Cuba, Ecuador, Guatemala, Honduras, Mexico, Nicaragua, Paraguay, Peru, El Salvador, Uruguay, Venezuela

Brazil: population increase 1920-80
1920 1940 1950 1960 1970 1980

□ **Social revolution** Fundamental change (attempted or achieved) in economic and social structure by nationalist or Marxist movements

◯ **Reformism** Moderate socio-economic change or modernisation by democratic or other process

☆ **Populism** Interventionist state based on multi-class alliance for policy of development

◇ **Christian Democracy** Radical socio-economic change by Christian Democrat parties

▽ **Unreformed militarism** Military dictatorship of the right, without social or modernising programme

⬡ **Indigenous guerrilla movements** Urban guerrillas from late 1960s following failure of Cuban-inspired rural guerrillas

The development of the United States from 1940

THE New Deal administrations of President Franklin Roosevelt, from 1933 to 1940, failed to restore American employment and industrial production to their 1929 levels; but by public investment and wholesale restructuring of the economy, above all by accustoming the people to economic leadership from Washington, they prepared the country for the actively predominant world role thrust upon it by the Second World War, which brought complete economic recovery and a massive victory.

The requirements of wartime production solved the unemployment problem at last. Economic output, to meet the needs of the army, the navy and the allies, was gigantic. This performance demonstrated economic possibilities which, when realised, were to create an epoch of unprecedented prosperity and power.

Peace brought no serious interruption to the upward trend for more than twenty years, and gross national product nearly trebled in real terms between 1950 and 1980, while income per head almost doubled. A number of factors brought this about: population increase, technological advances and the emergence of new things to buy, the stimulus given to the economy by re-conversion from war to peace and the sudden spending of wartime savings (1945-8), then the rearmament programmes connected with the Cold War and the Korean War (1948-53). Affluence seemed wholly normal. Business confidence was never more buoyant. On this basis of wealth and hope the American people began to transform their entire way of life.

Rising expectations were a genuinely revolutionary force. There was a "baby boom", a huge stimulus to demand, that started in the Second World War. There was a second great migration to the West, and immigration rose steadily after 1945. By the 1980s Spanish-speaking immigrants were the dominant population group in many parts of the South and the South-West, and Miami had become a Latin American city. But perhaps the most noticeable change of all in this period was the expansion of the suburbs. Easy credit, cheap fuel (whether for homes or automobiles), mass production of housing and cars, and the giant road-building programmes of the federal and state governments were among the factors encouraging Americans by their millions to move off the farms and out of the cities into endless miles of suburbs. So although the population of the central cities grew from 48 million to 64 million between 1950 and 1970 that of their urban fringes grew from 21 million to 55 million. The total population rose from 132 million in 1940 to 226 million in 1980.

Underpinning the national prosperity was a strong dollar, vast national resources within the continental United States and an economic system which was far in advance of any other in the world, at least until the 1960s. Undermining it were the insatiable appetites of American consumer society; the marked tendency of American capitalists to spend their profits rather than reinvest them, and of American industrial workers to claim higher wages and easier conditions of work, without regard to the effect of such claims (if successful) on prices and on the international competitiveness of the American industrial machine; and the growing inability of this most pampered nation to believe that things could ever be different. This last trait bred a recklessness in many policy-makers and citizens which put the whole position of the USA in danger. The Vietnam War (1965-73) would in any case have been inflationary; it was made much more so by the refusal of the Johnson and Nixon administrations to impose any curb on civilian incomes and consumption. The result was the great crisis of 1973, when the cartel of oil-exporting nations (OPEC), first imposed an oil embargo and then took advantage of the apparently unquenchable American demand to increase oil prices by nearly 250 per cent. American industry allowed itself increasingly to be undersold by more efficient foreign competitors, so that exports steadily sank against imports. Defeat in Vietnam and economic uncertainty made the later 1970s a troubling time for Americans. Nationalism, a tax-payers' revolt, and a widespread wish to be reassured elected Ronald Reagan to the Presidency in 1980. With the cheerful acquiescence of the voters he began to accelerate all the disturbing trends of the previous decade. He cut taxes by a third, thereby releasing a flood of spending power on to the market. He vastly increased expenditure on armaments, so creating the biggest national deficit in history. He did nothing about the structural defects of American industry, so the new purchasing power went overwhelmingly on imports, creating an equally unprecedented trade deficit. At the same time the Federal Reserve Board's successful efforts to curb inflation by imposing high interest rates meant that foreign capital poured into the United States, financing the deficits and maintaining a boom in national and international trade.

By the mid-1980s the USA was living on credit. With the collapse of the century's longest-running bull market on 'Black Monday', 19 October 1987 there was a run on the dollar and share-holder panic set in. There was strong nationalist resentment against Japan and the EEC for their protectionist outlook. But the crisis proved only temporary. The US economy continued to expand, and there were foreign policy successes in Grenada, Panama and the Gulf War in 1991. The collapse of Communism produced a growing assertiveness in America's dealings with the outside world.

The most notable achievements of post-war America contributed to this revival of America's 'manifest destiny'. Soviet expansionism had been resisted successfully without direct war, through rearmament, alliances and economic assistance, as in the Marshall Programme (launched 1947). The civil rights movement had triumphed in the Civil Rights Act of 1964 and the Voting Rights Act of 1965, which gave black American citizens effective political and social equality for the first time (although economic equality had to wait). And prosperity had made possible the space exploration programme.

The superior technology *(above)* and management techniques which helped maintain her position as the world's most sophisticated industrial power were shown by the speed with which the US responded to the early Soviet lead in rocketry. The first men to walk on the moon (20 July 1969) were launched by the Saturn V rocket.

3 and 4/Urban growth *(below and right)* Suburban growth has seen great development, and in several areas this has had the effect of joining up formerly separate urban areas to create "super cities", nowhere more dramatically than in the Los Angeles region (map 4). In the '70s, however, perhaps for the first time in US history the population in rural areas grew as fast as the population as a whole. An interstate system of highways totalling about 40,000 miles by 1980 facilitated long-distance movement of people and the rise of complex networks of residence and work (map 3).

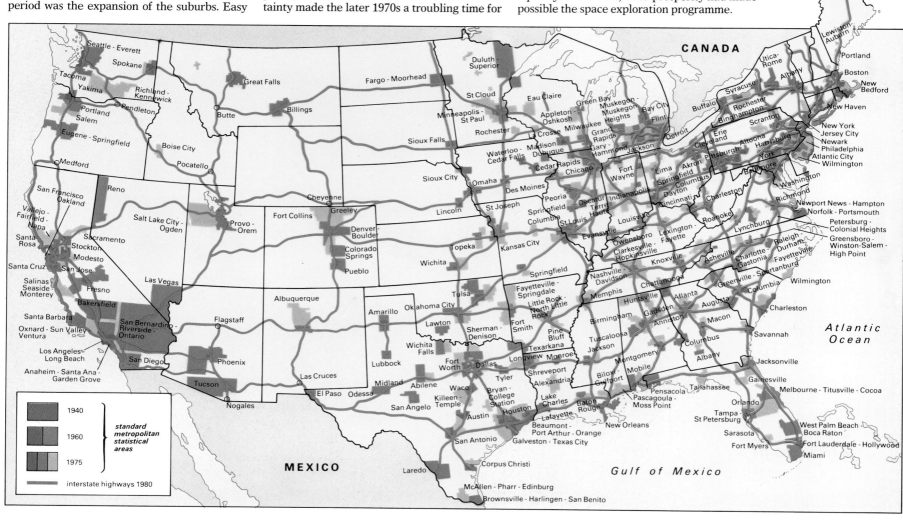

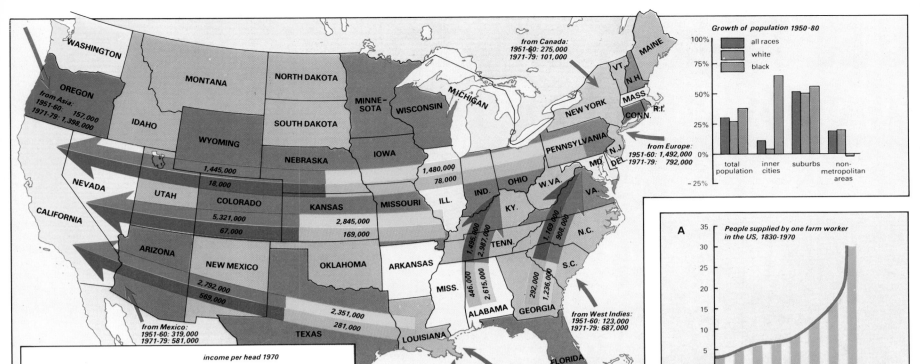

WASHINGTON
OREGON
from Asia:
1951-60: 157,000
1971-79: 1,398,000
MONTANA
NORTH DAKOTA
MINNE-SOTA
WISCONSIN
MICHIGAN
from Canada:
1951-60: 275,000
1971-79: 101,000
MAINE
VT **N.H.**
NEW YORK
MASS.
CONN. **R.I.**
IDAHO
WYOMING
SOUTH DAKOTA
IOWA
NEVADA
1,445,000
18,000
1,480,000
78,000
PENNSYLVANIA
N.J. **DEL.**
from Europe:
1951-60: 1,492,000
1971-79: 792,000
UTAH
COLORADO
5,321,000
67,000
NEBRASKA
KANSAS
2,845,000
169,000
MISSOURI
ILL.
IND.
OHIO
W.VA.
MD
CALIFORNIA
ARIZONA
NEW MEXICO
2,792,000
569,000
OKLAHOMA
ARKANSAS
1,495,800
2,587,000
KY.
TENN.
1,169,000
908,000
VA.
N.C.
S.C.
446,000
2,615,000
292,000
1,236,000
MISS.
ALABAMA
GEORGIA
from West Indies:
1951-60: 123,000
1971-79: 687,000
TEXAS
2,351,000
281,000
LOUISIANA
FLORIDA
from Mexico:
1951-60: 319,000
1971-79: 581,000
from Central America:
1951-60: 45,000
1971-79: 111,000
from South America:
1951-60: 72,000
1971-79: 245,000
Gulf of Mexico

Legend:
1930-60	1965-79	movement of white population
1930-60	1965-79	movement of black population
→		immigrants

income per head 1970
under $3000 | $4000-4500
$3000-3500 | $4500-4750
$3500-4000 | over $4750
(USA average $3943)

Growth of population 1950-80
all races
white
black
total population | inner cities | suburbs | non-metropolitan areas

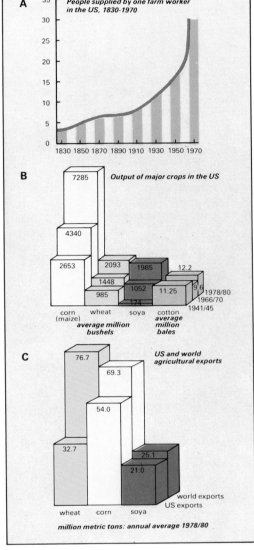

A People supplied by one farm worker in the US, 1830-1970
1830 1850 1870 1890 1910 1930 1950 1970

B Output of major crops in the US
7285
4340
2653
2093 1985 12.2
1448 1052 9.0 1978/80
985 174 11.25 1966/70
corn (maize) | wheat | soya | cotton 1941/45
average million bushels | average million bales

C US and world agricultural exports
76.7
69.3
54.0
32.7
25.1
21.0
wheat | corn | soya
world exports / US exports
million metric tons: annual average 1978/80

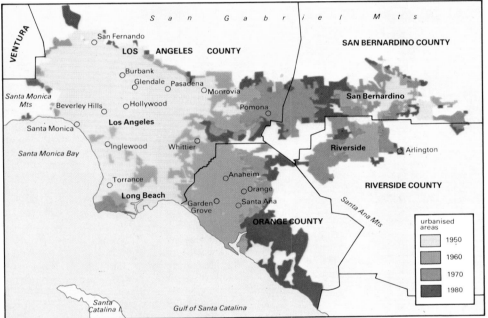

VENTURA
San Gabriel Mts
LOS ANGELES COUNTY
SAN BERNARDINO COUNTY
San Fernando
Burbank
Glendale Pasadena
Monrovia
San Bernardino
Santa Monica Mts
Beverley Hills
Hollywood
Pomona
Los Angeles
Inglewood
Whittier
Riverside
Arlington
Santa Monica Bay
Santa Monica
Torrance
Anaheim
RIVERSIDE COUNTY
Long Beach
Garden Grove
Orange
Santa Ana
Santa Ana Mts
ORANGE COUNTY
Santa Catalina I.
Gulf of Santa Catalina

urbanised areas
1950
1960
1970
1980

2 Wealth and population *(above)*
Since the Second World War there has been a striking migration of population to the far West; California is now the most populous state. The industrial states have the highest average incomes and the Dakotas, Arkansas and Mississippi have fared worst as regards both income and population growth. The black population has grown faster than the white (see graph) and the blacks have moved heavily into the big cities.

Farm efficiency *(right)* The farming population fell from 30.5 million in 1940 to 9 million in 1974, yet because of remarkable increases in productivity the US remain the world's greatest food supplier (see graphs A, B, C).

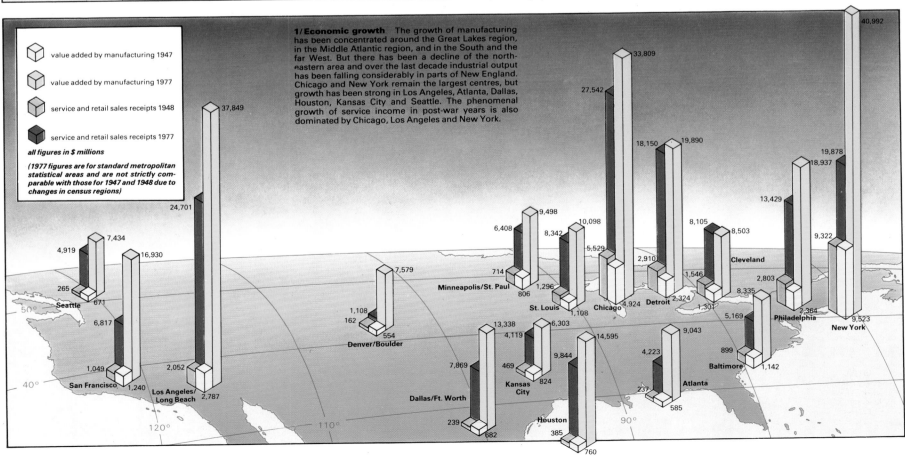

1/Economic growth The growth of manufacturing has been concentrated around the Great Lakes region, in the Middle Atlantic region, and in the South and the far West. But there has been a decline of the north-eastern area and over the last decade industrial output has been falling considerably in parts of New England. Chicago and New York remain the largest centres, but growth has been strong in Los Angeles, Atlanta, Dallas, Houston, Kansas City and Seattle. The phenomenal growth of service income in post-war years is also dominated by Chicago, Los Angeles and New York.

value added by manufacturing 1947
value added by manufacturing 1977
service and retail sales receipts 1948
service and retail sales receipts 1977
all figures in $ millions
(1977 figures are for standard metropolitan statistical areas and are not strictly comparable with those for 1947 and 1948 due to changes in census regions)

Seattle 4,919 7,434 265 671
San Francisco 24,701 37,849 16,930 6,817 1,049 1,240
Los Angeles/Long Beach 2,052 2,787
Denver/Boulder 7,579 1,108 162 554
Minneapolis/St. Paul 6,408 9,498 8,342 714 806
St. Louis 10,098 5,529 1,296 1,108
Dallas/Ft. Worth 13,338 4,119 7,869 239 682
Kansas City 6,303 9,844 469 824
Houston 14,595 9,043 385 760
Atlanta 4,223 237 899 585 1,142
Chicago 27,542 33,809 4,924 2,910
Detroit 18,150 19,890 1,546 2,324 1,301
Cleveland 8,105 8,503 5,169
Baltimore 8,335 2,803 2,364
Philadelphia 13,429 18,937 19,878 9,322
New York 40,992 19,878 9,523

50°
40°
120° 110° 90°

The development of the Soviet Union after 1926

BY 1926 it was clear that the Bolshevik regime was going to survive, in spite of the immense problems still facing it. Civil war, foreign intervention, chaos and famine followed the Revolution, and Russia became an isolated nation. After Lenin's death in 1924, Trotsky and Stalin struggled for the leadership, which was decided by Trotsky's expulsion from the Communist Party in 1927. Trotsky's aim had been to spread communism to other countries; Stalin's triumph meant, instead, concentration on domestic problems, and the first five-year plan of industrialisation was introduced in 1928. Russia looked inwards to the resources of her own vast territories: self-sufficiency was to be the new economic goal. One great weakness however, was the supply of food. Soviet towns had serious shortages in 1927, 1928 and again in 1929. It is now accepted that these were caused by the regime's serious misunderstanding of agriculture, but at the time they were blamed on supposedly capitalist farmers, 'kulaks', who allegedly withheld grain to force up prices. Late in 1929 Stalin decided to expropriate all private farms, with a process known as the Collectivisation of Agriculture. It was a disaster. Peasants, unable to feed their animals, slaughtered them; their own seed-corn was requisitioned and dumped on the world market to pay for foreign machinery. The result was a great famine in 1932-33, particularly affecting the Ukraine, and causing the death of uncounted millions. The collective farms did not function as expected, there was not nearly enough machinery (only 278,000 tractors in use in 1934), and the peasants were badly paid and demoralised: it was not until 1951 that yields returned to their level of 1928.

The convulsions in the countryside caused forty million people to move to the towns in the 1930s. The fresh labour was used mainly for construction which makes the growth-rates of the Soviet economy in the years of the first and second five-year plans startling and unique. Underpinning the economy were the existing industries and skills which had grown up in the last generation of Tsarist times, when Russia was already the fourth economic power in the world. However, a crash programme for technical skills was shortly implemented. Foreign machinery was acquired by grain-exports and such devices as the sale of forty paintings from the Hermitage to American millionaires. In the 1930s the Germans and the Americans were relatively generous with credits. The result was a great growth in iron, coal and steel industries. In 1928 there had been an iron industry in the Ukraine and in the central Urals. By 1940 both had been expanded and modernised. Two new large iron and steel bases were established: one near a massive iron ore deposit in the southern Urals at the new town of Magnitogorsk; the other on the Kuzbass coalfield at Stalinsk (Novokuznetsk).

All of this required a coercive machinery and Yeshov, head of the NKVD, or 'People's Commissariat of Internal Affairs', launched, in 1936, a wave of terror known as 'the Great Purge' which carried off millions to labour-camps or execution. It killed off a large part of the Soviet officer-corps and seriously weakened the Red Army before its great war with Hitler.

In 1941, when Germany attacked, virtually no-one expected Russia to survive for more then a few weeks. However, much of the industrialisation of the first five-year plans had taken place in eastern regions beyond the reach of the Germans in the 1941-45 war, and this was a vital factor in Soviet survival. During the war the industrialisation of these strategically safe regions was greatly speeded up, but the western parts of the country were devastated. Agriculture suffered from the destruction of farm buildings and equipment.

Nevertheless, there was remarkable economic reconstruction. After 1950 the output of heavy industry continued to grow, and light industry, neglected during the Stalinist period (1928-53), also progressed. Siberian reserves of oil, gas and mineral ores were discovered and exploited, and powerful hydro-electric and coal-fired generating stations built in eastern Siberia and Kazakhstan. The Soviet economy was joined up with those of the countries of eastern Europe which came under Soviet control after the war, and their high-quality engineering products proved to be of immense value to the USSR's technological progress.

Stalin's successors were forced to recognise the immensity of the agricultural problem. A growing population was expecting the oft-promised increase in the level of living but agriculture was scarcely more productive than before the revolution. There was an increase in grain production under Khrushchev and after 1965 much was done under Brezhnev to improve the collective farmer's lot.

By 1980 the Soviet Union, like the United States, was recognised as a 'superpower', with a comparable degree of military strength. Although Soviet gross national product still fell well short of America's, the USSR overtook the USA in the production of iron ore, cement, steel and oil, and was rapidly developing the world's largest reserves of natural gas. Despite this, the Soviet economy began to enter a crisis in the later 1970s. Increasingly, the USSR could afford the arms-race less easily than the USA, and there were alarms when the USA threatened to introduce a defence-system against missiles, known as 'Star Wars'. In 1985 a new leader, M. S. Gorbachov, came to power with a programme of reform, 'a revolution within the revolution'.

Plans for economic reform proved difficult to implement successfully. Price-rises and shortages occurred in the cities; dependence on the

2/Changes in republican status (below) Autonomous Soviet Socialist Republics (ASSRs) were created for important nationalities within. Union Republics (SSRs). Since 1941 the Karelo-Finnish Republic has become an ASSR, the Crimean ASSR has been incorporated in the Ukrainian SSR and the Volga-German ASSR has been dissolved.

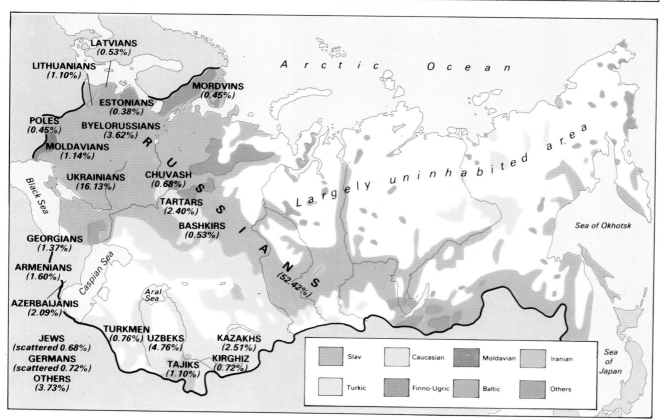

4/The different nationalities in the USSR (left) The Soviet Union comprises many different ethnic groups, languages, religions and cultures. The majority of the population are of Slavic origin. This includes the Russians and Ukrainians who are the first and second largest national groups. Russian is the official language and most people in the USSR are bi- or even tri-lingual in an attempt to retain their ethnic origins. Some groups, such as the Azerbaijanis, the Armenians and the Baltic states, are keen not only to retain their national origins but to establish their independence from the Soviet Union.

west for food and technical assistance increased. Gorbachev reduced the role of the Communist Party, became executive President and increased presidential powers. New legislative bodies for the Soviet republics provided growing opposition to state power, making economic reform even more difficult to implement. Demands by non-Russian peoples for greater autonomy or independence led to crises in the Baltic states and the Caucasus Republics and protests were violently repressed. By 1991 the Soviet Union faced its greatest internal crisis since the 1920s.

3/The movement of population (right) From 1926 to 1939 major population growth was in Moscow and Leningrad; early Soviet industrial expansion was concentrated here. The second period (1939-59) included the war, and reflects the eastward movement of industry and urban population away from the war zones. More urban growth took place in the west during the years 1959-70.

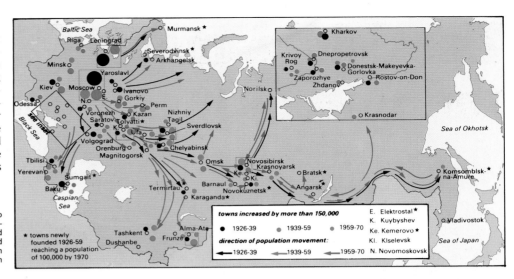

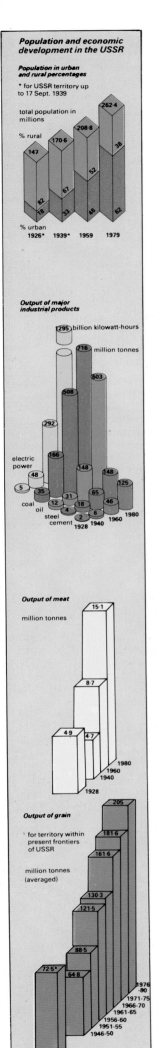

Population and economic development in the USSR

Population in urban and rural percentages

*for USSR territory up to 17 Sept. 1939

total population in millions

Output of major industrial products

Output of meat

million tonnes

Output of grain

for territory within present frontiers of USSR

million tonnes (averaged)

1/The Soviet Union after 1926 (right) In this period Russia was transformed from a backward peasant economy to a highly industrialised, militarily powerful state, second only to the USA; it was also, in the early years, a period of immense human suffering which was intensified by the German invasion.

The Cold War from 1949

Soviet territorial gains since 1939
Warsaw Pact allies
Polish gains from Germany
air corridors for Western access to Berlin
Western autobahn to Berlin

WITH the elimination of Germany, Japan and Italy and the weakening of Great Britain and France in the Second World War, the USA and the USSR emerged as the two 'superpowers'. The Cold War was the expression of their political and ideological confrontation.

Already visible at the Yalta Conference (February 1945), their conflict of interests became more acute after the death of Franklin D. Roosevelt and the succession of Harry S. Truman as President of the United States (12 April 1945). The American monopoly of the A-bomb, first successfully detonated on 16 July 1945, increased tension, and after the inconclusive Potsdam Conference of July-August 1945, the Soviet Union under Stalin decided to consolidate Communist control of eastern Europe. In 1947, Soviet-dominated governments were set up in Albania, Hungary, Poland, Bulgaria, Romania, and finally (in February 1948) in Czechoslovakia; only Yugoslavia retained some independence. When civil war and an attempted Communist takeover occurred in Greece in December 1947, and the Russians threatened in April 1948 to freeze out the western sectors of Berlin and incorporate the whole city in the German Democratic Republic (established on 7 October 1949), the USA reacted vigorously. Even earlier, the Truman Doctrine and Marshall Plan (1947) had been established as the American reply to the alleged Russian threat.

Starting as a conflict over central Europe and divided Germany, the Cold War spread to Asia following the Communist victory in China (1949), and soon developed into a global conflict. For the United States, the Korean War (1950) was evidence of a world-wide Communist conspiracy, although in fact the Chinese only intervened in the Korean War (October 1950) when the US advance to the Yalu river seemed to threaten their territorial security. Even then, the USSR remained in US eyes the main threat, and though Japan was built up as an American bastion against China (1951) and Okinawa retained as an American missile base, and links with the Chinese nationalists in Taiwan strengthened, the main aim of United States policy was to 'contain' the USSR by a series of encircling alliances and bases around its frontiers from west to east. First was NATO (North Atlantic Treaty Organisation, 1949), followed by SEATO (South-East Asia Treaty Organisation, 1954) and CENTO (Central Treaty Organisation, 1959, replacing the Baghdad Pact of 1955). By this time the United States had over 1400 foreign bases in 31 countries, including 275 bases for nuclear bombers. For its own defence, after the USSR had acquired nuclear weapons (A-bomb 1949, H-bomb 1953), it constructed the so-called 'DEW

2/Europe *(left)* Soviet control in eastern Europe was established gradually between 1945 and 1948. Although it was evident that Allied victory over Germany would bring a major westward expansion of Soviet influence, Stalin at first proceeded cautiously. 'Bourgeois' parties were tolerated and elections in 1945 and 1946 were relatively free, but by February 1948 eastern Europe was ruled by communist or communist-controlled 'socialist unity' parties. Subsequently 'national communists' (Gomulka 1949, Kádár 1950) were removed, thus assuring full Soviet control, except in Yugoslavia, where Marshal Tito broke with Moscow in 1948.

line' (a Distant Early Warning system of radar posts across the Arctic Circle from Alaska through Canada to Baffin Island). But this became obsolete after the Soviet launching of the satellite Sputnik in 1957 and the advent of the intercontinental ballistic missile (ICBM).

The most intensive phase of the Cold War occurred during the period 1949-59, when Dean Acheson and John Foster Dulles were United States secretaries of state. After 1955 (Baghdad Pact) it spilled over into the Middle East (Eisenhower Doctrine, 1957; United States intervention in Lebanon, 1958), where it proved a divisive force, some countries seeking Soviet, others American, support. But by this time conditions were changing, the two monolithic blocks were showing signs of strain. Uprisings in Hungary and Poland (1956) shook Soviet self-confidence; unrest in Latin America and Soviet attempts to strike up relationships there (1958) were scarcely less disturbing for the United States. Both parties seem to have concluded that they had more to lose than to gain by the conflict, and after the settlement of the Cuban crisis in 1962, Soviet-American tension gradually relaxed. A first sign of this was the signature of a nuclear test treaty in 1963.

The focus of the Cold War now shifted to South-East Asia, where the United States had been increasingly involved in Indo-China since 1954. The greater moderation of Soviet policy after the fall of Khrushchev in 1964, accumulating evidence of Sino-Soviet conflict, and the Chinese acquisition of nuclear potential (1964), all seemed to point to China as the centre of militant Communism. The 'Domino Theory' led the United States to ever-increasing military intervention in Laos, Cambodia, and particularly Vietnam, which reached its peak under President Johnson (1963-68): ultimately more than 543,000 American troops were committed.

At this stage a revulsion set in. The failure to destroy Vietnamese resistance without recourse to nuclear weapons, involving the possibility of Chinese intervention and the outbreak of a third world war, but above all the financial strain imposed both by the war and by the costly American system of alliances, imposed a halt. The new Republican President, Richard M. Nixon, promised in 1969 to reduce and finally (1973) to withdraw United States ground troops from Vietnam. When in 1971 he followed up this reversal by overtures to Communist China and later visited Peking and Moscow, the relaxation of tension seemed to mark the beginning of a new era in international relations; and a similar change occurred in Europe with the conclusion of a Four-Power Agreement on Berlin in 1971 and détente between East and West Germany. But the underlying tensions remained unresolved, particularly in the field of nuclear armaments, and in spite of continuing discussion of limitation and control in the so-called SALT negotiations of 1972 and later, both the Soviet Union and the United States continued to build up new and more powerful strategic weapon systems. The atmosphere of détente, or 'thaw', was at least outwardly maintained up to 1979; but from the beginning of the 1980s the unresolved tensions came to the surface again, especially following the Soviet invasion of Afghanistan (1979), and a more repressive atmosphere as regards human rights in the Soviet Union. The tempo of the arms race was stepped up on both sides and only in December 1987, with a new

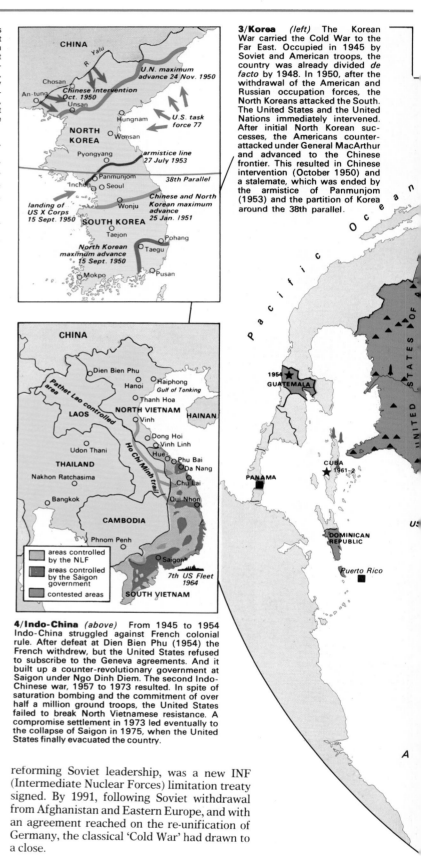

3/Korea *(left)* The Korean War carried the Cold War to the Far East. Occupied in 1945 by Soviet and American troops, the country was already divided *de facto* by 1948. In 1950, after the withdrawal of the American and Russian occupation forces, the North Koreans attacked the South. The United States and the United Nations immediately intervened. After initial North Korean successes, the Americans counter-attacked under General MacArthur and advanced to the Chinese frontier. This resulted in Chinese intervention (October 1950) and a stalemate, which was ended by the armistice of Panmunjom (1953) and the partition of Korea around the 38th parallel.

areas controlled by the NLF
areas controlled by the Saigon government
contested areas

4/Indo-China *(above)* From 1945 to 1954 Indo-China struggled against French colonial rule. After defeat at Dien Bien Phu (1954) the French withdrew, but the United States refused to subscribe to the Geneva agreements. And it built up a counter-revolutionary government at Saigon under Ngo Dinh Diem. The second Indo-Chinese war, 1957 to 1973 resulted. In spite of saturation bombing and the commitment of over half a million ground troops, the United States failed to break North Vietnamese resistance. A compromise settlement in 1973 led eventually to the collapse of Saigon in 1975, when the United States finally evacuated the country.

reforming Soviet leadership, was a new INF (Intermediate Nuclear Forces) limitation treaty signed. By 1991, following Soviet withdrawal from Afghanistan and Eastern Europe, and with an agreement reached on the re-unification of Germany, the classical 'Cold War' had drawn to a close.

members of Baghdad Pact
countries opposed to Baghdad Pact
major pipelines of the Iraq Petroleum Company and Aramco
major oil fields
areas occupied by Israel after the 1967 war

decline of British influence:
(1) evacuation of Canal Zone 1954
(2) dismissal of General Glubb 1956
(3) Iraqi revolution, assassination of Nuri es-Said 1958
(4) withdrawal from Aden, 1968

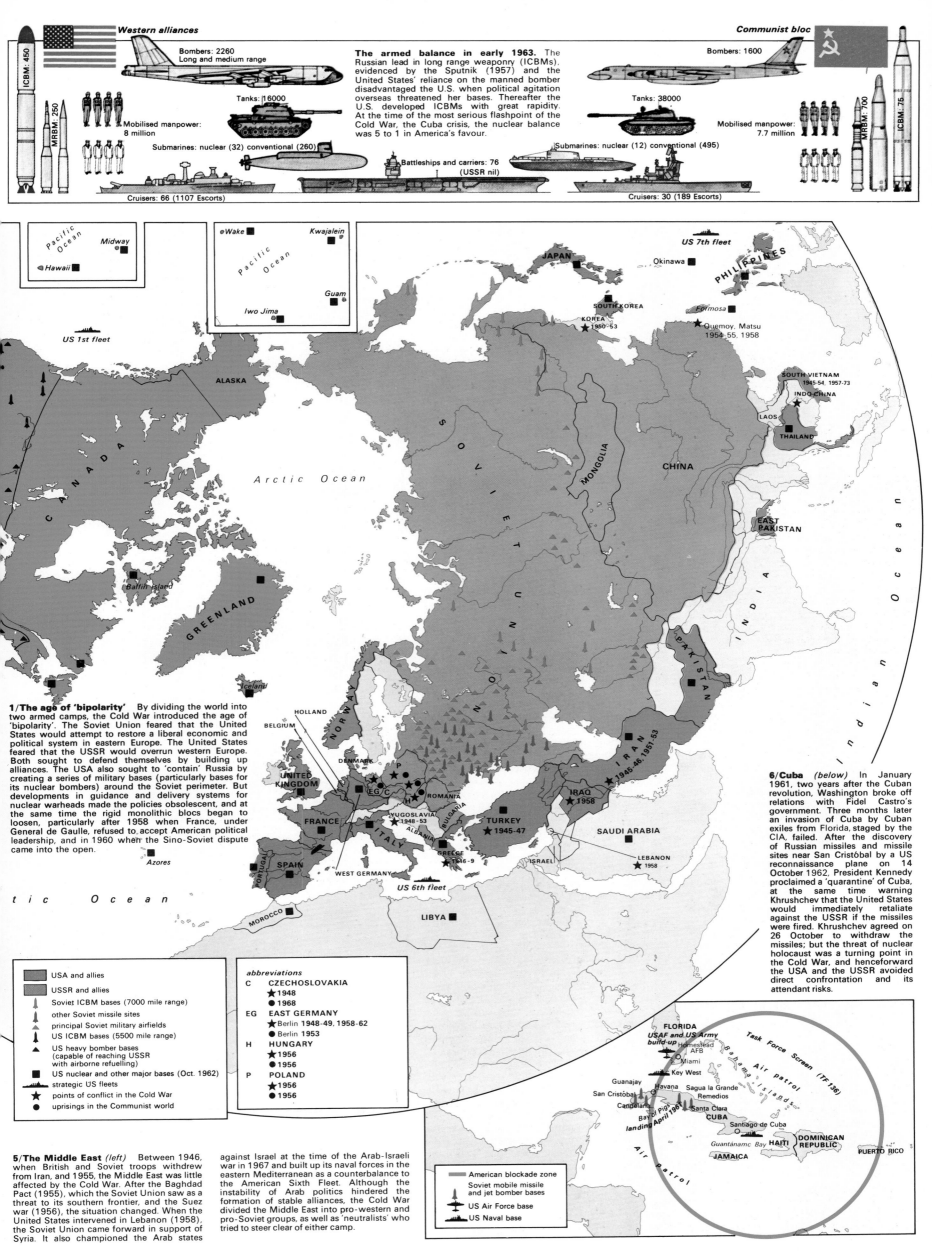

Western alliances — Bombers: 2260 Long and medium range | ICBM: 450 | MRBM: 250

Mobilised manpower: 8 million | Tanks: 16000 | Submarines: nuclear (32) conventional (260) | Battleships and carriers: 76 (USSR nil) | Cruisers: 66 (1107 Escorts)

The armed balance in early 1963. The Russian lead in long range weaponry (ICBMs), evidenced by the Sputnik (1957) and the United States' reliance on the manned bomber disadvantaged the U.S. when political agitation overseas threatened her bases. Thereafter the U.S. developed ICBMs with great rapidity. At the time of the most serious flashpoint of the Cold War, the Cuba crisis, the nuclear balance was 5 to 1 in America's favour.

Communist bloc — Bombers: 1600 | MRBM: 700 | ICBM: 75

Tanks: 38000 | Mobilised manpower: 7.7 million | Submarines: nuclear (12) conventional (495) | Cruisers: 30 (189 Escorts)

1/The age of 'bipolarity' By dividing the world into two armed camps, the Cold War introduced the age of 'bipolarity'. The Soviet Union feared that the United States would attempt to restore a liberal economic and political system in eastern Europe. The United States feared that the USSR would overrun western Europe. Both sought to defend themselves by building up alliances. The USA also sought to 'contain' Russia by creating a series of military bases (particularly bases for its nuclear bombers) around the Soviet perimeter. But developments in guidance and delivery systems for nuclear warheads made the policies obsolescent, and at the same time the rigid monolithic blocs began to loosen, particularly after 1958 when France, under General de Gaulle, refused to accept American political leadership, and in 1960 when the Sino-Soviet dispute came into the open.

6/Cuba (below) In January 1961, two years after the Cuban revolution, Washington broke off relations with Fidel Castro's government. Three months later an invasion of Cuba by Cuban exiles from Florida, staged by the CIA, failed. After the discovery of Russian missiles and missile sites near San Cristóbal by a US reconnaissance plane on 14 October 1962, President Kennedy proclaimed a 'quarantine' of Cuba, at the same time warning Khrushchev that the United States would immediately retaliate against the USSR if the missiles were fired. Khrushchev agreed on 26 October to withdraw the missiles; but the threat of nuclear holocaust was a turning point in the Cold War, and henceforward the USA and the USSR avoided direct confrontation and its attendant risks.

Legend:
- USA and allies
- USSR and allies
- Soviet ICBM bases (7000 mile range)
- other Soviet missile sites
- principal Soviet military airfields
- US ICBM bases (5500 mile range)
- US heavy bomber bases (capable of reaching USSR with airborne refuelling)
- US nuclear and other major bases (Oct. 1962)
- strategic US fleets
- ★ points of conflict in the Cold War
- ● uprisings in the Communist world

abbreviations
C CZECHOSLOVAKIA ★1948 ●1968
EG EAST GERMANY ★Berlin 1948-49, 1958-62 ●Berlin 1953
H HUNGARY ★1956 ●1956
P POLAND ★1956 ●1956

5/The Middle East (left) Between 1946, when British and Soviet troops withdrew from Iran, and 1955, the Middle East was little affected by the Cold War. After the Baghdad Pact (1955), which the Soviet Union saw as a threat to its southern frontier, and the Suez crisis (1956), the situation changed. When the United States intervened in Lebanon (1958), the Soviet Union came forward in support of Syria. It also championed the Arab states against Israel at the time of the Arab-Israeli war in 1967 and built up its naval forces in the eastern Mediterranean as a counterbalance to the American Sixth Fleet. Although the instability of Arab politics hindered the formation of stable alliances, the Cold War divided the Middle East into pro-western and pro-Soviet groups, as well as 'neutralists' who tried to steer clear of either camp.

Cuba inset legend:
- American blockade zone
- Soviet mobile missile and jet bomber bases
- US Air Force base
- US Naval base

The world in the 1980s

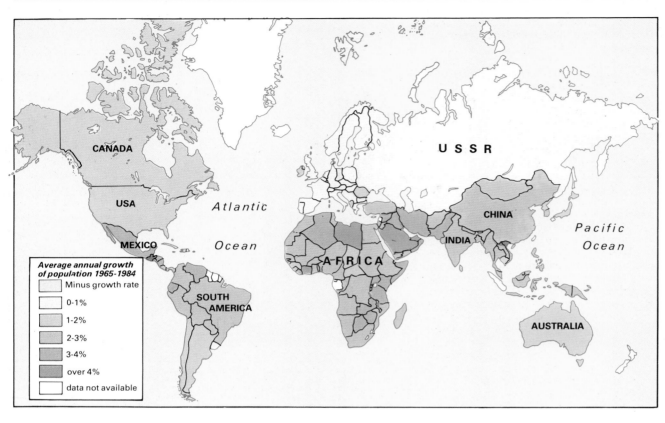

monopoly position to increase oil prices dramatically to bring about some redistribution in the divide between rich and poor nations. This produced an economic slump in 1973-75, and one even more severe in 1979-83. In turn the rising prosperity of the richer·states left large surpluses to invest in the developing areas. This led to high levels of indebtedness. In 1973 the developing world owed $130 billion, rising to $1,000 billion in 1987. These figures were in addition to the foreign aid provided directly by richer states. The effect was to produce a very unstable world financial system and by 1979 many poorer or developing states were unable to meet their debt repayments. The IMF set up a special fund to help them reschedule their payments, but of the 30 states whose debts were rescheduled, 24 were unable to cope. By 1987 Peru, Brazil, Poland, Sudan, Zaire, Bolivia and Nicaragua were in default, while others faced serious crisis. The leading banks in Europe, Japan and the United States wrote off much of the debt because the price of squeezing the money out of the debtor nations would have

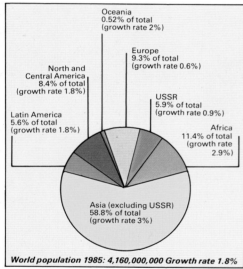

World population 1985: 4,160,000,000 Growth rate 1.8%

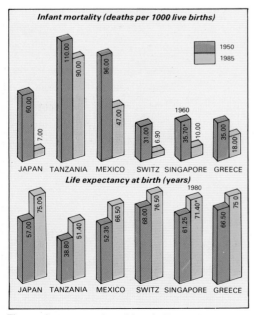

The gap between nations *(above)* The graphs illustrate the discrepancies between developed and developing countries in infant mortality and life expectancy. Although infant mortality is shockingly high in the poorest countries, there is not such a pronounced discrepancy between life expectancies in rich and poor countries. However, the population continues to grow faster in the poorer countries and therefore contributes to all their problems.

AFTER the Second World War two developments dominated global history: an unprecedented expansion of wealth and income and an enormous increase in the world's population. The course of economic growth was almost continuous; though there were short slumps, there was nothing to compare with the great depression of the 1930s. Economic growth was the primary goal of every state, and the economy was better managed and regulated as a result. Every part of the world benefitted from the expansion, but the gap betweeen the rich, industrially developed countries and the poorer, developing countries, was as great as ever. In 1981 2.2 billion people in the 'low-income' developing states had an average annual income of $275 each whereas the 700 million living in the industrial world had an average of $11,100.

The gulf between the rich and poor states can be expressed in other ways. In 1960 the exports of the developing world amounted to two-thirds of the value of exports from the developed world; in 1981 the proportion was only a quarter. The poorer states could not afford the same levels of education or welfare provision needed to make good the gap. In 1980 the number of people per doctor ranged from 520 in the United States to 58,000 in Ethiopia; literacy rates for adults by the 1980s were much lower in the developing countries than the industrialised world – 56 per cent on average, but only 30 per cent in Africa. Although the poorer economies grew throughout the period up to the 1980s, the gains were all but eroded by the increase in population. High rates of population growth created enormous problems. Health improvements kept people alive longer – life expectancy in the developing world in the late 1980s was 60 years against only 45 in 1960 – but the weak economies could not cope with the numbers. Most people in the poorer states were peasants extracting a meagre living. In the United States only 2 per cent worked in agriculture while in China the figure was 69 per cent and for most of Africa and Asia the figure rose to between 75-93 per cent. High levels of economic growth produced rich élites in the poorer states, but did not correct the imbalance of the world's wealth and prosperity.

The survival of these inequalities brought problems even for the rich parts of the world. In the 1970s the oil-producing states used their

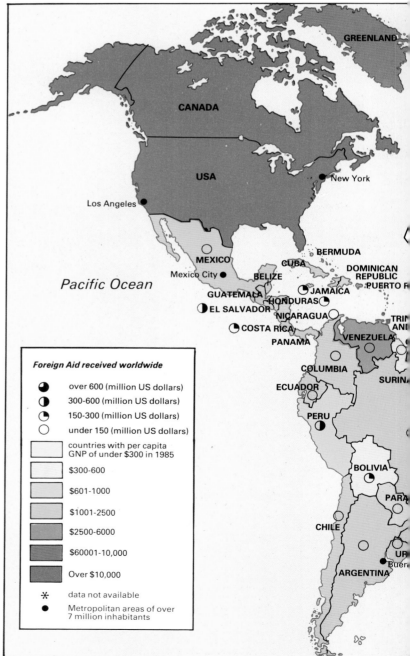

been political upheaval and the severe dislocation of the world economy.

The instability caused by problems over oil and debts brought a major business crisis in the early 1980s. The world economy in the 1980s had grown more slowly than in the previous thirty years, but was still growing at an average of 2-3 per cent a year. The developing countries suffered most, with falling commodity prices, high unemployment and austerity programmes to cope with debt. The wealthy élites, however, sent their money out of the country to avoid the economic crisis. By 1987 the 'flight capital' from the major debtor states was equivalent to almost half the total debt owed. The richer states recovered during the 1980s. Unemployment began to fall, productivity increased again with the application of new communications technology, and the rapid growth of service industries. Capitalism was 'managed' more successfully than in the 1930s, and levels of co-operation were much higher. By 1992 the countries of western Europe will be united in a single economic bloc. The major industrial states meet regularly to co-ordinate policy.

Part of the success of the economy in the 1980s may be attributed to the rise of right-wing governments committed to growth and 'enterprise', and the decline of trade union power, or left-wing politics. In the United States, Britain, West Germany and Japan the new ethos of aggressive capitalism began to erode some of the welfare gains of the years since 1945, but higher per capita income produced broad support for the new strategies. The survival of western capitalism also encouraged the eastern Communist bloc to move away from state-managed 'command' economies to more flexible, mixed economies, with market mechanisms. In China, the Soviet Union and much of eastern Europe this led to a political revolution. In the Soviet Union the new leader, Mikhail Gorbachov, trans-

3/Origins of migrant workers (right) In many poorer countries the growth in the post-war population was not matched by increasing employment opportunities. Thousands of people left their homes to find work in other, richer, countries, where they were welcomed as cheap labour until the industrial depression hit the West in the 70s. This caused high levels of unemployment and hostility towards the immigrant workers who were often accused of taking jobs away from local people.

formed Soviet politics after 1985, introducing more participation in order to encourage a more open economy, with greater individual initiative. But capitalism was embraced with most success in the Far East. Around the Pacific 'rim' Japan, South Korea, Taiwan, Singapore and Indonesia, became areas of high economic growth, less burdened by debt, and able to discipline their workforces to accept work practices and conditions that had been unacceptable in the west for many years. By the 1980s the balance of the world economy and of economic power had already begun to shift from the United States and Europe, towards eastern Asia. The old bi-polarity between an American-dominated west and a Soviet-dominated east disappeared.

The problems of the late 1980s arose from the wider implications of forty years of unparalleled industrial and population growth. Many natural resources became scarce; industry produced high levels of pollution; high population growth produced regular famine, particularly in Africa. By the 1990s, however, there were signs that the world was becoming freer, more responsible and more co-operative as dictatorships crumbled in the wake of powerful demands for democracy; apartheid was being dismantled in South Africa and the communist world was in turmoil. Nevertheless, war, poverty, famine, and oppression continued to confront the world of the 1990s.

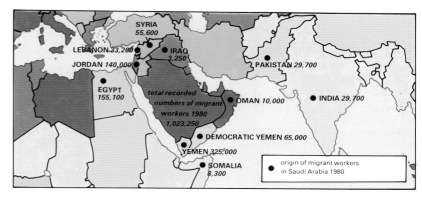

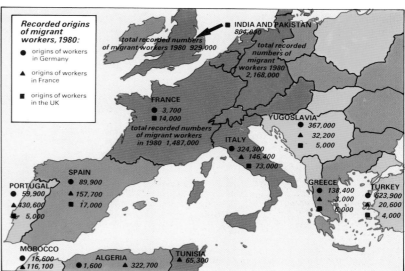

1/Rich nations and poor nations (below) The peoples of the world are here divided into categories according to Gross National Product per head and the amount of foreign aid received. Per capita GNP is a useful but inaccurate index of wealth which often hides gross inequalities between different segments of the population within a single country. Nevertheless, there is a close correlation between low per capita GNP and other indices of poverty and deprivation, such as how much foreign aid a country receives. For example, most of the countries in Africa receiving foreign aid have a GNP below $1000 which indicates poverty.

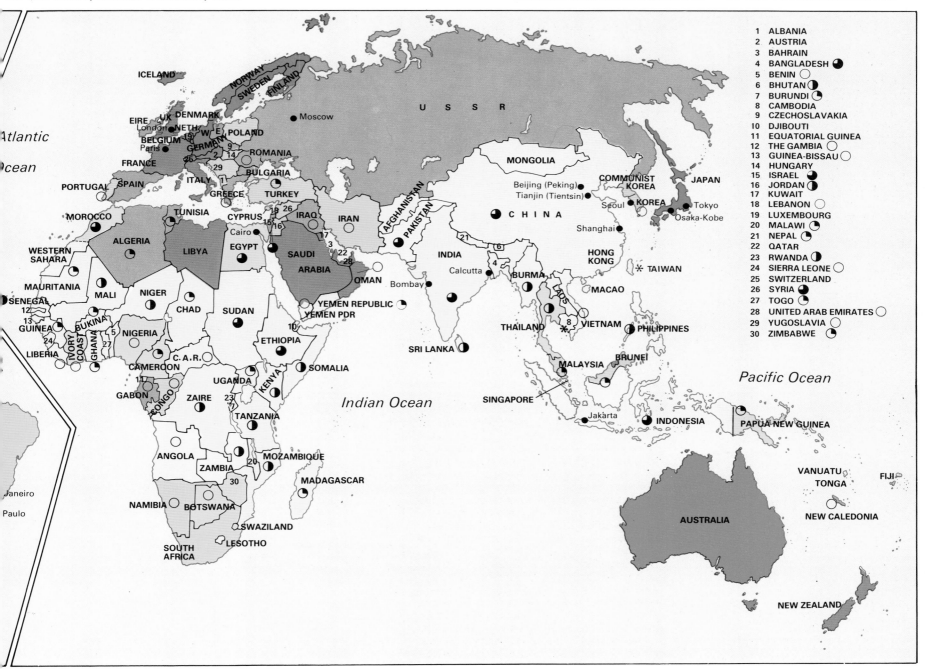

1 ALBANIA
2 AUSTRIA
3 BAHRAIN
4 BANGLADESH
5 BENIN
6 BHUTAN
7 BURUNDI
8 CAMBODIA
9 CZECHOSLAVAKIA
10 DJIBOUTI
11 EQUATORIAL GUINEA
12 THE GAMBIA
13 GUINEA-BISSAU
14 HUNGARY
15 ISRAEL
16 JORDAN
17 KUWAIT
18 LEBANON
19 LUXEMBOURG
20 MALAWI
21 NEPAL
22 QATAR
23 RWANDA
24 SIERRA LEONE
25 SWITZERLAND
26 SYRIA
27 TOGO
28 UNITED ARAB EMIRATES
29 YUGOSLAVIA
30 ZIMBABWE

Acknowledgements

Acknowledgments and Bibliography: Maps

We have pleasure in acknowledging the following:
Map 4, page 37, is based, with kind permission, on Professor P.A. Martin *American Population Explosion* Science Magazine 1973.

Map 4, page 55, is based, with permission, on a map on page 51 in W.H. McNeill, M.R. Buske, A.W. Roehm, *The World.....its History in Maps*, Chicago 1969 © Denoyer-Geppert

Map 3, page 278, is based with permission on material reproduced from *Population Change in China* by Paul White, page 3, The Geographical Magazine, London, January 1984.

Map 4, page 289, is based with permission on *The Slowing of Urbanization in the US* by Larry Long and Diana DeAre, page 35, Scientific American, July 1983.

Among the large number of works consulted by contributors, the following contain valuable maps and other data that have been particularly useful:

I. History Atlases

Atlas zur Geschichte 2 vols. Leipzig 1976
Bazilevsky, K.V., Golubtsov, A., Zinoviev, M.A. *Atlas Istorii SSR*, Moscow 1952
Beckingham, C.F. *Atlas of the Arab World and the Middle East*, London 1960
Bertin, J. (et al) *Atlas of Food Crops*, Paris 1971
Bjørklund, O., Holmboe, H., Røhr, A. *Historical Atlas of the World*, Edinburgh 1970
Cappon, L. (et al) *Atlas of Early American History*, Chicago 1976
Darby, H.C., Fullard, H. (eds.) *The New Cambridge Modern History* vol. XIV: Atlas, Cambridge 1970
Davies, C.C. *An Historical Atlas of the Indian Peninsula*, London 1959
Engel, J. (ed.) *Grosser Historischer Weltatlas* 3 vols. Munich 1953–70
Fage, J.D. *An Atlas of African History*, London 1958
Gilbert, M. *Russian History Atlas*, London 1972
Gilbert, M. *Recent History Atlas 1860–1960*, London 1966
Gilbert, M. *First World War Atlas*, London 1970
Gilbert, M. *Jewish History Atlas*, London 1969
Hazard, H.W. *Atlas of Islamic History*, Princeton 1952
Herrmann, A. *Historical and Commercial Atlas of China*, Harvard 1935
Herrmann, A. *An Historical Atlas of China*,. Edinburgh 1966
Jedin, H., Latourette, K.S., Martin, J. *Atlas zur Kirchengeschichte*, Freiburg 1970
Kinder, H., Hilgermann, W. *DTV Atlas zur Weltgeschichte* 2 vols. Stuttgart 1964 (published in English as *The Penguin Atlas of World History*, London 1974 & 1978)
Matsui and Mori *Ajiarekishi chizu*, Tokyo 1965
May, H.G. (ed.) *Oxford Bible Atlas*, Oxford 1974
McNeill, W.H. Buske, M.R., Roehm, A.W. *The World.....its History in Maps*, Chicago 1969
Nelson's Atlas of the Early Christian World, London 1959
Nelson's Atlas of the Classical World, London 1959
Nelson's Atlas of World History, London 1965
Nihon rekishi jiten Atlas vol., Tokyo 1959
Palmer, R.R. (ed.) *Atlas of World History*, Chicago 1965
Paullin, C.O. *Atlas of the Historical Geography of the United States*, Washington 1932
Ragi al Faruqi, I. (ed.) *Historical Atlas of the Religions of the World*, New York 1974
Roolvink, R. *Historical Atlas of the Muslim Peoples*, London 1957
Schwartzberg, J.E. (ed.) *A Historical Atlas of South Asia*, Chicago 1978
Shepherd, W.R. *Historical Atlas*, New York 1964
Toynbee, A.J., Myers, E.D. *A Study of History, Historical Atlas and Gazetteer*, Oxford 1959
Treharne, R.F., Fullard, H. (eds.) *Muir's Historical Atlas*, London 1966
Van der Heyden, A.M., Scullard, H.H. *Atlas of the Classical World*, London 1959
Wesley, E.B. *Our United States.....its History in Maps*, Chicago 1977
Westermann *Grosser Atlas zur Weltgeschichte*, Brunswick 1976
Whitehouse, D. & R. *Archaeological Atlas of the World*, London 1975
Wilgus, A.C. *Latin America in Maps*, New York 1943

II. General Works

Ahzweiler, H. *L'Asie Mineure et les Invasions Arabes*, Revue Historique 1962
Ajayi, J.F.A., Crowder, M. *History of West Africa* vols. 1 & 2 London 1974
Allchin, B. & R. *The Birth of Indian Civilisation*, London 1968
Australia, Commonwealth of, Department of National Development, *Atlas of Australian Resources*
Barraclough, G. *Medieval Germany*, Oxford 1938
Basham, A.L. *The Wonder that was India*, London 1967
Beresford, M. *New Towns of the Middle Ages*, London 1967
Berney, M. (ed.) *Australia*, Sydney 1965
Bloch, M. *Les Caractères Originaux de l'Histoire Rurale Française*, Oslo 1931
Boisselier, J. *La Statuaire du Champa*, Paris 1963
Braudel, F. *The Mediterranean and the Mediterranean World at the time of Philip II*, London 1972
Bury, J.B., Cook, S.A., Adcock, F.E. (eds.) *The Cambridge Ancient History*, Cambridge 1923–
Bury, J.B. Gwatkin, H.M. Whitney, J.P. (eds.) *The Cambridge Medieval History*, Cambridge 1911
Bussagli, M. *Paintings of Central Asia*, Geneva 1963
Chang, K.C. *The Archaeology of Ancient China*, New Haven & London 1968
Cheng Te-k'un *Archaeology in China*, Cambridge 1959
Churchill, Winston S. *The Second World War*, London 1948–53
Coedès, G. *Les Etats Hindouisés de l'Indochine et d'Indonésie*, Paris 1964
Cook, M.A. (ed.) *A History of the Ottoman Empire to 1730*, Cambridge 1974
Cresswell, K.A.C. *A Short Account of Early Muslim Architecture*, Oxford 1958
Crowder, M. *West Africa under Colonial Rule*, London 1968
Cumberland, K.B. *Aotearoa Maori: New Zealand about 1780*, Geographical Review no.39
Curtin, P. de A. *The Atlantic Slave Trade*, Wisconsin 1969
Dalton, B.J. *War and Politics in New Zealand 1855–1870*, Sydney 1967
Darby, H.C. (ed.) *An Historical Geography of England before AD 1800*, Cambridge 1936 & 1960
Despois, J., Raynal, R. *Géographie de l'Afrique du Nord*, Paris 1967
Dyos, H.J. Aldcroft, D.H. *British Transport*, Leicester 1969
East, W.G. *The Geography behind History*, London 1965
East, W.G. *An Historical Geography of Europe*, London 1966
Edwardes, M. *A History of India*, London 1961
Evans, B.L. *Agricultural and Pastoral Statistics of New Zealand 1861–1954*, Wellington 1956
Ferguson, J. *The Heritage of Hellenism*, London 1973
Fisher, C.A. *South-East Asia*, London 1964
Fletcher, A. *Tudor Rebellions*, London 1968
Fowler, K. *The Age of Plantagenet and Valois*, New York 1967
Fourquin G. *Histoire Economique de l'Occident Médiéval*, Paris 1969
Ganshof, F.L. *Etude sur le Développement des Villes entre Loire et Rhin au Moyen Age*, Paris–Brussels 1943
Geelan, P.J.M., Twitchett, D.C. (eds.) *The Times Atlas of China*, London 1974
Gernet, J. *Le Monde Chinois*, Paris 1969
Grousset, R. *The Empire of the Steppes: A History of Central Asia*, New Brunswick N.J. 1970
Guillermaz, J. *Histoire du Parti Communiste Chinois*, Paris 1968
Hall, D.G.E. *A History of South-East Asia*, London 1968
Harlan, J.R. *The Plants and Animals that Nourish Man*, Scientific American 1976
Harlan, J.R., Zohary, D. *The Distribution of Wild Wheats and Barleys*, Science 1966
Hatton, R.M. *Europe in the age of Louis XIV*, London 1969
Henderson, W.O. *Britain and Industrial Europe 1750–1870*, Liverpool 1954
Hopkins A.G. *Economic History of West Africa*, London 1973
Inalcik, H. *The Ottoman Empire: The Classical Age 1300–1600*, London 1973
Jeans, D.N. *An Historical Geography of New South Wales to 1901*, Sydney 1972
Kennedy, J. *A History of Malaya 1400–1959*, London 1962
Kjölstad, T., Rystad, G. *5000 år: Epoker och utvecklingslinjer*, Lund 1973
Konigsberger, H., Mosse, G.L. *Europe in the sixteenth century*, London 1968
Laird, C.E. *Language in America*, New York 1970
Langer, W.L. *An Encyclopedia of World History*, London 1972
La Roncière (et al) *L'Europe au Moyen Age*, Paris 1969
Lattimore, O. *Inner Asian Frontiers of China*, New York 1951
Lyashchenko, P.I. *History of the National Economy of Russia to the 1917 Revolution*, New York 1949
Majumdar, R.C. *The Vedic Age*, Bombay 1951
Majumdar R.C. *History and Culture of the Indian People, Age of Imperial Unity*, Bombay 1954
Macmillan's Atlas of South-East Asia, London 1964
McBurney, C.B.M. *Proceedings of the British Academy LXI* 1975
McIntyre, W.D., Gardner, W.J. *Speeches and Documents on New Zealand History*, Oxford 1970
McNeill, W.H., *A World History*, New York 1971
Meinig, D.W. *On the Margins of the Good Earth*, New York 1962, London 1963
Mellaart, J. *The Neolithic of the Near East*, London 1975
Ministry of Works *A Survey of New Zealand Population*, Wellington 1960
Miquel, A. *L'Islam et sa Civilisation*, Paris 1968
Morrell, W.P., Hall, D.O.W. *A History of New Zealand Life*, Christchurch 1957
Moss, H. St. L.B. *The Birth of the Middle Ages*, Oxford 1935
Mulvaney, D.J. *The Prehistory of Australia*, London 1975
Musset, L. *Les Invasions: Les Vagues Germaniques*, Paris 1965
Musset, L. *Les Invasions: Le Second Assaut contre l'Europe Chrétienne*, Paris 1971
The National Atlas of the United States of America, Washington DC 1970
Neatby, H. *Quebec, The Revolutionary Age 1760–1791*, London 1966
New Zealand Official Yearbook, Wellington 1893–
Ogot, B.A. (ed.) *Zamani, A Survey of East African History* , London 1974–1976
Oliver, R., Fagan, B. *Africa in the Iron Age c.500 BC–AD 1400*, Cambridge 1975
Oliver, R., Atmore, A. *Africa since 1800*, Cambridge 1972
Ostrogorsky, G. *History of the Byzantine State*, Oxford 1956
Parker, W.H. *An Historical Geography of Russia*, London 1968
Piggott, S. *Prehistoric India to 1000 BC*, London 1962
Pitcher, D.E. *An Historical Geography of the Ottoman Empire*, Leiden 1973
Roberts, J.M. *The Hutchinson History of the World*, London 1976
Sanders, W.T., Marino, J. *New World Prehistory: Archaeology of the American Indian*, Englewood Cliffs, N.J. 1970
Saum, L.O. *The Fur Trader and the Indian*, London 1965
Seltzer, L.E. (ed.) *The Columbia Lippincott Gazetteer of the World*, New York 1952
Simkin, C.F. *The Traditional Trade of Asia*, Oxford 1968
Smith, C.T. *An Historical Geography of Western Europe before 1800*, London & New York 1960
Smith, W.S. *The Art and Architecture of Ancient Egypt*, London 1965
Snow, D. *The American Indians: their Archaeology and Prehistory*, London 1976
Stavrianos, L.S. *The World to 1500*, Englewood Cliffs, N.J. 1975
Stein, Sir Aurel *Travels in Central Asia*, London 1935
Stoye, J. *The Siege of Vienna*, London 1964
Stratos, A.N. *Byzantium in the seventh century*, Athens 1965
Tarn, W.W. *Alexander the Great*, Cambridge 1948
Tate, D.J.M. *The Making of South-East Asia*, Kuala Lumpur 1971
Thapar, R. *A History of India*, London 1967
The Times Atlas of the World, Comprehensive Edition, London 1976
Toynbee, A.J. (ed.) *Cities of Destiny*, London 1967
Toynbee, A.J. *Mankind and Mother Earth*, Oxford 1976
U.S. Strategic Bombing Survey, Summary Report (Pacific War), Washington 1946
Van Alstyne, R.W. *The Rising American Empire*, Oxford 1960
Van Heekeren, H.R. *The Stone Age of Indonesia*, The Hague 1957
Wadham, S., Wilson, R.K., Wood, J. *Land Utilization in Australia*, Melbourne 1964
Watters, R.F. *Land and Society in New Zealand*, Wellington 1965
Wheatley, P. *The Golden Khersonese*, Kuala Lumpur 1961
Wheeler, M. *Early India and Pakistan to Ashoka*, London 1968
Willey, G. *An Introduction to American Archaeology* vols. 1 & 2 Englewood Cliffs, N.J. 1970
Williams, M. *The Making of the South Australian Landscape*, London 1974
Wilson, M., Thompson, L. *Oxford History of South Africa* vols. 1 & 2 Oxford 1969, 1971

Acknowledgements: Illustrations

Unless stated to the contrary all the illustrations in this book are the work of the following artists: Peter Sullivan, David Case, John Grimwade, Tom Stimpson, Chris Fen, Chee Chai, Chris Burke, Ken Tan.

The publishers would like to thank the following museums, publishers and picture agencies for permission to base illustrations upon their photographs or to reproduce them. Where there is no such acknowledgement we have been unable to trace the source, or the illustration is a composition by our illustrators and contributors.

p.32 illustration based on a cave painting at Gargas, France
p.34 from K.P. Oakley *Man the Tool-Maker*, reproduced with kind permission of the Trustees of the British Museum (Natural History), London
p.35 from Cueva de los Caballos, near Castellón, Spain
p.37 The Times Picture Library
p.40 National Archaeological Musuem, Athens
p.42 Hungarian National Museum, Budapest
p.47 University Museum, Philadelphia
p.53 a reconstruction by Seton Lloyd, *The Art of the Ancient Near East*, London 1961
p.55 Archive Photographique, Musée du Louvre, Paris
p.56 reproduced courtesy of the Trustees of the British Museum, London
p.59 The Cooper-Bridgeman Library, London (photograph)
p.63 *The Genius of China*, London 1973
p.65 National Museum of Pakistan, Karachi
p.70 Musée Guimet, Paris
p.75 National Archaeological Museum, Athens
p.81 *The Genius of China*, London 1973
p.86 Professor H.H. Scullard
p.102 from The Arch of Titus, Rome
p.106 Bibliothèque Municipale Classée de Cambrai, France
p.109 from Bernet Kempers *Ancient Indonesian Art*, Harvard University Press, 1959
p.116 Nationalmuseet, Copenhagen, Denmark
p.132 from D.G.E. Hall *A History of South-East Asia*, London 1968
p.134 Kunsthistorisches Museum, Vienna
p.136 from Abraham Cresques *Catalan Atlas* 1375 (Bibliothèque Nationale, Paris)
p.138 Turkish miniature from the *Hünername*
p.141 from a woodcut from Schedel's *World Chronicle of 1493*, provided courtesy of the Czech Embassy, London
p.142 John Freeman, London
p.144 *Arvhiv der Hansestadt*, Lübeck 1256
p.145 Fugger Museum, Babanhausen, Germany
p.146 courtesy of Dr. P. Whitehouse, British School of Archaeology, Rome
p.148 top: reproduced courtesy of the Trustees of the British Museum, London
middle: American Museum of Natural History, New York
bottom: from L.C. Wyman *Sandpaintings of the Navaho Shootingway and the Walcott Collection*, Washington 1970, courtesy of the Department of Anthropology, Smithsonian Institution, Washington DC
p.157 The Cooper-Bridgeman Library, London
p.159 Museum für Völkerkunde, Vienna
p.162 from *Istoriya SSSR*, vol. 3, Moscow 1967
p.164 from A.F. Frezier *A Voyage to the South Seas and along the Coasts of Chile and Peru*, 1717
p.166 Holle Bildarchiv, Baden-Baden, Germany
p.170 Topkapi Saray Museum, Istanbul
p.173 The Chester Beatty Library and Gallery of Oriental Art, Dublin
p.177 National Portrait Gallery, London
p.180 *Scripta Mercaturae*, Munich 1972
p.183 Radio Times Hulton Picture Library, London
p.185 Larousse, Paris
p.190 Metropolitan Museum of Art, New York
p.201 left: Radio Times Hulton Picture Library, London
right: by courtesy, Science Musuem, London
p.208 from *The Illustrated London News*, 1892
p.211 by courtesy, Science Museum, London
p.212 from *The Illustrated London News*, 1867
p.216 Statue, Hamburg, Germany
p.221 from a contemporary American painting
p.235 from Hutchinson's *Story of the British Nation*, London 1924/5?
p.242 provided by the Historiographical Institute, Tokyo
p.246 from *The New York Journal*, 1898 (Radio Times Hulton Picture Library)
p.248 Church Missionary Society, London
p.252 Imperial War Museum, London (photograph)
p.258 Popperfoto, London
p.269 top: Musée de l'Affiche, Paris
bottom: Museo Civico Luigi Bailo, Salce Collection, Treviso, Italy
p.272 based on a photograph by Yevgeni Khaldei
p.288 photograph by NASA/Space Frontiers

For the revised edition: Maps

We have pleasure in acknowledging the following:

Map 3, page 280, is based with permission on material reproduced from *A Historical Atlas of South Asia*, by Joseph E. Schwartzberg (ed.), Chicago 1978.

Illustrations

pp.30-31 Susan Griggs Agency
p.48 Rock Art Archives of the Frobenius Institute, Frankfurt/Main
pp.50-51 Robert Harding Picture Library
pp.68-69 The Photographers' Library
pp.96-97 Robert Harding Picture Library
pp.152-153 Robert Harding Picture Library
pp.206-207 Robert Harding Picture Library
pp.254-255 Susan Griggs Agency
p.271 Imperial War Museum, London

Aachen–Alborán Island

Index

1 HISTORICAL PLACE NAMES

Geographical names vary with time and with language, and there is some difficulty in treating them consistently in an historical atlas which covers the whole world from the beginning of human prehistory, especially for individual maps within whose time span the same place has been known by many different names. We have aimed at the simplest possible approach to the names on the maps, using the index to weld together the variations.

On the maps forms of names will be found in the following hierarchy of preference:-

a English conventional names or spellings, in the widest sense, for all principal places and features, e.g., Moscow, Vienna, Munich, Danube (including those that today might be considered obsolete when these are appropriate to the context, e.g., Leghorn).

b Names that are contemporary in terms of the maps concerned. There are here three broad categories:-

i names in the ancient world, where the forms used are classical, e.g., Latin or latinized Greek, but extending also to Persian, Sanskrit, etc.

ii names in the post-mediaeval modern world, which are given in the form (though not necessarily the spelling) current at the time of the map (e.g., St. Petersburg before 1914, not Leningrad); whose language reflects the sovereignty then existing, e.g., Usküb (Turkish) rather than Skoplje (Serbian) or Skopje (Macedonian) in maps showing Ottoman rule.

iii names in the present-day world, where the spelling generally follows that of *The Times Atlas of the World,* though in the interests of simplicity there has been a general omission of diacritics in spellings derived by transliteration from non-roman scripts, e.g., Sana rather than Şan'ā'.

On the spelling of Chinese names, readers will be increasingly aware of the Pinyin romanizations that have come into use over the last ten years (e.g. Beijing, Qin dynasty) but the atlas continues to spell Chinese names in the conventional forms and Wade-Giles romanizations that are still more generally found in historical contexts (e.g. Peking, Ch'in dynasty). However, all Chinese names that occur as main entries in the index give the Pinyin spelling in brackets, and there are cross-references from all Pinyin forms to the traditional spellings used in the atlas.

Alternative names and spellings have occasionally been shown in brackets on the maps to aid in identification.

2 THE INDEX

The index does not include every name shown on the maps. In general only those names are indexed which are of places, features, regions or countries where "something happens", i.e., which carry a date or symbol or colour explained in the key, or which are mentioned in the text.

Where a place is referred to by two or more different names in the course of the atlas, there will be a corresponding number of main entries in the index. The variant names in each case are given in brackets at the beginning of the entry, their different forms and origins being distinguished by such words as *now, later, formerly* and others included in the list of abbreviations *(right).*

"Istanbul (*form.* Constantinople, *anc.* Byzantium)" means that the page references to that city on maps dealing with periods when it was known as Istanbul follow that entry, but the page references pertaining to it when it had other names will be found under those other names.

Places are located generally by reference to the country in which they lie (exceptionally by reference to island groups or sea areas), this being narrowed down where necessary by location as E(ast), N(orth), C(entral), etc. The reference will normally be to the modern state in which the place now falls unless (a) there is a conventional or historical name which conveniently avoids the inevitably anachronistic ring of some modern names, e.g., Anatolia rather than Turkey, Mesopotamia rather than Iraq, or (b) the modern state is little known or not delineated on the map concerned, e.g., many places on the Africa plates can only be located as W.,E., Africa, etc.

Though page references are generally kept in numerical order, since this corresponds for the most part with chronological order, they have been rearranged occasionally where the chronological sequence would be obviously wrong, or in the interests of grouping appropriate references under a single sub-heading.

All variant names and spellings are cross-referenced in the form "Bourgogne (Burgundy)", except those which would immediately precede or follow the main entries to which they refer. The bracketed form has been chosen so that such entries may also serve as quick visual indications of equivalence. Thus Bourgogne (Burgundy) means not only "see under Burgundy" but also that Burgundy is another name for Bourgogne.

Reference is generally to page number/map number (e.g., 114/2) unless the subject is dealt with over the plate as a whole, when the reference occurs as 114-5 (i.e., pages 114 and 115). All entries with two or more references have been given sub-headings where possible, e.g., Civil War 268/3. Battles are indicated by the symbol ✕.

3 ABBREVIATIONS

a/c also called
AD Autonomous District
Alb. Albanian
anc. ancient
AO Autonomous Okrug
Ar. Arabic
a/s also spelled
ASSR Autonomous Soviet Socialist Republic
Bibl. Biblical
Bulg. Bulgarian
C Century (when preceded by 17,18 etc.)
C Central
Cat. Catalan
Chin. Chinese
Cz. Czech
Dan. Danish
Dut. Dutch
E. East(ern)
Eng. English
Est. Estonian
f/c formerly called
Finn. Finnish
form. former(ly)
Fr. French
f/s formerly spelled
Ger. German
Gr. Greek
Heb. Hebrew
Hung. Hungarian
Indon. Indonesian
Ir. Irish
Is. Island
It. Italian
Jap. Japanese
Kor. Korean
Lat. Latin
Latv. Latvian
Lith. Lithuanian
Maced. Macedonian
Mal. Malay
med. mediaeval
mod. modern
Mong. Mongolian
N. North(ern)
n/c now called
Nor. Norwegian
n/s now spelled
NT New Testament
obs. obsolete
O.E. Old English
OT Old Testament
Pers. Persian
Pol. Polish
Port. Portuguese
Rom. Romanian
Russ. Russian
S. South(ern)
s/c sometimes called
Skr. Sanskrit
Som. Somali
Sp. Spanish
S. Cr. Serbo-Croat
SSR Soviet Socialist Republic
Sw. Swedish
Turk. Turkish
Ukr. Ukrainian
US(A) United States (of America)
var. variant
W. West(ern)
Wel. Welsh
W/G Wade-Giles
WW1 The First World War
WW2 The Second World War

Aachen (*Fr.* Aix-la-Chapelle *anc.* Aquisgranum) W Germany Frankish royal residence 107/3; imperial city 190/1,2: industrial development 212/1; WW1 253/3
Aargau Switzerland Reformation 183/1
Aarhus (*n/s* Aårhus) Denmark bishopric 101/2; archbishopric 116/2
Abadan SW Iran oil terminal 285/3
Abaj Takalik Mexico Maya site 46/2
Abasgia region of Caucasus 113/1
Abarshahr (*mod.* Nishapur *Pers.* Neyshabur) NE Persia town of Sasanian Empire 79/3
Abbasid Caliphate 108-9, 134-5
Abbasids Muslim dynasty 135/1
Abbeville N France 17C revolt 185/1
Abdera NE Greece Greek colony 75/1
Abellinum (*mod.* Avellino) C Italy 87/1
Abemama Gilbert Is WW2 270-271
Abenaki NE Canada Indian tribe 149/1
Abhisara NW India kingdom 77/1, 82/3
Abilene C USA cow town 220/1
Abipon Argentina Indian tribe 149/1
Abkhaz ASSR Caucasus 290/2
Abodrites Germany tribe 98/3, 118/3, 140/2
Aborigines N Australia modern hunters and gatherers 35/2
Aboukir Bay Egypt ✕ 194/2
Abqaiq (*Ar.* Buqayq) E Arabia oilfield 285/3
Abr Nahr Syria Achaemenid province 79/1
Abrotonum (Sabrata)
Abu Aweigila Sinai captured by Israel 284/2
Abu Dhabi United Arab Emirates 284/1, 285/3
Abu Rudeis Sinai Israeli capture 285/2
Abu Safa Saudi Arabia oilfield 285/3
Abu Simbel Upper Egypt temple 59/3
Abusina S Germany Roman fort 88/2
Abydus W Turkey Persian War 74/3; Dorian colony 75/1; Byzantine Empire 113/1
Abydus Upper Egypt 59/1
Abyssinia (*now* Ethiopia) 218/1, 245/1
Acadia (Nova Scotia)
Acalan Mexico Maya state 148/2
Acancéh E Mexico Maya site 46/2
Acapulco Mexico early trade 145/4, 158/1, 199/1
Acarnania country of ancient Greece 76/4
Accho (Acre)
Accra Ghana early European settlement 166/1; British settlement 239/1
Aceh (Achin)
Achaea (*a/s* Achaia) Greek parent state 74/3, 75/1; League 76/4; Roman province 89/1; Venetian principality 141/1
Achaemenid Empire Persia 79/1
Achaia (Achaea)
Acheh (Achin)
Achin (*mod.* Aceh *var.* Acheh, Atjeh) N Sumatra early trade 161/1
Açores (Azores)
Acquebouille C France mediaeval *villeneuve* 121/7
Acragas (*Lat.* Agrigentum *mod.* Agrigento) Sicily Dorian colony 75/1
'Acre (*OT* Accho *NT* Ptolemais *Fr.* St. Jean-d'Acre *Heb.* Akko) Palestine Muslim reconquest 134/3; early trade 146/1
Actium W Greece ✕ 86/3; 89/1
Acton SE USA ✕ 221/4
Adab Mesopotamia 54/1
Adal E Africa early state 137/1, 167/1, 239/1
Adamawa W Africa 239/1
Adamgarh C India site 64/2
Adan (Aden)
Adana W Turkey Jewish community 103/1; Byzantine Empire 113/1; revolt against Ottoman rule 170/1; Ottoman Empire 229/1
Ad Dawhah (Doha)
Ad Decimum Tunisia ✕ 99/1
Addis Ababa Ethiopia Italian penetration 241/1
Adelaide S Australia founded 237/5; industry 218/1
Aden (*Chin.* Adan *W/G* A-tan) S Arabia Muslim trade 135/1; early trade with China 146/1; Portuguese in 147/2; early town 159/1; Ottoman Empire 171/1, 229/1; taken by British 239/1; British base 277/2; 284/1
Aden Protectorate (*successively renamed* Protectorate of South Arabia, Federation of South Arabia, People's Republic of South Yemen, People's Democratic Republic of Yemen) British protectorate 245/1, 260/1, 277/1
Adhur Gushnasp NW Persia town of Sasanian Empire 79/3
Adiabene region of Assyria 103/1
Adichanallur S India site 64/2
Admiralty Islands S Pacific Japanese attack 271/1
Adowa N Ethiopia ✕ 241/1
Adramyttium (*mod.* Edremit) W Turkey 113/5
Adrianople (*anc.* Adrianopolis *mod.* Edirne) W Turkey ✕ 99/1, 108/1; Byzantine Empire 113/1, 135/2; Ottoman centre 170/1; 16C urban development 180/1; 18C urban development 181/2; occupied by Greece 265/1
Adrianopolis (*mod.* Edirne *Eng.* Adrianople) W Turkey archbishopric 93/1
Adriatic early trade routes 52/1
Adulis Red Sea port 71/1, 82/4, 137/1
Adyge AD Caucasus 290/2
Adzhar ASSR Caucasus 290/2
Aeclanum C Italy early town 87/1
Aegean early movements of people 67/1
Aegospotamus (*Turk.* Karaova Suyu) NW Turkey ✕ 74/4
Aegyptus (*mod.* Egypt) Roman province 89/1, 91/2
Aelana (*a/c* Aela *mod.* Aqaba) N Arabia port 71/1, 82/4; Roman Empire 91/1
Aelia Capitolina (*mod.* Jerusalem) Judaea Roman city 91/1
Aenus (*mod.* Enez) W Turkey Aeolian colony 75/1
Aesernia (*mod.* Isernia) C Italy Latin colony 87/1
Aesis (*mod. Iesi*) N Italy 87/1
Aetolia ancient country of C Greece 74/3
Aetolian League military confederation of ancient Greece 76/4
Afars and Issas, French Territory of (*form.* French Somaliland *now* Rep. of Djibouti) NE Africa 295/1
Afghanistan under Abbasid sovereignty 135/1; under Mughal rule 173/1; independent sultanate 229/1; Anglo-Afghan war 261/1; territorial claim against Pakistan 281/3; establishment of republic 284/1; economy 218/1, 295/1; Soviet occupation 281/3, 284/1
Africa early man 33/1,4; agricultural origins 39/1; early cultures 44-5; expansion of Christianity 100/1; Portuguese exploration 147/2; early trade 154; early European voyages of discovery 157/1; slave trade 166/2; early empires 167/1; 18C trade 199/1; European exploration 238/2; before partition 239/1; colonial strategy 240/3; partition 240-41; colonial empires 245/1; anti-colonial resistance 249/2; decolonisation 276/2; modern political developments 282-3
Africa (*mod.* Tunisia and Libya) Roman province 86/3, 91/2; conversion to Christianity 72/1; Byzantine province 112/1
Africa Nova (*mod.* Tunisia) Roman province 86/3
Aga Buryat-Mongol AD E USSR 290/2
Agadès (*var.* Agadez) W Africa 63/2, 136/2, 137/1, 154/2, 167/1, 241/1
Agathe (*mod.* Agde) SW France Ionian colony 75/1
Agathopolis Bulgaria Byzantine Empire 112/4
Agau tribe of NE Africa 137/1
Agde (Agathe)
Aggersborg N Denmark circular fortification 116/2
Aghlabids Muslim dynasty of N Africa 108/1, 135/1
Agincourt (*mod.* Azincourt) N France ✕ 142/4
Aglar (Aquileia)
Agra N India region 173/1; centre of Mutiny 234/1
Agram (Zagreb)
Agrigentum (*Gr.* Acragas *mod.* Agrigento) Sicily Roman Empire 86/2,3, 89/1, 91/1
Agropoli S Italy Saracen occupation 111/1
Aguascalientes state of C Mexico 227/1
Aguntum (*mod.* San Candido) N Italy 92/1
Ahar NW India site 64/2,3
Ahicchatra N India 64/2,3, 83/1, 131/3
Ahmadabad (Ahmedabad)
Ahmadi Kuwait oil terminal 285/3
Ahmadnagar W India sultanate 130/4; state 173/1
Ahmedabad (*n/s* Ahmadabad) W India industry 218/1, 235/3; Hindu- Muslim clashes 281/3
Ahvenanmaa (Åland islands)
Ahwaz (*a/s* Ahvaz) W Persia 82/3; oilfield 285/3
Aichi prefecture of C Japan 218/2; industry 242/1
Aigues-Mortes S France Mediterranean trade 144/1
Aigun (*n/c* Heihe *a/c* Aigui) NE China treaty port 232/2
Ain Jalut Palestine ✕ 128/1, 135/1
Ain Salah NW Africa Saharan trade 136/2, 146/1, 167/1
Ainu tribe of N Japan 35/2
Air early state of W Africa 137/1, 167/1
Aire NW France fort 193/1
Aisne *river* NE France WW1 252-3
Aix (*or* Aix-en-Provence *anc.* Aquae Sextiae) S France archbishopric 106/3; St Bartholomew Massacre 182/3; parlement 193/1
Aix-la-Chapelle (*Ger.* Aachen) W Germany Carolingian capital 109/6
Aizu N Japan 175/4
Ajanta C India Buddhist site 73/1
Ajayameru (*mod.* Ajmer) C India 83/1
Ajman United Arab Emirates 284/1
Ajmer (*form.* Ajayameru) N India Mughal province 173/1; British rule 234/1; industry 235/3
Ajnadain Palestine ✕ 105/1
Akamagaseki (*n/c* Shimonoseki) W Japan 174/4
Akan W Africa early state 137/1
Akaroa S island, New Zealand French colony 236/1
Akashi C Japan 175/4
Akhisar (Thyatira)
Akhtiar (Sevastopol)
Akita town and prefecture of N Japan 218/2; industry 243/1
Akizuki W Japan 174/4
Akjoujt W Africa stone age site 45/1
Akkadians people of Mesopotamia 54/3
Akkerman (*from 1946* Belgorod-Dnestrovskiy *anc.* Tyras *Rom.* Cetatea Alba) S Russia Ottoman conquest 139/1; Ottoman control 170/1
'Akko (Acre)
Akkoyunlu Muslim dynasty of Anatolia 135/1
Ak-Mechet (Kzyl-Orda, Simferopol)
Akmolinsk (Tselinograd)
A-k'o-su (Aksu)
Akrotiri S Aegean Cretan colony 67/1
Aksai-Chin district of N India territorial dispute with China 281/3
Akşehir (Philomelium)
Aksu (*a/s* Aqsu *W/G* A-k'o-su) Sinkiang trade 71/2; Muslim insurrection against China 175/1
Aktyubinsk Kazakhstan 230/2, 291/1
Alabama state of SE USA Civil War 233/1; 19C politics 225/2,3; Depression 267/1; income and population 289/2
Alacaluf Indian tribe of S Chile 149/1
Alagoas state of E Brazil 227/1
Alalakh (*a/c* Atchana) Syria 54/1, 57/1, 67/1
Alalia (*or* Aleria) Corsica Ionian colony 75/1
Alamannia (Alemannia)
Alamgirpur India stone age and Harappan site 64/2, 65/1
Åland Islands (*Finn.* Ahvenanmaa) SW Finland acquired by Russia 163/1; neutralised 265/1
Alans (*Lat.* Alani) E and W Europe, Africa tribal movements 89/1; 98-99
Alarcos S Spain ✕ 124/3
Alaşehir (Philadelphia)
Alashiya (*mod.* Cyprus) early trade 54/1; under Hittite Empire 57/1; 59/2
Alaska state of USA purchase from Russia 230/2, 244/1; border dispute with Canada 246/3; income and population 289/2
Alatri (Aletrium)
Alawites people of NW Syria, uprising 261/2
Alba Fucens C Italy 87/1
Alba Iulia (*anc.* Apulum *Hung.* Gyulafehérvár *Ger.* Karlsburg) Romania Mithraic site 72/1
Albania Slav settlement 112/4; Black Death 143/1; Ottoman control 187/1; principality 215/2; Ottoman province 229/1; WW1 252-3; Muslim insurrection 267/2; inter-war alliances 264/2, 268/2; annexed by Italy 269/4; WW2 269/5, 272/1, 273/3; withdraws from Warsaw Pact 275/3; Cold War 274/1, 293/1; economy 295/1; 275/4
Albania ancient country of Caucasus vassal of Parthian Empire 79/3; 86/3, 89/1, 113/1
Albany (*form.* Fort Orange) NE USA surrenders to Dutch 161/2
Albany W Australia founded 237/5
Albazinsk SE Siberia founded 162/3
Alberta province of Canada economic development 219/3
Albertville (*now* Kalémié) E Belgian Congo 282/2
Alborán Island Morocco Spanish occupation 251/2

Ålborg–Artajona

Ålborg N Denmark flint mine 42/2
Albret region of SW France 151/4
Alcalá S Portugal site 42/2
Alcazarquivir (Al-Kasr-al-Kabir)
Aldeigjuborg (Staraya Ladoga)
Aleksandropol (Leninakan)
Alemanni tribe of C Europe 99/1
Alemannia region of C Europe 160/1, 107/3
Alençon N France fief annexed by France 151/4; provincial capital 193/1
Alep (Aleppo)
Aleppo (*anc.* Beroea *a/c* Yamkhad *Fr.* Alep *Ar.* Halab) Syria 54/1; bishopric 101/1; Byzantine Empire 113/1,5; early trade 135/1; conquest by Ottomans 139/1; Ottoman centre 170/1; economy 285/1
Aleria (Alalia)
Alesia (*mod.* Alise-Sainte-Reine) C France 86/3
Alessandria N Italy Lombard League 119/2; mediaeval city 123/4; Signorial domain 124/2
Aletum NW France monastery 93/3
Aletrium (*mod.* Alatri) C Italy 87/1
Aleut tribe of Alaska 35/2
Aleutian Islands W Alaska 247/1; WW2 270-271
Alexander's Empire 76-77; 82/3
Alexandreschata (Alexandria Eschata)
Alexandretta (*mod.* Iskenderun) E Turkey Achaemenid Empire 79/1; ceded to Turkey 265/1
Alexandria (*Ar.* Al Iskandariyah) Egypt spread of Christianity 72/1; Alexander's route 76/1; Persian Empire 79/1; Roman Empire 86/3, 89/1, 91/1; Christian centre 92-3; patriarchate 101/2; trade 71/1, 82/4, 135/1, 144/1, 146/1, 154/2; early Jewish community 103/1; Arab conquest 105/1; conquered by Ottomans 139/1; WW2 273/3
Alexandria NW India Alexander's route 77/1
Alexandria (*mod.* Gulashkird) S Persia Alexander's route 77/1
Alexandria (*mod.* Charikar) Afghanistan 82/3
Alexandria (*mod.* Ghazni) Alexander's Route 77/1; 82/3
Alexandria (*later* Merv *since 1937* Mary) C Asia 77/1
Alexandria ad Caucasum Afghanistan Alexander's route 77/1
Alexandria Arachoton (*mod* Qandahar *Eng.* Kandahar) Afghanistan Alexander's route 77/1; Achaemenid Empire 79/1; 82/3
Alexandria Areion (*mod.* Herat) Afghanistan Alexander's route 77/1; Achaemenid Empire 79/1; 82/3
Alexandria Eschata (*a/c* Alexandreschata) C Asia Alexander's route 77/1; Achaemenid Empire 79/1; 82/3
Alexandria Opiana NW India Alexander's route 77/1
Alexandria Prophthasia (*mod.* Farah) Afghanistan Alexander's route 77/1; Achaemenid Empire 79/1
Alexandria Troas W Anatolia Roman Empire 89/1
Al Fas (Fez)
Alger (Algiers)
Algeria under the Almohads 134/1; vassalised by Turks 186/1; Spanish conquests 186/2; economy under French rule 218/1; Ottoman province 228/1; French invasion 239/1; French colonisation 240-41, 244/1; immigration from France 209/2; overseas province of France 260/1; under Vichy control 269/5; civil war 282/3; independence 276/2; political development 283/1; economy 294-295
Algiers (*Fr.* Alger *Sp.* Argel *Ar.* Al Jaza'ir *anc.* Icosium) N Algeria Saharan trade 136/2; Mediterranean trade 144/1; Corsair city 167/1; Ottoman rule 170/1, 228/1; Spanish occupation 186/2; Allied landing WW2 273/3; 283/1
Algonkin (*a/s* Algonquin) Indian tride of C Canada 35/2, 149/1
Al Hadhr (Hatra)
Al Hira Mesopotamia town of Parthian Empire 78/3
Al Hoceima (Alhucemas)
Alhucemas (*n/s* Al Hoceima) N Morocco Spanish occupation 251/2
Al Hudaydah (Hodeida)
Alice Springs C Australia 237/5
Aligarh N India centre of Mutiny 234/1
Ali Kosh Mesopotamia early village 40/1
Ali Murad NW India Harappan site 65/1
Alise-Sainte-Reine (Alesia)
Al Iskandariyah (Alexandria)
Al Jaza'ir (Algiers)
Al-Kasr-al-Kabir (*Sp.* Alcazarquivir *a/c* Battle of the Three Kings) Morocco × 167/1 (inset), 187/2
Al Khalil (Hebron)
Allahabad NE India Mughal province 173/1; industry 218/1; Hindu-Muslim clashes 281/3
Allahdino NW India pre-Harappan site 65/1
Allenstein (*Pol.* Olsztyn) W Poland acquired by Germany after plebiscite 265/1
Allifae C Italy early town 87/1
Alma-Ata (*until 1921* Vernyy) C Asia urban growth 290/3; industry 291/1
Al Madinah (Medina)
Al Mahdiya Tunisia Mediterranean trade 134/1
Al Makkah (Mecca)
Almalyk Mongolia bishopric 101/1
Almanaza Spain × 192/3
Al Mawsil (Mosul)
Almería S Spain Mediterranean trade 120/2, 134/1, 144/1
Almizaraque S Spain site 42/2
Almoravids Muslim dynasty of Morocco 135/1; North African empire 137/1
Almohads Muslim dynasty and empire of North Africa 134-5; 137/1
Alpes Cottiae Roman province, France/Italy, 89/1
Alpes Maritimae Roman province, France/Italy 89/1
Alpes Penninae Roman province, France/Italy 89/1
Alpirsbach SW Germany monastery 121/3
Al Qadisiya Mesopotamia × 78/3, 105/1
Al Qahirah (Cairo)
Al Quds (Jerusalem)
Al Raydaniyya N Egypt × 139/1
Alsace (*anc.* Alsatia *Ger.* Elsass) Magyar invasions 111/1; in German Empire 123/5; acquired by Habsburgs 150/2; Burgundian possession 151/3; acquired by French 192-3; customs union 217/1; WW1 252/2
Alsace-Lorraine (*Ger.* Elsass-Lothringen) region of E France annexed by German Empire 216/3; ceded to France 265/1
Alsatia (Alsace)
Alsium (*mod.* Palo) C Italy Roman colony 87/1
Altendorf W Germany Megalithic site 42/2
Altmark region of E Germany 119/1
Altona N Germany customs union 217/1
Altun Ha E Mexico Maya site 46/2
Alwa early Christian kingdom of the Sudan 137/1
Amalfi S Italy Byzantine port 120/2
Amara NW India pre-Harappan site 65/1
Amarapura C Burma early trade centre 177/1
Amasela N Turkey early archbishopric 93/1
Amasia (*mod.* Amasya) E Anatolia Roman Empire 89/1; Byzantine Empire 112/3
Amastris (*earlier* Sesamus) N Anatolia Byzantine Empire 112/3
Amasya (*anc.* Amasia) C Turkey Ottoman town 170/1
Amathus Cyprus ancient Greek colony 75/1
Ambianum (Amiens)
Amboina C Indonesia massacre of English 176/2; trade centre 177/1; WW2 271/2
Ambracia NW Greece 76/4
Ambriz Angola Portuguese settlement 239/1
Amchitka Aleutian Is, Alaska US air base 271/2
Amecameca Mexico on Cortés' route 159/2
America, Central (*a/c* Mesoamerica) early peoples 36-7; agricultural origins 38/1; early civilisations 46/2, 47/1; Aztec Empire 148/2; Indian tribes 149/1; early voyages of discovery 156/2; colonial expansion 165/1; 18C trade 199/1; exports and foreign investment 226/3; population 226/4; recent development 286-7
America, North early man 33/1, 36-7, 37/4; agricultural origins 38/1; early cultures 46/3, 47/1; Indian tribes 149/1; early voyages of discovery 156/1; colonial expansion, 164-5; European colonial rivalry 194-5; 18C trade 199/1; immigration from Europe 209/2; industrialisation 219/1; range of buffalo 221/5; Peyote drug cult 221/6; Ghost dance 221/6. See also Canada, United States
America, South early peoples 36-7; agricultural origins 38/1; early civilisations 47/1,4,5; Indian tribes 149/1; Inca Empire 149/3; early voyages of discovery 156/1; colonial expansion 165/1,2; 18C trade 199/1; revolts against Spain 202/1; industrialisation 219/1; Independence 226-7; immigration from Europe 209/2; economic development 286/2; modern politics 287/1; population 287/3
American Colonies trade 199/1
American Samoa (*f/c* Eastern Samoa) S Pacific 247/1, 277/2 (inset)
Amida (*mod.* Diyarbakır) E Anatolia 78/3; 89/1; archbishopric and monastery 93/1,3; trade 135/1
Amiens (*anc.* Samarobriva *later* Ambianum) N France bishopric 117/1; Burgundian possession 151/3; 17C revolt 185/1; provincial capital 193/1; French Revolution 203/2; industrial development 210/1; WW1 252-3
Amisus (*mod.* Samsun) N Anatolia Ionian colony 75/1; Roman Empire 86/3; early archbishopric 93/1; Byzantine Empire 112/3
Amiternum C Italy 87/1
Amman (*Bibl.* Rabbath Ammon *anc.* Philadelphia) Jordan 229/1, 285/1
Ammon, Sanctuary of Egypt Alexander's route 76/1
Amnisos Crete Mycenaean settlement 67/1,2
Amöneburg W Germany monastery 100/3
Amorites people of Arabia, migrations 54/3; kingdom 55/2
Amorium C Anatolia Byzantine Empire, 112-3
Amoy (*n/s* Xiamen *W/G* Hsia-men) S China early trade 147/1, 161/1; industry 218/1; treaty port 232/2; Anglo-French attacks 233/1; Japanese influence 243/2; occupied by Japanese 263/3, 268/3, 271/2
Amphipolis N Greece × 74/4, 78/3; Roman Empire 91/1; early church 93/1
Amri NW India Harappan site 65/1
Amritsar N India town of Punjab 235/3, 280/1, 281/3; political disturbances under British rule 261/1; police action against Sikh insurgents 281/3
Amselfeld (Kosovo)
Amsterdam Netherlands trading port 180/3; 16C urban development 180/1; 18C financial centre 181/2; imperial trade 198-9; industrial development 210/1, 212/1
Amud Palestine site of early man 32/2
Amur River (*Chin.* Heilong Jiang *W/G* Hei-lung Chiang) Russia/China border 162/3; Russian conflict with Japan 268/2; border conflict with China 279/1
Anadyrsk E Siberia founded 162/3
Anagnia (*mod.* Anagni) C Italy early town 87/1
Anantapur S India ceded to Britain 172/3
Anatolia early settlement 41/1; early trade routes 54/1; ethnic movements 54/3; Muslim conquest 135/2; Ottoman conquest 139/1; Black Death 143/1 See also Asia Minor
Anatolic Theme Anatolia district of Byzantine Empire 112/3
Anazarbus SW Anatolia early archbishopric 93/1; early Jewish community 103/1; Byzantine Empire 112/3
Ancona N Italy Roman Empire 87/1, 91/1
Ancyra (*mod.* Ankara *obs. Eng.* Angora) W Anatolia Alexander's route 76/1; Roman Empire 86/3, 89/1, 91/1; early archbishopric 93/1; Byzantine Empire 112-3
Åndalsnes C Norway WW2 269/5
Andalusia (*Sp.* Andalucía) region of S Spain reconquest by Castile 124/3
Andaman and Nicobar Islands Indian territory of Bay of Bengal 235/3, 245/1
Andegavum (*earlier* Juliomagus *mod.* Angers) W France 92/1
Anderab Afghanistan Alexander's route 82/3
Andernach (*anc.* Antunnacum) W Germany × 118/3
Andhra region of E India 65/1
Andhra Pradesh state of S India 281/3
Anding (An-ting)
Andover S England Industrial Revolution 201/1
Anegray E France early monastery 100/3
Anga region of NE India 65/1, 83/1,2
Angarsk S Siberia urban growth 290/3; industry 291/1
Angers (*anc.* Juliomagus *med.* Andegavum) W France 17C revolt 185/1; French Revolution 203/2
Anghelu Ruju Sardinia burial site 43/1
Angkor Cambodia Buddhist site 73/1
Angkor Borei S Cambodia Hindu-Buddhist remains 133/2
Angkor Wat Cambodia temple complex 133/2
Angles tribe of NW Europe, migrations 94/1, 98/1
Anglo-Egyptian Sudan Ottoman territory under British control 245/1; condominium 240/2, 260/1, 276/1
Angola SW Africa Portuguese discovery 147/2; early Portuguese trade 159/1; source of slaves 166/2; Portuguese colonisation 218/1, 240-41, 245/1; anti-Portuguese risings 249/2; independence 276/2; political development 283/1; economy 295/1
Angora (Ankara)
Angostura Venezuela 226/2
Angoulême (*anc.* Iculisma) C France provincial capital 193/1
Angoumois C France region annexed to France 151/4
Anguilla island of West Indies settled by English 160/3; independence 277/2 (inset)
Anhalt C Germany principality and duchy 119/1, 191/1; Reformation 182/2; 216/3
An-hsi (*n/s* Anxi) N China trading port 71/1
Anhui (Anhwei)
Anhwei (*n/s* Anhui) province of E China under the Ming 169/1; Manchu expansion 175/1; T'ai-p'ing control 233/1
Ani Persia Byzantine Empire 113/1
Anjira NW India pre-Harappan site 65/1
Anjou region of NW France British possession 125/1; annexed by France 150/1, 151/4; province of France 193/1
Ankara (*anc.* Ancyra *obs. Eng.* Angora) W Turkey × 128/4, 139/1; revolt against Ottoman rule 170/1; Ottoman Empire 229/3
Ankole Uganda kingdom 167/1, 239/1
Annaba (Bône, Hippo Regius)
Annam N Indo-China under T'ang control 127/2; under Mongol control 129/1; expansion and early trade 177/1; anti-French resistance in 19C 248/1; French protectorate 261/1
Annapolis (*until 1694* Anne Arundel Town *earlier* Providence) NE USA 161/2
Annesoi NW Anatolia early monastery 93/3
An-p'ing (*n/s* Anping) NE China Han prefecture 81/2
Ansbach S Germany Reformation 183/1; margraviate 191/1
An-shan (*n/s* Anshan) Manchuria Russo-Japanese War 242/3; industry 263/3, 278/3
Anta da Marquesa Portugal Megalithic site 42/2
Anta dos Gorgiones Portugal Megalithic site 42/2
Antakya (*anc.* Antioch *Lat.* Antiochia) E Turkey Ottman centre 170/1
Antalya (Attalia)
Antananarivo (Tananarive)
Antibes (Antipolis)
Antietam (*a/c* Sharpsburg) NE USA × 223/1
Antigua island of West Indies settlement by British 160/3; colony 227/1; independence 277/2 (inset)
An-ting (*n/s* Anding) NW China Han commanderie 81/2
Antioch (*Lat.* Antiochia *mod.* Antakya) E Anatolia Mediterranean trade 71/1, 82/4, 135/1; spread of Christianity 72/1; Persian Empire 79/1; Roman Empire 86/3; patriarchate 93/1; archbishopric 101/2; Jewish community 103/1; Byzantine rule 112-3, 121/2; principality 134/3
Antioch C Anatolia early archbishopric 93/1
Antiochia (*anc.* Antioch *mod.* Antakya) E Anatolia fortified Roman town 88/3, 91/1
Antiochia Margiana Persia trade 82/4
Antipolis (*mod.* Antibes) SE France Ionian colony 75/1
Antium *mod.* Anzio) C Italy Roman colony 87/1
Antofagasta region of N Chile dispute with Peru and Bolivia 227/5
Antrim N Ireland massacre of Catholics 184/2
An-tung (*n/c* Dandong *W/G* Tan-tung) Manchuria treaty port 232/2; Russo-Japanese war 242/3; industry 263/3
Antunnacum (Andernach)
Antwerp (*Fr.* Anvers *Dut.* Antwerpen) Belgium Hansa city 144/1, 145/3; trade 154/2; 16C and 18C financial centre 180/1, 181/2; town of Spanish Netherlands 185/1; industrial development 212/1; WW1 252-3; WW2 273/3
Anuradhapura Ceylon Buddhist site 73/1
Anvers (Antwerp)
Anxi (An-hsi)
Anxur (*later* Tarracina *mod.* Terracina) C Italy 86/2
An-yang (*n/s* Anyang) N China early urban settlement 53/1; Shang city 62/2
Anyer Lor W Java Iron Age site 132/1
Anzio (*anc.* Antium) C Italy WW2 273/3
Aocang (Ao-ts'ang)
Aomori N Japan town and prefecture 243/1; industry 243/1
Aornos (*mod.* Tash-Kurghan) Afghanistan Alexander's route 77/1
Ao-ts'ang (*n/s* Aocang) C China Han prefecture 81/2
Aozou Strip N Chad occupied by Libya 283/1
Apache Indian tribe of SW USA, 35/2, 149/1
Apache Pass SW USA on trail west 220/1
Apamea Syria Peace of 77/3; Roman Empire 88/3, 91/1; early archbishopric 93/1
Apesokari Crete site 67/2
Aphrodisias SW France Ionian colony 75/1
Apodhoulou Crete site 67/2
Apollonia NE Greece Dorian colony 75/1; Roman Empire 86/3, 89/1, 91/1; early church 93/1
Apollonia (*mod.* Sozopol) Bulgaria Ionian colony 75/1
Apollonia Libya Greek colony 75/1; Roman Empire 91/1; Byzantine Empire 113/1
Apollinopolis (Edfu)
Apologos Persian Gulf port 71/1, 78/2, 79/3
Appenwihr W Germany Hallstatt site 84/1
Appenzell Switzerland Reformation 183/1
Appian Way (Via Appia)
Appomattox SE USA Confederates surrender 223/1
Apremont E France Hallstatt site 84/1
Apulia region of SE Italy unification with Naples 124/2
Apulum (*mod.* Alba Iulia) Romania Roman Empire 89/1, 91/1
Aqaba (*anc.* Aela *or* Aelana) Jordan WW1 253/4
Aqsu (Aksu)
Aquae Sextiae (*mod.* Aix) France Roman Empire 86/3
Aquileia (*med.* Aglar) N Italy Mediterranean trade 71/1; Latin colony 87/1; Roman Empire 86/3, 89/1, 91/1; early archbishopric 92/1, 107/3; monastery 93/3; invaded by Goths 99/1; Byzantine Empire 112/1
Aquincum (*mod.* Budapest) Hungary Roman Empire 89/1, 91/1
Aquino (Aquinum)
Aquinum (*mod.* Aquino) C Italy early town 87/1
Aquisgranum (Aachen)
Aquitaine (*anc.* Aquitania *mod.* Guyenne) region of SW France English possession 125/1; Black Death 143/1
Aquitania (*mod.* Aquitaine *later* Guyenne) Roman province of Gaul 89/1; invasion by Vandals 98/1; Visigothic territory conquered by Franks 106/1,3; 111/1
Arabaya Arabia satrapy of Achaemenid Empire 79/1
Arabia early trade 71/1, 146/1; spread of Judiasm 72/1; early Christian activity 100/1; centre of Islam 105/1; under Abbasid Caliphate 108/1; Egyptian expedition 239/1; WW1 253/4
Arabia Eudaemon S Arabia port 82/4
Arabian Gulf (Persian Gulf)
Arabia Petraea Roman province of N Arabia, 89/1
Arabissos E Anatolia Byzantine Empire 113/1
Arabs (of Mansura) NW India 131/1
Arabs (of Multan) NW India 131/1
Arachosia (*a/c* Harauvatish) Afghanistan ancient province of Persian and Alexander's Empires, 77/1, 82/3, 83/1
Aradus (*Bibl.* Arvad *later* Arwad *Fr.* Rouad) Syria Phoenician city 75/1; Alexander's route 76/1; early Jewish community 103/1
Arago S France site of early man 32/2
Aragon (*Sp.* Aragón) region of E Spain at time of Reconquista 124/3; rural uprisings 143/1; acquired by Habsburgs 150/1,2; kingdom 186/2
Arakan district of SW Burma Islamic state 133/2,3; British control 177/1; annexed by British 234/2; 281/3
Aralsk C Asia 291/1
Aramaeans people of Syria, 56/3, 60-1
Arapaho C USA Plains Indian tribe 149/1
Arash N Caucasus conquered by Ottomans 171/1
Araucanian S America Andean Indian Tribe 149/1
Arausio (*mod.* Orange) S France 92/1
Arawak S America Indian tribe 149/1
Arbailu (*a/c* Arbela *mod.* Arbil) Mesopotamia 54/1
Arbela (*a/c* Arbailu *mod.* Arbil) Mesopotamia Alexander's route 76/1; town of Parthian Empire 78/3; under Alexander 82/3; early archbishopric 93/1, 101/1
Arcadiopolis Bulgaria Byzantine Empire 113/1
Archangel (*Russ.* Arkhangelsk) N Russia founded 157/1, 163/1; Revolution and Allied occupation 259/1; WW2 273/3; growth 290/3; industry 291/1
Arcole N Italy × 205/1
Arcot S India ceded to British 172/3; × 194/2
Arcy-sur-Cure C France site of early man 32/2
Ardabil Azerbaijan early trade 135/1
Ardea N Italy ancient town 87/1
Ardennes *forest* Belgium/France WW1 252-3; WW2 × 273/3
Ardmore Ireland early bishopric 92/1
Arelate (*mod.* Arles) S France Roman Empire 89/1, 90/1; archbishopric 92/1
Arène Candide SE France site 43/1
Arequipa Peru early Spanish city 158/1
Arezzo (*anc.* Arretium) C Italy mediaeval city 124/2
Argel (Algiers)
Argentina independence from Spain 226-7, 244/1; exports and foreign investment 226/3; population 226/4; industrialisation and economy 219/1; 286-7, 294-295
Argentoratum (*mod.* Strasbourg) E France Mithraic site 72/1
Arghun early kingdom of NW India 130/4
Arginusae islands of the Aegean × 74/4
Argissa Greece site 43/1
Argonne NE France WW1 253/3 (inset)
Argos S Greece 74/3
Arguin island off NW Africa Portuguese settlement 147/2, 166/1
Århus (*a/s* Aarhus) C Denmark early bishopric 101/2, 116/2
Aria (*a/c* Haraiva) ancient region of Afghanistan 77/1, 82/3
Arica Peru trading post 158/1
Arickara E USA × 221/4
Ariha (Jericho)
Arikamadur S India site 64/3
Ariminum (*mod.* Rimini) N Italy Latin colony 87/1; archbishopric 92/1
Arizona state of USA Depression 267/1; income and population 289/2
Arjunayanas tribe of N India 82/5
Arkansas state of C USA 19C politics 225/2,3; Depression 267/1; income and population 289/2
Arkhanes Crete settlement and palace 67/1,2
Arkhangelsk (Archangel)
Arlberg Austria tunnel 257/2
Arles (*anc.* Arelate *or* Arelas) S France early archbishopric 106/3; mediaeval kingdom 119/1; mediaeval trade 120/1
Armagh N Ireland archbishopric 92/1, 117/1; monastery 100/3
Armagnac region of SW France under English rule 125/1; annexed to France 151/4
Armenia (*anc.* Urartu) country of Caucasus spread of Christianity 72/1; Alexander's Empire 76/1, 82/3; part of Kushan Empire 78/3; Roman province 89/1, 86/3, 91/2; Muslim conquest 105/1; Ottoman Empire 229/1; Independence after WW1 265/1; Soviet Socialist Republic 290/2
Armenia, Lesser region of Asia Minor 134/3
Armeniac Theme Anatolia division of Byzantine Empire 112/3
Armenians emigration from Turkey 265/3; in USSR 290/4
Armenoi Crete site 67/2
Armorica (*mod.* Brittany *and* Normandy) region of NW France, settlement by Britons 98/1
Arnhem Land N Australia Pleistocene site 48/2
Arpachiyah N Mesopotamia early settlement 41/1
Arpi C Italy early town 87/1
Arpino (Arpinum)
Arpinum (*mod.* Arpino) C Italy early town 87/1
Arrapkha Mesopotamia trading town 54/1
Arras (*anc.* Nemetocenna) N France early bishopric 117/1; fort 193/1; French Revolution 203/2; WW1 252-3
Arretium (*mod.* Arezzo) C Italy Etruscan city 75/1, 86/2; Roman Empire 91/1
Arsamosata E Anatolia city of Kushan Empire 78/3
Arsinoe (*older* Crocodilopolis) Egypt trade 82/4; Roman Empire 89/1; early Jewish community 103/1
Arsinoe Libya ancient town 89/1
Artacoana Afghanistan Alexander's route 77/1
Artajona N Spain Megalithic site 42/2

Ártánd–Bear Paw Mountains

Ártánd Hungary Thracian/Scythian site 85/1
Artashat Caucasus patriarchate 93/1
Artaxata Armenia Kushan Empire 78/3; Roman Empire 89/1
Artemision (Cape Artemisium)
Artois region of NE France Burgundian possession 151/3,4; province of France 193/1; WW1 252-3
Aruba island of Dutch West Indies 227/1, 244/1, 277/2 (inset)
Arunachal Pradesh (*form.* North East Frontier Agency) NE India
frontier dispute with China 279/1, 281/3
Arvad (Arwad)
Arvernis C France monastery 93/3
Arwad (*anc.* Aradus *Bibl.* Arvad *Fr.* Rouad) Syria Assyrian Empire 57/2; Crusader states 134/3
Asaak Persia town of Parthian Empire 79/3
Asab Abu Dhabi oilfield 285/4
Asahikawa N Japan 243/1
Asante W Africa early state 166/1, 239/1
Ascalon (*mod.* Ashqelon) S Palestine Egyptian Empire 58/2; Philistine city 75/1; early church 93/1; Venetian naval victory 121/2
Ascension Island S Atlantic British colony 244/1, 276/1,2
Ascoli Piceno (Asculum)
Ascoli Satriano (Ausculum)
Asculum (*a/c* Asculum Picenum *mod.* Ascoli Piceno) N Italy 87/1
Ashdod (*Lat.* Azotus) Palestine Philistine city 75/1
Ash Hollow C USA × 221/4
Ashkhabad (*from 1919-27* Poltoratsk) SW Central Asia industry 291/1
Ashqelon (Ascalon)
Ash Sham (Damascus)
Ash Shariqah (Sharjah)
Ashtishat Caucasus monastery 93/3
Ashur (*mod.* Sharqat) Mesopotamia early urban centre 52/1; early trade 54/1; Assyrian Empire 56-7
Asia early man 33/1,4, 34-5, 37/1; agricultural origins 39/1; early trade routes 70-1, 146-7; tribal movements 94-5; expansion of Christianity 101/1; early empires 108-9; Chinese expansion 80/3, 127/2, 175/1; Mongol expansion 128-9; religious distribution 133/3; early voyages of discovery 157/1; Russian expansion 162/3; 18C trade 199/1; industrialisation 218/1; colonial empires 245/1; anti-colonial resistance 248/1
Asia (*Byzantine name* Asiana) Roman province of Anatolia 86/3, 89/1
Asiago N Italy WW1 253/3
Asia Minor spread of civilisation 52/1; conversion to Christianity 72/1, 101/2; Ottoman control 170/1 See also Anatolia
Asiana (Asia)
Asir SW Arabia Ottoman Empire 229/1
Asisium (*mod.* Assisi) N Italy 87/1
Asmaka ancient kingdom of S India 83/2
Asoka's Empire India 82-3
Aspanvar Mesopotamia town of Sasanian Empire 79/3
Aspendus SW Anatolia Dorian colony 75/1
Aspern/Essling Austria × 205/1
Aspromonte S Italy × 217/2
Assam state of NE India Mongol control 129/1; conquered by Burmese 177/1; British control 232/2; 234/2, 235/3, 280/2, 281/3,4
Assos (*Lat.* Assus) W Anatolia Aeolian colony 75/1; early church 93/1
Assyria empire 56-7; Roman province 89/1
Assyrians people of Middle East 60-61; risings in N Iraq 261/2
Astacus (*mod.* Izmit) NW Anatolia Dorian colony 75/1
Astarac SW France independent fief 151/4
Asti N Italy Lombard League 119/1
Astorga (Asturica Augusta)
Astoria NW USA fur station 220/1
Astrabad Ardashir Mesopotamia town of Sasanian Empire 79/3
Astrakhan S Russia occupied by Mongols 128/4; economy 162/2, 231/1; Tartar khanate 163/1; urban growth 231/1; Bolshevik seizure 259/1; WW2 273/3
Asturias region of N Spain kingdom 106/3, 108/1; part of Castile 124/3; political unrest 264/2
Asturica Augusta (*mod.* Astorga) N Spain Roman Empire 88/1; bishopric 92/1
Asunción Paraguay early Spanish settlement 158/1; 227/1
Asuristan Mesopotamia province of Achaemenid Empire 79/3
Asyut (*anc.* Lycopolis) S Egypt trade 135/1; 284/1
Atacama (*Sp.* Atacameño) S America Andean Indian tribe 47/4, 149/1
Atacama Desert Chile/Peru War of Pacific 227/5
Atacameño (Atacama)
A-tan (*n/s* Adan *Eng.* Aden) S Arabia early trade with China 146/1
Atapuerca N Spain site of early man 32/2
Atchana (Alakakh)
Athabaskan Indian tribe of Canada 35/2
Athenae (*Eng.* Athens *mod. Gr.* Athinai) Greece Roman Empire 86/3, 89/1, 91/1
Athenopolis SE France Ionian colony 75/1
Athens (*Lat.* Athenae *mod. Gr.* Athinai) Greece Mycenaean palace 67/1; Greek parent state 75/1; cultural centre 74/2; Persian wars 74/3; war with Sparta 74/4; 76/1,4; bishopric 93/1; invaded by Goths 99/1; early Jewish community 103/1; Byzantine Empire 112-3; WW1 253/3; WW2 269/5, 273/3
Athinai (Athens)
Athribis N Egypt early Jewish community 103/1
Athura Mesopotamia satrapy of Achaemenid Empire 79/1
Atjeh (*n/s* Aceh *var.* Acheh *a/s* Achin) N Sumatra Islamic state 133/2,3; early trade 176/2
Altanta SE USA × 223/1; strike 267/1; industry 289/1
Atlantic Ocean Viking voyages 111/4; U-Boat warfare WW2 273/2
Atropatene (Azerbaijan)
Attalia (*mod.* Antalya) S Anatolia early church 93/1; Byzantine Empire 112-3
Attica ancient state of SE Greece 74/3, 76/4, 91/2
Attigny NE France Frankish royal residence 106/3
Attirampakkan and Gudiyam Cave S India Stone Age site 64/2
Attleborough E England rebellion 185/1
Attu Island Aleutians, W Alaska WW2 270-271
Auch (*anc.* Elimberrum *later* Augusta Auscorum) SE France *parlement 193/1*
Auckland N Island, New Zealand province and second capital 236/1
Audenarde (Oudenaarde)
Auerstädt E Germany 205/1
Aufidena C Italy early town 87/1
Augila (*n/a* Awjilah) Libya early trade 137/1
Augsburg (*anc.* Augusta Vindelicorum) S Germany town of Swabia 118/1; mediaeval trade centre 145/3; 16C financial centre 180/1; imperial city 191/1
Augusta W Australia early settlement 237/5
Augusta Auscorum (Auch)
Augusta Rauricorum (*mod.* Augst) Switzerland Roman Empire 90/1
Augusta Taurinorum (*mod.* Turin) N Italy early bishopric 92/1
Augusta Treverorum (*mod.* Trier *Eng. Treves*) W Germany Mithraic site 72/1; Roman Empire 89/1, 90/1; archbishopric 92/1; early Jewish community 103/1
Augusta Vindelicorum (*mod.* Augsburg) S Germany Roman Empire 89/1, 91/1
Augustodunum (*mod.* Autun) C France Roman Empire 89/1, 90/1; early bishopric 92/1
Augustów NE Poland WW1 253/3
Auliye-Ata (Dzhambul)
Aulon (*later* Avlona *mod.* Vlorë) Albania Dorian colony 75/1
Auranitis region of Judaea 102/2
Aurelian Way (Via Aurelia)
Aurunci early tribe of C Italy, 86/2
Auschwitz (*correctly* Auschwitz - Birkenau *Pol.* Oświęcim) concentration camp 272/1
Ausculum (*a/c* Ausculum Apulum *mod.* Ascoli Satriano) C Italy early town 87/1
Austerlitz (*mod.* Slavkov) Czechoslovakia × 205/1
Australia (*originally called* New Holland) before the Europeans 48/1,2; early voyages of discovery and exploration 157/3, 237/2,3; early trade 237/4; settlement and development 237/5; emergence of Commonwealth 245/1; dominion status 277/1; economy and industrialisation 218/1, 266/3, 278/2, 295/1; WW2 270-271
Austrasia the eastern Frankish Empire 107/1
Austria (*Ger.* Österreich) German settlement 119/1; Black Death 143/1; acquired by Habsburgs 141/1, 150/1,2; attacked by Ottomans 170/1; early industry 190/2; archduchy 191/1; Habsburg conquests 196/1, 197/3; opposition to Napoleon 204-5; Alpine tunnels and railways 257/2; inter-war alliances 264/2, 268/1; socio-political change 267/2; annexed by Germany 269/4, 272/1; Allied occupation zones 274/1; EFTA 275/3; economy , 295/1
Austro-Hungarian Empire agriculture and peasant emancipation 178/1; military Frontier with Ottoman Empire 197/3; population growth 208/3,4; industrial revolution 210/1, 213/1; customs frontier abolished 211/2; ethnic composition 214/1; in Crimean War 230/4; growth in armaments 250; European alliances 250-51; overseas trade 256-7; WW1 252-3; dismantled 265/1
Autesiodorum (*mod.* Auxerre) C France monastery 93/3, 106/3
Autun (Augustodunum)
Auvergne region of C France English possession 125/1; annexed to France 150/1, 151/4; French province 193/1
Auvernier W Switzerland early settlement 43/1
Auxerre (*anc.* Autesiodorum) C France mediaeval town 120/1, 121/4
Auximum N Italy Roman colony 87/1
Ava C Burma political centre 133/2,3; old capital 177/1
Avanti region of C India 83/1,2
Avaricum (*mod.* Bourges) C France Roman Empire 86/3
Avaris (*a/c* Tanis) Lower Egypt Hyksos capital 58/1
Avars (*Chin.* Juan-juan) ancient people of Asia and Europe 94/1, 98-9; kingdom destroyed 107/3
Avellino (Abellinum)
Avenio (Avignon)
Avennes N France flint mine 42/2
Avesnes N France fort 193/1
Avignon (*anc.* Avenio) S France in Great Schism 143/1 (inset); Papal enclave 193/1; annexed by France 203/3
Ávila C Spain expulsion of Jews 102/3
Avlona (*Gr.* Aulon *mod.* Vlorë *It.* Valona) Albania Byzantine Empire 112-3; Ottoman conquest 139/1
Avranches NW France 17C revolt 185/1
Awdaghost W Africa trans-Saharan trade 136/1,2, 167/1
Awjilah (Augila)
Axel S Netherlands town of Dutch Republic 185/1
Axim Ghana early Dutch settlement 166/1 (inset)
Axum ancient kingdom of NE Africa, 45/1, 71/1, 105/1, 137/1
Ayacucho Peru × 226/2
Aydhab Sudan early trade 135/1
Aydin W Anatolia emirate 138/2, 139/1
Ayia Irini W Aegean ancient site 67/1
Ayia Pelagia Crete site 67/2
Ayia Triadha Crete Mycenean village and palace 67/1,2
Aylesbury S England Industrial Revolution 201/1
Aymará Andean Indian tribe of S America, 149/1
Ayodhya (*earlier* Saketa) NC India site 64/3; town of Kosala 83/1; Hindu-Muslim clashes 281/3
Ayutthaya (*a/s* Ayuthia *properly* Phra Nakhon Si Ayutthaya) S Thailand early political centre 133/2,3; early trade 177/1
Ayyubids Muslim dynasty, Egypt 135/1; Arabia 137/1
Azad Kashmir district of Pakistan 280/1
Azak (*mod.* Azov) S Russia Ottoman conquest 139/1
Azerbaijan (*anc.* Atropatene) country of the Caucasus province of Achaemenid Empire 79/3; Muslim conquest 105/1; under Abbasid sovereignty 135/1; Ottoman conquest 171/1; acquired by Russia 163/1, 229/1; independence after WW1 265/1; Soviet Socialist Republic 290/2
Azerbaijanis 290/4
Azincourt (Agincourt)
Azores (*Port.* Açores) islands of N Atlantic Portuguese discovery 147/2; trade 158/1; Portuguese colony 244/1
Azotus (*mod.* Ashdod) Palestine bishopric 93/1; in Judaea 102/2
Azov (*Turk.* Azak) S Russia Ottoman town 170/1
Aztalan C USA Hopewell site 46/3
Aztec Empire Mexico growth 148/2; early economy 155/1; conquest by Spain 159/2
Ba (Pa)
Baalbek (Heliopolis)
Babirush Mesopotamia satrapy of Achaemenid Empire 79/1
Babylon Mesopotamia early urban settlement 52/1; centre of Amorite kingdom 55/2; town of Parthian Empire 71/1; Achaemenid Empire 79/1; Alexander's route 77/1, 82/3; Jewish community 103/1
Babylonia ancient country of Mesopotamia fall of 56-7; under Alexander 77/1, 82/3
Baçaim (Bassein)
Bactra (*a/c* Zariaspa *mod.* Balkh) Afghanistan silk route 70/2; Alexander's route 77/1, 82/3,4
Bactria (*a/c* Bactriana *Pers.* Bakhtrish *Chin.* Ta-hsia) ancient country of Afghanistan 71/71, 77/1, 82/3
Badajoz SW Spain × 204/1
Badakhshan district of Bactria in N Afghanistan early trade 55/1; under Uzbek khans 171/1
Bad Axe N USA × 221/4
Bad Cannstatt W Germany late Hallstatt site 85/1
Baddegama Ceylon early trade 147/1
Baden S Germany margraviate 191/1,4; state 216/3; German customs union 217/1; 275/2
Baden-Württemberg region of SW Germany 275/2
Badli-ki-Serai N India centre of Mutiny 234/1
Badr W Arabia × 105/1
Baecula SW Spain × 86/3
Baetica S Spain Roman province 88/1
Baffin Island N Canada discovery 156/1
Baghdad Mesopotamia early archbishopric 101/1; Abbasid capital 109/4; Mongol conquest 128/4; early trade 135/1, 146/1, 154/2; under Ottoman rule 171/1, 229/1; WW1 253/4; anti-British uprising 260/1; oil pipeline 285/3
Bagirmi NC Africa early state 137/1
Bagneux N France Megalithic site 42/2
Bagrationovsk (Eylau)
Bahadarabad NW India site 64/2
Bahal C India site 64/3
Bahamas islands of N Caribbean discovery 156/1; British colony 160/3, 165/1, 199/1, 227/1, 224/1; independence 277/2 (inset)
Bahawalpur native state of NW India under British rule 234/1; joins Pakistan at Partition 280/1
Bahçesaray (Bakhchesaray)
Bahia E Brazil Portuguese control 158/1, 165/1; port 199/1; province 227/1
Bahrain (*f/s* Bahrein *Ar.* Al Bahrayn) island of Persian Gulf Sasanian Empire 79/3; Ottoman siege 171/1; independent sheikhdom 229/1; British control 260/1; independence 277/2; 285/3
Bahr al Ghazal district of C Sudan 239/1
Baile Atha Cliath (Dublin)
Bailén S Spain × 204/1
Baiovarii tribe of S Germany 99/1
Bairat (*a/c* Bhabra) N India site 64/2, 82/3
Bakhchesaray (*Turk.* Bahçesaray) Crimea Ottoman Empire 139/1
Bakhtrish (Bactria) Afghanistan Achaemenid province 79/1
Baku Azerbaijan early trade 135/1; conquered by Ottomans 171/1; Congress of Peoples of the East 258/3; British occupation 259/1; urban growth 231/1, 290/3; Russian Revolution 259/1; WW2 273/3; industry 213/1, 231/1, 291/1
Bakusu tribe of C Belgian Congo 282/2
Balagansk SC Siberia founded 162/3
Balaklava S Russia Crimean War 230/4
Bala-Kot NW India Harappan site 65/1
Balambangan district of Java Dutch control 176/3
Balanovo C Russia early settlement 52/1
Balboa Panama 246/2
Bâle (Basle)
Baleares Insulae (*mod.* Baleares *Eng.* Balearic Islands) W Mediterranean Roman province 86/3; Byzantine Empire 112/1
Balearic Islands W Mediterranean attacked by Saracens 111/1; conquest by Pisa 120/2; reconquered by Aragon 124/3
Balikpapan E Borneo recaptured from Japanese 271/2
Balkans rise of nationalism 215/2; alliances 250-51
Balkh (*anc.* Bactra *a/c* Zariaspa) Afghanistan Sasanian Empire 79/3; early bishopric 101/1; Muslim conquest 105/1; Empire of Ghazni 130/2; early trade 135/1
Balkhash C Asia 291/1
Ballarat SE Australia goldfield 237/5
Ballinamuck Ireland × 194/3
Ballynagilly Ireland site 43/1
Baltic Viking trade 110/3; Swedish settlement 111/1; 188-9
Baltic States (Estonia, Latvia, Lithuania)
Baltimore E USA industry 289/1
Balts Indo-European tribe 61/1
Baluba tribe of C and S Belgian Congo, 282/2
Baluchistan region of NW India tribal agency 235/3; joins Pakistan after Partition 280/1, 281/3
Balunda tribe of S Belgian Congo 282/2
Bamako W Africa reached by Mungo Park 238/2; occupied by French 241/1
Bamangwato tribe of S Africa 238/3
Bambala tribe of N Belgian Congo 282/2
Bambara tribe of W Africa 239/1
Bamberg S Germany bishopric 101/2, 117/1, 191/1; mediaeval trade 120/1
Bamiyan region of NW India 131/3
Bamongo tribe of W Belgian Congo 282/2
Banat region of Hungary/Romania/Yugoslavia conquered by Habsburgs 196/1, 197/3; WW1 253/3
Banbury C England Industrial Revolution 201/1
Ban Chiang N Siam early site 132/1
Bancorna Wales early bishopric 92/1
Banda Islands East Indies early trade 147/1
Bandar Abbas (*form.* Gombroon) SW Persia early trade 161/1; Ottoman siege 171/1
Bandjarmasin (*n/s* Banjarmasin) S Borneo Islamic town 133/3; early trading centre 177/1; WW2 271/2
Bangala tribe of N Belgian Congo 282/2
Bangalore S India industry 218/1
Bangarh E India site 64/3
Banghazi (Benghazi)
Bangka island E Sumarta Dutch settlement 177/1
Bangkok (*Thai.* Krung Thep) S Thailand early trade centre 177/1; captured by Japanese 270/2
Bangladesh (*form.* East Pakistan *or* East Bengal) part of Pakistan 280/2; independence 277/2; 281/3; economy 295/1
Bangor N Ireland monastery 100/3
Bangor Wales monastery 93/3, 100/3; bishopric 117/1
Banjarmasin (Bandjarmasin)
Banjul (Bathurst)
Ban Kao SW Thailand early site 132/1
Bannockburn C Scotland × 125/1, 142/2
Bannu (*form.* Edwardesabad) NW Pakistan industry 218/1
Bañolas NE Spain site of early man 32/2
Banpo (Pan-p'o)
Bantam (*form.* Banten) Java Islamic town 133/3; early trade 145/4, 147/1, 161/1, 177/1; sultanate under Dutch control 176/3
Banten (Bantam)
Banyu (Pan-yü)
Banzart (Bizerta)
Bao'an (Pao-an)
Baoji (Pao-chi)
Baotou (Pao-t'ou)
Bapaume NW France fort 193/1
Bapende tribe of W Belgian Congo, 282/2
Bar region of NE France/W Germany Burgundian possession 151/3; independent fief 151/4; duchy 190/1
Baranovichi (*Pol.* Baranowicze) W Russia WW1 253/3
Barbados island of West Indies settled by English 160/3; British colony 227/1, 244/1; independence 277/2 (inset)
Barbalissus Syria × 78/3; Roman fort 88/3
Barbaricum port of NW India 71/1, 82/4
Barbuda island of West Indies settled by English 160/3; dependency of Antigua 277/2 (inset)
Barca Libya × 78/1
Barcelona (*anc.* Barcino) NE Spain Mediterranean trade 120/2, 134/1, 144/1, 146/1; urban revolt 143/1; 16C financial centre 180/1; trading port 180/3; 18C urban development 181/2; × 204/1; industrial development 210/1; Civil War 268/3
Barcelonette SE France fort 193/1
Barcino (*mod.* Barcelona) NE Spain early bishopric 92/1
Bardaa NW Persia early archbishopric 101/1
Bardia (*n/s* Bardiyah) Libya WW2 273/3
Bardsey Wales monastery 93/3
Barduli (Barletta)
Bareilly N India Mutiny 234/1
Barguzinsk (*now* Barguzin) SC Siberia founded 162/3
Bari (*anc.* Barium) S Italy Saracen occupation 111/1; captured by Normans 120/2; WW2 273/3
Barium (*mod.* Bari) S Italy Roman Empire 87/1; Jewish community 103/1
Bar-le-Duc E France 190/1
Barletta (*anc.* Barduli) S Italy mediaeval city 119/1
Barmen-Elberfeld (*since 1930* Wuppertal) W Germany industrial development 210/1, 212/1
Barnard Castle N England × 185/1
Barnaul C Asia founded 162/3; industry 290/3, 291/1
Barnsley C England Industrial Revolution 201/1
Baroda C India industry 218/1
Barotseland SC Africa early state 239/1
Bar-sur-Aube C France mediaeval fair 120/1
Barygaza (*Skt.* Bhrigukaccha *mod.* Broach *n/s* Bharuch) NW India trading centre 71/1, 82/4, 83/1
Basel (*Fr.* Bâle *Eng.* Basle) Switzerland centre of religious dissent 122/1; bishopric 191/1
Bashkir ASSR C Russia 290/2
Bashkirs Turkic people of C Russia 163/1, 290/4
Basingstoke S England Industrial Revolution 201/1
Basle (*Fr.* Bâle *Ger.* Basel) Switzerland mediaeval trade 120/1; Reformation 183/1; bishopric 191/1; industrial development 210/1, 212/1
Basonge tribe of C Belgian Congo 282/2
Basque Provinces N Spain reconquest by Castile 124/3
Basque Republic N Spain autonomy 264/1
Basques people of N Spain and SW France 99/2, 214/1
Basra (*Ar.* Al Basrah) Mesopotamia early archbishopric 101/1; × 105/1; trade 135/1; Ottoman conquest 171/1; British control 228/2, 229/1; oil terminal 285/3; WW1 253/4
Bassano N Italy × 205/1
Bassein Burma early trade centre 177/1
Bassein (*Port.* Baçaim) W India Portuguese settlement 161/1, 173/1
Basse-Yutz E France La Tène site 84/1
Basti district of N India ceded to Britain 172/3
Basutoland (*now* Lesotho) S Africa state 238/3; British colony 240/2, 245/1, 276/1
Batanaea district of Judaea 102/2
Batavi tribe of the Netherlands 89/1
Batavia (*form.* Sunda Kalapa, *since 1949* Jakarta *f/s* Djakarta) Java early trade 161/1, 177/1; Dutch control 176/3; port 199/1; WW2 270-271
Batavian Republic (*mod.* Netherlands) state established by French Revolution 203/3
Batelela tribe of N Belgian Congo 282/2
Bath W England Industrial Revolution 201/1
Bathnae E Anatolia monastery 93/3
Bathurst SE Australia founded 237/5
Bathurst (*now* Banjul) Gambia, W Africa British settlement 238/1; 283/1
Bato Caves C Philippines early site 132/1
Baton Rouge S USA × 222/1
Batshokwe tribe of S Belgian Congo 282/2
Batumi (*f/s* Batum) Caucasus British occupation 259/1; economy 291/1
Baudouinville Zaire Congo crisis 282/2
Bautzen E Germany × 205/1
Bavaria (*Ger.* Bayern) conversion to Christianity 100/3; part of Frankish Empire 107/3, 123/4,5; Magyar invasions 111/1; Wittelsbach territory 150/1; Electorate 191/1; German Empire 216/3; customs union 217/1; short-lived soviet republic 258/2; 275/2
Bawit Egypt monastery 100/1
Baxter Spring C USA cow town 220/1
Bayern (Bavaria)
Bayeux N France Scandinavian settlement 110/2; bishopric 117/1
Bayonne (*anc.* Lapurdum) SW France 18C financial centre 181/2; 193/1
Bayreuth S Germany margraviate 191/1
Bayrut (Beirut)
Beachy Head S England Dutch naval victory 185/1
Beans Store C USA cow town 220/1
Bear Island Spitsbergen discovered 157/1
Béarn region of SW France under English rule 125/1; acquired by France 151/4
Bear Paw Mountains C USA × 221/4

Bear Valley–Bubastis

Bear Valley W USA mining site 220/1
Beas Valley NW India site 64/2
Beaucaire S France mediaeval fair 144/1
Beaulieu S England Industrial Revolution 201/1
Beauvais N France bishopric 117/1; 17C revolt 185/1
Beaver NW Canada sub-arctic Indian tribe 149/1
Beç (Vienna)
Becan E Mexico Maya site 46/2
Bechuanaland (*now* Botswana) country of S Africa, British protectorate 218/1, 238/3, 240/2, 245/1, 276/1
Bedford S England Industrial Revolution 201/1
Bedsa Karli)
Beersheba (*Heb.* Beer Sheva) S Israel WW1 253/4
Beidha S Palestine early village 41/1
Beihai (Pakhoi)
Beijing (Peking)
Beilngries W Germany early Hallstatt site 85/1
Beiqu (Pei-ch'ü)
Beira SE Africa Portuguese occupation 241/1
Beirut (*anc.* Berytus *Fr.* Beyrouth *Ar.* Bayrut) Lebanon Mediterranean trade 135/1, 145/1; French control 229/1; disturbances under French mandate 261/2; civil war 285/4
Beisamoun S Syria early village 41/1
Beiyu (Pei-yü)
Beizhou (Pei-chou)
Bejaia (*anc.* Saldae *Fr.* Bougie *Sp.* Bugia) Algeria Mediterranean trade 144/1
Bekaa Valley Lebanon occupied by Syria 285/4
Belchete NE Spain Civil War 268/3
Belfast N Ireland industrial development 212/1
Belfort E France fort 193/1
Belgian Congo (*form.* Congo Free State *now* Zaire) economy 218/1; colony 240/2, 245/1; uprising 249/2; independence 276/1,2
Belgica Roman province of NE France 89/1
Belgium (*form.* Spanish Netherlands *or* Southern Netherlands) industrial revolution 210/1, 212/1; colonial empire 245/1; WW1 252-3; overseas trade 256-7; acquisition of Eupen and Malmédy 265/1; economic and social development 1929-39 266/3, 267/2; inter-war alliances 268/1; WW2 269/5, 272-3; EEC and NATO 274-275, 293/1; economy 295/1
Belgorod S Russia founded 163/1; early bishopric 101/2; WW2 273/5; industry 291/1
Belgorod-Dnestrovskiy (Akkerman)
Belgrade (*anc.* Singidunum *S. Cr.* Beograd) C Yugoslavia × 129/1; Ottoman conquest 170/1; 18C urban development 180/1; WW1 253/3; WW2 269/5, 272-3
Belize city of C America founded by British 160/3, 165/1
Belize (*form.* British Honduras) independence 277/2 (inset); economy 295/1
Bellary district of S India ceded to Britain 172/3
Belleau Wood NE France WW1 253/3 (inset)
Belostok (*now* Białystok) Poland in Russian Empire 231/1
Belsen (*correctly* Bergen-Belsen) N Germany concentration camp 272/1
Belzec S Poland concentration camp 272/1
Bemba tribe of Rhodesia 167/1, 239/1
Benares (*anc.* Kasi *now* Varanasi) N India 83/1, 130-31, 172/3; Hindu-Muslim clashes 281/3
Bender (*mod.* Bendery *Rom.* Tighina) S Russia Ottoman conquest 170/1
Bendigo SE Australia goldfield 237/5
Benevento (*anc.* Beneventum) C Italy 111/1; dukedom under Byzantine Empire 113/1; × 123/5, 124/2
Beneventum (*mod.* Benevento) C Italy Roman Empire 87/1, 89/1
Bengal country of E India 130/4; under Mughal Empire 171/1, 173/1; under British rule 172/3, 194/2, 235/3; anti-colonial revolt 248/1, 261/1; partition between India and Pakistan 280/2, 281/3
Benghazi (*anc.* Berenice *Ar.* Banghazi) Libya Ottoman rule 229/1,239/1; Italian occupation 241/1; WW2 269/5, 273/3
Benguela Angola Portugese settlement 167/1, 239/1, 241/1
Benin early state of Nigeria 137/1, 166/1, 239/1
Benin (*form.* Dahomey) country of W Africa independence 276/2; economy 295/1
Benkulen Sumatra trading post 177/1
Benqi (Penki)
Bentheim W Germany country 191/1
Bentonville E USA × 223/1
Bent's Fort C USA fur station 220/1
Beograd (Belgrade)
Beothuk Newfoundland Indian tribe 149/1
Berar C India sultanate 130/4, 173/1; tribal territory 235/3
Berbera Somalia Muslim Colony 137/1; British occupation 241/1
Berbers people of NW Africa, attack Roman Africa 94/1; incursions into Morocco 134/1
Berenice Red Sea early trading port 71/1, 82/4; Roman Empire 91/1
Berenice (*mod.* Benghazi) Libya city of Roman Empire 89/1, 91/1; early bishopric 93/1
Berezina river of W Russia × 205/1
Berezov (*now* Berezovo) W Siberia founded 163/1
Berg W Germany Reformation 182/2; duchy 191/1,4
Bergama (Pergamum)
Bergamo (*anc.* Bergomum) N Italy mediaeval city 119/1, 123/4
Bergen Norway bishopric 101/2; Hanseatic trading post 144/1; WW2 269/5
Bergen (Mons)
Bergen Belsen (Belsen)
Bergomum (*mod.* Bergamo) N Italy invaded by Huns 99/1
Beringia N Pacific land bridge 37/4
Bering Strait N Pacific European discovery 157/3
Berlin Germany Hanseatic city 144/1; 18C urban development 181/2; urban development 190/2; population growth 209; industrial development 210/1, 212/1; WW1 253/3; Communist uprising 258/2, 264/2; WW2 272-3; divided 275/2; Cold War 292/2
Bermuda British colony in W Atlantic, 244/1
Bern (*Fr.* Berne) Switzerland Zähringen town 121/6; early canton 142/3; Reformation 183/1; industrial development 212/1
Beroea (*mod.* Veroia) N Greece bishopric 93/1; Jewish community 103/1
Beroea (*mod.* Aleppo) Syria Roman fort 88/3
Berri E Arabia oilfield 285/3
Berry region of C France Frankish Royal domain 125/1, 151/4; province 193/1
Bersham N England Industrial Revolution 201/1
Berytus (*mod.* Beirut) Lebanon Roman Empire 89/1, 91/1; early bishopric 93/1
Besançon (*anc.* Vesontio) E France archbishopric 106/3; mediaeval fair 144/1; gained by France 192/2; French Revolution 203/2
Beshbalik W Mongolia 129/1,3
Besigheim W Germany Mithraic site 72/1
Bessarabia region of Romania/Russia acquired by Russia 163/1; Ottoman province 229/1; lost to Romania 259/1; regained by Russia 265/1, 269/5, 292/2
Besseringen W Germany La Tène site 84/1
Beth Katraye SE Arabia early bishopric 101/1
Bethlehem Palestine bishopric 93/1
Béthune N France fort 193/1
Betsileo Kingdom Madagascar 239/1
Beverley NE England Industrial Revolution 201/1
Bewdley W England Industrial Revolution 201/1
Beyrouth (Beirut)
Bhabra (Bairat)
Bhagatrav NW India Harappan site 65/1
Bhaja (Karli)
Bhakra-Nangal N India dam 281/3
Bharuch (Broach)
Bhilai C India steel plant 281/3
Bhonsla state of C India 172/3; alliance with Britain 194/2 (inset)
Bhopal C India chemical plant 281/3
Bhota (*mod.* Tibet) 83/2
Bhrigukaccha (Broach)
Bhutan Himalayan kingdom 235/3, 281/3; end of Chinese tributary status 232/2; British influence 277/1; economy 295/1
Biache-Saint-Vaast N France site of early man 32/2
Biafra E Nigeria civil war 283/1
Białystok (Belostok)
Biak NW New Guinea captured by US 271/2
Bianzhou (Pien-chou)
Bibi Hakimeh W Iran oilfield 285/3
Bibracte C France Roman Empire 86/3
Bidar sultanate of S India, 130/4
Big Bell W Australia gold town 237/5
Big Hole NW USA × 221/4
Big Mound N USA × 221/4
Bigorre region of SW France under English rule 125/1; independent fief 151/4
Bihar state of E India Muslim expansion 104/2; Sultanate of Delhi 131/3; Mughal Empire 173/1; under British control 172/3, 194/2; 235/3, 281/3
Bijapur sultanate of SW India, 130/4, 173/1
Bilá Hora (White Mountain)
Bilbao N Spain 18C financial centre 181/2; industrial development 210/1, 212/1; Civil War 268/3
Billungmark district of N Germany 117/1
Bilma W Africa early trade 136/2, 167/1; occupied by French 241/1
Biloxi S USA fur station 220/1
Bilston C England Industrial Revolution 200/3
Bilzingsleben Germany site of early man 32/2
Bimlipatan NE India Dutch settlement 173/1
Bingen W Germany Mithraic site 72/1
Binh Dinh (Vijaya)
Bioko (Fernando Po)
Bird Creek C USA × 221/4
Birka E Sweden Viking trade centre 110/3
Birkenhead N England Industrial Revolution 200/3
Birmingham C England 18C urban development 181/2; Industrial Revolution 200/3, 201/1; industrial development 210/1, 212/1; bombed in WW2 269/5
Birmingham SE USA industry 218/1
Birten N Germany × 118/3
Bisa tribe of C Africa, 239/1
Bishapur S Persia town of Parthian Empire 79/3
Bishopbridge E England Industrial Revolution 201/1
Bishop's Stortford S England Industrial Revolution 201/1
Bisitun W Persia town of Achaemenid Empire 79/1
Bist Sasanian town 79/3
Biterrae S France bishopric 92/1
Bithynia ancient country of NW Anatolia 75/1, 76/1; Roman province 86/3, 91/2; Byzantine Empire 113/1
Bithynia and Pontus Anatolia Roman province 89/1
Bitlis E Anatolia Byzantine Empire 113/1
Bitolj (*n/s* Bitola *Turk.* Manastır *a/s* Monastir) S Yugoslavia Ottoman control 139/1
Bituricae C France archbishopric 92/1
Biysk Russ. C Asia founded 162/3
Bizerta (*anc.* Hippo Zarytus *Fr.* Bizerte *Ar.* Banzart) Tunisia Mediterranean trade 134/1; Spanish occupation 186/2; WW2 273/3
Bjerre N Denmark Megalithic site 42/2
Blackburn NE England Industrial Revolution 200/3
Blackburn S Africa Iron Age site 45/1
Blackfoot W Canada Plains Indian tribe 149/1
Black Forest SW Germany colonisation 121/3; 18C industrial growth 190/2
Blackheath S England × 185/1
Black Patch S England Megalithic site 42/2
Black Sea early trade 52/1
Blagoveshchensk Russ. Far East 231/2; industry 291/1
Blekinge region of S Sweden under Danish rule 116/2; acquired by Sweden 188-9
Blenheim (*Ger.* Blindheim) W Germany × (called Höchstädt by French and Germans) 192/3
Blenheim S Island, New Zealand founded 236/1
Blois region of N France 151/4
Bloody Brook NE USA × 221/4
Bloody Ridge NE USA × 221/4
Bloody Run NE USA × 221/4
Blue Turks tribe of Mongolia 95/1
Bluff S Island, New Zealand aluminium 236/1
Bobangi early state of C Africa 239/1
Bobbio N Italy monastery 100/3, 107/3
Bobriki (Novomoskovsk)
Bodh Gaya NE India Buddhist site 73/1
Bodiam SE England Industrial Revolution 201/1
Bodo E Africa site of early man 32/4
Bodrum (Halicarnassus)
Boeotia ancient country of C Greece, Persian influence 74/3; League 76/4
Boer Republic S Africa 238/3
Boğazköy (*anc.* Hattushash *Gr.* Pteria) C Anatolia site 67/3,4
Boğdan (*Eng. Moldavia*) vassal state of Ottoman Empire 139/1
Bohai (Po-hai)
Bohemia (*Ger.* Böhmen) W part of mod. Czechoslovakia occupied by Poland 117/3; mediaeval German Empire 118/3, 119/1, expansion 141/1; Black Death 143/1; acquired by Habsburgs 150/1,2, 197/3; Thirty Years War 182/2; Reformation 183/1; 18C industrial growth 190/2; kingdom within Holy Roman Empire 190-91; conquest by Prussia 196/4; Austro-Hungarian Empire 197/3, 265/1
Bohemians Slav tribe of C Europe 98/3
Bohuslän province of S Sweden acquired from Denmark 188-9
Bojador, Cape W Africa Portuguese exploration 147/2
Bolgar (*a/c* Bulgar) C Russia city of the Volga Bulgars 114/4, 115/1, 128/1; Viking trade 110/3
Bolivia country of S America independence 226-7, 244/1; exports and foreign investments 226/3; population 226/4; 20C revolutions 286-7; economy 219/1, 295/1
Bologna (*anc.* Felsina *later* Bononia) N Italy Mithraic site 72/1; mediaeval city 119/1, 124/2; 18C urban development 181/2
Bolsheretsk Russ. Far East founded 162/3
Bolton N England Industrial Revolution 200/3, 201/1
Bombay W India early trade 147/1, 161/1, 172/2, 199/1; British settlement 173/1; industry 218/1, 235/3; British rule 234/1; Shiv Sena disturbances and Hindu-Muslim clashes 281/3
Bombo Kaburi E Africa Iron Age site 45/1
Bona (*mod.* Annaba *Fr.* Bône) N Algeria acquired by Habsburgs 150/1,2; Spanish occupation 186/2
Bonaire island of Dutch West Indies 227/1, 244/1, 277/2 (inset)
Bonampak E Mexico Maya site 46/2
Bondu early state of W Africa 238/1
Bône (*mod.* Annaba *Sp.* Bona *anc.* Hippo Regius) N Algeria Pisan raids 120/2; Mediterranean trade 144/1; French invasion 239/1
Bonin Islands (*a/c* Ogasawara Islands) N Pacific annexed by Japan 243/2; WW2 270-271
Bonn W Germany capital of Federal Republic 275/2
Bonna (*mod.* Bonn) W Germany Roman Empire 90/1
Bononia (*earlier* Felsina *mod.* Bologna) N Italy Roman Empire 87/1, 89/1
Bophuthatswana S Africa independent Bantustan 283/1
Bordeaux (*anc.* Burdigala) SW France early archbishopric 106/3; occupied by English 142/4; mediaeval fair 144/1; 16C urban development 180/1; trading port 180/3; 18C financial centre 181/2; St Bartholomew Massacre 182/3; Ormée revolt 185/1; industry 193/1; overseas trade 198/3; French Revolution 203/2
Border Cave S Africa site of early man 33/4
Borger Holland site 42/2
Borgu States W Africa 167/1
Borneo (*Indon. Kalimantan*) island of East Indies Muslim expansion 104/3, 133/3; Dutch trade 177/1; Dutch and British colonisation 245/1; WW2 270-271
Bornhöved N Germany × 119/1
Borno Nigeria early state 167/1, 239/1
Borobudur C Java Buddhist site 73/1; political centre 133/2
Borodino W Russia × 205/1
Bororo forest Indian tribe of S Brazil 149/1
Bosna Saray (*n/c* Sarajevo) C Yugoslavia captured by Ottomans 139/1
Bosnia country of C Yugoslavia vassal state of Ottoman Empire 139/1; under Hungarian Kingdom 141/1; Black Death 143/1
Bosnia-Herzegovina (*S. Cr.* Bosna i Hercegovina) region of S Yugoslavia part of Austria-Hungary 215/2; under Ottoman rule 228/1; Balkan alliances 250-51; after WW1 265/1
Bosnians people of C Yugoslavia 265/3
Bosporan Kingdom S Russia 86/3, 89/1
Boston E England mediaeval trade 144/1; Industrial Revolution 201/1
Boston NE USA founded 161/2; British naval base 194/1; trade and industry 199/1; 219/1
Boston Post Road NE USA 220/1
Bostra S Syria Roman fort 88/3, 91/1; early archbishopric 93/1
Botany Bay SE Australia penal settlement 237/5
Botocudo Indian tribe of S Brazil 149/1
Botswana (*form. Bechuanaland*) S Africa independence 276/2; political development 283/1; economy 295/1
Bouchain N France fort 193/1
Bougainville one of Solomon Islands, W Pacific WW2 270-271
Bougie (*anc.* Saldae *Sp.* Bugia *mod.* Bejaia) N Algeria Genoese raids 120/2; Spanish occupation 186/2
Bougon N France Megalithic site 42/2
Boulogne (*anc.* Gesoriacum) N France fort 193/1
Boulonnais region of NE France Burgundian possession 151/3
Bouqras SE Syria early village 41/1
Bourbon (*now.* Réunion) island of Indian Ocean French possession 194/2
Bourbon (Bourbonnais)
Bourbonnais (*a/c* Bourbon) region of C France Royal domain 125/1; annexed to France 150/1, 151/4
Boure early state of W Africa 136/1
Bourges (*anc.* Avaricum) C France St Bartholomew Massacre 182/3; 193/1
Bourg-la-Reine C France mediaeval *villeneuve* 121/7
Bourgogne (Burgundy)
Bourg-St Andéol S France Mithraic site 72/1
Bourne E England Industrial Revolution 201/1
Boussargues S France early settlement 43/1
Bouvines NE France × 119/1, 125/1
Boyacá Colombia × 226/2
Bozeman Trail and Pass NW USA 220/1
Brabant region of Belgium/Holland mediaeval German Empire 119/1, 125/1; Burgundian possession 151/3
Bracara (*mod.* Braga) Portugal archbishopric 92/1, 101/2
Bradford N England Industrial Revolution 201/1
Braga (Bracara)
Brahmagiri S India site 64/3
Branč Czechoslovakia burial site 43/1
Branco, Cape W Africa Portuguese exploration 147/2
Brandenburg region of E Germany margraviate under German Empire 117/1; Black Death 143/1; Hohenzollern territory 150/1; Reformation 182/2, 183/1; Electorate 190-91; 18C industrial growth 190/2; part of Prussia 216/3
Brass Nigeria early European settlement 239/1
Bratislava (*Ger.* Pressburg *Hung.* Pozsony) Slovakia WW1 253/3
Bratsk SC Siberia founded 162/3; industry 290/3, 291/1
Braunschweig (Brunswick)
Brazil discovered 157/1; early trade 145/4; Portuguese colony 158/1, 165/1; independent Empire 227/1, 244/1; immigration from Europe 209/2; exports and foreign investment 226/3; population 226/4; industrialisation and economy 219/1, 266/3, 286-7, 294-295
Brecon W Wales Industrial Revolution 201/1
Brega E Ireland early kingdom 117/1
Breisach W Germany gained by France 192/2
Breitenfeld E Germany × 182/2
Bremen N Germany bishopric 100/3; archbishopric 117/1, 191/1; Hanseatic city 144/1; Reformation 182/2, 183/1; urban development 190/2; industrial development 210/1; German customs union 217/1; WW1 253/3; short-lived Soviet Republic 258/2; WW2 273/3; city-state 275/2
Bremen and Verden region of N Germany lost by Sweden 188-9
Bremerhaven N Germany WW1 253/3; city-state 275/2
Brenner Austria tunnel 257/2
Brenta, River N Italy × 111/1
Brescia (*anc.* Brixia) N Italy mediaeval city 119/1, 124/2; religious dissent 122/1
Breslau (*n/c* Wrocław) W Poland Hanseatic city 144/1; 18C financial centre 181/2; Reformation 183/1; urban and industrial development 190/2, 211/1, 213/1; WW1 253/3
Brest NW France English base for 100 Years War 142/4; fort 193/1; naval base 195/1; French Revolution 203/2
Brest (*a/c* Brest-Litovsk *Pol.* Brześć nad Bugiem) W Russia 231/1, 259/1; WW1 253/3
Bretagne (Brittany)
Bretons Celtic people of NW France, 106/1, 214/1
Bretteville-le-Rabet N France Megalithic site 42/2
Briançon SE France fort 193/1
Bridgnorth W England Industrial Revolution 201/1
Bridgwater W England Industrial Revolution 201/1
Brieg (*Pol.* Brzeg) W Poland Reformation 182/2
Brigantes Britain early tribe 88/1
Brigetio Hungary Mithraic site 72/1; Roman Empire 91/1
Brihuega C Spain × 192/3
Brindisi (*anc.* Brundisium) S Italy captured by Normans 120/2; WW1 253/3
Briocum NW France monastery 93/3
Brisbane E Australia founded 237/5
Bristol W England trading port 180/3; 18C urban development 181/2; industrial development 198/3, 201/1, 212/1; bombed in WW2 269/5
Britain conversion to Christianity 72/1; invasion by Germanic tribes 98/1. See also England, United Kingdom
Britannia (*mod.* Britain) Roman Empire 91/2
Britannia Inferior Roman province of N England, 88/1
Britannia Superior Roman province of S England 88/1
British Bechuanaland S Africa 241/1
British Cameroons (*now part of* Cameroon) W Africa protectorate 276/1
British Columbia province of W Canada economic development 219/3; joins Confederation 244/1; border dispute with Alaska 246/3
British East Africa (*now* Kenya) colony 240/2, 241/1, 245/1, 249/2
British Empire 245/1
British Guiana (*now* Guyana) S America colony 219/1, 227/1, 244/1
British Honduras (*now* Belize) C America colony 227/1, 244/1, 247/4
British North Borneo (*now* Sabah) protectorate 261/1, 277/1
British Somaliland (*now part of* Somalia) E Africa protectorate 218/1, 240/2, 245/1, 260/1, 277/2
Britons tribe of SW England, movement to Brittany 99/1
Brittany (*Fr.* Bretagne) NW France on borders of Frankish Empire 106/3; duchy 117/1; conquered by Normans 125/1; Hundred Years War 142/4; Black Death 143/1; annexed to France 151/4
Brivas C France monastery 93/3
Brixia (*mod.* Brescia) N Italy attacked by Goths 99/1
Brno (*Ger.* Brünn) Moravia WW1 253/3
Broach (*anc.* Barygaza *mod.* Bharuch) NW India ceded to Britain 172/2
Brody SE Poland WW1 253/3
Brogne Belgium centre of monastic reform 122/2
Broken Hill SE Australia mining 237/5
Broome W Australia early settlement 237/5
Broseley C England Industrial Revolution 200/3, 201/1
Brouage W France port 193/1
Bruges (*Dut.* Brugge) Belgium mediaeval city 119/1, 120/1; urban revolt 143/1; Hanseatic city 144/1, 145/3; 16C urban development 180/1; town of Spanish Netherlands 185/1; WW1 252-3
Brundisium (*mod.* Brindisi) S Italy Latin colony 87/1; Roman Empire 89/1, 91/1; Byzantine Empire 113/1
Brunei sultanate of N Borneo spread of Islam 104/3, 133/3; early trade 177/1; recaptured from Japanese 271/2; independence 277/2; British troops 278/2; economy 295/1
Brunete C Spain Civil War 268/3
Brünn (*Cz.* Brno) Czechoslovakia urban and industrial development 190/2, 213/1
Brunswick (*Ger.* Braunschweig) N Germany early city and duchy 119/1; urban revolt 143/1; Hanseatic city 144/1; German state 216/3; WW1 253/3
Brunswick-Lüneburg duchy of N Germany Reformation 183/1; 191/1
Brunswick-Wolfenbüttel duchy of N Germany 191/1
Brusa (Bursa)
Brussels (*Fr.* Bruxelles *Dut.* Brussel) Belgium 16C urban development 180/1; 18C urban development 181/2; city of Spanish Netherlands 185/1, 190/1; industrial development 210/1, 212/1; WW1 252-3; WW2 269/5, 273/3
Bruttii ancient tribe of S Italy 86/2
Bruttium ancient district of S Italy 91/2
Bruxelles (Brussels)
Bryansk W Russia bishopric 101/2; town of Novgorod-Seversk 115/1; WW2 273/3,5; industry 291/1
Brzeg (Brieg)
Bubastis Lower Egypt 58/1; Jewish community 103/1

Ch'ang-chou–Cork

Ch'ang-chou (*n/s* Changzhou) E China T'ang prefecture 126/1
Ch'ang-ch'un (*n/s* Changchun) Manchuria treaty port 232/2; railway 242/3, 263/3; industry 278/2
Chang-i (*n/s* Changyi) NW China Han commanderie 81/2
Changkufeng Manchuria Russo-Japanese conflict 268/2
Ch'ang-sha (*n/s* Changsha) C China Han principality 81/2; treaty town 232/2; captured by Kuomintang 262/1; captured by Japanese 270/1; industry 218/1, 263/3, 278/3
Chang-yeh (*n/s* Zhangye) NW China conquered by Han 80/3
Changyi (Ch'ang-i)
Changzhou (Ch'ang-chou)
Chanhu-Daro N India Harappan site 65/1
Channel Islands WW2 273/6
Chansen N Thailand Iron Age site 132/1
Chao (*n/s* Zhao) early state of N China 80/1
Chao-ming (*n/s* Zhaoming) N Korea Han prefecture 81/2
Characene early kingdom of Mesopotamia 78/2; vassal state of Parthian Empire 79/1
Charax early port on Persian Gulf, 71/1, 82/4
Charcas N Mexico Spanish centre 158/1
Chard SW England Industrial Revolution 201/1
Chardzhou (*until 1940* Chardzhuy) Russ. C Asia industry 291/1
Charikar (Alexandria)
Charleroi Belgium industrial development 210/1; WW1 253/3 (inset)
Charles Town Path SE USA settlers' route 220/1
Charleville E Australia railway 237/5
Charolais region of E France Habsburg possession 151/4, 185/1
Charrúa Indian tribe of Argentina 149/1
Charsinian Theme Byzantine province of C Anatolia, 112/3
Charsianum C Anatolia Byzantine Empire 112/3
Chartres C France WW1 253/3
Château-sur-Salins E France late Hallstatt site 84/1
Château-Thierry N France × 205/1; WW1 252/2, 253/3 (inset)
Chatham SE England Dutch naval raid 185/1; naval base 195/1; Industrial Revolution 201/1; WW1 253/3
Chattanooga SE USA × 223/1
Chatti Germanic tribe of Roman Empire 89/1
Chauci Germanic tribe of Roman Empire 89/1
Chaul W India Portuguese settlement 173/1
Chavín C Andes site 47/1
Chechen-Ingush ASSR Caucasus 290/2
Che-chiang (Chekiang)
Chedi early kingdom of N India 65/1, 83/2
Chekiang (*n/s* Zhejiang *W/G* Che-chiang) province of E China Ming economy 168/2; Manchu expansion 175/1; T'ai-p'ing control 233/1; Hsin-hai revolution 233/3
Chełm (Kholm)
Chelmno Poland concentration camp 272/1
Chelmsford (*anc.* Caesaromagus) E England Industrial Revolution 201/1
Chelyabinsk C Russia industry 231/1, 290/2, 291/1; urban growth 290/3
Chemin des Dames NE France WW1 253/3 (inset)
Chemnitz (*since 1953* Karl-Marx-Stadt) E Germany industrial development 210/1, 212/1; WW1 253/3
Chemulpo (Inchon)
Ch'en (*n/s* Chen) N China Chou domain 63/4
Chencang (Ch'en-ts'ang)
Cheng (*n/s* Zheng) N China Late Chou domain 63/4
Cheng-chou (*n/s* Zhengzhou *a/s* Chengchow) N China Shang city 62/2; on railway 263/3
Ch'eng-tu (*n/s* Chengdu) W China on trade route 71/1; Han prefecture 81/2; T'ang prefecture 126/1; Ming provincial capital 169/1; industry 278/3
Ch'eng-tu Fu (*n/s Chengdufu*) W China Sung province 127/5
Chenstokhov (*Pol.* Częstochowa) C Poland in European Russia 231/1
Chen-ting-fu (*n/s* Zhendingfu) N China Sung provincial capital 127/5
Ch'en-ts'ang (*n/s* Chencang) C China Han prefecture 81/2
Chepstow W England Industrial Revolution 201/1
Chera (*mod.* Kerala) region of S India 83/1
Cherbourg N France English base in Hundred Years War 142/4; French naval base 195/1; WW1 253/3; WW2 273/3,6
Cherchell (Caesarea)
Cherchen (*Chin.* Ch'ieh-mo) Chin. C Asia silk route 71/2
Cheremkhovo S Siberia industry 291/1
Cherepovets NW Russia industry 291/1
Cheribon (*Dut.* Tjeribon *n/s* Ceribon) district of Java Dutch control 176/3
Cherkess AD Caucasus 290/2
Chernigov Ukraine bishopric 101/2; principality 115/1
Chernovtsy (Czernowitz)
Cherokee Indian tribe of SE USA 149/1
Cherokees SE USA × 221/4
Chersonesus Crimea Ionian colony 75/1; bishopric 93/1
Cherusci Germanic tribe of Roman Empire 89/1
Chesowanja E Africa site of early man 33/4
Chester (*anc.* Deva) C England county palatine 125/1; Industrial Revolution 201/1
Cheyenne plains Indian tribe of C USA 49/1
Ch'i (*n/s* Qi) NE China Chou domain 62/3, 63/4; state 80/1, 126/3
Chia (*n/s* Jia) NW China Western Chou domain 62/3
Chia-mu-ssu (Kiamusze)
Ch'iang (*n/s* Qiang) border people of NW China 63/4
Chiang-hsi (Kiangsi)
Chiang-hsia (*n/s* Jiangxia) C China Han commanderie 81/2
Chiang-hsi-an (*n/s* Jiangxi'an) S China early settlement 62/1
Chiang-hsi Nan (*n/s* Jiangxi Nan) C China Sung province 127/5
Chiang-ling (*n/s* Jiangling) C China Western Chou site 62/3; T'ang prefecture 126/1; Sung provincial capital 127/5
Chiang Mai (Chiengmai)
Chiang-nan Hsi-tao (*n/s* Jiangnan Xidao) S China T'ang province 126/1
Chiang-nan Tung (*n/s* Jiangnan Dong) E China Sung province 127/5
Chiang-nan Tung-tao (*n/s* Jiangnan Dongdao) SE China T'ang province 126/1
Chiang-ning-fu (*n/s* Jiangningfu) E China Sung provincial capital 127/5
Chiang-su (Kiangsu)
Chiao (*n/s* Jiao) N China Western Chou domain 62/3
Chiao-chih (*n/s* Jiaozhi) China-Vietnam Han commanderie 81/2
Chiao-ho (*n/s* Jiaohe) Chin. C Asia Han expansion 80/3
Chiao-hsien (Kiaochow)
Chiao-li (*n/s* Jiaoli) NE China Han prefecture 81/2
Chiapa de Corzo C Mexico early site 46/2
Chiapas province of S Mexico 227/1
Chiba C Japan city and prefecture 218/2; industry 243/1
Chibcha Andean Indian tribe 149/1
Chicago N USA industry 219/1, 289/1
Chichén Itzá Mexico Maya site 46/2; Toltec domination 148/2
Chichester S England Industrial Revolution 201/1
Ch'i-ch'i-ha-erh (Tsitsihar)
Chi-chou (*n/s* Jizhou) NE China T'ang prefecture 126/1; Ming military post 169/1
Ch'i-ch'un (*n/s* Qichun) C China Western Chou site 62/3
Chickamauga SE USA × 223/1
Chickasaw Indian tribe of SE USA 149/1, 221/4
Ch'ieh-mo (*n/s* Qiemo *a/c* Qarqan *n/s* Cherchen) Chin. C Asia Han expansion 80/3
Ch'ien-ch'eng (*n/s* Qiancheng) NE China Han prefecture 81/2
Chien-chou (*n/s* Jianzhou) NE China Ming military post 169/1
Ch'ien-chung (*n/s* Qianzheng) SW China T'ang province 126/1
Chiengmai (*n/s* Chiang Mai) N Thailand early political centre 133/2,3
Chien-nan (*n/s* Jiannan) W China T'ang province 126/1
Ch'ien-t'ang (*n/s* Qiantang) E China Han prefecture 81/2
Chietao district of Manchuria occupied by Russia 242/3
Chien-wei (*n/s* Jianwei) W China Han commanderie 81/2
Chieti (Teate)
Chihli former province of N China Manchu expansion 175/1; Boxer uprising 233/1
Chi-hsi (*n/s* Jixi) Manchuria industry 278/3
Chihuahua province of N Mexico 227/1; US military action 247/4
Chile Spanish colony 158/1, 165/1; 226-7; independence from Spain 244/1; 286-7; exports and foreign investment 226/3; population 226/4; economy 219/1, 294-295
Chilia-Nouă (Kilia)
Chi-lin (Kirin)
Chimkent Russ. C Asia industry 291/1
Chimú Andean Indian tribe 149/1,3
Chin (*n/s* Jin) N China Chou domain 62/3, 63/4; state 126/3; empire conquered by Mongols 129/1
Ch'in (*n/s* Qin) NW China Chou domain 62/3, 63/4; empire 80/1,2,3
China agricultural origins 39/1, 62/1; development of writing 53; beginnings of civilisation 62-3; early trade routes 71/1; silk route 71/1; Buddhism and Taoism 73/1; Han expansion 80/3; population growth 80/4, 127/4; early Christianity 101/1; T'ang and Sung 109/1; 126-7; Mongol conquests 129/1,3; Ming Empire 155/1; 168/9; early trade 147/1, 154/2, 161/1, 177/1; Ch'ing 174/2,3; Manchu expansion 175/1; 18C overseas trade 199/1; Manchu Empire 232-3; Russo-Japanese war 242/3; Japanese influence 243/2; European spheres of influence 245/1; Boxer rebellion 248/1; Empire overthrown 279/1; Communist Party founded 258/3; Japanese occupation 268/2, 270/1, 271/2; Revolution 262-263; Cold War 291/3; emigration to USA 209/2; industry and economy 218/1, 278/2,3, 295/1; conflict with Vietnam 279/1; conflict with India 281/3
Chi-nan (*n/s* Jinan *a/s* Tsinan) N China Ming provincial capital 169/1; industry 218/1
Chin-ch'eng (*n/s* Jincheng) NW China Han commanderie 81/2
Chin-chiang (Chinkiang)
Chin-chou (*n/s* Jinzhou) NE China Ming military post 169/1
Ch'in-feng (*n/s* Qinfeng) NW China Sung province 127/5
Ching-chao-fu (*n/s* Jingzhaofu) N China Sung provincial capital 127/5
Ching-chi (*n/s* Jingji) N China T'ang province 126/1
Ch'ing-chiang (*n/s* Qingjiang) SW China Sung provincial capital 127/5
Ch'ing-chou (*n/s* Qingzhou) NE China Sung provincial capital 127/5
Chinghai (Tsinghai)
Ching-hsi Nan (*n/s* Jingxi Nan) C China Sung province 127/5
Ching-hsi Pei (*n/s* Jingxi Bei) C China Sung province 127/5
Ching-hu Nan (*n/s* Jinghu Nan) SW China Sung province 127/5
Ching-hu Pei (*n/s* Jinghu Bei) Sung province 127/5
Ching-kang Shan (*n/s* Jinggang Shan) SE China early Communist soviet 263/3
Chingleput SE India ceded to Britain 172/3
Ching-nan (*n/s* Jingnan) early state of C China 126/3
Ch'ing-tao (*n/s* Qingdao *a/s* Tsingtao) E China industry 278/3
Ching-tung Hsi (*n/s* Jingdong Xi) N China Sung province 127/5
Ching-tung Tung (*n/s* Jingdong Dong) NE China Sung province 127/5
Chinkiang (*n/s* Jinjiang *W/G* Chin-chiang) E China treaty port 232/2
Chinkultic E Mexico Maya site 46/2
Chin-men (Quemoy)
Chinnampo N Korea Russo-Japanese war 242/3
Chinook coast Indian tribe of W Canada, 149/1
Chin Special Division administrative territory of W Burma 281/3
Chinsura Bengal Dutch settlement 161/1, 173/1
Chin-t'ien (*n/s* Jintian) S China T'ai-p'ing rebellion 233/1
Chin-yang (*n/s* Jinyang) N China Late Chou city site 63/4
Chios (*mod. Gk.* Khios) island of E Aegean bishopric 93/1; Byzantine Empire 112/3; to Genoa 139/1, 151/1; gained by Turks 187/1; ceded to Greece 215/2
Chipewyan sub-arctic Indian tribe of N Canada, 149/1
Chisholm Trail C USA cattle trail 220/1
Chishima-retto (Kurile Islands)
Chisimaio (Kismayu)
Chişinău (Kishinev)
Chita E Siberia Trans-Siberian railway 230/2; capital of Far Eastern Republic 258/3; industry 291/1
Chittagong SE Bangladesh trade 147/1, 235/3, 281/3
Chiu-chang (*n/s* Jiuzhang) E China Han commanderie 81/2
Chiu-chen (*n/s* Jiuzhen) N Indo-China Han commanderie 81/2
Chiu-chiang (Kiukiang)
Chiu-ch'üan (*n/s* Jiuquan) NW China conquered by Han 80/3; Han commanderie 81/2
Chiu-hua Shan (*n/s* Jiuhua Shan) mountain of E China Buddhist site 73/1
Ch'iung-chou (*n/s* Qiongzhou) S China treaty port 232/2
Chiusi (Clusium)
Chi-yang (*n/s* Jiyang) C China Han prefecture 81/2
Chlum Czechoslovakia La Tène site 85/1
Chocó Indian tribe of S America 149/1
Choctaw Indian tribe of S USA 149/1, 221/4
Choga Mami Mesopotamia site 41/1
Chola ancient country of S India 83/1
Cholas dynasty of S India and Ceylon 130/2, 131/1
Cholet W France French Revolution 203/2
Cholula C Mexico early site 46/2; Aztec site 148/2; on Cortés' route 159/2
Chongqing (Chungking)
Chorasmia (*a/c* Khiva, Khwarizm) country of C Asia 82/3
Chorasmii people of C Asia 77/1
Chosen (Korea)
Chotin (*n/s* Khotin) Ukraine Thracian site 85/1
Chou (*n/s* Zhou) NC China Western Chou domain 62/3; warring state 80/1
Chou-k'ou-tien (*n/s* Zhoukoudian) N China site 33/1, 37/1, 62/1
Christchurch S Island, New Zealand founded 236/1
Christiania (*mod.* Oslo) Norway 189/1
Christiansborg Gold Coast early Danish settlement 166/1 (inset)
Chu (*n/s* Zhu) N China Western Chou domain 62/3
Ch'u (*n/s* Chu) C China Chou domain 62/3, 63/4; warring state 80/1
Ch'u (*n/s* Chu) NE China Western Chou domain 62/3
Ch'u (*n/s* Chu) state of SW China 126/3
Ch'üan-chou (*n/s* Quanzhou) S China Ming trade 168/2
Chud (*a/c* Chudi) early tribe of N Russia 101/2, 115/1
Chudskoye Ozero (Lake Peipus)
Chukchi tribe of NE Siberia, 162/3
Chukchi AD NE Siberia 290/2
Chü-lu (*n/s* Julu) N and S China Han prefectures 81/2
Chumash Indian tribe of W USA 149/1
Chün (*n/s* Jun) C China Western Chou domain 62/3
Chün (*n/s* Jun) N China Western Chou site 62/3
Ch'ung-ch'ing (Chungking)
Chungking (*n/s* Chongqing *W/G* Ch'ung-ch'ing) C China treaty town 232/2; industry 263/3, 278/3; capital during WW2 268/2,3
Ch'ü-sou (*n/s* Qusou) N China Han prefecture 81/2
Chustenahlah C USA × 221/4
Chuvash ASSR C Russia 290/2
Chuvashi tribe of C Russia, conquered 163/1; 290/4
Ch'u-wo (*n/s* Chuwo) N China Late Chou city site 63/4
Chu-yai (*n/s* Zhuya) S China Han prefecture 81/2
Chü-yen (*n/s* Juyan) NW China administrative centre of later Han 80/3
Ciboney Indian tribe of the Caribbean 149/1
Cibyrrhaeot Theme Byzantine province of S Anatolia, 112/3
Cieszyn (Teschen)
Cilicia (*Hittite name* Kizzuwadna) region of S Anatolia 54/1; Hittite Empire 57/1; early trade 66/4; Persian Empire 75/1; Alexander's Empire 76/1, 82/3; Achaemenid Empire 79/1; Roman province 86/3, 89/1; Byzantine Empire 113/1
Cimmerians people of Asia Minor 56/3, 61/1
Cincinnati N USA industry 219/1
Circassia (*Turk.* Çerkes) region of Caucasus 139/1
Circeii C Italy Latin colony 87/1
Cirencester (*anc.* Corinium) W England Industrial Revolution 201/1
Cirene (Cyrene)
Cirrha C Greece early site 67/1
Cirta (*mod.* Constantine) N Algeria Roman Empire 86/3, 89/1, 90/1; early bishopric 92/1
Cisalpine Gaul (Gallia Cisalpina)
Cisalpine Republic N Italy state established by French Revolution 203/3
Cishan (Tz'u-shan)
Ciskei S Africa independent Bantustan 283/1
Cissbury S England Megalithic site 42/2
Citium (*OT* Kittim) Phoenician colony 75/1
Ciudad de México (Mexico City)
Civita Castellana (Falerii)
Civitas Nemetum (Speyer)
Clava N Scotland Megalithic tomb 42/2
Clearwater NW USA × 221/4
Cleveland N USA industry 219/1, 289/1
Cleves (*Ger.* Kleve) NW Germany Reformation 182/2; duchy 191/1
Clonard Ireland monastery 93/3, 100/3
Cloncurry N Australia copper mining 237/5
Clonfert Ireland monastery 100/3
Clonmacnoise Ireland monastery 100/3
Clontarf E Ireland × 117/1
Clontibret NE Ireland × 185/1
Cloyne Ireland bishopric 92/1
Cluny C France centre of monastic reform 122/2
Clusium (*mod.* Chiusi) N Italy Etruscan city 86/2
Clysma Red Sea early port 70/1; Roman Empire 91/1
Cnossus (*Gr.* Knossos) Crete Roman Empire 89/1, 91/1
Coahuila province of N Mexico 227/1; US military action 247/4
Coahuiltec Indian tribe of N Mexico 149/1
Coalbrookdale C England Industrial Revolution 200/3
Coba Mexico Maya site 46/2
Coblenz (*n/s* Koblenz) W Germany WW1 253/3, 275/2
Cochimi Indian tribe of W Mexico 149/1
Cochin (*early Chin.* Ko-chih) region of S India early trade 147/1; Portuguese rule 159/1; Dutch settlement 161/1, 173/1; 18C trade 199/1; British rule 234/1
Cochin-China region of S Indo-China expansion into Cambodia 177/1; French control 244/1 (inset), 261/1; claimed by Cambodia 279/1
Cocos Islands (*now* under Australian administration *called* Cocos-Keeling Islands) Indian Ocean British control 245/1
Coele Roman province of SE Anatolia 89/1
Colchester (Camulodunum)
Colchis ancient country of the Caucasus, Ionian colonisation 75/1, 76/1; 89/1
Coldizzi Slav tribe of SE Germany 140/2
Colima province of C Mexico 227/1
Colle di Tenda NW Italy tunnel 257/2
Cologne (*anc.* Colonia Agrippina *Ger.* Köln) W Germany mediaeval city 118/3, 119/1, 120/1, 121/8; centre of religious dissent 122/1; Hanseatic city 141/1; archbishopric 107/3, 117/1, 191/1; 18C urban development 180/1; 18C urban development 210/1, 212/1; WW1 253/3; WW2 273/3
Colombia independence from Spain 226-7, 244/1; exports and foreign investment 226/3; population 226/4; political development 286-7; economy 219/1, 294-295
Colombo Ceylon early trade 147/1; Portuguese trade 159/1; Dutch trade 161/1; Dutch settlement 173/1; capital of British colony 235/3
Colón Panama Canal Zone 246/2
Colonia Agrippina (*a/c* Colonia Agrippinensis *mod.* Köln *Eng.* Cologne) NW Germany Mithraic site 72/1; Roman Empire 89/1, 90/1; bishopric 92/1; Jewish community 103/1
Colonia Julia Fenestris (Fanum Fortunae)
Colonian Theme Byzantine province of E Anatolia 112/3
Colorado state of W USA 1896 election 225/3; Depression 267/1; income and population 289/2
Colossae W Anatolia town of Achaemenid Empire 78/1
Columbia SE USA burned 223/1
Comacchio N Italy captured by Venice 120/2
Comalcalco Mexico Maya site 46/2
Comana ancient city of E Anatolia 112/3
Comanche plains Indian tribe of S USA 149/1
Comisene region of N Persia vassal state of Parthian Empire 79/3
Commagene region of SE Anatolia state 86/3; Roman province 89/1
Commendah W Africa early British settlement 166/1 (inset)
Commercy C France industrial development 210/1
Comminges independent fief of SW France 151/4
Como N Italy Lombard League 119/1
Comoro Islands E Africa spread of Islam 167/1; French colonisation 245/1, 277/1; independence 277/2, 283/1
Compiègne NE France WW1 252/2
Comtat Venaissin S France Papal site 151/4
Conakry W Africa occupied by French 241/1
Condatomagus (*mod.* La Graufesenque) S France Roman Empire 90/1
Confederate States of America 222/3
Confederation of the Rhine 204/2, 205/1
Congo (*form.* Middle Congo *or* French Congo) region of C Africa source of slaves 166/2; independence 276/2; political development 283/1; economy 295/1
Congo Free State (*later* Belgian Congo *now* Zaire) 241/1
Connaught (*a/s* Connacht) region of W Ireland early kingdom 117/1; Norman-Angevin overlordship 125/1; Presidency 185/1
Connecticut NE USA colony 161/2, 164/3; 19C politics 224/1,2,3; Depression 267/1; income and population 289/1
Connell's Prairie NW USA × 221/4
Constance (*anc.* Constantia *Ger.* Konstanz) S Germany Frankish Kingdom 118/3
Constanța (*anc.* Tomi *Turk.* Küstence) E Romania WW1 253/3
Constantia (Salamis)
Constantine (*anc.* Cirta) N Algeria Ottoman Empire 228/1
Constantinople (*anc.* Byzantium *Norse* Mikligard *mod.* Istanbul) NW Turkey centre of early Christianity 72/1, 92/2; patriarchate 93/1, 101/2; Arab attacks 105/1; Byzantine Empire 108/3, 113/1,5; conquered 135/2; trade 110/3, 144/1, 146/1, 154/2; 16C urban development 180/1; 18C urban development 181/2; WW1 253/3
Cooch Behar former state of NE India joins India at partition 280/2
Cooks Islands S Pacific early Polynesian settlement 49/1; New Zealand possession 277/2 (inset)
Cook Strait New Zealand rail ferry 236/1
Cooktown E Australia early settlement 237/5
Coorg state of British India 235/3
Copán E Mexico Maya site 46/2
Copenhagen (*Dan.* København) Denmark 183/1; 189/1; × 194/3; WW1 253/3; WW2 273/3
Coppa Nevigata S Italy site 43/1
Copts Christian people of Egypt, 100/1
Coptus Lower Egypt trading centre 82/4; Roman Empire 89/1, 91/1; bishopric 93/1
Coquilhatville (*now* Mbandaka) NW Belgian Congo 282/2
Cora C Italy Latin colony 87/1
Cora Indian tribe of C Mexico 149/1
Coracesium S Anatolia 75/1
Coral Sea S Pacific × 271/2
Corbie N France monastery 106/3
Corcyra (*mod.* Corfu *Gr.* Kerkira) island of NW Greece Dorian colony 75/1
Cordilleran ice-sheet N America 37/4
Córdoba (*anc.* Corduba) S Spain Muslim conquest 104/1; Umayyad Caliphate and Muslim city 109/5, 120/2; reconquered from Muslims 124/3; Mediterranean trade 134/1; 16C urban development 180/1; 18C urban development 181/2; Civil War 268/3
Corduba (*mod.* Córdoba) S Spain Roman Empire 86/3, 89/1, 90/1; bishopric 92/1; Jewish community 103/1
Corfinium S Italy Roman Empire 89/1
Corfu (*anc.* Corcyra *mod.* Kerkira) island of W Greece Byzantine Empire 113/5; under Venetian rule 138/1, 141/1, 187/3; Ottoman siege 170/1; 1923 incident 265/1
Corinium (Cirencester)
Corinth (*Lat.* Corinthus *Gr.* Korinthos) C Greece parent state 75/1; archbishopric 93/1; Jewish community 103/1; Byzantine Empire 113/1,5; WW2 269/5
Corinth SE USA × 223/1
Corinthus (*Gr.* Korinthos *Eng.* Corinth) C Greece town of Roman Empire 89/1, 91/1
Cork S Ireland monastery 100/3; Scandinavian settlement 110/2, 111/1; bishopric under Scandinavian control 117/1

Guiyang–Hupeh

Guiyang (Kuei-yang)
Guizhou (Kweichow)
Guizi (Kuei-tzu)
Gujarat (*f/s* Gujerat) state of W India 281/3
Gujerat (*n/s* Gujarat) region of W India under Delhi Sultanate 131/3; Mughal conquest 171/1, 173/1; under British rule 234/1
Gulashkird (Alexandria)
Gulja (Kuldja)
Gumbinnen E Prussia × WW1 253/3
Gumma prefecture of C Japan 218/2, 243/1
Gümmenen C Switzerland Zähringen town 121/6
Gumu (Ku-mu)
Güns (*Hung.* Köszeg) Hungary Ottoman siege 170/1
Günük (Xanthus)
Gupta Empire India 83/1; destroyed by White Huns 95/1
Gurage region of NE Africa 239/1
Gurgan (*a/s* Gorgan *anc.* Hyrcania) city and region of N Persia Sasanian Empire 79/3; Muslim conquest 105/1
Gurjara-Pratiharas dynasty of N India 131/1
Guryev *Russ.* C Asia founded 163/1; industry 291/1
Gusev (Gumbinnen)
Guyana (*form.* British Guiana) S America 286-7; economy 295/1
Guyenne (*a/c* Aquitaine *anc.* Aquitania) region of SW France English possession 125/1; French Royal domain 151/4; province of France 193/1
Guyuan (Ku-yüan)
Gwadar (*f/s* Gwador) Pakistan Alexander's route 77/1; Alexander's Empire 82/3; ceded by Muscat 281/3
Gwalior former state of C India 234/1, 235/3
Gwynedd early Welsh principality 117/1, 125/1
Gyulafehérvár (Alba Iulia)
Haarlem Netherlands 16C urban development; 18C urban development 181/2
Habomai island of N Japan occupied by Russia, claimed by Japan 279/1
Hacilar W Anatolia site 41/1, 43/1
Hadar Ethiopia site of early man 33/1
Hadhramaut region of S Arabia Muslim expansion 105/1
Hadria C Italy Latin colony 87/1
Hadrumetum (*mod.* Sousse) Tunisia Phoenician city 74/1; Roman Empire 89/1
Ha-erh-pin (Harbin)
Haervej land route of Jutland, Denmark 116/2
Hafrsfjord S Norway × 117/1
Hafsids Muslim dynasty of Tunisia 135/1
Haåga E Sweden Megalithic site 42/2
Hagen W Germany industrial development 210/1
Hagi W Japan 174/4
Hagmatana (*a/c* Ecbatana) Persia 79/1
Haida coast Indian tribe of NW Canada 149/1
Hailar (*W/G* Hai-la-erh) Manchuria on railway 263/3
Hailufeng SE China Soviet under P'eng P'ai 263/3
Hainan *island* S China early trade 177/1; railway soviet 263/2; WW2 270-271
Hainaut (*Dut.* Henegouwen) district of Belgium under mediaeval German Empire 119/1, 125/1; Burgundian possession 151/3
Haiphong N Vietnam early trade 177/1; railway 232/2; Vietnamese war 292/4
Haithabu (Hedeby)
Haiti Toussaint l'Ouverture's revolt 202/1; French rule 205/3; independence 227/1; US intervention 247/4; political development 286-7; economy 295/1; See also **Hispaniola**
Hakodate city of N Japan 175/4, 243/1
Halab (Aleppo)
Halberstadt N Germany bishopric 117/1, 191/1
Halicarnassus (*mod.* Bodrum) W Anatolia Alexander's route 76/1; Byzantine Empire 113/1
Halidon Hill NE USA × 142/2
Halifax N England Industrial Revolution 201/1
Halifax E Canada British naval base 195/1; growth 219/3
Halin N Burma Hindu-Buddhist remains 133/2
Halland province of SW Sweden under Danish rule 116/2; regained from Denmark 188-9
Halle C Germany WW1 253/3; 275/2
Hallein-Dürnberg Austria La Tène site 85/1
Haller's Defeat NW USA × 221/4
Hallstatt Austria early site 35/1
Halwan Mesopotamia early archbishopric 101/1
Halys River C Anatolia × 79/1
Hama (Hamath)
Hamadan (*anc.* Ecbatana) W Persia trade 55/1; Mongol conquest 128/4, 135/1; Empire of Ghazni 130/2; Ottoman control 171/1
Hamamatsu C Japan 175/4
Haman's Defeat NE USA × 221/4
Hamath (*mod.* Hama) Syria site 67/3
Hamburg N Germany bishopric 101/2; bishopric 117/1; Hanseatic city 144/1; 16C urban development 180/1; 18C financial centre 181/2; industrial development 210/3, 212/1; German customs union 217/1; WW1 253/3; Communist uprising 258/2; WW2 273/3; city-state 275/2
Hamdanids Muslim dynasty of Syria 135/1
Ha-mi (Kumul)
Hamid early Turkoman principality of SW Anatolia 138-9
Hamilton C Canada growth 219/3
Hammadids Muslim dynasty of Algeria 135/1
Hamwic (*a/s* Hamwih *mod.* Southampton) 110/3, 111/1
Han NW China Western Chou domain 62/3; warring state 80/1; expansion 80/3; Empire 81/2, 95/1
Hana sub-arctic Indian tribe of Alaska, 149/1
Hanau W Germany × 205/1
Han-chung (*n/s* Hanzhong) C China Han commanderie 81/2
Handan (Han-tan)
Hang-chou (*n/s* Hangzhou *a/c* Hangchow) E China provincial capital 127/5, 169/1
Hangchow (*n/s* Hangzhou *W/G* Hang-chou) C China early trade 147/1, 154/2; captured by Kuomintang 262/1; industry 218/1, 263/3, 278/3
Hang Gon S Vietnam Iron Age site 132/1
Hangzhou (Hang-chou)
Hankow (*n/s* Hankou *W/G* Han-k'ou) C China industry 218/1; treaty town 232/2
Hannover (Hanover)
Hanoi (*form.* Thang Long) N Vietnam trade centre 177/1; Japanese occupation 268/2; 1945-75 war 292/4
Hanover (*Ger.* Hannover) former state of N Germany cession of Swedish territory 188-9; 191/4; industrial development 212/1; unification with Germany 216/3, 217/1; WW1 253/3; WW2 273/3; 275/2
Hanseatic League N Europe 144/1
Han-tan (*n/s* Handan) N China Late Chou site 63/4
Han-yang-hsiang C China Han prefecture 81/2
Hanzhong (Han-chung)
Hao C China Western Chou capital 62/3
Haraiva (*a/c* Aria) region of Afghanistan satrapy of Achaemenid Empire 79/1
Haran (Harran)
Harappa N India early urban settlement 52/1, 64/2, 65/1
Harauvatish (*a/c* Arachosia) region of C Afghanistan satrapy of Achaemenid Empire 79/1
Harbin (*W/G* Ha-erh-pin) Manchuria railway 230/2; Russian occupation 232/2; Russo-Japanese war 242/3; industry 263/3, 278/3
Hardaway N America site 47/1
Hare sub-arctic Indian tribe of NW Canada, 149/1
Harfleur N France 142/4
Härjedalen region of C Sweden 188-9
Harmozia (*later* Ormuz *or* Hormuz) S Persia Alexander's Empire 77/1, 82/3
Harran (*a/s* Haran *anc.* Carrhae) E Anatolia town of Persian Empire 79/1
Harris Bison Runs N America site 47/1
Hartalyangar N India site of early man 33/1
Hartlepool N England WW1 253/3
Harwich E England Industrial Revolution 201/1; WW1 253/3
Haryana state of N India 281/3
Hasa Ottoman province of E Arabia, 229/1; annexed by Arabia 253/4
Hasuike W Japan 174/4
Hassuna C Mesopotamia early settlement 41/1
Hatra (*mod.* Al Hadhr) Mesopotamia city state of Parthian Empire 78/3; Roman Empire 89/1
Hatten Germany La Tène site 85/1
Hattin Palestine × 134/3
Hattushash (*mod.* Boğazköy) C Anatolia early urban settlement 52/1; trade 54/1; Hittite Empire 57/1
Hausa States (*a/c* Hausaland) Nigeria 137/1, 167/1, 239/1
Havana (*Sp.* La Habana) Cuba imperial trade 158/1, 199/1; Spanish base captured by British 194/1
Havelberg N Germany bishopric 117/1
Havelte Holland Megalithic site 42/2
Hawaii state of USA income and population 289/2; military base 293/1 (inset)
Hawaiian Islands (*f/c* Sandwich islands) C Pacific early Polynesian settlement 49/1; annexed by US 247/1; war in the Pacific 271/1
Hawkes Bay province of N Island, New Zealand 236/1
Hay W England Industrial Revolution 201/1
Hebei (Hopeh)
Hebei Dong (Ho-pei Tung)
Hebei Xi (Ho-pei Hsi)
Hebrides (*form. Nor.* Sudreyar) Scandinavian settlement 110/1, 111/1
Hebron (*Ar.* Al Khalil) Palestine city of Judaea 102/2; disturbances under British mandate 261/2; West Bank 284/2
Hecatompylos (*a/c* Qumis) ancient city of Persia 71/1; Alexander's route 77/1
Hedeby (a/c Haithabu) N Germany Viking town 110/3, 116/2
Hedong (Ho-tung)
Hehe tribe of E Africa 239/1
Heidelberg S Germany Reformation 183/1
Heihe (Aigun)
Heijo (Pyongyang)
Heilong Jiang (Amur River)
Hei-lung Chiang (Amur River)
Hejaz (*Ar.* Hijaz) region of W Arabia centre of Islam 105/1; under Abbasid sovereignty 135/1; Ottoman sovereignty 229/1; Arab revolt in WW1 253/4
Helenopolis W Anatolia Byzantine Empire 113/1
Heliopolis (*mod.* Baalbek) Syria monastery 93/3
Heliopolis (*Bibl.* On) Lower Egypt 58/1; Alexander's route 76/1; conquered by Arabs 105/1
Hellespont (Dardanelles)
Hellespontine Phrygia country of NW Anatolia 76/1
Helluland Viking name of part of NE Canada 111/4
Helmantica (Salamantica)
Helsinki (*Sw.* Helsingfors) S Finland Swedish port 189/1; WW2 273/3
Helvetia (Swiss Confederation)
Helvetic Republic (*mod.* Switzerland) state under French protection 203/3, 204-5
Hembury SW England site 43/1
Hemeroscopium (*a/s* Hemeroskopeion) SE Spain Greek colony 75/1
Hemudu (Ho-mu-tu)
Henan (Honan)
Henegouwen (Hainaut)
Heng-yang (*n/s* Hengyang) SE China industry 263/3
Heptanesus (Ionian Islands)
Hepu (Ho-p'u)
Heraclea S Italy Roman Empire 87/1
Heraclea Pontica (*mod.* Ereğli) N Anatolia Greek colony 75/1
Heracleopolis Lower Egypt early urban settlement 52/1, 58/1
Heraeumteichos W Turkey Greek colony 75/1
Herat (*anc.* Alexandria Areion) C Persia town of Sasanian Empire 79/1; early archbishopric 101/1; Muslim conquest 105/1; early trade 135/1; Safavid conquest 171/1
Herculis Monoeci (Portus Herculis Monoeci)
Hereford W England bishopric 117/1; Industrial Revolution 201/1
Herero people of SW Africa 239/1
Heri NW France monastery 93/3
Hermopolis Egypt Roman Empire 89/1
Hermunduri western Germanic tribe 89/1
Hersfeld C Germany early city 119/1; 191/1
Herstal W Germany Frankish royal residence 106/3
Hertford S England Industrial Revolution 201/1
Heruli tribe of N Borders of Roman Empire 89/4
Herzegovina SE Europe Ottoman vassal state 139/1
Hesse (*Ger.* Hessen) Electorate and Duchy of N Germany 191/4; Reformation 183/1; unification with Germany 216/3, 217/1; 275/2
Hesse-Darmstadt Landgraviate of C Germany 191/1
Hesse-Kassel Landgraviate of C Germany 191/1; Reformation 182/2
Heuneburg Germany Hallstatt site 85/1
Hevelli early Slav tribe of Germany 118/3, 140/2
Hexham N England bishopric 100/3; × 185/1
Hexhamshire franchise of N England 142/2
Hibernia (*mod.* Ireland) Roman Empire 88/1, 90/1
Hidalgo province of C Mexico 227/1
Hieraconpolis Egypt 59/1
Hierapolis W Anatolia archbishopric 93/1
Hiero Sicily early kingdom 77/2
Hierosolyma (*Eng.* Jerusalem *Heb.* Yerushalayim *Ar.* Al Quds) Palestine Roman Empire 86/3, 89/1
Hiiumaa (Ösel)
Hijaz (Hejaz)
Hikone C Japan 175/4
Hildesheim N Germany bishopric 117/1, 191/1
Himachal Pradesh state of N India 281/3
Himeji W Japan 175/4, 242/1
Himera Sicily Greek colony 75/1; Roman Empire 86/2,3
Hims (Homs)
Hippo Dhiarrhytus (*a/s* Hippo Zarytus *mod.* Bizerta) Tunisia Phoenician city 74/1
Hipponium (*mod.* Vibo Valentia) S Italy Greek colony 75/1
Hippo Regius (*Sp.* Bona *Fr.* Bône *mod.* Annaba) Algeria Phoenician city 74/1; Roman Empire 89/1, 90/1; early bishopric 92/1
Hippo Zarytus (Hippo Dhiarrhytus)
Hirado W Japan 174/4
Hirah Mesopotamia early bishopric 101/1
Hirosaki N Japan 175/4
Hiroshima city and prefecture of W Japan 175/4, 242/1; bombed by US 271/2
Hirsau SW Germany monastery 107/3; centre of monastic reform 122/2
Hisai C Japan 175/4
Hispalis (*mod.* Seville) S Spain Roman Empire 88/1, 90/1; archbishopric 92/1
Hispania (*mod.* Spain and Portugal) Roman Empire 91/2
Hispania Citerior E Spain Roman province 86/3
Hispania Ulterior W Spain Roman province 86/3
Hispaniae Roman province 89/4
Hispaniola (*mod.* Dominican Republic *and* Haiti) island of West Indies early exploration 156/2; settled by French and Spanish 160/3; early trade 199/1
Hit Mesopotamia early trade 54/1
Hittite Empire Asia Minor 57/1
Hittites tribe of Asia Minor 54/3, 61/1, 67/3
Hjaltland (Shetland)
Hlučin (Hultschin)
Hobart Tasmania penal settlement 237/5
Ho Chi Minh Trail Vietnam/Laos 292/4
Höchstädt W Germany × 192/3
Hodeida (*Ar.* Al Hudaydah) Yemen early trade 135/1; Red Sea port 285/1
Hódmezövásárhely Hungary site 43/1
Ho-fei C China Han trade centre 81/2
Hoggar region of N Africa 45/1
Hogup Cave N America site 47/1
Hohenfriedeberg (*mod.* Dąbromierz) W Poland × 196/4
Hohenlinden S Germany × 205/1
Hohenlohe country of C Germany 191/1
Hojo clan territory of C Japan 168/4
Hokitika S Island, New Zealand founded 236/1
Hokkaido (*form.* Ezo *a/s* Yezo) N Island of Japan 218/2 (inset), industry 243/1
Hole-in-the-Wall C USA × 221/4
Holkar region of C India Maratha site 172/3; in alliance with Britain 194/2
Holkham E England agricultural revolution 201/2
Holland early settlement 42-43; Black Death 143/1; Burgundian possession 151/3; province of Dutch Republic 185/1; kingdom under French protection 204/2; WW1 252-3; inter-war alliances 268/1; WW2 269/5, 272-3. See also **Netherlands**
Hollandia (*n/c* Jayapura) N Guinea WW2 271/2
Holme C England Industrial Revolution 201/1
Holme's Bonfire North Sea English naval victory 185/1
Holstein region of N Germany mediaeval German Empire 119/1; under Danish rule 150/1; Reformation 183/1; in German Confederation 216/3
Holstein-Glückstadt former state of N Germany 191/1
Holstein-Gottorp former state of N Germany 191/1
Holt N England Industrial Revolution 201/1
Holyhead NW Wales port 201/1
Holy Roman Empire Mongol invasion 128/2; Black Death 143/1; reign of Charles V 150/1; Thirty Years War 182/2
Homestead Florida US Air Force base 293/6
Homildon Hill N England × 142/2
Homs (Emsea, Hims)
Ho-mu-tu (*n/s* Hemudu) N China early settlement 62/1
Honan (*n/s* Henan *W/G* Ho-nan) region of C China T'ang province 126/1; Ming province 168/2, 169/1; Nien rebels 233/1; Hsin-hai revolution 233/3
Hondschoote NE France × 203/2
Honduras country of C America early exploration 156/2; independence 227/1; political development 286-7; economy 294/1
Hong Kong acquired by Britain 232/2, 233/1; occupied by Japanese 268/2, 270/1; British colony and base 277/2, 279/1; trade and industry 218/1, 219/1, 263/3, 295/1
Hongdong (Hung-tung)
Hongnong (Hung-nung)
Hongzhao (Hung-chao)
Honjo N Japan 175/4
Honshu the main island of Japan 242-3
Hooghly (*Port.* Ugolim) E India Portuguese settlement 159/1, 173/1
Hopeh (*n/s* Hebei *W/G* Ho-pei) region of N China T'ang province 126/1
Ho-pei Hsi (*n/s* Hebei Xi) N China Sung province 127/5
Ho-pei Tung (*n/s* Hebei Dong) N China Sung province 127/5
Hopewell early Indian culture, USA, 46/3, 47/1
Hopi Indian tribe of SW USA 149/1
Ho-p'u (*n/s* Hepu) S China Han commanderie 81/2
Horákov Czechoslovakia Hallstatt site 85/1
Hormuz (*a/s* Ormuz *anc.* Harmozia) S Persia early trade 145/4
Horn, Cape S America first rounded 156/1
Horncastle N England rebellion 185/1; Industrial Revolution 201/1
Horseshoe Bend SE USA × 221/4
Hotan (Khotan)
Ho-t'ien (Khotan)
Hotin (Khotin)
Hottentots people of S Africa 238/3
Ho-tung (*n/s* Hedong) N China T'ang province 126/1; Sung province 127/5
Hou-ma (*n/s* Houma) N China Late Chou city site 63/4
Housesteads (Vercovicium)
Houston S USA industry 219/1, 289/1
Hov N Denmark Megalithic site 42/2
Hova early state of Madagascar 167/1
Hoya country of N Germany 191/1
Hoysalas dynasty of C India 131/3
Hradenín Czechoslovakia Hallstatt site 85/1
Hradiště Czechoslovakia La Tène site 85/1
Hrvatska (Croatia)
Hsi (*n/s* Xi) C China Western Chou domain 62/3
Hsia (*n/s* Xia) N China Late Chou city site 63/4
Hsia-hsiang (*n/s* Xiaxiang) NE China Han prefecture 81/2
Hsia-men (Amoy)
Hsi-an (*n/s* Xi'an *a/s* Sian) N China Western Chou site 62/3; Ming provincial capital 169/1; industry 278/3
Hsiang-chou (*n/s* Xiangzhou) C China T'ang prefecture 126/1
Hsiang-fen (*n/s* Xiangfen) N China Late Chou city site 63/4
Hsiang-yang (*n/s* Xiangyang) C China Han prefecture 81/2
Hsia-p'i (*n/s* Xiapi) NE China Han prefecture 81/1
Hsien (*n/s* Xian) C China Western Chou domain 62/3
Hsien-jen-tung (*n/s* Xianrendong) SE China early settlement 62/1
Hsien-pi (*n/s* Xianbi) tribe of NE Asia, invade China 95/1
Hsien-yang (*n/s* Xianyang) NW China Late Chou city site 63/4
Hsi-hsia (*n/s* Xixia) NW China Tangut kingdom 127/5
Hsi-lan (*Eng.* Ceylon) early Chinese trade 147/1
Hsin-chiang (Sinkiang)
Hsing (*n/s* Xing) N China Western Chou domain 62/3
Hsing-t'ai (*n/s* Xingtai) N China Shang city 62/2
Hsing-yüan (*n/s Xingyuan) NW China* Sung provincial capital 127/5
Hsi-ning (*n/s* Xining *a/s* Sining) NW China Ming military post 169/1
Hsin-kan (*n/s* Xingan) C China Han prefecture 81/2
Hsi-sha Chün-tao (Paracel Islands)
Hsiung-nu (*n/s* Xiongnu *a/s* Hiung-mi) tribe on northern borders of China 80/1,3: 95/1
Hsiu-t'u (*n/s* Xiulu) NW China Han prefecture 81/2
Hsü (*n/s* Xu) E China Western Chou domain 62/3
Hsüan-fu (*n/s* Xuantu) N China Ming frontier defence area 169/1
Hsüan-t'u (*n/s* Xuantu) NE China Han Commanderie 81/2
Hsü-i (*n/s* Xuyi) E China Han commanderie 81/2
Hsün (*n/s* Xun) N China Western Chou domain 62/3; Late Chou domain 63/4
Huai-nan (*n/s* Huainan) E China T'ang province 126/1
Huai-nan Hsi (*n/s* Huainan Xi) C China Sung province 127/5
Huai-nan Tung (*n/s* Huainan Dong) E China Sung province 127/5
Huai-yang (*n/s* Huaiyang) C China Western Chou site 62/3
Huamachuco Peru on Pizarro's route 158/3
Huamanga Peru on Pizarro's route 158/3
Huan E China Western Chou domain 62/3
Huancayo Peru on Pizarro's route 158/3
Huang C China Western Chou domain 62/3
Huang Ho (*n/s* Huang He *Eng.* Yellow River) Shang sites 62/2
Huaraz Peru on Pizarro's route 158/3
Huari Empire C Andes 47/1,5
Huastec Indian tribe of N Mexico 46/2, 149/1
Hua-yin (*n/s* Huayin) C China Han prefecture 81/2
Hubei (Hupeh)
Huddersfield N England Industrial Revolution 201/1
Hudson Bay N Canada exploration 156/1
Hudson's Bay Company N Canada 164/3
Hue S Vietnam 1945-75 war 292/4
Huelva SW Spain Civil War 268/3
Huichal Indian tribe of C Mexico 149/1
Hui-hsien (*n/s* Huixian) N China Shang cty 62/2
Hui-p'u (*n/s* Huipu) E China Han prefecture 81/2
Hu-kuang (*n/s* Huguang) C China Ming province 168/2, 169/1
Hull N England mediaeval trade 144/1; Industrial Revolution 201/1
Hu-lun-tao (*n/s* Hulundao) Manchuria Russo-Japanese war 242/3
Hu-meng (*n/s* Humeng) N China Han prefecture 81/2
Hunan (*W/G* Hu-nan) province of C China under the Ming 169/1; Manchu expansion 175/1; T'ai-p'ing advance 233/1; Hsin-hai revolution 233/3; under warlord control 262/2
Hun-ch'un (*n/s* Hunchun) NE China treaty port 232/2
Hungarians migration after WW1 265/3
Hungary conversion to Christianity 101/2; early kingdom 117/3, 141/1; Mongol invasion 128/2; mediaeval Christian state 138-9; Black Death 143/1; empire of Mathias Corvinus 150/1; acquired by Habsburgs 150/2; Reformation 183/1; under Ottoman control 170/1, 187/1; Habsburg-Ottoman frontier 197/3; movement for independence 202/1; short-lived Soviet Republic 258/2; independence after WW1 265/1; inter-war alliances 264/2, 268/1; economic and socio-political development 266/3, 267/2; Axis satellite 269/5; occupation of SE Czechoslovakia 269/4; WW2 272/3; Warsaw Pact and Comecon 275/3, 292/2; anti-Communist uprising 293/1; economy 295/1; 275/4. See also Austro-Hungarian Empire.
Hung-chao (*n/s* Hongzhao) N China Western Chou site 62/3
Hungnam N Korea 1950-53 war 292/3
Hung-nung (*n/s* Hongnong) C China Han prefecture 81/2
Hung-tung (*n/s* Hongdong) N China Late Chou city site 63/4
Huns tribe, invasion of Europe 94/1, 99/1
Hupeh (*n/s* Hubei *W/G* Hu-pei) province of C China palaeolithic site 62/1; under the Ming 169/1; Manchu

Huron–Kandy

expansion 175/1; T'ai-p'ing control 233/1; Hsin-hai revolution 233/3
Huron Indian tribe of NE Canada 149/1
Hurri country of ancient Near East 57/1
Hurrians people of Mesopotamia 54/3
Hydaspes Afghanistan × 79/1
Hyderbad (*f/c* Nizam's Dominions) former state of C India, 234/1, 235/3
Hyogo prefecture of W Japan 175/4, 218/2; industry 242/1
Hyrcania (*anc. Pers.* Varkana *mod.* Gorgan *a/s* Gurgan) region of N Persia Alexander's Empire 77/1; Achaemenid Empire 79/1; vassal state of Parthian Empire 79/3; on borders of Roman Empire 91/2
Iadera (*mod.* Zadar *It.* Zara) Yugoslavia Byzantine Empire 113/1
Iapyges ancient tribe of S Italy 86/2
Iaşi (Jassy)
Ibadan S Nigeria 239/1, 241/1
Ibaraki prefecture of C Japan 218/2; industry 243/1
Ibbenbüren N Germany industrial development 210/1
Iberia ancient country of Caucasus 79/3, 86/3, 113/3
Ibero-Celts early people of Spain 75/1
Ibiza Balearic Islands Spanish Civil War 268/3
Ibo people of Nigera, 167/1, 239/1, 241/1
Iboina tribe of N Madagascar 239/1
Iceland Norse settlement 111/1,4; joins Union of Kalmar 150/1; Reformation 182/1; independence from Denmark 264/1 (inset); NATO and EFTA 275/3; economy 295/1
Iceni ancient tribe of Britain 89/1
Ichang C China treaty town 232/2
I-ch'eng (*n/s* Yicheng) N China Western Chou site 62/3
I-chou (*n/s* Yizhou) SW China Han commanderie 81/2
Ichpaatun Mexico fortified site 148/2
Iconium (*mod.* Konya) C Anatolia early trade 52/1; Roman Empire 89/1, 91/1; early archbishopric 93/1; Jewish community 103/1;, Byzantine Empire 113/1
Icosium (*mod.* Algiers *Fr.* Alger *Sp.* Argel) Algeria Roman Empire 89/1
Iculisma (Angoulême)
Idaho state of W USA 1896 election 225/3; Depression 267/1; income and population 289/2
Idalium (*mod.* Dhali) Cyprus Phoenician city 75/1
Idfu (Edfu)
Idrisids Muslim dynasty of Morocco 108/1, 135/1
Ieper (Ypres)
Iesi (Aesis)
Ife Nigeria Iron Age site 45/1; bronze sculpture site 137/1, 167/1
Ifni region of NW Africa ceded to Morocco 276/2
Igbo-Ukwu Nigeria Iron Age site 45/1
Iguvium (*mod.* Gubbio) N Italy Roman Empire 87/1
I-hsün (*n/s* Yixun) Sinkiang Han expansion 80/3
Ilchester SW England Industrial Revolution 201/1
Ilebo (Port-Francqui)
Ile-de-France region of N France 125/1, 193/1
Ilerda (*mod.* Lérida) N Spain Roman Empire 86/3
Ileret E Africa site of early man 33/4
Ili region of C Asia Chinese protectorate 175/1; ceded to Russia 232/2
Ilici (*mod.* Elche) E Spain Roman Empire 88/1
I-ling (*n/s* Yiling) C China Han prefecture 81/2
Ilipa Spain × 86/3
Ilium (Troy)
Il-Khan Empire Persia 129/3, 138/1
Ilkhandis Mongol dynasty of Persia 135/1
Illahun Lower Egypt 58/1
Iliberris (*mod.* Elne) S France bishopric 92/1
Illinois state of C USA 19C politics 225/2,3; Depression 267/1; income and population 289/2
Illinois Indian tribe of C USA, 149/1
Illyria ancient country of Adriatic 76/1
Illyrian Provinces Adriatic under French protection 204-5
Illyrians ancient people of Adriatic 61/1, 75/1
Illyricum Roman province of Adriatic 86/3, 89/1, 91/2
Ilmen Slavs E Slav tribe 115/1
Ilorin early state of Nigeria 241/1
Ilva (*mod.* Elba) island of W Italy Etruscan city 75/1; Roman Empire 86/2, 87/1
Imagawa clan territory of C Japan 168/4
Imbangala early state of WC Africa 239/1
Imola C Italy member of 1167 League 117/1
Inca Empire Peru 149/3; 155/1; conquest by Spain 158/3
Inchon (*a/c* Chemulpo *Jap.* Jinsen) S Korea Russo-Japanese war 242/3; US landing in Korean war 292/3
India early urban centres 53/1; early civilisations 64-5; centre of Buddhism and Hinduism 73/1; invaded by Alexander 77/1; early empires 82-3; introduction of Christianity 101/1; spread of Islam 104/2; under Sultanate of Delhi 130/3; first seaborne European visit 157/1; Mughal Empire 171/1, 172-3; Anglo-French rivalry 194/2; trade 71/1, 147/1, 154/2, 161/1, 199/1; emigration to South Africa 209/1; industrialisation 218/1; under British rule 234-5, 245/1; anti-British uprisings 248/1, 261/1; Japanese support for independence movements 268/2; independence 277/2; partition 280-81; boundary dispute with China 281/3; languages 281/4; economy 294-295
Indiana state of C USA 19C politics 225/2,3; Depression 277/1; income and population 289/2
Indianapolis C USA industry 219/1
Indian Ocean early trade routes 146/1; European discovery 157/1; British control 245/2
Indo-Aryans early people of India 61/1
Indo-China French colony 245/1, 248/1, 261/1; occupied by Japanese 268/2, 271/1; 1945-75 war 292/4
Indo-European tribes movement 61/1
Indonesia (*form.* Dutch East Indies) independence 277/2, 279/1; economy 278/2, 294-295
Indore C India 235/3
Indus civilisation 61/1
Ingalik Arctic Indian tribe of Alaska, 149/1
Ingelheim W Germany Frankish royal residence 107/3
Ingermanland (*a/c* Ingria) region of Baltic Russia under Swedish rule 189/1
Ingombe Ilede early state of SC Africa 137/1
Ingria (Ingermanland)
I-ning (Kuldja)
Inner Mongolia N China Manchu expansion 175/1
Innsbruck Austria industrial development 212/1
Inönü W Turkey × 229/3
In Salah S Algeria occupied by French 241/1
Interamna (*mod.* Teramo) N Italy Roman Empire 87/1
Interior Provinces New Spain C America, 165/1
Invercargill S Island, New Zealand founded 236/1
Iona island of W Scotland monastery 93/3, 100/3, 101/2; Scandinavian settlement 111/1
Ionia ancient region of W Anatolia 74/3
Ionian Islands (anc. Heptanesus) W Greece occupied by France 203/3; occupied by Britain 205/1; ceded to Greece 215/2
Iowa state of NW USA 19C politics 225/2,3; Depression 267/1; income and population 289/2
Ipswich E England mediaeval trade 144/1; Industrial Revolution 201/1
Iraklion (Candia)
Iran (*f/c* Persia) economy 218/1; 285/1; WW2 272/1; Baghdad Pact 292/5, 293/1; economy 294-295; war with Iraq 284/1; oil 285
Iranian tribes 61/1
Iraq (*form.* Mesopotamia) under Abbasid sovereignty 135/1; conquered by Ottomans 171/1; British mandate 260/1; political disturbances 261/2; independence 277/2; war with Iran 284/1; Baghdad Pact 292/5, 293/1; oil 285
Ireland (*anc.* Hibernia *Ir.* Eire *a/c* Irish Republic) expansion of Christianity 100/3; Scandinavian settlement 110/2, 111/1, 117/1; English and Norman overlordship 125/1; Black Death 143/1; English kingdom 150/1; Reformation 183/1; invaded by Parliamentary forces 184/2; English control 185/1; attempted French invasion 194/3; revolt against England 202/1; trade and industry 180-81, 210/1; socio-political change 267/2; neutral in WW2 272/1; EEC 275/3; economy 295/1. See also Irish Free State
Irian Jaya (Dutch New Guinea, West Irian)
Irish Free State (1922-37 *since 1949* Republic of Ireland) 265/1
Irish Republic (Ireland)
Irkutsk Siberia founded 162/3; 203/2; industry 291/1
Iroquois Indian tribe of NE USA 149/1
Isandhlwana Zululand, SE Africa × 238/2
Isaura C Anatolia Byzantine Empire 112/3
Isauria C Anatolia district of Byzantine Empire 113/1
Isca (*mod.* Caerleon) S Wales Mithraic site 72/1; Roman Empire 88/1; 90/1
Isenburg county of C Germany 191/1
Isernia (Aesernia)
Isfahan (*f/s* Ispahan *properly* Esfahan) C Persia Alexander's Empire 82/3; early bishopric 101/1; Mongol conquest 128/4; Empire of Ghazni 130/2; early trade 135/1, 146/1, 154/2; 285/1
Ishikawa prefecture of C Japan 218/2, 242/1
Ishim Russ. C Asia founded 162/3
Isiro (Paulis)
Iskenderun (*Eng.* Alexandretta) E Turkey Ottoman trade 170/1; to Turkey 265/1
Islamabad capital of Pakistan 281/3
Island Arawak Indian tribe of the Caribbean 149/1
Island Carib Indian tribe of the Caribbean 149/1
Island No 10 C USA × 223/1
Ismail (*n/s* Izmail) SW Ukraine Ottoman control 170/1
Isonzo (*S. Cr.* Soča) *river* Italy-Yugoslavia battles of WW1 253/3
Ispahan (Isfahan)
Israel (*form. part of* Palestine) independence 277/2; war with Arab States 284/1; 285/2,4; 295/5; 293/5; economy 294-295
Issus E Anatolia × 76/1, 79/1
Istakhr SW Persia town of Sasanian Empire 79/3
Istanbul (*form.* Constantinople *anc.* Byzantium *Norse* Mikligard) W Turkey Ottoman Empire 139/1, 170/1, 229/1
Istria region of NW Yugoslavia Byzantine Empire 113/1; Habsburg acquisition 197/3; disputed between Italy and Yugoslavia 275/4
Istrus Bulgaria Greek colony 75/1
Italia Roman province of S Italy, 86/3, 89/1
Italian East Africa union of colonies, 277/1
Italians inter-war emigration to France 265/3
Italian Somaliland (*now S part of* Somalia) colony 218/1, 241/1, 245/1, 260/1, 269/4 (inset) 277/2
Italics early tribe of C Europe, 60/1
Italy early settlement 42-43; early peoples 86/2; Greek colonisaton 75/1; growth of Roman power 87/1; Visigothic and Ostrogothic invasion 99/1; conversion to Christianity 72/1; Saracen and Magyar invasions 111/1; in mediaeval German Empire 119/1; Norman kingdom in south 120/2; monastic reform 122/2; imperial expeditions 123/4,5; disunity 124/2; Black Death 143/1; peasant emancipation 178/1; states established by Revolutionary France 204/2; under Napoleon 204/1; industrial revolution 210/1, 212/1; unification 217/2; population growth 208/3,4; emigration 209/1,2; colonial empire 245/1; growth in armaments 250; WW1 253/3; overseas trade 256-7; Alpine tunnels and railways 257/2; inter-war alliances 264/2, 268/1; S Tyrol regained 265/1; socio-political devleopment 266/3, 267/2; expansion 1934-39 269/4; WW2 269/5, 272-3; territorial losses to Yugoslavia 274/1; NATO 275/3, 293/1; economy, 294-295
Itil N Caspian Khazar city 108/1; 115/1; 146/1
Itj-towy (El Lisht)
Ivanovo W Russia Russian Revolution 259/1; urban growth 290/3
Ivory Coast (*Fr.* Côte d'Ivoire) country of W Africa French colony 241/1, 244/1; independence 276/2; political development 283/1; economy 294-295
Ivuna early state of SE Africa 137/1
Iwate prefecture of N Japan 218/2; industry 243/1
Iwo Jima Japanese island of N Pacific WW2 271/2; US base 293/1 (inset)
Iximiché Guatemala Maya Kingdom 148/2
Ixtacmaxtitlan Mexico on Cortés' route 159/2
I-yang (*n/s* Yiyang) N China Late Chou site 63/4
Izhevsk C Russia Russian Revolution 259/1
Izmail (Ismail)
Izmir (*form.* Smyrna) W Turkey 229/3
Izmit (*anc.* Astacus *later* Nicomedia) W Anatolia Ottoman Empire 139/1
Iztapalapa Mexico on Cortés' route 159/2
Jablines N France Megalithic site 42/2
Jackson SE USA × 222/1
Jaffa (*anc.* Joppa *Ar.* Yafa *Heb.* Yafo) Palestine disturbances under British mandate 261/2
Jaffna N Ceylon Tamil stronghold 281/4
Jaipur E India 218/1, 235/3
Jajce Bosnia acquired by Ottomans 139/1
Jajnagar (*now* Orissa) region of E India 131/3
Jakarta (Batavia, Djakarta)
Jalapa Mexico on Cortés' route 159/2
Jalisco province of C Mexico 227/1
Jalula Mesopotamia × 78/3, 105/1
Jamaica island of West Indies captured from Spain 160/3; British colony 165/1, 227/1, 244/1; imperial trade 199/1; independence 277/2 (inset); economy 295/1
James Island Gambia, W Africa British settlement 166/1
Jamestown E USA × 164/3
Jammu and Kashmir native state of British India 235/2; disputed with Pakistan 280/1, 281/3
Jamshedpur NE India industry 235/3, 281/3
Jämtland old province of E Sweden acquired from Norway 188
Jankau (*n/s* Jankov) Bohemia × 182/2
Japan Buddhism and Shintoism 73/1; early empire 109/1; Chinese cultural influence 127/2; attacked by Mongols 129/1; early trade 145/4, 161/1; 15-16C civil war 168/4; invasion of Korea and China 169/1; period of isolation 175/4; emigration to USA 209/2; industrialisation 218/1,2; Russo-Japanese war 242/3; modern development 242-3, 266/3; British investment 245/1; US influence 246/1; in Great Depression 266/3; expansion in Asia 268/2; WW2 270-71; 278-9; US bases 293/1; economy 295/1
Jarmo N Mesopotamia early village 41/1
Jarrama C Spain Civil War 268/3
Jarrow N England monastery 100/3
Jarvis Island British island of C Pacific 277/2 (inset)
Jassy (*Rom.* Iaşi *Turk.* Yaş) NE Romania Ottoman attack 170/1; WW2 273/3
Jats people of N India, revolt against Mongols 173/1
Jauja Peru × 158/3
Java (*Indon.* Jawa) island of C Indonesia early man 33/1; early sites 132/1; Muslim expansion 129/1; spread of Buddhism and Hinduism 73/1, 133/3; Mongol expedition 129/1; early trade 147/1, 199/1; Dutch possession 245/1; anti-colonial rebellion 248/1, 261/1; WW2 270-271
Java Sea WW2 × 270/1
Jay Sasanian town 79/3
Jazira (Jezira)
Jebel Druze region of S Syria revolt against French mandate 261/2
Jebel Irhoud Morocco site of early man 33/1
Jedda (Jiddah, Jidda *early Chin.* Shih-ta) W Arabia Red Sea trade 135/1; early Chinese voyages 146/1; Portuguese exploration 147/2; Ottoman Empire 171/1
Jehol former province of Manchuria Boxer uprising 233/1; occupied by Japanese 262/2
Jemappes Belgium × 203/2
Jena E Germany × 205/1; WW1 253/3
Jenne (*Fr.* Djenné) W Africa town of Mali Empire 137/1; town of Masina state 239/1
Jenny Lind W USA mining site 220/1
Jericho (*Ar.* Ariha) Palestine site of early village 41/1; town of Judaea 102/2
Jersey City NE USA urban growth 208
Jerusalem (*anc.* Hierosolyma *Roman* Aelia Capitolina *Heb.* Yerushalayim *Ar.* Al Quds) Israel under Alexander 82/3; centre of Christianity 72/1; patriarchate 101/2; town of Judaea 102/2; early Jewish community 103/1; Muslim conquest 105/1; Byzantine Empire 112/2; Kingdom of 134/3; early trade 146/1; Ottoman Empire 139/1, 229/1; WW1 253/4; disturbances under British mandate 261/2; in Arab-Israeli conflict 285/2, (inset)
Jessore Bangladesh 281/3
Jewish AD Far E. USSR 290/2
Jews in USSR 290/4
Jeypore district of E India cession to Britain 172/3
Jezira (*a/s* Jazira) region of NE Syria under Abbasid sovereignty 135/1; disturbances under French mandate 261/2
Jhansi N India Indian Mutiny 234/1
Jia (Chia)
Jiamusi (Kiamusze)
Jiangling (Chiang-ling)
Jiangnan Dong (Chiang-nan Tung)
Jiangnan Dongdao (Chiang-nan Tung-tao)
Jiangnan Xidao (Chiang-nan Hsi-tao)
Jiangningfu (Chiang-ning-fu)
Jiangsu (Kiangsu)
Jiangxi (Kiangsi)
Jiangxia (Chiang-hsia)
Jiangxi'an (Chiang-hsi-an)
Jiangxi Nan (Chiang-hsi Nan)
Jiannan (Chien-nan)
Jianwei (Chien-wei)
Jianzhou (Chien-chou)
Jiao (Chiao)
Jiaohe (Chiao-ho)
Jiaoli (Chiao-li)
Jiaoxian (Kiaochow)
Jiaozhi (Chiao-chih)
Jibuti (Djibouti)
Jidda (Jedda)
Jih-le (*n/s Rile) NW China* Han prefecture 81/2
Jih-nan (*n/s* Rinan) N Indo-China Han commanderie 81/2
Jilin (Kirin)
Jimma early state of C Ethiopia 239/1
Jin (Chin)
Jinan (Tsinan)
Jincheng (Chin-ch'eng)
Jingdong Dong (Ching-tung Tung)
JingdongXi (Ching-tung Hsi)
Jinggang Shan (Ching-kang Shan)
Jinghu Bei (Ching-hu Pei)
Jinghu Nan (Ching-hu Nan)
Jingji (Ching-chi)
Jingjiang (Chinkiang)
Jingnan (Ching-nan)
Jingxi Bei (Ching-hsi Pei)
Jingxi Nan (Ching-hsi Nan)
Jingzhaofu (Ching-chao-fu)
Jinjiang (Kinkiang)
Jinsen (Inchon)
Jintian (Chin-t'ien)
Jinyang (Ching-yang)
Jinzhou (Chin-chou)
Jiruft Sasanian town 79/3
Jiuhua Shan (Chiu-hua Shan)
Jiuquan (Chiu-ch'üan)
Jiuzhang (Chiu-chang)
Jiuzhen (Chiu-chen)
Jivaro forest Indian tribe of S America 149/1
Jixi (Chi-hsi)
Jiyang (Chi-yang)
Jizhou (Chi-chou)
Jo (*n/s* Ruo) C China Western Chou domain 62/3
Jodphur NW India 218/1
Jogjakarta (*n/s* Yogyakarta) district of Java Dutch control 176/3
Johannesburg S Africa industry 218/1
Johore state of Malaya 176/4
Joppa (*mod.* Jaffa *Ar.* Yafa *Heb.* Yafo) Palestine Philistine city 75/1; early bishopric 93/1; town of Judaea 102/2
Jordan independence 277/2, 284/1; Middle East conflicts 285/2, 292/5, 293/1; economy 295/1. See also Transjordan
Jordhøj N Denmark Megalithic site 42/2
Juan-juan (*n/s* Ruanruan *a/c* Avars) tribe of N China 95/1
Judaea Palestine Roman province 89/1; independent Jewish state 102/2; Israeli settlements 285/2
Judeirjo-Daro N India Harappan site 65/1
Jui (*n/s* Rui) N China Western Chou domain 62/3
Jui-ch'eng (*n/s* Ruicheng) N China Late Chou city site 63/4
Jui-chin (*n/s* Ruijin *a/s* Juikin) S China centre of Kiangsu Soviet 263/3
Jülich duchy of W Germany 191/1
Juliomagus (Angers)
Julu (Chü-lu)
Jun (Chün)
Ju-nan (*n/s* Runan) C China Han commanderie, 81/2
Jun-chou (*n/s* Runzhou) E China T'ang prefecture 126/1
Junction City C USA cow town 220/1
Jund-i Shapur NW Persia early archbishopric 101/1
Juneau Alaska 246/3
Jung (*n/s* Rong) border people of NW China 63/4
Jung-yang (*n/s* Rongyang) C China Han prefecture 81/2
Juno Beach NW France invasion point 273/6
Jutes Germanic tribe, invasion of Britain 98/1
Jutland Denmark × 253/3
Juyan (Chü-yen)
Ju-yin (*n/s* Ruyin) C China Han prefecture 81/2
Juzjan N Persia province of Ghazni Empire 130/2
Kaarta early state of W Africa 167/1, 238/1
Kabah Mexico Maya site 46/2
Kabardino-Balkar ASSR Caucasus, 290/2
Kabul (*anc.* Ortospana) Afghanistan Achaemenid Empire 79/1; Parthian Empire 79/3; Alexander's Empire 82/1; Muslim conquest 105/1; Mongol conquest 128/4, 135/1, 171/1; Akbar's Empire 173/1
Kachin State N Burma 279/1, 281/3
Kadambas tribe of India 82/5
Kadiköy (Chalcedon)
Kaesong C Korea Russo-Japanese war 242/3
Kafa early state of C Ethiopia 239/1
Kaffa (*It.* Caffa *Turk.* Kefe *anc.* Theodosia *mod.* Feodosiya) Crimea Mongol conquest 128/4, 129/3; Ottoman administrative centre 170/1
Kafiristan region of Afghanistan Empire of Ghazni 130/2
Kagawa prefecture of W Japan 242/1
Kagoshima city and prefecture of W Japan 174/4, 218/2, 242/1
K'ai-feng (*n/s* Kaifeng) N China Sung capital 127/5; Ming provincial capital 169/1; industry 278/2
Kaingang Indian tribe of S Brazil 149/1
Kairouan Tunisia Muslim conquest 104/1; Mediterranean trade 134/1
Kakegawa C Japan 175/4
Kalanay C Philippines Iron Age site 132/1
Kalemie (Albertville)
Kalenberg duchy of N Germany 191/1
Kalenderberg Germany Hallstatt site 85/1
Kalgan (*n/s* Zhangjiakou *W/G* Chang-chia-k'ou) N China 232/2, 263/3
Kalgoorlie W Australia goldfield 237/5
Kalhu (Calah)
Kalibangan N India Harappan site 64/2, 65/1
Kalimantan (Borneo)
Kalinga region of E India 83/1, 130/2, 131/1
Kalinin (*until 1932* Tver) C Russia industry 291/1
Kaliningrad (*form.* Königsberg) W Russia industry 291/1, 292/2
Kalisz (*Ger.* Kalisch) C Poland 140/2
Kalka S Russia × 114/4, 128/1
Kalmyks (*Russ.* Kalmyki) tribe of C Asia 171/1; conquered by Russia 163/1
Kalmyk ASSR S Russia 290/2
Kalpi N India Indian Mutiny 234/1
Kaluga W Russia Russia Bolshevik seizure 259/1; industry 291/1
Kalumba E Africa Iron Age site 45/1
Kalundu S Africa Iron Age site 45/1
Kalyani C India Rashtrakuta capital 131/1
Kamarupa region of NE India under Guptas 82/5
Kamba tribe of E Africa, 239/1
Kamboja early kingdom of N India 83/2
Kamchadali native people of Kamchatka 162/3
Kamchatka territory of E Russia 162/3
Kamenets (*later* Kamenets-Podolskiy) Ukraine 115/1
Kamerun (Cameroon)
Kameyama C Japan 175/4
Kamień Pomorski (Cammin)
Kamina Zaire Congo crisis 282/2
Kaminaljuyú E Mexico Maya site 46/2
Kammin (*a/s* Cammin) NE Germany bishopric 191/1
Kamnama E Africa Iron Age site 45/1
Kampala Uganda Speke's jouney 238/2; taken by British 241/1; 283/1
Kampen Netherlands Hanseatic town 144/1
Kampuchea (Cambodia)
Kanaga (Luluabourg)
Kanagawa city and prefecture of C Japan 175/4, 218/2; industry 243/1
Kanara district of SW India ceded to Britain 172/3
Kanauj (*a/c* Kanyakubja) N India city and district of Delhi Sultanate, 131/3
Kanazawa city of C Japan 175/4, 242/1
Kan-chou (*n/s* Ganzhou) NW China early bishopric 101/1; state 126/3; Ming fronier defence area 169/1
Kandahar (*a/s* Qandahar *anc.* Alexandria Arachoton) Afghanistan trade 135/1; Tamil majority 281/4
Kandy Ceylon Buddhist site 73/1; Tamil majority 281/4

Kwangsi–Lucerne

Kwangsi (*n/s* Guangxi *W/G* Kuang-hsi) province of SW China Mesolithic sites 62/1; under Ming 168/2, 169/1; rebellion against Ch'ing 174/2; Manchu expansion 175/1; T'ai-p'ing rebellion 233/1; Hsin-hai revolution 233/3; warlords 262/1
Kwangtung (*n/s* Guangdong *W/G* Kuang-tung) province of S China Mesolithic sites 62/1; under Ming 168/2, 169/1; rebellion against Ch'ing 174/2; Manchu expansion 175/1; Hakka-Cantonese war 233/1; Hsin-hai revolution 233/3; autonomous 262/2
Kwantung Leased Territory NE China 243/2
Kwararafa early state of W Africa 137/1, 167/1
Kweichow (*n/s* Guizhou *W/G* Kuei-chou) province of SW China under Ming 168/2, 169/1; rebellion against Ch'ing 174/2; Manchu expansion 175/1; Miao tribal rising 233/1; Hsin-hai revolution 233/3; independent 262/2
Kwidzyn (Marienwerder)
Kyakhta S Siberia Russian trade with China 175/1
Kyongju S Korea Buddhist site 73/1
Kyoto C Japan Buddhist site 73/1; city and prefecture 175/4, 218/2; industry 242/1
Kypros (Cyprus)
Kyushu W Island of Japan 218/2, 242/1
Kzyl-Orda (*form.* Perovsk *earlier* Ak-Mechet) Russ. C Asia industry 291/1
Laang Spean Cambodia early site 132/1
Labici C Italy Latin colony 87/1
Labrador region of NE Canada rediscovered 156/1; to Newfoundland 219/3
Labuan N Borneo British colony 244/1 (inset)
Laccadive Islands (*n/c* Lakshadweep) SW India conversion to Islam 104/2; gained by British 194/2
Lacedaemon (*a/c* Sparta) S Greece Byzantine Empire 113/1
La Chaise W France site of early man 32/2
La Chapelle-aux-Saints C France site of early man 32/2
La Chaussée-Tirancourt N France Megalithic site 42/2
Laconia ancient country of S Greece, 74/3, 76/4
La Coruña (*Eng.* Corunna) NW Spain Civil War 268/3
Ladhiqiyah (Latakia)
Ladoga, Lake (*Russ.* Ladozhskoye Ozero) NW Russia waterway trade route 115/1
Ladrones (Marianas)
Lae SE New Guinea retaken by Allies 271/2
Laetolil E Africa site of early man 33/4
La Fère Champenoise NE France × 205/1
La Ferrassie S France site of early man 32/2
La Ferté-Bernard N France French Revolution 203/2
La Florida S Peru early site 47/1
La Forêt-le-Roi C France mediaeval *villeneuve* 121/7
La Forêt-Sainte-Croix C France mediaeval *villeneuve* 127/1
La Frebouchere NW France Megalithic site 42/2
Lagash (*a/c* Shipurla) ancient city of Mesopotamia, trade 55/1
Lagny C France mediaeval fair 120/1
La Goletta (*Fr.* La Goulette) Tunisia Spanish occupation 186/2
La Gorge Meillet N France La Tène site 84/1
Lagos S Portugal × 195/1
Lagos Nigeria Slave Coast 167/1; taken by British 239/1; British colony 245/1
La Goulette (La Goletta)
La Graufesengue (Condatomagus)
Laguna de los Cerros C Mexico Olmec site 46/2
La Habana (Havana)
La Halliade SW France Megalithic site 42/2
La Hogue English Channel Megalithic site 42/2; English naval victory 185/1
Lahore NW India in Delhi Sultanate 131/3; trade 172/3; 173/1; industry in British India 235/3; capital of Pakistan Punjab 281/3
Lake Albert W USA × 221/4
Lake Mungo Australia site of early man 33/1
Lake of the Woods (Fort Charles)
Lake Okeechobee SE USA × 221/4
Lakhnauti N India district of Delhi Sultanate 131/3
Lalibela Ethiopia monastery 100/1
La Madeleine C France site of early man 22/2
Lamaghan Afghanistan district of Ghazni Empire 130/2
Lamanai E Mexico Maya site 46/2, 148/2
Lambaesis (*mod.* Tazoult) Algeria Mithraic site 72/1; Roman Empire 89/1
Lampaka ancient country of NW India 83/1
Lampsacus (*mod.* Lâpseki) NW Anatolia Greek colony 75/1; early bishopric 93/1; Byzantine Empire 112/3
Lamu Kenya Muslim colony 137/1
Lamuts Siberian tribe 162/3
Lancarvan Wales monastery 93/3
Lanchow (*n/s* Lanzhou *W/G* Lan-chou) NW China early trade 71/1; T'ang prefecture 126/1; Sung provincial capital 127/5; industry 218/1, 263/3, 278/3
Landau W Germany gained by France 192/2; French Revolution 203/2
Langobardi early tribe of NW Germany 89/1. See also Lombards
Lang-t'an-tung (*n/s* Langtandong) E China site of early man 33/1
Languedoc region of S France French Royal domain 125/1, 151/4; province of France 193/1
Lanka (Ceylon)
L'Anse aux Meadows Newfoundland Norse colony 47/1
Lan-t'ien (*n/s* Lantian) C China prehistoric site 33/1; Late Chou site 62/3; Han prefecture 81/2
Lanzhou (Lanchow)
Laodicea (*mod.* Denizli) W Anatolia Roman Empire 89/1; one of seven churches of Asia 93/1; Jewish community 103/1; Byzantine Empire 112/3
Laodicea (*mod.* Latakia *Fr.* Lattaquié) Syria Byzantine Empire 112/3, 113/1
Laodicea in Media (Nehavend)
Laon N France bishopric 117/1; × 205/1
Laos country of SE Asia 133/2; kingdom of Luang Prabang 177/1; end of Chinese tributary status 232/2; French protectorate 261/1; independence 277/2, 279/1; Pathet Lao 292/4; economy 295/1
Lapland region of Swedish Empire 189/1
Lapps people of N Russia 101/2
Lâpseki (Lampsacus)
Lapurdum (Bayonne)
La Quina SW France site of early man 32/2
Larache Morocco Spanish colony 251/2
Laranda (Karaman)
Lardavif Wales bishopric 92/1
Larisa (*a/s* Larissa *Turk.* Yenişehir) C Greece archbishopric 93/1; Jewish community 103/1; Byzantine Empire 113/1,5
La Rochelle W France 16-17C revolts 185/1; commercial harbour 193/1; imperial trade 198-9
Larsa (*Bibl.* Ellasar) Mesopotamia trade 54/1; Amorite kingdom 55/2
Las Bela NW India Alexander's Empire 82/3
Las Haldas N Peru early site 47/1
Lashio E Burma WW2 270/2
Las Navas de Tolosa S Spain × 124/3, 134/1
La Starza S Italy early settlement 43/1
Latakia (*anc.* Laodicea *Fr.* Lattaquié *Ar.* Ladhiqiyah) Syria Mediterranean trade 135/1
La Tène E France site 84/1,3
Later Liang dynasty of N China 126/3
Latin America (America, South)
Latini early tribe of Italy, 86/2
Latin Way (Via Latina)
Lattaquié (Latakia)
Latvia country of the Baltic corn shipments 181/4; independence from Russia 259/1, 265/1; inter-war alliances 264/2, 268/1; socio-political change 267/2; WW2 272-3; annexed by Russia 269/5, 274/1; Soviet Socialist Republic 290/2, 292/2; 275/4
Latvians emigration from Russia 265/3; in USSR 290/4
Lauenburg principality of N Germany 191/1
Launceston W England 16C riots 185/1
Launceston Tasmania gold 237/5
Laupen W Switzerland Zähringen town 121/6; × 142/3
Laurentide ice-sheet N America 37/4
Lausanne Switzerland 1924 Conference 265/1
Lausitz (*Eng.* Lusatia) region of E Germany acqired by Poland 117/3
Lava Beds W USA × 221/4
Laval NW France 17C revolts 185/1
Lavan Island S Iran oil terminal 285/3
Lavenham E England rebellion against Henry VIII, 185/1
La Venta C Mexico Olmec site 46/2
Lavinium C Italy Roman Empire 87/1
Lazaret S France site of early man 32/2
Lazica early country of the Caucasus 113/1
Lebanon district of Ottoman Empire 229/1; French mandate 260/1; political disturbances 261/2; independence 277/2, 284/1; US landing 292/5; Middle East conflict 285/4, 293/1; economy 295/1
Lebda (Leptis Magna)
Lechfeld S Germany × 111/1, 118/3
Le Creusot C France industrial development 210/1, 212/1
Ledosus (*mod.* Lezoux) C France Roman Empire 90/1
Leeds N England industrial development 200/3, 201/1, 210/1
Leek C England Industrial Revolution 201/1
Leeward Islands West Indies British and French settlement 160/3
Leghorn (Livorno)
Legionum Urbs Wales early bishopric 92/1
Legnica (Liegnitz)
Le Havre N France trading port 180/3; forfitied naval port 193/1; French Revolution 203/2; industrial development 210/1, 212/1; WW2 273/6
Leicester (*anc.* Ratae) C England Scandinavian settlement 110/2, 111/1; Industrial Revolution 201/1
Leiden (Leyden)
Leinster province of SE Ireland early kingdom 117/1; conquered by Normans 125/1
Leipzig E Germany mediaeval fair 144/1; 18C financial centre 181/2; industrial development 210/1, 212/1; WW1 253/3; Communist insurrection 258/2
Leipzig (Battle of the Nations) E Germany × 205/1
Le Kef (Sicca Veneria)
Leling (Lo-ling)
Le Mans NW France bishopric 117/1; French Revolution 203/2; industrial development 210/1
Lemberg (*Pol.* Lwów *now* Lvov) N Austria-Hungary mediaeval trade 144/1; WW1 253/3; E Germany WW2 273/3
Lemnos island of the Aegean Byzantine naval victory 120/2; ceded to Greece 215/2
Le Moustier S France site of early man 32/2
Lenca Indian tribe of central America 149/1
Leng-hui NW China oilfield 278/3
Leninakan (*until 1924* Aleksandropol) Armenian SSR industry 291/1
Leningrad (*form.* St Petersburg *Russ.* Sankt-Peterburg, *between 1914 and 1923* Petrograd) NW Russia WW2 269/1, 273/3; urban growth 290/3; industry 291/1
Lens NE France WW1 253/3 (inset)
Lenzen N Germany × 118/3
León early kingdom of C Spain 124/3; city of N Spain, Civil War 268/3
Leontopolis N Egypt early Jewish community 103/1
Léopoldville (*now* Kinshasa) W Belgian Congo 282/2
Lepanto (*mod. Gr.* Navapaktos) C Greece × 170/1, 187/3
Leptis N Libya Stone Age site 45/1; Phoenician city 74/1
Leptis Magna (*a/s* Lepcis Magna *mod.* Lebda) N Libya Mithraic site 72/1; Carthaginian city 86/3; Roman Empire 89/1, 91/1; early bishopric 93/1
Le Puiset C France mediaeval *villeneuve* 121/7
Lérida (Ilerda)
Lerinum S France monastery 93/3
Lerna C Greece early site 67/1
Leros S Aegean WW2 273/3
Les Bolards C France Mithraic site 72/1
Lesbos (*mod. Gr.* Lesvos *a/c* Mytilene) island of E Aegean Greek parent state 75/1; acquired by Turks 151/1; ceded to Greece 215/2
Lesotho (*form.* Basutoland) S Africa independence 276/2; political development 283/1; economy 295/1
Letts people of Latvia, NW Russia 259/1
Leubuzzi Slav tribe of C Germany 140/2
Leucas (*mod. Gr.* Levkas *It.* Santa Maura) W Greece Greek colony 75/1
Leucecome early port of W Arabia 71/1
Leucos Limen Red Sea Roman Empire 91/1
Leuthen (*Pol.* Lutynia) SW Poland × 196/4
Leuven (*Fr.* Louvain) town of Sp. Netherlands 185/1
Leu Wiliang W Java early site 132/1
Levkandi E Greece early site 67/1
Levkas (*anc.* Leucas *It.* Santa Maura) W Greece Venetian fort 187/3
Lewes S England × 125/1
Lexington NE USA × 164/3
Leyden (*n/s* Leiden) Netherlands 16C urban development 180/1; 18C urban development 181/2
Leyte SE Philippines US landing 271/2
Lezetxiki N Spain site of early man 32/2
Lezoux (Ledosus)
Lhasa Tibet early trade 71/1; Buddhist site 73/1; seat of Lamaistic patriarch 175/1
Liang NW China Western Chou domain 62/3
Liang-che (*n/s* Liangzhe) E China Sung province 127/5
Liang-chou (*n/s* Liangzhou) NW China early state 126/3; Ming military post 169/1
Liao (Khitan)
Liao-hsi (*n/s* Liaoxi) NE China Han commanderie 81/2
Liao-tung (*n/s* Liaodong) NE China Ming frontier defence area 169/1
Libau (*Latv.* Liepāja) W Russia WW1 253/3; port of Latvian SSR 231/1
Liberia country of W Africa founded 238/1; independent state 240/2, 244/1, 276/1,2, 283/1; economy 295/1
Libya Arab conquest 104/1; under the Almohads 134/1; under Ottoman Empire 229/1; Italian colony 218/1, 240/2, 245/1, 260/1; anti-colonial rebellion 249/2; WW2 269/5, 272-3; independence 276/2; political development 283/1; US base 293/1; economy 295/1
Lichfield E England bishopric 117/1
Li-chou (*n/s* Lizhou) W China Sung province 127/5
Liège Belgium bishopric 117/1, 190/1; urban revolt 143/1; 16C urban development 180/1; 18C urban development 181/2; Prince-Bishop expelled 202/1; industrial development 210/1, 212/1; WW1 252-3
Liegnitz (*Pol.* Legnica) W Poland × 128/2, 196/4; Reformation 182/2; industrial development 211/1
Liepāja (*Ger.* Libau) Latvian SSR industry 291/1
Ligny Belgium × 205/1
Ligor S Thailand Hindu-Buddhist remains 133/2
Ligures early tribe of N Italy, 86/2
Liguria country of NW Italy 217/2
Ligurian Republic NW Italy state established by French Revolution 203/3
Lille NE France mediaeval fair 120/1, 144/1; 18C financial centre 181/2; gained by France 192/2; industrial development 193/1, 210/1; WW1 252/2, 253/3 (inset)
Lilybaeum (*mod.* Marsala) Sicily Phoenician city 75/1
Lima Peru early people 47/4; colonised 158/1, 165/1; imperial state 199/2; attack on 226/2
Limanowa N Austria-Hungary WW1 253/3
Limatambo C Andes Inca site 149/3
Limburg region of Belgium/Holland Burgundian possession 151/3; country 191/1
Limerick Ireland Scandinavian control 111/1;, 117/1
Limoges C France annexed to France 151/4; industrial development 193/1, 210/1
Limonum (Poitiers)
Limousin region of C France under English rule 125/1; French province 193/1
Li Muri Sardinia Megalithic site 42/2
Lincoln (*anc.* Lindum) E England Danish Viking base 110/2, 111/1; rebellion against Henry VIII 185/1; Industrial Revolution 201/1
Lindisfarne (*a/c* Holy Island) N England monastery 100/3, 101/2; Viking attack 111/1
Lindum (*mod.* Lincoln) E England Roman Empire 83/1, 90/1; bishopric 92/1
Ling N China Ming prefecture 169/1
Lingen district of NW Germany Burgundian possession 151/3; country 191/1
Ling-fang (*n/s* Lingfang) S China Han prefecture 81/2
Ling-ling (*n/s* Lingling) S China Han commanderie 81/2
Ling-nan (*n/s* Lingnan) S China T'ang province 126/1
Ling-yüan (*n/s* Lingyuan) NE China Western Chou site 62/3
Lin-t'ao (*n/s* Lintao) NW China Han prefecture 81/2
Lin-t'ung (*n/s* Lintong) NW China Late Chou city site 63/4
Lin-tzu (*n/s* Linzi) NE China Late Chou city site 63/4; Han trade centre 81/2
Linyanti S Africa on Livingstone's route 238/2
Linz Austria mediaeval fair 144/1; WW2 273/3
Lipara (*n/s* Lipari) island of S Italy early settlement 43/1; 74/4
Lippe country of N Germany Reformation 182/2; 191/1, 216/3
Lisala Zaire Congo crisis 282/2
Lisbon (*Port.* Lisboa *anc.* Olisipo) Portugal Muslim conquest 104/1; early trade 145/4, 147/2, 154/2; colonial trade 159/1, 198-9; trading port 180/3; 16C and 18C financial centre 180/1, 181/2; × 204/1
Liscuis N France Megalithic site 42/2
Lismore S Ireland Scandinavian settlement 111/1
Lissa (*S.Cr.* Vis) C Adriatic × 217/2
Listem C Ukraine × 115/1
Liternum C Italy Roman colony 87/1
Lithuania country of NW USSR conversion to Christianity 101/2; Christian empire 138/2; early expansion 141/1; Black Death 143/1; empire of Casimir IV 151/1; acquired by Russia 163/1; corn shipments 181/4; Reformation 183/1; independence 259/1, 265/1; inter-war alliances 264/3, 268/1; socio-political change 267/2; loses Memel territory to Germany 269/4; WW2 272-3; retaken by Russia 269/4, 275/1; Soviet Socialist Republic 290/2, 292/2; 275/4
Lithuanians (*earlier* Litva) people of N Europe 98/3; emigration from Russia 265/3; in USSR 290/4
Little Armenia early Christian state of S Anatolia 138/2
Little Big Horn N USA × 221/4
Littlehampton S England Industrial Revolution 201/1
Little Poland 117/3
Little Preslav Bulgaria early settlement 112/4
Litva (*mod.* Lithuanians) people of NW Russian border 115/1
Liu C China Western Chou domain 62/3
Liu-ch'eng (*n/s* Liucheng) NE China Han prefecture 81/2
Liverpool N England trading port 180/3; imperial trade 198-9; industrial development 201/1, 210/1, 212/1; WW2 269/5
Livonia region of E Baltic occupied by Teutonic Knights 140-1, 151/1; conquered by Russia 163/1; Reformation 183/1; under Swedish rule 189/1
Livonian Order NW Russia 115/1
Livorno (*obs. Eng.* Leghorn) C Italy 18C financial centre 181/2; WW2 273/3
Lixus (*mod.* Larache) Morocco Roman Empire 88/1
Li-yang (*n/s* Liyang) E China Han prefecture 81/2
Lizhou (Li-chou)
Ljubljana (Emona)
Llangollen N Wales Industrial Revolution 201/1
Llantwit Wales monastery 93/3
Lo C China Western Chou domain 62/3
Lobositz (*mod.* Lovosice) Bohemia × 196/4
Locarno Switzerland 1925 Conference 265/1
Loch Garman (Wexford)
Lochhill SW Scotland Megalithic site 42/2
Locri Epizephyrii S Italy Greek colony 75/1, 86/2
Locris W Greece parent state 75/1
Lodi N Italy Lombard League 119/3; Signorial domain 124/2; × 205/1
Lodomeria (Vladimir) region of W Ukraine acquired by Habsburgs 197/3
Lodz (*Pol.* Łódź) Poland industrial development 211/1, 213/1; in Russia 231/1; urban growth 231/1; WW1 253/3
Logan's Fort NE USA × 221/4
Lohumjo-Daro N India Harappan site 65/1
Lo-i (*n/s* Luoyi) N China Western Chou capital 62/3
Lokoja Nigeria taken by British 241/1
Lo-lan Sinkiang Han prefecture 80/3
Lo-lang N Korea Han commanderie 81/2
Lo-ling (*n/s* Leling) NE China Han prefecture 81/2
Lombards early tribe of S Germany 89/4, 99/1. See also Langobardi
Lombardy region of N Italy kingdom under Frankish dominion 107/3; under mediaeval German Empire 119/1, 123/4,5; mediaeval trade 120/1; 124/2; acquired by Habsburgs 150/2; unification of Italy 217/2
Lonato N Italy × 205/1
Londinium (*mod.* London) S England Mithraic site 72/1; Roman Empire 88/1, 90/1; bishopric 92/1
London (*anc.* Londinium) S England bishopric 100/3, 117/1; urban unrest 143/1; Hansa trading post 144/1; mediaeval trade 145/3; trade and industry 16C and 18C 180-81; in Civil War 184/2; 1641 riots 185/1; imperial trade 198-9; industrial development 200/3, 201/1, 210/1, 212/1; WW1 253/3; in Depression 267/2; WW2 269/5, 273/3
London C Canada growth 219/3
Longreach E Australia railway 237/5
Longwy NE France fort 203/2
Longxi (Lung-hsi)
Longxingfu (Lung-hsing-fu)
Longyu (Lung-yu)
Longzhou (Lungchow)
Loochoo Islands (Ryukyu Islands)
Lookout Mountain S USA × 223/1
Loos NE France WW1 253/3 (inset)
Lopera S Spain Civil War 268/3
Lord Howe Island W Pacific Australian possession 277/2 (inset)
Lorient NW France 193/1
Lorraine (*a/c* Lotharingia *Ger.* Lothringen) region of NE France Magyar invasions 111/1; part of mediaeval German Empire 118-9; conflict of Church and state 123/3; Black Death 143/1, 150/2; Burgundian possession 151/3; German duchy 191/1; Holy Roman Empire 193/1; German Empire 216/3; WW1 252/2
Lorsch W Germany monastery 107/3
Los Angeles W USA foundation 165/1; industry 289/1; urban development 289/3
Los Millares S Spain site 43/1, 52/1
Lostwithiel SW England × 184/2
Lothagam E Africa site of early man 33/4
Lothal N India early urban settlement 53/1; Harappan site 65/1
Lotharingia (Lorraine)
Lothringen (Lorraine)
Lötschberg Switzerland tunnel 257/2
Loudoun Hill C Scotland × 142/2
Loughborough C England Industrial Revolution 201/1
Louhans E France French Revolution 203/2
Louisbourg Nova Scotia captured by British 195/1
Louisiana region of C North America French rule 160/3, 161/2, 165/1, 205/3; Spanish rule 164/3; purchased by USA 220/3
Louisiana state of S USA Civil War 223/1,3; 19C politics 225/2,3; Depression 267/1; income and population 289/2
Lou-lan (*n/s* Loulan) NW China early trade 71/2
Lourenço Marques (Maputo)
Louth E England rebellion against Henry VIII 185/1: Industrial Revolution 201/1
Louth Ireland bishopric 92/1
Louvain (Leuven)
Lovewell's Fight NE USA × 221/4
Lovosice (*Ger.* Lobositz) Czechoslovakia Hallstatt site 85/1
Lower Burma annexed by British 234/2
Lower California province of N Mexico 227/1
Lower Ob Gasfield N Siberia 291/1
Lower Palatinate W Germany Reformation 182/2
Lower Saxony (*Ger.* Niedersachsen) region of West Germany 275/2
Lowestoft E England English naval victory 185/1; WW1 253/3
Lo-yang (*n/s* Luoyang) N China Shang city 62/2; Chou site 62/3; 63/4; early trade 71/1; Han prefecture 81/2; sacked by Hsiung-nu 95/1; T'ang city 126/1; industry 278/3
Lozi tribe of C Africa, 239/1
Lu E China Chou domain 62/3, 63/4; Han prefecture 81/2
Lü C China Western Chou domain 62/3
Luanda Angola early trade 159/1; Portuguese settlement 167/1, 239/1, 241/1
Luango early state of W Africa 167/1, 239/1
Luang Prabang SE Asia early political centre 133/2; kingdom 177/1
Luba people of C Africa 137/1, 167/1, 239/1
Lubaantún E Mexico Maya site 46/2
Lübeck N Germany urban revolt 143/1; Hanseatic city 144/1; 16C urban development 180/1; Reformation 183/1; bishopric 191/1; WW1 253/3; WW2 273/3
Lublin Poland mediaeval fair 144/1; WW1 253/3
Lubumbashi (Elisabethville)
Lubusi S Africa Iron Age site 45/1
Lucani early people of S Italy 86/2
Lucania region of S Italy kingdom of Naples 124/2
Lucca N Italy Republican commune 124/2; independent republic 150/1, 187/1, 203/3
Lucerne (*Ger.* Luzern) early Swiss canton 142/3

Pinsk–Riom

Pinsk W Russia town of Turov-Pinsk 115/1; WW1 253/3
Piombino N Italy Mediterranean trade 144/1; French rule 205/1
Piqillacta C Andes early site 47/5
Pirna E Germany × 196/4
Piro forest Indian tribe of S America 149/1
Pisa (*anc.* Pisae) N Italy mediaeval city 119/1; Mediterranean trade 120/1, 134/1, 146/1; raids and conquests 120/2; Republican commune 124/2; 150/1
Pisae (*mod.* Pisa) N Italy Roman Empire 87/1, 89/1; bishopric 92/1
Pisaurum (*mod.* Pesaro) N Italy Roman colony 87/1
Piscataway Fort NE USA × 221/4
Pishpek (Frunze)
Pisidia ancient country of C Anatolia 76/1, 113/1
Pistoia (*anc.* Pistoriae) N Italy Roman Empire 87/1; mediaeval city 119/1
Pitcairn Island C Pacific British colony 277/2 (inset)
Pithecusa S Italy Greek colony 75/1
Pit River W USA × 221/4
Pittsburgh E USA industry 219/1
Pittsburg Landing (Shiloh)
Pityus Caucasus Greek colony 75/1; early bishopric 93/1
Placentia (*mod.* Piacenza) N Italy Latin colony 87/1
Plassey E India × 172/3, 19/2 (inset)
Plataea C Greece × 74/3, 78/1
Plate River (*Sp.* Rio de la Plata) Argentina explored 156/1
Platěnice Czechoslovakia Hallstatt site 85/1
Plevna (*now* Pleven) Bulgaria WW1 253/3
Pliska Bulgaria early city 108/1
Pločnik S Yugoslavia early settlement 43/1
Ploeşti (*n/s* Ploieşti) Romania WW2 273/3
Plovdiv (Philippopolis)
Plymouth SW England naval base 195/1; Industrial Revolution 201/1; WW1 253/3; WW2 269/5
Plymouth NE USA founded 161/2
Plzeň (Pilsen)
Poço da Gateira S Portugal Megalithic site 42/2
Podolia region of S Ukraine acquired by Lithuania 141/1
Poduca S India early port 71/1
Poetovio (*mod.* Ptuj *Ger.* Pettau) N Yugoslavia Mithraic site 72/1; Roman Empire 89/1; early bishopric 93/1
Po-hai (*n/s* Bohai *Kor.* Parhae *mod.* Manchuria) NE China early state 127/2
Pohang S Korea 1950-53 war 292/3
Point of Rocks C USA × 221/4
Poitiers (*anc.* Limonum) C France × 104/1, 125/1; × 142/4; monastery 106/3; 17C revolts 185/1; seat of intendant 193/1; centre of French Revolution 203/2
Poitou region of W France English possession 125/1; French Royal domain 151/4; province of France 193/1
Pola (*mod.* Pula) N Yugoslavia Roman Empire 89/1; WW1 253/3
Polabii Slavic tribe of N Germany 118/3, 140/2
Poland conversion to Christianity 101/2; under Boleslav Chrobry 117/3; Mongol invasion 128/2; union with Lithuania 141/1; Black Death 143/1; Empire of Casimir IV 151/1; acquired by Russia 163/1; agriculture and peasant emancipation 178/1; Reformation 183/1; Baltic trade 189/1; Partitions 196/1; 197/5; revolt against Russia 202/1; industry under Russian rule 231/1; independence after WW1 259/1, 265/1; socio-political development 266/3, 267/2; WW2 269/5; Warsaw Pact and Comecon 275/3, 292/2; anti-Communist uprising 293/1; economy 294-295; 275/4
Poles post-WW1 migration to Poland 265/3; post-WW2 migration to West 274/1
Polish Corridor 265/1
Polochanye NW Russia E Slav tribe 115/1
Polotsk W Russia bishopric 101/2; early city and principality 115/1; Hanseatic trading post 144/1
Polovtsy (*a/c* Cumans) tribe of C Russia 114-5
Poltava Ukraine town of Pereyaslavl 115/1; industry and urban growth 231/1; Bolshevik seizure 259/1
Poltoratsk (Ashkhabad)
Polyane Slav tribe of the Ukraine, 115/1
Polynesia island group of C Pacific early settlement 49/1
Pomerania (*Ger.* Pommern *Pol.* Pomorze) region of N Europe acquired by Poland 117/3; mediaeval German Empire 119/1; Black Death 143/1; Reformation 183/1; unification of Germany 216/3; 275/2
Pomerania, East part of Germany 191/1
Pomerania, Swedish 196/4; ceded to Prussia 215/3
Pomerania, West to Sweden 188-9, 191/1,4
Pomeranians Slav tribe of N Europe 140/2
Pomerelia (*Ger.* Pommerellen) region of N Europe occupied by Teutonic Knights 140/3
Pomo Indian tribe of NW USA 149/1
Pompeii S Italy Jewish community 103/1
Pompeiopolis S Anatolia Roman Empire 89/1
Pondicherry (*Fr.* Pondichéry) SE India French settlement 161/1, 173/1; captured by British 194/2 (inset); imperial trade 199/1; French enclave 235/3; returned to India 277/2
Pondo region of SE Africa British administration 238/3
Pons Saravi E France Mithraic site 72/1
Ponthieu region of NE France Frankish royal residence 106/3; under English rule 125/1; Burgundian possession 151/3
Pontia (Ponza)
Pontiae (*a/c* Pontine Islands *mod.* Isole Ponziane) C Italy Roman Empire 87/1
Pontianak W Borneo Dutch settlement 177/1
Pontine Islands (Pontiae)
Pontnewydd N Wales early man 32/2
Pontus district of N Anatolia 77/3; Roman province 86/3, 89/4; Byzantine Empire 113/1
Ponza (Pontia) *island* C Italy Mithraic site 72/1
Ponziane, Isole (Pontiae)
Poona W India industry 218/1, 235/3
Populonia N Italy Etruscan city 75/1, 86/2
Porolissensis Roman province of E Europe 89/1
Porolissum Romania Roman Empire 89/1
Portage la Prairie (Fort La Reine)
Port Arthur (*Chin.* Lüshun *Jap.* Ryojun) Manchuria ceded to Russia and Japan 230/2, 232/2, Russo-Japanese war 242/3; 263/3
Port Arthur (*now* Thunder Bay) C Canada growth 219/3
Port Arthur Tasmania penal settlement 237/5
Port Augusta S Australia settlement 237/5
Port Chalmers S Island, New Zealand 236/1
Port Elizabeth SE Africa British settlement 238/3
Port Essington N Australia founded 237/5
Port-Francqui (*now* Ilebo) C Belgian Congo 282/2
Port Hedland W Australia early settlement 237/5
Port Hudson S USA × 222/1
Port Jackson (Sydney)
Portland S England WW1 253/3
Portland SE Australia founded 237/5
Port Lincoln S Australia settlement 237/5
Port Macquarie SE Australia penal settlement 237/5
Port Moresby SE New Guinea Allied base in WW2 271/1
Portobello Panama port 199/1
Porto Novo SE India × 194/2
Porto-Novo W Africa French settlement 239/1
Porto Pisano N Italy Mediterranean trade 144/1
Port Pirie S Australia settlement 237/5
Port Royal Jamaica British naval base 194/1
Port Said N Egypt Egyptian-Israeli war 285/2
Portsmouth S England naval base 195/1; Industrial Revolution 201/1; WW1 253/3
Portsmouth NE USA settlement 161/2
Portugal (*anc.* Lusitania) early settlement 42-43; Jewish migration 102/3; Muslim conquest 104/1; reconquest 124/3; voyages of discovery 147/2, 150/1,2; 156-7; expansion overseas 158-9; annexed to Spain 186/1; agriculture 179/1; trade and industry 180-81, 198-9; population growth 208/3,4; emigration 209/1; railway development 212/1; colonial empire 245/1; 19C alliances 250-51; WW1 252/1; inter-war alliances 264/2; general strike 267/2; NATO and EEC 275/3, 274/2; US bases 293/1; economy 294-295
Portuguese East Africa (*now* Mozambique) 245/1
Portuguese Guinea (*now* Guinea-Bissau) W Africa Portuguese colony 240/2, 244/1, 276/1; independence 276/2
Portuguese Timor E Indies annexed by Indonesia 277/2, 279/1
Portus Herculis Monoeci (*a/c* Herculis Monoeci *mod.* Monaco) S France Greek colony 75/1
Porus early kingdom of NW India 77/1
Poseidonia (*later* Paestum *mod.* Pesto) S Italy Greek colony 75/1
Posen (*Pol.* Poznań) W Poland mediaeval fair 144/1; industrial development 211/1; North German Confederation 216/3; WW1 253/3; ceded by Germany 265/1
Potaissa Romania Roman Empire 91/1
Potawatomi Indian tribe of C USA 149/1
Potentia (*mod.* Potenza) N Italy Roman colony 87/1
Potidaea N Greece Dorian colony 75/1
Potosí Peru Spanish silver mine 158/1
Potsdam E Germany 275/2
Poverty Point N America site 47/1
Powhatan Indian tribe of E USA 149/1
Pozsony (Bratislava)
Poznań (*Ger.* Posen) W Poland bishopric 117/3; 141/1
Pozzuoli (Puteoli)
Praeneste (*mod.* Palestrina) C Italy Roman Empire, 87/1
Prague (*Cz.* Praha) Czechoslovakia bishopric 101/2, 117/3; mediaeval trade 120/1; Hanseatic trade 144/1; 16C urban development 180/1; × 196/4; industrial development 210/1, 213/1; communist coup 292/2
Praia das Maçãs C Portugal burial site 43/1
Prambanan C Java Hindu-Buddhist temple 133/2
Pratiharas early dynasty of N India 130/2
Pravdinsk (Friedland)
Preah Vihear district of Cambodia claimed by Thailand 279/1
Preanger district of Java Dutch control 176/3
Předmostí Czechoslovakia site of early man 32/2
Preslav Bulgaria early city 108/1
Pressburg (*mod.* Bratislava) 111/1
Preston N England × 184/1; Industrial Revolution 201/1
Prestonpans S Scotland Industrial Revolution 200/3
Pretoria S Africa on Boer trek 238/3
Preussen (Prussia)
Preussisch-Eylau (Eylau)
Preveza C Greece × 170/1; Venetian fort 187/3
Prilep S Yugoslavia mediaeval fair 144/1
Primorskiy Kray (Maritime Province)
Prince Edward Island (St. Jean)
Prince's Town Ghana early French settlement 166/1 (inset)
Principe *island* W Africa Portuguese settlement 167/1, 241/1
Prizren Serbia WW1 253/3
Procolitia (*mod.* Carrawburgh) N Britain Mithraic site 72/1
Prome C Burma Buddhist site 73/1
Provence region of S France Frankish Empire 106/1,3; mediaeval German Empire 119/1, 125/1; Arabs expelled 120/2; annexed to France 151/4; province of France 193/1
Providence NE USA founded 161/2
Provins C France mediaeval fair 120/1
Prusa (*mod.* Bursa) W Anatolia Byzantine Empire 113/1
Prussia (*Ger.* Preussen) region of E Germany conquest by Teutonic Knights 140/3; Reformation 183/1; Baltic trade 189/1; rise of 190/3; Duchy 191/1; Kingdom 191/4; conquests in Europe 196/1,4; 197/1; opposition to Napoleon 204-5; unification of Germany 216-7
Przemyśl Austria-Hungary WW1 253/3
Pskov W Russia town of Novgorod Empire 115/1, 163/1; Hanseatic trading post 144/1; acquired by Muscovy 151/1; Russian Revolution 259/1
Pteria (*mod.* Boğazköy) C Anatolia × 79/1
Ptolemais Egypt Roman Empire 89/1
Ptolemais (*mod.* Tulmaythah *It.* Tolmeta) Libya Roman Empire 89/1, 91/1; early archbishopric 93/1
Ptolemais (*Eng.* Acre *mod.* 'Akko) Palestine early archbishopric 93/1
Ptuj (Poetovio)
Puebla C Mexico early Spanish city 158/1; province 227/1
Pueblo Indian tribe of SW USA 149/1; 46/3
Pueblo Bonito N America site 47/1
Puelche Indian tribe of Argentina 149/1
Puerto Rico W Indies Spanish settlement 160/3; imperial trade 199/1; conquered by US 227/1, 247/4
Puig Roig NE Spain Megalithic site 42/2
Pukow (*n/s* Pukou *W/G* P'u-k'ou) E China British influence 232/2
Pula (Pola)
Pulicat SE India Dutch settlement 173/1
Pumbedita Mesopotamia early Jewish community 103/1
Pundra region of E India 83/1
Punjab region of NW India Muslim expansion 105/1; limit of Abbasid sovereignty 135/1; state of British India 235/3; partition between India and Pakistan 281/1, 282/3; water dispute with Haryana 281/3
Puri district of NE India cession to Britain 172/3
Purushkhaddum early town of C Anatolia 54/1
Pusan (*Jap.* Fusan) S Korea Russo-Japanese war 242/3; 1950-53 war 292/2
P'u-shan (*n/s* Pushan) Sinkiang Han expansion 80/3
Pushkari W USSR site of early man 32/2
Putaya Libya satrapy of Achaemenid Empire 78/1
Puteoli (*mod.* Pozzuoli) C Italy Roman colony 87/1; Roman Empire 91/1; early bishopric 93/1
P'u-t'o Shan (*n/s* Putuo Shan) *mountain* E China Buddhist site 73/1
Pyatigorsk Caucasus 163/1
Pydna C Greece × 77/3; Roman Empire 86/3
Pygmies people of C Africa 35/2
Pylos (*a/s* Pilos *It.* Navarino) SW Greece Mycenaean palace site 66/1
Pyongyang (*Jap.* Heijo) N Korea Russo-Japanese war 242/3; 1950-53 war 292/3
Pyramid Lake W USA × 221/4
Pyrgi C Italy Roman colony 87/1
Pyu S Burma Buddhist kingdom 127/2
Qadi Burhaneddi Turcoman principality of C Anatolia 138/2
Qandahar (Kandahar)
Qarabagh region of the Caucasus conquered by Ottomans 171/1
Qarakhanids (*a/s* Karakhanids) Muslim dynasty of Central Asia 135/1
Qarqan (Ch'ieh-mo)
Qatar sheikhdom of Persian Gulf 229/1, 285/3, 295/1
Qatif E Arabia oilfield 285/3
Qatna Syria Amorite kingdom 55/2
Qi (Ch'i)
Qiancheng (Ch'ien-ch'eng)
Qiang (Ch'iang)
Qiantong (Ch'ien-t'ang)
Qianzhong (Ch'ien-chung)
Qichun (Ch'i-ch'un)
Qiemo (Ch'ieh-mo)
Qin (Ch'in)
Qinfeng (Ch'in-feng)
Qingdao (Tsingtao)
Qinghai (Tsinghai)
Qingjiang (Ch'ing-chiang)
Qingzhou (Ch'ing-chou)
Qiongzhou (Ch'iung-chou)
Qiqihar (Tsitsihar)
Quadi Germanic tribe 89/1
Quanterness N Scotland Megalithic site 42/2
Quanzhou (Ch'üan-chou)
Quebec city, E Canada capital of New France 161/2; captured by British 194/1
Quebec province, E Canada 164/5; joins Confederation 244/1; economic development 219/3
Quechua Andean Indian tribe of S America, 149/1
Queen Adelaide Province SE Africa 238/3
Queensland state of NE Australia 237/5; 244/1 (inset)
Quelimane Mozambique Portuguese settlement 167/1, 239/2, 241/1
Quemoy (*W/G* Chin-men) *island* SE China Nationalist outpost 279/1, 293/1
Quentovic (*a/s* Quentowic) N France 110/3
Querétaro state of C Mexico 227/1
Quetta Pakistan 235/3, 281/3
Quiberon Bay W France × 195/1
Quierzy N France Frankish royal residence 106/3
Quillon S India early trade 147/1
Quimper NW France bishopric 117/1
Qui Nhon S Vietnam 1945-75 war 292/4
Quiriguá E Mexico Maya site 46/2
Quito Ecuador Inca Empire 148/3; colonised 158/1, 165/1
Qumis (*a/c* Hecatompylos) city of Parthian Empire 79/3
Qunaytirah SW Syria Arab-Israeli war 285/2
Qusou (Ch'ü-sou)
Rabat Morocco early trade 136/2; French occupation 251/2
Rabaul Papua New Guinea Japanese base in WW2 271/1
Rabbath Ammon (Amman)
Rabih's State C Africa 241/1
Radimichi W Russia E Slav tribe 115/1
Rafah (*anc.* Raphia) Sinai Egyptian-Israeli war 285/2
Raffles Bay N Australia settlement 237/1
Rages (Rai)
Ragusa (*now* Dubrovnik) W Yugoslavia Byzantine Empire 113/5; Venetian conquest 120/2, 139/1; in Reformation 183/1; Ottman vassal republic 187/1; under French rule 205/1
Rai (*anc.* Rhagae *Bibl.* Rages *Gr.* Europus) N Persia early archbishopric 101/1; Muslim conquest 105/1; Mongol conquest 128/4; early trade 135/1
Rainy Lake (Fort Pierre)
Rajasthan (*form.* Rajputana Agency) state of N India 281/3
Rajputana region of NW India Muslim expansion 104/2; Mughal conquest 171/1; in alliance with Britain 194/2
Rajputana Agency (*now* Rajasthan) state of British India 235/3
Rajput Confederacy NW India 130/4
Rajputs people of NW India, 173/1
Raleigh E USA Civil War × 223/1
Ram Hormizd W Persia town of Sasanian Empire 79/3
Ramillies Belgium × 192/3
Ramla Palestine × 105/1
Ramsbury S England bishopric 117/1
Ramsey E England Industrial Revolution 201/1
Ramshög S Sweden Megalithic site 42/2
Randelia E Anatolia Roman Empire 89/1
Rangiriri N Island, New Zealand × 236/1
Rangoon (*anc.* Dagon) Burma Buddhist site 73/1; early trade centre 177/1; industry 235/3; WW2 270/1; 271/2; capital of independent state 281/3
Rangpur NW India Harappan site 65/1
Ranians E Germany Slavonic tribe 140/2
Rann of Kutch region of W India boundary dispute with Pakistan 280/1, 281/3
Rapallo N Italy 1922 Conference 265/1
Raphanea Syria Roman Empire 91/1
Raphia (*mod.* Rafah) N Sinai Roman Empire 86/3
Raqqa (*anc.* Nicephorium) Syria 139/1
Ras al Khaimah United Arab Emirates Persian Gulf 285/3
Ras el-'Amiya C Mesopotamia early settlement 41/1
Ras Hafun Somalia Muslim colony 137/1
Rashtrakutas dynasty of C India 130/2, 131/1
Ras Shamra (*anc.* Ugarit) Syria early village 41/1; early trade 66/4; destroyed 67/3
Ras Tanura E Arabia oil terminal 285/3
Rasulids Muslim dynasty of SW Arabia 135/1
Ratae (*mod.* Leicester) C England Roman Empire 88/1
Ratiaria Bulgaria early archbishopric 93/1
Ratisbon (*Ger.* Regensburg) S Germany × 205/1
Ravenna N Italy Roman Empire 91/1; early archbishopric 93/1; 107/3; Byzantine occupation 99/1; exarchate 113/1; captured by Venice 120/2; mediaeval city 124/2
Ravensberg N Germany Burgundian possession 151/3; county 190/3, 191/1
Ravensbrück N Germany concentration camp 272/1
Raynham E England agrarian revolution 201/2
Reading S England Industrial Revolution 201/1
Reate (*mod.* Rieti) N Italy Roman Empire 87/1
Rechitsa W Russia town of Turov-Pinsk 115/1
Recife (Pernambuco)
Recuay early people of C Andes 47/4
Redarii N Germany Slav tribe 11/3, 140/2
Redwood Ferry E USA × 221/4
Regensburg (*anc.* Casra Regina *obs. Eng.* Ratisbon) S Germany bishopric 100/3, 191/1; Frankish royal residence 107/3; 120/1
Reggio (*a/c* Reggio di Calabria *anc.* Rhegium) S Italy Norman conquest 120/2; Ottoman siege 170/1
Reggio (*a/c* Reggio Emilia *anc.* Regium Lepidum) N Italy Republican commune 124/2
Regina C Canada growth 219/3
Regium Lepidum (Reggio Emilia)
Reichenau S Germany monastery 107/3
Reii S France early bishopric 92/1
Reims (Rheims)
Remedello N Italy burial site 43/1
Remi (*mod.* Rheims) N France early bishopric 92/1
Remojadas C Mexico early site 46/2
Rennes NW France bishopric 117/1; 17C revolt 185/1; French Revolution 203/2
Rethel NE France independent fief 151/4
Réunion (*form.* Bourbon) *island* Indan Ocean French colony 205/3, 245/1
Reval (*Russ.* Revel *mod. Est.* Tallinn) E Baltic German colonisation 140/3, Hanseatic city 144/1; Swedish Empire 189/1; Russian Empire 231/1; Russian Revolution 259/1
Rewardashur Persia early archbishopric 93/1, 101/1
Rhaeti early tribe of N Italy 86/2
Rhaetia (*mod.* Switzerland) Roman province 89/1; Frankish Empire 106/1
Rhagae (*Per.* Rai *Bibl.* Rages *Gr.* Europus) N Persia Alexander's Empire 77/1, 79/1; early trade 82/4
Rhambacia NW India early trade 82/4
Rhegium (*mod.* Reggio di Calabria) N Italy Greek colony 75/1; Roman Empire 87/1, 89/1, 91/1
Rheims (*Fr.* Reims *anc.* Durocortorum *later* Remi) N France sacked by Vandals 99/1; archbishopric 106/3, 117/1; French Revolution 203/2; × 205/1; industrial development 210/1; WW1 252-3; WW2 273/3
Rheinheim Germany La Tène site 84/1
Rheinland (Rhineland)
Rhenish Prussia W Germany unification of Germany 216/3
Rhesaenae E Anatolia Roman Empire 91/1
Rhine, Confederation of the Napoleonic creation 191/4, 204/2, 205/1
Rhineland (*Ger.* Rheinland) region of W Germany 18C industrial growth 190/2; remilitarised 265/1, 269/4
Rhineland Palatinate (*Ger.* Rheinland-Pfalz) region of NW Germany 275/2
Rhode Island state of NE USA colony 161/2, 164/3; 19C politics 224/1, 225/2,3; Depression 267/1; income and population 289/2
Rhodes (*mod. Gr.* Rodhos *Lat.* Rhodus *It.* Rodi) *island* SE Aegean Greek state 75/1, 77/2,3; archbishopric 93/1; × 105/1; under Knights of St John 139/1; Ottoman conquest 170/1; gained by Turks 187/1. See also Dodecanese
Rhodesia (*form.* Southern Rhodesia *n/c* Zimbabwe) Matabele/Mashona revolt 249/2; independence (UDI) 276/2; 283/1; economy 295/1. See also Zimbabwe
Rhodus (*mod. Gr.* Rodhos *Eng.* Rhodes) *island* SE Aegean Roman Empire 86/3, 89/1, 91/1
Riade C Germany × 117/1
Ribe Denmark bishopric 101/2, 116/2
Rich Bar W USA mining site 220/1
Richmond N England rebellion against Henry VIII 185/1
Richmond E USA burned 223/1; industry 219/1
Ricken Switzerland tunnel 257/2
Ricomagus (Riom)
Rieti (Reate)
Rif mountain region of Morocco resistance to French 260/1
Riga Latvia, NW USSR founded by Teutonic Knights 140/3; Hanseatic city 144/1; early trade 146/1; early bishopric 101/2; Swedish Empire 189/1; Russian Empire 231/1; urban growth 231/1; short-lived Communist control 258/2; WW2 272-3; industry 291/1
Rijeka (Fiume)
Rijkholt S Holland Megalithic site 42/2
Rile (Jih-le)
Rimini (*anc.* Ariminum) N Italy Lombard League 119/1; Signorial domination 124/2; WW2 273/3
Rinaldone C Italy early settlement 43/1
Rinan (Jih-nan)
Rio Barbate Spain × 104/1
Rio de Janeiro Brazil colonised 165/1; imperial trade 199/1; industry 219/1; state 227/1
Rio de la Plata (*mod.* Argentina) early Spanish colony 165/1; vice-royalty in rebellion against Spain 202/1
Rio de Oro (*later* Spanish Sahara *now* Western Sahara) NW Africa Spanish colony 240/1,2, 244/1, 260/1
Rio Grande do Norte state of N Brazil Confederation of the Equator 227/1
Rio Grande do Sul state of S Brazil 227/1
Riom (*anc.* Ricomagus) C France seat of intendant 193/1

Soviet Union–Tazoult

Soviet Union (USSR)
Sowerby Bridge N England Industrial Revolution 201/1
Soweto S Africa 283/1
Sozopol (Apollonia)
Spa Belgium 1920 Conference 265/1
Spain (*anc.* Hispania) early settlement 42-43; Celtic penetration 84/3; early invasions 98/1; conversion to Christianity 72/1, 92-3, 101/2; Jewish migrations 102/1; Muslim conquest 104/1; Umayyad caliphate 108/1; Reconquista 124/3; south under Almohads 134/1; Union of Castile and Aragon 150/1; Habsburg possession 150/2; voyages of discovery 157/1; overseas expansion 158-9; overseas settlements 160-1, 168-9; colonisation of America 194-5; imperial trade 158/1, 198-9; Ottoman attack 170/1; Reformation 183/1; expansion in Europe 186/1; expansion in the Maghreb 186/2; War of the Spanish Succession 192/3; opposition to Napoleon 202/1, 204/1; agriculture and society 178-9; trade and industry 180-81, 210/1, 212/1; population growth and emigration 208-9; colonial empire 245/1; 19C alliances 250/51; overseas trade 256-7; 20C socio-political change 267/2; Civil War 268/3; joins EEC 275/3; US bases 293/1; economy 295/1
Spalato (*anc.* Spalatum *mod.* Split) Yugoslavia Byzantine Empire 113/1; Venetian fort 187/3; WW1 253/3
Spalding E England Industrial Revolution 201/1
Spalding's Mission NW USA 220/1
Spanish Guinea (*now* Equatorial Guinea) W Africa colony 244/1 (inset)
Spanish March Frankish Empire 106/3
Spanish Morocco NW Africa incorporated into Morocco 276/1
Spanish Road W Europe Habsburg military road 150/2
Spanish Sahara (*a/c* Western Sahara *includes* Rio de Oro) NW Africa Spanish colony 241/1; partition between Morocco and Mauritania 276/2, 283/1; economy 218/1, 295/1
Sparda (*Lat.* Lydia) region of W Anatolia satrapy of Achaemenid Empire 78/1
Sparta (*a/c* Lacedaemon) S Greece Mycenaean palace site 67/1; Peloponnesian War 74/4; Roman Empire 86/3; 91/1; Jewish community 103/1
Spartalos N Greece × 74/4
Spasinou Charax Mesopotamia town of Achaemenid Empire 79/1
Speyer (*Eng.* Spires *anc.* Civitas Nemetum) W Germany bishopric 117/1
Sphacteria S Greece × 74/4
Spice Islands (*mod.* Moluccas *Dut.* Molukken *Indon.* Maluku) E Indies early trade 161/1
Spiennes N France Megalithic site 42/2
Spires (Speyer)
Spirit Cave N Siam early site 132/1
Spiro C USA early site 46/3
Split (Spalato)
Spokane House NW USA fur station 220/1
Spoletium (*mod.* Spoleto) N Italy Latin colony 87/1; Dukedom 113/1
Spotsylvania E USA × 223/1
Spy Belgium site of early man 32/2
Sredets (*now* Sofia *anc.* Serdica) Bulgaria Slav settlement 112/4
Sredne-Kolymsk NE Siberia founded 162/3
Srem (Syrmia)
Sri Ksetra S Burma Hindu-Buddhist remains 133/2
Sri Lanka (*a/c* Ceylon) economy 295/1
Srinagar N India capital of Kashmir 235/3, 281/3
Srivijaya E Indies early empire 133/2
Ssu-ch'uan (Szechwan)
Ssu-mao (Szemao)
Stabroek (*now* Georgetown) Guyana Dutch settlement 160/3
Stafford C England Industrial Revolution 201/1
Stalin (Varna)
Stalinabad (Dushanbe)
Stalingrad (*until 1925* Tsaritsyn *since 1961* Volograd) S Russia WW2 273/3,4
Stalino (Donetsk)
Stalinogorsk (Novomoskovksiy)
Stalinsk (Novokuznetsk)
Stamford C England Scandinavian settlement 110/2, 111/1; Industrial Revolution 201/1
Stanleyville (*now* Kisangani) S Belgian Congo Congo crisis 282/2
Staraya Ladoga (*Norse* Aldeigjuborg) N Russia Viking trade 110/3, 111/1
Starčevo Yugoslavia early site 43/1
Stargard E Germany Hanseatic trade 144/1
Staroselye S USSR site of early man 32/2
Stato dei Presidi C Italy Spanish Habsburg territory 187/1
Stavanger S Norway WW2 269/5
Stavelot NE France early city 119/1
Stavropol (*1940-44* Voroshilovsk) S Russia industry 231/1
Stavropol C Russia (Tolyatti)
Stębark (Tannenberg)
Steiermark (Styria)
Steinheim Germany site of early man 32/2
Steptoe Butte NW USA × 221/4
Sterkfontein S Africa site of early man 33/4
Stettin (*now* Szczecin) N Poland Hanseatic city 144/1; Swedish Empire 188-9; WW1 253/3; WW2 273/3
Steyr Austria industrial development 210/1, 212/1
Stična Yugoslavia Hallstatt site 85/1
Stillman's Defeat N USA × 221/4
Stirling Bridge C Scotland × 142/2
Stobi S Yugoslavia Roman Empire 89/1; early archbishopric 93/1; Jewish community 103/1
Stockholm Sweden Hanseatic city 144/1; 18C urban development 181/2; in Swedish Empire 188-9
Stockport N England Industrial Revolution 200/3, 201/1
Stockstadt W Germany Mithraic site 72/1
Stoke-on-Trent C England Industrial Revolution 200/3, 201/1
Stonehenge S England early site 52/1
Stone Tower S Asia trading route 71/2
Stony Lake N USA × 221/4
Stourbridge W England mediaeval fair 144/1; Industrial Revolution 201/1
Stowmarket England Industrial Revolution 201/1
Stralsund N Germany founded 140/2; Hanseatic city 144/1
Strasbourg (*Ger.* Strassburg *anc.* Argentoratum) E France French Revolution 203/2; industrial development 210/1
Strassburg (*Fr.* Strasbourg) SW Germany royal mint 118/3; early mediaeval settlement 121/3; on Emperor's travels 118/2; mediaeval fair 144/1; 18C urban development 181/2; Reformation 183/1; gained by France 192/2; bishopric 191/1; WW1 253/3; 275/2
Stratford-on-Avon C England Industrial Revolution 201/1
Strathclyde N Britain mediaeval kingdom 100/3, 117/1
Stratonicea W Anatolia Roman Empire 89/1
Stresa N Italy 1935 Conference 265/1
Stupava Czechoslovakia La Tène site 85/1
Stuttgart S Germany industrial development 210/1, 212/1; WW1 253/3; 275/2
Stutthof (*now Pol.* Sztutowo) NE Germany concentration camp 272/1
Styria (*Ger.* Steiermark) province of SE Austria mediaeval German Empire 118-9; acquired by Habsburgs 141/1, 150/1,2; 197/3; Duchy 191/1
Suakin E Sudan Ottoman settlement 167/1, 170/1; occupied by Egypt 239/1
Suceava (Suczawa)
Su-chou NW China Ming military post 169/1
Su-chou (Soochow)
Suczawa (*n/s* Suceava) Romania under Ottoman control 139/1, 170/1
Sudan region of N Africa 239/1
Sudan (*form.* Anglo-Egyptian Sudan) Mahdist state 241/1, 248-9; British control 229/1; Anglo-Egyptian condominium 241/1, 260/1; independence 276/2; civil war 283/1; economy 218/1, 294-295
Sudan, Western W Africa invaded by Morocco 166/1
Sudbury E England revolt against Henry VIII 185/1; Industrial Revolution 201/1
Sudbury NE USA × 221/4
Sudetenland C Europe German annexation 269/4
Sudr Sinai oilfield 285/3
Sudreyjar (*mod.* Hebrides) islands of NW Scotland under Earldom of Orkney 117/1
Suebi (Sueves)
Suessa Aurunca (*mod.* Sessa Aurunca) C Italy Latin colony 87/1
Sueves (*Lat.* Suebi) early tribe of SW Europe 98-9
Suez (*Ar.* As Suways) N Egypt Ottoman port 170/1; Egyptian-Israeli war 285/2
Suez Canal N Egypt opening 239/1, 257/1; Egyptian-Israeli war 285/2; WW1 253/4; Anglo-French attack 283/1
Sugambri early tribe of NW Europe 89/1
Suguda (*a/c* Sogdia *or* Sogdiana) C Asia satrapy of Achaemenid Empire 79/1
Suhar E Arabia Muslim conquest 105/1
Sui C China Western Chou domain 62/3
Sui-fen (*n/s* Suifen) NE China treaty port 232/2
Suiyuan former province of N China 262/2
Sukhothai C Thailand Buddhist site 73/1; major political centre 133/2
Sukhum-Kale (*mod.* Sukhumi *anc.* Dioscurias) Caucasus conquered by Russia 163/1
Sukumu tribe of E Africa 239/1
Sulawesi (Celebes)
Sulmo (*mod.* Sulmona) C Italy Roman Empire 87/1
Sumatra (*Indon.* Sumatera) E Indies spread of Buddhism 73/1; Muslim expansion 104/3, 133/3; early sites 132/1; early trade 147/1, 176-7, 199/1; Dutch possession 245/1; anti-colonial war 248/1; WW2 270-271
Sumerians ancient people of Mesopotamia 54/3
Sumpu (*now* Shizuoka) C Japan 175/4
Sunda Kalapa (*mod.* Jakarta) Java Islamic town 133/3
Sunderland NE England Industrial Revolution 201/1
Sung (*n/s* Song) N China Chou domain 62/3, 63/4; warring state 80/1
Sung-chiang (Sungkiang)
Sung-chou (*n/s* Songzhou) C China T'ang prefecture 126/1
Sung Empire China 127/5; conquered by Mongols 129/1
Sungir C USSR site of early man 32/2
Sungkiang (*n/s* Songjiang *W/G* Sung-chiang) E China British attack 233/1
Suomussalmi C Finland WW2 269/5
Sura Syria Jewish community 103/1
Surabaya (*Dut.* Soerabaia) Java trading centre 177/1
Surakarta district of Java Dutch control 176/3
Surasena early kingdom of N India 83/2
Surashtra early state of W India 82-3
Surat NW India Mughal port 161/1; Ottoman siege 171/1; trade 147/1, 199/1; industry 235/3
Surgut W Siberia founded 162/3
Surinam (*Dut.* Suriname *form.* Dutch Guiana) country of S America 286-7; economy 295/1
Susa SW Persia early urban settlement 52/1; Assyrian Empire 57/1,2; early trade 55/1, 71/1; Alexander's route 77/1; Persian Royal Road 79/1
Susiana (*a/c* Elam *mod.* Khuzistan) region of SW Persia province of Alexander's Empire 77/1, 82/3
Susquehannock Indian tribe of NE USA 149/1
Sussex early kingdom of S England 100/3
Sutkagen-Dor NW India Harappan site 65/1
Sutrium N Italy Latin colony 87/1
Suvar E Russia early town 115/1
Suzhou (Soochow)
Suzdal C Russia town of Vladimir-Suzdal 115/1
Sverdlovsk (*until 1924* Yekaterinburg) C Russia urban growth 290/3; industry 291/1
Sveta Lucija Yugoslavia Hallstatt site 85/1
Swabia (*Ger.* Schwaben) region of S Germany Magyar invasions 111/1; province of mediaeval German Empire 117/1, 118-9, 123/4,5
Swakopmund SW Africa German settlement 241/1
Swanscombe England site of early man 32/2
Swansea S Wales Industrial Revolution 201/1
Swartkrans S Africa site of early man 33/4
Swatow (*W/G* Shan-t'ou) S China treaty port 232/2; industry 263/3; Japanese occupation 268/2
Swazi tribe of SE Africa 238/3, 239/1
Swaziland country of SE Africa British protectorate 240/2, 245/1; independence 277/2, 283/1; economy 295/1
Sweden conversion to Christianity 101/2; Viking expansion 111/1; emergence as a state 117/1; Black Death 143/1; Union of Kalmar 150/1; Thirty Years War 182/2; Reformation 183/1; empire in the Baltic 188-9; losses to Russia and Prussia 196/1; population and emigration 208-9; industry 180-81, 211/1; customs union 211/3, 213/1; loss of Denmark and Norway 215/3; 20C economic and socio-political development 266/3, 267/2; EFTA 275/3; economy 295/1
Swift Creek/Santa Rosa Group early Indians of USA 46/3
Swindon W England Industrial Revolution 201/1
Swiss Confederaton (*a/c* Helvetia) formation 142/3; agriculture and peasant emancipation 178/1
Switzerland early settlement 42/2; Zähringen towns 121/6; mediaeval cantons 150/1; Reformation 183/1; Industrial Revolution 210/1, 212/1; neutral in WW1 253/3; Alpine tunnels and railways 257/2; socio-political change 267/2: EFTA 275/3; economy 295/1; neutral in WW2 269/5, 272-3. See also Swiss Confederation
Sword Beach NW France Allied invasion point 273/6
Sybaris S Italy Greek colony 75/1, 86/2
Sycae S Anatolia Byzantine Empire 112/3
Sydney (*form.* Port Jackson) SE Australia founded 237/5; industry 218/1
Sydney Nova Scotia growth 219/3
Syene (*mod.* Aswan) Upper Egypt 59/1
Syktyvkar (*until 1930* Ust-Sysolsk) N Russia industry 291/1
Sylhet district of Bengal votes to join Pakistan 280/2
Synnada W Anatolia early archbishopric 93/1; Byzantine Empire 112/3
Syracusa (*a/s* Syracusae *mod.* Siracusa *Eng.* Syracuse) Sicily Greek colony 74/1; 74/4; Roman Empire 86/3, 89/1, 91/1; bishopric 93/1; Byzantine Empire 113/1; Norman conquest 120/2; Mediterranean trade 144/1
Syria earliest settlements 41/1, 52/1; centre of ancient civilisations 56-7; at time of Alexander 76/1; Roman Empire 86/3, 91/2; expansion of Christianity 101/1; Arab conquest 105/1; under Abbasids 134/3; conquered by Turks 187/1; Ottoman province 229/1; French attack on 205/3; WW1 253/4; French mandate 260/1; political disturbances 261/1; WW2 272/1; independence 277/2; war with Israel 285/2, 292/5; occupation of Lebanon 285/4; economy 295/1
Syriam S Burma early trade centre 177/1
Syrmia (*S Cr.* Srem *Hung.* Szerém *Ger.* Sirmien) district of Austria-Hungary *now part of* Serbia WW1 253/3
Syzran C Russia founded 163/1
Szczecin (Stettin)
Szechwan (*n/s* Sichuan *W/G* Ssu-ch'uan) province of W China under Ming 168-9; rebellion against Ch'ing 174/2; Manchu expansion 175/1; T'ai-p'ing rebellion 233/1,3; politically fragmented 262/1; Nationalist control 262/2; industry 278/3
Szemao (*n/s* Simao *W/G* Ssu-mao) SW China treaty town 232/2
Szentes-Vekerzug Hungary Thracian site 85/1
Szentgotthárd (St. Gotthard)
Szerém (Syrmia)
Sztutowo (Stutthof)
Tabasco state of S Mexico 227/1
Tabennesis Egypt monastery 100/1
Tabert Algeria Arab conquest 104/1
Tábor Moravia Hussite centre 143/1
Tabora E Africa Livingstone's travels 238/2
Tabriz NW Persia early archbishopric 101/1; occupied by Mongols 128/4; early trade 135/1, 146/1; conquered by Ottomans 139/1, 171/1
Tabun C Israel site of early man 32/2
Ta-ching Manchuria oilfield 278/3
Tadcaster N England Industrial Revolution 201/1
Tadmekka NW Africa early town 136/2, 137/1; trade 167/1
Tadmor (Palmyra)
Tadzhik SSR (Tajik SSR)
Taegu S Korea 1950-53 war 292/2
Taejon S Korea 1950-53 war 292/2
Taganrog Crimea acquired by Muscovy 163/1
Taghaza (*n/c* Terhazza) NW Africa trans-Saharan trade 136/2, 137/1, 167/1
Tagliacozzo C Italy × 119/1, 123/5, 124/2
Tahiti *island* S Pacific Polynesian settlement 49/1; European discovery 157/3
Ta-hsia (Bactria)
Tai (*n/s* Dai) N China Han prefecture 81/2
Taimyr AO C Siberia 290/2
T'ai-hsi-ts'un (*n/s* Taixicun) N China Shang city 62/2
Taira N Japan 175/4
Taiwan (*a/c* Formosa) Mesolithic sites 62/1; Japanese pirate invasions 169/1; occupied by Ch'ing 174/2; rising of aboriginals 175/1; acquired by Japan 232/2, 243/2, 262/1,2, 268/2; conflict with mainland China 279/1; economy 294-295
Taixicun (T'ai-hsi-ts'un)
T'ai-yüan (*n/s* Taiyuan) N China; early bishopric 101/1; T'ang city 126/1; Sung provincial capital 127/5; Ming provincial capital 169/1; French railway 232/2; industry 263/1, 278/3
Taizz Yemen trade 135/1
Tajik SSR (*a/s* Tadzhik) C Asia 290/2,4
Takada C Japan 175/2
Takamatsu W Japan 175/4
Takasaki C Japan 175/4
Takeda C Japan clan territory 168/4
Takedda NW Africa trans-Saharan trade 136/2
Takeshima (*Kor.* Tok-do) *island* Sea of Japan claimed by Korea 279/1
Takht-i-Sulaiman (Adhur Gushnasp)
Takkola Malaya early trade 71/1
Takla Makan Desert 71/1,2
Takoradi W Africa early Dutch settlement 166/1 (inset)
Takrur early empire of W Africa 136/1
Takua Pa S Thailand Hindu-Buddhist remains 133/2
Talas *river* C Asia × 105/1, 109/1, 127/2
Talavera S Spain × 204/1
Talgai SE Australia site of early man 33/1
Ta-li (*n/s* Dali) N China site of early man 33/1
Ta-lien (Dairen)
Tallinn (*Ger.* Reval *Russ.* Revel) Estonian SSR industry 291/1
Talladega SE USA × 221/4
Tamanrasset S Algeria Saharan trade 136/2, 166/1; French occupation 241/1
Tamar (Palmyra)
Tamaulipas state of N Mexico 227/1
Tambov C Russia founded 163/1; Bolshevik seizure 259/1
Tambo Viejo C Andes early site 47/4
Tamil Nadu (*form.* Madras) state of S India 281/3
Tamils people of Ceylon 281/5
Ta-ming-fu (*n/s* Dumingfu) N China Sung provincial capital 127/5
Tamsui (*W/G* Tan-shui) N Taiwan treaty port 232/2; Anglo-French attacks 233/1
Tamuín Mexico Huastec site 148/2
T'an (*n/s* Tan) E China Chou domain 62/3, 63/4
Tana S Russia Mongol conquest 128/4, 129/3; early trade 146/1
Tanais S Russia Greek colony 75/1
Tanakura N Japan 175/4
Tanana sub-artic Indian tribe of Alaska 149/1
Tananarive (*n/s* Antananarivo) Madagascar centre of Merina kingdom 239/1, 241/1
Tancáh Mexico Maya site 46/2
T'an-chou (*n/s* Tanzhou) C China Sung provincial capital 127/5; T'ang prefecture 126/1
Tan-erh (*n/s* Dan'er) S China Han prefecture 81/2
Tanga E Africa Arab-Swahili settlement 239/1
Tanganyika (*form.* German East Africa *now part of* Tanzania) 239/1; anti-German rising 249/1; British mandate 277/1; industry 218/1; independence 277/2; political development 283/1
T'ang Empire China 109/1, 126-7
Tangier (*a/c* Tangiers *Fr.* Tangier *Sp.* Tánger *Ar.* Tanjah *anc.* Tingis) Morocco early trade 134/1, 136/2, 147/2; transferred from Portugal to Britain 186/2; French and Spanish influence 251/2; international control 260/1
T'ang-shan (*n/s* Tangshan) NE China industry 263/1, 278/3
Tanguts tribe of S Mongolia 129/1
Tani Spain early trade 147/1
Tanis (*a/c* Avaris) Lower Egypt 58/1
Tanjah (Tangier)
Tanjore district of S India ceded to Britain 172/3
Tannenberg (*Pol.* Stębark) E Prussia × Teutonic Knights defeated 140/3; × 253/3
Tannu Tuva (*now* Tuvinskaya ASSR) C Asia independence from China 232/2; People's Republic under Soviet protection 258/3
Tan-shui (Tamsui)
Tanta Egypt mediaeval fair 145/1
Tan-t'u (*n/s* Dantu) E China Western Chou site 62/3
Tan-yang (*n/s* Danyang) E China Han commanderie 81/2
Tan-Zam Railway E Africa 283/1
Tanzania (formed by amalgamation of Tanganyika and Zanzibar) 277/2, 283/1, 295/1. See also German East Africa
Tanzhou (T'an-chou)
Tao (*n/s* Dao) C China Western Chou domain 62/3
T'ao-chou (*n/s* Taozhou) W China Ming military post 169/1
Taodeni (*a/s* Taoudenni) NW Africa trade 137/1; French occupation 241/1
Taprobane (Ceylon)
Tara W Siberia founded 162/3
Tarabulus al Gharb (Tripoli)
Tarabulus ash Sham (Tripoli)
Tarahumara Indian tribe of N Mexico 149/1
Tarakan NE Borneo recaptured from Japanese 271/2
Taranaki (*a/c* New Plymouth) province of N Island, New Zealand 236/1
Taranto (*anc.* Tarentum) S Italy Saracen occupation 111/1; WW2 273/3
Tarapaca S Peru acquired by Chile 227/5
Tarapur NE India atomic energy plant 281/3
Tarasco Indian tribe of C Mexico 149/1
Tarawa Gilbert Islands, S Pacific × 271/2
Tarentaise SE France archbishopric 107/3
Tarentum (*mod.* Taranto) S Italy Greek colony 75/1; Roman Empire 86/3, 87/1, 89/1, 91/1
Tarim Basin C Asia occupied by China 127/2
Tarnopol (*now Russ.* Ternopol) E Austria-Hungary WW1 253/3; WW2 273/3
Tarnow (*now Pol.* Tarnów) E Austria-Hungary WW1 253/3
Tarquinii (*later* Corneto *mod.* Tarquinia) C Italy Etruscan city 75/1
Tarracina (*earlier* Axur *mod.* Terracina) C Italy Roman colony 87/1, 91/2
Tarraco (*mod.* Tarragona) NE Spain Greek colony 75/1; Roman Empire 86/3, 89/1, 90/1; Jewish community 103/1
Tarraconensis Roman province of N Spain 88/1
Tarragona (*anc.* Tarraco) NE Spain Civil War 268/3
Tarsus S Anatolia early trade 52/1, 54/1; Assyrian Empire 57/2; Alexander's route 76/1; Achaemenid Empire 79/1; Roman Empire 89/1;, 91/1; early archbishopric 93/1; Jewish community 103/1; Byzantine Empire 113/1
Tărtăria C Rumania early settlement 43/1
Tartars (*a/s* Tatars) Turkic people of E Russia, 129/1, 151/1, 162/3, 196/1, 290/4
Tartu (Dorpat)
Taruga C Africa Iron Age site 45/1
Tarvisium (Treviso)
Tashi-lhunpo S Tibet seat of Lamaistic patriarch 175/1
Tashkent Russ. C Asia silk route 71/2; on Alexander's journey 77/1; Mongol conquest 128/4; centre of Bolshevik activity 258/3; industry 291/1; urban growth 290/3
Tash-Kurghan (*a/s* Tashkurgan *anc.* Aornos) C Asia early trade 82/4
Tasmania (*until 1856* Van Diemen's Land) island state of SE Australia settlement and development 237/5 (inset), 244/1 (inset)
Tatanagar NE India industry 281/1
Tatar ASSR C Russia 290/2
Tatars (Tartars)
Tatebayashi C Japan 175/4
Tatsuno W Japan 175/4
Ta-t'ung (*n/s* Datong) N China Ming frontier defence area 169/1; railway 263/3; industry 278/3
Tauern Austria Alpine tunnel 257/2
Taungs S Africa site of early man 33/4
Taunum W Germany Mithraic site 72/1
Ta-wen-k'ou (*n/s* Dawenkou) NE China early settlement 62/1
Taurasia (Turin)
Taxila (*Skt.* Takshasila) NW India Alexander's route 77/1; early trade 71/1, 82/3,4, 83/1,2
Taxiles early kingdom of NW India 82/3
Tayadirt N Morocco Megalithic site 42/2
Tazoult (Lambaesis)